PALMER'S COMPANY LAW: ANNOTATED GUIDE TO THE COMPANIES ACT 2006

THOMSON

SWEET & MAXWELL

AUSTRALIA
Law Book Co.
Sydney

CANADA and USA
Carswell
Toronto

HONG KONG
Sweet & Maxwell Asia

NEWZEALAND
Bookers
Wellington

SINGAPORE and MALAYSIA
Sweet & Maxwell Asia
Singapore and Kuala Lumpur

PALMER'S COMPANY LAW: ANNOTATED GUIDE TO THE COMPANIES ACT 2006

FIRST EDITION

By

GEOFFREY MORSE, LL.B.
of Lincoln's Inn, Barrister;
Professor ot Corporate and Tax Law,
University of Birmingham

PAUL DAVIES, M.A., LL.M., F.B.A.
Cassel Professor of Commercial Law,
London School of Economics

SARAH WORTHINGTON, B.Sc., LL.B., LL.M. (Melb), Ph.D. (Cantab)
Professor of Law
London School of Economics and Political Science

RICHARD MORRIS, B.A., M.Sc., F.C.A.
Emeritus Professor of Accounting, University of Liverpool

DAVID A. BENNETT, M.A. LL.B., (Edinburgh) W.S.
Solicitor,
Gillespie Macandrew, W.S.,
Solicitors, Edinburgh
Professor of Company Law,
The University of Edinburgh

ALASTAIR HUDSON, LL.B., LL.M., Ph.D. (London)
of Lincoln's Inn, Barrister;
Professor of Equity & Law,
Queen Mary,
University of London

STEPHEN GIRVIN, B.A., LL.B., LL.M. (Natal), Ph.D. (Aberdeen)
Advocate, High Court, South Africa
Associate Professor,
University of Birmingham

SANDRA FRISBY, LL.B., Ph.D. (Nottingham)
Norton Rose Lecturer in Corporate and Financial Law,
University of Nottingham

JENNIFER PAYNE, M.A. (Cantab)
Solicitor, Travers Smith
Lecturer in Corporate Finance Law,
University of Oxford

KEITH WALMSLEY, LL.B., FCIS
Barrister, Head of Legal Services,
The London Law Agency Ltd.

ANTHONY MACAULAY, B.A. (Oxon)
Solicitor,
Partner at Herbert Smith LLP

JANE TUCKLEY
Partner,
Travers Smith Braithwaite

EILÍS FERRAN, M.A. (Cantab), Ph.D. (Cantab)
Professor of Company and Securities Law,
University of Cambridge

LONDON
SWEET & MAXWELL
2007

Published in 2007 by
Sweet & Maxwell Limited of 100 Avenue Road, London,
http://www.sweetandmaxwell.co.uk
Typeset by Sweet and Maxwell Limited
Printed and bound in Great Britain by
Ashford Colour Press

No natural forests were destroyed to make this product;
only farmed timber was used and re-planted.

British Library Cataloguing in Publication Data

*A CIP catalogue record for this book
is available from the British Library*

ISBN 978-1-847-03001-6

CONTENTS

CONTENTS

COMPANIES ACT 2006

(2006 c.46)

CONTENTS

PART 1
GENERAL INTRODUCTORY PROVISIONS

Companies and Companies Acts

Types of company

PART 2
COMPANY FORMATION

General

Requirements for registration

Registration and its effect

PART 3
A COMPANY'S CONSTITUTION

CHAPTER 1
INTRODUCTORY

CHAPTER 2
ARTICLES OF ASSOCIATION

General

Part 8
A Company's Members

CHAPTER 4
PROHIBITION ON SUBSIDIARY BEING MEMBER OF ITS HOLDING COMPANY

General prohibition

Subsidiary acting as personal representative or trustee

Subsidiary acting as dealer in securities

Supplementary

PART 9
EXERCISE OF MEMBERS' RIGHTS

Effect of provisions in company's articles

Information rights

Exercise of rights where shares held on behalf of others

PART 10
A COMPANY'S DIRECTORS

CHAPTER 1
APPOINTMENT AND REMOVAL OF DIRECTORS

Requirement to have directors

CHAPTER 2
GENERAL DUTIES OF DIRECTORS

CHAPTER 3
DECLARATION OF INTEREST IN EXISTING TRANSACTION OR ARRANGEMENT

Chapter 4
TRANSACTIONS WITH DIRECTORS REQUIRING APPROVAL OF MEMBERS

CHAPTER 5
DIRECTORS' SERVICE CONTRACTS

CHAPTER 6
CONTRACTS WITH SOLE MEMBERS WHO ARE DIRECTORS

CHAPTER 7
DIRECTORS' LIABILITIES

Provision protecting directors from liability

Ratification of acts giving rise to liability

CHAPTER 8
DIRECTORS' RESIDENTIAL ADDRESSES: PROTECTION FROM DISCLOSURE

CHAPTER 9
SUPPLEMENTARY PROVISIONS

Provision for employees on cessation or transfer of business

Records of meetings of directors

Meaning of Idirector I and Ishadow director I

Other definitions

CHAPTER 2
WRITTEN RESOLUTIONS

General provisions about written resolutions

Circulation of written resolutions

Agreeing to written resolutions

Supplementary

CHAPTER 3
RESOLUTIONS AT MEETINGS

General provisions about resolutions at meetings

Calling meetings

Notice of meetings

CHAPTER 6
RECORDS OF RESOLUTIONS AND MEETINGS

CHAPTER 7
SUPPLEMENTARY PROVISIONS

PART 14
CONTROL OF POLITICAL DONATIONS AND EXPENDITURE

Introductory

Donations and expenditure to which this Part applies

Authorisation required for donations or expenditure

Remedies in case of unauthorised donations or expenditure

Exemptions

CHAPTER 12
SUPPLEMENTARY PROVISIONS

PART 16
AUDIT

CHAPTER 1
REQUIREMENT FOR AUDITED ACCOUNTS

CHAPTER 2
APPOINTMENT OF AUDITORS

CHAPTER 3
FUNCTIONS OF AUDITOR

Liability limitation agreements

CHAPTER 7
SUPPLEMENTARY PROVISIONS

PART 17
A COMPANY'S SHARE CAPITAL

CHAPTER 1
SHARES AND SHARE CAPITAL OF A COMPANY

Shares

Share capital

CHAPTER 2
ALLOTMENT OF SHARES: GENERAL PROVISIONS

Power of directors to allot shares

Prohibition of commissions, discounts and allowances

Registration of allotment

Return of allotment

Supplementary provisions

CHAPTER 3
ALLOTMENT OF EQUITY SECURITIES: EXISTING SHAREHOLDERS' RIGHT OF PRE-EMPTION

CHAPTER 4
PUBLIC COMPANIES: ALLOTMENT WHERE ISSUE NOT FULLY SUBSCRIBED

CHAPTER 5
PAYMENT FOR SHARES

CHAPTER 8
ALTERATION OF SHARE CAPITAL

CHAPTER 9
CLASSES OF SHARE AND CLASS RIGHTS

CHAPTER 10
REDUCTION OF SHARE CAPITAL

CHAPTER 11
MISCELLANEOUS AND SUPPLEMENTARY PROVISIONS

PART 18
ACQUISITION BY LIMITED COMPANY OF ITS OWN SHARES

CHAPTER 1
GENERAL PROVISIONS

Chapter 2
FINANCIAL ASSISTANCE FOR PURCHASE OF OWN SHARES

Introductory

Circumstances in which financial assistance prohibited

Exceptions from prohibition

Supplementary

Chapter 3
REDEEMABLE SHARES

Chapter 4
PURCHASE OF OWN SHARES

General provisions

Authority for purchase of own shares

Authority for off-market purchase

CHAPTER 5
REDEMPTION OR PURCHASE BY PRIVATE COMPANY OUT OF CAPITAL

Introductory

CHAPTER 6
TREASURY SHARES

PART 22

INFORMATION ABOUT INTERESTS IN A COMPANY'S SHARES

Introductory

Notice requiring information about interests in shares

Orders imposing restrictions on shares

Power of members to require company to act

Register of interests disclosed

Meaning of interest in shares

Other supplementary provisions

PART 23

DISTRIBUTIONS

CHAPTER 1

RESTRICTIONS ON WHEN DISTRIBUTIONS MAY BE MADE

Introductory

General rules

Distributions by investment companies

CHAPTER 2

JUSTIFICATION OF DISTRIBUTION BY REFERENCE TO ACCOUNTS

Justification of distribution by reference to accounts

Requirements applicable in relation to relevant accounts

Application of provisions to successive distributions etc

CHAPTER 3

SUPPLEMENTARY PROVISIONS

Accounting matters

Distributions in kind

Consequences of unlawful distribution

PART 24
A COMPANY'S ANNUAL RETURN

PART 25
COMPANY CHARGES

CHAPTER 1
COMPANIES REGISTERED IN ENGLAND AND WALES OR IN NORTHERN IRELAND

Requirement to register company charges

Special rules about debentures

Charges in other jurisdictions

Orders charging land: Northern Ireland

The register of charges

Avoidance of certain charges

Companies' records and registers

CHAPTER 4
SUPPLEMENTARY PROVISIONS

Expert's report and related matters

Powers of the court

Liability of transferee companies

Interpretation

PART 28
TAKEOVERS ETC

CHAPTER 1
THE TAKEOVER PANEL

The Panel and its rules

Information

Co-operation

CHAPTER 2
PROPERTY OF DISSOLVED COMPANY

Property vesting as bona vacantia

Effect of Crown disclaimer: England and Wales and Northern Ireland

Effect of Crown disclaimer: Scotland

Supplementary provisions

CHAPTER 3
RESTORATION TO THE REGISTER

Administrative restoration to the register

Restoration to the register by the court

Supplementary provisions

PART 32
COMPANY INVESTIGATIONS: AMENDMENTS

PART 36

OFFENCES UNDER THE COMPANIES ACTS

Liability of officer in default

Offences under the Companies Act 1985

General provisions

Production and inspection of documents

Supplementary

PART 37
COMPANIES: SUPPLEMENTARY PROVISIONS

PART 38
COMPANIES: INTERPRETATION

PART 39
COMPANIES: MINOR AMENDMENTS

PART 40
COMPANY DIRECTORS: FOREIGN DISQUALIFICATION ETC

Introductory

Power to disqualify

Power to make persons liable for company's debts

Power to require statements to be sent to the registrar of companies

PART 41
BUSINESS NAMES

CHAPTER 1
RESTRICTED OR PROHIBITED NAMES

Introductory

Sensitive words or expressions

Misleading names

Supplementary

CHAPTER 2
DISCLOSURE REQUIRED IN CASE OF INDIVIDUAL OR PARTNERSHIP

Introductory

Disclosure requirements

Consequences of failure to make required disclosure

CHAPTER 3
SUPPLEMENTARY

PART 42
STATUTORY AUDITORS

CHAPTER 1
INTRODUCTORY

CHAPTER 2
INDIVIDUALS AND FIRMS

Eligibility for appointment

Independence requirement

Effect of appointment of a partnership

Supervisory bodies

Professional qualifications

Information

Enforcement

CHAPTER 3
AUDITORS GENERAL

Eligibility for appointment

Conduct of audits

The Independent Supervisor

Supervision of Auditors General

Reporting requirement

PART 43
TRANSPARENCY OBLIGATIONS AND RELATED MATTERS

PART 44
MISCELLANEOUS PROVISIONS

An Act to reform company law and restate the greater part of the enactments relating to companies; to make other provision relating to companies and other forms of business organisation; to make provision about directors' disqualification, business names, auditors and actuaries; to amend Part 9 of the Enterprise Act 2002; and for connected purposes. [8th November 2006]

PROGRESS OF THE BILL

The Bill, initially named the Company Law Reform Bill, was introduced in the House of Lords on November 1, 2005, HL Bill 34 (*Hansard*, HL Vol.675, col.127). It went for its second reading in the House of Lords on January 11, 2006 (*Hansard*, HL Vol.677, cols 180-249). The Committee stage of the Bill was before a House of Lords' Grand Committee, taken in a committee room. A motion for approval was made on January 18, 2006 (*Hansard*, HL Vol.677, col.665). The Bill entered Grand Committee on January 30, 2006 and was subsequently debated in Grand Committee for almost three months, from January 30 to April 25, 2006 (*Hansard*, HL Vol.678, cols.1-GC64, 119-GC176, 321-GC382; Vol.679, cols.124-GC62, 340-GC188, 744-GC324, 1212-GC466, 467-GC532; Vol.680, cols 128-GC70, 285-GC356, 357-GC440; Vol.681, cols GC61-GC100). The Bill was reprinted after the Grand Committee, HL Bill 98.

The Bill then moved to the Report stage in the House of Lords on May 9, 2006 (*Hansard*, HL Vol.681, cols 777-898, 912-1034; Vol.682, cols 141-253). The Bill completed its initial passage in the House of Lords on May 16, 2006, and was reprinted again, HL Bill 108. The third reading took place in the House of Lords on May 23, 2006 (*Hansard* HL Vol.682, cols 709-797).

After entering the House of Commons with its first Reading on May 24, 2006 (and reprinted, HL Bill 190) the Bill had its second reading on June 6, 2006 (*Hansard*, HC Vol.447, cols 122-223). It entered the Committee stage of the House of Commons (Standing Committee D) on June 15, 2006. The Bill was debated in Standing Committee D until July 21, 2006, a considerably shorter period than the three months that the Bill remained in Grand Committee. The Bill was reprinted again to reflect the amendments made in the House of Commons' Committee, HL Bill 218. By this point the Bill (now renamed the Companies Bill) had grown to 1264 clauses and 16 schedules.

The Report and third reading in the House of Commons took place on October 17-19, 2006 (*Hansard*, HC Vol.450, cols 743-838, 881-980 and 1030-1108). The House of Lords' consideration of the Commons amendments took place on November 3, 2006 (*Hansard*, HL Vol.686, cols 428-510). The House of Lords' reasons for insisting on certain of their amendments to which the Commons had disagreed were considered by the House of Commons on November 6, 2006 (*Hansard*, HC Vol.451, cols. 667-676).

The Companies Bill obtained Royal Assent on November 8, 2006.

INTRODUCTION AND GENERAL NOTE

The Company Law Review

In March 1998, the DTI launched a fundamental review of company law. This review, the Company Law Review ("CLR"), was led by an independent Steering Group whose aim was to develop a simple, modern, efficient and cost effective framework for carrying out business activity in Britain for the twenty-first century. The Steering Group was formed of those with particular knowledge and expertise in company law matters to oversee the management of the CLR.

The remit of the CLR Steering Group was to conduct a wide ranging and thorough review of company law. It was felt that many of the key features of existing company law provisions were out-dated, being based on arrangements put in place in the middle of the nineteenth century, and had not kept up with the pace of change. An additional pressure for change was felt to be the increasing globalization of the UK economy. When the CLR was established it had been nearly 40 years since the last broad review of company law, carried out by the Jenkins Committee (1962). Although there had been numerous changes and additions to company law in that period, this had created a patchwork of regulation that was immensely complex and out of date. Particular problems raised for consideration by the CLR were the overly formal language and excessive detail of the existing law (there was a suggestion that company law legislation should be rewritten in plain English) as well as its complexity and the dangers of over-regulation. The resulting costs and problems were felt to be "real and substantial". The object of the CLR was to "bring forward proposals for a modern law for the modern world" (*Modern Company Law for a Competitive Economy*, cl.2.1).

Once established, the CLR Steering Group went about its work with considerable energy. Fundamental principles guiding the review were mapped out in *The Strategic Framework* in February 1999 (URN 99/654). Early papers were produced suggesting that significant reform was on the way, particularly with regard to the law on share capital, shareholder communication and company formation (see e.g. *Company Formation and Capital Maintenance*, URN 99/1145; *Company General Meetings and Shareholder Communication*, URN 99/1144). Other papers dealt with the law on company charge registration and the regulatory regime governing overseas companies (*Registration of Company Charges*, URN 00/1213; and *Reforming the Law Concerning Overseas Companies*, URN 99/1146). A more general paper published in March 2000 and entitled *Developing the Framework* (URN 00/656) gave the CLR Steering Group the opportunity to float key ideas for wide consultation and comment. These were built upon in the *Completing the Structure* document of November 2000 (URN 00/1335).

After three years of deliberation the *Final Report* of the CLR was published on July 26, 2001. The finished product consisted of two volumes (URN 01/942 and URN 01/943) and included amongst the recommendations were suggested draft clauses for a future Companies Bill. As one might expect, the *Final Report* contained few surprises given the substantive nature of the consultation process which had gone before. Adopting the "Think Small First" injunction, the CLR proposed a substantial dose of deregulation for small private companies. The CLR recommended that private companies need not hold any AGMs, lay accounts in general meeting, appoint auditors or be required to have a company secretary. The *Final Report* also included the recommendation that directors' duties be contained in a clear statutory statement. This statutory statement included the recommendation that although the primary role for directors should be to promote the success of the company for the benefit of its shareholders as a whole, nevertheless directors should also recognize the wider relationships (such as suppliers, customers and the local community) which are essential to the success of the company. In its *Final Report*, the CLR favoured incorporation of companies via a single document, instead of using separate memoranda and articles of association (see paragraph 9.4). The proposals on minority shareholders in the *Final Report* broadly followed the recommendations for reform put forward by the Law Commission (see Law Com. Report No 246). A statutory derivative action was favoured (para.7.46) and the ruling in *O'Neill v Phillips* [1999] 1 W.L.R. 1092 was allowed to stand in spite of some reservations (para.7.41). In addition the *Final Report* acknowledged that, even if its proposals were implemented, there would remain a continuing need to keep corporate law under review. It therefore recommended the establishment of standing bodies to undertake that task (Ch.5). A Company Law and Reporting Commission would be given the lead role in this respect that would be supported by a Private Companies Committee and a new Standards Board whose remit it would be to make rules on company accounts and reporting.

Not all of the recommendations made in the *Final Report* found their way into a final version of the Act. For example, the *Final Report* recognized that the presentation of the law in a user-friendly manner would be critical to the success of any new regime. Whilst some attempt has been made to keep the language of the Act simple (as compared to that found in the Companies Act 1985, for example), the new Act has not been written in the plain English style suggested by the CLR. In addition, in the *Final Report* the CLR recommended a specific duty of care for directors in favour of creditors where insolvency threatens (see para.3.13). This did not find favour with the Government and is not to be found in the Act. Likewise, the recommendation that a duty based on s.214 of the Insolvency Act 1986 should be included in any statutory statement of directors' duties was not favored by the Government.

One other issue deserves special mention here. Chapter 8 of the *Final Report* recommended the creation of an Operating and Financial Review ("OFR") to improve the quality of company reporting. This recommendation was subsequently introduced in the Companies Act 1985 (Operating and Financial Review and Directors' Report etc) Regulations 2005 (SI 2005/1011). However, on November 28, 2005 the Chancellor of the Exchequer abolished the requirement for companies to produce a statutory OFR, citing over-regulation as the reason for this change. The mandatory nature of the OFR was then removed by the Companies Act 1985 (Operating and Financial Review) (Repeal) Regulations 2005 (SI 2005/3442) with effect from January 12, 2006. The relevant provisions in the Companies Bill implementing the OFR were also removed. This change of policy has proved controversial. The OFR was already regarded as good practice for listed companies and formed a cornerstone of the narrative reporting requirement changes recommended by the Company Law Review, endorsed by the DTI White Paper, Modernising Company Law (Cm.5553, July 2002). The OFR is replaced by a "business review" as a part of the directors' report of quoted companies and introduced via the new Act (see s.417 of the 2006 Act). The contents of the business review cover much of the ground covered in the OFR but in less prescriptive form and will not have the additional audit requirement specified for the OFR.

The Government's Response

The Government published an eagerly awaited White Paper, *Modernising Company Law*, on 16 July 2002. This White Paper (in two volumes, Cm.5553-I and Cm.5553-II) was the first part of the Government's response to the *Final Report*. Volume 2 of the White Paper included some 200 draft clauses of a proposed Companies Bill for consideration. This was followed by a further White Paper, in March 2005, followed by further draft clauses and explanatory material in July, September and October 2005. These documents together set out the Government's response to the CLR's proposals. Although all in all the Government's response was favourable there were areas in which the Government rejected the CLR proposals. Some of these have been mentioned already. Others include the fact that the Government did not support the *Final Report's* proposals to allow corporate migration to take place (*Modernising Company Law*, paras 6.21-6.22), due to concerns about lost tax revenues, and the proposal that there might be value in an independent professional review as an alternative to audit for some small company accounts was rejected.

These White papers were followed quickly, in November 2005, by a Company Law Reform Bill. The Bill was introduced in the House of Lords on November 1, 2005, with 885 sections and 15 schedules. The Bill initially envisaged that approximately two thirds of the 1985 Act would be repealed and one third would remain in place. Schedule 15 of the Bill contained a list of provisions to be repealed within the Companies Act 1985 and other legislative provisions. The Bill amended and restated many of the provisions of the Companies Act 1985 and made specific amendments to other legislation. The Bill also implemented some EC directives.

The Bill entered a Grand Committee of the House of Lords on January 30, 2006. A huge number of changes were introduced during this stage. Undoubtedly the single biggest change was the entire removal of Pt 31 of the Bill as it was originally drafted. This Part had contained the controversial company law reform power, ie a power to reform company law for the future by delegated legislation. Another important shift at this stage, which occurred on the last day of the Grand Committee was an opposition proposal to introduce a clause to require the Government to consolidate the new Act with the Companies Act 1985, the Companies Act 1989 and the Companies (Audit, Investigations and Community Enterprise) Act 2004 within two years of Royal Assent

The CLR's initial proposals envisaged a single, consolidated Companies Act to replace and update existing legislation. However the Bill as initially published left substantial portions of this older legislation in place, to co-exist with the new Act. The opposition proposal on the last day of Grand Committee was designed to avoid this confusing plethora of partially repealed statutes standing alongside the new Act. Unsurprisingly, the Government did not support this proposal, but it did sympathise with the idea and agreed that certain remaining provisions in the three older Acts would be considered for inclusion in the Bill. Of course, with the removal of the proposed general company law reform power, further amendments to the statutes would be much more difficult than originally envisaged (and would require primary legislation) so to agree to do as much as possible at this point made some sense. Indeed it is a shame that this process was begun only part way through the Bill's passage through Parliament. There were a number of downsides to this decision. First, the consolidation would not be complete: sections from the three older Acts would still be relevant and therefore those dealing with companies would need to continue to refer to all four Acts. Second, the new Bill would now be much longer, and indeed this Bill had the dubious honour of being the largest that had ever been debated. Third, the provisions from the older Acts to be consolidated into the Bill were restatements - but subject to redrafting in a style appropriate for the Bill. Hence some changes of language were introduced, raising questions as to whether the substance of the older provisions had been preserved. However, the benefits of legislation which is more consolidated than envisaged by the Bill as published were clear.

Having completed the Committee Stage in the House of Lords on April 25, 2006, the Bill went on to the Report Stage of the House of Lords on May 9. More amendments followed at this stage, in particular the statutory statement of directors' duties came under review again, as did derivative actions and the shape of the new business review which replaced the scrapped OFR. In addition, guidance was still being sought at this stage on matters which were expected to be included in the Bill. In particular, the Insolvency Service and the DTI respectively asked for comments on two specific areas: on the provision for the statutory reversal of the decision in *Buchler v Talbot* [2004] UKHL 9; [2004] B.C.C. 214 and on proposed new provisions for the execution of documents by individuals (other than directors or the company secretary) on behalf of companies. It is not unfair to say that the Bill was still very much a moving target at this point.

The Bill completed its initial passage in the House of Lords on May 16, 2006, and was ordered to be reprinted again. After entering the House of Commons with its First Reading on May 24, the Bill had its second reading on June 6. In the Second Reading the Secretary of State for Trade and Industry reiterated the intention to consolidate the majority of the remaining provisions of the Companies Acts 1985 and 1989 into the Bill. The Government refused an opposition proposal that the House of Commons Committee Stage be divided into two parts: the first to consider only the existing 925 clauses of the Bill (in the Bill as ordered to be printed on May 24), and a second stage after the summer recess to consider the consolidating provisions. As these consolidation measures were not intended to amend the existing law, they were not to be debated in Parliament. The DTI published a series of these consolidating clauses on June 30 and July 6, 2006, including clauses dealing with takeover offers (ss.428-430F of the 1985 Act), share capital and financial assistance (ss.89-179 and Sch.2 paras 3-5 of the 1985 Act), debentures (ss.190-197 of the 1985 Act), distributions (ss.263-281 of the 1985 Act) and protection against unfair prejudice (ss.459-461). Comments were sought within a short space of time (by September 8) in order to allow these clauses to be consolidated into the Bill in time for the anticipated autumn Royal Assent.

The second development in the Second Reading was the introduction of a "Programme Motion" seeking a "Programme Order" (a relatively modern method of House of Commons procedure to curtail the length of the Committee Stage) for the Committee Stage to run provisionally from June 15 to July 13 - a massive reduction compared with the Grand Committee in the House of Lords which lasted for almost three months. As a result, very little time was set aside for the Committee stage of the House of Commons, but one significant change did take place at this stage, namely the change of title of the Bill from "Company Law Reform Bill" to "Companies Bill", to bring it into line with previous company law legislation.

On emerging from House of Commons' Committee the Bill was reprinted again on July 28. Over the summer of 2006, extra-parliamentary scrutiny of the restated provisions suggested by the DTI took place, by the Law Societiey and other interested parties. The DTI considered comments on the consolidation and restatement clauses and indeed continued to publish further restatement clauses, the last being published on October 4. The DTI also published draft model articles for public companies for comment, having previously published draft model articles for private companies. It also published for comment a paper describing its general approach to the transitional application of the Bill to existing companies (DTI, *Companies Bill: A paper seeking views on the application of the Companies Bill to existing companies*, August 2006).

With the commencement of the autumn parliamentary calendar, the Bill then moved quite swiftly through its final stages. Although over 800 amendments were tabled at the Report stage of the House of Commons, most of these were technical in nature, but some had more substance. For example, the proposed new "authorised signatory" regime was removed. This regime had been designed to enable companies to appoint one or more authorised signatories who, by virtue of such appointment, would be authorised to sign documents of any description on behalf of the company.

The Bill eventually received Royal Assent on November 8, 2006.

The Shape of the Companies Act 2006

At 1300 sections and 16 schedules, and 760 pages in length, the Companies Act 2006 is believed to be the longest piece of legislation ever passed in the United Kingdom. It was eight years in the making and went through over 3,000 amendments in the final 12 months alone. A substantial portion of the Act is a restatement of the previous law. It replaces the company law provisions of the Companies Act 1985, the Companies Act 1989 and the Companies (Audit, Investigations and Community Enterprise) Act 2004, except for the self-standing provisions on community interest companies and provisions on investigations, which are of wider application than companies. The 1300 clauses of the Companies Act 2006 are divided into 47 Parts. Parts 1-7 deal with the fundamentals of what a company is, how it can be formed and what it can be called. Parts 8-12 deal with the members and officers of a company, including the duties owed by directors, and the new statutory derivative action. Parts 13 and 14 deal with how companies may take decisions. Parts 15 and 16 deal with the safeguards for ensuring that the officers of a company are accountable to its members, namely the requirements for accounts and reports, and audit. Parts 17-28 deal with various matters to do with the company's capital, including raising capital, distributions, company charges and takeovers. Parts 29-31 contain some miscellaneous restatements of the provisions of the Companies Act 1985. Parts 32-40 contain a number of provisions dealing with the regulatory framework of company law such as company investigations, offences under the Companies Act and the registrar of companies. Parts 41 and 42 deal with business names and statutory auditors respectively. Part 43 introduces a number of provisions which allow the UK to implement the Transparency Directive (2004/ 109/ EC). Parts 44-47 contain a number of miscellaneous and general provisions.

Parts 1-7: The fundamentals of what a company is, how it can be formed and what it can be called

Part 1 contains general introductory provisions, providing definitions of a "company" (s.1) and "the Companies Acts" (s.2) and setting out the different types of company that can exist. No new types of company are created by this Act. Part 1 retains all of the existing forms of company. Part 2 deals with how companies are formed and replaces equivalent provisions in the 1985 Act. A number of changes are introduced, including the ability of a single person to form any kind of company, not just a private company, as under the 1985 Act (s.7 of the 2006 Act), and a new and more limited role for the memorandum of association (s.8). Part 3 deals with various matters relating to the company's constitution and replaces similar provisions in the 1985 Act. A new (non-exhaustive) definition of "a company's constitution" is included (s.17). Provision is made regarding the main constituent parts of a company's constitution such as the articles of association, including their juridical effect (s.33 of the 2006 Act, replacing s.14 of the 1985 Act), how they may be altered (s.21 of the 2006 Act, replacing s.9 of the 1985 Act) and the effect of alteration. New sections allow members of a company to entrench provisions within the articles (ss.22-24). Resolutions and agreements affecting a company's constitution are also dealt with (ss.29-30). One important change within this Part is that companies will be assumed to have unlimited objects unless their objects are specifically restricted by the company's articles (s.31).

In Pt 4 various matters to do with the company's capacity are tackled. In particular, s.39 of the 2006 Act replaces s.35 of the 1985 Act, reproducing s.35(1) but not s.35(2) and 35(3), thereby effectively removing any need to consider whether a company has acted ultra vires its objects (although see s.42 as regards charities). In addition, ss.40-41 replace s.35A and s.322A of the 1985 Act respectively. Part 5 deals with the name under which a company is registered, and regulates the choice of a corporate name. Part 6 deals with the requirements for a company's registered office. Part 7 deals with the re-registration of companies and replaces the provisions in Pt 2 of the 1985 Act.

Parts 8-12: The members and officers of a company, including directors' duties and the new statutory derivative action

Part 8 deals with members of a company. Much of this material retains the existing law, although some changes of detail are introduced, e.g. in relation to the register of members a new provision makes it clear that joint holders of a share fall to be treated as a single member, although all of the names must be entered on the register: s.113(5). A new provision (s.120), implemented on the recommendation of the CLR (*Final Report*, para.11.43), requires companies to advise anyone exercising their right to inspect the register of members of their right to demand a copy of the index detailing whether the information is up-to-date and if not the date to which it has been made up. Part 9 deals with the exercise of members' rights and introduces new provisions enabling companies to extend certain rights to investors holding through intermediaries. This follows the recommendations of the CLR (*Final Report*, Ch.7). These provisions allow companies to enfranchise persons identified by the registered member to enjoy and exercise some or all of certain governance rights, detailed in this Part.

Part 10 concerns company directors. It deals with the appointment and removal of directors, introducing, amongst other things, a new requirement that there be at least one director who is a natural person (s.155) and a new minimum age requirement for directors of 16 (s.157). This Part also introduces a new statutory statement of directors' general duties to the company. This statutory statement, particularly s.172 dealing with the duty to promote the success of the company, in combination with the new statutory derivative action (see Pt 11), prompted a lot of discussion and debate as the Bill progressed through Parliament. Part 10 also sets out detailed rules governing directors' conflicts of interest, replacing Pt 10 of the 1985 Act, but with a number of changes. Sections 309A-C of the 1985 Act regarding directors' liability are restated in Ch.7 of Pt 10. A new provision is included at s.239 which reverses *North-West Transportation Co Ltd v Beatty* (1887) L.R. 12 App. Cas. 589 and requires that the ratification of conduct by a director amounting to negligence, default, breach of duty or breach of trust is passed only if the necessary majority is obtained "disregarding votes in favour of the resolution by the director (if a member of the company) and any member connected with him". New provisions allow directors to file a service address on the public register and to put their residential addresses on a separate secure register to which access is restricted (Ch.8 of Pt 10).

Part 11 introduces a new statutory derivative action, largely implementing the recommendations of the Law Commission (*Shareholder Remedies*, Law Com Report No 246), as recommended by the CLR. This Part does not formulate a substantive rule to replace the rule in *Foss v Harbottle* (1843) 2 Hare 461, 67 E.R. 189, but rather introduces a new procedure for bringing such an action. Detailed procedural rules are laid down as regards bringing a derivative claim in England, Wales or Northern Ireland (Ch.1 of Pt 11) or a derivative action in Scotland (Ch.2 of Pt 11). Part 12 deals with company secretaries and introduces some changes to the existing law eg a private company is not required to have a secretary (see *Final Report*, para.4.7).

Parts 13 and 14: How companies may take decisions

Part 13 deals with resolutions and meetings and makes a number of changes to the existing law. Two general changes are the fact that the Act makes the existing "elective" regime the default for private companies and that the new provisions assume that many private companies will not take their decisions by way of general meetings. Instead new procedures for decisions to be taken by written resolution are introduced (Ch.2 of Pt 13). Part 13 deals first with private companies and then adds in additional requirements for public and quoted companies. Part 14 deals with the control of political donations and expenditure, and restates Pt 10A of the 1985 Act, with some changes e.g. to allow private companies to authorize donations by written resolution rather than requiring a general meeting (s.366).

Parts 15 and 16: The requirements for accounts and report and audit

Part 15 deals with accounts and reports and replaces Pt 7 of the 1985 Act relating to accounts and reports (the provisions of Pt 7 of the 1985 Act relating to audit are replaced by Pt 16 of the 2006 Act). Part 15 has adopted the "Think Small First" strategy and where possible provisions applying to small companies appear before the provisions applying to other companies. Another change is to allow the Secretary of State to replace the detailed Schedules to Pt 7 of the 1985 Act by regulations. This Part also introduces substantive changes e.g. reductions in the time limits for private and public companies to file their accounts, and in the case of public companies to lay full financial statements before the company (s.442), and new requirements for quoted companies to publish their annual accounts and reports on a website (s.430). Part 16 deals with audit, bringing together various provisions on the audit of companies from the 1985 Act and introducing a number of significant changes to the law on auditing.

Parts 17-28: The company's capital, including raising capital, distributions, company charges and takeovers

Part 17 deals with a company's share capital and includes provisions governing the allotment of shares (Ch.2); pre-emption rights (Ch.3); the rules governing the payment for shares (Ch.5), including a requirement for an independent valuation for non-cash consideration received for shares by public companies (Ch.6); and how share capital may be altered (Ch.8). Provisions dealing with the variation of class rights are included, as are provisions dealing with reductions of capital. These provisions replace equivalent provisions in the 1985 Act. Some new provisions are inserted, eg a new definition of classes of shares is introduced (s.629). There are also changes to the existing law, following some of the recommendations made by the CLR, e.g. the introduction of a new method for reducing capital for private companies (that sits alongside the usual court order method) which requires a solvency statement from the directors (ss.642-644 and see *Final Report*, para.10.6).

Part 18 deals with the acquisition of a limited company of its own shares, including financial assistance for the purchase of a company's own shares and provisions dealing with redeemable shares. It replaces the provisions of the 1985 Act in this regard, introducing numerous small changes and some more major changes to the existing regime, e.g. the effective abolition of the prohibition on the giving of financial assistance by a private company for the purchase of its own shares (Ch.2), as recommended by the CLR (*Final Report*, para.10.6). This Part also deals with Treasury Shares (Ch.6). Part 19 deals with debentures and restates the provisions of the 1985 Act, with small changes. Part 20 deals with private and public companies, replacing the provisions of the 1985 Act in this regard. The prohibition on private companies offering their shares or debentures (or any securities of the company) to the public is maintained (s.755). The minimum capital requirement for public companies of £50,000 for public companies is also retained (Ch.2). Part 21 deals with the certification and transfer of securities. Chapter 2 allows the Secretary of State and the Treasury either separately or jointly to make regulations to enable title to securities to be evidenced and transferred without a written instrument. Part 22 deals with information about interests in a company's shares and replaces equivalent provisions in Pt 6 of the 1985 Act. There are a number of small changes to the existing regime and one major change, namely that the automatic disclosure obligations previously contained in ss.198-211 of the 1985 Act need to be repealed and replaced in order to implement the Transparency Directive (see Pt 43 of the 2006 Act).

Part 23 deals with distributions and replaces the provisions in Pt 8 of 1985 Act dealing with this issue. Part 24 deals with a company's annual return and replaces Ch.3 of Pt 11 of the 1985 Act. Part 25 deals with company charges and replaces Pt 12 of the 1985 Act. It is divided between companies registered in England, Wales or Northern Ireland (Ch.1) and companies registered in Scotland (Ch.2). Part 26 deals with arrangements and reconstructions while Pt 27 deals with mergers and divisions of public companies. These two Parts, taken together, replace Pt 13 of the 1985 Act. Part 28 deals with takeovers. It implements the European Directive on Takeover Bids (2004/25/EC) which was adopted on April 21, 2004. This directive required implementation by May 20, 2006, and so the Takeovers Directive (Interim Implementation) Regulations 2006 were passed to fill the gap. This Part also replaces the "squeeze-out" and "sell-out" rules found in Pt 13A of the 1985 Act, in part to implement the Directive but also to implement changes recommended by the CLR (*Final Report*, Ch.13).

Parts 29-31: Miscellaneous restatements of the provisions of the Companies Act 1985

Part 29 deals with fraudulent trading and contains a single section restating s.458 of the 1985 Act. Part 30 deals with the protection of members from unfair prejudice and restates Pt 17 of the 1985 Act, i.e. ss.459-461 of the Companies Act 1985. Part 31 deals with the dissolution of companies and their restoration to the register and replaces Pt 20 of the 1985 Act.

Parts 32-40: The regulatory framework

Part 32 deals with company investigations and provides some amendments to Pt 14 of the 1985 Act, which will remain in force subject to those amendments. This Part makes some changes to the existing regime. In particular the Secretary of State is given new powers to bring to an end an investigation when it is no longer in the public interest to continue with it; to revoke the appointment of an inspector, and to issue directions about the scope of an investigation, its duration and certain other matters (ss.1035 and 1036 of the 2006 Act, inserting new ss.446A, B and C into the 1985 Act). Part 33 deals with United

Kingdom companies not formed under the Companies Acts. These include companies not formed under the Companies Act but authorized to register and unregistered companies. Part 34, and the regulations made under it, deal with overseas companies and replace Pt 23 and Schs.21A-D of the 1985 Act. Regulations made under this Part will continue to implement the requirements of the Eleventh Company Law Directive (89/66/EEC) which imposes disclosure requirements on overseas companies that set up branches in the UK. This implements some of the CLR's recommended changes to the pre-existing regime (*Final Report*, paras 11.21-11.33).

Part 35 deals with the registrar of companies, and largely replaces Pt 24 of the 1985 Act. It sets out the basic functions of the registrar of companies. New sections implement a number of CLR recommendations eg the Secretary of State will have a new power to provide for electronic-only delivery of classes of document (s.1069). Part 36 deals with offences under the Companies Act. In the light of recommendations made by the CLR, that a reformed Companies Act must be underpinned by effective and proportionate sanctions and enforcement, this Part makes a number of changes to the existing regime. In particular it refines the "officer in default" framework in order to make it clearer which individuals may be liable for a breach, and in what circumstances. It also removes criminal liability from the company itself in some circumstances. Part 37 introduces a number of supplementary provisions regarding companies. These include company records; service addresses; sending or supplying documents or information, in particular the facilitation of communication by companies by electronic means; and some additional requirements regarding independent valuations required under ss.93, 593 or 599 of the 2006 Act. New provisions requiring notice of appointment of certain officers are included, eg the appointment of a judicial factor in Scotland, together with some provisions concerning courts and legal proceedings, including a restatement of s.727 of the 1985 Act (concerning the power of the court to give relief in certain cases) as s.1157 of the 2006 Act. Part 38 provides a number of important interpretative sections, including definitions for "parent" and "subsidiary" and related expressions, and introduces the index of defined expressions in Sch.8 of the Act. Part 39 deals with some minor amendments to pre-existing companies legislation. Part 40 deals with the situation in which directors are subject to disqualification under the law of a country or territory outside the UK.

Parts 41-42: Business names and statutory auditors

Part 41 deals with business names and the provisions of this Part replace the Business Names Act 1985. Part 41 widens the coverage of the controls over business names beyond that covered by the Business Names Act so that eg the controls under the 2006 Act apply to all overseas companies carrying on business in the UK. Part 42 deals with statutory auditors. It replaces Pt 2 of the Companies Act 1989 and equivalent Northern Ireland provisions, by restating those provisions with some modifications. In particular this Part extends the category of auditors that are subject to regulation and makes provision for the registration and regulation of auditors in countries outside the EC, who audit companies that are incorporated outside the EC, but are listed in the UK (see registered third country auditors in Ch.5).

Part 43 Implementation of the Transparency Directive

The UK is under an obligation to implement the Transparency Directive (2004/109/EC), which governs periodic financial reporting, disclosure of major shareholdings and provision of information to shareholders and investors generally, by January 2007. This Part introduces a number of provisions which will be inserted into the Financial Services and Markets Act 2000 to enable the United Kingdom to comply with this obligation. Provisions in this Part are some of the few provisions within the Act to come into force Royal Assent (s.1300).

Parts 44-47: Miscellaneous and general

Part 44 deals with a number of miscellaneous matters. These include the regulation of actuaries (amending ss.16-18 of the Companies (Audit, Investigations and Community Enterprise) Act 2004); a power for the Treasury or Secretary of State to make regulations requiring certain institutions, broadly institutional investors, to provide information about the exercise of their voting rights attached to certain shares (ss.1277-1280); and provisions regarding the disclosure of information under the Enterprise Act 2002 (amending Pt 9 of the Enterprise Act 2002). Part 44 also includes a provision regarding the expenses of winding up which is designed to reverse the House of Lord's decision in *Buchler v Talbot* [2004] UKHL 9 (s.1282); and a provision amending para.3(1) of Sch.3 to the Commonhold and Leasehold Reform Act 2002 (s.1283).

Part 45 deals with Northern Ireland. Prior to the 2006 Act, the Companies Acts extended to Great Britain only. This Part extends the Companies Acts to the whole of the United Kingdom, including Northern Ireland. Part 46 provides general supplementary provisions, including sections providing that regulations and orders made under the Act are to be made by statutory instrument, and defining "negative resolution procedure" and "affirmative resolution procedure" for the purposes of the Act. It includes a power to make consequential amendments (s.1294), a power to make transitional provision and savings, and introduces Sch.16, the repeal schedule. Part 47 provides for the short title for the Act, includes a provision explaining the extent of the Act (the whole of the United Kingdom: s.1299) and the commencement of the Act (s.1300).

The Schedules

Schedule 1 deals with the definition of connected persons for the purposes of ss.254 and 255. Schedule 2 deals with various definitions (e.g. specified persons, descriptions of disclosures) for the purposes of s.948. Schedule 3 deals with amendments to some of the provisions of the Companies Act 1985 relating to offences for the purposes of s.1124. Schedule 4 deals with documents and information sent or supplied to a company (s.1144(1)). Schedule 5 deals with communications by a company (s.1144(2)). Schedule 6 deals a number of definitions (e.g. "subsidiary") for the purposes of s.1159. Schedule 7 deals with the meaning of parent and subsidiary undertakings for the purposes of s.1162. Schedule 8 provides an index of defined expressions. Schedule 9 provides for the removal of special provisions about accounts and audit of charitable companies (s.1175). Schedule 10 deals with recognised supervisory bodies (s.1217). Schedule 11 deals with recognised professional qualifications (s.1220). Schedule 12 deals with arrangements in which registered third country auditors are required to participate (s.1242). Schedule 13 deals with supplementary provisions with respect to a delegation order under s.1252. Schedule 14 deals with statutory auditors (s.1264). Schedule 15 deals with transparency obligations and related matters (s.1272). Schedule 16 is the repeals schedule.

COMMENCEMENT

Section 1300 of the Act sets out a small number of matters which came into force on Royal Assent, on November 8, 2006. These are: (i) the majority of Pt 43 of the Act concerning transparency obligations and related matters; (ii) two sections from Pt 44, namely s.1274 (grants to bodies concerned with actuarial standards etc), and s.1276 (the amendment of ss.16 and 66 of the Companies (Audit, Investigations and Community Enterprise) Act 2004 regarding the application of those provisions to Scotland and Northern Ireland); (iii) most of Pt 46, except s.1295 and Sch.16 (repeals); and (iv) all of Pt 47 of the Act.

As regards the rest of the Act, s.1300 provides that "[t]he other provisions of this Act come into force on such day as may be appointed by order of the Secretary of State or the Treasury" (s.1300(2)). A number of other provisions were intended to be brought into force very shortly after Royal Assent (see *Hansard*, HL Vol.686, cols 432-433 (November 2, 2006)). The first commencement order to the 2006 Act, the Companies Act 2006 (Commencement No. 1, Transitional Provisions and Savings) Order 2006 (SI 2006/3428), was made on December 20, 2006 and laid before Parliament on December 21, 2006. It brings into force specific provisions of the Companies Act 2006 (see http://www.opsi.gov.uk/si/si2006/20063428.htm). It also repeals a number of free-standing provisions of the Companies Act 1985. The provisions brought into force by this Order fall into three categories:

(i) The first batch of provisions came into effect on January 1, 2007 (see s.2 of the Order). These are necessary to implement the First Company Law Amendment Directive (2003/58/EC), which updates the First Company Law Directive by reflecting the use of information technology and the use of electronic communications. The First Company Law Amendment Directive required implementation by January 1, 2007. In this regard see the Companies (Registrar, Languages and Trading Disclosures) Regulations 2006 (SI 2006/3429) (http://www.opsi.gov.uk/si/si2006/20063429.htm), in force January 1, 2007. The DTI "regrets" that these Regulations, and certain provisions in the Order, came into force less than 21 days after they had been laid before Parliament, but felt that it was "highly unlikely" that anyone would be put at a disadvantage as a result of this non-compliance with the 21-day rule (see Explanatory memorandum accompanying the Order and Regulations at http://www.opsi.gov.uk/si/em2006/uksiem_20063429_en.pdf, para 3).

(ii) The second batch of provisions came into effect on January 20, 2007 (see s.3 of the Order). These are primarily necessary for the Government to give effect to the Transparency Obligations Directive (Directive 2004/109/EC), which required implementation by January 20, 2007. The provisions coming into effect on this date include provisions on company communications to shareholders and others and provisions facilitating electronic communication; provisions concerning a public company's right to investigate who has an interest in its shares; and s.463 of the Act, which sets out a statutory basis of directors' liability to the company in relation to the Directors' Report (including the Business Review) and the Directors' Remuneration Report. The provisions in the Companies Act 2006 enabling the exercise of powers to make orders or regulations by statutory instrument are also commenced on January 20, 2007.

(iii) The third batch of provisions come into effect on April 6, 2007 (see s.4 of the Order). These include: s.1063, which relates to fees payable to the Registrar of Companies, and s.1281, which amends Pt 9 of the Enterprise Act 2002 to enable public authorities, in certain circumstances, to disclose information where the information is to be used in civil proceedings or otherwise for the purpose of establishing, enforcing or defending legal rights.

As regards the commencement of the rest of the Act, in a statement to the House of Lords on November 2, 2006 (*Hansard*, HL Vol.686, col.432), Lord Sainsbury stated that the Government is committed to bring the remaining provisions of the Act into effect "by October 2008". The Government has promised to consult in February 2007 on its detailed implementation plans. The extended implementation period is necessary because there remains a great deal of work to be done before the complete package of new companies legislation is available. In particular many detailed provisions still need to be laid down in secondary legislation. These include, for example, rules on the form and content of company accounts. Regulations such as these have yet to be drafted and consulted on. The DTI is considering whether existing statutory instruments made under the Companies Act 1985 should be kept as they are or should be amended or replaced. The Act also provides for new forms of model articles to serve as default articles. There will be different forms for public and private companies, and for companies limited by guarantee. Although some initial consultation has taken place, further consultation on these documents is expected.

PART 1

GENERAL INTRODUCTORY PROVISIONS

GENERAL NOTE

Part 1 concerns the fundamentals of what constitutes a company. These clauses are largely a restatement of the existing law with adjustments to reflect both changes in the law which have arisen since the 1985 Act, such as the arrival of Community Interest Companies (see s.6 of the 2006 Act), and some of the general changes introduced by the 2006 Act. There are two primary changes which fall into this latter category. First is the fact that the Act creates a single company law regime for the whole of the United Kingdom (see Pt 45 of the 2006 Act) i.e. it covers Northern Ireland companies as well as GB companies. Second is the fact that the Act introduces changes regarding what is included in a company's memorandum of association (see s.8 of the 2006 Act).

Companies and Companies Acts

1.   Companies

(1) In the Companies Acts, unless the context otherwise requires-
"company" means a company formed and registered under this Act, that is-
   (a) a company so formed and registered after the commencement of this Part, or
   (b) a company that immediately before the commencement of this Part-
       (i) was formed and registered under the Companies Act 1985 (c. 6) or the Companies (Northern Ireland) Order 1986 (S.I. 1986/1032 (N.I. 6)), or
       (ii) was an existing company for the purposes of that Act or that Order,
   (which is to be treated on commencement as if formed and registered under this Act).

(2) Certain provisions of the Companies Acts apply to-
   (a) companies registered, but not formed, under this Act (see Chapter 1 of Part 33), and
   (b) bodies incorporated in the United Kingdom but not registered under this Act (see Chapter 2 of that Part).

(3) For provisions applying to companies incorporated outside the United Kingdom, see Part 34 (overseas companies).

GENERAL NOTE

Subsection (1)

This replaces s.735(1)(a) and (b) of the 1985 Act. It sets out the definitions of "company" for the purposes of the Companies Acts. This section is effectively a repetition of the previous provisions but with one significant change: the 2006 Act creates a single company law regime for the whole of the United Kingdom. Companies Acts since 1929 have extended to Great Britain only, although Northern Ireland companies legislation has followed changes in GB companies legislation very closely. The 2006 Act extends GB company law to Northern Ireland, although company law will remain in formal terms a transferred matter. As a result of the 2006 Act companies will be United Kingdom companies rather than GB companies or Northern Ireland companies. This is dealt with in detail in Pt 45 of the 2006 Act. As a consequence of this extension the definition of a "company" in s.1(1) includes a company that immediately before the commencement of this Part was formed or registered under the Companies (Northern Ireland) Order 1986 (S.I. 1986/1032 (N.I.6)) or was an existing company for the purposes of that Order (s.1(1)(b)(ii)).

Subsection (2)

This section directs attention to provisions in the 2006 Act which relate to companies which are registered but not formed under the 2006 Act (s.1(2)(a)) and unregistered companies (s.1(2)(b)). These companies are dealt with in Ch.1 (ss.1040-1042) and Ch.2 (s.1043) of Pt 33 of the 2006 Act respectively.

Subsection (3)

This section directs attention to provisions in Pt 34 of the 2006 Act which relate to overseas companies (defined at s.1044 of the 2006 Act)..

2. The Companies Acts

(1) In this Act "the Companies Acts" means-
  (a) the company law provisions of this Act,
  (b) Part 2 of the Companies (Audit, Investigations and Community Enterprise) Act 2004 (c. 27) (community interest companies), and
  (c) the provisions of the Companies Act 1985 (c. 6) and the Companies Consolidation (Consequential Provisions) Act 1985 (c. 9) that remain in force.
(2) The company law provisions of this Act are-
  (a) the provisions of Parts 1 to 39 of this Act, and
  (b) the provisions of Parts 45 to 47 of this Act so far as they apply for the purposes of those Parts.

GENERAL NOTE

The original intention behind the Company Law Review project was not only to get rid of unnecessary and outdated restrictions, but also to put in place a new Companies Act bringing together all the company law requirements for private and public companies which would be written in plain English and would be simpler to understand for companies and their advisers. The 2006 Act is only partially successful in this regard. Although some simplification in language has been undertaken within the Act, it is not written in plain English. In addition, although some consolidation of company law legislation has been achieved, it is not true to say that companies and advisers will only have to consult the 2006 Act in the future. During the progress of the Bill through Parliament, many company law provisions from, e.g. the 1985 Act and the Companies (Audit, Investigations and Community Enterprise) Act 2004 were brought into ("restated in") the Bill. However, the 2006 Act does not wholly repeal these Acts, and provisions within these Acts remain in force (see Sch.16 of the 2006 Act). These Acts may therefore still need to be consulted (see, e.g. the provisions on company investigations which remain within Pt 14 of the 1985 Act, amended by Pt 32 of the 2006 Act). In addition other relevant legislation (e.g. Insolvency Act 1986, ss.213-214) is not restated in the 2006 Act. Despite the enormous size of the 2006 Act companies and their advisers will therefore still need to have regard to other legislation. In addition, of course, despite some codification of the common law regarding companies, most notably the new statutory statement of directors' duties (see Ch.2 of Pt 10 of the 2006 Act), companies and their advisers will still have to have regard to the common law to fully appreciate the company law requirements for public and private companies.

Subsection (1)

This section makes it clear that any reference to "Companies Acts" in the 2006 Act includes not only the company law provisions of the 2006 Act (defined in s.2(2)) but also Pt 2 of the Companies (Audit, Investigations and Community Enterprise) Act 2004 which introduced community interest companies, and, more importantly, all of the provisions of the 1985 Act and the Companies Consolidation (Consequential Provisions) Act 1985 that remain in force. The 2006 Act amends and restates many of the provisions of the 1985 Act, and repeals a substantial amount of the 1985 Act (see Sch.16 of the 2006 Act), although the amount left in place is not insignificant.

Subsection (2)

This section provides a definition of the company law provisions of the 2006 Act.

Types of company

GENERAL NOTE

The Company Law Review recommended that the law should provide for the formation of new companies of each of the types that were already available (*Final Report*, para.9.2). This recommendation is implemented by ss.3-6 of the 2006 Act which retain all of the current forms of companies.

3. Limited and unlimited companies

(1) A company is a "limited company" if the liability of its members is limited by its constitution.

It may be limited by shares or limited by guarantee.

(2) If their liability is limited to the amount, if any, unpaid on the shares held by them, the company is "limited by shares".

(3) If their liability is limited to such amount as the members undertake to contribute to the assets of the company in the event of its being wound up, the company is "limited by guarantee".

(4) If there is no limit on the liability of its members, the company is an "unlimited company".

GENERAL NOTE

This section replaces ss.1(2)(a), (b) and (c) of the 1985 Act. In broad terms the law is left unchanged. However, what were three definitions (a company limited by shares, a company limited by guarantee and an unlimited company), now become four, with the inclusion of a separate definition for a limited company (s.3(1) of the 2006 Act). This is intended to clarify the existing definition rather than to introduce any change to the law. The only change to the law in this section arises from the need to reflect the changes to what is now included in a company's memorandum of association (discussed in relation to subs.(1) below).

Subsection (1)

There was no specific definition of a "limited company" in s.1(2) of the 1985 Act, which this section replaces. The inclusion of this definition is intended to clarify the law. The definition of a "limited company" reflects the changes to what is to be included in a company's memorandum of association (see s.8 of the 2006 Act), so that rather than the company being a limited company if liability of the members is limited "by the memorandum..." (s.1(2)(a) and (b) of the 1985 Act) the company is a limited company if the liability of its members is "limited by its constitution". It is stated that a limited company may take two forms: it may be limited by shares (see subs.(2)) or by guarantee (subs.(3))

Subsection (2)

This section, when combined with subs.(1), replaces s.1(2)(a) of the 1985 Act. The only substantive change reflects the changes to the company's memorandum, as described in subs.(1) above.

Subsection (3)

This section, when combined with subs.(1), replaces s.1(2)(b) of the 1985 Act. Again, the only substantive change reflects the changes to the company's memorandum, as described in subs.(1) above.

Subsection (4)

This replaces s.1(2)(c) of the 1985 Act. It states that where there is no limit on the liability of the company's members, a company is an "unlimited company". This follows the form of the 1985 Act. By reference back to subs.(1), the definition of an unlimited company is also updated to reflect the changes to the company's memorandum, so that an investigation of any limits on the liability of members in the company's constitution must take place in order to determine whether the company is limited (limits are found) or unlimited (no limits are found).

4. Private and public companies

(1) A "private company" is any company that is not a public company.

(2) A "public company" is a company limited by shares or limited by guarantee and having a share capital-

   (a) whose certificate of incorporation states that it is a public company, and

   (b) in relation to which the requirements of this Act, or the former Companies Acts, as to registration or re-registration as a public company have been complied with on or after the relevant date.

(3) For the purposes of subsection (2)(b) the relevant date is-

(a) in relation to registration or re-registration in Great Britain, 22nd December 1980;

(b) in relation to registration or re-registration in Northern Ireland, 1st July 1983.

(4) For the two major differences between private and public companies, see Part 20.

GENERAL NOTE

This section replaces s.1(3) and s.735(2) of the 1985 Act, and provides definitions of private and public companies.

Subsection (1)

This provides a negative definition of a private company, i.e. a private company is any company that is not a public company. A public company is then defined in subss.(2) and (3). This repeats the form of the 1985 Act, in which a private company is also negatively defined. This repetition is unfortunate. Company law developed mainly with the public company in mind. The provisions that apply to private companies have often been expressed as exceptions to the provisions applying to public companies, making them difficult to understand. This was highlighted in the company law reform process. The 2002 White Paper, *Modernising Company Law*, made it clear that the company law reform process primarily sought to address the specific needs of small companies. The Government has constantly reiterated a "Think Small First" principle in relation to this company law reform process, and this approach has been adopted in some aspects of the 2006 Act, e.g. the requirements on accounts and reports (Pt 15 of the 2006 Act) where possible provisions applying to small companies appear before the provisions applying to other companies. It is therefore unfortunate that an individual will still need to analyse the definition of a public company to ascertain whether their company is a private company or not. This analysis is made more difficult by the way in which the definition of a "public company" has been organised in the 2006 Act (see subs.(2) below).

Subsection (2)

This states that a public company is a company whose certificate of incorporation states that it is a public company. To obtain this certificate the company will need to comply with the provisions of the Companies Acts, or the former Companies Acts (see s.1171 of the 2006 Act), as regards registration or re-registration as a public company. This is effectively a repetition of the existing law (see s.1(3) of the 1985 Act) with changes to include Northern Ireland companies (see subs.(3) below). This provision also reflects the changes to the memorandum of association (see s.8 of the 2006 Act), as the document in which a company is stated to be a public company will be its certificate of incorporation (s.4(2)(a)) of the 2006 Act) rather than its memorandum (s.1(3)(a) of the 1985 Act). There is a minimum share capital requirement for public companies, which was £50,000 prior to the Act, and remains unchanged in the 2006 Act, although reference must be made to s.761 of the 2006 Act to discover this information. It is also notable that the Company Law Review came to the conclusion in its *Final Report* that the most important difference between public and private companies is that private companies may not offer their shares to the public, yet this is not referred to in s.4 at all (although a pointer is made to these provisions in subs.(4)). This makes the application of the definition of a "public company", and by extension the definition of a private company" (see subs.(1) above), more awkward to apply than might have been hoped.

Subsection (3)

This provides the definition of the "relevant date" for the purposes of subs.(2). This updates the pre-existing law to include a reference to Northern Ireland companies (s.4(3)(b)) to reflect the extension of GB company law to Northern Ireland (see s.1(1)(b) and Pt 45 of the 2006 Act).

Subsection (4)

This provides a pointer to the key differences between public and private companies, which are set out at Pt 20 of the 2006 Act.

5. Companies limited by guarantee and having share capital

(1) A company cannot be formed as, or become, a company limited by guarantee with a share capital.

(2) Provision to this effect has been in force-

(a) in Great Britain since 22nd December 1980, and

(b) in Northern Ireland since 1st July 1983.

(3) Any provision in the constitution of a company limited by guarantee that purports to divide the company's undertaking into shares or interests is a provision for a share capital.

This applies whether or not the nominal value or number of the shares or interests is specified by the provision.

GENERAL NOTE

Subsection (1)

This clause replaces s.1(4) of the 1985 Act. It retains the existing position, that a company can not be formed (or re-register) as a company limited by guarantee and with a share capital, but extends s.1(4) of the 1985 Act by reference to the position in Northern Ireland (see subs.(2)).

Subsection (2)

This provides the dates from which a provision to the effect of subs.(1) has been in force. The inclusion of subs.2(b) reflects the extension of GB company law to Northern Ireland (see s.1(1)(b) and Pt 45 of the 2006 Act).

Subsection (3)

This clarifies the fact that any provision in the constitution of a company limited by guarantee that purports to divide the company's undertaking into shares or interests is a provision for capital, whether or not the nominal value or number of shares or interests is specified in the provision.

6. Community interest companies

(1) In accordance with Part 2 of the Companies (Audit, Investigations and Community Enterprise) Act 2004 (c. 27)-

    (a) a company limited by shares or a company limited by guarantee and not having a share capital may be formed as or become a community interest company, and

    (b) a company limited by guarantee and having a share capital may become a community interest company.

(2) The other provisions of the Companies Acts have effect subject to that Part.

GENERAL NOTE

The Companies (Audit, Investigations and Community Enterprise) Act 2004 came fully into force on July 1, 2005. Part 2 of that Act created a new company vehicle, the "community interest company" which is designed for use by social enterprises.

Subsection (1)

This provides a signpost to the provisions of the Companies (Audit, Investigations and Community Enterprise) Act 2004 which enable a company to be formed as, or to become, a community interest company.

Subsection (2)

Community interest companies are registered under the same legislation as other registered companies, but have to complete certain additional formalities and are subject to certain additional elements of regulation. Subsection (2) highlights the fact that in some respects the requirements imposed on community interest companies are different from the requirements imposed on other registered companies.

PART 2

COMPANY FORMATION

GENERAL NOTE

This Part of the Act is concerned with the methods by which a company may be formed under the Act. It replaces and largely modifies equivalent provisions in Pt I of the Companies Act 1985. The central aim of the modifications is to make formation of a company a simpler procedure, as stated by Lord Sainsbury of Turville when introducing the Bill to the House of Lords (See *Hansard*, Vol.677, col.182 (January 1, 2006)). Part 1 of the Companies Act 2006 (see above) deals with the various types of companies (e.g. a company limited by shares, or by guarantee) that may be registered under Pt 2 so that the latter Part deals entirely with the requirements for formation by registration.

One method of simplifying the incorporation by registration regime is to allow for electronic incorporation, and many of the changes to the law have been devised with that possibility in mind. It is envisaged that, from January 1, 2007, such a facility will be made available by the registrar of companies, following a recent amendment to the First Company Law Directive (68/151/EEC) which, in Art.3, now requires that certain corporate documents be deliverable electronically.

General

7. Method of forming company

(1) A company is formed under this Act by one or more persons-
    (a) subscribing their names to a memorandum of association (see section 8), and
    (b) complying with the requirements of this Act as to registration (see sections 9 to 13).
(2) A company may not be so formed for an unlawful purpose.

GENERAL NOTE

This section replaces s.1 of the 1985 Act. Subsections (2)-(4) of that Act dealt with the question of what type of companies could be formed under the Companies Act 1985. These matters are now addressed in Pt 1 of the Companies Act 2006 (see above).

Subsection (1)

The *Final Report* of the Company Law Review, at para.9.2, recommended that a single person should now be able to form a public limited company, as well as a private limited company, as was provided for in s.1(3A) of the Companies Act 1985. A person or persons may now therefore form a public or a private company by (a) subscribing their name(s) to a memorandum of association and (b) complying with the requirements for registration found in ss.9-13 of the 2006 Act.

Subsection (2)

This subsection states that a company may not be formed for an unlawful purpose. An explicit statement of the "purpose" for which a company was formed could, under the 1985 Act, have been found in the objects clause of the memorandum of association, which was a compulsory clause under s.2(1)(c) of that Act. The 2006 Act takes an entirely different approach to the question of a company's objects (see below, at note to s.31). However, the requirement that the company be formed for a lawful purpose remains, having originally been found in s.1(1) of the 1985 Act.

8. Memorandum of association

(1) A memorandum of association is a memorandum stating that the subscribers-
    (a) wish to form a company under this Act, and
    (b) agree to become members of the company and, in the case of a company that is to have a share capital, to take at least one share each.
(2) The memorandum must be in the prescribed form and must be authenticated by each subscriber.

GENERAL NOTE

The memorandum of association, in accordance with the ethos of simplification, is a significantly abridged document under the 2006 Act. Under s.2 of the 1985 Act the memorandum required a statement of the company's name (s.2(1)(a)), whether its registered office was to be situated in England and Wales or in Scotland (s.2(1)(b)) and a statement of the company's objects (s.2(1)(c)). Statements as the whether the company was to be limited by shares or by guarantee, of the extent of each member's guarantee (where relevant), of the registered share capital and division of share capital into shares of a fixed amount, and of the number of shares taken by each subscriber to the memorandum were also compulsory elements of the memorandum under s.2(3), (4) and (5) of the 1985 Act. These matters are now dealt with as part of the registration requirements under ss.9-13 of the 2006 Act. In the case of existing companies, when the Act comes into force these provisions will be treated as provisions of the Articles of Association (see s.28, below).

This attenuation of the memorandum of association reflects the recommendation of the Company Law Review, at para.9.4, that there should in future be a single constitutional document for companies. The memorandum now performs the function of evidencing the intention of the subscribers to it to form a company and to take at least one share each in that company. In accordance with this, the memorandum of a company formed under the 2006 Act will no longer be subject to alteration, amendment or update.

Subsection (1)

The subscribers to the memorandum must state that they wish to form a company under the Act and that, where the company in question is to have a share capital, that they agree to take at least one share each. This latter requirement reproduces the position under the Companies Act 1985 s.2(5)(b) that no subscriber to the memorandum may take less than one share.

Subsection (2)

The memorandum must be in the prescribed form and authenticated by each subscriber. The registrar of companies is empowered by s.1068(1) (see below) to prescribe the form, authentication and manner of delivery of documents. Given that the memorandum (and the articles of association: see below) are documents subject to the "Directive disclosure requirements" in Art.3 of the First Company Law Directive (68/151/EEC), the registrar must, as from January 1, 2007, secure that these are deliverable by electronic means (s.1068(5)).

Requirements for registration

9. Registration documents

(1) The memorandum of association must be delivered to the registrar together with an application for registration of the company, the documents required by this section and a statement of compliance.

(2) The application for registration must state-

 (a) the company's proposed name,

 (b) whether the company's registered office is to be situated in England and Wales (or in Wales), in Scotland or in Northern Ireland,

 (c) whether the liability of the members of the company is to be limited, and if so whether it is to be limited by shares or by guarantee, and

 (d) whether the company is to be a private or a public company.

(3) If the application is delivered by a person as agent for the subscribers to the memorandum of association, it must state his name and address.

(4) The application must contain-

 (a) in the case of a company that is to have a share capital, a statement of capital and initial shareholdings (see section 10);

 (b) in the case of a company that is to be limited by guarantee, a statement of guarantee (see section 11);

 (c) a statement of the company's proposed officers (see section 12).

(5) The application must also contain-

 (a) a statement of the intended address of the company's registered office; and

 (b) a copy of any proposed articles of association (to the extent that these are not supplied by the default application of model articles: see section 20).

(6) The application must be delivered-

 (a) to the registrar of companies for England and Wales, if the registered office of the company is to be situated in England and Wales (or in Wales);

 (b) to the registrar of companies for Scotland, if the registered office of the company is to be situated in Scotland;

 (c) to the registrar of companies for Northern Ireland, if the registered office of the company is to be situated in Northern Ireland.

GENERAL NOTE

This section replaces ss.2 and 10 of the 1985 Act and prescribes the documents and information that must be delivered to the registrar of companies, along with the memorandum of association as described in s.8, on an application for registration. Much of the information required to be delivered by this section would previously have been contained in the memorandum of association. These documents must also be accompanied by a statement of compliance. The method of delivery is also prescribed by this section. Sections 10-13 of the Companies Act 2006 (see below) amplify upon the requirements in relation to the documents mentioned in this section.

In future it will be possible to comply with the requirements for formation of a company online, so that it will be possible for the documents and information required by this section to be supplied on a web-based form.

Subsection (1)

This subsection requires the memorandum of association, together with an application for registration of the company, the documents prescribed by the following subsections and a statement of compliance to be delivered to the registrar of companies.

Subsection (2)

The application for registration must state the company's proposed name (subs.(2)(a)), its location (England and Wales (or Wales), Scotland or Northern Ireland (subs.(2)(b)), whether the member's liability is to be limited, and, if so, whether by shares or by guarantee (subs.(2)(c)), and whether the company is to be a private or a public company (subs.(2)(d)). This information would previously have been contained in the memorandum of association (see Companies Act 1985, s.2(1), (2) and (3)). There is no longer any requirement that the objects of the company be identified in the memorandum of association, or, indeed, in any of the registration documents, as the new approach taken by the 2006 Act is to treat companies as having unlimited objects unless its incorporators choose to restrict the objects (see below, at note to s.31).

Subsection (3)

Where the application for registration is delivered by any person as agent for the subscribers to the memorandum of association, the application must state that person's name and address.

Subsection (4)

The application for registration must, in the case of a company that is to have a share capital, contain a statement of capital and initial shareholdings, the precise details of this requirement being amplified in s.10 (see below). In the case of a company to be limited by guarantee, a statement of the guarantee must be provided (see below, at note to s.11). All applications for registration must contain a statement of the proposed company's officers, the precise requirements of this aspect being contained in s.12 (see below).

Subsection (5)

The application for registration must contain a statement of the intended address of the company's registered office (subs.(5)(a)). This is in addition to the statement, in subs.(2)(b), of the jurisdiction in which the registered office is to be located. Where the company does not intend to adopt all or any part of model articles of association prescribed by the Secretary of State (as to which see below, at notes to ss.19-20), the application for registration must contain a copy of the proposed articles of association.

Subsection (6)

This subsection deals with the question of where the application for registration is to be delivered. The location of the company's registered office determines this matter: if it is to be in England and Wales (or Wales) the application must be delivered to the registrar of companies for England and Wales, if in Scotland to the registrar of companies for Scotland, and if in Northern Ireland, to the registrar of companies for Northern Ireland.

10. Statement of capital and initial shareholdings

(1) The statement of capital and initial shareholdings required to be delivered in the case of a company that is to have a share capital must comply with this section.

(2) It must state-

    (a) the total number of shares of the company to be taken on formation by the subscribers to the memorandum of association,

    (b) the aggregate nominal value of those shares,

(c) for each class of shares-
    (i) prescribed particulars of the rights attached to the shares,
    (ii) the total number of shares of that class, and
    (iii) the aggregate nominal value of shares of that class, and
(d) the amount to be paid up and the amount (if any) to be unpaid on each share (whether on account of the nominal value of the share or by way of premium).
(3) It must contain such information as may be prescribed for the purpose of identifying the subscribers to the memorandum of association.
(4) It must state, with respect to each subscriber to the memorandum-
    (a) the number, nominal value (of each share) and class of shares to be taken by him on formation, and
    (b) the amount to be paid up and the amount (if any) to be unpaid on each share (whether on account of the nominal value of the share or by way of premium).
(5) Where a subscriber to the memorandum is to take shares of more than one class, the information required under subsection (4)(a) is required for each class.

GENERAL NOTE

This provision refers to the statement of capital and initial shareholdings required to be delivered with the application for registration in s.9(4) (above). It replaces s.2(5)(a) and (c), (6) and (6A) of the Companies Act 1985 and, in accordance with the recommendation in para.10.6 of the Company Law Review, abolishes the current requirement in that section for a statement in the memorandum of association of the company's "authorised share capital". That statement currently comprises the amount of share capital with which the company is to be registered, and the nominal amount of each share, and that ceiling is now therefore abolished. Section 121 of the 1985 Act, which allowed for the authorised share capital to be increased by ordinary resolution, will be repealed.

This new statement of capital and initial shareholdings is described in the Explanatory Notes as a "snapshot" of the company's share capital at the point of registration. The point is also made that it implements, as far as public companies are concerned, Art.2 of the Second Company Law Directive (77/91/EC) which requires, as a minimum, the amount of subscribed capital. It is thought appropriate that the substance of Art.2 should apply to private, as well as public companies, in order to ensure that the register contains accurate and up-to-date information. Whilst it might be objected that the provision of a "snapshot" of capital on formation will be of little informative value in that it may well rapidly become out of date, provisions elsewhere in the Act require a statement of capital whenever an alteration to share capital is made.

Subsection (1)

This subsection requires the statement of capital and initial shareholdings to be in compliance with s.10.

Subsection (2)

The statement of capital and initial shareholdings must state the total number of shares to be taken by the subscribers to the memorandum of association and the aggregate nominal value of those shares (subs.(2)(a)(b)). This corresponds only in part to the position in s.2(5) of the Companies Act 1985, which required a statement in the memorandum of association of the amount of share capital with which the company proposed to be registered and the division of that capital into shares of a fixed amount. Subsection (2)(c) requires a statement, for each class of shares, of the prescribed particulars of the rights attached to the shares, the total number of shares of the class and the aggregate nominal value of the shares of the class. These latter two are self-explanatory. The reference to prescribed particulars of the rights attached to each class of shares is to any particulars prescribed by the Secretary of State by statutory instrument. Subsection (2)(d) requires that the amount to be paid up and the amount to remain unpaid (whether in relation to the nominal value of each share or by way of premium) be stated in the statement of capital. This goes beyond what was called for in the "capital clause" of the memorandum of association under s.2(5) of the Companies Act 1985 in that it provides information on the respective amounts of paid up and uncalled capital.

Subsection (3)

The statement of initial capital and shareholdings must contain such information as prescribed (by the Secretary of State by statutory instrument) for the purpose of identifying the subscribers to the memorandum of association. The Explanatory Notes suggest that where the requirement is for an address for the subscribers to the memorandum, this need not be the subscriber's home address and that a contact address will be sufficient.

Subsection (4)

The statement of initial capital and shareholdings must state, for each subscriber to the memorandum of association, information about his shareholding at the point of formation. The information required is the number of shares to be taken, the nominal value of each share, the class of shares to be taken (assuming that there are to be different classes of shares) and the amount to be paid up (or left unpaid) either on account of the nominal value of the share or by way of premium.

Subsection (5)

Where a subscriber to the memorandum takes shares of more than one class the statement must specify the number and nominal value, for each class, of the shares taken by the subscriber. There appears to be no requirement to specify, for each class, the amount to be paid or left unpaid on the shares in each class. That requirement is found in subs.(4)(b) (above) in respect to the entire shareholding (of all classes of shares) of each subscriber.

11. Statement of guarantee

(1) The statement of guarantee required to be delivered in the case of a company that is to be limited by guarantee must comply with this section.

(2) It must contain such information as may be prescribed for the purpose of identifying the subscribers to the memorandum of association.

(3) It must state that each member undertakes that, if the company is wound up while he is a member, or within one year after he ceases to be a member, he will contribute to the assets of the company such amount as may be required for-

(a) payment of the debts and liabilities of the company contracted before he ceases to be a member,

(b) payment of the costs, charges and expenses of winding up, and

(c) adjustment of the rights of the contributories among themselves,

not exceeding a specified amount.

GENERAL NOTE

This section replaces s.2(4) of the Companies Act 1985, which required that each subscriber to the memorandum of association must state the amount he agreed to contribute to the assets of the company should it be wound up for payment of the debts and liabilities of the company contracted before he ceased to be a member, for the costs and expenses of the winding up, and for the adjustment of the rights of the contributories between themselves. This information will now be contained in the statement of guarantee required to be delivered to the registrar of companies with the application for registration required by s.(9) (see above).

The statement of guarantee is an undertaking given by the subscribers to the memorandum, and one which will be expected of new members of the company, to contribute up to a specified amount on the company's winding up. The guarantee is, in one sense, the equivalent to the consideration provided by shareholders in return for their shares in the company, in that it represents a fund to which creditors of the company have access on its winding up.

Subsection (2)

The statement of guarantee must contain such information as prescribed (by the Secretary of State by statutory instrument) for the purpose of identifying the subscribers to the memorandum of association (see also above, at note to subs.(10)(3)).

Subsection (3)

The statement of guarantee must provide that each member of the company undertakes that if the company is wound up whilst he is a member, or within one year after he ceases to be a member he will contribute to its assets, such amount as may be required for payment of the debts and liabilities of the company contracted before he ceased to be a member, for the costs and expenses of the winding up, and for the adjustment of the rights of the contributories between themselves. It therefore reproduces the information required to be included in the memorandum of association under s.2(4) of the Companies Act 1985.

12.   Statement of proposed officers

(1) The statement of the company's proposed officers required to be delivered to the registrar must contain the required particulars of-

(a) the person who is, or persons who are, to be the first director or directors of the company;

(b) in the case of a company that is to be a private company, any person who is (or any persons who are) to be the first secretary (or joint secretaries) of the company;

(c) in the case of a company that is to be a public company, the person who is (or the persons who are) to be the first secretary (or joint secretaries) of the company.

(2) The required particulars are the particulars that will be required to be stated-

(a) in the case of a director, in the company's register of directors and register of directors' residential addresses (see sections 162 to 166);

(b) in the case of a secretary, in the company's register of secretaries (see sections 277 to 279).

(3) The statement must also contain a consent by each of the persons named as a director, as secretary or as one of joint secretaries, to act in the relevant capacity.

If all the partners in a firm are to be joint secretaries, consent may be given by one partner on behalf of all of them.

GENERAL NOTE

This section replaces s.10(2), (2A), (4) and (5) of the 1985 Act. Whilst it is no longer a requirement for a private company to appoint a secretary (see the recommendation of the Company Law Review *Final Report* that the decision whether to appoint a secretary should "be made by the market rather than by law" (para.4.7)), provision continues to be made for those private companies that do appoint one to provide particulars to the registrar of that person or persons. the directors named in the statement of proposed officers may opt to have their residential addresses treated as "protected information".

Subsection (1)

A statement of proposed officers of the company is required to be delivered to the registrar of companies with the application for registration under s.9(4)(c) of the 2006 Act. The statement must contain required particulars of any person who is to be a first director of the company and any persons who are to be the first secretary or joint secretaries of a private or public company.

Subsection (2)

The required particulars referred to in subs.(1) are, for directors, the information required to be stated in the company's register of directors and register of directors' residential addresses. Where a director is an individual, s.163(1) applies (see below), and requires entry of the name (or former name) of the director, a service address, a statement of usual residence, nationality, business occupation and date of birth. For corporate directors or firms, s.164 applies (see below) and requires, inter alia, entry of the company or firm name and its registered office or principal address. Requirements in relation to the company's register of directors' residential addresses are found in s.165 (see below). This may, at the option of the director in question, be treated as protected information (see note to s.240(1), (2) below), in accordance with the recommendation of the Company Law Review's *Final Report* (see paras 11.46-11.48).

The required particulars for the secretary or secretaries of a private or a public company are those stated in the company's register of secretaries under ss.277-279 (see below), which are, basically, a name and service address.

Subsection (3)

The statement of proposed officers must contain a consent by named directors and secretaries to act in that capacity. Where all partners in a firm are to be joint secretaries of a company, this consent may be given by one partner on behalf of them all.

13.   Statement of compliance

(1) The statement of compliance required to be delivered to the registrar is a statement that the requirements of this Act as to registration have been complied with.

(2) The registrar may accept the statement of compliance as sufficient evidence of compliance.

GENERAL NOTE

The 1985 Act, in s.12(3) and (3A), required a statutory declaration, in paper or electronic form, made by a solicitor engaged in the formation of the company or a director or secretary of the company that the requirements of the Act in respect of registration had been complied with. Section 13 of the 2006 Act replaces s.12(3) and (3A) and requires, instead of a witnessed statutory declaration, a statement that the requirements of that Act as to registration have been complied with. This accords with the recommendation of The Company Law Review *Final Report* that the statutory declaration in the s.12 of the 1985 Act (and others required in other parts of the 2006 Act), be replaced by a statement of compliance (*Final Report*, para.9.5)

Subsection (1)

This subsection describes the statement of compliance as a statement that the requirements of the Act as to registration have been met. The form, authentication and manner of delivery of this statement is a matter for the registrar of companies under s.1068 of the Act, although it is for the Secretary of State to prescribe that delivery must be made in electronic form (s.1069). The registrar must ensure that, by January 1, 2007, documents subject to the disclosure requirements of Art.3 of the First Company Law Directive (68/151/EEC) may be delivered in electronic form. These include, for the purposes of this Part of the Act, the company's memorandum and articles of association and the statement of the proposed officers of the company. It will be an offence under s.1112 of the Act for any person delivering any document to the registrar to make a statement in that document which is false, misleading or deceptive in any material particular.

Subsection (2)

As under s.12(3) of the Companies Act 1985, the registrar is entitled to treat the statement of compliance as sufficient evidence of compliance.

Registration and its effect

14. Registration

If the registrar is satisfied that the requirements of this Act as to registration are complied with, he shall register the documents delivered to him.

GENERAL NOTE

This section replaces and substantially re-enacts s.12(1) of the Companies Act 1985. Where the registrar of companies is satisfied that the registration requirements of the 2006 Act have been complied with he will register the delivered documents and issue a certificate of incorporation under s.15.

15. Issue of certificate of incorporation

(1) On the registration of a company, the registrar of companies shall give a certificate that the company is incorporated.

(2) The certificate must state-
    (a) the name and registered number of the company,
    (b) the date of its incorporation,
    (c) whether it is a limited or unlimited company, and if it is limited whether it is limited by shares or limited by guarantee,
    (d) whether it is a private or a public company, and
    (e) whether the company's registered office is situated in England and Wales (or in Wales), in Scotland or in Northern Ireland.

(3) The certificate must be signed by the registrar or authenticated by the registrar's official seal.

(4) The certificate is conclusive evidence that the requirements of this Act as to registration have been complied with and that the company is duly registered under this Act.

GENERAL NOTE

This provision replaces s.13(1), (2), (6) and (7) of the Companies Act 1985. Under that Act the registrar of companies, on registration of the company's memorandum of association issues a certificate of incorporation, as now provided for in s.15(1). The certificate is conclusive evidence that the requirements of the Act as to registration have been complied with and that the company is duly registered under the Act (s.15(4)).

Subsection (2)

The certificate of incorporation must state the information contained in this subsection. The information in question is the name and registered number of the company, the date of its incorporation, whether it is a limited or unlimited company and, if limited, whether by shares or guarantee and whether it is a private or public company. Subsection 15(2)(e) is a new addition to the information required to be stated in the certificate of incorporation. It calls for a statement of whether the company's registered office is situated in England or Wales (or in Wales), or in Scotland or in Northern Ireland.

Subsection (3)

This subsection requires, as did s.13(3) of the Companies Act 1985, the certificate of incorporation to be signed by the registrar of companies or authenticated by the registrar's official seal.

16.   Effect of registration

(1) The registration of a company has the following effects as from the date of incorporation.

(2) The subscribers to the memorandum, together with such other persons as may from time to time become members of the company, are a body corporate by the name stated in the certificate of incorporation.

(3) That body corporate is capable of exercising all the functions of an incorporated company.

(4) The status and registered office of the company are as stated in, or in connection with, the application for registration.

(5) In the case of a company having a share capital, the subscribers to the memorandum become holders of the shares specified in the statement of capital and initial shareholdings.

(6) The persons named in the statement of proposed officers-

    (a) as director, or

    (b) as secretary or joint secretary of the company,

are deemed to have been appointed to that office.

GENERAL NOTE

Section 16 replaces s.13(3), (4) and (5) of the Companies Act 1985 without any substantive changes to those provisions. Subsections (3) and (4) of the section are self-explanatory.

Subsection (2)

This subsection substantially reproduces s.13(3) of the Companies Act 1985. It has the effect that the subscribers to the memorandum, on registration of the company, and any future members of the company, are a body corporate by the name stated in the certificate of incorporation. In effect, therefore, this provision establishes the company as having a legal personality separate from that of its members.

Subsections (5) and (6)

Registration of the company has the effect that the subscribers to the memorandum become the holders of those shares specified in the statement of capital and initial shareholdings (see note to s.10, above), and that the persons named as the proposed officers of the company, whether as director or as secretary, are deemed to have been appointed to the office in question (see note to s.12, above).

PART 3

A COMPANY'S CONSTITUTION

GENERAL NOTE

In accordance with the recommendations of the Company Law Review *Final Report* (see para.9.4), this Part deals with the question of which documents are to be treated as constitutional documents of a company. Constitutional documents are essentially those which will govern the internal aspects of corporate activity. As noted above, the memorandum of association was originally treated as a part of the corporate constitution, but that document is now required to be submitted, on an application for registration, in a substantially abridged form (see general note to s.8, above). Part 3 comprises four Chapters, the first an introduction to the meaning of a company's constitution, Ch.2 dealing with provisions governing the articles of association, Ch.3 with resolutions and other agreements affecting a company's constitution, and Ch.4 containing supplementary and miscellaneous provisions.

CHAPTER I

INTRODUCTORY

17.   A company's constitution

Unless the context otherwise requires, references in the Companies Acts to a company's constitution include-

    (a) the company's articles, and

    (b) any resolutions and agreements to which Chapter 3 applies (see section 29).

GENERAL NOTE

This new provision specifies the elements of a company's constitution, and defines them as the company's articles of association and any resolutions and agreements to which Ch.3 of Pt 2 applies. This latter is dealt with in s.29 of the 2006 Act, which lists all "resolutions and agreements affecting a company's constitution" (see below). All references to a company's constitution in the Companies Acts will therefore, unless the context otherwise requires, include these two elements. In certain circumstances, the definition of a company's constitution may be expanded or restricted, according to the terms of particular provisions.

CHAPTER 2

ARTICLES OF ASSOCIATION

General

18.   Articles of association

(1) A company must have articles of association prescribing regulations for the company.

(2) Unless it is a company to which model articles apply by virtue of section 20 (default application of model articles in case of limited company), it must register articles of association.

(3) Articles of association registered by a company must-

    (a) be contained in a single document, and

    (b) be divided into paragraphs numbered consecutively.

(4) References in the Companies Acts to a company's "articles" are to its articles of association.

GENERAL NOTE

This provision replaces s.7 of the Companies Act 1985. It prescribes that all companies must have articles of association prescribing regulations for the company. Once registered, the articles amount to a statutory contract between the members and the company, and the members inter se in their capacity of members. Thus, terms in the articles may be enforced by the members against the company (see *Wood v Odessa Waterworks Co* (1889) 42 Ch. D) and by the company against the members (see *Hickman v Kent or Romney Sheepbreeders Association* [1915] 1 Ch. 881). A member, to enforce provisions in the articles, must act in his capacity as member (see *Eley v The Positive Government Security Life Assurance Company* (1876) 1 Ex. D. 88).

Subsections (1) and (2)

These two subsections enact the requirements that all companies must have articles of association prescribing regulations for the company and that all companies must register articles of association unless the company in question is one to which s.20 applies. Essentially, if a company is a "limited" company, if it does not register articles of association then Model Articles as prescribed by the Secretary of State (see s.19, below) will constitute its articles of association. Only unlimited companies, therefore, will be subject to the requirement for registration of articles of association. This amends the existing law in s.7(1) of the Companies Act 1985 that companies limited by guarantee must register articles of association.

Subsections (3)

This subsection prescribes the form of the articles of association. They must be contained in a single document and be divided into consecutively numbered paragraphs, as previously provided in s.7(3) of the 1985 Act. As the articles of association are a document to which Art.3 of First Company Law Directive (68/151/EEC) apply, facilities to deliver them electronically must be made (see s.1068(5)). The requirement in s.7(3) that the articles be printed is therefore abolished, as, it appears, is the requirement that articles in legible form (i.e. not delivered electronically under s.7(3A) of the Companies Act 1985) be signed by each subscriber to the memorandum of association, that signature being witnessed.

19.   Power of Secretary of State to prescribe model articles

(1) The Secretary of State may by regulations prescribe model articles of association for companies.

(2) Different model articles may be prescribed for different descriptions of company.

(3) A company may adopt all or any of the provisions of model articles.

(4) Any amendment of model articles by regulations under this section does not affect a company registered before the amendment takes effect.

"Amendment" here includes addition, alteration or repeal.

(5) Regulations under this section are subject to negative resolution procedure.

GENERAL NOTE

This section replaces s.8 of the Companies Act 1985 (see also, in this regard, s.20 below). The Company Law Review recommended that the Secretary of State should have power to prescribe Model Articles to a wider range of companies than provided for in the 1985 Act and this recommendation is implemented by s.19(2) and certain provisions of s.20 (see below). As pointed out in the Explanatory Notes certain special types of companies are subject to regulations made under the Acts of Parliament creating them and these will continue to apply. The present set of Model Articles are contained in the Companies (Tables A-F) Regulations 1985 (SI 1985/805). It is only in relation to a company limited by shares that the Secretary of State is able to prescribe "default" articles, which will apply to the extent that, on registration, a company does not register its own articles or does not exclude the articles contained in SI 1985/805. This provision, in conjunction with s.20 (below), allows for default articles to be prescribed for a wider range of companies.

Subsections (1) and (2)

Section 19(1) and 19(2) enacts the basic power of the Secretary of State to prescribe model articles of association for companies and that there may be different model articles for different companies, as recommended by the Company Law Review (*Company Formation and Capital Maintenance*, para.2.22).

Subsection (3)

Section 19(3) provides that a company may adopt all or any of the model articles. As observed in the Explanatory Notes, adoption by reference is common and allows a company to incorporate such provisions in model articles as it thinks fit simply by noting which are to be adopted on registration.

Subsection (4)

This subsection maintains the *status quo* for companies registered before the amendment of model articles, amendment including an addition to, or alteration or repeal of, model articles as prescribed by the Secretary of State. As stated in the Explanatory Notes to the Act, the model articles in force at the time of registration of any given company will continue to apply to that company. The vast majority of registered companies are private companies limited by shares, and, as prescribed by this subsection, Table A of the Companies (Tables A to F) Regulations 1985 (SI 1985/ 805) will continue to apply to them (except, of course, to the extent that a company has registered articles which exclude or modify the model articles in Table A). However, existing registered companies, by virtue of s.19(3) will be free to adopt all or any of the model articles prescribed by the Secretary of State for companies registered under the 2006 Act. Indeed, and as observed in the Explanatory Notes (at para.71), existing companies may adopt any of the prescribed model articles, so that an existing private company limited by shares may, if it chooses, adopt model articles for a public company limited by shares. In such event, the company in question will have to follow the procedure for alteration of its articles as prescribed in s.21 (below).

Subsection (5)

Regulations prescribing model articles are subject to negative resolution procedure. This procedure requires a statutory instrument in question to be laid before Parliament. The House before which it is laid may then, within 40 days, proceed to have the instrument annulled.

20. Default application of model articles

(1) On the formation of a limited company-
   (a) if articles are not registered, or
   (b) if articles are registered, in so far as they do not exclude or modify the relevant model articles,

the relevant model articles (so far as applicable) form part of the company's articles in the same manner and to the same extent as if articles in the form of those articles had been duly registered.

(2) The "relevant model articles" means the model articles prescribed for a company of that description as in force at the date on which the company is registered.

GENERAL NOTE

This provision reproduces the effect of s.8(2) of the Companies Act 1985, and extends that effect to companies other than those limited by shares. Section 20, in conjunction with s.19 (above), provides freedom for companies to select appropriate articles of association, s.19 providing for adoption of any model articles prescribed by the Secretary of State and s.20 providing that such shall apply in the event that a company either does not register its own articles (s.20(1)(a)) or, if it does register articles, those articles do not exclude or modify the model articles for a company of that type. This provision, according to the Explanatory Notes, acts as a safety net which will provide for decision-making in the event that, on registration, a company fails to register articles or to include articles which do not deal with any particular matter.

Subsection (2)

The applicable (or "relevant") model articles are those in force at the time the company is formed and registered.

Alteration of articles

21. Amendment of articles

(1) A company may amend its articles by special resolution.
(2) In the case of a company that is a charity, this is subject to-
   (a) in England and Wales, section 64 of the Charities Act 1993 (c. 10);
   (b) in Northern Ireland, Article 9 of the Charities (Northern Ireland) Order 1987 (S.I. 1987/ 2048 (N.I. 19)).
(3) In the case of a company that is registered in the Scottish Charity Register, this is subject to-
   (a) section 112 of the Companies Act 1989 (c. 40), and

(b) section 16 of the Charities and Trustee Investment (Scotland) Act 2005 (asp 10).

GENERAL NOTE

Section 9 of the Companies Act 1985 provides that a company may amend its articles be special resolution and s.21(1) replaces s.9 and reproduces this power. Any amendment to the articles must be by special resolution.

Subsections (2) and (3)

The general power of alteration in s.21(1) is modified in the case of a company that is a charity. An alteration to either the memorandum or the articles of association in such a case will require the consent of the Commissioners, and subss.(2) and (3) reflect this in relation to charitable companies in England and Wales, in Northern Ireland and in Scotland.

22.   Entrenched provisions of the articles

(1) A company's articles may contain provision ("provision for entrenchment") to the effect that specified provisions of the articles may be amended or repealed only if conditions are met, or procedures are complied with, that are more restrictive than those applicable in the case of a special resolution.

(2) Provision for entrenchment may only be made-

(a) in the company's articles on formation, or

(b) by an amendment of the company's articles agreed to by all the members of the company.

(3) Provision for entrenchment does not prevent amendment of the company's articles-

(a) by agreement of all the members of the company, or

(b) by order of a court or other authority having power to alter the company's articles.

(4) Nothing in this section affects any power of a court or other authority to alter a company's articles.

GENERAL NOTE

The Company Law Review *Final Report* recommended that companies should be able to choose to "entrench" provisions of their constitutions in their articles. These are referred to in this section as "entrenched provisions". Section 17(2)(b) of the Companies Act 1985 provided for entrenchment where items that could have been contained in the articles of association were instead contained in the memorandum, but, given the provisions of s.8 (above), the memorandum will now be an unsuitable medium for this.

Subsection (1)

"Entrenched" provisions of the articles are those that may only be amended or repealed if specified conditions are met or procedures followed, these being more restrictive than those applicable in the case of a special resolution. Thus, entrenching provisions does not render the articles unalterable but rather alterable only according to the conditions or procedures specified, which will be stricter than the 75 per cent majority required for the passing of a special resolution. The subsection itself refers, without elaboration, to conditions that must be met or procedures that must be followed. It would seem, therefore, that these might include a higher majority threshold or, indeed, the consent of certain specified members (as, for example, in the case of *Russell v Northern Bank Development Corp* [1992] 3 All E.R. 161) or, perhaps, directors. It appears that it is for the company to determine what conditions or procedures are considered appropriate in this regard.

Subsection (2)

Provision for entrenchment may only be made in the articles on formation of the company (s.22(2)(a)) or, after formation, by amending the articles to entrench provisions with the consent of all the members of the company (s.22(2)(b)).

Subsection (3) and (4)

This provision states that a provision for entrenchment does not prevent the company's articles being amended by unanimous agreement of the members. It therefore reinforces the point that entrenchment cannot render articles unalterable. Further, provision for entrenchment does not prevent the company's articles being amended by order of the court or any other authority with power to order such an alteration, or, indeed, to make the alteration.

23. Notice to registrar of existence of restriction on amendment of articles

(1) Where a company's articles-
- (a) on formation contain provision for entrenchment,
- (b) are amended so as to include such provision, or
- (c) are altered by order of a court or other authority so as to restrict or exclude the power of the company to amend its articles,

the company must give notice of that fact to the registrar.

(2) Where a company's articles-
- (a) are amended so as to remove provision for entrenchment, or
- (b) are altered by order of a court or other authority-
    - (i) so as to remove such provision, or
    - (ii) so as to remove any other restriction on, or any exclusion of, the power of the company to amend its articles,

the company must give notice of that fact to the registrar.

GENERAL NOTE

This new provision prescribes the formalities required on the entrenchment of elements of the articles of association (see note to s.22, above). Whether such items are entrenched in the articles on formation or subsequently by amendment the company must give notice to the registrar (s.23(1)(a), (b)). Where a company's articles are altered by court (or other) order so as to restrict or exclude the company's power to amend its articles, the company must give notice to the registrar (s.23(1)(c)). Where articles containing a provision for entrenchment are amended so as to remove that provision, either by the company or by court or other order, the company must notify the registrar (s.23(2)).

24. Statement of compliance where amendment of articles restricted

(1) This section applies where a company's articles are subject-
- (a) to provision for entrenchment, or
- (b) to an order of a court or other authority restricting or excluding the company's power to amend the articles.

(2) If the company-
- (a) amends its articles, and
- (b) is required to send to the registrar a document making or evidencing the amendment,

the company must deliver with that document a statement of compliance.

(3) The statement of compliance required is a statement certifying that the amendment has been made in accordance with the company's articles and, where relevant, any applicable order of a court or other authority.

(4) The registrar may rely on the statement of compliance as sufficient evidence of the matters stated in it.

GENERAL NOTE

This new provision supplements ss.22 and 23. It applies where a company's articles are subject to provision for entrenchment or where a court or other order restricts or excludes the company's power to amend its articles. If an amendment to the articles is made which is required to be sent to the registrar, the document making or evidencing the amendment must be accompanied by a statement of compliance (subs.(2)), which must certify that the amendment has been made in accordance with the company's articles and, where appropriate, a court or other order (subs.(3)). This statement may be relied upon by the registrar as sufficient evidence of the matters stated in it (subs.(4)).

25. Effect of alteration of articles on company's members

(1) A member of a company is not bound by an alteration to its articles after the date on which he became a member, if and so far as the alteration-

    (a) requires him to take or subscribe for more shares than the number held by him at the date on which the alteration is made, or

    (b) in any way increases his liability as at that date to contribute to the company's share capital or otherwise to pay money to the company.

  (2) Subsection (1) does not apply in a case where the member agrees in writing, either before or after the alteration is made, to be bound by the alteration.

GENERAL NOTE

This section replaces s.16 of the Companies Act 1985 without substantive amendment. With the articles of association now substantially replacing the memorandum of association as the source of the company's constitution, it provides that an alteration of the articles will only be effective to require a member of the company at the date of the alteration to take more shares in the company or to increase his liability to contribute to the company's share capital (or otherwise pay money to it) if that member agrees in writing, either before or after the alteration, to by bound by it.

26.   Registrar to be sent copy of amended articles

  (1) Where a company amends its articles it must send to the registrar a copy of the articles as amended not later than 15 days after the amendment takes effect.

  (2) This section does not require a company to set out in its articles any provisions of model articles that-

    (a) are applied by the articles, or

    (b) apply by virtue of section 20 (default application of model articles).

  (3) If a company fails to comply with this section an offence is committed by-

    (a) the company, and

    (b) every officer of the company who is in default.

  (4) A person guilty of an offence under this section is liable on summary conviction to a fine not exceeding level 3 on the standard scale and, for continued contravention, a daily default fine not exceeding one-tenth of level 3 on the standard scale.

GENERAL NOTE

This provision replaces s.18(2) of the Companies Act 1985. As a company's articles of association are subject to the disclosure requirements of the First Company Law Directive (68/151/EEC), being "statutes" of constitution, any amendment to them must be disclosed (Art. 2(1)(b)).

Subsection (1)

Where articles of association are amended the company must, not more than 15 days after the amendment takes place, send a copy of the amended articles to the registrar.

Subsection (2)

Where provisions of the model articles as prescribed by the Secretary of State are applied by the company's own articles or by default under s.20, an amendment to the articles does not require the setting out in the articles any provisions of the model articles. It should be noted that Art.2(1)(d) of Directive 68/151/EEC requires, after amendment of the "statutes" (i.e. the articles) disclosure of "... the complete text of the instrument or statutes as amended to date".

Subsections (3) and (4)

Failure to comply with the requirements of this section constitutes an offence which is committed by the company and every one of its officers who is in default, the penalty for which is set out in subs.(4).

27.   Registrar's notice to comply in case of failure with respect to amended articles

  (1) If it appears to the registrar that a company has failed to comply with any enactment requiring it-

(a) to send to the registrar a document making or evidencing an alteration in the company's articles, or
(b) to send to the registrar a copy of the company's articles as amended,

the registrar may give notice to the company requiring it to comply.

(2) The notice must-
  (a) state the date on which it is issued, and
  (b) require the company to comply within 28 days from that date.

(3) If the company complies with the notice within the specified time, no criminal proceedings may be brought in respect of the failure to comply with the enactment mentioned in subsection (1).

(4) If the company does not comply with the notice within the specified time, it is liable to a civil penalty of £200.

This is in addition to any liability to criminal proceedings in respect of the failure mentioned in subsection (1).

(5) The penalty may be recovered by the registrar and is to be paid into the Consolidated Fund.

GENERAL NOTE

This is a new provision which allows the registrar of companies, on becoming aware of a failure on the part of the company to comply with the requirement in s.26 (or in any other enactment, for example, s.18(2) of the Companies Act 1985) to issue a notice to the company requiring compliance. Failure to comply with this notice renders the company liable to a civil penalty of £200 in addition to any criminal liability arising under s.26(3). The company is, however, afforded a chance to avoid criminal proceedings under that section by complying with the registrar's notice within 28 days of its issue. If compliance occurs then no criminal proceedings may be brought under s.26(3) (s.27(3)).

Supplementary

28. Existing companies: provisions of memorandum treated as provisions of articles

(1) Provisions that immediately before the commencement of this Part were contained in a company's memorandum but are not provisions of the kind mentioned in section 8 (provisions of new-style memorandum) are to be treated after the commencement of this Part as provisions of the company's articles.

(2) This applies not only to substantive provisions but also to provision for entrenchment (as defined in section 22).

(3) The provisions of this Part about provision for entrenchment apply to such provision as they apply to provision made on the company's formation, except that the duty under section 23(1)(a) to give notice to the registrar does not apply.

GENERAL NOTE

This is a new provision which addresses the fact that companies formed and registered before the coming into force of the 2006 Act will, in their memorandum of association, have recorded information that, for companies formed and registered under the 2006 Act, will be recorded in the articles of association. The section provides that such information ("provisions of the memorandum") will be treated as provisions of the articles, and so subject to any provision of the 2006 Act relating to the articles of association.

Subsection (1)

This subsection enacts the basic rule that any provisions of the memorandum (other than those provisions in s.8 (see above)) immediately before the commencement of Pt 3, are, after the coming into force of Pt 3, to be treated as provisions of the articles.

Subsection (2)

It may be that the memorandum contains what are now termed "provisions for entrenchment" (see note to s.22, above). Where this is the case, such entrenched provisions fall to be treated as provisions of the articles under the basic rule in subs.(1).

Subsection (3)

Provisions of the memorandum which are to be treated as entrenched provisions of the articles are to be subject to ss.22-24 of the Act. This subsection appears to be directed towards relieving the company of the obligation, in s.23 of the Act, to notify the registrar of any amendment to the articles to include an entrenching provision. An amendment removing an entrenched provision (of the memorandum, which is now treated as an entrenched provision of the articles) will now subject to the notification requirement under s.24 (see above).

Chapter 3

Resolutions and Agreements Affecting a Company's Constitution

29. Resolutions and agreements affecting a company's constitution

(1) This Chapter applies to-
  (a) any special resolution;
  (b) any resolution or agreement agreed to by all the members of a company that, if not so agreed to, would not have been effective for its purpose unless passed as a special resolution;
  (c) any resolution or agreement agreed to by all the members of a class of shareholders that, if not so agreed to, would not have been effective for its purpose unless passed by some particular majority or otherwise in some particular manner;
  (d) any resolution or agreement that effectively binds all members of a class of shareholders though not agreed to by all those members;
  (e) any other resolution or agreement to which this Chapter applies by virtue of any enactment.
(2) References in subsection (1) to a member of a company, or of a class of members of a company, do not include the company itself where it is such a member by virtue only of its holding shares as treasury shares.

GENERAL NOTE

This provision is the first of Ch.3 of Pt 3 and records all those resolutions and agreements that affect the corporate constitution. It replaces s.380(4) of the Companies Act 1985.

30. Copies of resolutions or agreements to be forwarded to registrar

(1) A copy of every resolution or agreement to which this Chapter applies, or (in the case of a resolution or agreement that is not in writing) a written memorandum setting out its terms, must be forwarded to the registrar within 15 days after it is passed or made.
(2) If a company fails to comply with this section, an offence is committed by-
  (a) the company, and
  (b) every officer of it who is in default.
(3) A person guilty of an offence under this section is liable on summary conviction to a fine not exceeding level 3 on the standard scale and, for continued contravention, a daily default fine not exceeding one-tenth of level 3 on the standard scale.
(4) For the purposes of this section, a liquidator of the company is treated as an officer of it.

GENERAL NOTE

This provision replaces s.380(1), (5) and (7) of the Companies Act 1985. Where any resolution is passed, or agreement made, which falls under s.29 a copy of the resolution or agreement (or, where the resolution or agreement is not in writing, a written memorandum setting out its terms) must be delivered to the registrar within 15 days after the resolution is passed or the agreement made (s.30(1)). Failure to comply with the requirements of this section constitutes an offence committed by the company and by every officer of the company who is in default (including a liquidator of the company, but not an administrator (s.30(2), (4)). The penalty for an offence under this section is set out in subs.(3).

CHAPTER 4

MISCELLANEOUS AND SUPPLEMENTARY PROVISIONS

Statement of company's objects

31. Statement of company's objects

(1) Unless a company's articles specifically restrict the objects of the company, its objects are unrestricted.

(2) Where a company amends its articles so as to add, remove or alter a statement of the company's objects-

   (a) it must give notice to the registrar,

   (b) on receipt of the notice, the registrar shall register it, and

   (c) the amendment is not effective until entry of that notice on the register.

(3) Any such amendment does not affect any rights or obligations of the company or render defective any legal proceedings by or against it.

(4) In the case of a company that is a charity, the provisions of this section have effect subject to-

   (a) in England and Wales, section 64 of the Charities Act 1993 (c. 10);

   (b) in Northern Ireland, Article 9 of the Charities (Northern Ireland) Order 1987 (S.I. 1987/2048 (N.I. 19)).

(5) In the case of a company that is entered in the Scottish Charity Register, the provisions of this section have effect subject to the provisions of the Charities and Trustee Investment (Scotland) Act 2005 (asp 10).

GENERAL NOTE

Under s.2(1)(c) of the Companies Act 1985, all companies were required, in s.3 of the memorandum of association, to state the company's objects. Section 3A of that Act provides that a company may state that its object is to carry on business as a general commercial company, which means that the object is to carry on any trade or business whatsoever, with power to do all such things incidental or conducive to that object. This provision, inserted by s.110(1) of the Companies Act 1989, was intended to avoid the problems caused by the *ultra vires* doctrine, which regarded the statement of a company's objects as limiting its capacity to activities in pursuit of those objects. This doctrine was inconvenient for members, who would have to effect an alteration to the memorandum of association if it was considered expedient for the company to pursue new objects, ratification of what was a nullity being impossible. It was also potentially prejudicial for those dealing with the company, who were taken to have constructive notice of the provisions of the memorandum and who might therefore find themselves unable to enforce against the company obligations which the company, by virtue of the *ultra vires* doctrine, has no capacity to incur (see, for example, *Ashbury Railway Carriage and Iron Company v Hector Riche* (1874-75) L.R. 7 H.L. 653; *Jon Beauforte (London) Ltd, Re* [1953] Ch. 131).

The 2006 Act takes a different approach to the question of corporate capacity. Rather than *allowing* companies to adopt what in effect are unrestricted objects (by recourse to s.3A, for example) it provides that, unless the company chooses to restrict its objects, those objects will be unlimited. This approach is based on a recommendation of the Company Law Review. Where no restriction is made, as the Company Law Review points out: "Those doing business with such a company would no longer need to concern themselves with the question whether the company has capacity to enter into a transaction ..." (*Final Report*, para.9.10). The position of members of such a company is safeguarded in two ways. They may, on formation, restrict the company's capacity by specifying objects in its articles of association. Whilst this will not be effective to prevent third parties from enforcing against the company a transaction not within its capacity (see note to s.39, below), the members will nevertheless be able to pursue the company's directors for any loss or damage resulting from their failure to observe to corporate constitution (see note to s.171, below).

Subsection (1)

This provision enacts the basic principle that a company will have unlimited objects unless its articles specifically restrict its objects. It will apply to companies formed and registered after the 2006 Act comes into force. For companies formed and registered under the Companies Act 1985 (or any preceding enactment), the objects clause in the memorandum of association will now be treated as a provision of the articles (see note to s.28, above) and to the extent that the company has not stated that its object is to carry on business as a general commercial company (under s.3A Companies Act 1985 (see General Note, above)) will continue to restrict the company's capacity.

Subsection (2)

A company may alter or amend its articles so as to add or remove a statement of the company's objects. If this occurs, notice must be given to the registrar of companies who, on receipt of the notice, is required to register it. The amendment does not take effect until the notice is entered on the register.

Subsection (3)

Any amendment of the objects of the company takes effect prospectively only. Thus, to the extent that a company amends its articles to restrict its objects, this has no effect on obligations it has already incurred or on any legal proceedings already issued against it. Equally, any amendment does not affect any pre-existing rights of the company, or proceedings issued by it.

Subsections (4) and (5)

Companies which are charities are subject to additional requirements when they propose to amend their constitution in any way. In general, such an alteration requires the consent of the Commissioners and will be ineffective unless such consent is acquired (s.64(2)(a) of the Charities Act 1993, and see the corresponding provisions for companies which are charities in Northern Ireland and in Scotland). These subsections preserve these requirements.

Other provisions with respect to a company's constitution

32. Constitutional documents to be provided to members

(1) A company must, on request by any member, send to him the following documents-
    (a) an up-to-date copy of the company's articles;
    (b) a copy of any resolution or agreement relating to the company to which Chapter 3 applies (resolutions and agreements affecting a company's constitution) and that is for the time being in force;
    (c) a copy of any document required to be sent to the registrar under-
        (i) section 34(2) (notice where company's constitution altered by enactment), or
        (ii) section 35(2)(a) (notice where order of court or other authority alters company's constitution);
    (d) a copy of any court order under section 899 (order sanctioning compromise or arrangement) or section 900 (order facilitating reconstruction or amalgamation);
    (e) a copy of any court order under section 996 (protection of members against unfair prejudice: powers of the court) that alters the company's constitution;
    (f) a copy of the company's current certificate of incorporation, and of any past certificates of incorporation;
    (g) in the case of a company with a share capital, a current statement of capital;
    (h) in the case of a company limited by guarantee, a copy of the statement of guarantee.
(2) The statement of capital required by subsection (1)(g) is a statement of-
    (a) the total number of shares of the company,
    (b) the aggregate nominal value of those shares,
    (c) for each class of shares-
        (i) prescribed particulars of the rights attached to the shares,

    (ii) the total number of shares of that class, and

    (iii) the aggregate nominal value of shares of that class, and

  (d) the amount paid up and the amount (if any) unpaid on each share (whether on account of the nominal value of the share or by way of premium).

(3) If a company makes default in complying with this section, an offence is committed by every officer of the company who is in default.

(4) A person guilty of an offence under this section is liable on summary conviction to a fine not exceeding level 3 on the standard scale.

GENERAL NOTE

This provision replaces s.19 of the Companies Act 1985, which makes provision for members to require the company to send to them a copy of the memorandum and the articles of association, and a copy of any Act of Parliament which alters the memorandum. Section 32 expands upon the documents that a member may call for and removes the right of the company to levy a (maximum) charge of 5p for a copy of the memorandum and the articles.

Subsection (1)

A member may now require to company to send to him, free of charge, an up-to-date copy of the company's articles, copies of any of the resolutions or agreements to which Ch.3 applies, a copy of any document required to be sent to the registrar under s.34(2) or s.35(2)(a), a copy of the company's current certificate of incorporation, and of any past certificates of incorporation, a current statement of capital or a statement of guarantee (depending upon whether the company is limited by shares or by guarantee). A member may also require copies of court orders made under ss.899, 900 and 996 (sanctioning compromises or arrangements, facilitating reconstructions or amalgamations or protecting members against unfair prejudice respectively).

Subsection (2)

This subsection expands upon what is meant by a "current statement of capital" in subs.(1)(g). It corresponds roughly to the statement of capital required to be delivered to the registrar with an application for registration (see note to s.10, above) but must obviously be up-to-date.

Subsections (3) and (4)

Failure to comply with this provision is an offence on the part of the company and any officer in default, the penalty being prescribed by subs.(4).

33. Effect of company's constitution

(1) The provisions of a company's constitution bind the company and its members to the same extent as if there were covenants on the part of the company and of each member to observe those provisions.

(2) Money payable by a member to the company under its constitution is a debt due from him to the company.

In England and Wales and Northern Ireland it is of the nature of an ordinary contract debt.

GENERAL NOTE

This provision replaces s.14 of the Companies Act 1985 and reproduces its general effect that the constitutional documents of the company (which were, under that Act, the memorandum and articles of association) constitute a "statutory" or "special" contract the terms of which bind the company and its members (see, e.g. *Welton v Saffery* [1897] A.C. 299 at 315, per Lord Herschell). The explanatory notes state that this contract is one that is enforceable *only* by the company and its members (in their capacity as members) and so is excepted from the general principle in s.1 of the Contracts (Rights of Third Parties) Act 1999. Further, the notes state explicitly that the new wording of the section is not intended to alter the existing principles established by case law.

Subsection (1)

The reference in this subsection to "the provisions of a company's constitution" replaces the reference to "the memorandum and articles" in its predecessor, s.14 of the Companies Act 1985. This reflects the fact that the company's constitution is now largely contained in the articles and other constitutional documents as prescribed by the Act.

Subsection (2)

Any money due from a member of the company to the company under its constitution is, in England and Wales and Northern Ireland, a debt in the nature of an ordinary contract debt. This subsection replaces s.14(2) of the Companies Act 1985.

34. Notice to registrar where company's constitution altered by enactment

(1) This section applies where a company's constitution is altered by an enactment, other than an enactment amending the general law.

(2) The company must give notice of the alteration to the registrar, specifying the enactment, not later than 15 days after the enactment comes into force.

In the case of a special enactment the notice must be accompanied by a copy of the enactment.

(3) If the enactment amends-

     (a) the company's articles, or

     (b) a resolution or agreement to which Chapter 3 applies (resolutions and agreements affecting a company's constitution),

the notice must be accompanied by a copy of the company's articles, or the resolution or agreement in question, as amended.

(4) A "special enactment" means an enactment that is not a public general enactment, and includes-

     (a) an Act for confirming a provisional order,

     (b) any provision of a public general Act in relation to the passing of which any of the standing orders of the House of Lords or the House of Commons relating to Private Business applied, or

     (c) any enactment to the extent that it is incorporated in or applied for the purposes of a special enactment.

(5) If a company fails to comply with this section an offence is committed by-

     (a) the company, and

     (b) every officer of the company who is in default.

(6) A person guilty of an offence under this section is liable on summary conviction to a fine not exceeding level 3 on the standard scale and, for continued contravention, a daily default fine not exceeding one-tenth of level 3 on the standard scale.

GENERAL NOTE

This section makes provision for the possibility that a company's constitution may be altered by an enactment other than a public general act. The Explanatory Notes give, as examples of provisions in public general acts affecting a company's constitution, a provision in a new Companies Act rendering certain types of article void (a provision of general relevance to all companies) or new commonhold legislation changing the provisions to be included in the articles of commonhold associations. These would be "enactments amending the general law" (s.34(1)) and this section does not apply where a company's constitution is altered by such an enactment.

In contrast, certain Acts of Parliament, described as "special enactments" in subs.(4) of this section, will be of relevance only to a specific company (the example given in the explanatory notes is of a private Act of Parliament amending the articles of a specific company established by an earlier Act). This section requires a company whose constitution is amended by a "special enactment" to send to the registrar a notice of the alteration to the registrar, specifying the enactment and a copy of the special enactment. The company must comply with the requirement not later than 15 days after the enactment comes into force. The rationale behind distinguishing between enactments amending the general law and special enactments is that, whilst it is thought appropriate that those searching the register of companies be kept informed of any constitutional amendments, a balance has to be struck between complete transparency and "inundating the registrar and searchers with mountains of paper which will be of little use to them" (Explanatory Notes). As enactments amending the general law will, in any event, be in the public domain, it is thought reasonable to exempt companies from having to send a notice of alteration to the registrar under this section. It only applies, therefore, in the case of "special enactments" as defined by subs.(4).

Failure to comply with the requirements of this section constitutes an offence by the company and every one of its officers who is in default under subs.(5). The penalty for the offence is prescribed in subs.(6).

35.   Notice to registrar where company's constitution altered by order

(1) Where a company's constitution is altered by an order of a court or other authority, the company must give notice to the registrar of the alteration not later than 15 days after the alteration takes effect.

(2) The notice must be accompanied by-

    (a) a copy of the order, and

    (b) if the order amends-

        (i) the company's articles, or

        (ii) a resolution or agreement to which Chapter 3 applies (resolutions and agreements affecting the company's constitution),

    a copy of the company's articles, or the resolution or agreement in question, as amended.

(3) If a company fails to comply with this section an offence is committed by-

    (a) the company, and

    (b) every officer of the company who is in default.

(4) A person guilty of an offence under this section is liable on summary conviction to a fine not exceeding level 3 on the standard scale and, for continued contravention, a daily default fine not exceeding one-tenth of level 3 on the standard scale.

(5) This section does not apply where provision is made by another enactment for the delivery to the registrar of a copy of the order in question.

GENERAL NOTE

As well as a company's constitution being amended by a general or special enactment under s.34 (above), such an alteration may occur by court order or by the order of some other authority (for example, the Charity Commissioners). This new provision requires the company to notify the registrar of such an alteration not later than 15 days after it takes effect. It does not apply where another enactment provides for delivery of a copy of the order to the registrar (subs.(5)).

Subsection (2)

This subsection requires the notice to the registrar required under subs.(1) to be accompanied by a copy of the order in question and, if it amends the company's articles or any resolution or agreement to which Ch.3 applies (see, for details of these, note to s.29 above), a copy of the amended articles, resolution or agreement as the case may be.

Subsections (3) abd (4)

Failure to comply with the requirements of this section constitutes an offence by the company and every one of its officers who is in default under subs.(3). The penalty for the offence is prescribed in subs.(4).

36.   Documents to be incorporated in or accompany copies of articles issued by company

(1) Every copy of a company's articles issued by the company must be accompanied by-

    (a) a copy of any resolution or agreement relating to the company to which Chapter 3 applies (resolutions and agreements affecting a company's constitution),

    (b) where the company has been required to give notice to the registrar under section 34(2) (notice where company's constitution altered by enactment), a statement that the enactment in question alters the effect of the company's constitution,

    (c) where the company's constitution is altered by a special enactment (see section 34(4)), a copy of the enactment, and

    (d) a copy of any order required to be sent to the registrar under section 35(2)(a) (order of court or other authority altering company's constitution).

(2) This does not require the articles to be accompanied by a copy of a document or by a statement if-

    (a) the effect of the resolution, agreement, enactment or order (as the case may be) on the company's constitution has been incorporated into the articles by amendment, or

(b) the resolution, agreement, enactment or order (as the case may be) is not for the time being in force.

(3) If the company fails to comply with this section, an offence is committed by every officer of the company who is in default.

(4) A person guilty of an offence under this section is liable on summary conviction to a fine not exceeding level 3 on the standard scale for each occasion on which copies are issued, or, as the case may be, requested.

(5) For the purposes of this section, a liquidator of the company is treated as an officer of it.

GENERAL NOTE

This section specifies which documents are to be incorporated in or accompany any copies of its articles issued by the company (whether to its members or otherwise). These are copies of resolutions or agreements affecting the company's constitution to which Ch.3 applies, copies of any notice required by s.34(2) or (4) and any order required by s.35(2)(a) (subs.(1)). There is no requirement for documents to be sent with the articles where the effect of the resolution, agreement enactment or order has already been incorporated in the articles or has yet to come into force (subs.(2)). Failure to comply with the requirements of this section constitutes an offence by the company and every one of its officers who is in default under subs.(3) and the penalty for the offence is prescribed in subs.(4). A liquidator of the company (but not an administrator) is treated as an officer of the company for the purposes of the section (subs.(5)).

Supplementary provisions

37. Right to participate in profits otherwise than as member void

In the case of a company limited by guarantee and not having a share capital any provision in the company's articles, or in any resolution of the company, purporting to give a person a right to participate in the divisible profits of the company otherwise than as a member is void.

GENERAL NOTE

This provision replaces s.15 of the Companies Act 1985. It applies only to a company limited by guarantee and not having a share capital and provides that any provision in the articles or any resolution of the members of the company which purports to give a person (including a member other than in his capacity as a member) a right to share in the company's divisible profits is void.

38. Application to single member companies of enactments and rules of law

Any enactment or rule of law applicable to companies formed by two or more persons or having two or more members applies with any necessary modification in relation to a company formed by one person or having only one person as a member.

GENERAL NOTE

As provided by s.7(1) of the Act (see above), it is now possible for a single person to form any type of company provided for in Pt 1 of the Act. This provision states that any enactment or rule of law applicable to companies formed by two or more persons now applies, with any necessary modification, to "single-member companies". As observed in the Explanatory Notes, this is already provided for in the case of private limited companies in the Companies (Single Member Private Limited Companies) Regulations 1992 (SI 1992/1699).

PART 4

A COMPANY'S CAPACITY AND RELATED MATTERS

GENERAL NOTE

This Part of the Act replaces various provisions of Ch.3 of Pt 1 of the Companies Act 1985, and makes some substantive changes to the rules of law contained therein. It is largely concerned with the effect of provisions in the corporate constitution which limit the company's capacity and with the effect of provisions in the constitution which purport to limit the power of corporate directors to commit the company to legally enforceable obligations. It also deals with the formalities of doing business under the law of England and Wales, Northern Ireland and Scotland as far as these relate to the authority of corporate agents, the affixation of the company's seal to corporate documents and the execution of deeds. Finally, it addresses the question of the use of the company's common seal abroad, the effect of pre-incorporation contracts and the endorsement, on behalf of the company, of bills of exchange and promissory notes.

Capacity of company and power of directors to bind it

39. A company's capacity

(1) The validity of an act done by a company shall not be called into question on the ground of lack of capacity by reason of anything in the company's constitution.

(2) This section has effect subject to section 42 (companies that are charities).

GENERAL NOTE

This provision replaces s.35(1) of the Companies Act 1985. The original text of s.35(1) referred to "anything in the company's memorandum", as it was the memorandum that called for a statement of the company's objects which, as noted above (see note to s.31), could operate to limit corporate capacity. The requirement to specify corporate objects has been replaced by an option to do so. If a company chooses to state its objects this statement will now be found in the company's articles, hence the change in wording in s.39(1) of the Companies Act 2006, which refers to anything in "the company's constitution".

In effect, however, the two provisions are substantially the same. If there is any limitation on corporate capacity (which may be as to the company's objects or, indeed, as to the kinds of transactions it can enter into) it will not render any act by the company carried out in contravention of the limitation invalid. Thus, a counterparty will be able to enforce an obligation incurred by the company even where the company acts in contravention of its constitution.

A more noteworthy change to the law contained in the Companies Act 1985 is the omission of any provision equivalent to s.35(2). This provision allowed a member of the company to bring proceedings to restrain what would, but for s.35(1), amount to an ultra vires act. The internal consequence of the objects clause was thereby preserved and, in effect, s.35(2) enabled members to make a "pre-emptive strike" against proposed acts that would be beyond the company's capacity. The s.35(2) entitlement could not be invoked in respect of acts done in fulfilment of legal obligations already incurred. Section 39 contains no corresponding provision. According to the Explanatory Notes, this was considered unnecessary for two main reasons. Firstly, a statement of objects is no longer a legal requirement in the formation of a company and, unless the company positively elects to include a statement of objects in its articles it will be taken to have unlimited capacity (see note to s.31, above). Secondly, directors under the Companies Act 2006 will be subject to a statutory duty to act in accordance with the company's constitution (see note to s.171, below). Thus, to the extent that a company opts to include a statement of its objects in its articles, and to the extent that the company's directors are in any way involved in causing the company to act in contravention of this or any other provision in the constitution which limits the company's capacity, they will have committed a breach of statutory duty and will be in breach of their duty to the company. Section 171 stands in, therefore, for s.35(3) of the Companies Act 1985, for which this Part of the 2006 Act contains no equivalent. It is also probably worth remarking that the ability of members to bring derivative claims in respect of a breach of duty of this nature is probably rendered a more straightforward matter by s.260 of the 2006 Act, so that a breach of the duty to observe the company's constitution may be more easy to pursue than previously.

One further point should be made here. Under s.35(3) of the Companies Act 1985 it was open to members to ratify the ultra vires act by special resolution and to relieve the directors from liability by a separate special resolution. No such explicit provision appears in this Part of the Act, and whilst s.39(1) allows that an ultra vires act on the part of the company is enforceable against it, it says nothing of the internal implications.

Subsection (4)

The general principle in subs.(1) is subject to s.42 (see below).

40. Power of directors to bind the company

(1) In favour of a person dealing with a company in good faith, the power of the directors to bind the company, or authorise others to do so, is deemed to be free of any limitation under the company's constitution.

(2) For this purpose-

    (a) a person "deals with" a company if he is a party to any transaction or other act to which the company is a party,

    (b) a person dealing with a company-

        (i) is not bound to enquire as to any limitation on the powers of the directors to bind the company or authorise others to do so,

        (ii) is presumed to have acted in good faith unless the contrary is proved, and

        (iii) is not to be regarded as acting in bad faith by reason only of his knowing that an act is beyond the powers of the directors under the company's constitution.

(3) The references above to limitations on the directors' powers under the company's constitution include limitations deriving-

    (a) from a resolution of the company or of any class of shareholders, or

    (b) from any agreement between the members of the company or of any class of shareholders.

(4) This section does not affect any right of a member of the company to bring proceedings to restrain the doing of an action that is beyond the powers of the directors.

But no such proceedings lie in respect of an act to be done in fulfilment of a legal obligation arising from a previous act of the company.

(5) This section does not affect any liability incurred by the directors, or any other person, by reason of the directors' exceeding their powers.

(6) This section has effect subject to-

section 41 (transactions with directors or their associates), and

section 42 (companies that are charities).

GENERAL NOTE

This section replaces s.35A Companies Act 1985 and is intended, as was s.35A, to protect third parties dealing with the company in good faith from any internal restrictions contained in (usually) the articles of association which limited the power of the board to act on the company's behalf. For example, where the articles contained a provision to the effect that contracts over a certain value required the unanimous consent of the board, and a contract of that nature was entered into without unanimous consent, the counterparty could rely on s.35A to enforce the contract against the company as long as he was dealing with the company in good faith. Equally, where the authorisation of another person to act on behalf of the company required, say, the unanimous consent of the board, a third party in good faith could rely on the section to "cure" consent defectively delivered. The section therefore reflected, and to some degree extended, the "indoor management rule" from *Royal British Bank v Turquand* (1856) All E.R. Rep 435. This rule effectively states that a person dealing in good faith with a company is entitled to assume that any internal procedures contained in the constitution had been properly complied with.

Subsection (1)

This provision replaces, and virtually reproduces, s.35A(1) of the Companies Act 1985. There is, however, a change in the wording. Section 35A(1) refers to "the power of the *board of directors* to bind the company", whereas s.40(1) refers to "the power of the *directors* to bind the company". There is nothing in the explanatory notes or any Parliamentary debates to amplify on the intention, if any, behind this change of wording. It may simply reflect a general desire to simplify drafting style, but this is perhaps unlikely considering that the reference to the power *of the board of directors* is hardly complex. A more likely explanation is that the reference to the power of the *directors* reflects the explicit view of Robert Walker L.J. in *Smith v Henniker-Major & Co* [2002] EWCA Civ 762 to the effect that a third party who deals with an inquorate board may nevertheless rely on s.35A, the quorum provision simply being a limitation contained in the company's constitution (*cf.* the decision of Rimer J., at first instance, who considered that a decision of a quorate board was a condition precedent to reliance on s.35A).

The reference to directors in the plural might be taken to exclude the acts of individual directors acting otherwise than in accordance with the constitution from the protective effect of s.40(1). However, it might also conceivably be argued that, by virtue of s.40, each *individual director* now has effectively unlimited power to commit the company to obligations if the party with whom he transacts on behalf of the company deals with it in good faith. This would represent a significant change in the current law, which calls for such a third party to demonstrate that an individual director has *apparent authority* to commit its corporate principal to an obligation (see, for example, *Freeman & Lockyer v Buckhurst Park Properties (Mangal) Ltd* [1964] 1 All E.R. 630). With no explicit statement to this effect in debates or the explanatory notes, this is perhaps an ambitious construction of the section, but arguably not entirely outlandish. Section 35A was enacted in order to give effect to Art.9(2) of the First Company Law Directive (68/151/EEC), which provides that "The limits on the powers of the organs of the company, arising under the statutes or from a decision of the competent organs, may never be relied on as against third parties, even if they have been disclosed." Section 35A treats the board of directors as one of the "organs" of the company, and therefore the question arises whether each of its directors, acting individually, is for the future to be treated in the same way by virtue of s.40(1). As noted above, this is certainly implausible, but perhaps not impossible.

Subsection (2)

Subsection 2(a) reproduces exactly s.35A(2)(a) of the 1985 Act. It defines when a person can be said to be "dealing" with the company for the purposes of s.40(1). In relation to s.35A(2)(a) it has been held that a shareholder receiving bonus shares from the company does not "deal" with it: see *EIC Services Ltd v Phipps* [2004] EWCA Civ 1069. This same case also raises, without definitively answering, the question of whether a member of the company can ever be "a person" dealing with the company for the purposes of the section. Given that s.40(2)(a) is in the exact same terms as s.35A(2)(a), this can be taken to remain good law.

Subsection 2(b)(i) replaces s.35B of the Companies Act 1985. It absolves a person dealing with the company from any duty to enquire as to the existence of limitations on the powers of directors to bind the company or authorise others to do so. Again, the wording here refers to the power of *the directors* rather than the power of the board, as in s.35B. Subsection 2(b)(ii) and (iii) replaces subsection 35A(2)(b) and (c) of the 1985 Act, and provides for a rebuttable presumption that a party dealing with a company acts in good faith, and that the presumption is not rebutted by knowledge on the part of that party that the act to which he is a counterparty is beyond the powers of the directors under the company's constitution. It is not entirely clear in what circumstance the presumption of good faith will be rebutted if knowledge of the directors' want of power is inadequate in this regard. It is tentatively suggested that what is required is evidence of conduct on the third party's part that might amount to knowing assistance in a breach of trust, or, if property passes to the third party under the agreement, knowing receipt of trust property (see, for possible support for this contention, *Criterion Properties Plc v Stratford UK Properties LLC* [2004] UKHL 28).

Subsection (3)

This subsection replaces the equivalent s.35A(3) of the Companies Act 1985. Whilst limitations on directors' powers would usually be found in the articles of association, this provision makes it clear that the protective effect of s.40 extends to circumstances where the limitation in question derives from corporate resolutions, from any class of shareholders or from any shareholder agreement, whether of the members generally or of a class of shareholders.

Subsection (4)

This subsection replaces s.35A(4) of the Companies Act 1985. It retains the right of members of the company to bring proceedings to restrain corporate directors from acting beyond their powers under the corporate constitution, but only where such action has not already given rise to a legal obligation on the part of the company. In other words, only a pre-emptive action is possible.

Subsection (5)

This is an equivalent provision to s.35A(5) of the 1985 Act, which in terms retained the internal consequences of the directors acting beyond their powers. To the extent that the directors exceed their constitutional powers they will be in breach of s.171 (see below) and liable accordingly.

41. Constitutional limitations: transactions involving directors or their associates

(1) This section applies to a transaction if or to the extent that its validity depends on section 40 (power of directors deemed to be free of limitations under company's constitution in favour of person dealing with company in good faith).

Nothing in this section shall be read as excluding the operation of any other enactment or rule of law by virtue of which the transaction may be called in question or any liability to the company may arise.

(2) Where-
   (a) a company enters into such a transaction, and
   (b) the parties to the transaction include-
      (i) a director of the company or of its holding company, or
      (ii) a person connected with any such director,
the transaction is voidable at the instance of the company.

(3) Whether or not it is avoided, any such party to the transaction as is mentioned in subsection (2)(b)(i) or (ii), and any director of the company who authorised the transaction, is liable-

    (a) to account to the company for any gain he has made directly or indirectly by the transaction, and

    (b) to indemnify the company for any loss or damage resulting from the transaction.

(4) The transaction ceases to be voidable if-

    (a) restitution of any money or other asset which was the subject matter of the transaction is no longer possible, or

    (b) the company is indemnified for any loss or damage resulting from the transaction, or

    (c) rights acquired bona fide for value and without actual notice of the directors' exceeding their powers by a person who is not party to the transaction would be affected by the avoidance, or

    (d) the transaction is affirmed by the company.

(5) A person other than a director of the company is not liable under subsection (3) if he shows that at the time the transaction was entered into he did not know that the directors were exceeding their powers.

(6) Nothing in the preceding provisions of this section affects the rights of any party to the transaction not within subsection (2)(b)(i) or (ii).

But the court may, on the application of the company or any such party, make an order affirming, severing or setting aside the transaction on such terms as appear to the court to be just.

(7) In this section-

    (a) "transaction" includes any act; and

    (b) the reference to a person connected with a director has the same meaning as in Part 10 (company directors).

GENERAL NOTE

This section retains the substantive effect of s.322A Companies Act 1985. It operates where a company enters into a transaction to which s.40 (above) applies (i.e. a transaction to which the company's directors commit it in excess of their powers under the company's constitution) and the other party to the transaction is a director of the company or its holding company or a person connected with such a director. In such circumstances the transaction, which might otherwise be enforceable under s.40, is voidable at the instance of the company, subject to certain exceptions as provided. Thus, where the company's directors enter into an agreement without having powers under the constitution to do so, and the other party to the agreement is an "insider", that insider cannot rely on s.40(1) to enforce the agreement.

Subsection (1)

This subsection determines the scope of the section. It applies to transactions which depend for their validity on the operation of s.40. It reproduces the effect of s.322A(4) of the Companies Act 1985, so that the provision itself does not exclude the operation of any other enactment or that of the general law which might call into question the validity of the transaction or render any person liable to the company. Therefore, notwithstanding that a company which could avoid a transaction under this section determines not to do so, provisions of other enactments, or principles or rules of the general law, may still operate to render the transaction invalid. An example of the provisions of another enactment are the avoidance provisions of the Insolvency Act 1986. An example of rules of the general law that might be applicable here are the equitable rules imposing liability for knowing assistance in a breach of fiduciary duty or for knowing receipt of trust property.

Subsection (2)

This subsection re-enacts the substance of parts of s.322A(1) and (2). Where a transaction to which subs.(1) applies is entered into and the counterparties include either a director of the company or its holding company or a person connected with such a director the company may avoid the transaction. The definition of a person connected with a director is now to be found in ss.252 and 253 of the Companies Act 2006. These sections provide an exhaustive list of persons falling into this category (see notes to ss.252 and 253 below).

Subsection (3)

This subsection replaces s.322A(3) of the Companies Act 1985. It provides that, whether or not a transaction to which s.41(1) applies has been avoided by the company, the counterparties mentioned in subs.2(b)(i) and (ii) remain liable to account to the company for any direct or indirect gain from the transaction or to indemnify the company for any loss or damage resulting from it. This liability extends to any director (other than the counterparty) who authorised the transaction.

Subsection (4)

This subsection replaces s.322A(5) of the Companies Act 1985. It details circumstances when the company's power to avoid the transaction as conferred by subs.(1) ceases to be exercisable. These are: when the restitution of the subject matter of the contract (whether money or an asset) is no longer possible (s.41(4)(a)); when the company has been indemnified against loss or damage (but *not* where the counterparty has accounted for any direct or indirect benefit under subs.(3): s.41(4)(b)); where a third party, acting bona fide and without actual notice of the directors' lack of authority, has acquired rights for value which would be prejudiced by avoidance (s.41(4)(c)); and; where the company affirms the transaction (s.41(4)(d)).

Subsection (5)

This provision replicates s.322A(6) of the Companies Act 1985. Where the counterparty to the transaction is not a director of the company, he will not be liable under subs.(3) if he can demonstrate that, at the time the transaction was entered into, he was unaware that the directors were exceeding their powers. This subsection therefore applies to transactions involving directors of a holding company and to persons connected with directors. It absolves them of liability to account or to indemnify, but has no effect on the company's power to avoid the transaction.

Subsection (6)

This subsection replaces s.322A(7) of the Companies Act 1985. It concerns cases where the parties to the transaction in question include both "insiders" (i.e. those parties mentioned in subs.(2)(b)(i) and (ii) and ("outsiders" who may rely on s.40 to validate the transaction). The rights of these "outsiders" are not affected by s .41, but the court may, on the application of the company of an outsider, make an order affirming the transaction, severing it or setting it aside on whatever terms it thinks fit.

42. Constitutional limitations: companies that are charities

(1) Sections 39 and 40 (company's capacity and power of directors to bind company) do not apply to the acts of a company that is a charity except in favour of a person who-
   (a) does not know at the time the act is done that the company is a charity, or
   (b) gives full consideration in money or money's worth in relation to the act in question and does not know (as the case may be)-
      (i) that the act is not permitted by the company's constitution, or
      (ii) that the act is beyond the powers of the directors.

(2) Where a company that is a charity purports to transfer or grant an interest in property, the fact that (as the case may be)-
   (a) the act was not permitted by the company's constitution, or
   (b) the directors in connection with the act exceeded any limitation on their powers under the company's constitution,
does not affect the title of a person who subsequently acquires the property or any interest in it for full consideration without actual notice of any such circumstances affecting the validity of the company's act.

(3) In any proceedings arising out of subsection (1) or (2) the burden of proving-
   (a) that a person knew that the company was a charity, or
   (b) that a person knew that an act was not permitted by the company's constitution or was beyond the powers of the directors,
lies on the person asserting that fact.

(4) In the case of a company that is a charity the affirmation of a transaction to which section 41 applies (transactions with directors or their associates) is ineffective without the prior written consent of-
   (a) in England and Wales, the Charity Commission;
   (b) in Northern Ireland, the Department for Social Development.

(5) This section does not extend to Scotland (but see section 112 of the Companies Act 1989 (c. 40)).

GENERAL NOTE

This section reproduces the substance of s.65 of the Charities Act 1993. It effectively modifies the operation of ss.39 and 40 of the Companies Act 2006 where the company in question is a charity *unless* the counterparty to a transaction with the company does not know that it is a charity *or* does not know that that the transaction is not permitted by the company's constitution or is beyond the powers' of the directors and gives full consideration in money or money's worth in relation to the act in question (subs.(1)). Where the transaction in question involves the transfer of or granting of an interest in property of the company, subs.(2) preserves the rights of anyone who subsequently acquires the property in question for full consideration, *provided* that that person did not have actual notice of the circumstances giving rise to the potential invalidity of the act. In all cases under these subsections, where it is alleged that a person knew the company was a charity or that the act in question was not permitted by the companies constitution or was beyond its directors powers, the burden of proof is with the party making such an allegation (subs.(3)). Any affirmation by the company will be ineffective without the prior written consent of the Charity Commission (in England and Wales) or the Department for Social Development (in Northern Ireland) (subs.(4)). The section does not extend to Scotland (subs.(5)), but its effect is largely reproduced by s.112(3), (4) and (5) of the Companies Act 1989.

Formalities of doing business under the law of England and Wales or Northern Ireland

43.   Company contracts

(1) Under the law of England and Wales or Northern Ireland a contract may be made-
    (a) by a company, by writing under its common seal, or
    (b) on behalf of a company, by a person acting under its authority, express or implied.

(2) Any formalities required by law in the case of a contract made by an individual also apply, unless a contrary intention appears, to a contract made by or on behalf of a company.

GENERAL NOTE

This section re-enacts s.36 of the Companies Act 1985 and describes how a company can make a contract. The first is in writing under the common seal (see below) and the second is through human agency. Where, under the general law, formalities apply to the making of a contract by an individual, the same formalities will apply to a contract made by a company, unless a contrary intention appears. As an example, the requirement in the Law of Property (Miscellaneous Provisions) Act 1989 that a contract granting an estate or interest in land be in writing will apply just as much to such a contract where one of the parties to it is a company.

44.   Execution of documents

(1) Under the law of England and Wales or Northern Ireland a document is executed by a company-
    (a) by the affixing of its common seal, or
    (b) by signature in accordance with the following provisions.

(2) A document is validly executed by a company if it is signed on behalf of the company-
    (a) by two authorised signatories, or
    (b) by a director of the company in the presence of a witness who attests the signature.

(3) The following are "authorised signatories" for the purposes of subsection (2)-
    (a) every director of the company, and
    (b) in the case of a private company with a secretary or a public company, the secretary (or any joint secretary) of the company.

(4) A document signed in accordance with subsection (2) and expressed, in whatever words, to be executed by the company has the same effect as if executed under the common seal of the company.

(5) In favour of a purchaser a document is deemed to have been duly executed by a company if it purports to be signed in accordance with subsection (2).
A "purchaser" means a purchaser in good faith for valuable consideration and includes a lessee, mortgagee or other person who for valuable consideration acquires an interest in property.

(6) Where a document is to be signed by a person on behalf of more than one company, it is not duly signed by that person for the purposes of this section unless he signs it separately in each capacity.

(7) References in this section to a document being (or purporting to be) signed by a director or secretary are to be read, in a case where that office is held by a firm, as references to its being (or purporting to be) signed by an individual authorised by the firm to sign on its behalf.

(8) This section applies to a document that is (or purports to be) executed by a company in the name of or on behalf of another person whether or not that person is also a company.

GENERAL NOTE

This provision replaces s.36A Companies Act 1986 and deals with the methods by which a company may execute a document. There are two methods of executing a document, the first by affixing the company's common seal (s.44(1)(a): see below as to the common seal), and the second by signature in accordance with the section (s.44(1)(b)).

Subsections (2)

Execution of a document by signature is validly achieved if the document in question is signed by two authorised signatories or by a director of the company in the presence of a witness who attests the signature. "Authorised signatory" is defined in subs.(3) as any director of the company and a secretary of a company.

Subsection (3)

Where the requirements of subs.(2) are satisfied and the document is expressed to be executed by the company (which will be a question of construction according to the words used), the signature will have the same effect as if the document was executed under the common seal of the company.

Subsection (4)

This subsection replaces s.36A(6) of the Companies Act 1985. In relation to purchasers (including lessees, mortgagees and persons acquiring an interest in the company's property for valuable consideration) who act in good faith, any document purporting to be signed in accordance with subs.(2) is deemed to have been duly executed by the company.

Subsection (5)

Subsection (5) replaces s.36A(4A) of the Companies Act 1985. It provides for the situation where an authorised signatory of more than one company signs a document and makes it clear that the document will not be duly signed for the purposes of s.44 unless the signatory signs it separately in each capacity.

Subsections (6) and (7)

These subsections replace s.36A(7), (8) of the 1985 Act. Subsection (6) addresses the situation where a director or secretary of the company is a firm and signs a document on behalf of a company as authorised signatory. In such a case, references in s.44 to a document being signed (or purporting to be signed) by an authorised signatory are to be read as references to the document being signed (or purporting to be signed) by an individual authorised to sign on its behalf by the firm in question. Section 44 applies to a document that is (or purports to be) executed by a company in the name or on behalf of another person, whether that person is a company or not.

45. Common seal

(1) A company may have a common seal, but need not have one.

(2) A company which has a common seal shall have its name engraved in legible characters on the seal.

(3) If a company fails to comply with subsection (2) an offence is committed by-
  (a) the company, and
  (b) every officer of the company who is in default.

(4) An officer of a company, or a person acting on behalf of a company, commits an offence if he uses, or authorises the use of, a seal purporting to be a seal of the company on which its name is not engraved as required by subsection (2).

(5) A person guilty of an offence under this section is liable on summary conviction to a fine not exceeding level 3 on the standard scale.

(6) This section does not form part of the law of Scotland.

GENERAL NOTE

This subsection, which does not form part of the law of Scotland, replaces ss.36A(3) and 350 Companies Act 1985. There is no requirement for a company to have a common seal (s.45(1)), but if it does the company's name must be engraved upon it in legible characters (s.45(2)). Failure to comply with subs.(2) is an offence committed by the company and every officer in default (s.45(3)) and use of the seal (or the authorisation of its use) by any officer of the company or person acting in its behalf also constitutes an offence if the requirements of subs.(2) are breached (s.45(4)). The penalty for the offence is set out in subs.(5) of s.45.

46.   Execution of deeds

(1) A document is validly executed by a company as a deed for the purposes of section 1(2)(b) of the Law of Property (Miscellaneous Provisions) Act 1989 (c. 34) and for the purposes of the law of Northern Ireland if, and only if-

(a) it is duly executed by the company, and

(b) it is delivered as a deed.

(2) For the purposes of subsection (1)(b) a document is presumed to be delivered upon its being executed, unless a contrary intention is proved.

GENERAL NOTE

This section re-enacts s.36AA Companies Act 1985. That section was inserted into the 1985 Act by the Regulatory Reform (Execution of Deeds and Documents) Order 2005 (SI 2005/1906). Section 1(2)(b) of the Law of Property Act (Miscellaneous Provisions) Act 1989 states that an instrument shall not be a deed unless it is executed as a deed. This section deals with deeds executed by companies and their validity depends upon them being validly executed and delivered as a deed. The question of whether a document has been delivered is dealt with in subs.(2) with a rebuttable presumption that delivery occurs upon execution. The presumption is rebutted by proof of a contrary intention.

47.   Execution of deeds or other documents by attorney

(1) Under the law of England and Wales or Northern Ireland a company may, by instrument executed as a deed, empower a person, either generally or in respect of specified matters, as its attorney to execute deeds or other documents on its behalf.

(2) A deed or other document so executed, whether in the United Kingdom or elsewhere, has effect as if executed by the company.

GENERAL NOTE

This section replaces s.38 of the Companies Act 1985. It reproduces the express power of a company to empower any person to act as its attorney in respect of the execution of deeds or other documents. The empowerment must be made by an instrument in writing, but it may be either general or specific to certain matters. Where the person empowered executes a deed or document, whether in the United Kingdom or elsewhere, that execution takes effect as though the company had executed the deed or document.

Formalities of doing business under the law of Scotland

48.   Execution of documents by companies

(1) The following provisions form part of the law of Scotland only.

(2) Notwithstanding the provisions of any enactment, a company need not have a company seal.

(3) For the purposes of any enactment-

(a) providing for a document to be executed by a company by affixing its common seal, or

(b) referring (in whatever terms) to a document so executed,

a document signed or subscribed by or on behalf of the company in accordance with the provisions of the Requirements of Writing (Scotland) Act 1995 (c. 7) has effect as if so executed.

GENERAL NOTE

This section is headed "Formalities of Doing Business under the Law of Scotland" and replaces s.36B of the Companies Act 1985 which is repealed by the Companies Act 2006, s.1295 and Sch.16.

Subsection (1)

Section 48 applies only where the formal validity of a document executed by a company is to be determined under Scots law. If that is the case, it is immaterial whether the company is incorporated in Scotland or elsewhere.

Subsection (2)

This repeats s.36B(1) of the Companies Act 1985. "Enactment" was defined in s.36B(3) of the 1985 Act as including an enactment contained in a statutory instrument. The (expanded) definition now appears as s.1293 of the Companies Act 2006.

Subsection (3)

This re-enacts s.36B(2) of the Companies Act 1985. The Requirements of Writing (Scotland) Act 1995 provides in Sch.2, para.3(1) that :

"Except where an enactment expressly provides otherwise, where a granter of a document is a company, the document is signed by the company if it is signed on its behalf by a director, or by the secretary, of the company or by a person authorised to sign the document on its behalf."

Other matters

49. Official seal for use abroad

(1) A company that has a common seal may have an official seal for use outside the United Kingdom.

(2) The official seal must be a facsimile of the company's common seal, with the addition on its face of the place or places where it is to be used.

(3) The official seal when duly affixed to a document has the same effect as the company's common seal.

This subsection does not extend to Scotland.

(4) A company having an official seal for use outside the United Kingdom may-

(a) by writing under its common seal, or

(b) as respects Scotland, by writing subscribed in accordance with the Requirements of Writing (Scotland) Act 1995,

authorise any person appointed for the purpose to affix the official seal to any deed or other document to which the company is party.

(5) As between the company and a person dealing with such an agent, the agent's authority continues-

(a) during the period mentioned in the instrument conferring the authority, or

(b) if no period is mentioned, until notice of the revocation or termination of the agent's authority has been given to the person dealing with him.

(6) The person affixing the official seal must certify in writing on the deed or other document to which the seal is affixed the date on which, and place at which, it is affixed.

GENERAL NOTE

This section replaces s.39 of the Companies Act 1985 and describes the circumstances and methods by which a company may use a seal outside of the United Kingdom.

Subsections (1)-(3)

In order that a company may have an official seal for use abroad it must have a common seal (see note to s.45, above). Under the predecessor s.39(1), the company's objects must have required or comprised the transaction of business in foreign countries, but s.31 now states that, unless a company adopts to limit its objects, they will be unlimited and therefore this part of the provision is now of less importance. It would appear from the wording of s.49 that the previous requirement of authorisation in the articles of association for the use of an official seal is no longer required. The official seal must be in the form described in subs.(2). The affixation of an official seal has the same effect as the affixation of the company's common seal (subs.(3)), although that subsection does not extend to Scotland.

Subsections (4) and (5)

These subsection replaces s.39(3) and (4) of the 1985 Act. Where a company has an official seal for use outside the United Kingdom it may, by writing under its common seal (or, in Scotland, in accordance with Requirements of Writing (Scotland) Act 1995) authorise any person for the purpose of using the official seal outside the United Kingdom to affix the official seal to deeds or documents to which the company is a party. Where any person deals with a person so authorised, that authority continues for the period mentioned in the written instrument conferring it or, where no period is specified, until notice of revocation or termination of the agent's authority is provided to that person.

Subsection (6)

This subsection re-enacts s.39(5) of the Companies Act 1985.

50.   Official seal for share certificates etc

(1) A company that has a common seal may have an official seal for use-
    (a) for sealing securities issued by the company, or
    (b) for sealing documents creating or evidencing securities so issued.
(2) The official seal-
    (a) must be a facsimile of the company's common seal, with the addition on its face of the word "Securities", and
    (b) when duly affixed to the document has the same effect as the company's common seal.

GENERAL NOTE

This section re-enacts s.40 of the Companies Act 1985. It provides for the use by a company which has a common seal an official seal for use in sealing securities issued by it, or documents creating or evidencing securities so issued. Subsection (2) described the form of such an official seal, and prescribes that the effect of affixing it is the same as affixing the company's common seal.

51.   Pre-incorporation contracts, deeds and obligations

(1) A contract that purports to be made by or on behalf of a company at a time when the company has not been formed has effect, subject to any agreement to the contrary, as one made with the person purporting to act for the company or as agent for it, and he is personally liable on the contract accordingly.
(2) Subsection (1) applies-
    (a) to the making of a deed under the law of England and Wales or Northern Ireland, and
    (b) to the undertaking of an obligation under the law of Scotland,
as it applies to the making of a contract.

GENERAL NOTE

This provision re-enacts s.36C Companies Act 1985. It deals with the situation where a contract is entered into by a person purporting to act on behalf of a company which has not yet been incorporated. As such, the contract cannot be enforced by or against the company even after incorporation, as it has been made on behalf of a non-existent principal.

Subsection (1)

A contract made on behalf of a company prior to incorporation has effect as a contract made with the person purporting to act for the company and, in the absence of any agreement to the contrary, he is personally liable on that contract. Any contrary agreement must be express, in that the "agent" must clearly exclude his personal liability, and this will not be implied from the fact that the "agent" purports to enter the contract on behalf of the company (*Phonogram Ltd v Lane* [1982] Q.B. 938). It appears from *Braymist v Wise Finance Co Ltd* [2002] EWCA Civ 127 that the person purporting to enter the agreement on behalf of the company may enforce it post-incorporation unless the counterparty can demonstrate that he would not have entered into the agreement on the basis that it was to be enforceable by the agent in question. This will probably involve the counterparty demonstrating some special attribute of the *company* (perhaps, for example, the fact that a certain person was to be involved in its management) that is no longer present post-incorporation.

It is perhaps surprising that no provision is made under the Companies Act 2006 for ratification of a pre-incorporation contract by the company, once formed. For the company to become a party to such an agreement, novation of the contract must occur, although such novation may be express or implied.

52. Bills of exchange and promissory notes

A bill of exchange or promissory note is deemed to have been made, accepted or endorsed on behalf of a company if made, accepted or endorsed in the name of, or by or on behalf or on account of, the company by a person acting under its authority.

GENERAL NOTE

Section 52 re-enacts s.37 of the Companies Act 1985. Both bills of exchange and promissory notes are required to be in writing (see Bills of Exchange Act 1882, ss.3(1) and 17(2)). The former is an unconditional order requiring a person to whom it is addressed to pay a third person (either on demand or at some fixed or determinable future time) a sum of money. The third person may be named on the face of the bill, or it may be an order to pay "the bearer". A promissory note is an unconditional promise made by the maker of the note to pay (either on demand or at some fixed or determinable future time) a sum of money to a specific person or to the bearer of the promissory note. This provision specifies that where any person authorised by the company makes, accepts or endorses a bill of exchange or promissory note on behalf of the company that instrument is deemed to have been made, accepted or endorsed by the company itself.

PART 5

A COMPANY'S NAME

CHAPTER I

GENERAL REQUIREMENTS

GENERAL NOTE

This Part of the 2006 Act is concerned with the name with which a company is registered. It comprises six Chapters, Ch.1 dealing generally with certain prohibited names by which a company cannot be formed and other expressions and characters which require permission to be used as part of a company's name. Chapter 2 prescribes the use of certain indications of the corporate form in the company's name and Ch.3 deals with circumstances where a company proposes to be formed with a name that is the same as or similar to a company already registered. Chapter 4 provides for the exercise by the Secretary of State of powers to direct the change of name of a company, and Ch.5 with the methods by which a company may change its name. Chapter 6 contains provisions requiring the company's name to be disclosed. The general objective behind the provisions of this Part is to ensure that third parties dealing with companies are not misled by the name with which it is registered, although certain of them may also protect existing companies in that they prevent the use of a similar or identical name.

Prohibited names

53. Prohibited names

A company must not be registered under this Act by a name if, in the opinion of the Secretary of State-

(a) its use by the company would constitute an offence, or

(b) it is offensive.

GENERAL NOTE

This section replaces s.26(1)(d) and (e) of the Companies Act 1985. It re-enacts the basic rule that a company must not be registered by a name if, in the opinion of the Secretary of State, that name would constitute an offence or is offensive.

Sensitive words and expressions

54. Names suggesting connection with government or public authority

(1) The approval of the Secretary of State is required for a company to be registered under this Act by a name that would be likely to give the impression that the company is connected with-

(a) Her Majesty's Government, any part of the Scottish administration or Her Majesty's Government in Northern Ireland,

(b) a local authority, or

(c) any public authority specified for the purposes of this section by regulations made by the Secretary of State.

(2) For the purposes of this section-

"local authority" means-

(a) a local authority within the meaning of the Local Government Act 1972 (c. 70), the Common Council of the City of London or the Council of the Isles of Scilly,

(b) a council constituted under section 2 of the Local Government etc. (Scotland) Act 1994 (c. 39), or

(c) a district council in Northern Ireland;

"public authority" includes any person or body having functions of a public nature.

(3) Regulations under this section are subject to affirmative resolution procedure.

GENERAL NOTE

Section 54 replaces s.26(2) of the Companies Act 1985. It provides that the approval of the Secretary of State is required for the registration of a company with a name that would be likely to give the impression that the company is connected with local or national government, whether in England and Wales, Scotland or Northern Ireland, any local authority or any public authority specified by regulations made by the Secretary of State. "Local authority" is defined in subs.2 as a local authority within the meaning of Local Government Act 1972, the Common Council of the City of London or the Council of the Isles of Scilly, a council constituted under s.2 of the Local Government etc. (Scotland) Act 1994 or a district council in Northern Ireland. "Public authority" is defined in the same subsection as including any person or body having functions of a public nature.

55. Other sensitive words or expressions

(1) The approval of the Secretary of State is required for a company to be registered under this Act by a name that includes a word or expression for the time being specified in regulations made by the Secretary of State under this section.

(2) Regulations under this section are subject to approval after being made.

GENERAL NOTE

This section replaces s.26(2)(b) and s.29(1)(a) of the Companies Act 1985. It provides that the approval of the Secretary of State is required for the registration of a company with a name that includes a word or expression specified by the Secretary of State in regulations made under the section. Regulations made under this section are subject to approval after being made. Regulations currently specifying words or expressions include the Company and Business Names Regulations 1981 (SI 1981/1685). Some of the words and expressions listed therein are association, benevolent, charitable, duke, her majesty, king, midwife, patent and royal.

56. Duty to seek comments of government department or other specified body

(1) The Secretary of State may by regulations under-

    (a) section 54 (name suggesting connection with government or public authority), or

    (b) section 55 (other sensitive words or expressions),

require that, in connection with an application for the approval of the Secretary of State under that section, the applicant must seek the view of a specified Government department or other body.

    (2) Where such a requirement applies, the applicant must request the specified department or other body (in writing) to indicate whether (and if so why) it has any objections to the proposed name.

    (3) Where a request under this section is made in connection with an application for the registration of a company under this Act, the application must-

        (a) include a statement that a request under this section has been made, and

        (b) be accompanied by a copy of any response received.

    (4) Where a request under this section is made in connection with a change in a company's name, the notice of the change sent to the registrar must be accompanied by-

        (a) a statement by a director or secretary of the company that a request under this section has been made, and

        (b) a copy of any response received.

    (5) In this section "specified" means specified in the regulations.

GENERAL NOTE

Section 56 replaces s.29(1)(b), (2), (3) and (4) of the 1985 Act. Where the Secretary of State makes regulations under ss.55 or 56 he may by regulations, on an application for approval of a name suggesting a connection with government or containing a sensitive word or expression, require the applicant to seek the view of a specified government department or other body. Examples contained in the Company and Business Names Regulations 1981 (SI 1981/1685) include the Home Office or Scottish Ministers in connection with the use of the terms "her majesty" or "royal" and the Charity Commission or the Scottish Ministers in connection with the use of the term "charitable".

Subsections (2) and (3)

In circumstance where the section applies, the applicant must write to the specified department or body requesting an indication as to whether it objects to the proposed name and, where such a request is made in connection with an application for registration under the Act, the applicant must, on an application for registration, include a statement that a request under s.56 was made and a copy of any response received.

Subsection (4)

The requirement to consult departments or bodies specified by the Secretary of State applies also where it is proposed to change to company's name to one which falls within ss.55 or 56. The methods by which a company may change its name are dealt with in Ch.5 of Pt 5 (see below). Where the company changes its name to one which falls within ss.55 or 56 a director or secretary of the company must, on an application to the registrar of companies to register the change of name, include a statement that a request under s.56 was made and a copy of any response received.

Permitted characters etc

57. Permitted characters etc

(1) The Secretary of State may make provision by regulations-
   (a) as to the letters or other characters, signs or symbols (including accents and other diacritical marks) and punctuation that may be used in the name of a company registered under this Act; and
   (b) specifying a standard style or format for the name of a company for the purposes of registration.
(2) The regulations may prohibit the use of specified characters, signs or symbols when appearing in a specified position (in particular, at the beginning of a name).
(3) A company may not be registered under this Act by a name that consists of or includes anything that is not permitted in accordance with regulations under this section.
(4) Regulations under this section are subject to negative resolution procedure.
(5) In this section "specified" means specified in the regulations.

GENERAL NOTE

This is a new provision and empowers the Secretary of State to provide by regulations (which are subject to negative resolution procedure) which letters, characters, signs and symbols may be used in the name of a company registered under the Act. The regulations may specify a standard style or format for the company's name and may prohibit the use of specified characters, signs and symbols appearing in a specified position in the company's name. A company may not be registered under the Act if its name includes or consists of anything not permitted in accordance with regulations made under the section. The Explanatory Notes, in relation to the specifying of a standard style or format, give the example of regulations proscribing the use of superscript or subscript in the company's name.

CHAPTER 2

INDICATIONS OF COMPANY TYPE OR LEGAL FORM

Required indications for limited companies

58. Public limited companies

(1) The name of a limited company that is a public company must end with "public limited company" or "p.l.c.".
(2) In the case of a Welsh company, its name may instead end with "cwmni cyfyngedig cyhoeddus" or "c.c.c.".
(3) This section does not apply to community interest companies (but see section 33(3) and (4) of the Companies (Audit, Investigations and Community Enterprise) Act 2004 (c. 27)).

GENERAL NOTE

This section replaces s.25(1) and s.27(4)(b) and (d) of the Companies Act 1985. Where a company is a public company, its name must end with the appropriate term as prescribed in subs.(1) and (2). As with all the provisions in this Chapter, the section addresses the objective that a company's name should accurately describe its particular status under the Act, in this case a public limited company. With this in mind, the provision does not apply to community interest companies, these being governed in this respect by s.33(3) and (4) of the Companies (Audit, Investigations and Community Enterprise) Act 2004.

59. Private limited companies

(1) The name of a limited company that is a private company must end with "limited" or "ltd.".

(2) In the case of a Welsh company, its name may instead end with "cyfyngedig" or "cyf.".

(3) Certain companies are exempt from this requirement (see section 60).

(4) This section does not apply to community interest companies (but see section 33(1) and (2) of the Companies (Audit, Investigations and Community Enterprise) Act 2004).

GENERAL NOTE

This section replaces s.25(2) and s.27(4)(a) and (c) of the 1985 Act. The name of a private limited company must end with the appropriate term as prescribed in subs.(1) and (2). Section 60 (see below) exempts certain companies from this requirement, which does not apply to community interest companies, these being governed in this respect by s.33(1) and (2) of the Companies (Audit, Investigations and Community Enterprise) Act 2004.

60. Exemption from requirement as to use of "limited"

(1) A private company is exempt from section 59 (requirement to have name ending with "limited" or permitted alternative) if-

(a) it is a charity,

(b) it is exempted from the requirement of that section by regulations made by the Secretary of State, or

(c) it meets the conditions specified in-

section 61 (continuation of existing exemption: companies limited by shares), or

section 62 (continuation of existing exemption: companies limited by guarantee).

(2) The registrar may refuse to register a private limited company by a name that does not include the word "limited" (or a permitted alternative) unless a statement has been delivered to him that the company meets the conditions for exemption.

(3) The registrar may accept the statement as sufficient evidence of the matters stated in it.

(4) Regulations under this section are subject to negative resolution procedure.

GENERAL NOTE

This section replaces s.30 Companies Act 1985, which exempted certain companies from using the term "limited" (or an equivalent) at the end of their names.

Subsection (1)

This subsection specifies which private companies are exempted from the requirement in s.59. These are a company that is a charity (s.61(1)(a)), a company exempted by regulations (subject to negative resolution procedure - subs.(4)) made by the Secretary of State (s.61(1)(b)) or a company meeting the conditions specified in s.61 or 62 (see below).

Subsections (2) and (3)

Where an application for registration is made in relation to a private limited company whose name does not include the word limited (or a permitted equivalent term as prescribed by s.59(1) or (2)), the registrar of companies may refuse to register the company if a statement that the company meets the conditions for exemption has not been delivered to him. Any such statement may be accepted by the registrar as sufficient evidence of the matters stated in it.

61. Continuation of existing exemption: companies limited by shares

(1) This section applies to a private company limited by shares-

(a) that on 25th February 1982-

(i) was registered in Great Britain, and

      (ii) had a name that, by virtue of a licence under section 19 of the Companies Act 1948 (c. 38) (or corresponding earlier legislation), did not include the word "limited" or any of the permitted alternatives, or

  (b) that on 30th June 1983-

      (i) was registered in Northern Ireland, and

      (ii) had a name that, by virtue of a licence under section 19 of the Companies Act (Northern Ireland) 1960 (c. 22 (N.I.)) (or corresponding earlier legislation), did not include the word "limited" or any of the permitted alternatives.

(2) A company to which this section applies is exempt from section 59 (requirement to have name ending with "limited" or permitted alternative) so long as-

  (a) it continues to meet the following two conditions, and

  (b) it does not change its name.

(3) The first condition is that the objects of the company are the promotion of commerce, art, science, education, religion, charity or any profession, and anything incidental or conducive to any of those objects.

(4) The second condition is that the company's articles-

  (a) require its income to be applied in promoting its objects,

  (b) prohibit the payment of dividends, or any return of capital, to its members, and

  (c) require all the assets that would otherwise be available to its members generally to be transferred on its winding up either-

      (i) to another body with objects similar to its own, or

      (ii) to another body the objects of which are the promotion of charity and anything incidental or conducive thereto,

(whether or not the body is a member of the company).

GENERAL NOTE

  This section replaces s.30(2) and (3) of the Companies Act 1985 to the extent that that provision applies to private companies limited by shares. It preserves the existing exemption for such companies from the requirement that their names include the word "limited" (or a permitted equivalent) in so far as they continue to satisfy the conditions in subss.(3) and (4). Such companies would have enjoyed the privilege of exemption immediately prior to the coming into force of s.25(1)(a) of the Companies Act 1981 (on February 26, 1982).

Subsection (1)

  This subsection specifies those companies to which the exemption noted above applies. They must have enjoyed the exemption by virtue of a licence under previous legislation in Great Britain or Northern Ireland.

Subsections (2)-(4)

  Subsection (2) preserves the exemption to include the term limited (or its equivalent) in its name for those companies specified in subs.(1) on condition that the conditions in subss.(3) and (4) continue to be fulfilled *and* so long as the company does not change its name. The condition in subs.(3) relates to the objects of the company, which must be the promotion of commerce, art, science, education, religion, charity or any profession, and anything incidental or conducive to any of those objects. The condition in subs.(4) relates to the income and assets of the company. Its articles must require income to be applied for the promotion of its objects, they must prohibit the payment of dividends or capital to members and, on winding up, the articles must provide for any surplus assets to be transferred to another body with similar objects or whose objects are the promotion of charity. Assets may not, therefore, be returned to members.

62. Continuation of existing exemption: companies limited by guarantee

(1) A private company limited by guarantee that immediately before the commencement of this Part-

  (a) was exempt by virtue of section 30 of the Companies Act 1985 (c. 6) or Article 40 of the Companies (Northern Ireland) Order 1986 (S.I. 1986/ 1032 (N.I. 6)) from the requirement to have a name including the word "limited" or a permitted alternative, and

(b) had a name that did not include the word "limited" or any of the permitted alternatives,

is exempt from section 59 (requirement to have name ending with "limited" or permitted alternative) so long as it continues to meet the following two conditions and does not change its name.

(2) The first condition is that the objects of the company are the promotion of commerce, art, science, education, religion, charity or any profession, and anything incidental or conducive to any of those objects.

(3) The second condition is that the company's articles-

    (a) require its income to be applied in promoting its objects,

    (b) prohibit the payment of dividends to its members, and

    (c) require all the assets that would otherwise be available to its members generally to be transferred on its winding up either-

        (i) to another body with objects similar to its own, or

        (ii) to another body the objects of which are the promotion of charity and anything incidental or conducive thereto,

(whether or not the body is a member of the company).

GENERAL NOTE

This section replaces s.30(2) and (3) of the Companies Act 1985 to the extent that that provision applies to private companies limited by guarantee. Under that section such companies were granted exemption from using the word "limited" (or a permitted alternative) in their names provided that their objects were the promotion of commerce, art, science, education, religion, charity or any profession, and anything incidental or conducive to any of those objects, and that their memorandum or articles provided that profits or income be applied in the promotion of the objects, prohibited the payment of dividends to members and, on winding up, provided for any surplus assets to be transferred to another body with similar objects or whose objects were the promotion of charity. This exemption continues to operate by virtue of s.62.

63. Exempt company: restriction on amendment of articles

(1) A private company-

    (a) that is exempt under section 61 or 62 from the requirement to use "limited" (or a permitted alternative) as part of its name, and

    (b) whose name does not include "limited" or any of the permitted alternatives,

must not amend its articles so that it ceases to comply with the conditions for exemption under that section.

(2) If subsection (1) above is contravened an offence is committed by-

    (a) the company, and

    (b) every officer of the company who is in default.

For this purpose a shadow director is treated as an officer of the company.

(3) A person guilty of an offence under this section is liable on summary conviction to a fine not exceeding level 5 on the standard scale and, for continued contravention, a daily default fine not exceeding one-tenth of level 5 on the standard scale.

(4) Where immediately before the commencement of this section-

    (a) a company was exempt by virtue of section 30 of the Companies Act 1985 (c. 6) or Article 40 of the Companies (Northern Ireland) Order 1986 (S.I. 1986/1032 (N.I. 6)) from the requirement to have a name including the word "limited" (or a permitted alternative), and

    (b) the company's memorandum or articles contained provision preventing an alteration of them without the approval of-

        (i) the Board of Trade or a Northern Ireland department (or any other department or Minister), or

        (ii) the Charity Commission,

that provision, and any condition of any such licence as is mentioned in section 61(1)(a)(ii) or (b)(ii) requiring such provision, shall cease to have effect. This does not apply if, or to the extent that, the provision is required by or under any other enactment.

(5) It is hereby declared that any such provision as is mentioned in subsection (4)(b) formerly contained in a company's memorandum was at all material times capable, with the appropriate approval, of being altered or removed under section 17 of the Companies Act 1985 or Article 28 of the Companies (Northern Ireland) Order 1986 (S.I. 1986/1032 (N.I. 6)) (or corresponding earlier enactments).

GENERAL NOTE

This provision replaces s.31(1) and (5) of the Companies Act 1985 and, as did those provisions, prevents a private company that is exempted under ss.62 and 63 from using the word "limited" (or a permitted alternative) in its name from amending its articles in such a way that it ceases to satisfy the conditions for exemption. It should be noted that there is no prohibition on such a company from amending the provisions of its memorandum, and in companies pre-dating the 2006 Act the objects clause will be found in the memorandum of association rather than in the articles. However, s.28 of the Companies Act 2006 provides that provisions in the memorandum of existing companies are to be treated as provisions in the articles, and therefore any amendment to the objects so that they cease to comply with the conditions in ss.61(3) and 62(2) will still breach the prohibition in s.63(1). As under s.31(5), breach of the section renders the company and any officer in default liable to a fine (subs.(2)) at the level prescribed in subs.(3). This section, unlike its predecessor, treats any shadow director of the company as an officer.

Subsections (4) and (5)

These two subsection address the position of those companies which, under previous legislation in Great Britain or Northern Ireland, were required to include in their memorandum a provision requiring the consent of the Board of Trade (or a variation of it) of the Charity Commission for any alteration to the memorandum. Such a provision, by virtue of these subsections, now ceases to have any effect.

64. Power to direct change of name in case of company ceasing to be entitled to exemption

(1) If it appears to the Secretary of State that a company whose name does not include "limited" or any of the permitted alternatives-
(a) has ceased to be entitled to exemption under section 60(1)(a) or (b), or
(b) in the case of a company within section 61 or 62 (which impose conditions as to the objects and articles of the company)-
  (i) has carried on any business other than the promotion of any of the objects mentioned in subsection (3) of section 61 or, as the case may be, subsection (2) of section 62, or
  (ii) has acted inconsistently with the provision required by subsection (4)(a) or (b) of section 61 or, as the case may be, subsection (3)(a) or (b) of section 62,
the Secretary of State may direct the company to change its name so that it ends with "limited" or one of the permitted alternatives.

(2) The direction must be in writing and must specify the period within which the company is to change its name.

(3) A change of name in order to comply with a direction under this section may be made by resolution of the directors.
This is without prejudice to any other method of changing the company's name.

(4) Where a resolution of the directors is passed in accordance with subsection (3), the company must give notice to the registrar of the change.
Sections 80 and 81 apply as regards the registration and effect of the change.

(5) If the company fails to comply with a direction under this section an offence is committed by-
(a) the company, and
(b) every officer of the company who is in default.

(6) A person guilty of an offence under this section is liable on summary conviction to a fine not exceeding level 5 on the standard scale and, for continued contravention, a daily default fine not exceeding one-tenth of level 5 on the standard scale.

(7) A company that has been directed to change its name under this section may not, without the approval of the Secretary of State, subsequently change its name so that it does not include "limited" or one of the permitted alternatives.

This does not apply to a change of name on re-registration or on conversion to a community interest company.

GENERAL NOTE

This section replaces s.31(2), (3), (4) and (6) of the Companies Act 1985. It empowers the Secretary of State to direct a company to change its name if that name does not include the word "l;imited" (or a permitted alternative) *and* it appears that the company in question has ceased to be entitled to the exemption under s.61 or, having been exempt under ss.61 or 62, has ceased to comply with the conditions for exemption therein.

Subsections (2)-(4)

Any direction given by the Secretary of State under this section must be in writing and must specify the period in which the company must change its name. The change of name can be effected by a resolution of the directors and the company must give notice to the registrar of companies (in accordance with s.80 and subject to s.81 of the Companies Act 2006 (see below)).

Subsection (5) and (6)

A failure to comply with a direction under s.64 constitutes an offence committed by the company and every officer in default. The penalty for the offence is prescribed in subs.(6).

Subsection (7)

Where a company has been directed to change its name under s.64, a subsequent change of name to one which does not include "limited" (or a permitted alternative) requires the approval of the Secretary of State. This subsection does not apply where the company changes its name on re-registration (see below) or where it is converted to a community interest company.

Inappropriate use of indications of company type or legal form

65. Inappropriate use of indications of company type or legal form

(1) The Secretary of State may make provision by regulations prohibiting the use in a company name of specified words, expressions or other indications-
   (a) that are associated with a particular type of company or form of organisation, or
   (b) that are similar to words, expressions or other indications associated with a particular type of company or form of organisation.

(2) The regulations may prohibit the use of words, expressions or other indications-
   (a) in a specified part, or otherwise than in a specified part, of a company's name;
   (b) in conjunction with, or otherwise than in conjunction with, such other words, expressions or indications as may be specified.

(3) A company must not be registered under this Act by a name that consists of or includes anything prohibited by regulations under this section.

(4) In this section "specified" means specified in the regulations.

(5) Regulations under this section are subject to negative resolution procedure.

GENERAL NOTE

This provision replaces s.26(1)(a), (b), (bb) and (bbb) of the Companies Act 1985. It empowers the Secretary of State to make provision by regulations (subject to negative resolution procedure) to prohibit the use in a company name of specified words, expressions or other indicators. Such words, etc. must be associated with particular types of companies or other form of organisation or similar to words, expressions or characters associated with such. Examples from the 1985 Act include the use of the term "limited" in a company name, other than at the end of it, and use of the terms "limited liability partnership", "open-ended investment company" and their Welsh equivalents. Where regulations are made specifying prohibited words, etc., or restricting their use, the registrar of companies must not register a company whose name includes such a word in contravention to the regulations.

CHAPTER 3

SIMILARITY TO OTHER NAMES

Similarity to other name on registrar's index

66.   Name not to be the same as another in the index

(1) A company must not be registered under this Act by a name that is the same as another name appearing in the registrar's index of company names.

(2) The Secretary of State may make provision by regulations supplementing this section.

(3) The regulations may make provision-

   (a) as to matters that are to be disregarded, and

   (b) as to words, expressions, signs or symbols that are, or are not, to be regarded as the same,

for the purposes of this section.

(4) The regulations may provide-

   (a) that registration by a name that would otherwise be prohibited under this section is permitted-

      (i) in specified circumstances, or

      (ii) with specified consent, and

   (b) that if those circumstances obtain or that consent is given at the time a company is registered by a name, a subsequent change of circumstances or withdrawal of consent does not affect the registration.

(5) Regulations under this section are subject to negative resolution procedure.

(6) In this section "specified" means specified in the regulations.

GENERAL NOTE

   This provision replaces s.26(1)(c) and (3) of the Companies Act 1985. It re-enacts the prohibition in that section on registration of a company under a name that is the same as another name appearing in the registrar's index of names, but also empowers to Secretary of State to make regulations (subject to negative resolution procedure: subs.(5)) providing matters to be disregarded and words, expressions, signs or symbols that are (or are not) to be regarded as the same for the purposes of s.66. Subsection 26(3)(a), (b) and (c) of the 1985 Act provided that the definite article (when it was the first word of the company's name) and a series of words and expressions (such as "company", "limited" and "unlimited") could be disregarded for the purpose of comparing a proposed name with one already on the register. Section 26(3)(d) provided that type and case of letters, accents, spaces between letters and punctuation marks, were to be regarded as the same, as were the word "and" and the symbol "&".

Subsection (4)

   This new provision allows for exceptions to the prohibition on registration of a name that is the same to one already on the register to be provided for by the making of regulations. These regulations may permit registration of an otherwise prohibited name in specified circumstances or with specified consent (subs.(4)(a)(i), (ii)). They may also provide that if a company is registered with a particular name in either of these situations, the fact of a subsequent change of circumstance or withdrawal of consent does not affect the that registration (subs.(4)(b)).

67. Power to direct change of name in case of similarity to existing name

(1) The Secretary of State may direct a company to change its name if it has been registered in a name that is the same as or, in the opinion of the Secretary of State, too like-

  (a) a name appearing at the time of the registration in the registrar's index of company names, or

  (b) a name that should have appeared in that index at that time.

(2) The Secretary of State may make provision by regulations supplementing this section.

(3) The regulations may make provision-

  (a) as to matters that are to be disregarded, and

  (b) as to words, expressions, signs or symbols that are, or are not, to be regarded as the same,

for the purposes of this section.

(4) The regulations may provide-

  (a) that no direction is to be given under this section in respect of a name-

    (i) in specified circumstances, or

    (ii) if specified consent is given, and

  (b) that a subsequent change of circumstances or withdrawal of consent does not give rise to grounds for a direction under this section.

(5) Regulations under this section are subject to negative resolution procedure.

(6) In this section "specified" means specified in the regulations.

GENERAL NOTE

This section replaces s.28(2) of the Companies Act 1985. It is aimed at protecting the public from confusion caused by two companies having very similar names, and empowers the Secretary of State to direct a company to change its registered name in such circumstances.

Subsection (1)

Where a company is registered with a name which, in the opinion of the Secretary of State, is too like a name already appearing on the registrar's index of names at the time of the registration, or to a name that *should* have appeared on that index, the Secretary of State may direct that company (the most recently registered) to change its name.

Subsections (2)-(5)

These subsections empower the Secretary of State to supplement the section by the making of regulations (subs.(2)) (subject to negative resolution procedure (subs.(5)). The regulations in question correspond to those seen in s.66(3) and (4) (above). Thus they may specify matters to be disregarded when comparing names, and for which words, expressions, signs or symbols that are, or are not, the be regarded as the same for the purposes of the section (subs.(3)). Equally, the regulations may provide that no direction is to be given under the section in specified circumstances or where specified consent is given (subs.(4)).

68. Direction to change name: supplementary provisions

(1) The following provisions have effect in relation to a direction under section 67 (power to direct change of name in case of similarity to existing name).

(2) Any such direction-

  (a) must be given within twelve months of the company's registration by the name in question, and

  (b) must specify the period within which the company is to change its name.

(3) The Secretary of State may by a further direction extend that period. Any such direction must be given before the end of the period for the time being specified.

(4) A direction under section 67 or this section must be in writing.

(5) If a company fails to comply with the direction, an offence is committed by-

  (a) the company, and

(b) every officer of the company who is in default.

For this purpose a shadow director is treated as an officer of the company.

(6) A person guilty of an offence under this section is liable on summary conviction to a fine not exceeding level 3 on the standard scale and, for continued contravention, a daily default fine not exceeding one-tenth of level 3 on the standard scale.

GENERAL NOTE

This section replaces s.28(4) and (5) of the Companies Act 1985. Where the Secretary of State makes a direction (in writing - subs.(4)) under s.67 that a company change its name on the grounds that it is too similar to a name already on the registrar's index of names he must specify a time period within which the direction should be complied with (s.68(2)(b)). That period is extendable by the Secretary of State (subs.(3)). The direction itself must be given within 12 months of the company's registration with the name in question (subs.2(a): the recommendation of the Company Law Review, in para.11.50 of the *Final Report* that this period be extended to 15 months has not been implemented). Failure to comply with a direction within the stated time period constitutes an offence committed by the company and every officer in default, including a shadow director, who is treated as an officer for the purposes of this section (subs.(5)). The penalty for the commission of this offence is set out in subs.(6).

Similarity to other name in which person has goodwill

69.   Objection to company's registered name

(1) A person ("the applicant") may object to a company's registered name on the ground-
   (a) that it is the same as a name associated with the applicant in which he has goodwill, or
   (b) that it is sufficiently similar to such a name that its use in the United Kingdom would be likely to mislead by suggesting a connection between the company and the applicant.

(2) The objection must be made by application to a company names adjudicator (see section 70).

(3) The company concerned shall be the primary respondent to the application. Any of its members or directors may be joined as respondents.

(4) If the ground specified in subsection (1)(a) or (b) is established, it is for the respondents to show-
   (a) that the name was registered before the commencement of the activities on which the applicant relies to show goodwill; or
   (b) that the company-
      (i) is operating under the name, or
      (ii) is proposing to do so and has incurred substantial start-up costs in preparation, or
      (iii) was formerly operating under the name and is now dormant;
      or
   (c) that the name was registered in the ordinary course of a company formation business and the company is available for sale to the applicant on the standard terms of that business; or
   (d) that the name was adopted in good faith; or
   (e) that the interests of the applicant are not adversely affected to any significant extent.

If none of those is shown, the objection shall be upheld.

(5) If the facts mentioned in subsection (4)(a), (b) or (c) are established, the objection shall nevertheless be upheld if the applicant shows that the main purpose of the respondents (or any of them) in registering the name was to obtain money (or other consideration) from the applicant or prevent him from registering the name.

(6) If the objection is not upheld under subsection (4) or (5), it shall be dismissed.

(7) In this section "goodwill" includes reputation of any description.

GENERAL NOTE

This is a new provision inserted to give effect to the recommendation of the Company Law Review (*Final Report*, para.11.50) that provision should be made for a person to apply to court for a direction that a company change its name on the basis that the name is similar to a name used by that person and in which he has goodwill. Goodwill is defined in s.69(7) as including reputation of any description.

Subsections (1)-(3)

Subsection (1) allows a person (the applicant) to object to the registered name of a company on the ground that it is the same name as one associated with him and in which he has goodwill, or that it is sufficiently similar to such a name so that its use in the United Kingdom would be likely to mislead by suggesting that the company is in some way connected to the applicant. The objection must be made by application to the company names adjudicator (subs.(2)), and see note to s.70, below). Subsection (3) specifies that the company with the same or similar name is to be the primary respondent to the application, and that any of its directors or members may be joined as respondents.

Subsection (4)

This subsection contains a number of grounds which might be described as "defences" to the application. If the applicant has established either of the grounds in subs.(1), the burden is on the respondent company to demonstrate one or more of these grounds. They are: that the name was registered prior to the commencement of the activities on which the applicant relies to show goodwill (subs.4(a)); that the company is already operating under the name in question, or is proposing to so operate and has incurred substantial start-up costs in preparation, or formally operated under the name in question and is now dormant (subs.(4)(b)(i), (ii), (iii)); that the registration of the name in question was registered in the ordinary course of formation and that the company is available to sale to the applicant on the standard terms of that business (subs.(4)(c)); that the name was adopted in good faith (subs.(4)(d)); that the applicant's interests are not significantly adversely affected (subs.(4)(e)). If none of these can be established by the respondent company, the objection will be upheld.

Subsection (5)

Even if the company is able to establish one of the defences in subs.(4)(a), (b) or (c) (but not if it successfully relies on subs.(4)(d) or (e)), the objection will be upheld where the applicant can show that the main purpose of the respondent in registering the name in question was to obtain money or other consideration from him or the prevent him from registering the name.

70. Company names adjudicators

(1) The Secretary of State shall appoint persons to be company names adjudicators.

(2) The persons appointed must have such legal or other experience as, in the Secretary of State's opinion, makes them suitable for appointment.

(3) An adjudicator-

   (a) holds office in accordance with the terms of his appointment,

   (b) is eligible for re-appointment when his term of office ends,

   (c) may resign at any time by notice in writing given to the Secretary of State, and

   (d) may be dismissed by the Secretary of State on the ground of incapacity or misconduct.

(4) One of the adjudicators shall be appointed Chief Adjudicator.

He shall perform such functions as the Secretary of State may assign to him.

(5) The other adjudicators shall undertake such duties as the Chief Adjudicator may determine.

(6) The Secretary of State may-

   (a) appoint staff for the adjudicators;

   (b) pay remuneration and expenses to the adjudicators and their staff;

   (c) defray other costs arising in relation to the performance by the adjudicators of their functions;

   (d) compensate persons for ceasing to be adjudicators.

GENERAL NOTE

This is a new provision. It enables the Secretary of State to appoint persons to the office of "company names adjudicator". Appointees must have legal or other experience which, in the opinion of the Secretary of State, qualifies them for appointment, and one of their number is to be appointed as Chief Adjudicator. The Chief Adjudicator, whose functions are to be assigned to him by the Secretary of State, determines the duties of other adjudicators. The Secretary of State is empowered to appoint staff for the adjudicators, to remunerate them and their staff, to defray costs arising from the performance of their functions and to compensate them for ceasing to be adjudicators. Clearly, the primary function of such adjudicators will be to hear applications under s.69 (above).

71.   Procedural rules

(1) The Secretary of State may make rules about proceedings before a company names adjudicator.

(2) The rules may, in particular, make provision-
  (a) as to how an application is to be made and the form and content of an application or other documents;
  (b) for fees to be charged;
  (c) about the service of documents and the consequences of failure to serve them;
  (d) as to the form and manner in which evidence is to be given;
  (e) for circumstances in which hearings are required and those in which they are not;
  (f) for cases to be heard by more than one adjudicator;
  (g) setting time limits for anything required to be done in connection with the proceedings (and allowing for such limits to be extended, even if they have expired);
  (h) enabling the adjudicator to strike out an application, or any defence, in whole or in part-
    (i) on the ground that it is vexatious, has no reasonable prospect of success or is otherwise misconceived, or
    (ii) for failure to comply with the requirements of the rules;
  (i) conferring power to order security for costs (in Scotland, caution for expenses);
  (j) as to how far proceedings are to be held in public;
  (k) requiring one party to bear the costs (in Scotland, expenses) of another and as to the taxing (or settling) the amount of such costs (or expenses).

(3) The rules may confer on the Chief Adjudicator power to determine any matter that could be the subject of provision in the rules.

(4) Rules under this section shall be made by statutory instrument which shall be subject to annulment in pursuance of a resolution of either House of Parliament.

GENERAL NOTE

This new provision supplements ss.69 and 70. The office of company names adjudicator, and the possibility of objecting to a company name by application to the adjudicator are innovations in the 2006 Act, and this section enables the Secretary of State to make procedural rules for proceedings before the adjudicators. Subsection (2) contains a non-exhaustive list of matters about which rules made under subs.(1) may make provision, including the form of any application, the fees to be charged, the service of documents and the manner in which evidence is to be given, time limits to apply and the striking out of applications or defences. Rules under s.71 are to be made by statutory instrument, which shall be subject to annulment in pursuance of a resolution of either the House of Commons or the House of Lords.

72.   Decision of adjudicator to be made available to public

(1) A company names adjudicator must, within 90 days of determining an application under section 69, make his decision and his reasons for it available to the public.

(2) He may do so by means of a website or by such other means as appear to him to be appropriate.

GENERAL NOTE

This new section requires publication (within 90 days of determining an application) of any decision of the company names adjudicator and his reasons for making it. The method of publication is left to the adjudicator.

73. Order requiring name to be changed

(1) If an application under section 69 is upheld, the adjudicator shall make an order-

    (a) requiring the respondent company to change its name to one that is not an offending name, and

    (b) requiring all the respondents-

        (i) to take all such steps as are within their power to make, or facilitate the making, of that change, and

        (ii) not to cause or permit any steps to be taken calculated to result in another company being registered with a name that is an offending name.

(2) An "offending name" means a name that, by reason of its similarity to the name associated with the applicant in which he claims goodwill, would be likely-

    (a) to be the subject of a direction under section 67 (power of Secretary of State to direct change of name), or

    (b) to give rise to a further application under section 69.

(3) The order must specify a date by which the respondent company's name is to be changed and may be enforced-

    (a) in England and Wales or Northern Ireland, in the same way as an order of the High Court;

    (b) in Scotland, in the same way as a decree of the Court of Session.

(4) If the respondent company's name is not changed in accordance with the order by the specified date, the adjudicator may determine a new name for the company.

(5) If the adjudicator determines a new name for the respondent company he must give notice of his determination-

    (a) to the applicant,

    (b) to the respondents, and

    (c) to the registrar.

(6) For the purposes of this section a company's name is changed when the change takes effect in accordance with section 81(1) (on the issue of the new certification of incorporation).

GENERAL NOTE

    This new provision expands upon the previous three sections by providing for the consequences of an application under s.70 being upheld. In such circumstances, the adjudicator is required to make an order that the respondent company change its name to one that is not an "offending name", and requiring all the respondents (which, it will be recalled, may include the company's directors or members joined as respondents under s.69(3)) to take steps to make that change or facilitate the making of that change. Further, the respondents, by that order, must not cause or permit steps to be taken which are calculated to result in another company being registered with an "offending" name (s.73(1)(a), (b)(i) and (ii)). An "offending name" is defined in subs.(2) as one which, because of its similarity to the name associated with the applicant, be subject to a direction under s.68 or an application under s.69. The order must specify a date by which the change of name is to take place, and if it is not changed by that date the adjudicator may determine a new name for the company (subss.(3) and (4)). Where the adjudicator exercises this power he must notify the applicant, the respondent and the registrar (subs.(5)).

74. Appeal from adjudicator's decision

(1) An appeal lies to the court from any decision of a company names adjudicator to uphold or dismiss an application under section 69.

(2) Notice of appeal against a decision upholding an application must be given before the date specified in the adjudicator's order by which the respondent company's name is to be changed.

(3) If notice of appeal is given against a decision upholding an application, the effect of the adjudicator's order is suspended.

(4) If on appeal the court-

(a) affirms the decision of the adjudicator to uphold the application, or

(b) reverses the decision of the adjudicator to dismiss the application,

the court may (as the case may require) specify the date by which the adjudicator's order is to be complied with, remit the matter to the adjudicator or make any order or determination that the adjudicator might have made.

(5) If the court determines a new name for the company it must give notice of the determination-

(a) to the parties to the appeal, and

(b) to the registrar.

GENERAL NOTE

This section, which again is a new provision, allows for an appeal against a decision of a company names adjudicator to uphold or to dismiss an application under s.70. Such an appeal may be made by the applicant (where the adjudicator has dismissed the application) or by the respondent company (where he has upheld it). If the court affirms a decision of the adjudicator to uphold an application, or reverses his decision to dismiss it, the court may specify a date by which the adjudicator's order is to be complied with, remit the matter to the adjudicator or may itself make any order that the adjudicator could make. Notice must be given to the parties to the appeal and to the registrar if the court determines a new name for the company.

CHAPTER 4

OTHER POWERS OF THE SECRETARY OF STATE

75. Provision of misleading information etc

(1) If it appears to the Secretary of State-

(a) that misleading information has been given for the purposes of a company's registration by a particular name, or

(b) that an undertaking or assurance has been given for that purpose and has not been fulfilled,

the Secretary of State may direct the company to change its name.

(2) Any such direction-

(a) must be given within five years of the company's registration by that name, and

(b) must specify the period within which the company is to change its name.

(3) The Secretary of State may by a further direction extend the period within which the company is to change its name.

Any such direction must be given before the end of the period for the time being specified.

(4) A direction under this section must be in writing.

(5) If a company fails to comply with a direction under this section, an offence is committed by-

(a) the company, and

(b) every officer of the company who is in default.

For this purpose a shadow director is treated as an officer of the company.

(6) A person guilty of an offence under this section is liable on summary conviction to a fine not exceeding level 3 on the standard scale and, for continued contravention, a daily default fine not exceeding one-tenth of level 3 on the standard scale.

GENERAL NOTE

This section replaces s.28(3) of the Companies Act 1985. The Secretary of State may direct a company to change its name if it appears to him that either misleading information has been given for the purposes of the company's registration by a particular name or that some undertaking or assurance given for the purpose of the company's registration by a particular name has not been fulfilled (subs.(1)). As under s.28(3), a direction under the section must be in writing (subs.(4)) and must be given within five years of the company's registration by that name and must specify the period within which the change of name must take place (subs.(2)). This period may be extended by a further direction (subs.(3)). Failure to comply with a direction under the section constitutes an offence by the company and every officer in default (including a shadow director of the company) (subs.(5)). The penalty for the offence is set out in subs.(6).

76. Misleading indication of activities

(1) If in the opinion of the Secretary of State the name by which a company is registered gives so misleading an indication of the nature of its activities as to be likely to cause harm to the public, the Secretary of State may direct the company to change its name.

(2) The direction must be in writing.

(3) The direction must be complied with within a period of six weeks from the date of the direction or such longer period as the Secretary of State may think fit to allow.

This does not apply if an application is duly made to the court under the following provisions.

(4) The company may apply to the court to set the direction aside.

The application must be made within the period of three weeks from the date of the direction.

(5) The court may set the direction aside or confirm it.

If the direction is confirmed, the court shall specify the period within which the direction is to be complied with.

(6) If a company fails to comply with a direction under this section, an offence is committed by-

(a) the company, and

(b) every officer of the company who is in default.

For this purpose a shadow director is treated as an officer of the company.

(7) A person guilty of an offence under this section is liable on summary conviction to a fine not exceeding level 3 on the standard scale and, for continued contravention, a daily default fine not exceeding one-tenth of level 3 on the standard scale.

GENERAL NOTE

This section replaces s.32 of the Companies Act 1985. It re-enacts the power of the Secretary of State to direct a company (in writing - subs.(2)) to change its name if, in his opinion, that name gives a misleading indication of the nature of the company's activities which is likely to cause harm to the public (subs.(1)). The direction may be given at any time following registration and must be complied with within six weeks (or such period as the Secretary of State allows (subs.(3)). On receiving such a direction, the company may, within three weeks of the date of the direction, apply to court to have it set aside and the court may do so or may confirm the direction, in which case it must specify the period within which it is to be complied with (subss.(4) and (5)). Failure to comply with a direction under the section constitutes an offence by the company and every officer in default (including a shadow director of the company) (subs.(7)). The penalty for the offence is set out in subs.(7).

An example of the kind of circumstance to which this section will apply can be found in *Association of Certified Public Accountants v Secretary of State* [1998] 1 W.L.R. 164. Jacob J. upheld a direction of the Secretary of State made on the basis that the use of the word "certified" in the name was likely to mislead the public (because it suggested, erroneously, that rigorous entry qualifications applied to the association) and to harm the public because they would expect a high level of expertise by virtue of that suggestion.

CHAPTER 5

CHANGE OF NAME

77. Change of name

(1) A company may change its name-

(a) by special resolution (see section 78), or

(b) by other means provided for by the company's articles (see section 79).

(2) The name of a company may also be changed-

(a) by resolution of the directors acting under section 64 (change of name to comply with direction of Secretary of State under that section);

  (b) on the determination of a new name by a company names adjudicator under section 73 (powers of adjudicator on upholding objection to company name);

  (c) on the determination of a new name by the court under section 74 (appeal against decision of company names adjudicator);

  (d) under section 1033 (company's name on restoration to the register).

GENERAL NOTE

This section replaces s.28(1) of the Companies Act 1985 and adds a new method by which a company may change its name and a new circumstance in which it may change its name.

Subsection (1)

This subsection re-enacts the rule that a company may change its name by special resolution and adds the new method of changing the company's name by other means provided for by the company's articles (see also note to s.79 below). This will allow a company to register articles providing for other, most likely less stringent methods by which its name may be changed

Subsection (2)

This subsection re-enacts the rule that the company's name may be changed by a resolution of the directors in compliance with a direction that the company change its name made by the Secretary of State under s.64 (see above). It adds provision for the company's name to be changed by order of a company name adjudicator under s.73 (above) or by the court under s.74 (above) and on the company's restoration to the register under s.1033 (below).

78. Change of name by special resolution

  (1) Where a change of name has been agreed to by a company by special resolution, the company must give notice to the registrar.

This is in addition to the obligation to forward a copy of the resolution to the registrar.

  (2) Where a change of name by special resolution is conditional on the occurrence of an event, the notice given to the registrar of the change must-

  (a) specify that the change is conditional, and

  (b) state whether the event has occurred.

  (3) If the notice states that the event has not occurred-

  (a) the registrar is not required to act under section 80 (registration and issue of new certificate of incorporation) until further notice,

  (b) when the event occurs, the company must give notice to the registrar stating that it has occurred, and

  (c) the registrar may rely on the statement as sufficient evidence of the matters stated in it.

GENERAL NOTE

This is a new provision requiring notice of a change of name by special resolution to be given to the registrar. This might appear superfluous, given that s.26 of the Companies Act 2006 requires a company to send a copy of any amended articles to the registrar but, as subs.(1) makes clear, the obligation to notify the registrar of a special resolution changing the name of the company is in addition to that requirement.

Subsections (2) and (3)

These provisions are intended to deal with the situation where a change of name by special resolution is conditional upon the occurrence of a particular event. The Explanatory Notes give the example of a change of name to take place once a merger has occurred. If a resolution to this effect has been passed the registrar must be notified of that fact, but also that the change is conditional and the notice must state whether the event upon which the change of name is conditional has occurred (subs.(2)). If the notice states that the event has not occurred the registrar need not act under s.80 (see below) until further notice. The company must then further notify the registrar when the event occurs (subs.(3)(a) and (b)). The registrar may rely on that statement as sufficient evidence of the matters states in it (subs.(3)(c)).

79.   Change of name by means provided for in company's articles

(1) Where a change of a company's name has been made by other means provided for by its articles-

(a) the company must give notice to the registrar, and

(b) the notice must be accompanied by a statement that the change of name has been made by means provided for by the company's articles.

(2) The registrar may rely on the statement as sufficient evidence of the matters stated in it.

GENERAL NOTE

This new provision supplements s.77(1)(b), which provides that a company may change its name by means other than a special resolution provided for by its articles. Where such a change takes place, the company must notify the registrar and include a statement that the change has been made by a method provided for by the articles (s.79(1)). This statement may be relied on by the registrar as sufficient evidence of the matters stated in it (s.79(2)).

80.   Change of name: registration and issue of new certificate of incorporation

(1) This section applies where the registrar receives notice of a change of a company's name.

(2) If the registrar is satisfied-

(a) that the new name complies with the requirements of this Part, and

(b) that the requirements of the Companies Acts, and any relevant requirements of the company's articles, with respect to a change of name are complied with,

the registrar must enter the new name on the register in place of the former name.

(3) On the registration of the new name, the registrar must issue a certificate of incorporation altered to meet the circumstances of the case.

GENERAL NOTE

This subsection replaces parts of s.28(6) of the 1985 Act, and applies when the registrar is notified of a change of a company's name. If the registrar is satisfied that the new name complies with the requirements of Pt 5 and with the Companies Act, and also with any relevant requirements of the company's articles, he must replace the former name with the new name on his index of names. On that registration, the issue a certificate of incorporation altered to meet the circumstance of the case.

81.   Change of name: effect

(1) A change of a company's name has effect from the date on which the new certificate of incorporation is issued.

(2) The change does not affect any rights or obligations of the company or render defective any legal proceedings by or against it.

(3) Any legal proceedings that might have been continued or commenced against it by its former name may be continued or commenced against it by its new name.

GENERAL NOTE

This section replaces, in part, s.28(6) of the Companies Act 1985 and s.28(7) of that Act. Where a company changes its name, the new name has effect from the date at which the new certificate of incorporation is issued under s.80(3). Subsection (2) re-enacts the rule that the change of name does not affect existing rights or obligations of the company or any legal proceedings issued by or against it. Subsection (3) re-enacts the rule that legal proceedings commenced or continued against the company under its former name may be continued or commenced against it by its new name.

CHAPTER 6

TRADING DISCLOSURES

82.   Requirement to disclose company name etc

(1) The Secretary of State may by regulations make provision requiring companies-
   (a) to display specified information in specified locations,
   (b) to state specified information in specified descriptions of document or communication, and
   (c) to provide specified information on request to those they deal with in the course of their business.

(2) The regulations-
   (a) must in every case require disclosure of the name of the company, and
   (b) may make provision as to the manner in which any specified information is to be displayed, stated or provided.

(3) The regulations may provide that, for the purposes of any requirement to disclose a company's name, any variation between a word or words required to be part of the name and a permitted abbreviation of that word or those words (or vice versa) shall be disregarded.

(4) In this section "specified" means specified in the regulations.

(5) Regulations under this section are subject to affirmative resolution procedure.

GENERAL NOTE
   This section replaces ss.348(1), 349(1), 351(1) and (2) of the Companies Act 1985 and, in so far as it applies to companies, s.4(1) of the Business Names Act 1985. It is concerned with the disclosure of the company name in a number of circumstances and empowers the Secretary of State to make provision by regulations (which will be subject to affirmative resolution procedure - subs.(4)) for that disclosure.

Subsection (1)
   The regulations may provide that a company is required to display specified (in the regulations - subs.(4)) information in specified locations (subs.(1)(a)). Under s.348(1) of the Companies Act 1985 this would include painting or affixing the company name, in easily legible letters, in a conspicuous position outside every office or place in which it carries out its business. They may also provide that the company states specified information in specified documents or communications (subs.(1)(b)), which corresponds to s.349(1) of the Companies Act 1985. This requires that the company mentions its name, in legible characters, on all business letters, notices and other official publications, bills of exchange, promissory notes, endorsements, cheques and other orders for money or goods purporting to be signed by or on behalf of the company, and on all its bills of parcels, invoices, receipts and letters of credit. Finally, provision may be made for the company to provide specified information on request to those it deals with in the course of its business (subs.(1)(b)). This is a new provision.

Subsections (2) and (3)
   Regulations under this section must in every case require disclosure of the company's name. They may further make provision for the manner in which any element of the specified information is to be displayed, stated or provided. By subs.(3), where a company's name is required to be disclosed, the regulations may provide that any variation between a word or words required to be part of the name and a permitted abbreviation of that word or those words (or vice versa) shall be disregarded.

83.   Civil consequences of failure to make required disclosure

(1) This section applies to any legal proceedings brought by a company to which section 82 applies (requirement to disclose company name etc) to enforce a right arising out of a contract made in the course of a business in respect of which the company was, at the time the contract was made, in breach of regulations under that section.

(2) The proceedings shall be dismissed if the defendant (in Scotland, the defender) to the proceedings shows-

(a) that he has a claim against the claimant (pursuer) arising out of the contract that he has been unable to pursue by reason of the latter's breach of the regulations, or

(b) that he has suffered some financial loss in connection with the contract by reason of the claimant's (pursuer's) breach of the regulations,

unless the court before which the proceedings are brought is satisfied that it is just and equitable to permit the proceedings to continue.

(3) This section does not affect the right of any person to enforce such rights as he may have against another person in any proceedings brought by that person.

GENERAL NOTE

This section replaces s.349(4) of the Companies Act 1985 and s.5 of the Business Names Act 1985 in so far as it applies to companies. The Company Law Review, in its *Final Report* (at para.11.57) noted that s.349(4) could operate unduly harshly, imposing as it did personal liability to the holder of any bill of exchange, promissory note, cheque or order for money or goods on any officer of the company who signed or authorised to be signed on behalf of the company any such instrument on which the company's name was not mentioned as required by subs.349(1)(c). The courts have taken an almost consistently strict approach to s.349(4), so that officers were held liable even where the company's name was misstated to a relatively minor degree (see, e.g. *Lindholst & Co A/S v Fowler* [1988] B.C.L.C. 166 (company's name stated as "The Corby Chicken Co" instead of "The Corby Chicken Co Ltd" on a bill of exchange), although where the misstatement could be attributed to the holder of the instrument, that holder was estopped from holding the company's signatory liable (*Durham Fancy Goods Ltd v Michael Jackson (Fancy Goods) Ltd* [1968] 2 All E.R. 987). This approach did not require the holder of the instrument to demonstrate that he had in fact been misled, and, as noted by the Company Law Review, could lead to disproportionate penalising of junior employees of the company.

Section 83 implements the Company Law Review's recommendation that the civil sanction in s.349(4) be considerably narrowed by adopting the approach of s.5 of the Business Names Act 1985, which it replaces in respect of companies. Where a company is seeking to enforce a right arising out of a contract made in the course of a business in which it was in breach of the requirement of disclosure under s.82, any legal proceedings will be dismissed if the defendant to the action can show that he has a claim against the company which he has been unable to pursue because of the breach or that the company's breach has cause him to suffer financial loss.

84. Criminal consequences of failure to make required disclosures

(1) Regulations under section 82 may provide-

(a) that where a company fails, without reasonable excuse, to comply with any specified requirement of regulations under that section an offence is committed by-

(i) the company, and

(ii) every officer of the company who is in default;

(b) that a person guilty of such an offence is liable on summary conviction to a fine not exceeding level 3 on the standard scale and, for continued contravention, a daily default fine not exceeding one-tenth of level 3 on the standard scale.

(2) The regulations may provide that, for the purposes of any provision made under subsection (1), a shadow director of the company is to be treated as an officer of the company.

(3) In subsection (1)(a) "specified" means specified in the regulations.

GENERAL NOTE

This section replaces ss.348(2), 349(2), (3), and 351(5) of the Companies Act 1985 and s.7 of the Business Names Act 1985 in so far as it applies to companies. Regulations made under s.82 may provide that failure to comply with the requirements of those regulations constitutes an offence committed by the company and any officer in default (subs.(1)(a)), the penalty being specified in subs.(1)(b). The same regulations may make provision for treating a shadow director as an officer of the company (subs.(2)).

85.   Minor variations in form of name to be left out of account

(1) For the purposes of this Chapter, in considering a company's name no account is to be taken of-
    (a) whether upper or lower case characters (or a combination of the two) are used,
    (b) whether diacritical marks or punctuation are present or absent,
    (c) whether the name is in the same format or style as is specified under section 57(1)(b) for the purposes of registration,

provided there is no real likelihood of names differing only in those respects being taken to be different names.

(2) This does not affect the operation of regulations under section 57(1)(a) permitting only specified characters, diacritical marks or punctuation.

GENERAL NOTE

This new provision allows that, when considering a company's name for the purposes of the disclosure requirements of Ch.6, certain minor variations in the form of that name need not be considered. Thus, for example, where a company discloses its name in upper case characters when its registered name is in lower case characters, that minor variation will not be a breach of s.82 unless there is a real likelihood that that variation will lead to the name being taken to be a different name.

PART 6

A COMPANY'S REGISTERED OFFICE

General

86.   A company's registered office

A company must at all times have a registered office to which all communications and notices may be addressed.

GENERAL NOTE

This section re-enacts s.287(1) of the Companies Act 1985. Every company must have a registered office, and that office is to be the company's address for the purposes of all communications and notices. Section 1139 of the 2006 Act provides that a document may be served on a company by leaving it at, or posting it to, the company's registered office.

87.   Change of address of registered office

(1) A company may change the address of its registered office by giving notice to the registrar.

(2) The change takes effect upon the notice being registered by the registrar, but until the end of the period of 14 days beginning with the date on which it is registered a person may validly serve any document on the company at the address previously registered.

(3) For the purposes of any duty of a company-
    (a) to keep available for inspection at its registered office any register, index or other document, or
    (b) to mention the address of its registered office in any document,

a company that has given notice to the registrar of a change in the address of its registered office may act on the change as from such date, not more than 14 days after the notice is given, as it may determine.

(4) Where a company unavoidably ceases to perform at its registered office any such duty as is mentioned in subsection (3)(a) in circumstances in which it was not practicable to give prior notice to the registrar of a change in the address of its registered office, but-

(a) resumes performance of that duty at other premises as soon as practicable, and

(b) gives notice accordingly to the registrar of a change in the situation of its registered office within 14 days of doing so,

it is not to be treated as having failed to comply with that duty.

GENERAL NOTE

This section deals with the situation where a company changes the address of its registered office. It replaces s.287(3), (4), (5) and (6) of the Companies Act 1985.

Subsections (1) and (2)

These subsections re-enact s.287(3) and (4) of the 1985 Act. A company may change the address of its registered office by notifying the registrar of companies. Whilst the change takes effect when the registrar registers the notice, any person may validly serve a document on the company at its old address for a period of 14 days after registration of the notice. During this time, service at either the old or the new address will be valid.

Subsection (3)

Companies are under certain duties to keep items such as registers, indexes and other documents available for inspection at their registered office and to mention that address of the registered office in documents. This subsection, replacing s.287(5), provides that a company which gives notice to the registrar of a change to the address of its registered office has a 14 day period to make such changes as are necessary to comply with these duties (for example, to alter its letterheads containing its address, or to move registers and indexes to the new address). The Explanatory Notes point out that this is necessary to avoid a company becoming criminally liable under s.82 and other sections imposing criminal liability.

Subsection (4)

This subsection replaces s.287(6) and deals with the situation where, by reason of some kind of emergency (the Explanatory Notes give the example of a fire at the company's registered office), the company has to change its registered office unexpectedly. In such circumstances it will obviously be difficult or impossible to comply with the duty referred to in subs.3(a) (to keep available for inspection at its registered office any register, index or other document), and therefore this subsection treats it as in compliance if it resumes performance of the duty at other premises as soon as is practicable and notifies the registrar of the change to the situation of its registered office within 14 days of doing so. Again, this provision avoids criminal liability attaching to the company in circumstance beyond its control.

Welsh companies

88. Welsh companies

(1) In the Companies Acts a "Welsh company" means a company as to which it is stated in the register that its registered office is to be situated in Wales.

(2) A company-

(a) whose registered office is in Wales, and

(b) as to which it is stated in the register that its registered office is to be situated in England and Wales,

may by special resolution require the register to be amended so that it states that the company's registered office is to be situated in Wales.

(3) A company-

(a) whose registered office is in Wales, and

(b) as to which it is stated in the register that its registered office is to be situated in Wales,

may by special resolution require the register to be amended so that it states that the company's registered office is to be situated in England and Wales.

(4) Where a company passes a resolution under this section it must give notice to the registrar, who shall-

(a) amend the register accordingly, and

(b) issue a new certificate of incorporation altered to meet the circumstances of the case.

GENERAL NOTE

This section defines a "Welsh company" as one which the register records as having a registered office situated in Wales. Subsection (2) provides that a company whose registered office is in Wales but which the register records as to have its registered office situation in England and Wales may, by special resolution, require the register to be amended to record that its registered office is to be situated in Wales (so fulfilling the definition of "Welsh company"). Subsection (3) provides for the opposite circumstance: a "Welsh company" may, be special resolution, require the register to be amended to record that its registered office is to be situated in England and Wales. Where such a resolution is passed the company must notify the registrar, who shall amend the register and issue a new certificate of incorporation.

PART 7

RE-REGISTRATION AS A MEANS OF ALTERING A COMPANY'S STATUS

GENERAL NOTE

Part II of the Companies Act 1985 provides for a number of ways in which a company of one status (e.g. a private company limited by shares) could, by re-registration, alter that status to another (e.g. a public company limited by shares). The Company Law Review, in its *Final Report*, recommended retention of the existing possibilities for a change of status through re-registration and, further, to extend them. One of the recommended extensions (see *Final Report*, para.11.16) is implemented in this Part, in that it will now be possible for a public company to re-register as a private unlimited company without having first to re-register as a private limited company. The Company Law Review also recommended that feasibility studies be carried out to determine whether private companies limited by shares should be permitted to re-register as private companies limited by guarantee, and vice versa. This Part has not made any such provision. Where no provision is made for re-registration by the act the alternative is for the company in question to undergo liquidation and then to be reformed under the Act in the status of its choice.

Part 7 deals with five circumstance in which a company's status can be altered by re-registration. Sections 90-96 addresses a private company becoming a public company, ss.97-101 a public company becoming a private company, ss.102-104 a private limited company becoming an unlimited company, ss.105-107 an unlimited private company becoming limited and ss.108-111 a public company becoming private and unlimited.

Introductory

89. Alteration of status by re-registration

A company may by re-registration under this Part alter its status-
(a) from a private company to a public company (see sections 90 to 96);
(b) from a public company to a private company (see sections 97 to 101);
(c) from a private limited company to an unlimited company (see sections 102 to 104);
(d) from an unlimited private company to a limited company (see sections 105 to 108);
(e) from a public company to an unlimited private company (see sections 109 to 111).

GENERAL NOTE

This introductory section lists the five possible permutations for re-registration.

Private company becoming public

90. Re-registration of private company as public

(1) A private company (whether limited or unlimited) may be re-registered as a public company limited by shares if-
(a) a special resolution that it should be so re-registered is passed,
(b) the conditions specified below are met, and
(c) an application for re-registration is delivered to the registrar in accordance with section 94, together with-

    (i) the other documents required by that section, and

    (ii) a statement of compliance.

(2) The conditions are-

  (a) that the company has a share capital;

  (b) that the requirements of section 91 are met as regards its share capital;

  (c) that the requirements of section 92 are met as regards its net assets;

  (d) if section 93 applies (recent allotment of shares for non-cash consideration), that the requirements of that section are met; and

  (e) that the company has not previously been re-registered as unlimited.

(3) The company must make such changes-

  (a) in its name, and

  (b) in its articles,

as are necessary in connection with its becoming a public company.

(4) If the company is unlimited it must also make such changes in its articles as are necessary in connection with its becoming a company limited by shares.

GENERAL NOTE

This section sets out the basic requirements for a private company to be re-registered as a public company under this part. It replaces s.43(1)(a), (2) and s.48 of the Companies Act 1985. The requirements are that the company passes a special resolution for re-registration as a public company and delivers to the registrar an application for re-registration in accordance with the requirements of s.94 (see below). By subs.(2), the company applying for re-registration must have a share capital (so that a private company limited by guarantee and not having a share capital cannot re-register has a public company (subs.2(a)), and compliance with the requirements of ss.91, 92 and 93 is required (subs.(2)(b), (c), (d)). The company itself must not previously have been *re-registered* as unlimited (subs.(2)(e)). A company applying to re-register under this section must change its name (i.e. to include the denomination "plc" or a permitted alternative) and its articles where such changes are necessary in connection with its becoming a public company (subs.(3)) and, if the company is unlimited, it must alter its articles in the same way (subs.(4)). These subsections will be particularly relevant to private and unlimited companies formed under the 2006 Act, as any model articles they may adopt under s.19 or which apply by default under s.20 will have been drafted with the private or unlimited form in mind and so will be inappropriate to the public form.

91. Requirements as to share capital

(1) The following requirements must be met at the time the special resolution is passed that the company should be re-registered as a public company-

  (a) the nominal value of the company's allotted share capital must be not less than the authorised minimum;

  (b) each of the company's allotted shares must be paid up at least as to onequarter of the nominal value of that share and the whole of any premium on it;

  (c) if any shares in the company or any premium on them have been fully or partly paid up by an undertaking given by any person that he or another should do work or perform services (whether for the company or any other person), the undertaking must have been performed or otherwise discharged;

  (d) if shares have been allotted as fully or partly paid up as to their nominal value or any premium on them otherwise than in cash, and the consideration for the allotment consists of or includes an undertaking to the company (other than one to which paragraph (c) applies), then either-

    (i) the undertaking must have been performed or otherwise discharged, or

    (ii) there must be a contract between the company and some person pursuant to which the undertaking is to be performed within five years from the time the special resolution is passed.

(2) For the purpose of determining whether the requirements in subsection (1)(b), (c) and (d) are met, the following may be disregarded-

  (a) shares allotted-

(i) before 22nd June 1982 in the case of a company then registered in Great Britain, or

(ii) before 31st December 1984 in the case of a company then registered in Northern Ireland;

(b) shares allotted in pursuance of an employees' share scheme by reason of which the company would, but for this subsection, be precluded under subsection (1)(b) (but not otherwise) from being re-registered as a public company.

(3) No more than one-tenth of the nominal value of the company's allotted share capital is to be disregarded under subsection (2)(a).

For this purpose the allotted share capital is treated as not including shares disregarded under subsection (2)(b).

(4) Shares disregarded under subsection (2) are treated as not forming part of the allotted share capital for the purposes of subsection (1)(a).

(5) A company must not be re-registered as a public company if it appears to the registrar that-

(a) the company has resolved to reduce its share capital,

(b) the reduction-

(i) is made under section 626 (reduction in connection with redenomination of share capital),

(ii) is supported by a solvency statement in accordance with section 643, or

(iii) has been confirmed by an order of the court under section 648, and

(c) the effect of the reduction is, or will be, that the nominal value of the company's allotted share capital is below the authorised minimum.

GENERAL NOTE

Public companies are subject to more stringent requirements as to the raising and maintenance of their share capital than are private companies. This section, which replaces ss.45 and 47(3) of the Companies Act 1985, is designed to ensure that the newly re-registered public company complies with those requirements.

Subsection (1)

At the time of the passing of the special resolution to re-register a private company as a public company the nominal value of the company's allotted share capital must not be less than the authorised minimum (subs.(1)(a)) which remains as £50,000 (see s.s.763(1)(a)). Each of the allotted shares must have been paid up at least as to one quarter of its nominal value and all of any premium (subs.(1)(b)) and if any shares have been fully or partly paid by an undertaking given by any person that work or services shall be performed (for the company or any other person), that undertaking must have been performed or otherwise discharged (subs.(1)(b)). This reflects the requirement in s.585 that public companies must not accept, as consideration for their shares, an undertaking to do work or provide services. Where the company applying for re-registration as a public company has allotted shares other than for cash and the consideration consists of or includes an undertaking other than to do work or provide services, then that undertaking must have already been performed or their must exist a contractual obligation owed to the company to perform the undertaking within five years of the special resolution to re-register as a public company being passed (subs.(1)(d)). This reflects the requirements imposed upon public companies by s.587.

Subsections (2)-(4)

This subsection specifies that shares allotted before 22 June 1982 (in relation to companies then registered in Great Britain) or before 31 December 1984 (in relation to companies then registered in Northern Ireland) are to be disregarded for the purposes of compliance with the requirements of subs.(1)(b), (c) and (d) (subs.(2)(a)). However, no more than one-tenth of the nominal value of the company's allotted share capital may be disregarded under this subsection (subs.(3)). Shares allotted under an employees' shares scheme are to be disregarded for the purpose of determining whether the requirement of subs.(1)(b)) is satisfied. Any shares disregarded under subs.(2) are not treated as forming part of the company's allotted share capital under subs.(1)(a), and so cannot count towards the authorised minimum capital.

Subsection (5)

This subsection replaces s.47(3) of the Companies Act 1985. It prevents re-registration where the company has already resolved to reduce its capital and that the effect of the reduction is or will be that the nominal value of the allotted capital falls under the authorised minimum of £50,000.

92.   Requirements as to net assets

(1) A company applying to re-register as a public company must obtain-
   (a) a balance sheet prepared as at a date not more than seven months before the date on which the application is delivered to the registrar,
   (b) an unqualified report by the company's auditor on that balance sheet, and
   (c) a written statement by the company's auditor that in his opinion at the balance sheet date the amount of the company's net assets was not less than the aggregate of its called-up share capital and undistributable reserves.
(2) Between the balance sheet date and the date on which the application for reregistration is delivered to the registrar, there must be no change in the company's financial position that results in the amount of its net assets becoming less than the aggregate of its called-up share capital and undistributable reserves.
(3) In subsection (1)(b) an "unqualified report" means-
   (a) if the balance sheet was prepared for a financial year of the company, a report stating without material qualification the auditor's opinion that the balance sheet has been properly prepared in accordance with the requirements of this Act;
   (b) if the balance sheet was not prepared for a financial year of the company, a report stating without material qualification the auditor's opinion that the balance sheet has been properly prepared in accordance with the provisions of this Act which would have applied if it had been prepared for a financial year of the company.
(4) For the purposes of an auditor's report on a balance sheet that was not prepared for a financial year of the company, the provisions of this Act apply with such modifications as are necessary by reason of that fact.
(5) For the purposes of subsection (3) a qualification is material unless the auditor states in his report that the matter giving rise to the qualification is not material for the purpose of determining (by reference to the company's balance sheet) whether at the balance sheet date the amount of the company's net assets was not less than the aggregate of its called-up share capital and undistributable reserves.
(6) In this Part "net assets" and "undistributable reserves" have the same meaning as in section 831 (net asset restriction on distributions by public companies).

GENERAL NOTE
   This section replaces, without substantive change, s.43(3)(b), (c) and (4) of the Companies Act 1985. It is concerned with ensuring that the requirement imposed on public companies that their net assets should not fall below the aggregate of their called-up share capital and undistributable reserves (as defined in s.831 of the Companies Act 2006 - (subs.(6)). Thus, on applying for re-registration as a public company, the company must obtain a balance sheet prepared not more than seven months before the application, and unqualified auditor's report (as defined in subs.(3)) on that balance sheet and a written statement from its auditor stating his opinion that, at the balance sheet date, the amount of the company's net assets was not less than the aggregate of its called-up share capital and undistributable reserves (subs.(1)). This position must obtain between the date of the balance sheet and the application (subs.(2)).

93.   Recent allotment of shares for non-cash consideration

(1) This section applies where-
   (a) shares are allotted by the company in the period between the date as at which the balance sheet required by section 92 is prepared and the passing of the resolution that the company should re-register as a public company, and
   (b) the shares are allotted as fully or partly paid up as to their nominal value or any premium on them otherwise than in cash.
(2) The registrar shall not entertain an application by the company for reregistration as a public company unless-

    (a) the requirements of section 593(1)(a) and (b) have been complied with (independent valuation of non-cash consideration; valuer's report to company not more than six months before allotment), or

    (b) the allotment is in connection with-

        (i) a share exchange (see subsections (3) to (5) below), or

        (ii) a proposed merger with another company (see subsection (6) below).

  (3) An allotment is in connection with a share exchange if-

    (a) the shares are allotted in connection with an arrangement under which the whole or part of the consideration for the shares allotted is provided by-

        (i) the transfer to the company allotting the shares of shares (or shares of a particular class) in another company, or

        (ii) the cancellation of shares (or shares of a particular class) in another company; and

    (b) the allotment is open to all the holders of the shares of the other company in question (or, where the arrangement applies only to shares of a particular class, to all the holders of the company's shares of that class) to take part in the arrangement in connection with which the shares are allotted.

  (4) In determining whether a person is a holder of shares for the purposes of subsection (3), there shall be disregarded-

    (a) shares held by, or by a nominee of, the company allotting the shares;

    (b) shares held by, or by a nominee of-

        (i) the holding company of the company allotting the shares,

        (ii) a subsidiary of the company allotting the shares, or

        (iii) a subsidiary of the holding company of the company allotting the shares.

  (5) It is immaterial, for the purposes of deciding whether an allotment is in connection with a share exchange, whether or not the arrangement in connection with which the shares are allotted involves the issue to the company allotting the shares of shares (or shares of a particular class) in the other company.

  (6) There is a proposed merger with another company if one of the companies concerned proposes to acquire all the assets and liabilities of the other in exchange for the issue of its shares or other securities to shareholders of the other (whether or not accompanied by a cash payment).

"Another company" includes any body corporate.

  (7) For the purposes of this section-

    (a) the consideration for an allotment does not include any amount standing to the credit of any of the company's reserve accounts, or of its profit and loss account, that has been applied in paying up (to any extent) any of the shares allotted or any premium on those shares; and

    (b) "arrangement" means any agreement, scheme or arrangement, (including an arrangement sanctioned in accordance with-

        (i) Part 26 of this Act (arrangements and reconstructions), or

        (ii) section 110 of the Insolvency Act 1986 (c. 45) or Article 96 of the Insolvency (Northern Ireland) Order 1989 (S.I. 1989/2405 (N.I. 19)) (liquidator in winding up accepting shares as consideration for sale of company's property)).

GENERAL NOTE

  This section replaces, without substantive amendment, s.44 of the Companies Act 1985. It is concerned with an application for re-registration as a public company by a private company that has, between the time when it prepares a balance sheet as required by s.92 and the passing of the resolution for re-registration, allotted shares as fully or partly paid up in return for a non-cash consideration. In such circumstances, the registrar shall not entertain the application unless the consideration has been valued in accordance with the provisions of s.593 or the allotment is in connection with a share exchange (as defined in subs.(3)-(5)) or a proposed merger (as amplified by subs.(6)): subs.(1), (2).

94. Application and accompanying documents

(1) An application for re-registration as a public company must contain-
   (a) a statement of the company's proposed name on re-registration; and
   (b) in the case of a company without a secretary, a statement of the company's proposed secretary (see section 95).
(2) The application must be accompanied by-
   (a) a copy of the special resolution that the company should re-register as a public company (unless a copy has already been forwarded to the registrar under Chapter 3 of Part 3);
   (b) a copy of the company's articles as proposed to be amended;
   (c) a copy of the balance sheet and other documents referred to in section 92(1); and
   (d) if section 93 applies (recent allotment of shares for non-cash consideration), a copy of the valuation report (if any) under subsection (2)(a) of that section.
(3) The statement of compliance required to be delivered together with the application is a statement that the requirements of this Part as to re-registration as a public company have been complied with.
(4) The registrar may accept the statement of compliance as sufficient evidence that the company is entitled to be re-registered as a public company.

GENERAL NOTE

This clause replaces s.43(1)(b), (2)(a), (3)(a) and (e) and (3A) of the Companies Act 1985 and prescribes the the contents of an application for re-registration of a private company as a public company. The application must contain a statement of the company's proposed name on re-registration and a statement of the company's secretary (see s.95) (subs.(1)). With the application must be sent a copy of the special resolution for re-registration, a copy of the company's articles as proposed to be amended to reflect the new status, a copy of the balance sheet and documents referred to in s.92 and, if the company has recently allotted shares for a non-cash consideration, a copy of the valuation report as required by s.93(2)(a) (subs.(2)). The statement of compliance referred to in s.90 (above) will be in the new form specified in s.13 (above) and must accompany the application (subs.(3)), and the registrar may accept that statement as sufficient evidence that the company is entitled to be re-registered as a public company (subs.(4)).

95. Statement of proposed secretary

(1) The statement of the company's proposed secretary must contain the required particulars of the person who is or the persons who are to be the secretary or joint secretaries of the company.
(2) The required particulars are the particulars that will be required to be stated in the company's register of secretaries (see sections 277 to 279).
(3) The statement must also contain a consent by the person named as secretary, or each of the persons named as joint secretaries, to act in the relevant capacity. If all the partners in a firm are to be joint secretaries, consent may be given by one partner on behalf of all of them.

GENERAL NOTE

This section is a new provision reflecting the fact that private companies need no longer appoint a secretary. Where it is proposed that a private company without a secretary re-register as a public company, an application for re-registration must contain a statement of the company's proposed secretary. This section requires that statement to contain the required particulars of the person or persons who is or are to be the company's secretary or joint secretary (subs.(1)), these particulars being those prescribed by ss.277-279 for the company's register of secretaries (subs.(2)). The named person or persons must consent to act as secretary or secretaries, and a statement of consent must be included in the application for re-registration, and if all partners in a firm are to be joint secretaries the consent of one may be given on behalf of all (subs.(3)).

96.   Issue of certificate of incorporation on re-registration

(1) If on an application for re-registration as a public company the registrar is satisfied that the company is entitled to be so re-registered, the company shall be re-registered accordingly.

(2) The registrar must issue a certificate of incorporation altered to meet the circumstances of the case.

(3) The certificate must state that it is issued on re-registration and the date on which it is issued.

(4) On the issue of the certificate-

    (a) the company by virtue of the issue of the certificate becomes a public company,

    (b) the changes in the company's name and articles take effect, and

    (c) where the application contained a statement under section 95 (statement of proposed secretary), the person or persons named in the statement as secretary or joint secretary of the company are deemed to have been appointed to that office.

(5) The certificate is conclusive evidence that the requirements of this Act as to reregistration have been complied with.

GENERAL NOTE

This section replaces s.47 of the Companies Act 1985. Where a private company applies for re-registration as a public company, and the registrar is satisfied that the company is entitled to be so re-registered, he shall re-register it accordingly and issue an altered certificate of incorporation, which must state that it is issued on re-registration and the date on which it is issued (subs.(1), (2) and (3)). The issue of the new certificate of incorporation has the effect that the company becomes a public company, its new name and articles take effect, and any person or persons named as secretary or joint secretaries of the company in accordance with s.95 are deemed to have been appointed to that office (subs.(4)). The certificate is conclusive evidence that the requirements of the Act as to re-registration have been complied with (subs.(5)).

Public company becoming private

97.   Re-registration of public company as private limited company

(1) A public company may be re-registered as a private limited company if-

    (a) a special resolution that it should be so re-registered is passed,

    (b) the conditions specified below are met, and

    (c) an application for re-registration is delivered to the registrar in accordance with section 100, together with-

        (i) the other documents required by that section, and

        (ii) a statement of compliance.

(2) The conditions are that-

    (a) where no application under section 98 for cancellation of the resolution has been made-

        (i) having regard to the number of members who consented to or voted in favour of the resolution, no such application may be made, or

        (ii) the period within which such an application could be made has expired, or

    (b) where such an application has been made-

        (i) the application has been withdrawn, or

        (ii) an order has been made confirming the resolution and a copy of that order has been delivered to the registrar.

(3) The company must make such changes-

    (a) in its name, and

    (b) in its articles,

as are necessary in connection with its becoming a private company limited by shares or, as the case may be, by guarantee.

GENERAL NOTE

Section 97 replaces s.53 of the Companies Act 1985. It provides for a public company to re-register as a private company and states the basic requirements for re-registration, these being supplemented in the following four sections. The company must have passed a special resolution for re-registration as a private company and there must either be no possibility of an application under s.98 (below) to cancel the resolution being made or, where such an application has been made, it must have been withdrawn or an order confirming the resolution must have been made and a copy of it delivered to the registrar (sub-s.(1)(a)(b), subs.(2)(a)(b)). The application for re-registration must be delivered to the registrar with such documents as are required by s.100 (below) and a statement of compliance (subs.(1)(c)), and the company must make changes to its name (i.e. to include the term "ltd" or a permitted alternative) and to its articles, the changes being those required in connection with its becoming a private company limited by shares or by guarantee (subs.(3)).

98. Application to court to cancel resolution

(1) Where a special resolution by a public company to be re-registered as a private limited company has been passed, an application to the court for the cancellation of the resolution may be made-

    (a) by the holders of not less in the aggregate than 5% in nominal value of the company's issued share capital or any class of the company's issued share capital (disregarding any shares held by the company as treasury shares);

    (b) if the company is not limited by shares, by not less than 5% of its members; or

    (c) by not less than 50 of the company's members;

but not by a person who has consented to or voted in favour of the resolution.

(2) The application must be made within 28 days after the passing of the resolution and may be made on behalf of the persons entitled to make it by such one or more of their number as they may appoint for the purpose.

(3) On the hearing of the application the court shall make an order either cancelling or confirming the resolution.

(4) The court may-

    (a) make that order on such terms and conditions as it thinks fit,

    (b) if it thinks fit adjourn the proceedings in order that an arrangement may be made to the satisfaction of the court for the purchase of the interests of dissentient members, and

    (c) give such directions, and make such orders, as it thinks expedient for facilitating or carrying into effect any such arrangement.

(5) The court's order may, if the court thinks fit-

    (a) provide for the purchase by the company of the shares of any of its members and for the reduction accordingly of the company's capital; and

    (b) make such alteration in the company's articles as may be required in consequence of that provision.

(6) The court's order may, if the court thinks fit, require the company not to make any, or any specified, amendments to its articles without the leave of the court.

GENERAL NOTE

This section replaces s.54(1), (2), (3), (5), (6) and (8) of the Companies Act 1985 and deals with an application by a pre-scribed proportion of the company's members to apply to court for the cancellation of a special resolution to re-register the company as a private company. The holders of not less than 5 per cent in nominal value of the issued share capital of any class, or 5 per cent of its members if it is not limited by shares, or not less than 50 of its members may make such an application (but not any person who voted in favour of the resolution) (subs.(1)). Any such application must be made within 28 days of the passing of the resolution (subs.(2)) and the court is required to make an order either confirming or cancelling it (subs.(3)). The court may make the order on such terms and conditions as it thinks fit, and may adjourn proceedings so that the dissentient applicants' shares may be purchased (subs.(4)), and it may order that the company purchase those shares and reduce its capital accordingly (subs.(5)).

99.   Notice to registrar of court application or order

(1) On making an application under section 98 (application to court to cancel resolution) the applicants, or the person making the application on their behalf, must immediately give notice to the registrar.
This is without prejudice to any provision of rules of court as to service of notice of the application.

(2) On being served with notice of any such application, the company must immediately give notice to the registrar.

(3) Within 15 days of the making of the court's order on the application, or such longer period as the court may at any time direct, the company must deliver to the registrar a copy of the order.

(4) If a company fails to comply with subsection (2) or (3) an offence is committed by-
   (a) the company, and
   (b) every officer of the company who is in default.

(5) A person guilty of an offence under this section is liable on summary conviction to a fine not exceeding level 3 on the standard scale and, for continued contravention, a daily default fine not exceeding one-tenth of level 3 on the standard scale.

GENERAL NOTE

This section replaces s.54(4), (7) and (10) of the Companies Act 1985 and provides for the situation where an application to cancel the special resolution to re-register the company as a private company is made under s.98. In such circumstance, the company, on being served with notice of the application, must immediately notify the registrar, and, within 15 days of the court making an order, must deliver a copy of that order to the registrar (subs.(2), (3)). Failure to comply with these subsections constitutes an offence committed by the company and every officer in default (subs.(4), the penalty for which is prescribed by subs.(5).

100.   Application and accompanying documents

(1) An application for re-registration as a private limited company must contain a statement of the company's proposed name on re-registration.

(2) The application must be accompanied by-
   (a) a copy of the resolution that the company should re-register as a private limited company (unless a copy has already been forwarded to the registrar under Chapter 3 of Part 3); and
   (b) a copy of the company's articles as proposed to be amended.

(3) The statement of compliance required to be delivered together with the application is a statement that the requirements of this Part as to re-registration as a private limited company have been complied with.

(4) The registrar may accept the statement of compliance as sufficient evidence that the company is entitled to be re-registered as a private limited company.

GENERAL NOTE

Section 100 replaces s.53(1)(b) of the Companies Act 1985 and prescribes the contents of an application for re-registration of a public company as a private company. These are a statement of the company's proposed name on re-registration (subs.(1)), a copy of the special resolution that the company should re-register as a private limited company and a copy of the amended articles (subs.(2)) and a statement of compliance attesting to the fact that the requirements for re-registration as a private company have been complied with (subs.(3)). The registrar is entitled to treat this statement as sufficient evidence that the company is entitled to be re-registered as a private limited company (subs.(4)).

101. Issue of certificate of incorporation on re-registration

(1) If on an application for re-registration as a private limited company the registrar is satisfied that the company is entitled to be so re-registered, the company shall be re-registered accordingly.

(2) The registrar must issue a certificate of incorporation altered to meet the circumstances of the case.

(3) The certificate must state that it is issued on re-registration and the date on which it is issued.

(4) On the issue of the certificate-

    (a) the company by virtue of the issue of the certificate becomes a private limited company, and

    (b) the changes in the company's name and articles take effect.

(5) The certificate is conclusive evidence that the requirements of this Act as to reregistration have been complied with.

GENERAL NOTE

  This section replaces s.5 of the Companies Act 1985. If the registrar is satisfied that the company is entitled to be re-registered as a private limited company she shall re-register it and issue an appropriately altered certificate of incorporation, which must state that it is issued on re-registration and the date of its issue (subs.(1), (2), (3)). On the issue of the certificate the company becomes a private limited company and the changes to its name and articles take effect (subs.(4)). The certificate is conclusive evidence that the Act's requirements as to re-registration have been complied with.

Private limited company becoming unlimited

102. Re-registration of private limited company as unlimited

(1) A private limited company may be re-registered as an unlimited company if-

    (a) all the members of the company have assented to its being so reregistered,

    (b) the condition specified below is met, and

    (c) an application for re-registration is delivered to the registrar in accordance with section 103, together with-

        (i) the other documents required by that section, and

        (ii) a statement of compliance.

(2) The condition is that the company has not previously been re-registered as limited.

(3) The company must make such changes in its name and its articles-

    (a) as are necessary in connection with its becoming an unlimited company; and

    (b) if it is to have a share capital, as are necessary in connection with its becoming an unlimited company having a share capital.

(4) For the purposes of this section-

    (a) a trustee in bankruptcy of a member of the company is entitled, to the exclusion of the member, to assent to the company's becoming unlimited; and

    (b) the personal representative of a deceased member of the company may assent on behalf of the deceased.

(5) In subsection (4)(a), "a trustee in bankruptcy of a member of the company" includes-

    (a) a permanent trustee or an interim trustee (within the meaning of the Bankruptcy (Scotland) Act 1985 (c. 66)) on the sequestrated estate of a member of the company;

    (b) a trustee under a protected trustee deed (within the meaning of the Bankruptcy (Scotland) Act 1985) granted by a member of the company.

GENERAL NOTE

  This section replaces s.49(1), (2) and (9) of the Companies Act 1985 and permits, as previously, a company limited by shares or by guarantee to re-register as an unlimited company. All the members of the company must assent to the re-registration (subs.(1)(a)) and the application must comply with the requirements of s.103 (below) and be accompanied by a statement of compliance (subs.(1)(c)). The company must not have previously been re-registered as a limited company (subs.(2)) and must make the necessary changes to its name and articles as are necessary in connection with it becoming an unlimited company (subs.(3)). As far as the assent of the members is concerned, a trustee in bankruptcy of a member is entitled to assent to the exclusion of the member and the personal representative of a deceased member may assent on behalf of the deceased (subs.(4)). Subsection (5) expands the definition of trustee in bankruptcy to include a permanent or interim trustee or a trustee under a protected trust deed in Scotland.

103.   Application and accompanying documents

(1) An application for re-registration as an unlimited company must contain a statement of the company's proposed name on re-registration.

(2) The application must be accompanied by-
   (a) the prescribed form of assent to the company's being registered as an unlimited company, authenticated by or on behalf of all the members of the company;
   (b) a copy of the company's articles as proposed to be amended.

(3) The statement of compliance required to be delivered together with the application is a statement that the requirements of this Part as to re-registration as an unlimited company have been complied with.

(4) The statement must contain a statement by the directors of the company-
   (a) that the persons by whom or on whose behalf the form of assent is authenticated constitute the whole membership of the company, and
   (b) if any of the members have not authenticated that form themselves, that the directors have taken all reasonable steps to satisfy themselves that each person who authenticated it on behalf of a member was lawfully empowered to do so.

(5) The registrar may accept the statement of compliance as sufficient evidence that the company is entitled to be re-registered as an unlimited company.

GENERAL NOTE

This section replaces s.49(4)-(8A) of the Companies Act 1985 and prescribes the contents of an application for re-registration of a private limited company as unlimited. The application must contain a statement of the proposed name of the company on re-registration (subs.(1)) and the application must be accompanied by a copy of the articles as proposed to be amended and a form of assent, authenticated by or on behalf of the members, to the company's being so re-registered (subs.(2)). The statement of compliance required by s.102(1)(c)(ii) must contain a statement by the directors of the company that the persons by whom or on behalf the form of assent is authenticated constitute the whole membership of the company (subs.(4)(a)). Where the assent is authenticated on behalf of a member, the directors' statement must attest that the directors have taken all reasonable steps to satisfy themselves that the person so assenting was lawfully empowered to do so (subs.(4)(b)). This is an important protection for members whose liability for the debts of the company will, on re-registration, be unlimited. The statement of compliance may be treated by the registrar as sufficient evidence that the company is entitled to be re-registered as an unlimited company (subs.(5)).

104.   Issue of certificate of incorporation on re-registration

(1) If on an application for re-registration of a private limited company as an unlimited company the registrar is satisfied that the company is entitled to be so re-registered, the company shall be re-registered accordingly.

(2) The registrar must issue a certificate of incorporation altered to meet the circumstances of the case.

(3) The certificate must state that it is issued on re-registration and the date on which it is issued.

(4) On the issue of the certificate-
   (a) the company by virtue of the issue of the certificate becomes an unlimited company, and

(b) the changes in the company's name and articles take effect.

(5) The certificate is conclusive evidence that the requirements of this Act as to reregistration have been complied with.

GENERAL NOTE

Section 104 replaces s.50 of the Companies Act 1985. If the registrar is satisfied that a private limited company is entitled to be re-registered as an unlimited company he shall re-register it accordingly and issue an appropriately altered certificate of incorporation (subss.(1) and (2)). The certificate must state that it is issued on re-registration and the date on which it is issued (subs.(3)). On the issue of the amended certificate of incorporation the company becomes unlimited and the changes to its name and articles take effect, and the certificate is conclusive evidence that the requirements of the Act as to re-registration have been complied with (subss.(4) and (5)).

Unlimited private company becoming limited

105. Re-registration of unlimited company as limited

(1) An unlimited company may be re-registered as a private limited company if-
    (a) a special resolution that it should be so re-registered is passed,
    (b) the condition specified below is met, and
    (c) an application for re-registration is delivered to the registrar in accordance with section 106, together with-
        (i) the other documents required by that section, and
        (ii) a statement of compliance.

(2) The condition is that the company has not previously been re-registered as unlimited.

(3) The special resolution must state whether the company is to be limited by shares or by guarantee.

(4) The company must make such changes-
    (a) in its name, and
    (b) in its articles,
as are necessary in connection with its becoming a company limited by shares or, as the case may be, by guarantee.

GENERAL NOTE

This section replaces s.51(1), (2), (3) and (6) of the Companies Act 1985 and specifies conditions for the re-registration of an unlimited company as a private limited company. The company must pass a special resolution (stating whether the company is to be limited by shares or by guarantee (subs.(3)) in favour of re-registration and deliver to the registrar an application for re-registration accompanied by a statement of compliance (subss.(1)(a) and (c)). The company must not previously have been re-registered as unlimited (subss.(1)(b) and (2)). Necessary changes must be made to the company's name and its articles to reflect its new status as a company limited by shares or by guarantee (subs.(4)).

106. Application and accompanying documents

(1) An application for re-registration as a limited company must contain a statement of the company's proposed name on re-registration.

(2) The application must be accompanied by-
    (a) a copy of the resolution that the company should re-register as a private limited company (unless a copy has already been forwarded to the registrar under Chapter 3 of Part 3);
    (b) if the company is to be limited by guarantee, a statement of guarantee;
    (c) a copy of the company's articles as proposed to be amended.

(3) The statement of guarantee required to be delivered in the case of a company that is to be limited by guarantee must state that each member undertakes that, if the company is wound

up while he is a member, or within one year after he ceases to be a member, he will contribute to the assets of the company such amount as may be required for-

    (a) payment of the debts and liabilities of the company contracted before he ceases to be a member,

    (b) payment of the costs, charges and expenses of winding up, and

    (c) adjustment of the rights of the contributories among themselves,

not exceeding a specified amount.

    (4) The statement of compliance required to be delivered together with the application is a statement that the requirements of this Part as to re-registration as a limited company have been complied with.

    (5) The registrar may accept the statement of compliance as sufficient evidence that the company is entitled to be re-registered as a limited company.

GENERAL NOTE

    This section replaces s.51(3), (4) and (5) of the Companies Act 1985 and prescribes the content of an application for re-registration of an unlimited company as a private limited company and the content of the documents required to be delivered to the registrar. The application must state the company's proposed name on re-registration (which will have to contain the term "limited" or a permitted alternative) (subs.(1)). The documents are a copy of the resolution for re-registration, a statement of guarantee (if the company is to be re-registered as a company limited by guarantee) and a copy of the articles as proposed to be amended (subs.(2)). Subsection (3) prescribes the form of the statement of guarantee, which is equivalent to that required by s.11 (see above). The statement of compliance, as defined in subs.(4), must be delivered to the registrar with the application for re-registration and the registrar may accept it as sufficient evidence that the company is entitled to be re-registered as a limited company (subs.(5)).

107. Issue of certificate of incorporation on re-registration

    (1) If on an application for re-registration of an unlimited company as a limited company the registrar is satisfied that the company is entitled to be so reregistered, the company shall be re-registered accordingly.

    (2) The registrar must issue a certificate of incorporation altered to meet the circumstances of the case.

    (3) The certificate must state that it is issued on re-registration and the date on which it is so issued.

    (4) On the issue of the certificate-

    (a) the company by virtue of the issue of the certificate becomes a limited company, and

    (b) the changes in the company's name and articles take effect.

    (5) The certificate is conclusive evidence that the requirements of this Act as to reregistration have been complied with.

GENERAL NOTE

    Section 107 replaces s.52 of the Companies Act 1985. If the registrar is satisfied that an unlimited company is entitled to be re-registered as a limited company he shall re-register it accordingly and issue an appropriately altered certificate of incorporation (subss.(1) and (2)). The certificate must state that it is issued on re-registration and the date on which it is issued (subs.(3)). On the issue of the amended certificate of incorporation the company becomes limited and the changes to its name and articles take effect, and the certificate is conclusive evidence that the requirements of the Act as to re-registration have been complied with (subss.(4) and (5)).

108. Statement of capital required where company already has share capital

    (1) A company which on re-registration under section 107 already has allotted share capital must within 15 days after the re-registration deliver a statement of capital to the registrar.

    (2) This does not apply if the information which would be included in the statement has already been sent to the registrar in-

    (a) a statement of capital and initial shareholdings (see section 10), or

    (b) a statement of capital contained in an annual return (see section 856(2)).

(3) The statement of capital must state with respect to the company's share capital on re-registration-

    (a) the total number of shares of the company,

    (b) the aggregate nominal value of those shares,

    (c) for each class of shares-

        (i) prescribed particulars of the rights attached to the shares,

        (ii) the total number of shares of that class, and

        (iii) the aggregate nominal value of shares of that class, and

    (d) the amount paid up and the amount (if any) unpaid on each share (whether on account of the nominal value of the share or by way of premium).

(4) If default is made in complying with this section, an offence is committed by-

    (a) the company, and

    (b) every officer of the company who is in default.

(5) A person guilty of an offence under this section is liable on summary conviction to a fine not exceeding level 3 on the standard scale and, for continued contravention, a daily default fine not exceeding one-tenth of level 3 on the standard scale.

GENERAL NOTE

Section 108 applies to a company which, on re-registration, already has allotted share capital. Subsection (1) requires the company to deliver to the registrar, within 15 days of re-registration, a statement of capital unless a statement of capital and initial shareholdings under s.10 (see above) or an annual return containing a statement of capital (under s.856(2) - see below) has already been sent to the registrar (subs.(2)). The statement of capital must state information corresponding to that in a statement of capital and initial shareholdings under s.10(2) (subs.(3)), and failure to comply with this requirement constitutes an offence committed by the company and every one of its officers in default (subs.(4)). The penalty for the offence is set out in subs.(5).

Public company becoming private and unlimited

109. Re-registration of public company as private and unlimited

(1) A public company limited by shares may be re-registered as an unlimited private company with a share capital if-

    (a) all the members of the company have assented to its being so reregistered,

    (b) the condition specified below is met, and

    (c) an application for re-registration is delivered to the registrar in accordance with section 110, together with-

        (i) the other documents required by that section, and

        (ii) a statement of compliance.

(2) The condition is that the company has not previously been re-registered-

    (a) as limited, or

    (b) as unlimited.

(3) The company must make such changes-

    (a) in its name, and

    (b) in its articles,

as are necessary in connection with its becoming an unlimited private company.

(4) For the purposes of this section-

    (a) a trustee in bankruptcy of a member of the company is entitled, to the exclusion of the member, to assent to the company's re-registration; and

    (b) the personal representative of a deceased member of the company may assent on behalf of the deceased.

(5) In subsection (4)(a), "a trustee in bankruptcy of a member of the company" includes-

(a) a permanent trustee or an interim trustee (within the meaning of the Bankruptcy (Scotland) Act 1985 (c. 66)) on the sequestrated estate of a member of the company;

(b) a trustee under a protected trustee deed (within the meaning of the Bankruptcy (Scotland) Act 1985) granted by a member of the company.

GENERAL NOTE

Section 109 is a new provision and implements the recommendation of the Company Law Review that a public company should be enabled to re-register as a private unlimited company in a single process (i.e. instead of first having to re-register as a private company and then having to re-register as an unlimited company: see Company Law Review *Final Report*, para.11.6). To take advantage of this possibility the members of the company must assent to its re-registration (subs.(1)(a): assent may be given on behalf of a bankrupt member by his trustee in bankruptcy to the exclusion of the member, and the personal representative of a deceased member may give assent on behalf of the deceased (subs.(4)). For the position in Scotland as regards a trustee in bankruptcy see subs.(5)). The company in question must not have previously re-registered as either limited or unlimited (subs.(2)) and must make changes to its name and articles necessary to reflect its new unlimited status (subs.(3)).

110.   Application and accompanying documents

(1) An application for re-registration of a public company as an unlimited private company must contain a statement of the company's proposed name on reregistration.

(2) The application must be accompanied by-

  (a) the prescribed form of assent to the company's being registered as an unlimited company, authenticated by or on behalf of all the members of the company, and

  (b) a copy of the company's articles as proposed to be amended.

(3) The statement of compliance required to be delivered together with the application is a statement that the requirements of this Part as to re-registration as an unlimited private company have been complied with.

(4) The statement must contain a statement by the directors of the company-

  (a) that the persons by whom or on whose behalf the form of assent is authenticated constitute the whole membership of the company, and

  (b) if any of the members have not authenticated that form themselves, that the directors have taken all reasonable steps to satisfy themselves that each person who authenticated it on behalf of a member was lawfully empowered to do so.

(5) The registrar may accept the statement of compliance as sufficient evidence that the company is entitled to be re-registered as an unlimited private company.

GENERAL NOTE

This provision is a new one, prescribing the contents of an application for re-registration of a public company as a private unlimited company. The application must contain a statement of the company's proposed new name on re-registration (subs.(1)) and must be accompanied by the prescribed form of assent to re-registration authenticated by or on behalf of all the company's members (subs.(2)(a)). Where the assent is authenticated on behalf of a member, the directors' statement must attest that the directors have taken all reasonable steps to satisfy themselves that the person so assenting was lawfully empowered to do so (subs.(4)(b)). This is an important protection for members whose liability for the debts of the company will, on re-registration, be unlimited. The application must also be accompanied by a copy of the appropriately amended articles of the company (subs.(2)(b)) and the necessary statement of compliance (subs.(3)). The statement of compliance may be treated by the registrar as sufficient evidence that the company is entitled to be re-registered as an unlimited company (subs.(5)).

111.   Issue of certificate of incorporation on re-registration

(1) If on an application for re-registration of a public company as an unlimited private company the registrar is satisfied that the company is entitled to be so re-registered, the company shall be re-registered accordingly.

(2) The registrar must issue a certificate of incorporation altered to meet the circumstances of the case.

(3) The certificate must state that it is issued on re-registration and the date on which it is so issued.

(4) On the issue of the certificate-

(a) the company by virtue of the issue of the certificate becomes an unlimited private company, and

(b) the changes in the company's name and articles take effect.

(5) The certificate is conclusive evidence that the requirements of this Act as to reregistration have been complied with.

GENERAL NOTE

The final provision of this part, s.111 provides that where, on a public company's application to be re-registered as an unlimited private company, the registrar is satisfied that the company is entitled to be so re-registered he shall re-register it accordingly (subs.(1)) and issue an appropriately amended certificate of incorporation. The certificate must state its date of issue and that it is issued on re-registration (subs.(3)). On the issue if the amended certificate the company becomes an unlimited private company and the changes in its name and articles take effect (subs.(4)). The certificate is conclusive evidence that the requirements of the Act as to re-registration have been complied with (subs.(5)).

PART 8

A COMPANY'S MEMBERS

GENERAL NOTE

This Part of the Act restates many of the existing provisions of the 1985 Act. However, in a better overall arrangement, it draws together provisions which, in the 1985 Act, were concerned with membership and the register. Thus, included within Pt 8 of this new Act are most of the provisions of Ch.2 of Pt 11 of the 1985 Act.

CHAPTER I

THE MEMBERS OF A COMPANY

112. The members of a company

(1) The subscribers of a company's memorandum are deemed to have agreed to become members of the company, and on its registration become members and must be entered as such in its register of members.

(2) Every other person who agrees to become a member of a company, and whose name is entered in its register of members, is a member of the company.

GENERAL NOTE

Subsection (1) essentially repeats the wording of s.22(1) of the 1985 Act. The new subsection however makes it clear that, on registration, the subscribers must be entered as members on the company's register of members. Subsection (2) is in the same terms as s.22(2) of the 1985 Act.

CHAPTER 2

REGISTER OF MEMBERS

General

113.   Register of members

(1) Every company must keep a register of its members.

(2) There must be entered in the register-
   (a) the names and addresses of the members,
   (b) the date on which each person was registered as a member, and
   (c) the date at which any person ceased to be a member.

(3) In the case of a company having a share capital, there must be entered in the register, with the names and addresses of the members, a statement of-
   (a) the shares held by each member, distinguishing each share-
      (i) by its number (so long as the share has a number), and
      (ii) where the company has more than one class of issued shares, by its class, and
   (b) the amount paid or agreed to be considered as paid on the shares of each member.

(4) If the company has converted any of its shares into stock, and given notice of the conversion to the registrar, the register of members must show the amount and class of stock held by each member instead of the amount of shares and the particulars relating to shares specified above.

(5) In the case of joint holders of shares or stock in a company, the company's register of members must state the names of each joint holder. In other respects joint holders are regarded for the purposes of this Chapter as a single member (so that the register must show a single address).

(6) In the case of a company that does not have a share capital but has more than one class of members, there must be entered in the register, with the names and addresses of the members, a statement of the class to which each member belongs.

(7) If a company makes default in complying with this section an offence is committed by-
   (a) the company, and
   (b) every officer of the company who is in default.

(8) A person guilty of an offence under this section is liable on summary conviction to a fine not exceeding level 3 on the standard scale and, for continued contravention, a daily default fine not exceeding one-tenth of level 3 on the standard scale.

GENERAL NOTE

This section largely replaces s.352(1)-(5) of the 1985 Act. Like the previous s.352, it specifies what information is required to be kept in the company's register of members. Subsections (1) and (2) contain almost exactly similar wording to s.352(1)(2) of the 1985 Act. They specify first that there is a statutory obligation on the company to keep a register of its members and second the information which must be entered. This information includes both the names and address of the members as well as the date on which each person was registered as a member. A record must also be kept of the date on which any person ceased to be a member. Subsection (3), likewise, is in the same terms as s.352(3)(a) of the 1985 Act. It spells out additional information which must be stated in the case of a company which has a share capital. This additional information required includes the number of each share (assuming that the share has a number), its class (where the company has more than one class of issued shares) and the amount paid-up on each share. Subsection (4) is in the same terms as s.352(3)(b) of the 1985 Act and provides that the register of members must show the amount and class of those shares which the company has converted into stock, showing the amount and class of stock held by each member. Subsection (5), on the other hand, is a new provision. It makes it clear that the register must state, in the case of joint holders of shares or stock, the names of each joint holder. In all other respects, for the purposes of the Chapter, joint holders of a share fall to be treated as a single member. Subsection (6) is the same as s.352(4) of the 1985 Act and provides that if a company does not have a share capital but has more than one class of members, the class of each must be entered on the register. Subsection (7) and

(8) impose criminal penalties for contravention of the preceding sections. Subsection (7) essentially reproduces s.352(5) while the details of the penalties are spelled out in subs.(8).

114. Register to be kept available for inspection

(1) A company's register of members must be kept available for inspection-
   (a) at its registered office, or
   (b) at a place specified in regulations under section 1136.
(2) A company must give notice to the registrar of the place where its register of members is kept available for inspection and of any change in that place.
(3) No such notice is required if the register has, at all times since it came into existence (or, in the case of a register in existence on the relevant date, at all times since then) been kept available for inspection at the company's registered office.
(4) The relevant date for the purposes of subsection (3) is-
   (a) 1st July 1948 in the case of a company registered in Great Britain, and
   (b) 1st April 1961 in the case of a company registered in Northern Ireland.
(5) If a company makes default for 14 days in complying with subsection (2), an offence is committed by-
   (a) the company, and
   (b) every officer of the company who is in default.
(6) A person guilty of an offence under this section is liable on summary conviction to a fine not exceeding level 3 on the standard scale and, for continued contravention, a daily default fine not exceeding one-tenth of level 3 on the standard scale.

GENERAL NOTE

This section replaces s.353 of the 1985 Act. The former position was that the register of members was required to be kept at the registered office of the company, except that if the company had appointed a third party to maintain or update the register, it might be kept at the office where that work is done, subject to that office being in the jurisdiction (either England and Wales or Scotland) where the company is registered. Subsections (1) and (2) make it mandatory for the register of members to be kept available for inspection at the company's registered office or at any other place where the company is registered. The registrar must be kept informed of the place where the register is located. Under subss.(3) amd (4) no notice is required to the registrar if the register has been kept available for inspection at the company's registered office. The relevant dates for these purposes are specified in subs.(4). Subsections (5) and (6) impose criminal penalties for contravention of the preceding provisions.

115. Index of members

(1) Every company having more than 50 members must keep an index of the names of the members of the company, unless the register of members is in such a form as to constitute in itself an index.
(2) The company must make any necessary alteration in the index within 14 days after the date on which any alteration is made in the register of members.
(3) The index must contain, in respect of each member, a sufficient indication to enable the account of that member in the register to be readily found.
(4) The index must be at all times kept available for inspection at the same place as the register of members.
(5) If default is made in complying with this section, an offence is committed by-
   (a) the company, and
   (b) every officer of the company who is in default.
(6) A person guilty of an offence under this section is liable on summary conviction to a fine not exceeding level 3 on the standard scale and, for continued contravention, a daily default fine not exceeding one-tenth of level 3 on the standard scale.

GENERAL NOTE

This section is in similar terms to s.354 of the 1985 Act. It requires that any company with more than 50 members must keep an up-to-date index of the names of those members and this must be kept available for inspection at the same place as the register. There are criminal penalties for default (subss.(5) and (6)).

116. Rights to inspect and require copies

(1) The register and the index of members' names must be open to the inspection-
- (a) of any member of the company without charge, and
- (b) of any other person on payment of such fee as may be prescribed.

(2) Any person may require a copy of a company's register of members, or of any part of it, on payment of such fee as may be prescribed.

(3) A person seeking to exercise either of the rights conferred by this section must make a request to the company to that effect.

(4) The request must contain the following information-
- (a) in the case of an individual, his name and address;
- (b) in the case of an organisation, the name and address of an individual responsible for making the request on behalf of the organisation;
- (c) the purpose for which the information is to be used; and
- (d) whether the information will be disclosed to any other person, and if so-
  - (i) where that person is an individual, his name and address,
  - (ii) where that person is an organisation, the name and address of an individual responsible for receiving the information on its behalf, and
  - (iii) the purpose for which the information is to be used by that person.

GENERAL NOTE

This clause essentially replaces s.356 of the 1985 Act. In its *Final Report*, the CLR recommended that information in a company's register of members should be made available only for certain specified purposes (see para.11.44). This clause essentially follows this recommendation. Subsections (1) and (2) provide for the index to be open for inspection without charge to any member of the company, although a charge may be levied to any other person. Any person is entitled to a copy of the register of members or any part of it, on payment of the relevant fee. Under subss.(3) and (4) any person seeking to inspect or to be provided with a copy of the register of members must provide their names and addresses, the purpose for which the information will be used, and, if the access is sought on behalf of others, similar information for them. The request must also indicate whether the information will be disclosed to others and, if so, the purpose for which the information will be used by that person.

117. Register of members: response to request for inspection or copy

(1) Where a company receives a request under section 116 (register of members: right to inspect and require copy), it must within five working days either-
- (a) comply with the request, or
- (b) apply to the court.

(2) If it applies to the court it must notify the person making the request.

(3) If on an application under this section the court is satisfied that the inspection or copy is not sought for a proper purpose-
- (a) it shall direct the company not to comply with the request, and
- (b) it may further order that the company's costs (in Scotland, expenses) on the application be paid in whole or in part by the person who made the request, even if he is not a party to the application.

(4) If the court makes such a direction and it appears to the court that the company is or may be subject to other requests made for a similar purpose (whether made by the same person or different persons), it may direct that the company is not to comply with any such request.

The order must contain such provision as appears to the court appropriate to identify the requests to which it applies.

(5) If on an application under this section the court does not direct the company not to comply with the request, the company must comply with the request immediately upon the court giving its decision or, as the case may be, the proceedings being discontinued.

GENERAL NOTE

This is an entirely new section. Under subss.(1) and (2) a company which receives a request under s.116 must comply with the request or apply to the court within five days. If the latter course is intended then the person making the request must be notified by the company. In response to such an application, subss.(3) and (4) provide that if the court is not satisfied that the application is sought for a proper purpose, it may direct the company not to comply with the request and order that the requestor pay the company's costs, in whole or in part. The court can also direct that the company need not comply with other requests made for a similar purpose, whether by the same person, or different persons. Finally, subs.(5) indicates that if the court finds against the company in an application then the company must immediately comply with the request.

118. Register of members: refusal of inspection or default in providing copy

(1) If an inspection required under section 116 (register of members: right to inspect and require copy) is refused or default is made in providing a copy required under that section, otherwise than in accordance with an order of the court, an offence is committed by-
   (a) the company, and
   (b) every officer of the company who is in default.

(2) A person guilty of an offence under this section is liable on summary conviction to a fine not exceeding level 3 on the standard scale and, for continued contravention, a daily default fine not exceeding one-tenth of level 3 on the standard scale.

(3) In the case of any such refusal or default the court may by order compel an immediate inspection or, as the case may be, direct that the copy required be sent to the person requesting it.

GENERAL NOTE

This section is also new and must be read in the light of s.116. It provides for the consequences of a refusal of inspection or default in providing copy. By subs.(1), if an inspection is required and there is any default, an offence is committed by both the company and also every officer of the company (such as the company secretary) who is in default. The relevant penalties are spelt out in subs.(2). Finally, subs.(3) provides that where there has been a refusal or a default, the court can, by order, compel an immediate inspection or direct that the copy required is sent to the person who has requested it.

119. Register of members: offences in connection with request for or disclosure of information

(1) It is an offence for a person knowingly or recklessly to make in a request under section 116 (register of members: right to inspect or require copy) a statement that is misleading, false or deceptive in a material particular.

(2) It is an offence for a person in possession of information obtained by exercise of either of the rights conferred by that section-
   (a) to do anything that results in the information being disclosed to another person, or
   (b) to fail to do anything with the result that the information is disclosed to another person,

knowing, or having reason to suspect, that person may use the information for a purpose that is not a proper purpose.

(3) A person guilty of an offence under this section is liable-
   (a) on conviction on indictment, to imprisonment for a term not exceeding two years or a fine (or both);
   (b) on summary conviction-

(i) in England and Wales, to imprisonment for a term not exceeding twelve months or to a fine not exceeding the statutory maximum (or both);

(ii) in Scotland or Northern Ireland, to imprisonment for a term not exceeding six months, or to a fine not exceeding the statutory maximum (or both).

GENERAL NOTE

This section is entirely new. Subsection (1) provides for offences in connection with requests made under s.116. Thus, where a request is made and a person knowingly or recklessly makes a statement which is misleading, false, or deception, this is an offence. It will also be an offence if a person does anything which results in the information being disclosed to another person or if he fails to doing anything with the result that the information is disclosed to another person, and where he knows or has reason to suspect that person may use the information for an improper purpose (subs.(2)). Subsection (3) spells out the relevant penalties.

120.   Information as to state of register and index

(1) When a person inspects the register, or the company provides him with a copy of the register or any part of it, the company must inform him of the most recent date (if any) on which alterations were made to the register and there were no further alterations to be made.

(2) When a person inspects the index of members' names, the company must inform him whether there is any alteration to the register that is not reflected in the index.

(3) If a company fails to provide the information required under subsection (1) or (2), an offence is committed by-

(a) the company, and

(b) every officer of the company who is in default.

(4) A person guilty of an offence under this section is liable on summary conviction to a fine not exceeding level 3 on the standard scale.

GENERAL NOTE

This section is also new and is also based on the recommendation of the CLR in its *Final Report* (para.11.43). Subsection (1) provides that the company must, when providing an individual with a copy of the register (or any part of it), inform him of the most recent date on which any alterations were made to the register. Likewise, under subs.(2), when a person inspects the index, there is again a requirement that the company must inform the individual whether there is any alteration which is not reflected in the index. Failure by the company under the preceding subsections constitutes an offence for both the company and every officer in default. On summary conviction, there is a fine (subss.(3) and (4)).

121.   Removal of entries relating to former members

An entry relating to a former member of the company may be removed from the register after the expiration of ten years from the date on which he ceased to be a member.

GENERAL NOTE

This section replaces s.352(6) of the 1985 Act and is also based on a recommendation by the CLR in its *Final Report* (para.11.40). In essence it reduces the period for which the entry of a past member must be kept from 20 years to ten years.

Special cases

122.   Share warrants

(1) On the issue of a share warrant the company must-

(a) enter in the register of members-

(i) the fact of the issue of the warrant,

      (ii) a statement of the shares included in the warrant, distinguishing each share by its number so long as the share has a number, and

      (iii) the date of the issue of the warrant,

  and

  (b) amend the register, if necessary, so that no person is named on the register as the holder of the shares specified in the warrant.

(2) Until the warrant is surrendered, the particulars specified in subsection (1)(a) are deemed to be those required by this Act to be entered in the register of members.

(3) The bearer of a share warrant may, if the articles of the company so provide, be deemed a member of the company within the meaning of this Act, either to the full extent or for any purposes defined in the articles.

(4) Subject to the company's articles, the bearer of a share warrant is entitled, on surrendering it for cancellation, to have his name entered as a member in the register of members.

(5) The company is responsible for any loss incurred by any person by reason of the company entering in the register the name of a bearer of a share warrant in respect of the shares specified in it without the warrant being surrendered and cancelled.

(6) On the surrender of a share warrant, the date of the surrender must be entered in the register.

GENERAL NOTE

This section replaces s.355 of the 1985 Act and implements a CLR recommendation in its paper, *Completing the Structure* (see para.5.41). Subsection (1) provides for entry of a share warrant in the register of members on its issue. The information required includes the fact of issue and a statement of the shares included in the warrant. The company is required to amend the register so that no person is named on the register as the holder of the shares specified. By subs.(2) it is provided that, until such time as the warrant is surrendered, the particulars specified in the previous subsection will be deemed to be those required by the Act to be entered in the register. Subsection (3) provides for the holder of a share warrant to be deemed a member of the company, if the articles of the company so provide, while subs.(4) provides that the holder of a share warrant is entitled, on surrender of the warrant for cancellation, to have his name entered on the register as a member. The company is responsible for any loss incurred by any person where the company enters in the register the name of a bearer of a share warrant, without the warrant being surrendered (subs.(5)). The date of surrender must be entered in the register (subs.(6)).

123. Single member companies

(1) If a limited company is formed under this Act with only one member there shall be entered in the company's register of members, with the name and address of the sole member, a statement that the company has only one member.

(2) If the number of members of a limited company falls to one, or if an unlimited company with only one member becomes a limited company on reregistration, there shall upon the occurrence of that event be entered in the company's register of members, with the name and address of the sole member-

  (a) a statement that the company has only one member, and

  (b) the date on which the company became a company having only one member.

(3) If the membership of a limited company increases from one to two or more members, there shall upon the occurrence of that event be entered in the company's register of members, with the name and address of the person who was formerly the sole member-

  (a) a statement that the company has ceased to have only one member, and

  (b) the date on which that event occurred.

(4) If a company makes default in complying with this section, an offence is committed by-

  (a) the company, and

  (b) every officer of the company who is in default.

(5) A person guilty of an offence under this section is liable on summary conviction to a fine not exceeding level 3 on the standard scale and, for continued contravention, a daily default fine not exceeding one-tenth of level 3 on the standard scale.

GENERAL NOTE

This section replaces s.352A of the 1985 Act, which implemented the Twelfth Company Law Directive (89/667/EEC) on single member private limited liability companies. Subsections (1) and (2) provide that where a limited company has a single member, a statement to this effect must be entered in the company's register. There is a similar requirement where the number of members falls to one, or if an unlimited company with one member becomes a limited company on re-registration. Subsection (3) provides that where is an increase in the company's membership to two or more, then the company's register must contain a statement to that effect, together the date of its occurrence. Finally, subss.(4) and (5) lay down penalties for default. Both the company and every officer of the company who is in default will be guilty of an offence.

124. Company holding its own shares as treasury shares

(1) Where a company purchases its own shares in circumstances in which section 724 (treasury shares) applies-
    (a) the requirements of section 113 (register of members) need not be complied with if the company cancels all of the shares forthwith after the purchase, and
    (b) if the company does not cancel all of the shares forthwith after the purchase, any share that is so cancelled shall be disregarded for the purposes of that section.
(2) Subject to subsection (1), where a company holds shares as treasury shares the company must be entered in the register as the member holding those shares.

GENERAL NOTE

This section is intended to replace s.352(3A) of the Companies Act 1985. In particular, the section specifies the entries which must be made in the register of members where a company holds treasury shares. Thus, subs.(1) provides that where treasury shares are purchased the requirements as to the register do not need to be complied with if the company cancels all the shares after the purchase. If, on the other hand, the company does not cancel all the shares after the purchase, any share which is cancelled will be disregarded for the purposes of s.113. Subsection (2) simply provides that the company holds treasury shares, it must be entered in the register as the member holding the relevant shares.

Supplementary

125. Power of court to rectify register

(1) If-
    (a) the name of any person is, without sufficient cause, entered in or omitted from a company's register of members, or
    (b) default is made or unnecessary delay takes place in entering on the register the fact of any person having ceased to be a member,
the person aggrieved, or any member of the company, or the company, may apply to the court for rectification of the register.
(2) The court may either refuse the application or may order rectification of the register and payment by the company of any damages sustained by any party aggrieved.
(3) On such an application the court may decide any question relating to the title of a person who is a party to the application to have his name entered in or omitted from the register, whether the question arises between members or alleged members, or between members or alleged members on the one hand and the company on the other hand, and generally may decide any question necessary or expedient to be decided for rectification of the register.
(4) In the case of a company required by this Act to send a list of its members to the registrar of companies, the court, when making an order for rectification of the register, shall by its order direct notice of the rectification to be given to the registrar.

GENERAL NOTE

This section is intended to replace s.359 of the 1985 Act, although there are no real changes of substance. Thus, under subs.(1) if the name of any person is, without sufficient cause, entered or omitted from the register or default is made or unnecessary delay takes place in entering on the register the fact of any person having ceased to be a member, then the aggrieved person, or any member of the company, or the company, may apply to court for the register to be rectified. The court is empowered under subs.(2) to refuse the application or may order rectification of the register and award damages for any loss sustained by the aggrieved party. The court may decide any question relating to the title of a person who is a party to the application, whether this arises between members and alleged members, or between members or alleged members on the one hand and the company on the other. Indeed, the court may generally decide any question necessary or expedient to be decided for rectification of the register (subs.(3)). Where a company is required to send a list of its members to the registrar, the court in making an order for rectification shall direct notice of the rectification to be given to the registrar (subs.(4)).

126. Trusts not to be entered on register

No notice of any trust, expressed, implied or constructive, shall be entered on the register of members of a company registered in England and Wales or Northern Ireland, or be receivable by the registrar.

GENERAL NOTE

This section replaces s.360 of the 1985 Act and provides, as that section did, that no notice of any trust is to be entered on the register or to be receivable by the registrar. The effect of the section is extended to Northern Ireland.

127. Register to be evidence

The register of members is prima facie evidence of any matters which are by this Act directed or authorised to be inserted in it.

GENERAL NOTE

This section replaces s.361 of the 1985 Act but the scope is the same, namely that the register is *prima facie* evidence of those matters which are inserted in it.

128. Time limit for claims arising from entry in register

   (1) Liability incurred by a company-
      (a) from the making or deletion of an entry in the register of members, or
      (b) from a failure to make or delete any such entry,
is not enforceable more than ten years after the date on which the entry was made or deleted or, as the case may be, the failure first occurred.
   (2) This is without prejudice to any lesser period of limitation (and, in Scotland, to any rule that the obligation giving rise to the liability prescribes before the expiry of that period).

GENERAL NOTE

This section replaces s.352(7) of the 1985 Act. Based on a recommendation by the CLR (*Final Report*, para.11.40), it reduces the time limit for claims relating to entries in the register from 20 years to ten years (subs.(1)), although this is without prejudice to any lesser period of limitation (subs.(2)).

CHAPTER 3

OVERSEAS BRANCH REGISTERS

129. Overseas branch registers

   (1) A company having a share capital may, if it transacts business in a country or territory to which this Chapter applies, cause to be kept there a branch register of members resident there (an "overseas branch register").
   (2) This Chapter applies to-

    (a) any part of Her Majesty's dominions outside the United Kingdom, the Channel Islands and the Isle of Man, and

    (b) the countries or territories listed below.

Bangladesh	Malaysia
Cyprus	Malta
Dominica	Nigeria
The Gambia	Pakistan
Ghana	Seychelles
Guyana	Sierra Leone
The Hong Kong Special Administrative Region of the People's Republic of China	Singapore
India	South Africa
Ireland	Sri Lanka
Kenya	Swaziland
Kiribati	Trinidad and Tobago
Lesotho	Uganda
Malawi	Zimbabwe

    (3) The Secretary of State may make provision by regulations as to the circumstances in which a company is to be regarded as keeping a register in a particular country or territory.

    (4) Regulations under this section are subject to negative resolution procedure.

    (5) References-

      (a) in any Act or instrument (including, in particular, a company's articles) to a dominion register, or

      (b) in articles registered before 1st November 1929 to a colonial register,

are to be read (unless the context otherwise requires) as a reference to an overseas branch register kept under this section.

GENERAL NOTE

This part of the Act integrates provisions which were previously in s.362 of and Sch.14 to the 1985 Act. Subsection (1), which is in similar terms to s.362(1) of the 1985 Act, permits a company to keep a branch register of those members of a country in which it transacts business. Subsection (2) is in *pari materia* with Sch.14, Pt I of the 1985 Act and lists those countries to which this Part of the Act applies. Subsection (3) enables the Secretary of State to make provision, by regulation, as to those circumstances in which a company will be regarded as keeping a register in a particular country and the regulations so made are subject to the negative resolution procedure (subs.(4)). A savings provision indicates that reference to a dominion register or to a colonial register are to be read as references to an overseas branch register (subs.(5)).

130.   Notice of opening of overseas branch register

    (1) A company that begins to keep an overseas branch register must give notice to the registrar within 14 days of doing so, stating the country or territory in which the register is kept.

    (2) If default is made in complying with subsection (1), an offence is committed by-

      (a) the company, and

      (b) every officer of the company who is in default.

(3) A person guilty of an offence under subsection (2) is liable on summary conviction to a fine not exceeding level 3 on the standard scale and, for continued contravention, a daily default fine not exceeding one-tenth of level 3 on the standard scale.

GENERAL NOTE

This section lays down the period for the giving of notice to the registrar where the company begins to keep an overseas branch register - within 14 days (subs.(1)). In the event of default, the company and every officer of the company commits an offence (subs.(2)) for which there are penalties (subs.(3)).

131. Keeping of overseas branch register

(1) An overseas branch register is regarded as part of the company's register of members ("the main register").
(2) The Secretary of State may make provision by regulations modifying any provision of Chapter 2 (register of members) as it applies in relation to an overseas branch register.
(3) Regulations under this section are subject to negative resolution procedure.
(4) Subject to the provisions of this Act, a company may by its articles make such provision as it thinks fit as to the keeping of overseas branch registers.

GENERAL NOTE

This section of the Act contains information previously found in Sch.14 of the 1985 Act. The essential points are that such a register is to be regarded as part of the company's register of members - the so-called "main register" (subs.(1)). Regulations which may be made by the Secretary of State modifying any provision of this Part relating to the register of members (subs.(2)) are also subject to the negative resolution procedure (subs.(3)). Finally, it is provided that the company may, by its articles, make such provision as it thinks fit as to the keeping of overseas branch registers (subs.(4)).

132. Register or duplicate to be kept available for inspection in UK

(1) A company that keeps an overseas branch register must keep available for inspection-
   (a) the register, or
   (b) a duplicate of the register duly entered up from time to time,
at the place in the United Kingdom where the company's main register is kept available for inspection.
(2) Any such duplicate is treated for all purposes of this Act as part of the main register.
(3) If default is made in complying with subsection (1), an offence is committed by-
   (a) the company, and
   (b) every officer of the company who is in default.
(4) A person guilty of an offence under subsection (3) is liable on summary conviction to a fine not exceeding level 3 on the standard scale and, for continued contravention, a daily default fine not exceeding one-tenth of level 3 on the standard scale.

GENERAL NOTE

In much the same way as the provisions relating to the main register, this section provide that a company which has an overseas branch register must keep this, or a duplicate, available for inspection (subs.(1)). Any duplicate will be regarded a part of the main register (subs.(2)). There are penalties for default and the company and every officer who is in default commits an offence (subss.(3) and (4)).

133. Transactions in shares registered in overseas branch register

(1) Shares registered in an overseas branch register must be distinguished from those registered in the main register.

(2) No transaction with respect to shares registered in an overseas branch register may be registered in any other register.

(3) An instrument of transfer of a share registered in an overseas branch register-

    (a) is regarded as a transfer of property situated outside the United Kingdom, and

    (b) unless executed in a part of the United Kingdom, is exempt from stamp duty.

GENERAL NOTE

  This section of the Act makes it mandatory for shares in the overseas branch register to be distinguished from those in the main register (subs.(1)) and provides emphatically that no transaction concerning shares registered in an overseas branch register may be registered in any other register (subs.(2)). Subsection (3) provides that any transfer of a share registered in an overseas branch is to be regarded as a transfer of property outside the United Kingdom and, as such, does not attract stamp duty.

134. Jurisdiction of local courts

(1) A competent court in a country or territory where an overseas branch register is kept may exercise the same jurisdiction as is exercisable by a court in the United Kingdom-

    (a) to rectify the register (see section 125), or

    (b) in relation to a request for inspection or a copy of the register (see section 117).

(2) The offences-

    (a) of refusing inspection or failing to provide a copy of the register (see section 118), and

    (b) of making a false, misleading or deceptive statement in a request for inspection or a copy (see section 119),

may be prosecuted summarily before any tribunal having summary criminal jurisdiction in the country or territory where the register is kept.

(3) This section extends only to those countries and territories to which paragraph 3 of Schedule 14 to the Companies Act 1985 (c. 6) (which made similar provision) extended immediately before the coming into force of this Chapter.

GENERAL NOTE

  This section provides that a competent court in a country or territory is empowered to rectify the register (under s.125) and also to act in relation to a request for inspection or a copy of the register, pursuant to s.117 (subs.(1)). Such a court is also empowered to exercise its powers summarily in relation to the offences connected with this jurisdiction (subs.(2)). Subsection (3) limits this section only to those countries and territories to which Sch.4, para.3 to the Companies Act 1985 extended immediately prior to the coming into the force of this Part of the Act (subs.(3)).

135. Discontinuance of overseas branch register

(1) A company may discontinue an overseas branch register.

(2) If it does so all the entries in that register must be transferred-

    (a) to some other overseas branch register kept in the same country or territory, or

    (b) to the main register.

(3) The company must give notice to the registrar within 14 days of the discontinuance.

(4) If default is made in complying with subsection (3), an offence is committed by-

    (a) the company, and

    (b) every officer of the company who is in default.

(5) A person guilty of an offence under subsection (4) is liable on summary conviction to a fine not exceeding level 3 on the standard scale and, for continued contravention, a daily default fine not exceeding one-tenth of level 3 on the standard scale.

GENERAL NOTE

  This section of the Act makes provision for the discontinuation of an overseas branch register (subs.(1)). However, when it does so, all the entries in that register are required to be transferred to another overseas branch register or to the main register (subs.(2)). The company is required to give notice to the registrar, within 14 days, of any such discontinuance (subs.(3)). There are penalties for default (subss.(4) and (5)).

CHAPTER 4

PROHIBITION ON SUBSIDIARY BEING MEMBER OF ITS HOLDING COMPANY

General prohibition

136. Prohibition on subsidiary being a member of its holding company

(1) Except as provided by this Chapter-
   (a) a body corporate cannot be a member of a company that is its holding company, and
   (b) any allotment or transfer of shares in a company to its subsidiary is void.

(2) The exceptions are provided for in-
   section 138 (subsidiary acting as personal representative or trustee), and
   section 141 (subsidiary acting as authorised dealer in securities).

GENERAL NOTE

This section is based on s.23(1) of the 1985 Act and provides that a body corporate may not be a member of a company which is its holding company, save in two instances, namely those specified in s.138 and in s.141 (subs.(2)). Any allotment or transfer which is made in breach of the section is void (subs.1)).

137. Shares acquired before prohibition became applicable

(1) Where a body corporate became a holder of shares in a company-
   (a) before the relevant date, or
   (b) on or after that date and before the commencement of this Chapter in circumstances in which the prohibition in section 23(1) of the Companies Act 1985 or Article 33(1) of the Companies (Northern Ireland) Order 1986 (S.I. 1986/1032 (N.I. 6)) (or any corresponding earlier enactment), as it then had effect, did not apply, or
   (c) on or after the commencement of this Chapter in circumstances in which the prohibition in section 136 did not apply,
it may continue to be a member of the company.

(2) The relevant date for the purposes of subsection (1)(a) is-
   (a) 1st July 1948 in the case of a company registered in Great Britain, and
   (b) 1st April 1961 in the case of a company registered in Northern Ireland.

(3) So long as it is permitted to continue as a member of a company by virtue of this section, an allotment to it of fully paid shares in the company may be validly made by way of capitalisation of reserves of the company.

(4) But, so long as the prohibition in section 136 would (apart from this section) apply, it has no right to vote in respect of the shares mentioned in subsection (1) above, or any shares allotted as mentioned in subsection (3) above, on a written resolution or at meetings of the company or of any class of its members.

GENERAL NOTE

In certain circumstances where the body corporate became a holder of a shares in a company it may continue to do so. These are specified in subs.(1). The relevant date specified for the purpose of subs.(1) is July 1, 1948 in the case of companies registered in Great Britain and April 1, 1961, in the case of a company registered in Northern Ireland. Subsection (3) provides that, so long as permitted under the section, any allotment to it of fully paid shares in the company may validly be made by way of a capitalisation of reserves of the company. In cases where the prohibition in the preceding section applies, the body corporate has no right to vote in respect of shares mentioned in subs.(1) or on shares allotted in subs.(2).

Subsidiary acting as personal representative or trustee

138.   Subsidiary acting as personal representative or trustee

(1) The prohibition in section 136 (prohibition on subsidiary being a member of its holding company) does not apply where the subsidiary is concerned only-

(a) as personal representative, or

(b) as trustee,

unless, in the latter case, the holding company or a subsidiary of it is beneficially interested under the trust.

(2) For the purpose of ascertaining whether the holding company or a subsidiary is so interested, there shall be disregarded-

(a) any interest held only by way of security for the purposes of a transaction entered into by the holding company or subsidiary in the ordinary course of a business that includes the lending of money;

(b) any interest within-

section 139 (interests to be disregarded: residual interest under pension scheme or employees' share scheme), or

section 140 (interests to be disregarded: employer's rights of recovery under pension scheme or employees' share scheme);

(c) any rights that the company or subsidiary has in its capacity as trustee, including in particular-

(i) any right to recover its expenses or be remunerated out of the trust property, and

(ii) any right to be indemnified out of the trust property for any liability incurred by reason of any act or omission in the performance of its duties as trustee.

GENERAL NOTE

   This section is based on s.23(4) of the 1985 Act. Thus, the prohibition in s.136, will not apply where the subsidiary is concerned only as a personal representative or as a trustee, unless the holding company or a subsidiary of it is beneficially interested under the trust (subs.(1)). Subsection (2) identifies those interests which may be disregarded.

139.   Interests to be disregarded: residual interest under pension scheme or employees' share scheme

(1) Where shares in a company are held on trust for the purposes of a pension scheme or employees' share scheme, there shall be disregarded for the purposes of section 138 any residual interest that has not vested in possession.

(2) A "residual interest" means a right of the company or subsidiary ("the residual beneficiary") to receive any of the trust property in the event of-

(a) all the liabilities arising under the scheme having been satisfied or provided for, or

(b) the residual beneficiary ceasing to participate in the scheme, or

(c) the trust property at any time exceeding what is necessary for satisfying the liabilities arising or expected to arise under the scheme.

(3) In subsection (2)-

(a) the reference to a right includes a right dependent on the exercise of a discretion vested by the scheme in the trustee or another person, and

(b) the reference to liabilities arising under a scheme includes liabilities that have resulted, or may result, from the exercise of any such discretion.

(4) For the purposes of this section a residual interest vests in possession-

(a) in a case within subsection (2)(a), on the occurrence of the event mentioned there (whether or not the amount of the property receivable pursuant to the right is ascertained);

(b) in a case within subsection (2)(b) or (c), when the residual beneficiary becomes entitled to require the trustee to transfer to him any of the property receivable pursuant to the right.

(5) In this section "pension scheme" means a scheme for the provision of benefits consisting of or including relevant benefits for or in respect of employees or former employees.

(6) In subsection (5)-

(a) "relevant benefits" means any pension, lump sum, gratuity or other like benefit given or to be given on retirement or on death or in anticipation of retirement or, in connection with past service, after retirement or death; and

(b) "employee" shall be read as if a director of a company were employed by it.

GENERAL NOTE

This section is concerned with residual interests under pension schemes or employees share schemes. Subsection (1) provides that where shares are held on trust for the purposes of a pension scheme or employees share scheme, any residual interest which has not vested in possession should be disregarded. The meaning of a residual interest is amplified in subss.(2) and (3) and pension scheme in subss.(5) and (6).

140. Interests to be disregarded: employer's rights of recovery under pension scheme or employees' share scheme

(1) Where shares in a company are held on trust for the purposes of a pension scheme or employees' share scheme, there shall be disregarded for the purposes of section 138 any charge or lien on, or set-off against, any benefit or other right or interest under the scheme for the purpose of enabling the employer or former employer of a member of the scheme to obtain the discharge of a monetary obligation due to him from the member.

(2) In the case of a trust for the purposes of a pension scheme there shall also be disregarded any right to receive from the trustee of the scheme, or as trustee of the scheme to retain, an amount that can be recovered or retained, under section 61 of the Pension Schemes Act 1993 (c. 48) or section 57 of the Pension Schemes (Northern Ireland) Act 1993 (c. 49) (deduction of contributions equivalent premium from refund of scheme contributions) or otherwise, as reimbursement or partial reimbursement for any contributions equivalent premium paid in connection with the scheme under Part 3 of that Act.

(3) In this section "pension scheme" means a scheme for the provision of benefits consisting of or including relevant benefits for or in respect of employees or former employees.

"Relevant benefits" here means any pension, lump sum, gratuity or other like benefit given or to be given on retirement or on death or in anticipation of retirement or, in connection with past service, after retirement or death.

(4) In this section "employer" and "employee" shall be read as if a director of a company were employed by it.

GENERAL NOTE

This section is concerned with employer's rights of recovery under pension schemes or employees' share schemes. In particular, where shares are held on trust for the purposes of either type of scheme, any charge or lien or set-off against any benefit or other right or interest for the purpose of enabling the employer or former employer of a member of the scheme to obtain the discharge of a monetary obligation due to him from the member, is to be disregarded (subs.(1)). Subsection (2) deals with specific cases of trusts. Subsection (3) provides definitions of pension scheme and relevant benefits. Finally, subs.(4) elaborates that the terms employer and employee are to be read as if a director of a company were employed by it.

Subsidiary acting as dealer in securities

141. Subsidiary acting as authorised dealer in securities

(1) The prohibition in section 136 (prohibition on subsidiary being a member of its holding company) does not apply where the shares are held by the subsidiary in the ordinary course of its business as an intermediary.

(2) For this purpose a person is an intermediary if he-

(a) carries on a bona fide business of dealing in securities,

(b) is a member of or has access to a regulated market, and

(c) does not carry on an excluded business.

(3) The following are excluded businesses-

(a) a business that consists wholly or mainly in the making or managing of investments;

(b) a business that consists wholly or mainly in, or is carried on wholly or mainly for the purposes of, providing services to persons who are connected with the person carrying on the business;

(c) a business that consists in insurance business;

(d) a business that consists in managing or acting as trustee in relation to a pension scheme, or that is carried on by the manager or trustee of such a scheme in connection with or for the purposes of the scheme;

(e) a business that consists in operating or acting as trustee in relation to a collective investment scheme, or that is carried on by the operator or trustee of such a scheme in connection with and for the purposes of the scheme.

(4) For the purposes of this section-

(a) the question whether a person is connected with another shall be determined in accordance with section 839 of the Income and Corporation Taxes Act 1988 (c. 1);

(b) "collective investment scheme" has the meaning given in section 235 of the Financial Services and Markets Act 2000 (c. 8);

(c) "insurance business" means business that consists in the effecting or carrying out of contracts of insurance;

(d) "securities" includes-

(i) options,

(ii) futures, and

(iii) contracts for differences,

and rights or interests in those investments;

(e) "trustee" and "the operator" in relation to a collective investment scheme shall be construed in accordance with section 237(2) of the Financial Services and Markets Act 2000 (c. 8).

(5) Expressions used in this section that are also used in the provisions regulating activities under the Financial Services and Markets Act 2000 have the same meaning here as they do in those provisions. See section 22 of that Act, orders made under that section and Schedule 2 to that Act.

GENERAL NOTE

The prohibition in s.136 would not apply in cases where the shares are held by the subsidiary in the ordinary course of its business as an intermediary (subs.(1)). Subsection (2) defines intermediary and subs.(3) sets out those businesses which are excluded. Subsection (4) sets out various definitions and subs.(5) provides that expressions used in this part of the Act are intended to have the same meaning as provisions used in the Financial Services and Markets Act 2000.

142. Protection of third parties in other cases where subsidiary acting as dealer in securities

(1) This section applies where-

(a) a subsidiary that is a dealer in securities has purportedly acquired shares in its holding company in contravention of the prohibition in section 136, and

(b) a person acting in good faith has agreed, for value and without notice of the contravention, to acquire shares in the holding company-

(i) from the subsidiary, or

(ii) from someone who has purportedly acquired the shares after their disposal by the subsidiary.

(2) A transfer to that person of the shares mentioned in subsection (1)(a) has the same effect as it would have had if their original acquisition by the subsidiary had not been in contravention of the prohibition.

GENERAL NOTE

This section is concerned with those situations where the subsidiary acts as a dealer in securities. Thus, under subs.(1), the section will apply where the subsidiary which is a dealer in securities purportedly acquires shares in its holding company in contravention of the prohibition in s.136 and where a person who is acting in good faith has agreed, for value and without notice of any contravention, to acquire shares in the holding company from the subsidiary or from someone who has purportedly acquired the shares after their disposal by the subsidiary. Subsection (2) provides that a transfer of the shares has the same effect as it would have had if the original acquisition by the subsidiary has not been in contravention of the prohibition.

Supplementary

143. Application of provisions to companies not limited by shares

In relation to a company other than a company limited by shares, the references in this Chapter to shares shall be read as references to the interest of its members as such, whatever the form of that interest.

GENERAL NOTE

This section provides that references in this part of the Act to companies limited by shares are to be read as references to the interest of its members as such, whatever the form of that interest.

144. Application of provisions to nominees

The provisions of this Chapter apply to a nominee acting on behalf of a subsidiary as to the subsidiary itself.

GENERAL NOTE

This section provides that the Chapter is to apply to a nominee acting on behalf of a subsidiary as much as to the subsidiary itself.

PART 9

EXERCISE OF MEMBERS' RIGHTS

GENERAL NOTE

This part of the Act is entirely new and is concerned with the exercise of members' rights.

Effect of provisions in company's articles

145. Effect of provisions of articles as to enjoyment or exercise of members' rights

(1) This section applies where provision is made by a company's articles enabling a member to nominate another person or persons as entitled to enjoy or exercise all or any specified rights of the member in relation to the company.

(2) So far as is necessary to give effect to that provision, anything required or authorised by any provision of the Companies Acts to be done by or in relation to the member shall instead be done, or (as the case may be) may instead be done, by or in relation to the nominated person (or each of them) as if he were a member of the company.

(3) This applies, in particular, to the rights conferred by-

  (a) sections 291 and 293 (right to be sent proposed written resolution);

  (b) section 292 (right to require circulation of written resolution);

  (c) section 303 (right to require directors to call general meeting);

  (d) section 310 (right to notice of general meetings);

  (e) section 314 (right to require circulation of a statement);

  (f) section 324 (right to appoint proxy to act at meeting);

  (g) section 338 (right to require circulation of resolution for AGM of public company); and

  (h) section 423 (right to be sent a copy of annual accounts and reports).

(4) This section and any such provision as is mentioned in subsection (1)-

  (a) do not confer rights enforceable against the company by anyone other than the member, and

  (b) do not affect the requirements for an effective transfer or other disposition of the whole or part of a member's interest in the company.

GENERAL NOTE

This section of the Act is concerned with the effect of provision made in the articles as to the enjoyment or exercise of members' rights. Accordingly, subs.(1) provides that, where provision is made by the company's articles for a member to nominate another person or persons as entitled to enjoy or exercise all or any specified rights of the member in relation to the company, the section will apply. Under subs.(2) anything which may be done by a member may instead be done by or in relation to the nominated person, or each of them, as if he were a member of the company. The rights affected are those listed in subs.(3). Subsection (4) confirms that it is only members who have rights which are enforceable against the company. Further, the requirements for an effective transfer or other disposition of the whole or part of a member's interest in the company are not affected by this section.

Information rights

146. Traded companies: nomination of persons to enjoy information rights

(1) This section applies to a company whose shares are admitted to trading on a regulated market.

(2) A member of such a company who holds shares on behalf of another person may nominate that person to enjoy information rights.

(3) "Information rights" means-

(a) the right to receive a copy of all communications that the company sends to its members generally or to any class of its members that includes the person making the nomination, and

(b) the rights conferred by-

    (i) section 431 or 432 (right to require copies of accounts and reports), and

    (ii) section 1145 (right to require hard copy version of document or information provided in another form).

(4) The reference in subsection (3)(a) to communications that a company sends to its members generally includes the company's annual accounts and reports. For the application of section 426 (option to provide summary financial statement) in relation to a person nominated to enjoy information rights, see subsection (5) of that section.

(5) A company need not act on a nomination purporting to relate to certain information rights only.

GENERAL NOTE

This new section is concerned with the nomination of persons to enjoy information rights.

Specifically, as enumerated in subs.(1), the section will apply to those companies whose shares are admitted to trading on a regulated market. The gist of the section is in subs.(2), namely that a member of a company holding shares on behalf of another may nominate that person to enjoy information rights. Information rights are defined in subs.(3) as the right to receive a copy of all communications that the company sends to its members generally or to any class of its members (including the person making the nomination). It also includes rights to require copies of accounts and reports (ss.431 and 432) and the right to require hard copy versions of documents or information provided in another form (s.1145). Finally, subs.(4) provides that a company is not obliged to act on a nomination which purports to relate to certain information rights only.

147. Information rights: form in which copies to be provided

(1) This section applies as regards the form in which copies are to be provided to a person nominated under section 146 (nomination of person to enjoy information rights).

(2) If the person to be nominated wishes to receive hard copy communications, he must-

    (a) request the person making the nomination to notify the company of that fact, and

    (b) provide an address to which such copies may be sent.

This must be done before the nomination is made.

(3) If having received such a request the person making the nomination-

    (a) notifies the company that the nominated person wishes to receive hard copy communications, and

    (b) provides the company with that address,

the right of the nominated person is to receive hard copy communications accordingly.

(4) This is subject to the provisions of Parts 3 and 4 of Schedule 5 (communications by company) under which the company may take steps to enable it to communicate in electronic form or by means of a website.

(5) If no such notification is given (or no address is provided), the nominated person is taken to have agreed that documents or information may be sent or supplied to him by the company by means of a website.

(6) That agreement-

    (a) may be revoked by the nominated person, and

    (b) does not affect his right under section 1145 to require a hard copy version of a document or information provided in any other form.

GENERAL NOTE

This new section is concerned with the form in which copies are to be provided (subs.(1)) to a person nominated under the previous section. A nominated person who wishes to receive hard copy communications must request the nominator to inform the company of this fact and provide an address to which copies may be sent. This request must be made before the nomination is made (subs.(2)). Provided these steps are followed, subs.(3) provides that the nominated person has the right to receive hard copy communications. The preceding provisions are, however, made subject to the provisions of Sch.5

to the Act, which makes it possible for the company to take steps to enable it to communicate in electronic form or by means of a website (subs.(4)). If no notification is given - or where no address is provided - the nominated person will be taken to have agreed that the documents or information may be supplied to him by the company by its website (subs.(5)). Under subs.(6) the agreement may be revoked by the nominated person and it will not affect his right under s.1145 to require a hard copy version of a document or information provided in any other form.

148. Termination or suspension of nomination

(1) The following provisions have effect in relation to a nomination under section 146 (nomination of person to enjoy information rights).

(2) The nomination may be terminated at the request of the member or of the nominated person.

(3) The nomination ceases to have effect on the occurrence in relation to the member or the nominated person of any of the following-

    (a) in the case of an individual, death or bankruptcy;

    (b) in the case of a body corporate, dissolution or the making of an order for the winding up of the body otherwise than for the purposes of reconstruction.

(4) In subsection (3)-

    (a) the reference to bankruptcy includes-

        (i) the sequestration of a person's estate, and

        (ii) a person's estate being the subject of a protected trust deed (within the meaning of the Bankruptcy (Scotland) Act 1985 (c. 66)); and

    (b) the reference to the making of an order for winding up is to-

        (i) the making of such an order under the Insolvency Act 1986 (c. 45) or the Insolvency (Northern Ireland) Order 1989 (S.I. 1989/2405 (N.I. 19)), or

        (ii) any corresponding proceeding under the law of a country or territory outside the United Kingdom.

(5) The effect of any nominations made by a member is suspended at any time when there are more nominated persons than the member has shares in the company.

(6) Where-

    (a) the member holds different classes of shares with different information rights, and

    (b) there are more nominated persons than he has shares conferring a particular right,

the effect of any nominations made by him is suspended to the extent that they confer that right.

(7) Where the company-

    (a) enquires of a nominated person whether he wishes to retain information rights, and

    (b) does not receive a response within the period of 28 days beginning with the date on which the company's enquiry was sent,

the nomination ceases to have effect at the end of that period.

Such an enquiry is not to be made of a person more than once in any twelvemonth period.

(8) The termination or suspension of a nomination means that the company is not required to act on it.

It does not prevent the company from continuing to do so, to such extent or for such period as it thinks fit.

GENERAL NOTE

    This section is concerned with the termination or suspension of the nomination made under s.146 (subs.(1)). Thus, the nomination may be terminated at the request of the member or of the nominated person (subs.(2)). It will cease to have effect, in relation to the member or the nominated person, in the case of death or bankruptcy of a member and in the case of the dissolution or the making of an order for the winding up of a body corporate (subs.(3)). These terms are explained in subs.(4). Under subs.(5) the effect of any nominations made by a member will be suspended at any time where there are more nominated persons than the member has shares in the company. In the case of the member holding different classes of shares with different information rights and more nominated persons than that member has shares conferring a particular right, subs.(6) provides that the effect of any nominations are suspended to the extent that they confer that right. Subsection (7) provides that where the company makes an enquiry of the nominated person whether he wishes to retain information rights and does not receive a response with 28 days of the day of the enquiry, the nomination will cease to have effect at the end of that period. It is also provided that such an enquiry should not be made of a person more than once in any 12 month period. Finally, under subs.(8) the termination or suspension of a nomination has the effect that the company is not required to act on it, although it does not prevent the company continuing to do so, for such period as it thinks fit.

149. Information as to possible rights in relation to voting

(1) This section applies where a company sends a copy of a notice of a meeting to a person nominated under section 146 (nomination of person to enjoy information rights)

(2) The copy of the notice must be accompanied by a statement that-

    (a) he may have a right under an agreement between him and the member by whom he was nominated to be appointed, or to have someone else appointed, as a proxy for the meeting, and

    (b) if he has no such right or does not wish to exercise it, he may have a right under such an agreement to give instructions to the member as to the exercise of voting rights.

(3) Section 325 (notice of meeting to contain statement of member's rights in relation to appointment of proxy) does not apply to the copy, and the company must either-

    (a) omit the notice required by that section, or

    (b) include it but state that it does not apply to the nominated person.

GENERAL NOTE

This section is concerned with those occasions where the company sends a copy of a notice of a meeting to a person nominated under s.146 (subs.(1)). Subsection (2) provides that the copy of the notice must be accompanied by a statement that the nominated person or someone else may have a right to be appointed as a proxy for the meeting under an agreement between him and the person by whom he was nominated. If he has no such right or does not wish to exercise it, the subsection goes on to say that he may have a right under such an agreement to give instructions to the member as to the exercise of voting rights. Subsection (3) provides that s.325 does not apply to the copy and the company is required to either omit the notice required or include it, in that case stating that it does not apply to the nominated person.

150. Information rights: status of rights

(1) This section has effect as regards the rights conferred by a nomination under section 146 (nomination of person to enjoy information rights).

(2) Enjoyment by the nominated person of the rights conferred by the nomination is enforceable against the company by the member as if they were rights conferred by the company's articles.

(3) Any enactment, and any provision of the company's articles, having effect in relation to communications with members has a corresponding effect (subject to any necessary adaptations) in relation to communications with the nominated person.

(4) In particular-

    (a) where under any enactment, or any provision of the company's articles, the members of a company entitled to receive a document or information are determined as at a date or time before it is sent or supplied, the company need not send or supply it to a nominated person-

        (i) whose nomination was received by the company after that date or time, or

        (ii) if that date or time falls in a period of suspension of his nomination; and

    (b) where under any enactment, or any provision of the company's articles, the right of a member to receive a document or information depends on the company having a current address for him, the same applies to any person nominated by him.

(5) The rights conferred by the nomination-

    (a) are in addition to the rights of the member himself, and

    (b) do not affect any rights exercisable by virtue of any such provision as is mentioned in section 145 (provisions of company's articles as to enjoyment or exercise of members' rights).

(6) A failure to give effect to the rights conferred by the nomination does not affect the validity of anything done by or on behalf of the company.

(7) References in this section to the rights conferred by the nomination are to-

(a) the rights referred to in section 146(3) (information rights), and

(b) where applicable, the rights conferred by section 147(3) (right to hard copy communications) and section 149 (information as to possible voting rights).

GENERAL NOTE

This new section is concerned with the status of the rights conferred by a nominated person (subs.(1)). Thus, under subs.(2) the enjoyment by the nominated person of the rights conferred by the nomination is enforceable against the company by the member as if they were rights conferred by the articles of the company. Under subs.(3), any enactment and provision of the company's articles which has effect in relation to communications with members has a corresponding effect on nominated persons. Where under any enactment or provision of the articles the members are entitled to receive a document or information determined as at a date or time before it is sent or supplied, subs.(4) provides that the company need not send or supply it to a nominated person whose nomination was received by the company after that date or time or if that date or time falls in a period of suspension of the nomination and where under any enactment or provision of the company's articles, the right of a member to receive a document or information depends on the company having a current address for him or any person nominated by him. Subsection (5) provides that the rights conferred by the nomination are in addition to the rights of the member himself and will not affect any rights exercisable by virtue of any such provision mentioned in s.145. A failure to give effect to the rights conferred by the nomination will not affect the validity of anything done by or on behalf of the company (subs.(6)). Finally, subs.(7) provides that the right conferred by the nomination are to those rights referred to in s.146(3) and, where applicable, those rights conferred by s.147(3)) and s.149.

151. Information rights: power to amend

(1) The Secretary of State may by regulations amend the provisions of sections 146 to 150 (information rights) so as to-

(a) extend or restrict the classes of companies to which section 146 applies,

(b) make other provision as to the circumstances in which a nomination may be made under that section, or

(c) extend or restrict the rights conferred by such a nomination.

(2) The regulations may make such consequential modifications of any other provisions of this Part, or of any other enactment, as appear to the Secretary of State to be necessary.

(3) Regulations under this section are subject to affirmative resolution procedure.

GENERAL NOTE

This section enables the Secretary of State to make regulations amending the preceding sections so as to extend the classes of companies to which ss.146-150 applies, make other provision as to the circumstances in which a nomination may be made under that section, or extend or restrict the rights conferred by any nomination (subs.(1)). Subsection (2) provides that the regulations may also make consequential amendments to any other provisions or this Part of the Act or any other enactment. Subsection (3) provides that any regulations made are subject to the affirmative resolution procedure.

Exercise of rights where shares held on behalf of others

152. Exercise of rights where shares held on behalf of others: exercise in different ways

(1) Where a member holds shares in a company on behalf of more than one person-

(a) rights attached to the shares, and

(b) rights under any enactment exercisable by virtue of holding the shares,

need not all be exercised, and if exercised, need not all be exercised in the same way.

(2) A member who exercises such rights but does not exercise all his rights, must inform the company to what extent he is exercising the rights.

(3) A member who exercises such rights in different ways must inform the company of the ways in which he is exercising them and to what extent they are exercised in each way.

(4) If a member exercises such rights without informing the company-

    (a) that he is not exercising all his rights, or

    (b) that he is exercising his rights in different ways,

the company is entitled to assume that he is exercising all his rights and is exercising them in the same way.

GENERAL NOTE

    Subsection (1) provides that rights attached to shares and rights under any enactment exercisable by virtue of holding shares need not all be exercised and, if exercised, need not all be exercised in the same way. Subsection (2) provides that a person who exercises such rights, but does not exercise all his rights, must inform the company to what extent he is doing so. Under subs.(3) a member who exercises such rights in different ways must inform the company of the ways in which he is exercising them and to what extent they are exercised in each way. If the member exercises such rights without informing the company, the company is entitled to assume that he is exercising all his rights and is exercising them in the same way (subs.(4)).

153. Exercise of rights where shares held on behalf of others: members' requests

(1) This section applies for the purposes of-

    (a) section 314 (power to require circulation of statement),

    (b) section 338 (public companies: power to require circulation of resolution for AGM),

    (c) section 342 (power to require independent report on poll), and

    (d) section 527 (power to require website publication of audit concerns).

(2) A company is required to act under any of those sections if it receives a request in relation to which the following conditions are met-

    (a) it is made by at least 100 persons;

    (b) it is authenticated by all the persons making it;

    (c) in the case of any of those persons who is not a member of the company, it is accompanied by a statement-

        (i) of the full name and address of a person ("the member") who is a member of the company and holds shares on behalf of that person,

        (ii) that the member is holding those shares on behalf of that person in the course of a business,

        (iii) of the number of shares in the company that the member holds on behalf of that person,

        (iv) of the total amount paid up on those shares,

        (v) that those shares are not held on behalf of anyone else or, if they are, that the other person or persons are not among the other persons making the request,

        (vi) that some or all of those shares confer voting rights that are relevant for the purposes of making a request under the section in question, and

        (vii) that the person has the right to instruct the member how to exercise those rights;

    (d) in the case of any of those persons who is a member of the company, it is accompanied by a statement-

        (i) that he holds shares otherwise than on behalf of another person, or

        (ii) that he holds shares on behalf of one or more other persons but those persons are not among the other persons making the request;

    (e) it is accompanied by such evidence as the company may reasonably require of the matters mentioned in paragraph (c) and (d);

    (f) the total amount of the sums paid up on-

        (i) shares held as mentioned in paragraph (c), and

        (ii) shares held as mentioned in paragraph (d),

    divided by the number of persons making the request, is not less than £100;

(g) the request complies with any other requirements of the section in question as to contents, timing and otherwise.

GENERAL NOTE

This section applies to certain limited sections listed in subs.(1). Under subs.(2) the company is required to act under any of those sections where the conditions listed are met.

PART 10

A COMPANY'S DIRECTORS

GENERAL NOTE

Part 10 is concerned with company directors and replaces Pt 10 of the Companies Act 1985, the sections relating to directors in Pt 9, and the sections relating to confidentiality orders in Pt 25.

The most important changes are contained in Ch.2 which introduces for the first time a statutory statement of directors' duties and the concept of "enlightened shareholder value". The statutory statement of directors' duties is for the most part a codification of the common law, although there are some potentially troublesome elaborations. Another important change is contained in Ch.8 concerning the protection of directors' home addresses. Under the new scheme the default position is that directors' residential addresses will be kept off the public register.

Part 10 has nine Chapters. Chapter 1 concerns the appointment and removal of directors; Ch.2 contains the codified general duties of directors; Ch.3 concerns declarations of interest in existing transactions or arrangements; Ch.4 relates to transactions with directors requiring approval of members; Ch.5 contains rules on the availability for inspection of directors' service contracts; Ch.6 applies to contracts with sole members who are directors; Ch.7 concerns directors' liabilities; Ch.8 provides a new framework for the protection of directors' residential addresses; and Ch.9 provides supplementary provisions.

CHAPTER 1

APPOINTMENT AND REMOVAL OF DIRECTORS

Requirement to have directors

154. Companies required to have directors

(1) A private company must have at least one director.

(2) A public company must have at least two directors.

DEFINITIONS

"Private Company" and "Public Company": see s.4 (Private and public companies).

GENERAL NOTE

This section replaces s.282 of the 1985 Act. It removes the exception in s.282(2) of the Companies Act 1985 that public companies registered before November 1, 1929 only require one director.

155. Companies required to have at least one director who is a natural person

(1) A company must have at least one director who is a natural person.

(2) This requirement is met if the office of director is held by a natural person as a corporation sole or otherwise by virtue of an office.

GENERAL NOTE

This new section requires every company to have at least one director who is a natural person. Previously all directors could be companies or other corporations (*Bulawayo Market and Offices Co Ltd, Re* [1907] 2 Ch. 58). The change is intended to improve the enforceability of directors' obligations and to solve the difficulty of pursuing corporate directors.

Subsection (2)

Provides that the requirement is fulfilled if a corporation sole (e.g. the Archbishop of Canterbury) is appointed as the only director. It is not envisaged that this subsection will allow companies to avoid the requirement of having a director who is a natural person (See HC Report Stage, October 17, 2006 col.813).

156. Direction requiring company to make appointment

(1) If it appears to the Secretary of State that a company is in breach of-

section 154 (requirements as to number of directors), or

section 155 (requirement to have at least one director who is a natural person),

the Secretary of State may give the company a direction under this section.

(2) The direction must specify-

(a) the statutory requirement the company appears to be in breach of,

(b) what the company must do in order to comply with the direction, and

(c) the period within which it must do so.

That period must be not less than one month or more than three months after the date on which the direction is given.

(3) The direction must also inform the company of the consequences of failing to comply.

(4) Where the company is in breach of section 154 or 155 it must comply with the direction by-

(a) making the necessary appointment or appointments, and

(b) giving notice of them under section 167,

before the end of the period specified in the direction.

(5) If the company has already made the necessary appointment or appointments (or so far as it has done so), it must comply with the direction by giving notice of them under section 167 before the end of the period specified in the direction.

(6) If a company fails to comply with a direction under this section, an offence is committed by-

(a) the company, and

(b) every officer of the company who is in default.

For this purpose a shadow director is treated as an officer of the company.

(7) A person guilty of an offence under this section is liable on summary conviction to a fine not exceeding level 5 on the standard scale and, for continued contravention, a daily default fine not exceeding one-tenth of level 5 on the standard scale.

DEFINITIONS

"Shadow Director": see s.251 ("Shadow director")

GENERAL NOTE

This provision makes it an offence not to comply with ss.154 and 155.

Subsection (1)

The provision gives the Secretary of State the power to issue a direction (see subs.(2)) to the company where it appears they are in breach of s.154 or s.155.

Subsection (2)

This provision states that the direction given by the Secretary of State must include: (a) a statement of the section the company is in breach of; (b) the action the company must take in order to comply; and (c) the period within which the company must comply with the direction. The Secretary of State must give a period of more than one month after the date of the direction, but less than three months (see also subs.(3)).

Subsections (4) and (5)

The company must give notice of the appointments made in order to comply with ss.154, 155 and 167 (duty to notify registrar of changes).

Subsections (6) and (7)

An offence is committed by the company and every officer in default, including shadow directors. Liability is specified in subs.(7).

Appointment

157. Minimum age for appointment as director

(1) A person may not be appointed a director of a company unless he has attained the age of 16 years.

(2) This does not affect the validity of an appointment that is not to take effect until the person appointed attains that age.

(3) Where the office of director of a company is held by a corporation sole, or otherwise by virtue of another office, the appointment to that other office of a person who has not attained the age of 16 years is not effective also to make him a director of the company until he attains the age of 16 years.

(4) An appointment made in contravention of this section is void.

(5) Nothing in this section affects any liability of a person under any provision of the Companies Acts if he-
  (a) purports to act as director, or
  (b) acts as a shadow director,
although he could not, by virtue of this section, be validly appointed as a director.

(6) This section has effect subject to section 158 (power to provide for exceptions from minimum age requirement).

GENERAL NOTE

This section enacts a new statutory minimum age of 16 for company directors and any appointment in contravention is void (subs.(4)). However, if an under-age director acts as a director in contravention of the section he will still be liable as a director (subs.(5)) and so must still comply with the directors' duties. This section was introduced to safeguard against those who appoint child directors "in order to exploit their immunity from prosecution or the reluctance of enforcement authorities to pursue young persons" (*Hansard*, HL GC Day 2, Vol.678, col.167 (February 1, 2006)). The minimum age requirement should not be considered a prescription of a minimum age of competence.

Also see ss.158 (Power to provide for exceptions from minimum age requirement), 159 (Existing under-age directors) and 161 (Validity of acts of directors).

158. Power to provide for exceptions from minimum age requirement

(1) The Secretary of State may make provision by regulations for cases in which a person who has not attained the age of 16 years may be appointed a director of a company.

(2) The regulations must specify the circumstances in which, and any conditions subject to which, the appointment may be made.

(3) If the specified circumstances cease to obtain, or any specified conditions cease to be met, a person who was appointed by virtue of the regulations and who has not since attained the age of 16 years ceases to hold office.

(4) The regulations may make different provision for different parts of the United Kingdom.
This is without prejudice to the general power to make different provision for different cases.

(5) Regulations under this section are subject to negative resolution procedure.

GENERAL NOTE
This section allows the Secretary of State by statutory instrument to make exceptions to s.157. It is envisaged by the Government that any exceptions made under this section would be made for classes of people rather than for individuals (HC Comm D, col.501 (October 17, 2006)).

Subsection (4)
This subsection allows the Secretary of State to make different exceptions to s.157 for different parts of the United Kingdom. The reason for including this subsection is to "provide for the differences in law on age in the various countries of the UK" (HC Comm D col.501 (July 6, 2006)).

159. Existing under-age directors

(1) This section applies where—
  (a) a person appointed a director of a company before section 157 (minimum age for appointment as director) comes into force has not attained the age of 16 when that section comes into force, or
  (b) the office of director of a company is held by a corporation sole, or otherwise by virtue of another office, and the person appointed to that other office has not attained the age of 16 years when that section comes into force,
and the case is not one excepted from that section by regulations under section 158.
(2) That person ceases to be a director on section 157 coming into force.
(3) The company must make the necessary consequential alteration in its register of directors but need not give notice to the registrar of the change.
(4) If it appears to the registrar (from other information) that a person has ceased by virtue of this section to be a director of a company, the registrar shall note that fact on the register.

GENERAL NOTE
This section is a transitional provision which provides that any under-age director not excepted under s.158 will cease to be a director on the coming into force of s.157 and that the company's register must be altered accordingly. Interestingly, the company need not notify the registrar, so the change will not appear on the register at Companies House until the registrar is alerted in some other way. The government intends to produce further transitional provisions to deal with special circumstances (HC Comm D, col.501 (July 6, 2006); HC Report Stage, col.815 (October 17, 2006)).
Also see s.161 (Validity of acts of directors).

160. Appointment of directors of public company to be voted on individually

(1) At a general meeting of a public company a motion for the appointment of two or more persons as directors of the company by a single resolution must not be made unless a resolution that it should be so made has first been agreed to by the meeting without any vote being given against it.
(2) A resolution moved in contravention of this section is void, whether or not its being so moved was objected to at the time.
But where a resolution so moved is passed, no provision for the automatic reappointment of retiring directors in default of another appointment applies.
(3) For the purposes of this section a motion for approving a person's appointment, or for nominating a person for appointment, is treated as a motion for his appointment.
(4) Nothing in this section applies to a resolution amending the company's articles.

GENERAL NOTE
This section is derived from s.292 of the 1985 Act. This statutory rule applies only to public companies. It overrides any contrary provisions in the company's constitution, although those provisions and the Main Principle A.4 of the Combined Code for listed companies may supply additional requirements that must be met in the appointments process.

The fact that the appointments of directors of a company are deemed void by s.160(2) does not bring into operation any provision in the company's constitution or elsewhere for the automatic reappointment of retiring directors in default of another appointment.

Also see s.161 (Validity of acts of directors).

161. Validity of acts of directors

(1) The acts of a person acting as a director are valid notwithstanding that it is afterwards discovered-
    (a) that there was a defect in his appointment;
    (b) that he was disqualified from holding office;
    (c) that he had ceased to hold office;
    (d) that he was not entitled to vote on the matter in question.

(2) This applies even if the resolution for his appointment is void under section 160 (appointment of directors of public company to be voted on individually).

GENERAL NOTE

This provision replaces s.285 of the 1985 Act. The purpose of the provision is to protect third parties against a company relying on a person's lack of entitlement in order to avoid obligations. The predecessor section, s.285 of the Companies Act 1985, referred only to "any defect that may afterwards be discovered in his appointment or qualification", and specifically mentioning void resolutions to appoint (as in the new subs.(2)). That wording had been interpreted narrowly so as to apply only when there is a procedural defect in the appointment, not when there has been no appointment at all (*Morris v Kanssen* [1946] AC 459), or where a director had vacated office but continued to act. The new section is explicitly more expansive, and, for example, appears to cover acts of under-age directors notwithstanding that their appointment is void (by virtue of subs.(1)(b)) or that they have been removed from office as a consequence of s.159 (by virtue of subs.(1)(c)).

Section 285 of the Companies Act 1985 could only be relied upon by third parties acting in good faith (*Channel Collieries Trust Ltd v Dover, St Margaret's and Martin Mill Light Rwy Co* [1914] 2 Ch. 506, CA; *British Asbestos Co Ltd v Boyd* [1903] 2 Ch. 439). The material words in the new section are identical, so presumably the same limitation will apply.

Register of directors, etc

162. Register of directors

(1) Every company must keep a register of its directors.
(2) The register must contain the required particulars (see sections 163, 164 and 166) of each person who is a director of the company.
(3) The register must be kept available for inspection-
    (a) at the company's registered office, or
    (b) at a place specified in regulations under section 1136.
(4) The company must give notice to the registrar-
    (a) of the place at which the register is kept available for inspection, and
    (b) of any change in that place,
unless it has at all times been kept at the company's registered office.
(5) The register must be open to the inspection-
    (a) of any member of the company without charge, and
    (b) of any other person on payment of such fee as may be prescribed.
(6) If default is made in complying with subsection (1), (2) or (3) or if default is made for 14 days in complying with subsection (4), or if an inspection required under subsection (5) is refused, an offence is committed by-
    (a) the company, and
    (b) every officer of the company who is in default.
For this purpose a shadow director is treated as an officer of the company.

(7) A person guilty of an offence under this section is liable on summary conviction to a fine not exceeding level 5 on the standard scale and, for continued contravention, a daily default fine not exceeding one-tenth of level 5 on the standard scale.

(8) In the case of a refusal of inspection of the register, the court may by order compel an immediate inspection of it.

DEFINITIONS

"in default": see s.1121 (Liability of officer in default) which provides a definition of "in default"

GENERAL NOTE

This section replaces those parts of s.288 of the 1985 Act relating to the register of directors. The reason for applying registration requirements to directors is that "it is essential that the identities of those who control companies ... should have their record in the public domain" (HC Comm D, cols 515-518 (July 6, 2006)) and "to prevent the easy evasion of the legislation by persons who control companies but who either do not wish to be appointed to the board or, more typically, cannot be appointed because they are undischarged bankrupts or the subject of disqualification orders" (*Hansard*, HL GC Day 2, Vol.678, col.170, (February 1, 2006)).

Subsection (6)

This subsection makes it an offence not to comply with subss.(1), (2) or (3), or to fail for 14 days in complying with subs.(4), or to refuse an inspection required under subs.(5). The offence is committed by the company and every officer of the company who is in default, including any shadow directors.

Subsection (7)

This subsection sets out the liability for default. In addition, the extent of a director's responsibility for any failure to comply with this section is a matter to which the court must have regard in deciding whether that person's conduct as a director or shadow director makes him unfit to be concerned in the management of a company (Company Directors' Disqualification Act 1986, s.9 and Sch.1, para.4(c)).

163. Particulars of directors to be registered: individuals

(1) A company's register of directors must contain the following particulars in the case of an individual-

(a) name and any former name;

(b) a service address;

(c) the country or state (or part of the United Kingdom) in which he is usually resident;

(d) nationality;

(e) business occupation (if any);

(f) date of birth.

(2) For the purposes of this section "name" means a person's Christian name (or other forename) and surname, except that in the case of-

(a) a peer, or

(b) an individual usually known by a title,

the title may be stated instead of his Christian name (or other forename) and surname or in addition to either or both of them.

(3) For the purposes of this section a "former name" means a name by which the individual was formerly known for business purposes.

Where a person is or was formerly known by more than one such name, each of them must be stated.

(4) It is not necessary for the register to contain particulars of a former name in the following cases-

(a) in the case of a peer or an individual normally known by a British title, where the name is one by which the person was known previous to the adoption of or succession to the title;

(b) in the case of any person, where the former name-

      (i) was changed or disused before the person attained the age of 16 years, or

      (ii) has been changed or disused for 20 years or more.

(5) A person's service address may be stated to be "The company's registered office".

GENERAL NOTE

    This provision is derived from s.289 of the 1985 Act. The three significant changes from the 1985 Act are that the director's address need not be a residential address but must be a service address; particulars of any other directorships held are no longer required to be registered; and there is no longer an exception for married women's maiden names. In addition, this register is only a register of directors, not directors and secretaries. The new Act only requires public companies to keep a register of secretaries, and that register is now separate from the register of directors (see s.275).

    See further Pt 10, Ch.8 (Directors' residential addresses: protection from disclosure).

164.   Particulars of directors to be registered: corporate directors and firms

    A company's register of directors must contain the following particulars in the case of a body corporate, or a firm that is a legal person under the law by which it is governed-

    (a) corporate or firm name;

    (b) registered or principal office;

    (c) in the case of an EEA company to which the First Company Law Directive (68/151/ EEC) applies, particulars of-

      (i) the register in which the company file mentioned in Article 3 of that Directive is kept (including details of the relevant state), and

      (ii) the registration number in that register;

    (d) in any other case, particulars of-

      (i) the legal form of the company or firm and the law by which it is governed, and

      (ii) if applicable, the register in which it is entered (including details of the state) and its registration number in that register.

GENERAL NOTE

    This section replaces s.289(1)(b) of the 1985 Act and implements the CLR recommendation requiring EEA companies to state where the company is registered and the registration number in that register (see CLR *Final Report*, para.11.38; Company Law Reform Bill 190 Explanatory Notes, at para.273).

165.   Register of directors' residential addresses

(1) Every company must keep a register of directors' residential addresses.

(2) The register must state the usual residential address of each of the company's directors.

(3) If a director's usual residential address is the same as his service address (as stated in the company's register of directors), the register of directors' residential addresses need only contain an entry to that effect.

    This does not apply if his service address is stated to be "The company's registered office".

(4) If default is made in complying with this section, an offence is committed by-

    (a) the company, and

    (b) every officer of the company who is in default.

    For this purpose a shadow director is treated as an officer of the company.

(5) A person guilty of an offence under this section is liable on summary conviction to a fine not exceeding level 5 on the standard scale and, for continued contravention, a daily default fine not exceeding one-tenth of level 5 on the standard scale.

(6) This section applies only to directors who are individuals, not where the director is a body corporate or a firm that is a legal person under the law by which it is governed.

GENERAL NOTE

    This is a new provision requiring companies to keep a register of individual directors' residential addresses, although this register is not open for inspection. This separate register is necessary as directors' residential addresses no longer have to be included in the company's register of directors (see s.163(1)(b)). Subsection (4) makes it a criminal offence not to comply with this section, and liability extends to shadow directors.

See further s.167 (Duty to notify registrar of changes) and Ch.8 (Directors' Residential Addresses: Protection from Disclosure) provisions.

166. Particulars of directors to be registered: power to make regulations

(1) The Secretary of State may make provision by regulations amending-

> section 163 (particulars of directors to be registered: individuals),
>
> section 164 (particulars of directors to be registered: corporate directors and firms), or
>
> section 165 (register of directors' residential addresses),

so as to add to or remove items from the particulars required to be contained in a company's register of directors or register of directors' residential addresses.

(2) Regulations under this section are subject to affirmative resolution procedure.

GENERAL NOTE

This is a new provision giving the Secretary of State power to amend the particulars required to be registered in ss.163, 164 and 165.

Re. subs.(2), see s.1290 (affirmative resolution procedure).

167. Duty to notify registrar of changes

(1) A company must, within the period of 14 days from-

    (a) a person becoming or ceasing to be a director, or

    (b) the occurrence of any change in the particulars contained in its register of directors or its register of directors' residential addresses,

give notice to the registrar of the change and of the date on which it occurred.

(2) Notice of a person having become a director of the company must-

    (a) contain a statement of the particulars of the new director that are required to be included in the company's register of directors and its register of directors' residential addresses, and

    (b) be accompanied by a consent, by that person, to act in that capacity.

(3) Where-

    (a) a company gives notice of a change of a director's service address as stated in the company's register of directors, and

    (b) the notice is not accompanied by notice of any resulting change in the particulars contained in the company's register of directors' residential addresses,

the notice must be accompanied by a statement that no such change is required.

(4) If default is made in complying with this section, an offence is committed by-

    (a) the company, and

    (b) every officer of the company who is in default.

For this purpose a shadow director is treated as an officer of the company.

(5) A person guilty of an offence under this section is liable on summary conviction to a fine not exceeding level 5 on the standard scale and, for continued contravention, a daily default fine not exceeding one-tenth of level 5 on the standard scale.

GENERAL NOTE

This provision replaces s.288(2) of the 1985 Act in so far as it relates to directors.

Subsection (3)

In line with the underlying policies of protecting directors' residential addresses whilst safeguarding against directors seeking to evade liability, subs.(3) requires any change in a directors' service address to be accompanied by a confirmation of the director's residential address.

Shadow directors are treated as officers of the company for the purposes of liability under subs.(4).

Removal

168. Resolution to remove director

(1) A company may by ordinary resolution at a meeting remove a director before the expiration of his period of office, notwithstanding anything in any agreement between it and him.

(2) Special notice is required of a resolution to remove a director under this section or to appoint somebody instead of a director so removed at the meeting at which he is removed.

(3) A vacancy created by the removal of a director under this section, if not filled at the meeting at which he is removed, may be filled as a casual vacancy.

(4) A person appointed director in place of a person removed under this section is treated, for the purpose of determining the time at which he or any other director is to retire, as if he had become director on the day on which the person in whose place he is appointed was last appointed a director.

(5) This section is not to be taken-

    (a) as depriving a person removed under it of compensation or damages payable to him in respect of the termination of his appointment as director or of any appointment terminating with that as director, or

    (b) as derogating from any power to remove a director that may exist apart from this section.

GENERAL NOTE

Earlier cases will remain relevant. See, e.g. the effective enhanced voting clause in *Bushell v Faith* [1970] A.C. 1099, although these clauses are unlikely to be acceptable in public company constitutions. On the other hand, the *Duomatic* principle (from *Duomatic Ltd, Re* [1969] 2 Ch. 365 at 373, Buckley J.) of effective unanimous informal assent or informed acquiescence (i.e. assent/acquiescence without a meeting) is unlikely to operate in the context of s.168 decisions. This is because the formal procedure is designed for the protection of the impugned directors, not for the protection of voting members. It follows that only the directors can waive the protection, not the voting members (see *New Cedos Engineering Co Ltd, Re* [1994] 1 B.C.L.C. 797; *Wright v Atlas Wright (Europe) Ltd* [1999] 2 B.C.L.C. 310 at 314-15 CA).

169. Director's right to protest against removal

(1) On receipt of notice of an intended resolution to remove a director under section 168, the company must forthwith send a copy of the notice to the director concerned.

(2) The director (whether or not a member of the company) is entitled to be heard on the resolution at the meeting.

(3) Where notice is given of an intended resolution to remove a director under that section, and the director concerned makes with respect to it representations in writing to the company (not exceeding a reasonable length) and requests their notification to members of the company, the company shall, unless the representations are received by it too late for it to do so-

    (a) in any notice of the resolution given to members of the company state the fact of the representations having been made; and

    (b) send a copy of the representations to every member of the company to whom notice of the meeting is sent (whether before or after receipt of the representations by the company).

(4) If a copy of the representations is not sent as required by subsection (3) because received too late or because of the company's default, the director may (without prejudice to his right to be heard orally) require that the representations shall be read out at the meeting.

(5) Copies of the representations need not be sent out and the representations need not be read out at the meeting if, on the application either of the company or of any other person who claims to be aggrieved, the court is satisfied that the rights conferred by this section are being abused.

(6) The court may order the company's costs (in Scotland, expenses) on an application under subsection (5) to be paid in whole or in part by the director, notwithstanding that he is not a party to the application.

GENERAL NOTE

This section is derived from s.304 of the 1985 Act. It sets out the formal procedure to be followed by companies an their directors in relation to proposed resolutions under s.168.

CHAPTER 2

GENERAL DUTIES OF DIRECTORS

GENERAL NOTE

This chapter represents one of the most significant changes in the new Companies Act. It purports to codify the equitable principles of fiduciary duty and the common law of negligence as they apply to directors. Codification was recommended by the Law Commission and the Scottish Law Commission in *Company Directors: Regulating Conflicts of Interests and Formulating a Statement of Duties* (Law Com. No.261, Cm.4436), Pt 4. The CLR published a draft version of codified rules in *Modern Company Law for a Competitive Economy: Final Report*, Vol.1 (URN 01/942), Annex C, with extensive commentary. The primary reason for recommending codification was to make the rules accessible. The 2002 White Paper indicates that the government will produce plain language guidance explaining the statutory duties (*Company Law Reform*, para.3.3). This was confirmed by the Attorney-General (*Hansard* HL, col.GC249 (February 6, 2006)).

Introductory

170. Scope and nature of general duties

(1) The general duties specified in sections 171 to 177 are owed by a director of a company to the company.

(2) A person who ceases to be a director continues to be subject-

    (a) to the duty in section 175 (duty to avoid conflicts of interest) as regards the exploitation of any property, information or opportunity of which he became aware at a time when he was a director, and

    (b) to the duty in section 176 (duty not to accept benefits from third parties) as regards things done or omitted by him before he ceased to be a director.

To that extent those duties apply to a former director as to a director, subject to any necessary adaptations.

(3) The general duties are based on certain common law rules and equitable principles as they apply in relation to directors and have effect in place of those rules and principles as regards the duties owed to a company by a director.

(4) The general duties shall be interpreted and applied in the same way as common law rules or equitable principles, and regard shall be had to the corresponding common law rules and equitable principles in interpreting and applying the general duties.

(5) The general duties apply to shadow directors where, and to the extent that, the corresponding common law rules or equitable principles so apply.

GENERAL NOTE

The Explanatory Notes accompanying Ch.2 of the Company Law Reform Bill 190 began "the general duties form a code of conduct, which sets out how directors are expected to behave; it does not tell them in terms what to do" (at para.280).

For remedies see s.178 (Civil consequences of breach of general duties).

See also s.239 (Ratification of acts of directors) and Pt 10, Ch.7 (Liability of directors).

Subsection (1)

This provision states the fundamental principle that directors' duties are owed to the company. Unless there are very special circumstances, directors do not owe duties to the members of the company, to creditors, or to other directors (*Multinational Gas and Petrochemical Co v Multinational Gas and Petrochemical Services Ltd* [1983] Ch. 258 CA). It follows that it is only the company that can bring an action for a breach of a duty. Such an action can be initiated on behalf of the company by the board of directors, a liquidator, or by means of a derivative action (see Pt 11).

Section 250 defines "director" as including "any person occupying the position of director, by whatever name called". It follows that the general duties of directors apply equally to de facto directors. It is less clear to what extent the general duties are also owed by shadow directors (see subs.(5), below).

Subsection (2)

This subsection makes it clear that certain directors' duties continue after a person has ceased to be a director. The duty to avoid conflicts of interest and the duty not to accept benefits from third parties continue to apply to former directors *to the extent stated* in subs.(2)(a) and (b). The wording "subject to any necessary adaptation" signals to the court that it may be more flexible when interpreting and applying these duties to former directors as opposed to current directors. Existing case law is likely to remain relevant, although subs.(2) clarifies some of the underlying uncertainties (see, e.g. *Industrial Development Consultants Ltd v Cooley* [1972] 1 W.L.R. 443; *CMS Dolphin Ltd v Simonet* [2001] 2 B.C.L.C. 704).

Subsection (3)

Subsection (3) explains that the statutory duties described in Ch.2 have been put in place to replace the common law rules and equitable principles from which they are derived. It follows that actions against directors will have to be based on breaches of statutory provisions, not breaches of related common law rules and equitable principles (but see subs.(4) below).

Subsection (4)

Subsection (4) applies to all of Ch.2 (General duties of directors), and provides a new way of interpreting and applying a statute. The provision requires the court to have regard to the existing interpretation and the continuing development of the common law rules and equitable principles on which the statutory statement is based when interpreting and applying the statutory statement. This is not normally allowed in interpreting the words of a statute. In Grand Committee Lord Goldsmith explained the Government's intention:

> "Although the duties in relation to directors have developed in a distinctive way, they are often manifestations of more general principles. Subsection (4) is intended to enable the courts to continue to have regard to developments in the common law rules and equitable principles applying to these other types of fiduciary relationship. The advantage of that is that it will enable the statutory duties to develop in line with relevant developments in the law as it applies elsewhere" (*Hansard*, HL GC Day 3, Vol.678, cols 243-245 (February 6, 2006)).

This was developed in more detail by David Howarth:

> "It was clear throughout the Company Law Review, and in the Law Commission's report on the same matters, that the statutory statement of directors' duties was intended to reflect a refined version of where the case law has got to. Because part of our intention in passing the statute is to put into statutory form what already exists in some other form in case law, it would be legitimate to refer back to existing case law, because that would tend to clarify, rather than make more confusing, what we are doing" (HC Comm D cols 531-537 (July 6, 2006)).

Whether this intention is consistent with the text is a matter of debate (see comments in HC Third Reading, col.1104 (October 19, 2006)). The practical effect of subss.(3) and (4), however, is that reference must be made to the statutory statement of duties, but that in order to understand and apply these duties the surrounding case law must also be read. Practitioners and judges will therefore continue to be required to "refer back to a bundle of cases" (see Solicitor-General's comments, HC Comm D, cols 531-537 (July 6, 2006)).

Subsection (5)

This subsection indicates that shadow directors are subject to these general statutory duties to the same extent that, before the Act, they were subject to the corresponding common law rules and equitable principles. The difficult decision is thus left to the courts to determine, based on precedent and particular circumstances. For example, the mere fact that a person is a shadow director, and exercises indirect influence, is not enough to impose fiduciary duties: the facts must go further and suggest that there is a fiduciary relationship (*Ultraframe (UK) Ltd v Fielding* [2005] EWHC 1638 Ch, at [1284] and [1289]-[1291])

The general duties

171. Duty to act within powers

A director of a company must-

  (a) act in accordance with the company's constitution, and

  (b) only exercise powers for the purposes for which they are conferred.

DEFINITIONS

"Company's constitution": see s.17 (company constitution). See also s.172 (Duty to promote the success of the company)

GENERAL NOTE

This section codifies the general duty of a director to act in accordance with the company's constitution and to exercise powers for a proper purpose.

The company's constitution is commonly regarded as relevant in limiting a director's authority to act. This has potential ramifications for third parties dealing with the company. Section 171(a) makes it clear that non-compliance with these constitutional limitations is a breach of duty by the director. A director who acts in breach of s.171(a) is liable to compensate the company for any loss that the company suffers as a result of the breach. The validity of an act that is not in accordance with the company's constitution depends upon rules of agency (see *Hely Hutchinson v Brayhead Ltd* [1968] 1 Q.B. 549, CA; *Freeman and Lockyer v Buckhurst Park Properties (Mangal) Ltd* [1964] 2 Q.B. 480 CA).

Section 171(b) codifies the proper purposes doctrine as it applies to directors. This subsection therefore puts to rest earlier debates about whether such a duty exists. The precursor equitable duty to "act bona fide in what they (i.e. the directors) consider - not what a court may consider -is in the interests of the company, and not for any collateral purpose" (*Smith and Fawcett Ltd, Re* [1942] Ch. 304 at 306, Lord Greene M.R.) was variously urged as imposing either one duty or two. The new Act separates the two limbs, with the proper purposes aspect appearing here in s.171, and the "interests of the company", reformulated as the "duty to promote the success of the company", appearing in s.172. This recognition that there are two duties follows *Punt v Symons & Co Ltd* [1903] 2 Ch. 506; *Hogg v Cramphorn Ltd* [1967] Ch. 254 (Buckley J.), and *Howard Smith Ltd v Ampol Petroleum Ltd* [1974] A.C. 821 (PC, Lord Wilberforce). The separation, and the objective test embraced by the proper purposes doctrine, allows for greater judicial intervention in corporate decision-making that might otherwise be the case.

The positive formulation of the proper purposes obligation in s.171(b) (a director "must ... exercise powers for ... [proper] purposes") as opposed to the negative version in *Smith and Fawcett* (a director must not act for any collateral purpose) also aligns the duty more closely with the common law version that is familiar in public and administrative law (*Associated Provincial Picture Houses Ltd v Wednesbury Corp* [1948] 1 K.B. 223, Lord Greene M.R.). This alignment has been advocated in certain recent cases (*Hunter v Senate Support Services Ltd* [2004] EWHC 1085 Ch; [2005] 1 B.C.L.C. 175; *Edge v Pensions Ombudsman* [2000] Ch 602 at 627-8 CA).

It is not easy to determine the proper purposes for which a power can be exercised; context is crucial (*Howard Smith Ltd v Ampol Petroleum Ltd* at 835; *Peskin v Anderson* [2001] 1 B.C.L.C. 372; *Criterion Properties plc v Stratford UK Properties Plc* [2004] UKHL 28; [2004] 1 W.L.R. 1846). In many cases, powers are exercised for a variety of purposes, only some of which may be improper. In these circumstances, the exercise will be tainted only if the improper purpose is the 'moving cause' (*Hindle v John Cotton Ltd* (1919) 56 S.L.R. 625 at 631). Other jurisdictions describe this as the "substantial" or "dominant" purpose (*Whitehouse v Carlton Hotel Pty Ltd* (1987) 162 C.L.R. 285 Aust HCt at 294; also see *Mills v Mills* (1938) 60 CLR 150 at 186). An exercise of power for improper purposes is voidable, not void (*Howard Smith Ltd v Ampol Petroleum Ltd* [1974] A.C. 821).

Nominee directors in particular are at risk of breaching this duty: they may use their powers to advance the interests of their nominator, not the interests of the company itself (*Scottish Cooperative Wholesale Society Ltd v Meyer* [1959] A.C. 324; *Kuwait Asia Bank EC v National Mutual Life Nominees Ltd* [1991] 1 A.C. 187 at 222 PC).

172. Duty to promote the success of the company

(1) A director of a company must act in the way he considers, in good faith, would be most likely to promote the success of the company for the benefit of its members as a whole, and in doing so have regard (amongst other matters) to-

    (a) the likely consequences of any decision in the long term,

    (b) the interests of the company's employees,

    (c) the need to foster the company's business relationships with suppliers, customers and others,

    (d) the impact of the company's operations on the community and the environment,

    (e) the desirability of the company maintaining a reputation for high standards of business conduct, and

    (f) the need to act fairly as between members of the company.

(2) Where or to the extent that the purposes of the company consist of or include purposes other than the benefit of its members, subsection (1) has effect as if the reference to promoting the success of the company for the benefit of its members were to achieving those purposes.

(3) The duty imposed by this section has effect subject to any enactment or rule of law requiring directors, in certain circumstances, to consider or act in the interests of creditors of the company.

GENERAL NOTE

This section is one of the more important and controversial provisions in the Act and took up much of the discussion through the various stages of the Bill.

In adopting the approach seen here, the Act purports to end the debate that has raged for years over the meaning of "in the interests of the company" (see *Smith and Fawcett Ltd* [1942] Ch. 304 at 306, Lord Greene M.R.: directors are required to "act bona fide in what they consider - not what a court may consider - is in the interests of the company, and not for any collateral purpose"). The Act specifies that the director's duty is to the company (s.170), and it is to promote the success of the company for the benefit of its members as a whole (not for the benefit of other constituencies). The Act therefore rejects the "pluralist approach" and adopts the "enlightened shareholder value" recommendations of the Company Law Review Steering Group (Company Law Reform Bill - White Paper 2005, para.3.3; CLR, *Modern Company Law for a Competitive Economy: A Strategic Framework*, at para.5). One important reason for this choice is that the pluralist view risks leaving directors accountable to no one, since there is no clear yardstick for judging their performance (Committee on Corporate Governance, *Final Report*, para.1.17).

Subsection (1)

This subsection enshrines a number of important elements:

(i) "*The success of the company for the benefit of its members as a whole*". This statement relates the success of the company to the interests of its members as a whole. This approach was advocated by the CLR (CLR, *Modern Company Law for a Competitive Economy: Developing the Framework* (URN 00/656), para.3.51):

> "We believe there is value in inserting a reference to the success of the company, since what is in view is not the individual interests of members, but their interests as members of an association with the purposes and the mutual arrangements embodied in the constitution; the objective is to be achieved by the directors successfully managing the complex of relationships and resources which comprise the company's undertaking."

The primacy of the company is significant. If the interests of the company as a separate entity are in conflict with the interests of the members as a whole, or at least some of them, it would appear that the interests of the company should be preferred (*Mutual Life Assurance Co of New York v Rank Organisation Ltd* [1985] B.C.L.C. 11 at 21 (Goulding J.); *BSB Holdings Ltd (No.2), Re* [1996] 1 B.C.L.C. 155 at 251 (Arden J.)).

(ii) *Directors and members to decide what "success" means.* Directors' good faith business judgements must be calculated to promote the success of the company. "Success" is to be determined on a company-by-company basis. The Attorney-General, Lord Goldsmith, explained further:

> "The starting point is that it is essentially for the members of the company to define the objectives that they wish to achieve. Success means what the members collectively want the company to achieve" (*Hansard*, HL GC Day 3, Vol.678, cols 255-256 (February 6, 2006)).

It is then for the directors to interpret these objectives and make practical decisions about how best to achieve them. At its simplest, success may often mean the long-term increase in financial value of the company, but even this has its difficulties. It is not clear, e.g. whether the directors should favour increased dividend rates, market price for the shares, or long-term growth and stability of the company.

(iii) *Success for the members as a whole*. The directors must make decisions that are calculated to be for the long-term benefit of the members as a whole. It follows that promoting sectional interests would be a breach of the duty to promote the success of the company (see *Mills v Mills* (1938) 60 CLR 150 Aust HCt). The Attorney General, Lord Goldsmith, explained the practical effect of this element:

> "What is meant by 'members as a whole'? The duty is to promote the success for the benefit of the members as a whole - that is, for the members as a collective body - not only to benefit the majority shareholders, or any particular shareholder or section of shareholders, still less the interests of directors who might happen to be shareholders themselves. That is an important statement of the way in which the directors need to look at this judgment that they have to make" (*Hansard* HL GC Day 3, Vol.678, cols 255-256 (February 6, 2006)).

(iv) *Directors to make decisions - subjective test*. The essential principle is that it is for directors to make decisions, in good faith, as to how to promote the success of the company for the benefit of the members as a whole. This test repeats the common law rule from which it is derived (*Smith and Fawcett Ltd* [1942] Ch 304 at 306, Lord Greene M.R.). It follows that a court will not inquire whether, objectively, the decision was the best decision for the company (*Howard Smith Ltd v Ampol Petroleum Ltd* [1974] A.C. 821 at 832 (PC, Lord Wilberforce); *Regentcrest Plc v Cohen* [2001] 2 B.C.L.C. 80 at 105), nor whether the director's honestly held belief was a reasonable one (*Smith v Fawcett* [1942] 1 Ch. 304 at 306; *Bristol & West Building Society v Mothew* [1998] Ch. 1 at 18; *Regentcrest Plc v Cohen* [2001] 2 B.C.L.C. 80 at 105).

At Report Stage in the House of Commons, an amendment was tabled which would have changed the wording of this section from "have regard ... to" to "endeavour to". The amendment was rejected, but the discussion sheds some light on the nature of the duty:

> "Whereas 'have regard ... to' is a subjective test - a director can say that he has thought about the six secondary duties listed in clause [172] ... and may or may not have done more about them - 'must endeavour to' is an objective test, requiring some evidence of having sought to abide by those duties before deciding whether it was in the best interests of the company to do so" (Patrick Hall, HC Report Stage 1, col 763 (October 17, 2006)).

Leaving aside the comment regarding secondary duties, this highlights the fact that it is for *directors* to make decisions and decide what success means. Although Parliament cannot determine how a "good faith business judgment" will be interpreted by the courts, it is not expressly subject to any 'reasonableness' test (also see *Extrasure Travel Insurance Ltd v Scattergood* [2003] 1 B.C.L.C. 598 at [90] and [97]).

(v) *Regard to the specified factors*. Subsection (1), especially when read with s.170, makes it clear that the duty imposed on directors to consider the interests of persons other than the company (e.g. employees, suppliers, customers, the community) does not indicate that directors owe a duty directly to those persons. A director's duties are owed to the company alone (s.170).

(vi) *Conflicting factors*. Where consideration of different "factors" suggests conflicting courses of action, what is required? Margaret Hodge explained in Committee Stage of the House of Commons that "a director will not be required to consider any of the factors beyond the point at which to do so would conflict with the overarching duty to promote the success of the company" (HC Comm D cols 591-593 (July 7, 2006)). The emphasis is simply on directors taking "good faith business decisions".

(vii) *Failure to have regard to the specified matters*. If a director acts *without* adopting the form of consideration required by subs.(1), how will a court respond? If there is no basis on which a director could reasonably have concluded that the action was likely to promote the success of the company, a court is likely to find the director in breach of this duty (see *Item Software (UK) Ltd v Fassihi* [2004] EWCA Civ 1244 at [44]). But if a reasonable director, giving due consideration, might well have concluded that the action was likely to promote the success of the company, the court's reaction is not so clear. Assuming the director acted bona fide, perhaps a court will find there has been no breach of duty (see *Charterbridge Corp Ltd v Lloyds Bank Ltd* [1970] Ch. 62 at 74), or at least that the breach has caused no harm. In favour of this approach, the Attorney-General, Lord Goldsmith, said (*Hansard* HL col 846 (May 9, 2006)):

> "We want the director to give such consideration to the factors identified as is necessary for the decision that he has to take, and no more than that. We do not intend a director to be required to do more than good faith and the duty of skill and care would require, nor do we want it to be possible for a director acting in good faith to be held liable for a process failure where it could not have affected the outcome."

However, on a strict legal interpretation it is also possible that the decision may be subjected to review, and deemed voidable because it has been made without taking into account all material considerations (see the note to s.171, above, and *Associated Provincial Picture Houses Ltd v Wednesbury Corp* [1948] 1 K.B. 223, Lord Greene MR). Subsection (1) effectively specifies some (not all) of the matters deemed to be relevant to decisions made by directors. Setting out such a list may expand the grounds for judicial review of directors' decision-making.

(viii) *No need for a paper trail.* Concerns were expressed during the legislative process that this section would require directors to keep a "paper trail" of all business judgements made and that the section would lead to an increase in litigation. The concerns are linked in so far as an increase in litigation would require directors to undertake more defensive practices and procedures, and, conversely, the lower the threat of litigation the less the requirement for paper trails. The government strongly denied that this section introduced a "tick-box culture" whereby directors would be required to consider each factor one by one. The list of factors is non-exclusive and is intended to illustrate elements of the wider principle that directors are required to make good faith business judgements to promote the success of the company for the benefit of its members as a whole. As such directors should not be liable for a "process failure".

On the other hand, s.417 (Contents of directors' report: business review) sets out the requirements for the contents of directors' reports. Subsection (2) of that section, which states the purpose of the business review, was introduced in Report Stage of the House of Lords as a response to stakeholders and interest groups. Lord Sainsbury gave two reasons for introducing the subsection. First, it makes it clear that "the business review is designed for the benefit of members as a whole so they may exercise their governance rights more effectively". Secondly:

> "We want to make an express link between the business review and the directors' duties under [s.172: Duty to promote the success of the company]. That clause ... embodies the concept of enlightened shareholder value. That is relevant to reporting on matters such as the environment and employees in the business review ... As we explained with regard to [s.172], the Company Law Review concluded that the success of the company could only be promoted taking due account of such factors, which reflect wider expectation of responsible business behaviour. By making the link to directors' duties, it helps to make clear that those factors contribute to the success of the company for the benefit of members as a whole, and it is in that context that directors are being asked to report on them" (HL Report Stage, col.920 (May 10, 2006)).

(ix) *No risk of increased litigation.* The second fear expressed was that a failure to take into account specific factors may lead to increased litigation. This fear was said to be over-exaggerated (see HC Comm D, cols 568-575 (July 11, 2006)). The only duty at stake is the duty to promote the success of the company, and so long as directors have made good faith business judgements with reasonable care, skill and diligence they are unlikely to be in breach of this duty (see *Hansard*, HL Vol.681, cols 845-846 (May 9, 2006)). In Committee Stage in the House of Commons, David Howarth made the important additional observation that the class of potential litigants is limited, and that it will also often be difficult to identify any loss. Without these two factors, the risk of litigation is minimal. The class of potential litigants is limited to the board, a majority of shareholders, a minority of shareholders under Pt 11, and liquidators acting on behalf of an insolvent company. It is only during a takeover that a board or a majority of shareholders is likely to bring an action against a director; in most cases there are far better remedies available against directors, e.g. removal of the director. Further, a derivative action under Pt 11 is extremely difficult to advance against the wishes of the majority of shareholders. In reality, it is only during takeovers and liquidation proceedings that the section is likely to be utilised. Moreover, an action will only be useful where there is a loss to the company; a breach of the duty to promote the success of the company is unlikely, alone, to give rise to significant calculable financial loss.

(x) *A defence rather than duty?* Although the "enlightened shareholder value" approach was designed to avoid the problems of director accountability inherent in the "pluralist approach", it is not clear that this ambition is achieved. Subsection (1) sets out proper considerations for director decision-making, but these considerations will allow directors to justify almost any bona fide approach to delivering the success of the company. Where directors have made a good faith business judgment to favour employees' interests over short-term financial gain, for example, in order to promote the success of the company for the benefits of its members as a whole, then this legitimate decision cannot be challenged (see *Welfab Engineers Ltd, Re* (1990) B.C.L.C. 833). Similarly, directors are not compelled to make decisions according to the wider interests of community and the environment, but they are protected from reproach if they choose to do so.

(xi) *Duty to disclose misconduct?* The controversial finding in *Item Software (UK) Ltd v Fassihi* [2004] EWCA Civ 1244 at [44], may be embraced by the terms of s.172. *Fassihi* suggests that a director who acts in breach of his or her fiduciary duty is under a further duty to disclose the breach to the company if disclosure is required by the general equitable duty to act bona fide in what the director considers to be the interests of the company. The analogy with the statutory duty in s.172(1) is obvious. It is difficult to see when it would not be in the company's interest to know of a breach of duty, and on that basis any breach of duty will always involve a further breach in failing to disclose. The further breach may result in loss of employment benefits (e.g. termination rights, share options, pension benefits), and may provide justification for summary dismissal (*Tesco Stores Ltd v Pook* [2003] EWHC 823 Ch; *Fulham Football Club (1987) Ltd v Tigana* [2004] EWHC 2585 QB). On the other hand, this aspect of the *Fassihi* decision represents a radical extension of the traditional equitable duties owed by directors, and the approach to these statutory rules advocated in s.170 may argue against its acceptance.

Less controversially, a director also has an equitable duty to disclose breaches of duty by fellow directors if this is what the director, acting bona fide, considers to be in the best interests of the company (*British Midland Tool Ltd v Midland Inter-*

national Tooling Ltd [2003] EWHC 466 Ch; [2003] 2 B.C.L.C. 523). Again, the analogy with the statutory duty in s.172(1) is apparent.

Subsection (1) (a)

The first factor that directors ought to consider is the long-term consequences of any decision. This subsection effects a clear change from the version published in the government White Paper (*Company Law Reform*, Cm.6456 (2005)), which required a director to take into account "the likely consequences (short and long term) of the actions open to the director". The change highlights the importance that Government places on introducing 'long-termism' to modern company law. *Subsectioon (1) (b)*

This replaces s.309 of the 1985 Act. The wording of subss.(1) and (1)(b) makes it clear that the interests of employees are secondary to promoting the success of the company for the benefit of its members as a whole. This clear statement follows the recommendations of the CLR (CLR, *Modern Company Law for a Competitive Economy*: The Strategic Framework, 1999, paras 5.1.20-5.1.23).

However, also see the power to make provision for employees on cessation or transfer of business (s.247). Subsection (2) of that section states that this latter power "is exercisable notwithstanding the general duty imposed by s.172".

Subsection (2)

Where the purposes of the company are, or include, purposes other than the benefit of members, then subs.(1) must be read as a duty to promote the success of the company in achieving those purposes (see *CAS (Nominees) Ltd v Nottingham Forest FC Plc* [2002] 1 B.C.L.C. 613). This aspect is likely to become increasingly important as investors select companies that take into account social, environmental and ethical considerations.

Subsection (3)

The duty to promote the success of the company for the benefit of the members as a whole is subject to any enactment or rule of law requiring directors to consider or act in the interests of creditors of the company.

This subsection requires directors to comply with the Insolvency Act 1986, s.214 (wrongful trading). Under this section, a director or shadow director of a company in liquidation may be liable to contribute to the assets of the insolvent company if the director knew or ought to have known that the company had no reasonable prospect of avoiding insolvency and the director did not take every step to minimise the potential loss to company creditors.

The scope of the common law duty requiring directors to consider the interests of creditors is more controversial. Cases support a variety of propositions, but the better accepted view is that a duty is owed by directors to the company (and not to the creditors themselves: *Kuwait Asia Bank EC v National Mutual Life Nominees Ltd* [1991] 1 A.C. 187 at 217 PC; *Yukong Line Ltd v Rendsburg Investments Corp (No.2)* [1998] 1 W.L.R. 294), and this duty requires directors of insolvent or borderline insolvent companies to have regard to the interests of the company's creditors (*West Mercia Safetywear Ltd v Dodd* [1988] B.C.L.C. 250 CA). The duty does not seem to require directors to act to the best advantage of creditors, but merely not to act in a way that would leave the creditors in a worse position than on liquidation (*Weldfab Engineers Ltd, Re* [1990] B.C.L.C. 833, Hoffmann J.). Although the duty is relatively easy to state, the boundary between acceptable entrepreneurial risk-taking and unacceptable breaches of duties to creditors in the lead up to insolvency is not clear-cut, especially without the benefit of hindsight (*Facia Footwear Ltd v Hinchcliffe* [1998] 1 B.C.L.C. 218 at 228).

173. Duty to exercise independent judgment

(1) A director of a company must exercise independent judgment.

(2) This duty is not infringed by his acting-

    (a) in accordance with an agreement duly entered into by the company that restricts the future exercise of discretion by its directors, or

    (b) in a way authorised by the company's constitution.

GENERAL NOTE

This provision codifies the equitable principles that directors must exercise their powers independently and must not fetter their discretion. Clearly directors can rely on the advice of others, but they must make the judgment their own:

> "The duty is about directors having to make their own judgments and not following blindly the views of another without considering the interests of the company. In other words, the role of a director is to exercise independent judgment for the benefit of the company" (HC Comm D, col.599 (July 11, 2006)).

The duty applies equally to nominee directors. As such, nominee directors cannot blindly follow the judgment of those who appointed them, although they may rely on their advice provided they make the judgment their own.

This provision reflects the current law in so far as directors will not breach the duty in subs.(1) if the company fetters directors' discretion or authorises the director to delegate his or her discretion. A director may only delegate his or her discretion to the extent that the company gives him the power to do so.

Case law: *Kregor v Hollins* (1913) 109 L.T. 225; *Fulham Football Club Ltd v Cabra Estates Plc* [1994] 1 B.C.L.C. 363; *Scottish Co-operative Wholesale Society Ltd v Meyer* [1959] A.C. 324; *Kuwait Asia Bank EC v National Mutual Life Nominees Ltd* [1991] 1 A.C. 187.

174.   Duty to exercise reasonable care, skill and diligence

(1) A director of a company must exercise reasonable care, skill and diligence.

(2) This means the care, skill and diligence that would be exercised by a reasonably diligent person with-

    (a) the general knowledge, skill and experience that may reasonably be expected of a person carrying out the functions carried out by the director in relation to the company, and

    (b) the general knowledge, skill and experience that the director has.

GENERAL NOTE

This provision mirrors the subjective/objective test found in s.214(4) of the Insolvency Act 1986. It thus codifies the still somewhat controversial approach found in more recent case law, and marks an end to the subjective test enunciated in *City Equitable Fire Insurance Co Ltd, Re* [1925] Ch 407 at 428 (Romer J.). The approach adopts as the minimum standard that objectively expected of persons in the directors' position; that standard may be raised by the subjective element of the test if the particular director has any special knowledge, skill and experience.

The Act does not indicate whether this duty is a common law or equitable duty, but it is not fiduciary (see s.178). The duty is owed to the company (s.170), not to the members. Members have no right, e.g. to expect a reasonable standard of general management from the company's managing director: management quality is one of the normal risks of investing (*Elgindata Ltd, Re* [1991] B.C.L.C. 959 at 994).

As well as liability to the company in tort or in equity, breach of this duty may show unfitness to be concerned in the management of the company and so lead to disqualification under the Company Directors Disqualification Act 1986, s.6.

Case law: On the subjective/objective test: *D'Jan of London Ltd* [1994] 1 B.C.L.C. 561; *Base Metal Trading Ltd v Shamurin* [2005] 1 W.L.R. 1157 (*per* Arden L.J., dissenting). On reliance on other officials and employees: *Dovey v Cory* [1901] A.C. 477; *Barings Plc (No.6), Re* [2000] 1 BCLC 523 at 536 (a disqualification case); *Queens Moat House Plc (No.2)* [2004] EWHC 1730 Ch, [2005] 1 B.C.L.C. 136; *Equitable Life Assurance Society v Bowley* [2003] EWHC 2263 (Comm), [2004] 1 B.C.L.C. 180. On the duty to take positive action and keep informed: *Westmid Packing Services Ltd, Re* [1998] 2 All E.R. 124; *Barings Plc (No.5)* [2000] 1 B.C.L.C. 523 at 535-6 (a disqualification case); *Continental Assurance Co of London Plc* [1997] 1 B.C.L.C. 48.

175.   Duty to avoid conflicts of interest

(1) A director of a company must avoid a situation in which he has, or can have, a direct or indirect interest that conflicts, or possibly may conflict, with the interests of the company.

(2) This applies in particular to the exploitation of any property, information or opportunity (and it is immaterial whether the company could take advantage of the property, information or opportunity).

(3) This duty does not apply to a conflict of interest arising in relation to a transaction or arrangement with the company.

(4) This duty is not infringed-

    (a) if the situation cannot reasonably be regarded as likely to give rise to a conflict of interest; or

    (b) if the matter has been authorised by the directors.

(5) Authorisation may be given by the directors-

(a) where the company is a private company and nothing in the company's constitution invalidates such authorisation, by the matter being proposed to and authorised by the directors; or

(b) where the company is a public company and its constitution includes provision enabling the directors to authorise the matter, by the matter being proposed to and authorised by them in accordance with the constitution.

(6) The authorisation is effective only if-

(a) any requirement as to the quorum at the meeting at which the matter is considered is met without counting the director in question or any other interested director, and

(b) the matter was agreed to without their voting or would have been agreed to if their votes had not been counted.

(7) Any reference in this section to a conflict of interest includes a conflict of interest and duty and a conflict of duties.

GENERAL NOTE

This section is the first of three general sections that address the equitable duties owed by directors to their companies (also see Ch.4 on specific transactions between directors and the company and Pt 14 on political donations and expenditure). This section replaces the equitable no-conflict rule as it applies to conflicts of interest arising from third party dealings by a director.

i   the statutory general duty to avoid conflicts of interest does not address conflicts of interest arising in relation to transactions or arrangements *with* the company (see subs.(3)). This change is perhaps a statutory acknowledgement that companies' articles routinely permit their directors to have interests in company transactions, provided they are declared. Instead, these transactions will merely have to be declared (see Ch.3), unless the transaction is a substantial transaction requiring the approval of members (as defined in Ch.4).

ii The statutory duty to avoid conflicts of interest replaces the equitable no-conflict and no-profit rules by a single rule. The Explanatory Notes to the Bill as introduced in the House of Commons, para.320, indicate that the no-profit rule is included within the general duty, in so far as making a profit gives rise to a conflict of interest. This approach, where the no-profit rule is regarded as part of the no-conflict rule, is evident in *Bray v Ford* [1896] A.C. 44 at 51-2, and *Boardman v Phipps* [1967] 2 A.C. 46 at 123. But other cases have regarded the two rules as distinct, although overlapping, so that a breach of the no-profit rule cannot always be readily analysed as a conflict of duty and interest (see, e.g. *Regal (Hastings) Ltd v Gulliver* [1967] 2 A.C. 134 at153 and 159). To the extent (if any) that the no-conflict rule fails to cover the no-profit rule, the new statutory regime deviates from existing equitable rules.

iii The statutory duty modifies the equitable rules with regard to authorisation of conflicts of interest (see subss.(4)(b), (5) and (6)).

iv The statutory duty covers both conflicts of interest and duty and conflicts of duties (see subs.(7)). The precise implications and remedial consequences of this bundling may need further working out.

v   Also see s.170(2). This makes it clear that a person who ceases to be a director will continue to be subject to the duty to avoid conflicts of interest as regards the exploitation of any property, information or opportunity of which he became aware at a time when he was a director.

Subsection (1) and (4) (a)

The general rule in subs.(1) is a reformulation of the statement of the rule in *Aberdeen Railway Co v Blaikie Bros* (1854) 1 Macq 461 at 471 (Lord Cranworth L.C.) (*Hansard*, HL col GC 288, Attorney-General, Lord Goldsmith (February 6, 2006)). It comprehends actual and potential conflicts. Interestingly, the formulation bars unauthorised conflicts of personal interest with the interests of the company, not with *duties* to the company (as in the formulation in *Bray v Ford* [1896] A.C. 44 at 51-2). The former approach is often regarded as too wide, and the narrower formulation is preferred. Subsection (4)(a) may render this concern academic. Also see subs.(7). But the wider formulation may make it easier, especially in relation to corporate opportunities, to argue that pursuit of the opportunity involves a conflict. Cases on the equitable rule vary in their approach, some taking a narrow view of which opportunities are caught (*Balston Ltd v Headline Filters Ltd* [1990] F.S.R. 385 at 412; *Industrial Development Consultants Ltd v Cooley* [1972] 1 W.L.R. 443 at 451), and some a wider view (*Bhullar v Bhullar* [2003] EWCA Civ 424, [2003] 2 B.C.L.C. 241 at [28] and [41]).

Subsection (4)(a) indicates the duty is not infringed if the situation cannot reasonably be regarded as likely to give rise to a conflict of interest. This, too, reflects the equitable rule (*Queensland Mines Ltd v Hudson* (1978) 52 A.L.J.R. 399 PC; *Boardman v Phipps* [1967] 2 A.C. 46 at 124 (Lord Upjohn, dissenting); *Bhullar v Bhullar* [2003] EWCA Civ 424; [2003] 2 B.C.L.C. 241). On this basis, it may now be the case that if a company considers a new venture and concludes, on a properly informed and bona fide basis, that it will not pursue the venture, then the company's directors will be free to pursue the venture on their own account (see the controversial Canadian decision to this effect, *Peso Silver Mines Ltd (NPL) v Cropper* (1966) 58 D.L.R. (2d) 1).

The company's articles may include exemption clauses preventing a conflict of interest arising in the first place. Whether such a restriction on the liability of directors will be valid is left to the common law. See s.232 (Provisions protecting directors from liability). The government's stated intention "is that everything that may currently be done in the articles for authorising or dealing with conflicts of interest will remain valid and can continue to be done in the future" (*Hansard*, HL Third Reading, Vol.682, col.722 (May 25, 2006)). *Subsection (2)*

This repeats the equitable rule that it is immaterial whether the company could take advantage of the property, information or opportunity exploited by the defaulting director. The inclusion of this subsection must also indicate that this element is immaterial in deciding whether a situation can reasonably be regarded as likely to give rise to a conflict of interest (sub-s.(4)(a)). This accords with the equitable rule (see *Keech v Sandford* (1726) Sel. Cas. Ch. 61; *Regal (Hastings) Ltd v Gulliver* [1967] 2 A.C. 134).

Subsection (3)

Conflicts of interest arising as a consequence of transactions or arrangements with the company are not dealt with by this section, but by s.177 and Chs 3 and 4.

Subsections (4) (b), (5) and (6)

Subs (4)(b) states that the duty is not infringed if the matter has been authorised by the directors, and subs.(5) describes how and when such authorisation may be given by the directors. Subsection (5) distinguishes between private and public companies. Authorisation may be given by the directors of a private company so long as the constitution does not contain any provision to the contrary, whereas authorisation may only be given by the directors of a public company if the constitution contains a provision enabling the directors to authorise the matter and they do so in accordance with this provision.

Subsection (6) apparently states the minimum procedural requirements for an authorisation to be effective. It appears to override any more lenient approaches to disapplication of the conflicts rules set out in a company's articles (so, e.g. the approach in *Boulting v Association of Cinematograph, Television and Allied Technicians* [1963] 2 Q.B. 606 at 636 is not longer relevant). In Grand Committee, Lord Goldsmith explained that this kept in place any constitutional rules or rules of the common law:

> "[A]ny requirements under the common law for what is necessary for a valid authorisation remain in force. I draw the Committee's attention to [s.175](6), which says: 'The authorisation is effective only if'. It then sets out certain specific requirements. It deliberately does not say that if those requirements are met the authorisation is effective. There might be other conditions in relation to the authorisation that would be required - for example, the company's constitution may have some specific provision with which it would be necessary to comply. Those formalities and those conditions need to be complied with as well" (*Hansard*, HL GC Day 4, Vol.678, col.326 (February 9, 2006)).

For example, the common law indicates that any authorisation must be "informed authorisation" in order to be effective.

Finally, note that a breach of the duty to avoid conflicts may be ratified by a majority of shareholders in general meeting, although the statutory rules on this (see s.180(4)(a) (Consent, approval and authorisation by members), effect several important changes when compared with the common law (e.g. *North-West Transportation Co Ltd v Beatty* (1887) 12 App. Cas. 589 PC). Ratification may be useful where the board has either failed or refused to authorise a conflict of interest.

Subsection (7)

This provision makes it clear that a conflict of interest includes conflicts of interest and duty and conflicts of duties. In relation to conflicts of duties, the equitable rule prohibits a fiduciary from entering into a position which imposes conflicting fiduciary duties to another person without the informed consent of both principals (*Clark Boyce v Mouat* [1994] 1 A.C. 428). The statutory formulation adopts this equitable rule (see, e.g. *In Plus Group Ltd v Pyke* [2002] EWCA Civ 370; [2002] 2 B.C.L.C. 201), and discards the controversial approach found in *London and Mashonaland Exploration Co Ltd v New Mashonaland Exploration Co Ltd* [1891] W.N. 165; *Bell v Lever Bros Ltd* [1932] A.C. 161 at 195; and *Item Software (UK) Ltd v Fassihi* [2004] EWCA Civ 1244; [2005] ICR 450 at [63] (Arden L.J., *obiter*). These latter cases suggested that a director of one company may be a director of competing companies unless prohibited by contract. This is inconsistent with the equitable rule on conflict of duties.

Subsection (7) means that conflicting multiple directorships will be caught by the duty to avoid conflicts of interest. It would seem to follow that these appointments will need to be authorised according to the process outlined in subss.(5) and (6).

176. Duty not to accept benefits from third parties

(1) A director of a company must not accept a benefit from a third party conferred by reason of-
   (a) his being a director, or
   (b) his doing (or not doing) anything as director.

(2) A "third party" means a person other than the company, an associated body corporate or a person acting on behalf of the company or an associated body corporate.

(3) Benefits received by a director from a person by whom his services (as a director or otherwise) are provided to the company are not regarded as conferred by a third party.

(4) This duty is not infringed if the acceptance of the benefit cannot reasonably be regarded as likely to give rise to a conflict of interest.

(5) Any reference in this section to a conflict of interest includes a conflict of interest and duty and a conflict of duties.

DEFINITIONS

"Associated body corporate": see s.256 (Associated bodies corporate)

GENERAL NOTE

This provision reformulates and replaces the equitable principle that fiduciaries, including directors, must not accept bribes or secret commissions (*A-G for Hong Kong v Reid* [1994] 1 A.C. 324 PC). This provision does not embrace the broader equitable 'no-profit' rule, which is subsumed in s.175 above.

Note that under this section there is no provision for authorisation by the board of directors. However, it appears that the company's articles may contain specific provisions concerning benefits from third parties (see s.232(4) (provisions protecting directors from liability)). Alternatively, the members the may give consent (s.180(4) (Consent, approval and authorisation by members) and s.239 (Ratification of acts of directors)).

Subsection (1)

During this section's passage through Parliament there was some debate as to the meaning of 'benefit'. The Solicitor-General suggested that the starting point ought to be the dictionary definition of the word:

> "In using the word 'benefit', we intend the ordinary dictionary meaning of the word. The 'Oxford English Dictionary' defines it as a favourable or helpful factor, circumstance, advantage or profit"
> (HC Comm D, 11/7/06 Cols 621-622)

A benefit may be financial or non-financial, of any shape or size. Subsection (4) ensures that trivial benefits are not caught by the provision.

Subsection (2)

A benefit received from the company or an associated body corporate or from a person acting for either of these is not a benefit from a third party.

Subsection (3)

The Attorney General, Lord Goldsmith explained the meaning of this subsection in Grand Committee:

> "If the director's services are provided to the company by another person, benefits received by the director from that other person are also excluded from this clause - for example, if the director provides his services through his own company, which is not an uncommon event" (*Hansard*, GC Day 4, Vol.678, col.330 (February 9, 2006)).

Subsection (4)

The duty is not infringed if there is no reasonable likelihood that acceptance of the benefit will give rise to a conflict.

177. Duty to declare interest in proposed transaction or arrangement

(1) If a director of a company is in any way, directly or indirectly, interested in a proposed transaction or arrangement with the company, he must declare the nature and extent of that interest to the other directors.

(2) The declaration may (but need not) be made-
    (a) at a meeting of the directors, or
    (b) by notice to the directors in accordance with-
        (i) section 184 (notice in writing), or
        (ii) section 185 (general notice).

(3) If a declaration of interest under this section proves to be, or becomes, inaccurate or incomplete, a further declaration must be made.

(4) Any declaration required by this section must be made before the company enters into the transaction or arrangement.

(5) This section does not require a declaration of an interest of which the director is not aware or where the director is not aware of the transaction or arrangement in question.

For this purpose a director is treated as being aware of matters of which he ought reasonably to be aware.

(6) A director need not declare an interest-
    (a) if it cannot reasonably be regarded as likely to give rise to a conflict of interest;
    (b) if, or to the extent that, the other directors are already aware of it (and for this purpose the other directors are treated as aware of anything of which they ought reasonably to be aware); or
    (c) if, or to the extent that, it concerns terms of his service contract that have been or are to be considered-
        (i) by a meeting of the directors, or
        (ii) by a committee of the directors appointed for the purpose under the company's constitution.

DEFINITIONS

"Service contract": see s.227 (Directors' service contracts)

"Persons connected with a director": see s.252 (Persons connected with a director), see also ss.182 and 183 and the notes to those sections.

GENERAL NOTE

This provision is the third of the general provisions designed to reformulate and codify the equitable duties owed by directors. The provision deals with situations of conflict of interest and duty in proposed transactions or arrangements with the company. It replaces both s.317 of the 1985 Act and the equitable rules (including the company law version of the "self-dealing" rule, although this provision is wider than that rule). It abolishes the application of the equitable no-conflict and no-profit rules (*Aberdeen Railway Co v Blaikie Bros* (1854) 1 Macq. 461 at 471, Lord Cranworth L.C.), but preserves the duty to declare such an interest. This formally adopts the practical rule that most companies put in place via their articles (e.g. Companies Act 1985, Table A, Art 85), in derogation from the strict equitable rule.

Section 177 does not adopt the criminal sanctions found in Companies Act 1985, s.317 (but see s.182 in relation to *existing* transactions or arrangements). To the extent that this duty is breached, the sanctions are the equitable sanctions described in s.178.

Section 180 makes it clear that, subject to the company's constitution, if directors comply with s.177, the transaction is not liable to be set aside by virtue of the usual equitable rule requiring the consent of the company's members. But precedents dealing with the exclusion of the equitable no-conflict and no-profit rules by the articles, not by statute, suggest that such an exclusion does not give directors complete freedom to act for their own benefit in these transactions and arrangements. Directors remain subject to other fiduciary duties imposed upon them (*Neptune (Vehicle Washing Equipment) Ltd v Fitzgerald (No.2)* [1995] B.C.C. 1000 at 1016-17). By analogy, under the new statutory rules, directors will remain subject to the duties imposed in ss.171 and 172. Nevertheless, it is difficult to imagine a situation where s.177 has been complied with, yet a breach of either s.171 or s.172 can be established.

Members of a company are free to impose stricter requirements in the company's articles than the duty to declare an interest in this section.

Subsection (1)

Note that the director need not be a party to the transaction or arrangement; the section will apply if the director is interested, either directly or indirectly.

The director must declare to the other directors the nature and extent of any interest, unless it is an interest, or involves a transaction, of which the director is unaware. The director is treated as being aware of matters of which he ought to be aware (subs.(5)). Also see subs.(3).

The section is deliberately limited to *proposed* transaction and arrangements (subs.(4)), as the Attorney General, Lord Goldsmith, explained in Grand Committee:

> "Different consequences flow from not disclosing an interest in a proposed transaction and failing to disclose an interest in an existing transaction, which one gets to under s.182 (Declaration of interest in existing transaction of arrangement). There is a difference in fact, in principle and in business sense because, if a company is told that a director has an interest in a proposed transaction, it can decide whether to enter into the transaction, on what terms and with what safeguards, whereas, if the transaction has already taken place, we are in a very different position" (*Hansard*, HL GC Day 4, Vol.678, cols 333-334 (February 9, 2006)).

Existing transactions are dealt with in Ch.3.

Subsection (2)

Although this section does not impose rules on how the disclosure of any interest must be made, subs.(2) states that it may be made at a meeting of directors, by notice in writing, or by general notice. The articles may impose further requirements.

Subsections (3) and (4)

The declaration must be made before the company enters into the transaction or arrangement, and must be, and remain, an accurate and complete declaration in order to discharge the duty. Declarations must be updated if necessary.

This statutory standard of full disclosure reflects the common law rule (*Bentinck v Fenn* (1887) 12 App. Cas. 652 at 661; *JJ Harrison (Properties) Ltd v Harrison* [2001] 1 B.C.L.C. 158; *Gwembe Valley Development Co Ltd v Koshy (No.3)* [2003] EWCA Civ 1478; [2004] 1 B.C.L.C. 131 CA), although at common law the disclosure was to the members, not to the other directors.

Subsection (5)

For the duty to apply, the director must be aware of the relevant interest and the relevant transaction. The section imposes a subjective and objective test, so the director is treated as being aware of matters of which he ought reasonably to be aware. This repeats Companies Act 1985, Table A, Art 86(b).

Subsection (6)

This subsection makes a number of exceptions to the duty to declare an interest, all reflected in existing common law rules. These apply where there is no reasonable likelihood of a conflict (*Cowan de Groot Properties Ltd v Eagle Trust Plc* [1991] B.C.L.C. 1045); where the other directors are already aware or ought reasonably to be aware of the interest; and where the interest concerns service contracts which have been or are to be considered by a meeting of directors or by a remuneration committee (*Runciman v Walter Runciman Plc* [1992] B.C.L.C. 1084). A fourth exception, not included in the section but recognised in s.186, is that the director of a company with only one director is not required to make a declaration to himself.

Supplementary provisions

178. Civil consequences of breach of general duties

(1) The consequences of breach (or threatened breach) of sections 171 to 177 are the same as would apply if the corresponding common law rule or equitable principle applied.

(2) The duties in those sections (with the exception of section 174 (duty to exercise reasonable care, skill and diligence)) are, accordingly, enforceable in the same way as any other fiduciary duty owed to a company by its directors.

GENERAL NOTE

The remedies available for breach of the fiduciary duties have not been subject to codification, despite the recommendations of the Law Commissions. This provision states that same consequences and remedies as are currently available should apply to the statutory general duties. Where the statutory duty departs from its equitable equivalent, the court must identify the equivalent rule and apply the same consequences and remedies. The Solicitor-General summarised the position as follows:

> "The consequences of a breach of the fiduciary duty can include damages, compensation, restoration of a company's property, rescission of a transaction or a requirement of a director to

account for any profits made as a result. They may also include injunctions or declarations, although those methods are primarily employed when a breach is threatened but has not yet occurred. The consequences of a breach of the duty of care and skill may include the court awarding compensation or damages" (HC Comm D, col 627 (July 11, 2007)).

Also see s.1157 (Power of court to grant relief in certain circumstances) (replacing Companies Act 1985, s.727).

Subsection (2)

This subsection may indicate that remedies for breach of s.174 (duty to exercise reasonable care, skill and diligence) will be assessed on common law, not equitable, principles, thus laying to rest the debates in that area (*Henderson v Merrett Syndicates Ltd* [1995] 2 A.C. 145; *Bristol & West Building Society v Mothew* [1998] Ch. 1).

Relevant cases:

General issues: *Murad v Al-Saraj* [2005] EWCA Civ 959, noting the irrelevance of the fact that the company could not have made the profit ([59]-[66]) or that the company would have given consent if requested ([71]), noting also the deterrence function ([72]-[74], [108]) and the objective to strip profits ([56], [58], [108]), and problems in identifying relevant profits ([77]-[79], [111]-[112]); *Gwembe Valley Development Co Ltd v Koshy (No.3)* [2003] EWCA Civ 1478; [2004] 1 B.C.L.C. 131 at [142] (identifying relevant profits).

Profits held on trust: *JJ Harrison (Properties) Ltd v Harrison* [2001] EWCA Civ 1467; [2002] 1 B.C.L.C. 162.

Equitable allowance to the director: restrictive approach in *Murad v Al-Saraj* [2005] EWCA Civ 959; *Quarter Master UK Ltd v Pyke* [2004] EWHC 1815 Ch; [2005] 1 B.C.L.C. 245 at [76]-[77]; *Guinness Plc v Saunders* [1990] 2 A.C. 663 HL; more lenient approach in *Patel v Brent LBC* [2003] EWHC 3081 Ch at [29]; *Warman International Ltd v Dwyer* (1995) 182 CLR 544 Aust HCt; *Boardman v Phipps* [1967] 2 A.C. 46 (a trustee case).

When an account of profits is *not* available: *North West Transportation Co Ltd v Beatty* (1887) 12 App. Cas. 589; *Burland v Earle* [1902] A.C. 83; also see *Cook v Deeks* [1916] 1 AC 554.

Rescission: *Hely-Hutchinson v Brayhead Ltd* [1968] 1 Q.B. 549 (impugned transaction with the company is not void, but is voidable at the option of the company if the general conditions for rescission are met); *Logicrose Ltd v Southend United Football Club Ltd* [1988] 1 W.L.R. 1256 (rescission against a third party); *Bentinck v Fenn* (1887) 12 App. Cas. 652 (rescission denied, *restutio in integrum* impossible).

Extent of liability for profits: *Regal (Hastings) Ltd v Gulliver* [1967] 2 A.C. 134; *Ultraframe (UK) Ltd v Fielding* [2005] EWHC 1638 Ch (director only liable for profits made personally, not for profits made by others, unless the claim can be brought under some other head of liability, e.g. knowing receipt, dishonest assistance, partnership law, etc.).

Equitable compensation: the orthodox view is that equitable compensation is not available for breach of the equitable no-conflict and no-profit rules, but is only available to compensate for losses caused by breach of the equitable duty of care (if this duty exists distinct from the common law duty) and the equitable duties to exercise powers independently, bona fide and for proper purposes (i.e. the equitable equivalents of ss.171-4). Note that misuse of the company's property may involve a conflict of duty and interest (for which profits are recoverable) *and* a breach of the duty to act bona fide and for proper purposes (for which equitable compensation is recoverable, even if the director has not made a profit from the misuse (*Extrasure Travel Insurance Ltd v Scattergood* [2003] 1 B.C.L.C. 598; *Gwembe Valley Development Co Ltd v Koshy (No.3)* [2003] EWCA Civ 1478; [2004] 1 BCLC 131, and note [143] which raises but does not answer the question whether compensation is available if the only breach is of the no-conflict or no-profit rules). If equitable compensation is available, the loss is measured at the time of the trial and must be causally related to the breach (*Target Holdings Ltd v Redferns* [1996] 1 A.C. 421, a case concerning fiduciary obligations of solicitors, not directors).

Limitation periods: the normal limitation period for breach of equitable fiduciary duties is six years, unless the Limitation Act 1980, s.21(1) applies, in which case there is no limitation (e.g. *JJ Harrison (Properties) Ltd v Harrison* [2001] EWCA Civ 1467; [2002] 1 B.C.L.C. 162; *Gwembe Valley Development Co Ltd v Koshy (No.3)* [2003] EWCA Civ 1478; [2004] 1 B.C.L.C. 131).

179.   Cases within more than one of the general duties

Except as otherwise provided, more than one of the general duties may apply in any given case.

GENERAL NOTE

This section is for the avoidance of doubt.

180.   Consent, approval or authorisation by members

(1)   In a case where-

   (a)   section 175 (duty to avoid conflicts of interest) is complied with by authorisation by the
         directors, or

   (b)   section 177 (duty to declare interest in proposed transaction or arrangement) is
         complied with,

the transaction or arrangement is not liable to be set aside by virtue of any common law rule or
equitable principle requiring the consent or approval of the members of the company.

This is without prejudice to any enactment, or provision of the company's constitution, requiring
such consent or approval.

(2)   The application of the general duties is not affected by the fact that the case also falls
      within Chapter 4 (transactions requiring approval of members), except that where that
      Chapter applies and-

   (a)   approval is given under that Chapter, or

   (b)   the matter is one as to which it is provided that approval is not needed,

it is not necessary also to comply with section 175 (duty to avoid conflicts of interest) or section
176 (duty not to accept benefits from third parties).

(3)   Compliance with the general duties does not remove the need for approval under any
      applicable provision of Chapter 4 (transactions requiring approval of members).

(4)   The general duties-

   (a)   have effect subject to any rule of law enabling the company to give authority, specifically
         or generally, for anything to be done (or omitted) by the directors, or any of them, that
         would otherwise be a breach of duty, and

   (b)   where the company's articles contain provisions for dealing with conflicts of interest,
         are not infringed by anything done (or omitted) by the directors, or any of them, in
         accordance with those provisions.

(5)   Otherwise, the general duties have effect (except as otherwise provided or the context
      otherwise requires) notwithstanding any enactment or rule of law.

GENERAL NOTE

This provision deals with the ways in which directors can avoid liability for breaches of their general statutory duties by
making the appropriate declaration or obtaining the appropriate consent, approval or authorisation from either the directors
or the members.

This provision also deals with the interaction between the general statutory duties in this Chapter and the specific duties
in Ch.4.

Subsection (1)

This subsection deals only with directors' avoidance of liability in respect of breaches of ss.175 and 177 (the statutory enactment of the no-conflict and no-profit rules, but excluding the rule against bribes and secret commissions). These sections
provide their own authorisation and disclosure mechanisms, respectively. Subsection (1) indicates that these mechanisms replace the equitable rule which requires the members, not the directors, to authorise these types of breaches of duty.

This is subject to any contrary enactment (e.g. Ch.4), or any provision in the company's constitution imposing additional
demands.

Subsection (2) and (3)

These two subsections indicate that the general duties contained in Ch.2 apply even in a case also covered by Ch.4, but
that the approval provisions in Ch.4 have priority.

In particular, compliance with the general duties (Ch.2) does not remove the need to comply with the approval requirements in Ch.4 (subs.(3)); and if the specific approval requirement in Ch.4 have been met, or found to be unnecessary in
the circumstances, then there is no need to comply with the further approval requirements in Ch.2.

Note that subs.(2) specifically refers to compliance with ss.175 (duty to avoid conflicts of interest) and 176 (duty not to
accept benefits from third parties), but the latter seems to be an error, and in order to make sense ought to refer to s.177 (duty
to declare interest in proposed transaction or arrangement) rather than s.176).

Subsection (4)

This provision retains the equitable and common law rules which allow companies to authorise what would otherwise be a breach of duty by the directors, and to make provision in their articles for dealing with conflicts of interest in specific ways.

Subsection (4)(a) makes the general duties subject to any rule of law enabling the company to give authority, specifically or generally, for anything to be done/omitted by the directors that would otherwise be a breach of duty. The equitable rules indicate that authorisation must be given by the members, not the directors (*Furs Ltd v Tomkies* (1936) 54 C.L.R. 583 at 590 and 599), unless the members and the directors are the same persons (*Queensland Mines Ltd v Hudson* (1978) 18 A.L.R. 1; 52 A.L.J.R. 399 PC). The authorisation may be given either in advance or retrospectively (*Hogg v Cramphorn Ltd* [1967] Ch. 254 at 269), but is effective only if consent is proper and fully informed (*Kaye v Croydon Tramways Co* [1898] 1 Ch. 358; *Knight v Frost* [1999] 1 B.C.L.C. 364), and if the decision of the members is not a fraud on the creditors (*Halt Garage (1964) Ltd, Re* [1982] 3 All E.R. 1016) or (it seems) a fraud on the minority or an abuse of power (*North West Transportation Co Ltd v Beatty* (1887) 12 App Cas 569 at 593-4). This last aspect is controversial (*Burland v Earle* [1902] A.C. 83; *Cook v Deeks* [1916] 1 A.C. 554; *Prudential Assurance Co Ltd v Newman Industries Ltd (No.2)* [1981] Ch. 257 at 307; *Smith v Croft (No.2)* [1988] Ch 114). It is sometimes alleged that authorisation or ratification of negligence is more controversial, but arguably the same rules apply - companies, like other individuals, can waive the duty of care and forgive past acts of negligence (but see *Pavlides v Jensen* [1956] Ch. 565; *Daniels v Daniels* [1978] Ch. 406; *Horsley and Weight Ltd, Re* [1982] Ch. 442, CA; *Multinational Gas and Petrochemical Co v Multinational Gas and Petrochemical Services Ltd* [1983] Ch. 258 CA).

Subsection (5)

This provision makes it clear that the general duties now provide the default rules for directors' duties, and have effect (subject to s.180) notwithstanding any enactment or rule of law, unless otherwise provided or the context otherwise requires.

181. Modification of provisions in relation to charitable companies

(1) In their application to a company that is a charity, the provisions of this Chapter have effect subject to this section.

(2) Section 175 (duty to avoid conflicts of interest) has effect as if-

    (a) for subsection (3) (which disapplies the duty to avoid conflicts of interest in the case of a transaction or arrangement with the company) there were substituted-

        "(3) This duty does not apply to a conflict of interest arising in relation to a transaction or arrangement with the company if or to the extent that the company's articles allow that duty to be so disapplied, which they may do only in relation to descriptions of transaction or arrangement specified in the company's articles.";

    (b) for subsection (5) (which specifies how directors of a company may give authority under that section for a transaction or arrangement) there were substituted-

        "(5) Authorisation may be given by the directors where the company's constitution includes provision enabling them to authorise the matter, by the matter being proposed to and authorised by them in accordance with the constitution.".

(3) Section 180(2)(b) (which disapplies certain duties under this Chapter in relation to cases excepted from requirement to obtain approval by members under Chapter 4) applies only if or to the extent that the company's articles allow those duties to be so disapplied, which they may do only in relation to descriptions of transaction or arrangement specified in the company's articles.

(4) After section 26(5) of the Charities Act 1993 (c. 10) (power of Charity Commission to authorise dealings with charity property etc) insert-

        "(5A) In the case of a charity that is a company, an order under this section may authorise an act notwithstanding that it involves the breach of a duty imposed on a director of the company under Chapter 2 of Part 10 of the Companies Act 2006 (general duties of directors).".

(5) This section does not extend to Scotland.

It was thought inappropriate to relax in any general way the no-conflict and no-profit rules as they apply to charities, including relaxation in relation to proposed transactions with the company and relaxation in relation to authorisation of conflicts of interest by the directors (see *Hansard*, HL GC Day 4, Vol.678, cols 867-868 (February 9, 2006)). This section therefore reinstates the stringent no-conflict rules for charitable companies. The default rule for charities is that conflict situations cannot be authorised by the board but must be authorised by the members, and proposed transactions or arrangements with the company must be authorised by the members, not merely disclosed to the directors. However, charitable companies may adopt more lenient rules by express provisions in their articles (although note the specific form required by subs.(2)(a)).

CHAPTER 3

DECLARATION OF INTEREST IN EXISTING TRANSACTION OR ARRANGEMENT

182. Declaration of interest in existing transaction or arrangement

(1) Where a director of a company is in any way, directly or indirectly, interested in a transaction or arrangement that has been entered into by the company, he must declare the nature and extent of the interest to the other directors in accordance with this section.

This section does not apply if or to the extent that the interest has been declared under section 177 (duty to declare interest in proposed transaction or arrangement).

(2) The declaration must be made-

    (a) at a meeting of the directors, or

    (b) by notice in writing (see section 184), or

    (c) by general notice (see section 185).

(3) If a declaration of interest under this section proves to be, or becomes, inaccurate or incomplete, a further declaration must be made.

(4) Any declaration required by this section must be made as soon as is reasonably practicable.

Failure to comply with this requirement does not affect the underlying duty to make the declaration.

(5) This section does not require a declaration of an interest of which the director is not aware or where the director is not aware of the transaction or arrangement in question.

For this purpose a director is treated as being aware of matters of which he ought reasonably to be aware.

(6) A director need not declare an interest under this section-

    (a) if it cannot reasonably be regarded as likely to give rise to a conflict of interest;

    (b) if, or to the extent that, the other directors are already aware of it (and for this purpose the other directors are treated as aware of anything of which they ought reasonably to be aware); or

    (c) if, or to the extent that, it concerns terms of his service contract that have been or are to be considered-

        (i) by a meeting of the directors, or

        (ii) by a committee of the directors appointed for the purpose under the company's constitution.

DEFINITIONS

"Service contract": see s.227 (Directors' service contracts)

GENERAL NOTE

This provision replaces s.317 of the 1985 Act with regard to existing transactions and arrangements. The section does not apply if the director has already declared the interest under s.177 (Duty to declare interest in proposed transaction or arrangement). If a director enters into a transaction or arrangement with the company without declaring his interest under s.177 (Duty to declare interest in proposed transaction or arrangement), he will be under an immediate obligation to declare that interest and failure to do so will constitute a criminal offence (see s.183 (Offence of failure to declare interest)). Even in these circumstances, however, it seems that the director is given a reasonable amount of time in which to comply with the duty in s.182 (see subs.(4)).

Subsections (2) and (3)

Unlike s.177 (Duty to declare interest in proposed transaction or arrangement), this subsection makes it clear that directors must use one of the three prescribed methods of declaration. Presumably a failure to make a declaration in the prescribed manner will render the declaration either a nullity or incomplete, and a further declaration will be required (subs.(3)). How this requirement will be reconciled with subs.(6)(b), indicating that the duty does not apply if the other directors are already aware of the interest or ought to be aware of the interest, is unclear.

Subsection (5)

This subsection was not present in the old Companies Act 1985, s.317, and was introduced to lighten the burden on company directors. The provision, as with s.177 (Duty to declare interest in proposed transaction or arrangement), makes it a condition of the duty applying that the director is aware (or ought to be aware) of the existence of his interest and of the transaction:

> "[D]irectors are not expected to disclose things that they do not know. One of the purposes of the clause is to ensure that the board is aware of anything that might influence a director's decision. The director can disclose only what he is aware of, and if he is aware of it, he ought to declare it" (HC Comm D col 628 (July 11, 2006)).

Subsection (6)

As with s.177 (and see the notes to that section), a director need not declare an interest where there is no reasonable likelihood of a conflict; where the other directors are already aware or ought reasonably to be aware of the interest; or where the interest concerns service contracts which have been or are to be considered by a meeting of directors or by a remuneration committee.

183.   Offence of failure to declare interest

(1) A director who fails to comply with the requirements of section 182 (declaration of interest in existing transaction or arrangement) commits an offence.

(2) A person guilty of an offence under this section is liable-

    (a) on conviction on indictment, to a fine;

    (b) on summary conviction, to a fine not exceeding the statutory maximum.

GENERAL NOTE

Unlike the duty to declare an interest in a *proposed* transaction or arrangement (s.177), it is a criminal offence not to comply with the duty to declare an interest in an existing transaction or arrangement. The Attorney General, Lord Goldsmith, in Grand Committee explained the rationale behind this:

> "... because one is here concerned with an existing transaction or arrangement, the failure to declare cannot affect the validity of the transaction or give rise to any other civil consequences. That is to be contrasted with the position where there is a failure to disclose an interest in relation to a proposed transaction where the law can say that as a result of the failure to disclose that interest - and the company then enters into the transaction in ignorance of that - consequences follow. The transaction may be voidable, to be set aside. The company may wish to claim financial redress in one form or another as a result of what has taken place. But, as I say, that is different from a failure to declare an interest in an existing transaction where those considerations probably cannot arise. That is why a criminal offence is created" (*Hansard*, HL GC Day 4, Vol.678, col.338 (February 9, 2006)).

This does not appear to be an accurate description of the differences between these two provisions. If a director *complies* with s.177, then the company can decide on a fully informed basis whether to proceed with the proposed transaction or arrangement. Section 180 indicates that this declaration replaces the need for the approval of the company's members under the equitable rules, although any additional requirements imposed by the articles will still have to be met. Assuming these requirements (if any) have also been met, the transaction cannot be impugned for breach of s.177 or for breach of the no-conflict and no-profit rules in relation to transactions with the company (although the deal might nevertheless be a breach of some other general statutory duty, and give rise to an action for a remedy under some other head - availability of the relevant remedies in the particular circumstances will then need to be assessed in the usual way).

On the other hand, if s.177 is *not* complied with, and the company nevertheless enters into the proposed transaction or arrangement, then the director will be in breach of s.177 and, if the breach continues, will also be in breach of s.182. The equitable remedies for breach of the general statutory duty can be pursued against the defaulting director (and, again, an assessment will have to be made about the availability of various remedies - e.g. rescission will not be available against a bona fide third party purchaser, but will be available against other parties not protected by this equitable rule, including the director). In addition, the director will also be liable for the criminal offence described in s.183. Put this way, there is no logical divide between the remedies available for breach of ss.177 and 182; indeed, if s.177 is breached, and the proposed arrangement is pursued, s.182 will also be breached so long as the director fails to declare the interest. Section 177 is therefore not a provision designed to *impose* liability on directors, but a provision designed to afford protection to those who comply with it.

In this sense, there is the same relationship between ss.183 and 178 (as influenced by s.180) as between Companies Act 1985, s.317 and the equitable consequences of breach of the no-conflict and no-profit rules (as influenced by any relevant consents given by the members or given in the way allowed by the articles). See *Guinness Plc v Saunders* [1990] 2 A.C. 663 at 697 (Lord Goff); *Coleman Taymar Ltd v Oakes* [2001] 2 B.C.L.C. 749.

184. Declaration made by notice in writing

(1) This section applies to a declaration of interest made by notice in writing.

(2) The director must send the notice to the other directors.

(3) The notice may be sent in hard copy form or, if the recipient has agreed to receive it in electronic form, in an agreed electronic form.

(4) The notice may be sent-
   (a) by hand or by post, or
   (b) if the recipient has agreed to receive it by electronic means, by agreed electronic means.

(5) Where a director declares an interest by notice in writing in accordance with this section-
   (a) the making of the declaration is deemed to form part of the proceedings at the next meeting of the directors after the notice is given, and
   (b) the provisions of section 248 (minutes of meetings of directors) apply as if the declaration had been made at that meeting.

GENERAL NOTE

This provision describes one of the three means of giving the notice required by s.182. The director must send the notice to the other directors, either by hand, by post, or electronically (but the last only if previously agreed). The notice must declare the nature and extent of any interest in order to comply with s.182. The declaration will form part of the proceedings of the next meeting of directors and as such will be entered in the minutes.

185. General notice treated as sufficient declaration

(1) General notice in accordance with this section is a sufficient declaration of interest in relation to the matters to which it relates.

(2) General notice is notice given to the directors of a company to the effect that the director-
   (a) has an interest (as member, officer, employee or otherwise) in a specified body corporate or firm and is to be regarded as interested in any transaction or arrangement that may, after the date of the notice, be made with that body corporate or firm, or
   (b) is connected with a specified person (other than a body corporate or firm) and is to be regarded as interested in any transaction or arrangement that may, after the date of the notice, be made with that person.

(3) The notice must state the nature and extent of the director's interest in the body corporate or firm or, as the case may be, the nature of his connection with the person.

(4) General notice is not effective unless-
   (a) it is given at a meeting of the directors, or
   (b) the director takes reasonable steps to secure that it is brought up and read at the next meeting of the directors after it is given.

DEFINITIONS

"Persons connected with a director": see s.252 (Persons connected with a director)

GENERAL NOTE

This provision describes another of the three means of giving the notice required by s.182. It replaces s.317(3) and (4) of the 1985 Act and states that general notice is sufficient declaration. The significant change is that the general notice must state the nature and extent of the director's interest in any body corporate or firm, or the nature of his association with any connected person (subs.(3)). Subsection (4) indicates that a general notice will not be effective unless certain conditions are met. It does not seem necessary for the notice to be in writing.

186. Declaration of interest in case of company with sole director

(1) Where a declaration of interest under section 182 (duty to declare interest in existing transaction or arrangement) is required of a sole director of a company that is required to have more than one director-
   (a) the declaration must be recorded in writing,
   (b) the making of the declaration is deemed to form part of the proceedings at the next meeting of the directors after the notice is given, and
   (c) the provisions of section 248 (minutes of meetings of directors) apply as if the declaration had been made at that meeting.
(2) Nothing in this section affects the operation of section 231 (contract with sole member who is also a director: terms to be set out in writing or recorded in minutes).

GENERAL NOTE

This provision requires a sole director of a company that ought to have two or more directors (e.g. a public company: see s.154 (Companies required to have directors)) to formally record in writing the nature and extent of any interest he has in an existing transaction or arrangement with the company. This will protect the director from criminal liability and, more importantly, help to inform the company effectively of the issues of conflict.

187. Declaration of interest in existing transaction by shadow director

(1) The provisions of this Chapter relating to the duty under section 182 (duty to declare interest in existing transaction or arrangement) apply to a shadow director as to a director, but with the following adaptations.
(2) Subsection (2)(a) of that section (declaration at meeting of directors) does not apply.
(3) In section 185 (general notice treated as sufficient declaration), subsection (4) (notice to be given at or brought up and read at meeting of directors) does not apply.
(4) General notice by a shadow director is not effective unless given by notice in writing in accordance with section 184.

GENERAL NOTE

This section extends the provisions of the Chapter to shadow directors. The significant change is that an effective declaration by a shadow director can only be made by notice in writing or by general notice. This provision is derived from s.317(8) of the 1985 Act.

CHAPTER 4

TRANSACTIONS WITH DIRECTORS REQUIRING APPROVAL OF MEMBERS

Service contracts

188. Directors' long-term service contracts: requirement of members' approval

(1) This section applies to provision under which the guaranteed term of a director's employment-

    (a) with the company of which he is a director, or

    (b) where he is the director of a holding company, within the group consisting of that company and its subsidiaries,

is, or may be, longer than two years.

(2) A company may not agree to such provision unless it has been approved-

    (a) by resolution of the members of the company, and

    (b) in the case of a director of a holding company, by resolution of the members of that company.

(3) The guaranteed term of a director's employment is-

    (a) the period (if any) during which the director's employment-

        (i) is to continue, or may be continued otherwise than at the instance of the company (whether under the original agreement or under a new agreement entered into in pursuance of it), and

        (ii) cannot be terminated by the company by notice, or can be so terminated only in specified circumstances, or

    (b) in the case of employment terminable by the company by notice, the period of notice required to be given,

or, in the case of employment having a period within paragraph (a) and a period within paragraph (b), the aggregate of those periods.

(4) If more than six months before the end of the guaranteed term of a director's employment the company enters into a further service contract (otherwise than in pursuance of a right conferred, by or under the original contract, on the other party to it), this section applies as if there were added to the guaranteed term of the new contract the unexpired period of the guaranteed term of the original contract.

(5) A resolution approving provision to which this section applies must not be passed unless a memorandum setting out the proposed contract incorporating the provision is made available to members-

    (a) in the case of a written resolution, by being sent or submitted to every eligible member at or before the time at which the proposed resolution is sent or submitted to him;

    (b) in the case of a resolution at a meeting, by being made available for inspection by members of the company both-

        (i) at the company's registered office for not less than 15 days ending with the date of the meeting, and

        (ii) at the meeting itself.

(6) No approval is required under this section on the part of the members of a body corporate that-

    (a) is not a UK-registered company, or

    (b) is a wholly-owned subsidiary of another body corporate.

(7) In this section "employment" means any employment under a director's service contract.

DEFINITIONS

"Director's service contract": see s.227 (Director's service contract)

GENERAL NOTE

Recall that directors have no *prima facie* entitlement to remuneration (*Hutton v West Cork Railway Co* (1883) 23 Ch. D. 654 at 672; *Guinness Plc v Saunders* [1990] 2 A.C. 663). Provision for payment is therefore usually made in the articles, and the appropriate decision-making process is as determined there. This section and the next limit the company's power to determine its own procedures. Directors' long-term service contracts (i.e. two years or more) require the approval of the company's members.

This section and the next (s.189 (Director's long-term service contracts: civil consequences of contravention)) replace s.319 of the 1985 Act. The provision applies to contract of service and contracts for services (as did Companies Act 1985, s.319). The significant change is that approval is now required for service contracts longer than two years, as opposed to five as it was previously. The change is designed to bring the statutory rule into line with modern corporate governance recommendations that directors' contracts to be renewed annually or at least bi- or tri-annually (Law Commissions, *Company Directors: Regulating Conflicts of Interest and Formulating a Statement of Duties*, Law Com. No.261, Cm.4436, paras 9.26-9.34, recommending a three year rule and careful treatment of rolling contracts; CLR, *Modern Company Law for a Competitive Economy: Final Report*, Vol.1, URN 01/942, paras 6.10-6.14; Combined Code, in respect of listed companies, provision B.1.6). This provision, like its predecessor, is intended to ensure that the power of dismissal in s.168 is not unduly constrained by the qualification in s.168(5) (removal of a director not to affect compensation rights).

In proposing these service contracts, directors are subject to the general duties applying to all their activities, and failure in this regard may indicate grounds for disqualification (*Secretary of State for Trade and Industry v Van Hengel* [1995] 1 B.C.L.C. 545). For listed companies, also note Combined Code Main Principle B.2.

Note that the provision also applies to shadow directors: s.223(1)(a).

Subsection (2)

This subsection indicates that the provision must be approved before the contract is made (*Wright v Atlas Wright (Europe) Ltd* [1999] 2 B.C.L.C. 310, 314).

Subsection (5)

See Pt 13 Ch.2.

Subsection (6)

This subsection applies the section to all United Kingdom-registered companies except wholly owned subsidiaries. Agreements for employment of directors of wholly owned subsidiaries are treated as the responsibility of the directors of the holding company; the directors of subsidiaries are treated as managers. If the director of the subsidiary is also a director of the holding company, the contract will be caught by subs.(2)(b). Note, however, that s.228(1)(a) (Copy of contract or memorandum of terms to be available for inspection) extends to contracts of service of directors of subsidiaries.

189. Directors' long-term service contracts: civil consequences of contravention

If a company agrees to provision in contravention of section 188 (directors' long-term service contracts: requirement of members' approval)-

    (a) the provision is void, to the extent of the contravention, and

    (b) the contract is deemed to contain a term entitling the company to terminate it at any time by the giving of reasonable notice.

GENERAL NOTE

This provision reproduces s.319(6) of the 1985 Act without substantive change, and ensures that provisions in contravention of s.188 are void to the extent of the contravention, and that the company can terminate the service contract at any time by the giving of reasonable notice.

Substantial property transactions

190. Substantial property transactions: requirement of members' approval

(1) A company may not enter into an arrangement under which-

    (a) a director of the company or of its holding company, or a person connected with such a director, acquires or is to acquire from the company (directly or indirectly) a substantial non-cash asset, or

    (b) the company acquires or is to acquire a substantial non-cash asset (directly or indirectly) from such a director or a person so connected,

unless the arrangement has been approved by a resolution of the members of the company or is conditional on such approval being obtained.

For the meaning of "substantial non-cash asset" see section 191.

  (2) If the director or connected person is a director of the company's holding company or a person connected with such a director, the arrangement must also have been approved by a resolution of the members of the holding company or be conditional on such approval being obtained.

  (3) A company shall not be subject to any liability by reason of a failure to obtain approval required by this section.

  (4) No approval is required under this section on the part of the members of a body corporate that-

    (a) is not a UK-registered company, or

    (b) is a wholly-owned subsidiary of another body corporate.

  (5) For the purposes of this section-

    (a) an arrangement involving more than one non-cash asset, or

    (b) an arrangement that is one of a series involving non-cash assets,

shall be treated as if they involved a non-cash asset of a value equal to the aggregate value of all the non-cash assets involved in the arrangement or, as the case may be, the series.

  (6) This section does not apply to a transaction so far as it relates-

    (a) to anything to which a director of a company is entitled under his service contract, or

    (b) to payment for loss of office as defined in section 215 (payments requiring members' approval).

DEFINITIONS

    "Connected person": see s.252 (Persons connected with a director)

    "Directors' service contracts": see s.227 (Directors' service contracts)

    "Non-cash asset": see s.1163, and also the note to subs.(1) below

    "Substantial": see s.191 (meaning of "substantial")

GENERAL NOTE

    This provision replaces s.320(1) of the 1985 Act, and makes minor amendments. An "arrangement" includes an agreement or understanding that does not have contractual effect (*Duckwari Plc (No.2), Re* [1999] Ch. 253). Note the exceptions in ss.192-4 below.

    The civil consequences are described in s.195, below.

    Note that this section and related sections (i.e. ss.190-196 - property transactions) apply equally to shadow directors: s.223(1)(b).

Subsection (1)

    This subsection changes the current law in that it permits substantial property transactions provided they are approved by the members. This change is designed to alleviate practical difficulties and commercial disadvantages that possibly arose under the old provisions (see Law Com No 261, at paras 10.8-10.10). Failure to obtain the necessary authorisation will not result in any liability for the company (subs.(3)).

    On non-cash assets (valuation and property law issues), see *Ultraframe (UK) Ltd v Fielding* [2005] EWHC 1638 Ch at [1362]-[1410].

Subsection (5)

    This new subsection introduces a change to the current law whereby the value of more than one cash asset or a series of cash assets will be their aggregate value. The purpose of this change is to prevent abuse of the provisions and to further the general objective of preventing asset-stripping by directors.

Subsection (6)

For the avoidance of doubt this section excludes payments under directors' service contracts and payments for loss of office. This new provision is based upon a recommendation by the Law Commission (see Law Com. No. 261, at paras 10.11-10.13).

191.   Meaning of "substantial"

(1) This section explains what is meant in section 190 (requirement of approval for substantial property transactions) by a "substantial" non-cash asset.

(2) An asset is a substantial asset in relation to a company if its value-
  (a) exceeds 10% of the company's asset value and is more than £5,000, or
  (b) exceeds £100,000.

(3) For this purpose a company's "asset value" at any time is-
  (a) the value of the company's net assets determined by reference to its most recent statutory accounts, or
  (b) if no statutory accounts have been prepared, the amount of the company's called-up share capital.

(4) A company's "statutory accounts" means its annual accounts prepared in accordance with Part 15, and its "most recent" statutory accounts means those in relation to which the time for sending them out to members (see section 424) is most recent.

(5) Whether an asset is a substantial asset shall be determined as at the time the arrangement is entered into.

GENERAL NOTE

This section is derived from s.320(2) of the 1985 Act. The only substantive change is that the minimum value regarded as substantial has been raised to £5,000. The Secretary of State has the power to raise financial limits under s.258 (Power to increase financial limits).

192.   Exception for transactions with members or other group companies

Approval is not required under section 190 (requirement of members' approval for substantial property transactions)-
  (a) for a transaction between a company and a person in his character as a member of that company, or
  (b) for a transaction between-
    (i) a holding company and its wholly-owned subsidiary, or
    (ii) two wholly-owned subsidiaries of the same holding company.

DEFINITIONS
  "Holding company": see ss.1159, 1160 and Sch.6
  "Wholly owned subsidiary": see ss.1159, 1160 and Sch.6

GENERAL NOTE

This section restates s.321(2)(a) and (3) of the 1985 Act. The only substantive change is that the exception in subs.(a) is expanded to include acquisition of assets from a member by the company.

193.   Exception in case of company in winding up or administration

(1) This section applies to a company-
  (a) that is being wound up (unless the winding up is a members' voluntary winding up), or
  (b) that is in administration within the meaning of Schedule B1 to the Insolvency Act 1986 (c. 45) or the Insolvency (Northern Ireland) Order 1989 (S.I. 1989/ 2405 (N.I. 19)).

(2) Approval is not required under section 190 (requirement of members' approval for substantial property transactions)-

    (a) on the part of the members of a company to which this section applies, or

    (b) for an arrangement entered into by a company to which this section applies.

GENERAL NOTE

This provision is derived from s.321(2)(b) of the 1985 Act but makes two changes, which Lord Sainsbury explained at Report Stage in the House of Lords:

> "First, the circumstances in which the exception applies have been widened to include administration. That implements a recommendation of the Law Commissions. Secondly, there has been a change in the operation of the exception. In the Companies Act 1985, the exception applies to arrangements entered into by a company that is being wound up. Section [193 (Exception in case of company in winding up or administration)] operates differently by removing the need for approval on the part of the members of a company that is being wound up" (*Hansard*, HL Report Stage, Vol.681, col 870 (May 9, 2006)).

The recommendation of the Law Commissions was based on the consideration that "the conflict of interest which a director faces in substantial property transactions does not arise when an administrator contracts on behalf of the company", and the need to alleviate the concerns caused by the decision in *Demite Ltd v Protec Health Ltd* [1998] B.C.C. 638 (Law Com. No.261, at paras 10.17-10.18).

The rationale for the exception was explained by Lord Sainsbury as follows:

> "The point of the exception is that when a company is being wound up or is in administration, the conduct of the company's affairs is no longer in the hands of the members. If a liquidator or administrator is content with the substantial property transaction, it is not appropriate to require approval under [s.190 (Substantial property transactions: requirement of members' approval)], either by the members of the company being wound up or in administration, or by the members of its holding company" (*Hansard*, HL Report Stage, Vol.681, col 870 (May 9, 2006)).

194. Exception for transactions on recognised investment exchange

(1) Approval is not required under section 190 (requirement of members' approval for substantial property transactions) for a transaction on a recognised investment exchange effected by a director, or a person connected with him, through the agency of a person who in relation to the transaction acts as an independent broker.

(2) For this purpose-

    (a) "independent broker" means a person who, independently of the director or any person connected with him, selects the person with whom the transaction is to be effected; and

    (b) "recognised investment exchange" has the same meaning as in Part 18 of the Financial Services and Markets Act 2000 (c. 8).

GENERAL NOTE

This provision is derived from s.321(4) of the 1985 Act (added by Companies Act 1989 as amended by the Financial Services and Markets Act 2000). This provision excludes the requirement for member approval with regard to transactions on an investment exchange by directors or connected persons through an independent broker. The Current Law Statutes annotations accompanying the 1989 amendment give an example of when the exception will apply:

> "[This subsection] will apply to the case, e.g. of a director of a holding company in a financial services group which includes a market maker who buys shares from that market maker through a broker without being aware of it" (Currrent Law Statutes Companies Act 1989 Annotations, pp.40-347/Sch.19).

195. Property transactions: civil consequences of contravention

(1) This section applies where a company enters into an arrangement in contravention of section 190 (requirement of members' approval for substantial property transactions).

(2) The arrangement, and any transaction entered into in pursuance of the arrangement (whether by the company or any other person), is voidable at the instance of the company, unless-

(a) restitution of any money or other asset that was the subject matter of the arrangement or transaction is no longer possible,

(b) the company has been indemnified in pursuance of this section by any other persons for the loss or damage suffered by it, or

(c) rights acquired in good faith, for value and without actual notice of the contravention by a person who is not a party to the arrangement or transaction would be affected by the avoidance.

(3) Whether or not the arrangement or any such transaction has been avoided, each of the persons specified in subsection (4) is liable-

(a) to account to the company for any gain that he has made directly or indirectly by the arrangement or transaction, and

(b) (jointly and severally with any other person so liable under this section) to indemnify the company for any loss or damage resulting from the arrangement or transaction.

(4) The persons so liable are-

(a) any director of the company or of its holding company with whom the company entered into the arrangement in contravention of section 190,

(b) any person with whom the company entered into the arrangement in contravention of that section who is connected with a director of the company or of its holding company,

(c) the director of the company or of its holding company with whom any such person is connected, and

(d) any other director of the company who authorised the arrangement or any transaction entered into in pursuance of such an arrangement.

(5) Subsections (3) and (4) are subject to the following two subsections.

(6) In the case of an arrangement entered into by a company in contravention of section 190 with a person connected with a director of the company or of its holding company, that director is not liable by virtue of subsection (4)(c) if he shows that he took all reasonable steps to secure the company's compliance with that section.

(7) In any case-

(a) a person so connected is not liable by virtue of subsection (4)(b), and

(b) a director is not liable by virtue of subsection (4)(d),

if he shows that, at the time the arrangement was entered into, he did not know the relevant circumstances constituting the contravention.

(8) Nothing in this section shall be read as excluding the operation of any other enactment or rule of law by virtue of which the arrangement or transaction may be called in question or any liability to the company may arise.

GENERAL NOTE

"This provision is derived from s.322 of the Companies Act 1985 and is not intended to make any substantive change save in respect of s.322(2)(c) of that Act, which is now replaced by [s.196 (Property transactions: effect of subsequent affirmation)]" (*Hansard*, HL GC Day 4, Vol.678, col.347 (February 9, 2006)).

The remedies provided by this section enlarge both the types of recovery (including recovery of losses, not only profits) and the persons against whom recovery is available, when compared with the remedies available in equity for breach of fiduciary duty in entering into transactions involving a conflict of interest.

Case law:

Rescission/affirmation: *Ultraframe (UK) Ltd v Fielding* [2005] EWHC 1638 Ch at[1441]; *Demite Ltd v Protec Health Ltd* [1998] B.C.C. 638; *Ciro Citterio Menswear Plc* [2002] EWHC 662; [2002] 1 W.L.R. 2217 (no constructive trust before rescission). Also see s.196, below. Loss or damage: *Duckwari Plc (No.2), Re* [1999] Ch. 253; *Duckwari Plc (No.3), Re* [1999] Ch. 268; *Murray v Leisureplay Plc* [2005] EWCA Civ 963.

Also see s.1157 (Power of court to grant relief in certain circumstances) (replacing Companies Act 1985, s.727).

196. Property transactions: effect of subsequent affirmation

Where a transaction or arrangement is entered into by a company in contravention of section 190 (requirement of members' approval) but, within a reasonable period, it is affirmed-

(a) in the case of a contravention of subsection (1) of that section, by resolution of the members of the company, and

(b) in the case of a contravention of subsection (2) of that section, by resolution of the members of the holding company,

the transaction or arrangement may no longer be avoided under section 195.

GENERAL NOTE

This section is derived from s.322(2)(c) of the 1985 Act without substantive change. Where a substantive property transaction entered into by a company is affirmed by the members of the company within a reasonable period it is expressly no longer voidable under s.195 (Property transactions: civil consequences of contravention), and presumably is also to be treated in other respects as if the approval were properly given in a timely fashion, so that the other remedies in s.195(3) no longer apply.

Loans, quasi-loans and credit transactions

197. Loans to directors: requirement of members' approval

(1) A company may not-

(a) make a loan to a director of the company or of its holding company, or

(b) give a guarantee or provide security in connection with a loan made by any person to such a director,

unless the transaction has been approved by a resolution of the members of the company.

(2) If the director is a director of the company's holding company, the transaction must also have been approved by a resolution of the members of the holding company.

(3) A resolution approving a transaction to which this section applies must not be passed unless a memorandum setting out the matters mentioned in subsection (4) is made available to members-

(a) in the case of a written resolution, by being sent or submitted to every eligible member at or before the time at which the proposed resolution is sent or submitted to him;

(b) in the case of a resolution at a meeting, by being made available for inspection by members of the company both-

(i) at the company's registered office for not less than 15 days ending with the date of the meeting, and

(ii) at the meeting itself.

(4) The matters to be disclosed are-

(a) the nature of the transaction,

(b) the amount of the loan and the purpose for which it is required, and

(c) the extent of the company's liability under any transaction connected with the loan.

(5) No approval is required under this section on the part of the members of a body corporate that-

(a) is not a UK-registered company, or

(b) is a wholly-owned subsidiary of another body corporate.

DEFINITIONS

"Company": see ss.1 (Companies); and 1158 (United Kingdom registered company)

"Connected persons": see s.252 (Persons connected with a director)

"Director": see s.250 (Director)

"Guarantee": see s.331(2) of the Companies Act 1985

"Holding company": see ss.1159, and 1160 and Sch.6

"Quasi-loan": see s.199 (Meaning of "quasi-loan" and related expressions)

"Subsidiary": see ss.1159, 1160 and Sch.6

"Wholly owned subsidiary": ss.1159, 1160 and Sch.6

GENERAL NOTE

This section is derived from s.330(2) of the 1985 Act. The significant change is that loans to directors and connected persons are no longer generally prohibited but are subject to the requirement of member approval, and sometimes also approval of the members of its holding company. The provisions relating to loans apply to all United Kingdom-registered companies, with the exception of wholly-owned subsidiaries (subs.(5)). This is in contrast to the provisions for quasi-loans and credit transactions which only apply to public companies and associated companies (see ss.198 (Quasi-loans to directors: requirement of members' approval) and 201 (Credit transactions: requirement of members' approval), below). See other related restrictions (ss.198-203).

This and related sections (i.e. ss.197-214, on loans, etc) apply equally to shadow directors: s.223(1)(c).

The requirement for member approval in subs.(1) is subject to the exceptions in ss.204-209 inclusive (exception for expenditure on company business, on defending proceedings etc, in connection with regulatory action or investigation, for minor and business transactions, for intra-group transactions and for money-lending companies. Of these, the most general is s.207, which sets the minimum threshold value for transactions requiring the approval of members (£10,000 for loans, etc.; £15,000 for credit transactions).

For remedies see s.213 (Loans, etc.: civil consequences of contravention). For subsequent affirmation, see s.214 (Loans etc.: effect of subsequent affirmation).

Subsection (4)

The amount of the loan or quasi-loan should be calculated in accordance with s.211 (The value of transactions and arrangements).

198.   Quasi-loans to directors: requirement of members' approval

(1) This section applies to a company if it is-
    (a) a public company, or
    (b) a company associated with a public company.
(2) A company to which this section applies may not-
    (a) make a quasi-loan to a director of the company or of its holding company, or
    (b) give a guarantee or provide security in connection with a quasi-loan made by any person to such a director,
unless the transaction has been approved by a resolution of the members of the company.
(3) If the director is a director of the company's holding company, the transaction must also have been approved by a resolution of the members of the holding company.
(4) A resolution approving a transaction to which this section applies must not be passed unless a memorandum setting out the matters mentioned in subsection (5) is made available to members-
    (a) in the case of a written resolution, by being sent or submitted to every eligible member at or before the time at which the proposed resolution is sent or submitted to him;
    (b) in the case of a resolution at a meeting, by being made available for inspection by members of the company both-
        (i) at the company's registered office for not less than 15 days ending with the date of the meeting, and
        (ii) at the meeting itself.
(5) The matters to be disclosed are-
    (a) the nature of the transaction,
    (b) the amount of the quasi-loan and the purpose for which it is required, and
    (c) the extent of the company's liability under any transaction connected with the quasi-loan.
(6) No approval is required under this section on the part of the members of a body corporate that-
    (a) is not a UK-registered company, or
    (b) is a wholly-owned subsidiary of another body corporate.

GENERAL NOTE

GENERAL NOTE
Note that this section applies only to public companies or companies associated with a public company. Quasi-loans are defined in s.199. The section was introduced at Report Stage in the House of Commons and is derived from s.330(3) of the 1985 Act. Initially the provisions concerning loans, quasi-loans and credit transactions applied to all United Kingdom-registered companies. However, after further consultation with stakeholders the government amended the sections concerned with quasi-loans and credit transactions, limiting their application to public companies and associated companies (see HC Report Stage, col.798 (October 17, 2006)). Private companies are not prohibited from making quasi-loans to directors under this section. However, directors of private companies must ensure they comply with their general duties in Ch.2.

The section and related sections (i.e. ss.197-214, on loans, etc.) apply equally to shadow directors: s.223(1)(c). Note, too, the exceptions (ss.204-209), especially s.207, which sets the minimum threshold value for transactions requiring the approval of members (£10,000 for loans, etc.). The amount of the loan or quasi-loan is calculated in accordance with s.211 (The value of transactions and arrangements). For remedies see s.213 (Loans etc: civil consequences of contravention). For subsequent affirmation, see s.214 (Loans etc: effect of subsequent affirmation).

199. Meaning of "quasi-loan" and related expressions

(1) A "quasi-loan" is a transaction under which one party ("the creditor") agrees to pay, or pays otherwise than in pursuance of an agreement, a sum for another ("the borrower") or agrees to reimburse, or reimburses otherwise than in pursuance of an agreement, expenditure incurred by another party for another ("the borrower")-

(a) on terms that the borrower (or a person on his behalf) will reimburse the creditor; or

(b) in circumstances giving rise to a liability on the borrower to reimburse the creditor.

(2) Any reference to the person to whom a quasi-loan is made is a reference to the borrower.

(3) The liabilities of the borrower under a quasi-loan include the liabilities of any person who has agreed to reimburse the creditor on behalf of the borrower.

GENERAL NOTE
This section restates s.331(3) and (4) of the 1985 Act without substantive change.

200. Loans or quasi-loans to persons connected with directors: requirement of members' approval

(1) This section applies to a company if it is-

(a) a public company, or

(b) a company associated with a public company.

(2) A company to which this section applies may not-

(a) make a loan or quasi-loan to a person connected with a director of the company or of its holding company, or

(b) give a guarantee or provide security in connection with a loan or quasi-loan made by any person to a person connected with such a director,

unless the transaction has been approved by a resolution of the members of the company.

(3) If the connected person is a person connected with a director of the company's holding company, the transaction must also have been approved by a resolution of the members of the holding company.

(4) A resolution approving a transaction to which this section applies must not be passed unless a memorandum setting out the matters mentioned in subsection (5) is made available to members-

(a) in the case of a written resolution, by being sent or submitted to every eligible member at or before the time at which the proposed resolution is sent or submitted to him;

(b) in the case of a resolution at a meeting, by being made available for inspection by members of the company both-

  (i) at the company's registered office for not less than 15 days ending with the date of the meeting, and

  (ii) at the meeting itself.

(5) The matters to be disclosed are-

(a) the nature of the transaction,

(b) the amount of the loan or quasi-loan and the purpose for which it is required, and

(c) the extent of the company's liability under any transaction connected with the loan or quasi-loan.

(6) No approval is required under this section on the part of the members of a body corporate that-

(a) is not a UK-registered company, or

(b) is a wholly-owned subsidiary of another body corporate.

DEFINITIONS

"Connected persons": see s.252 (Persons connected with a director)

GENERAL NOTE

This section was introduced in Report Stage in the House of Commons and is derived from s.330(3)(b) of the 1985 Act. The section prohibits public companies and associated companies, not private companies, from making loans or quasi-loans to persons connected with the directors unless the transaction has been approved by resolution of the members of the company. Although private companies are not prohibited from making loans or quasi-loans to connected persons under this section, their directors must ensure they comply with their general duties under Ch.2.

The section applies equally to those connected with shadow directors: s.223(1)(c). Note the exceptions (ss.204-209), especially s.207, which sets the minimum threshold value for transactions requiring the approval of members (£10,000 for loans, etc). The amount of the loan or quasi-loan is calculated in accordance with s.211 (The value of transactions and arrangements). For remedies, see s.213 (Loans etc.: civil consequences of contravention). For subsequent affirmation, see s.214 (Loans etc.: effect of subsequent affirmation).

201. Credit transactions: requirement of members' approval

(1) This section applies to a company if it is-

(a) a public company, or

(b) a company associated with a public company.

(2) A company to which this section applies may not-

(a) enter into a credit transaction as creditor for the benefit of a director of the company or of its holding company, or a person connected with such a director, or

(b) give a guarantee or provide security in connection with a credit transaction entered into by any person for the benefit of such a director, or a person connected with such a director,

unless the transaction (that is, the credit transaction, the giving of the guarantee or the provision of security, as the case may be) has been approved by a resolution of the members of the company.

(3) If the director or connected person is a director of its holding company or a person connected with such a director, the transaction must also have been approved by a resolution of the members of the holding company.

(4) A resolution approving a transaction to which this section applies must not be passed unless a memorandum setting out the matters mentioned in subsection (5) is made available to members-

(a) in the case of a written resolution, by being sent or submitted to every eligible member at or before the time at which the proposed resolution is sent or submitted to him;

(b) in the case of a resolution at a meeting, by being made available for inspection by members of the company both-

  (i) at the company's registered office for not less than 15 days ending with the date of the meeting, and

(ii) at the meeting itself.

(5) The matters to be disclosed are-

   (a) the nature of the transaction,

   (b) the value of the credit transaction and the purpose for which the land, goods or services sold or otherwise disposed of, leased, hired or supplied under the credit transaction are required, and

   (c) the extent of the company's liability under any transaction connected with the credit transaction.

(6) No approval is required under this section on the part of the members of a body corporate that-

   (a) is not a UK-registered company, or

   (b) is a wholly-owned subsidiary of another body corporate.

DEFINITIONS

"Company": see ss.1 (Companies) and 1158 (United Kingdom registered company)

"Connected persons": see s.252 (Persons connected with a director)

"Credit transaction": see s.202 (meaning of "credit transaction")

"Director": see s.250 (Director)

"Guarantee": see s.331(2) of the Companies Act 1985

"Holding company": see ss.1159, 1160 and Sch.6

"Subsidiary": see ss.1159, 1160 and Sch.6

"Wholly owned subsidiary": see ss.1159, 1160 and Sch.6

GENERAL NOTE

This section applies only to public companies or companies associated with a public company. It replaces s.330(4) of the 1985 Act. The substantive change is that, subject to member approval, credit transactions, guarantees and the provision of security are no longer prohibited, but are subject to member approval.

The section applies equally to shadow directors: s.223(1)(c). Note the exceptions (ss.204-208), especially s.207, which sets the minimum threshold value for transactions requiring the approval of members (£15,000 for credit transactions). For remedies, see s.213 (Loans etc.: civil consequences of contravention). For subsequent affirmation, see s.214 (Loans etc.: effect of subsequent affirmation).

Subsection (4)

The value of the credit transaction should be calculated in accordance with s.211 (The value of transactions and arrangements).

202. Meaning of "credit transaction"

(1) A "credit transaction" is a transaction under which one party ("the creditor")-

   (a) supplies any goods or sells any land under a hire-purchase agreement or a conditional sale agreement,

   (b) leases or hires any land or goods in return for periodical payments, or

   (c) otherwise disposes of land or supplies goods or services on the understanding that payment (whether in a lump sum or instalments or by way of periodical payments or otherwise) is to be deferred.

(2) Any reference to the person for whose benefit a credit transaction is entered into is to the person to whom goods, land or services are supplied, sold, leased, hired or otherwise disposed of under the transaction.

(3) In this section-

"conditional sale agreement" has the same meaning as in the Consumer Credit Act 1974 (c. 39); and

"services" means anything other than goods or land.

GENERAL NOTE

This section restates s.331(7), (8), (9)(b) and (10) of the 1985 Act without substantive change.

203.   Related arrangements: requirement of members' approval

(1) A company may not-
    (a) take part in an arrangement under which-
        (i) another person enters into a transaction that, if it had been entered into by the company, would have required approval under section 197, 198, 200 or 201, and
        (ii) that person, in pursuance of the arrangement, obtains a benefit from the company or a body corporate associated with it, or
    (b) arrange for the assignment to it, or assumption by it, of any rights, obligations or liabilities under a transaction that, if it had been entered into by the company, would have required such approval,
  unless the arrangement in question has been approved by a resolution of the members of the company.

(2) If the director or connected person for whom the transaction is entered into is a director of its holding company or a person connected with such a director, the arrangement must also have been approved by a resolution of the members of the holding company.

(3) A resolution approving an arrangement to which this section applies must not be passed unless a memorandum setting out the matters mentioned in subsection (4) is made available to members-
    (a) in the case of a written resolution, by being sent or submitted to every eligible member at or before the time at which the proposed resolution is sent or submitted to him;
    (b) in the case of a resolution at a meeting, by being made available for inspection by members of the company both-
        (i) at the company's registered office for not less than 15 days ending with the date of the meeting, and
        (ii) at the meeting itself.

(4) The matters to be disclosed are-
    (a) the matters that would have to be disclosed if the company were seeking approval of the transaction to which the arrangement relates,
    (b) the nature of the arrangement, and
    (c) the extent of the company's liability under the arrangement or any transaction connected with it.

(5) No approval is required under this section on the part of the members of a body corporate that-
    (a) is not a UK-registered company, or
    (b) is a wholly-owned subsidiary of another body corporate.

(6) In determining for the purposes of this section whether a transaction is one that would have required approval under section 197, 198, 200 or 201 if it had been entered into by the company, the transaction shall be treated as having been entered into on the date of the arrangement.

GENERAL NOTE
  This section replaces s.330(6) and (7) of the 1985 Act. The substantive change is that, subject to member approval, a company can now enter into related transactions and arrangements. These are defined widely, so care must be taken to ensure that the necessary approvals are obtained in appropriate cases. Comments on s.330(6) and (7) of the 1985 Act may still prove useful:

      "These are drafted in wide terms. The transaction is the particular business conducted between the two parties, such as the transfer of the money by way of loan or the granting of a mortgage. An arrangement is wider and may cover a number of transactions and involve a number of parties. An assignment would occur if the company purchased the right to repayment of a loan made by a third party to a director of the company. Liability would be assumed if the company took over the guarantee of a debt due by the director to a third party. Subsection (7) [i.e. Companies Act 1985, s.330(7), now s.203(1)(a) ((Related transactions: requirement of members' approval)] catches, in particular, back-to-back arrangements where a company agrees to make loans to the directors of another company in return for loans to its directors. It would also apply where, in return for the company's business, a director obtains a loan from a bank on favourable terms"

Lord Sainsbury explained the rationale of this section in Grand Committee:

"Section [203 (Related arrangements: requirement of members' approval)] is an anti-avoidance provision. It prevents a company from evading the requirements for member approval by entering into an arrangement whereby another person gives the director a loan, quasi-loan or credit transaction, and in return that person obtains a benefit from a company or subsidiary of the company" (*Hansard*, HL GC Day 4, Vol.678, cols 349-350 (February 9, 2006)).

This section applies equally to shadow directors: s.223(1)(c).

204. Exception for expenditure on company business

(1) Approval is not required under section 197, 198, 200 or 201 (requirement of members' approval for loans etc) for anything done by a company-

  (a) to provide a director of the company or of its holding company, or a person connected with any such director, with funds to meet expenditure incurred or to be incurred by him-

    (i) for the purposes of the company, or

    (ii) for the purpose of enabling him properly to perform his duties as an officer of the company, or

  (b) to enable any such person to avoid incurring such expenditure.

(2) This section does not authorise a company to enter into a transaction if the aggregate of-

  (a) the value of the transaction in question, and

  (b) the value of any other relevant transactions or arrangements,

exceeds £50,000.

GENERAL NOTE

This section replaces s.337 of the 1985 Act which made an exception to the prohibition on loans, quasi-loans and credit transactions under s.330 of that Act for funding directors' expenditure on company business. This section removes the stringent requirements imposed by s.337 of the 1985 Act. The thing done requiring expenditure no longer requires prior member approval, and as such there is no longer a requirement to pay back the loan, quasi-loan or credit transaction if member approval is not forthcoming and nor is there any disclosure requirement.

This section applies equally to shadow directors: s.223(1)(c).

Lord Sainsbury explained this section in Grand Committee:

"This section contains an exception from the requirement for member approval under sections [197-198 (Loans or quasi-loans: requirement of members' approval)] or [s 201 (Credit transactions: requirement of members' approval)] where a loan, quasi-loan or credit transaction is intended to provide a director with funds to meet expenditure on company business. The exception is subject to a limit of £50,000. In calculating whether the limit has been reached, it is necessary to add up the transaction in question and any other relevant existing transactions or arrangement. Section [210 (Other relevant transactions or arrangements)] explains what is meant by 'other relevant existing transactions or arrangements' for the purpose of this exception" (*Hansard*, HL GC Day 4, Vol.678 (Feruary 9, 2006)).

Subsection (2)

The maximum amount of a transaction that can be entered into without authorisation has been raised from £20,000 to £50,000. This amount is subject to the Secretary of State's power to increase financial limits (see s.258 (Power to increase financial limits)).

205. Exception for expenditure on defending proceedings etc

(1) Approval is not required under section 197, 198, 200 or 201 (requirement of members' approval for loans etc) for anything done by a company-

  (a) to provide a director of the company or of its holding company with funds to meet expenditure incurred or to be incurred by him-
    (i) in defending any criminal or civil proceedings in connection with any alleged
     negligence, default, breach of duty or breach of trust by him in relation to the
     company or an associated company, or
    (ii) in connection with an application for relief (see subsection (5)), or
  (b) to enable any such director to avoid incurring such expenditure,
if it is done on the following terms.

 (2) The terms are-
  (a) that the loan is to be repaid, or (as the case may be) any liability of the company
   incurred under any transaction connected with the thing done is to be discharged, in the
   event of-
    (i) the director being convicted in the proceedings,
    (ii) judgment being given against him in the proceedings, or
    (iii) the court refusing to grant him relief on the application; and
  (b) that it is to be so repaid or discharged not later than-
    (i) the date when the conviction becomes final,
    (ii) the date when the judgment becomes final, or
    (iii) the date when the refusal of relief becomes final.

 (3) For this purpose a conviction, judgment or refusal of relief becomes final-
  (a) if not appealed against, at the end of the period for bringing an appeal;
  (b) if appealed against, when the appeal (or any further appeal) is disposed of.

 (4) An appeal is disposed of-
  (a) if it is determined and the period for bringing any further appeal has ended, or
  (b) if it is abandoned or otherwise ceases to have effect.

 (5) The reference in subsection (1)(a)(ii) to an application for relief is to an application for
  relief under-
   section 661(3) or (4) (power of court to grant relief in case of acquisition of shares by
    innocent nominee), or
   section 1157 (general power of court to grant relief in case of honest and reasonable
    conduct).

GENERAL NOTE

 This section replaces s.337A of the 1985 Act, inserted by the Companies (Audit, Investigations and Community Enterprise) Act 2004. Its function is clear.

 This section applies equally to shadow directors: s.223(1)(c).

Subsection (1)

 This section was amended at Report Stage in the House of Commons to allow loans to be granted to directors to enable
them to defend themselves in proceedings relating to associated companies as well as the director's own company (the same
amendment was also made to s.206 (Exception for expenditure in connection with regulatory action or investigation)). This
exception was considered to be a matter of convenience for group situations:

  "We recognise, in a group situation, it might be more convenient for the loan to be made by a
  different company in the group" (Margaret Hodge HC Report Stage, col.799 (October 17, 2006)).

 Margaret Hodge went on to emphasise that the exception to the rules requiring member approval "should only be used
for matters that are properly connected to the company. It would be inappropriate for the exceptions to be available for company funds to be used without member approval to defend a director against proceedings unconnected with company business" (HC Report Stage 17, col.799 (October 17, 2006)).

 It is not clear that the section delivers these aims. If the director is a director of the associated company, but not of the
company granting the loan, then the general restriction (in s.197, etc.) does not apply and the exemption (in s.205) is not
needed. If the director is a director of the company making the loan, but the loan is intended to assist the director defend
proceeding in relation to the associated company, then the loan will have to be on the terms specified in s.205(2) if there is no
members' approval, or perhaps on other terms if members' approval is given (s.197, etc.), but in either case the directors
agreeing/proposing the loan will have to do so in compliance with their general duties in Ch.2, including the duty to act
within powers (and in particular for proper purposes, s.171) and to promote the success of the company (s.172). Compliance
with these requirements is possible even if the funding is to assist in defending proceedings in relation to an associated com-

pany, but caution is warranted (see, e.g. *Scottish Cooperative Wholesale Society Ltd v Meyer* [1959] A.C. 324; *Kuwait Asia Bank EC v National Mutual Life Nominees Ltd* [1991] 1 A.C. 187 PC).

On the question whether or not this exception from the requirement for authorisation also covers regulatory proceedings and investigations, Lord Sainsbury suggested:

> "The preliminary stages of action by a regulatory body for non-compliance with a requirement of a regulatory nature might not constitute formal 'proceedings'. But in that case a loan to a director would be permitted under subs.(1)(b). One of the purposes of defending regulatory proceedings and investigations is to prevent the imposition of a penalty and thus to avoid incurring expenditure in defending any civil proceedings brought to enforce payment of the penalty" (*Hansard*, HL GC Day 4, Vol.678, cols 351-352 (February 9, 2006)).

Nevertheless, for the avoidance of doubt, s.206 (Exception for expenditure in connection with regulatory action or investigation) was also introduced at Report Stage in the House of Lords. Also see s.234 (Qualifying third party indemnity insurance).

Subsection (2)

This subsection specifies the terms that must be agreed to attract the exemption from the requirement for members' approval. Clearly the loan, etc., may be on different terms if members' authorisation is obtained, as required under the relevant section.

206. Exception for expenditure in connection with regulatory action or investigation

Approval is not required under section 197, 198, 200 or 201 (requirement of members' approval for loans etc) for anything done by a company-

(a) to provide a director of the company or of its holding company with funds to meet expenditure incurred or to be incurred by him in defending himself-

(i) in an investigation by a regulatory authority, or

(ii) against action proposed to be taken by a regulatory authority,

in connection with any alleged negligence, default, breach of duty or breach of trust by him in relation to the company or an associated company, or

(b) to enable any such director to avoid incurring such expenditure.

GENERAL NOTE

This section was introduced at Report Stage in the House of Lords for the avoidance of doubt and in response to concerns that the exception in s.205 (Exception for expenditure on defending proceedings, etc.) would not cover expenditure in connection with regulatory action or investigation.

This section applies equally to shadow directors: s.223(1)(c).

207. Exceptions for minor and business transactions

(1) Approval is not required under section 197, 198 or 200 for a company to make a loan or quasi-loan, or to give a guarantee or provide security in connection with a loan or quasi-loan, if the aggregate of-

(a) the value of the transaction, and

(b) the value of any other relevant transactions or arrangements,

does not exceed £10,000.

(2) Approval is not required under section 201 for a company to enter into a credit transaction, or to give a guarantee or provide security in connection with a credit transaction, if the aggregate of-

(a) the value of the transaction (that is, of the credit transaction, guarantee or security), and

(b) the value of any other relevant transactions or arrangements,

does not exceed £15,000.

(3) Approval is not required under section 201 for a company to enter into a credit transaction, or to give a guarantee or provide security in connection with a credit transaction, if-

(a) the transaction is entered into by the company in the ordinary course of the company's business, and

(b) the value of the transaction is not greater, and the terms on which it is entered into are not more favourable, than it is reasonable to expect the company would have offered to, or in respect of, a person of the same financial standing but unconnected with the company.

GENERAL NOTE

This section replaces s.332, 334 and 335 of the 1985 Act. The substantive change is that the exception for small loans is extended to include small quasi-loans, and also to include connected persons. The financial limits have been raised from £5,000 for loans, etc, to £10,000; and from £10,000 for credit transactions to £15,000. These amounts are subject to the Secretary of State's power to increase financial limits (see s.258 (Power to increase financial limits).

This section applies equally to shadow directors: s.223(1)(c).

208. Exceptions for intra-group transactions

(1) Approval is not required under section 197, 198 or 200 for-
    (a) the making of a loan or quasi-loan to an associated body corporate, or
    (b) the giving of a guarantee or provision of security in connection with a loan or quasi-loan made to an associated body corporate.
(2) Approval is not required under section 201-
    (a) to enter into a credit transaction as creditor for the benefit of an associated body corporate, or
    (b) to give a guarantee or provide security in connection with a credit transaction entered into by any person for the benefit of an associated body corporate.

DEFINITIONS

"Associated body corporate": see s.256 (Associated bodies corporate)

GENERAL NOTE

This section replaces ss.333 and 336 of the 1985 Act. The exception is widened.

This section applies equally to shadow directors: s.223(1)(c).

209. Exceptions for money-lending companies

(1) Approval is not required under section 197, 198 or 200 for the making of a loan or quasi-loan, or the giving of a guarantee or provision of security in connection with a loan or quasi-loan, by a money-lending company if-
    (a) the transaction (that is, the loan, quasi-loan, guarantee or security) is entered into by the company in the ordinary course of the company's business, and
    (b) the value of the transaction is not greater, and its terms are not more favourable, than it is reasonable to expect the company would have offered to a person of the same financial standing but unconnected with the company.
(2) A "money-lending company" means a company whose ordinary business includes the making of loans or quasi-loans, or the giving of guarantees or provision of security in connection with loans or quasi-loans.
(3) The condition specified in subsection (1)(b) does not of itself prevent a company from making a home loan-
    (a) to a director of the company or of its holding company, or
    (b) to an employee of the company,
if loans of that description are ordinarily made by the company to its employees and the terms of the loan in question are no more favourable than those on which such loans are ordinarily made.
(4) For the purposes of subsection (3) a "home loan" means a loan-

(a) for the purpose of facilitating the purchase, for use as the only or main residence of the person to whom the loan is made, of the whole or part of any dwelling-house together with any land to be occupied and enjoyed with it,

(b) for the purpose of improving a dwelling-house or part of a dwelling-house so used or any land occupied and enjoyed with it, or

(c) in substitution for any loan made by any person and falling within paragraph (a) or (b).

GENERAL NOTE

This section replaces s.338 of the 1985 Act. The significant changes are the abolition of a maximum amount permitted under the exception and the widening of the exception for 'home loans' to those connected persons who are employees (subs.(3)). Lord Sainsbury explains the rationale in his proposal for making the change:

"Section [209 (Exceptions for money lending companies)] contains various exceptions for money-lending companies from the requirements for member approval of loans and quasi-loans ... Subsection (3) contains a particular exception enabling money-lending companies to make home loans to directors. The purpose of this exception is to allow directors to take advantage of any employee home loan schemes operated by the money-lending company on the same terms as are offered to employees. This exception is derived from s.338(6) of the Companies Act 1985. In a change from that section, the £100,000 limit has not been retained. However, as in that section, the money-lending company can take advantage of the exception only if the loan is for the purpose of facilitating the purchase, for use as the director's only or main residence, of the whole or part of any dwelling house. This means that in practice only a director can take advantage of the exception. The exception is not available in case of a home loan to a person connected to a director, even if that person happens to be an employee of the company. We consider that preventing employees from taking advantage of an employee home loan scheme operated by the company simply because they happen to be connected to a director of the company, while the director is not similarly prevented from taking advantage of the scheme, is unfair" (*Hansard*, HL GC Day 4, Vol.678 cols 352-353 (February 9, 2006)).

This section applies equally to shadow directors: s.223(1)(c).

210. Other relevant transactions or arrangements

(1) This section has effect for determining what are "other relevant transactions or arrangements" for the purposes of any exception to section 197, 198, 200 or 201.

In the following provisions "the relevant exception" means the exception for the purposes of which that falls to be determined.

(2) Other relevant transactions or arrangements are those previously entered into, or entered into at the same time as the transaction or arrangement in question in relation to which the following conditions are met.

(3) Where the transaction or arrangement in question is entered into-

(a) for a director of the company entering into it, or

(b) for a person connected with such a director,

the conditions are that the transaction or arrangement was (or is) entered into for that director, or a person connected with him, by virtue of the relevant exception by that company or by any of its subsidiaries.

(4) Where the transaction or arrangement in question is entered into-

(a) for a director of the holding company of the company entering into it, or

(b) for a person connected with such a director,

the conditions are that the transaction or arrangement was (or is) entered into for that director, or a person connected with him, by virtue of the relevant exception by the holding company or by any of its subsidiaries.

(5) A transaction or arrangement entered into by a company that at the time it was entered into-

(a) was a subsidiary of the company entering into the transaction or arrangement in question, or

(b) was a subsidiary of that company's holding company,

is not a relevant transaction or arrangement if, at the time the question arises whether the transaction or arrangement in question falls within a relevant exception, it is no longer such a subsidiary.

GENERAL NOTE

This section is derived from s.339 of the 1985 Act.

This section applies equally to shadow directors: s.223(1)(c).

Subsections (3) and (4)

Lord Sainsbury made the following statement in Grand Committee:

"Section [210 (Other relevant transactions or arrangements)] (3) and (4) determine what transactions or arrangements are 'other relevant transactions or arrangements' for the purposes of working out whether the company may make further use of a particular exception to the requirement for member approval to a loan, quasi-loan or credit transaction under sections [ss.197, 198 and 200 (Loans or quasi-loans: requirements of members' approval)] or [s.201 (Credit transaction: requirement of members' approval)]. Section [210 (Other relevant transactions or arrangements)](3) deals with those cases where the transaction or arrangement is entered into for a director of the company, or a person connected with such a director. Section [210 (Other relevant transactions or arrangements)](4) deals with those cases where the transaction or arrangement is entered into for a director of the company's holding company, or a person connected with such a director" (*Hansard*, HL GC Day 4, Vol.678 cols 353-354 (February 9, 2006)).

211.   The value of transactions and arrangements

(1) For the purposes of sections 197 to 214 (loans etc)-
   (a) the value of a transaction or arrangement is determined as follows, and
   (b) the value of any other relevant transaction or arrangement is taken to be the value so determined reduced by any amount by which the liabilities of the person for whom the transaction or arrangement was made have been reduced.
(2) The value of a loan is the amount of its principal.
(3) The value of a quasi-loan is the amount, or maximum amount, that the person to whom the quasi-loan is made is liable to reimburse the creditor.
(4) The value of a credit transaction is the price that it is reasonable to expect could be obtained for the goods, services or land to which the transaction relates if they had been supplied (at the time the transaction is entered into) in the ordinary course of business and on the same terms (apart from price) as they have been supplied, or are to be supplied, under the transaction in question.
(5) The value of a guarantee or security is the amount guaranteed or secured.
(6) The value of an arrangement to which section 203 (related arrangements) applies is the value of the transaction to which the arrangement relates.
(7) If the value of a transaction or arrangement is not capable of being expressed as a specific sum of money-
   (a) whether because the amount of any liability arising under the transaction or arrangement is unascertainable, or for any other reason, and
   (b) whether or not any liability under the transaction or arrangement has been reduced,
its value is deemed to exceed £50,000.

GENERAL NOTE

This section replaces ss.339(6) and 340 of the 1985 Act and does not make any substantive changes.

This section applies equally to shadow directors: s.223(1)(c).

212.   The person for whom a transaction or arrangement is entered into

For the purposes of sections 197 to 214 (loans etc) the person for whom a transaction or arrangement is entered into is-
   (a) in the case of a loan or quasi-loan, the person to whom it is made;

(b) in the case of a credit transaction, the person to whom goods, land or services are supplied, sold, hired, leased or otherwise disposed of under the transaction;

(c) in the case of a guarantee or security, the person for whom the transaction is made in connection with which the guarantee or security is entered into;

(d) in the case of an arrangement within section 203 (related arrangements), the person for whom the transaction is made to which the arrangement relates.

GENERAL NOTE

This section replaces s.331(9)(a)-(d) of the 1985 Act without substantive change.

This section applies equally to shadow directors: s.223(1)(c).

213. Loans etc: civil consequences of contravention

(1) This section applies where a company enters into a transaction or arrangement in contravention of section 197, 198, 200, 201 or 203 (requirement of members' approval for loans etc).

(2) The transaction or arrangement is voidable at the instance of the company, unless-

(a) restitution of any money or other asset that was the subject matter of the transaction or arrangement is no longer possible,

(b) the company has been indemnified for any loss or damage resulting from the transaction or arrangement, or

(c) rights acquired in good faith, for value and without actual notice of the contravention by a person who is not a party to the transaction or arrangement would be affected by the avoidance.

(3) Whether or not the transaction or arrangement has been avoided, each of the persons specified in subsection (4) is liable-

(a) to account to the company for any gain that he has made directly or indirectly by the transaction or arrangement, and

(b) (jointly and severally with any other person so liable under this section) to indemnify the company for any loss or damage resulting from the transaction or arrangement.

(4) The persons so liable are-

(a) any director of the company or of its holding company with whom the company entered into the transaction or arrangement in contravention of section 197, 198, 201 or 203,

(b) any person with whom the company entered into the transaction or arrangement in contravention of any of those sections who is connected with a director of the company or of its holding company,

(c) the director of the company or of its holding company with whom any such person is connected, and

(d) any other director of the company who authorised the transaction or arrangement.

(5) Subsections (3) and (4) are subject to the following two subsections.

(6) In the case of a transaction or arrangement entered into by a company in contravention of section 200, 201 or 203 with a person connected with a director of the company or of its holding company, that director is not liable by virtue of subsection (4)(c) if he shows that he took all reasonable steps to secure the company's compliance with the section concerned.

(7) In any case-

(a) a person so connected is not liable by virtue of subsection (4)(b), and

(b) a director is not liable by virtue of subsection (4)(d),

if he shows that, at the time the transaction or arrangement was entered into, he did not know the relevant circumstances constituting the contravention.

(8) Nothing in this section shall be read as excluding the operation of any other enactment or rule of law by virtue of which the transaction or arrangement may be called in question or any liability to the company may arise.

GENERAL NOTE

This section is derived from s.341 of the 1985 Act. The remedies for breach of ss.197, 198, 200, 201 or 203 are the same as those for breach of s.190 (Substantial property transactions: requirement of members' approval) under s.195 (Property transactions: civil consequences of contravention). See the notes to that section.

The significant change from the 1985 Act is that there are no longer any criminal penalties for breach of the provisions. This section applies equally to shadow directors: s.223(1)(c).

Also see s.1157 (Power of court to grant relief in certain circumstances) (replacing Companies Act 1985, s.727).

214.   Loans etc: effect of subsequent affirmation

Where a transaction or arrangement is entered into by a company in contravention of section 197, 198, 200, 201 or 203 (requirement of members' approval for loans etc) but, within a reasonable period, it is affirmed-

> (a) in the case of a contravention of the requirement for a resolution of the members of the company, by a resolution of the members of the company, and
>
> (b) in the case of a contravention of the requirement for a resolution of the members of the company's holding company, by a resolution of the members of the holding company,

the transaction or arrangement may no longer be avoided under section 213.

GENERAL NOTE

This new provision allows for the subsequent affirmation of loans, quasi-loans, credit-transactions and related transactions and arrangements within a reasonable amount of time. This brings the provisions concerned with loans, quasi-loans and credit transactions into line with the provisions on substantial property transactions. See note accompanying s.196 (Property transactions: effect of subsequent affirmation).

Payments for loss of office

215.   Payments for loss of office

> (1) In this Chapter a "payment for loss of office" means a payment made to a director or past director of a company-
>
> (a) by way of compensation for loss of office as director of the company,
>
> (b) by way of compensation for loss, while director of the company or in connection with his ceasing to be a director of it, of-
>
> > (i)   any other office or employment in connection with the management of the affairs of the company, or
> >
> > (ii) any office (as director or otherwise) or employment in connection with the management of the affairs of any subsidiary undertaking of the company,
>
> (c) as consideration for or in connection with his retirement from his office as director of the company, or
>
> (d) as consideration for or in connection with his retirement, while director of the company or in connection with his ceasing to be a director of it, from-
>
> > (i)   any other office or employment in connection with the management of the affairs of the company, or
> >
> > (ii) any office (as director or otherwise) or employment in connection with the management of the affairs of any subsidiary undertaking of the company.
>
> (2) The references to compensation and consideration include benefits otherwise than in cash and references in this Chapter to payment have a corresponding meaning.
>
> (3) For the purposes of sections 217 to 221 (payments requiring members' approval)-
>
> (a) payment to a person connected with a director, or
>
> (b) payment to any person at the direction of, or for the benefit of, a director or a person connected with him,

is treated as payment to the director.

(4) References in those sections to payment by a person include payment by another person at the direction of, or on behalf of, the person referred to.

GENERAL NOTE

This new provision defines for the purpose of this Chapter 'payment for loss of office'. It extends the provisions to include not only payments for loss of office as director but also payments for any loss of office or employment in connection with management of the company or a subsidiary. The provisions are also extended to include payments to connected persons, bringing the provisions into line with the other provisions in the chapter. These provisions implement certain Law Commission recommendations (see Law Com. No.261, at Pt 7).

Subsection (1)

It is made clear that the provisions apply equally to payments to former directors:

"It does not matter if the director ceased to be a director at the time that they payment is made. What matters is the reason for payment ... It is not possible to evade the provisions simply by the device of resignation prior to payment. As the Law Commission pointed out, it would expect the court to treat the resignation and the payment as part of a single operation" (*Hansard*, HL GC Day 4 Vol.678, cols 355-356 (February 9, 2006)).

Subsection (2)

"Benefits": see s.176 (Duty not to accept benefits from third parties) and accompanying notes.

216. Amounts taken to be payments for loss of office

(1) This section applies where in connection with any such transfer as is mentioned in section 218 or 219 (payment in connection with transfer of undertaking, property or shares) a director of the company-

  (a) is to cease to hold office, or

  (b) is to cease to be the holder of-

    (i) any other office or employment in connection with the management of the affairs of the company, or

    (ii) any office (as director or otherwise) or employment in connection with the management of the affairs of any subsidiary undertaking of the company.

(2) If in connection with any such transfer-

  (a) the price to be paid to the director for any shares in the company held by him is in excess of the price which could at the time have been obtained by other holders of like shares, or

  (b) any valuable consideration is given to the director by a person other than the company,

the excess or, as the case may be, the money value of the consideration is taken for the purposes of those sections to have been a payment for loss of office.

GENERAL NOTE

This section is derived from s.316(2) of the 1985 Act and concerns amounts taken to be payments for loss office in relation to ss.218 (Payment in connection with transfer of undertaking etc: requirement of members' approval) and 219 (Payment in connection with share transfer: requirement of members' approval). The section deems an excessive payment for a transfer of undertaking or shares to a director in relation to loss of office as director or loss of office or employment in relation to the management of the company or its subsidiary to be a payment for loss of office.

217. Payment by company: requirement of members' approval

(1) A company may not make a payment for loss of office to a director of the company unless the payment has been approved by a resolution of the members of the company.

(2) A company may not make a payment for loss of office to a director of its holding company unless the payment has been approved by a resolution of the members of each of those companies.

(3) A resolution approving a payment to which this section applies must not be passed unless a memorandum setting out particulars of the proposed payment (including its amount) is made available to the members of the company whose approval is sought-

    (a) in the case of a written resolution, by being sent or submitted to every eligible member at or before the time at which the proposed resolution is sent or submitted to him;

    (b) in the case of a resolution at a meeting, by being made available for inspection by the members both-

        (i) at the company's registered office for not less than 15 days ending with the date of the meeting, and

        (ii) at the meeting itself.

(4) No approval is required under this section on the part of the members of a body corporate that-

    (a) is not a UK-registered company, or

    (b) is a wholly-owned subsidiary of another body corporate.

DEFINITIONS

"Payment for loss of office": see s.215 (Payments for loss of office). Also see s.216 (Amounts taken to be payments for loss of office)

GENERAL NOTE

This section replaces s.312 of the 1985 Act. The requirement of members' approval of payments for loss of office is extended to cover payments to a director of a holding company (subs.(2)).

Note that this requirement for approval does not extend to bona fide payments made in order to discharge existing legal obligations, or by way of damages for breach of such obligations, settlement or compromise of claims, or pension payments (s.220(1)).

Remedies: see s.222 (Payments made without approval: civil consequences).

218. Payment in connection with transfer of undertaking etc: requirement of members' approval

(1) No payment for loss of office may be made by any person to a director of a company in connection with the transfer of the whole or any part of the undertaking or property of the company unless the payment has been approved by a resolution of the members of the company.

(2) No payment for loss of office may be made by any person to a director of a company in connection with the transfer of the whole or any part of the undertaking or property of a subsidiary of the company unless the payment has been approved by a resolution of the members of each of the companies.

(3) A resolution approving a payment to which this section applies must not be passed unless a memorandum setting out particulars of the proposed payment (including its amount) is made available to the members of the company whose approval is sought-

    (a) in the case of a written resolution, by being sent or submitted to every eligible member at or before the time at which the proposed resolution is sent or submitted to him;

    (b) in the case of a resolution at a meeting, by being made available for inspection by the members both-

        (i) at the company's registered office for not less than 15 days ending with the date of the meeting, and

        (ii) at the meeting itself.

(4) No approval is required under this section on the part of the members of a body corporate that-

    (a) is not a UK-registered company, or

(b) is a wholly-owned subsidiary of another body corporate.

(5) A payment made in pursuance of an arrangement-

    (a) entered into as part of the agreement for the transfer in question, or within one year before or two years after that agreement, and

    (b) to which the company whose undertaking or property is transferred, or any person to whom the transfer is made, is privy,

is presumed, except in so far as the contrary is shown, to be a payment to which this section applies.

DEFINITIONS

"Payment for loss of office": see s.215 (Payments for loss of office). Also see s.216 (Amounts taken to be payments for loss of office)

GENERAL NOTE

This section is derived from ss.313(1) and 316(1) of the 1985 Act.

Subsection (2)

This subsection extends the provision to cover the transfer of a subsidiary company's undertaking or property.

Subsection (5)

This subsection maintains the "suspect period" found in s.316(1) of the 1985 Act of one year before the agreement for the transfer in question or the offer leading to it, and two years after that agreement or offer. Payments made to a director during this period in pursuance of the relevant transfer arrangements are presumed, except in so far as the contrary is shown, to be payments to which the section applies.

Remedies: see s.222 (Payments made without approval: civil consequences).

219. Payment in connection with share transfer: requirement of members' approval

(1) No payment for loss of office may be made by any person to a director of a company in connection with a transfer of shares in the company, or in a subsidiary of the company, resulting from a takeover bid unless the payment has been approved by a resolution of the relevant shareholders.

(2) The relevant shareholders are the holders of the shares to which the bid relates and any holders of shares of the same class as any of those shares.

(3) A resolution approving a payment to which this section applies must not be passed unless a memorandum setting out particulars of the proposed payment (including its amount) is made available to the members of the company whose approval is sought-

    (a) in the case of a written resolution, by being sent or submitted to every eligible member at or before the time at which the proposed resolution is sent or submitted to him;

    (b) in the case of a resolution at a meeting, by being made available for inspection by the members both-

        (i) at the company's registered office for not less than 15 days ending with the date of the meeting, and

        (ii) at the meeting itself.

(4) Neither the person making the offer, nor any associate of his (as defined in section 988), is entitled to vote on the resolution, but-

    (a) where the resolution is proposed as a written resolution, they are entitled (if they would otherwise be so entitled) to be sent a copy of it, and

    (b) at any meeting to consider the resolution they are entitled (if they would otherwise be so entitled) to be given notice of the meeting, to attend and speak and if present (in person or by proxy) to count towards the quorum.

(5) If at a meeting to consider the resolution a quorum is not present, and after the meeting has been adjourned to a later date a quorum is again not present, the payment is (for the purposes of this section) deemed to have been approved.

(6) No approval is required under this section on the part of shareholders in a body corporate that-

    (a) is not a UK-registered company, or

    (b) is a wholly-owned subsidiary of another body corporate.

(7) A payment made in pursuance of an arrangement-

    (a) entered into as part of the agreement for the transfer in question, or within one year before or two years after that agreement, and

    (b) to which the company whose shares are the subject of the bid, or any person to whom the transfer is made, is privy,

is presumed, except in so far as the contrary is shown, to be a payment to which this section applies.

DEFINITIONS

"Payment for loss of office": see s.215 (Payments for loss of office). Also see s.216 (Amounts taken to be payments for loss of office)

GENERAL NOTE

This section is derived from ss.314 and 315 of the 1985 Act.

Subsection (1)

The duty to disclose details of a share transfer to target shareholders has been replaced with a requirement for approval.

> "The Bill does not retain the duty placed on the director to take all reasonable steps to secure that particulars of the proposed payment are sent with any notice of the offer made for the shares. The criminal offence of failing to comply with that duty has also been dropped ... [T]he requirement seems over-regulatory, given that the shareholders must approve the payment in any event. The section ensures that they are informed of the payment either by details being available at the meeting and for inspection at the company's registered office, or by the details being circulated with a written resolution to approve payment" (*Hansard*, HL GC Day 4, Vol.678, cols 358-359 (February 9, 2006)).

The provision is also extended to cover transfers of all company and subsidiary shares resulting from a takeover bid. The rationale is "to avoid the risk that directors may obtain advantageous payments from the persons launching the takeover bid which should in fact go towards the members in return for their shares" (*Hansard*, HL GC Day 4, Vol.678, cols 358-359 (February 9, 2006)).

Subsection (4)

"Another change made by the section is that neither the person making the offer, nor any associate of his, may vote on the resolution to approve the payment to the director. This implements a recommendation of the Law Commission. We believe that this is the right approach as it provides essential protection for shareholders" (*Hansard*, HL GC Day 4, Vol.678 col.359 (February 9, 2006)).

Remedies: see s.222 (Payments made without approval: civil consequences).

220. Exception for payments in discharge of legal obligations etc

(1) Approval is not required under section 217, 218 or 219 (payments requiring members' approval) for a payment made in good faith-

    (a) in discharge of an existing legal obligation (as defined below),

    (b) by way of damages for breach of such an obligation,

    (c) by way of settlement or compromise of any claim arising in connection with the termination of a person's office or employment, or

    (d) by way of pension in respect of past services.

(2) In relation to a payment within section 217 (payment by company) an existing legal obligation means an obligation of the company, or any body corporate associated with it, that was not entered into in connection with, or in consequence of, the event giving rise to the payment for loss of office.

(3) In relation to a payment within section 218 or 219 (payment in connection with transfer of undertaking, property or shares) an existing legal obligation means an obligation of the person making the payment that was not entered into for the purposes of, in connection with or in consequence of, the transfer in question.

(4) In the case of a payment within both section 217 and section 218, or within both section 217 and section 219, subsection (2) above applies and not subsection (3).

(5) A payment part of which falls within subsection (1) above and part of which does not is treated as if the parts were separate payments.

GENERAL NOTE

This provision is derived from s.316(3) of the 1985 Act and extends the exception to the discharge of existing legal obligations.

Subsection (1)

"Pension" is not defined in this section, although presumably it will include "any superannuation allowance, superannuation gratuity or similar payment", as defined in the second paragraph of s.316(3) of the 1985 Act.

Subsections (2) and (3)

An "existing legal obligation" for the purposes of s.217 (Payment by a company: requirement of members' approval) is an obligation not related to the event giving rise to the loss of office, and for the purposes of ss.218 (Payment in connection with transfer of undertaking etc: requirement of members' approval) and 219 (Payment in connection with share transfer: requirement of members' approval) is an obligation not related to the transfer in question.

221. Exception for small payments

(1) Approval is not required under section 217, 218 or 219 (payments requiring members' approval) if-
   (a) the payment in question is made by the company or any of its subsidiaries, and
   (b) the amount or value of the payment, together with the amount or value of any other relevant payments, does not exceed £200.

(2) For this purpose "other relevant payments" are payments for loss of office in relation to which the following conditions are met.

(3) Where the payment in question is one to which section 217 (payment by company) applies, the conditions are that the other payment was or is paid-
   (a) by the company making the payment in question or any of its subsidiaries,
   (b) to the director to whom that payment is made, and
   (c) in connection with the same event.

(4) Where the payment in question is one to which section 218 or 219 applies (payment in connection with transfer of undertaking, property or shares), the conditions are that the other payment was (or is) paid in connection with the same transfer-
   (a) to the director to whom the payment in question was made, and
   (b) by the company making the payment or any of its subsidiaries.

GENERAL NOTE

This section creates a new exception for small payments, currently set at under £200. The Secretary of State has the power to raise this limit (see s.258 (Power to increase financial limits)).

222. Payments made without approval: civil consequences

(1) If a payment is made in contravention of section 217 (payment by company)-
   (a) it is held by the recipient on trust for the company making the payment, and
   (b) any director who authorised the payment is jointly and severally liable to indemnify the company that made the payment for any loss resulting from it.

(2) If a payment is made in contravention of section 218 (payment in connection with transfer of undertaking etc), it is held by the recipient on trust for the company whose undertaking or property is or is proposed to be transferred.

(3) If a payment is made in contravention of section 219 (payment in connection with share transfer)-

(a) it is held by the recipient on trust for persons who have sold their shares as a result of the offer made, and

(b) the expenses incurred by the recipient in distributing that sum amongst those persons shall be borne by him and not retained out of that sum.

(4) If a payment is in contravention of section 217 and section 218, subsection (2) of this section applies rather than subsection (1).

(5) If a payment is in contravention of section 217 and section 219, subsection (3) of this section applies rather than subsection (1), unless the court directs otherwise.

GENERAL NOTE

This section is derived from ss.313(2) and 315(1) of the 1985 Act and clarifies the civil consequences of breach of the payment for loss of office provisions. The significant change from that Act is that there are no longer any criminal penalties. Lord Sainsbury provides the following explanation:

"We have removed all the criminal offences applying in this chapter as the civil consequences of breach seem sufficient. For example, in section [219 (Payment in connection with a share transfer: requirement of members' approval)] if a payment is made to a director without the required approval from the shareholders, the payment is held on trust for those persons who have sold their shares as a result of the offer made, and the expenses incurred by the director in distributing that sum among those persons are to be borne by the director" (*Hansard*, HL GC Day 4, Vol.678, cols 358-359 (February 9, 2006)).

Also see s.1157 (Power of court to grant relief in certain circumstances) (replacing Companies Act 1985, s.727).

Subsections (4) and (5)

These sections resolve the conflict between remedies where more than one provision applies.

Supplementary

223. Transactions requiring members' approval: application of provisions to shadow directors

(1) For the purposes of-

(a) sections 188 and 189 (directors' service contracts),

(b) sections 190 to 196 (property transactions),

(c) sections 197 to 214 (loans etc), and

(d) sections 215 to 222 (payments for loss of office),

a shadow director is treated as a director.

(2) Any reference in those provisions to loss of office as a director does not apply in relation to loss of a person's status as a shadow director.

DEFINITIONS

"Director": see s.250 ("Director")
"Shadow director": see s.251 ("Shadow director")

GENERAL NOTE

For the purpose of this Chapter all references to director are to include shadow director. However, loss of status as shadow director is not to be construed as a loss of office as a director (subs.(2)).

224. Approval by written resolution: accidental failure to send memorandum

(1) Where-
   (a) approval under this Chapter is sought by written resolution, and
   (b) a memorandum is required under this Chapter to be sent or submitted to every eligible member before the resolution is passed,
any accidental failure to send or submit the memorandum to one or more members shall be disregarded for the purpose of determining whether the requirement has been met.

(2) Subsection (1) has effect subject to any provision of the company's articles.

DEFINITIONS
"Written resolutions": see Pt 13 Ch.2

GENERAL NOTE
This new section was introduced at Report Stage in the House of Lords to make it clear that accidental failure to send a memorandum should not necessarily invalidate any approval:

"In most cases, where approval is to be given by written resolutions, the sections [in this chapter] require certain information relating to the transaction to be sent to the members eligible to vote on the written resolution. A memorandum containing the required information must be sent to eligible members before, or at the same time as, the written resolution is sent to them. This is so that the members have the necessary information before them when they vote. In Committee, we explained our intention that accidental failure to send the memorandum to each and every eligible member should not necessarily invalidate the approval given by the members" (HL Report Stage col.871 (May 9, 2006)).

In the unlikely circumstance of an accidental failure to send a memorandum to any members, or even a majority of shareholders, it is unclear whether this provision will still apply. There will be a failure in the required procedure, but if the vote can be shown to be a properly informed vote, it may be that the procedural failure can be ignored.

225. Cases where approval is required under more than one provision

(1) Approval may be required under more than one provision of this Chapter.
(2) If so, the requirements of each applicable provision must be met.
(3) This does not require a separate resolution for the purposes of each provision.

GENERAL NOTE
It is possible that a transaction may be characterised as requiring approval under more than one section in Ch.4. This new section, introduced in Grand Committee in the House of Lords, makes it clear that each set of rules will apply unless otherwise provided. Lord Sainsbury gives an example of how this should work:

"So, for example, if the transaction involves both a loan and a substantial property transaction, approval should be required under section [190 (Substantial property transactions: requirement of members' approval)] and section [197 (Loans or quasi-loans: requirement of members' approval)], unless in each case a relevant exemption applies. On the other hand, if the transaction is both a payment for loss of office and a substantial property transaction, section [190 (Substantial property transactions: requirement of members' approval)] (6)(b) provides that the rules on substantial property transactions should not apply, but the rules on payment for loss of office should apply in the usual manner" (*Hansard*, HL GC Day 4, Vol.678, cols 360-361 (February 9, 2006)).

226. Requirement of consent of Charity Commission: companies that are charities

For section 66 of the Charities Act 1993 (c. 10) substitute-

66. "Consent of Commission required for approval etc by members of charitable companies

(1) Where a company is a charity-

(a) any approval given by the members of the company under any provision of Chapter 4 of Part 10 of the Companies Act 2006 (transactions with directors requiring approval by members) listed in subsection (2) below, and

(b) any affirmation given by members of the company under section 196 or 214 of that Act (affirmation of unapproved property transactions and loans),

is ineffective without the prior written consent of the Commission.

(2) The provisions are-

    (a) section 188 (directors' long-term service contracts);

    (b) section 190 (substantial property transactions with directors etc);

    (c) section 197, 198 or 200 (loans and quasi-loans to directors etc);

    (d) section 201 (credit transactions for benefit of directors etc);

    (e) section 203 (related arrangements);

    (f) section 217 (payments to directors for loss of office);

    (g) section 218 (payments to directors for loss of office: transfer of undertaking etc).

66A   Consent of Commission required for certain acts of charitable company

(1) A company that is a charity may not do an act to which this section applies without the prior written consent of the Commission.

(2) This section applies to an act that-

    (a) does not require approval under a listed provision of Chapter 4 of Part 10 of the Companies Act 2006 (transactions with directors) by the members of the company, but

    (b) would require such approval but for an exemption in the provision in question that disapplies the need for approval on the part of the members of a body corporate which is a wholly-owned subsidiary of another body corporate.

(3) The reference to a listed provision is a reference to a provision listed in section 66(2) above.

(4) If a company acts in contravention of this section, the exemption referred to in subsection (2)(b) shall be treated as of no effect in relation to the act.".

GENERAL NOTE

This section was introduced in the House of Commons. Lord Sainsbury explained the amendment to the Lords as follows:

"Companies legislation requires prior authorisation by the members for certain transactions; for example, loans or payments for loss of office between the company and a director. Section 66 of the Charities Act 1993 renders prior authorisation by the members for transactions such as payments for loss of office invalid unless the Charity Commissioners have given their prior written consent. That reflects concerns that in some cases the members of a charitable company are not independent of the directors, and that requiring their approval would not provide sufficient protection for the charity. Chapter 4 of Pt 10 makes various changes to the provisions on the requirements for prior shareholder authorisation. Amendment No. 157 inserts two new sections into the Charities Act 1993, in place of s.66 of that Act, to reflect the changes made by the Bill" (*Hansard*, HL col.440 (November 2, 2006)).

CHAPTER 5

DIRECTORS' SERVICE CONTRACTS

227. Directors' service contracts

(1) For the purposes of this Part a director's "service contract", in relation to a company, means a contract under which-

(a) a director of the company undertakes personally to perform services (as director or otherwise) for the company, or for a subsidiary of the company, or

(b) services (as director or otherwise) that a director of the company undertakes personally to perform are made available by a third party to the company, or to a subsidiary of the company.

(2) The provisions of this Part relating to directors' service contracts apply to the terms of a person's appointment as a director of a company.

They are not restricted to contracts for the performance of services outside the scope of the ordinary duties of a director.

GENERAL NOTE

This provision defines what is meant by "directors' service contract" for the purposes of Pt 10. Unlike the 1985 Act, a definition common to the whole Part is provided.

Subsection (1)

Lord Sainsbury makes further comments on the changes introduced by this section:

"In line with the recommendations of the Law Commissioners and the Company Law Review, the definition of 'service contracts' is expressly extended so that, in addition to covering contracts of service and contracts for services, it includes letters of appointment to the office of director. As a result, it covers the terms under which a director is appointed to that office alone. The section operates as follows; subs.(1)(a) covers contracts of service such as any employment contract that the director may hold with a company or a subsidiary of the company of which he is director, for example, as an executive director, or any contract for services that he personally undertakes to perform as such. Subsection (1)(b) covers the case where those services are made available to the company through a third party such as a personal services company. In either case, the contract must require the director personally to perform the service or services in question" (*Hansard*, HL GC Day 4, Vol.678, cols 361-362 (February 9, 2006)).

Subsection (2)

"Subsection (2) brings within the definition of a service contract letters of appointment to the office of director. Many directors will have no contract of service or for services with the company. Historically ... an office has been regarded as a kind of property, with the fees attaching to that office being regarded as incident of that office. The second sentence of subs.(2) ensures that the definition of 'service contracts' includes arrangements under which the director performs duties within the scope of the ordinary duties of the director, as well as contracts to perform duties outside the scope of the ordinary duties of a director. Without that, the term 'service contract' might be interpreted as applying only to the latter type of contract" (*Hansard*, HL GC Day 4, Vol.678, cols 361-362 (February 9, 2006)).

228. Copy of contract or memorandum of terms to be available for inspection

(1) A company must keep available for inspection-

(a) a copy of every director's service contract with the company or with a subsidiary of the company, or

(b) if the contract is not in writing, a written memorandum setting out the terms of the contract.

(2) All the copies and memoranda must be kept available for inspection at-

(a) the company's registered office, or

(b) a place specified in regulations under section 1136.

(3) The copies and memoranda must be retained by the company for at least one year from the date of termination or expiry of the contract and must be kept available for inspection during that time.

(4) The company must give notice to the registrar-

(a) of the place at which the copies and memoranda are kept available for inspection, and

(b) of any change in that place,

unless they have at all times been kept at the company's registered office.

(5) If default is made in complying with subsection (1), (2) or (3), or default is made for 14 days in complying with subsection (4), an offence is committed by every officer of the company who is in default.

(6) A person guilty of an offence under this section is liable on summary conviction to a fine not exceeding level 3 on the standard scale and, for continued contravention, a daily default fine not exceeding one-tenth of level 3 on the standard scale.

(7) The provisions of this section apply to a variation of a director's service contract as they apply to the original contract.

GENERAL NOTE

This section and the following two replace s.318 of the 1985 Act. The Explanatory Notes to the Bill state that "the exemption for contracts requiring a director to work outside the United Kingdom (s.318(5) of the 1985 Act) and the exemption for contracts with less than 12 months to run (s.318(11)) have not been retained" (Explanatory Notes, para.396; see further Law Com. No. 261, at paras 9.12-9.17).

Subsection (1)

As with s.318 of the 1985 Act, if a director's contract of service is not in writing a company is obliged to keep a written memorandum setting out the terms of the contract. This caused some concern in the House of Lords as it was unclear why the term "memorandum" should be used. Lord Sainsbury explained the rationale for subs.(1)(b) and the meaning of "memorandum":

> "This seems to be an anti-avoidance provision. Without it, the disclosure requirements imposed by this section could be avoided simply by the director having an unwritten service contract. Section 318 of the Companies Act 1985 was considered by the Law Commissioners, and they did not note any difficulty with this particular requirement. A memorandum is nothing more than a proper written record of the terms of the contract or agreement" (*Hansard*, HL GC Day 4, Vol.678, cols 362-363 (February 9, 2006)).

Subsection (3)

A new section requiring service contracts to be kept available for inspection for one year following termination or expiry.

Subsection (4)

Breach of subss.(1)-(3) results in an offence committed by every officer of the company. Unlike s.318(8) of the 1985 Act, the company itself is no longer liable.

229.   Right of member to inspect and request copy

(1) Every copy or memorandum required to be kept under section 228 must be open to inspection by any member of the company without charge.

(2) Any member of the company is entitled, on request and on payment of such fee as may be prescribed, to be provided with a copy of any such copy or memorandum.

The copy must be provided within seven days after the request is received by the company.

(3) If an inspection required under subsection (1) is refused, or default is made in complying with subsection (2), an offence is committed by every officer of the company who is in default.

(4) A person guilty of an offence under this section is liable on summary conviction to a fine not exceeding level 3 on the standard scale and, for continued contravention, a daily default fine not exceeding one-tenth of level 3 on the standard scale.

(5) In the case of any such refusal or default the court may by order compel an immediate inspection or, as the case may be, direct that the copy required be sent to the person requiring it.

GENERAL NOTE

This section replaces s.318(7)-(9) of the 1985 Act.

Subsection (2)

This section introduces a new right for members to obtain a copy of any contract or memorandum on payment of a fee.

See s.1137 (Regulations about inspection of records and provision of copies).

Subsection (3)

As with s.228(4) (Copy of contract or memorandum of terms to be available for inspection), an offence is no longer committed by the company itself if an inspection is refused.

230. Directors' service contracts: application of provisions to shadow directors

A shadow director is treated as a director for the purposes of the provisions of this Chapter.

GENERAL NOTE

This section replaces s.318(6) of the 1985 Act.

CHAPTER 6

CONTRACTS WITH SOLE MEMBERS WHO ARE DIRECTORS

231. Contract with sole member who is also a director

(1) This section applies where-
   (a) a limited company having only one member enters into a contract with the sole member,
   (b) the sole member is also a director of the company, and
   (c) the contract is not entered into in the ordinary course of the company's business.
(2) The company must, unless the contract is in writing, ensure that the terms of the contract are either-
   (a) set out in a written memorandum, or
   (b) recorded in the minutes of the first meeting of the directors of the company following the making of the contract.
(3) If a company fails to comply with this section an offence is committed by every officer of the company who is in default.
(4) A person guilty of an offence under this section is liable on summary conviction to a fine not exceeding level 5 on the standard scale.
(5) For the purposes of this section a shadow director is treated as a director.
(6) Failure to comply with this section in relation to a contract does not affect the validity of the contract.
(7) Nothing in this section shall be read as excluding the operation of any other enactment or rule of law applying to contracts between a company and a director of the company.

GENERAL NOTE

This section replaces s.322B of the 1985 Act which implements Art.5 of the 12th Company Law Directive (89/667/ EEC). The Explanatory Notes explain that the purpose of this section is

"... to ensure that records are kept in those cases where there is a high risk of the lines becoming blurred between where a person acts in his personal capacity and when he acts on behalf of the company. This may be of particular interest to a liquidator should the company become insolvent" (Explanatory Notes, para.400).

Subsection (1)

The Explanatory Notes accompanying the Bill state that "as the Bill will permit public companies to have a single shareholder, this section applies to both private and public limited companies" (Explanatory Notes, para.401), whilst Companies Act 1985, s.322B(1) explicitly applied only to private limited companies.

Subsection (4)

As with the provisions in Ch.5, liability for breach no longer attaches to the company but only to the officers of the company in default.

Subsection (5)

This subsection extends the provision to impose liability on all shadow directors (see subs.(3)), as opposed to shadow directors who are also sole members (as in s.322B(3) of the 1985 Act).

CHAPTER 7

DIRECTORS' LIABILITIES

Provision protecting directors from liability

232. Provisions protecting directors from liability

(1) Any provision that purports to exempt a director of a company (to any extent) from any liability that would otherwise attach to him in connection with any negligence, default, breach of duty or breach of trust in relation to the company is void.

(2) Any provision by which a company directly or indirectly provides an indemnity (to any extent) for a director of the company, or of an associated company, against any liability attaching to him in connection with any negligence, default, breach of duty or breach of trust in relation to the company of which he is a director is void, except as permitted by-
   (a) section 233 (provision of insurance),
   (b) section 234 (qualifying third party indemnity provision), or
   (c) section 235 (qualifying pension scheme indemnity provision).

(3) This section applies to any provision, whether contained in a company's articles or in any contract with the company or otherwise.

(4) Nothing in this section prevents a company's articles from making such provision as has previously been lawful for dealing with conflicts of interest.

DEFINITIONS

"Associated company": see s.256 (Associated bodies corporate)

GENERAL NOTE

This section replaces s.309A of the 1985 Act, introduced by the Companies (Audit, Investigations and Community Enterprise) Act 2004, without significant change. The difficult relationship between this section and Art.85 of the Table A articles (Companies Act 1985) (and see Companies Act 2006, s.18) is maintained by this section: see subss.(1) and (4). In *Movitex Ltd v Bulfield* [1988] B.C.L.C. 104, it was suggested the problem could be solved by introducing a distinction between duties and disabilities, so that the articles did not provide an exemption from liability for a breach of duty, but redefined a disability. That analysis has been rejected by the Court of Appeal as 'a needless complication' in - *Gwembe Valley Development Co Ltd v Koshy (No.3)* [2003] EWCA Civ 1478, [2004] 1 BCLC 131 at [104]-[109]. So far as the Act in concerned, it too in its statutory statement of directors' duties abandons the distinction between duties and disabilities. This means the problem remains.

The factors that this section must balance are the need to encourage people to undertake the office of directorship whilst protecting company shareholders from loss created by the company director (see *Hansard*, HL GC Day 4, Vol.678, col.363 (February 9, 2006)).

Also see s.1157 (Power of court to grant relief in certain circumstances) (replacing Companies Act 1985, s.727).

Subsection (2)

This subsection extends the exceptions to the prohibition on indemnity insurance to qualifying pension scheme indemnity insurance (subs.(2)(c): see s.235 (Qualifying pension scheme indemnity insurance)). The subsection prevents companies indemnifying directors of other companies in the group, including wholly-owned subsidiaries. Lord Goldsmith explains the reason for this prohibition:

"The 2004 Act, to which I have already drawn attention, closed an important loophole concerning the indemnification of directors by third parties. It used to be the practice in some groups that one group company would indemnify the director of another group company. It was possible thereby in effect to circumvent the rule that the company could not indemnify its own directors. We take the view that that should continue to apply and that what we consider is an important prohibition - to continue to make directors properly accountable for what they do in relation to the company - should stand. I turn to the slightly narrower category in which the director of one group company is indemnified not just by another group company but by the parent of that company. That is a narrower category, but in our view there remains scope for potential mischief there. We are not therefore persuaded that it would be right to provide a carve-out in that category of case" (see *Hansard*, HL GC Day 4, Vol.678, cols 365-367 (February 9, 2006, 2006)).

The Solicitor-General in Committee Stage of the House of Commons went as far as to suggest that "such exemption might even encourage the setting up of artificial group structures to take advantage of it" (HC Comm D, col 640 (July 11, 2006)).

Subsection (3)

This subsection makes it clear that the section applies to provisions found in company articles. Mr Djanogly in the House of Commons, for the Opposition, comments on the inclusion of indemnity provisions in company articles, and in doing so also explains the rationale behind the catch-all 'or otherwise' at the end of subs.(3):

"In light of the changes [to ratification], companies will probably want to consider entering into individual indemnity agreements with directors and to check their articles of association. Most companies have indemnity provisions in favour of the company's directors in their articles of association. However, although the articles in effect form a binding commitment between the company and its members, a director is not a party to that arrangement and may not therefore be able to enforce directly an indemnity in his favour. In *Globalink Telecommunications Ltd v Wilmbury Ltd* [[2002] EWHC 1988 (QB)], it was held that a company's articles of association were not automatically binding as between the company and its officers, but could expressly or impliedly be incorporated into a contract between the company and a director. To mitigate the risk of not being able to enforce an indemnity in the company's articles, directors are therefore increasingly seeking protection of stand-alone indemnities. Many directors already have the benefit of indemnities in contracts with the company - for example, in their service contracts, letters of appointment or stand-alone deeds of indemnity - and companies may want to consider amending the relevant indemnities provide the increased protection permitted as a result of the changes introduced by the 2004 Act" (HC Comm D cols 636-640 (July 11, 2006)).

Subsection (4)

This new section leaves it to the courts to develop the law regarding the relationship between the articles and the Act in relation to conflict of interest clauses. See further s.175 (Duty to avoid conflicts of interest).

233. Provision of insurance

Section 232(2) (voidness of provisions for indemnifying directors) does not prevent a company from purchasing and maintaining for a director of the company, or of an associated company, insurance against any such liability as is mentioned in that subsection.

GENERAL NOTE

This section replaces without substantive change s.309A(5) of the 1985 Act.

234. Qualifying third party indemnity provision

(1) Section 232(2) (voidness of provisions for indemnifying directors) does not apply to qualifying third party indemnity provision.

(2) Third party indemnity provision means provision for indemnity against liability incurred by the director to a person other than the company or an associated company.

Such provision is qualifying third party indemnity provision if the following requirements are met.

(3) The provision must not provide any indemnity against-

    (a) any liability of the director to pay-

        (i) a fine imposed in criminal proceedings, or

   (ii) a sum payable to a regulatory authority by way of a penalty in respect of non-compliance with any requirement of a regulatory nature (however arising); or
   (b) any liability incurred by the director-
       (i) in defending criminal proceedings in which he is convicted, or
       (ii) in defending civil proceedings brought by the company, or an associated company, in which judgment is given against him, or
       (iii) in connection with an application for relief (see subsection (6)) in which the court refuses to grant him relief.
(4) The references in subsection (3)(b) to a conviction, judgment or refusal of relief are to the final decision in the proceedings.
(5) For this purpose-
   (a) a conviction, judgment or refusal of relief becomes final-
       (i) if not appealed against, at the end of the period for bringing an appeal, or
       (ii) if appealed against, at the time when the appeal (or any further appeal) is disposed of; and
   (b) an appeal is disposed of-
       (i) if it is determined and the period for bringing any further appeal has ended, or
       (ii) if it is abandoned or otherwise ceases to have effect.
(6) The reference in subsection (3)(b)(iii) to an application for relief is to an application for relief under-
   section 661(3) or (4) (power of court to grant relief in case of acquisition of shares by innocent nominee), or
   section 1157 (general power of court to grant relief in case of honest and reasonable conduct).

GENERAL NOTE
This section replaces without substantive change s.309B of the 1985 Act.

235. Qualifying pension scheme indemnity provision

(1) Section 232(2) (voidness of provisions for indemnifying directors) does not apply to qualifying pension scheme indemnity provision.
(2) Pension scheme indemnity provision means provision indemnifying a director of a company that is a trustee of an occupational pension scheme against liability incurred in connection with the company's activities as trustee of the scheme.
Such provision is qualifying pension scheme indemnity provision if the following requirements are met.
(3) The provision must not provide any indemnity against-
   (a) any liability of the director to pay-
       (i) a fine imposed in criminal proceedings, or
       (ii) a sum payable to a regulatory authority by way of a penalty in respect of non-compliance with any requirement of a regulatory nature (however arising); or
   (b) any liability incurred by the director in defending criminal proceedings in which he is convicted.
(4) The reference in subsection (3)(b) to a conviction is to the final decision in the proceedings.
(5) For this purpose-
   (a) a conviction becomes final-
       (i) if not appealed against, at the end of the period for bringing an appeal, or
       (ii) if appealed against, at the time when the appeal (or any further appeal) is disposed of; and
   (b) an appeal is disposed of-
       (i) if it is determined and the period for bringing any further appeal has ended, or

(ii) if it is abandoned or otherwise ceases to have effect.

(6) In this section "occupational pension scheme" means an occupational pension scheme as defined in section 150(5) of the Finance Act 2004 (c. 12) that is established under a trust.

GENERAL NOTE

This new provision was introduced as a consequence of Opposition pressure in both the House of Lords and House of Commons. The Opposition considered that s.232 (Provisions protecting directors from liability) went too far in preventing companies from indemnifying the directors of corporate trustees of their occupational pension schemes, especially as there was already a dearth of protection available. The section was introduced by the Government in Committee Stage in the House of Commons:

"The amendments concern the indemnification of a director of a company acting as a trustee of an occupational pension scheme. They deal with worries that were raised in another place. It was said that such directors perform a vital role, often for little direct financial regard, and that directors' and officers' liability insurance policies currently available afford limited protection. We made it clear in another place that the Government attach importance to the work of such directors and that we were aware that it can sometimes be difficult to recruit high-quality directors for companies to indemnify the directors of associated companies acting as trustees of occupational pension schemes. That is what the Government amendments would provide" (*Hansard*, HC Comm D cols 636-637 (July 11, 2006)).

Subsections (2), (3) and (6)

Subsection (2) defines 'third party indemnity provision' as any provision indemnifying a director of a company against liabilities incurred in connection with the company's activities as trustee of an occupational pension scheme. The prohibition on indemnity provisions is narrower in this section than those in s.234 (Qualifying third party indemnity provision).

Under subs.(3), the provisions must not provide an indemnity against any liability of a director to pay a fine or penalty in respect of criminal or regulatory proceedings, or any liability incurred in defending criminal proceedings in which the director is convicted. Unlike s.234 (Qualifying third party indemnity provision), there may be provisions indemnifying a director against any liability incurred in defending civil proceedings brought by the company or an associated company in which judgment is given against him, or in connection with an application for relief.

For the purposes of this section, "occupational pension scheme" is defined as a pension scheme established under a trust "by an employer or employers and having or capable of having effect so as to provide benefits to or in respect of any or all of the employees" of either that or those employers, or any other employers (subs.(6) and s.150(5) of the Finance Act 2004).

236. Qualifying indemnity provision to be disclosed in directors' report

(1) This section requires disclosure in the directors' report of-
   (a) qualifying third party indemnity provision, and
   (b) qualifying pension scheme indemnity provision.
Such provision is referred to in this section as "qualifying indemnity provision".

(2) If when a directors' report is approved any qualifying indemnity provision (whether made by the company or otherwise) is in force for the benefit of one or more directors of the company, the report must state that such provision is in force.

(3) If at any time during the financial year to which a directors' report relates any such provision was in force for the benefit of one or more persons who were then directors of the company, the report must state that such provision was in force.

(4) If when a directors' report is approved qualifying indemnity provision made by the company is in force for the benefit of one or more directors of an associated company, the report must state that such provision is in force.

(5) If at any time during the financial year to which a directors' report relates any such provision was in force for the benefit of one or more persons who were then directors of an associated company, the report must state that such provision was in force.

DEFINITIONS

"Directors' Report": see Pt 15, Ch.5

GENERAL NOTE

This section replaces s.309C(1)-(3) of the 1985 Act. The section is extended to include qualifying pension scheme indemnity provisions.

237.   Copy of qualifying indemnity provision to be available for inspection

(1) This section has effect where qualifying indemnity provision is made for a director of a company, and applies-
   (a) to the company of which he is a director (whether the provision is made by that company or an associated company), and
   (b) where the provision is made by an associated company, to that company.

(2) That company or, as the case may be, each of them must keep available for inspection-
   (a) a copy of the qualifying indemnity provision, or
   (b) if the provision is not in writing, a written memorandum setting out its terms.

(3) The copy or memorandum must be kept available for inspection at-
   (a) the company's registered office, or
   (b) a place specified in regulations under section 1136.

(4) The copy or memorandum must be retained by the company for at least one year from the date of termination or expiry of the provision and must be kept available for inspection during that time.

(5) The company must give notice to the registrar-
   (a) of the place at which the copy or memorandum is kept available for inspection, and
   (b) of any change in that place,
unless it has at all times been kept at the company's registered office.

(6) If default is made in complying with subsection (2), (3) or (4), or default is made for 14 days in complying with subsection (5), an offence is committed by every officer of the company who is in default.

(7) A person guilty of an offence under this section is liable on summary conviction to a fine not exceeding level 3 on the standard scale and, for continued contravention, a daily default fine not exceeding one-tenth of level 3 on the standard scale.

(8) The provisions of this section apply to a variation of a qualifying indemnity provision as they apply to the original provision.

(9) In this section "qualifying indemnity provision" means-
   (a) qualifying third party indemnity provision, and
   (b) qualifying pension scheme indemnity provision.

GENERAL NOTE

This section replaces s.309C(4)-(5) of the 1985 Act. The section is extended to include qualifying pension scheme indemnity provisions.

Subsection (4)

This new section requires all qualifying indemnity provisions to be retained by the company and available for inspection for at least one year from the date of termination or expiry of the provision.

Subsection (6)

This section makes failure to comply with the requirements of this section a criminal offence committed by all officers of the company in default. An offence will no longer be committed by the company itself.

238.   Right of member to inspect and request copy

(1) Every copy or memorandum required to be kept by a company under section 237 must be open to inspection by any member of the company without charge.

(2) Any member of the company is entitled, on request and on payment of such fee as may be prescribed, to be provided with a copy of any such copy or memorandum.

The copy must be provided within seven days after the request is received by the company.

(3) If an inspection required under subsection (1) is refused, or default is made in complying with subsection (2), an offence is committed by every officer of the company who is in default.

(4) A person guilty of an offence under this section is liable on summary conviction to a fine not exceeding level 3 on the standard scale and, for continued contravention, a daily default fine not exceeding one-tenth of level 3 on the standard scale.

(5) In the case of any such refusal or default the court may by order compel an immediate inspection or, as the case may be, direct that the copy required be sent to the person requiring it.

GENERAL NOTE

This section, which gives the members the right to inspect copies of the qualifying indemnity provisions without charge, and to request copies of these upon payment of a prescribed fee. This mirrors s.229 (Right of member to inspect and request copy) in relation to directors' service contracts.

Also see s.1137 (Regulations about inspection of records and provision of copies).

Subsection (3)

An offence is no longer committed by the company itself if an inspection is refused.

Ratification of acts giving rise to liability

239. Ratification of acts of directors

(1) This section applies to the ratification by a company of conduct by a director amounting to negligence, default, breach of duty or breach of trust in relation to the company.

(2) The decision of the company to ratify such conduct must be made by resolution of the members of the company.

(3) Where the resolution is proposed as a written resolution neither the director (if a member of the company) nor any member connected with him is an eligible member.

(4) Where the resolution is proposed at a meeting, it is passed only if the necessary majority is obtained disregarding votes in favour of the resolution by the director (if a member of the company) and any member connected with him.

This does not prevent the director or any such member from attending, being counted towards the quorum and taking part in the proceedings at any meeting at which the decision is considered.

(5) For the purposes of this section-
   (a) "conduct" includes acts and omissions;
   (b) "director" includes a former director;
   (c) a shadow director is treated as a director; and
   (d) in section 252 (meaning of "connected person"), subsection (3) does not apply (exclusion of person who is himself a director).

(6) Nothing in this section affects-
   (a) the validity of a decision taken by unanimous consent of the members of the company, or
   (b) any power of the directors to agree not to sue, or to settle or release a claim made by them on behalf of the company.

(7) This section does not affect any other enactment or rule of law imposing additional requirements for valid ratification or any rule of law as to acts that are incapable of being ratified by the company.

DEFINITIONS

"Connected persons": see s.252 (Persons connected with a director)
"Shadow directors": see s.251 ("Shadow directors"). See Pt 13 (Resolutions and meetings)

GENERAL NOTE

This important provision settles new minimum requirements for effective ratification. The provision draws on existing equitable rules, but imposes more stringent demands. To the extent (if any) that the statutory version is more lenient than the equitable rules, the latter rules - and rules in any other enactment - remain effective to supplement or enhance the statutory requirements (subs.(7)).

Also see s.1157 (Power of court to grant relief in certain circumstances) (replacing Companies Act 1985, s.727).

Subsection (1)

This subsection makes it clear that the provision is designed to afford a mechanism for the company, via its members, to forgive a defaulting director for conduct amounting to negligence, default, breach of duty or breach of trust in relation to the company (i.e. the provision includes all the wrongs which are the subject of Pt 10, including negligence, and not simply fiduciary wrongs).

Subsection (2)

This subsection insists that the ratification must be by resolution of the members of the company. This minimum requirement will apply regardless of any more lenient alternative provided by company's articles, or by existing general law (although these alternative sources can supplement the minimum requirements set by s.239 - see subs.(7)).

Subsections (3) and (4)

These important new subsections indicate that ratification is effective only if the resolution is passed without votes in favour of the resolution by the director (if a member of the company) and any member connected with him.

This changes the law as expressed in *North West Transportation Co Ltd v Beatty* (1887) 12 App. Cas. 589; *Burland v Earle* [1902] A.C.83; and *Pavlides v Jensen* [1956] Ch. 565, but adopts the approach advocated in *Atwool v Merryweather* (1868) L.R. 5 Eq. 464; *Cook v Deeks* [1916] 1 A.C. 554; *Hogg v Cramphorn* [1967] Ch 254; *Bamford v Bamford* [1970] Ch. 212; *Howard Smith Ltd v Ampol Petroleum Ltd* [1975] A.C. 821 PC; *Daniels v Daniels* [1978] Ch. 406; *Prudential Assurance Co Ltd v Newman Industries Ltd (No.2)* [1982] Ch. 204; and *Smith v Croft (No.2)* [1988] Ch 114 at 139.

The Attorney-General, Lord Goldsmith, explained the rationale for the change that this section is intended to bring about:

> "[W]hat we are trying to do in this section ... is disregard the votes, or at least the votes in favour of a resolution, of those who have a personal interest in the ratification. So the intention is to capture those members who are motivated or influenced by personal advantage or gain arising from a vote in favour of ratification. It is intended to be a narrower test than just having an interest in the resolution because, arguably, all the shareholders will have an interest in the resolution" (*Hansard*, HL GC Day 4, Vol.678, col.369 (February 9, 2006)).

Lord Goldsmith was referring here to an earlier version of the section which would have excluded from the ratification procedure all members with a direct or indirect interest. This approach was dropped due to the problems that were envisaged with such wording and the wide-sweeping nature of the section. The section was narrowed to its current format which applies to directors and connected persons. Explaining the change, the Attorney General, Lord Goldsmith, stated the following:

> "It seeks to exclude the votes of the wrongdoer and those persons most likely to be biased in favour of the director or under his influence - namely, the persons connected with him - and makes it easier to identify those persons when the votes are counted" (*Hansard*, HL Report Stage, cols 872-873 (May 9, 2006)).

However, a number of concerns were expressed by the Opposition, which provide a useful illustration of the practical effect that the section may have:

> "The advance of the common law position will place a signification restriction on the actions of directors, make it more difficult to achieve the majority required for ratification, and might lead to an increase in the number of derivative actions taken against company directors. For instance, what if the majority of shares in a company are held by directors, which the norm for smaller family-type companies? In such a situation, their votes will be disregarded for ratification purposes, giving much more power to small shareholders, who will then have leverage over the owners, which will not necessarily serve the best interests of the company. What if the minority shareholder owns say only 1 per cent of the company? Should they still have that veto over ratification?" (*Hansard*, HC Comm D, cols 648-650 (July 13, 2006)).

On the other hand, it is difficult to see why wrongdoers should be able to vote to forgive themselves.

Subsection (5)

This subsection indicates that the section is available for the protection of former directors and shadow directors.

Subsection (6)

The Explanatory Notes accompanying this subsection state:

"*Subsection (6)* makes clear that nothing in this clause changes the law on unanimous consent, so the restrictions imposed by this clause as to who may vote on a ratification resolution will not apply when every members votes (informally or otherwise) in favour of the resolution. The subsection also makes clear that nothing in this clause removes any powers of the directors that they may have to manage the affairs of the company" (Explanatory Notes, para.423).

On unanimous consent, see: *Duomatic Ltd, Re* [1969] 2 Ch. 365 at 373 (need the agreement of every member entitled to vote); *D'Jan of London Ltd, Re* [1994] 1 B.C.L.C. 561 (confirming that all members must actually apply their minds to the question and decide in favour of the proposal); *Demite Ltd v Protec Health Ltd* [1998] B.C.C. 638 (illustrating the potential problems with informal voting if the members themselves are companies); *Bailey Hay and Co Ltd* [1971] 1 WLR 1357 (acquiescence as an alternative to assent).

Subsection (6)(b) also makes it clear that directors retain the power to agree not to sue, or to settle or release a claim made on behalf of the company. The validity of any such actions will be determined by the general law (eg, whether consideration is necessary), the authority of the directors, and the effect of any failure to comply with the statutory duties set out in this Part (especially Chs 2-4).

Subsection (7)

The Attorney General, Lord Goldsmith, indicated that this subsection is intended to make it clear that "the requirements of this section are additional and not alternative to any other requirements as to ratification imposed by statute or under the common law" (*Hansard*, HL Report Stage, col.873 (May 9, 2006)).

For example, the members cannot, either unanimously or by the required statutory majority, overcome prohibitions imposed on the company by the general law, the Companies Act or the company's articles. In addition, any agreement must be fully informed if it is to be effective (*Kaye v Croydon Tramways Co* [1898] 1 Ch. 358; *Baillie v Oriental Telephone and Electric Co Ltd* [1915] 1 Ch. 503; *Knight v Frost* [1999] 1 BCLC 364).

CHAPTER 8

DIRECTORS' RESIDENTIAL ADDRESSES: PROTECTION FROM DISCLOSURE

240. Protected information

(1) This Chapter makes provision for protecting, in the case of a company director who is an individual-

    (a) information as to his usual residential address;

    (b) the information that his service address is his usual residential address.

(2) That information is referred to in this Chapter as "protected information".

(3) Information does not cease to be protected information on the individual ceasing to be a director of the company.

References in this Chapter to a director include, to that extent, a former director.

GENERAL NOTE

Chapter 8 replaces ss.723B-723E of the 1985 Act, introduced by the Criminal Justice and Police Act 2001. These sections introduced a discretionary system of confidentiality orders to protect certain directors from illegal harassment and intimidation by certain protestors. The change in the law was a recommendation of the Company Law Review which "considered that there should not be any discretion as to whether particular addresses should or should not be placed on the public record" (Explanatory Notes, para.427). The provisions in Ch.8 underwent a shift in emphasis at Report Stage in the House of Lords. Initially the clauses would have introduced an "opt-in" system whereby all directors had the option of obtaining a non-disclosure certificate. However, on the basis of a suggestion by the Association of the British Pharmaceutical Industry, an "opt-out" scheme was adopted and the Bill was substantially amended. Lord Sainsbury explained the change as follows:

"Where, under the old clauses, directors would have to apply for a confidentiality certificate to have their home addresses kept off the public record, the new drafting means that all directors will have to make a conscious decision if they want to use their home addresses as their public service addresses. This cuts out the application process and provides a better way of affording protection to people who are not normally troubled by animal rights extremists or other protestors using similar tactics, but may find that a particular contract puts them at risk. This seems a better way of tackling the same problem that was addressed by the earlier clauses" (*Hansard*, HL Report Stage, cols 873-874 (May 9, 2006)).

Lord Sainsbury also commented on the relationship between Ch.8 and the Data Protection Act 1998, in particular liability for breach of the provisions:

"To the extent that home addresses are kept off the public record under the provisions being introduced by the Bill, the main exemption in the 1998 Act, which applies in respect of records kept under the Companies Act 1985, will cease to apply. Consequently, the range of sanctions under the 1998 Act will be available. They include a criminal offence in the case of unauthorised disclosure, and enforcement notices ..." (*Hansard*, HL Report Stage, cols 873-874 (May 9, 2006)).

Subsection (3)

This section makes it clear that former directors' addresses are also "protected information" and therefore within the Ch.8 measures. As such, "protection does not end with employment" (HC Comm D 23/5/06 Col 725). The reason for this section is that "it is no good giving a director of a company the right to withhold his private address if it is already public property when he has been the director of another company" (*Hansard*, HL Report Stage, cols 874-876 (May 9, 2006)).

241. Protected information: restriction on use or disclosure by company

(1) A company must not use or disclose protected information about any of its directors, except-
    (a) for communicating with the director concerned,
    (b) in order to comply with any requirement of the Companies Acts as to particulars to be sent to the registrar, or
    (c) in accordance with section 244 (disclosure under court order).
(2) Subsection (1) does not prohibit any use or disclosure of protected information with the consent of the director concerned.

GENERAL NOTE

This section prohibits a company from using or disclosing protected information unless it either falls within the exceptions in subs.(1) or the director concerned has consented to the information being used or disclosed.

242. Protected information: restriction on use or disclosure by registrar

(1) The registrar must omit protected information from the material on the register that is available for inspection where-
    (a) it is contained in a document delivered to him in which such information is required to be stated, and
    (b) in the case of a document having more than one part, it is contained in a part of the document in which such information is required to be stated.
(2) The registrar is not obliged-
    (a) to check other documents or (as the case may be) other parts of the document to ensure the absence of protected information, or
    (b) to omit from the material that is available for public inspection anything registered before this Chapter comes into force.
(3) The registrar must not use or disclose protected information except-
    (a) as permitted by section 243 (permitted use or disclosure by registrar), or
    (b) in accordance with section 244 (disclosure under court order).

GENERAL NOTE

This section restricts the use or disclosure of protected information by the registrar to the exceptions found in ss.243 (Permitted use or disclosure by the registrar) and 244 (Disclosure under court order). However, subs.(2) makes it clear that the registrar's obligation is not onerous. The registrar is not obliged to check other documents or parts of documents to ensure that protected information is not disclosed, nor to omit from the material that is available for public inspection anything registered before this Chapter comes into force. The reason for the latter exception is that to act otherwise would be impractical and of minimal benefit as the information is already in the public domain.

243.   Permitted use or disclosure by the registrar

(1) The registrar may use protected information for communicating with the director in question.

(2) The registrar may disclose protected information-
  (a) to a public authority specified for the purposes of this section by regulations made by the Secretary of State, or
  (b) to a credit reference agency.

(3) The Secretary of State may make provision by regulations-
  (a) specifying conditions for the disclosure of protected information in accordance with this section, and
  (b) providing for the charging of fees.

(4) The Secretary of State may make provision by regulations requiring the registrar, on application, to refrain from disclosing protected information relating to a director to a credit reference agency.

(5) Regulations under subsection (4) may make provision as to-
  (a) who may make an application,
  (b) the grounds on which an application may be made,
  (c) the information to be included in and documents to accompany an application, and
  (d) how an application is to be determined.

(6) Provision under subsection (5)(d) may in particular-
  (a) confer a discretion on the registrar;
  (b) provide for a question to be referred to a person other than the registrar for the purposes of determining the application.

(7) In this section-
  "credit reference agency" means a person carrying on a business comprising the furnishing of information relevant to the financial standing of individuals, being information collected by the agency for that purpose; and
  "public authority" includes any person or body having functions of a public nature.

(8) Regulations under this section are subject to negative resolution procedure.

GENERAL NOTE

Subsection (2) and (3)

In Grand Committee Lord McKenzie explained why this section allows the registrar to disclose protected information to credit reference agencies:

> "The Government's concern is that a lack of information about the home addresses of a company's directors may have a negative impact on the company's ability to obtain credit. In its response to consultation last year, the Institute of Credit Management urged that: 'This would have a particularly adverse effect on business start-ups - restricting the amount of credit available to them'. In the case of a small company, the credit-worthiness of its directors is relevant to its credit rating. Credit reference agencies need directors' addresses to check, for example, whether there are any court orders against them" (*Hansard*, HL GC Day 4, Vol.678, cols 374-376 (February 9, 2006)).

The disclosure of information by registrars to credit reference agencies is not an open power, but may be subject to conditions laid down by the Secretary of State under subs.(3).

244. Disclosure under court order

(1) The court may make an order for the disclosure of protected information by the company or by the registrar if-

   (a) there is evidence that service of documents at a service address other than the director's usual residential address is not effective to bring them to the notice of the director, or

   (b) it is necessary or expedient for the information to be provided in connection with the enforcement of an order or decree of the court,

and the court is otherwise satisfied that it is appropriate to make the order.

(2) An order for disclosure by the registrar is to be made only if the company-

   (a) does not have the director's usual residential address, or

   (b) has been dissolved.

(3) The order may be made on the application of a liquidator, creditor or member of the company, or any other person appearing to the court to have a sufficient interest.

(4) The order must specify the persons to whom, and purposes for which, disclosure is authorised.

GENERAL NOTE

   The Explanatory Notes indicate that:

   "This clause provides for two circumstances in which the court may require the company to disclose protected information. The first is that the service address is not effective; the second is that the home address is needed for the enforcement of an order or decree of the court. If the company cannot provide the address, the court may require the registrar to reveal it. Subsection (3) provides that the application for the order may be made not only by a liquidator, creditor or member of the company but also by anyone with sufficient interest" (Explanatory Notes, para.433).

245. Circumstances in which registrar may put address on the public record

(1) The registrar may put a director's usual residential address on the public record if-

   (a) communications sent by the registrar to the director and requiring a response within a specified period remain unanswered, or

   (b) there is evidence that service of documents at a service address provided in place of the director's usual residential address is not effective to bring them to the notice of the director.

(2) The registrar must give notice of the proposal-

   (a) to the director, and

   (b) to every company of which the registrar has been notified that the individual is a director.

(3) The notice must-

   (a) state the grounds on which it is proposed to put the director's usual residential address on the public record, and

   (b) specify a period within which representations may be made before that is done.

(4) It must be sent to the director at his usual residential address, unless it appears to the registrar that service at that address may be ineffective to bring it to the individual's notice, in which case it may be sent to any service address provided in place of that address.

(5) The registrar must take account of any representations received within the specified period.

(6) What is meant by putting the address on the public record is explained in section 246.

GENERAL NOTE

   The Explanatory Notes indicate:

   "This clause provides that if a service address is not effective, then the home address can be put on the public record. It provides for the registrar to send a warning notice, with a specified period for representations before the intended revocation, both to the director and to every company of which he is a director. The registrar must take account of any representations made within the specified period in deciding whether to proceed as provided by the next clause" (Explanatory Notes, para.434).

246. Putting the address on the public record

(1) The registrar, on deciding in accordance with section 245 that a director's usual residential address is to be put on the public record, shall proceed as if notice of a change of registered particulars had been given-
  (a) stating that address as the director's service address, and
  (b) stating that the director's usual residential address is the same as his service address.
(2) The registrar must give notice of having done so-
  (a) to the director, and
  (b) to the company.
(3) On receipt of the notice the company must-
  (a) enter the director's usual residential address in its register of directors as his service address, and
  (b) state in its register of directors' residential addresses that his usual residential address is the same as his service address.
(4) If the company has been notified by the director in question of a more recent address as his usual residential address, it must-
  (a) enter that address in its register of directors as the director's service address, and
  (b) give notice to the registrar as on a change of registered particulars.
(5) If a company fails to comply with subsection (3) or (4), an offence is committed by-
  (a) the company, and
  (b) every officer of the company who is in default.
(6) A person guilty of an offence under subsection (5) is liable on summary conviction to a fine not exceeding level 5 on the standard scale and, for continued contravention, a daily default fine not exceeding one-tenth of level 5 on the standard scale.
(7) A director whose usual residential address has been put on the public record by the registrar under this section may not register a service address other than his usual residential address for a period of five years from the date of the registrar's decision.

GENERAL NOTE

This section provides that if a director decides to place a director's residential address on the public record he must proceed as if a notice of a change of registered particulars had been given. A company receiving notice of the registrar placing a director's residential address on the public record must amend its register of directors as appropriate (subs.(3)) or notify the registrar of a more recent usual residential address of the director (subs.(4)). Subsection (5) makes it an offence committed by both the company and all officers in default to fail to comply with subss.(3) or (4). A director whose residential address is placed on the public record cannot register a service address other than his or her usual residential address for a period of five years from the date of the registrar's decision (subs.(7)).

CHAPTER 9

SUPPLEMENTARY PROVISIONS

Provision for employees on cessation or transfer of business

247. Power to make provision for employees on cessation or transfer of business

(1) The powers of the directors of a company include (if they would not otherwise do so) power to make provision for the benefit of persons employed or formerly employed by the

company, or any of its subsidiaries, in connection with the cessation or the transfer to any person of the whole or part of the undertaking of the company or that subsidiary.

(2) This power is exercisable notwithstanding the general duty imposed by section 172 (duty to promote the success of the company).

(3) In the case of a company that is a charity it is exercisable notwithstanding any restrictions on the directors' powers (or the company's capacity) flowing from the objects of the company.

(4) The power may only be exercised if sanctioned-
    (a) by a resolution of the company, or
    (b) by a resolution of the directors,
in accordance with the following provisions.

(5) A resolution of the directors-
    (a) must be authorised by the company's articles, and
    (b) is not sufficient sanction for payments to or for the benefit of directors, former directors or shadow directors.

(6) Any other requirements of the company's articles as to the exercise of the power conferred by this section must be complied with.

(7) Any payment under this section must be made-
    (a) before the commencement of any winding up of the company, and
    (b) out of profits of the company that are available for dividend.

GENERAL NOTE

This section replaces s.719 of the 1985 Act. The only significant change is the inclusion of subs.(3) relating to charities. This subsection renders the power exercisable by a charity notwithstanding any restrictions on the directors' powers or the company's capacity flowing from the objects of the company. However, this is still subject to the company's articles (subs.(6)).

Subsection 5(b)

This subsection makes it clear that the power to make provision for employees cannot be used to avoid the no-conflict duties. This is a change from s.719 of the 1985 Act: "The CLR recommended that directors should be prevented from abusing the power by making excessive payments to themselves" (Explanatory Notes, at para.440).

See s.172 (Duty to promote the success of the company).

See also s.187 of the Insolvency Act 1986 (power to make provision for employees once the company has commenced winding up).

Records of meetings of directors

248.   Minutes of directors' meetings

(1) Every company must cause minutes of all proceedings at meetings of its directors to be recorded.

(2) The records must be kept for at least ten years from the date of the meeting.

(3) If a company fails to comply with this section, an offence is committed by every officer of the company who is in default.

(4) A person guilty of an offence under this section is liable on summary conviction to a fine not exceeding level 3 on the standard scale and, for continued contravention, a daily default fine not exceeding one-tenth of level 3 on the standard scale.

GENERAL NOTE

This section and the next replaces s.382 of the 1985 Act concerning records of meetings of directors.

Subsection (2)

Lord McKenzie explains this new provision, and why ten years was chosen as a time, rather than 12 years as under the Limitation Act:

"Subsection (2) contains a new provision, introducing a minimum period for keeping these records, so as to make it clear that they are not required to be kept in perpetuity. Ten years has been chosen as the period for keeping records of shareholder resolutions and meetings (Records of meetings and resolutions etc). There are advantages in terms of consistency in taking the same approach. We concluded that it would not necessarily help to tie the period that these records should be kept to any particular limitation period. For example, the limitation period for breach of contract runs from the breach, and if minutes prove evidence of a contract, they may date from some years before the breach. Companies may keep the records for longer if they wish to do so. It seems to us that within ten years the company - its directors and others - should have a sense of whether the minutes need too be kept for posterity" (*Hansard*, HL GC Day 4, Vol.678, cols 377-378 (February 9, 2006)).

Subsection (3)

Liability is restricted to every officer of the company in default. The company itself is no longer liable for contravention.

See Pt 37 (Companies: supplementary provisions) on the form in which company records may be kept.

249. Minutes as evidence

(1) Minutes recorded in accordance with section 248, if purporting to be authenticated by the chairman of the meeting or by the chairman of the next directors' meeting, are evidence (in Scotland, sufficient evidence) of the proceedings at the meeting.

(2) Where minutes have been made in accordance with that section of the proceedings of a meeting of directors, then, until the contrary is proved-

    (a) the meeting is deemed duly held and convened,

    (b) all proceedings at the meeting are deemed to have duly taken place, and

    (c) all appointments at the meeting are deemed valid.

GENERAL NOTE

This section replaces those parts of s.382 of the 1985 Act relating to the evidential value of the minutes of directors' meetings without significant change.

Meaning of "director" and "shadow director"

250. "Director"

In the Companies Acts "director" includes any person occupying the position of director, by whatever name called.

GENERAL NOTE

This section restates s.741(1) of the 1985 Act.

251. "Shadow director"

(1) In the Companies Acts "shadow director", in relation to a company, means a person in accordance with whose directions or instructions the directors of the company are accustomed to act.

(2) A person is not to be regarded as a shadow director by reason only that the directors act on advice given by him in a professional capacity.

(3) A body corporate is not to be regarded as a shadow director of any of its subsidiary companies for the purposes of-

Chapter 2 (general duties of directors),

Chapter 4 (transactions requiring members' approval), or

Chapter 6 (contract with sole member who is also a director), by reason only that the directors of the subsidiary are accustomed to act in accordance with its directions or instructions.

GENERAL NOTE

This section restates the definition of "shadow director" found in s.741(2) and (3) of the 1985 Act. The same definition is given in the Insovency Act 1986, s.251 and Company Directors Disqualification Act 1986, s.22(5).

See *Kuwait Asia Bank EC v National Mutual Life Nominees Ltd* [1991] A.C. 187 at 223; *Secretary of State for Trade and Industry v Deverell* [2001] Ch. 304; *Ultraframe (UK) Ltd v Fielding* [2005] EWHC 1638 Ch at [1262]-[1279].

Other definitions

252. Persons connected with a director

(1) This section defines what is meant by references in this Part to a person being "connected" with a director of a company (or a director being "connected" with a person).

(2) The following persons (and only those persons) are connected with a director of a company-

(a) members of the director's family (see section 253);

(b) a body corporate with which the director is connected (as defined in section 254);

(c) a person acting in his capacity as trustee of a trust-

(i) the beneficiaries of which include the director or a person who by virtue of paragraph (a) or (b) is connected with him, or

(ii) the terms of which confer a power on the trustees that may be exercised for the benefit of the director or any such person,

other than a trust for the purposes of an employees' share scheme or a pension scheme;

(d) a person acting in his capacity as partner-

(i) of the director, or

(ii) of a person who, by virtue of paragraph (a), (b) or (c), is connected with that director;

(e) a firm that is a legal person under the law by which it is governed and in which-

(i) the director is a partner,

(ii) a partner is a person who, by virtue of paragraph (a), (b) or (c) is connected with the director, or

(iii) a partner is a firm in which the director is a partner or in which there is a partner who, by virtue of paragraph (a), (b) or (c), is connected with the director.

(3) References in this Part to a person connected with a director of a company do not include a person who is himself a director of the company.

GENERAL NOTE

This section and the following three replace s.346 of the 1985 Act. The rules determining whether a director or a connected person is interested in shares or debentures of a company are contained in Sch.1 (Connected persons: references to an interest in shares or debentures).

Subsection (3)

This section does not apply in so far as the section applies to ratification of acts of directors under s.239 (Ratification of acts of directors).

253. Members of a director's family

(1) This section defines what is meant by references in this Part to members of a director's family.

(2) For the purposes of this Part the members of a director's family are-

(a) the director's spouse or civil partner;

(b) any other person (whether of a different sex or the same sex) with whom the director lives as partner in an enduring family relationship;

(c) the director's children or step-children;

(d) any children or step-children of a person within paragraph (b) (and who are not children or step-children of the director) who live with the director and have not attained the age of 18;

(e) the director's parents.

(3) Subsection (2)(b) does not apply if the other person is the director's grandparent or grandchild, sister, brother, aunt or uncle, or nephew or niece.

GENERAL NOTE

This section replaces those aspects of s.346 of the 1985 relating to a director's spouse, child or step-child. The section significantly extends "connected persons" in relation to a director's family to cover a director's spouse or civil-partner, children and step-children, any person with whom the director lives as partner in an enduring family relationship (which must be read in conjunction with subs.(3)), children and step-children of the person with whom the director lives in an enduring family relationship who are under eighteen and live with the director, and the director's parents. The changes implement the Law Commission's recommendations, with the exception that "connected persons" has not been extended to cover directors' siblings (see Law Com. No. 261, at Pt 14).

Lord Freeman made the following comment on the extension of 'connected persons' to adult children and step-children and to directors' parents:

"Children, even adult children, and parents again seem very much the sorts of people where questions of commonality of interest can arise. The Law Commission thought so and made the recommendation that they should be covered, and it was supported on consultation" (< Hansard, HL GC Day 4, Vol.678, cols 379-380 (February 9, 2006)).

254. Director "connected with" a body corporate

(1) This section defines what is meant by references in this Part to a director being "connected with" a body corporate.

(2) A director is connected with a body corporate if, but only if, he and the persons connected with him together-

(a) are interested in shares comprised in the equity share capital of that body corporate of a nominal value equal to at least 20% of that share capital, or

(b) are entitled to exercise or control the exercise of more than 20% of the voting power at any general meeting of that body.

(3) The rules set out in Schedule 1 (references to interest in shares or debentures) apply for the purposes of this section.

(4) References in this section to voting power the exercise of which is controlled by a director include voting power whose exercise is controlled by a body corporate controlled by him.

(5) Shares in a company held as treasury shares, and any voting rights attached to such shares, are disregarded for the purposes of this section.

(6) For the avoidance of circularity in the application of section 252 (meaning of "connected person")-

(a) a body corporate with which a director is connected is not treated for the purposes of this section as connected with him unless it is also connected with him by virtue of subsection (2)(c) or (d) of that section (connection as trustee or partner); and

(b) a trustee of a trust the beneficiaries of which include (or may include) a body corporate with which a director is connected is not treated for the purposes of this section as connected with a director by reason only of that fact.

GENERAL NOTE

This section replaces s.346(4), (6)-(8) of the 1985 Act without substantive change.

255. Director "controlling" a body corporate

(1) This section defines what is meant by references in this Part to a director "controlling" a body corporate.

(2) A director of a company is taken to control a body corporate if, but only if-
   (a) he or any person connected with him-
      (i) is interested in any part of the equity share capital of that body, or
      (ii) is entitled to exercise or control the exercise of any part of the voting power at any general meeting of that body, and
   (b) he, the persons connected with him and the other directors of that company, together-
      (i) are interested in more than 50% of that share capital, or
      (ii) are entitled to exercise or control the exercise of more than 50% of that voting power.

(3) The rules set out in Schedule 1 (references to interest in shares or debentures) apply for the purposes of this section.

(4) References in this section to voting power the exercise of which is controlled by a director include voting power whose exercise is controlled by a body corporate controlled by him.

(5) Shares in a company held as treasury shares, and any voting rights attached to such shares, are disregarded for the purposes of this section.

(6) For the avoidance of circularity in the application of section 252 (meaning of "connected person")-
   (a) a body corporate with which a director is connected is not treated for the purposes of this section as connected with him unless it is also connected with him by virtue of subsection (2)(c) or (d) of that section (connection as trustee or partner); and
   (b) a trustee of a trust the beneficiaries of which include (or may include) a body corporate with which a director is connected is not treated for the purposes of this section as connected with a director by reason only of that fact.

GENERAL NOTE
This section replaces s.346(5)-(8) of the 1985 Act without substantive change.

256. Associated bodies corporate

For the purposes of this Part-
   (a) bodies corporate are associated if one is a subsidiary of the other or both are subsidiaries of the same body corporate, and
   (b) companies are associated if one is a subsidiary of the other or both are subsidiaries of the same body corporate.

GENERAL NOTE
This new section defines "associated bodies corporate" for the purpose of this Part. The Explanatory Notes indicate:
"A holding company is associated with all its subsidiaries, and a subsidiary is associated with its holding company and all the other subsidiaries of its holding company" (Explanatory Notes, para.454).

257. References to company's constitution

(1) References in this Part to a company's constitution include-
   (a) any resolution or other decision come to in accordance with the constitution, and
   (b) any decision by the members of the company, or a class of members, that is treated by virtue of any enactment or rule of law as equivalent to a decision by the company.

(2) This is in addition to the matters mentioned in section 17 (general provision as to matters contained in company's constitution).

GENERAL NOTE

This new section is to avoid doubt as to the meaning of references in this Part to a company's constitution. See further Pt 3 (A company's constitution).

General

258. Power to increase financial limits

(1) The Secretary of State may by order substitute for any sum of money specified in this Part a larger sum specified in the order.

(2) An order under this section is subject to negative resolution procedure.

(3) An order does not have effect in relation to anything done or not done before it comes into force.

Accordingly, proceedings in respect of any liability incurred before that time may be continued or instituted as if the order had not been made.

GENERAL NOTE

This section restates s.345 of the 1985 Act without substantive change.

259. Transactions under foreign law

For the purposes of this Part it is immaterial whether the law that (apart from this Act) governs an arrangement or transaction is the law of the United Kingdom, or a part of it, or not.

GENERAL NOTE

This section restates s.347 of the 1985 Act.

PART 11

DERIVATIVE CLAIMS AND PROCEEDINGS BY MEMBERS

GENERAL NOTE

Part 11 identifies a procedure whereby a member of the company may seek to institute a derivative claim (in England and Wales or Northern Ireland) or derivative proceedings (in Scotland), i.e. an action seeking relief on behalf of the company in respect of a wrong done to it (see ss.260(1) and 265(1) and (7)(a)). Henceforward, derivative actions may be brought only under this Part or as a result of a court order under the unfair prejudice provisions of the Act (see Pt 30 of the Act) (ss.260(2) and 265(2) and (6)(b)). However, not all wrongs done to the company may be the subject of a derivative action under Pt 11. Only acts or omissions by directors may give rise to derivative actions and where those acts or omissions (actual or proposed) involve 'negligence, default, breach of duty or breach of trust' (ss.260(3) and 265(3)). However, where a cause of action arises out of such acts or omissions on the part of the director, the derivative action may be brought against a third party (as well as or instead of the director), for example, where a third party has knowingly received corporate property as a result of a breach of duty by a director (ss.260(3) and 265(4)).

Thus, the theory behind this Part appears to be that the normal decision-making processes of the company may be left to operate when the wrong to the company has been done by someone other than a director, that process typically being that the decision whether to sue or not is one for the board, as provided in the company's articles. However, because of the potential for a conflict of interest where the alleged wrongdoers include a director, giving the right of decision to the board alone is unsafe. Of course, the shareholders in general meeting might bring litigation in the company's name; and neither this Part nor any other provision of the Act expressly addresses the somewhat vexed question of the circumstances in which and the procedure by which the general meeting may initiate litigation on the company's behalf where the board is unable or unwilling to do so. See *Alexander Ward & Co Ltd v Samyang Navigation Co Ltd* [1975] 1 W.L.R. 673 and *Breckland Group Holdings Ltd v London & Suffolk Properties Ltd* [1989] B.C.L.C. 100. However, the common law always recognised that, in limited circumstances, reliance on the general meeting to bring litigation was likely to be unrealistic and so permitted an individual shareholder in those circumstances to bring a derivative action. Those common law rules, associated with the case of *Foss v Harbottle* (1843) 2 Hare 461 in England and Wales, are now replaced by Pt 11. However, it should be noted that *Foss v Harbottle* and associated cases may continue to be relevant, at least in England and Wales, where the shareholder seeks to enforce a right vested in himself rather than in the company. That such an action is not caught by the new statutory procedure is expressly recognised for Scotland by s.265(6)(a), but the same conclusion would seem to follow for England and Wales (and Northern Ireland) from the definition of a derivative action in s.260(1) as being one where the cause of action is "vested in the company". Nevertheless, where a shareholder seeks to enforce a right vested in himself but derived from the company's articles, the English courts have sometimes seen the *Foss* line of cases as relevant. See *MacDougall v Gardiner* (1875) 1 Ch. D. 13 (Court of Appeal). This line of authority, to the extent that it is persuasive, is not affected by the provisions of Ch.11.

The "rule in *Foss v Harbottle*" identified the situations in which a member could bring a derivative action by reference to three factors: the nature of the wrong committed by the directors (in particular, whether it was ratifiable); the question of whether the alleged wrongdoers had control of the general meeting; and, more recently, the views of the majority of the non-involved shareholders (whether they favoured the litigation). These three tests represented cumulative hurdles for prospective derivative claimants and it was generally agreed that the result was that derivative actions were available only in a narrow set of circumstances. There was also widespread agreement that rules were in some important respects unclear. In 1997 the English Law Commission recommended reform (*Shareholder Remedies*, Cm.3769 (1997)). That reform proposal involved using a significantly different legal technique to identify the availability of the derivative action. Instead of a set of rules which defined when the derivative action was to be available (which is what the rule in *Foss v Harbottle* attempted), the Commission proposed vesting a discretion in the court whether to allow a derivative action. This proposal involved building on a development in the English Civil Procedure Rules which had already occurred as a result of the decision of the Court of Appeal in *Prudential Insurance Co Ltd v Newman Industries (No.2)* [1982] Ch. 204. There the Court of Appeal had insisted upon the importance of determining whether the member had *locus standi* to bring a derivative action in advance of and separately from the hearing on the substantive merits of the claim. Consequently, what is now CPR 19.9 requires a derivative claimant, after the claim form has been issued, to apply to the court for permission to continue the proceedings. At this point the claimant's standing to bring the claim can be considered, if contested. Thus, given the courts' involvement at a preliminary stage under the existing procedure, it was thought to be straightforward to give the court a discretion at this stage in place of an examination of whether the *Foss* rules had been complied with. Moreover, the factors to which the court was to have regard in exercising its discretion were, in part, factors already familiar as constituents of the existing standing rules. In a further, but not necessarily linked proposal, the Commission recommended that the rules governing the exercise of the judicial discretion should be set out in revised Civil Procedure Rules, of which Appendix B to its Report contained a draft.

The Report mentioned above was that of the English and Welsh Commission only. However, in its Appendix D the Scottish Law Commission made recommendations which, it said, were aimed to achieve "a similar practical result" to those proposed for England and Wales. However, the major difference between the jurisdictions, in the Scottish Commissioners' view, was that the rules on derivative actions were in Scotland part of substantive, not procedural, law, so that the proposal to give effect to the reforms mainly through changes to the equivalent of the CPR was not acceptable, and delegated legislation would be needed instead. In fact, this difference over the method of implementing the reforms has become much less important over time. Because of the controversial nature of the underlying proposal to substitute a (constrained) judicial discretion for a set of rules, Pt 11 sets out much more of the framework within which the discretion is to be exercised than had been contemplated by the Law Commission (which envisaged only one clause dealing with English law and one with Scottish law). Moreover, in response to outside representations, that framework was made more elaborate during the Bill's passage through Parliament. See *Hansard*, HL Vol.681, col. col.882 *et seq.*, May 9, 2006. Consequently, much less is left to be dealt with elsewhere, whether in the CPR or delegated legislation. It is in any event controversial even in England and Wales whether the rule in *Foss v Harbottle* is to be regarded as purely procedural law. See *Konamaneni v Rolls Royce Industrial Power (India) Ltd* [2002] 1 W.L.R.1269 at [50].

CHAPTER I

DERIVATIVE CLAIMS IN ENGLAND AND WALES OR NORTHERN IRELAND

Sections 260 to 264 set out the legislative framework for derivative claims in England and Wales and Northern Ireland. They create a procedure whereby the claimant who brings a derivative claim must apply to the court for permission to continue it and set out criteria to guide the court on whether to grant permission.

260.   Derivative claims

(1) This Chapter applies to proceedings in England and Wales or Northern Ireland by a member of a company-

(a) in respect of a cause of action vested in the company, and

(b) seeking relief on behalf of the company.

This is referred to in this Chapter as a "derivative claim".

(2) A derivative claim may only be brought-

(a) under this Chapter, or

(b) in pursuance of an order of the court in proceedings under section 994 (proceedings for protection of members against unfair prejudice).

(3) A derivative claim under this Chapter may be brought only in respect of a cause of action arising from an actual or proposed act or omission involving negligence, default, breach of duty or breach of trust by a director of the company.

The cause of action may be against the director or another person (or both).

(4) It is immaterial whether the cause of action arose before or after the person seeking to bring or continue the derivative claim became a member of the company.

(5) For the purposes of this Chapter-

(a) "director" includes a former director;

(b) a shadow director is treated as a director; and

(c) references to a member of a company include a person who is not a member but to whom shares in the company have been transferred or transmitted by operation of law.

GENERAL NOTE

This section defines what is meant by a derivative claim (1), makes the statutory rules exclusive (2), sets out the circumstances in which a derivative claim may be brought (3), allows claims by current members in relation to prior events (4) and contains definitions (5).

Subsection (1)

This subsection defines a derivative claim for the purposes of the law of England and Wales and Northern Ireland as an action by a member (whether a shareholder or not - defined in s.112) in respect of a cause of action vested in the company and seeking relief on behalf of the company. For the extension of the term member to a person who is not in fact a member (because, for example the directors have refused to enter the transferee's name in the register of members), but to whom shares in the company have been transferred or transmitted by operation of law, for example on the death of the previous holder, see subs.(5)(c). This produces a parallel definition of a member to that to be found in Pt 30 of the Act, dealing with unfair prejudice (see s.994(2)). As both the derivative action and the unfair prejudice remedy are minority shareholder protection remedies, such parallelism is to be welcomed.

Subsection (2)

As recommended by the Law Commission, this section makes the new statutory remedy the exclusive procedure for bringing a derivative action, with the exception of an order by the court for derivative proceedings to be brought as a remedy in a successful unfair prejudice action (see s.996(2)(c)). To this extent the rule in *Foss v Harbottle* is displaced (see the general note to this chapter).

Subsection (3)

A derivative claim may be brought to assert the company's rights only in respect of the category of wrongs listed in this subsection. Only wrongs committed or proposed by directors are included, but the term "director" includes former and shadow directors (subs.(5)). However, not all the wrongs which a director could conceivably commit against the company are within the section, but the included wrongs do encompass breaches of the general duties set out in Ch.2 of Pt 10 of the Act. In particular, derivative claims can now be brought in respect of breaches of the duty of care, normally not permitted under the *Foss* rule. However, it should be noted that the inclusion of former and shadow directors in s.260 does not override the limitations on the circumstances in which the general duties apply to former directors (see s.170(2)) or shadow directors (s.170(5)). However, the phrase "breach of duty" seems to be wider than just the general duties and would encompass, for example, other breaches of duty on the part of the director to the company under the Act, as well as breaches of common law duties not within the statute at all. Provided, however, that the cause of action is in respect of a relevant breach by a director, third parties may be made defendants in the derivative claim, either in lieu of or as well as the director. The general rules which determine whether the company has a claim against third parties in respect of breaches of duty by directors are not set out in the Act, but are to be found in the common law rules relating to knowing assistance in breach of duty by a director or knowing receipt of corporate property in breach of trust.

Subsection (4)

This retains the common law rule that a member may complain of events that occurred before he became a member, but a former member cannot bring a claim even in relation to events occurring when he was a member. This reflects the economic position when a person purchases or sells a share: if the company secures a windfall from previous events just after a shareholder disposes of shares, it is the new holder who takes the benefit - or suffers the detriment if the company suffers an unexpected loss arising out of events before he became a member.

261. Application for permission to continue derivative claim

(1) A member of a company who brings a derivative claim under this Chapter must apply to the court for permission (in Northern Ireland, leave) to continue it.

(2) If it appears to the court that the application and the evidence filed by the applicant in support of it do not disclose a prima facie case for giving permission (or leave), the court-

    (a) must dismiss the application, and

    (b) may make any consequential order it considers appropriate.

(3) If the application is not dismissed under subsection (2), the court-

    (a) may give directions as to the evidence to be provided by the company, and

    (b) may adjourn the proceedings to enable the evidence to be obtained.

(4) On hearing the application, the court may-

    (a) give permission (or leave) to continue the claim on such terms as it thinks fit,

    (b) refuse permission (or leave) and dismiss the claim, or

    (c) adjourn the proceedings on the application and give such directions as it thinks fit.

GENERAL NOTE

This section lays down the procedure which a claimant who has initiated a derivative action must follow in order to obtain the court's permission to continue the action. It thus represents the statutory refinement of the procedure currently contained in the Civil Procedure Rules. The criteria the court should have regard to in determining whether to allow the claim to proceed are set out in s.263.

Subsection (1)

This lays down the basic control that a person bringing a derivative action cannot proceed with it without the permission (or, in Northern Ireland, leave) of the court. The "court" in either jurisdiction means the High Court but may include a county court in England and Wales, subject to the power of the Lord Chancellor to re-define the jurisdictions of the county courts for the purposes of the Companies Acts (s.1156).

Subsection (2)

This subsection deals with the additional procedural stage, introduced after debate in the Lords, in order to reduce the burden on directors in defending unmeritorious cases. See *Hansard*, HL Vol.681, col.883 (May 9, 2006). The subsection contemplates a first stage in which the court considers only the application and evidence submitted by the claimant in order to decide whether it establishes a *prima facie* case for giving permission. However, the section does not appear to make the hearing ex parte, so that the defendants may appear and submit arguments against permission being granted, but are not at this stage required to produce evidence on their side. Presumably, the *prima facie* case for permission would require the court to be satisfied, on a *prima facie* basis, both that the directors have committed the wrong alleged against the company and that permission to continue the case should be given on the criteria set out in s.263. If the court is not so satisfied it must dismiss the application and may make a consequential order (such as an order for costs or an order restraining the applicant from bringing further proceedings).

Subsection (3)

This applies where a *prima facie* case is made out. The court is encouraged to take an active role through its power to give directions about the evidence to be provided by the company. It may and presumably normally will adjourn proceedings for the evidence to be obtained.

Subsection (4)

This subsection refers to the hearing at which the court determines whether permission should be given to continue the action, on the criteria set out in s.263, assuming that the case has survived the *prima facie* scrutiny. This is likely to be a hearing subsequent to the one at which the *prima facie* strength of the case is assessed, though the section does not require this. Presumably, the court will have before it the evidence of the claimant, the company (certainly if so requested by the court and probably in any event) and that of the defendant directors. It thus appears that there could be three preliminary stages: one in which the court has before it only the claimant's evidence; a second in which the court has before it also the evidence it has requested the company to produce but not that of the defendants; and a third in which the claimant's, company's and defendants' evidence are all before it. The court is given three courses of action to choose between, which seem to cover all the available options. It may refuse leave and dismiss the claim. It may adjourn proceedings, with directions, for example, where it requires further evidence. Or it may give permission to continue the claim on such terms as it thinks fit. In this third case the court's powers presumably will include, as under the present CPR 19.9(7), an order that the company indemnify the claimant against the costs incurred in the claim, on the ground that the claim is being brought for the benefit of the company. The criteria governing the court's choice of action are set out in s.263.

262. Application for permission to continue claim as a derivative claim

(1) This section applies where-
    (a) a company has brought a claim, and
    (b) the cause of action on which the claim is based could be pursued as a derivative claim under this Chapter.
(2) A member of the company may apply to the court for permission (in Northern Ireland, leave) to continue the claim as a derivative claim on the ground that-
    (a) the manner in which the company commenced or continued the claim amounts to an abuse of the process of the court,
    (b) the company has failed to prosecute the claim diligently, and
    (c) it is appropriate for the member to continue the claim as a derivative claim.
(3) If it appears to the court that the application and the evidence filed by the applicant in support of it do not disclose a prima facie case for giving permission (or leave), the court-
    (a) must dismiss the application, and
    (b) may make any consequential order it considers appropriate.
(4) If the application is not dismissed under subsection (3), the court-
    (a) may give directions as to the evidence to be provided by the company, and
    (b) may adjourn the proceedings to enable the evidence to be obtained.
(5) On hearing the application, the court may-
    (a) give permission (or leave) to continue the claim as a derivative claim on such terms as it thinks fit,
    (b) refuse permission (or leave) and dismiss the application, or
    (c) adjourn the proceedings on the application and give such directions as it thinks fit.

GENERAL NOTE

This deals with the case where the company itself has instituted a claim which could be pursued as a derivative claim. It might be thought that in such a case the member has nothing to worry about, for the burden of action is being taken up by the company which will obtain the benefit of any relief. However, it is possible that the directors will have caused the company to take up the claim in order to forestall a derivative action. In such circumstances, the member may be able to take over the company's claim as a derivative one and this section deals with the circumstances in which this is possible. Whether at common law a member could take over an action begun by the company seems never to have been determined. Unless the requirements of this section are satisfied, however, the implication is that action by the member is excluded where the company has commenced litigation.

Subsection (1)

This sets out the situation with which the section deals: the claim has been brought by the company but it could have been brought as a derivative claim within the Chapter.

Subsection (2)

This subsection sets out the grounds upon which the member may seek to take over the company's claim. The first is that the manner of its conduct by the company amounts to an abuse of the process of the court - a rather strict test. The second is that the company has not prosecuted the claim diligently. The third is the very open-ended ground that it is appropriate for the claim to be continued as a derivative claim.

These subsections repeat what is stated in subss.(2)-(4) of s.261. Thus, the statutory structure is that, even if, for example, the company has not prosecuted the claim diligently, the member may not take over the claim unless the court would grant the member leave to commence the action if it were being brought as an original derivative action. Subsection (2) and subss.(3)-(5) thus create two hurdles, both of which the member must surmount if he wishes to take over claim commenced by the company. That subss.(3)-(5) require the court to apply the criteria it would apply to a claim being commenced as a derivative action is made clear by s.263(1).

263. Whether permission to be given

(1) The following provisions have effect where a member of a company applies for permission (in Northern Ireland, leave) under section 261 or 262.

(2) Permission (or leave) must be refused if the court is satisfied-
    (a) that a person acting in accordance with section 172 (duty to promote the success of the company) would not seek to continue the claim, or
    (b) where the cause of action arises from an act or omission that is yet to occur, that the act or omission has been authorised by the company, or
    (c) where the cause of action arises from an act or omission that has already occurred, that the act or omission-
        (i) was authorised by the company before it occurred, or
        (ii) has been ratified by the company since it occurred.

(3) In considering whether to give permission (or leave) the court must take into account, in particular-
    (a) whether the member is acting in good faith in seeking to continue the claim;
    (b) the importance that a person acting in accordance with section 172 (duty to promote the success of the company) would attach to continuing it;
    (c) where the cause of action results from an act or omission that is yet to occur, whether the act or omission could be, and in the circumstances would be likely to be-
        (i) authorised by the company before it occurs, or
        (ii) ratified by the company after it occurs;
    (d) where the cause of action arises from an act or omission that has already occurred, whether the act or omission could be, and in the circumstances would be likely to be, ratified by the company;
    (e) whether the company has decided not to pursue the claim;
    (f) whether the act or omission in respect of which the claim is brought gives rise to a cause of action that the member could pursue in his own right rather than on behalf of the company.

(4) In considering whether to give permission (or leave) the court shall have particular regard to any evidence before it as to the views of members of the company who have no personal interest, direct or indirect, in the matter.

(5) The Secretary of State may by regulations-
    (a) amend subsection (2) so as to alter or add to the circumstances in which permission (or leave) is to be refused;
    (b) amend subsection (3) so as to alter or add to the matters that the court is required to take into account in considering whether to give permission (or leave).

(6) Before making any such regulations the Secretary of State shall consult such persons as he considers appropriate.

(7) Regulations under this section are subject to affirmative resolution procedure.

GENERAL NOTE

This section contains the heart of the new procedure because it identifies the criteria the court should use when determining whether to grant permission for the member to continue a derivative action or take over as a derivative an action started by the company. The section contains two types of criteria: those laid out in subs.(2) which require the court to refuse leave to commence or continue the claim and those set out in subs.(3). The latter contains a list of factors which the court must take into account if it does not refuse permission under subs.(2).

Subsection (2)

If any of the conditions set out in (a)-(c) of this subsection is satisfied, the court must refuse permission or leave. (b) and (c) are perhaps straight forward. If the proposed or actual act has been authorised or ratified by the company, the court must refuse permission. This is to be expected: if the act has been authorised or ratified, it no longer constitutes a wrong on the part of the director and the company cannot complain of it, whether through a derivative action or otherwise. Of course, the authorisation or ratification must have been duly effected, a matter which is not dealt with in this section but elsewhere in the Act. See, for example, s.175 on authorisation of conflicts of interest, s.180(4) preserving the common law rules on authorisation generally or s.239 on ratification of acts of directors. Nor does this section purport to answer the question of whether the act in question is capable of authorisation or ratification. Indeed, s.239(7) preserves the common law rules on non-ratifiable breaches of duty and s.180(4) implicitly does the same for authorisation.

Subsection (2)(a) addresses the central issue in granting permission. The member is permitted to sue derivatively, not because it is for the benefit of that member, but because it is for the benefit of the company. Consequently, the crucial issue is whether it is in the interests of 'the company' for such litigation to be brought. The section requires the court to address that question by reference to the definition of the directors' core duty of loyalty in s.172 of the Act. If a director acting to promote the success of the company would not seek to bring the litigation, permission must be denied. Note that this test seems requires the court itself to decide whether the litigation is required to promote the success of the company, by reference to the test of what a hypothetical director would decide in such a case.

These three matters constitute the only complete bars to the court giving permission to the member to continue the derivative claim. In the Parliamentary debates attempts were made to introduce others, but they were resisted by the Government. Consequently, a good faith decision by the board not to sue on behalf of the company is not a bar to a derivative claim (though it is a factor to be taken into account under subs.(3) nor is probability of ratification of the act by the general meeting, though again this is a factor to be taken into account under subs.(3).

Subsection (3)

If the negative proposition debated under subs.(2)(a) cannot be established - i.e. the court cannot say that a director acting in accordance with s.172 would decide not to bring the action - it appears, nevertheless, from subs.(3) that the court is not required in such a case to give permission. Rather, the court has a discretion whether to give permission and must take into account the factors listed in subs.(3) in exercising that discretion. The issue of whether a director acting in accordance with s.172 would be in favour of the litigation is one factor the court must take into account (see (3)(b)), but not the only one. Thus, it appears that the court could refuse permission if it concluded the member was not acting in good faith ((3)(a)), even if it also concluded that a hypothetical director acting in accordance with s.172 would be in favour of the litigation. It is somewhat curious that the court's discretion is formulated in this way (i.e. that the s.172 test is not given overriding or even predominant importance) but it can be said that the factors listed in (c)-(f) are simply factors which a director would take into account in deciding the overall question of whether the success of the company would be promoted by the litigation. The list of factors in subs.(3) is not exclusive, for the court must "take into account in particular" the listed factors.

Subsection (4)

This subsection requires the court to "have particular regard" to the views of the members with no personal interest, direct or indirect, in the matter. The phrase 'particular regard' seems to attach to this factor a significance above that accorded to the factors listed in subs.(3), as indeed does its setting out in a separate sub-section. It builds upon the decision of Knox J. in *Smith v Croft (No.2)* [1988] Ch. 114.

Subsections (5)-(7)

These sub-sections permit the Secretary of State by regulation, approved by affirmative resolution, and after consultation to alter (including presumably remove) or add to the circumstances mentioned in sub-sections (2) and (3), but not, seemingly, to alter the architecture of the sections, for example, by prioritising the factors laid out in subs.(3).

264. Application for permission to continue derivative claim brought by another member

(1) This section applies where a member of a company ("the claimant")-
   (a) has brought a derivative claim,
   (b) has continued as a derivative claim a claim brought by the company, or
   (c) has continued a derivative claim under this section.

(2) Another member of the company ("the applicant") may apply to the court for permission (in Northern Ireland, leave) to continue the claim on the ground that-

    (a) the manner in which the proceedings have been commenced or continued by the claimant amounts to an abuse of the process of the court,

    (b) the claimant has failed to prosecute the claim diligently, and

    (c) it is appropriate for the applicant to continue the claim as a derivative claim.

(3) If it appears to the court that the application and the evidence filed by the applicant in support of it do not disclose a prima facie case for giving permission (or leave), the court-

    (a) must dismiss the application, and

    (b) may make any consequential order it considers appropriate.

(4) If the application is not dismissed under subsection (3), the court-

    (a) may give directions as to the evidence to be provided by the company, and

    (b) may adjourn the proceedings to enable the evidence to be obtained.

(5) On hearing the application, the court may-

    (a) give permission (or leave) to continue the claim on such terms as it thinks fit,

    (b) refuse permission (or leave) and dismiss the application, or

    (c) adjourn the proceedings on the application and give such directions as it thinks fit.

GENERAL NOTE

    This section envisages a member seeking permission to take over a derivative claim already commenced by another member or a derivative claim taken over by another member from the company or a derivative claim previously taken over by the other member under this section (subs.(1)). The grounds (set out in subs.(2)) upon which the member may seek to take this step and the procedure (set out in subss.(3)-(5)) to be followed are the same as those set out for the taking over of an action commenced by the company (see s.262). The major difference between this section and s.262, however, is that the court is not formally required to take the further step of exercising its discretion under s.263 (which does not refer to s.264). This is presumably because, the action which the member is seeking to take over being in derivative form, the requirements of s.263 have already been satisfied. However, the section does not appear to state that, if one of the grounds set out in subs.(2) is satisfied, the court must give the member leave to take over the claim. Subsection (5) appears to confer upon the court a discretion as to the action it takes once one or more of the grounds is made out, but the Act does not give the court any further guidance as to how it should exercise that discretion.

CHAPTER 2

DERIVATIVE PROCEEDINGS IN SCOTLAND

GENERAL NOTE

    Scots law has always recognised that a member of a company may, in appropriate circumstances, bring proceedings in the name of the company to recover a loss suffered by the company where its directors cannot take proceedings in the name of the company itself, or refuse to do so, such as where it is established that the board of directors is effectively under the control of the alleged wrong-doer (*Anderson v Hogg* 2000 S.L.T. 634 and (on appeal) 2002 SLT 354; *Wilson v Inverness Retail and Business Park Ltd* 2003 SLT 301). Chapter 2 of Pt 11 of the 2006 Act replaces the common law with a statutory basis for such "derivative proceedings". It also introduces into Scots law the requirement that such proceedings may be raised only with the leave of the court and specifies the conditions which require to be satisfied for the granting of such leave. This is not catered for by the rules of court in Scotland as they currently stand; appropriate amendments will have to be made by Scottish Statutory Instrument before these provisions are commenced.

265.   Derivative proceedings

(1) In Scotland, a member of a company may raise proceedings in respect of an act or omission specified in subsection (3) in order to protect the interests of the company and obtain a remedy on its behalf.

(2) A member of a company may raise such proceedings only under subsection (1).

(3) The act or omission referred to in subsection (1) is any actual or proposed act or omission involving negligence, default, breach of duty or breach of trust by a director of the company.

(4) Proceedings may be raised under subsection (1) against (either or both)-

(a) the director referred to in subsection (3), or

(b) another person.

(5) It is immaterial whether the act or omission in respect of which the proceedings are to be raised or, in the case of continuing proceedings under section 267 or 269, are raised, arose before or after the person seeking to raise or continue them became a member of the company.

(6) This section does not affect-

(a) any right of a member of a company to raise proceedings in respect of an act or omission specified in subsection (3) in order to protect his own interests and obtain a remedy on his own behalf, or

(b) the court's power to make an order under section 996(2)(c) or anything done under such an order.

(7) In this Chapter-

(a) proceedings raised under subsection (1) are referred to as "derivative proceedings",

(b) the act or omission in respect of which they are raised is referred to as the "cause of action",

(c) "director" includes a former director,

(d) references to a director include a shadow director, and

(e) references to a member of a company include a person who is not a member but to whom shares in the company have been transferred or transmitted by operation of law.

GENERAL NOTE

Subsections (1) and (2)

These prohibit a member of a company from raising proceedings to obtain a remedy on its behalf except under subs.(1), which provides the statutory basis for such proceedings in place of the common law referred to in the General Note above.

Siubsections (3) and (4)

Proceedings under subs.(1) may be raised in respect of any actual or proposed act or omission involving negligence, default, breach of duty or breach of trust by a director, but proceedings may be against either or both of the director in question and any other person alleged to be liable to compensate the company as a result of that act or omission.

Subsection (5)

A member may bring proceedings even if the act or omission complained of occurred before he became a member of the company.

Subsection (6)

This preserves any right a member may have in respect of a loss suffered by him personally, whether or not the company also has a right to recover loss in respect of the same act or omission. The Scottish courts may be expected to follow the line of authorities in England which prevents a shareholder from recovering, as a personal claim, the loss in value of his shareholding which is merely "reflective" of the loss recoverable by derivative proceedings (See *Prudential Assurance Co Ltd v Newman Industries Ltd (No.2)* [1981] Ch. 257; *Giles v Rhind* [2002] 4 All E.R. 977, CA and the discussion in *Palmer's Company Law,* paras 8.809-810.1). Section 265 is also without prejudice to the right of a member to bring proceedings in respect of "unfair prejudice" under Pt 30 of the Act (formerly ss.459-461 of the Companies Act 1985).

Subsection (7)

This defines the proceedings referred to in ss.265-269 as "derivative proceedings". The act or omission in respect of which they are raised is referred to as the "cause of action" and the references to "directors" extend to a former director or a shadow director, and those to a "member" include a person to whom shares have been transferred or have transmitted by operation of law although not yet registered as a member of the company.

266.   Requirement for leave and notice

(1) Derivative proceedings may be raised by a member of a company only with the leave of the court.

(2) An application for leave must-

   (a) specify the cause of action, and

   (b) summarise the facts on which the derivative proceedings are to be based.

(3) If it appears to the court that the application and the evidence produced by the applicant in support of it do not disclose a prima facie case for granting it, the court-

   (a) must refuse the application, and

   (b) may make any consequential order it considers appropriate.

(4) If the application is not refused under subsection (3)-

   (a) the applicant must serve the application on the company,

   (b) the court-

   (i) may make an order requiring evidence to be produced by the company, and

   (ii) may adjourn the proceedings on the application to enable the evidence to be obtained, and

   (c) the company is entitled to take part in the further proceedings on the application.

(5) On hearing the application, the court may-

   (a) grant the application on such terms as it thinks fit,

   (b) refuse the application, or

   (c) adjourn the proceedings on the application and make such order as to further procedure as it thinks fit.

GENERAL NOTE

Subsection (1)

Leave of the court is required before derivative proceedings may be commenced. "The court" is defined in s.1156(1)(b) as the Court of Session or the Sheriff Court. Section 1156(2) preserves "any enactment or rule of law relating to the allocation of jurisdiction ... between courts". Accordingly, the Scottish Rules of Court determine whether the Sheriff Court has concurrent jurisdiction with the Court of Session for the purposes of granting leave to commence derivative proceedings.

Subsection (2)

Amendments to the Scottish Rules of Court will presumably specify the form which an application for leave to commence derivative proceedings must take. Subsection (2) requires the petition or initial writ to specify the act or omission in respect of which it is to be raised and to aver the material facts. Subsection (3) implies that this must be accompanied by "evidence", presumably in the form of productions, which the Rules of Court will require to specify.

Subsection (3)

If the court considers that the application and evidence produced do not disclose a *prima facie* case for granting the remedy sought, the court must refuse the application and may make any consequential order it considers appropriate (e.g. with respect to expenses).

Subsection (4)

No provision is made for intimating an application for leave to commence derivative proceedings under s.266(2) to the company or to any person whose act or omission is alleged to give rise to the cause of action. If, however, the application is not refused under subs.(3), it must then be served on the company. No provision is made in s.266 for service of the proceedings on any person alleged to be responsible for the cause of action. Such a requirement may, however, be provided for in the Rules of Court when these have been amended to take account of s.266.

Subs. (4) confers upon the court the power to require the production of evidence by the company. It is also provided that the company has locus to enter the process. While no provision is made in s.266 for the person whose act or omission is alleged to give rise to the cause of action to enter the process, it must be assumed that such a person can state an interest in the proceedings and lodge answers to the application accordingly.

Subsection (5)

Upon hearing the application, the court may grant it on such terms as it thinks fit, refuse the application or adjourn the proceedings and make such order as the court thinks appropriate.

267. Application to continue proceedings as derivative proceedings

(1) This section applies where-
    (a) a company has raised proceedings, and
    (b) the proceedings are in respect of an act or omission which could be the basis for derivative proceedings.
(2) A member of the company may apply to the court to be substituted for the company in the proceedings, and for the proceedings to continue in consequence as derivative proceedings, on the ground that-
    (a) the manner in which the company commenced or continued the proceedings amounts to an abuse of the process of the court,
    (b) the company has failed to prosecute the proceedings diligently, and
    (c) it is appropriate for the member to be substituted for the company in the proceedings.
(3) If it appears to the court that the application and the evidence produced by the applicant in support of it do not disclose a prima facie case for granting it, the court-
    (a) must refuse the application, and
    (b) may make any consequential order it considers appropriate.
(4) If the application is not refused under subsection (3)-
    (a) the applicant must serve the application on the company,
    (b) the court-
        (i) may make an order requiring evidence to be produced by the company, and
        (ii) may adjourn the proceedings on the application to enable the evidence to be obtained, and
    (c) the company is entitled to take part in the further proceedings on the application.
(5) On hearing the application, the court may-
    (a) grant the application on such terms as it thinks fit,
    (b) refuse the application, or
    (c) adjourn the proceedings on the application and make such order as to further procedure as it thinks fit.

GENERAL NOTE

Subsections (1) and (2)

Section 267 applies where the company has already commenced proceedings alleging a cause of action which could have founded derivative proceedings by a member. In such a case a member may apply to the court to be substituted as pursuer or petitioner, and for proceedings to continue as if they were "derivative proceedings" on the basis that he alleges that the company's conduct of the proceedings amounts to an abuse of process, or that the company has failed to prosecute them diligently and that it is appropriate for the member to be substituted for the company in the proceedings. Abuse of process or want of diligence are the only grounds upon which this may be granted.

The form of such an application and the evidence and productions that support it will require to be specified in amended rules of court.

Subsection (3)

The court is required to determine whether the application and the evidence produced disclose a *prima facie* case for granting the application. If not, it must refuse the application and may make any consequential order it considers appropriate.

Subsection (4)

If the application is not refused, it must be served by the applicant on the company. The court may order the company to produce additional evidence and may adjourn proceedings for this purpose. The company may continue to participate in the proceedings.

As with an application to raise derivative proceedings, the Act does not require an application to substitute a member for the company to be served on any other person, such as the director alleged to be responsible for the cause of action. This may, however, be provided for in rules of court.

Subsection (5)

On hearing the application the court has discretion to grant it on such terms as it thinks fit, to refuse it or to adjourn for further procedure.

268. Granting of leave

(1) The court must refuse leave to raise derivative proceedings or an application under section 267 if satisfied-

    (a) that a person acting in accordance with section 172 (duty to promote the success of the company) would not seek to raise or continue the proceedings (as the case may be), or

    (b) where the cause of action is an act or omission that is yet to occur, that the act or omission has been authorised by the company, or

    (c) where the cause of action is an act or omission that has already occurred, that the act or omission-

        (i) was authorised by the company before it occurred, or

        (ii) has been ratified by the company since it occurred.

(2) In considering whether to grant leave to raise derivative proceedings or an application under section 267, the court must take into account, in particular-

    (a) whether the member is acting in good faith in seeking to raise or continue the proceedings (as the case may be),

    (b) the importance that a person acting in accordance with section 172 (duty to promote the success of the company) would attach to raising or continuing them (as the case may be),

    (c) where the cause of action is an act or omission that is yet to occur, whether the act or omission could be, and in the circumstances would be likely to be-

        (i) authorised by the company before it occurs, or

        (ii) ratified by the company after it occurs,

    (d) where the cause of action is an act or omission that has already occurred, whether the act or omission could be, and in the circumstances would be likely to be, ratified by the company,

    (e) whether the company has decided not to raise proceedings in respect of the same cause of action or to persist in the proceedings (as the case may be),

    (f) whether the cause of action is one which the member could pursue in his own right rather than on behalf of the company.

(3) In considering whether to grant leave to raise derivative proceedings or an application under section 267, the court shall have particular regard to any evidence before it as to the views of members of the company who have no personal interest, direct or indirect, in the matter.

(4) The Secretary of State may by regulations-

    (a) amend subsection (1) so as to alter or add to the circumstances in which leave or an application is to be refused,

    (b) amend subsection (2) so as to alter or add to the matters that the court is required to take into account in considering whether to grant leave or an application.

(5) Before making any such regulations the Secretary of State shall consult such persons as he considers appropriate.

(6) Regulations under this section are subject to affirmative resolution procedure.

GENERAL NOTE

Subsection (1)

The court is not allowed to grant leave to commence derivative proceedings or to substitute a member for the company as pursuer or petitioner if the cause of action was authorised or ratified by the company. The Act does not explain what it means by "ratified by the company". Presumably, the intention is that the common law rules on what constitutes valid ratification will apply, including the exclusion from a vote in favour of ratification of the alleged wrongdoer and those associated with him. The question of whether the cause of action has been validly ratified will be a matter for the court to determine after taking such considerations into account. The court will also have to consider whether the cause of action is a breach of duty by a director (which can in principle be ratified by ordinary resolution) or ultra vires the company (which requires a special resolution).

The court is also required to refuse an application to commence derivative proceedings if it considers that a person acting in accordance with s.172 (which requires a director to exercise his or her powers to promote the success of the company) would not seek to raise or continue the proceedings. This is likely to require the court to make a commercial judgement on the merits of the act or omission to which the proposed proceedings relates, which, historically, the courts have been reluctant to undertake.

Subsection (2)

This sets out the considerations which (if the proceedings are not barred by subs.(1)) the court must take into account in considering whether to grant leave, and which therefore must be addressed in the application and evidence produced. The court requires to take into account whether the applicant is acting in good faith, whether the proceedings would contribute to "the success of the company", whether the cause of action has been or is likely to be ratified, whether the company is already pursuing the same cause of action and whether the member has an independent right of recovery in his or her own name. Apart from addressing the issues specified in subs.(2) this again requires the court to exercise its commercial judgement and, where relevant, to anticipate the judgement of a majority of the disinterested members of the company.

Subsection (3)

The court is also required to take into account the views of members who have no personal interest in the matter, in so far as these have been made available. The views of such persons will no doubt be of considerable assistance to the court in exercising its judgement under subss.(1) and (2).

Subsections (4)-(6)

The Secretary of State is authorised to amend subss.(1) and (2) after appropriate consultation, by Statutory Instrument, subject to affirmative resolution procedure.

269. Application by member to be substituted for member pursuing derivative proceedings

(1) This section applies where a member of a company ("the claimant")-
    (a) has raised derivative proceedings,
    (b) has continued as derivative proceedings raised by the company, or
    (c) has continued derivative proceedings under this section.

(2) Another member of the company ("the applicant") may apply to the court to be substituted for the claimant in the action on the ground that-
    (a) the manner in which the proceedings have been commenced or continued by the claimant amounts to an abuse of the process of the court,
    (b) the claimant has failed to prosecute the proceedings diligently, and
    (c) it is appropriate for the applicant to be substituted for the claimant in the proceedings.

(3) If it appears to the court that the application and the evidence produced by the applicant in support of it do not disclose a prima facie case for granting it, the court-
    (a) must refuse the application, and
    (b) may make any consequential order it considers appropriate.

(4) If the application is not refused under subsection (3)-
    (a) the applicant must serve the application on the company,
    (b) the court-

       (i) may make an order requiring evidence to be produced by the company, and

       (ii) may adjourn the proceedings on the application to enable the evidence to be obtained, and

    (c) the company is entitled to take part in the further proceedings on the application.

  (5) On hearing the application, the court may-

    (a) grant the application on such terms as it thinks fit,

    (b) refuse the application, or

    (c) adjourn the proceedings on the application and make such order as to further procedure as it thinks fit.

GENERAL NOTE

Subsections (1) and (2)

Where a member is petitioner or pursuer in derivative proceedings, another member may apply to be substituted on the grounds that the conduct of the proceedings is an abuse of process, is being inadequately prosecuted or that, in any case, it is appropriate for the applicant to be substituted as pursuer or petitioner.

Subsection (3)

The court is required to refuse an application if it, together with the evidence produced in support, does not disclose a *prima facie* case for granting it. The court may make any consequential order it considers appropriate.

Subsection (4)

If the court does not refuse the application it must be served on the company. Presumably, the rules of court will also require it to be served upon the member whom the applicant seeks to replace, and upon any person whose alleged act or omission is the cause of action. The company is entitled to take part in further proceedings, and the court will presumably allow any other person with an interest in the matter to do so.

Subsection (5)

On hearing a application under s.269, the court may grant it on such terms as it thinks fit, refuse it or adjourn the proceedings on such terms as it thinks fit.

PART 12

COMPANY SECRETARIES

GENERAL NOTE

Part 12 is concerned with company secretaries, replacing ss.283-290 of the Companies Act 1985. In addition to many detailed changes, the major difference is that private companies will no longer be required to appoint a company secretary. This change was recommended by the CLR in Ch.4 (para.4.7) of their *Final Report* (2001), having consulted on this issue in their papers: *Developing the Framework* (March 2000) (paras 7.34-7.36) and Completing the Structure (November 2000) (paras 2.18-2.22). Additional consultation followed in the White Paper of March 2005 (Cm 6456) (para.4.5). The CLR stressed that this recommendation would not of course remove the obligation on the company to carry out the functions that a company normally carries out. Further, a private company would continue to be able to appoint a company secretary if that was its wish and the appointee would be able to carry out the functions of that office with the full authority that a company secretary has hitherto had under Companies Act 1985.

The requirement to appoint a secretary will now apply only to public companies and s.272 gives the Secretary of State a new power to direct a public company which is in breach of this requirement to appoint a secretary.

As was the case under the 1985 Act, the secretary (including the secretary of a private company which has one) is an officer of the company, see s.1173(1).

Private companies

270. Private company not required to have secretary

  (1) A private company is not required to have a secretary.

(2) References in the Companies Acts to a private company "without a secretary" are to a private company that for the time being is taking advantage of the exemption in subsection (1); and references to a private company "with a secretary" shall be construed accordingly.

(3) In the case of a private company without a secretary-

    (a) anything authorised or required to be given or sent to, or served on, the company by being sent to its secretary-

        (i) may be given or sent to, or served on, the company itself, and

        (ii) if addressed to the secretary shall be treated as addressed to the company; and

    (b) anything else required or authorised to be done by or to the secretary of the company may be done by or to-

        (i) a director, or

        (ii) a person authorised generally or specifically in that behalf by the directors.

GENERAL NOTE

Subsection (1)

This new provision excludes private companies from the requirement to appoint a secretary (now applicable only to public companies - see s.271). A private company may continue to appoint a secretary if that is its wish - in which event the provisions of the remaining subsections of s.270 and ss.274-280 will apply to such a secretary. Also, when this subs.(1) comes into force, any appointment of a secretary of a private company then in force would not be affected by this provision but would continue in force until brought to an end in the usual manner (e.g. by resignation of the secretary or by decision of the directors).

Private company - see s.4.

Subsection (2)

This new provision defines the expressions: *private company without a secretary* and *private company with a secretary* which are used in other provisions of this Act (in particular s.44 (execution of documents) and s.270(3), below).

Subsection (3)

This new provision sets out the manner in which, in the case of a company which does not have a secretary, (a) documents may be sent to or served on the company and (b) anything else to be done by or to the secretary may be done.

Public companies

271. Public company required to have secretary

A public company must have a secretary.

GENERAL NOTE

This section restates s.283(1) of the 1985 Act but this requirement for a company to have a secretary only now applies to public companies.

Public company - see s.4.

272. Direction requiring public company to appoint secretary

(1) If it appears to the Secretary of State that a public company is in breach of section 271 (requirement to have secretary), the Secretary of State may give the company a direction under this section.

(2) The direction must state that the company appears to be in breach of that section and specify-

    (a) what the company must do in order to comply with the direction, and

    (b) the period within which it must do so.

That period must be not less than one month or more than three months after the date on which the direction is given.

(3) The direction must also inform the company of the consequences of failing to comply.
(4) Where the company is in breach of section 271 it must comply with the direction by-
    (a) making the necessary appointment, and
    (b) giving notice of it under section 276,
before the end of the period specified in the direction.
(5) If the company has already made the necessary appointment, it must comply with the direction by giving notice of it under section 276 before the end of the period specified in the direction.
(6) If a company fails to comply with a direction under this section, an offence is committed by-
    (a) the company, and
    (b) every officer of the company who is in default.
For this purpose a shadow director is treated as an officer of the company.
(7) A person guilty of an offence under this section is liable on summary conviction to a fine not exceeding level 5 on the standard scale and, for continued contravention, a daily default fine not exceeding one-tenth of level 5 on the standard scale.

GENERAL NOTE

This is a new provision supporting the requirement in s.271 for public companies to have a secretary. If it appears to the Secretary of State that a public company is in breach of that provision, the Secretary of State may give a direction to the company which requires the company to appoint a secretary and to notify that appointment to the registrar under s.276.

Subsection (5) deals with the situation if the company has already appointed a secretary when a direction under this section is made - in which case the company is just required to notify the appointment to the registrar under s.276.

273. Qualifications of secretaries of public companies

(1) It is the duty of the directors of a public company to take all reasonable steps to secure that the secretary (or each joint secretary) of the company-
    (a) is a person who appears to them to have the requisite knowledge and experience to discharge the functions of secretary of the company, and
    (b) has one or more of the following qualifications.
(2) The qualifications are-
    (a) that he has held the office of secretary of a public company for at least three of the five years immediately preceding his appointment as secretary;
    (b) that he is a member of any of the bodies specified in subsection (3);
    (c) that he is a barrister, advocate or solicitor called or admitted in any part of the United Kingdom;
    (d) that he is a person who, by virtue of his holding or having held any other position or his being a member of any other body, appears to the directors to be capable of discharging the functions of secretary of the company.
(3) The bodies referred to in subsection (2)(b) are-
    (a) the Institute of Chartered Accountants in England and Wales;
    (b) the Institute of Chartered Accountants of Scotland;
    (c) the Association of Chartered Certified Accountants;
    (d) the Institute of Chartered Accountants in Ireland;
    (e) the Institute of Chartered Secretaries and Administrators;
    (f) the Chartered Institute of Management Accountants;
    (g) the Chartered Institute of Public Finance and Accountancy.

GENERAL NOTE

This section restates s.286 of the 1985 Act without substantial amendment.

Subsection (2)

The specified qualifications are the same as were specified in s.286(1) of the 1985 Act but now omit a transitional qualification of having held on December 22, 1980 the office of secretary or assistant or deputy secretary of the company.

Subsection (3)

The bodies specified are the same bodies as were specified in s.286(2) of the 1985 Act, but their names have been updated to those current at the date of enactment of the 2006 Act.

Provisions applying to private companies with a secretary and to public companies

274. Discharge of functions where office vacant or secretary unable to act

Where in the case of any company the office of secretary is vacant, or there is for any other reason no secretary capable of acting, anything required or authorised to be done by or to the secretary may be done-

    (a) by or to an assistant or deputy secretary (if any), or

    (b) if there is no assistant or deputy secretary or none capable of acting, by or to any person authorised generally or specifically in that behalf by the directors.

GENERAL NOTE

This section restates without substantial amendment s.283(3) of the 1985 Act.

This section is expressed to apply to "any company" but the cross heading before ss.274-280 indicates that these provisions apply only to private companies with a secretary and to public companies. This ambiguity is unfortunate as the contents of this provision would clearly be of assistance to a private company without a secretary in complying with any requirement which assumes that the company has a secretary.

275. Duty to keep register of secretaries

(1) A company must keep a register of its secretaries.

(2) The register must contain the required particulars (see sections 277 to 279) of the person who is, or persons who are, the secretary or joint secretaries of the company.

(3) The register must be kept available for inspection-

    (a) at the company's registered office, or

    (b) at a place specified in regulations under section 1136.

(4) The company must give notice to the registrar-

    (a) of the place at which the register is kept available for inspection, and

    (b) of any change in that place,

unless it has at all times been kept at the company's registered office.

(5) The register must be open to the inspection-

    (a) of any member of the company without charge, and

    (b) of any other person on payment of such fee as may be prescribed.

(6) If default is made in complying with subsection (1), (2) or (3), or if default is made for 14 days in complying with subsection (4), or if an inspection required under subsection (5) is refused, an offence is committed by-

    (a) the company, and

    (b) every officer of the company who is in default.

For this purpose a shadow director is treated as an officer of the company.

(7) A person guilty of an offence under this section is liable on summary conviction to a fine not exceeding level 5 on the standard scale and, for continued contravention, a daily default fine not exceeding one-tenth of level 5 on the standard scale.

(8) In the case of a refusal of inspection of the register, the court may by order compel an immediate inspection of it.

GENERAL NOTE

This section restates s.288(1) and (3)-(5) of the 1985 Act, though that provision related to a register of directors and secretaries (for the register of directors see now s.162). The 1985 provision required the register to be kept at the registered office but subs.(3) now allows an alternative of the register being kept at a place specified in regulations under s.1136.

This section is expressed to apply to "any company" but the cross heading before ss.274-280 indicates that these provisions apply only to private companies with a secretary and to public companies. It is not clear whether a private company which does not have secretary is required to keep a register of secretaries but this is unlikely to be a practical issue as printed register books and company secretarial software will usually automatically provide such a register.

Subsection (4)

This is a new provision - the need for notice to be given of the place at which the register is kept arises because, while the 1985 Act required the register to be kept at the registered office, subs.(3) now allows an alternative of the register being kept at a place specified in regulations under s.1136.

Registered office - see s.86.

276. Duty to notify registrar of changes

(1) A company must, within the period of 14 days from-
   (a) a person becoming or ceasing to be its secretary or one of its joint secretaries, or
   (b) the occurrence of any change in the particulars contained in its register of secretaries,
give notice to the registrar of the change and of the date on which it occurred.

(2) Notice of a person having become secretary, or one of joint secretaries, of the company must be accompanied by a consent by that person to act in the relevant capacity.

(3) If default is made in complying with this section, an offence is committed by every officer of the company who is in default. For this purpose a shadow director is treated as an officer of the company.

(4) A person guilty of an offence under this section is liable on summary conviction to a fine not exceeding level 5 on the standard scale and, for continued contravention, a daily default fine not exceeding one-tenth of level 5 on the standard scale.

GENERAL NOTE

This section restates without substantial amendment s.288(2) of the 1985 Act, though that provision related to changes to a register of directors and secretaries (for changes to the register of directors see now s.167).

277. Particulars of secretaries to be registered: individuals

(1) A company's register of secretaries must contain the following particulars in the case of an individual-
   (a) name and any former name;
   (b) address.

(2) For the purposes of this section "name" means a person's Christian name (or other forename) and surname, except that in the case of-
   (a) a peer, or
   (b) an individual usually known by a title,
the title may be stated instead of his Christian name (or other forename) and surname or in addition to either or both of them.

(3) For the purposes of this section a "former name" means a name by which the individual was formerly known for business purposes.

Where a person is or was formerly known by more than one such name, each of them must be stated.

(4) It is not necessary for the register to contain particulars of a former name in the following cases-

(a) in the case of a peer or an individual normally known by a British title, where the name is one by which the person was known previous to the adoption of or succession to the title;

(b) in the case of any person, where the former name-

(i) was changed or disused before the person attained the age of 16 years, or

(ii) has been changed or disused for 20 years or more.

(5) The address required to be stated in the register is a service address.

This may be stated to be "The company's registered office".

GENERAL NOTE

This section (taken together with s.278) restates with amendments s.290 of the 1985 Act which lays down the particulars of secretaries which must be entered in the register of directors and notified to the registrar.

Subsection (3)

"Former name" means a name or names by which a person was formerly known for business purposes - the 1985 Act did not include the limitation of the provision to names used for business purposes.

Subsection (4)

Under this new provision (based on s.289(2) of the 1985 Act, which applied only to directors) former names need not be given (i) of a secretary who is a peer or who is known by a British title and (ii) where the name has not been used for 20 years or since the secretary attained the age of 16 years (the 1985 Act specified the age of 18 years). Unlike the 1985 Act provision, there is now no exclusion for former names by which married women were known prior to marriage.

Subsection (5)

The address to be shown for the secretary is required to be a service address (see s.1141) (the 1985 Act provision required the usual residential address to be shown). The address may be stated as "The company's registered office".

278. Particulars of secretaries to be registered: corporate secretaries and firms

(1) A company's register of secretaries must contain the following particulars in the case of a body corporate, or a firm that is a legal person under the law by which it is governed-

(a) corporate or firm name;

(b) registered or principal office;

(c) in the case of an EEA company to which the First Company Law Directive (68/151/EEC) applies, particulars of-

(i) the register in which the company file mentioned in Article 3 of that Directive is kept (including details of the relevant state), and

(ii) the registration number in that register;

(d) in any other case, particulars of-

(i) the legal form of the company or firm and the law by which it is governed, and

(ii) if applicable, the register in which it is entered (including details of the state) and its registration number in that register.

(2) If all the partners in a firm are joint secretaries it is sufficient to state the particulars that would be required if the firm were a legal person and the firm had been appointed secretary.

GENERAL NOTE

This section restates with amendments provisions which were contained in s.290 of the 1985 Act; which lays down the particulars which must be entered in the register of directors and notified to the registrar concerning secretaries which are bodies corporate or firms.

Subsection (1)

Items (c) and (d) are new requirements concerning the particulars of secretaries which are EEA companies and requiring in any other case particulars to be given of the legal form and governing law and of any relevant registration.

EEA company - see s.1170.

279.   Particulars of secretaries to be registered: power to make regulations

(1) The Secretary of State may make provision by regulations amending-
    section 277 (particulars of secretaries to be registered: individuals), or
    section 278 (particulars of secretaries to be registered: corporate secretaries and firms),
  so as to add to or remove items from the particulars required to be contained in a company's
register of secretaries.
  (2) Regulations under this section are subject to affirmative resolution procedure.

GENERAL NOTE
   Affirmative resolution procedure - see s.1290.

280.   Acts done by person in dual capacity

A provision requiring or authorising a thing to be done by or to a director and the secretary of
a company is not satisfied by its being done by or to the same person acting both as director and
as, or in place of, the secretary.

GENERAL NOTE
   This section restates s.284 of the 1985 Act without amendment. The 1985 Act provision was considered to be effectively
an extension of the principle in s.283(2) of the 1985 Act that a sole director may not also be a secretary but that provision has
been repealed by, and not reenacted in the 2006 Act.

PART 13

RESOLUTIONS AND MEETINGS

CHAPTER I

GENERAL PROVISIONS ABOUT RESOLUTIONS

281.   Resolutions

(1) A resolution of the members (or of a class of members) of a private company must be
     passed-
     (a) as a written resolution in accordance with Chapter 2, or
     (b) at a meeting of the members (to which the provisions of Chapter 3 apply).
(2) A resolution of the members (or of a class of members) of a public company must be
     passed at a meeting of the members (to which the provisions of Chapter 3 and, where
     relevant, Chapter 4 apply).
(3) Where a provision of the Companies Acts-
     (a) requires a resolution of a company, or of the members (or a class of members) of a
          company, and
     (b) does not specify what kind of resolution is required,
 what is required is an ordinary resolution unless the company's articles require a higher majority
(or unanimity).
     (4) Nothing in this Part affects any enactment or rule of law as to-
     (a) things done otherwise than by passing a resolution,
     (b) circumstances in which a resolution is or is not treated as having been passed, or
     (c) cases in which a person is precluded from alleging that a resolution has not been duly
          passed.

GENERAL NOTE

Part 13 is concerned with resolutions and meetings of companies, replacing ss.366-383 of the Companies Act 1985. In addition to many detailed changes, the major differences are that: (i) private companies will no longer be required to hold any formal meetings (including an AGM) but may instead use written resolutions. Partly as a consequence, the elective resolution regime has been discontinued; (ii) extraordinary resolutions have been dropped; and (iii) quoted companies will be subject to the right to demand an independent audit of any poll conducted by the company.

The changes are based mainly on the CLR's recommendations in Chs 2, 6 and 7 of their *Final Report* (2001), having consulted on these issues in their paper *Company General Meetings and Shareholder Communications* (URN 99/1144). Additional consultations followed in the White Papers of July 2002 (Cm.5553-1) and March 2005 (Cm 6456). Some of the sections were also drafted with the proposed directive on *The exercise of voting rights by shareholders of companies having their registered office in a Member State and whose shares are admitted to trading on a regulated market* (COM(2005) 685 final, January 5, 2006) in mind. In particular the draft directive is concerned with electronic voting and equal treatment of shareholders, including the counting of all votes.

Part 13 has seven Chapters. Chapter 1 applies general rules to the passing of all resolutions; Ch.2 contains the modified written resolution procedure for private companies; Ch.3 applies to formal meetings of any company; Ch.4 applies additional rules for AGMs of public companies; Ch.5 introduces the new poll audit provisions for quoted companies; Ch.6 is concerned with record keeping; and Ch.7 is supplementary.

Subsection (1)

This new provision allows private companies the choice of passing resolutions at a meeting or (except for those dismissing a director or an auditor) by the modified written resolution procedure in Ch.2. In fact they may also still continue to use the informal consent or *Duomatic* principle (see subs.(4)).

Subsection (2)

This new provision provides that public companies cannot use the written resolution procedure, they must hold meetings under the procedures set out in Ch.3. This is partly because the Second Directive (79/91/EEC) requires certain resolutions to be taken in general meeting, and the consultations produced little enthusiasm for public companies being able to opt out of AGMs (a CLR recommendation). In theory, however, the *Duomatic* principle also applies to public companies.

Subsection (3)

This new provision provides a default position where the type of resolution required under a provision of the Act is not specified (if it is so specified, it is usually as a special resolution). In such cases it is to be taken to be an ordinary resolution (as defined in the next section), unless the articles of the company provide for a higher majority or unanimity. This new right to provide for a higher majority in the articles cannot apply where an ordinary resolution is expressly provided for in this Act, e.g. on a resolution to dismiss a director under s.168, since in that case the type of resolution is specified.

Subsection (4)

Derived from s.381C(2) of the 1985 Act, this preserves the unanimous consent or *Duomatic* principle as a general alternative to both the written resolution and formal resolution procedures. That principle, encapsulated in *Duomatic Ltd, Re* [1969] 2 Ch. 365, applies to most but not all resolutions (generally excluding those which are required for the protection of interests other than those of the shareholders). Its flexibility persuaded the Government not to codify the principle - see the 2005 White Paper (Cm.6456), paras 2.31-2.35.

282. Ordinary resolutions

(1) An ordinary resolution of the members (or of a class of members) of a company means a resolution that is passed by a simple majority.

(2) A written resolution is passed by a simple majority if it is passed by members representing a simple majority of the total voting rights of eligible members (see Chapter 2).

(3) A resolution passed at a meeting on a show of hands is passed by a simple majority if it is passed by a simple majority of-

(a) the members who, being entitled to do so, vote in person on the resolution, and

(b) the persons who vote on the resolution as duly appointed proxies of members entitled to vote on it.

(4) A resolution passed on a poll taken at a meeting is passed by a simple majority if it is passed by members representing a simple majority of the total voting rights of members who (being entitled to do so) vote in person or by proxy on the resolution.

(5) Anything that may be done by ordinary resolution may also be done by special resolution.

GENERAL NOTE

This new section in effect codifies the common law definition of an ordinary resolution (see *Bushell v Faith* [1970] AC 1099). This is the default resolution under the Act (see the previous section).

Subsection (2)

This looks forward to the fact that written resolutions no longer need be unanimous but only require the appropriate majority.

Subsection (3)

For potential problems arising from the appointment of multiple proxies, see s.284.

283.   Special resolutions

(1) A special resolution of the members (or of a class of members) of a company means a resolution passed by a majority of not less than 75%.

(2) A written resolution is passed by a majority of not less than 75% if it is passed by members representing not less than 75% of the total voting rights of eligible members (see Chapter 2).

(3) Where a resolution of a private company is passed as a written resolution-
   (a) the resolution is not a special resolution unless it stated that it was proposed as a special resolution, and
   (b) if the resolution so stated, it may only be passed as a special resolution.

(4) A resolution passed at a meeting on a show of hands is passed by a majority of not less than 75% if it is passed by not less than 75% of-
   (a) the members who, being entitled to do so, vote in person on the resolution, and
   (b) the persons who vote on the resolution as duly appointed proxies of members entitled to vote on it.

(5) A resolution passed on a poll taken at a meeting is passed by a majority of not less than 75% if it is passed by members representing not less than 75% of the total voting rights of the members who (being entitled to do so) vote in person or by proxy on the resolution.

(6) Where a resolution is passed at a meeting-
   (a) the resolution is not a special resolution unless the notice of the meeting included the text of the resolution and specified the intention to propose the resolution as a special resolution, and
   (b) if the notice of the meeting so specified, the resolution may only be passed as a special resolution.

GENERAL NOTE

This section is derived from s.378(1), (2), (3) and (5) of the 1985 Act. The concept of an extraordinary resolution has been discontinued. Special resolutions will continue to require a 75 per cent majority, but will no longer require 21 days' notice. The text of a written resolution or the notice of the meeting must state that the resolution is proposed as a special resolution and it can then only be passed as such (subss.(3) and (6)).

Subsection (2)

This reflects the fact that written resolutions no longer require unanimous consent, only the requisite majority.

Subsection (4)

For potential problems arising from the appointment of multiple proxies, see s.284.

284. Votes: general rules

(1) On a vote on a written resolution-
    (a) in the case of a company having a share capital, every member has one vote in respect of each share or each £10 of stock held by him, and
    (b) in any other case, every member has one vote.

(2) On a vote on a resolution on a show of hands at a meeting-
    (a) every member present in person has one vote, and
    (b) every proxy present who has been duly appointed by a member entitled to vote on the resolution has one vote.

(3) On a vote on a resolution on a poll taken at a meeting-
    (a) in the case of a company having a share capital, every member has one vote in respect of each share or each £10 of stock held by him, and
    (b) in any other case, every member has one vote.

(4) The provisions of this section have effect subject to any provision of the company's articles.

GENERAL NOTE

This section sets out the general default voting rights of shareholders whether on a written resolution, a show of hands or a poll. It is derived from s.370(6) and para.54 of Table A. Its main thrust is to ensure equality of voting either by one vote per share (on a written resolution or a poll) or one vote per person (on a show of hands) - see Art.14 of the draft directive, Com(2005)865 final. The provisions are subject to contrary provisions in the articles, thus preserving, e.g. weighted voting (*Bushell v Faith* [1970] A.C. 1099) or restricted-voting preference shares - but see the following section. As to challenges to voting rights, see s.294.

Subsection (1) and (3)

Under this Act, companies will no longer be able to issue stock; but the current position formerly in s.370(6) of the 1985 Act is preserved because stock may still be held in fractional amounts.

Subsection (2)

The provision allowing one vote on a show of hands per duly appointed proxy by each member is designed to apply to pool nominees, i.e. where several members appoint the same proxy. That proxy will be able to cast one vote for each appointing member.

But it seems to have an unintended consequence where one member, with say ten shares, appoints ten proxies, one for each share, which he is entitled to do under s.324. In such a case it seems that each proxy will have one vote on a show of hands, since they will have been duly appointed, giving ten in all; whereas if the member had voted in person he would only have had one vote (cf. s.285(2)). In practice, however, the right to demand a poll (one vote per share) will then be important.

285. Votes: specific requirements

(1) Where a member entitled to vote on a resolution has appointed one proxy only, and the company's articles provide that the proxy has fewer votes in a vote on a resolution on a show of hands taken at a meeting than the member would have if he were present in person-
    (a) the provision about how many votes the proxy has on a show of hands is void, and
    (b) the proxy has the same number of votes on a show of hands as the member who appointed him would have if he were present at the meeting.

(2) Where a member entitled to vote on a resolution has appointed more than one proxy, subsection (1) applies as if the references to the proxy were references to the proxies taken together.

(3) In relation to a resolution required or authorised by an enactment, if a private company's articles provide that a member has a different number of votes in relation to a resolution when it is passed as a written resolution and when it is passed on a poll taken at a meeting-

(a) the provision about how many votes a member has in relation to the resolution passed on a poll is void, and

(b) a member has the same number of votes in relation to the resolution when it is passed on a poll as he has when it is passed as a written resolution.

GENERAL NOTE

This new section, corresponding in part to Art.10 of the draft directive, COM(2005)865 final, provides that members appointing proxies cannot be disadvantaged in voting terms by anything in a company's articles. Any such article is void and proxies are given the same voting rights as if the member were present.

Subsection (2)

This wording avoids the problem of the appointment of multiple proxies by one member, found in s.284.

Subsection (3)

The extension of the section to written resolutions reflects the fact that unanimous approval is no longer required. But note that it only applies to resolutions required or authorised by an enactment, which would not as such apply to those required purely by the articles or the common law with no statutory purpose or link.

286. Votes of joint holders of shares

(1) In the case of joint holders of shares of a company, only the vote of the senior holder who votes (and any proxies duly authorised by him) may be counted by the company.

(2) For the purposes of this section, the senior holder of a share is determined by the order in which the names of the joint holders appear in the register of members.

(3) Subsections (1) and (2) have effect subject to any provision of the company's articles.

GENERAL NOTE

This section enacts, as a default provision, what was para.55 of Table A. In HC Committee D, col.300, the minister confirmed that there was no intention to change the accepted way in which this section will operate. That is that the vote of the most senior named shareholder who votes will be counted. Thus, e.g. if the first named person on the register does not vote but the second and third ones do, the second named person will take priority.

There is no intention to limit the number of joint holders of shares, either in statute or the default articles. For challenges to the right to vote, see s.287.

287. Saving for provisions of articles as to determination of entitlement to vote

Nothing in this Chapter affects-

(a) any provision of a company's articles-

(i) requiring an objection to a person's entitlement to vote on a resolution to be made in accordance with the articles, and

(ii) for the determination of any such objection to be final and conclusive, or

(b) the grounds on which such a determination may be questioned in legal proceedings.

GENERAL NOTE

This new section preserves both the rights of companies to provide in their articles a procedure as to how any right to vote may be challenged and for the determination of such a challenge. It also continues the existing law on the limited grounds for any possible legal challenge to such a determination, e.g. fraud or misconduct.

CHAPTER 2

WRITTEN RESOLUTIONS

General provisions about written resolutions

288. Written resolutions of private companies

(1) In the Companies Acts a "written resolution" means a resolution of a private company proposed and passed in accordance with this Chapter.

(2) The following may not be passed as a written resolution-

   (a) a resolution under section 168 removing a director before the expiration of his period of office;

   (b) a resolution under section 510 removing an auditor before the expiration of his term of office.

(3) A resolution may be proposed as a written resolution-

   (a) by the directors of a private company (see section 291), or

   (b) by the members of a private company (see sections 292 to 295).

(4) References in enactments passed or made before this Chapter comes into force to-

   (a) a resolution of a company in general meeting, or

   (b) a resolution of a meeting of a class of members of the company,

have effect as if they included references to a written resolution of the members, or of a class of members, of a private company (as appropriate).

(5) A written resolution of a private company has effect as if passed (as the case may be)-

   (a) by the company in general meeting, or

   (b) by a meeting of a class of members of the company,

and references in enactments passed or made before this section comes into force to a meeting at which a resolution is passed or to members voting in favour of a resolution shall be construed accordingly.

GENERAL NOTE

The following 13 sections replace ss.381A, 381B and 381C of the 1985 Act on the written resolution procedure for private companies, introduced by the 1989 Act and as amended by SI 1996/1471. They continue the trend of relaxation of the rules and follow recommendations of the CLR, *Final Report*, paras 4.2 and 7.26, and para.32 of the 2005 White Paper (Cm.6456).

The major changes are: (i) no need for unanimous consent, just the appropriate majority; (ii) no auditor involvement; (iii) no necessity for hard copy; (iv) no provision to allow an alternative written resolution procedure under the articles for statutory resolutions; and (v) closer alignment with the procedures for formal resolutions - that is consequent on the abolition of the unanimity rule. However, note that the procedure still cannot be used for dismissing a director or an auditor. Otherwise the procedure cannot, so far as statutory procedures are concerned, be negated by the articles: s.300.

The decision not to allow companies to provide an alternative written resolution procedure under their articles was taken deliberately in so far as statutory resolutions are concerned. However, the informal passing of a resolution within the parameters of the *Duomatic* principle has been retained by virtue of s.281(4). Following an alternative written procedure, however, might amount to a de facto resolution under the *Duomatic* principle in some cases.

This section replaces, in part, s.381A and a small part of Sch.15A to the 1985 Act. It provides for the possibility of such resolutions being proposed either by the directors or members of a private company.

Subsection (2)

This preserves the exceptions for the dismissal of a director or auditor.

Subsections (4) and (5)

These subsections not only provide for the effectiveness of written resolutions but also allow for their use in class meetings (*quaere* whether it will be used in a scheme of arrangement).

289.   Eligible members

(1) In relation to a resolution proposed as a written resolution of a private company, the eligible members are the members who would have been entitled to vote on the resolution on the circulation date of the resolution (see section 290).

(2) If the persons entitled to vote on a written resolution change during the course of the day that is the circulation date of the resolution, the eligible members are the persons entitled to vote on the resolution at the time that the first copy of the resolution is sent or submitted to a member for his agreement.

GENERAL NOTE

Based on s.381A of the 1985 Act, this section defines the members entitled to vote on a written resolution as those entitled to vote on the circulation date. It also makes provision for the situation where those persons change on that date. In certain cases the resolution can be sent electronically or even posted on a website.

Circulation date - s.290.

Circulation of written resolutions

290.   Circulation date

References in this Part to the circulation date of a written resolution are to the date on which copies of it are sent or submitted to members in accordance with this Chapter (or if copies are sent or submitted to members on different days, to the first of those days).

GENERAL NOTE

This section, also based on s.381A of the 1985 Act, defines the circulation date of a written resolution. The resolution can be sent or submitted in hard copy, electronically or even on a website: see ss.298 and 299.

291.   Circulation of written resolutions proposed by directors

(1) This section applies to a resolution proposed as a written resolution by the directors of the company.

(2) The company must send or submit a copy of the resolution to every eligible member.

(3) The company must do so-

   (a) by sending copies at the same time (so far as reasonably practicable) to all eligible members in hard copy form, in electronic form or by means of a website, or

   (b) if it is possible to do so without undue delay, by submitting the same copy to each eligible member in turn (or different copies to each of a number of eligible members in turn),

or by sending copies to some members in accordance with paragraph (a) and submitting a copy or copies to other members in accordance with paragraph (b).

(4) The copy of the resolution must be accompanied by a statement informing the member-

   (a) how to signify agreement to the resolution (see section 296), and

   (b) as to the date by which the resolution must be passed if it is not to lapse (see section 297).

(5) In the event of default in complying with this section, an offence is committed by every officer of the company who is in default.

(6) A person guilty of an offence under this section is liable-

   (a) on conviction on indictment, to a fine;

   (b) on summary conviction, to a fine not exceeding the statutory maximum.

(7) The validity of the resolution, if passed, is not affected by a failure to comply with this section.

GENERAL NOTE

Derived from s.381A of the 1985 Act, this section provides the mechanism for circulation of a written resolution by the directors. Circulation can be effected by sending a separate copy to each of the eligible members simultaneously or (if there is no undue delay) by sending the same or a separate copy to each member consecutively, or by a combination of any of these. Since the resolution must be passed within 28 days of the sending out of the first copy (s.297) any delay which materially affects compliance with that, would surely be regarded as unreasonable.

Circulation can be effected by hard copy, email or on a website. In addition to the terms of the resolution, additional information is required by subs.(4).

eligible member - s.289.

Subsections (5)-(7)

The sanction for any breach of the section is criminal and not civil. The intention is to preserve commercial certainty, although deliberate failure to circulate a member might well amount to unfairly prejudicial conduct since that depends on conduct and not the validity of the resolution as such.

292. Members' power to require circulation of written resolution

(1) The members of a private company may require the company to circulate a resolution that may properly be moved and is proposed to be moved as a written resolution.

(2) Any resolution may properly be moved as a written resolution unless-

    (a) it would, if passed, be ineffective (whether by reason of inconsistency with any enactment or the company's constitution or otherwise),

    (b) it is defamatory of any person, or

    (c) it is frivolous or vexatious.

(3) Where the members require a company to circulate a resolution they may require the company to circulate with it a statement of not more than 1,000 words on the subject matter of the resolution.

(4) A company is required to circulate the resolution and any accompanying statement once it has received requests that it do so from members representing not less than the requisite percentage of the total voting rights of all members entitled to vote on the resolution.

(5) The "requisite percentage" is 5% or such lower percentage as is specified for this purpose in the company's articles.

(6) A request-

    (a) may be in hard copy form or in electronic form,

    (b) must identify the resolution and any accompanying statement, and

    (c) must be authenticated by the person or persons making it.

GENERAL NOTE

This new section is modelled on s.314 of the 1985 Act which allows members of a public company to propose a resolution at an AGM. It provides for the right of members holding at least 5 per cent of the relevant voting rights to request and so require that a written resolution be circulated (under the terms of following section). They may also require circulation of a statement not exceeding 1,000 words on the subject matter of the resolution. The form of the request(s) is set out in subs.(6).

Subsection (2)

There is a limit to this power on the grounds of the resolution being ineffective, defamatory, frivolous or vexatious. The section itself provides no specific mechanism for the resolution of any dispute on these points. Although there are no equivalent restrictions on the right to have the accompanying statement circulated, s.295 applies so as to allow the court to stop the circulation of any statement where the rights under this section are being abused, which must surely include such matters.

293.   Circulation of written resolution proposed by members

(1) A company that is required under section 292 to circulate a resolution must send or submit to every eligible member-

    (a) a copy of the resolution, and

    (b) a copy of any accompanying statement.

This is subject to section 294(2) (deposit or tender of sum in respect of expenses of circulation) and section 295 (application not to circulate members' statement).

(2) The company must do so-

    (a) by sending copies at the same time (so far as reasonably practicable) to all eligible members in hard copy form, in electronic form or by means of a website, or

    (b) if it is possible to do so without undue delay, by submitting the same copy to each eligible member in turn (or different copies to each of a number of eligible members in turn),

or by sending copies to some members in accordance with paragraph (a) and submitting a copy or copies to other members in accordance with paragraph (b).

(3) The company must send or submit the copies (or, if copies are sent or submitted to members on different days, the first of those copies) not more than 21 days after it becomes subject to the requirement under section 292 to circulate the resolution.

(4) The copy of the resolution must be accompanied by guidance as to-

    (a) how to signify agreement to the resolution (see section 296), and

    (b) the date by which the resolution must be passed if it is not to lapse (see section 297).

(5) In the event of default in complying with this section, an offence is committed by every officer of the company who is in default.

(6) A person guilty of an offence under this section is liable-

    (a) on conviction on indictment, to a fine;

    (b) on summary conviction, to a fine not exceeding the statutory maximum.

(7) The validity of the resolution, if passed, is not affected by a failure to comply with this section.

GENERAL NOTE

This new section is consequent on the exercise of the rights of members in the previous section. Subject to an application to the court not to circulate the statement under s.302 and the provision of expenses by the requisitionists under s.294 the company must circulate the resolution and statement to all eligible members.

This must be done in the same format and by the same methods as if it were a resolution proposed by the directors under s.291. Additional information is required by subs.(4).

eligible member - s.289.

Subsection (3)

The resolution must be circulated within 21 days of the requirement to do so arising. Note that if the resolution is circulated to the members on different days, only the first copy need comply with that time limit. There is no specific time limit on subsequent copies sent to other members, although under subs.2(b) there must be no unreasonable delay. Since s.297 requires any written resolution to be passed within 28 days of that first date, any late circulation beyond or marginal to that time will surely be regarded as unreasonable.

Subsections (5)-(7)

The penalty for breach of this section is criminal for those officers in default and not civil. That will ensure commercial certainty, but it should not affect the possibility of a remedy for unfairly prejudicial conduct in appropriate circumstances since that is based on conduct and not the validity of the resolution as such.

294.   Expenses of circulation

(1) The expenses of the company in complying with section 293 must be paid by the members who requested the circulation of the resolution unless the company resolves otherwise.

(2) Unless the company has previously so resolved, it is not bound to comply with that section unless there is deposited with or tendered to it a sum reasonably sufficient to meet its expenses in doing so.

GENERAL NOTE

This new section (mirroring s.316 in respect of meetings) provides that the costs of circulating a written resolution proposed by the members must be met by the requisitionists unless the company resolves otherwise. Further, again subject to contrary resolution, the company need not circulate the members' resolution until a sum has been deposited or tendered to meet those expenses.

In the HC Comm D, col.316, the minister stated that if the directors asked for an unreasonable sum they would not be complying with their obligation under the previous section to circulate the resolution and so would be committing an offence.

295.   Application not to circulate members' statement

(1) A company is not required to circulate a members' statement under section 293 if, on an application by the company or another person who claims to be aggrieved, the court is satisfied that the rights conferred by section 292 and that section are being abused.

(2) The court may order the members who requested the circulation of the statement to pay the whole or part of the company's costs (in Scotland, expenses) on such an application, even if they are not parties to the application.

GENERAL NOTE

This new section, which mirrors s.317 in respect of meetings, allows the company to ask the court to allow it not to circulate a statement attached to a requisitioned written resolution. The court may do so if the right to have a resolution circulated is being abused, with an appropriate order as to costs (or expenses) being made against the requisitionists whether or not they are parties to the application.

An application can also be brought by any other person who claims to be aggrieved (see HC Comm D, col.317).

Agreeing to written resolutions

296.   Procedure for signifying agreement to written resolution

(1) A member signifies his agreement to a proposed written resolution when the company receives from him (or from someone acting on his behalf) an authenticated document-
   (a) identifying the resolution to which it relates, and
   (b) indicating his agreement to the resolution.

(2) The document must be sent to the company in hard copy form or in electronic form.

(3) A member's agreement to a written resolution, once signified, may not be revoked.

(4) A written resolution is passed when the required majority of eligible members have signified their agreement to it.

GENERAL NOTE

Based on s.381A of the 1985 Act, this section is designed to enable private companies to be sure as to when the requisite number of agreements has been received. The agreement, as set out in subs.(1), may take either hard copy or electronic form (unless either the company does nor permit such electronic communications or is not deemed to do so under s.298 - see Sch.4). Revocations are not allowed. Guidance as to how to signify agreement to the resolution must be sent out with the resolution when it is circulated: ss.291(4)(a) and 293(4)(a).

Subsection (1)

The document must be authenticated. As to that and the authenticity of the sender, see s.1146.

297. Period for agreeing to written resolution

(1) A proposed written resolution lapses if it is not passed before the end of-
   (a) the period specified for this purpose in the company's articles, or
   (b) if none is specified, the period of 28 days beginning with the circulation date.
(2) The agreement of a member to a written resolution is ineffective if signified after the expiry of that period.

GENERAL NOTE

This new section makes it clear that, subject to the articles, there is a default rule that a written resolution lapses if insufficient agreements are not signified within 28 days, beginning with the circulation date. Out of time agreements are not counted.

Circulation date - s.290.

Supplementary

298. Sending documents relating to written resolutions by electronic means

(1) Where a company has given an electronic address in any document containing or accompanying a proposed written resolution, it is deemed to have agreed that any document or information relating to that resolution may be sent by electronic means to that address (subject to any conditions or limitations specified in the document).
(2) In this section "electronic address" means any address or number used for the purposes of sending or receiving documents or information by electronic means.

GENERAL NOTE

This new section, taken together with Pt 3 of Sch.4 to the Act, provides that if the company has given an electronic address (as defined in subs.(2)) in any document containing or accompanying a written resolution, the members may in turn signify their agreements electronically.

299. Publication of written resolution on website

(1) This section applies where a company sends-
   (a) a written resolution, or
   (b) a statement relating to a written resolution,
to a person by means of a website.
(2) The resolution or statement is not validly sent for the purposes of this Chapter unless the resolution is available on the website throughout the period beginning with the circulation date and ending on the date on which the resolution lapses under section 297.

GENERAL NOTE

This new section allows a company in certain situations to circulate a written resolution by means of a website rather than individually to each member. Temporary website failure is dealt with in Sch.5.

Circulation date - s.290.

Subsection (2)

The resolution must be available on the website during the whole of the period when the resolution is open for agreements.

300. Relationship between this Chapter and provisions of company's articles

A provision of the articles of a private company is void in so far as it would have the effect that a resolution that is required by or otherwise provided for in an enactment could not be proposed and passed as a written resolution.

GENERAL NOTE

This new section makes it clear that a company cannot by its articles create an alternative written resolution procedure or require meetings instead in respect of statutory procedures. In some cases, using such an alternative written procedure could take effect as a *de facto* resolution under the *Duomatic* principle.

CHAPTER 3

RESOLUTIONS AT MEETINGS

General provisions about resolutions at meetings

301. Resolutions at general meetings

A resolution of the members of a company is validly passed at a general meeting if-
  (a) notice of the meeting and of the resolution is given, and
  (b) the meeting is held and conducted,
in accordance with the provisions of this Chapter (and, where relevant, Chapter 4) and the company's articles.

GENERAL NOTE

This Chapter sets out the rules relating to meetings, whether held by public or private companies. It replaces ss.376-377, 379 and 381 of the 1985 Act. Section 367 of the 1985 Act (power of Secretary of State to order an AGM) has not been continued. Chapter 4 separates out those parts applicable to AGMs (see, e.g. s.338) which now only apply to public companies.

This section applies the principle, formerly applied to special resolutions by s.378(6) of the 1985 Act, that to be valid a resolution must be passed in accordance with the mandatory provisions of the Act (e.g. s.324) and any additional requirements imposed by the company's articles.

Calling meetings

302. Directors' power to call general meetings

The directors of a company may call a general meeting of the company.

GENERAL NOTE

This section enacts para.37 of the former Table A. It leaves to the articles the procedure whereby the directors can exercise this power.

303. Members' power to require directors to call general meeting

(1) The members of a company may require the directors to call a general meeting of the company.
(2) The directors are required to call a general meeting once the company has received requests to do so from-
  (a) members representing at least the required percentage of such of the paid-up capital of the company as carries the right of voting at general meetings of the company (excluding any paid-up capital held as treasury shares); or

    (b) in the case of a company not having a share capital, members who represent at least the required percentage of the total voting rights of all the members having a right to vote at general meetings.

(3) The required percentage is 10% unless, in the case of a private company, more than twelve months has elapsed since the end of the last general meeting-

    (a) called in pursuance of a requirement under this section, or

    (b) in relation to which any members of the company had (by virtue of an enactment, the company's articles or otherwise) rights with respect to the circulation of a resolution no less extensive than they would have had if the meeting had been so called at their request,

in which case the required percentage is 5%.

(4) A request-

    (a) must state the general nature of the business to be dealt with at the meeting, and

    (b) may include the text of a resolution that may properly be moved and is intended to be moved at the meeting.

(5) A resolution may properly be moved at a meeting unless-

    (a) it would, if passed, be ineffective (whether by reason of inconsistency with any enactment or the company's constitution or otherwise),

    (b) it is defamatory of any person, or

    (c) it is frivolous or vexatious.

(6) A request-

    (a) may be in hard copy form or in electronic form, and

    (b) must be authenticated by the person or persons making it.

GENERAL NOTE

    This section, together with the two following sections, re-enact, with modifications, s.368 of the 1985 Act, giving the members of a company the right to require the directors to call a meeting, with power to do so themselves in default. There are corresponding provisions in ss.292-295 relating to written resolutions. There is a major difference, however, in that this power now extends to including, within limits, circulation of the text of a resolution to be moved at the meeting (see subss.(4)(b) and (5)).

Subsections (2) and (3)

    The power requires a minimum number of requisitionists calculated by reference to those representing voting rights in relation to the paid up capital (or total voting rights if there is no capital). For public companies this remains at ten per cent. For private companies, the threshold is lowered to 5 per cent if there has been no exercise of the power in the past year (and no meeting held in that period giving the members equivalent rights as to circulating a resolution). This was a compromise between reducing the threshold for private companies generally, since there need be no AGM, and not unduly burdening private companies into maybe holding more meetings than before.

Subsection (6)

    This subsection allows for the requisition to be in electronic form - see Sch.4.

304.   Directors' duty to call meetings required by members

(1) Directors required under section 303 to call a general meeting of the company must call a meeting-

    (a) within 21 days from the date on which they become subject to the requirement, and

    (b) to be held on a date not more than 28 days after the date of the notice convening the meeting.

(2) If the requests received by the company identify a resolution intended to be moved at the meeting, the notice of the meeting must include notice of the resolution.

(3) The business that may be dealt with at the meeting includes a resolution of which notice is given in accordance with this section.

(4) If the resolution is to be proposed as a special resolution, the directors are treated as not having duly called the meeting if they do not give the required notice of the resolution in accordance with section 283.

GENERAL NOTE

This section, re-enacting part of s.368 of the 1985 Act, continues the existing time limits on the board calling and holding a meeting requisitioned by the members.

Subsections (2)-(4)

These subsections provide for the situation where a resolution is also specified in the requisition. Notice of the resolution must be given. If it is a special resolution, the formalities associated with such resolutions in s.283 must be complied with, so that the actual text, rather than the general nature of the business, will have to be included.

305. Power of members to call meeting at company's expense

(1) If the directors-
    (a) are required under section 303 to call a meeting, and
    (b) do not do so in accordance with section 304,
the members who requested the meeting, or any of them representing more than one half of the total voting rights of all of them, may themselves call a general meeting.

(2) Where the requests received by the company included the text of a resolution intended to be moved at the meeting, the notice of the meeting must include notice of the resolution.

(3) The meeting must be called for a date not more than three months after the date on which the directors become subject to the requirement to call a meeting.

(4) The meeting must be called in the same manner, as nearly as possible, as that in which meetings are required to be called by directors of the company.

(5) The business which may be dealt with at the meeting includes a resolution of which notice is given in accordance with this section.

(6) Any reasonable expenses incurred by the members requesting the meeting by reason of the failure of the directors duly to call a meeting must be reimbursed by the company.

(7) Any sum so reimbursed shall be retained by the company out of any sums due or to become due from the company by way of fees or other remuneration in respect of the services of such of the directors as were in default.

GENERAL NOTE

This section re-enacts that part of s.368 of the 1985 Act allowing the requisitionists to call a meeting themselves if the directors default under the previous two sections. In line with the amendments in those sections, this power extends to any resolution included in the requisition.

Otherwise the provisions are the same, including the three months time limit, the nature of the meeting and the reimbursement of reasonable expenses by the company, to be withheld from sums due for services to the defaulting directors. The wording seems wide enough to include such sums due to a director's service company.

306. Power of court to order meeting

(1) This section applies if for any reason it is impracticable-
    (a) to call a meeting of a company in any manner in which meetings of that company may be called, or
    (b) to conduct the meeting in the manner prescribed by the company's articles or this Act.

(2) The court may, either of its own motion or on the application-
    (a) of a director of the company, or
    (b) of a member of the company who would be entitled to vote at the meeting,
order a meeting to be called, held and conducted in any manner the court thinks fit.

(3) Where such an order is made, the court may give such ancillary or consequential directions as it thinks expedient.

(4) Such directions may include a direction that one member of the company present at the meeting be deemed to constitute a quorum.

(5) A meeting called, held and conducted in accordance with an order under this section is deemed for all purposes to be a meeting of the company duly called, held and conducted.

GENERAL NOTE

This section directly re-enacts s.371 of the 1985 Act with no changes. As to the meaning of impractical, see e.g. *el Sombrero Ltd, Re* [1958] Ch. 900; *Ross v Telford* [1998] 1 B.C.L.C. 82; *Opera Photographic Ltd, Re* [1989] 1 WLR 634; *Woven Rugs Ltd, Re* [2002] 1 B.C.L.C. 324; *Union Music Ltd v Watson* [2001] 1 B.C.L.C. 453; *Might SA v Redbus Interhouse Plc* [2004] 2 B.C.L.C. 449.

Notice of meetings

307.   Notice required of general meeting

(1) A general meeting of a private company (other than an adjourned meeting) must be called by notice of at least 14 days.

(2) A general meeting of a public company (other than an adjourned meeting) must be called by notice of-

(a) in the case of an annual general meeting, at least 21 days, and

(b) in any other case, at least 14 days.

(3) The company's articles may require a longer period of notice than that specified in subsection (1) or (2).

(4) A general meeting may be called by shorter notice than that otherwise required if shorter notice is agreed by the members.

(5) The shorter notice must be agreed to by a majority in number of the members having a right to attend and vote at the meeting, being a majority who-

(a) together hold not less than the requisite percentage in nominal value of the shares giving a right to attend and vote at the meeting (excluding any shares in the company held as treasury shares), or

(b) in the case of a company not having a share capital, together represent not less than the requisite percentage of the total voting rights at that meeting of all the members.

(6) The requisite percentage is-

(a) in the case of a private company, 90% or such higher percentage (not exceeding 95%) as may be specified in the company's articles;

(b) in the case of a public company, 95%.

(7) Subsections (5) and (6) do not apply to an annual general meeting of a public company (see instead section 337(2)).

GENERAL NOTE

This section re-enacts with modifications part of s.369 of the 1985 Act. See also Art.5 of the draft directive COM(2005)865 final. The period of notice for all meetings is 14 days except for an AGM of a public company when it is 21 days. The articles may provide for longer periods. See also s.312 on resolutions requiring special notice.

That 14 day period is exclusive is exclusive in that it does not include either the date when the notice is given or when the meeting is held - see s.360.

Subsections (4)-(6)

The notice period can be shortened for private companies if 90 per cent (reduced from the existing figure of 95 per cent) of the owners of the nominal value of the voting capital (or votes if there is no capital) agree. The articles may raise this figure, but not above 95 per cent. For public company meetings other than AGMs, the figure remains at 95 per cent. Public company AGMs are governed by s.344(2) which requires 100 per cent agreement for shorter notice.

308.   Manner in which notice to be given

Notice of a general meeting of a company must be given-
  (a) in hard copy form,
  (b) in electronic form, or
  (c) by means of a website (see section 309),
or partly by one such means and partly by another.

GENERAL NOTE

This new section allowing for electronic and website methods of giving notice must be read in conjunction with Sch.5 to the Act. There is a general distinction in this area between traded and non-traded companies. See also the following section.

309.   Publication of notice of meeting on website

(1) Notice of a meeting is not validly given by a company by means of a website unless it is given in accordance with this section.
(2) When the company notifies a member of the presence of the notice on the website the notification must-
  (a) state that it concerns a notice of a company meeting,
  (b) specify the place, date and time of the meeting, and
  (c) in the case of a public company, state whether the meeting will be an annual general meeting.
(3) The notice must be available on the website throughout the period beginning with the date of that notification and ending with the conclusion of the meeting.

GENERAL NOTE

This section re-enacts the provisions of s.369 of the 1985 Act in relation to websites. In addition, reference should be made to para.13 of Sch.5 which requires companies to notify intended recipients directly of the posting of documents and information on a website and deals with temporary website failure. See also art 5(3) of the draft directive, COM(2005)683 final.

310.   Persons entitled to receive notice of meetings

(1) Notice of a general meeting of a company must be sent to-
  (a) every member of the company, and
  (b) every director.
(2) In subsection (1), the reference to members includes any person who is entitled to a share in consequence of the death or bankruptcy of a member, if the company has been notified of their entitlement.
(3) In subsection (2), the reference to the bankruptcy of a member includes-
  (a) the sequestration of the estate of a member;
  (b) a member's estate being the subject of a protected trust deed (within the meaning of the Bankruptcy (Scotland) Act 1985 (c. 66)).
(4) This section has effect subject to-
  (a) any enactment, and
  (b) any provision of the company's articles.

GENERAL NOTE

This section enacts part of para.38 of the former Table A. See also Art.7 of the draft directive COM(2005)863 final. It details all those who must be sent notice of a meeting, including those entitled to shares by transmission on a death or bankruptcy. Auditors are also entitled to notices of meetings: s.502.

Surprisingly perhaps the articles may limit this section, without any restrictions (*quaere* - the effect on the draft directive?). One possibility is to exclude those persons for whom the company has no address, but it could in theory exclude anyone.

311.   Contents of notices of meetings

(1) Notice of a general meeting of a company must state-
    (a) the time and date of the meeting, and
    (b) the place of the meeting.
(2) Notice of a general meeting of a company must state the general nature of the business to be dealt with at the meeting.

This subsection has effect subject to any provision of the company's articles.

GENERAL NOTE

This section enacts another part of para.38 of the former Table A. It deals with the salient points relating to the meeting. Note that the requirement as to the general nature of the business to be discussed is subject to the articles.

This section must be read together with s.325 as to the appointment of proxies.

312.   Resolution requiring special notice

(1) Where by any provision of the Companies Acts special notice is required of a resolution, the resolution is not effective unless notice of the intention to move it has been given to the company at least 28 days before the meeting at which it is moved.
(2) The company must, where practicable, give its members notice of any such resolution in the same manner and at the same time as it gives notice of the meeting.
(3) Where that is not practicable, the company must give its members notice at least 14 days before the meeting-
    (a) by advertisement in a newspaper having an appropriate circulation, or
    (b) in any other manner allowed by the company's articles.
(4) If, after notice of the intention to move such a resolution has been given to the company, a meeting is called for a date 28 days or less after the notice has been given, the notice is deemed to have been properly given, though not given within the time required.

GENERAL NOTE

This section re-enacts, with one modification, s.379 of the 1985 Act. It sets out the requirement for special notice resolutions. These are required for: removal of a director, s.168; removal of an auditor, s.510; and failure to reappoint auditor, s.514. Since these cannot be effected by a written resolution, this section only applies to formal resolutions.

The period of notice remains 28 days prior to the meeting (excluding both the date when the notice is given and the date of the meeting itself - see s.367), but if it is impracticable to give notice of the resolution at the same time as notice of the meeting there is a change to the pre-existing alternative route. Notice must still be given in a newspaper advertisement (or under the articles), but only 14 days prior to the meeting and not 21 days. This is intended to reflect the general 14 day-notice period in the Act.

Subsection (1)

The reference to the Companies Acts is intended to refer only to this Act (see *Hansard* HL GC122, Vol.679 (March 1, 2006); HC Comm col.326).

313.   Accidental failure to give notice of resolution or meeting

(1) Where a company gives notice of-
    (a) a general meeting, or

(b) a resolution intended to be moved at a general meeting,
any accidental failure to give notice to one or more persons shall be disregarded for the purpose of determining whether notice of the meeting or resolution (as the case may be) is duly given.

(2) Except in relation to notice given under-

(a) section 304 (notice of meetings required by members),

(b) section 305 (notice of meetings called by members), or

(c) section 339 (notice of resolutions at AGMs proposed by members),

subsection (1) has effect subject to any provision of the company's articles.

GENERAL NOTE

This section enacts and expands para.39 of the former Table A. In the interests of certainty, accidental failure to give a notice of a meeting or resolution is to be disregarded, unless the articles provide otherwise. That default rule is, however, mandatory in respect of notice of meetings called or required by the members or for resolutions proposed by the members at an AGM.

Members' statements

314. Members' power to require circulation of statements

(1) The members of a company may require the company to circulate, to members of the company entitled to receive notice of a general meeting, a statement of not more than 1,000 words with respect to-

(a) a matter referred to in a proposed resolution to be dealt with at that meeting, or

(b) other business to be dealt with at that meeting.

(2) A company is required to circulate a statement once it has received requests to do so from-

(a) members representing at least 5% of the total voting rights of all the members who have a relevant right to vote (excluding any voting rights attached to any shares in the company held as treasury shares), or

(b) at least 100 members who have a relevant right to vote and hold shares in the company on which there has been paid up an average sum, per member, of at least £100.

See also section 153 (exercise of rights where shares held on behalf of others).

(3) In subsection (2), a "relevant right to vote" means-

(a) in relation to a statement with respect to a matter referred to in a proposed resolution, a right to vote on that resolution at the meeting to which the requests relate, and

(b) in relation to any other statement, a right to vote at the meeting to which the requests relate.

(4) A request-

(a) may be in hard copy form or in electronic form,

(b) must identify the statement to be circulated,

(c) must be authenticated by the person or persons making it, and

(d) must be received by the company at least one week before the meeting to which it relates.

GENERAL NOTE

This section, together with the following three sections, re-enacts, with modifications, those parts of ss.376 and 377 of the 1985 Act which relate to members' statements. (The other parts of those sections relate to resolutions to be proposed at an AGM and are now in ss.338-340 in Ch.4 of this Part of the Act.)

The basic provisions are the same in that a percentage of the members may require circulation of a statement of up to 1,000 words in respect of a resolution or other business of any meeting. (There are equivalent provisions in ss.292 and 294 in relation to written resolutions.)

Although the required percentage of members remains at either holders of 5 per cent of the voting rights or 100 such holders of voting rights holding at least £100 paid up capital on average, the voting rights in question now relate to the right to vote on the resolution (if the statement relates to one) rather than at the meeting generally. See also s.153 which allows requests by those whose shares are held by others.

Electronic requests are also now provided for. The one-week notice period in subs.(7) is exclusive of both the date when the request is made and the date of the meeting itself - see s.360.

315.   Company's duty to circulate members' statement

(1) A company that is required under section 314, to circulate a statement must send a copy of it to each member of the company entitled to receive notice of the meeting-
    (a) in the same manner as the notice of the meeting, and
    (b) at the same time as, or as soon as reasonably practicable after, it gives notice of the meeting.
(2) Subsection (1) has effect subject to section 316(2) (deposit or tender of sum in respect of expenses of circulation) and section 317 (application not to circulate members' statement).
(3) In the event of default in complying with this section, an offence is committed by every officer of the company who is in default.
(4) A person guilty of an offence under this section is liable-
    (a) on conviction on indictment, to a fine;
    (b) on summary conviction, to a fine not exceeding the statutory maximum.

GENERAL NOTE

This section re-enacts the method of the company complying with its obligation to circulate the statement under the previous section. Default remains a criminal offence. It is subject to the following two sections which allow a company to avoid the obligation in two circumstances.

316.   Expenses of circulating members' statement

(1) The expenses of the company in complying with section 315 need not be paid by the members who requested the circulation of the statement if-
    (a) the meeting to which the requests relate is an annual general meeting of a public company, and
    (b) requests sufficient to require the company to circulate the statement are received before the end of the financial year preceding the meeting.
(2) Otherwise-
    (a) the expenses of the company in complying with that section must be paid by the members who requested the circulation of the statement unless the company resolves otherwise, and
    (b) unless the company has previously so resolved, it is not bound to comply with that section unless there is deposited with or tendered to it, not later than one week before the meeting, a sum reasonably sufficient to meet its expenses in doing so.

GENERAL NOTE

This section provides the most important change from ss.376 and 377 of the 1985 Act. Although, in general, the requisitionists remain liable for the costs of circulating the statement unless the company resolves otherwise (as with written resolutions), that will not be the case if the request relates to a public company's AGM and the request threshold is met before the end of the preceding financial year.

If the members are liable for the costs there is no obligation to circulate the statement until a reasonable sum has been tendered or deposited with the company. The minister stated in the HC Comm D, col.316, that asking for an unreasonable sum would mean that the directors were not complying with their obligation under the sections and so would be committing a criminal offence. The one-week period specified in subs.(2)(b) is exclusive of both the date of the deposit or tender and the date of the meeting itself - see s.360.

317. Application not to circulate members' statement

(1) A company is not required to circulate a members' statement under section 315 if, on an application by the company or another person who claims to be aggrieved, the court is satisfied that the rights conferred by section 314 and that section are being abused.

(2) The court may order the members who requested the circulation of the statement to pay the whole or part of the company's costs (in Scotland, expenses) on such an application, even if they are not parties to the application.

GENERAL NOTE

This section re-enacts s.377(3) of the 1985 Act and allows the company to apply to the courts to be excused of its obligation under the previous three sections on the grounds that the right under those sections is being abused. Subsection (2) deals with costs or expenses of the application.

This section (mirroring s.295 on written resolutions) would, inter alia, prevent the circulating of defamatory material.

Procedure at meetings

318. Quorum at meetings

(1) In the case of a company limited by shares or guarantee and having only one member, one qualifying person present at a meeting is a quorum.

(2) In any other case, subject to the provisions of the company's articles, two qualifying persons present at a meeting are a quorum, unless-

  (a) each is a qualifying person only because he is authorised under section 323 to act as the representative of a corporation in relation to the meeting, and they are representatives of the same corporation; or

  (b) each is a qualifying person only because he is appointed as proxy of a member in relation to the meeting, and they are proxies of the same member.

(3) For the purposes of this section a "qualifying person" means-

  (a) an individual who is a member of the company,

  (b) a person authorised under section 323 (representation of corporations at meetings) to act as the representative of a corporation in relation to the meeting, or

  (c) a person appointed as proxy of a member in relation to the meeting.

GENERAL NOTE

This section replaces, with modifications, s.370(4) and 370A of the 1985 Act. In a single member company the quorum for a meeting is one qualifying person, in other cases the default rule is two.

A qualifying person means an individual member, the representative of a corporate member (s.323) or a proxy appointed in relation to the meeting (s.324). However, other than in single member companies, the default rule is that a quorum cannot consist only of such representatives or proxies.

319. Chairman of meeting

(1) A member may be elected to be the chairman of a general meeting by a resolution of the company passed at the meeting.

(2) Subsection (1) is subject to any provision of the company's articles that states who may or may not be chairman.

GENERAL NOTE

This section re-enacts s.370(5) of the 1985 Act. It provides a default rule as to the election of a chairman at a meeting by resolution.

320.   Declaration by chairman on a show of hands

(1) On a vote on a resolution at a meeting on a show of hands, a declaration by the chairman that the resolution-
   (a) has or has not been passed, or
   (b) passed with a particular majority,
is conclusive evidence of that fact without proof of the number or proportion of the votes recorded in favour of or against the resolution.

(2) An entry in respect of such a declaration in minutes of the meeting recorded in accordance with section 355 is also conclusive evidence of that fact without such proof.

(3) This section does not have effect if a poll is demanded in respect of the resolution (and the demand is not subsequently withdrawn).

GENERAL NOTE

   The section re-enacts 378(4) of the 1985 Act, modified to absorb para.47 of the former Table A. Its intention, on the grounds of commercial certainty, is to prevent any challenge to a chairman's declaration as to the passing or otherwise of any resolution on a show of hands unless a poll has been demanded and not withdrawn. Another change is that the minutes of the meeting are also conclusive evidence of the chairman's declaration.

   At common law, a chairman must call for a poll on any contentious resolution where he considers that the result on a poll (generally one vote per share) would be different from that on a show of hands (one vote per person). The position on advisory resolutions is less clear, but the government indicated that it intended to leave good practice to evolve (HC Comm D, col.329).

321.   Right to demand a poll

(1) A provision of a company's articles is void in so far as it would have the effect of excluding the right to demand a poll at a general meeting on any question other than-
   (a) the election of the chairman of the meeting, or
   (b) the adjournment of the meeting.

(2) A provision of a company's articles is void in so far as it would have the effect of making ineffective a demand for a poll on any such question which is made-
   (a) by not less than 5 members having the right to vote on the resolution; or
   (b) by a member or members representing not less than 10% of the total voting rights of all the members having the right to vote on the resolution (excluding any voting rights attached to any shares in the company held as treasury shares); or
   (c) by a member or members holding shares in the company conferring a right to vote on the resolution, being shares on which an aggregate sum has been paid up equal to not less than 10% of the total sum paid up on all the shares conferring that right (excluding shares in the company conferring a right to vote on the resolution which are held as treasury shares).

GENERAL NOTE

   This section re-enacts, without any major substantive changes, the important limitations on a company's ability to restrict the right to demand a poll in its articles.

Subsection (1)

   The pre-existing exemptions for electing a chairman and an adjournment resolution are maintained. The Government resisted attempts to remove the latter: see *Hansard* HL GC Day 6, Vol.679, col.125 (March 1, 2006); HC Comm D, col.331 (June 29, 2006).

Subsection (2)

   The three pre-existing thresholds for the right to demand a poll are maintained but in calculating those various thresholds the right to vote on the resolution replaces the former criterion of the right to vote at the meeting. Proxies, including multiple proxies, also have rights to demand a poll: see s.329.

322. Voting on a poll

On a poll taken at a general meeting of a company, a member entitled to more than one vote need not, if he votes, use all his votes or cast all the votes he uses in the same way.

GENERAL NOTE

This section directly re-enacts s.374 of the 1985 Act and allows for members holding shares on behalf of more than one client to vote differently according to instructions.

323. Representation of corporations at meetings

(1) If a corporation (whether or not a company within the meaning of this Act) is a member of a company, it may by resolution of its directors or other governing body authorise a person or persons to act as its representative or representatives at any meeting of the company.

(2) Where the corporation authorises only one person, he is entitled to exercise the same powers on behalf of the corporation as the corporation could exercise if it were an individual member of the company.

(3) Where the corporation authorises more than one person, any one of them is entitled to exercise the same powers on behalf of the corporation as the corporation could exercise if it were an individual member of the company.

(4) Where the corporation authorises more than one person and more than one of them purport to exercise a power under subsection (3)-
  (a) if they purport to exercise the power in the same way, the power is treated as exercised in that way,
  (b) if they do not purport to exercise the power in the same way, the power is treated as not exercised.

GENERAL NOTE

This section re-enacts s.375 of the 1985 Act, giving a representative all the powers of an individual member of the corporate member, but with an additional clarification where a corporate member appoints more than one representative to the meeting (see CLR's *Developing the Framework*, para.4.55).

Subsections (3) and (4)

Multiple appointments could be made under the previous section, but it was unclear as to the position if they voted differently. In such a case the corporate member is deemed to have abstained. If that situation is a real possibility the company should appoint proxies, who may vote differently with different blocks of shares.

Proxies

324. Rights to appoint proxies

(1) A member of a company is entitled to appoint another person as his proxy to exercise all or any of his rights to attend and to speak and vote at a meeting of the company.

(2) In the case of a company having a share capital, a member may appoint more than one proxy in relation to a meeting, provided that each proxy is appointed to exercise the rights attached to a different share or shares held by him, or (as the case may be) to a different £10, or multiple of £10, of stock held by him.

GENERAL NOTE

This section replaces s.372(1) and (2) of the 1985 Act, following the CLR's *Final Report* paras 7.4 and 7.13. Se also Art.11 of the draft directive, COM(2005) 685 final. The major difference is that all its basic rights are mandatory and not subject to restrictions in the articles, although they can be extended by them - see s.338. Thus the right to appoint a proxy who can attend, speak and vote at a meeting is absolute. As to voting rights, see ss.284 and 285.

Provision is made for the appointment of more than one proxy provided each is identified with a share, block of shares or £10 of stock (which can still be held in fractional amounts, even if no longer issued). Each duly appointed proxy will then have a vote on a show of hands - see note on s.284(3).

325.   Notice of meeting to contain statement of rights

(1) In every notice calling a meeting of a company there must appear, with reasonable prominence, a statement informing the member of-
    (a) his rights under section 324, and
    (b) any more extensive rights conferred by the company's articles to appoint more than one proxy.
(2) Failure to comply with this section does not affect the validity of the meeting or of anything done at the meeting.
(3) If this section is not complied with as respects any meeting, an offence is committed by every officer of the company who is in default.
(4) A person guilty of an offence under this section is liable on summary conviction to a fine not exceeding level 3 on the standard scale.

GENERAL NOTE
This section re-enacts s.372(3) and (4) of the 1985 Act, modified to take account of the extension of the rights in the previous section. Thus the notice of a meeting must now also include not only the statutory rights to appoint a proxy, etc. but also any more extensive rights in the articles to appoint more than one proxy.

It is further made clear, for the sake of commercial certainty, that there are no civil consequences for the meeting of a breach of this section, but it remains a criminal offence in default. This does not preclude any possible action based on unfairly prejudicial conduct or breach of contract.

326.   Company-sponsored invitations to appoint proxies

(1) If for the purposes of a meeting there are issued at the company's expense invitations to members to appoint as proxy a specified person or a number of specified persons, the invitations must be issued to all members entitled to vote at the meeting.
(2) Subsection (1) is not contravened if-
    (a) there is issued to a member at his request a form of appointment naming the proxy or a list of persons willing to act as proxy, and
    (b) the form or list is available on request to all members entitled to vote at the meeting.
(3) If subsection (1) is contravened as respects a meeting, an offence is committed by every officer of the company who is in default.
(4) A person guilty of an offence under this section is liable on summary conviction to a fine not exceeding level 3 on the standard scale.

GENERAL NOTE
This section, replacing s.372(6) of the 1985 Act, provides that if a proxy form is sent out specifying a particular proxy or proxies, forms must be sent to all those eligible to vote at the meeting.

The exception where a member requests such a form identifying a specific proxy or list of potential proxies is maintained in subs.(2). The criminal sanction in default is also retained, although nothing is said as to the effect of a breach on the validity of the meeting (cf. the previous section above).

327.   Notice required of appointment of proxy etc

(1) This section applies to-

    (a) the appointment of a proxy, and

    (b) any document necessary to show the validity of, or otherwise relating to, the appointment of a proxy.

(2) Any provision of the company's articles is void in so far as it would have the effect of requiring any such appointment or document to be received by the company or another person earlier than the following time-

    (a) in the case of a meeting or adjourned meeting, 48 hours before the time for holding the meeting or adjourned meeting;

    (b) in the case of a poll taken more than 48 hours after it was demanded, 24 hours before the time appointed for the taking of the poll;

    (c) in the case of a poll taken not more than 48 hours after it was demanded, the time at which it was demanded.

(3) In calculating the periods mentioned in subsection (2) no account shall be taken of any part of a day that is not a working day.

GENERAL NOTE

    This section re-enacts s.372(5) of the 1985 Act. It retains the maximum 48-hour cut-off point for lodging proxies prior to a meeting or adjourned meeting, but in subs.(3) now provides that in calculating that period no account is to be taken of any non-working day, i.e. weekends and bank holidays. Thus if, say, a meeting is scheduled for 10.00 on a Monday, the cut-off point cannot now be earlier than 10.00 on the previous Friday and not, as under the former provision, on the previous Saturday.

    Subsection (2) also applies the cut-off rules where a poll is not taken immediately on demand at the meeting. If it is held within 48 hours, the earliest cut-off date is when the poll was demanded. If the delay is more than 48 hours, the earliest cut-off is 24 hours before the poll is taken. Again, in this case, a non-working day is ignored.

328. Chairing meetings

(1) A proxy may be elected to be the chairman of a general meeting by a resolution of the company passed at the meeting.

(2) Subsection (1) is subject to any provision of the company's articles that states who may or who may not be chairman.

GENERAL NOTE

    This new section applies a default rule that a proxy can be elected as chairman of a meeting.

329. Right of proxy to demand a poll

(1) The appointment of a proxy to vote on a matter at a meeting of a company authorises the proxy to demand, or join in demanding, a poll on that matter.

(2) In applying the provisions of section 321(2) (requirements for effective demand), a demand by a proxy counts-

    (a) for the purposes of paragraph (a), as a demand by the member;

    (b) for the purposes of paragraph (b), as a demand by a member representing the voting rights that the proxy is authorised to exercise;

    (c) for the purposes of paragraph (c), as a demand by a member holding the shares to which those rights are attached.

GENERAL NOTE

    This section re-enacts s.373(2) of the 1985 Act and provides that a proxy may demand or join in the demanding of a poll.

    If there is a single proxy appointed, then that proxy has exactly the same rights as the appointing member in calculating the thresholds under s.321 required to successfully demand a poll; e.g. a proxy may count as one of the five required members.

If, as there can be, there are multiple proxies appointed by one member, then, for the purposes of calculating the thresholds in s.321(2)(b)(c) based on voting rights or shares, each proxy counts according to the shares (or stock) he represents. But there seems no reason on the wording of subs.(2)(a) why each such proxy cannot count as a separate member for that purpose. Thus if a member, having five shares, appoints five proxies, one per share, and all five then demand a poll, the requirements of s.321(2)(a) would appear to have been fulfilled.

330.   Notice required of termination of proxy's authority

(1) This section applies to notice that the authority of a person to act as proxy is terminated ("notice of termination").

(2) The termination of the authority of a person to act as proxy does not affect-
   (a) whether he counts in deciding whether there is a quorum at a meeting,
   (b) the validity of anything he does as chairman of a meeting, or
   (c) the validity of a poll demanded by him at a meeting,
unless the company receives notice of the termination before the commencement of the meeting.

(3) The termination of the authority of a person to act as proxy does not affect the validity of a vote given by that person unless the company receives notice of the termination-
   (a) before the commencement of the meeting or adjourned meeting at which the vote is given, or
   (b) in the case of a poll taken more than 48 hours after it is demanded, before the time appointed for taking the poll.

(4) If the company's articles require or permit members to give notice of termination to a person other than the company, the references above to the company receiving notice have effect as if they were or (as the case may be) included a reference to that person.

(5) Subsections (2) and (3) have effect subject to any provision of the company's articles which has the effect of requiring notice of termination to be received by the company or another person at a time earlier than that specified in those subsections.
This is subject to subsection (6).

(6) Any provision of the company's articles is void in so far as it would have the effect of requiring notice of termination to be received by the company or another person earlier than the following time-
   (a) in the case of a meeting or adjourned meeting, 48 hours before the time for holding the meeting or adjourned meeting;
   (b) in the case of a poll taken more than 48 hours after it was demanded, 24 hours before the time appointed for the taking of the poll;
   (c) in the case of a poll taken not more than 48 hours after it was demanded, the time at which it was demanded.

(7) In calculating the periods mentioned in subsections (3)(b) and (6) no account shall be taken of any part of a day that is not a working day.

GENERAL NOTE

   This section enacts para.63 of the former Table A to provide a partial default rule in subss.(2) and (3) that the termination of a person's authority to act as a proxy does not affect the validity of his counting towards the quorum of a meeting, his or her actions as chairman of a meeting, any poll demanded by him or any votes cast by him, unless the company has notice of that termination before the commencement of the meeting. If there is a poll taken more than 48 hours after it has been demanded, the notice must be received by the time that the poll is taken.

   This is subject to any provisions in the articles either allowing for a termination notice to be given to a person other than the company, when such notice will count as notice to the company (subs.(4)), or providing for an earlier notification date (subs.(5)).

   But this earlier notification date is limited by subs.(6) in the same way as the date for effective notification of an appointment of a proxy is limited in s.334. Thus the earliest date can be no more than 48 hours before the meeting or adjourned meeting, with adjustments for polls not taken immediately after they have been demanded. Non-working days are excluded in that calculation (subs.(7)). See the note on s.327 above.

331. Saving for more extensive rights conferred by articles

Nothing in sections 324 to 330 (proxies) prevents a company's articles from conferring more extensive rights on members or proxies than are conferred by those sections.

GENERAL NOTE

This new section allows the mandatory provisions in the Act on proxies to be extended by the articles.

Adjourned meetings

332. Resolution passed at adjourned meeting

Where a resolution is passed at an adjourned meeting of a company, the resolution is for all purposes to be treated as having been passed on the date on which it was in fact passed, and is not to be deemed passed on any earlier date.

GENERAL NOTE

This section directly reproduces the effect of s.381 of the 1985 Act as to the date of a resolution passed at an adjourned meeting.

Electronic communications

333. Sending documents relating to meetings etc in electronic form

(1) Where a company has given an electronic address in a notice calling a meeting, it is deemed to have agreed that any document or information relating to proceedings at the meeting may be sent by electronic means to that address (subject to any conditions or limitations specified in the notice).

(2) Where a company has given an electronic address-

    (a) in an instrument of proxy sent out by the company in relation to the meeting, or

    (b) in an invitation to appoint a proxy issued by the company in relation to the meeting,

it is deemed to have agreed that any document or information relating to proxies for that meeting may be sent by electronic means to that address (subject to any conditions or limitations specified in the notice).

(3) In subsection (2), documents relating to proxies include-

    (a) the appointment of a proxy in relation to a meeting,

    (b) any document necessary to show the validity of, or otherwise relating to, the appointment of a proxy, and

    (c) notice of the termination of the authority of a proxy.

(4) In this section "electronic address" means any address or number used for the purposes of sending or receiving documents or information by electronic means.

GENERAL NOTE

This new section, which will comply with Arts 8, 9 and 11 of the draft directive, COM(2005)865 final, must be read with Sch.4 to the Act. In effect where the company has given an electronic address in a notice calling a meeting or on a proxy form or invitation, the member may communicate with the company by e mail to that address on all matters relating to that meeting or appointment, e.g. in appointing or terminating the appointment of a proxy.

Application to class meetings

334. Application to class meetings

(1) The provisions of this Chapter apply (with necessary modifications) in relation to a meeting of holders of a class of shares as they apply in relation to a general meeting.
This is subject to subsections (2) and (3).

(2) The following provisions of this Chapter do not apply in relation to a meeting of holders of a class of shares-
  (a) sections 303 to 305 (members' power to require directors to call general meeting), and
  (b) section 306 (power of court to order meeting).

(3) The following provisions (in addition to those mentioned in subsection (2)) do not apply in relation to a meeting in connection with the variation of rights attached to a class of shares (a "variation of class rights meeting")-
  (a) section 318 (quorum), and
  (b) section 321 (right to demand a poll).

(4) The quorum for a variation of class rights meeting is-
  (a) for a meeting other than an adjourned meeting, two persons present holding at least one-third in nominal value of the issued shares of the class in question (excluding any shares of that class held as treasury shares);
  (b) for an adjourned meeting, one person present holding shares of the class in question.

(5) For the purposes of subsection (4), where a person is present by proxy or proxies, he is treated as holding only the shares in respect of which those proxies are authorised to exercise voting rights.

(6) At a variation of class rights meeting, any holder of shares of the class in question present may demand a poll.

(7) For the purposes of this section-
  (a) any amendment of a provision contained in a company's articles for the variation of the rights attached to a class of shares, or the insertion of any such provision into the articles, is itself to be treated as a variation of those rights, and
  (b) references to the variation of rights attached to a class of shares include references to their abrogation.

GENERAL NOTE
   This section, derived in part from s.125(6) of the 1985 Act, applies the provisions, of this Chapter, suitably modified, to class meetings, i.e. of members of a class of shares.

Subsection (2)
   This excludes the rights of members to require the directors to call a meeting, and the power of the court to order a meeting, from applying to class meetings.

Subsections (3)-(7)
   These provisions apply to meetings to vary class rights. On those generally see ss.630 and 633. They provide for modifications to the quorum and poll provisions. Subsection (7) is replicated in s.630(6).

335. Application to class meetings: companies without a share capital

(1) The provisions of this Chapter apply (with necessary modifications) in relation to a meeting of a class of members of a company without a share capital as they apply in relation to a general meeting.
This is subject to subsections (2) and (3).

(2) The following provisions of this Chapter do not apply in relation to a meeting of a class of members-

    (a) sections 303 to 305 (members' power to require directors to call general meeting), and

    (b) section 306 (power of court to order meeting).

(3) The following provisions (in addition to those mentioned in subsection (2)) do not apply in relation to a meeting in connection with the variation of the rights of a class of members (a "variation of class rights meeting")-

    (a) section 318 (quorum), and

    (b) section 321 (right to demand a poll).

(4) The quorum for a variation of class rights meeting is-

    (a) for a meeting other than an adjourned meeting, two members of the class present (in person or by proxy) who together represent at least one-third of the voting rights of the class;

    (b) for an adjourned meeting, one member of the class present (in person or by proxy).

(5) At a variation of class rights meeting, any member present (in person or by proxy) may demand a poll.

(6) For the purposes of this section-

    (a) any amendment of a provision contained in a company's articles for the variation of the rights of a class of members, or the insertion of any such provision into the articles, is itself to be treated as a variation of those rights, and

    (b) references to the variation of rights of a class of members include references to their abrogation.

GENERAL NOTE

This new section replicates the previous section in respect of companies without shares but which have different classes of members. On those see ss.631 and 634.

CHAPTER 4

PUBLIC COMPANIES: ADDITIONAL REQUIREMENTS FOR AGMS

336. Public companies: annual general meeting

(1) Every public company must hold a general meeting as its annual general meeting in each period of 6 months beginning with the day following its accounting reference date (in addition to any other meetings held during that period).

(2) A company that fails to comply with subsection (1) as a result of giving notice under section 392 (alteration of accounting reference date)-

    (a) specifying a new accounting reference date, and

    (b) stating that the current accounting reference period or the previous accounting reference period is to be shortened,

shall be treated as if it had complied with subsection (1) if it holds a general meeting as its annual general meeting within 3 months of giving that notice.

(3) If a company fails to comply with subsection (1), an offence is committed by every officer of the company who is in default.

(4) A person guilty of an offence under this section is liable-

    (a) on conviction on indictment, to a fine;

    (b) on summary conviction, to a fine not exceeding the statutory maximum.

GENERAL NOTE

This Chapter provides for additional rules for public companies' AGMs. A private company need no longer have an AGM - see the CLR's *Final Report*, paras 7.6 and 7.8; 2005 White Paper (Cm.6456), para.31. It may, of course, still hold meetings, but it will be subject only to the provisions of the previous Chapter and not this one, whether or not the meeting is styled as an AGM. The concept of an EGM has been discontinued in this Act.

This section replaces s.366 of the Companies Act 1985, except that it only applies to public companies. The other change is that the time limits for holding an AGM are different. An AGM must now be held within six months of the end of a public company's financial year (see ss.390 and 391). A breach remains a criminal offence by any officer in default.

Subsection (2)

This makes provision for the case where a company gives a notice under s.390 shortening its current or prior financial reporting period. The time limit is then three months from the date of giving that notice.

337.   Public companies: notice of AGM

(1) A notice calling an annual general meeting of a public company must state that the meeting is an annual general meeting.

(2) An annual general meeting may be called by shorter notice than that required by section 307(2) or by the company's articles (as the case may be), if all the members entitled to attend and vote at the meeting agree to the shorter notice.

GENERAL NOTE

This section re-enacts part of s.366 and s.369(3)(a) of the 1985 Act. The actual period of notice for a public company AGM is 21 days minimum as fixed by s.307. Shorter notice is possible, but only with the unanimous consent of those entitled to attend and vote at the meeting. See the CLR's *Final Report*, para.7.10.

If a private company decides to hold an AGM, then under s.307 the minimum period would be 14 days.

338.   Public companies: members' power to require circulation of resolutions for AGMs

(1) The members of a public company may require the company to give, to members of the company entitled to receive notice of the next annual general meeting, notice of a resolution which may properly be moved and is intended to be moved at that meeting.

(2) A resolution may properly be moved at an annual general meeting unless-

   (a) it would, if passed, be ineffective (whether by reason of inconsistency with any enactment or the company's constitution or otherwise),

   (b) it is defamatory of any person, or

   (c) it is frivolous or vexatious.

(3) A company is required to give notice of a resolution once it has received requests that it do so from-

   (a) members representing at least 5% of the total voting rights of all the members who have a right to vote on the resolution at the annual general meeting to which the requests relate (excluding any voting rights attached to any shares in the company held as treasury shares), or

   (b) at least 100 members who have a right to vote on the resolution at the annual general meeting to which the requests relate and hold shares in the company on which there has been paid up an average sum, per member, of at least £100.

See also section 153 (exercise of rights where shares held on behalf of others).

(4) A request-

   (a) may be in hard copy form or in electronic form,

   (b) must identify the resolution of which notice is to be given,

   (c) must be authenticated by the person or persons making it, and

   (d) must be received by the company not later than-

      (i) 6 weeks before the annual general meeting to which the requests relate, or

      (ii) if later, the time at which notice is given of that meeting.

GENERAL NOTE

This section, together with the following two sections, re-enacts, with some significant modifications, those parts of ss.376 and 377 of the Companies Act 1985 on a members' right to circulate resolutions at a public company's AGM. The corresponding rights in the former sections to have statements circulated in relation to any company meeting are set out in ss.314 and 315. See Arts 6(1)-(3) of the draft directive, COM(2005)685 final.

There is, curiously, no corresponding statutory right to have a resolution circulated at any meeting other than a public company's AGM, although there is a right to have a written resolution circulated under that procedure for private companies - see s.292.

Subsection (2)

These specific limits replace the former requirement that the resolution must be one which it is "proper" to move. Any dispute will have to be resolved either by the articles or litigation.

Subsection (3)

This subsection re-enacts the previous thresholds, but the numbers in both cases are to be calculated by reference to those entitled to vote on the resolution rather than those entitled to attend the meeting. See also s.153, which allows requests by those whose shares are held on their account by others.

Subsection (4)

Requests may be in electronic form. The six-week period specified is exclusive of both the date when the request is made and the date of the meeting itself - see s.360.

339. Public companies: company's duty to circulate members' resolutions for AGMs

(1) A company that is required under section 338 to give notice of a resolution must send a copy of it to each member of the company entitled to receive notice of the annual general meeting-
   (a) in the same manner as notice of the meeting, and
   (b) at the same time as, or as soon as reasonably practicable after, it gives notice of the meeting.
(2) Subsection (1) has effect subject to section 340(2) (deposit or tender of sum in respect of expenses of circulation).
(3) The business which may be dealt with at an annual general meeting includes a resolution of which notice is given in accordance with this section.
(4) In the event of default in complying with this section, an offence is committed by every officer of the company who is in default.
(5) A person guilty of an offence under this section is liable-
   (a) on conviction on indictment, to a fine;
   (b) on summary conviction, to a fine not exceeding the statutory maximum.

GENERAL NOTE

This section re-enacts parts of ss.376 and 377 of the 1985 Act as to how a company must comply with a valid requisition under the previous section. It is subject to a right to refuse compliance under the following section.

340. Public companies: expenses of circulating members' resolutions for AGM

(1) The expenses of the company in complying with section 339 need not be paid by the members who requested the circulation of the resolution if requests sufficient to require the company to circulate it are received before the end of the financial year preceding the meeting.
(2) Otherwise-
   (a) the expenses of the company in complying with that section must be paid by the members who requested the circulation of the resolution unless the company resolves otherwise, and
   (b) unless the company has previously so resolved, it is not bound to comply with that section unless there is deposited with or tendered to it, not later than-

    (i) six weeks before the annual general meeting to which the requests relate, or
    (ii) if later, the time at which notice is given of that meeting,
a sum reasonably sufficient to meet its expenses in complying with that section.

GENERAL NOTE

    This section makes a major change from s.377(1)(b) of the 1985 Act. If a valid requisition under s.345 is made before the end of the company's financial year preceding the meeting then the expenses of circulating the resolution need not be paid by the requisitionists. A similar change was made in s.316 on the circulation of members' statements but not in s.294 in respect of written resolutions.

    Otherwise the pre-existing position applies and the company, unless it resolves otherwise, may refuse to circulate the resolution unless sufficient monies are deposited or tendered by the requisitionists to defray the costs. The six week period specified is exclusive of both the dates when the sum is deposited or tendered and the date of the meeting itself - see s.360.

    See also the note to s.316.

CHAPTER 5

ADDITIONAL REQUIREMENTS FOR QUOTED COMPANIES

Website publication of poll results

341. Results of poll to be made available on website

(1) Where a poll is taken at a general meeting of a quoted company, the company must ensure that the following information is made available on a website-
    (a) the date of the meeting,
    (b) the text of the resolution or, as the case may be, a description of the subject matter of the poll,
    (c) the number of votes cast in favour, and
    (d) the number of votes cast against.
(2) The provisions of section 353 (requirements as to website availability) apply.
(3) In the event of default in complying with this section (or with the requirements of section 353 as it applies for the purposes of this section), an offence is committed by every officer of the company who is in default.
(4) A person guilty of an offence under subsection (3) is liable on summary conviction to a fine not exceeding level 3 on the standard scale.
(5) Failure to comply with this section (or the requirements of section 353) does not affect the validity of-
    (a) the poll, or
    (b) the resolution or other business (if passed or agreed to) to which the poll relates.
(6) This section only applies to polls taken after this section comes into force.

GENERAL NOTE

    This Chapter sets out two new obligations on quoted companies only. A quoted company is defined in s.361 by reference to s.385. In essence it includes all listed companies in the United Kingdom, the EEA, the New York Stock Exchange and the Nasdaq.

    This section sets out the first new obligation and implements Art.15 of the draft directive COM(2005)685 final, in advance. See also the CLR's *Final Report* para.6.39(ii). It will be a criminal offence not to publish the required details of a poll on a website (see s.353), although there is no time limit for compliance specified in the section. Failure will not, however, affect the validity of the poll or the underlying resolution or business.

Subsection (6)

    This section will not operate retrospectively on polls demanded but not taken before this section comes into force.

Independent report on poll

342. Members' power to require independent report on poll

(1) The members of a quoted company may require the directors to obtain an independent report on any poll taken, or to be taken, at a general meeting of the company.

(2) The directors are required to obtain an independent report if they receive requests to do so from-

    (a) members representing not less than 5% of the total voting rights of all the members who have a right to vote on the matter to which the poll relates (excluding any voting rights attached to any shares in the company held as treasury shares), or

    (b) not less than 100 members who have a right to vote on the matter to which the poll relates and hold shares in the company on which there has been paid up an average sum, per member, of not less than £100.

See also section 153 (exercise of rights where shares held on behalf of others).

(3) Where the requests relate to more than one poll, subsection (2) must be satisfied in relation to each of them.

(4) A request-

    (a) may be in hard copy form or in electronic form,

    (b) must identify the poll or polls to which it relates,

    (c) must be authenticated by the person or persons making it, and

    (d) must be received by the company not later than one week after the date on which the poll is taken.

GENERAL NOTE

This second obligation, to submit on request to an independent report on the conduct of any poll taken, was introduced on the recommendation of the CLR, *Final Report*, para.6.39(iv), and after positive responses to the 2002 and 2005 White Papers (Cm.5333-1 and Cm.6456). It was also backed by Paul Myners' *Review of impediments to voting United Kingdom shares*. The concept was the subject of considerable political debate. See in particular: *Hansard*, HL GC Day 6, Vol.679, col.134 (March 1, 2006); *Hansard*, HL Report, Vol.682, cols 731 *et seq* (May 9, 2006) and HC Comm D, cols 336 *et seq*.

The reason for introducing this right was a perceived lack of confidence in the integrity and effectiveness of the counting of proxies - in particular in registering voting instructions. It is seen as a method of obtaining transparency. However, an adverse report will not legally affect the result of the poll.

Subsection (1)

This right applies to any meeting of a quoted company and not just the AGM.

Subsection (2)

These thresholds are similar to those entitled to circulate a resolution at a public company's AGM or a statement at any meeting. The denominator is those entitled to vote on the matter to which the poll relates. The threshold must be met in relation to each poll (subs.(3)). See also s.153, which allows requests from those whose shares are held on their account by others.

Subsection (4)

The request for an independent report can be made in advance of the meeting (giving the assessor the right to attend the meeting - see s.348) even in advance of the demand for a poll. Since the thresholds for both are similar that will not be a problem in practice. The request may also be made up to one week after the date of the poll, although the effectiveness of the assessor may be less in such cases. There is no time limit for the preparation of the report.

343. Appointment of independent assessor

(1) Directors who are required under section 342 to obtain an independent report on a poll or polls must appoint a person they consider to be appropriate (an "independent assessor") to prepare a report for the company on it or them.

(2) The appointment must be made within one week after the company being required to obtain the report.

(3) The directors must not appoint a person who-
  (a) does not meet the independence requirement in section 344, or
  (b) has another role in relation to any poll on which he is to report (including, in particular, a role in connection with collecting or counting votes or with the appointment of proxies).

(4) In the event of default in complying with this section, an offence is committed by every officer of the company who is in default.

(5) A person guilty of an offence under this section is liable on summary conviction to a fine not exceeding level 5 on the standard scale.

(6) If at the meeting no poll on which a report is required is taken-
  (a) the directors are not required to obtain a report from the independent assessor, and
  (b) his appointment ceases (but without prejudice to any right to be paid for work done before the appointment ceased).

GENERAL NOTE

An independent assessor requested under the previous section must be appointed by the directors within one week of a valid request. The section provides that no-one connected with the voting process can be appointed. It was suggested by the minister in HC Committee D, col 342, that the registrar of another company would be a good choice which suggests that the lack of confidence in voting procedures may not be very deep. Failure to appoint will be a criminal offence by those officers of the company in default.

For what is meant by independent - see the following section.

Subsection (6)

Given the similarity between the thresholds for demanding a poll and for requiring a report, this is not a likely scenario.

344. Independence requirement

(1) A person may not be appointed as an independent assessor-
  (a) if he is-
    (i) an officer or employee of the company, or
    (ii) a partner or employee of such a person, or a partnership of which such a person is a partner;
  (b) if he is-
    (i) an officer or employee of an associated undertaking of the company, or
    (ii) a partner or employee of such a person, or a partnership of which such a person is a partner;
  (c) if there exists between-
    (i) the person or an associate of his, and
    (ii) the company or an associated undertaking of the company,
  a connection of any such description as may be specified by regulations made by the Secretary of State.

(2) An auditor of the company is not regarded as an officer or employee of the company for this purpose.

(3) In this section-
  "associated undertaking" means-

    (a) a parent undertaking or subsidiary undertaking of the company, or

    (b) a subsidiary undertaking of a parent undertaking of the company; and

"associate" has the meaning given by section 345.

  (4) Regulations under this section are subject to negative resolution procedure.

GENERAL NOTE

This section provides a number of categories of persons who would not be regarded as independent for the purposes of the previous section. They include officers and employees of either the company or an associated undertaking (see subs.(3)), partners of either of those (*quaere* limited partners in a limited partnership?), and those with such links to be decided on by regulations as between anyone or his associate and the company or associated undertaking.

    Associate - s.345.

Subsection (2)

Auditors are not excluded by virtue of being regarded as either an officer or employee of the company (*quaere* auditors of an associated undertaking?)

345. Meaning of "associate"

  (1) This section defines "associate" for the purposes of section 344 (independence requirement).

  (2) In relation to an individual, "associate" means-

    (a) that individual's spouse or civil partner or minor child or step-child,

    (b) any body corporate of which that individual is a director, and

    (c) any employee or partner of that individual.

  (3) In relation to a body corporate, "associate" means-

    (a) any body corporate of which that body is a director,

    (b) any body corporate in the same group as that body, and

    (c) any employee or partner of that body or of any body corporate in the same group.

  (4) In relation to a partnership that is a legal person under the law by which it is governed, "associate" means-

    (a) any body corporate of which that partnership is a director,

    (b) any employee of or partner in that partnership, and

    (c) any person who is an associate of a partner in that partnership.

  (5) In relation to a partnership that is not a legal person under the law by which it is governed, "associate" means any person who is an associate of any of the partners.

  (6) In this section, in relation to a limited liability partnership, for "director" read "member".

GENERAL NOTE

This section defines who is an associate for the purposes of the previous section. It covers associates of individuals, bodies corporate (including LLPs), United Kingdom partnerships (Scottish ones have legal personality) and overseas partnerships, with or without legal personality.

It is not clear whether the wording of subs.(5) includes associates of limited partners in a United Kingdom limited partnership.

346. Effect of appointment of a partnership

  (1) This section applies where a partnership that is not a legal person under the law by which it is governed is appointed as an independent assessor.

  (2) Unless a contrary intention appears, the appointment is of the partnership as such and not of the partners.

  (3) Where the partnership ceases, the appointment is to be treated as extending to-

    (a) any partnership that succeeds to the practice of that partnership, or

(b) any other person who succeeds to that practice having previously carried it on in partnership.

(4) For the purposes of subsection (3)-

(a) a partnership is regarded as succeeding to the practice of another partnership only if
the members of the successor partnership are substantially the same as those of the
former partnership, and

(b) a partnership or other person is regarded as succeeding to the practice of a partnership
only if it or he succeeds to the whole or substantially the whole of the business of the
former partnership.

(5) Where the partnership ceases and the appointment is not treated under subsection (3) as
extending to any partnership or other person, the appointment may with the consent of the
company be treated as extending to a partnership, or other person, who succeeds to-

(a) the business of the former partnership, or

(b) such part of it as is agreed by the company is to be treated as comprising the appointment.

GENERAL NOTE

This section is required because, with the exception of Scotland, United Kingdom partnerships and limited partnerships
do not have legal personality. As is often the case, the section ignores that and provides for a partnership appointed as an
independent assessor to be treated as an entity and so as the appointee. Elaborate provisions are then necessary in subss.(3)-
(5) to provide for continuity where the partnership ceases, which technically happens on every change of partner.

347.   The independent assessor's report

(1) The report of the independent assessor must state his opinion whether-

(a) the procedures adopted in connection with the poll or polls were adequate;

(b) the votes cast (including proxy votes) were fairly and accurately recorded and counted;

(c) the validity of members' appointments of proxies was fairly assessed;

(d) the notice of the meeting complied with section 325 (notice of meeting to contain
statement of rights to appoint proxy);

(e) section 326 (company-sponsored invitations to appoint proxies) was complied with in
relation to the meeting.

(2) The report must give his reasons for the opinions stated.

(3) If he is unable to form an opinion on any of those matters, the report must record that fact
and state the reasons for it.

(4) The report must state the name of the independent assessor.

GENERAL NOTE

This section details the minimum information required to be in an assessor's report and so provides a guide as to what
the process is intended to check.

The quality audit so required relates to conduct procedures, vote counting, proxies, notices and proxy forms. Reasons
must be given, including where the assessor was unable to form an opinion on any matter. In making this report the assessor
has the rights to attend meetings and obtain information as provided by the following two sections.

348.   Rights of independent assessor: right to attend meeting etc

(1) Where an independent assessor has been appointed to report on a poll, he is entitled to
attend-

(a) the meeting at which the poll may be taken, and

(b) any subsequent proceedings in connection with the poll.

(2) He is also entitled to be provided by the company with a copy of-

(a) the notice of the meeting, and

(b) any other communication provided by the company in connection with the meeting to persons who have a right to vote on the matter to which the poll relates.

(3) The rights conferred by this section are only to be exercised to the extent that the independent assessor considers necessary for the preparation of his report.

(4) If the independent assessor is a firm, the right under subsection (1) to attend the meeting and any subsequent proceedings in connection with the poll is exercisable by an individual authorised by the firm in writing to act as its representative for that purpose.

GENERAL NOTE

This section gives an assessor qualified rights to attend and receive documentation relating to the meeting where the poll will be taken and of any subsequent proceedings relating to the poll. This will be of limited use if the assessor is appointed after the meeting.

Subsection (3)

Although this qualifies the rights, the test is essentially a subjective one.

Subsection (4)

The concept of a partnership used in s.346 has here been replaced by a "firm", which is certainly wide enough to include all United Kingdom partnerships, limited partnerships and LLPs. There seems to be nothing in the legislation to prevent the appointment of a company as assessor (unless a contrary intention is divined), but does this subsection extend to them?

349. Rights of independent assessor: right to information

(1) The independent assessor is entitled to access to the company's records relating to-
    (a) any poll on which he is to report;
    (b) the meeting at which the poll or polls may be, or were, taken.

(2) The independent assessor may require anyone who at any material time was-
    (a) a director or secretary of the company,
    (b) an employee of the company,
    (c) a person holding or accountable for any of the company's records,
    (d) a member of the company, or
    (e) an agent of the company,
to provide him with information or explanations for the purpose of preparing his report.

(3) For this purpose "agent" includes the company's bankers, solicitors and auditor.

(4) A statement made by a person in response to a requirement under this section may not be used in evidence against him in criminal proceedings except proceedings for an offence under section 350 (offences relating to provision of information).

(5) A person is not required by this section to disclose information in respect of which a claim to legal professional privilege (in Scotland, to confidentiality of communications) could be maintained in legal proceedings.

GENERAL NOTE

This section gives the assessor the rights to access company records (see Ch.6 of this Part) on the relevant poll and meetings. It also imposes an obligation on various categories of persons (set out in subss.(2) and (3)) linked to the company to provide him with information or explanations for the purpose of the report. The definition of agent is non-inclusive.

Subsection (4)

There are criminal offences in the next section for breach of these requirements, although any information given cannot be used as evidence against the informant for any other offence.

Subsection (5)

There is a general exception for legal privilege.

350. Offences relating to provision of information

(1) A person who fails to comply with a requirement under section 349 without delay commits an offence unless it was not reasonably practicable for him to provide the required information or explanation.

(2) A person guilty of an offence under subsection (1) is liable on summary conviction to a fine not exceeding level 3 on the standard scale.

(3) A person commits an offence who knowingly or recklessly makes to an independent assessor a statement (oral or written) that-

    (a) conveys or purports to convey any information or explanations which the independent assessor requires, or is entitled to require, under section 349, and

    (b) is misleading, false or deceptive in a material particular.

(4) A person guilty of an offence under subsection (3) is liable-

    (a) on conviction on indictment, to imprisonment for a term not exceeding two years or a fine (or both);

    (b) on summary conviction-

        (i) in England and Wales, to imprisonment for a term not exceeding twelve months or to a fine not exceeding the statutory maximum (or both);

        (ii) in Scotland or Northern Ireland, to imprisonment for a term not exceeding six months, or to a fine not exceeding the statutory maximum (or both).

(5) Nothing in this section affects any right of an independent assessor to apply for an injunction (in Scotland, an interdict or an order for specific performance) to enforce any of his rights under section 348 or 349.

GENERAL NOTE

This section creates two offences. The first in subss.(1) and (2) is triggered by the non-compliance with a request (without delay) by anyone covered by the previous section. It is subject to a defence of not reasonably practical.

The second offence, in subss.(3) and (4), concerns the making of false, misleading or deceptive statements to assessors in response to a request under the previous section.

Subsection (5)

This subsection preserves an independent assessor's right to obtain an injunction or an order for specific performance.

351. Information to be made available on website

(1) Where an independent assessor has been appointed to report on a poll, the company must ensure that the following information is made available on a website-

    (a) the fact of his appointment,

    (b) his identity,

    (c) the text of the resolution or, as the case may be, a description of the subject matter of the poll to which his appointment relates, and

    (d) a copy of a report by him which complies with section 347.

(2) The provisions of section 353 (requirements as to website availability) apply.

(3) In the event of default in complying with this section (or with the requirements of section 353 as it applies for the purposes of this section), an offence is committed by every officer of the company who is in default.

(4) A person guilty of an offence under subsection (3) is liable on summary conviction to a fine not exceeding level 3 on the standard scale.

(5) Failure to comply with this section (or the requirements of section 353) does not affect the validity of-

    (a) the poll, or

    (b) the resolution or other business (if passed or agreed to) to which the poll relates.

GENERAL NOTE

This section (which must be read with s.353) requires any company subject to the appointment of an assessor to publish that fact, the details of both the assessor and the poll, and the report, on a website.

There are criminal penalties in default, but no civil consequences as to the validity of the poll or the underlying resolution or business.

Supplementary

352. Application of provisions to class meetings

(1) The provisions of-

section 341 (results of poll to be made available on website), and

sections 342 to 351 (independent report on poll),

apply (with any necessary modifications) in relation to a meeting of holders of a class of shares of a quoted company in connection with the variation of the rights attached to such shares as they apply in relation to a general meeting of the company.

(2) For the purposes of this section-

    (a) any amendment of a provision contained in a company's articles for the variation of the rights attached to a class of shares, or the insertion of any such provision into the articles, is itself to be treated as a variation of those rights, and

    (b) references to the variation of rights attached to a class of shares include references to their abrogation.

GENERAL NOTE

This section applies both of the obligations imposed on quoted companies by this Chapter to polls taken at class meetings with regard to the variation of class rights.

Subsection (2)

This is the standard expansion of the concept of a variation of class rights - see s.630(6).

353. Requirements as to website availability

(1) The following provisions apply for the purposes of-

section 341 (results of poll to be made available on website), and

section 351 (report of independent observer to be made available on website).

(2) The information must be made available on a website that-

    (a) is maintained by or on behalf of the company, and

    (b) identifies the company in question.

(3) Access to the information on the website, and the ability to obtain a hard copy of the information from the website, must not be conditional on the payment of a fee or otherwise restricted.

(4) The information-

    (a) must be made available as soon as reasonably practicable, and

    (b) must be kept available throughout the period of two years beginning with the date on which it is first made available on a website in accordance with this section.

(5) A failure to make information available on a website throughout the period specified in subsection (4)(b) is disregarded if-

    (a) the information is made available on the website for part of that period, and

    (b) the failure is wholly attributable to circumstances that it would not be reasonable to have expected the company to prevent or avoid.

GENERAL NOTE

This section sets out the minimum criteria for the website on which the results of a poll and/or the assessor's appointment and report must be displayed under s.351.

So long as the company is identified, the site may be maintained by a website service provider.

The information must be kept on the site for at least two years, although subs.(5) makes provision for partial website failure.

354. Power to limit or extend the types of company to which provisions of this Chapter apply

(1) The Secretary of State may by regulations-
    (a) limit the types of company to which some or all of the provisions of this Chapter apply, or
    (b) extend some or all of the provisions of this Chapter to additional types of company.
(2) Regulations under this section extending the application of any provision of this Chapter are subject to affirmative resolution procedure.
(3) Any other regulations under this section are subject to negative resolution procedure.
(4) Regulations under this section may-
    (a) amend the provisions of this Chapter (apart from this section);
    (b) repeal and re-enact provisions of this Chapter with modifications of form or arrangement, whether or not they are modified in substance;
    (c) contain such consequential, incidental and supplementary provisions (including provisions amending, repealing or revoking enactments) as the Secretary of State thinks fit.

GENERAL NOTE

Although there was no demand in the responses to the 2002 White Paper (Cm.5533-1), this section allows for regulations to make future changes to the scope of this Chapter.

First by extending the companies subject to it beyond those currently included, e.g. other companies with a wide shareholder base. Secondly, if there is such an extension, it will be possible to limit the application of some of the provisions to certain categories of company. The former regulations require the affirmative procedure (see s.1290), the latter, the negative procedure (see s.1189).

CHAPTER 6

RECORDS OF RESOLUTIONS AND MEETINGS

355. Records of resolutions and meetings etc

(1) Every company must keep records comprising-
    (a) copies of all resolutions of members passed otherwise than at general meetings,
    (b) minutes of all proceedings of general meetings, and
    (c) details provided to the company in accordance with section 357 (decisions of sole member).
(2) The records must be kept for at least ten years from the date of the resolution, meeting or decision (as appropriate).
(3) If a company fails to comply with this section, an offence is committed by every officer of the company who is in default.
(4) A person guilty of an offence under this section is liable on summary conviction to a fine not exceeding level 3 on the standard scale and, for continued contravention, a daily default fine not exceeding one-tenth of level 3 on the standard scale.

GENERAL NOTE

This Chapter replaces ss.318(2), 382A, 382B and 383 of the 1985 Act requiring companies to keep records of meetings and resolutions. Additional requirements as to the keeping of company records generally are in Pt 37 of this Act. The only changes of substance are that there is now a ten year minimum for keeping these records rather than an obligation to keep them forever and that the rules apply to class meetings. The parts of the 1985 Act relating to directors' meetings are now in Pt 10 of this Act.

This section re-enacts the obligation to keep records of all informal resolutions (written or effected under the *Duomatic* principle), minutes of general meetings and decisions of a sole member (see s.357). A new ten year minimum period is introduced. Failure to do so remains a criminal offence by those officers in default.

356. Records as evidence of resolutions etc

(1) This section applies to the records kept in accordance with section 355.

(2) The record of a resolution passed otherwise than at a general meeting, if purporting to be signed by a director of the company or by the company secretary, is evidence (in Scotland, sufficient evidence) of the passing of the resolution.

(3) Where there is a record of a written resolution of a private company, the requirements of this Act with respect to the passing of the resolution are deemed to be complied with unless the contrary is proved.

(4) The minutes of proceedings of a general meeting, if purporting to be signed by the chairman of that meeting or by the chairman of the next general meeting, are evidence (in Scotland, sufficient evidence) of the proceedings at the meeting.

(5) Where there is a record of proceedings of a general meeting of a company, then, until the contrary is proved-

   (a) the meeting is deemed duly held and convened,

   (b) all proceedings at the meeting are deemed to have duly taken place, and

   (c) all appointments at the meeting are deemed valid.

GENERAL NOTE

This section re-enacts the principle that the records of resolutions and the minutes of meetings kept under the previous section are evidence either that the resolution was passed (and in the case of a written resolution also that the procedure under the Act was complied with) or of the proceedings of the meeting, as appropriate. The copy of a resolution kept as a record must only purport to be signed by a director or the company secretary, if there is one.

Further, as in the 1985 Act, the minutes of a meeting are presumed to be accurate as to the holding of the meeting, its proceedings and any appointments made there unless the contrary can be proved.

357. Records of decisions by sole member

(1) This section applies to a company limited by shares or by guarantee that has only one member.

(2) Where the member takes any decision that-

   (a) may be taken by the company in general meeting, and

   (b) has effect as if agreed by the company in general meeting,

he must (unless that decision is taken by way of a written resolution) provide the company with details of that decision.

(3) If a person fails to comply with this section he commits an offence.

(4) A person guilty of an offence under this section is liable on summary conviction to a fine not exceeding level 2 on the standard scale.

(5) Failure to comply with this section does not affect the validity of any decision referred to in subsection (2).

GENERAL NOTE

This section directly re-enacts s.382B of the 1985 Act (added by SI 1992/1699) relating to the recording of decisions of a sole member. The effect is that there must be a written record of any decision which has the same effect as a resolution, with a criminal sanction but no civil consequences with regard to the effectiveness of the decision in default.

358.   Inspection of records of resolutions and meetings

(1) The records referred to in section 355 (records of resolutions etc) relating to the previous ten years must be kept available for inspection-
   (a) at the company's registered office, or
   (b) at a place specified in regulations under section 1136.
(2) The company must give notice to the registrar-
   (a) of the place at which the records are kept available for inspection, and
   (b) of any change in that place,
unless they have at all times been kept at the company's registered office.
(3) The records must be open to the inspection of any member of the company without charge.
(4) Any member may require a copy of any of the records on payment of such fee as may be prescribed.
(5) If default is made for 14 days in complying with subsection (2) or an inspection required under subsection (3) is refused, or a copy requested under subsection (4) is not sent, an offence is committed by every officer of the company who is in default.
(6) A person guilty of an offence under this section is liable on summary conviction to a fine not exceeding level 3 on the standard scale and, for continued contravention, a daily default fine not exceeding one-tenth of level 3 on the standard scale.
(7) In a case in which an inspection required under subsection (3) is refused or a copy requested under subsection (4) is not sent, the court may by order compel an immediate inspection of the records or direct that the copies required be sent to the persons who requested them.

GENERAL NOTE

This section re-enacts, with modifications, the rights of members to inspect, without charge, and to obtain a copy of the records of resolutions and meetings which companies are required to keep under s.357.

Subsections (1) and (2)

The records may now be kept either at the company's registered office or at a place to be specified in regulations made under s.1137. This has the consequence of imposing an obligation on the company to notify the registrar as to where the records are in fact kept and of any change.

Subsections (3)-(7)

As before, there is a prescribed charge for obtaining a copy. Failure to comply with the new notification obligations to the registrar under subs.(2) within 14 days or a refusal to allow inspection or failure to provide a copy under subs.(1) are criminal offences by those officers in default and the court may also order an inspection or the production of a copy.

359.   Records of resolutions and meetings of class of members

The provisions of this Chapter apply (with necessary modifications) in relation to resolutions and meetings of-
   (a) holders of a class of shares, and
   (b) in the case of a company without a share capital, a class of members,
as they apply in relation to resolutions of members generally and to general meetings.

GENERAL NOTE

This new section applies the previous sections in this Chapter to meetings of a class of shareholders or members as appropriate.

CHAPTER 7

SUPPLEMENTARY PROVISIONS

360. Computation of periods of notice etc: clear day rule

(1) This section applies for the purposes of the following provisions of this Part-

    section 307(1) and (2) (notice required of general meeting),

    section 312(1) and (3) (resolution requiring special notice),

    section 314(4)(d) (request to circulate members' statement),

    section 316(2)(b) (expenses of circulating statement to be deposited or tendered before meeting),

    section 338(4)(d)(i) (request to circulate member's resolution at AGM of public company), and

    section 340(2)(b)(i) (expenses of circulating statement to be deposited or tendered before meeting).

(2) Any reference in those provisions to a period of notice, or to a period before a meeting by which a request must be received or sum deposited or tendered, is to a period of the specified length excluding-

    (a) the day of the meeting, and

    (b) the day on which the notice is given, the request received or the sum deposited or tendered.

GENERAL NOTE

This new section makes it clear that, in the cases specified, where the Act provides a notice period for a meeting or resolution, or the lodging of a request or the depositing or tendering of a sum, that period does not include either the day of the meeting or the day when the notice was given, the request made or the sum tendered or deposited. Thus the notice periods, etc. are exclusive of either date.

361. Meaning of "quoted company"

In this Part "quoted company" has the same meaning as in Part 15 of this Act.

GENERAL NOTE

This new section defines what is meant by a quoted company for the purposes of the new obligations to publish the results of a poll on a website and for the appointment of an independent assessor to report on a poll. It imports the definition used in s.385 in Pt 15 of the Act. This means officially listed companies in the United Kingdom, the EEA and New York (including the Nasdaq).

PART 14

CONTROL OF POLITICAL DONATIONS AND EXPENDITURE

Introductory

362. Introductory

This Part has effect for controlling-

    (a) political donations made by companies to political parties, to other political organisations and to independent election candidates, and

    (b) political expenditure incurred by companies.

DEFINITIONS

"Political donation": see s.364 (Meaning of "political donation")

"Political expenditure": see s.365 (Meaning of "political expenditure")

"Political parties": see s.363(1) (Political parties, organisations etc to which this Part applies)

"Political organisation": see s.363(2) Political parties, organisations etc to which this Part applies)

"Independent election candidate": see s.363(3) (Political parties, organisations etc to which this Part applies)

GENERAL NOTE

This provision replaces s.347A(1) of the 1985 Act, introduced by the Political Parties, Elections and Referendums Act 2000.

    Lord McKenzie, in the House of Lords, gave an overview of this Part of the Act:

    "In October 1998, the Committee on Standards in Public Life presented to the Prime Minister its report on the funding of political parties in the United Kingdom. The report recommended that any company that intended to make a donation either in cash or in kind - including any sponsorship, loans or transactions at favourable rates - to a political party or organisation should be required to have the prior authority of its shareholders. The Government accepted that recommendation and implemented it through the Political Parties, Elections and Referendums Act 2000, by inserting a new regime for control of political donations and expenditure into the Companies Act 1985 as Pt XA of that Act.

    [Part14] ... largely restates the provisions of Part XA in a style consistent with the other clauses. In particular, companies will continue to be prohibited from making a donation to a political party or other political organisation and incurring political expenditure unless the donation or expenditure has been authorised -typically, by the members of the company. A political donation will continue to be defined by reference to ss.50-52 of the Act. However, the Bill makes some important changes to the current regime in the light of representations that we have received from companies and business organisations. In particular, [Pt 14] introduces greater flexibility for companies. The Bill will, for example, permit holding companies to seek authorisation for donations and expenditure in respect of both the holding company itself and one or more subsidiaries through a single approval resolution" (*Hansard*, HL GC Day 6, Vol.678, cols 139-140 (March 1, 2006)).

    Lord McKenzie went on to state the rationale for this Part as follows:

    "[T]he wider company law rationale for this part is to regulate conflicts of interest. We do not believe that it is acceptable for directors to support political parties that promote policies with which they personally agree, rather than policies that will benefit the company" (*Hansard*, HL GC Day 6, Vol.678, cols 139-140 (March 1, 2006)).

Donations and expenditure to which this Part applies

363.   Political parties, organisations etc to which this Part applies

    (1) This Part applies to a political party if-

        (a) it is registered under Part 2 of the Political Parties, Elections and Referendums Act 2000 (c. 41), or

        (b) it carries on, or proposes to carry on, activities for the purposes of or in connection with the participation of the party in any election or elections to public office held in a member State other than the United Kingdom.

    (2) This Part applies to an organisation (a "political organisation") if it carries on, or proposes to carry on, activities that are capable of being reasonably regarded as intended-

        (a) to affect public support for a political party to which, or an independent election candidate to whom, this Part applies, or

        (b) to influence voters in relation to any national or regional referendum held under the law of the United Kingdom or another member State.

    (3) This Part applies to an independent election candidate at any election to public office held in the United Kingdom or another member State.

(4) Any reference in the following provisions of this Part to a political party, political organisation or independent election candidate, or to political expenditure, is to a party, organisation, independent candidate or expenditure to which this Part applies.

GENERAL NOTE

This section replaces s.347A(6), (7) and (9) of the 1985 Act.

364. Meaning of "political donation"

(1) The following provisions have effect for the purposes of this Part as regards the meaning of "political donation".

(2) In relation to a political party or other political organisation-
  (a) "political donation" means anything that in accordance with sections 50 to 52 of the Political Parties, Elections and Referendums Act 2000-
    (i) constitutes a donation for the purposes of Chapter 1 of Part 4 of that Act (control of donations to registered parties), or
    (ii) would constitute such a donation reading references in those sections to a registered party as references to any political party or other political organisation,
  and
  (b) section 53 of that Act applies, in the same way, for the purpose of determining the value of a donation.

(3) In relation to an independent election candidate-
  (a) "political donation" means anything that, in accordance with sections 50 to 52 of that Act, would constitute a donation for the purposes of Chapter 1 of Part 4 of that Act (control of donations to registered parties) reading references in those sections to a registered party as references to the independent election candidate, and
  (b) section 53 of that Act applies, in the same way, for the purpose of determining the value of a donation.

(4) For the purposes of this section, sections 50 and 53 of the Political Parties, Elections and Referendums Act 2000 (c. 41) (definition of "donation" and value of donations) shall be treated as if the amendments to those sections made by the Electoral Administration Act 2006 (which remove from the definition of "donation" loans made otherwise than on commercial terms) had not been made.

GENERAL NOTE

This provision replaces s.347A(4) of the 1985 Act. The significant change is that it extends the definition to include independent election candidates.

On the question of whether a payment to a political party for the promotion or advertising of that company's product or services would be construed as a political donation Lord McKenzie stated:

"Part IV of the Political Parties, Elections and Referendums Act 2000 already recognises that companies may interact with political parties on commercial terms. It is also important to remember that s.50(2)(a) of that Act states that 'donation' means 'any gift to the party of money or other property'. A payment to a political party for the purposes of promoting or advertising the products or services of the company will not be treated as a gift if it is genuinely commensurate with the value of the service provided by the political party" (*Hansard*, HL GC Day 6, Vol.678, cols 145-146 (March 1, 2006)).

Subsection (4)

Lord McKenzie explained the meaning of this section at Report Stage in the House of Lords:

"This clause refers to the definition of 'political donation' set out in the Political Parties, Elections and Referendums Act 2000. Changes to this definition have recently been agreed by way of amendments to the Electoral Administration Bill in this House relating to loans made to political parties. The amendment to clause [364 (Meaning of 'political donation')] ensures that the scope of this provision is not altered by the changes to the Political Parties, Elections and Referendums Act 2000 made by the Electoral Administration Bill. In other words, [Pt 14] of this Bill will continue to apply only to political donations, which are defined as including loans at a non-commercial rate. It remains the case that [Pt 14] does not apply to loans at a commercial rate" (*Hansard*, HL Report Stage, col.912 (May 10, 2006)).

365. Meaning of "political expenditure"

(1) In this Part "political expenditure", in relation to a company, means expenditure incurred by the company on-
  (a) the preparation, publication or dissemination of advertising or other promotional or publicity material-
      (i) of whatever nature, and
      (ii) however published or otherwise disseminated,
  that, at the time of publication or dissemination, is capable of being reasonably regarded as intended to affect public support for a political party or other political organisation, or an independent election candidate, or
  (b) activities on the part of the company that are capable of being reasonably regarded as intended-
      (i) to affect public support for a political party or other political organisation, or an independent election candidate, or
      (ii) to influence voters in relation to any national or regional referendum held under the law of a member State.
(2) For the purposes of this Part a political donation does not count as political expenditure.

GENERAL NOTE
This provision replaces s.347A(5) of the 1985 Act.

Authorisation required for donations or expenditure

366. Authorisation required for donations or expenditure

(1) A company must not-
  (a) make a political donation to a political party or other political organisation, or to an independent election candidate, or
  (b) incur any political expenditure,
unless the donation or expenditure is authorised in accordance with the following provisions.
(2) The donation or expenditure must be authorised-
  (a) in the case of a company that is not a subsidiary of another company, by a resolution of the members of the company;
  (b) in the case of a company that is a subsidiary of another company by-
      (i) a resolution of the members of the company, and
      (ii) a resolution of the members of any relevant holding company.
(3) No resolution is required on the part of a company that is a wholly-owned subsidiary of a UK-registered company.
(4) For the purposes of subsection (2)(b)(ii) a "relevant holding company" means a company that, at the time the donation was made or the expenditure was incurred-
  (a) was a holding company of the company by which the donation was made or the expenditure was incurred,
  (b) was a UK-registered company, and
  (c) was not a subsidiary of another UK-registered company.
(5) The resolution or resolutions required by this section-
  (a) must comply with section 367 (form of authorising resolution), and
  (b) must be passed before the donation is made or the expenditure incurred.

(6) Nothing in this section enables a company to be authorised to do anything that it could not lawfully do apart from this section.

GENERAL NOTE

This provision replaces s.347C(1) and (6) and s.347D of the 1985 Act. There are three significant changes. First, a donation or expenditure by a subsidiary must be authorised by the members of the company and also a resolution of any relevant holding company. A "relevant holding company" is a United Kingdom holding company that is not the subsidiary of any other company (subs.(5)). Second,ly a resolution is not required for donation or expenditure by a wholly-owned subsidiary of a United Kingdom company, only from the relevant holding company. Thirdly, the section no longer prohibits retrospective ratification of any breach of the rules (which presumably must be effected in accordance with s.239). Lord McKenzie made the following comment on this third change:

> "It is our intention - and we believe the effect of these clauses - that members will be able to ratify an unauthorised donation or political expenditure and that, in such cases, the director will not continue to have any liability for the failure to obtain authorisation. Similarly, Part [14 (Control of political donations and expenditure)] will not prevent a director applying for relief under section [1157 (Power of court to grant relief in certain cases)] from the court" (*Hansard*, HL GC Day 6, Vol.678, col.149 (March 1, 2006))).

A question that was repeatedly raised during this Part's passage through Parliament was why a director cannot make a political donation or incur political expenditure without a resolution if he considers that it would promote the success of the company, or why board authorisation is not sufficient. Lord McKenzie gave the following response:

> "It is important that donations and expenditure are authorised by the company's members, not by the board of directors. The reforms introduced in 2000 that implemented a recommendation by the Committee on Standards in Public Life reflected the view that it is important to regulate political donations that might be seen to reflect the director's personal viewpoint rather than the interests of the company. That is the nuisance that we are seeking to avoid, and the requirement for member authorisation is needed to achieve that ... [I]t has long been accepted that where the possibility of a conflict of interest is particular acute there should be a requirement for shareholder consent" (*Hansard*, HL GC Day 6, Vol.678, col.149 (March 1, 2006)).

To this extent, the requirement of member authorisation for political donations and expenditure is no different from the specific no-conflict rules in Ch.4 of Pt 10.

See s.367 (Form of authorising resolution).

367. Form of authorising resolution

(1) A resolution conferring authorisation for the purposes of this Part may relate to-
    (a) the company passing the resolution,
    (b) one or more subsidiaries of that company, or
    (c) the company passing the resolution and one or more subsidiaries of that company.

(2) A resolution may be expressed to relate to all companies that are subsidiaries of the company passing the resolution-
    (a) at the time the resolution is passed, or
    (b) at any time during the period for which the resolution has effect,
without identifying them individually.

(3) The resolution may authorise donations or expenditure under one or more of the following heads-
    (a) donations to political parties or independent election candidates;
    (b) donations to political organisations other than political parties;
    (c) political expenditure.

(4) The resolution must specify a head or heads-
    (a) in the case of a resolution under subsection (2), for all of the companies to which it relates taken together;
    (b) in the case of any other resolution, for each company to which it relates.

(5) The resolution must be expressed in general terms conforming with subsection (2) and must not purport to authorise particular donations or expenditure.

(6) For each of the specified heads the resolution must authorise donations or, as the case may be, expenditure up to a specified amount in the period for which the resolution has effect (see section 368).

(7) The resolution must specify such amounts-

(a) in the case of a resolution under subsection (2), for all of the companies to which it relates taken together;

(b) in the case of any other resolution, for each company to which it relates.

GENERAL NOTE

This provision replaces s.347C(2) and (4) of the 1985 Act with two substantive changes, set out by Lord McKenzie in Grand Committee:

"The Bill introduces two important reforms. A holding company will be permitted to seek authorisation of donations and expenditure in respect of both itself and one or more of its subsidiaries, including non-wholly-owned subsidiaries, in a single approval resolution. Nothing in the clause would prevent authorisation covering all a company's subsidiaries; a company may pass separate approval resolutions in respect of donations to political parties and donations to other political organisations" (*Hansard*, HL GC Day 4, Vol.678, cols 150-151 (March 1, 2006)).

Lord McKenzie went on to explain the government's intention:

"It is our intention to provide flexibility. We believe, for example, that a holding company should be permitted to state one aggregate amount to cover the total amounts paid or incurred by all the companies for, on the one hand, political donations and, on the other, political expenditure" (*Hansard*, HL GC Day 4, Vol.678, cols 150-151 (March 1, 2006)).

368. Period for which resolution has effect

(1) A resolution conferring authorisation for the purposes of this Part has effect for a period of four years beginning with the date on which it is passed unless the directors determine, or the articles require, that it is to have effect for a shorter period beginning with that date.

(2) The power of the directors to make a determination under this section is subject to any provision of the articles that operates to prevent them from doing so.

GENERAL NOTE

This provision restates s.347C(3)(b) of the 1985 Act without substantive change.

Remedies in case of unauthorised donations or expenditure

369. Liability of directors in case of unauthorised donation or expenditure

(1) This section applies where a company has made a political donation or incurred political expenditure without the authorisation required by this Part.

(2) The directors in default are jointly and severally liable-

(a) to make good to the company the amount of the unauthorised donation or expenditure, with interest, and

(b) to compensate the company for any loss or damage sustained by it as a result of the unauthorised donation or expenditure having been made.

(3) The directors in default are-

(a) those who, at the time the unauthorised donation was made or the unauthorised expenditure was incurred, were directors of the company by which the donation was made or the expenditure was incurred, and

(b) where-

(i) that company was a subsidiary of a relevant holding company, and

(ii) the directors of the relevant holding company failed to take all reasonable steps to prevent the donation being made or the expenditure being incurred,

the directors of the relevant holding company.

(4) For the purposes of subsection (3)(b) a "relevant holding company" means a company that, at the time the donation was made or the expenditure was incurred-

(a) was a holding company of the company by which the donation was made or the expenditure was incurred,

(b) was a UK-registered company, and

(c) was not a subsidiary of another UK-registered company.

(5) The interest referred to in subsection (2)(a) is interest on the amount of the unauthorised donation or expenditure, so far as not made good to the company-

(a) in respect of the period beginning with the date when the donation was made or the expenditure was incurred, and

(b) at such rate as the Secretary of State may prescribe by regulations.

Section 379(2) (construction of references to date when donation made or expenditure incurred) does not apply for the purposes of this subsection.

(6) Where only part of a donation or expenditure was unauthorised, this section applies only to so much of it as was unauthorised.

GENERAL NOTE

This provision replaces s.347F of the 1985 Act. The provision introduces two changes. First, only directors of the company and any relevant holding company will be liable. This is said to reflect the new rules for authorisation under s.366 (Authorisation required for donations or expenditure). Margaret Hodge explained that the underlying policy intention of the section "is to ensure that if, for example, the directors of a holding company use the controlling voting rights that they have in a subsidiary to pass a resolution authorising the subsidiary to make a political donation without an authorising resolution from the members of the holding company, they, as well as the directors of the subsidiary, are liable" (HC Comm D, col.363 (June 29, 2006)). Second, a director will be permitted to apply to the court for relief under Power of the court to grant relief in certain cases. As such, directors of a relevant holding company who do not know of any unauthorised political donations or expenditure can apply for relief.

The Explanatory Notes state that the conditions for exemption from liability found in the 1985 Act have not been reproduced in the new Act. "However, directors of the 'relevant holding company' will not be liable for an unauthorised political donation or unauthorised political expenditure by a subsidiary if they took 'all reasonable steps to prevent the donation being made or the expenditure being incurred'" (Explanatory Notes, at para.599).

Also see s.1157 (Power of court to grant relief in certain circumstances) (replacing Companies Act 1985, s.727).

370. Enforcement of directors' liabilities by shareholder action

(1) Any liability of a director under section 369 is enforceable-

(a) in the case of a liability of a director of a company to that company, by proceedings brought under this section in the name of the company by an authorised group of its members;

(b) in the case of a liability of a director of a holding company to a subsidiary, by proceedings brought under this section in the name of the subsidiary by-

(i) an authorised group of members of the subsidiary, or

(ii) an authorised group of members of the holding company.

(2) This is in addition to the right of the company to which the liability is owed to bring proceedings itself to enforce the liability.

(3) An "authorised group" of members of a company means-

(a) the holders of not less than 5% in nominal value of the company's issued share capital,

(b) if the company is not limited by shares, not less than 5% of its members, or

(c) not less than 50 of the company's members.

(4) The right to bring proceedings under this section is subject to the provisions of section 371.

(5) Nothing in this section affects any right of a member of a company to bring or continue proceedings under Part 11 (derivative claims or proceedings).

GENERAL NOTE

This provision is derived from s.347I of the 1985 Act without substantive change.

Subsection (1)

Margaret Hodge explained this section as follows:

"[C]lause [369 (Liability of directors in case of unauthorised donation or expenditure)] imposes liability on the directors of the subsidiary donor company and its relevant holding company. Clause [370 (Enforcement of directors' liabilities by shareholder action)] gives conduct of legal proceedings to enforce the liability to members of the company. In that case, 'the company' means the donor company, not the relevant holding company. However, if the company is a wholly-owned subsidiary, it will not have any members with an interest in pursuing the action. Accordingly, the action must be capable of being brought in the name of the donor company by members of the relevant holding company, and, arguably, by members of any intermediate holding company, too" (*Hansard*, HC Comm D cols 364-365 (June 29, 2006)).

As originally drafted this section did not achieve this result. Consequently a number of amendments were accepted at Report Stage in the House of Commons:

"[T]he amendments address the problem by giving the right to bring proceedings to shareholders of the subsidiary and the shareholders of the holding company. That will ensure that the directors of the holding company can be held to account by their shareholders if they use subsidiaries that they control to make unauthorised donations" (Margaret Hodge HC Report Stage, col.961 (October 18, 2006, 2006)).

371. Enforcement of directors' liabilities by shareholder action: supplementary

(1) A group of members may not bring proceedings under section 370 in the name of a company unless-
  (a) the group has given written notice to the company stating-
    (i) the cause of action and a summary of the facts on which the proceedings are to be based,
    (ii) the names and addresses of the members comprising the group, and
    (iii) the grounds on which it is alleged that those members constitute an authorised group; and
  (b) not less than 28 days have elapsed between the date of the giving of the notice to the company and the bringing of the proceedings.

(2) Where such a notice is given to a company, any director of the company may apply to the court within the period of 28 days beginning with the date of the giving of the notice for an order directing that the proposed proceedings shall not be brought, on one or more of the following grounds-
  (a) that the unauthorised amount has been made good to the company;
  (b) that proceedings to enforce the liability have been brought, and are being pursued with due diligence, by the company;
  (c) that the members proposing to bring proceedings under this section do not constitute an authorised group.

(3) Where an application is made on the ground mentioned in subsection (2)(b), the court may as an alternative to directing that the proposed proceedings under section 370 are not to be brought, direct-
  (a) that such proceedings may be brought on such terms and conditions as the court thinks fit, and
  (b) that the proceedings brought by the company-
    (i) shall be discontinued, or
    (ii) may be continued on such terms and conditions as the court thinks fit.

(4) The members by whom proceedings are brought under section 370 owe to the company in whose name they are brought the same duties in relation to the proceedings as would be owed by the company's directors if the proceedings were being brought by the company.

But proceedings to enforce any such duty may be brought by the company only with the permission of the court.

(5) Proceedings brought under section 370 may not be discontinued or settled by the group except with the permission of the court, which may be given on such terms as the court thinks fit.

DEFINITIONS

"Authorised group": see s.370(3) (Enforcement of directors' liabilities by shareholder action)

GENERAL NOTE

This section was introduced at Report Stage in the House of Commons to give further clarification of the procedure for shareholder action under s.370 (Enforcement of directors' liabilities by shareholder action) and gives the court a supervisory role in relation to course of the proceedings.

Subsection (1)

This subsection makes it a prerequisite to a shareholder action that the group has written to the company more than 28 days before the bringing of proceedings stating the cause of action, the alleged facts, the names and addresses of the members of the group, and the grounds on which those members constitute an authorised group.

Subsections (2) and (3)

This subsection allows the directors of the company to stop proceedings if the unauthorised amount has been made good, the company is pursuing the matter with due diligence, or the members do not constitute an authorised group. If the company is pursuing the matter, then the court has the power under subs.(3) to direct that the shareholder action may be brought on such terms as it thinks fit, including that the proceedings be discontinued.

372. Costs of shareholder action

(1) This section applies in relation to proceedings brought under section 370 in the name of a company ("the company") by an authorised group ("the group").

(2) The group may apply to the court for an order directing the company to indemnify the group in respect of costs incurred or to be incurred by the group in connection with the proceedings.

The court may make such an order on such terms as it thinks fit.

(3) The group is not entitled to be paid any such costs out of the assets of the company except by virtue of such an order.

(4) If no such order has been made with respect to the proceedings, then-

    (a) if the company is awarded costs in connection with the proceedings, or it is agreed that costs incurred by the company in connection with the proceedings should be paid by any defendant, the costs shall be paid to the group; and

    (b) if any defendant is awarded costs in connection with the proceedings, or it is agreed that any defendant should be paid costs incurred by him in connection with the proceedings, the costs shall be paid by the group.

(5) In the application of this section to Scotland for "costs" read "expenses" and for "defendant" read "defender".

GENERAL NOTE

This provision replaces s.347J of the 1985 Act without substantive change.

373. Information for purposes of shareholder action

(1) Where proceedings have been brought under section 370 in the name of a company by an authorised group, the group is entitled to require the company to provide it with all information relating to the subject matter of the proceedings that is in the company's possession or under its control or which is reasonably obtainable by it.

(2) If the company, having been required by the group to do so, refuses to provide the group with all or any of that information, the court may, on an application made by the group, make an order directing-

(a) the company, and

(b) any of its officers or employees specified in the application,

to provide the group with the information in question in such form and by such means as the court may direct.

GENERAL NOTE

This provision replaces s.347K of the 1985 Act without substantive change.

Exemptions

374.   Trade unions

(1) A donation to a trade union, other than a contribution to the union's political fund, is not a political donation for the purposes of this Part.

(2) A trade union is not a political organisation for the purposes of section 365 (meaning of "political expenditure").

(3) In this section-

"trade union" has the meaning given by section 1 of Trade Union and Labour Relations (Consolidation) Act 1992 (c. 52) or Article 3 of the Industrial Relations (Northern Ireland) Order 1992 (S.I. 1992/807 (N.I. 5));

"political fund" means the fund from which payments by a trade union in the furtherance of political objects are required to be made by virtue of section 82(1)(a) of that Act or Article 57(2)(a) of that Order.

GENERAL NOTE

This provision, together with the following four, sets out five exceptions to the requirement for shareholder authorisation of political donations and expenditure. This new provision provides that a donation to a trade union otherwise than to its political fund is not a political donation for the purposes of this Part, and therefore does not require shareholder authorisation.

Apparently "companies asked specifically that trade unions not be treated as political organisations when companies decide on political donations" (HC Comm D, col 375 (July 4, 2006)). Margaret Hodge continued:

"That is because we all know ... that companies provide a range of crucial facilities to trade unions ranging from meeting rooms to employee time off, which should not be regarded as a donation to a political party ... The purpose of the clause is to make things simpler for companies to reduce their administrative overheads. That is an underlying theme of the Bill ... Providing companies with a long list of approved trade union activities that they must cross-reference before deciding whether they can legitimately expend resources or time, or allow rooms to be used, would be inconsistent with the principle that runs through the Bill" (*Hansard*, HC Comm D, cols 376-378 (July 4, 2006)).

This provision initially deemed trade unions not to be political organisations for the purposes of this Part. This suggestion was criticised as contrary to the truth. More importantly, David Howarth that recognised that this approach might provide a loophole through which a company could evade the provisions of the Act: "It could give money to a political party through a trade union, and so undermine the law" (HC Comm D, cols 374-375 (July 4, 2006)). Consequently, an amendment was introduced at Report Stage in the House of Commons which provided an exception for trade unions in relation to non-political donations. This was explained by Margaret Hodge:

"Our new clause will prevent companies from circumventing the controls of the Bill. If they wish to donate to the political fund of a trade union, they must seek shareholder authorisation. If they donate to trade union funding in other ways - such as providing free meeting room facilities - they will not need to seek authorisation. In the latter case, there is no danger of such funds being redirected to political parties, because the Trade Union and Labour Relations (Consolidation) Act 1992 prevents trade unions from making payments to political parties, except through their political fund. That Act also prohibits trade unions from redirecting money received from third parties into the political fund unless the money is given as a contribution to the political fund"

(*Hansard*, HC Report Stage, cols 960-961 (October 18, 2006)).

375. Subscription for membership of trade association

(1) A subscription paid to a trade association for membership of the association is not a political donation for the purposes of this Part.

(2) For this purpose-

"trade association" means an organisation formed for the purpose of furthering the trade interests of its members, or of persons represented by its members, and

"subscription" does not include a payment to the association to the extent that it is made for the purpose of financing any particular activity of the association.

GENERAL NOTE

This provision replaces s.347B(1) and (2) of the 1985 Act without substantive change.

376. All-party parliamentary groups

(1) An all-party parliamentary group is not a political organisation for the purposes of this Part.

(2) An "all-party parliamentary group" means an all-party group composed of members of one or both of the Houses of Parliament (or of such members and other persons).

GENERAL NOTE

This provision replaces s.347B(3) of the 1985 Act without substantive change.

377. Political expenditure exempted by order

(1) Authorisation under this Part is not needed for political expenditure that is exempt by virtue of an order of the Secretary of State under this section.

(2) An order may confer an exemption in relation to-

(a) companies of any description or category specified in the order, or

(b) expenditure of any description or category so specified (whether framed by reference to goods, services or other matters in respect of which such expenditure is incurred or otherwise),

or both.

(3) If or to the extent that expenditure is exempt from the requirement of authorisation under this Part by virtue of an order under this section, it shall be disregarded in determining what donations are authorised by any resolution of the company passed for the purposes of this Part.

(4) An order under this section is subject to affirmative resolution procedure.

GENERAL NOTE

This provision replaces s.347B(8)-(11) of the 1985 Act without substantive change. The Explanatory Notes states that power under s.347B has to date been only used once "to exempt business activities such as the publication of newspapers which, by their very nature, involve the publication or dissemination of material which seeks to influence the views of members of the public" (Explanatory Notes, para.603).

378. Donations not amounting to more than £5,000 in any twelve month period

(1) Authorisation under this Part is not needed for a donation except to the extent that the total amount of-

    (a) that donation, and

    (b) other relevant donations made in the period of 12 months ending with the date on which that donation is made,

exceeds £5,000.

  (2) In this section-

    "donation" means a donation to a political party or other political organisation or to an independent election candidate; and

    "other relevant donations" means-

        (a) in relation to a donation made by a company that is not a subsidiary, any other donations made by that company or by any of its subsidiaries;

        (b) in relation to a donation made by a company that is a subsidiary, any other donations made by that company, by any holding company of that company or by any other subsidiary of any such holding company.

  (3) If or to the extent that a donation is exempt by virtue of this section from the requirement of authorisation under this Part, it shall be disregarded in determining what donations are authorised by any resolution passed for the purposes of this Part.

GENERAL NOTE

  This provision replaces s.347B(4)-(7) of the 1985 Act without substantive change. Lord McKenzie explained the reason for the exception and why it does not apply to political expenditure:

> "We believe there is a strong case for exempting small donations, not least because we accept that a company may make some forms of donation - for example, attendance at a fund-raising dinner - for reasons other than an intent to fund a political party or organisation. We do not think the same is true of political expenditure. For example, a company is unlikely to incur expenditure on an advertising campaign which is capable of being reasonably regarded as intended to affect public support for a political party without having considered the issues carefully. Direct involvement by a company in political activities is a major step which we believe should always be subject to member authorisation" (*Hansard*, HL GC Day 4, Vol.678, col.156 (March 1, 2006)).

Margaret Hodge explained that a group cannot "tot-up" its political donation "points":

> "In earlier clauses, we have tightened up provisions relating to subsidiaries to ensure that directors of holding companies do not circumvent their obligations. In the same spirit, we now include subsidiaries in the annual total, so the annual total for all companies is £5,000; it cannot be £15,000, and one cannot tot it up, with the subsidiaries underneath" (HC Comm D, col.392 (July 4, 2006)).

Supplementary provisions

379. Minor definitions

  (1) In this Part-

    "director" includes shadow director; and

    "organisation" includes any body corporate or unincorporated association and any combination of persons.

  (2) Except as otherwise provided, any reference in this Part to the time at which a donation is made or expenditure is incurred is, in a case where the donation is made or expenditure incurred in pursuance of a contract, any earlier time at which that contract is entered into by the company.

GENERAL NOTE

  This provision replaces s.347A(3), (8) and (10) of the 1985 Act without substantive change.

ACCOUNTS AND REPORTS

GENERAL NOTE

This Part replaces Pt 7 of the 1985 Act where the provisions of the latter related to accounts and reports. Part 16 of the new Act replaces the provisions of Pt 7 of the 1985 Act that related to the statutory audit.

More generally, following a proposal in the March 2005 White Paper, "Company Law Reform", the provisions in this Part have been reordered and redrafted to make it easier for companies of whatever size to find the requirements relevant to them. This is in contrast to Pt 7 of the 1985 Act, where the provisions applying to small companies were generally expressed as modifications of the provisions applying to large companies. In the new Act, where provisions do not apply to all kinds of company, those relating to small companies are set out before those applying to other companies; those relating to private companies appear before those applying to public companies; and those relating to quoted companies appear after those applying to other companies.

A further change in the legislation enables the Secretary of State to replace the detailed schedules to Pt 7 of the 1985 Act by regulations. The aim is to give greater flexibility in arranging the material previously in Schedules, which should make it easier to follow the requirements relating to different types of company. In framing the legislation, the view taken is that it is not only unnecessary, but also undesirable to have parallel and duplicative regimes in primary legislation that focus on the detail for different types of company. Rather, it is preferable to have parallel sets of regulations for different sizes and types of company.

The Secretary of State has power under this Part of the Act to issue the following regulations:

- Provisions applying to quoted and unquoted companies (s.385);
- Companies Act individual accounts (s.396);
- Companies Act group accounts (s.404);
- Information about related undertakings (s.409);
- Information about directors' benefits (remuneration, pensions and compensation for loss of office) (s.412);
- Content of directors' report (s.416);
- Content of directors' remuneration report (s.421);
- Option to provide summary financial statement (s.426);
- Form and contents of summary financial statement: unquoted companies (s.427);
- Form and contents of summary financial statement: quoted companies (s.428);
- Filing obligations of companies subject to the "small companies" regime (s.444);
- Filing obligations of medium-sized companies (s.445);
- Civil penalties for failing to file accounts and reports (s.453);
- Revised accounts and reports (s.454);
- Accounting standards (s.464);
- General power to make further provision about accounts and reports (s.468); and
- Power to apply provisions to banking partnerships (s.470).

Section 473 specifies the Parliamentary procedure that must be followed in connection with nine of these sets of regulations. In addition, the Secretary of State is empowered to issue orders under s.457 (Other persons authorised to apply to the court) and s.462 (Power to amend categories of disclosure).

The detailed schedules to Pt 7 of the 1985 Act dealing with accounts and reports that will be affected are:

- Schedule 4: Form and Content of Company Accounts;
- Schedule 4A: Form and Content of Group Accounts;
- Schedule 5: Disclosure of Information: Related Undertakings;
- Schedule 6: Disclosure of Information: Emoluments and Other Benefits of Directors and Others;
- Schedule 7: Matters to be dealt with in Directors' Report;
- Schedule 7A: Directors' Remuneration Report;
- Schedule 7B: Specified Persons, Descriptions of Disclosures, etc. for the Purposes of s.245G;
- Schedule 8: Form and Content of Accounts Prepared by Small Companies;
- Schedule 8A: Form and Content of Abbreviated Accounts of Small Companies Delivered to Registrar;
- Schedule 9: Special Provisions for Banking Companies and Groups;
- Schedule 9A: Special Provisions for Insurance Companies and Groups; and

• Schedule 10A: Parent and Subsidiary Undertakings: Supplementary Provisions.

Overall, the main substantive changes in this Part of the Act are:

• a reduction in the time limit for private companies to file their accounts from ten months to nine months after the year end (s.442);

• a reduction in the time limit for public companies to lay full financial statements before the company in general meeting and file them from seven months to six months after the year end (s.442);

• new requirements for quoted companies to publish their annual accounts and reports on a website (s.430); and

• replacement of the general power of the Secretary of State to alter accounting requirements in s.257 of the 1985 Act by a general power of amendment by regulations (s.468) and more specific powers in relation to specific sections.

The Accounting Standards Board ("ASB"), which is part of the Financial Reporting Council ("FRC"), issues financial reporting standards ("FRSs") for the accounting profession in the United Kingdom and Ireland. These are modelled on international financial reporting standards (IFRSs) and international accounting standards ("IASs"), issued by the International Accounting Standards Board ("IASB"). Under Regulation 1606/2002 of the European Parliament and of the Council of July 19, 2002 (known as "The International Accounting Standards (IAS) Regulation") (see [2002] O.J. L243), these international standards have had to be used from 2005 onwards by listed companies within the European Union when preparing their consolidated accounts. The texts of the ASB's FRSs, and other standards in force, as well as statements of recommended practice ("SORPs") that apply to companies in specific industries, can be accessed at www.frc.org.uk/asb/; while those of the IASB's FRSs and IASs, as well as interpretations of standards, can be accessed at www.iasb.org.

Definitions

Definitions of frequently used terms in this Part of the Act can be found in Pt 38, "Companies: interpretation", ss.1158-1174. Terms covered include "UK-registered company" (s.1158); "subsidiary", "wholly-owned subsidiary", "holding company" and "company" (ss.1159-1160 and Sch.6); "undertaking", and "fellow subsidiary" (s.1161); "parent" and "subsidiary undertakings" (s.1162 and Sch.7); "non-cash asset" (s.1163); "banking company" and "banking group" (s.1164); "insurance company", "authorised insurance company", "insurance group" and "insurance market activity" (s.1165); "employees' share scheme" (s.1166); "prescribed" by order or by regulations (s.1167); "hard copy", "electronic form" and related expressions (s.1168); "dormant" and "significant accounting transaction" (s.1169); "EEA state" and related expressions (s.1170); "former Companies Acts" and the "Joint Stock Companies Acts" (s.1171); and "body corporate", "corporation", "credit institution", "financial institution", "firm", "the Gazette", "hire-purchase agreement", "officer", "parent company", "regulated activity", "regulated market" and "working day" (s.1173).

Further definitions relating to this Part of the Act are given in s.474, including "e-money issuer", "group", "IAS Regulation", "consolidation" (with respect to accounts), "international accounting standards" (often referred to by the acronym "IAS"), "ISD investment firm", "profit and loss account", "regulated activity" (under the Financial Services and Markets Act 2000), "turnover", "UCITS management company", and "an income and expenditure account".

Schedule 8 further provides an alphabetical "Index of defined expressions", giving cross references to sections where individual terms are defined.

CHAPTER I

INTRODUCTION

General

380. Scheme of this Part

(1) The requirements of this Part as to accounts and reports apply in relation to each financial year of a company.

(2) In certain respects different provisions apply to different kinds of company.

(3) The main distinctions for this purpose are-

    (a) between companies subject to the small companies regime (see section 381) and companies that are not subject to that regime; and

    (b) between quoted companies (see section 385) and companies that are not quoted.

(4) In this Part, where provisions do not apply to all kinds of company-
  (a) provisions applying to companies subject to the small companies regime appear before the provisions applying to other companies,
  (b) provisions applying to private companies appear before the provisions applying to public companies, and
  (c) provisions applying to quoted companies appear after the provisions applying to other companies.

GENERAL NOTE

This is a new section introducing this Part of the Act.

Subsections (1)-(4)

This is an introductory section (subs.(1)), which indicates the main way in which the structure of this Part differs from that of Pt 7 of the 1985 Act (subs.(2)). In particular, new distinctions are drawn for companies subject to the "small companies regime" (s.381) and for "quoted companies" (s.385) (subs.(3)). Where provisions do not apply to all kinds of company: (i) those relating to small companies are set out before those applying to other companies; (ii) those relating to private companies appear before those applying to public companies; and (iii) those relating to quoted companies appear after those applying to other companies (subs.(4)).

Companies subject to the small companies regime

GENERAL NOTE

Sections 381-384 set out which companies, parent companies or groups fall within the "small companies regime" (i.e. those that qualify as small companies or groups and are not excluded from the regime for one of the reasons set out in s.384). With one minor change, the conditions for qualification as a small company are unchanged from ss.247, 247A and 249 of the 1985 Act, as substituted, inserted or amended by the 1989 Act and subsequent SIs. The change is that, whereas s.247A(2) of the 1985 Act provides that a group is ineligible if any of its members is a body corporate other than a company having power to offer its shares or debentures to the public, the reference in s.384(2)(b) is now to such a body corporate whose securities are admitted to trading on a "regulated market" in an EEA state. (The term "regulated market" is defined in s.1173.) This reflects changes made by the Accounts Modernisation Directive (2003/51/EEC).

381. Companies subject to the small companies regime

The small companies regime for accounts and reports applies to a company for a financial year in relation to which the company-
  (a) qualifies as small (see sections 382 and 383), and
  (b) is not excluded from the regime (see section 384).

GENERAL NOTE

This is another new section, which indicates that the "small companies regime" applies to a company for a financial year in which it qualifies as small (ss.382-383) and where it is not excluded from the regime (s.384).

382. Companies qualifying as small: general

(1) A company qualifies as small in relation to its first financial year if the qualifying conditions are met in that year.
(2) A company qualifies as small in relation to a subsequent financial year-
  (a) if the qualifying conditions are met in that year and the preceding financial year;
  (b) if the qualifying conditions are met in that year and the company qualified as small in relation to the preceding financial year;
  (c) if the qualifying conditions were met in the preceding financial year and the company qualified as small in relation to that year.
(3) The qualifying conditions are met by a company in a year in which it satisfies two or more of the following requirements-

1. Turnover	Not more than £5.6 million
2. Balance sheet total	Not more than £2.8 million
3. Number of employees	Not more than 50

(4) For a period that is a company's financial year but not in fact a year the maximum figures for turnover must be proportionately adjusted.

(5) The balance sheet total means the aggregate of the amounts shown as assets in the company's balance sheet.

(6) The number of employees means the average number of persons employed by the company in the year, determined as follows-

    (a) find for each month in the financial year the number of persons employed under contracts of service by the company in that month (whether throughout the month or not),

    (b) add together the monthly totals, and

    (c) divide by the number of months in the financial year.

(7) This section is subject to section 383 (companies qualifying as small: parent companies).

GENERAL NOTE

This section is largely derived from s.247 of the 1985 Act, as inserted by s.13(1) of the 1989 Act and subsequently amended by SIs 1992/2452, 1996/189, 2004/16 and 2004/2947.

Subsections (1) and (2)

A company qualifies as small in its first financial year if the qualifying conditions are met (subs.(1)). For subsequent financial years it qualifies as small if (i) the qualifying conditions are met for that year and the preceding financial year; (ii) if the qualifying conditions are met for that year and the company qualified as small in the preceding financial year; or (iii) if the qualifying conditions were met for the preceding financial year and the company qualified as small for that year (subs.(2)).

Subsections (3)-(6)

The qualifying conditions to be classified as small company restate those in s.247(3) of the 1985 Act, as inserted by s.13(1) of the 1989 Act and most recently amended with respect to the size criteria by SI 2004/16, reg.2(1)-(2). Briefly these are that it must meet two or more of the requirements that: (i) [annual] turnover should not exceed £5.6m; (ii) the end-year balance sheet total should not exceed £2.8m; and (iii) the number of employees should not exceed 50 (subs.(3)). With respect to criterion (i), turnover [defined in s.474(1) in similar terms to s.262 of the 1985 Act, as inserted by s.22 of the 1989 Act] should, where appropriate, be annualised (e.g. where the accounting reporting period is greater or less than a year) (subs.(4)). With regard to criterion (ii), the "balance sheet total" means the aggregate of the amounts shown as assets in the balance sheet [which will be determined by the prescribed format adopted for presenting the accounts] (subs.(5)). With respect to criterion (iii), the rules for determining the number of employees are spelt out in subs.(6): namely, the monthly totals of persons employed under contracts of service for the whole of that period or just a part of it should be aggregated and be divided by the number of months in the financial reporting period.

Subsection (7)

The provisions of this section are subject to s.383, below, which deals with small parent companies.

383. Companies qualifying as small: parent companies

(1) A parent company qualifies as a small company in relation to a financial year only if the group headed by it qualifies as a small group.

(2) A group qualifies as small in relation to the parent company's first financial year if the qualifying conditions are met in that year.

(3) A group qualifies as small in relation to a subsequent financial year of the parent company-

    (a) if the qualifying conditions are met in that year and the preceding financial year;

(b) if the qualifying conditions are met in that year and the group qualified as small in relation to the preceding financial year;

(c) if the qualifying conditions were met in the preceding financial year and the group qualified as small in relation to that year.

(4) The qualifying conditions are met by a group in a year in which it satisfies two or more of the following requirements-

1. Aggregate turnover	Not more than £5.6 million net (or £6.72 million gross)
2. Aggregate balance sheet total	Not more than £2.8 million net (or £3.36 million gross)
3. Aggregate number of employees	Not more than 50

(5) The aggregate figures are ascertained by aggregating the relevant figures determined in accordance with section 382 for each member of the group.

(6) In relation to the aggregate figures for turnover and balance sheet total-
"net" means after any set-offs and other adjustments made to eliminate group transactions-

(a) in the case of Companies Act accounts, in accordance with regulations under section 404,

(b) in the case of IAS accounts, in accordance with international accounting standards; and

"gross" means without those set-offs and other adjustments.

A company may satisfy any relevant requirement on the basis of either the net or the gross figure.

(7) The figures for each subsidiary undertaking shall be those included in its individual accounts for the relevant financial year, that is-

(a) if its financial year ends with that of the parent company, that financial year, and

(b) if not, its financial year ending last before the end of the financial year of the parent company.

If those figures cannot be obtained without disproportionate expense or undue delay, the latest available figures shall be taken.

GENERAL NOTE

This section derives from s.247A(3), as inserted into the 1985 Act, and from s.249 of the Act, as substituted by s.13(1) of the 1989 Act and subsequently amended by SIs 1992/2452 and 2004/16.

Subsection (1)

A parent company qualifies as a small company only if the group headed by it qualifies as a "small group".

Subsections (2) and (3)

A group qualifies as small in its first financial year if the qualifying conditions are met (subs.(2)). For subsequent financial years it qualifies as small if: (i) the qualifying conditions are met for that year and the preceding financial year; (ii) if the qualifying conditions are met for that year and the group qualified as small in the preceding financial year; or (iii) if the qualifying conditions were met for the preceding financial year and the group qualified as small for that year (subs.(3)).

Subsections (4)-(6)

The qualifying conditions to be classified as a small group restate those in s.249(3) of the 1985 Act, as inserted by s.13(1) of the 1989 Act and most recently amended with respect to the size criteria by SI 2004/16, reg.3(1)-(2). Briefly these are that it must meet two or more of the requirements that: (i) [annual] turnover should not exceed £5.6m net (or £6.72m gross); (ii) the end-year balance sheet total should not exceed £2.8m net (or £3.36m gross); and (iii) the number of employees should not exceed 50 (subs.(4)). The aggregate figures are to be determined by adding together the relevant figures for individual companies within the group as described in s.382, above (i.e. with respect to turnover, balance sheet total and number of employees) (subs.(5)). Subsection (6) defines the meaning of "net" and "gross" with respect to set-offs and other adjustments in relation to "turnover" and "balance sheet total", both for Companies Act group accounts covered by s.404 and to IAS group accounts prepared according to the provisions of s.406.

Subsection (7)

The figures from each subsidiary to be aggregated are to be those for the relevant financial year. If this is not coterminous with that of the parent company, they should be those in its last financial year ending before that of the parent company. If the necessary figures cannot be determined without undue expense or delay, the latest figures should be used.

384.   Companies excluded from the small companies regime

(1) The small companies regime does not apply to a company that is, or was at any time within the financial year to which the accounts relate-
    (a) a public company,
    (b) a company that-
        (i) is an authorised insurance company, a banking company, an e-money issuer, an ISD investment firm or a UCITS management company, or
        (ii) carries on insurance market activity, or
    (c) a member of an ineligible group.
(2) A group is ineligible if any of its members is-
    (a) a public company,
    (b) a body corporate (other than a company) whose shares are admitted to trading on a regulated market in an EEA State,
    (c) a person (other than a small company) who has permission under Part 4 of the Financial Services and Markets Act 2000 (c. 8) to carry on a regulated activity,
    (d) a small company that is an authorised insurance company, a banking company, an e-money issuer, an ISD investment firm or a UCITS management company, or
    (e) a person who carries on insurance market activity.
(3) A company is a small company for the purposes of subsection (2) if it qualified as small in relation to its last financial year ending on or before the end of the financial year to which the accounts relate.

GENERAL NOTE

This section derives from ss.247A(1)-(2) and 248(2), as inserted into the 1985 Act and subsequently amended.

Subsections (1)-(3)

The "small companies regime" does not apply to: (i) a public company; (ii) an authorised insurance company, a banking company, an e-money issuer, an ISD investment firm, a UCITS management company, or a company engaging in insurance market activity; or (iii) a member of an ineligible group (subs.(1)). With regard to the latter, a group is ineligible if any of its members is (i) a public company; (ii) a body corporate (other than a company) whose shares are traded on a regulated market in an EEA state; (iii) a person (other than a small company) carrying on a regulated activity; (iv) a small company that is an authorised insurance company, a banking company, an e-money issuer, an ISD investment firm or a UCITS management company; or (iv) a person who carries on insurance market activity (subs.(2)). For the purposes of subs.(2), a company is a small company if it was so qualified on or before the end of the financial year to which its accounts relate (subs.(3)).

The expressions "insurance market activity" and "regulated activity" are defined in s.474(1) in similar terms to the definitions given in s.262 of the 1985 Act, as substituted by s.22 of the 1989 Act and subsequently amended by reg.17(1) of SI 2005/2280. The terms "authorised insurance company", a "banking company", an "e-money issuer", an "ISD investment firm", and a "UCITS management company" are also defined in s.474.

Quoted and unquoted companies

385. Quoted and unquoted companies

(1) For the purposes of this Part a company is a quoted company in relation to a financial year if it is a quoted company immediately before the end of the accounting reference period by reference to which that financial year was determined.

(2) A "quoted company" means a company whose equity share capital-

    (a) has been included in the official list in accordance with the provisions of Part 6 of the Financial Services and Markets Act 2000 (c. 8), or

    (b) is officially listed in an EEA State, or

    (c) is admitted to dealing on either the New York Stock Exchange or the exchange known as Nasdaq.

In paragraph (a) "the official list" has the meaning given by section 103(1) of the Financial Services and Markets Act 2000.

(3) An "unquoted company" means a company that is not a quoted company.

(4) The Secretary of State may by regulations amend or replace the provisions of subsections (1) to (2) so as to limit or extend the application of some or all of the provisions of this Part that are expressed to apply to quoted companies.

(5) Regulations under this section extending the application of any such provision of this Part are subject to affirmative resolution procedure.

(6) Any other regulations under this section are subject to negative resolution procedure.

GENERAL NOTE

The definition of a quoted company in this section is similar to the definition of "quoted company" in subs.(1) of s.262 of the 1985 Act, as substituted by s.22 of the 1989 Act and subsequently inserted by reg.10 of SI 2002/1986.

Subsections (1) and (2)

A "quoted company" for this Part of the Act is one which was such immediately before the end of the accounting reference period (as determined in s.391) that is used to determine the relevant financial year (as specified in s.390) (subs.(1)). The term means a company whose share capital has been included in the Official List under the Financial Services and Markets Act 2000 or is officially listed in an EEA state or on the New York Stock Exchange or the Nasdaq (subs.(2)).

Subsection (3)

An "unquoted company" is any company that is not a "quoted company".

Subsections (4)-(6)

The definition of "quoted company" under subss.(1)-(2) can be amended by regulations. However, if the regulations extend the application of this Part of the Act, they will be subject to the affirmative resolution procedure (see s.1290). Otherwise they are subject to the negative resolution procedure (see s.1289).

CHAPTER 2

ACCOUNTING RECORDS

GENERAL NOTE

Sections 386-389 replace ss.221-222 of the 1985 Act, as inserted by s.2 of the 1989 Act and subsequently amended by SI 2004/2947, paras 4(a) and (5)(a). They set out a company's general duty to keep accounting records and specify where and for how long such records are to be kept. Their purpose is to ensure that businesses have the right information to make informed decisions and to prepare accounts which comply with the Companies Act and, where relevant, with International Accounting Standards.

There is no specific definition of the term "accounting records" as they will differ depending on the nature and complexity of the business. For a simple business, they may just comprise bank statements, purchase orders, sales and purchase invoices. In a larger and more complex business they will typically comprise books kept on the double-entry system and be held electronically.

386.   Duty to keep accounting records

(1) Every company must keep adequate accounting records.
(2) Adequate accounting records means records that are sufficient-
    (a) to show and explain the company's transactions,
    (b) to disclose with reasonable accuracy, at any time, the financial position of the company at that time, and
    (c) to enable the directors to ensure that any accounts required to be prepared comply with the requirements of this Act (and, where applicable, of Article 4 of the IAS Regulation).
(3) Accounting records must, in particular, contain-
    (a) entries from day to day of all sums of money received and expended by the company and the matters in respect of which the receipt and expenditure takes place, and
    (b) a record of the assets and liabilities of the company.
(4) If the company's business involves dealing in goods, the accounting records must contain-
    (a) statements of stock held by the company at the end of each financial year of the company,
    (b) all statements of stocktakings from which any statement of stock as is mentioned in paragraph (a) has been or is to be prepared, and
    (c) except in the case of goods sold by way of ordinary retail trade, statements of all goods sold and purchased, showing the goods and the buyers and sellers in sufficient detail to enable all these to be identified.
(5) A parent company that has a subsidiary undertaking in relation to which the above requirements do not apply must take reasonable steps to secure that the undertaking keeps such accounting records as to enable the directors of the parent company to ensure that any accounts required to be prepared under this Part comply with the requirements of this Act (and, where applicable, of Article 4 of the IAS Regulation).

GENERAL NOTE
   This section derives from ss.221(1)-(4) of the 1985 Act, as inserted by s.2 of the 1989 Act.

Subsections (1)-(4)
   Every company must keep adequate accounting records (subs.(1)) that are sufficient (i) to show and explain transactions; (ii) to disclose at any time the company's financial position; and (iii) to enable the directors to prepare accounts required by provisions of the Act (subs.(2)). In particular, they must contain entries relating to all money transactions and provide a record of the company's assets and liabilities (subs.(3)). Where the company trades in goods, they must also contain statements of year-end inventories, records of stocktakings, and apart from normal retail trade details of all goods purchased and sold, including the buyers and sellers (subs.(4)).

Subsection (5)
   A parent company that has a subsidiary to which the above provisions do not apply (e.g. because it is an overseas company) must take reasonable steps to ensure that it keeps accounting records sufficient to enable the directors to prepare group accounts as required under the provisions of the Act.

387.   Duty to keep accounting records: offence

(1) If a company fails to comply with any provision of section 386 (duty to keep accounting records), an offence is committed by every officer of the company who is in default.
(2) It is a defence for a person charged with such an offence to show that he acted honestly and that in the circumstances in which the company's business was carried on the default was excusable.

(3) A person guilty of an offence under this section is liable-
- (a) on conviction on indictment, to imprisonment for a term not exceeding two years or a fine (or both);
- (b) on summary conviction-
    - (i) in England and Wales, to imprisonment for a term not exceeding twelve months or to a fine not exceeding the statutory maximum (or both);
    - (ii) in Scotland or Northern Ireland, to imprisonment for a term not exceeding six months, or to a fine not exceeding the statutory maximum (or both).

GENERAL NOTE

This section replaces subss.(5)-(6) of s.221 of the 1985 Act, as inserted by s.2 of the 1989 Act.

Subsections (1) and (2)

A criminal offence is committed by each defaulting officer if a company fails to keep adequate accounting records as required by s.386(1). However, it is a defence show that he acted honestly and in the circumstances the default was excusable (subs.(2)).

Subsection (3)

This subsection lists the penalties in relation to the offence referred to in subs.(1): i.e. imprisonment or a fine, or both.

388. Where and for how long records to be kept

(1) A company's accounting records-
- (a) must be kept at its registered office or such other place as the directors think fit, and
- (b) must at all times be open to inspection by the company's officers.

(2) If accounting records are kept at a place outside the United Kingdom, accounts and returns with respect to the business dealt with in the accounting records so kept must be sent to, and kept at, a place in the United Kingdom, and must at all times be open to such inspection.

(3) The accounts and returns to be sent to the United Kingdom must be such as to-
- (a) disclose with reasonable accuracy the financial position of the business in question at intervals of not more than six months, and
- (b) enable the directors to ensure that the accounts required to be prepared under this Part comply with the requirements of this Act (and, where applicable, of Article 4 of the IAS Regulation).

(4) Accounting records that a company is required by section 386 to keep must be preserved by it-
- (a) in the case of a private company, for three years from the date on which they are made;
- (b) in the case of a public company, for six years from the date on which they are made.

(5) Subsection (4) is subject to any provision contained in rules made under section 411 of the Insolvency Act 1986 (c. 45) (company insolvency rules) or Article 359 of the Insolvency (Northern Ireland) Order 1989 (S.I. 1989/2405 (N.I. 19)).

GENERAL NOTE

This section replaces s.222(1)-(5) of the 1985 Act, as inserted by s.2 of the 1989 Act, and subsequently amended by SI 2004/2947 (Sch.1, para.5(a)). Although subs.(4) only requires private companies to keep their accounting records for three years and public companies theirs for six years, the Taxes Management Act 1970 effectively requires a six year retention period for accounting records, while in order to cover against possible actions for negligence under the Limitation Act 1980 (as amended) the retention period would have to be as long as 15 years.

Subsections (1)-(3)

A company's accounting records must be kept at its registered office or at another place as the directors see fit. They should also be open at all times for inspection by the company's officers (subs.(1)). Where it operates outside the United Kingdom, accounts and returns relating to such business should be kept in the United Kingdom and be available at all times for inspection by the company's officers (subs.(2)). These returns must be sufficient to disclose with reasonable accuracy the financial position of the business at intervals no greater than six months and enable the directors to prepare accounts in accordance with the requirements of the Act (subs.(3)).

Subsections (4) and (5)

Private companies must keep their records for at least three years after they originate and public companies for six years (subs.(4)). However, this is subject to provisions in regulations made under s.411 of the Insolvency Act 1986 and art.359 of the Insolvency (Northern Ireland) Order 1989 (SI 1989/2405 (NI 19)) (subs.(5)).

389.   Where and for how long records to be kept: offences

(1) If a company fails to comply with any provision of subsections (1) to (3) of section 388 (requirements as to keeping of accounting records), an offence is committed by every officer of the company who is in default.

(2) It is a defence for a person charged with such an offence to show that he acted honestly and that in the circumstances in which the company's business was carried on the default was excusable.

(3) An officer of a company commits an offence if he-
  (a) fails to take all reasonable steps for securing compliance by the company with subsection (4) of that section (period for which records to be preserved), or
  (b) intentionally causes any default by the company under that subsection.

(4) A person guilty of an offence under this section is liable-
  (a) on conviction on indictment, to imprisonment for a term not exceeding two years or a fine (or both);
  (b) on summary conviction-
    (i) in England and Wales, to imprisonment for a term not exceeding twelve months or to a fine not exceeding the statutory maximum (or both);
    (ii) in Scotland or Northern Ireland, to imprisonment for a term not exceeding six months, or to a fine not exceeding the statutory maximum (or both).

GENERAL NOTE

This section replaces subss.(4) and (6) of s.222 the 1985 Act, as inserted by s.2 of the 1989 Act. It makes similar provision to s.387, but in relation to a failure to comply with the requirements of s.388.

Subsections (1) and (2)

A criminal offence is committed by each defaulting officer if a company fails to keep accounting records as required by s.388. However, it is a defence show that he acted honestly and in the circumstances the default was excusable (subs.(2)).

Subsection (3)

An officer of a company commits an offence if he fails to take all reasonable steps to ensure that the accounting records are kept for the periods specified in subs.(4) of s.388: namely, at least three years after they originate for private companies and six years for public companies. He also commits an offence if he intentionally causes default on the part of the company.

Subsection (4)

This subsection lists the penalties in relation to the offence referred to in subs.(1): i.e. imprisonment or a fine, or both.

CHAPTER 3

A COMPANY'S FINANCIAL YEAR

GENERAL NOTE

This Chapter replaces ss.223-225 of the 1985 Act.

390. A company's financial year

(1) A company's financial year is determined as follows.

(2) Its first financial year-

   (a) begins with the first day of its first accounting reference period, and

   (b) ends with the last day of that period or such other date, not more than seven days before or after the end of that period, as the directors may determine.

(3) Subsequent financial years-

   (a) begin with the day immediately following the end of the company's previous financial year, and

   (b) end with the last day of its next accounting reference period or such other date, not more than seven days before or after the end of that period, as the directors may determine.

(4) In relation to an undertaking that is not a company, references in this Act to its financial year are to any period in respect of which a profit and loss account of the undertaking is required to be made up (by its constitution or by the law under which it is established), whether that period is a year or not.

(5) The directors of a parent company must secure that, except where in their opinion there are good reasons against it, the financial year of each of its subsidiary undertakings coincides with the company's own financial year.

GENERAL NOTE

This section replaces s.223 of the 1985 Act. A company's financial year is the period for which its accounts and reports must be prepared.

Subsections (1)-(3)

A company's financial year is determined (subs.(1)) as follows:

- in the case of its first financial year, from the first day of its first "accounting reference period" (see s.391 below) and ends on the last day of that period (or on a day within seven days before or after that date, as the directors may determine) (subs.(2)); and

- in the case of subsequent financial years, from a date immediately after the end of the company's previous financial year and ends on the last day of its next accounting reference period (or on a day within seven days before or after that date, as the directors may determine) (subs.(3)).

Subsection (4)

Where an undertaking is not a company, references to "a financial year" are to be taken as relating to a period for which it prepares a profit and loss account.

Subsection (5)

The directors of a parent company are required to secure (except where there are good reasons otherwise) each subsidiary to have a financial year coinciding with that of the parent company.

391.   Accounting reference periods and accounting reference date

(1) A company's accounting reference periods are determined according to its accounting reference date in each calendar year.

(2) The accounting reference date of a company incorporated in Great Britain before 1st April 1996 is-

    (a) the date specified by notice to the registrar in accordance with section 224(2) of the Companies Act 1985 (c. 6) (notice specifying accounting reference date given within nine months of incorporation), or

    (b) failing such notice-

        (i) in the case of a company incorporated before 1st April 1990, 31st March, and

        (ii) in the case of a company incorporated on or after 1st April 1990, the last day of the month in which the anniversary of its incorporation falls.

(3) The accounting reference date of a company incorporated in Northern Ireland before 22nd August 1997 is-

    (a) the date specified by notice to the registrar in accordance with article 232(2) of the Companies (Northern Ireland) Order 1986 (S.I. 1986/1032 (N.I. 6)) (notice specifying accounting reference date given within nine months of incorporation), or

    (b) failing such notice-

        (i) in the case of a company incorporated before the coming into operation of Article 5 of the Companies (Northern Ireland) Order 1990 (S.I. 1990/593 (N.I. 5)), 31st March, and

        (ii) in the case of a company incorporated after the coming into operation of that Article, the last day of the month in which the anniversary of its incorporation falls.

(4) The accounting reference date of a company incorporated-

    (a) in Great Britain on or after 1st April 1996 and before the commencement of this Act,

    (b) in Northern Ireland on or after 22nd August 1997 and before the commencement of this Act, or

    (c) after the commencement of this Act,

is the last day of the month in which the anniversary of its incorporation falls.

(5) A company's first accounting reference period is the period of more than six months, but not more than 18 months, beginning with the date of its incorporation and ending with its accounting reference date.

(6) Its subsequent accounting reference periods are successive periods of twelve months beginning immediately after the end of the previous accounting reference period and ending with its accounting reference date.

(7) This section has effect subject to the provisions of section 392 (alteration of accounting reference date).

GENERAL NOTE

  This section replaces s.224 of the 1985 Act, as amended by SIs 1990/355 and 1996/189.

Subsection (1)

  A company's "accounting reference period" is determined according to its "accounting reference date".

Subsections (2)-(4)

  These subsections preserve the "accounting reference dates" and "accounting reference periods" of companies incorporated in Great Britain before April 1, 1996 (subs.(2)), and of companies incorporated in Northern Ireland before August 22, 1997 (subs.(3)). In both cases, if it is not the date given in a notice specifying the "accounting reference date" lodged with the appropriate registrar, it is to be taken as March 31 for companies incorporated before April 1, 1990 (Great Britain) or before the coming into operation of Art.5 of SI 1990/593 (NI. 5). Otherwise, a company's accounting reference date is the last day of the month in which the anniversary of its incorporation falls (subs.(4)).

Subsection (5)

A company's first "accounting reference period" is a period of more than six months, but not more than 18 months, beginning with the date of incorporation and ending with the "accounting reference date" (subs.(5)) (unless the company changes the date on which its accounting reference period ends in accordance with s.392, below).

Subsection (6)

Subsequent "accounting reference periods" (and hence "financial years") are successive periods of 12 months, beginning immediately after the end of the previous "accounting reference period", but again subject to any alteration of the "accounting reference date".

Subsection (7)

The provisions of this section are subject to those in s.392, which deals with alterations in the "accounting reference date".

392. Alteration of accounting reference date

(1) A company may by notice given to the registrar specify a new accounting reference date having effect in relation to-

    (a) the company's current accounting reference period and subsequent periods, or

    (b) the company's previous accounting reference period and subsequent periods.

A company's "previous accounting reference period" means the one immediately preceding its current accounting reference period.

(2) The notice must state whether the current or previous accounting reference period-

    (a) is to be shortened, so as to come to an end on the first occasion on which the new accounting reference date falls or fell after the beginning of the period, or

    (b) is to be extended, so as to come to an end on the second occasion on which that date falls or fell after the beginning of the period.

(3) A notice extending a company's current or previous accounting reference period is not effective if given less than five years after the end of an earlier accounting reference period of the company that was extended under this section.

This does not apply-

    (a) to a notice given by a company that is a subsidiary undertaking or parent undertaking of another EEA undertaking if the new accounting reference date coincides with that of the other EEA undertaking or, where that undertaking is not a company, with the last day of its financial year, or

    (b) where the company is in administration under Part 2 of the Insolvency Act 1986 (c. 45) or Part 3 of the Insolvency (Northern Ireland) Order 1989 (S.I. 1989/2405 (N.I. 19)), or

    (c) where the Secretary of State directs that it should not apply, which he may do with respect to a notice that has been given or that may be given.

(4) A notice under this section may not be given in respect of a previous accounting reference period if the period for filing accounts and reports for the financial year determined by reference to that accounting reference period has already expired.

(5) An accounting reference period may not be extended so as to exceed 18 months and a notice under this section is ineffective if the current or previous accounting reference period as extended in accordance with the notice would exceed that limit.

This does not apply where the company is in administration under Part 2 of the Insolvency Act 1986 (c. 45) or Part 3 of the Insolvency (Northern Ireland) Order 1989 (S.I. 1989/2405 (N.I. 19)).

(6) In this section "EEA undertaking" means an undertaking established under the law of any part of the United Kingdom or the law of any other EEA State.

GENERAL NOTE

This section replaces s.225 of the 1985 Act, as inserted by the 1985 Act, and amended by SIs 1996/189 and 2003/2093 and Sch.17, para.4(b), of the Enterprise Act 2003.

Subsections (1)-(3)

A company may give notice to the registrar specifying a new "accounting reference date" in relation to the current and subsequent periods or the previous and subsequent periods (subs.(1)). The notice must state whether the current or previous "accounting reference period" is to be shortened or lengthened (subs.(2)). A notice extending the current or previous "accounting reference period" is not effective if given within five years of a previous extension to the "accounting reference period", except where (i) the company is a subsidiary of another EEA undertaking (defined in subs.(6)) and the change is made to ensure financial years within the group coincide; (ii) the company is in administration under the relevant insolvency legislation in Great Britain or in Northern Ireland; or where the Secretary of State directs (subs.(3)).

Subsection (4)

A company is not permitted to change its "accounting reference date" if the period allowed for *delivering* accounts and reports to the registrar for that period has already expired.

This is slightly different from the provisions in s.225(5) of the 1985 Act, as inserted by s.3 of the 1989 Act and subsequently amended by SI 1996/189. This stated that the company could not change the date "if the period allowed for *laying and delivering* accounts and reports in relation to that period has already expired".

Under the new Act, under s.437 only public companies will be required to lay their accounts at a general meeting. However, previously a private company could by elective resolution in accordance with s.379A of the 1985 Act dispense with presenting before the company in general meeting its annual accounts and the directors' report, together with (where relevant) the auditors' report. Such a resolution related to the financial statements for the year in which it was made, and the election carried over to subsequent financial years. However, the financial statements still had to be circulated to members, and references in the Act to the laying of accounts were therefore to be interpreted as referring to the documents so circulated (s.252 of the 1985 Act). Essentially the situation is the same under the new Act as under s.423, below, a company has a duty to circulate copies of its accounts and reports to shareholders, debenture holders and everyone who is entitled to receive notice of general meetings.

Subsection (5)

An accounting reference period cannot be extended to exceed 18 months. However, this does not apply if the company is in administration under the relevant insolvency legislation in Great Britain or Northern Ireland.

Subsection (6)

This subsection defines the term "EAA undertaking" for the purpose of this section.

CHAPTER 4

ANNUAL ACCOUNTS

General

393. Accounts to give true and fair view

(1) The directors of a company must not approve accounts for the purposes of this Chapter unless they are satisfied that they give a true and fair view of the assets, liabilities, financial position and profit or loss-
    (a) in the case of the company's individual accounts, of the company;
    (b) in the case of the company's group accounts, of the undertakings included in the consolidation as a whole, so far as concerns members of the company.
(2) The auditor of a company in carrying out his functions under this Act in relation to the company's annual accounts must have regard to the directors' duty under subsection (1).

GENERAL NOTE

This section is derived from ss.226A and 227A of the 1985 Act, as substituted by SI 2004/2947, reg.2.

Subsection (1)

There is an overriding obligation on directors, as preparers of accounts, not to approve accounts unless they are satisfied that they give "a true and fair view" of the profit or loss for a period and the financial position of the company and, in the case of group accounts, the group. This provision reflects the underlying legal duty already expressed in Community law.

Subsection (2)

An auditor is equally obliged in carrying out his duties to ensure that the accounts give "a true and fair view" of the profit or loss for a period and the financial position of the company (and, if relevant, the group) when giving an opinion on the accounts. This requirement supplements the functions of an auditor set out in s.495 below.

Individual accounts

GENERAL NOTE

Sections 394-397, which replace ss.226, 226A and 226B of the 1985 Act, as substituted by SI 2004/2947, reg.2, concern the duty of the directors to prepare individual accounts. The individual accounts may either be prepared under the Act (when they are referred to as "Companies Act individual accounts") or (unless the company is a charity) in accordance with international accounting standards (IAS) adopted under the IAS Regulation (when they are known as "IAS individual accounts").

The terms "IAS Regulation" and "international accounting standards" are defined in s.474. Once a company has switched to IAS individual accounts, all subsequent individual accounts must be prepared in accordance with IAS unless there is a relevant change of circumstance (see s.395(3)-(5)). The provisions concerning the form and content of Companies Act accounts previously to be found in the Schedules to Pt 7 to the 1985 Act will in future be contained in regulations to be made by the Secretary of State (s.396(3)). The Parliamentary procedure for such regulations is set out in s.473.

394. Duty to prepare individual accounts

The directors of every company must prepare accounts for the company for each of its financial years.

Those accounts are referred to as the company's "individual accounts".

GENERAL NOTE

This section is derived from s.226(1) of the 1985 Act, as substituted by s.4 of the 1989 Act and subsequently amended by reg.2 of SI 2004/2947.

The section states that a company's directors are required to prepare its "individual accounts" for each financial year.

395. Individual accounts: applicable accounting framework

(1) A company's individual accounts may be prepared-
   (a) in accordance with section 396 ("Companies Act individual accounts"), or
   (b) in accordance with international accounting standards ("IAS individual accounts").

This is subject to the following provisions of this section and to section 407 (consistency of financial reporting within group).

(2) The individual accounts of a company that is a charity must be Companies Act individual accounts.

(3) After the first financial year in which the directors of a company prepare IAS individual accounts ("the first IAS year"), all subsequent individual accounts of the company must be prepared in accordance with international accounting standards unless there is a relevant change of circumstance.

(4) There is a relevant change of circumstance if, at any time during or after the first IAS year-
   (a) the company becomes a subsidiary undertaking of another undertaking that does not prepare IAS individual accounts,
   (b) the company ceases to be a company with securities admitted to trading on a regulated market in an EEA State, or

(c) a parent undertaking of the company ceases to be an undertaking with securities admitted to trading on a regulated market in an EEA State.

(5) If, having changed to preparing Companies Act individual accounts following a relevant change of circumstance, the directors again prepare IAS individual accounts for the company, subsections (3) and (4) apply again as if the first financial year for which such accounts are again prepared were the first IAS year.

GENERAL NOTE

This section restates the provisions of subss.(2)-(6) of s.226 of the 1985 Act, as substituted by s.4 of the 1989 Act and subsequently amended by reg.2 of SI 2004/2947.

Subsections (1) and (2)

A company's individual accounts may either be prepared under s.396 as "Companies Act individual accounts" or in accordance with international accounting standards as "IAS individual accounts", so long as there is consistency within a group (see s.407) (subs.(1)). However, the individual accounts of a charity must be prepared as "Companies Act individual accounts" (subs.(2)).

Subsections (3)-(5)

Once a company prepares "IAS individual accounts", it cannot switch back to preparing "Companies Act individual accounts", except where is a "relevant change of circumstance" (subs.(3)). The latter would arise if the company became a subsidiary of a company that does not prepare "IAS individual accounts", or the company or its parent ceases to have its securities traded in a regulated market in an EEA state (subs.(4)). Where such a change back to preparing "Companies Act individual accounts" occurs, and the directors subsequently prepare "IAS individual accounts", the provisions of subss.(3)-(4) once again apply (subs.(5)).

396.   Companies Act individual accounts

(1) Companies Act individual accounts must comprise-
    (a) a balance sheet as at the last day of the financial year, and
    (b) a profit and loss account.
(2) The accounts must-
    (a) in the case of the balance sheet, give a true and fair view of the state of affairs of the company as at the end of the financial year, and
    (b) in the case of the profit and loss account, give a true and fair view of the profit or loss of the company for the financial year.
(3) The accounts must comply with provision made by the Secretary of State by regulations as to-
    (a) the form and content of the balance sheet and profit and loss account, and
    (b) additional information to be provided by way of notes to the accounts.
(4) If compliance with the regulations, and any other provision made by or under this Act as to the matters to be included in a company's individual accounts or in notes to those accounts, would not be sufficient to give a true and fair view, the necessary additional information must be given in the accounts or in a note to them.
(5) If in special circumstances compliance with any of those provisions is inconsistent with the requirement to give a true and fair view, the directors must depart from that provision to the extent necessary to give a true and fair view.
Particulars of any such departure, the reasons for it and its effect must be given in a note to the accounts.

GENERAL NOTE

This section restates the provisions of s.226A of the 1985 Act, as inserted by SI 2004/2947, reg.2, and it applies to companies preparing "Companies Act individual accounts". Subsection (3) gives the Secretary of State power to issue regulations prescribing the form and content of the balance sheet and profit and loss account, as well as additional information to be provided by way of notes to the accounts. These regulations will replace the previous requirements contained in Sch.4 to the 1985 Act, and they are subject to the Parliamentary procedure described in s.473, below.

Subsections (1)-(3)

"Companies Act individual accounts" comprise a profit and loss account and end-year balance sheet (subs.(1)). The former must give "a true and fair view" of the profit or loss for the year and the latter "a true and fair view" of the state of the company's financial affairs at the year end (subs.(2)). The accounts must comply with regulations issued by the Secretary of State with respect to the form and content of the profit and loss account and balance sheet and additional information required to be shown in the form of notes to the accounts (subs.(3)).

Subsections (4) and (5)

If compliance with provisions of the Act or regulations would be insufficient to give "a true and fair view", the necessary additional information to achieve that must be given in the accounts or in notes thereto (subs.(4)). Similarly, if compliance with provisions of the Act or regulations is inconsistent with the requirement to ensure the financial statements give "a true and fair view", the directors must depart from them. However, they must indicate in a note the particulars of such a departure, as well as the reasons for it and the effect on the accounts (subs.(5)).

397. IAS individual accounts

Where the directors of a company prepare IAS individual accounts, they must state in the notes to the accounts that the accounts have been prepared in accordance with international accounting standards.

GENERAL NOTE

This section restates the provisions of s.226B of the 1985 Act, as inserted by SI 2004/2947, reg.2.

The section states that where IAS individual accounts are prepared, this must be disclosed in a note to the financial statements.

Group accounts: small companies

398. Option to prepare group accounts

If at the end of a financial year a company subject to the small companies regime is a parent company the directors, as well as preparing individual accounts for the year, may prepare group accounts for the year.

GENERAL NOTE

This section restates subs.(1) of s.248 of the 1985 Act, as substituted by s.13(3) of the 1989 Act and subsequently amended by SIs 1996/189 and 2001/3649, art.12. It gives parent companies that are subject to the small companies regime the option to prepare group accounts in addition to individual accounts.

The previous exemption in s.248 of the 1985 Act from preparation of group accounts by parent companies heading medium-sized groups has been abolished, following the substantial increase in the financial thresholds for medium-sized groups in 2004.

Briefly, the section provides that a company, which is subject to the small companies regime and is a parent company, is not required to prepare group accounts in addition to its individual accounts. However, it may nevertheless choose to do so.

Group accounts: other companies

GENERAL NOTE

The sections relating to group accounts have been reorganised to make them easier to follow. Sections 399-402 re-enact various sections of the 1985 Act, as amended: namely ss.227(1) and (8) (as substituted by SI 2004/2947), 228 (as inserted by s.5(3) of the 1989 Act and subsequently amended by SIs 1992/3178 and 1993/3246, the Welsh Language Act 1993, and SI 2004/2947, Sch.7, para.4(3)), 228A (as inserted by SI 2004/2947, reg.4) and 229(5) (as inserted by s.5(3) of the 1989 Act).

399. Duty to prepare group accounts

(1) This section applies to companies that are not subject to the small companies regime.

(2) If at the end of a financial year the company is a parent company the directors, as well as preparing individual accounts for the year, must prepare group accounts for the year unless the company is exempt from that requirement.

(3) There are exemptions under-

    section 400 (company included in EEA accounts of larger group),

    section 401 (company included in non-EEA accounts of larger group), and

    section 402 (company none of whose subsidiary undertakings need be included in the consolidation).

(4) A company to which this section applies but which is exempt from the requirement to prepare group accounts, may do so.

GENERAL NOTE

    This section, derived from subss.(1) and (8) of s.227 of the 1985 Act, as substituted by reg.2 of SI 2004/2947, concerns the requirements and exemptions from requirements in relation to group accounts. Parent companies not subject to the small companies regime have the duty to prepare consolidated accounts unless exempt from having to do so under ss.400-402.

Subsections (1)-(3)

    Companies not subject to the "small companies regime" under s.381, above (subs.(1)), that are parent companies at the end of a financial year are required to prepare group accounts in addition to individual company accounts (subs.(2)). There are, however, exceptions: namely: (i) under s.400 (company included in EEA accounts of a larger group); (ii) under s.401 (company included in non-EEA accounts of a larger group); and (iii) under s.402 (company none of whose subsidiary undertakings need be included in consolidation) (subs.(3)).

Subsection (4)

    A company that is exempt from the requirement to prepare group accounts may nevertheless choose to do so.

400. Exemption for company included in EEA group accounts of larger group

(1) A company is exempt from the requirement to prepare group accounts if it is itself a subsidiary undertaking and its immediate parent undertaking is established under the law of an EEA State, in the following cases-

    (a) where the company is a wholly-owned subsidiary of that parent undertaking;

    (b) where that parent undertaking holds more than 50% of the allotted shares in the company and notice requesting the preparation of group accounts has not been served on the company by shareholders holding in aggregate-

        (i) more than half of the remaining allotted shares in the company, or

        (ii) 5% of the total allotted shares in the company.

    Such notice must be served not later than six months after the end of the financial year before that to which it relates.

(2) Exemption is conditional upon compliance with all of the following conditions-

    (a) the company must be included in consolidated accounts for a larger group drawn up to the same date, or to an earlier date in the same financial year, by a parent undertaking established under the law of an EEA State;

    (b) those accounts must be drawn up and audited, and that parent undertaking's annual report must be drawn up, according to that law-

        (i) in accordance with the provisions of the Seventh Directive (83/349/EEC) (as modified, where relevant, by the provisions of the Bank Accounts Directive (86/635/EEC) or the Insurance Accounts Directive (91/674/EEC)), or

        (ii) in accordance with international accounting standards;

    (c) the company must disclose in its individual accounts that it is exempt from the obligation to prepare and deliver group accounts;

    (d) the company must state in its individual accounts the name of the parent undertaking that draws up the group accounts referred to above and-

(i) if it is incorporated outside the United Kingdom, the country in which it is incorporated, or

(ii) if it is unincorporated, the address of its principal place of business;

(e) the company must deliver to the registrar, within the period for filing its accounts and reports for the financial year in question, copies of-

(i) those group accounts, and

(ii) the parent undertaking's annual report,

together with the auditor's report on them;

(f) any requirement of Part 35 of this Act as to the delivery to the registrar of a certified translation into English must be met in relation to any document comprised in the accounts and reports delivered in accordance with paragraph (e).

(3) For the purposes of subsection (1)(b) shares held by a wholly-owned subsidiary of the parent undertaking, or held on behalf of the parent undertaking or a wholly-owned subsidiary, shall be attributed to the parent undertaking.

(4) The exemption does not apply to a company any of whose securities are admitted to trading on a regulated market in an EEA State.

(5) Shares held by directors of a company for the purpose of complying with any share qualification requirement shall be disregarded in determining for the purposes of this section whether the company is a wholly-owned subsidiary.

(6) In subsection (4) "securities" includes-

(a) shares and stock,

(b) debentures, including debenture stock, loan stock, bonds, certificates of deposit and other instruments creating or acknowledging indebtedness,

(c) warrants or other instruments entitling the holder to subscribe for securities falling within paragraph (a) or (b), and

(d) certificates or other instruments that confer-

(i) property rights in respect of a security falling within paragraph (a), (b) or (c),

(ii) any right to acquire, dispose of, underwrite or convert a security, being a right to which the holder would be entitled if he held any such security to which the certificate or other instrument relates, or

(iii) a contractual right (other than an option) to acquire any such security otherwise than by subscription.

GENERAL NOTE

This section, derived from s.228 of the 1985 Act, as substituted by s.5(3) of the 1989 Act and subsequently amended, provides an exemption from preparing group accounts for companies whose accounts are consolidated in EEA group accounts of a larger group.

Subsection (1)

A company that is itself a subsidiary and its immediate parent is established in the EEA is *prima facie* exempt from preparing group accounts. The exception arises if it is not wholly owned by the immediate parent, and more than half the minority shareholders, or holders of at least 5 per cent of the total allotted shares, serve notice requesting the preparation of group accounts. Such a notice must be issued within six months of the subsidiary's financial year end.

Subsection (2)

The following further conditions must be met to secure exemption from preparing group accounts: (i) the company's accounts must be included in the consolidated accounts for the relevant year of a group headed by a parent undertaking established in the EEA; (ii) the group's accounts must be prepared according to the requirements of the European Union's relevant group accounts directive or in accordance with international accounting standards; (iii) the company must disclose in a note to its individual accounts that it is exempt from the requirement to prepare and deliver group accounts; (iv) the company must disclose in its individual accounts the name of the parent undertaking preparing group accounts, stating the country in which it is incorporated if it is not the United Kingdom, or, if it is unincorporated, the address of its principal place of business; (v) the company must file with the registrar copies of the group accounts and the ultimate parent's annual report, together with the auditor's report; and (vi) the company must file a certified translation into English, where relevant, complying with the provisions of ss.1102-1107.

Subsections (3)-(6)

Subsections (3)-(6) deal with various matters that clarify the meaning of subss.(1)-(2). Thus shares held by or on behalf of the parent or wholly-owned subsidiaries are to be treated as if held by the parent undertaking (subs.(3)). The exemption covered by s.400 does not apply to a company whose securities (as defined in subs.(6)) are admitted to trading on a regulated market in an EEA state (subs.(4)). Shares held by directors for share qualification purposes are to be disregarded for the purpose of s.400 in determining whether or not a subsidiary is wholly owned (subs.(5)).

401. Exemption for company included in non-EEA group accounts of larger group

(1) A company is exempt from the requirement to prepare group accounts if it is itself a subsidiary undertaking and its parent undertaking is not established under the law of an EEA State, in the following cases-

    (a) where the company is a wholly-owned subsidiary of that parent undertaking;

    (b) where that parent undertaking holds more than 50% of the allotted shares in the company and notice requesting the preparation of group accounts has not been served on the company by shareholders holding in aggregate-

        (i) more than half of the remaining allotted shares in the company, or

        (ii) 5% of the total allotted shares in the company.

    Such notice must be served not later than six months after the end of the financial year before that to which it relates.

(2) Exemption is conditional upon compliance with all of the following conditions-

    (a) the company and all of its subsidiary undertakings must be included in consolidated accounts for a larger group drawn up to the same date, or to an earlier date in the same financial year, by a parent undertaking;

    (b) those accounts and, where appropriate, the group's annual report, must be drawn up-

        (i) in accordance with the provisions of the Seventh Directive (83/ 349/ EEC) (as modified, where relevant, by the provisions of the Bank Accounts Directive (86/ 635/ EEC) or the Insurance Accounts Directive (91/ 674/ EEC)), or

        (ii) in a manner equivalent to consolidated accounts and consolidated annual reports so drawn up;

    (c) the group accounts must be audited by one or more persons authorised to audit accounts under the law under which the parent undertaking which draws them up is established;

    (d) the company must disclose in its individual accounts that it is exempt from the obligation to prepare and deliver group accounts;

    (e) the company must state in its individual accounts the name of the parent undertaking which draws up the group accounts referred to above and-

        (i) if it is incorporated outside the United Kingdom, the country in which it is incorporated, or

        (ii) if it is unincorporated, the address of its principal place of business;

    (f) the company must deliver to the registrar, within the period for filing its accounts and reports for the financial year in question, copies of-

        (i) the group accounts, and

        (ii) where appropriate, the consolidated annual report,

    together with the auditor's report on them;

    (g) any requirement of Part 35 of this Act as to the delivery to the registrar of a certified translation into English must be met in relation to any document comprised in the accounts and reports delivered in accordance with paragraph (f).

(3) For the purposes of subsection (1)(b), shares held by a wholly-owned subsidiary of the parent undertaking, or held on behalf of the parent undertaking or a wholly-owned subsidiary, are attributed to the parent undertaking.

(4) The exemption does not apply to a company any of whose securities are admitted to trading on a regulated market in an EEA State.

(5) Shares held by directors of a company for the purpose of complying with any share qualification requirement shall be disregarded in determining for the purposes of this section whether the company is a wholly-owned subsidiary.

(6) In subsection (4) "securities" includes-

    (a) shares and stock,

    (b) debentures, including debenture stock, loan stock, bonds, certificates of deposit and other instruments creating or acknowledging indebtedness,

    (c) warrants or other instruments entitling the holder to subscribe for securities falling within paragraph (a) or (b), and

    (d) certificates or other instruments that confer-

        (i) property rights in respect of a security falling within paragraph (a), (b) or (c),

        (ii) any right to acquire, dispose of, underwrite or convert a security, being a right to which the holder would be entitled if he held any such security to which the certificate or other instrument relates, or

        (iii) a contractual right (other than an option) to acquire any such security otherwise than by subscription.

GENERAL NOTE

This section is derived from s.228A of the 1985 Act, as inserted by reg.4 of SI 2004/2947.

The section gives a similar exemption to that available in s.400 for companies included in non-EEA group accounts of a larger group.

Subsection (1)

A company that is itself a subsidiary and its immediate parent is not established in the EEA is *prima facie* exempt from preparing group accounts. The exception arises if it is not wholly owned by the immediate parent, and more than half the minority shareholders, or holders of at least 5 per cent of the total allotted shares, serve notice requesting the preparation of group accounts. Such a notice must be issued within six months of the subsidiary's financial year-end.

Subsection (2)

The following further conditions must be met to secure exemption from preparing group accounts: (i) the company's accounts must be included in the consolidated accounts for the relevant year of a group headed by a parent undertaking; (ii) the group's accounts must be prepared according to the requirements of the EU's relevant group accounts directives or in an equivalent manner; (iii) the group accounts must be audited by persons legally authorised to do so; (iv) the company must disclose in a note to its individual accounts that it is exempt from the requirement to prepare and deliver group accounts; (v) the company must disclose in its individual accounts the name of the parent undertaking preparing group accounts, stating the country in which it is incorporated if it is not the United Kingdom, or, if it is unincorporated, the address of its principal place of business; (vi) the company must file with the registrar copies of the group accounts and the annual report on the consolidated accounts, together with the auditor's report; and (vii) the company must file a certified translation into English, where relevant, complying with the provisions of ss.1102-1107.

Subsections (3)-(6)

Subsections (3)-(6) deal with various matters that clarify the meaning of subss.(1)-(2). Thus shares held by or on behalf of the parent or wholly owned subsidiaries are to be treated as if held by the parent undertaking (subs.(3)). The exemption covered by s.401 does not apply to a company whose securities (as defined in subs.(6)) are admitted to trading on a regulated market in an EEA state (subs.(4)). Shares held by directors for share qualification purposes are to be disregarded for the purpose of s.401 in determining whether or not a subsidiary is wholly owned (subs.(5)).

402. Exemption if no subsidiary undertakings need be included in the consolidation

A parent company is exempt from the requirement to prepare group accounts if under section 405 all of its subsidiary undertakings could be excluded from consolidation in Companies Act group accounts.

GENERAL NOTE

This section derives from s.229(5) of the 1985 Act, as substituted by s.5(3) of the 1989 Act and subsequently amended by Sch.1, para.7(c) of SI 2004/2947.

The section states that a parent company is also exempt from the requirement to prepare group accounts when under s.405 all the company's subsidiary undertakings can be excluded from consolidation in Companies Act group accounts.

Group accounts: general

403.   Group accounts: applicable accounting framework

(1) The group accounts of certain parent companies are required by Article 4 of the IAS Regulation to be prepared in accordance with international accounting standards ("IAS group accounts").

(2) The group accounts of other companies may be prepared-
    (a) in accordance with section 404 ("Companies Act group accounts"), or
    (b) in accordance with international accounting standards ("IAS group accounts").
This is subject to the following provisions of this section.

(3) The group accounts of a parent company that is a charity must be Companies Act group accounts.

(4) After the first financial year in which the directors of a parent company prepare IAS group accounts ("the first IAS year"), all subsequent group accounts of the company must be prepared in accordance with international accounting standards unless there is a relevant change of circumstance.

(5) There is a relevant change of circumstance if, at any time during or after the first IAS year-
    (a) the company becomes a subsidiary undertaking of another undertaking that does not prepare IAS group accounts,
    (b) the company ceases to be a company with securities admitted to trading on a regulated market in an EEA State, or
    (c) a parent undertaking of the company ceases to be an undertaking with securities admitted to trading on a regulated market in an EEA State.

(6) If, having changed to preparing Companies Act group accounts following a relevant change of circumstance, the directors again prepare IAS group accounts for the company, subsections (4) and (5) apply again as if the first financial year for which such accounts are again prepared were the first IAS year.

GENERAL NOTE
    This section replaces subss.(2)-(7) of s.227 of the 1985 Act, as substituted by s.5 of the 1989 Act and subsequently amended by reg.2 of SI 2004/2947.

Subsections (1)-(3)
    Parent companies whose securities are publicly traded must prepare group accounts ("IAS group accounts") in accordance with the IAS Regulation (subs.(1)). Other parent companies (with the exception of charitable parent companies, which under subs.(3) must prepare "Companies Act group accounts") have the choice whether to prepare group accounts in accordance with s.404 (below) under the Companies Act ("Companies Act group accounts") or in accordance with international accounting standards ("IAS group accounts") (sub.(2)).

Subsections (4)-(6)
    After a company has switched to preparing "IAS group accounts", all subsequent group accounts must be prepared in accordance with international accounting standards (IAS) unless there is "a relevant change of circumstance" (subs.(4)). The latter would arise if the company became a subsidiary of another undertaking that does not prepare "IAS group accounts", or the company or it parent ceases to have its securities traded on a regulated market in an EEA state (subs.(5)). Where such a change back to preparing "Companies Act group accounts" occurs, and the directors subsequently prepare "IAS group accounts", the provisions of subss.(4)-(5) once again apply (subs.(6)).

404. Companies Act group accounts

(1) Companies Act group accounts must comprise-
  (a) a consolidated balance sheet dealing with the state of affairs of the parent company and its subsidiary undertakings, and
  (b) a consolidated profit and loss account dealing with the profit or loss of the parent company and its subsidiary undertakings.

(2) The accounts must give a true and fair view of the state of affairs as at the end of the financial year, and the profit or loss for the financial year, of the undertakings included in the consolidation as a whole, so far as concerns members of the company.

(3) The accounts must comply with provision made by the Secretary of State by regulations as to-
  (a) the form and content of the consolidated balance sheet and consolidated profit and loss account, and
  (b) additional information to be provided by way of notes to the accounts.

(4) If compliance with the regulations, and any other provision made by or under this Act as to the matters to be included in a company's group accounts or in notes to those accounts, would not be sufficient to give a true and fair view, the necessary additional information must be given in the accounts or in a note to them.

(5) If in special circumstances compliance with any of those provisions is inconsistent with the requirement to give a true and fair view, the directors must depart from that provision to the extent necessary to give a true and fair view.

Particulars of any such departure, the reasons for it and its effect must be given in a note to the accounts.

GENERAL NOTE

This section restates s.227A of the 1985 Act, as inserted by SI 2004/2947, reg.2, and it applies to companies preparing "Companies Act group accounts". Subsection (3) gives the Secretary of State power to issue regulations prescribing the form and content of the consolidated balance sheet and consolidated profit and loss account, as well as additional information to be provided by way of notes to the accounts. These regulations will replace the previous requirements contained in Sch.4A to the 1985 Act, and they are subject to the Parliamentary procedure described in s.473, below.

Subsections (1)-(3)

"Companies Act group accounts" comprise a consolidated profit and loss account and a consolidated end-year balance sheet (subs.(1)). The former must give "a true and fair view" of the group profit or loss for the year and the latter "a true and fair view" of the state of the group's financial affairs at the year end (subs.(2)). The accounts must comply with regulations issued by the Secretary of State with respect to the form and content of the consolidated profit and loss account and consolidated balance sheet and additional information required to be shown in the form of notes to the accounts (subs.(3)).

Subsections (4)-(5)

If compliance with provisions of the Act or regulations would be insufficient to give "a true and fair view", the necessary additional information to achieve that must be given in the accounts or in notes thereto (subs.(4)). Similarly, if compliance with provisions of the Act or regulations is inconsistent with the requirement to ensure the group financial statements give "a true and fair view", the directors must depart from them. However, they must indicate in a note the particulars of such a departure, as well as the reasons for it and the effect on the accounts (subs.(5)).

405. Companies Act group accounts: subsidiary undertakings included in the consolidation

(1) Where a parent company prepares Companies Act group accounts, all the subsidiary undertakings of the company must be included in the consolidation, subject to the following exceptions.

(2) A subsidiary undertaking may be excluded from consolidation if its inclusion is not material for the purpose of giving a true and fair view (but two or more undertakings may be excluded only if they are not material taken together).

(3) A subsidiary undertaking may be excluded from consolidation where-

    (a) severe long-term restrictions substantially hinder the exercise of the rights of the parent company over the assets or management of that undertaking, or

    (b) the information necessary for the preparation of group accounts cannot be obtained without disproportionate expense or undue delay, or

    (c) the interest of the parent company is held exclusively with a view to subsequent resale.

(4) The reference in subsection (3)(a) to the rights of the parent company and the reference in subsection (3)(c) to the interest of the parent company are, respectively, to rights and interests held by or attributed to the company for the purposes of the definition of "parent undertaking" (see section 1162) in the absence of which it would not be the parent company.

GENERAL NOTE

This section replaces subss.(1)-(3) of s.229 of the 1985 Act, a section inserted by s.5(3) of the 1989 Act and subsequently amended by Sch.1, para.7(c), of SI 2004/2947. It requires all subsidiary undertakings to be included in the consolidated accounts, subject to certain permitted exclusions.

Subsections (1)-(3)

All subsidiary undertakings must be included when a parent prepares "Companies Act group accounts" (subs.(1)), subject to the following exceptions: (i) one or more subsidiaries may be excluded if their inclusion individually and together is not material in giving a true and fair view (subs.(2)): (ii) a subsidiary may be excluded from consolidation where (a) long-term restrictions impede managerial control by the parent, (b) information necessary for the preparation of group accounts can only be obtained with undue expense or delay, or (c) the investment in the subsidiary is held for resale (subs.(3)).

Subsection (4)

This subsection defines the meaning of "rights" and "the interest" of the parent company as used in subs.(3). It also clarifies the meaning of "parent company" and "parent undertaking" in this context.

406.   IAS group accounts

Where the directors of a company prepare IAS group accounts, they must state in the notes to those accounts that the accounts have been prepared in accordance with international accounting standards.

GENERAL NOTE

This section re-enacts s.227B of the 1985 Act, as inserted by reg.2 of SI 2004/2947.

The section provides that where group accounts are prepared in accordance with international accounting standards ("IAS group accounts"), this must be stated in the notes to the accounts.

407.   Consistency of financial reporting within group

(1) The directors of a parent company must secure that the individual accounts of-

    (a) the parent company, and

    (b) each of its subsidiary undertakings,

are all prepared using the same financial reporting framework, except to the extent that in their opinion there are good reasons for not doing so.

(2) Subsection (1) does not apply if the directors do not prepare group accounts for the parent company.

(3) Subsection (1) only applies to accounts of subsidiary undertakings that are required to be prepared under this Part.

(4) Subsection (1) does not require accounts of undertakings that are charities to be prepared using the same financial reporting framework as accounts of undertakings which are not charities.

(5) Subsection (1)(a) does not apply where the directors of a parent company prepare IAS group accounts and IAS individual accounts.

GENERAL NOTE

This section restates s.227C of the 1985 Act, as inserted by reg.2 of SI 2004/2947. If a parent company prepares both consolidated and individual accounts under IAS, it is not required to ensure that all its subsidiary undertakings also use IAS. However, it must otherwise ensure that its individual accounts and those of all its subsidiary undertakings use the same financial reporting framework, unless there are good reasons for not doing so.

Subsections (1)-(5)

The directors of a parent company must ensure that the individual accounts of the parent and each subsidiary are prepared using the same accounting framework, except where there are good reasons why this should not be so (subs.(1)). However, the requirement of subs.(1) does not apply (i) if the directors do not prepare group accounts (subs.(2)); (ii) if subsidiary undertakings are not required to prepare accounts (subs.(3)); (iii) if the undertaking is a charity (see ss.395(2) and 403(3)) (subs.(4)); and (iv) where the directors of a parent company prepare IAS group accounts and IAS individual accounts (subs.(5)).

408. Individual profit and loss account where group accounts prepared

(1) This section applies where—
    (a) a company prepares group accounts in accordance with this Act, and
    (b) the notes to the company's individual balance sheet show the company's profit or loss for the financial year determined in accordance with this Act.

(2) The profit and loss account need not contain the information specified in section 411 (information about employee numbers and costs).

(3) The company's individual profit and loss account must be approved in accordance with section 414(1) (approval by directors) but may be omitted from the company's annual accounts for the purposes of the other provisions of the Companies Acts.

(4) The exemption conferred by this section is conditional upon its being disclosed in the company's annual accounts that the exemption applies.

GENERAL NOTE

This section replaces most of s.230 of the 1985 Act, a section substituted by s.5(4) of the 1989 Act and subsequently amended by Sch.1, para.8 of SI 2004/2947.

A parent company that prepares group accounts and meets specific criteria may, subject to the individual profit and loss account being approved by the directors, dispense with the inclusion of such a profit and loss account in the company's accounts (e.g. when delivered to the registrar of companies). However, notes to the individual balance sheet must show the company's profit or loss for the year. The profit and loss account may also omit the information on employee numbers and costs required by s.411. The exemption, previously provided for in s.230(2) of the 1985 Act for certain information required by provisions of Sch.4 to that Act, will be available under regulations to be issued by the Secretary of State under s.396, above.

Subsections (1) and (2)

Where in accordance with the Act a company prepares group accounts, and the notes to the company's individual balance sheet show its (individual) profit or loss for the financial year (subs.(1)), the profit and loss account need not contain the information about employee numbers and costs specified in s.411, below (subs.(2)).

Subsection (3)

The company's individual profit and loss account must be approved by the directors under s.414(1), but it may otherwise be omitted from the company's annual accounts.

Subsection (4)

The company's accounts must disclose in a note that the exemption applies.

Information to be given in notes to the accounts

409. Information about related undertakings

(1) The Secretary of State may make provision by regulations requiring information about related undertakings to be given in notes to a company's annual accounts.

(2) The regulations-

    (a) may make different provision according to whether or not the company prepares group accounts, and

    (b) may specify the descriptions of undertaking in relation to which they apply, and make different provision in relation to different descriptions of related undertaking.

(3) The regulations may provide that information need not be disclosed with respect to an undertaking that-

    (a) is established under the law of a country outside the United Kingdom, or

    (b) carries on business outside the United Kingdom,

if the following conditions are met.

(4) The conditions are-

    (a) that in the opinion of the directors of the company the disclosure would be seriously prejudicial to the business of-

        (i) that undertaking,

        (ii) the company,

        (iii) any of the company's subsidiary undertakings, or

        (iv) any other undertaking which is included in the consolidation;

    (b) that the Secretary of State agrees that the information need not be disclosed.

(5) Where advantage is taken of any such exemption, that fact must be stated in a note to the company's annual accounts.

GENERAL NOTE

This section replaces subss.(1)-(4) of s.231 of the 1985 Act, as substituted by s.6(1) of the 1989 Act and subsequently amended by SI 1993/1820.

This section gives the Secretary of State a new power to make regulations requiring information about related undertakings to be given in notes to a company's annual accounts. The requirement to disclose information about such undertakings in the notes to a company's annual accounts applies whether or not the company has to produce group accounts, but there are different disclosure requirements in each case. There are grounds for exemption, detailed in subss.(3)-(5), with respect to related undertakings established and/or operating overseas, but only a very small number of companies seek such concessions each year.

The regulations will replace the provisions of Sch.5 to the 1985 Act, but are subject to the Parliamentary procedure described in s.473.

Subsections (1) and (2)

Regulations may be issued by the Secretary of State requiring information to be given about "related undertakings" in notes to a company's annual accounts (subs.(1)). The regulations may make different provisions for companies preparing group accounts and differentiate the requirements relating to various types of undertaking (subs.(2)).

Subsections (3)-(5)

The regulations, like s.231(3) of the 1985 Act, may provide that information need not be disclosed about an undertaking that is established abroad or carries on business outside the United Kingdom (subs.(3)). However, this is subject to conditions: first, that the directors are of the opinion that disclosure would be seriously prejudicial to the business of the undertaking, the company itself and any of its subsidiaries, and of any other undertaking included in the consolidated accounts; and, secondly, that the Secretary of State agrees that the information should be omitted (subs.(4)). The fact that advantage is taken of such exemption must be stated in a note to the company's annual accounts (subs.(5)).

410. Information about related undertakings: alternative compliance

(1) This section applies where the directors of a company are of the opinion that the number of undertakings in respect of which the company is required to disclose information under any provision of regulations under section 409 (related undertakings) is such that compliance with that provision would result in information of excessive length being given in notes to the company's annual accounts.

(2) The information need only be given in respect of-

    (a) the undertakings whose results or financial position, in the opinion of the directors, principally affected the figures shown in the company's annual accounts, and

    (b) where the company prepares group accounts, undertakings excluded from consolidation under section 405(3) (undertakings excluded on grounds other than materiality).

(3) If advantage is taken of subsection (2)-

    (a) there must be included in the notes to the company's annual accounts a statement that the information is given only with respect to such undertakings as are mentioned in that subsection, and

    (b) the full information (both that which is disclosed in the notes to the accounts and that which is not) must be annexed to the company's next annual return.

For this purpose the "next annual return" means that next delivered to the registrar after the accounts in question have been approved under section 414.

(4) If a company fails to comply with subsection (3)(b), an offence is committed by-

    (a) the company, and

    (b) every officer of the company who is in default.

(5) A person guilty of an offence under subsection (4) is liable on summary conviction to a fine not exceeding level 3 on the standard scale and, for continued contravention, a daily default fine not exceeding one-tenth of level 3 on the standard scale.

GENERAL NOTE

This section replaces subss.(5)-(7) of s.231 of the 1985 Act, as substituted by s.6(1) of the 1989 Act and subsequently amended by SI 1996/189 and Sch.7, para.5 of SI 2004/2947.

Directors may give more limited information about related undertakings where they are numerous and the directors believe that full disclosure would result in information of excessive length in the notes to the accounts. However, there is a minimum level of information that must be disclosed about such undertakings, and full information about them has to be submitted with the next annual return (for which, see ss.854-859).

Subsections (1)-(3)

Where a company has numerous "related undertakings" and the directors are of the opinion that compliance with the regulations issued under s.409, above, would result in an excessively lengthy note to the accounts (subs.(1)), information need only be given with respect to: (i) those undertakings whose financial position principally affects the figures shown in the company's annual accounts; and (ii) undertakings excluded from consolidation in any group accounts under s.405(3) (subs.(2)). However, the fact that information is not being given in respect of all related undertakings must be made clear in the notes to the accounts, and information about all related undertakings must be annexed to the next annual return (subs.(3)).

Subsections (4) and (5)

The company and every defaulting officer commits an offence if full information about all related undertakings is not annexed to the next annual return (subs.(4)), the penalties for which are set out in subs.(5).

411. Information about employee numbers and costs

(1) In the case of a company not subject to the small companies regime, the following information with respect to the employees of the company must be given in notes to the company's annual accounts-

    (a) the average number of persons employed by the company in the financial year, and

    (b) the average number of persons so employed within each category of persons employed by the company.

(2) The categories by reference to which the number required to be disclosed by subsection (1)(b) is to be determined must be such as the directors may select having regard to the manner in which the company's activities are organised.

(3) The average number required by subsection (1)(a) or (b) is determined by dividing the relevant annual number by the number of months in the financial year.

(4) The relevant annual number is determined by ascertaining for each month in the financial year-

    (a) for the purposes of subsection (1)(a), the number of persons employed under contracts of service by the company in that month (whether throughout the month or not);

    (b) for the purposes of subsection (1)(b), the number of persons in the category in question of persons so employed;

and adding together all the monthly numbers.

(5) In respect of all persons employed by the company during the financial year who are taken into account in determining the relevant annual number for the purposes of subsection (1)(a) there must also be stated the aggregate amounts respectively of-

    (a) wages and salaries paid or payable in respect of that year to those persons;

    (b) social security costs incurred by the company on their behalf; and

    (c) other pension costs so incurred.

This does not apply in so far as those amounts, or any of them, are stated elsewhere in the company's accounts.

(6) In subsection (5)-

    "pension costs" includes any costs incurred by the company in respect of-

        (a) any pension scheme established for the purpose of providing pensions for persons currently or formerly employed by the company,

        (b) any sums set aside for the future payment of pensions directly by the company to current or former employees, and

        (c) any pensions paid directly to such persons without having first been set aside;

    "social security costs" means any contributions by the company to any state social security or pension scheme, fund or arrangement.

(7) Where the company prepares group accounts, this section applies as if the undertakings included in the consolidation were a single company.

GENERAL NOTE

    This section, concerning staff particulars, replaces s.231A of the 1985 Act, as inserted by Sch.1, para.9 of SI 2004/2947. (The provisions were previously in the Schedules to Pt 7 of the 1985 Act, and the amendment was made in 2004 to ensure that the provisions applied both to companies preparing Companies Act accounts and to those preparing IAS accounts.)

Subsections (1) and (2)

    Companies other than those subject to the "small companies regime" (s.381) must give details in notes to their accounts of the average number of persons employed in the year by various categories (subs.(1)), the latter to be determined by the directors having regard to the way in which the company's activities are organised (subs.(2)).

Subsections (3) and (4)

    Subsections (3) and (4) respectively give instructions on calculating the average number of persons employed and the relevant annual number.

Subsections (5) and (6)

    Details are also to be disclosed of the aggregate amounts paid or payable in respect of each of the following: wages and salaries; social security costs; and other pension costs (subs.(5)), definitions of the latter two items being given in subs.(6).

Subsection (7)

Where group accounts are prepared, the information has to be in respect of the group rather than to individual undertakings.

412. Information about directors' benefits: remuneration

(1) The Secretary of State may make provision by regulations requiring information to be given in notes to a company's annual accounts about directors' remuneration.

(2) The matters about which information may be required include-
  (a) gains made by directors on the exercise of share options;
  (b) benefits received or receivable by directors under long-term incentive schemes;
  (c) payments for loss of office (as defined in section 215);
  (d) benefits receivable, and contributions for the purpose of providing benefits, in respect of past services of a person as director or in any other capacity while director;
  (e) consideration paid to or receivable by third parties for making available the services of a person as director or in any other capacity while director.

(3) Without prejudice to the generality of subsection (1), regulations under this section may make any such provision as was made immediately before the commencement of this Part by Part 1 of Schedule 6 to the Companies Act 1985 (c. 6).

(4) For the purposes of this section, and regulations made under it, amounts paid to or receivable by-
  (a) a person connected with a director, or
  (b) a body corporate controlled by a director,
are treated as paid to or receivable by the director.
The expressions "connected with" and "controlled by" in this subsection have the same meaning as in Part 10 (company directors).

(5) It is the duty of-
  (a) any director of a company, and
  (b) any person who is or has at any time in the preceding five years been a director of the company,
to give notice to the company of such matters relating to himself as may be necessary for the purposes of regulations under this section.

(6) A person who makes default in complying with subsection (5) commits an offence and is liable on summary conviction to a fine not exceeding level 3 on the standard scale.

GENERAL NOTE

This section, together with s.413, replaces s.232 of the 1985 Act, as substituted by s.6(3) of the 1989 Act and subsequently amended by reg.2 of SI 2002/1986.

Under s.232 of the 1985 Act, information on directors' remuneration specified in Pt 1 of Sch.6 had to be given in notes to a company's annual accounts. Small companies could be exempt from some of the disclosures required by Sch.6, while quoted companies were subject to separate requirements on the disclosure of directors' remuneration under Sch.7A. Section 412 of the new Act gives the Secretary of State power to make provision by regulations requiring information about directors' remuneration to be given in notes to a company's annual accounts. Regulations under this section are subject to the Parliamentary procedure described in s.473.

Subsections (1)-(3)

The Secretary of State is empowered to make regulations concerning disclosure of information about directors' remuneration in notes to a company's annual accounts (subs.(1)). These may continue the provisions in Pt 1 of Sch.6 to the 1985 Act (subs.(3)). The matters about which information may be required include gains on the exercise of share options; benefits receivable under long-term incentive schemes; compensation for loss of office (as defined in s.215); contributions and benefits receivable with respect to past services; and consideration receivable by third parties for making available the services of a director (subs.(2)).

Subsection (4)

The information given is to include benefits receivable by a person "connected with" a director or a body corporate "controlled by" a director, these terms being interpreted in accordance with the provisions of ss.254 and 255, above.

Subsections (5) and (6)

It is the duty of a director, or someone who has been a director within the past five years, to give details of the necessary information to the company (subs.(5)), and failure to do so makes the defaulting party *prima facie* guilty of an offence, the penalty for which is a fine (subs.(6)).

413. Information about directors' benefits: advances, credit and guarantees

(1) In the case of a company that does not prepare group accounts, details of-
    (a) advances and credits granted by the company to its directors, and
    (b) guarantees of any kind entered into by the company on behalf of its directors,
must be shown in the notes to its individual accounts.

(2) In the case of a parent company that prepares group accounts, details of-
    (a) advances and credits granted to the directors of the parent company, by that company or by any of its subsidiary undertakings, and
    (b) guarantees of any kind entered into on behalf of the directors of the parent company, by that company or by any of its subsidiary undertakings,
must be shown in the notes to the group accounts.

(3) The details required of an advance or credit are-
    (a) its amount,
    (b) an indication of the interest rate,
    (c) its main conditions, and
    (d) any amounts repaid.

(4) The details required of a guarantee are-
    (a) its main terms,
    (b) the amount of the maximum liability that may be incurred by the company (or its subsidiary), and
    (c) any amount paid and any liability incurred by the company (or its subsidiary) for the purpose of fulfilling the guarantee (including any loss incurred by reason of enforcement of the guarantee).

(5) There must also be stated in the notes to the accounts the totals-
    (a) of amounts stated under subsection (3)(a),
    (b) of amounts stated under subsection (3)(d),
    (c) of amounts stated under subsection (4)(b), and
    (d) of amounts stated under subsection (4)(c).

(6) References in this section to the directors of a company are to the persons who were a director at any time in the financial year to which the accounts relate.

(7) The requirements of this section apply in relation to every advance, credit or guarantee subsisting at any time in the financial year to which the accounts relate-
    (a) whenever it was entered into,
    (b) whether or not the person concerned was a director of the company in question at the time it was entered into, and
    (c) in the case of an advance, credit or guarantee involving a subsidiary undertaking of that company, whether or not that undertaking was such a subsidiary undertaking at the time it was entered into.

(8) Banking companies and the holding companies of credit institutions need only state the details required by subsections (3)(a) and (4)(b).

GENERAL NOTE

This section, which deals with the disclosure of directors' benefits in the form of advances, credit and guarantees, together with s.412 replaces s.232 of the 1985 Act, as substituted by s.6(3) of the 1989 Act and subsequently amended by reg.2 of SI 2002/1986.

Under s.232 of the 1985 Act, in an extension of s.317 of that Act, dealing with the duty of directors to disclose an interest in contracts, information had to be given in notes to a company's annual accounts giving details of: (i) loans, quasi-loans, credit transactions and related guarantees and security between a company and its directors or connected persons; and (ii) any other transactions or arrangements in which a director, indirectly or directly, had a material interest. Part 2 of Sch.6 to the 1985 Act provided details of the disclosures required in respect of these areas, while Pt 3 imposed similar disclosure requirements with respect to such transactions between the company and its other officers. The Act repeals Pts 2 and 3 of Sch.6.

Section 413 sets out the new disclosure requirements in respect of (a) advances and credits granted by the company to its directors, and (b) guarantees of any kind entered into by the company on behalf of its directors. The wording of s.413 is similar to that of Arts 43(1)(13) and 34(13) of the Fourth (78/660/EEC) and Seventh (83/349/EEC) Company Law Directives, which deal with these matters.

The provisions of s.396(3)(b) ("Companies Act individual accounts") and s.404(3)(b) ("Companies Act group accounts") enable the Secretary of State to issue regulations that will be used to require the disclosure of information about certain related party transactions in the notes to Companies Act accounts. However, companies will no longer be required to disclose transactions made between the company and officers other than directors.

Further changes have been made with respect to disclosures by banks and credit institutions. In the light of the simplified disclosure regime for advances, credit and guarantees in s.413, ss.343 and 344 of the 1985 Act, which made special provision for financial institutions, are repealed.

Subsections (1) and (2)

Details of advances and credits to directors and of guarantees entered into on their behalf must be shown in notes to the accounts. Where a company does not prepare group accounts, the information relates to the company itself and is to be shown in notes to its individual company accounts (subs.(1)). However, where a company prepares group accounts, the information to be shown in a note to the group accounts relates to directors of the parent company and advances, credits, and guarantees entered into with them by any member of the group (subs.(2)).

Subsections (3) and (5)

The details to be disclosed with respect to an advance or credit are its amount, the interest rate, the main conditions, and any amounts repaid (subs.(3)). With respect to guarantees entered into, the details that have to be disclosed are the main terms, the maximum liability that may be incurred, and any amounts paid or liable to be paid as a result of entering into the guarantee (subs.(4)). The notes must also state the totals of the amounts advanced or credits granted to directors and any amounts repaid; and the amounts of the maximum liability incurred with respect to all guarantees entered into on behalf of directors, together with the total of amounts paid and liabilities incurred in relation to such guarantees (subs.(5)).

Subsections (6) and (7)

Subsection (6) indicates that the provisions apply to anyone who was a director for part of the financial year to which the accounts relate; while subs.(7) makes it clear it is immaterial when precisely the arrangements were made, whether or not the person concerned was a director when they were entered into, or indeed whether or not a subsidiary was a group member when the arrangement was made.

Subsection (8)

Banks and the holding companies of credit institutions need only state (i) the amount of an advance or credit; and (ii) in relation to a guarantee, the amount of the maximum liability that may be incurred by the company (or its subsidiary).

Approval and signing of accounts

414. Approval and signing of accounts

(1) A company's annual accounts must be approved by the board of directors and signed on behalf of the board by a director of the company.

(2) The signature must be on the company's balance sheet.

(3) If the accounts are prepared in accordance with the provisions applicable to companies subject to the small companies regime, the balance sheet must contain a statement to that effect in a prominent position above the signature.

(4) If annual accounts are approved that do not comply with the requirements of this Act (and, where applicable, of Article 4 of the IAS Regulation), every director of the company who-

    (a) knew that they did not comply, or was reckless as to whether they complied, and

    (b) failed to take reasonable steps to secure compliance with those requirements or, as the case may be, to prevent the accounts from being approved,

commits an offence.

(5) A person guilty of an offence under this section is liable-

    (a) on conviction on indictment, to a fine;

    (b) on summary conviction, to a fine not exceeding the statutory maximum.

GENERAL NOTE

This section replaces s.233 of the 1985 Act, as substituted by s.7 of the 1989 Act and subsequently amended by Sch.1, para.10 of SI 2004/2947, as well as s.246(8) (as substituted by SI 1997/220) and s.248A(5) (as inserted by SI 1997/220).

The criminal offence of approving accounts that do not comply with the requirements of the Act (or, where applicable, of art.4 of the IAS Regulation) is re-enacted in subs.(4). However, subs.(4) of s.233 of the 1985 Act, which required that a director of the company should sign the copy of the balance sheet delivered to the registrar, has not been reproduced as this requirement would have hampered developments in the electronic delivery of accounts.

Subsections (1) and (2)

A company's annual accounts (both its individual accounts and any group accounts) must be approved by the board of directors (subs.(1)), and the balance sheet must be signed by a director (subs.(2)).

Subsection (3)

The balance sheet of accounts prepared in accordance with the "small companies regime" (s.381) must carry a statement to that effect in a prominent position above the signature. (This re-enacts ss.246(8) and 248A(5) of the 1985 Act, as substituted and inserted respectively by SI 1997/220.)

Subsections (4) and (5)

Where annual accounts are approved when they do not comply with the requirements of the Act (or, where appropriate, Art.4 of the IAS Regulation [a term identified in s.474]), every director, who: (i) knew that they did not comply or who was reckless as to whether or not they complied; and (ii) failed to take reasonable steps to ensure compliance or prevent the accounts being approved, commits an offence (subs.4)), the penalty for which is a fine (subs.(5)).

CHAPTER 5

DIRECTORS' REPORT

GENERAL NOTE

Sections 415-419 concern the duty to prepare a directors' report, its content, approval and signature. They replace ss.234, 234ZZA, 234ZZB, 234ZA, 234A, 246(4)(a), 246A(2A) and 246(8) of the 1985 Act, as variously inserted and/or amended by s.8(1) of the 1989 Act, SI 1997/220, s.9(3) of the Companies (Audit, Investigations and Community Enterprise) Act 2004, and regs 2 and 4 of SI 2005/1011, as subsequently amended by SI 2005/3442 .

Directors' report

415.   Duty to prepare directors' report

(1) The directors of a company must prepare a directors' report for each financial year of the company.

(2) For a financial year in which-

(a) the company is a parent company, and

(b) the directors of the company prepare group accounts,

the directors' report must be a consolidated report (a "group directors' report") relating to the undertakings included in the consolidation.

(3) A group directors' report may, where appropriate, give greater emphasis to the matters that are significant to the undertakings included in the consolidation, taken as a whole.

(4) In the case of failure to comply with the requirement to prepare a directors' report, an offence is committed by every person who-

(a) was a director of the company immediately before the end of the period for filing accounts and reports for the financial year in question, and

(b) failed to take all reasonable steps for securing compliance with that requirement.

(5) A person guilty of an offence under this section is liable-

(a) on conviction on indictment, to a fine;

(b) on summary conviction, to a fine not exceeding the statutory maximum.

GENERAL NOTE

This section replaces s.234 of the 1985 Act, as substituted by reg.2 of SI 2005/1011 and subsequently amended by SI 2005/3442.

Subsections (1)-(3)

The directors of a company must prepare a directors' report for each financial year (subs.(1)), and where it is a parent company preparing group accounts a consolidated report (a "group directors' report") (subs.(2)). The latter may give greater emphasis to matters that affect the group as a whole (subs.(3)).

Subsections (4) and (5)

Every director immediately before the end of the period for filing accounts and who failed to take reasonable steps to ensure compliance with the provisions of subss.(1)-(3) commits an offence (subs.(4)), the penalty for which is a fine (subs.(5)).

416. Contents of directors' report: general

(1) The directors' report for a financial year must state-

(a) the names of the persons who, at any time during the financial year, were directors of the company, and

(b) the principal activities of the company in the course of the year.

(2) In relation to a group directors' report subsection (1)(b) has effect as if the reference to the company was to the undertakings included in the consolidation.

(3) Except in the case of a company subject to the small companies regime, the report must state the amount (if any) that the directors recommend should be paid by way of dividend.

(4) The Secretary of State may make provision by regulations as to other matters that must be disclosed in a directors' report.

Without prejudice to the generality of this power, the regulations may make any such provision as was formerly made by Schedule 7 to the Companies Act 1985.

GENERAL NOTE

This section is derived from s.243ZZA of the 1985 Act, as inserted by reg.2 of SI 2005/1011 and subsequently amended by SI 2005/3442, as well as s.246(4) of the 1985 Act, as amended by SI 1997/220.

Subsections (1) and (2)

The directors' report must state the names of persons who were directors during the financial year and the company's (or group's: subs.(2)) principal activities (subs.(1)).

Subsection (3)

Except where the company is subject to the "small companies regime" (s.381), the report must state the amount of dividend proposed, if any.

Subsection (4)

The Secretary of State is empowered to issue regulations as to other matters that must be disclosed in the directors' report. These regulations, which are subject to the Parliamentary procedure outlined in s.473, may repeat the provisions formerly in Sch.7 to the 1985 Act, which they replace.

417. Contents of directors' report: business review

(1) Unless the company is subject to the small companies' regime, the directors' report must contain a business review.

(2) The purpose of the business review is to inform members of the company and help them assess how the directors have performed their duty under section 172 (duty to promote the success of the company).

(3) The business review must contain-
    (a) a fair review of the company's business, and
    (b) a description of the principal risks and uncertainties facing the company.

(4) The review required is a balanced and comprehensive analysis of-
    (a) the development and performance of the company's business during the financial year, and
    (b) the position of the company's business at the end of that year,
consistent with the size and complexity of the business.

(5) In the case of a quoted company the business review must, to the extent necessary for an understanding of the development, performance or position of the company's business, include-
    (a) the main trends and factors likely to affect the future development, performance and position of the company's business; and
    (b) information about-
        (i) environmental matters (including the impact of the company's business on the environment),
        (ii) the company's employees, and
        (iii) social and community issues,
    including information about any policies of the company in relation to those matters and the effectiveness of those policies; and
    (c) subject to subsection (11), information about persons with whom the company has contractual or other arrangements which are essential to the business of the company.
If the review does not contain information of each kind mentioned in paragraphs (b)(i), (ii) and (iii) and (c), it must state which of those kinds of information it does not contain.

(6) The review must, to the extent necessary for an understanding of the development, performance or position of the company's business, include-
    (a) analysis using financial key performance indicators, and
    (b) where appropriate, analysis using other key performance indicators, including information relating to environmental matters and employee matters.
"Key performance indicators" means factors by reference to which the development, performance or position of the company's business can be measured effectively.

(7) Where a company qualifies as medium-sized in relation to a financial year (see sections 465 to 467), the directors' report for the year need not comply with the requirements of subsection (6) so far as they relate to non-financial information.

(8) The review must, where appropriate, include references to, and additional explanations of, amounts included in the company's annual accounts.

(9) In relation to a group directors' report this section has effect as if the references to the company were references to the undertakings included in the consolidation.

(10) Nothing in this section requires the disclosure of information about impending developments or matters in the course of negotiation if the disclosure would, in the opinion of the directors, be seriously prejudicial to the interests of the company.

(11) Nothing in subsection (5)(c) requires the disclosure of information about a person if the disclosure would, in the opinion of the directors, be seriously prejudicial to that person and contrary to the public interest.

GENERAL NOTE

This section is derived from: s.234(1) of the 1985 Act; s.234ZZB of the 1985 Act, as inserted by reg.2 of SI 2005/1011 and subsequently amended by SI 2005/3442; s.246(4) of the 1985 Act, as amended by SI 1997/220; and s.246A(2A) of the 1985 Act, as inserted by SI 1997/220 and subsequently amended.

The section requires that all companies, other than small companies, should prepare and publish a business review, as required by the EU Accounts Modernisation Directive (2003/51/EEC).

Originally, listed companies were going to be required by SI 2005/1011 to publish a more prescriptive form of the business review, the "Operating and financial review" ("OFR") from 2005 onwards. However, in a surprise about turn, the government tabled a statutory instrument (SI 2005/3442) in December 2005 repealing SI 2005/1011, preferring a less prescriptive approach, which however would still have required large listed companies to include a "business review" in their directors' reports. This would report both on non-financial issues relevant to the development and performance of the business (including, for example, environmental matters and human capital management), but also identify the principal risks and uncertainties facing the business, as well as giving a balanced and comprehensive analysis of its activities and prospects.

By this time the Accounting Standards Board ("ASB") had already issued a reporting standard ("RS") in May 2005 covering the OFR. It required directors to set out their analysis of the business with a forward looking commentary, and to report on employee, environmental and social and community issues. Directors were also required to outline the nature, objectives and strategies of the business, as well as disclosing the names of persons with whom the company has contractual or other arrangements that are essential to its activities. In addition to outlining the resources available to it, directors were also obliged to comment on the company's financial position (including its capital structure, cash flow generation, liquidity and treasury policies) and to outline the principal risks and uncertainties facing it. It was also necessary for directors to report on the company's performance in relation to a series of quantified targets, applying "key performance indicators" (KPIs), the potential significance of which had to be explained, as well as the basis of their calculation. In light of the about turn in government policy, the ASB withdrew RS1 as a standard, but instead converted it into a statement of "best practice".

When the Bill was tabled, what is now subs.(5) did not include para.(c), requiring quoted companies to disclose information about persons with whom the company has contractual or other arrangements which are essential to its business. This was inserted at a late stage and - despite the fact that it replicates a former OFR requirement, mirrored and expanded upon in the ASB's RS - it generated heated debate, not only in the Commons and Lords, but also in the commercial and financial world outside, becoming one of the most contentious innovations in the new Act. In the end, the House of Lords succeeded in getting an amendment passed that waters down the requirement to give information about persons with whom the company has contractual or other arrangements. This has been achieved by inserting a new subsection, subs.(11), providing an exemption for "information about a person if the disclosure would, in the opinion of the directors, be seriously prejudicial to that person and contrary to the public interest". However, it has been suggested that it may be difficult to make use of this exemption as it requires disclosure to be both prejudicial to the person *and* against the public interest.

The relevant debates in Parliament were: Commons, October 18, 2006: http://www.publications.parliament.uk/pa/cm200506/cmhansrd/cm061018/debtext/61018-0003.htm#06101834000001 (Vol.450, cols 881-919) and Lords, November 2, 2006: http://www.publications.parliament.uk/pa/ld199697/ldhansrd/pdvn/lds06/text/61102-0008.htm#06110288001858 (Vol.686, cols 453-474).

Subsections (1) and (2)

Unless the company is subject to the "small companies regime" (s.381), the directors' report must contain a business review (subs.(1)). The aim of the latter is to inform members and help them assess how they have carried out their duties under s.172 promoting the success of the business (subs.(2)). (In this context, it should perhaps be noted that s.172 imposes a single duty on directors to work for the benefit of shareholders - and not a separate set of duties in relation to the stakeholders who are referred in that section (e.g. employees, customers, suppliers, and the community in general).)

Subsections (3) and (4)

The business review should contain a fair review of the company's business and a description of the principal risks and uncertainties facing the company (subs.(3)). In so doing, it should, given the size and complexity of the business, provide a balanced and comprehensive analysis of the development and performance of the company's activities during the year and its business position at the year-end (subs.(4)).

Subsection (5)

The business review of a quoted company must, so far as is necessary for an understanding of the business's development, performance or position, include (a) the main trends and factors likely to affect its future; (b) information on and the company's policies concerning environmental matters, employees and social and community issues; and (c) subject to subs.(11), below, information about persons with whom the company has contractual or other arrangements which are essential to its business. Where directors of quoted companies have nothing to report on one or other of environmental, employee or social and community matters, or information about persons with whom the company has contractual or other arrangements which are essential to its business, their review must say so.

Subsection (6)

Where necessary for an understanding of the business's development, performance or position, the review should include an analysis of quantified financial and other "key performance indicators", including those relating to environmental and employee matters (subs.(6)).

Subsection (7)

Following the EU directive, companies qualifying as medium-sized companies (see ss.465-467, below), need not comply with the requirements of subs.(6) so far as they relate to non-financial information.

Subsection (8)

The review must, where appropriate, include references to, and explanations of, figures in the accounts.

Subsection (9)

Where appropriate, the review should relate to a group rather than an individual company.

Subsection (10)

Directors are permitted not to disclose information about impending developments or negotiations if, in their opinion, this would seriously prejudice the interests of the company.

Subsection (11)

As explained above, this subsection was inserted at a late stage to make the disclosures required by subs.(5)(c) less onerous to companies. It provides an exemption for information to be disclosed about a person with whom the company has contractual or other arrangements that are essential to the business if such disclosure would, in the opinion of the directors, "be seriously prejudicial to that person and contrary to the public interest".

418.   Contents of directors' report: statement as to disclosure to auditors

(1) This section applies to a company unless-
    (a) it is exempt for the financial year in question from the requirements of Part 16 as to audit of accounts, and
    (b) the directors take advantage of that exemption.
(2) The directors' report must contain a statement to the effect that, in the case of each of the persons who are directors at the time the report is approved-
    (a) so far as the director is aware, there is no relevant audit information of which the company's auditor is unaware, and
    (b) he has taken all the steps that he ought to have taken as a director in order to make himself aware of any relevant audit information and to establish that the company's auditor is aware of that information.
(3) "Relevant audit information" means information needed by the company's auditor in connection with preparing his report.
(4) A director is regarded as having taken all the steps that he ought to have taken as a director in order to do the things mentioned in subsection (2)(b) if he has-
    (a) made such enquiries of his fellow directors and of the company's auditors for that purpose, and
    (b) taken such other steps (if any) for that purpose,

as are required by his duty as a director of the company to exercise reasonable care, skill and diligence.

(5) Where a directors' report containing the statement required by this section is approved but the statement is false, every director of the company who-

(a) knew that the statement was false, or was reckless as to whether it was false, and

(b) failed to take reasonable steps to prevent the report from being approved,

commits an offence.

(6) A person guilty of an offence under subsection (5) is liable-

(a) on conviction on indictment, to imprisonment for a term not exceeding two years or a fine (or both);

(b) on summary conviction-

(i) in England and Wales, to imprisonment for a term not exceeding twelve months or to a fine not exceeding the statutory maximum (or both);

(ii) in Scotland or Northern Ireland, to imprisonment for a term not exceeding six months, or to a fine not exceeding the statutory maximum (or both).

GENERAL NOTE

This section restates the substance of s.234ZA of the 1985 Act, as inserted by s.9(3) of the Companies (Audit, Investigations and Community Enterprise) Act 2004. However, it corrects one aspect that affected charitable companies. Section 234ZA did not apply to companies exempt from audit under ss.249A(1) or 249AA(1) of the 1985 Act, as inserted respectively by SIs 1994/1935 and 2000/1430, but not for charitable companies exempt by virtue of having a report prepared by a reporting accountant under s.249C of that Act, as inserted by SI 1994/1935 and subsequently amended by SIs 1997/220, 2000/1430 and 2004/2947. The re-drafted provision exempts all companies exempt from audit under Pt 16 of the Act, including charitable companies. (The audit of small charitable companies is now dealt with in ss.30-32 of the Charities Act 2006: see www.opsi.gov.uk/acts/acts2006/20060050.htm#aofs; and s.1175 and Sch.9, which remove the special provisions in the 1985 Act relating to the accounts and audit of charitable companies).

Subsections (1)-(3)

Except where a company is exempt from the requirements with respect to a statutory audit in Pt 16 (see ss.477-481, below), and the directors take advantage of that exemption (subs.(1)), the directors' report must state that, so far as they are individually aware, there is no "relevant audit information" (as defined in subs.(3)) of which the auditor is not apprised, and each director has taken all "relevant steps" to ensure that the auditor is fully informed (subs.(2)).

Subsection (4)

A director has taken "all relevant steps" if he has made suitable enquiries of his fellow directors and the auditors with respect to what the latter might reasonably expect to know, as well as any other action required of a director exercising reasonable care, diligence and skill.

Subsections (5) and (6)

Where a directors' report contains a statement that there is no "relevant audit information" of which the auditor is not aware, but that statement is untrue, every director knowing that, or who acted in a reckless manner with respect to its veracity, and who failed to take the necessary steps to prevent the report being approved, commits an offence (subs.(5)), the penalty for which is a fine or imprisonment, or both (subs.(6)).

419. Approval and signing of directors' report

(1) The directors' report must be approved by the board of directors and signed on behalf of the board by a director or the secretary of the company.

(2) If the report is prepared in accordance with the small companies regime, it must contain a statement to that effect in a prominent position above the signature.

(3) If a directors' report is approved that does not comply with the requirements of this Act, every director of the company who-

(a) knew that it did not comply, or was reckless as to whether it complied, and

(b) failed to take reasonable steps to secure compliance with those requirements or, as the case may be, to prevent the report from being approved, commits an offence.

(4) A person guilty of an offence under this section is liable-

    (a) on conviction on indictment, to a fine;

    (b) on summary conviction, to a fine not exceeding the statutory maximum.

GENERAL NOTE

This section is derived from s.234A of the 1985 Act, as inserted by s.8(1) of the 1989 Act, and from s.246(8) of the 1985 Act, as substituted by SI 1997/220.

Subsections (1) and (2)

The directors' report must be approved by the board of directors and be signed on their behalf by a director or the company secretary (subs.(1)). If the report is prepared under the "small companies regime" (s.381), it must contain a statement to that effect in a prominent position above the signature (subs.(2)).

Subsections (3) and (4)

Where a directors' report is approved when it does not comply with the Act's requirements, every director knowing that, or who acted in a reckless manner with respect to ensuring that it did comply, and who failed to take the necessary steps to ensure compliance or to prevent the report being approved, commits an offence (subs.(3)), the penalty for which is a fine (subs.(4)).

Chapter 6

Quoted Companies: Directors' Remuneration Report

GENERAL NOTE

Sections 420-422 replace ss.234B and 234C of the 1985 Act, as inserted by reg.3 of SI 2002/1986, "The Directors' Remuneration Report Regulations 2002". These three sections require quoted companies to: (i) publish a report on directors' remuneration as part of the company's annual report; and (ii) disclose within it details of individual directors' remuneration packages, the company's remuneration policy, and the role of the board and the remuneration committee.

420.   Duty to prepare directors' remuneration report

(1) The directors of a quoted company must prepare a directors' remuneration report for each financial year of the company.

(2) In the case of failure to comply with the requirement to prepare a directors' remuneration report, every person who-

    (a) was a director of the company immediately before the end of the period for filing accounts and reports for the financial year in question, and

    (b) failed to take all reasonable steps for securing compliance with that requirement,

commits an offence.

(3) A person guilty of an offence under this section is liable-

    (a) on conviction on indictment, to a fine;

    (b) on summary conviction, to a fine not exceeding the statutory maximum.

GENERAL NOTE

This section is derived from subss.(1), (3) and (4) of s.234B of the 1985 Act, as inserted by reg.3 of SI 2002/1986.

Subsections (1)-(3)

Each year the directors of a quoted company are required to prepare a "directors' remuneration report" (subs.(1)). Every director immediately before the end of the period for filing accounts and who failed to take reasonable steps to ensure compliance with the requirement to prepare such a report commits an offence (subs.(2)), the penalty for which is a fine (subs.(3)).

421. Contents of directors' remuneration report

(1) The Secretary of State may make provision by regulations as to-
- (a) the information that must be contained in a directors' remuneration report,
- (b) how information is to be set out in the report, and
- (c) what is to be the auditable part of the report.

(2) Without prejudice to the generality of this power, the regulations may make any such provision as was made, immediately before the commencement of this Part, by Schedule 7A to the Companies Act 1985 (c. 6).

(3) It is the duty of-
- (a) any director of a company, and
- (b) any person who is or has at any time in the preceding five years been a director of the company,

to give notice to the company of such matters relating to himself as may be necessary for the purposes of regulations under this section.

(4) A person who makes default in complying with subsection (3) commits an offence and is liable on summary conviction to a fine not exceeding level 3 on the standard scale.

GENERAL NOTE

This section is derived from subss.(1), (5) and (6) of s.234B of the 1985 Act, as inserted by reg.3 of SI 2002/1986.

Under the provisions of this section, the Secretary of State may issue regulations detailing the information that must be contained in a directors' remuneration report, specifying how it should be set out, and what elements are to be auditable. These matters were previously set out in Sch.7A to the 1985 Act, and regulations made under this section - which will be subject to the Parliamentary procedure described in s.473 - will replace the provisions in Sch.7A.

Subsections (1) and (2)

The Secretary of State is empowered to issue regulations specifying: (i) the information that must be contained in a directors' remuneration report; (ii) how it should be set out; and (ii) what parts of it are to be subject to audit (subs.(1)). The regulations may repeat provisions that appeared in Sch.7A to the 1985 Act, as amended (subs.(2)).

Subsections (3) and (4)

It is the duty of a director of the company, or anyone who has been a director within the previous five years, to disclose to the company matters relating to himself that may be necessary for the remuneration report to be properly prepared (subs.(3)), and if such a person fails to comply they are committing an offence, the penalty for which is a fine (subs.(4)).

422. Approval and signing of directors' remuneration report

(1) The directors' remuneration report must be approved by the board of directors and signed on behalf of the board by a director or the secretary of the company.

(2) If a directors' remuneration report is approved that does not comply with the requirements of this Act, every director of the company who-
- (a) knew that it did not comply, or was reckless as to whether it complied, and
- (b) failed to take reasonable steps to secure compliance with those requirements or, as the case may be, to prevent the report from being approved,

commits an offence.

(3) A person guilty of an offence under this section is liable-
- (a) on conviction on indictment, to a fine;
- (b) on summary conviction, to a fine not exceeding the statutory maximum.

GENERAL NOTE

This section is derived from subs.(1) of s.234C of the 1985 Act, as inserted by reg.3 of SI 2002/1986, and subss.(3)-(4) of s.234B of the 1985 Act, as inserted by reg.3 of SI 2002/1986.

Subsections (1)-(3)

The directors' remuneration report must be approved by the board and signed on its behalf by a director or the company secretary (subs.(1)). Where such a report is approved when it does not comply with the Act's requirements, every director knowing that, or who acted in a reckless manner with respect to ensuring that it did comply, and who failed to take the necessary steps to ensure compliance or to prevent the report being approved, commits an offence (subs.(2)), the penalty for which is a fine (subs.(3)).

CHAPTER 7

PUBLICATION OF ACCOUNTS AND REPORTS

GENERAL NOTE

Sections 423-425 effectively replace s.238 of the 1985 Act, as amended by SIs 2000/3373, art.12; 2002/1986, reg.10; and 2005/3442, Sch.1, para.5(b).

Duty to circulate copies of accounts and reports

423. Duty to circulate copies of annual accounts and reports

(1) Every company must send a copy of its annual accounts and reports for each financial year to-
    (a) every member of the company,
    (b) every holder of the company's debentures, and
    (c) every person who is entitled to receive notice of general meetings.
(2) Copies need not be sent to a person for whom the company does not have a current address.
(3) A company has a "current address" for a person if-
    (a) an address has been notified to the company by the person as one at which documents may be sent to him, and
    (b) the company has no reason to believe that documents sent to him at that address will not reach him.
(4) In the case of a company not having a share capital, copies need not be sent to anyone who is not entitled to receive notices of general meetings of the company.
(5) Where copies are sent out over a period of days, references in the Companies Acts to the day on which copies are sent out shall be read as references to the last day of that period.
(6) This section has effect subject to section 426 (option to provide summary financial statement).

GENERAL NOTE

This section is derived from subss.(1)-(3) and (6) of s.238 of the 1985 Act, as inserted by s.10 of the 1989 Act and subsequently amended, and from s.251(1) of the 1985 Act, as amended. The section primarily deals with the persons entitled to receive copies of the annual accounts and reports. General provisions about how to supply copies to joint holders are now in Pt 6 of Sch.5 (Communications by a company).

Subsections (1)-(3)

A company must send a copy of its annual accounts and reports (as defined in s.471, and including any relevant auditor's report) to every member and debenture holder of the company and to anyone who is entitled to receive notice of general meetings (subs.(1)). However, this does not apply where the company does not have a "current address" (subs.(2)), the latter being defined in subs.(3). This relieves companies from having to send copies of the annual accounts and reports to addresses from which correspondence has previously been returned marked "not known at this address" (or its electronic equivalent).

Subsection (4)

This subsection repeats subs.(3) of s.238 of the 1985 Act, indicating that companies without a share capital need not send copies of the annual accounts and reports to anyone who is not entitled to receive notices of general meetings.

Where copies are sent out over a period of days, references in the Act to the day on which the copies are sent are to be taken to the last day on which the accounts and reports were sent.

Subsection (6)

The provisions of s.423 are subject to s.426, below, which deals with the option enabling certain companies to provide a summary financial statement.

424. Time allowed for sending out copies of accounts and reports

(1) The time allowed for sending out copies of the company's annual accounts and reports is as follows.

(2) A private company must comply with section 423 not later than-
    (a) the end of the period for filing accounts and reports, or
    (b) if earlier, the date on which it actually delivers its accounts and reports to the registrar.

(3) A public company must comply with section 423 at least 21 days before the date of the relevant accounts meeting.

(4) If in the case of a public company copies are sent out later than is required by subsection (3), they shall, despite that, be deemed to have been duly sent if it is so agreed by all the members entitled to attend and vote at the relevant accounts meeting.

(5) Whether the time allowed is that for a private company or a public company is determined by reference to the company's status immediately before the end of the accounting reference period by reference to which the financial year for the accounts in question was determined.

(6) In this section the "relevant accounts meeting" means the accounts meeting of the company at which the accounts and reports in question are to be laid.

GENERAL NOTE

This section is derived from subss.(1) and (4) of s.238 of the 1985 Act, as inserted by s.10 of the 1989 Act and subsequently amended. It mainly deals with the time intervals within which annual accounts and reports must be sent to those persons entitled to receive them, making changes to the rules that previously existed.

Subsections (1)-(6)

The time intervals within which the annual accounts and reports must be distributed (subs.(1)) are as follows:

- For private companies, to send out their accounts and reports no later than the earlier of the date of actual delivery to the registrar or the deadline for delivery (subs.(2)). (Section 442, below, indicates the time limits for filing.) (This contrasts with the previous requirement that private companies - unless they opted out of the obligation - should lay their accounts at a general meeting and send their accounts and reports to members 21 days before that meeting. The change has been made because private companies are no longer required to hold a general meeting.); and

- Public companies must (as before) send out copies of the annual accounts and reports at least 21 days before the date of the general meeting at which the accounts and reports are to be laid (defined as the "relevant accounts meeting" in subs.(6)) (subs.(3)). However, if they are sent out later, and all the members at the "relevant accounts meeting" so agree, they will be deemed to have been properly sent (subs.(4)).

Whether a company is "private" or "public" for the purpose of sending out its annual accounts and reports depends on its status immediately before the end of the "accounting reference period" (see s.391, above) (subs.(5)).

425. Default in sending out copies of accounts and reports: offences

(1) If default is made in complying with section 423 or 424, an offence is committed by-
    (a) the company, and
    (b) every officer of the company who is in default.

(2) A person guilty of an offence under this section is liable-
    (a) on conviction on indictment, to a fine;
    (b) on summary conviction, to a fine not exceeding the statutory maximum.

GENERAL NOTE

This section is derived from subs.(5) of s.238 of the 1985 Act, as inserted by s.10 of the 1989 Act and subsequently amended. It deals with the penalties for not complying with the requirements of ss.423-424 in sending out copies of the annual accounts and reports, which are the same as previously.

Subsections (1) and (2)

The company and every defaulting officer commits an offence if there is a failure to comply with the provisions of ss.423-424 (subs.(1)), the penalty being a fine (subs.(2)).

Option to provide summary financial statement

GENERAL NOTE

Sections 426-429 restate s.251 of the 1985 Act, as amended by SIs 1992/2003, 2000/3373, 2001/3649, 2002/1986, 2004/2947, 2005/1001, and 2005/3442 (Sch.1, para.14).

426.   Option to provide summary financial statement

(1) A company may-
     (a) in such cases as may be specified by regulations made by the Secretary of State, and
     (b) provided any conditions so specified are complied with,
provide a summary financial statement instead of copies of the accounts and reports required to be sent out in accordance with section 423.

(2) Copies of those accounts and reports must, however, be sent to any person entitled to be sent them in accordance with that section and who wishes to receive them.

(3) The Secretary of State may make provision by regulations as to the manner in which it is to be ascertained, whether before or after a person becomes entitled to be sent a copy of those accounts and reports, whether he wishes to receive them.

(4) A summary financial statement must comply with the requirements of-
    section 427 (form and contents of summary financial statement: unquoted companies), or
    section 428 (form and contents of summary financial statement: quoted companies).

(5) This section applies to copies of accounts and reports required to be sent out by virtue of section 146 to a person nominated to enjoy information rights as it applies to copies of accounts and reports required to be sent out in accordance with section 423 to a member of the company.

(6) Regulations under this section are subject to negative resolution procedure.

GENERAL NOTE

This section is derived from subss.(1)-(2) and (5) of s.251 of the 1985 Act, as amended. It states that all companies specified by regulations issued by the Secretary of State have the option to provide summary financial statements instead of copies of the full accounts and reports.

Subsections (1)-(3)

A company meeting requirements specified in regulations issued by the Secretary of State may send out a "summary financial statement" instead of copies of the annual accounts and reports in accordance with s.423, above (subs.(1)). However, copies of the full accounts must be sent to a person entitled to receive them if they so request (subs.(2)), the rules for determining this being laid down in the regulations issued by the Secretary of State (subs.(3)).

Subsection (4)

A "summary financial statement" prepared by a company must comply with the requirements either of s.427 (for unquoted companies) or s.428 (quoted companies).

Subsection (5)

The provisions of s.426 apply to all persons entitled to receive copies of reports and accounts under s.423, above, including (for quoted companies) persons nominated by virtue of s.146.

Subsection (6)

The regulations issued by the Secretary of State are subject to the negative resolution procedure (see s.1289).

427. Form and contents of summary financial statement: unquoted companies

(1) A summary financial statement by a company that is not a quoted company must-
   (a) be derived from the company's annual accounts, and
   (b) be prepared in accordance with this section and regulations made under it.
(2) The summary financial statement must be in such form, and contain such information, as the Secretary of State may specify by regulations. The regulations may require the statement to include information derived from the directors' report.
(3) Nothing in this section or regulations made under it prevents a company from including in a summary financial statement additional information derived from the company's annual accounts or the directors' report.
(4) The summary financial statement must-
   (a) state that it is only a summary of information derived from the company's annual accounts;
   (b) state whether it contains additional information derived from the directors' report and, if so, that it does not contain the full text of that report;
   (c) state how a person entitled to them can obtain a full copy of the company's annual accounts and the directors' report;
   (d) contain a statement by the company's auditor of his opinion as to whether the summary financial statement-
      (i) is consistent with the company's annual accounts and, where information derived from the directors' report is included in the statement, with that report, and
      (ii) complies with the requirements of this section and regulations made under it;
   (e) state whether the auditor's report on the annual accounts was unqualified or qualified and, if it was qualified, set out the report in full together with any further material needed to understand the qualification;
   (f) state whether, in that report, the auditor's statement under section 496 (whether directors' report consistent with accounts) was qualified or unqualified and, if it was qualified, set out the qualified statement in full together with any further material needed to understand the qualification;
   (g) state whether that auditor's report contained a statement under-
      (i) section 498(2)(a) or (b) (accounting records or returns inadequate or accounts not agreeing with records and returns), or
      (ii) section 498(3) (failure to obtain necessary information and explanations),
   and if so, set out the statement in full.
(5) Regulations under this section may provide that any specified material may, instead of being included in the summary financial statement, be sent separately at the same time as the statement.
(6) Regulations under this section are subject to negative resolution procedure.

GENERAL NOTE

This section is derived in part from subss.(1), (3), (3A) and (4) of s.251 of the 1985 Act, as amended. It sets out the form and content requirements for summary financial statements prepared by unquoted companies. Subsection (5) provides a new power, enabling the regulations to provide that specified material be sent separately at the same time as the summary financial statement, rather than be included in it. This is to cover the requirements of the Takeovers Directive as to necessary explanatory material (see s.992, below).

Subsections (1)-(3)

The "summary financial statement" of an unquoted company must be derived from its accounts and be prepared in accordance with the provisions of s.427 and the Secretary of State's regulations (subs.(1)). The latter will specify the form and content, and they may require the statement to include information drawn from the directors' report (subs.(2)). However, an unquoted company may also, as it sees fit, include additional information derived from the accounts or the directors' report (subs.(3)).

Subsection (4)

The "summary financial statement" must (i) state that it is a summary derived from the full accounts; (ii) state that it contains information drawn from the directors' report, but is not the full text; (iii) state how a person can obtain the full accounts and directors' report; (iv) contain a statement from the auditor indicating, first, that the summary financial statement is consistent with the full accounts and directors' report, and, secondly, that it complies with the requirements of the Act and regulations; (v) state whether the auditor's report on the full accounts was qualified or unqualified - and if the former, reproduce the auditor's report, together with other information to understand the nature of the qualification; (vi) state whether the auditor's report was qualified or unqualified with respect to acknowledging the consistency between the directors' report and the accounts, as required by s.496; and (vii) indicate whether the auditor's report contained a statement concerning the adequacy of the accounting records and returns, their agreement with the final accounts, or failure to obtain necessary information and explanations.

Subsections (5) and (6)

The regulations which are subject to the negative resolution procedure (see s.1289) (subs.(6)) may provide that specified material may be sent separately with the "summary financial statement", rather than be included in it (subs.(5)).

428.   Form and contents of summary financial statement: quoted companies

(1) A summary financial statement by a quoted company must-
   (a) be derived from the company's annual accounts and the directors' remuneration report, and
   (b) be prepared in accordance with this section and regulations made under it.
(2) The summary financial statement must be in such form, and contain such information, as the Secretary of State may specify by regulations.
The regulations may require the statement to include information derived from the directors' report.
(3) Nothing in this section or regulations made under it prevents a company from including in a summary financial statement additional information derived from the company's annual accounts, the directors' remuneration report or the directors' report.
(4) The summary financial statement must-
   (a) state that it is only a summary of information derived from the company's annual accounts and the directors' remuneration report;
   (b) state whether it contains additional information derived from the directors' report and, if so, that it does not contain the full text of that report;
   (c) state how a person entitled to them can obtain a full copy of the company's annual accounts, the directors' remuneration report or the directors' report;
   (d) contain a statement by the company's auditor of his opinion as to whether the summary financial statement-
      (i) is consistent with the company's annual accounts and the directors' remuneration report and, where information derived from the directors' report is included in the statement, with that report, and
      (ii) complies with the requirements of this section and regulations made under it;
   (e) state whether the auditor's report on the annual accounts and the auditable part of the directors' remuneration report was unqualified or qualified and, if it was qualified, set out the report in full together with any further material needed to understand the qualification;
   (f) state whether that auditor's report contained a statement under-

(i) section 498(2) (accounting records or returns inadequate or accounts or directors' remuneration report not agreeing with records and returns), or

(ii) section 498(3) (failure to obtain necessary information and explanations),

and if so, set out the statement in full;

(g) state whether, in that report, the auditor's statement under section 496 (whether directors' report consistent with accounts) was qualified or unqualified and, if it was qualified, set out the qualified statement in full together with any further material needed to understand the qualification.

(5) Regulations under this section may provide that any specified material may, instead of being included in the summary financial statement, be sent separately at the same time as the statement.

(6) Regulations under this section are subject to negative resolution procedure.

GENERAL NOTE

This section is derived in part from subss.(1), (3), (3A), (4) and (5) of s.251 of the 1985 Act, as amended. It sets out the form and content requirements for summary financial statements prepared by quoted companies. As in s.427, subs.(5) provides a new power, enabling the regulations to provide that specified material be sent separately at the same time as the summary financial statement, rather than be included in it. This is to cover the requirements of the Takeovers Directive as to necessary explanatory material (see s.992, below).

Subsections (1)-(3)

The "summary financial statement" of a quoted company must be derived from its accounts and directors' remuneration report and be prepared in accordance with the provisions of s.428 and the Secretary of State's regulations (subs.(1)). The latter will specify the form and content, and they may require the statement to include information drawn from the directors' report (subs.(2)). However, a quoted company may also, as it sees fit, include additional information derived from the accounts, the directors' remuneration report or the directors' report (subs.(3)).

Subsection (4)

The "summary financial statement" must (i) state that it is a summary derived from the full accounts and the directors' remuneration report; (ii) state that it contains information drawn from the directors' report, but is not the full text; (iii) state how a person can obtain the full accounts, the directors' remuneration report or the directors' report; (iv) contain a statement from the auditor indicating, first, that the summary financial statement is consistent with the full accounts, the directors' remuneration report and the directors' report, and, secondly, that it complies with the requirements of the Act and regulations; (v) state whether the auditor's report on the full accounts and the auditable part of the directors' remuneration report (see s.421, above) was qualified or unqualified - and if the former, reproduce the auditor's report, together with other information to understand the nature of the qualification; (vi) indicate whether the auditor's report contained a statement concerning the adequacy of the accounting records and returns, their agreement with the final accounts, or failure to obtain necessary information and explanations; and (vii) state whether the auditor's report was qualified or unqualified with respect to acknowledging the consistency between the directors' report and the accounts, as required by s.496.

Subsections (5) and (6)

The regulations which are subject to the negative resolution procedure (see s.1289) (subs.(6)) may provide that specified material may be sent separately with the "summary financial statement", rather than be included in it (subs.(5)).

429. Summary financial statements: offences

(1) If default is made in complying with any provision of section 426, 427 or 428, or of regulations under any of those sections, an offence is committed by-

(a) the company, and

(b) every officer of the company who is in default.

(2) A person guilty of an offence under this section is liable on summary conviction to a fine not exceeding level 3 on the standard scale.

GENERAL NOTE

This section is derived from subs.(6) of s.251 of the 1985 Act, as amended. It deals with the penalties for not complying with the requirements of ss.426-428 in sending out copies of the annual accounts and reports. (In fact, they are the same as previously.)

Subsections (1) and (2)

The company and every defaulting officer commits an offence if there is a failure to comply with the provisions of ss.426-428 (subs.(1)), the penalty being a fine (subs.(2)).

Quoted companies: requirements as to website publication

GENERAL NOTE

Section 430 introduces new requirements on quoted companies (as defined in s.385, above) to put accounting information on a website. The provisions have been developed in the light of recommendations made by the Company Law Review Steering Group in para.8.86 of the *Final Report* that there should be mandatory website publication by quoted companies of any preliminary announcement and of the full annual financial statements.

430. Quoted companies: annual accounts and reports to be made available on website

(1) A quoted company must ensure that its annual accounts and reports-
    (a) are made available on a website, and
    (b) remain so available until the annual accounts and reports for the company's next financial year are made available in accordance with this section.

(2) The annual accounts and reports must be made available on a website that-
    (a) is maintained by or on behalf of the company, and
    (b) identifies the company in question.

(3) Access to the annual accounts and reports on the website, and the ability to obtain a hard copy of the annual accounts and reports from the website, must not be-
    (a) conditional on the payment of a fee, or
    (b) otherwise restricted, except so far as necessary to comply with any enactment or regulatory requirement (in the United Kingdom or elsewhere).

(4) The annual accounts and reports-
    (a) must be made available as soon as reasonably practicable, and
    (b) must be kept available throughout the period specified in subsection (1)(b).

(5) A failure to make the annual accounts and reports available on a website throughout that period is disregarded if-
    (a) the annual accounts and reports are made available on the website for part of that period, and
    (b) the failure is wholly attributable to circumstances that it would not be reasonable to have expected the company to prevent or avoid.

(6) In the event of default in complying with this section, an offence is committed by every officer of the company who is in default.

(7) A person guilty of an offence under subsection (6) is liable on summary conviction to a fine not exceeding level 3 on the standard scale.

GENERAL NOTE

This section is new and deals with the website publication of a company's annual accounts and reports. However, a quoted company will still have to send the full accounts and reports to its members under the provisions of s.423, above.

Originally it was proposed that quoted companies should post their preliminary announcements of annual results on their websites, but the clause requiring this was later dropped.

Subsections (1)-(5)

A quoted company is required to ensure that its annual accounts and reports are made available on a publicly available website and remain so until the following year's accounts and reports are posted (subs.(1)). The website should be maintained by or on behalf of the company (subs.(2)), and the accounts and reports should be available on it as soon as is reasonably practicable and must be kept available throughout the specified period (subs.(4)), subject only to circumstances beyond the company's control and so long as the information has been available for part of the relevant period (subs.(5)). Access to the website, and the ability to obtain hard copy, must be available to the public and not just to members, and there must be continuous access without charge. However, access and the ability to obtain a hard copy may be restricted by the company where necessary to comply with any statutory or regulatory requirement (e.g. of a United Kingdom or overseas regulator) (subs.(3)).

Subsections (6) and (7)

Every defaulting officer commits an offence if there is a failure to comply with the provisions of this section (subs.(6)), the penalty being a fine (subs.(7)).

Right of member or debenture holder to demand copies of accounts and reports

GENERAL NOTE

Sections 431-432 re-enact s.239 of the 1985 Act, as amended by SI 2000/3373, art.13, and SI 2005/3442, Sch.1, para.6(b), entitling a member or debenture holder to demand a copy of the company's last annual accounts and reports without charge.

431. Right of member or debenture holder to copies of accounts and reports: unquoted companies

(1) A member of, or holder of debentures of, an unquoted company is entitled to be provided, on demand and without charge, with a copy of-

  (a) the company's last annual accounts,

  (b) the last directors' report, and

  (c) the auditor's report on those accounts (including the statement on that report).

(2) The entitlement under this section is to a single copy of those documents, but that is in addition to any copy to which a person may be entitled under section 423.

(3) If a demand made under this section is not complied with within seven days of receipt by the company, an offence is committed by-

  (a) the company, and

  (b) every officer of the company who is in default.

(4) A person guilty of an offence under this section is liable on summary conviction to a fine not exceeding level 3 on the standard scale and, for continued contravention, a daily default fine not exceeding one-tenth of level 3 on the standard scale.

GENERAL NOTE

This section is derived from subss.(1)-(3) of s.239 of the 1985 Act, as amended.

Subsections (1) and (2)

A member or debenture holder of an unquoted company is entitled to obtain on demand and without charge an additional copy (subs.(2)) of the last annual accounts and directors' and auditor's reports (subs.(1)).

Subsections (3) and (4)

The company must comply with a demand within seven days of receipt of the request by the company, otherwise it and every defaulting officer commits an offence (subs.(3)), the penalty being a fine (subs.(4)).

432. Right of member or debenture holder to copies of accounts and reports: quoted companies

(1) A member of, or holder of debentures of, a quoted company is entitled to be provided, on demand and without charge, with a copy of-
    (a) the company's last annual accounts,
    (b) the last directors' remuneration report,
    (c) the last directors' report, and
    (d) the auditor's report on those accounts (including the report on the directors' remuneration report and on the directors' report).
(2) The entitlement under this section is to a single copy of those documents, but that is in addition to any copy to which a person may be entitled under section 423.
(3) If a demand made under this section is not complied with within seven days of receipt by the company, an offence is committed by-
    (a) the company, and
    (b) every officer of the company who is in default.
(4) A person guilty of an offence under this section is liable on summary conviction to a fine not exceeding level 3 on the standard scale and, for continued contravention, a daily default fine not exceeding one-tenth of level 3 on the standard scale.

GENERAL NOTE
    This section is derived from subss.(1)-(3) of s.239 of the 1985 Act, as amended.

Subsections (1) and (2)
    A member or debenture holder of a quoted company is entitled to obtain on demand and without charge an additional copy (subs.(2)) of the last annual accounts, the directors' remuneration report, and the directors' and auditor's reports (subs.(1)).

Subsections (3) and (4)
    The company must comply with a demand within seven days of receipt of the request by the company, otherwise it and every defaulting officer commits an offence (subs.(3)), the penalty being a fine (subs.(4)).

Requirements in connection with publication of accounts and reports

433. Name of signatory to be stated in published copies of accounts and reports

(1) Every copy of a document to which this section applies that is published by or on behalf of the company must state the name of the person who signed it on behalf of the board.
(2) In the case of an unquoted company, this section applies to copies of-
    (a) the company's balance sheet, and
    (b) the directors' report.
(3) In the case of a quoted company, this section applies to copies of-
    (a) the company's balance sheet,
    (b) the directors' remuneration report, and
    (c) the directors' report.
(4) If a copy is published without the required statement of the signatory's name, an offence is committed by-
    (a) the company, and
    (b) every officer of the company who is in default.
(5) A person guilty of an offence under this section is liable on summary conviction to a fine not exceeding level 3 on the standard scale.

GENERAL NOTE

This section brings together provisions scattered throughout Pt 7 of the 1985 Act (in ss.233(3) and (6), 234A(2) and (4), 234C(2) and (4), and 234AB(2) and (4), as amended) concerning statements of the name of the signatory in published accounts and reports.

Subsections (1)-(3)

Every copy of a document covered by s.433 that is published by or on behalf of a company must state the name of the person who signed it on behalf of the board (subs.(1)). For an unquoted company the relevant documents are the balance sheet and directors' report (subs.(2)), whereas for a quoted company in addition to these two documents the directors' remuneration report must also be signed (subs.(3)).

Subsections (4) and (5)

If a document is published without stating the signatory's name as required, the company and every defaulting officer commits an offence (subs.(4)), the penalty being a fine (subs.(5)).

434. Requirements in connection with publication of statutory accounts

(1) If a company publishes any of its statutory accounts, they must be accompanied by the auditor's report on those accounts (unless the company is exempt from audit and the directors have taken advantage of that exemption).

(2) A company that prepares statutory group accounts for a financial year must not publish its statutory individual accounts for that year without also publishing with them its statutory group accounts.

(3) A company's "statutory accounts" are its accounts for a financial year as required to be delivered to the registrar under section 441.

(4) If a company contravenes any provision of this section, an offence is committed by-
    (a) the company, and
    (b) every officer of the company who is in default.

(5) A person guilty of an offence under this section is liable on summary conviction to a fine not exceeding level 3 on the standard scale.

(6) This section does not apply in relation to the provision by a company of a summary financial statement (see section 426).

GENERAL NOTE

This section, concerning requirements in connection with the publication of statutory accounts, re-enacts s.240(1)-(2),(5)-(6) of the 1985 Act (as inserted by s.10 of the 1989 Act and subsequently amended by SI 1994/ 1935) and s.251(7) of the 1985 Act, as amended.

Subsection (1)

Any statutory accounts that are published must be accompanied by the auditor's report on those accounts (unless the company is exempt from audit).

Subsections (2) and (3)

A company that prepares "statutory group accounts" (ss.398-408) must not publish its "statutory individual accounts" (ss.394-397) without also publishing with them its group accounts (subs.(2)). ("Statutory accounts" are accounts for a financial year that are to be filed with the registrar under s.441, below (subs.(3).)

Subsections (4)-(5)

The company and every defaulting officer commits an offence if the provisions of this section are contravened (subs.(4)), the penalty being a fine (subs.(5)).

Subsection (6)

The provisions of this section do not apply with respect to summary financial statements (s.426).

435.   Requirements in connection with publication of non-statutory accounts

(1) If a company publishes non-statutory accounts, it must publish with them a statement indicating-
>   (a) that they are not the company's statutory accounts,
>   (b) whether statutory accounts dealing with any financial year with which the non-statutory accounts purport to deal have been delivered to the registrar, and
>   (c) whether an auditor's report has been made on the company's statutory accounts for any such financial year, and if so whether the report-
>>   (i) was qualified or unqualified, or included a reference to any matters to which the auditor drew attention by way of emphasis without qualifying the report, or
>>   (ii) contained a statement under section 498(2) (accounting records or returns inadequate or accounts or directors' remuneration report not agreeing with records and returns), or section 498(3) (failure to obtain necessary information and explanations).

(2) The company must not publish with non-statutory accounts the auditor's report on the company's statutory accounts.

(3) References in this section to the publication by a company of "non-statutory accounts" are to the publication of-
>   (a) any balance sheet or profit and loss account relating to, or purporting to deal with, a financial year of the company, or
>   (b) an account in any form purporting to be a balance sheet or profit and loss account for a group headed by the company relating to, or purporting to deal with, a financial year of the company,

otherwise than as part of the company's statutory accounts.

(4) In subsection (3)(b) "a group headed by the company" means a group consisting of the company and any other undertaking (regardless of whether it is a subsidiary undertaking of the company) other than a parent undertaking of the company.

(5) If a company contravenes any provision of this section, an offence is committed by-
>   (a) the company, and
>   (b) every officer of the company who is in default.

(6) A person guilty of an offence under this section is liable on summary conviction to a fine not exceeding level 3 on the standard scale.

(7) This section does not apply in relation to the provision by a company of a summary financial statement (see section 426).

GENERAL NOTE

This section, concerning requirements in connection with the publication of non-statutory accounts, re-enacts subss.(3),(5) and (6) of s.240 of the 1985 Act (as inserted by s.10 of the 1989 Act and subsequently amended by SI 1994/1935 and reg.8(b) of SI 2004/2947) and s.251(7) of the 1985 Act, as amended.

Subsection (1)

Any non-statutory accounts that are published must be accompanied by a statement indicating: (i) they are not the statutory accounts; (ii) whether the statutory accounts for the year in question have been delivered to the registrar; and (iii) whether an auditor's report has been made on those statutory accounts, and, if so, whether it was qualified or unqualified (the former to include a "matter of emphasis statement" in the report; or reference either to inadequate records or returns, or to a lack of agreement between the records and returns and the accounts and/or the directors' remuneration report; or a statement indicating a failure to obtain the necessary information and explanations).

Subsection (2)

A company must *not* publish the auditor's report on its statutory accounts with any non-statutory accounts it releases.

Subsections (3) and (4)

"Non-statutory accounts" are defined as an individual or group balance sheet or profit and loss account purporting to relate to a financial year that are not part of the statutory accounts (subs.(3)). (The meaning of "group" in this context is explained in subs.(4).)

Subsections (5) and (6)

The company and every defaulting officer commits an offence if the provisions of this section are contravened (subs.(5)), the penalty being a fine (subs.(6)).

Subsection (7)

The provisions of this section do not apply with respect to summary financial statements (s.426).

436. Meaning of "publication" in relation to accounts and reports

(1) This section has effect for the purposes of-

    section 433 (name of signatory to be stated in published copies of accounts and reports),

    section 434 (requirements in connection with publication of statutory accounts), and

    section 435 (requirements in connection with publication of non-statutory accounts).

(2) For the purposes of those sections a company is regarded as publishing a document if it publishes, issues or circulates it or otherwise makes it available for public inspection in a manner calculated to invite members of the public generally, or any class of members of the public, to read it.

GENERAL NOTE

This section is derived from subs.(4) of s.240 of the 1985 Act, as inserted by s.10 of the 1989 Act.

Subsections (1) and (2)

For the purpose of ss.433 (name of signatory to be stated in published copies and reports), 434 (requirements in connection with the publication of statutory accounts) and 435 (requirements in connection with the publication of non-statutory accounts) (subs.(1)), "publication" is defined to cover publication, issuing, circulating or otherwise making available a document for public inspection (subs.(2)).

CHAPTER 8

PUBLIC COMPANIES: LAYING OF ACCOUNTS AND REPORTS BEFORE GENERAL MEETING

GENERAL NOTE

Sections 437-438, on the laying of accounts and reports before the company in general meeting, re-enact s.241 of the 1985 Act, as inserted by s.11 of the 1989 Act and amended by Sch.1, para.7(b) of SI 2005/3442. However, application is restricted to public companies. Under the Act, private companies are under no statutory obligation to hold an AGM or to lay accounts and reports in general meetings. There is therefore no statutory link for them between the accounts and AGMs (although such a link might be provided for in the company's articles). Any AGM that a private company may hold pursuant to its articles will not be a statutory meeting. Public companies are still required to hold AGMs, and they must now hold them within six months of the end of the accounting reference period.

437. Public companies: laying of accounts and reports before general meeting

(1) The directors of a public company must lay before the company in general meeting copies of its annual accounts and reports.

(2) This section must be complied with not later than the end of the period for filing the accounts and reports in question.

(3) In the Companies Acts "accounts meeting", in relation to a public company, means a general meeting of the company at which the company's annual accounts and reports are (or are to be) laid in accordance with this section.

GENERAL NOTE

This section is derived from subs.(1) of s.241 of the 1985 Act (as inserted by s.11 of the 1989 Act and subsequently amended by Sch.1, para.7(b) of SI 2005/3442) and subs.(2) of s.241A of the 1985 Act, as inserted by reg.7 of SI 2002/1986.

Subsections (1) and (2)

The directors of a public company must lay copies of its annual accounts and reports before the company in general meeting (subs.(1)) not later than the end of the period for filing the accounts and related reports (subs.(2)).

Subsection (3)

The term "accounts meeting" for a public company means a general meeting at which its accounts and related reports are to be laid.

438.   Public companies: offence of failure to lay accounts and reports

(1) If the requirements of section 437 (public companies: laying of accounts and reports before general meeting) are not complied with before the end of the period allowed, every person who immediately before the end of that period was a director of the company commits an offence.

(2) It is a defence for a person charged with such an offence to prove that he took all reasonable steps for securing that those requirements would be complied with before the end of that period.

(3) It is not a defence to prove that the documents in question were not in fact prepared as required by this Part.

(4) A person guilty of an offence under this section is liable on summary conviction to a fine not exceeding level 5 on the standard scale and, for continued contravention, a daily default fine not exceeding one-tenth of level 5 on the standard scale.

GENERAL NOTE

This section is derived from subss.(2)-(4) of s.241 of the 1985 Act, as inserted by s.11 of the 1989 Act.

Subsections (1)-(4)

Where a public company's accounts are not laid before a general meeting as prescribed, every director at the end of the period permitted for so laying the accounts commits an offence (subs.(1)). However, it is a defence to prove that he took all reasonable steps to ensure compliance (subs.(2)), but this excludes a claim that the documents were not prepared as required (subs.(3)). The penalty for such an offence is a fine, and for continued contravention a daily default fine (subs.(4)).

CHAPTER 9

QUOTED COMPANIES: MEMBERS' APPROVAL OF DIRECTORS' REMUNERATION
REPORT

GENERAL NOTE

Sections 439-440 restate the requirements of s.241A of the 1985 Act, as inserted by reg.7 of SI 2002/1986: namely, that a quoted company must circulate a resolution approving the directors' remuneration report for the preceding financial year to its shareholders prior to its annual general meeting. The vote is advisory, inasmuch as it does not require directors to amend contractual entitlements, nor to change their remuneration policy. However, the result of the vote will send a strong signal to the directors about the level of support among shareholders for the board's remuneration policy. In practice, directors are likely to take the members' views into account and respond appropriately.

Every "existing director" (i.e. each person who, immediately before the general meeting, is a director of the company) has a responsibility to ensure that the resolution is put to the vote of the meeting. As such, the requirement does not apply to past directors (even if they served on the board or as members of the remuneration committee in the current financial year), but it does apply to "existing directors" who were, for whatever reason, not present at the general meeting.

439. Quoted companies: members' approval of directors' remuneration report

(1) A quoted company must, prior to the accounts meeting, give to the members of the company entitled to be sent notice of the meeting notice of the intention to move at the meeting, as an ordinary resolution, a resolution approving the directors' remuneration report for the financial year.

(2) The notice may be given in any manner permitted for the service on the member of notice of the meeting.

(3) The business that may be dealt with at the accounts meeting includes the resolution.
This is so notwithstanding any default in complying with subsection (1) or (2).

(4) The existing directors must ensure that the resolution is put to the vote of the meeting.

(5) No entitlement of a person to remuneration is made conditional on the resolution being passed by reason only of the provision made by this section.

(6) In this section-
"the accounts meeting" means the general meeting of the company before which the company's annual accounts for the financial year are to be laid; and
"existing director" means a person who is a director of the company immediately before that meeting.

GENERAL NOTE

This section is derived from subss.(2)-(8) and (12) of s.241A of the 1985 Act, as inserted by reg.7 of SI 2002/1986.

Subsections (1)-(6)

Before the "accounts meeting" (defined in subs.(6)), a quoted company is required to give members notice, in any permitted manner (subs.(2)), of its intention to put an ordinary resolution approving the directors' remuneration report for the financial year (subs.(1)). Such business can be put at the "accounts meeting" (subs.(3)), and the "existing directors" (defined in subs.(6)) must ensure that the resolution is put to the vote (subs.(4)). A person's remuneration is not made conditional on the resolution being passed by reason only of the provisions of this section (subs.(5)).

440. Quoted companies: offences in connection with procedure for approval

(1) In the event of default in complying with section 439(1) (notice to be given of resolution for approval of directors' remuneration report), an offence is committed by every officer of the company who is in default.

(2) If the resolution is not put to the vote of the accounts meeting, an offence is committed by each existing director.

(3) It is a defence for a person charged with an offence under subsection (2) to prove that he took all reasonable steps for securing that the resolution was put to the vote of the meeting.

(4) A person guilty of an offence under this section is liable on summary conviction to a fine not exceeding level 3 on the standard scale.

(5) In this section-
"the accounts meeting" means the general meeting of the company before which the company's annual accounts for the financial year are to be laid; and
"existing director" means a person who is a director of the company immediately before that meeting.

GENERAL NOTE

This section is derived from subss.(2) and (9)-(12) of s.241A of the 1985 Act, as inserted by reg.7 of SI 2002/1986.

Subsections (1)-(5)

An offence is committed by every defaulting officer if notice of a resolution under s.439(1) approving the directors' remuneration report is not sent to members (subs.(1)). It is equally an offence committed by every "existing director" (defined in subs.(5)) if the resolution is not put to the vote at the "accounts meeting" (defined in subs.(5)) (subs.(2)), although it is a defence to prove that all reasonable steps were taken to ensure that it was so put (subs.(3)). The penalty for such an offence is a fine (subs.(4)).

CHAPTER 10

FILING OF ACCOUNTS AND REPORTS

GENERAL NOTE

Sections 441-443 cover the general duty to file accounts and reports with the registrar of companies and the period allowed for filing accounts.

Duty to file accounts and reports

441. Duty to file accounts and reports with the registrar

(1) The directors of a company must deliver to the registrar for each financial year the accounts and reports required by-

    section 444 (filing obligations of companies subject to small companies regime),

    section 445 (filing obligations of medium-sized companies),

    section 446 (filing obligations of unquoted companies), or

    section 447 (filing obligations of quoted companies).

(2) This is subject to section 448 (unlimited companies exempt from filing obligations).

GENERAL NOTE

This is a new introductory section that identifies for each class of company the filing obligation previously in subs.(1) of s.242 of the 1985 Act, as inserted by s.11 of the 1989 Act and subsequently amended.

Subsections (1) and (2)

Under subs.(1), a company's directors are required to file its accounts and reports with the registrar for each financial year as required by:

  i   s.444: companies subject to the "small companies regime" (s.381);
  ii s.445: medium-sized companies (s.465);
  iii s.446: unquoted companies (s.385); and
  iv s.447: quoted companies (s.385).

However, unlimited companies are exempt under s.448 from having to comply with the filing obligations (subs.(2)).

442. Period allowed for filing accounts

(1) This section specifies the period allowed for the directors of a company to comply with their obligation under section 441 to deliver accounts and reports for a financial year to the registrar.

This is referred to in the Companies Acts as the "period for filing" those accounts and reports.

(2) The period is-

    (a) for a private company, nine months after the end of the relevant accounting reference period, and

    (b) for a public company, six months after the end of that period.

This is subject to the following provisions of this section.

(3) If the relevant accounting reference period is the company's first and is a period of more than twelve months, the period is-

    (a) nine months or six months, as the case may be, from the first anniversary of the incorporation of the company, or

   (b) three months after the end of the accounting reference period,
whichever last expires.

(4) If the relevant accounting reference period is treated as shortened by virtue of a notice given by the company under section 392 (alteration of accounting reference date), the period is-

   (a) that applicable in accordance with the above provisions, or

   (b) three months from the date of the notice under that section,
whichever last expires.

(5) If for any special reason the Secretary of State thinks fit he may, on an application made before the expiry of the period otherwise allowed, by notice in writing to a company extend that period by such further period as may be specified in the notice.

(6) Whether the period allowed is that for a private company or a public company is determined by reference to the company's status immediately before the end of the relevant accounting reference period.

(7) In this section "the relevant accounting reference period" means the accounting reference period by reference to which the financial year for the accounts in question was determined.

GENERAL NOTE

This section is derived from subss.(1)-(2) and (4)-(6) of s.244 to the 1985 Act, as inserted by s.11 of the 1989 Act. However, it reduces the period for filing accounts calculated from the end of the relevant accounting reference period from ten months to nine months for private companies and from seven months to six months for public companies. This is in line with the proposals of the *Final Report* of the Company Law Review Steering Group, published in 2001, which however proposed that private companies should be required to file within seven months, not nine, proposals that were subsequently endorsed in the White Papers "Modernising Company Law", published in July 2002, and "Company Law Reform", published in March 2005. The timetable for delivering accounts to the registrar was last amended in 1976, and the periods have been reduced to reflect improvements in technology and the increased rate at which information becomes out of date. Filing timescales in other countries are usually less generous than in the United Kingdom.

Subsections (1)-(5)

The "period for filing" accounts and reports with the registrar under s.441 (subs.(1)) is:

i   for a private company, nine months after the end of the relevant "accounting reference period" (s.391 and subs.(7), below); and

ii for a public company, six months after the end of the relevant "accounting reference period" (s.391 and subs.(7), below) (subs.(2)).

However, if the reporting period is the company's first and is for more than 12 months, the period is the later of:

i   (i) nine months or six months respectively for a private or public company after the first anniversary of incorporation; or

ii three months after the end of the "accounting reference period" (s.391 and subs.(7), below) (subs.(3)).

If the reporting period is shortened when the "accounting reference period" (s.391 and subs.(7), below) is altered under the provisions of s.392, above, the period is the later of:

i   that applicable in accordance with the above provisions; or

ii three months from the date of notice under s.392 (subs.(4)).

The Secretary of State may, as he sees fit, extend the period by giving written notice if the company applies to him before the expiry of the period otherwise allowed (subs.(5)).

Subsection (6)

Whether a company is private or public for the purpose of its filing obligations is determined by its status immediately before the end of the relevant "accounting reference period" (s.391 and subs.(7), below).

Subsection (7)

For the purpose of s.442, "the relevant accounting reference period" means the accounting reference period used to determine the financial year to which the accounts in question: see ss.390-392.

443.   Calculation of period allowed

(1) This section applies for the purposes of calculating the period for filing a company's accounts and reports which is expressed as a specified number of months from a specified date or after the end of a specified previous period.

(2) Subject to the following provisions, the period ends with the date in the appropriate month corresponding to the specified date or the last day of the specified previous period.

(3) If the specified date, or the last day of the specified previous period, is the last day of a month, the period ends with the last day of the appropriate month (whether or not that is the corresponding date).

(4) If-
    (a) the specified date, or the last day of the specified previous period, is not the last day of a month but is the 29th or 30th, and

    (b) the appropriate month is February,

the period ends with the last day of February.

(5) "The appropriate month" means the month that is the specified number of months after the month in which the specified date, or the end of the specified previous period, falls.

GENERAL NOTE

This is a new provision that explains how the periods allowed for filing accounts and reports should be calculated. Generally this will be the same date for the relevant number of calendar months later (e.g. if the end of the accounting reference period is April 5, then six months on is October 5). However, as months are of unequal length, there can be confusion as to whether six months from, say, April 30 is October 30 or October 31. Under the rule laid down in this section, six months from April 30 will be taken to be October 31. This reverses the "corresponding date rule" laid down by the House of Lords in *Dodds v Walker* [1981] 1 W.L.R. 1027.

Subsections (1)-(4)

The provisions of s.443 apply for calculating the period for filing accounts when that is expressed in terms of a number of months (subs.(1)). Normally the date itself will be the determinant (subs.(2)), but where the date is the last day of a calendar month, then the period for filing will end on the last day of "the appropriate month" (defined in subs.(5)) (subs.(3)). Where the end month date is the 29th or 30th, and the corresponding month is February, the appropriate date will be February 28, or February 29 in a leap year (subs.(4)).

Subsection (5)

The term "the appropriate month" means the specified number of months after the month in which the specified date falls.

Filing obligations of different descriptions of company

GENERAL NOTE

Sections 444-448 concern the filing obligations of different sizes and types of company: namely, small companies (s.444), medium-sized (s.445), unquoted (s.446), quoted (s.447) and unlimited (s.448). They effectively restructure the provisions in the 1985 Act, as amended. The general rules were set out in s.242, as inserted by s.11 of the 1989 Act and subsequently amended by SI 1992/1083, Sch.2; the Welsh Language Act 1993, s.30(4)(a); and SI 2005/3442, Sch.1, para.8(b). The specific rules relating to size and type of company were dealt with as follows: (i) small companies: s.246, as inserted by s.13 of the 1989 Act and subsequently substituted by SI 1997/220 and amended by SIs 1997/570; 2000/1430, reg.8(1); 2004/2947, Sch.1, para.12(3); 2005/1011, reg.4, as subsequently amended by SI 2005/3442; and 2005/2280, reg.12; (ii) medium-sized companies: s.246A, as inserted by SI 1997/220 and subsequently amended by SI 2004/2947, Sch.1, para.13; (iii) unquoted companies: s.242, as inserted by s.11 of the 1989 Act and subsequently amended; (iv) quoted companies: s.242, as inserted by s.11 of the 1989 Act and subsequently amended; (v) unlimited companies: s.254, as inserted by s.17 of the 1989 Act and subsequently amended by SIs 1991/2705, 1993/1820 and 1993/3246.

444. Filing obligations of companies subject to small companies regime

(1) The directors of a company subject to the small companies regime-

    (a) must deliver to the registrar for each financial year a copy of a balance sheet drawn up as at the last day of that year, and

    (b) may also deliver to the registrar-

        (i) a copy of the company's profit and loss account for that year, and

        (ii) a copy of the directors' report for that year.

(2) The directors must also deliver to the registrar a copy of the auditor's report on those accounts (and on the directors' report).

This does not apply if the company is exempt from audit and the directors have taken advantage of that exemption.

(3) The copies of accounts and reports delivered to the registrar must be copies of the company's annual accounts and reports, except that where the company prepares Companies Act accounts-

    (a) the directors may deliver to the registrar a copy of a balance sheet drawn up in accordance with regulations made by the Secretary of State, and

    (b) there may be omitted from the copy profit and loss account delivered to the registrar such items as may be specified by the regulations.

These are referred to in this Part as "abbreviated accounts".

(4) If abbreviated accounts are delivered to the registrar the obligation to deliver a copy of the auditor's report on the accounts is to deliver a copy of the special auditor's report required by section 449.

(5) Where the directors of a company subject to the small companies regime deliver to the registrar IAS accounts, or Companies Act accounts that are not abbreviated accounts, and in accordance with this section-

    (a) do not deliver to the registrar a copy of the company's profit and loss account, or

    (b) do not deliver to the registrar a copy of the directors' report,

the copy of the balance sheet delivered to the registrar must contain in a prominent position a statement that the company's annual accounts and reports have been delivered in accordance with the provisions applicable to companies subject to the small companies regime.

(6) The copies of the balance sheet and any directors' report delivered to the registrar under this section must state the name of the person who signed it on behalf of the board.

(7) The copy of the auditor's report delivered to the registrar under this section must-

    (a) state the name of the auditor and (where the auditor is a firm) the name of the person who signed it as senior statutory auditor, or

    (b) if the conditions in section 506 (circumstances in which names may be omitted) are met, state that a resolution has been passed and notified to the Secretary of State in accordance with that section.

GENERAL NOTE

    This section deals with the filing obligations of companies subject to the small companies regime in a greatly simplified manner. Previously this matter was dealt with in s.242(1) of the 1985 Act (as inserted by s.11 of the 1989 Act and subsequently amended) and subss.(1) and (5)-(7) of s.246 of the 1985 Act (as inserted by the 1989 Act and subsequently amended) and (with respect to abbreviated accounts) in Schedule 8A to the 1985 Act, as inserted.

    While small and medium sized companies ("SMEs") will continue to be able to file abbreviated accounts, the government's intention is that they should be required to disclose turnover. Presumably such a provision will be included in the relevant regulations when they are published.

Subsections (1) and (2)

    The directors of a company subject to the "small companies regime" (s.381) must file with the registrar a copy of the end-year balance sheet for a financial year, and they may also file copies of the profit and loss account and the directors' report for the year (subs.(1)). The accounts filed must be accompanied by the auditor's report, except where the company is exempt from audit and the directors have taken advantage of that exemption (subs.(2)).

Subsections (3) and (4)

Where a company prepares Companies Act accounts (ss.396 and 404), the directors may opt to file "abbreviated accounts" with the registrar in accordance with regulations issued by the Secretary of State (subs.(3)). In such circumstances, a "special auditor's report" (subs.(4)) must be filed instead of the full auditor's report (subs.(5)).

Subsection (5)

Where a company files IAS accounts (ss.397 and 406) or Companies Act accounts (ss.396 and 404) that are not "abbreviated accounts", but nevertheless does not file copies of the profit and loss account or the directors' report, the copy of the balance sheet delivered to the registrar must contain in a prominent position a statement that the financial statements have been prepared in accordance to the requirements of the "small companies regime" (s.381).

Subsection (6)

Copies of the balance sheet and any directors' report filed must state the name of the person who signed them on behalf of the board (see s.433, above).

Subsection (7)

The copies of the auditor's report filed with the registrar must state the name of the auditor (s.503) and, where the auditor is a firm, of the senior statutory auditor (ss.503-504). The company may, however, take advantage of the exemption in s.506, which permits the names not to be disclosed if this might put the auditors at undue risk, but if so, there must be a statement that the exemption is being used.

445.   Filing obligations of medium-sized companies

(1) The directors of a company that qualifies as a medium-sized company in relation to a financial year (see sections 465 to 467) must deliver to the registrar a copy of-
    (a) the company's annual accounts, and
    (b) the directors' report.
(2) They must also deliver to the registrar a copy of the auditor's report on those accounts (and on the directors' report).
This does not apply if the company is exempt from audit and the directors have taken advantage of that exemption.
(3) Where the company prepares Companies Act accounts, the directors may deliver to the registrar a copy of the company's annual accounts for the financial year-
    (a) that includes a profit and loss account in which items are combined in accordance with regulations made by the Secretary of State, and
    (b) that does not contain items whose omission is authorised by the regulations.
 These are referred to in this Part as "abbreviated accounts".
(4) If abbreviated accounts are delivered to the registrar the obligation to deliver a copy of the auditor's report on the accounts is to deliver a copy of the special auditor's report required by section 449.
(5) The copies of the balance sheet and directors' report delivered to the registrar under this section must state the name of the person who signed it on behalf of the board.
(6) The copy of the auditor's report delivered to the registrar under this section must-
    (a) state the name of the auditor and (where the auditor is a firm) the name of the person who signed it as senior statutory auditor, or
    (b) if the conditions in section 506 (circumstances in which names may be omitted) are met, state that a resolution has been passed and notified to the Secretary of State in accordance with that section.
(7) This section does not apply to companies within section 444 (filing obligations of companies subject to the small companies regime).

GENERAL NOTE

This section deals with the filing obligations of companies subject to the medium-sized companies regime in a greatly simplified manner. Previously this matter was dealt with in s.242(1) of the 1985 Act (as inserted by s.11 of the 1989 Act and subsequently amended) and subss.(1) and (3) of s.246A of the 1985 Act (as inserted and subsequently amended). It permits medium-sized companies (as defined in s.465) to file abbreviated accounts and gives the Secretary of State the power to make regulations concerning abbreviated accounts for such companies.

While small and medium sized companies will continue to be able to file abbreviated accounts, the government's intention is that they should be required to disclose turnover. Presumably this will included in the relevant regulations when they are published.

Subsections (1) and (2)

The directors of a company that qualifies as "medium-sized" (ss.465-467, below) must file with the registrar a copy of the end-year balance sheet for a financial year, its profit and loss account, and the directors' report for the year (subs.(1)). The accounts filed must be accompanied by the auditor's report, except where the company is exempt from audit and the directors have taken advantage of that exemption (subs.(2)).

Subsections (3) and (4)

Where the company prepares Companies Act accounts, the directors may file "abbreviated accounts" in which certain items are omitted as permitted by regulations issued by the Secretary of State and various items in the profit and loss account are combined (subs.(3)). Where such "abbreviated accounts" are filed, a "special auditor's report" (s.449) must be appended instead of the full auditor's report (subs.(4)).

Subsection (5)

Copies of the balance sheet and the directors' report filed must state the name of the person who signed them on behalf of the board (see s.433, above).

Subsection (6)

The copies of the auditor's report filed with the registrar must state the name of the auditor (s.503) and, where the auditor is a firm, of the senior statutory auditor (ss.503-504). The company may, however, take advantage of the exemption in s.506, which permits the names not to be disclosed if this might put the auditors at undue risk, but if so, there must be a statement that the exemption is being used.

Subsection (7)

The provisions of s.445 do not apply to companies subject to the "small companies regime" filing obligations (s.444).

446. Filing obligations of unquoted companies

(1) The directors of an unquoted company must deliver to the registrar for each financial year of the company a copy of-
    (a) the company's annual accounts, and
    (b) the directors' report.
(2) The directors must also deliver to the registrar a copy of the auditor's report on those accounts (and the directors' report).
This does not apply if the company is exempt from audit and the directors have taken advantage of that exemption.
(3) The copies of the balance sheet and directors' report delivered to the registrar under this section must state the name of the person who signed it on behalf of the board.
(4) The copy of the auditor's report delivered to the registrar under this section must-
    (a) state the name of the auditor and (where the auditor is a firm) the name of the person who signed it as senior statutory auditor, or
    (b) if the conditions in section 506 (circumstances in which names may be omitted) are met, state that a resolution has been passed and notified to the Secretary of State in accordance with that section.
(5) This section does not apply to companies within-
    (a) section 444 (filing obligations of companies subject to the small companies regime), or
    (b) section 445 (filing obligations of medium-sized companies).

GENERAL NOTE

This section deals with the filing obligations of unquoted companies in a greatly simplified manner. Previously this matter was not specifically dealt with, but was covered by s.242(1) of the 1985 Act (as inserted by s.11 of the 1989 Act and subsequently amended).

Subsections (1) and (2)

The directors of an unquoted company (s.385, above) must file with the registrar a copy of the end-year balance sheet for a financial year, its profit and loss account, and the directors' report for the year (subs.(1)). The accounts filed must be accompanied by the auditor's report, except where the company is exempt from audit and the directors have taken advantage of that exemption (subs.(2)).

Subsection (3)

Copies of the balance sheet and the directors' report filed must state the name of the person who signed them on behalf of the board (see s.433, above).

Subsection (4)

The copies of the auditor's report filed with the registrar must state the name of the auditor (s.503) and, where the auditor is a firm, of the senior statutory auditor (ss.503-504). The company may, however, take advantage of the exemption in s.506, which permits the names not to be disclosed if this might put the auditors at undue risk, but if so, there must be a statement that the exemption is being used.

Subsection (5)

The provisions of s.446 do not apply to companies subject to the "small companies regime" filing obligaions (s.444) or the "medium sized companies" filing requirements (s.445).

447. Filing obligations of quoted companies

(1) The directors of a quoted company must deliver to the registrar for each financial year of the company a copy of-
    (a) the company's annual accounts,
    (b) the directors' remuneration report, and
    (c) the directors' report.

(2) They must also deliver a copy of the auditor's report on those accounts (and on the directors' remuneration report and the directors' report).

(3) The copies of the balance sheet, the directors' remuneration report and the directors' report delivered to the registrar under this section must state the name of the person who signed it on behalf of the board.

(4) The copy of the auditor's report delivered to the registrar under this section must-
    (a) state the name of the auditor and (where the auditor is a firm) the name of the person who signed it as senior statutory auditor, or
    (b) if the conditions in section 506 (circumstances in which names may be omitted) are met, state that a resolution has been passed and notified to the Secretary of State in accordance with that section.

GENERAL NOTE

This section deals with the filing obligations of quoted companies in a greatly simplified manner. Previously, as with unquoted companies, this matter was not specifically dealt with, but was covered by s.242(1) of the 1985 Act (as inserted by s.11 of the 1989 Act and subsequently amended).

Subsections (1)-(3)

The directors of a quoted company (s.385, above) must file with the registrar a copy of the end-year balance sheet for a financial year, its profit and loss account, the directors' remuneration report, and the directors' report for the year (subs.(1)). The accounts filed must be accompanied by the auditor's report on the accounts, the directors' remuneration report and the directors' report (subs.(2)). Copies of all the accounts, the directors' remuneration report, and the directors' report must state the name of the person who signed them on behalf of the board (subs.(3)).

Subsection (4)

The copies of the auditor's report filed with the registrar must state the name of the auditor (s.503) and, where the auditor is a firm, of the senior statutory auditor (ss.503-504). The company may, however, take advantage of the exemption in s.506, which permits the names not to be disclosed if this might put the auditors at undue risk, but if so, there must be a statement that the exemption is being used.

448. Unlimited companies exempt from obligation to file accounts

(1) The directors of an unlimited company are not required to deliver accounts and reports to the registrar in respect of a financial year if the following conditions are met.

(2) The conditions are that at no time during the relevant accounting reference period-
   (a) has the company been, to its knowledge, a subsidiary undertaking of an undertaking which was then limited, or
   (b) have there been, to its knowledge, exercisable by or on behalf of two or more undertakings which were then limited, rights which if exercisable by one of them would have made the company a subsidiary undertaking of it, or
   (c) has the company been a parent company of an undertaking which was then limited.
The references above to an undertaking being limited at a particular time are to an undertaking (under whatever law established) the liability of whose members is at that time limited.

(3) The exemption conferred by this section does not apply if-
   (a) the company is a banking or insurance company or the parent company of a banking or insurance group, or
   (b) the company is a qualifying company within the meaning of the Partnerships and Unlimited Companies (Accounts) Regulations 1993 (S.I. 1993/1820).

(4) Where a company is exempt by virtue of this section from the obligation to deliver accounts-
   (a) section 434(3) (requirements in connection with publication of statutory accounts: meaning of "statutory accounts") has effect with the substitution for the words "as required to be delivered to the registrar under section 441" of the words "as prepared in accordance with this Part and approved by the board of directors"; and
   (b) section 435(1)(b) (requirements in connection with publication of non-statutory accounts: statement whether statutory accounts delivered) has effect with the substitution for the words from "whether statutory accounts" to "have been delivered to the registrar" of the words "that the company is exempt from the requirement to deliver statutory accounts".

(5) In this section the "relevant accounting reference period", in relation to a financial year, means the accounting reference period by reference to which that financial year was determined.

GENERAL NOTE

This section replaces s.254 of the 1985 Act, as inserted by s.17 of the 1989 Act and subsequently amended by SIs 1991/2705, 1993/1820 and 1993/3246. It exempts unlimited companies from the obligation to file accounts, subject to limitations set out in subss.(2) and (3).

Subsections (1) and (2)

The directors of an unlimited company are not required to file accounts and reports with the registrar (subs.(1)), so long as they meet the following conditions: namely, that at no time during the accounting reference period: (i) has the company been a subsidiary of an undertaking with limited liability; (ii) have two or more undertakings with unlimited liability had rights that if exercised would have made the company a subsidiary of one of them; or (iii) has the company been a parent of an undertaking with limited liability (subs.(2)).

Subsection (3)

The exemption from having to file accounts and reports does not apply if (i) the company is, or is a parent company of, a banking or insurance concern; or (ii) it is a qualifying company within the meaning of SI 1993/1820, the "Partnerships and Unlimited Companies (Accounts) Regulations 1993".

Subsection (4)

This subsection substitutes appropriate wording for their application to unlimited companies exempt from filing accounts and reports to the registrar into ss.434(3) and 435(1)(b). The former deals with requirements in connection with publication of statutory accounts (specifically defining the meaning of "statutory accounts"); and the latter with requirements in connection with the publication of non-statutory accounts (specifically a statement indicating whether statutory accounts have been delivered).

Subsection (5)

For the purpose of s.448, the "relevant accounting reference period" means the accounting reference period used to determine the financial year in question: see ss.390-392.

Requirements where abbreviated accounts delivered

449.   Special auditor's report where abbreviated accounts delivered

(1) This section applies where-
    (a) the directors of a company deliver abbreviated accounts to the registrar, and
    (b) the company is not exempt from audit (or the directors have not taken advantage of any such exemption).
(2) The directors must also deliver to the registrar a copy of a special report of the company's auditor stating that in his opinion-
    (a) the company is entitled to deliver abbreviated accounts in accordance with the section in question, and
    (b) the abbreviated accounts to be delivered are properly prepared in accordance with regulations under that section.
(3) The auditor's report on the company's annual accounts need not be delivered, but-
    (a) if that report was qualified, the special report must set out that report in full together with any further material necessary to understand the qualification, and
    (b) if that report contained a statement under-
        (i) section 498(2)(a) or (b) (accounts, records or returns inadequate or accounts not agreeing with records and returns), or
        (ii) section 498(3) (failure to obtain necessary information and explanations),
    the special report must set out that statement in full.
(4) The provisions of-
    sections 503 to 506 (signature of auditor's report), and
    sections 507 to 509 (offences in connection with auditor's report),
apply to a special report under this section as they apply to an auditor's report on the company's annual accounts prepared under Part 16.
(5) If abbreviated accounts are delivered to the registrar, the references in section 434 or 435 (requirements in connection with publication of accounts) to the auditor's report on the company's annual accounts shall be read as references to the special auditor's report required by this section.

GENERAL NOTE

This section replaces the provisions in s.247B of the 1985 Act, as inserted by SI 1997/220 and subsequently amended by reg.8(2) of SI 2000/1430. Section 247B required a "special auditor's report" to be filed when a company delivered "abbreviated accounts" to the registrar. There is no requirement for the "special auditor's report" where the company is entitled to exemption from audit and has taken advantage of this exemption.

Subsections (1) and (2)

Where a company (i) files "abbreviated accounts" (ss.444(3) and 445(3)) with the registrar; and (ii) is not exempt from audit (or the directors have not taken advantage of such exemption) (subs.(1)), the directors must file a special report by the auditor stating that in his or her opinion (i) the company is entitled to file "abbreviated accounts"; and (ii) such "abbreviated accounts" have been properly prepared in accordance with the Secretary of State's regulations (subs.(2)).

Subsection (3)

The auditor's report on the company's annual accounts, as required by s.495, below, need not be filed, except where it is qualified, in which case it must be set out in full in the special report, together with any information necessary to understand the qualification. Moreover, if the auditor's report contains a statement made under s.498(2)(a)-(b) that the accounts, records or returns are inadequate, or that the accounts do not agree with the records or returns, such a statement must be set out in full in the special auditor's report. There is also a similar requirement with respect to a statement in the auditor's report made under s.498(3) with regard to a failure in obtaining the necessary information and explanations required to carry out the audit.

Subsection (4)

The provisions of ss.503-506 relating to the signature on the auditor's report and of ss.507-509 with regard to offences in connection with an auditor's report apply equally to a "special auditor's report" prepared under s.449.

Subsection (5)

Where "abbreviated accounts" are filed with the registrar, references to the statutory auditor's report in ss.434-435, above, concerning publication of statutory and non-statutory accounts, apply equally to the "special auditor's report". In other words, published "abbreviated accounts" that comply with statutory requirements must be accompanied by the "special auditor's report"; however, if they do not so comply, and are therefore "non-statutory" abbreviated accounts, they must not be accompanied by "the special auditor's report".

450. Approval and signing of abbreviated accounts

(1) Abbreviated accounts must be approved by the board of directors and signed on behalf of the board by a director of the company.
(2) The signature must be on the balance sheet.
(3) The balance sheet must contain in a prominent position above the signature a statement to the effect that it is prepared in accordance with the special provisions of this Act relating (as the case may be) to companies subject to the small companies regime or to medium-sized companies.
(4) If abbreviated accounts are approved that do not comply with the requirements of regulations under the relevant section, every director of the company who-
  (a) knew that they did not comply, or was reckless as to whether they complied, and
  (b) failed to take reasonable steps to prevent them from being approved,
commits an offence.
(5) A person guilty of an offence under subsection (4) is liable-
  (a) on conviction on indictment, to a fine;
  (b) on summary conviction, to a fine not exceeding the statutory maximum.

GENERAL NOTE

This section replaces, first, subss.(7) and (8) of s.246 of the 1985 Act (as inserted by s.13(1) of the 1989 Act and subsequently substituted by SI 1997/220); and, secondly, subs.(4) of s.246A of the 1985 Act, as inserted by SI 1997/220. The matters concerned are the approval and signing of "abbreviated accounts".

Subsections (1)-(3)

"Abbreviated accounts" must be approved by the board and the balance sheet (subs.(2)) be signed on their behalf by a director (subs.(1)). The balance sheet must also contain in a prominent position above the signature a statement indicating that it is prepared in accordance with the relevant regulations relating to the "small companies regime" (ss.381 and 444) or to medium-sized companies (ss.465-467 and 445) (subs.(3)).

Subsections (4) and (5)

Where "abbreviated accounts" are approved when they do not comply with the requirements of the regulations issued by the Secretary of State, every director who: (i) knew that they did not comply or who was reckless as to whether or not they complied; and (ii) failed to take reasonable steps to ensure compliance or prevent such accounts being approved commits an offence (subs.4)), the penalty for which is a fine (subs.(5)).

Failure to file accounts and reports

GENERAL NOTE

Sections 451-452 re-enact sanctions for failing to file accounts and reports within the required periods, as set out in subss.(2)-(5) of s.242 of the 1985 Act, as inserted by s.11 of the 1989 Act.

451.   Default in filing accounts and reports: offences

(1) If the requirements of section 441 (duty to file accounts and reports) are not complied with in relation to a company's accounts and reports for a financial year before the end of the period for filing those accounts and reports, every person who immediately before the end of that period was a director of the company commits an offence.

(2) It is a defence for a person charged with such an offence to prove that he took all reasonable steps for securing that those requirements would be complied with before the end of that period.

(3) It is not a defence to prove that the documents in question were not in fact prepared as required by this Part.

(4) A person guilty of an offence under this section is liable on summary conviction to a fine not exceeding level 5 on the standard scale and, for continued contravention, a daily default fine not exceeding one-tenth of level 5 on the standard scale.

GENERAL NOTE

This section is derived from subss.(2), (4)-(5) of s.242 of the 1985 Act, as inserted by s.11 of the 1989 Act.

Subsections (1)-(4)

Every person who was a director before the end of the period for filing accounts and reports commits an offence if there is a failure to comply with the filing requirements specified in s.441 (subs.(1)). However, it is a defence to prove that he took all reasonable steps to ensure compliance (subs.(2)), but this excludes a claim that the documents were not prepared as required (subs.(3)). The penalty for such an offence is a fine, and for continued contravention a daily default fine (subs.(4)).

452.   Default in filing accounts and reports: court order

(1) If-

(a) the requirements of section 441 (duty to file accounts and reports) are not complied with in relation to a company's accounts and reports for a financial year before the end of the period for filing those accounts and reports, and

(b) the directors of the company fail to make good the default within 14 days after the service of a notice on them requiring compliance,

 the court may, on the application of any member or creditor of the company or of the registrar, make an order directing the directors (or any of them) to make good the default within such time as may be specified in the order.

(2) The court's order may provide that all costs (in Scotland, expenses) of and incidental to the application are to be borne by the directors.

GENERAL NOTE

This section is derived from subs.(3) of s.242 of the 1985 Act, as inserted by s.11 of the 1989 Act.

Subsections (1) and (2)

Where there is a failure to comply with the filing requirements specified in s.441 and the directors fail to make good the default within 14 days after service of a notice on them requiring compliance, the court may, on the application of a member, a creditor, or the registrar, make an order requiring them to make good the default within a specified time (subs.(1)). The court may order that the costs and expenses related to the action should be borne by the directors (subs.(2)).

453. Civil penalty for failure to file accounts and reports

(1) Where the requirements of section 441 are not complied with in relation to a company's accounts and reports for a financial year before the end of the period for filing those accounts and reports, the company is liable to a civil penalty.

This is in addition to any liability of the directors under section 451.

(2) The amount of the penalty shall be determined in accordance with regulations made by the Secretary of State by reference to-
  (a) the length of the period between the end of the period for filing the accounts and reports in question and the day on which the requirements are complied with, and
  (b) whether the company is a private or public company.

(3) The penalty may be recovered by the registrar and is to be paid into the Consolidated Fund.

(4) It is not a defence in proceedings under this section to prove that the documents in question were not in fact prepared as required by this Part.

(5) Regulations under this section having the effect of increasing the penalty payable in any case are subject to affirmative resolution procedure.

Otherwise, the regulations are subject to negative resolution procedure.

GENERAL NOTE

This section provides a civil penalty for failing to file accounts, restating most s.242A of the 1985 Act, as inserted by s.11 of the 1989 Act. However, there is one change: namely, rather than setting out the table of penalties in the legislation, subs.(2) provides for the Secretary of State to make regulations specifying both the relevant periods and the amounts of the penalties.

Subsections (1)-(5)

Where there is a failure to comply with the filing requirements specified in s.441, the company is liable to a civil penalty in addition to any liability incurred by the directors under s.451, above (subs.(1)). The penalty will be determined in accordance with regulations issued by the Secretary of State and will depend on the length of time the company is in breach of its statutory obligations and whether it is private or public (subs.(2)). It is not a defence to prove that the documents were not prepared as required (subs.(4)). Regulations that have the effect of increasing the penalty will be subject to the affirmative resolution procedure (s.1290). Otherwise, they will be subject to the negative resolution procedure (s.1289) (subs.(5)). The penalty may be recovered by the registrar and is to be paid into the Consolidated Fund (subs.(3)).

CHAPTER II

REVISION OF DEFECTIVE ACCOUNTS AND REPORTS

Voluntary revision

454. Voluntary revision of accounts etc

(1) If it appears to the directors of a company that-
  (a) the company's annual accounts,
  (b) the directors' remuneration report or the directors' report, or
  (c) a summary financial statement of the company,
did not comply with the requirements of this Act (or, where applicable, of Article 4 of the IAS Regulation), they may prepare revised accounts or a revised report or statement.

(2) Where copies of the previous accounts or report have been sent out to members, delivered to the registrar or (in the case of a public company) laid before the company in general meeting, the revisions must be confined to-

    (a) the correction of those respects in which the previous accounts or report did not comply with the requirements of this Act (or, where applicable, of Article 4 of the IAS Regulation), and

    (b) the making of any necessary consequential alterations.

(3) The Secretary of State may make provision by regulations as to the application of the provisions of this Act in relation to-

    (a) revised annual accounts,

    (b) a revised directors' remuneration report or directors' report, or

    (c) a revised summary financial statement.

(4) The regulations may, in particular-

    (a) make different provision according to whether the previous accounts, report or statement are replaced or are supplemented by a document indicating the corrections to be made;

    (b) make provision with respect to the functions of the company's auditor in relation to the revised accounts, report or statement;

    (c) require the directors to take such steps as may be specified in the regulations where the previous accounts or report have been-

        (i) sent out to members and others under section 423,

        (ii) laid before the company in general meeting, or

        (iii) delivered to the registrar,

  or where a summary financial statement containing information derived from the previous accounts or report has been sent to members under section 426;

    (d) apply the provisions of this Act (including those creating criminal offences) subject to such additions, exceptions and modifications as are specified in the regulations.

(5) Regulations under this section are subject to negative resolution procedure.

GENERAL NOTE

This section, providing for the voluntary revision of defective accounts and reports and summary financial statements, restates s.245 of the 1985 Act, as amended by SIs 1994/1935, 2002/1986, 2004/2947, 2005/2011 and 2005/3442 (Sch.1, para.9).

Subsections (1) and (2)

The directors may voluntarily prepare revised accounts, reports or statements if it appears to them that the annual accounts, the directors' remuneration report, the directors' report, or a summary financial statement do not comply with the requirements of the Act or (where appropriate) art.4 of the IAS Regulation (subs.(1)). However, where the accounts, reports or statements have been sent to members, filed with the registrar, or (in the case of a public company) laid before a general meeting, the revisions are limited to correcting matters that did not comply with requirements of the Act or art.4 of the IAS Regulation and any consequential alterations (subs.(2)).

Subsections (3) and (4)

The Secretary of State may issue regulations relating to the application of the Act to revised annual accounts, directors' remuneration reports, directors' reports, and summary financial statements (subs.(3)). Such regulations may: (i) make different requirements depending on whether the original documents are to be replaced or merely supplemented by a statement of corrections; (ii) make provision for the auditor to attest the revised documents; (iii) require the directors to take remedial steps as specified where the documents (including a summary financial statement) have been sent out to members, debenture holders, etc, laid before a general meeting or filed with the registrar; and (iv) apply the provisions of the Act, including those creating criminal offences, subject to additions and modifications made in the regulations (subs.(4)).

Subsection (5)

The regulations issued under the provisions of s.454 are subject to the negative resolution procedure (s.1289).

Secretary of State's notice

455. Secretary of State's notice in respect of accounts or reports

(1) This section applies where-
  (a) copies of a company's annual accounts or directors' report have been sent out under section 423, or
  (b) a copy of a company's annual accounts or directors' report has been delivered to the registrar or (in the case of a public company) laid before the company in general meeting,

and it appears to the Secretary of State that there is, or may be, a question whether the accounts or report comply with the requirements of this Act (or, where applicable, of Article 4 of the IAS Regulation).

(2) The Secretary of State may give notice to the directors of the company indicating the respects in which it appears that such a question arises or may arise.

(3) The notice must specify a period of not less than one month for the directors to give an explanation of the accounts or report or prepare revised accounts or a revised report.

(4) If at the end of the specified period, or such longer period as the Secretary of State may allow, it appears to the Secretary of State that the directors have not-
  (a) given a satisfactory explanation of the accounts or report, or
  (b) revised the accounts or report so as to comply with the requirements of this Act (or, where applicable, of Article 4 of the IAS Regulation),

the Secretary of State may apply to the court.

(5) The provisions of this section apply equally to revised annual accounts and revised directors' reports, in which case they have effect as if the references to revised accounts or reports were references to further revised accounts or reports.

GENERAL NOTE

This section re-enacts s.245A of the 1985 Act, as inserted by s.12 of the 1989 Act and subsequently amended by SIs 2004/2947, 2005/1011 and 2005/3442 (Sch.1, para.10). It concerns the Secretary of State giving notice to the directors of a company if there is, or may be, a question as to whether the annual accounts or directors' report comply with the requirements of the Act or the IAS Regulation (Regulation (EC) 1606/2002 on the application of international accounting standards).

Subsections (1)-(4)

Where copies of the accounts or directors' report have been sent out under s.423 or been filed with the registrar and there appears to the Secretary of State that they do not, or may not, comply with the requirements of the Act (or, where appropriate, art.4 of the IAS Regulation) (subs.(1)), he may give notice to the directors indicating the respects in which there is a *prima facie* breach of the requirements (subs.(2)). The notice must specify a period of not less than a month for the directors to offer an explanation or prepare revised accounts or reports (subs.(3)). If at the expiry of the specified time interval it appears to the Secretary of State that no satisfactory explanation has been offered or revised accounts been prepared, he may apply to the court (subs.(4)).

Subsection (5)

The provisions of s.455 equally apply to accounts and reports that have already been revised.

Application to court

GENERAL NOTE

Sections 456-457 concern applications to the court in respect of defective accounts or reports. They re-enact ss.245B and 245C of the 1985 Act, as inserted by s.12 of the 1989 Act and subsequently amended by SIs 1990/2569, 2002/1986, 2004/2947, 2005/1011 and 2005/3442 (Sch.1, paras 11-12).

456.   Application to court in respect of defective accounts or reports

(1) An application may be made to the court-
    (a) by the Secretary of State, after having complied with section 455, or
    (b) by a person authorised by the Secretary of State for the purposes of this section,
for a declaration (in Scotland, a declarator) that the annual accounts of a company do not comply, or a directors' report does not comply, with the requirements of this Act (or, where applicable, of Article 4 of the IAS Regulation) and for an order requiring the directors of the company to prepare revised accounts or a revised report.

(2) Notice of the application, together with a general statement of the matters at issue in the proceedings, shall be given by the applicant to the registrar for registration.

(3) If the court orders the preparation of revised accounts, it may give directions as to-
    (a) the auditing of the accounts,
    (b) the revision of any directors' remuneration report, directors' report or summary financial statement, and
    (c) the taking of steps by the directors to bring the making of the order to the notice of persons likely to rely on the previous accounts,
and such other matters as the court thinks fit.

(4) If the court orders the preparation of a revised directors' report it may give directions as to-
    (a) the review of the report by the auditors,
    (b) the revision of any summary financial statement,
    (c) the taking of steps by the directors to bring the making of the order to the notice of persons likely to rely on the previous report, and
    (d) such other matters as the court thinks fit.

(5) If the court finds that the accounts or report did not comply with the requirements of this Act (or, where applicable, of Article 4 of the IAS Regulation) it may order that all or part of-
    (a) the costs (in Scotland, expenses) of and incidental to the application, and
    (b) any reasonable expenses incurred by the company in connection with or in consequence of the preparation of revised accounts or a revised report,
are to be borne by such of the directors as were party to the approval of the defective accounts or report.
For this purpose every director of the company at the time of the approval of the accounts or report shall be taken to have been a party to the approval unless he shows that he took all reasonable steps to prevent that approval.

(6) Where the court makes an order under subsection (5) it shall have regard to whether the directors party to the approval of the defective accounts or report knew or ought to have known that the accounts or report did not comply with the requirements of this Act (or, where applicable, of Article 4 of the IAS Regulation), and it may exclude one or more directors from the order or order the payment of different amounts by different directors.

(7) On the conclusion of proceedings on an application under this section, the applicant must send to the registrar for registration a copy of the court order or, as the case may be, give notice to the registrar that the application has failed or been withdrawn.

(8) The provisions of this section apply equally to revised annual accounts and revised directors' reports, in which case they have effect as if the references to revised accounts or reports were references to further revised accounts or reports.

GENERAL NOTE

    This section re-enacts s.245B of the 1985 Act, as inserted by s.12 of the 1989 Act and subsequently amended by SIs 2002/1986, 2004/2947, 2005/1011 and 2005/3442 (Sch.1, para.12).

Subsections (1) and (2)

    After complying with the provisions of s.455, the Secretary of State or a person authorised by him can apply to the court for a declaration (or a declarator in Scotland) that the accounts or a directors' report do not comply with the requirements of the Act (or, where appropriate art.4 of the IAS Regulation) and for an order requiring the directors to prepare revised accounts or a revised report (subs.(1)). Notice of the application, indicating the matters at issue, has to be given to the registrar (subs.(2)).

Subsections (3) and (4)

Where the court orders the preparation of revised accounts, it may make directions with respect to: (i) the audit of such accounts; (ii) the revision of the directors' remuneration report, the directors' report, or the summary financial statement; and (iii) the steps that the directors should take to make persons likely to rely on the previous accounts aware of the order (subs.(3)). Similarly, it may make directions concerning a revised directors' report with respect to: (i) its review by the auditors; (ii) the revision of a summary financial statement; (iii) the steps that the directors should take to make persons likely to rely on the previous report aware of the order; and (iv) any other matters as the court sees fit (subs.(4)).

Subsections (5) and (6)

Where the court finds that the accounts or report did not comply with the requirements of the Act (or, where appropriate art.4 of the IAS Regulation), it may order all or part of the costs or expenses of the application, and reasonable costs incurred by the company in preparing revised accounts or a revised report, to be recovered from directors party to the approval of the defective documents. For this purpose, every director will be assumed to be party to the defective documents' approval unless he can show he took all reasonable steps to prevent that approval being given (subs.(5)). However, in making such an order, the court will have to consider whether the directors should have known that the accounts or report did not comply with the relevant requirements, and it may exempt directors from the order or require them to pay different amounts towards the costs or expenses (subs.(6)).

Subsection (7)

At the end of the proceedings, the applicant must send a copy of the court order to the registrar or give notice that the application has failed or been withdrawn.

Subsection (8)

The provisions of s.456 equally apply to accounts and reports that have already been revised.

457. Other persons authorised to apply to the court

(1) The Secretary of State may by order (an "authorisation order") authorise for the purposes of section 456 any person appearing to him-
   (a) to have an interest in, and to have satisfactory procedures directed to securing, compliance by companies with the requirements of this Act (or, where applicable, of Article 4 of the IAS Regulation) relating to accounts and directors' reports,
   (b) to have satisfactory procedures for receiving and investigating complaints about companies' annual accounts and directors' reports, and
   (c) otherwise to be a fit and proper person to be authorised.
(2) A person may be authorised generally or in respect of particular classes of case, and different persons may be authorised in respect of different classes of case.
(3) The Secretary of State may refuse to authorise a person if he considers that his authorisation is unnecessary having regard to the fact that there are one or more other persons who have been or are likely to be authorised.
(4) If the authorised person is an unincorporated association, proceedings brought in, or in connection with, the exercise of any function by the association as an authorised person may be brought by or against the association in the name of a body corporate whose constitution provides for the establishment of the association.
(5) An authorisation order may contain such requirements or other provisions relating to the exercise of functions by the authorised person as appear to the Secretary of State to be appropriate.
No such order is to be made unless it appears to the Secretary of State that the person would, if authorised, exercise his functions as an authorised person in accordance with the provisions proposed.
(6) Where authorisation is revoked, the revoking order may make such provision as the Secretary of State thinks fit with respect to pending proceedings.

(7) An order under this section is subject to negative resolution procedure.

GENERAL NOTE

This section re-enacts s.245C of the 1985 Act, as inserted by s.12 of the 1989 Act and subsequently amended by SIs 1990/2569, 2004/2947 (Sch.1, para.11(1)) and 2005/3442 (Sch.1, paras 11-12).

Section 457 gives the Secretary of State the power to authorise a person for the purposes of s.456 to apply to the courts to require the directors of companies to prepare revised accounts and reports where the original accounts or reports were defective. The Financial Reporting Review Panel ("FRRP") is the only authorised person under this provision to date (the Companies (Defective Accounts) (Authorised Person) Order 2005: SI 2005/699).

Subsections (1)-(4)

The Secretary of State may make an "authorisation order" for the purpose of s.456, nominating a person or body to act on his behalf where he/it has an interest in, and satisfactory procedures for, securing compliance with the requirements of the Act (or, where appropriate art.4 of the IAS Regulation) with respect to annual accounts and directors' reports; has satisfactory procedures for receiving and investigating complaints on such matters; and is a fit and proper person or body to be so authorised (subs.(1)). Such a person or body may be authorised generally or in respect of particular areas (subs.(2)), and the Secretary of State may refuse authorisation if others have been or are more likely to meet his requirements (subs.(3)). Subsection (4) deals with the situation where the person or body is an unincorporated association.

Subsections (5) and (6)

An "authorisation order" may specify certain requirements as the Secretary of State deems to be appropriate, and no such order is to be issued unless he is satisfied that the authorised person or body will carry out the functions in accordance with the proposed provisions (subs.(5)). Where the order is revoked, the revoking order may deal with the matter of pending proceedings (subs.(6)).

Subsection (7)

An "authorisation order" is subject to the negative resolution procedure (s.1289).

458. Disclosure of information by tax authorities

(1) The Commissioners for Her Majesty's Revenue and Customs may disclose information to a person authorised under section 457 for the purpose of facilitating-
  (a) the taking of steps by that person to discover whether there are grounds for an application to the court under section 456 (application in respect of defective accounts etc), or
  (b) a decision by the authorised person whether to make such an application.
(2) This section applies despite any statutory or other restriction on the disclosure of information.
Provided that, in the case of personal data within the meaning of the Data Protection Act 1998 (c. 29), information is not to be disclosed in contravention of that Act.
(3) Information disclosed to an authorised person under this section-
  (a) may not be used except in or in connection with-
    (i) taking steps to discover whether there are grounds for an application to the court under section 456, or
    (ii) deciding whether or not to make such an application,
   or in, or in connection with, proceedings on such an application; and
  (b) must not be further disclosed except-
    (i) to the person to whom the information relates, or
    (ii) in, or in connection with, proceedings on any such application to the court.
(4) A person who contravenes subsection (3) commits an offence unless-
  (a) he did not know, and had no reason to suspect, that the information had been disclosed under this section, or
  (b) he took all reasonable steps and exercised all due diligence to avoid the commission of the offence.
(5) A person guilty of an offence under subsection (4) is liable-

    (a) on conviction on indictment, to imprisonment for a term not exceeding two years or a fine (or both);

    (b) on summary conviction-

        (i) in England and Wales, to imprisonment for a term not exceeding twelve months or to a fine not exceeding the statutory maximum (or both);

        (ii) in Scotland or Northern Ireland, to imprisonment for a term not exceeding six months, or to a fine not exceeding the statutory maximum (or both).

GENERAL NOTE

This section re-enacts the substance of ss.245D and 245E of the 1985 Act, which were inserted by s.11(1) of the Companies (Audit, Investigations and Community Enterprise) Act 2004.

Subsections (1)-(3)

HM Revenue and Customs may disclose information to a person or body authorised under s.457 (currently the Financial Reporting Review Panel, FRRP) to enable him/it to decide whether or not to apply to the court under s.456 with respect to defective accounts and reports (subs.(1)). The only restrictions on the disclosure of information are (i) personal data covered by the Data Protection Act 1998 is not to be disclosed (subs.(2)); and (ii) the information must not be used for any other purpose than to decide whether or not to apply to the court under s.456, and it must not be further disclosed except to the party involved or in proceedings related to the court application (subs.(3)).

Subsections (4) and (5)

A person who misuses or improperly discloses such information commits a criminal offence, unless he/she can show that: (i) he/she did not know or suspect that it was disclosed under the provisions of s.458; or (ii) he/she took all reasonable steps to avoid committing such an offence (subs.(4)). The penalties for such an offence are imprisonment and/or fines (subs.(5)).

Power of authorised person to require documents etc

459. Power of authorised person to require documents, information and explanations

(1) This section applies where it appears to a person who is authorised under section 457 that there is, or may be, a question whether a company's annual accounts or directors' report comply with the requirements of this Act (or, where applicable, of Article 4 of the IAS Regulation).

(2) The authorised person may require any of the persons mentioned in subsection (3) to produce any document, or to provide him with any information or explanations, that he may reasonably require for the purpose of-

    (a) discovering whether there are grounds for an application to the court under section 456, or

    (b) deciding whether to make such an application.

(3) Those persons are-

    (a) the company;

    (b) any officer, employee, or auditor of the company;

    (c) any persons who fell within paragraph (b) at a time to which the document or information required by the authorised person relates.

(4) If a person fails to comply with such a requirement, the authorised person may apply to the court.

(5) If it appears to the court that the person has failed to comply with a requirement under subsection (2), it may order the person to take such steps as it directs for securing that the documents are produced or the information or explanations are provided.

(6) A statement made by a person in response to a requirement under subsection (2) or an order under subsection (5) may not be used in evidence against him in any criminal proceedings.

(7) Nothing in this section compels any person to disclose documents or information in respect of which a claim to legal professional privilege (in Scotland, to confidentiality of communications) could be maintained in legal proceedings.

(8) In this section "document" includes information recorded in any form.

GENERAL NOTE

This section re-enacts s.245F of the 1985 Act, as inserted by s.12(1) of the Companies (Audit, Investigations and Community Enterprise) Act 2004. Subsections (1)-(3) provide the Financial Reporting Review Panel ("FRRP") (as the person/body currently authorised under s.457) with a statutory power to require a company and its officers, employees and auditors to provide documents and information. Where a person refuses to provide information or documents to the FRRP, it may apply to the court for an order. The court may make an order requiring disclosure. Failure to comply with such an order would be contempt of court.

Subsections (1)-(5)

A person or body authorised under s.457, above, to act on behalf of the Secretary of State with respect to defective accounts and reports (subs.(1)) may require a company and its officers, employees or auditor, including those in office or employed at the time to which the information relates (subs.(3)), to provide such documents, information and explanations as are reasonably required to help him/it decide whether or not to make an application to the court under s.456 (subs.(2)). Where a person does not comply, the authorised body may apply to the court (subs.(4)), which in turn may order the person to take the necessary steps to provide the documents, information and explanations requested (subs.(5)).

Subsections (6) and (7)

Disclosures made in response to a request from the authorised body or the court cannot be used in evidence in criminal proceedings against that person (subs.(6)), and individuals are also not required to disclose information that would breach legally recognised professional privilege (subs.(7)).

Subsection (8)

This subsection defines "document" to include information recorded in any form.

460.   Restrictions on disclosure of information obtained under compulsory powers

(1) This section applies to information (in whatever form) obtained in pursuance of a requirement or order under section 459 (power of authorised person to require documents etc) that relates to the private affairs of an individual or to any particular business.

(2) No such information may, during the lifetime of that individual or so long as that business continues to be carried on, be disclosed without the consent of that individual or the person for the time being carrying on that business.

(3) This does not apply-
    (a) to disclosure permitted by section 461 (permitted disclosure of information obtained under compulsory powers), or
    (b) to the disclosure of information that is or has been available to the public from another source.

(4) A person who discloses information in contravention of this section commits an offence, unless-
    (a) he did not know, and had no reason to suspect, that the information had been disclosed under section 459, or
    (b) he took all reasonable steps and exercised all due diligence to avoid the commission of the offence.

(5) A person guilty of an offence under this section is liable-
    (a) on conviction on indictment, to imprisonment for a term not exceeding two years or a fine (or both);
    (b) on summary conviction-
        (i) in England and Wales, to imprisonment for a term not exceeding twelve months or to a fine not exceeding the statutory maximum (or both);

(ii) in Scotland or Northern Ireland, to imprisonment for a term not exceeding six months, or to a fine not exceeding the statutory maximum (or both).

GENERAL NOTE

This section re-enacts the provisions of subss.(1)-(3), (7)-(8) and (10) of s.245G of the 1985 Act, as inserted by s.12(1) the Companies (Audit, Investigations and Community Enterprise) Act 2004.

Subsections (1)-(3)

Information that relates to the private affairs of an individual or business obtained by the authorised body (currently the Financial Reporting Review Panel, FRRP) under the powers in s.459 (subs.(1)) may not be disclosed to anyone else without the consent of the party concerned (subs.(2)), except where permitted by s.461, below, or where it is otherwise publicly available (subs.(3)).

Subsections (4) and (5)

A person or body who breaches these requirements and discloses such private information commits a criminal offence, unless they can show that: (i) they did not know or suspect that it was disclosed under the provisions of s.459; or (ii) they took all reasonable steps to avoid committing such an offence (subs.(4)). The penalties for such an offence are imprisonment and/or fines (subs.(5)).

461. Permitted disclosure of information obtained under compulsory powers

(1) The prohibition in section 460 of the disclosure of information obtained in pursuance of a requirement or order under section 459 (power of authorised person to require documents etc) that relates to the private affairs of an individual or to any particular business has effect subject to the following exceptions.

(2) It does not apply to the disclosure of information for the purpose of facilitating the carrying out by the authorised person of his functions under section 456.

(3) It does not apply to disclosure to-

    (a) the Secretary of State,

    (b) the Department of Enterprise, Trade and Investment for Northern Ireland,

    (c) the Treasury,

    (d) the Bank of England,

    (e) the Financial Services Authority, or

    (f) the Commissioners for Her Majesty's Revenue and Customs.

(4) It does not apply to disclosure-

    (a) for the purpose of assisting a body designated by an order under section 46 of the Companies Act 1989 (c. 40) (delegation of functions of the Secretary of State) to exercise its functions under Part 2 of that Act;

    (b) with a view to the institution of, or otherwise for the purposes of, disciplinary proceedings relating to the performance by an accountant or auditor of his professional duties;

    (c) for the purpose of enabling or assisting the Secretary of State or the Treasury to exercise any of their functions under any of the following-

        (i) the Companies Acts,

        (ii) Part 5 of the Criminal Justice Act 1993 (c. 36) (insider dealing),

        (iii) the Insolvency Act 1986 (c. 45) or the Insolvency (Northern Ireland) Order 1989 (S.I. 1989/2405 (N.I. 19)),

        (iv) the Company Directors Disqualification Act 1986 (c. 46) or the Company Directors Disqualification (Northern Ireland) Order 2002 (S.I. 2002/3150 (N.I. 4)),

        (v) the Financial Services and Markets Act 2000 (c. 8);

    (d) for the purpose of enabling or assisting the Department of Enterprise, Trade and Investment for Northern Ireland to exercise any powers conferred on it by the enactments relating to companies, directors' disqualification or insolvency;

    (e) for the purpose of enabling or assisting the Bank of England to exercise its functions;

(f) for the purpose of enabling or assisting the Commissioners for Her Majesty's Revenue and Customs to exercise their functions;

(g) for the purpose of enabling or assisting the Financial Services Authority to exercise its functions under any of the following-

    (i) the legislation relating to friendly societies or to industrial and provident societies,

    (ii) the Building Societies Act 1986 (c. 53),

    (iii) Part 7 of the Companies Act 1989 (c. 40),

    (iv) the Financial Services and Markets Act 2000; or

(h) in pursuance of any Community obligation.

(5) It does not apply to disclosure to a body exercising functions of a public nature under legislation in any country or territory outside the United Kingdom that appear to the authorised person to be similar to his functions under section 456 for the purpose of enabling or assisting that body to exercise those functions.

(6) In determining whether to disclose information to a body in accordance with subsection (5), the authorised person must have regard to the following considerations-

(a) whether the use which the body is likely to make of the information is sufficiently important to justify making the disclosure;

(b) whether the body has adequate arrangements to prevent the information from being used or further disclosed other than-

    (i) for the purposes of carrying out the functions mentioned in that subsection, or

    (ii) for other purposes substantially similar to those for which information disclosed to the authorised person could be used or further disclosed.

(7) Nothing in this section authorises the making of a disclosure in contravention of the Data Protection Act 1998 (c. 29).

GENERAL NOTE

This section restates, with certain modifications, s.245G(3) of, and Sch.7B to, the 1985 Act, as inserted by s.12 of the Companies (Audit, Investigations and Community Enterprise) Act 2004.

Subsections (1)-(5)

The provisions of s.460 restricting onward disclosure of private information do not apply in the following circumstances (subs.(1)): (i) information obtained by an authorised body under s.456 (e.g. the Financial Reporting Review Panel, FRRP) with respect to defective accounts (subs.(2)); (ii) disclosures to the Secretary of State; the Department of Enterprise, Trade and Investment for Northern Ireland; the Treasury; the Bank of England; the Financial Services Authority ("FSA"); or HM Revenue and Customs (subs.(3)); (iii) disclosures to assist a body designated under s.46 of the 1989 Act (*cf.* the powers now available under s.1252 of the new Act) to carry out on behalf of the Secretary of State supervisory and other functions relating to the auditing profession; (iv) disclosures made in connection with disciplinary proceedings being undertaken against an accountant or auditor with respect to his professional duties; (v) information enabling the Secretary of State, the Department of Enterprise, Trade and Investment for Northern Ireland, or the Treasury to exercise their functions with respect to the Companies Acts, insider dealing legislation, insolvency legislation, legislation concerning the disqualification of directors, and the Financial Services and Markets Act 2000; (vi) information enabling the Bank of England, HM Revenue and Customs and the FSA to exercise their functions; and (vii) information in pursuance of any EU obligation (subs.(4)).

Subsections (5) and (6)

Information may also be disclosed to an overseas regulatory body carrying out similar functions to those exercised by the authorised body under s.456 (subs.(5)). However, when deciding whether to disclose information to such an overseas body, the authorised person or body in the United Kingdom must assess, first, whether the use to which the information is likely to be put is sufficiently important to justify its disclosure; and, secondly, whether there are adequate arrangements in place to prevent misuse of the information (subs.(6)).

Subsection (7)

The exceptions listed above do not override the provisions of the Data Protection Act 1998.

462. Power to amend categories of permitted disclosure

(1) The Secretary of State may by order amend section 461(3), (4) and (5).

(2) An order under this section must not-

(a) amend subsection (3) of that section (UK public authorities) by specifying a person unless the person exercises functions of a public nature (whether or not he exercises any other function);

(b) amend subsection (4) of that section (purposes for which disclosure permitted) by adding or modifying a description of disclosure unless the purpose for which the disclosure is permitted is likely to facilitate the exercise of a function of a public nature;

(c) amend subsection (5) of that section (overseas regulatory authorities) so as to have the effect of permitting disclosures to be made to a body other than one that exercises functions of a public nature in a country or territory outside the United Kingdom.

(3) An order under this section is subject to negative resolution procedure.

GENERAL NOTE

This section re-enacts subss.(4) and (6) of s.245G of the 1985 Act, as inserted by s.12 of the Companies (Audit, Investigations and Community Enterprise) Act 2004.

Subsections (1) and (2)

The Secretary of State may amend by order various disclosure provisions relating to information obtained by the authorised person or body: namely, subss.(3), (4) and (5) of s.461 (subs.(1)). However, restrictions on this power are specified in relation to each of the subsections of s.461 in subs.(2).

Subsection (3)

An order under the section is subject to the negative resolution procedure (s.1289).

CHAPTER 12

SUPPLEMENTARY PROVISIONS

Liability for false or misleading statements in reports

463. Liability for false or misleading statements in reports

(1) The reports to which this section applies are-

(a) the directors' report,

(b) the directors' remuneration report, and

(c) a summary financial statement so far as it is derived from either of those reports.

(2) A director of a company is liable to compensate the company for any loss suffered by it as a result of-

(a) any untrue or misleading statement in a report to which this section applies, or

(b) the omission from a report to which this section applies of anything required to be included in it.

(3) He is so liable only if-

(a) he knew the statement to be untrue or misleading or was reckless as to whether it was untrue or misleading, or

(b) he knew the omission to be dishonest concealment of a material fact.

(4) No person shall be subject to any liability to a person other than the company resulting from reliance, by that person or another, on information in a report to which this section applies.

(5) The reference in subsection (4) to a person being subject to a liability includes a reference to another person being entitled as against him to be granted any civil remedy or to rescind or repudiate an agreement.

(6) This section does not affect-
    (a) liability for a civil penalty, or
    (b) liability for a criminal offence.

GENERAL NOTE

This new section is concerned with the extent of directors' liability in relation to the statutory narrative reporting requirements under this Part of the Act ("accounts and reports").

Subsections (1)-(3)

A director is liable to compensate a company for any loss it incurs as a result of an untrue or misleading statement, or an omission (subs.(2)) from the directors' report (which includes the business review: s.417), the directors' remuneration report (s.420 *et seq.*) or summary financial statements derived from them (s.426 *et seq.*) (subs.(1)). However, a director will only be liable if an untrue or misleading statement is made deliberately or recklessly, or an omission amounts to dishonest concealment of a material fact (subs.(3)).

Subsections (4) and (5)

No person is liable to a party other than the company where such a third party has relied on information in a report (subs.(4)). Such liability includes a right to a civil remedy or rescission or repudiation of an agreement (subs.(5)). The effect is that third parties, such as auditors, will be liable to the company for negligence in preparing their own report.

Subsection (6)

The above liability provisions do not affect any liability for a civil penalty or for a criminal offence.

Accounting and reporting standards

464. Accounting standards

(1) In this Part "accounting standards" means statements of standard accounting practice issued by such body or bodies as may be prescribed by regulations.
(2) References in this Part to accounting standards applicable to a company's annual accounts are to such standards as are, in accordance with their terms, relevant to the company's circumstances and to the accounts.
(3) Regulations under this section may contain such transitional and other supplementary and incidental provisions as appear to the Secretary of State to be appropriate.

GENERAL NOTE

This section re-enacts s.256 of the 1985 Act, as inserted by s.19 of the 1989 Act and subsequently amended by para.1 of Sch.8 to the Companies (Audit, Investigations and Community Enterprise) Act 2004. Currently the Accounting Standards Board (ASB) is the body prescribed for the purposes of issuing accounting standards under SI 2005/697 (The Accounting Standards (Prescribed Body) Regulations 2005).

Subsections (1) and (2)

"Accounting standards" are defined as statements of standard accounting practice issued by bodies prescribed by regulations (subs.(1)), and references in Pt 15 of the Act are to such standards as are relevant to the company's circumstances (e.g. if is quoted or an entity subject to the "small companies regime") and to its financial statements (e.g. whether they are in the form of individual or consolidated accounts, or whether it engages in foreign exchange transactions) (subs.(2)).

Subsection (3)

The regulations referred to in subs.(1) may contain transitional and other supplementary and incidental provisions.

Companies qualifying as medium-sized

GENERAL NOTE

Medium-sized companies benefit from certain limited accounting and reporting exemptions. For example, s.417(7) exempts such companies from disclosing certain non-financial information in their directors' reports.

Sections 465-467 set out which companies or parent companies qualify as medium-sized. The conditions for qualification as a medium-sized company have been separated in the new Act from those relating to small companies to make them easier to follow. However, they are otherwise unchanged from the previous regime (s.247 of the 1985 Act, as inserted by s.13(1) of the 1989 Act and subsequently amended by SIs 1992/2452, 1996/189, 2004/16 and 2004/2947 (Sch.1, para.14); s.247A of the 1985 Act, inserted by reg.4 of SI 1997/220 and subsequently amended by reg.13 of SI 2005/2280; and s.249 of the 1985 Act, as substituted by s.13(3) of the 1989 Act and subsequently amended by SIs 1992/2452 and 2004/16, reg.3(3)(b)).

465. Companies qualifying as medium-sized: general

(1) A company qualifies as medium-sized in relation to its first financial year if the qualifying conditions are met in that year.

(2) A company qualifies as medium-sized in relation to a subsequent financial year-

    (a) if the qualifying conditions are met in that year and the preceding financial year;

    (b) if the qualifying conditions are met in that year and the company qualified as medium-sized in relation to the preceding financial year;

    (c) if the qualifying conditions were met in the preceding financial year and the company qualified as medium-sized in relation to that year.

(3) The qualifying conditions are met by a company in a year in which it satisfies two or more of the following requirements-

1. Turnover	Not more than £22.8 million
2. Balance sheet total	Not more than £11.4 million
3. Number of employees	Not more than 250

(4) For a period that is a company's financial year but not in fact a year the maximum figures for turnover must be proportionately adjusted.

(5) The balance sheet total means the aggregate of the amounts shown as assets in the company's balance sheet.

(6) The number of employees means the average number of persons employed by the company in the year, determined as follows-

    (a) find for each month in the financial year the number of persons employed under contracts of service by the company in that month (whether throughout the month or not),

    (b) add together the monthly totals, and

    (c) divide by the number of months in the financial year.

(7) This section is subject to section 466 (companies qualifying as medium-sized: parent companies).

GENERAL NOTE

This section is derived from s.247 of the 1985 Act, as inserted by s.13(1) of the 1989 Act and subsequently amended by SIs 1992/2452, 1996/189, 2004/16 and 2004/2947 (Sch.1, para.14); and subs.(3) of s.247A of the 1985 Act, inserted by reg.4 of SI 1997/220 and subsequently amended by reg.13 of SI 2005/2280.

Subsections (1) and (2)

A company qualifies as medium-sized in its first financial year if the qualifying conditions are met (subs.(1)). For subsequent financial years it qualifies as medium-sized if (i) the qualifying conditions are met for that year and the preceding financial year; (ii) if the qualifying conditions are met for that year and the company qualified as medium-sized in the preceding financial year; or (iii) if the qualifying conditions were met for the preceding financial year and the company qualified as medium-sized for that year (subs.(2)).

Subsections (3)-(6)

The qualifying conditions to be classified as a medium-sized company restate those in s.247(3) of the 1985 Act, as inserted by s.13(1) of the 1989 Act and most recently amended with respect to the size criteria by SI 2004/ 16, reg.2(1)-(3). Briefly these are that it must meet two or more of the requirements that: (i) [annual] turnover should not exceed £22.8m; (ii) the end-year balance sheet total should not exceed £11.4m; and (iii) the number of employees should not exceed 250 (subs.(3)). With respect to criterion (i), turnover [defined in s.474(1) in similar terms to s.262 of the 1985 Act, as inserted by s.22 of the 1989 Act] should, where appropriate, be annualised (subs.(4)). With regard to criterion (ii), the "balance sheet total" means the aggregate of the amounts shown as assets in the balance sheet [which will be determined by the prescribed format adopted for presenting the accounts] (subs.(5)). With respect to criterion (iii), the rules for determining the number of employees are spelt out in subs.(6): namely, the monthly totals of persons employed under contracts of service for the whole of that period or just a part of it should be aggregated and be divided by the number of months in the financial reporting period.

Subsection (7)

The provisions of the section are subject to s.466, below, which deals with parent companies that qualify as medium-sized.

466.   Companies qualifying as medium-sized: parent companies

(1) A parent company qualifies as a medium-sized company in relation to a financial year only if the group headed by it qualifies as a medium-sized group.

(2) A group qualifies as medium-sized in relation to the parent company's first financial year if the qualifying conditions are met in that year.

(3) A group qualifies as medium-sized in relation to a subsequent financial year of the parent company-

    (a) if the qualifying conditions are met in that year and the preceding financial year;

    (b) if the qualifying conditions are met in that year and the group qualified as medium-sized in relation to the preceding financial year;

    (c) if the qualifying conditions were met in the preceding financial year and the group qualified as medium-sized in relation to that year.

(4) The qualifying conditions are met by a group in a year in which it satisfies two or more of the following requirements-

1. Aggregate turnover	Not more than £22.8 million net (or £27.36 million gross)
2. Aggregate balance sheet total	Not more than £11.4 million net (or £13.68 million gross)
3. Aggregate number of employees	Not more than 250

(5) The aggregate figures are ascertained by aggregating the relevant figures determined in accordance with section 465 for each member of the group.

(6) In relation to the aggregate figures for turnover and balance sheet total-

    "net" means after any set-offs and other adjustments made to eliminate group transactions-

        (a) in the case of Companies Act accounts, in accordance with regulations under section 404,

        (b) in the case of IAS accounts, in accordance with international accounting standards; and

    "gross" means without those set-offs and other adjustments.

A company may satisfy any relevant requirement on the basis of either the net or the gross figure.

(7) The figures for each subsidiary undertaking shall be those included in its individual accounts for the relevant financial year, that is-

    (a) if its financial year ends with that of the parent company, that financial year, and

    (b) if not, its financial year ending last before the end of the financial year of the parent company.

If those figures cannot be obtained without disproportionate expense or undue delay, the latest available figures shall be taken.

GENERAL NOTE

This section is derived from subs.(3) of s.247A of the 1985 Act (inserted by reg.4 of SI 1997/220 and subsequently amended by reg.13 of SI 2005/2280) and from s.249 of the 1985 Act (as substituted by s.13(3) of the 1989 Act and subsequently amended by SIs 1992/2452 and 2004/16, reg.3(3)(b)).

Subsection (1)

A parent company qualifies as a medium-sized company only if the group headed by it qualifies as a "medium-sized group".

Subsections (2) and (3)

A group qualifies as medium-sized in its first financial year if the qualifying conditions are met (subs.(2)). For subsequent financial years it qualifies as medium-sized if (i) the qualifying conditions are met for that year and the preceding financial year; (ii) if the qualifying conditions are met for that year and the group qualified as medium-sized in the preceding financial year; or (iii) if the qualifying conditions were met for the preceding financial year and the group qualified as medium-sized for that year (subs.(3)).

Subsections (4)-(6)

The qualifying conditions to be classified as a medium-sized group restate those in s.249(3) of the 1985 Act, as inserted by s.13(1) of the 1989 Act and most recently amended with respect to the size criteria by SI 2004/16, reg.3(3)(b). Briefly these are that it must meet two or more of the requirements that (i) turnover should not exceed £22.8m net (or £27.36m gross); (ii) the end-year balance sheet total should not exceed £11.4m net (or £13.68m gross); and (iii) the number of employees should not exceed 250 (subs.(4)). The aggregate figures are to be determined by adding together the relevant figures for individual companies within the group as described in s.465, above (i.e. with respect to turnover, balance sheet total and number of employees) (subs.(5)). Subsection (6) defines the meaning of "net" and "gross" with respect to set-offs and other adjustments in relation to "turnover" and "balance sheet total", both for Companies Act group accounts covered by s.404 and to IAS group accounts prepared according to the provisions of s.406.

Subsection (7)

The figures from each subsidiary to be aggregated are to be those for the relevant financial year. If this is not coterminous with that of the parent company, they should be those in its last financial year ending before that of the parent company. If the necessary figures cannot be determined without undue expense or delay, the latest figures should be used.

467. Companies excluded from being treated as medium-sized

(1) A company is not entitled to take advantage of any of the provisions of this Part relating to companies qualifying as medium-sized if it was at any time within the financial year in question-

    (a) a public company,

    (b) a company that-

        (i) has permission under Part 4 of the Financial Services and Markets Act 2000 (c. 8) to carry on a regulated activity, or

        (ii) carries on insurance market activity, or

    (c) a member of an ineligible group.

(2) A group is ineligible if any of its members is-

    (a) a public company,

    (b) a body corporate (other than a company) whose shares are admitted to trading on a regulated market,

    (c) a person (other than a small company) who has permission under Part 4 of the Financial Services and Markets Act 2000 to carry on a regulated activity,

    (d) a small company that is an authorised insurance company, a banking company, an e-money issuer, an ISD investment firm or a UCITS management company, or

    (e) a person who carries on insurance market activity.

(3) A company is a small company for the purposes of subsection (2) if it qualified as small in relation to its last financial year ending on or before the end of the financial year in question.

GENERAL NOTE

This section re-enacts, with modifications, the provisions of subss.(1), (1B) and (2) of s.247A of the 1985 Act (inserted by reg.4 of SI 1997/220 and subsequently amended by reg.13 of SI 2005/2280).

Subsections (1)-(3)

The concessions available to medium-sized companies do not apply to (i) a public company; (ii) a financial services company carrying on a regulated activity or a company engaging in insurance market activity; or (iii) a member of an ineligible group (subs.(1)). With regard to the latter, a group is ineligible if any of its members is (i) a public company: (ii) a body corporate other than a company whose shares are traded on a regulated market; (iii) a person (other than a small company) carrying on a regulated activity; (iv) a small company that is an authorised insurance company, a banking company, an e-money issuer, an ISD investment firm or a UCITS management company; or (iv) a person who carries on insurance market activity (subs.(2)). For the purposes of subs.(2), a company is a small company if it was so qualified on or before the end of the financial year to which its accounts relate (subs.(3)).

The expressions "insurance market activity" and "regulated activity" are defined in s.474(1) in similar terms to the definitions given in s.262 of the 1985 Act, as substituted by s.22 of the 1989 Act and subsequently amended by reg.17(1) of SI 2005/2280. The terms "authorised insurance company", a "banking company", an "e-money issuer", an "ISD investment firm", and a "UCITS management company" are also defined in s.474.

General power to make further provision about accounts and reports

468. General power to make further provision about accounts and reports

(1) The Secretary of State may make provision by regulations about-

    (a) the accounts and reports that companies are required to prepare;

    (b) the categories of companies required to prepare accounts and reports of any description;

    (c) the form and content of the accounts and reports that companies are required to prepare;

    (d) the obligations of companies and others as regards-

        (i) the approval of accounts and reports,

        (ii) the sending of accounts and reports to members and others,

        (iii) the laying of accounts and reports before the company in general meeting,

        (iv) the delivery of copies of accounts and reports to the registrar, and

        (v) the publication of accounts and reports.

(2) The regulations may amend this Part by adding, altering or repealing provisions.

(3) But they must not amend (other than consequentially)-

    (a) section 393 (accounts to give true and fair view), or

    (b) the provisions of Chapter 11 (revision of defective accounts and reports).

(4) The regulations may create criminal offences in cases corresponding to those in which an offence is created by an existing provision of this Part. The maximum penalty for any such offence may not be greater than is provided in relation to an offence under the existing provision.

(5) The regulations may provide for civil penalties in circumstances corresponding to those within section 453(1) (civil penalty for failure to file accounts and reports). The provisions of section 453(2) to (5) apply in relation to any such penalty.

GENERAL NOTE

This is a new section and gives the Secretary of State a general power to amend Pt 15 by regulations in certain specified areas. Under the provisions of subss.(3)-(4) of s.473, below, regulations that are more onerous than existing requirements are subject to the affirmative resolution procedure (s.1290); otherwise the negative resolution procedure (s.1289) applies.

Subsection (1)

The Secretary of State may issue regulations concerning: (i) company accounts and reports; (ii) the categories of companies required to prepare accounts and reports; (iii) the form and contents of accounts and reports; (iv) the following obligations of companies and others with respect to accounts and reports: their approval, their distribution, laying them before a general meeting, filing them with the registrar, and their general publication (subs.(1)).

Subsections (2) and (3)

The regulations may amend Pt 15 by adding, altering or repealing provisions (subs.(2)), except for s.393 (accounts to represent "a true and fair view") and Ch.11 (revision of defective accounts and reports) (subs.(3)). This power, together with a number of specific powers in Pt 15 to enable the form and contents of accounts and reports to be prescribed by regulations, replaces the wider general power in s.257 of the 1985 Act.

Subsections (4) and (5)

The regulations may create criminal offences in cases corresponding to existing provisions for which there are similar offences, but the maximum penalty must not exceed that already in place (subs.(4)). The regulations may also provide for civil penalties in circumstances corresponding to those within s.453(1), concerning the failure to file accounts and reports, but in which case the provisions of subss.(2)-(5) of s.453 will apply.

Other supplementary provisions

469. Preparation and filing of accounts in euros

(1) The amounts set out in the annual accounts of a company may also be shown in the same accounts translated into euros.

(2) When complying with section 441 (duty to file accounts and reports), the directors of a company may deliver to the registrar an additional copy of the company's annual accounts in which the amounts have been translated into euros.

(3) In both cases-
  (a) the amounts must have been translated at the exchange rate prevailing on the date to which the balance sheet is made up, and
  (b) that rate must be disclosed in the notes to the accounts.

(4) For the purposes of sections 434 and 435 (requirements in connection with published accounts) any additional copy of the company's annual accounts delivered to the registrar under subsection (2) above shall be treated as statutory accounts of the company.

In the case of such a copy, references in those sections to the auditor's report on the company's annual accounts shall be read as references to the auditor's report on the annual accounts of which it is a copy.

GENERAL NOTE

This section re-enacts s.242B of the 1985 Act, as inserted by SI 1992/2452, but replacing references to "ECUs" with "euros".

Subsections (1)-(3)

Companies may additionally show amounts in their annual accounts in euros (subs.(1)), and the directors may file with the registrar an additional copy of their accounts translated into euros (subs.(2)). However, in both cases the translation must be made at the exchange rate prevailing on the date of the end-year balance sheet, and this rate must be disclosed in notes to the accounts (subs.(3)).

Subsection (4)

For the purposes of ss.434-435 (requirements in connection with published accounts), the additional copy filed with the registrar will be treated as statutory accounts, and references in the auditor's report to the accounts will be interpreted accordingly.

470.   Power to apply provisions to banking partnerships

(1) The Secretary of State may by regulations apply to banking partnerships, subject to such exceptions, adaptations and modifications as he considers appropriate, the provisions of this Part (and of regulations made under this Part) applying to banking companies.

(2) A "banking partnership" means a partnership which has permission under Part 4 of the Financial Services and Markets Act 2000 (c. 8).

But a partnership is not a banking partnership if it has permission to accept deposits only for the purpose of carrying on another regulated activity in accordance with that permission.

(3) Expressions used in this section that are also used in the provisions regulating activities under the Financial Services and Markets Act 2000 have the same meaning here as they do in those provisions.

See section 22 of that Act, orders made under that section and Schedule 2 to that Act.

(4) Regulations under this section are subject to affirmative resolution procedure.

GENERAL NOTE

This section re-enacts s.255D of the 1985 Act, as inserted by s.18(2) of the 1989 Act and subsequently amended by SI 2001/3649, art.16.

Subsections (1) and (2)

The Secretary of State may issue regulations modifying the accounting and reporting provisions of this Part of the Act that apply to banking companies in order that they may be applied to "banking partnerships" (being partnerships authorised under Pt 4 of the Financial Services and Markets Act 2000 and as otherwise defined in subs.(2)) (subs.(1)).

Subsection (3)

Expressions used in the Financial Services and Markets Act 2000 have the same meaning in s.470.

Subsection (4)

Regulations issued under this section are subject to the affirmative resolution procedure (s.1290).

471.   Meaning of "annual accounts" and related expressions

(1) In this Part a company's "annual accounts", in relation to a financial year, means-
    (a) the company's individual accounts for that year (see section 394), and
    (b) any group accounts prepared by the company for that year (see sections 398 and 399).

This is subject to section 408 (option to omit individual profit and loss account from annual accounts where information given in group accounts).

(2) In the case of an unquoted company, its "annual accounts and reports" for a financial year are-
    (a) its annual accounts,
    (b) the directors' report, and
    (c) the auditor's report on those accounts and the directors' report (unless the company is exempt from audit).

(3) In the case of a quoted company, its "annual accounts and reports" for a financial year are-
    (a) its annual accounts,

(b) the directors' remuneration report,

(c) the directors' report, and

(d) the auditor's report on those accounts, on the auditable part of the directors' remuneration report and on the directors' report.

GENERAL NOTE

This section replaces s.262(1) of the 1985 Act (as substituted by s.22 of the 1989 Act and subsequently amended) and s.238(1A) of the 1985 Act (as inserted by s.10 of the 1989 Act and subsequently amended by reg.10 of SI 2002/1986 and Sch.1, para.5(b), of SI 2005/3442). It provides definitions of the terms "annual accounts" and "annual accounts and reports" for the purpose of this Part of the Act, the meaning being different for unquoted (subs.(2)) and quoted companies (subs.(3)).

Subsection (1)

"Annual accounts" in this Part of the Act means a company's "individual accounts" (s.394) and any "group accounts" prepared by the company (ss.398-399). However, the latter is subject to the proviso in s.408, providing an option to omit an individual profit and loss account where the relevant information is included in group accounts.

Subsections (2) and (3)

The "annual accounts" for an unquoted company comprise: its annual accounts, the directors' report, and - except where the company is exempt from the statutory audit (s.477 *et seq.*) - the auditor's report on these two documents (subs.(2)). For a quoted company, the annual accounts comprise: its annual accounts, the directors' remuneration report, the directors' report, and the auditor's report on the accounts, the directors' report, and the auditable part of the directors' remuneration report (subs.(3)).

472. Notes to the accounts

(1) Information required by this Part to be given in notes to a company's annual accounts may be contained in the accounts or in a separate document annexed to the accounts.

(2) References in this Part to a company's annual accounts, or to a balance sheet or profit and loss account, include notes to the accounts giving information which is required by any provision of this Act or international accounting standards, and required or allowed by any such provision to be given in a note to company accounts.

GENERAL NOTE

This section, concerning the notes to a company's accounts, re-enacts s.261 of the 1985 Act, as inserted by s.22 of the 1989 Act and subsequently amended by Sch.1, para.19, of SI 2004/2947.

Subsections (1) and (2)

Information required by this Part of the Act to be disclosed in notes to a company's annual accounts can be disclosed within the accounts or in a separate annexed document (subs.(1)). More generally, references in this Part of the Act to the annual accounts, or to the balance sheet or profit and loss account, should be taken to include information that is required by the Act or (where relevant) international accounting standards to be disclosed within those financial statements and/or in notes thereto (subs.(2)).

473. Parliamentary procedure for certain regulations under this Part

(1) This section applies to regulations under the following provisions of this Part-

section 396 (Companies Act individual accounts),

section 404 (Companies Act group accounts),

section 409 (information about related undertakings),

section 412 (information about directors' benefits: remuneration, pensions and compensation for loss of office),

section 416 (contents of directors' report: general),

section 421 (contents of directors' remuneration report),

section 444 (filing obligations of companies subject to small companies regime), section 445 (filing obligations of medium-sized companies),

section 468 (general power to make further provision about accounts and reports).

(2) Any such regulations may make consequential amendments or repeals in other provisions of this Act, or in other enactments.

(3) Regulations that-

(a) restrict the classes of company which have the benefit of any exemption, exception or special provision,

(b) require additional matter to be included in a document of any class, or

(c) otherwise render the requirements of this Part more onerous,

are subject to affirmative resolution procedure.

(4) Otherwise, the regulations are subject to negative resolution procedure.

GENERAL NOTE

This section specifies the Parliamentary procedure that must be followed in connection with regulations made under the various provisions of this Part of the Act. These regulations replace the requirements as to the form and content of accounts and reports previously contained in Schedules to Pt 7 of the 1985 Act, "Accounts and Audit", (i.e. Schs 4-10A, as inserted and amended), and in relation to the general regulation-making power in s.468.

The section is new, but it follows s.257 of the 1985 Act, inserted by s.20 of the 1989 Act and subsequently amended by s.13 of the Companies (Audit, Investigations and Community Enterprise) Act 2004, in requiring the affirmative resolution procedure (s.1290) for regulations which add to the documents required to be prepared by companies, restrict the exemptions available to particular classes or types of company, add to the information to be included in any particular document, or otherwise make the requirements more onerous. Other regulations are subject to the negative resolution procedure (s.1289).

The Secretary of State also has power to issue eight further sets of regulations and two types of order, not covered by the provisions of s.473. (For details, see the "General Note" introducing Part 15, before s.380 above.)

Subsections (1) and (2)

Under subs.(1), regulations may be issued with respect to the following matters dealt with in this part of the Act:

- Companies Act individual accounts (s.396);
- Companies Act group accounts (s.404);
- information about related undertakings (s.409);
- information about directors' benefits (remuneration, pensions and compensation for loss of office) (s.412);
- content of directors' report (s.416);
- content of directors' remuneration report (s.421);
- filing obligations of companies subject to the "small companies regime" (s.444);
- filing obligations of medium-sized companies (s.445); and
- general power to make further provision about accounts and reports (s.468).

Such regulations can make consequential amendments or repeals (subs.(2)).

Subsections (3) and (4)

Regulations that make the requirements more onerous are subject to the affirmative resolution procedure (s.1290). Other regulations are subject to the negative resolution procedure (s.1289).

474. Minor definitions

(1) In this Part-

"e-money issuer" means a person who has permission under Part 4 of the Financial Services and Markets Act 2000 (c. 8) to carry on the activity of issuing electronic money within the meaning of article 9B of the Financial Services and Markets Act 2000 (Regulated Activities) Order 2001 (S.I. 2001/544);

"group" means a parent undertaking and its subsidiary undertakings;

"IAS Regulation" means EC Regulation No. 1606/ 2002 of the European Parliament and of the Council of 19 July 2002 on the application of international accounting standards;

"included in the consolidation", in relation to group accounts, or "included in consolidated group accounts", means that the undertaking is included in the accounts by the method of full (and not proportional) consolidation, and references to an undertaking excluded from consolidation shall be construed accordingly;

"international accounting standards" means the international accounting standards, within the meaning of the IAS Regulation, adopted from time to time by the European Commission in accordance with that Regulation;

"ISD investment firm" has the meaning given by the Glossary forming part of the Handbook made by the Financial Services Authority under the Financial Services and Markets Act 2000;

"profit and loss account", in relation to a company that prepares IAS accounts, includes an income statement or other equivalent financial statement required to be prepared by international accounting standards;

"regulated activity" has the meaning given in section 22 of the Financial Services and Markets Act 2000, except that it does not include activities of the kind specified in any of the following provisions of the Financial Services and Markets Act 2000 (Regulated Activities) Order 2001 (S.I. 2001/544)-

    (a) article 25A (arranging regulated mortgage contracts),

    (b) article 25B (arranging regulated home reversion plans),

    (c) article 25C (arranging regulated home purchase plans),

    (d) article 39A (assisting administration and performance of a contract of insurance),

    (e) article 53A (advising on regulated mortgage contracts),

    (f) article 53B (advising on regulated home reversion plans),

    (g) article 53C (advising on regulated home purchase plans),

    (h) article 21 (dealing as agent), article 25 (arranging deals in investments) or article 53 (advising on investments) where the activity concerns relevant investments that are not contractually based investments (within the meaning of article 3 of that Order), or

    (i) article 64 (agreeing to carry on a regulated activity of the kind mentioned in paragraphs (a) to (h));

"turnover", in relation to a company, means the amounts derived from the provision of goods and services falling within the company's ordinary activities, after deduction of-

    (a) trade discounts,

    (b) value added tax, and

    (c) any other taxes based on the amounts so derived;

"UCITS management company" has the meaning given by the Glossary forming part of the Handbook made by the Financial Services Authority under the Financial Services and Markets Act 2000 (c. 8).

(2) In the case of an undertaking not trading for profit, any reference in this Part to a profit and loss account is to an income and expenditure account.

References to profit and loss and, in relation to group accounts, to a consolidated profit and loss account shall be construed accordingly.

GENERAL NOTE

This section replaces subss.(1)-(2) of s.262 of the 1985 Act, as substituted by s.22 of the 1989 Act and subsequently amended. It contains various definitions relating to this Part of the Act.

Other definitions of frequently used terms can be found in Pt 38, "Companies: interpretation", ss.1158-1174. There is no direct equivalent for s.262A of the 1985 Act, as inserted by s.22 of the 1989 Act and subsequently amended, which gave an index of defined expressions used in the corresponding Part of the 1985 Act. However, Sch.8 to the new Act provides a comprehensive index of defined expressions used in the statute.

Subsections (1) and (2)

Subsection (1) provides various definitions, including "e-money issuer", "group", "IAS Regulation", "consolidation" (with respect to accounts), "international accounting standards" (often referred to by the acronym "IAS"), "ISD investment firm", "profit and loss account", "regulated activity" (under the Financial Services and Markets Act 2000), "turnover", and "UCITS management company". Subsection (2) indicates that for a not-for-profit entity the expression "an income and expenditure account" is more suitable than "profit and loss account", and references in this Part of the Act should be altered for such entities and be interpreted appropriately.

PART 16

AUDIT

GENERAL NOTE

This Part brings together various provisions on the audit of companies from the 1985 Act. It also introduces a number of significant changes to the law on auditing. Much of the law in this area reflects EU Company Law Directives, including parts of the Fourth (78/660/EEC) on company accounts and Seventh (83/349/EEC) on consolidated accounts, as well as the Eighth on audit. The former Eighth Directive (84/253/EEC) has recently been replaced by a new Company Law Directive on Audit (adopted and published in *The Official Journal of the European Communities* on June 9, 2006, its provisions coming into force from June 29, 2006: see [2006] O.J. L157/87, http://eur-lex.europa.eu/LexUriServ/site/en/oj/2006/l.157/l.15720060609en00870107.pdf). The application of its provisions was anticipated when the present Act was being drafted, so its requirements are accommodated in the new legislation.

The Auditing Practices Board ("APB"), which is part of the Financial Reporting Council ("FRC"), sets standards for the auditing profession in the United Kingdom and Ireland. From December 2004 onwards it has published a series of International Standards on Auditing ("ISAs"), modified to apply to the United Kingdom and Ireland. Simultaneously with the publication of the ISAs, the APB issued a "Glossary of terms" and an International Standard on Quality Control ("ISQC"), tailored to requirements in the British Isles. Subsequently it has also issued a series of ethical standards. The texts of the ISAs and accompanying statements can be accessed at www.frc.org.uk/apb/publications/isa.cfm. Also relevant are Bulletins and Practice Notes published by the APB, although these are persuasive rather than prescriptive. They can be accessed respectively at www.frc.org.uk/apb/publications/bulletins.cfm and www.frc.org.uk/apb/publications/practice.cfm. The APB has also issued a series of Investment Circular Reporting Standards (www.frc.org.uk/apb/publications/sicrs.cfm).

The government has to decide how to implement the various audit provisions required by the European Union's Eighth Directive, which has a deadline of June 29, 2008 and will therefore need to be brought in earlier than the October 2008 backstop date for the Act as a whole. Some of the Pt 16 provisions implement articles in the Eighth Directive, including some of the changes to the resignation statement requirements (s.519 of the Act; art.38 of the Directive) and the requirement for the "senior statutory auditor" to sign audit reports (ss.504-505 of the Act; art.28 of the Directive). It will presumably be necessary, therefore, (i) to amend the relevant provisions of the 1989 Act; or (ii) to introduce either parts or the whole of Pt 16 so that there is compliance with the Eighth Directive deadline of June 29, 2008.

Apart from the European Union's Eighth Directive requirements, the main changes to the audit provisions are:

- the introduction of a criminal offence for auditors where they "knowingly or recklessly" cause their report to include anything that is misleading, false or deceptive; or "knowingly or recklessly" cause their report to omit a statement indicating that there is a problem with the accounts (s.507);
- the introduction of liability limitation agreements (ss.532-538); and
- giving members of quoted companies the right to raise audit concerns at the general meeting at which the accounts are laid (ss.527-531).

The Secretary of State has power under this Part of the Act to issue the following regulations:

- general power of amendment of regulations (s.484);
- disclosure of terms of audit appointment (s.493);
- disclosure of services provided by auditor or associates and related remuneration (s.494);
- terms of liability limitation agreement (s.535); and
- disclosure of [liability limitation] agreement by company (s.538).

The Secretary of State is also empowered by s.504 to make an order appointing a body to oversee the identification and functions of the "senior statutory auditor". Section 483 gives Scottish ministers the power to make an order directing that a company operating in the public sector should have its accounts audited by the Auditor General for Scotland ("AGS").

Definitions

Minor definitions in this Part of the Act are given in s.539. The meanings of "appropriate audit authority" and "major audit" are given in s.525; and "quoted company" in s.531. Schedule 8 further provides an alphabetical "Index of defined expressions", giving cross references to sections where individual terms are defined.

CHAPTER I

REQUIREMENT FOR AUDITED ACCOUNTS

GENERAL NOTE

This chapter restates the existing requirement for companies to produce audited accounts, previously in s.235(1) of the 1985 Act; and the existing exemptions, previously in ss.249A-249E of that Act.

The main change from existing law in this Chapter is to make it possible for the United Kingdom Comptroller and Auditor General (or the public sector auditors associated with devolved administrations) to carry out public sector audits of the accounts of certain non-departmental public bodies that are registered companies. (See also Pt 42, s.1226 *et seq.*)

Originally it was also proposed to replace the reporting accountant with an independent examiner as the person who reports on the accounts of small charitable companies in lieu of audit. However, the clauses that would have implemented this change were removed from the Bill at a late stage and the role of the reporting accountant instead dealt with in the Charities Bill. Consequently, the special treatment of small charitable companies with respect to the audit of their accounts is now dealt with in ss.32-33 of the Charities Act 2006 (see www.opsi.gov.uk/acts/acts2006/20060050.htm#aofs; and Sch.9, which removes the special provisions in the 1985 Act relating to the accounts and audit of charitable companies).

Requirement for audited accounts

475. Requirement for audited accounts

(1) A company's annual accounts for a financial year must be audited in accordance with this Part unless the company-
  (a) is exempt from audit under-
    section 477 (small companies), or
    section 480 (dormant companies);
    or
  (b) is exempt from the requirements of this Part under section 482 (non-profit-making companies subject to public sector audit).
(2) A company is not entitled to any such exemption unless its balance sheet contains a statement by the directors to that effect.
(3) A company is not entitled to exemption under any of the provisions mentioned in subsection (1)(a) unless its balance sheet contains a statement by the directors to the effect that-
  (a) the members have not required the company to obtain an audit of its accounts for the year in question in accordance with section 476, and
  (b) the directors acknowledge their responsibilities for complying with the requirements of this Act with respect to accounting records and the preparation of accounts.
(4) The statement required by subsection (2) or (3) must appear on the balance sheet above the signature required by section 414.

GENERAL NOTE

This section sets out the requirement for companies to have their accounts audited. It broadly corresponds to s.235(1) and s.249B(4)-(5) of the 1985 Act, as amended.

Subsection (1)

This restates the requirement for each company to have its annual accounts audited, unless it takes advantage of one of the exemptions in subsequent sections (namely for small companies and dormant companies); or unless the company is exempt under s.482 because it is subject to a public sector audit.

Subsections (2)-(4)

Directors must state on the balance sheet if they are taking advantage of an exemption (subs.(2)). The company is not entitled to exemption unless the statement says that the members have not required an audit in accordance with s.476, and that the directors take responsibility for producing compliant accounts (subs.(3)). The statement required by subss.(2) or (3) must appear on the balance sheet above the signature required by s.414 (subs.(4)).

476.   Right of members to require audit

(1) The members of a company that would otherwise be entitled to exemption from audit under any of the provisions mentioned in section 475(1)(a) may by notice under this section require it to obtain an audit of its accounts for a financial year.
(2) The notice must be given by-
    (a) members representing not less in total than 10% in nominal value of the company's issued share capital, or any class of it, or
    (b) if the company does not have a share capital, not less than 10% in number of the members of the company.
(3) The notice may not be given before the financial year to which it relates and must be given not later than one month before the end of that year.

GENERAL NOTE

This section sets out the right of members to require an audit where a company is entitled to exemption from audit. It corresponds to s.249B(2) of the 1985 Act, as amended.

Subsection (1)

This section restates the right of shareholders to require an audit by giving notice, even if the company qualifies for one of the audit exemptions referred to in s.475(1).

Subsection (2)

The notice must be given by holders representing not less than ten per cent of the nominal capital of a company, or of any class of its shares, or - if it has no share capital - not less than ten per cent of its members.

Subsection (3)

The notice may not be given before the financial year to which it relates has commenced nor later than one month before its end.

Exemption from audit: small companies

GENERAL NOTE

Sections 477-479 restate the exemption from audit for small companies. A company must not only meet the general small company criteria in s.382, but its turnover and balance sheet totals must fall below £5.6m and £2.8m respectively.

477.   Small companies: conditions for exemption from audit

(1) A company that meets the following conditions in respect of a financial year is exempt from the requirements of this Act relating to the audit of accounts for that year.
(2) The conditions are-
    (a) that the company qualifies as a small company in relation to that year,
    (b) that its turnover in that year is not more than £5.6 million, and

    (c) that its balance sheet total for that year is not more than £2.8 million.

(3) For a period which is a company's financial year but not in fact a year the maximum figure for turnover shall be proportionately adjusted.

(4) For the purposes of this section-

    (a) whether a company qualifies as a small company shall be determined in accordance with section 382(1) to (6), and

    (b) "balance sheet total" has the same meaning as in that section.

(5) This section has effect subject to-

    section 475(2) and (3) (requirements as to statements to be contained in balance sheet),

    section 476 (right of members to require audit),

    section 478 (companies excluded from small companies exemption), and

    section 479 (availability of small companies exemption in case of group company).

GENERAL NOTE

This section sets out the conditions for a company to be exempt from the statutory audit. It broadly corresponds to s.249A of the 1985 Act, as amended.

Subsection (1)

A company that meets certain requirements (set out in subs.(2) and which does not meet the conditions referred to in s.478, below) is exempt from the audit requirements of the Act. (In practice, this means that public companies and some financial services companies, as well as large private companies are excluded from the exemption.)

Subsections (2) and (3)

The conditions for audit exemption are, first, that the company qualifies as a "small company" for the year and is not excluded by virtue of the requirements of s.384 (i.e. it is not a public company or engaged in the financial services or insurance industries); and, secondly, that its annual turnover does not exceed £5.6m, and its balance sheet total does not exceed £2.8m (subs.(2)). For periods other than a year, the figure for turnover should be adjusted pro rata (subs.(3)).

Subsection (4)

This section defines "balance sheet total" and "small company" in terms of the criteria applied in s.382.

Subsection (5)

The section is subject to s.475 (requirements as to statements to be contained in the balance sheet), s.476 (right of members to require an audit), s.478 (companies excluded from the small companies exemption) and s.479 (availability of small companies exemption in the case of a group company).

478. Companies excluded from small companies exemption

A company is not entitled to the exemption conferred by section 477 (small companies) if it was at any time within the financial year in question-

    (a) a public company,

    (b) a company that-

        (i) is an authorised insurance company, a banking company, an e-money issuer, an ISD investment firm or a UCITS management company, or

        (ii) carries on insurance market activity, or

    (c) a special register body as defined in section 117(1) of the Trade Union and Labour Relations (Consolidation) Act 1992 (c. 52) or an employers' association as defined in section 122 of that Act or Article 4 of the Industrial Relations (Northern Ireland) Order 1992 (S.I. 1992/807 (N.I. 5)).

GENERAL NOTE

This section identifies companies that are excluded from the small companies audit exemption and corresponds to parts of ss.248(2) and 249B of the 1985 Act, as amended, although with some changes.

A company is not entitled to the small companies exemption if it is a public company, a banking company, an e-money issuer, an ISD investment firm, a UCITS management company, carries on insurance market activity, or is a special register body as defined in the Trade Union and Labour Relations (Consolidation) Act 1992 or the Industrial Relations (Northern

Ireland) Order 1992 (SI 1992/807 (N.I. 5)). (The terms "insurance company" and "banking company" are respectively defined in ss.1165 and 1164; and "e-money issuer", "ISD investment firm", and "UCITS management company" in s.539.)

479. Availability of small companies exemption in case of group company

(1) A company is not entitled to the exemption conferred by section 477 (small companies) in respect of a financial year during any part of which it was a group company unless-
    (a) the conditions specified in subsection (2) below are met, or
    (b) subsection (3) applies.
(2) The conditions are-
    (a) that the group-
        (i) qualifies as a small group in relation to that financial year, and
        (ii) was not at any time in that year an ineligible group;
    (b) that the group's aggregate turnover in that year is not more than £5.6 million net (or £6.72 million gross);
    (c) that the group's aggregate balance sheet total for that year is not more than £2.8 million net (or £3.36 million gross).
(3) A company is not excluded by subsection (1) if, throughout the whole of the period or periods during the financial year when it was a group company, it was both a subsidiary undertaking and dormant.
(4) In this section-
    (a) "group company" means a company that is a parent company or a subsidiary undertaking, and
    (b) "the group", in relation to a group company, means that company together with all its associated undertakings.
 For this purpose undertakings are associated if one is a subsidiary undertaking of the other or both are subsidiary undertakings of a third undertaking.
(5) For the purposes of this section-
    (a) whether a group qualifies as small shall be determined in accordance with section 383 (companies qualifying as small: parent companies);
    (b) "ineligible group" has the meaning given by section 384(2) and (3);
    (c) a group's aggregate turnover and aggregate balance sheet total shall be determined as for the purposes of section 383;
    (d) "net" and "gross" have the same meaning as in that section;
    (e) a company may meet any relevant requirement on the basis of either the gross or the net figure.
(6) The provisions mentioned in subsection (5) apply for the purposes of this section as if all the bodies corporate in the group were companies.

GENERAL NOTE

   This section sets out the conditions for a company in a group qualifying for a small company exemption. The provisions broadly correspond to s.249AA of the 1985 Act, as amended, but removing the special treatment of charities.

Subsections (1) and (2)

   A group company is not entitled to the small companies exemption (subs.(1)) unless the group qualifies as small, its aggregate balance sheet total is not more than £2.8m net (or £3.36m gross) and group annual turnover does not exceed £5.6m net (or £6.72m gross) (subs.(2)).

Subsection (3)

   A group company may nevertheless be exempt if it is a subsidiary and has been dormant throughout the financial year.

Subsections (4)-(6)

These subsections define the meaning for this section of "group company", "the group" (subs.(4)), an "ineligible group", a group's aggregate turnover and its aggregate balance sheet total, and the use of the terms "net" and "gross" in this context, either being sufficient to qualify (subs.(5)). For the purpose of subs.(5), all the bodies corporate within a group are to be regarded as companies (subs.(6)). It also indicates that whether or not a group qualifies as small should be determined in accordance with the requirements of s.383 (subs.(5)).

Exemption from audit: dormant companies

GENERAL NOTE

Sections 480-481 restate the exemption from audit available to dormant companies under s.249AA of the 1985 Act, as inserted by the Companies Act 1985 (Audit Exemption)(Amendment) Regulations 2000 (SI 2000/1430, reg.3, and subsequently amended by SI 2001/3649, art.13). "Dormant" is defined in s.1169. Certain financial services companies are excluded from using the exemption, even if they are dormant.

480.   Dormant companies: conditions for exemption from audit

(1) A company is exempt from the requirements of this Act relating to the audit of accounts in respect of a financial year if-

    (a) it has been dormant since its formation, or

    (b) it has been dormant since the end of the previous financial year and the following conditions are met.

(2) The conditions are that the company-

    (a) as regards its individual accounts for the financial year in question-

        (i) is entitled to prepare accounts in accordance with the small companies regime (see sections 381 to 384), or

        (ii) would be so entitled but for having been a public company or a member of an ineligible group, and

    (b) is not required to prepare group accounts for that year.

(3) This section has effect subject to-

    section 475(2) and (3) (requirements as to statements to be contained in balance sheet),

    section 476 (right of members to require audit), and

    section 481 (companies excluded from dormant companies exemption).

GENERAL NOTE

This section sets out the conditions for a dormant company to be exempt from audit. Its provisions correspond in part to s.249AA of the 1985 Act, as amended.

Subsections (1) and (2)

A company that has been dormant since its foundation, or which has been dormant since the end of the previous financial year, is exempt from the Act's audit requirements (subs.(1)). However, to so qualify for exemption, the company has to be a "small company" under ss.381-384 or would have so qualified but for being a public company or a member of an ineligible group (subs.(2)).

Subsection (3)

The section is subject to the requirements regarding statements to be included in a balance sheet (s.475(2), (3)); the right of members to require an audit (s.476); and rules excluding companies from the dormant companies audit exemption (s.481, below).

481.   Companies excluded from dormant companies exemption

A company is not entitled to the exemption conferred by section 480 (dormant companies) if it was at any time within the financial year in question a company that-

(a) is an authorised insurance company, a banking company, an e-money issuer, an ISD investment firm or a UCITS management company, or

(b) carries on insurance market activity.

GENERAL NOTE

This section indicates what companies are excluded from the dormant companies audit exemption, its provisions corresponding in part to those of s.249AA of the 1985 Act, as amended.

A dormant company is not entitled to the audit exemption under s.480 if it is an authorised insurance company, a banking company, an e-money issuer, an ISD investment firm, a UCITS management company, or carries on insurance market activity. (The terms "insurance company" and "banking company" are respectively defined in ss.1165 and 1164; and "e-money issuer", "ISD investment firm", and "UCITS management company" in s.539).

Companies subject to public sector audit

GENERAL NOTE

Sections 482–483 contain the only wholly new provisions in this chapter. They are intended to enable a public sector auditor to audit non-commercial, public sector bodies that happen to be constituted as companies.

482. Non-profit-making companies subject to public sector audit

(1) The requirements of this Part as to audit of accounts do not apply to a company for a financial year if it is non-profit-making and its accounts-
  (a) are subject to audit-
    (i) by the Comptroller and Auditor General by virtue of an order under section 25(6) of the Government Resources and Accounts Act 2000 (c. 20), or
    (ii) by the Auditor General for Wales by virtue of section 96, or an order under section 144, of the Government of Wales Act 1998 (c. 38);
  (b) are accounts-
    (i) in relation to which section 21 of the Public Finance and Accountability (Scotland) Act 2000 (asp 1) (audit of accounts: Auditor General for Scotland) applies, or
    (ii) that are subject to audit by the Auditor General for Scotland by virtue of an order under section 483 (Scottish public sector companies: audit by Auditor General for Scotland); or
  (c) are subject to audit by the Comptroller and Auditor General for Northern Ireland by virtue of an order under Article 5(3) of the Audit and Accountability (Northern Ireland) Order 2003 (S.I. 2003/418 (N.I. 5)).

(2) In the case of a company that is a parent company or a subsidiary undertaking, subsection (1) applies only if every group undertaking is non-profit-making.

(3) In this section "non-profit-making" has the same meaning as in Article 48 of the Treaty establishing the European Community.

(4) This section has effect subject to section 475(2) (balance sheet to contain statement that company entitled to exemption under this section).

GENERAL NOTE

The provisions of this section, dealing with the audit of not-for-profit companies, are new.

Subsection (1)

Any non-departmental public body that is a company and is a not-for-profit entity is exempt from a Companies Act statutory audit, so long as it has been made subject by order to a public sector audit.

For most United Kingdom bodies, such an order can be made under the Government Resources and Accounts Act 2000, and the body in question will then be audited by the National Audit Office on behalf of the United Kingdom Comptroller and Auditor General. Under the Audit and Accountability (Northern Ireland) Order 2003, an order can make a body subject to audit by the Comptroller and Auditor General for Northern Ireland. And under ss.96 and 144 of the Government of Wales Act 1998, an order can make a body subject to audit by the Auditor General for Wales.

Some Scottish bodies are subject to public sector audit by the Auditor General for Scotland ("AGS") under statute, namely the Public Finance and Accountability (Scotland) Act 2000. But there is at present no order-making power to make further companies subject to audit by the AGS. Such a power is conferred by the following section.

The companies exempted by this section are not subject to the Fourth Company Law Directive. This Directive is based on Art.44(2)(g) (formerly 54(3)(g)) of the EC Treaty, and Art.48 of the Treaty excludes from the scope of Art.44 undertakings that are non-profit-making. That is why subs.(3) gives "non-profit-making" the same meaning as in the Treaty.

Subsection (2)

A group company can benefit from the exemption, but only if every company in the group is non-profit-making.

Subsection (3)

This subsection defines the meaning of "non-profit-making" - which is used instead of the preferable (and more accurate) term, "not-for-profit", presumably because it is the phrase used in the EC Treaty (see note to subs.(1) above).

Subsection (4)

In order to comply with s.475(2), the directors of a company that uses this exemption must make a statement on its balance sheet that the company is eligible for such exemption.

483.   Scottish public sector companies: audit by Auditor General for Scotland

(1) The Scottish Ministers may by order provide for the accounts of a company having its registered office in Scotland to be audited by the Auditor General for Scotland.

(2) An order under subsection (1) may be made in relation to a company only if it appears to the Scottish Ministers that the company-

    (a) exercises in or as regards Scotland functions of a public nature none of which relate to reserved matters (within the meaning of the Scotland Act 1998 (c. 46)), or

    (b) is entirely or substantially funded from a body having accounts falling within paragraph (a) or (b) of subsection (3).

(3) Those accounts are-

    (a) accounts in relation to which section 21 of the Public Finance and Accountability (Scotland) Act 2000 (asp 1) (audit of accounts: Auditor General for Scotland) applies,

    (b) accounts which are subject to audit by the Auditor General for Scotland by virtue of an order under this section.

(4) An order under subsection (1) may make such supplementary or consequential provision (including provision amending an enactment) as the Scottish Ministers think expedient.

(5) An order under subsection (1) shall not be made unless a draft of the statutory instrument containing it has been laid before, and approved by resolution of, the Scottish Parliament.

GENERAL NOTE

This new section creates a power whereby Scottish Ministers can provide that a company should have its accounts audited by the Auditor General for Scotland ("AGS"). If an order is made under this section providing that a company should have a public sector audit by the AGS, and if that company is non-profit making, then it will benefit from the exemption from this Part of the Act described in the previous section.

The Office of AGS was created by the Scotland Act 1998. The AGS is an independent official responsible for auditing, or arranging for the audit, of the accounts of bodies responsible for public expenditure.

Subsection (1)

The Scottish Ministers may, by Statutory Instrument, require the accounts of a company registered in Scotland and within subs.(2) to be audited by the AGS.

Subsections (2) and (3)

Whether or not companies should have their accounts audited by the AGS depends on their functions or their funding. Scottish Ministers can designate a company under this power if its functions are public functions that are all covered by the Scottish Parliament's responsibilities; or if the company receives all or most of its funding from a public body already audited by the AGS. In the case of the latter, the funding body may be audited by the AGS because it is covered by the Public Finance and Accountability (Scotland) Act 2000, s.21, or because it is itself a company that Scottish Ministers have made auditable by the AGS by a previous order under this section.

Subsection (4)

An order referring the accounts of a company to the AGS may include supplementary or consequential provisions, including the amendment of any enactment (as defined in s.1293).

Subsection (5)

An order remitting the accounts of a company to the AGS requires the submission of the relevant Statutory Instrument in draft to the Scottish Parliament and its approval by resolution of that Parliament.

General power of amendment by regulations

484.   General power of amendment by regulations

(1) The Secretary of State may by regulations amend this Chapter or section 539 (minor definitions) so far as applying to this Chapter by adding, altering or repealing provisions.
(2) The regulations may make consequential amendments or repeals in other provisions of this Act, or in other enactments.
(3) Regulations under this section imposing new requirements, or rendering existing requirements more onerous, are subject to affirmative resolution procedure.
(4) Other regulations under this section are subject to negative resolution procedure.

GENERAL NOTE

This section provides a power for the Secretary of State to change the provisions on the requirement for audited accounts in Ch.1. Taken together with s.468, it broadly restates the power in s.257 of the 1985 Act.

Subsection (1)

This subsection gives power to the Secretary of State to amend this Chapter or s.539 (containing minor definitions) by adding, altering or repealing provisions.

Subsections (2) and (3)

The regulations may make consequential changes to other legislation (subs.(2)), but these are subject to affirmative resolution (see s.1290) if they extend the requirements for audit, or otherwise make requirements more onerous (subs.(3)).

Subsection (4)

Other regulations and amendments thereto are subject to negative resolution (see s.1289).

CHAPTER 2

APPOINTMENT OF AUDITORS

GENERAL NOTE

This Chapter broadly restates the existing law in ss.384-388A of the 1985 Act on the way in which shareholders appoint a company's auditors, with some minor changes. The provisions are reorganised to deal with private and public companies separately. The Chapter also introduces a new power for the Secretary of State to require disclosure of the terms of audit appointments.

Private companies

GENERAL NOTE
Sections 485-488 restate the law on appointment of auditors of private companies, providing that auditors are generally to be appointed by shareholders by ordinary resolution. For any financial year other than the first, this will generally be done within 28 days of the circulation to a company's shareholders of the accounts for the previous year.

There are two changes. First, an auditor's term of office will typically run from the end of the 28 day period following circulation of the accounts until the end of the corresponding period in the following year. This will apply even if the auditor is appointed at a meeting where the company's accounts are laid. The second change is that an auditor is now deemed to be reappointed unless the company decides otherwise.

485. Appointment of auditors of private company: general

(1) An auditor or auditors of a private company must be appointed for each financial year of the company, unless the directors reasonably resolve otherwise on the ground that audited accounts are unlikely to be required.

(2) For each financial year for which an auditor or auditors is or are to be appointed (other than the company's first financial year), the appointment must be made before the end of the period of 28 days beginning with-

    (a) the end of the time allowed for sending out copies of the company's annual accounts and reports for the previous financial year (see section 424), or

    (b) if earlier, the day on which copies of the company's annual accounts and reports for the previous financial year are sent out under section 423.

This is the "period for appointing auditors".

(3) The directors may appoint an auditor or auditors of the company-

    (a) at any time before the company's first period for appointing auditors,

    (b) following a period during which the company (being exempt from audit) did not have any auditor, at any time before the company's next period for appointing auditors, or

    (c) to fill a casual vacancy in the office of auditor.

(4) The members may appoint an auditor or auditors by ordinary resolution-

    (a) during a period for appointing auditors,

    (b) if the company should have appointed an auditor or auditors during a period for appointing auditors but failed to do so, or

    (c) where the directors had power to appoint under subsection (3) but have failed to make an appointment.

(5) An auditor or auditors of a private company may only be appointed-

    (a) in accordance with this section, or

    (b) in accordance with section 486 (default power of Secretary of State).

This is without prejudice to any deemed re-appointment under section 487.

GENERAL NOTE

This section deals with the appointment of auditors with respect to private companies, its provisions being derived in part from ss.384, 385, 385A and 388 of the 1985 Act, as amended.

Subsection (1)

An auditor must be appointed by a private company unless its directors are of the view that it will be entitled to exemption from audit.

Subsection (2)

The "period for appointing auditors" (other than in the company's first financial year) is to be before the end of the period of 28 days beginning with the end of the period for sending out copies of the annual accounts for the previous financial year (s.424) or, if earlier, beginning with the day the accounts are circulated under s.423.

Subsections (3)-(5)

The appointment is to be made by the shareholders by ordinary resolution (subs.(4)), except that the directors can appoint the company's first auditor (or the first after a period of audit exemption), and can fill a casual vacancy (subs.(3)). Auditors of a private company can only be appointed in accordance with s.485 or by the Secretary of State under s.486 (subs.(5)).

486.   Appointment of auditors of private company: default power of Secretary of State

(1) If a private company fails to appoint an auditor or auditors in accordance with section 485, the Secretary of State may appoint one or more persons to fill the vacancy.

(2) Where subsection (2) of that section applies and the company fails to make the necessary appointment before the end of the period for appointing auditors, the company must within one week of the end of that period give notice to the Secretary of State of his power having become exercisable.

(3) If a company fails to give the notice required by this section, an offence is committed by-
    (a) the company, and
    (b) every officer of the company who is in default.

(4) A person guilty of an offence under this section is liable on summary conviction to a fine not exceeding level 3 on the standard scale and, for continued contravention, a daily default fine not exceeding one-tenth of level 3 on the standard scale.

GENERAL NOTE

This section, dealing with the power of the secretary of State to appoint an auditor for a private company when it has itself failed to appoint one, is derived from s.387 of the 1985 Act.

Subsection (1)

If a private company fails to appoint an auditor under s.485, the Secretary of State may fill the vacancy.

Subsections (2)-(4)

Where a private company fails to make an appointment within 28 days of the circulation of its accounts as required by s.485(2), it must inform the Secretary of State within a week (subs.(2)). Failure to give such notice renders the company and every officer in default *prima facie* guilty of an offence (subs.(3)). The penalties for such an offence are detailed in subs.(4).

487.   Term of office of auditors of private company

(1) An auditor or auditors of a private company hold office in accordance with the terms of their appointment, subject to the requirements that-
    (a) they do not take office until any previous auditor or auditors cease to hold office, and
    (b) they cease to hold office at the end of the next period for appointing auditors unless re-appointed.

(2) Where no auditor has been appointed by the end of the next period for appointing auditors, any auditor in office immediately before that time is deemed to be re-appointed at that time, unless-
    (a) he was appointed by the directors, or
    (b) the company's articles require actual re-appointment, or
    (c) the deemed re-appointment is prevented by the members under section 488, or
    (d) the members have resolved that he should not be re-appointed, or
    (e) the directors have resolved that no auditor or auditors should be appointed for the financial year in question.

(3) This is without prejudice to the provisions of this Part as to removal and resignation of auditors.

(4) No account shall be taken of any loss of the opportunity of deemed reappointment under this section in ascertaining the amount of any compensation or damages payable to an auditor on his ceasing to hold office for any reason.

GENERAL NOTE

This section, dealing with the term of office of an auditor of a private company, is derived in part from ss.385(2) and 385A(2) of the 1985 Act, as amended.

Subsection (1)

An auditor of a private company does not take up his post until a previous auditor ceases to hold office. In such circumstances, a new auditor's term will typically begin immediately after the expiry of the 28-day period for appointing auditors. More generally, unless reappointed, an auditor ceases to hold office at the end of the next 28-day period for appointing auditors.

Subsection (2)

An auditor will automatically be deemed to be reappointed at the end of his term of office, except where: (1) he was appointed by the directors; (2) the company's articles require actual reappointment; (3) enough members have given notice to the company under s.488; (4) there has been a resolution that the auditor should not be reappointed; or (5) the directors decide that no auditor should be appointed for the following year.

Subsection (3)

Subsection (2) is without prejudice to the powers under ss.510 and 516 as to removal and resignation of auditors.

Subsection (4)

This subsection states that no account shall be taken of loss of opportunity of deemed appointment in determining compensation or damages to an auditor when he ceases to hold office.

488. Prevention by members of deemed re-appointment of auditor

(1) An auditor of a private company is not deemed to be re-appointed under section 487(2) if the company has received notices under this section from members representing at least the requisite percentage of the total voting rights of all members who would be entitled to vote on a resolution that the auditor should not be re-appointed.
(2) The "requisite percentage" is 5%, or such lower percentage as is specified for this purpose in the company's articles.
(3) A notice under this section-
    (a) may be in hard copy or electronic form,
    (b) must be authenticated by the person or persons giving it, and
    (c) must be received by the company before the end of the accounting reference period immediately preceding the time when the deemed reappointment would have effect.

GENERAL NOTE

This section, dealing with the prevention of the deemed reappointment of an auditor of a private company by its members, is derived in part from ss.385(2) and 385A(2) of the 1985 Act, as amended.

Subsections (1) and (2)

Members representing at least 5 per cent of the voting rights in a private company may prevent an auditor being automatically reappointed by giving notice to the company. The company's articles can enable members to do this with less than 5 per cent of the voting rights, but cannot increase the required percentage.

Subsection (3)

A notice under this section excluding the reappointment of an auditor may be in hard copy or electronic form, but it must be authenticated and be received before the end of the financial year the accounts of which the auditor concerned is examining.

Public companies

GENERAL NOTE

Sections 489-491 restate the law on appointment of auditors of public companies, providing that auditors are generally to be appointed by shareholders by ordinary resolution in the general meeting before which the company's accounts are laid.

489.   Appointment of auditors of public company: general

(1) An auditor or auditors of a public company must be appointed for each financial year of the company, unless the directors reasonably resolve otherwise on the ground that audited accounts are unlikely to be required.

(2) For each financial year for which an auditor or auditors is or are to be appointed (other than the company's first financial year), the appointment must be made before the end of the accounts meeting of the company at which the company's annual accounts and reports for the previous financial year are laid.

(3) The directors may appoint an auditor or auditors of the company-
   (a) at any time before the company's first accounts meeting;
   (b) following a period during which the company (being exempt from audit) did not have any auditor, at any time before the company's next accounts meeting;
   (c) to fill a casual vacancy in the office of auditor.

(4) The members may appoint an auditor or auditors by ordinary resolution-
   (a) at an accounts meeting;
   (b) if the company should have appointed an auditor or auditors at an accounts meeting but failed to do so;
   (c) where the directors had power to appoint under subsection (3) but have failed to make an appointment.

(5) An auditor or auditors of a public company may only be appointed-
   (a) in accordance with this section, or
   (b) in accordance with section 490 (default power of Secretary of State).

GENERAL NOTE

This section deals with the appointment of auditors with respect to public companies, its provisions being derived in part from ss.384, 385 and 388 of the 1985 Act, as amended.

Subsection (1)

An auditor must be appointed by a public company unless its directors are of the view that audited accounts are unlikely to be required.

Subsection (2)

Apart from in its first financial year, the appointment of a company's auditor must be made before the end of the meeting at which the accounts for the previous financial year are laid before the members.

Subsection (3)

The directors can appoint the company's first auditors (or the first after a period of audit exemption), and can fill a casual vacancy.

Subsection (4)

Members may also appoint an auditor by ordinary resolution, normally at the general meeting at which the accounts are laid (the so-called "accounts meeting").

Subsection (5)

An auditor of a public company can only be appointed in accordance with s.489 or by using the default power of appointment given to the Secretary of State under s.490, below.

490. Appointment of auditors of public company: default power of Secretary of State

(1) If a public company fails to appoint an auditor or auditors in accordance with section 489, the Secretary of State may appoint one or more persons to fill the vacancy.

(2) Where subsection (2) of that section applies and the company fails to make the necessary appointment before the end of the accounts meeting, the company must within one week of the end of that meeting give notice to the Secretary of State of his power having become exercisable.

(3) If a company fails to give the notice required by this section, an offence is committed by-
    (a) the company, and
    (b) every officer of the company who is in default.

(4) A person guilty of an offence under this section is liable on summary conviction to a fine not exceeding level 3 on the standard scale and, for continued contravention, a daily default fine not exceeding one-tenth of level 3 on the standard scale.

GENERAL NOTE

This section restates the obligation in s.387 of the 1985 Act of a company to inform the Secretary of State if it has failed to appoint an auditor at the general meeting that considers the previous year's accounts (the so-called "accounts meeting"); and the Secretary of State's power to appoint an auditor in those circumstances.

Subsection (1)

The Secretary of State can appoint an auditor if the company fails to do so in accordance with s.489.

Subsections (2) and (3)

If the company fails to make an appointment before the end of its "accounts meeting", it must within a week give notice of that fact to the Secretary of State (subs.(2)). Failure to do so renders the company and its officers *prima facie* guilty of an offence (subs.(3)).

Subsection (4)

This subsection details the penalties for the offence referred to in subs.(3).

491. Term of office of auditors of public company

(1) The auditor or auditors of a public company hold office in accordance with the terms of their appointment, subject to the requirements that-
    (a) they do not take office until the previous auditor or auditors have ceased to hold office, and
    (b) they cease to hold office at the conclusion of the accounts meeting next following their appointment, unless re-appointed.

(2) This is without prejudice to the provisions of this Part as to removal and resignation of auditors.

GENERAL NOTE

This section restates the provision in s.385(2) of the 1985 Act, as substituted by s.119 of the 1989 Act, that, unless he is reappointed, an auditor of a public company holds office until the end of the meeting at which the accounts he is auditing are laid before members. Where there is a change of auditor, the term of office of the incoming auditor does not begin before the end of the previous auditor's term. The result is that a new auditor's term will typically begin immediately after the end of the so-called "accounts meeting".

Subsection (1)

An auditor of a public company holds office in accordance with the terms of his appointment. However, he does not take up his or her post until a previous auditor ceases to hold office. More generally, unless reappointed, an auditor ceases to hold office at the end of the accounts meeting next following his or her appointment.

Subsection (2)

This is without prejudice to the powers under ss.510 and 516 as to removal and resignation of auditors.

General provisions

GENERAL NOTE

Sections 492-494 apply to both private and public companies.

492.   Fixing of auditor's remuneration

(1) The remuneration of an auditor appointed by the members of a company must be fixed by the members by ordinary resolution or in such manner as the members may by ordinary resolution determine.
(2) The remuneration of an auditor appointed by the directors of a company must be fixed by the directors.
(3) The remuneration of an auditor appointed by the Secretary of State must be fixed by the Secretary of State.
(4) For the purposes of this section "remuneration" includes sums paid in respect of expenses.
(5) This section applies in relation to benefits in kind as to payments of money.

GENERAL NOTE

This section restates the provision in s.390A of the 1985 Act (as inserted by s.121 of the 1989 Act) concerning the fixing of the auditor's remuneration.

Subsection (1)

The members of a company determine, by ordinary resolution, the remuneration of an auditor that they appoint, or alternatively decide the method by which such remuneration should be determined.

Subsections (2) and (3)

If the auditor was appointed by someone other than the members, then it will be the directors (subs.(2)) or the Secretary of State (subs.(3)), as appropriate, who will determine his remuneration.

Subsections (4) and (5)

"Remuneration" is defined to include expenses (subs.(4)) and includes benefits in kind (subs.(5)).

493.   Disclosure of terms of audit appointment

(1) The Secretary of State may make provision by regulations for securing the disclosure of the terms on which a company's auditor is appointed, remunerated or performs his duties.
Nothing in the following provisions of this section affects the generality of this power.
(2) The regulations may-
    (a) require disclosure of-
        (i) a copy of any terms that are in writing, and
        (ii) a written memorandum setting out any terms that are not in writing;
    (b) require disclosure to be at such times, in such places and by such means as are specified in the regulations;
    (c) require the place and means of disclosure to be stated-

    (i) in a note to the company's annual accounts (in the case of its individual accounts) or in such manner as is specified in the regulations (in the case of group accounts),

    (ii) in the directors' report, or

    (iii) in the auditor's report on the company's annual accounts.

(3) The provisions of this section apply to a variation of the terms mentioned in subsection (1) as they apply to the original terms.

(4) Regulations under this section are subject to affirmative resolution procedure.

GENERAL NOTE

This section creates a new power for the Secretary of State to require companies to disclose information about the terms on which they engage their auditors.

Subsection (1)

The Secretary of State may by regulations secure disclosure of the terms of an auditor's appointment, including his or her remuneration and how he should carry out his duties.

Subsection (2)

This subsection provides examples of the detailed requirements that the Secretary of State could specify in regulations (e.g. require copies of written agreements or a written memorandum of an oral agreement to be disclosed; where such information should be lodged; and how it should be disclosed - for instance, in notes to the accounts, in the directors' report, or in the auditor's report).

Subsection (3)

The regulations can require disclosure of changes in terms, as well as the terms at the time of appointment.

Subsection (4)

The regulations are to be made by the affirmative resolution procedure (see s.1290).

494. Disclosure of services provided by auditor or associates and related remuneration

(1) The Secretary of State may make provision by regulations for securing the disclosure of-

    (a) the nature of any services provided for a company by the company's auditor (whether in his capacity as auditor or otherwise) or by his associates;

    (b) the amount of any remuneration received or receivable by a company's auditor, or his associates, in respect of any such services.

Nothing in the following provisions of this section affects the generality of this power.

(2) The regulations may provide-

    (a) for disclosure of the nature of any services provided to be made by reference to any class or description of services specified in the regulations (or any combination of services, however described);

    (b) for the disclosure of amounts of remuneration received or receivable in respect of services of any class or description specified in the regulations (or any combination of services, however described);

    (c) for the disclosure of separate amounts so received or receivable by the company's auditor or any of his associates, or of aggregate amounts so received or receivable by all or any of those persons.

(3) The regulations may-

    (a) provide that "remuneration" includes sums paid in respect of expenses;

    (b) apply to benefits in kind as well as to payments of money, and require the disclosure of the nature of any such benefits and their estimated money value;

    (c) apply to services provided for associates of a company as well as to those provided for a company;

    (d) define "associate" in relation to an auditor and a company respectively.

(4) The regulations may provide that any disclosure required by the regulations is to be made-

    (a) in a note to the company's annual accounts (in the case of its individual accounts) or in such manner as is specified in the regulations (in the case of group accounts),

    (b) in the directors' report, or

    (c) in the auditor's report on the company's annual accounts.

(5) If the regulations provide that any such disclosure is to be made as mentioned in subsection (4)(a) or (b), the regulations may require the auditor to supply the directors of the company with any information necessary to enable the disclosure to be made.

(6) Regulations under this section are subject to negative resolution procedure.

GENERAL NOTE

This section restates the previous power of the Secretary of State, in s.390B of the 1985 Act (as inserted by s.121 of the 1989 Act), to require disclosure of details of all the services supplied to a company by its auditor, and the remuneration involved.

Guidance on how companies and their auditors that are not small or medium-sized should implement the provisions set out in SI 2005/2417, "The Companies (Disclosure of Auditor Remuneration) Regulations 2005" - which were the rules in force when the new Act was passed - can be found in a technical release of the Institute of Chartered Accountants in England and Wales, TECH 04/06 "Disclosure of auditor remuneration" (www.icaew.co.uk/index.cfm?route=135101).

Subsection (1)

The Secretary of State may by regulations secure disclosure of the nature of services provided by an auditor or by his associates, whether in that capacity or otherwise, and details of remuneration of all services provided.

Subsections (2)-(4)

Illustrations of the detailed requirements that the Secretary of State can specify in regulations are given in these subsections. For example, subs.(2) relates to the degree of detail that should be disclosed for each separate service provided and the remuneration for each, distinguishing between the auditor and his associates. Subsection (3) indicates that the regulations may define "remuneration" and "associate", and they may also indicate that benefits in kind are covered, as well as direct money payments. Subsection (4) indicates how the regulations may provide where the relevant information should be disclosed (e.g. in notes to the accounts, or in the directors' or auditor's reports).

Subsection (5)

The regulations can require the auditor to supply the directors with any information that may be required (e.g. about the auditor's associates). This gets round the problem that the regulations might ask for disclosure in a document compiled by the company rather than the auditor.

Subsection (6)

The regulations are to be made by the negative resolution procedure (see s.1289).

CHAPTER 3

FUNCTIONS OF AUDITOR

GENERAL NOTE

Sections 495-497 restate with modifications the existing law, in s.235 of the 1985 Act (as inserted by s.9 of the 1989 Act and subsequently amended by SIs 2002/1986, reg.4, 2004/2947, reg.6(2) and 2005/3442, Sch.1, para.4), on what the auditor should include in his report on the accounts.

The content of the audit report is in practice largely determined by the requirements detailed in an International Standard on Auditing (United Kingdom and Ireland), ISA 700, "The auditor's report on financial statements" (www.frc.org.uk/images/uploaded/documents/ACFAB4.pdf), which amongst other things deals with audit qualifications (see s.495(4)). (Reference should also be made to Bulletins issued by the Auditing Practices Board ("APB") which give recommended wording for audit reports. The latest is Bulletin 6/2006, "Auditor's Reports on Financial Statements in the United Kingdom" (www.frc.org.uk/apb/publications/pub1170.html.)

Auditor's report

495. Auditor's report on company's annual accounts

(1) A company's auditor must make a report to the company's members on all annual accounts of the company of which copies are, during his tenure of office-
    (a) in the case of a private company, to be sent out to members under section 423;
    (b) in the case of a public company, to be laid before the company in general meeting under section 437.

(2) The auditor's report must include-
    (a) an introduction identifying the annual accounts that are the subject of the audit and the financial reporting framework that has been applied in their preparation, and
    (b) a description of the scope of the audit identifying the auditing standards in accordance with which the audit was conducted.

(3) The report must state clearly whether, in the auditor's opinion, the annual accounts-
    (a) give a true and fair view-
        (i) in the case of an individual balance sheet, of the state of affairs of the company as at the end of the financial year,
        (ii) in the case of an individual profit and loss account, of the profit or loss of the company for the financial year,
        (iii) in the case of group accounts, of the state of affairs as at the end of the financial year and of the profit or loss for the financial year of the undertakings included in the consolidation as a whole, so far as concerns members of the company;
    (b) have been properly prepared in accordance with the relevant financial reporting framework; and
    (c) have been prepared in accordance with the requirements of this Act (and, where applicable, Article 4 of the IAS Regulation).
Expressions used in this subsection that are defined for the purposes of Part 15 (see section 474) have the same meaning as in that Part.

(4) The auditor's report-
    (a) must be either unqualified or qualified, and
    (b) must include a reference to any matters to which the auditor wishes to draw attention by way of emphasis without qualifying the report.

GENERAL NOTE

In addition to his duties identified in this section - which is derived in part from subss.(1)-(2A) of s.235 of the 1985 Act, as amended - an auditor is required by s.393, above, to ensure that the accounts give "a true and fair view" of the profit or loss for a period and the financial position of a company (and, if relevant, a group).

Although the auditors have a duty to report to members (subs.(1)), they perform their duty by forwarding their report to the secretary. They are not responsible if the report is not put before the members (*Allen, Craig and Co (London) Ltd, Re* [1934] Ch. 483).

Subsection (1)

An auditor must make a report to members on all annual accounts prepared during his or her tenure of office that, in the case of a private company are circulated to members under s.423, and in the case of a public company are laid before the company in general meeting under s.437.

Subsection (2)

The auditor must identify the accounts to which his report relates and the financial reporting framework that has been applied in their preparation. He also has to indicate the scope of his audit and identify the auditing standards applied.

Subsection (3)

The auditor is required to state in his or her report his opinion on three overlapping matters: (i) whether the accounts provide a true and fair view, (ii) whether they comply with the appropriate reporting framework, and (iii) whether the accounts comply with the requirements in Pt 15 of the Act, "Accounts and Reports" (and, where applicable, with art.4 of the IAS Regulation (Regulation (EC) 1606/2002 on the application of international accounting standards)).

Subsection (4)

The audit report has to be either qualified or unqualified, although the auditor can also draw attention by way of emphasis to aspects of his audit without qualifying the report.

496.   Auditor's report on directors' report

The auditor must state in his report on the company's annual accounts whether in his opinion the information given in the directors' report for the financial year for which the accounts are prepared is consistent with those accounts.

GENERAL NOTE

This section restates the law in s.235(3) of the 1985 Act, as inserted by s.9 of the 1989 Act, on what the auditor should include in relation to the directors' report, namely that in his opinion the information given therein for the financial year is consistent with the accounts.

It may be relevant to consult section B of a revised version of ISA 720, published by the APB in April 2006. This deals with "The auditor's statutory reporting responsibility in relation to directors' reports" (www.frc.org.uk/images/uploaded/documents/ISA%20720%20web%20optimized1.pdf).

497.   Auditor's report on auditable part of directors' remuneration report

(1) If the company is a quoted company, the auditor, in his report on the company's annual accounts for the financial year, must-
   (a) report to the company's members on the auditable part of the directors' remuneration report, and
   (b) state whether in his opinion that part of the directors' remuneration report has been properly prepared in accordance with this Act.
(2) For the purposes of this Part, "the auditable part" of a directors' remuneration report is the part identified as such by regulations under section 421.

GENERAL NOTE

This section restates the law in s.235(4)-(5) of the 1985 Act, as inserted by s.121 of the 1989 Act and subsequently amended by SI 2002/1986, reg.4, on what the auditor should include in relation to the directors' remuneration report (see ss.420-422).

The APB published guidance in Bulletin 2002/2 in October 2002 (www.frc.org.uk/apb/publications/pub0444.html) indicating auditors' obligations in relation to the directors' remuneration reports that have had to be published by listed companies following the enactment of SI 2002/1986, the relevant legislation in force until the new Act was passed.

Subsections (1) and (2)

In his report on the annual accounts of a quoted company, an auditor must report on the "auditable part" of the directors' remuneration report and state whether that part has been properly been prepared in accordance with the Act (subs.(1)). Subsection (2) identifies this "auditable part" of the remuneration report as that described as such in regulations issued under s.421(1)(c).

Duties and rights of auditors

GENERAL NOTE

Sections 498-502 bring together and restate the existing law on the auditor's duties (previously in s.237 of the 1985 Act, as inserted by s.9 of the 1989 Act) in investigating, forming an opinion, and making his report; and on the auditor's rights (ss.389A-390 of the 1985 Act, as inserted/substituted by s.120 of the 1989 Act) to be provided with appropriate information.

498. Duties of auditor

(1) A company's auditor, in preparing his report, must carry out such investigations as will enable him to form an opinion as to-

    (a) whether adequate accounting records have been kept by the company and returns adequate for their audit have been received from branches not visited by him, and

    (b) whether the company's individual accounts are in agreement with the accounting records and returns, and

    (c) in the case of a quoted company, whether the auditable part of the company's directors' remuneration report is in agreement with the accounting records and returns.

(2) If the auditor is of the opinion-

    (a) that adequate accounting records have not been kept, or that returns adequate for their audit have not been received from branches not visited by him, or

    (b) that the company's individual accounts are not in agreement with the accounting records and returns, or

    (c) in the case of a quoted company, that the auditable part of its directors' remuneration report is not in agreement with the accounting records and returns,

the auditor shall state that fact in his report.

(3) If the auditor fails to obtain all the information and explanations which, to the best of his knowledge and belief, are necessary for the purposes of his audit, he shall state that fact in his report.

(4) If-

    (a) the requirements of regulations under section 412 (disclosure of directors' benefits: remuneration, pensions and compensation for loss of office) are not complied with in the annual accounts, or

    (b) in the case of a quoted company, the requirements of regulations under section 421 as to information forming the auditable part of the directors' remuneration report are not complied with in that report,

the auditor must include in his report, so far as he is reasonably able to do so, a statement giving the required particulars.

(5) If the directors of the company have prepared accounts and reports in accordance with the small companies regime and in the auditor's opinion they were not entitled so to do, the auditor shall state that fact in his report.

GENERAL NOTE

This section, which is derived from s.237 of the 1985 Act, as amended, sets out the duties of the auditor.

Auditors' responsibilities on accounting records have been brought into line with those of the directors. Consequently, they will now report on whether *adequate*, rather than *proper*, records have been kept.

Subsections (1) and (2)

In preparing his report, the auditor must carry out appropriate investigations to enable him to form an opinion on the adequacy of the accounting records of the company and its branch returns, and whether there is consistency between these and (i) the accounts and (ii) - for a quoted company - the appropriate part of the directors' remuneration report (subs.(1)). If in the auditor's opinion the records and/or returns are inadequate, and/or there is inconsistency between these and the financial statements and/or the auditable part of the remuneration report, the auditor must state this in his report (subs.(2)).

Subsection (3)

The auditor must state in his report if he has not been able to get all the information he needs for his audit.

Subsection (4)

If possible, the auditor should make good any deficiencies in the information relating to payments to directors under s.412 relating to remuneration, pensions and compensation for loss of office, and (for a quoted company) information that would be included in the "auditable part" of the directors' remuneration report.

Subsection (5)

The auditor is also required to report if he believes that the company is taking advantage of the small companies accounts regime without in his opinion being entitled to do so.

499.   Auditor's general right to information

(1) An auditor of a company-
  (a) has a right of access at all times to the company's books, accounts and vouchers (in whatever form they are held), and
  (b) may require any of the following persons to provide him with such information or explanations as he thinks necessary for the performance of his duties as auditor.
(2) Those persons are-
  (a) any officer or employee of the company;
  (b) any person holding or accountable for any of the company's books, accounts or vouchers;
  (c) any subsidiary undertaking of the company which is a body corporate incorporated in the United Kingdom;
  (d) any officer, employee or auditor of any such subsidiary undertaking or any person holding or accountable for any books, accounts or vouchers of any such subsidiary undertaking;
  (e) any person who fell within any of paragraphs (a) to (d) at a time to which the information or explanations required by the auditor relates or relate.
(3) A statement made by a person in response to a requirement under this section may not be used in evidence against him in criminal proceedings except proceedings for an offence under section 501.
(4) Nothing in this section compels a person to disclose information in respect of which a claim to legal professional privilege (in Scotland, to confidentiality of communications) could be maintained in legal proceedings.

GENERAL NOTE

This section restates the auditor's right under s.389A of the 1985 Act (as inserted by s.120 of the 1989 Act) to obtain information and explanations from the company and its United Kingdom subsidiaries, and from appropriate associated individuals.

Subsections (1)-(4)

The auditor has a right of access at all times to a company's books, accounts and vouchers (subs.(1)). He is entitled under subs.(1)(b) to obtain necessary information and explanations from an officer or employee of the company, any person holding the books and vouchers, and a subsidiary incorporated in the UK and its officers and employees (subs.(2)). A statement made by one of these persons cannot be used against them in criminal proceedings, except for an offence under s.501 (below) (subs.(3)). However, none of these persons is required to breach legal professional privilege in disclosing information (subs.(4)).

500.   Auditor's right to information from overseas subsidiaries

(1) Where a parent company has a subsidiary undertaking that is not a body corporate incorporated in the United Kingdom, the auditor of the parent company may require it to obtain from any of the following persons such information or explanations as he may reasonably require for the purposes of his duties as auditor.

(2) Those persons are-
   (a) the undertaking;
   (b) any officer, employee or auditor of the undertaking;
   (c) any person holding or accountable for any of the undertaking's books, accounts or vouchers;
   (d) any person who fell within paragraph (b) or (c) at a time to which the information or explanations relates or relate.

(3) If so required, the parent company must take all such steps as are reasonably open to it to obtain the information or explanations from the person concerned.

(4) A statement made by a person in response to a requirement under this section may not be used in evidence against him in criminal proceedings except proceedings for an offence under section 501.

(5) Nothing in this section compels a person to disclose information in respect of which a claim to legal professional privilege (in Scotland, to confidentiality of communications) could be maintained in legal proceedings.

GENERAL NOTE

This restates and expands s.389A(4) of the 1985 Act (as inserted by s.120 of the 1989 Act), setting out the corresponding right to require the company to obtain information or explanations from any subsidiaries that are not incorporated in the United Kingdom.

Subsection (1)

The auditor of a parent company incorporated in the United Kingdom may require it to obtain information and explanations relating to overseas subsidiaries that are necessary to carry out the audit.

Subsection (2)

The persons from whom information may be obtained are the overseas subsidiary, its officers, employees or its auditor, and any person holding its books and vouchers.

Subsection (3)

The parent company must take all reasonable steps to obtain the information and explanations required.

Subsections (4) and (5)

A statement made by one of the persons referred to in subs.(2) cannot be used against them in criminal proceedings, except for an offence under s.501 (below) (subs.(4)). However, none of these persons is required to breach legal professional privilege in disclosing information (subs.(5)).

501. Auditor's rights to information: offences

(1) A person commits an offence who knowingly or recklessly makes to an auditor of a company a statement (oral or written) that-
   (a) conveys or purports to convey any information or explanations which the auditor requires, or is entitled to require, under section 499, and
   (b) is misleading, false or deceptive in a material particular.

(2) A person guilty of an offence under subsection (1) is liable-
   (a) on conviction on indictment, to imprisonment for a term not exceeding two years or a fine (or both);
   (b) on summary conviction-
      (i) in England and Wales, to imprisonment for a term not exceeding twelve months or to a fine not exceeding the statutory maximum (or both);
      (ii) in Scotland or Northern Ireland, to imprisonment for a term not exceeding six months or to a fine not exceeding the statutory maximum (or both).

(3) A person who fails to comply with a requirement under section 499 without delay commits an offence unless it was not reasonably practicable for him to provide the required information or explanations.

(4) If a parent company fails to comply with section 500, an offence is committed by-
    (a) the company, and
    (b) every officer of the company who is in default.

(5) A person guilty of an offence under subsection (3) or (4) is liable on summary conviction to a fine not exceeding level 3 on the standard scale.

(6) Nothing in this section affects any right of an auditor to apply for an injunction (in Scotland, an interdict or an order for specific performance) to enforce any of his rights under section 499 or 500.

GENERAL NOTE

This section, which is derived from s.389B of the 1985 Act, as substituted by s.7 of the Companies (Audit, Investigations and Community Enterprise) Act 2004, sets out offences for those who supply inaccurate information to auditors or fail to respond to auditors' requests for information without delay.

Subsection (1)

A person who knowingly or recklessly makes a written or oral statement to an auditor with respect to information that the auditor may require under s.499 (auditor's general right to information) that is misleading, false or deceptive commits an offence.

Subsection (2)

A person guilty of such an offence is liable to receive a prison sentence of up to two years and/or a fine.

Subsections (3)-(5)

A person who delays complying with a request under s.499 (subs.(3)), or a parent and its officers that fail to comply with a request under s.500 (subs.(4)), are *prima facie* guilty of an offence, the penalty for which is specified in subs.(5).

Subsection (6)

Nothing in this section affects the right of an auditor to apply for an injunction (or its equivalent in Scotland) to enforce his rights under ss.499 and 500.

502. Auditor's rights in relation to resolutions and meetings

(1) In relation to a written resolution proposed to be agreed to by a private company, the company's auditor is entitled to receive all such communications relating to the resolution as, by virtue of any provision of Chapter 2 of Part 13 of this Act, are required to be supplied to a member of the company.

(2) A company's auditor is entitled-
    (a) to receive all notices of, and other communications relating to, any general meeting which a member of the company is entitled to receive,
    (b) to attend any general meeting of the company, and
    (c) to be heard at any general meeting which he attends on any part of the business of the meeting which concerns him as auditor.

(3) Where the auditor is a firm, the right to attend or be heard at a meeting is exercisable by an individual authorised by the firm in writing to act as its representative at the meeting.

GENERAL NOTE

This section restates the rights given in s.390 of the 1985 Act, as inserted by s.120 of the 1989 Act and subsequently amended by SIs 1996/1471 and 2000/3373, art.31.

Subsection (1)

A private company is required to send its auditor all the information about any written resolutions that it sends to its shareholders.

The auditor of any company public or private - is entitled to receive all notices and communications relating to a general meeting, and he has the right to attend such meetings and be allowed to speak on anything relevant to the audit (subs.(2)). Where the auditor is a firm rather than an individual, such rights pass to a representative of the firm who is authorised in writing to act on its behalf (subs.(3)).

Signature of auditor's report

503. Signature of auditor's report

(1) The auditor's report must state the name of the auditor and be signed and dated.

(2) Where the auditor is an individual, the report must be signed by him.

(3) Where the auditor is a firm, the report must be signed by the senior statutory auditor in his own name, for and on behalf of the auditor.

GENERAL NOTE

This section, dealing with the signing and dating of the auditor's report, restates s.236 of the 1985 Act, as amended by SI 2004/2947, reg.7.

Subsection (1)

The audit report submitted to a company by its auditor must be signed and dated.

Subsections (2) and (3)

The report must state the name of the audit firm (subs.(3)), or if an individual has been appointed as auditor, his name (subs.(2)). In the former case, a change has been made from the 1985 Act by requiring the "senior statutory auditor", as defined in s.504 below, to sign the report in his own name on behalf of the firm. This is to accommodate a new requirement introduced by the EU Audit Directive.

504. Senior statutory auditor

(1) The senior statutory auditor means the individual identified by the firm as senior statutory auditor in relation to the audit in accordance with-

    (a) standards issued by the European Commission, or

    (b) if there is no applicable standard so issued, any relevant guidance issued by-

        (i) the Secretary of State, or

        (ii) a body appointed by order of the Secretary of State.

(2) The person identified as senior statutory auditor must be eligible for appointment as auditor of the company in question (see Chapter 2 of Part 42 of this Act).

(3) The senior statutory auditor is not, by reason of being named or identified as senior statutory auditor or by reason of his having signed the auditor's report, subject to any civil liability to which he would not otherwise be subject.

(4) An order appointing a body for the purpose of subsection (1)(b)(ii) is subject to negative resolution procedure.

GENERAL NOTE

This section is innovatory and defines a new term, the "senior statutory auditor", for the individual who will be asked to sign his name on the report relating to an audit carried out by a firm.

Subsection (1)

The auditing firm will identify the individual who is the "senior statutory auditor" according to standards issued by the European Commission, or if there are no standards, to guidance issued either by the Secretary of State or by a body appointed by him.

Subsection (2)

The person identified as a senior statutory auditor of a company must be eligible to be appointed as auditor of the company.

Subsection (3)

An individual named as senior statutory auditor will not be exposed to any additional civil liability because of his nomination.

Subsection (4)

An order issued by the Secretary of State appointing a body under subs.(1) to issue guidance to senior statutory auditors is subject to the negative resolution procedure: see s.1289.

505. Names to be stated in published copies of auditor's report

(1) Every copy of the auditor's report that is published by or on behalf of the company must-
   (a) state the name of the auditor and (where the auditor is a firm) the name of the person who signed it as senior statutory auditor, or
   (b) if the conditions in section 506 (circumstances in which names may be omitted) are met, state that a resolution has been passed and notified to the Secretary of State in accordance with that section.

(2) For the purposes of this section a company is regarded as publishing the report if it publishes, issues or circulates it or otherwise makes it available for public inspection in a manner calculated to invite members of the public generally, or any class of members of the public, to read it.

(3) If a copy of the auditor's report is published without the statement required by this section, an offence is committed by-
   (a) the company, and
   (b) every officer of the company who is in default.

(4) A person guilty of an offence under this section is liable on summary conviction to a fine not exceeding level 3 on the standard scale.

GENERAL NOTE

This section, part of which is derived from subss.(3)-(4) of s.236 of the 1985 Act, as inserted by s.9 of the 1989 Act, requires a company either to ensure that the copies of its auditor's report it sends out include the name of the auditor and of the senior statutory auditor (if there is one), or to say that it is taking advantage of the exemption in s.506, below.

Subsection (1)

Every copy of the auditor's report that is published by a company must state the name of the auditor, and (if it is a firm) the name of the senior statutory auditor. If advantage is taken of s.506, which permits names to be omitted in certain circumstances if a resolution has been passed and the Secretary of State informed, a statement of that fact.

Subsection (2)

The copies of the auditor's report that are subject to subs.(1) include the version circulated to shareholders, as well as any others that would be expected to be seen by members of the public. It does not, however, cover copies sent to the registrar: these are dealt with by ss.444(7), 445(6), 446(4) and 447(4).

Subsections (3) and (4)

Subsection (3) restates the offence committed by a company and every defaulting officer (previously in s.236(4) of the 1985 Act, as inserted by s.9 of the 1989 Act) of not including in the report the auditor's name - and now also the senior statutory auditor's name, where appropriate. The penalty for being guilty of such an offence is detailed in subs.(4).

506. Circumstances in which names may be omitted

(1) The auditor's name and, where the auditor is a firm, the name of the person who signed the report as senior statutory auditor, may be omitted from-
    (a) published copies of the report, and
    (b) the copy of the report delivered to the registrar under Chapter 10 of Part 15 (filing of accounts and reports),
if the following conditions are met.

(2) The conditions are that the company-
    (a) considering on reasonable grounds that statement of the name would create or be likely to create a serious risk that the auditor or senior statutory auditor, or any other person, would be subject to violence or intimidation, has resolved that the name should not be stated, and
    (b) has given notice of the resolution to the Secretary of State, stating-
        (i) the name and registered number of the company,
        (ii) the financial year of the company to which the report relates, and
        (iii) the name of the auditor and (where the auditor is a firm) the name of the person who signed the report as senior statutory auditor.

GENERAL NOTE

This is a new section and provides an exemption from the requirements to include the names of the auditor in both the published and filed copies of the audit report.

Subsection (1)

A company may omit the name of the auditor (or in the case where the auditor is a firm, the name of the senior statutory auditor) from published copies of the report and the copy of the report filed with the registrar of companies.

Subsection (2)

This concession is available if the company passes a resolution not to reveal the names because it considers on reasonable grounds that revealing them would lead to a serious risk of violence or intimidation. It is also a condition of using the exemption that the company must inform the Secretary of State, giving details of the name of the auditor, and of the senior statutory auditor if there is one.

Offences in connection with auditor's report

507. Offences in connection with auditor's report

(1) A person to whom this section applies commits an offence if he knowingly or recklessly causes a report under section 495 (auditor's report on company's annual accounts) to include any matter that is misleading, false or deceptive in a material particular.

(2) A person to whom this section applies commits an offence if he knowingly or recklessly causes such a report to omit a statement required by-
    (a) section 498(2)(b) (statement that company's accounts do not agree with accounting records and returns),
    (b) section 498(3) (statement that necessary information and explanations not obtained), or
    (c) section 498(5) (statement that directors wrongly took advantage of exemption from obligation to prepare group accounts).

(3) This section applies to-
    (a) where the auditor is an individual, that individual and any employee or agent of his who is eligible for appointment as auditor of the company;
    (b) where the auditor is a firm, any director, member, employee or agent of the firm who is eligible for appointment as auditor of the company.

(4) A person guilty of an offence under this section is liable-

(a) on conviction on indictment, to a fine;

(b) on summary conviction, to a fine not exceeding the statutory maximum.

GENERAL NOTE

This new section creates a criminal offence in relation to inaccurate auditor's reports. The offence is committed by any individual eligible to be a statutory auditor who, first, knowingly or recklessly causes a report to include anything that is misleading, false or deceptive; or, secondly, omits a statement indicating (i) that the accounts do not agree with the records and returns, (ii) that the necessary information and explanations have not been obtained, or (iii) that the directors wrongly took advantage of an exemption from the obligation to prepare group accounts.

Attempts were made in the Commons to amend the wording in the original Bill, changing "knowingly and recklessly" to "dishonestly or fraudulently" (*Hansard*, cols 1046-1063 (October 19, 2006): www.publications.parliament.uk/pa/cm200506/cmhansrd/cm061019/debtext/61019-0004.htm#06101926002885). In opposing the change, the minister (Vera Baird, Q.C.) pointed out that "recklessness and negligence are well-established legal concepts" (col.1059) and that "to prove that someone has behaved recklessly, it is necessary to show that the auditor was aware that an action or failure to act - the latter is probably much more likely - carried risks, that they personally knew that the risks were not reasonable ones to take, and that, despite knowing that, they went ahead anyway" (col.1060). Despite this assurance, the accountancy profession is anxious that the guidance offered under s.508 (below) will provide greater clarity for auditors who might provide an incorrect audit opinion.

The criminal offence for auditors in relation to *accounting records* was amended to relate to the statement that the accounts are in agreement with the records (rather than being proper or adequate), which has reduced the risk exposure of smaller audit practitioners.

Subsection (1)

This subsection identifies the offence of commission, where the auditor knowingly or recklessly causes a report under s.495 to include anything that is misleading, false or deceptive.

Subsection (2)

This subsection identifies the offence of omission. The items whose omission by knowing or reckless action can be an offence are: (a) a statement that the company's accounts do not agree with accounting records and returns; (b) a statement that necessary information and explanations have not been obtained; and (c) a statement that the directors wrongly took advantage of the exemption from the obligation to prepare group accounts.

Subsection (3)

Individuals potentially caught by the offence are the auditor, as a sole practitioner, and his employees and agents; and the directors, members, employees and agents of an audit firm. However, the offence only applies to such an individual if he is an accountant who would be qualified to act as auditor of the company in his own right.

Subsection (4)

The maximum penalty for an offence under this section is an unlimited fine.

508. Guidance for regulatory and prosecuting authorities: England, Wales and Northern Ireland

(1) The Secretary of State may issue guidance for the purpose of helping relevant regulatory and prosecuting authorities to determine how they should carry out their functions in cases where behaviour occurs that-

(a) appears to involve the commission of an offence under section 507 (offences in connection with auditor's report), and

(b) has been, is being or may be investigated pursuant to arrangements-

(i) under paragraph 15 of Schedule 10 (investigation of complaints against auditors and supervisory bodies), or

(ii) of a kind mentioned in paragraph 24 of that Schedule (independent investigation for disciplinary purposes of public interest cases).

(2) The Secretary of State must obtain the consent of the Attorney General before issuing any such guidance.

(3) In this section "relevant regulatory and prosecuting authorities" means-

    (a) supervisory bodies within the meaning of Part 42 of this Act,

    (b) bodies to which the Secretary of State may make grants under section 16(1) of the Companies (Audit, Investigations and Community Enterprise) Act 2004 (c. 27) (bodies concerned with accounting standards etc),

    (c) the Director of the Serious Fraud Office,

    (d) the Director of Public Prosecutions or the Director of Public Prosecutions for Northern Ireland, and

    (e) the Secretary of State.

(4) This section does not apply to Scotland.

GENERAL NOTE

This section is innovatory and enables the Secretary of State to issue guidance about handling matters where the same behaviour by an auditor could give rise both to disciplinary proceedings by a regulatory body, and to prosecution for the new offence under s.507. However, it is likely that one of the most important aspects of the guidance would be to enable prosecutors to decide not to prosecute in a particular case that would be better handled through disciplinary proceedings.

Subsection (1)

The Secretary of State is empowered to issue guidance to help regulatory and prosecuting authorities where behaviour occurs that appears to give rise to an offence under s.507 and which is being investigated under the arrangements in paras 15 and 24 of Sch.10 (respectively investigation of complaints against auditors and supervisory bodies; and independent investigation for disciplinary purposes of public interest cases).

Subsection (2)

The Secretary of State must obtain the Attorney General's agreement to any guidance.

Subsection (3)

This subsection lists the regulatory and prosecuting authorities the guidance would be intended to help. The list includes the accountancy supervisory bodies, the Financial Reporting Council, the Director of the Serious Fraud Office and the Director of Public Prosecutions, as well as the Secretary of State himself.

Subsection (4)

The Secretary of State's guidance is limited to England, Wales and Northern Ireland.

509. Guidance for regulatory authorities: Scotland

(1) The Lord Advocate may issue guidance for the purpose of helping relevant regulatory authorities to determine how they should carry out their functions in cases where behaviour occurs that-

    (a) appears to involve the commission of an offence under section 507 (offences in connection with auditor's report), and

    (b) has been, is being or may be investigated pursuant to arrangements-

        (i) under paragraph 15 of Schedule 10 (investigation of complaints against auditors and supervisory bodies), or

        (ii) of a kind mentioned in paragraph 24 of that Schedule (independent investigation for disciplinary purposes of public interest cases).

(2) The Lord Advocate must consult the Secretary of State before issuing any such guidance.

(3) In this section "relevant regulatory authorities" means-

    (a) supervisory bodies within the meaning of Part 42 of this Act,

    (b) bodies to which the Secretary of State may make grants under section 16(1) of the Companies (Audit, Investigations and Community Enterprise) Act 2004 (c. 27) (bodies concerned with accounting standards etc), and

    (c) the Secretary of State.

(4) This section applies only to Scotland.

GENERAL NOTE

Like the previous section, this is innovatory and enables the Lord Advocate to issue guidance about handling matters in Scotland where the same auditor's report could give rise both to disciplinary proceedings by a regulatory body, and to prosecution for the new offence under s.507.

Subsection (1)

The Lord Advocate may issue guidance to help the relevant regulatory authorities decide how they should carry out their functions where behaviour occurs that appears to involve an offence in connection with the auditor's report under s.507 and which is being investigated under the arrangements in paras 15 and 24 of Sch.10 (respectively investigation of complaints against auditors and supervisory bodies; and independent investigation for disciplinary purposes of public interest cases).

Subsections (2) and (3)

The Lord Advocate must consult the Secretary of State before issuing guidance (subs.(2)). The regulatory bodies the guidance is intended to help are listed in subs.(3). The list includes the accountancy supervisory bodies, the FRC, and the Secretary of State.

Subsection (4)

This section only applies to Scotland.

CHAPTER 4

REMOVAL, RESIGNATION, ETC OF AUDITORS

GENERAL NOTE

This Chapter restates the law on the ways in which auditors can cease to hold office. The previous provisions were in s.388 of the 1985 Act, as substituted by s.119 of the 1989 Act, and ss.391-394A of the 1985 Act, as substituted/inserted by ss.122-123 of the 1989 Act. There have been some changes to the previous law resulting from changes elsewhere in the Act, making it easier to pass written resolutions. There are also changes in the requirements when auditors leave office: (i) increasing the range of cases in which there is a requirement for a statement explaining why they are leaving, and (ii) requiring copies of any statement to be sent to shareholders and to appropriate regulators.

Removal of auditor

510. Resolution removing auditor from office

(1) The members of a company may remove an auditor from office at any time.
(2) This power is exercisable only-
    (a) by ordinary resolution at a meeting, and
    (b) in accordance with section 511 (special notice of resolution to remove auditor).
(3) Nothing in this section is to be taken as depriving the person removed of compensation or damages payable to him in respect of the termination-
    (a) of his appointment as auditor, or
    (b) of any appointment terminating with that as auditor.
(4) An auditor may not be removed from office before the expiration of his term of office except by resolution under this section.

GENERAL NOTE

This section restates much of s.391 of the 1985 Act, indicating that the shareholders in a company always have the right to dismiss its auditor by ordinary resolution. As previously, in order to remove the auditor before the end of his term of office, even a private company will need to hold a general meeting to pass such a resolution.

Subsections (1) and (2)

Members of a company may remove an auditor at any time (subs.(1)). However, this can only be achieved by passing an ordinary resolution at a meeting after giving special notice: see s.511, below (subs.(2)).

Subsection (3)

This procedure does not prevent the auditor being entitled to compensation for termination of his appointment.

Subsection (4)

A resolution as described in this section is the only way in which an auditor can be removed before the end of his term of office.

511. Special notice required for resolution removing auditor from office

(1) Special notice is required for a resolution at a general meeting of a company removing an auditor from office.

(2) On receipt of notice of such an intended resolution the company must immediately send a copy of it to the auditor proposed to be removed.

(3) The auditor proposed to be removed may make with respect to the intended resolution representations in writing to the company (not exceeding a reasonable length) and request their notification to members of the company.

(4) The company must (unless the representations are received by it too late for it to do so)-

    (a) in any notice of the resolution given to members of the company, state the fact of the representations having been made, and

    (b) send a copy of the representations to every member of the company to whom notice of the meeting is or has been sent.

(5) If a copy of any such representations is not sent out as required because received too late or because of the company's default, the auditor may (without prejudice to his right to be heard orally) require that the representations be read out at the meeting.

(6) Copies of the representations need not be sent out and the representations need not be read at the meeting if, on the application either of the company or of any other person claiming to be aggrieved, the court is satisfied that the auditor is using the provisions of this section to secure needless publicity for defamatory matter.

The court may order the company's costs (in Scotland, expenses) on the application to be paid in whole or in part by the auditor, notwithstanding that he is not a party to the application.

GENERAL NOTE

This section restates the requirement in s.391A of the 1985 Act, as inserted by s.122 of the 1989 Act, that a resolution to dismiss an auditor needs special notice (i.e. 28 days before the general meeting, as defined in s.312). The company must send a copy to the auditor facing dismissal, and he then has the right to make a statement of his case. The company has to circulate his statement to the shareholders (or, if time does not allow, the statement can be read out at the meeting).

Subsections (1) and (2)

Special notice is required for a resolution at a general meeting to remove an auditor (subs.(1)), and a copy must be sent to the auditor concerned (subs.(2)).

Subsections (3)-(5)

The auditor can make written representations to the company of a reasonable length and ask for them to be circulated to members (subs.(3)). The company must then inform members in the notice of the resolution that representations have been made and circulate them (subs.(4)). If a copy of the representations is not sent, either because of a lack of time or through the company's fault, the auditor (without prejudice to his right to address the meeting) may demand that the representations be read out at the meeting (subs.(5)).

Subsection (6)

This subsection provides protection to the company from vexatious behaviour by the auditor if he is using the provision to have a statement circulated to secure needless publicity for defamatory material. The company, or someone else, can then apply to the court for it to determine whether the auditor is using the provision in such a way, in which case the company is not obliged to circulate the statement. The court can order the auditor to pay some or all of the costs of the proceedings.

512. Notice to registrar of resolution removing auditor from office

(1) Where a resolution is passed under section 510 (resolution removing auditor from office), the company must give notice of that fact to the registrar within 14 days.

(2) If a company fails to give the notice required by this section, an offence is committed by-

    (a) the company, and

    (b) every officer of it who is in default.

(3) A person guilty of an offence under this section is liable on summary conviction to a fine not exceeding level 3 on the standard scale and, for continued contravention, a daily default fine not exceeding one-tenth of level 3 on the standard scale.

GENERAL NOTE

This section restates the obligation in s.391(2) in the 1985 Act (as inserted by s.122 of the 1989 Act) which requires a company that has decided to dismiss its auditor to inform the registrar within 14 days.

Subsections (1)-(3)

A company must notify the registrar within 14 days when a resolution is passed removing an auditor from office under s.510 (subs.(1)). Failure to give such notice renders the company and the officers at fault *prima facie* guilty of an offence (subs.(2)), the penalties for which are spelt out in subs.(3).

513. Rights of auditor who has been removed from office

(1) An auditor who has been removed by resolution under section 510 has, notwithstanding his removal, the rights conferred by section 502(2) in relation to any general meeting of the company-

    (a) at which his term of office would otherwise have expired, or

    (b) at which it is proposed to fill the vacancy caused by his removal.

(2) In such a case the references in that section to matters concerning the auditor as auditor shall be construed as references to matters concerning him as a former auditor.

GENERAL NOTE

This section restates the right in s.391A of the 1985 Act (as inserted by s.122 of the 1989 Act) of a dismissed auditor to attend any meeting effecting his removal.

Subsections (1) and (2)

A auditor dismissed by a resolution under s.510 has the rights conferred by s.502(2) to attend general meetings of the company at which his term of office would otherwise have expired (i.e. a public company's accounts meeting) or at which it is proposed to replace him (subs.(1)). In such circumstances, references to the auditor in s.502(2) can be read as referring to him as a "former auditor" (subs.(2)).

Failure to re-appoint auditor

514. Failure to re-appoint auditor: special procedure required for written resolution

(1) This section applies where a resolution is proposed as a written resolution of a private company whose effect would be to appoint a person as auditor in place of a person (the "outgoing auditor") whose term of office has expired, or is to expire, at the end of the period for appointing auditors.

(2) The following provisions apply if-

    (a) no period for appointing auditors has ended since the outgoing auditor ceased to hold office, or

    (b) such a period has ended and an auditor or auditors should have been appointed but were not.

(3) The company must send a copy of the proposed resolution to the person proposed to be appointed and to the outgoing auditor.

(4) The outgoing auditor may, within 14 days after receiving the notice, make with respect to the proposed resolution representations in writing to the company (not exceeding a reasonable length) and request their circulation to members of the company.

(5) The company must circulate the representations together with the copy or copies of the resolution circulated in accordance with section 291 (resolution proposed by directors) or section 293 (resolution proposed by members).

(6) Where subsection (5) applies-

    (a) the period allowed under section 293(3) for service of copies of the proposed resolution is 28 days instead of 21 days, and

    (b) the provisions of section 293(5) and (6) (offences) apply in relation to a failure to comply with that subsection as in relation to a default in complying with that section.

(7) Copies of the representations need not be circulated if, on the application either of the company or of any other person claiming to be aggrieved, the court is satisfied that the auditor is using the provisions of this section to secure needless publicity for defamatory matter.

The court may order the company's costs (in Scotland, expenses) on the application to be paid in whole or in part by the auditor, notwithstanding that he is not a party to the application.

(8) If any requirement of this section is not complied with, the resolution is ineffective.

GENERAL NOTE

The provisions of this section are new and set out the procedure for changing auditor from one financial year to the next by written resolution (a procedure only available to private companies). This may be done (i) during the term of office of the outgoing auditor, or (ii) afterwards, if no replacement has been appointed. However, case (ii) will arise only if there is no automatic deemed reappointment for one of the five reasons given in s.487(2), above.

Subsections (1)-(3)

This section applies to private companies where there is a written resolution replacing an auditor (the "outgoing auditor") whose term of office is expiring or has expired (subs.(1)). Whether or not the period for appointing auditors has ended and a new auditor has not been appointed (subs.(2)), the company must send a copy of the proposed resolution both to the outgoing auditor and to his proposed replacement (subs.(3)).

Subsections (4)-(6)

The outgoing auditor then has 14 days to make written representations of reasonable length to the company, requesting that they be circulated to members (subs.(4)). The company must then circulate such representations with the resolution, regardless of whether it has been proposed by the directors under s.291 or by members under s.293 (subs.(5)), with the proviso that the period allowed for circulation under s.293(3) is to be 28 days rather than 21 (subs.(6)).

Subsection (7)

The company is afforded protection if the outgoing auditor is using the provision to have a statement circulated to secure needless publicity for defamatory material. It enables the company, or someone else, to apply to the court, and the court can then determine whether the auditor is using the provision in that way, in which case the company is not obliged to circulate the auditor's representations. The court can order the auditor to pay some or all of the costs or expenses of the proceedings.

Subsection (8)

Failure to comply with the rules in this section will make the resolution ineffective.

515. Failure to re-appoint auditor: special notice required for resolution at general meeting

(1) This section applies to a resolution at a general meeting of a company whose effect would be to appoint a person as auditor in place of a person (the "outgoing auditor") whose term of office has ended, or is to end-

    (a) in the case of a private company, at the end of the period for appointing auditors;

    (b) in the case of a public company, at the end of the next accounts meeting.

(2) Special notice is required of such a resolution if-

    (a) in the case of a private company-

        (i) no period for appointing auditors has ended since the outgoing auditor ceased to hold office, or

        (ii) such a period has ended and an auditor or auditors should have been appointed but were not;

    (b) in the case of a public company-

        (i) there has been no accounts meeting of the company since the outgoing auditor ceased to hold office, or

        (ii) there has been an accounts meeting at which an auditor or auditors should have been appointed but were not.

(3) On receipt of notice of such an intended resolution the company shall forthwith send a copy of it to the person proposed to be appointed and to the outgoing auditor.

(4) The outgoing auditor may make with respect to the intended resolution representations in writing to the company (not exceeding a reasonable length) and request their notification to members of the company.

(5) The company must (unless the representations are received by it too late for it to do so)-

    (a) in any notice of the resolution given to members of the company, state the fact of the representations having been made, and

    (b) send a copy of the representations to every member of the company to whom notice of the meeting is or has been sent.

(6) If a copy of any such representations is not sent out as required because received too late or because of the company's default, the outgoing auditor may (without prejudice to his right to be heard orally) require that the representations be read out at the meeting.

(7) Copies of the representations need not be sent out and the representations need not be read at the meeting if, on the application either of the company or of any other person claiming to be aggrieved, the court is satisfied that the auditor is using the provisions of this section to secure needless publicity for defamatory matter.

The court may order the company's costs (in Scotland, expenses) on the application to be paid in whole or in part by the outgoing auditor, notwithstanding that he is not a party to the application.

GENERAL NOTE

This section, derived from s.391A of the 1985 Act (as inserted by s.122 of the 1989 Act), details the procedure for changing auditor between one financial year and the next at a general meeting. This may be done by resolution at the meeting, but special notice is required if no deadline for appointing auditors has passed since the outgoing auditor left, or if the deadline has passed when an auditor should have been appointed without one being appointed. So, for example, if a public company chooses not to reappoint an auditor at its accounts meeting, but later (before the next accounts meeting) changes its mind, it would need to give special notice of any general meeting appointing replacement auditors.

Subsections (1)-(3)

The provisions of s.515 apply where a resolution is put to a general meeting to replace an existing auditor whose term of office has ended or is to end (subs.(1)). There are different sets of circumstances for private and public companies where special notice is required for such a resolution (subs.(2)). However, when it receives the proposed resolution, the company should immediately send a copy of it both to the outgoing auditor and to his proposed replacement (subs.(3)).

The outgoing auditor may forward written representations of a reasonable length to the company (subs.(4)), and in such circumstances the company, when the representations are received in time, must refer to this fact when giving notice of such a resolution and send a copy to each member (subs.(5)). When the representations are received too late, or where the company fails to circulate them as required, the outgoing auditor can (in addition to his general right to speak at the meeting) demand that they should be read out (subs.(6)).

Subsection (7)

This subsection provides protection to the company from vexatious behaviour by the auditor if he is using the provision to have a statement circulated to secure needless publicity for defamatory material. The company, or someone else, can then apply to the court for it to determine whether the auditor is using the provision in such a way, in which case the company is not obliged to circulate the statement. The court can order the auditor to pay some or all of the costs of the proceedings.

Resignation of auditor

516. Resignation of auditor

(1) An auditor of a company may resign his office by depositing a notice in writing to that effect at the company's registered office.
(2) The notice is not effective unless it is accompanied by the statement required by section 519.
(3) An effective notice of resignation operates to bring the auditor's term of office to an end as of the date on which the notice is deposited or on such later date as may be specified in it.

GENERAL NOTE

This section restates the right in s.392(1)-(2) of the 1985 Act (as inserted by s.122 of the 1989 Act) of an auditor to resign by written notice to the company.

Subsections (1)-(3)

An auditor may resign by depositing written notice of his intention at the company's registered office (subs.(1)). However, to be effective, it must be accompanied by the statement required by s.519 (statement by auditor to be deposited with company) (subs.(2)). The resignation is effective from the date it is delivered to the company's registered office, or from a later date, where specified (subs.(3)).

517. Notice to registrar of resignation of auditor

(1) Where an auditor resigns the company must within 14 days of the deposit of a notice of resignation send a copy of the notice to the registrar of companies.
(2) If default is made in complying with this section, an offence is committed by-
    (a) the company, and
    (b) every officer of the company who is in default.
(3) A person guilty of an offence under this section is liable-
    (a) on conviction on indictment, to a fine;
    (b) on summary conviction, to a fine not exceeding the statutory maximum and, for continued contravention, a daily default fine not exceeding one-tenth of the statutory maximum.

GENERAL NOTE

This section restates the obligation in s.392(3) of the 1985 Act (as inserted by s.122 of the 1989 Act) on a company whose auditor resigns to inform the registrar.

A company must forward a copy to the registrar of companies of notice of its auditor's resignation within 14 days of its receipt (subs.(1)). Default in complying with this requirement renders the company and every officer concerned *prima facie* guilty of an offence (subs.(2)), the penalties for which are spelt out in subs.(3).

518.   Rights of resigning auditor

(1) This section applies where an auditor's notice of resignation is accompanied by a statement of the circumstances connected with his resignation (see section 519).

(2) He may deposit with the notice a signed requisition calling on the directors of the company forthwith duly to convene a general meeting of the company for the purpose of receiving and considering such explanation of the circumstances connected with his resignation as he may wish to place before the meeting.

(3) He may request the company to circulate to its members-

    (a) before the meeting convened on his requisition, or

    (b) before any general meeting at which his term of office would otherwise have expired or at which it is proposed to fill the vacancy caused by his resignation,

a statement in writing (not exceeding a reasonable length) of the circumstances connected with his resignation.

(4) The company must (unless the statement is received too late for it to comply)-

    (a) in any notice of the meeting given to members of the company, state the fact of the statement having been made, and

    (b) send a copy of the statement to every member of the company to whom notice of the meeting is or has been sent.

(5) The directors must within 21 days from the date of the deposit of a requisition under this section proceed duly to convene a meeting for a day not more than 28 days after the date on which the notice convening the meeting is given.

(6) If default is made in complying with subsection (5), every director who failed to take all reasonable steps to secure that a meeting was convened commits an offence.

(7) A person guilty of an offence under this section is liable-

    (a) on conviction on indictment, to a fine;

    (b) on summary conviction to a fine not exceeding the statutory maximum.

(8) If a copy of the statement mentioned above is not sent out as required because received too late or because of the company's default, the auditor may (without prejudice to his right to be heard orally) require that the statement be read out at the meeting.

(9) Copies of a statement need not be sent out and the statement need not be read out at the meeting if, on the application either of the company or of any other person who claims to be aggrieved, the court is satisfied that the auditor is using the provisions of this section to secure needless publicity for defamatory matter.

The court may order the company's costs (in Scotland, expenses) on such an application to be paid in whole or in part by the auditor, notwithstanding that he is not a party to the application.

(10) An auditor who has resigned has, notwithstanding his resignation, the rights conferred by section 502(2) in relation to any such general meeting of the company as is mentioned in subsection (3)(a) or (b) above. In such a case the references in that section to matters concerning the auditor as auditor shall be construed as references to matters concerning him as a former auditor.

GENERAL NOTE

This section restates the right in s.392A of the 1985 Act (as inserted by s.122 of the 1989 Act) of an auditor who resigns to require the directors to convene a general meeting of the company so that members can consider his explanation of the circumstances that led to his decision to resign.

Subsections (1) and (2)

Where an auditor's notice of resignation is accompanied by a "statement of circumstances" under s.519 (below) (subs.(1)), he may send with his notice of resignation a signed requisition asking the directors to convene a general meeting to hear the reasons for his action (subs.(2)).

Subsections (3)-(7)

The auditor is also entitled to ask the company to send out a written statement (of reasonable length), explaining why he has resigned. Such a statement can be circulated either in advance of that meeting if he has requested one, or before the next appropriate general meeting (subs.(3)). When the written representations are received in time, the company must refer to the fact that it has received them when giving notice of the meeting and send a copy of the statement to each member (subs.(4)). The directors then have 21 days to send out a notice convening a meeting once a resigning auditor has requested it, and it must then be held within 28 days of the notice being given (subs.(5)). Every director who fails to comply with subs.(5) is *prima facie* guilty of an offence (subs.(6)), the penalty for which is specified in subs.(7).

Subsection (8)

Where the statement is not circulated, either because the representations are received too late, or where the company fails to circulate them as required, the outgoing auditor can (in addition to his general right to speak at the meeting) demand that they should be read out.

Subsection (9)

The company is protected from vexatious behaviour by the auditor if he is using the provision to have a statement circulated to secure needless publicity for defamatory material. The company, or someone else, can then apply to the court for it to determine whether the auditor is using the provision in such a way, in which case the company is not obliged to circulate the statement. The court can order the auditor to pay some or all of the costs or expenses of the application.

Subsection (10)

An auditor who has resigned enjoys similar rights with respect to requesting circulation of an explanation of the reasons for his action ahead of a general meeting at which his term of office would otherwise have expired or at which it is proposed to appoint another auditor.

Statement by auditor on ceasing to hold office

GENERAL NOTE

For unquoted companies, the requirements for a "statement of circumstances" are essentially unchanged. However, auditors of quoted companies will now always need to make a statement of the circumstances connected with their ceasing to hold office.

There is also a new requirement that the audit authorities should be notified when auditors cease to hold office, giving reasons. For listed and public interest companies, this applies whenever they cease to hold office. However, auditors of other companies only need to notify the authorities if they cease to hold office before the end of their term. Companies are also required to notify the authorities when they change auditors: i.e. there is a "double notification" regime.

519. Statement by auditor to be deposited with company

(1) Where an auditor of an unquoted company ceases for any reason to hold office, he must deposit at the company's registered office a statement of the circumstances connected with his ceasing to hold office, unless he considers that there are no circumstances in connection with his ceasing to hold office that need to be brought to the attention of members or creditors of the company.

(2) If he considers that there are no circumstances in connection with his ceasing to hold office that need to be brought to the attention of members or creditors of the company, he must deposit at the company's registered office a statement to that effect.

(3) Where an auditor of a quoted company ceases for any reason to hold office, he must deposit at the company's registered office a statement of the circumstances connected with his ceasing to hold office.

(4) The statement required by this section must be deposited-

> (a) in the case of resignation, along with the notice of resignation;
>
> (b) in the case of failure to seek re-appointment, not less than 14 days before the end of the time allowed for next appointing an auditor;
>
> (c) in any other case, not later than the end of the period of 14 days beginning with the date on which he ceases to hold office.

(5) A person ceasing to hold office as auditor who fails to comply with this section commits an offence.

(6) In proceedings for such an offence it is a defence for the person charged to show that he took all reasonable steps and exercised all due diligence to avoid the commission of the offence.

(7) A person guilty of an offence under this section is liable-

> (a) on conviction on indictment, to a fine;
>
> (b) on summary conviction, to a fine not exceeding the statutory maximum.

GENERAL NOTE

This section modifies the substance of ss.394(1)-(2) and 394A of the 1985 Act (as inserted by s.123 of the 1989 Act), concerning a statement to be lodged with a company by a departing auditor. Briefly, for quoted companies, this statement should explain the circumstances surrounding his departure; whereas for other public companies, and for all private companies, it should explain the circumstances unless the auditor thinks that it is unnecessary for them to be brought to the attention of the shareholders and/or creditors. However, even in the latter case, the statement should state that there are no such circumstances.

This reverses the previous position under s.394 of the 1985 Act, where auditors were only required to make a statement if they considered there were relevant circumstances that needed to be brought to the attention of members and/or creditors. It also now provides that auditors of quoted companies will always be required to make such a statement of the circumstances when they leave office.

Subsections (1) and (2)

An auditor of an unquoted company is required to deposit with the company a statement of the circumstances when he ceases to hold office, unless he considers that there are no matters that need to be brought to the attention of members or creditors (subs.(1)) - although even in the latter case he is required to state this in a statement to be lodged at the company's registered office (subs.(2)).

Subsection (3)

An auditor of a quoted company is similarly required to deposit with the company a statement of the circumstances when he ceases to hold office.

Subsection (4)

The statement of circumstances must be deposited, in the case of resignation, with the notice of resignation; in the case of failure to seek reappointment, not less than 14 days before the end of time allowed for appointing the next auditor; or, in any other case, within 14 days of his leaving office.

Subsections (5)-(7)

Following the substance of s.394A of the 1985 Act, a departing auditor who fails to comply with the provisions of this section commits an offence (subs.(5)), although it is a defence to show that all reasonable steps were taken to comply (subs.(6)). The penalties for committing such an offence are detailed in subs.(7).

520. Company's duties in relation to statement

(1) This section applies where the statement deposited under section 519 states the circumstances connected with the auditor's ceasing to hold office.

(2) The company must within 14 days of the deposit of the statement either-

> (a) send a copy of it to every person who under section 423 is entitled to be sent copies of the accounts, or
>
> (b) apply to the court.

(3) If it applies to the court, the company must notify the auditor of the application.

(4) If the court is satisfied that the auditor is using the provisions of section 519 to secure needless publicity for defamatory matter-

  (a) it shall direct that copies of the statement need not be sent out, and

  (b) it may further order the company's costs (in Scotland, expenses) on the application to be paid in whole or in part by the auditor, even if he is not a party to the application.

The company must within 14 days of the court's decision send to the persons mentioned in subsection (2)(a) a statement setting out the effect of the order.

(5) If no such direction is made the company must send copies of the statement to the persons mentioned in subsection (2)(a) within 14 days of the court's decision or, as the case may be, of the discontinuance of the proceedings.

(6) In the event of default in complying with this section an offence is committed by every officer of the company who is in default.

(7) In proceedings for such an offence it is a defence for the person charged to show that he took all reasonable steps and exercised all due diligence to avoid the commission of the offence.

(8) A person guilty of an offence under this section is liable-

  (a) on conviction on indictment, to a fine;

  (b) on summary conviction, to a fine not exceeding the statutory maximum.

GENERAL NOTE

This section restates much of the substance of subss.(3)-(4) and (6)-(7) of s.394 of the 1985 Act (as inserted by s.123 of the 1989 Act).

In *Jarvis Plc and Others v PricewaterhouseCoopers (a firm)* (2000) 150 New Law Journal 1109, the High Court ruled that where a company brought proceedings under s.394(3) of the Companies Act 1985 on the basis of allegations that, on resignation, its former auditor was using the statement of reasons for ceasing to hold office to obtain needless publicity for defamatory matter, it could bring them to an end by a notice of discontinuance. The court did not, in these circumstances, have to make a positive ruling that it was not satisfied that the auditor had been using the statement for that purpose. However, indemnity costs could have been awarded to the auditors.

Subsections (1) and (2)

Where a statement of circumstances is deposited under s.519 (subs.(1)), a company must send a copy of the statement within 14 days to every person to whom it is required to send the annual accounts under s.423 (subs.(2)).

Subsections (3)-(5)

If the company does not want to circulate the statement, it can apply to the court, but it must then notify the auditor of its action (subs.(3)). If the court then decides that the departing auditor is trying to secure needless publicity for defamatory material, it may require him to pay in whole or in part the costs or expenses of the application, and it may direct that the company need not circulate the statement. However, it must instead send notice of the effect of the court decision within 14 days to those to whom it would otherwise have sent the statement of circumstances (subs.(4). Otherwise, if the court makes no such direction or the proceedings are discontinued, the statement of circumstances must be circulated to those entitled to receive copies of the annual accounts under s.423 within 14 days of the court's ruling or of the discontinuance of proceedings (subs.(5)).

Subsections (6)-(8)

Failure to comply with the provisions of this section renders every defaulting officer of a company *prima facie* guilty of an offence (subs.(6)), although it is a defence to show that all reasonable steps were taken to comply (subs.(7)). The penalties for committing such an offence are detailed in subs.(8).

521. Copy of statement to be sent to registrar

(1) Unless within 21 days beginning with the day on which he deposited the statement under section 519 the auditor receives notice of an application to the court under section 520, he must within a further seven days send a copy of the statement to the registrar.

(2) If an application to the court is made under section 520 and the auditor subsequently receives notice under subsection (5) of that section, he must within seven days of receiving the notice send a copy of the statement to the registrar.

(3) An auditor who fails to comply with subsection (1) or (2) commits an offence.

(4) In proceedings for such an offence it is a defence for the person charged to show that he took all reasonable steps and exercised all due diligence to avoid the commission of the offence.

(5) A person guilty of an offence under this section is liable-
    (a) on conviction on indictment, to a fine;
    (b) on summary conviction, to a fine not exceeding the statutory maximum.

GENERAL NOTE

This section restates and expands subs.(5) of s.394 of the 1985 Act (as inserted by s.123 of the 1989 Act).

Subsection (1)

A departing auditor must send a copy of his statement of circumstances to the registrar of companies, normally within 28 days of depositing it with the company. However, he is not required to send it to the registrar if, within 21 days of depositing it, he hears that the company has applied to the court under s.520, seeking an order relieving it of the obligation to circulate the statement.

Subsection (2)

If the company lets the auditor know that its application under s.520 was unsuccessful, he must then send a copy of the statement of circumstances to the registrar within seven days of being informed.

Subsections (3)-(5)

Failure to comply with the provisions of this section renders the defaulting auditor *prima facie* guilty of an offence (subs.(3)), although it is a defence to show that all reasonable steps were taken to comply (subs.(4)). The penalties for committing such an offence are detailed in subs.(5).

522. Duty of auditor to notify appropriate audit authority

(1) Where-
    (a) in the case of a major audit, an auditor ceases for any reason to hold office, or
    (b) in the case of an audit that is not a major audit, an auditor ceases to hold office before the end of his term of office,
the auditor ceasing to hold office must notify the appropriate audit authority.

(2) The notice must-
    (a) inform the appropriate audit authority that he has ceased to hold office, and
    (b) be accompanied by a copy of the statement deposited by him at the company's registered office in accordance with section 519.

(3) If the statement so deposited is to the effect that he considers that there are no circumstances in connection with his ceasing to hold office that need to be brought to the attention of members or creditors of the company, the notice must also be accompanied by a statement of the reasons for his ceasing to hold office.

(4) The auditor must comply with this section-
    (a) in the case of a major audit, at the same time as he deposits a statement at the company's registered office in accordance with section 519;
    (b) in the case of an audit that is not a major audit, at such time (not being earlier than the time mentioned in paragraph (a)) as the appropriate audit authority may require.

(5) A person ceasing to hold office as auditor who fails to comply with this section commits an offence.

(6) If that person is a firm an offence is committed by-
    (a) the firm, and
    (b) every officer of the firm who is in default.

(7) In proceedings for an offence under this section it is a defence for the person charged to show that he took all reasonable steps and exercised all due diligence to avoid the commission of the offence.

(8) A person guilty of an offence under this section is liable-

(a) on conviction on indictment, to a fine;

(b) on summary conviction, to a fine not exceeding the statutory maximum.

GENERAL NOTE

A new obligation is introduced in this section on departing auditors. They are required to send copies of their s.519 "statements of circumstances" to an "appropriate audit authority" (as defined in s.525, below). It contains different rules depending on whether the company the auditor is leaving is classified as a "major audit", another term defined in s.525.

Subsections (1)-(4)

An auditor is required to notify the appropriate audit authority if he leaves office before the appointed time (i.e. if has resigned or been dismissed). However, with respect to "major audits", he must notify the appropriate audit authority if he leaves office for any reason (subs.(1)). The notice must be accompanied by a copy of the "statement of circumstances" lodged at the company's registered office (subs.(2)), and if in his view there are no circumstances that need to be brought to the attention of members and/or creditors, he must submit a statement giving the reasons why he ceased to hold office (subs.(3)). The auditor is required to comply with this section, in the case of a "major audit" at the same time as he lodges his "statement of circumstances" with the company, and in other cases as the appropriate audit authority may require (subs.(4)).

Subsections (5)-(8)

Failure to comply with the provisions of this section renders a defaulting auditor *prima facie* guilty of an offence (subs.(5)), and if the auditor is a firm, the firm and every defaulting officer (subs.(6)). However, it is a defence to show that all reasonable steps were taken to comply (subs.(7)). The penalties for committing such an offence are detailed in subs.(8).

523. Duty of company to notify appropriate audit authority

(1) Where an auditor ceases to hold office before the end of his term of office, the company must notify the appropriate audit authority.

(2) The notice must-

    (a) inform the appropriate audit authority that the auditor has ceased to hold office, and

    (b) be accompanied by-

        (i) a statement by the company of the reasons for his ceasing to hold office, or

        (ii) if the copy of the statement deposited by the auditor at the company's registered office in accordance with section 519 contains a statement of circumstances in connection with his ceasing to hold office that need to be brought to the attention of members or creditors of the company, a copy of that statement.

(3) The company must give notice under this section not later than 14 days after the date on which the auditor's statement is deposited at the company's registered office in accordance with section 519.

(4) If a company fails to comply with this section, an offence is committed by-

    (a) the company, and

    (b) every officer of the company who is in default.

(5) In proceedings for such an offence it is a defence for the person charged to show that he took all reasonable steps and exercised all due diligence to avoid the commission of the offence.

(6) A person guilty of an offence under this section is liable-

    (a) on conviction on indictment, to a fine;

    (b) on summary conviction, to a fine not exceeding the statutory maximum.

GENERAL NOTE

This section introduces a new duty on a company to notify the appropriate audit authority whenever an auditor leaves office before the end of his term: i.e. when he has resigned or is dismissed. The company has the choice of sending in the statement of circumstances made by the auditor under s.519, or of sending in its own statement of the reasons for his ceasing to hold office.

Subsections (1)-(3)

A company whose auditor leaves office before the appointed time has to notify the appropriate audit authority (subs.(1)), informing it that he has ceased to hold office. This should be accompanied by a statement from the company, giving the reasons for his ceasing to hold office. Where the auditor's "statement of circumstances" contains information that needs to be brought to the attention of the company's members and/or creditors, this too should be forwarded (subs.(2)). Notice under this section must be given by the company within 14 days of the departing auditor filing his "statement of circumstances" at the company's registered office (subs.(3)).

Subsections (4)-(6)

Failure to comply with the provisions of this section renders the company and its defaulting officers *prima facie* guilty of an offence (subs.(4)), although it is a defence to show that all reasonable steps were taken to comply (subs.(5)). The penalties for committing such an offence are detailed in subs.(6).

524.   Information to be given to accounting authorities

(1) The appropriate audit authority on receiving notice under section 522 or 523 of an auditor's ceasing to hold office-
   (a) must inform the accounting authorities, and
   (b) may if it thinks fit forward to those authorities a copy of the statement or statements accompanying the notice.
(2) The accounting authorities are-
   (a) the Secretary of State, and
   (b) any person authorised by the Secretary of State for the purposes of section 456 (revision of defective accounts: persons authorised to apply to court).
(3) If either of the accounting authorities is also the appropriate audit authority it is only necessary to comply with this section as regards any other accounting authority.
(4) If the court has made an order under section 520(4) directing that copies of the statement need not be sent out by the company, sections 460 and 461 (restriction on further disclosure) apply in relation to the copies sent to the accounting authorities as they apply to information obtained under section 459 (power to require documents etc).

GENERAL NOTE

This is another new provision, setting out the duty of the audit authorities to inform the accounting authorities about departing auditors. It also gives the audit authorities discretion to pass on the statements that they receive from departing auditors under s.522.

The accounting authorities are the Secretary of State and anyone the Secretary of State has authorised under Pt 15 to apply to the court in respect of the revision of defective accounts. Currently this is the Financial Reporting Review Panel ("FRRP"), which operates as part of the Financial Reporting Council ("FRC").

Subsection (1)

The appropriate audit authority on receiving notice under ss.522-523 must inform the relevant accounting authorities when an auditor ceases to hold office and may, if it thinks fit, forward copies of relevant statements (subs.(1)).

Subsection (2)

The relevant accounting authorities are identified as the Secretary of State or any person or body that he has authorised for the purposes of s.456, which deals with persons or bodies authorised to apply to the court with respect to defective accounts.

Subsection (3)

Where the same body is both an audit authority and an accounting authority, it is only necessary to comply with this section with regard to any other accounting authority.

Subsection (4)

If an accounting authority receives a statement that the court has determined need not be circulated to members under s.520(4), applying ss.459-462 it must treat the statement as confidential.

525. Meaning of "appropriate audit authority" and "major audit"

(1) In sections 522, 523 and 524 "appropriate audit authority" means-
    (a) in the case of a major audit-
        (i) the Secretary of State, or
        (ii) if the Secretary of State has delegated functions under section 1252 to a body whose functions include receiving the notice in question, that body;
    (b) in the case of an audit that is not a major audit, the relevant supervisory body.
"Supervisory body" has the same meaning as in Part 42 (statutory auditors) (see section 1217).
(2) In sections 522 and this section "major audit" means a statutory audit conducted in respect of-
    (a) a company any of whose securities have been admitted to the official list (within the meaning of Part 6 of the Financial Services and Markets Act 2000 (c. 8)), or
    (b) any other person in whose financial condition there is a major public interest.
(3) In determining whether an audit is a major audit within subsection (2)(b), regard shall be had to any guidance issued by any of the authorities mentioned in subsection (1).

GENERAL NOTE
  This section is new and defines two terms used in ss.522-524 in relation to the duty to inform the audit authority when an auditor ceases to hold office, namely "appropriate audit authority" and "major audit".

Subsection (1)
  In relation to a "major audit", the term "appropriate audit authority" means the Secretary of State, or the body to whom he has delegated functions in relation to the supervision of statutory auditors under ss.1252-1253, currently the Professional Oversight Board, which is part of the Financial Reporting Council. In relation to an audit which is not a "major audit", the term "appropriate audit authority" means the relevant supervisory body (as defined in s.1217).

Subsection (2)
  In ss.522 and 525, the term "major audit" refers to the audit of a listed company or of an entity in whose financial condition there is a major public interest.

Subsection (3)
  In determining whether there is a major public interest in the financial condition of an entity, regard should be had to guidance issued by the "appropriate audit authority": i.e. generally the Financial Reporting Council.

Supplementary

526. Effect of casual vacancies

If an auditor ceases to hold office for any reason, any surviving or continuing auditor or auditors may continue to act.

GENERAL NOTE
  This section restates s.388(2) of the 1985 Act, as inserted by s.119 of the 1989 Act. It states that where one of two or more joint auditors ceases to be an auditor, the remaining auditors should continue in office.

QUOTED COMPANIES: RIGHT OF MEMBERS TO RAISE AUDIT CONCERNS AT
ACCOUNTS MEETING

GENERAL NOTE

This Chapter introduces a new right for shareholders in a quoted company to raise questions about the work of the auditors.

Members of quoted companies who are able to gain the support of a substantial proportion of shareholders are given a new right to raise questions about that the annual audit at the accounts general meeting. They must notify the company of their intentions, and the company must publish the questions on its website. Quoted companies will therefore need to ensure that they include an invitation to members to put questions about the audit in their papers for the annual accounts meeting. They will also need to have a procedure for informing their auditors of any questions that are received.

527. Members' power to require website publication of audit concerns

(1) The members of a quoted company may require the company to publish on a website a statement setting out any matter relating to-
   (a) the audit of the company's accounts (including the auditor's report and the conduct of the audit) that are to be laid before the next accounts meeting, or
   (b) any circumstances connected with an auditor of the company ceasing to hold office since the previous accounts meeting,
that the members propose to raise at the next accounts meeting of the company.
(2) A company is required to do so once it has received requests to that effect from-
   (a) members representing at least 5% of the total voting rights of all the members who have a relevant right to vote (excluding any voting rights attached to any shares in the company held as treasury shares), or
   (b) at least 100 members who have a relevant right to vote and hold shares in the company on which there has been paid up an average sum, per member, of at least £100.
See also section 153 (exercise of rights where shares held on behalf of others).
(3) In subsection (2) a "relevant right to vote" means a right to vote at the accounts meeting.
(4) A request-
   (a) may be sent to the company in hard copy or electronic form,
   (b) must identify the statement to which it relates,
   (c) must be authenticated by the person or persons making it, and
   (d) must be received by the company at least one week before the meeting to which it relates.
(5) A quoted company is not required to place on a website a statement under this section if, on an application by the company or another person who claims to be aggrieved, the court is satisfied that the rights conferred by this section are being abused.
(6) The court may order the members requesting website publication to pay the whole or part of the company's costs (in Scotland, expenses) on such an application, even if they are not parties to the application.

GENERAL NOTE

This section creates a new right whereby shareholders in a quoted company - if they have a sufficiently large holding in the company, or there are enough of them - can request the company to publish a statement on a website dealing with their audit concerns.

Subsection (1)

Members of a quoted company may require the company to publish on a website a statement setting out any matter relating to the audit of the company's accounts that will be laid before the next accounts meeting or any circumstances relating to the auditor ceasing to hold office.

Subsections (2) and (3)

The company will have to accede to the members' request for such a statement to be published where they represent at least 5 per cent of those having the "relevant right to vote" at an accounts meeting or where there are at least 100 of them holding shares on which there has been paid up an average sum per member of at least £100 (subs.(2)). (The "relevant right to vote" is defined in subs.(3).)

Subsection (4)

A request may be sent to the company in hard copy or electronic form, must identify the statement to which it relates, must be authenticated by the persons sending it, and must be received by the company at least one week before the meeting.

Subsections (5) and (6)

A quoted company is afforded protection if members abuse the new right (e.g. by requesting a defamatory statement to be published). It, or someone else (such as the auditor) may apply to the court, which can then determine whether the right is being abused, in which case the company is not obliged to publish the statement (subs.(5)). The court may then order the shareholders who requested publication to pay some or all of the costs or expenses of the proceedings (subs.(6)).

528. Requirements as to website availability

(1) The following provisions apply for the purposes of section 527 (website publication of members' statement of audit concerns).

(2) The information must be made available on a website that-
    (a) is maintained by or on behalf of the company, and
    (b) identifies the company in question.

(3) Access to the information on the website, and the ability to obtain a hard copy of the information from the website, must not be conditional on the payment of a fee or otherwise restricted.

(4) The statement-
    (a) must be made available within three working days of the company being required to publish it on a website, and
    (b) must be kept available until after the meeting to which it relates.

(5) A failure to make information available on a website throughout the period specified in subsection (4)(b) is disregarded if-
    (a) the information is made available on the website for part of that period, and
    (b) the failure is wholly attributable to circumstances that it would not be reasonable to have expected the company to prevent or avoid.

GENERAL NOTE

This section is new and sets out the requirements which a quoted company must meet in making the shareholders' statements available on a website, in the same way as s.353 (requirements [for quoted companies] with respect to website availability) in Pt 13, "Resolutions and meetings".

Subsections (1) and (2)

For the purposes of s.527 (subs.(1)), information must be made available on a website that identifies a company and is maintained by or on its behalf (subs.(2)).

Subsections (3) and (5)

Access to the site and the ability to obtain hard copy must not be conditional on a fee payment (subs.(3)). Moreover, a statement of audit concerns under s.527 must be made available on the website within three working days of the company being required to publish it, and it must remain there until after the meeting to which it relates (subs.(4)). However, failure to comply with the requirements in subs.(4) can be disregarded if the statement has been made available on the website for part of the period, and there are unavoidable reasons why it has not been available throughout (subs.(5)).

529. Website publication: company's supplementary duties

(1) A quoted company must in the notice it gives of the accounts meeting draw attention to-
    (a) the possibility of a statement being placed on a website in pursuance of members' requests under section 527, and
    (b) the effect of the following provisions of this section.

(2) A company may not require the members requesting website publication to pay its expenses in complying with that section or section 528 (requirements in connection with website publication).

(3) Where a company is required to place a statement on a website under section 527 it must forward the statement to the company's auditor not later than the time when it makes the statement available on the website.

(4) The business which may be dealt with at the accounts meeting includes any statement that the company has been required under section 527 to publish on a website.

GENERAL NOTE

    This section is new and requires quoted companies to draw attention to the possibility of a website statement in the notice of the accounts meeting.

Subsection (1)

    A quoted company must draw attention in the notice it gives of its accounts meeting of the possibility that a statement of audit concerns (issued under s.527) will be posted on its website (subs.(1)).

Subsection (2)

    The company cannot require members who request website publication of a statement of audit concerns to meet its expenses in complying with the provisions of ss. 527 and 528, above.

Subsection (3)

    A company that publishes a statement of audit concerns on its website must at the same time forward a copy of the statement to its auditor.

Subsection (4)

    Matters raised in a statement of audit concerns can be dealt with along with other business at the accounts meeting.

530. Website publication: offences

(1) In the event of default in complying with
    (a) section 528 (requirements as to website publication), or
    (b) section 529 (companies' supplementary duties in relation to request for website publication),
an offence is committed by every officer of the company who is in default.

(2) A person guilty of an offence under this section is liable-
    (a) on conviction on indictment, to a fine;
    (b) on summary conviction, to a fine not exceeding the statutory maximum.

GENERAL NOTE

    In a new provision, failure to comply with the provisions of ss.528 and 529, above, renders every defaulting officer of the company *prima facie* guilty of an offence (subs.(1)), the penalties for which are detailed in subs.(2).

531. Meaning of "quoted company"

(1) For the purposes of this Chapter a company is a quoted company if it is a quoted company in accordance with section 385 (quoted and unquoted companies for the purposes of Part 15) in relation to the financial year to which the accounts to be laid at the next accounts meeting relate.

(2) The provisions of subsections (4) to (6) of that section (power to amend definition by regulations) apply in relation to the provisions of this Chapter as in relation to the provisions of that Part.

GENERAL NOTE

This section is new and defines the term "quoted company" for the purposes of Ch.5 of Pt 16 as being the same as the definition in s.385 in Pt 15 (subs.(1)), and that the power in subss.(4)-(6) of s.385 to amend the definition also applies here (subs.(2)).

CHAPTER 6

AUDITORS' LIABILITY

GENERAL NOTE

New provisions in this Chapter make it possible for auditors to limit their liability by agreement with a company. However, such an agreement will not be effective if it is not fair and reasonable.

The concept of a "liability limitation agreement" is introduced, whereby there is a contractual limitation of an auditor's liability to a company, but which has to be endorsed by members. Such agreements are an exception to the general prohibition on a company indemnifying its auditor in s.310 of the 1985 Act, a provision that is restated in the new Act in s.532. The court will be able to set aside a "liability limitation agreement" if it aims to limit liability to an amount that is not fair and reasonable in all the circumstances.

Auditors are allowed to limit their liability to a "fair and reasonable" amount through agreements providing for proportionate liability, capping and formulae. It is expected that the Financial Reporting Council ("FRC") will consult with investor groups and the accountancy profession with a view to issuing guidance as to what is "fair and reasonable" prior to the new provisions coming into force.

Voidness of provisions protecting auditors from liability

532. Voidness of provisions protecting auditors from liability

(1) This section applies to any provision-

     (a) for exempting an auditor of a company (to any extent) from any liability that would otherwise attach to him in connection with any negligence, default, breach of duty or breach of trust in relation to the company occurring in the course of the audit of accounts, or

     (b) by which a company directly or indirectly provides an indemnity (to any extent) for an auditor of the company, or of an associated company, against any liability attaching to him in connection with any negligence, default, breach of duty or breach of trust in relation to the company of which he is auditor occurring in the course of the audit of accounts.

(2) Any such provision is void, except as permitted by-

     (a) section 533 (indemnity for costs of successfully defending proceedings), or

     (b) sections 534 to 536 (liability limitation agreements).

(3) This section applies to any provision, whether contained in a company's articles or in any contract with the company or otherwise.

(4) For the purposes of this section companies are associated if one is a subsidiary of the other or both are subsidiaries of the same body corporate.

GENERAL NOTE

This section restates the existing general prohibition, previously in s.310 of the 1985 Act, against a company indemnifying its auditor against claims by the company in the case of negligence or other default. Any such indemnities are void and unenforceable except where permitted by ss.533-536.

Subsections (1)-(4)

Any arrangement whose aim is to exempt or indemnify an auditor of a company or of an associated company (i.e. a subsidiary or fellow subsidiary: subs.(4)), either directly or indirectly, from liability for negligence, breach of duty or breach of trust (subs.(1)) is void (subs.(2)). However, there are exceptions to this: namely where there is an indemnity for costs of successfully defending proceedings under s.533, below; or under the provisions relating to "liability limitation agreements" under ss.534-536 (subs.(2)). This applies to any arrangement - for example, whether it appears in a company's articles or in a contract (subs.(3)).

Indemnity for costs of defending proceedings

533.   Indemnity for costs of successfully defending proceedings

Section 532 (general voidness of provisions protecting auditors from liability) does not prevent a company from indemnifying an auditor against any liability incurred by him-

(a) in defending proceedings (whether civil or criminal) in which judgment is given in his favour or he is acquitted, or

(b) in connection with an application under section 1157 (power of court to grant relief in case of honest and reasonable conduct) in which relief is granted to him by the court.

GENERAL NOTE

This section restates s.310(3)(b) of the 1985 Act (as inserted by s.137 of the 1989 Act). This provides the exception in what is now s.532 permitting the company to indemnify the auditor against the costs of successfully defending himself against a claim. However, the previous exception in s.310(3)(a) of the 1985 Act (as inserted by s.137 of the 1989 Act) is not repeated. This allowed the company to buy insurance for its auditor.

Liability limitation agreements

534.   Liability limitation agreements

(1) A "liability limitation agreement" is an agreement that purports to limit the amount of a liability owed to a company by its auditor in respect of any negligence, default, breach of duty or breach of trust, occurring in the course of the audit of accounts, of which the auditor may be guilty in relation to the company.

(2) Section 532 (general voidness of provisions protecting auditors from liability) does not affect the validity of a liability limitation agreement that-

(a) complies with section 535 (terms of liability limitation agreement) and of any regulations under that section, and

(b) is authorised by the members of the company (see section 536).

(3) Such an agreement-

(a) is effective to the extent provided by section 537, and

(b) is not subject-

(i) in England and Wales or Northern Ireland, to section 2(2) or 3(2)(a) of the Unfair Contract Terms Act 1977 (c. 50);

(ii) in Scotland, to section 16(1)(b) or 17(1)(a) of that Act.

GENERAL NOTE

This new section deals with "liability limitation agreements", defining them, indicating how they are exempt from the general voidness of such agreements, and indicating how their effect may be restricted.

Subsection (1)

A "liability limitation agreement" is defined as an agreement that seeks to limit the liability of an auditor to a company whose accounts he has audited. The agreement can cover liability for negligence, default, breach of duty or breach of trust by the auditor in relation to the audit of accounts.

Subsection (2)

A "liability limitation agreement" is exempt from the general voidness of such agreements under s.532, above, so long as the agreement complies with the conditions set out s.535, below, and any regulations issued under that section. It must also have been endorsed by the company's members as specified in s.536, below.

Subsection (3)

The effect of a "liability limitation agreement" is restricted by s.537, which contains a test of fairness and reasonableness. Moreover, certain provisions of the Unfair Contracts Terms Act 1977 do not apply.

535. Terms of liability limitation agreement

(1) A liability limitation agreement-
   (a) must not apply in respect of acts or omissions occurring in the course of the audit of accounts for more than one financial year, and
   (b) must specify the financial year in relation to which it applies.
(2) The Secretary of State may by regulations-
   (a) require liability limitation agreements to contain specified provisions or provisions of a specified description;
   (b) prohibit liability limitation agreements from containing specified provisions or provisions of a specified description.
   "Specified" here means specified in the regulations.
(3) Without prejudice to the generality of the power conferred by subsection (2), that power may be exercised with a view to preventing adverse effects on competition.
(4) Subject to the preceding provisions of this section, it is immaterial how a liability limitation agreement is framed.
In particular, the limit on the amount of the auditor's liability need not be a sum of money, or a formula, specified in the agreement.
(5) Regulations under this section are subject to negative resolution procedure.

GENERAL NOTE

This section is new and contains rules and conditions concerning the terms of a "liability limitation agreement".

Subsection (1)

A "liability limitation agreement" must relate to the audit of a specified financial year.

Subsections (2) and (3)

The Secretary of State can issue regulations prescribing or prohibiting specified provisions or descriptions of provisions (subs.(2)). Moreover, he may exercise that power to prevent adverse effects on competition (subs.(3)).

Subsection (4)

The limitation on liability may be expressed in any terms, not necessarily as a sum of money or a formula.

Subsection (5)

The regulations referred to in subs.(2) are subject to the negative resolution procedure (see s.1289).

536.   Authorisation of agreement by members of the company

(1) A liability limitation agreement is authorised by the members of the company if it has been authorised under this section and that authorisation has not been withdrawn.

(2) A liability limitation agreement between a private company and its auditor may be authorised-

    (a) by the company passing a resolution, before it enters into the agreement, waiving the need for approval,

    (b) by the company passing a resolution, before it enters into the agreement, approving the agreement's principal terms, or

    (c) by the company passing a resolution, after it enters into the agreement, approving the agreement.

(3) A liability limitation agreement between a public company and its auditor may be authorised-

    (a) by the company passing a resolution in general meeting, before it enters into the agreement, approving the agreement's principal terms, or

    (b) by the company passing a resolution in general meeting, after it enters into the agreement, approving the agreement.

(4) The "principal terms" of an agreement are terms specifying, or relevant to the determination of-

    (a) the kind (or kinds) of acts or omissions covered,

    (b) the financial year to which the agreement relates, or

    (c) the limit to which the auditor's liability is subject.

(5) Authorisation under this section may be withdrawn by the company passing an ordinary resolution to that effect-

    (a) at any time before the company enters into the agreement, or

    (b) if the company has already entered into the agreement, before the beginning of the financial year to which the agreement relates.

Paragraph (b) has effect notwithstanding anything in the agreement.

GENERAL NOTE

The way in which members of a company must give their approval to a "liability limitation agreement" for it to be effective are set out in this new section.

Subsection (1)

To be effective, a "liability limitation agreement" has to be authorised by a company's members according to the provisions of this section.

Subsection (2)

With respect to a private company, members can pass a resolution (i) waiving the need for approval; (ii) approving its principal terms before an agreement is signed; or (iii) approving the agreement after it is signed.

Subsection (3)

With respect to a public company, members can pass a resolution (i) approving its principal terms before an agreement is signed; or (ii) approving the agreement after it is signed.

Subsection (4)

The "principal terms" of a liability limitation agreement are for this purpose the terms that specify, or enable determination of, (i) the kind of acts or omissions of the auditor that are covered; (ii) the financial year to which the agreement relates; and (iii) the limit to the auditor's liability.

Subsection (5)

Authorisation under this section may be withdrawn by members passing an ordinary resolution at any time before the agreement is entered into; or, if the company has already entered into the agreement, notwithstanding anything in it, before the beginning of the financial year to which it relates.

537.   Effect of liability limitation agreement

(1) A liability limitation agreement is not effective to limit the auditor's liability to less than such amount as is fair and reasonable in all the circumstances of the case having regard (in particular) to-
    (a) the auditor's responsibilities under this Part,
    (b) the nature and purpose of the auditor's contractual obligations to the company, and
    (c) the professional standards expected of him.

(2) A liability limitation agreement that purports to limit the auditor's liability to less than the amount mentioned in subsection (1) shall have effect as if it limited his liability to that amount.

(3) In determining what is fair and reasonable in all the circumstances of the case no account is to be taken of-
    (a) matters arising after the loss or damage in question has been incurred, or
    (b) matters (whenever arising) affecting the possibility of recovering compensation from other persons liable in respect of the same loss or damage.

GENERAL NOTE

This new provision indicates that a "liability limitation agreement" will not be effective in restricting an auditor's liability if the limitation would result in the company recovering an amount that was less than might be regarded as fair and reasonable.

Subsections (1) and (2)

A "liability limitation agreement" will not be effective in restricting an auditor's liability if the result would be that the company would recover less than a fair and reasonable sum, given the circumstances of the case. Such circumstances have to take into account the auditor's responsibilities, the nature and purpose of his contractual obligations, and the professional standards expected of him (subs.(1)). An agreement that purports to restrict the auditor's liability to less than a fair and reasonable sum will have effect as if it limits his liability to such an amount (subs.(2)).

Subsection (3)

In assessing what is fair and reasonable in the circumstances, no account should be taken of matters arising after the loss or damage in question has been incurred. Equally, no account should be taken of matters affecting the possibility of the company successfully claiming compensation from other people responsible for the same loss or damage.

538.   Disclosure of agreement by company

(1) A company which has entered into a liability limitation agreement must make such disclosure in connection with the agreement as the Secretary of State may require by regulations.

(2) The regulations may provide, in particular, that any disclosure required by the regulations shall be made-
    (a) in a note to the company's annual accounts (in the case of its individual accounts) or in such manner as is specified in the regulations (in the case of group accounts), or
    (b) in the directors' report.

(3) Regulations under this section are subject to negative resolution procedure.

GENERAL NOTE

This section contains a new provision requiring companies to disclose any liability limitation agreement they have made with their auditor.

Subsections (1) and (2)

A company that has entered into a limitation of liability agreement with its auditor must disclose details as required by regulations issued by the Secretary of State (subs.(1)). The regulations may require such disclosure to be (i) in a note to the company's individual annual accounts, (ii) as may be specified in group accounts, or (iii) in the directors' report (subs.(2)).

Subsection (3)

Such regulations are subject to the negative resolution procedure (see s.1289).

CHAPTER 7

SUPPLEMENTARY PROVISIONS

539. Minor definitions

In this Part-

"e-money issuer" means a person who has permission under Part 4 of the Financial Services and Markets Act 2000 (c. 8) to carry on the activity of issuing electronic money within the meaning of article 9B of the Financial Services and Markets Act 2000 (Regulated Activities) Order 2001 (S.I. 2001/544);

"ISD investment firm" has the meaning given by the Glossary forming part of the Handbook made by the Financial Services Authority under the Financial Services and Markets Act 2000;

"qualified", in relation to an auditor's report (or a statement contained in an auditor's report), means that the report or statement does not state the auditor's unqualified opinion that the accounts have been properly prepared in accordance with this Act or, in the case of an undertaking not required to prepare accounts in accordance with this Act, under any corresponding legislation under which it is required to prepare accounts;

"turnover", in relation to a company, means the amounts derived from the provision of goods and services falling within the company's ordinary activities, after deduction of-

    (a) trade discounts,

    (b) value added tax, and

    (c) any other taxes based on the amounts so derived;

"UCITS management company" has the meaning given by the Glossary forming part of the Handbook made by the Financial Services Authority under the Financial Services and Markets Act 2000.

GENERAL NOTE

This section corresponds to ss.262(1) and 744 and defines various terms used in this Part of the Act: namely, "e-money issuer", "ISD investment firm", "qualified" (in relation to an audit report), "turnover" and "UCITS management company".

PART 17

A COMPANY'S SHARE CAPITAL

GENERAL NOTE

Part 17 is concerned with the fundamentals of share capital. It replaces Pt IV and Pt V of the Companies Act 1985.

The changes in Pt 17 are based mainly on the CLR's recommendations in Chs 2 and 10 of their *Final Report* ((URN 01/942), having consulted on these issues in their paper *Company Formation and Capital Maintenance* (URN 99/1145). Additional consultations followed in the White Papers of July 2002 (Cm.5553-1) and March 2005 (Cm.6456).

CHAPTER I

SHARES AND SHARE CAPITAL OF A COMPANY

Shares

540. Shares

(1) In the Companies Acts "share", in relation to a company, means share in the company's share capital.

(2) A company's shares may no longer be converted into stock.

(3) Stock created before the commencement of this Part may be reconverted into shares in accordance with section 620.

(4) In the Companies Acts-

    (a) references to shares include stock except where a distinction between share and stock is express or implied, and

    (b) references to a number of shares include an amount of stock where the context admits of the reference to shares being read as including stock.

GENERAL NOTE

This Part relates to the general provisions governing shares and share capital - it should be read with the following Part on the acquisition, or assistance for the acquisition, of its own shares by a company This Part applies to shares, the allotment of shares, pre-emption rights on allotment, payment for shares, share premiums, the alteration of share capital, including the new statutory concept of redenomination of capital, the variation of class rights, and the reduction of capital. Whilst many of these provisions are amended from their 1985 Act equivalents as a result of the CLR recommendations, others are simply restatements of the 1985 Act. (For the history behind this mixed approach, see the General Note to this Act.)

Subsections (1) and (4)

These subsection restate the definition of a share in s.744 of the 1985 Act. For stock see also subss.(2) and (3).

Subsections (2) and (3)

Subsection (2) implements the recommendation of the CLR to abolish the ability of companies to convert shares into stock under s.121(2)(c) of the 1985 Act. Subsection (3) allows existing stock to be reconverted into shares under s.620, but imposes no obligation to do so.

541. Nature of shares

The shares or other interest of a member in a company are personal property (or, in Scotland, moveable property) and are not in the nature of real estate (or heritage).

GENERAL NOTE

This section restates s.182(1)(a) of the 1985 Act to the effect that shares are personal and not real property. In England they are *choses in action* or intangibles.

542. Nominal value of shares

(1) Shares in a limited company having a share capital must each have a fixed nominal value.

(2) An allotment of a share that does not have a fixed nominal value is void.

(3) Shares in a limited company having a share capital may be denominated in any currency, and different classes of shares may be denominated in different currencies.

But see section 765 (initial authorised minimum share capital requirement for public company to be met by reference to share capital denominated in sterling or euros).

(4) If a company purports to allot shares in contravention of this section, an offence is committed by every officer of the company who is in default.

(5) A person guilty of an offence under this section is liable-

    (a) on conviction on indictment, to a fine;

    (b) on summary conviction, to a fine not exceeding the statutory maximum.

GENERAL NOTE

This new section replaces the requirement, formerly in s.2(5)(a) of the 1985 Act, that companies have an authorised capital figure in the memorandum divided into shares of "a fixed amount". The concept of authorised capital has been discontinued but the requirement of a fixed nominal value has been continued. There are to be no "no par value" shares. This is mainly because the second EC Directive (Dir 77/91/EEC) requires a nominal value for all public company shares.

The power to denominate the shares in any currency is set out in subs.(3). This is subject, however, to the EC requirement that the amount needed for the authorised minimum capital of a public company must either be in sterling or euros. The subsection codifies existing practice and case law: see, e.g. *Scandinavian Bank Group Plc, Re* [1988] Ch. 87.

This Act also now provides a specific procedure for re-denominating shares without the need to use the reduction of capital procedure (see ss.622-628).

Subsections (2), (4) and (5)

Although the general theme of the Act is to provide criminal rather than civil sanctions in default, both are present here.

543. Numbering of shares

(1) Each share in a company having a share capital must be distinguished by its appropriate number, except in the following circumstances.

(2) If at any time-

    (a) all the issued shares in a company are fully paid up and rank *pari passu* for all purposes, or

    (b) all the issued shares of a particular class in a company are fully paid up and rank *pari passu* for all purposes,

none of those shares need thereafter have a distinguishing number so long as it remains fully paid up and ranks *pari passu* for all purposes with all shares of the same class for the time being issued and fully paid up.

GENERAL NOTE

This section restates s.182(2) of the 1985 Act as to the numbering of shares. There are no amendments. In practice, numbers are dispensed with under subs.(2).

544. Transferability of shares

(1) The shares or other interest of any member in a company are transferable in accordance with the company's articles.

(2) This is subject to-

    (a) the Stock Transfer Act 1963 (c. 18) or the Stock Transfer Act (Northern Ireland) 1963 (c.24 (N.I.)) (which enables securities of certain descriptions to be transferred by a simplified process), and

    (b) regulations under Chapter 2 of Part 21 of this Act (which enable title to securities to be evidenced and transferred without a written instrument).

(3) See Part 21 of this Act generally as regards share transfers.

This section restates s.182(1)(b) of the 1985 Act, with the addition of the Northern Irish legislation. There is a drafting addition in subs.(3) which refers to Pt 21 of this Act. That restates the 1985 Act provisions on transfer of shares in general and amends those relating to uncertificated shares.

545. Companies having a share capital

References in the Companies Acts to a company having a share capital are to a company that has power under its constitution to issue shares.

This new section is the first of four sections that define references in the Act to types of share capital.

The model articles of association for public companies provide constitutional power to issue shares (Art.46).

546. Issued and allotted share capital

(1) References in the Companies Acts-
    (a) to "issued share capital" are to shares of a company that have been issued;
    (b) to "allotted share capital" are to shares of a company that have been allotted.
(2) References in the Companies Acts to issued or allotted shares, or to issued or allotted share capital, include shares taken on the formation of the company by the subscribers to the company's memorandum.

This section explains references in the Companies Acts to "issued" and "allotted" share capital.

Subsection (1)

Shares are allotted when a person acquires the unconditional right to be included in the company's register of members in respect of those shares (see s.558). The Companies Act 2006 does not determine when shares are issued, but in the context of a taxing statute it has been held that shares are issued when the entire process of application, allotment and registration is complete: *National Westminster Bank Plc v Inland Revenue Commissioners* [1995] 1 A.C. 119.

Subsection (2)

This new provision provides certainty with regard to the shares taken on formation of a company by the subscribers to the memorandum (see s.8) who become members upon registration of the company (see s.112). These shares are included in references in the Companies Acts to allotted or issued shares even though the process of allotment and issue does not apply to shares taken on formation.

Share capital

547. Called-up share capital

In the Companies Acts-
    "called-up share capital", in relation to a company, means so much of its share capital as equals the aggregate amount of the calls made on its shares (whether or not those calls have been paid), together with-
        (a) any share capital paid up without being called, and
        (b) any share capital to be paid on a specified future date under the articles, the terms of allotment of the relevant shares or any other arrangements for payment of those shares; and

    "uncalled share capital" is to be construed accordingly.

GENERAL NOTE

This section re-enacts the definition previously found in s.737 of the Companies Act 1985.

The definition of "called-up share capital" is relevant for the calculations required by s.656 (Public companies: duty of directors to call meeting on serious loss of capital) and s.831 (Net asset restriction on distributions by public companies).

548.   Equity share capital

In the Companies Acts "equity share capital", in relation to a company, means its issued share capital excluding any part of that capital that, neither as respects dividends nor as respects capital, carries any right to participate beyond a specified amount in a distribution.

GENERAL NOTE

This section re-states, without substantive change, the definition of "equity share capital" that was previously in s.744 of the Companies Act 1985. It remains that case that non-participating preference shares and other shares which have limited rights as to capital and dividend do not fall within the term.

CHAPTER 2

ALLOTMENT OF SHARES: GENERAL PROVISIONS

GENERAL NOTE

The derivation of the "allotment code"

Chapters 2-6 of Part 17 of the Companies Act 2006 replace Pt IV of the Companies Act 1985, as amended, which dealt more generally with "Allotment of Shares and Debentures". When originally published as a bill, this legislation did not repeal the whole of the Companies Act 1985, with the effect that ss.89-94 (inclusive) and s.96 of the Companies Act 1985 were not to have been repealed (as was made clear in Schedule 16 of the Bill in its earlier stages). These provisions have, however, now been repealed, as is made clear in Schedule 16 to this Act.

As considered in the note at the beginning of Pt 17, the whole of Pt 17 is concerned with regulations concerning share capital of a company in general, the allotment of shares and other securities, share premiums, alteration of share capital, classes of shares and class rights, and reduction of share capital. This fascicule of Chs 2-6, dealing specifically with the allotment of shares and securities, is cross-referenced internally. For the purposes of this discussion these groups of provisions in Chs 2-6 are referred to here as the "allotment code" for ease of general reference.

The division between public companies and private companies

One of the more immediately noticeable features of Ch.2 is that it divides between provisions dealing with public companies and provisions dealing with private companies, as is the case more generally with s.4 of the 2006 Act. The 1985 Act had had introduced to it a new s.80A (by the Companies Act 1989) which provided separately for the allotment of shares in relation to private companies from that in relation to public companies. More precisely, the allotment code divides between private companies which have only one class of shares; private companies with more than one class of shares; and finally public companies. In effect, the power of directors to allot shares in the former type of company has been simplified by the Companies Act 2006. Nevertheless, the 2006 Act perpetuates the division between public and private companies which was found in the 1985 Act. In general terms, it is the same real-world subject matter with which the statute is dealing and therefore much of the detail is similar in effect to the Companies Act 1985, even if there are a number of differences in terms of form, organisation of provisions and numerous changes of detail. Chapter 3 deals with "Allotment of Equity Securities: Existing Shareholders' Right of Pre-emption"; Ch.4 deals with "Public Companies: Allotment where issue not fully subscribed"; Ch.5, "Payment for shares"; and Ch.6, "Public Companies: Independent valuation of non-cash consideration". Later Chapters in this Part then deal with share premiums and so forth, but that is outwith the scope of the allotment code.

The rationale underpinning the replacement of the policy in Part IV of the Companies Act 1985

Sections 82 and 83 were repealed because the Prospectus Directive and the Transparency Directive, as implemented by the Financial Services and Markets Act 2000, have made provision for the public offer of securities. Therefore, the allotment code in the Companies Act 2006 deals with the remaining matters relating to the allotment of securities.

The removal of the concept of authorised capital

Whereas s.80 of the Companies Act 1985 placed a limit on the number of shares which directors were entitled to allot by means of a maximum authorised capital, s.549 of the 2006 Act removes the need to provide such a maximum authorised capital in the company's constitution for private companies with only one class of shares. The approach taken in the 2006 Act is to permit an authorisation for a period of up to five years stating the maximum amount of shares which may be allotted by the directors.

Power of directors to allot shares

549. Exercise by directors of power to allot shares etc

(1) The directors of a company must not exercise any power of the company-
    (a) to allot shares in the company, or
    (b) to grant rights to subscribe for, or to convert any security into, shares in the company,
except in accordance with section 550 (private company with single class of shares) or section 551 (authorisation by company).

(2) Subsection (1) does not apply-
    (a) to the allotment of shares in pursuance of an employees' share scheme, or
    (b) to the grant of a right to subscribe for, or to convert any security into, shares so allotted.

(3) If this section applies in relation to the grant of a right to subscribe for, or to convert any security into, shares, it does not apply in relation to the allotment of shares pursuant to that right.

(4) A director who knowingly contravenes, or permits or authorises a contravention of, this section commits an offence.

(5) A person guilty of an offence under this section is liable-
    (a) on conviction on indictment, to a fine;
    (b) on summary conviction, to a fine not exceeding the statutory maximum.

(6) Nothing in this section affects the validity of an allotment or other transaction.

GENERAL NOTE

This section divides between private companies with one class of shares on the one hand, and private companies with more than one class of shares and public companies on the other hand. In effect, the powers of directors to allot shares in relation to private companies with one class of shares have been greatly simplified. This clause replaced s.80(1), (2), (9) and (10) of the Companies Act 1985.

Subsection (1)

There are five types of shares and rights for the purposes of this provision: first, shares in public companies; secondly, shares in private companies; thirdly, shares allotted pursuant to an employee share scheme; fourthly, rights to convert any security into an allotted share; and, fifthly, rights under convertible securities to acquire shares and rights to subscribe for shares. The third and fourth categories of share are exempted from the limitations which are imposed on the other two types of company by this section by subs.(2). Directors' powers to allot shares in public and in private companies respectively are subject to specific provisions considered below.

Subsection (2)

Two categories of shares are exempted from this provision: shares allotted pursuant to an employee share scheme; and rights to convert any security into an allotted share. This provision effectively re-enacts s.80(2) of the 1985 Act.

Subsection (3)

Further to the exemptions in subs.(2) above, there is a further exemption from the effect of this section in relation to rights under convertible securities to acquire shares and rights to subscribe for shares.

Subsection (4)

Failure to follow the prescribed codes for the third and fourth types of shares will render a director who knowingly contravenes or permits or authorises a contravention of those codes guilty of an offence. There is no statutory guidance on what constitutes a director acting "knowingly": whether that requires subjective appreciation that there was a contravention of the code, or alternatively whether an objective notion of knowing some factor which would have brought to the attention of a reasonable director that there had been a breach of the code or that would have caused him to inquire further into the matter. The concept of a person who acts "knowingly" in relation to the criminal law is discussed in detail in the note to s.572(2) below.

Subsection (6)

As a matter of private law, the validity of an allotment of a share is not affected by any failure of a director to comply with the provisions of this section. Such a validity may be contested under general law, for example on the basis of misrepresentation or deceit, over and above the provisions of this section: there is nothing in the provision to suggest to the contrary. Rather, it is only failure to comply with this provision which will not constitute an invalidity.

550. Power of directors to allot shares etc: private company with only one class of shares

Where a private company has only one class of shares, the directors may exercise any power of the company-

    (a) to allot shares of that class, or

    (b) to grant rights to subscribe for or to convert any security into such shares,

except to the extent that they are prohibited from doing so by the company's articles.

GENERAL NOTE

The directors of a private company with only one class of shares are given a power by statute to "exercise any power of the company" to allot shares or to grant rights to subscribe for shares in the company or to convert securities into shares in the company. This power may be restricted on two bases. First, the reference to the power of the directors to "exercise any power of the company" means that the directors may only exercise powers which the company itself has under its constitutional documents. Secondly, the proviso to this provision means that the directors may not make allotments if the company's articles of association prohibit them from so doing or to the extent that those articles prohibit them from so doing. This provision repeals the requirement in s.80 of the 1985 Act that the directors have a prior authorisation from the company's members for an allotment of shares, provided that the company is a private company with only one class of shares. This refinement was recommended by para.4.5 of the *Company Law Review*.

551. Power of directors to allot shares etc: authorisation by company

(1) The directors of a company may exercise a power of the company-

    (a) to allot shares in the company, or

    (b) to grant rights to subscribe for or to convert any security into shares in the company,

if they are authorised to do so by the company's articles or by resolution of the company.

(2) Authorisation may be given for a particular exercise of the power or for its exercise generally, and may be unconditional or subject to conditions.

(3) Authorisation must-

    (a) state the maximum amount of shares that may be allotted under it, and

    (b) specify the date on which it will expire, which must be not more than five years from-

        (i) in the case of authorisation contained in the company's articles at the time of its original incorporation, the date of that incorporation;

        (ii) in any other case, the date on which the resolution is passed by virtue of which the authorisation is given.

(4) Authorisation may-

    (a) be renewed or further renewed by resolution of the company for a further period not exceeding five years, and

    (b) be revoked or varied at any time by resolution of the company.

(5) A resolution renewing authorisation must-

    (a) state (or restate) the maximum amount of shares that may be allotted under the authorisation or, as the case may be, the amount remaining to be allotted under it, and

    (b) specify the date on which the renewed authorisation will expire.

(6) In relation to rights to subscribe for or to convert any security into shares in the company, references in this section to the maximum amount of shares that may be allotted under the

authorisation are to the maximum amount of shares that may be allotted pursuant to the rights.

(7) The directors may allot shares, or grant rights to subscribe for or to convert any security into shares, after authorisation has expired if-

    (a) the shares are allotted, or the rights are granted, in pursuance of an offer or agreement made by the company before the authorisation expired, and

    (b) the authorisation allowed the company to make an offer or agreement which would or might require shares to be allotted, or rights to be granted, after the authorisation had expired.

(8) A resolution of a company to give, vary, revoke or renew authorisation under this section may be an ordinary resolution, even though it amends the company's articles.

(9) Chapter 3 of Part 3 (resolutions affecting a company's constitution) applies to a resolution under this section.

GENERAL NOTE

This section replaces s.80(3)-(8) of the Companies Act 1985. It applies both to private companies with more than one class of shares as well as to other types of private company and to public companies; whereas s.550 preceding relates only to private companies with only one class of shares. The directors of a company are permitted to allot shares in the company, or to grant rights to subscribe for shares or to convert other securities, if the articles of association permit them so to do or if there has been a resolution of the company granting them that authorisation. The authorisation itself must specify the maximum number of shares which may be so allotted and the authorisation must not last for longer than five years.

Subsection (1)

Authorisation to allot shares, or to grant rights to subscribe for shares or to convert other securities, is conferred on the directors of the company. Such authorisation may be manifested in the articles of association or by means of any resolution of the company. The reference to "any resolution" of the company includes an ordinary resolution, as confirmed in subs.(8) below.

Subsection (2)

Authorisation is frequently given in general terms in the articles of association in many companies; however, it is possible for authorisation to be given in relation to a single allotment of shares or other rights under subs.(1). Such an authorisation may be made subject to the satisfaction of conditions by the directors or third parties, or it can be entirely unconditional so that the directors are left to act on their own cognisance.

Subsection (3)

There are two conditions for the validity of an authorisation under this section. Importantly the authorisation must state "the maximum amount of shares that may be allotted under it", or else such authorisation will not be valid and effectual. The reference to the "amount" of shares can, it is suggested, be read as a reference to a proportion of the total shareholding in the company from time-to-time and not simply as a given number of shares. Furthermore, the second condition is that the authorisation must "specify the date on which it will expire" and that date must be "not more than five years" either from the date of the company's incorporation if the authorisation is contained in those articles, or else from the date on which the resolution which granted the authorisation was passed. An expired authorisation can be renewed in accordance with subs.(4) below.

Subsection (4)

Further to subs.(3) above, an authorisation can be renewed for a first time or on further occasions by means of a resolution of the company: in either event, that renewal may not last for more than five years. Similarly, an existing authorisation can be revoked or alternatively varied at any stage by means of a resolution of the company. A variation of the authorisation could, therefore, vary any conditions attached to the authorisation as well as the amount of shares falling under the authorisation or the time limit for its expiry.

Subsection (5)

A renewal of an authorisation under subs.(4) must state the maximum amount of shares which may be allotted and must contain a specification of the date on which this renewed authorisation will expire. As to the expiry date, there is a requirement in subs.(4) above that the renewal of authorisation must expire within five years.

Subsection (6)

In subs.(3)(a) above, the reference to the requirement that there be a statement of the maximum amount of shares which may be allotted, is applied in relation to convertible securities by a need to identify the amount of shares into which the convertible security may be converted.

Subsection (7)

The deadline for expiry of the authorisation to allot is, more accurately put, a deadline for the authorisation for the directors to make offers or agreements for the allotment of shares or other rights referred to in subs.(1) above. Thus, if the offer is only taken up after the authorisation has expired, but if the offer or agreement were made before the expiry of that authorisation, then the directors may nevertheless allot those shares or other rights.

Subsection (8)

Even though a resolution of the company may be used to amend the company's articles for the purposes of this provision, there is no requirement that that resolution be anything other than a general resolution.

Prohibition of commissions, discounts and allowances

552. General prohibition of commissions, discounts and allowances

(1) Except as permitted by section 553 (permitted commission), a company must not apply any of its shares or capital money, either directly or indirectly, in payment of any commission, discount or allowance to any person in consideration of his-
  (a) subscribing or agreeing to subscribe (whether absolutely or conditionally) for shares in the company, or
  (b) procuring or agreeing to procure subscriptions (whether absolute or conditional) for shares in the company.
(2) It is immaterial how the shares or money are so applied, whether by being added to the purchase money of property acquired by the company or to the contract price of work to be executed for the company, or being paid out of the nominal purchase money or contract price, or otherwise.
(3) Nothing in this section affects the payment of such brokerage as has previously been lawful.

GENERAL NOTE

This provision replaces s.98 of the Companies Act 1985. The prohibition on discounted allotments replaces s.100 et seq. of the Companies Act 1985, as is considered in detail in relation to s.580 of this Companies Act 2006. The law on allotment prohibits the allotment of shares at a discount either directly or indirectly. The common law had prohibited such allotments at a discount, as was confirmed by Lord Macnaghten in *Ooregum Gold Mining Co of India Ltd v Roper; Walworth v Roper* [1892] A.C. 125 at 145. Among the means of allocating an indirect discount would be to pay an amount of money out of the company's capital to the subscriber for shares in consideration for acquiring the shares, or alternatively the subscriber could be awarded "free" shares on top of the number of shares which had been subscribed for at the full price so that the price of each share was effectively reduced. As is considered in this provision, the three principal means of carrying out these sorts of practices are by means of discounts, or by means of the payment of commissions, or by means of some other allowances, all done by means of payment out of the company's capital account or by means of allocating shares in the company. The only forms of permission which may be paid in this manner are set out in s.553 below.

Subsection (1)

This provision replaces the purpose of s.98(1) of the Companies Act 1985. No commission, discount or allowance may be paid out of the company's capital nor may such commission, discount or allowance be made by means of any application of the company's shares (whether by allotment or otherwise) to any person in consideration for his or her subscription for shares on a contingent or non-contingent basis, or in consideration for that person procuring or agreeing to procure shares in the company. Under the former prohibition a person is, for the most part, prohibited from acquiring shares at less than their face value. Under the latter prohibition a person may not be compensated for having acquired shares or for having procured another person to acquire shares in the company.

Subsection (2)

This provision replaces s.98(2) of the Companies Act 1985 and, while it is effectively the same as that provision, there are some changes in the organisation of the wording which leave the provision more clearly expressed than its predecessor.

Subsection (3)

This provision replaces s.98(3) of the Companies Act 1985. It is extremely open-ended as drafted. It is suggested that this provision should be interpreted to mean that any means of paying brokerage which was lawful *immediately before the enactment of the Companies Act 2006* and not any means of paying brokerage which was lawful *at some point in the past* (that is, before this form of statutory prohibition was first introduced or before the common law crystallised such a prohibition).

553. Permitted commission

(1) A company may, if the following conditions are satisfied, pay a commission to a person in consideration of his subscribing or agreeing to subscribe (whether absolutely or conditionally) for shares in the company, or procuring or agreeing to procure subscriptions (whether absolute or conditional) for shares in the company.

(2) The conditions are that-
  (a) the payment of the commission is authorised by the company's articles; and
  (b) the commission paid or agreed to be paid does not exceed-
    (i) 10% of the price at which the shares are issued, or
    (ii) the amount or rate authorised by the articles,
  whichever is the less.

(3) A vendor to, or promoter of, or other person who receives payment in money or shares from, a company may apply any part of the money or shares so received in payment of any commission the payment of which directly by the company would be permitted by this section.

GENERAL NOTE

Further to s.552, which prohibits the payment of commission out of capital account or by means of the allotment of shares, this provision identifies some contexts in which commissions may be paid. This provision is similar to s.97 of the Companies Act 1985 as it was amended by the Financial Services Act 1986, s.212(2) and by the Public Offers of Securities Regulations 1995: where those amendments repealed much of the provision leaving only those parts which are effectively re-enacted by subss.(1) and (2) of this provision. The amendments were to remove provisions as to the content of prospectuses, which is now dealt with under the Prospectus Rules, which have been created further to Pt 6 of the Financial Services and Markets Act 2000.

Subsection (1)

Thus, in spite of the prohibitions in s.552 on paying commissions, a commission may be paid, subject to the following subs.(2), in relation to a subscription for shares, an agreement to subscribe for shares, procurement of subscriptions from another person, or an agreement to procure subscriptions from another person, in the manner set out below.

Subsection (2)

The two conditions for the payment of commission out of capital or by means of allotment of shares in the company are that the payment of such commission must be permitted by the company's articles of association, and also that the commission which is to be paid does not exceed ten per cent of the price at which the shares are issued or else that the amount or rate is authorised by the articles of association.

Subsection (3)

This provision is similar to s.98(4) of the Companies Act 1985 in that it grants a power to the recipient of money or of shares from a company the power to use that property to pay a commission if the company itself would have been permitted so to do under the provisions of this section. The new wording achieves the same purpose in relation to vendors, promoters and other persons, but does so in a less wordy fashion.

554. Registration of allotment

(1) A company must register an allotment of shares as soon as practicable and in any event within two months after the date of the allotment.

(2) This does not apply if the company has issued a share warrant in respect of the shares (see section 779).

(3) If a company fails to comply with this section, an offence is committed by-
    (a) the company, and
    (b) every officer of the company who is in default.

(4) A person guilty of an offence under this section is liable on summary conviction to a fine not exceeding level 3 on the standard scale and, for continued contravention, a daily default fine not exceeding one-tenth of level 3 on the standard scale.

(5) For the company's duties as to the issue of share certificates etc, see Part 21 (certification and transfer of securities).

GENERAL NOTE

This provision is a new introduction under the Companies Act 2006, although it bears similarity to s.111(1) of the Companies Act 1985, and is different from the "return of allotment" provisions which had been in the Companies Act 1985 and which are effected under s.555 immediately below for the purposes of the 2006 Act. While the provision requires that a registration of an allotment be made, and provides that it is a criminal offence not to do so, the provision is nevertheless silent in itself as to the manner in which such registration is to be effected. While this fascicule of sections is somewhat opaquely drafted, there is a reference in s.555(2) to an obligation on the company to "register a return of the allotment", such that those two provisions may be read together, given that there is no further reference to registration of the allotment in this Part of this Act.

Subsection (1)

A company is required to register an allotment of shares. Such registration must take place in general terms "as soon as practicable", but in any event within a period of two months after the date of allotment.

Subsection (2)

Further to s.779, if the company has issued a share warrant, that warrant must state that the holder of the warrant is entitled "to the shares specified in it" on delivery of the warrant. Such a warrant must have been issued under the company's common seal under English law.

Subsection (3)

An offence is committed by two categories of person if the registration does not take place in accordance with subs.(1): first, the company itself and, secondly, "every officer of the company who is in default". As to the individuals who may commit an offence, liability is not limited to directors of the company, but equally liability will only attach to people who are in default. Identifying those persons who are at fault will encompass any officer of the company who is identified by the articles of association or, it is suggested, by their job description or contract of employment as being responsible for such registrations. However, in the absence of such clearly identified lines of responsibility, it is suggested that liability may attach more generally to any members of the board of directors or management more generally who ought to have taken responsibility either for the identification of such lines of responsibility or for effecting the registration itself.

Subsection (5)

Aspects of the general responsibilities of the company in relation to the registration of such allotments and in relation to the issue of share certificates in general are considered in relation to Pt 21 of the Act below.

Return of allotment

555. Return of allotment by limited company

(1) This section applies to a company limited by shares and to a company limited by guarantee and having a share capital.

(2) The company must, within one month of making an allotment of shares, deliver to the registrar for registration a return of the allotment.

(3) The return must-

    (a) contain the prescribed information, and

    (b) be accompanied by a statement of capital.

(4) The statement of capital must state with respect to the company's share capital at the date to which the return is made up-

    (a) the total number of shares of the company,

    (b) the aggregate nominal value of those shares,

    (c) for each class of shares-

        (i) prescribed particulars of the rights attached to the shares,

        (ii) the total number of shares of that class, and

        (iii) the aggregate nominal value of shares of that class, and

    (d) the amount paid up and the amount (if any) unpaid on each share (whether on account of the nominal value of the share or by way of premium).

GENERAL NOTE

This provision replaces s.88 of the Companies Act 1985 in relation to the requirement that a company make a "return of allotment" to the registrar.

Subsection (1)

This provision applies to two forms of company: a company limited by shares and a company limited by guarantee which also has a share capital.

Subsection (2)

Within one month of making an allotment of shares, the company is required to deliver a return of the allotment to the registrar for registration. The form of that return is considered in the next subsection.

Subsection (3)

Two things are required of the return: first, it must contain "the prescribed information" and, secondly, it must be "accompanied by a statement of capital". There is nothing to qualify what is meant by "the prescribed information" in this subsection, although the contents of the statement are set out in subs.(4). The contents of the statement of capital are set out in the next subsection.

Subsection (4)

The required contents of the statement of capital are, as of the date at which the return is made: the total number of shares in the company; the aggregate nominal value of those shares; the prescribed particulars of the rights attached to any particular class of shares; the total number of shares in any particular class; the aggregate nominal value of shares of each class; and, finally, the amount paid up and any amount remaining to be paid on each share.

556. Return of allotment by unlimited company allotting new class of shares

(1) This section applies to an unlimited company that allots shares of a class with rights that are not in all respects uniform with shares previously allotted.

(2) The company must, within one month of making such an allotment, deliver to the registrar for registration a return of the allotment.

(3) The return must contain the prescribed particulars of the rights attached to the shares.

(4) For the purposes of this section shares are not to be treated as different from shares previously allotted by reason only that the former do not carry the same rights to dividends as the latter during the twelve months immediately following the former's allotment.

GENERAL NOTE

Whereas the previous section related to companies with limited liability or to companies limited by guarantee with a share capital, this section relates to unlimited companies. It imposes an obligation on such companies to register a return of the allotment. There was no comparator to this provision in s.88 of the Companies Act 1985.

Subsection (1)

In relation to unlimited companies, where the obligations of shareholders are not limited, it is possible that shares which are allotted may not have identical rights attaching to them as had applied to other shares of the same class. Thus subs.(1) imposes an obligation to make a return of any allotment of shares on unlimited companies. The effect of this fact emerges in subs.(3) below.

Subsection (2)

Within one month of making an allotment of shares, the company is required to deliver a return of the allotment to the registrar for registration. The form of that return is described in the next subsection.

Subsection (3)

The return of the allotment which must be delivered to the registrar is required to contain "the prescribed particulars of the rights attached to the shares", given that shares of the same class may not contain the same rights and obligations as one another.

Subsection (4)

It is not enough to render shares different from shares previously allotted that shares allotted later have different rights to dividends declared over the previous 12 months.

557. Offence of failure to make return

(1) If a company makes default in complying with-
  section 555 (return of allotment of shares by limited company), or
  section 556 (return of allotment of new class of shares by unlimited company),
an offence is committed by every officer of the company who is in default.

(2) A person guilty of an offence under this section is liable-
  (a) on conviction on indictment, to a fine;
  (b) on summary conviction, to a fine not exceeding the statutory maximum and, for continued contravention, a daily default fine not exceeding one-tenth of the statutory maximum.

(3) In the case of default in delivering to the registrar within one month after the allotment the return required by section 555 or 556-
  (a) any person liable for the default may apply to the court for relief, and
  (b) the court, if satisfied-
    (i) that the omission to deliver the document was accidental or due to inadvertence, or
    (ii) that it is just and equitable to grant relief,
  may make an order extending the time for delivery of the document for such period as the court thinks proper.

GENERAL NOTE

This provision relates only to failures to make a return of allotment, and is different from failure to register under s.554.

Subsection (1)

Further to ss.555 and 556, an offence is committed by "every officer of the company who is in default" if the company fails to make a return. As to the individual officers who may commit an offence, liability is not limited to directors of the company, but equally liability will only attach to people who are in default. The reader is referred to the discussion of this concept in relation to the note under s.554(3) above.

Subsection (3)

Unlike the offence of failing to register an allotment, the offence of failure to make a return of allotment is capable of statutory relief under this subs.(3). Any person liable for the commission of the offence may apply to the court for relief under this provision. Relief will be available if the court can be satisfied that the omission to deliver the appropriate document was "accidental or due to inadvertence" or alternatively if the court is satisfied that it is "just and equitable to grant relief". The court's power, if it is satisfied as to either of these things, is to make an order extending the time for the delivery of the necessary document for such a period as the court considers appropriate. The commission of the offence is thus, impliedly, expunged from the record.

Supplementary provisions

558. When shares are allotted

For the purposes of the Companies Acts shares in a company are taken to be allotted when a person acquires the unconditional right to be included in the company's register of members in respect of the shares.

GENERAL NOTE

There is a difficult question as to the time at which a person becomes the owner of shares and also as to the time at which allotment is deemed to have taken place. This section provides that shares in a company are deemed to have been allotted "when a person acquired the unconditional right to be included in the company's register of members in respect of the shares". The question therefore arises out of the wording of the section as to the point in time that one acquires such an "unconditional right". An allotment of shares is a contractual process: on which see *Palmer's Company Law*, paras 5.501 *et seq.*, and therefore one might say that such an unconditional right is acquired once that contract is executed. It could be said that one acquires rights to be transferred shares on the completion of a binding contract to transfer shares because the right of specific performance acquired on completion of such a contract leads equity "to consider as done that which ought to have been done", such that an equitable interest in the shares passes automatically (*Oughtred v IRC* [1960] A.C. 206; *Neville v Wilson* [1996] 3 All E.R. 171). However, because specific performance is a discretionary equitable remedy, it could be argued that one does not have an *unconditional* right to the shares until the court chooses to make such an order. Nevertheless, on the authorities just cited, one acquires such a right in equity on completion of the contract of allotment.

559. Provisions about allotment not applicable to shares taken on formation

The provisions of this Chapter have no application in relation to the taking of shares by the subscribers to the memorandum on the formation of the company.

CHAPTER 3

ALLOTMENT OF EQUITY SECURITIES: EXISTING SHAREHOLDERS' RIGHT OF PRE-EMPTION

GENERAL NOTE

This chapter relates to the pre-emption rights of existing shareholders in relation to allotments of new shares. Under s.89 of the Companies Act 1985, companies proposing to allot equity securities were obliged to offer them first to existing shareholders in a proportion equivalent to their existing shareholding. This Ch.3 operates by identifying a central rule in s.561, to the effect that any proposed allotment of equity securities must first be offered to existing shareholders on a pre-emptive basis, and then sets out a number of exceptions to that general rule in subsequent provisions. The principal policy behind this provision is a primitive notion that no new shares may be allotted to third parties which may have the effect of disrupting the voting power within the company or the right to receive dividends, unless the existing shareholders have had the opportunity to acquire those new shares for themselves. This does not protect existing shareholders who do not have sufficient funds to acquire the necessary number of new securities: instead, their rights would require protection under provisions relating to minority shareholders' rights and so forth. It is worth noting that it was only in the final stages of the passage of the Act that all of the provisions of the Companies Act 1985 in this regard were repealed, having previously been expressly preserved from repeal.

Introductory

560. Meaning of "equity securities" and related expressions

(1) In this Chapter-
    "equity securities" means-
        (a) ordinary shares in the company, or
        (b) rights to subscribe for, or to convert securities into, ordinary shares in the company;

    "ordinary shares" means shares other than shares that as respects dividends and capital carry a right to participate only up to a specified amount in a distribution.
(2) References in this Chapter to the allotment of equity securities include-
        (a) the grant of a right to subscribe for, or to convert any securities into, ordinary shares in the company, and
        (b) the sale of ordinary shares in the company that immediately before the sale are held by the company as treasury shares.

GENERAL NOTE

The rights of original subscribers to the memorandum of association of the company have rights to acquire shares which stem from their subscription to the memorandum which do not fall within the scope of this chapter on the allotment of shares.

GENERAL NOTE

The definition of "equity securities" in the 2006 Act is much more concise than that in s.94 of the Companies Act 1985. There is no reference in the 2006 Act to the concept of "relevant share" from the 1985 Act (formerly s.94(5) of that Act), which excluded from the ambit of these provisions shares with a right to participate in a dividend only up to an identified level and shares acquired further to an employee share scheme. The 2006 Act therefore appears to cover all such forms of share, except to the extent that they are qualified by the definition of "ordinary shares" in subs.(1) of this provision.

Subsection (1)

There are three classes of right which fall under the allotment provisions relating to equity securities in Ch.3 of this Part: ordinary shares; rights to subscribe for ordinary shares; and rights to convert securities into ordinary shares, such as convertible bonds. The definition of an "ordinary share" excludes shares with a right to participate in a dividend only up to an identified level (an exclusion formerly contained in s.94(5)(a) of the Companies Act 1985).

Subsection (2)

The concept of "allotment" for these purposes includes, but is not limited to, the grant of rights to subscribe for ordinary shares or the grant of a right to convert securities into ordinary shares, and the sale of shares as ordinary shares which had previously been held as treasury shares. These categories of "allotment" for the purposes of the equity securities allotment code contained in Ch.3 are over-and-above ordinary transactions which would ordinarily be described as allotments.

Existing shareholders' right of pre-emption

561. Existing shareholders' right of pre-emption

(1) A company must not allot equity securities to a person on any terms unless-

    (a) it has made an offer to each person who holds ordinary shares in the company to allot to him on the same or more favourable terms a proportion of those securities that is as nearly as practicable equal to the proportion in nominal value held by him of the ordinary share capital of the company, and

    (b) the period during which any such offer may be accepted has expired or the company has received notice of the acceptance or refusal of every offer so made.

(2) Securities that a company has offered to allot to a holder of ordinary shares may be allotted to him, or anyone in whose favour he has renounced his right to their allotment, without contravening subsection (1)(b).

(3) If subsection (1) applies in relation to the grant of such a right, it does not apply in relation to the allotment of shares in pursuance of that right.

(4) Shares held by the company as treasury shares are disregarded for the purposes of this section, so that-

    (a) the company is not treated as a person who holds ordinary shares, and

    (b) the shares are not treated as forming part of the ordinary share capital of the company.

(5) This section is subject to-

    (a) sections 564 to 566 (exceptions to pre-emption right),

    (b) sections 567 and 568 (exclusion of rights of pre-emption),

    (c) sections 569 to 573 (disapplication of pre-emption rights), and

    (d) section 576 (saving for certain older pre-emption procedures).

GENERAL NOTE

It was a feature of the Companies Act 1985 that under s.89 a company wishing to allot equity securities was required to offer those securities first on the same or more favourable terms to existing shareholders. This is referred to as the existing shareholders having a right of pre-emption, that is a form of option to acquire these shares before they are allotted to other people. There are minor changes in wording, as identified below, between that provision and this provision of the 2006 Act, although in essence it is the same policy which is being effected. The meaning of the expression "holder of securities", which arises in numerous places in this provision, is explained in s.574.

Subsection (1)

A company in this provision "must not allot equity securities" whereas in the 1985 Act under s.89(1) it was provided that a company "shall not allot" equity securities. The change in wording is slight: however, it may raise a question as to the validity of any allotment made to a third party without first offering those shares to existing shareholders. That a company "shall not" allot suggests that there is no power to allot and a prohibition on such an allotment, whereas the words "must not" could be interpreted to connote a moral obligation not to allot, but which may nevertheless generate an allotment on which the third-party allottee may rely even if the company and its directors then owe other obligations of compensation to the existing shareholders. More likely, these provisions will be interpreted as having the same intention: that is, to preclude the company from having any such general power.

Otherwise the provisions of para.(a) achieve the same effect as s.89(1)(a) of the 1985 Act, except that the proportion to be offered to any shareholder is calculated by reference to his proportionate holding of the whole "ordinary share capital of the company" as opposed to "the aggregate of relevant shares and relevant employee shares".

The only alteration in para.(b) is one of detail, relating to the change from "shall not" to "must not" as aforesaid, otherwise the wording is effectively the same as that in s.89(1)(b) of the 1985, such that the company is permitted to make an allotment to a third party either because the time period relating to the pre-emptive offer has expired or because the company has received an acceptance or refusal of that pre-emptive offer in relation to every offer so made.

Subsection (2)

The effect of this provision is a saving provision, in effect, in that it saves an allotment to an existing shareholder from being held to be in breach of the time limits set out in subs.(1)(b) above.

Subsection (3)

At first glance this provision is confusingly drafted because the particular right which is envisaged by the draftsman by the reference to "such a right" is not made clear. It is suggested that subs.(3) must be taken to refer to the grant of any right to any person which requires an offer of that right to existing shareholders on a pre-emptive basis within subs.(1). The purpose of subs.(3) is, it is suggested, to remove the need for the procedure in subs.(1) to be complied with both in relation to a right to receive securities and then again once that right is converted or activated so as receive an allotment of securities.

Subsection (4)

With the introduction of treasury shares to United Kingdom company law, ss.89(6) and 94(3A) were introduced to the Companies Act 1985 by the Companies (Acquisition of Own Shares) (Treasury Shares) Regulations 2003, SI 2003/1116, so as to exclude a company's holding of treasury shares from the operation of the pre-emption provisions (s.89(6)), but so that sales of shares which had previously been held as treasury shares would fall within those provisions (s.94(3A)). This subs.(4) of the 2006 Act provides that the company's treasury shares do not constitute a part of the company's ordinary share capital in calculating the proportion of shares which any existing shareholder should be offered and also so as to exclude the company itself (as a holder of treasury shares) from needing to receive a pre-emptive offer of equity securities on a pre-emptive basis.

Subsection (5)

The foregoing provisions are subject to the exclusions contained in the following sections, much as the provisions of s.89 of the 1985 Act were subject to exclusions in ss.90 through 94.

562. Communication of pre-emption offers to shareholders

(1) This section has effect as to the manner in which offers required by section 561 are to be made to holders of a company's shares.

(2) The offer may be made in hard copy or electronic form.

(3) If the holder-

    (a) has no registered address in an EEA State and has not given to the company an address in an EEA State for the service of notices on him, or

    (b) is the holder of a share warrant,

the offer may be made by causing it, or a notice specifying where a copy of it can be obtained or inspected, to be published in the Gazette.

(4) The offer must state a period during which it may be accepted and the offer shall not be withdrawn before the end of that period.

(5) The period must be a period of at least 21 days beginning-

    (a) in the case of an offer made in hard copy form, with the date on which the offer is sent or supplied;

    (b) in the case of an offer made in electronic form, with the date on which the offer is sent;

    (c) in the case of an offer made by publication in the Gazette, with the date of publication.

(6) The Secretary of State may by regulations made by statutory instrument-

    (a) reduce the period specified in subsection (5) (but not to less than 14 days), or

    (b) increase that period.

(7) A statutory instrument containing regulations made under subsection (6) is subject to affirmative resolution procedure.

GENERAL NOTE

This provision replaces s.90 of the Companies Act 1985 for the purposes of the preceding section. The methodology for making the pre-emptive offer to existing shareholders which is required by the preceding section in relation to any offer to allot securities to any person (here "the pre-emptive offer"), is set out in this section. The pre-emptive offer may be made either electronically or in hard copy. The offer must state a period of not less than 21 days during which it may be accepted. The presence of such a time period is significant because the company is entitled to proceed with the allotment to a third party once the time period for the acceptance of the pre-emptive has elapsed, if the pre-emptive offer was not accepted, under s.561(1). Such an offer may not be withdrawn within that period. The period during which the offer may be accepted may be the subject of regulation by statutory instrument, and those regulations may alter the minimum length of the period.

In relation to share warrants the procedure is different: due to the nature of share warrants it may not be possible for the company to contact the holder of the warrant directly at any given time and therefore offers in relation to the holders of share warrants may be published in the Gazette with information as to how the terms of that offer can be viewed.

563. Liability of company and officers in case of contravention

(1) This section applies where there is a contravention of-
    section 561 (existing shareholders' right of pre-emption), or
    section 562 (communication of pre-emption offers to shareholders).

(2) The company and every officer of it who knowingly authorised or permitted the contravention are jointly and severally liable to compensate any person to whom an offer should have been made in accordance with those provisions for any loss, damage, costs or expenses which the person has sustained or incurred by reason of the contravention.

(3) No proceedings to recover any such loss, damage, costs or expenses shall be commenced after the expiration of two years-
    (a) from the delivery to the registrar of companies of the return of allotment, or
    (b) where equity securities other than shares are granted, from the date of the grant.

GENERAL NOTE

There are two different objectives achieved within this provision. First, it sets out the perameters of the personal liabilities of the company and of certain of its officers to compensate existing shareholders of the company for any breach of the two foregoing sections. Secondly, it places a time limit of two years on the bringing of such claims for compensation.

Subsection (1)

The following heads of liability apply both to breach of the requirement to make a pre-emptive offer of equity securities to existing shareholders, and also to the requirement that the procedure for making such offers be followed, as considered in relation to the two preceding sections of this Act.

Subsection (2)

The right to compensation may be enforced by any person to whom a pre-emptive offer of equity securities should have been made in accordance with s.561. The matters which may be compensated are "any loss, damage, costs or expenses which the [claimant] has sustained or incurred by reason of the contravention" of the two preceding sections. Thus the matters which may be compensated relate to some out of pocket loss which has actually been sustained or incurred at the time of making the claim for compensation. The claimant may not, it is suggested from a literal reading of the provision, recover any anticipated future loss which would either fall outside the time limit set out in subs.(3) or which is unliquidated at the time of making the claim. The nature of the matters which may be claimed are: "loss", which would include financial loss such as the devaluation of the market price of shares occasioned by the transfer; "damage", which would include liquidated harm suffered but not limited to financial loss, provided that it was caused, it is suggested, by the contravention of the two preceding provisions on ordinary common law terms; and "costs or expenses", which may include professional fees connected to the establishment of the level of loss incurred, and so forth, provided that they were caused by the contravention of the pre-emption provisions.

The people who are liable for the payment of this compensation are the company and also "every officer of [the company] who knowingly authorised or permitted the contravention". The company and the relevant officers are jointly and severally liable for this compensation. The principal question, then, is as to the identity of those officers who may be liable to pay compensation. Liability does not attach to the board of directors en masse nor to any other identified cadre of employees. Rather there is a two-stage test. First, it must be established who authorised or alternatively permitted the contravention. Notably there is no reference simply to anyone who "committed" the contravention.

This first step is connected to the second stage of the test: for a person to be liable they must also have authorised or permitted the contravention "knowingly". Thus, it is suggested, inadvertent commission of the contravention - for example, by allotting equity securities in ignorance either of this obligation or in ignorance of the obligation not having been performed - would not attract liability to pay compensation. The difficulty then surrounds the word "knowingly". In relation to fiduciary law in general, and the law on knowing receipt of property in relation to a breach of fiduciary duty specifically, the word "knowingly" has been defined to mean acting with actual knowledge, or wilfully and recklessly failing to make the inquiries which an honest person would have made, or wilfully shutting one's eyes to the obvious (*Montagu's Settlements, Re* [1987] Ch. 264, *per Megarry V.C., culled from Baden v Societe Generale* (1983) [1993] 1 W.L.R. 509 *per* Peter Gibson J.). Thus a person may be held not to have acted knowingly if he had genuinely forgotten what he was supposed to have done

(*Montagu's Settlements, Re* [1987] Ch. 264); although it is suggested that such an analysis would be particularly unfortunate in relation to the obligation of directors under the allotment provisions of the Companies Act whereby incompetence in forgetting one's legal duties would excuse one from the liabilities to compensate shareholders which are otherwise required by securities law.

Subsection (3)

There is a time limit on the bringing of an action for compensation under subs.(2) above. The limit is two years and it runs from the later of the date of the delivery to the registrar of the return of the allotment, and the grant of non-equity securities.

Exceptions to right of pre-emption

GENERAL NOTE

The purpose of this fascicle of sections is to set out the exceptions to the general rule that any proposed allotment of equity securities must first be offered to existing shareholders, as considered above. The obligation to make such an offer of equity securities to existing shareholders in proportion to their existing shareholdings is referred to here as the "pre-emptive offer".

564.   Exception to pre-emption right: bonus shares

Section 561(1) (existing shareholders' right of pre-emption) does not apply in relation to the allotment of bonus shares.

GENERAL NOTE

The right of pre-emption contained in s.561(1) does not apply in relation to "bonus shares" or the grant of a right either to subscribe for or to convert securities into bonus shares. The term "bonus shares" is not itself defined.

565.   Exception to pre-emption right: issue for non-cash consideration

Section 561(1) (existing shareholders' right of pre-emption) does not apply to a particular allotment of equity securities if these are, or are to be, wholly or partly paid up otherwise than in cash.

GENERAL NOTE

The right of pre-emption contained in s.561(1) does not apply in relation to a specific allotment, as suggested by the term "a particular allotment", if that allotment is to be "wholly or partly paid up otherwise that in cash". The provisions relating specifically to non-cash consideration are set out in Ch.6 of this Part of the Act, and considered below.

566.   Exception to pre-emption right: securities held under employees' share scheme

Section 561 (existing shareholders' right of pre-emption) does not apply to the allotment of securities that would, apart from any renunciation or assignment of the right to their allotment, be held under an employees' share scheme.

GENERAL NOTE

The right of pre-emption contained in s.561 generally does not apply in relation to securities which are held under an employees' share scheme, apart from any renunciation or assignment of the right of allotment.

Exclusion of right of pre-emption

GENERAL NOTE

The following fascicle of sections relates to the exclusion of the right of pre-emption considered hitherto, as opposed merely to providing exceptions to its general application.

567. Exclusion of requirements by private companies

(1) All or any of the requirements of-
   (a) section 561 (existing shareholders' right of pre-emption), or
   (b) section 562 (communication of pre-emption offers to shareholders)
may be excluded by provision contained in the articles of a private company.

(2) They may be excluded-
   (a) generally in relation to the allotment by the company of equity securities, or
   (b) in relation to allotments of a particular description.

(3) Any requirement or authorisation contained in the articles of a private company that is inconsistent with either of those sections is treated for the purposes of this section as a provision excluding that section.

(4) A provision to which section 568 applies (exclusion of pre-emption right: corresponding right conferred by articles) is not to be treated as inconsistent with section 561.

GENERAL NOTE

There is a general exclusion of the s.561 principle, requiring that an offer of an allotment of equity securities be made pre-emptively to existing shareholders (hereafter "the pre-emption principle"), in relation to a private company if the articles of association of such a company so provide. This provision re-enacts the principle in s.91 of the Companies Act 1985, although that predecessor provision permitted the exclusion to be contained in the articles or in the memorandum of association. Apart from subs.(3) below, the remainder of this provision is then additional to provisions contained in its predecessor.

Subsection (1)

As mentioned in the General Note, above, this subsection excludes the operation of the pre-emption offer principle from private companies where a private company has such an exclusion in its articles of association. The permitted nature of that exclusion emerges from the other subsections.

Subsection (2)

The exclusion referred to in subs.(1) may be either a general exclusion of the pre-emption principle or it may exclude the pre-emption principle only in relation to certain types of allotment.

Subsection (3)

It may be that the articles do not exclude the operation of the pre-emption principle in explicit language. However, provided that there are provisions of the articles which can be interpreted as being inconsistent with the pre-emption principle then those provisions may be deemed to be exclusions of the pre-emption principle within subs.(1), except to the extent provided in connection with subs.(4) and the exclusion of pre-emption rights under articles conferring corresponding rights.

568. Exclusion of pre-emption right: articles conferring corresponding right

(1) The provisions of this section apply where, in a case in which section 561 (existing shareholders' right of pre-emption) would otherwise apply-
   (a) a company's articles contain provision ("pre-emption provision") prohibiting the company from allotting ordinary shares of a particular class unless it has complied with the condition that it makes such an offer as is described in section 561(1) to each person who holds ordinary shares of that class, and
   (b) in accordance with that provision-
      (i) the company makes an offer to allot shares to such a holder, and
      (ii) he or anyone in whose favour he has renounced his right to their allotment accepts the offer.

(2) In that case, section 561 does not apply to the allotment of those shares and the company may allot them accordingly.

(3) The provisions of section 562 (communication of pre-emption offers to shareholders) apply in relation to offers made in pursuance of the pre-emption provision of the company's articles.

This is subject to section 567 (exclusion of requirements by private companies).

(4) If there is a contravention of the pre-emption provision of the company's articles, the company, and every officer of it who knowingly authorised or permitted the contravention, are jointly and severally liable to compensate any person to whom an offer should have been made under the provision for any loss, damage, costs or expenses which the person has sustained or incurred by reason of the contravention.

(5) No proceedings to recover any such loss, damage, costs or expenses may be commenced after the expiration of two years-

    (a) from the delivery to the registrar of companies of the return of allotment, or

    (b) where equity securities other than shares are granted, from the date of the grant.

GENERAL NOTE

A company's articles of association may exclude the operation of the pre-emption principle in s.561 above if those articles impose a prohibition on the company allotting ordinary shares unless it has made an offer of those securities to its existing shareholders in the manner described in s.561. The company may then allot those ordinary shares provided that it has complied with the obligation to make an offer of allotment to its existing shareholders and provided that they accept the offer. Interestingly, this condition precedent to allotment, does not correlate exactly with s.561 because it is not required that the shareholder has either accepted or refused the allotment or that the time period for the allotment has expired, instead it refers only to acceptance of the offer by the shareholder or by anyone in whose favour he has renounced his or her right to the allotment. This provision only refers to ordinary shares and does not apply to the other forms of right which fall within s.561. The methodology for communicating the offer to existing shareholders is that in s.561 above, except in relation to private companies where the provisions of s.567 apply instead. The meaning of the expression "holder of securities" is explained in s.574.

Subsection (4)

The liability for compensation is the same as that set out in s.563 and discussed above in detail in relation particularly to s.563(2).

Subsection (5)

The time period governing liability for compensation is the same as that set out in s.563 and discussed above in detail in relation particularly to s.563(3).

Disapplication of pre-emption rights

GENERAL NOTE

The following fascicle of sections disapply the pre-emption rights of existing shareholders, as set out in s.561 above, in the situations identified below. The first two categories of disapplication mirror the categories of disapplication of the general rule relating to the powers of directors to allot securities in s.551.

569. Disapplication of pre-emption rights: private company with only one class of shares

(1) The directors of a private company that has only one class of shares may be given power by the articles, or by a special resolution of the company, to allot equity securities of that class as if section 561 (existing shareholders' right of pre-emption)-

    (a) did not apply to the allotment, or

    (b) applied to the allotment with such modifications as the directors may determine.

(2) Where the directors make an allotment under this section, the provisions of this Chapter have effect accordingly.

GENERAL NOTE

The provisions relating to the existing shareholders' right of pre-emption in relation to offers to allot equity securities make frequent exception in relation to private companies. Under s.567 above there is an exclusion of the pre-emption obligations contained in s.561; in this provision those pre-emption rights are disapplied in relation to private companies. Further to the exclusion provided by s.567, what this section, and the sections which follow, achieve is the empowering of the directors of a private company in certain circumstances to allot shares.

Subsection (1)

This provision applies to private companies with only one class of shares: a category which receives distinct treatment under s.550 above in relation to directors' powers to allot shares. Section 561, containing the existing shareholders' pre-emption rights, may not apply to private companies with only one class of shares. If the company's articles contain a power for the directors to allot shares, or if a special resolution of the company has been passed empowering the directors to allot shares, then s.561 will not apply, or will not apply to the extent specified by the articles or that special resolution as appropriate.

Subsection (2)

Where an allotment is made, the remaining provisions of Ch.3 of this Part of the Act will have effect as appropriate.

570. Disapplication of pre-emption rights: directors acting under general authorisation

(1) Where the directors of a company are generally authorised for the purposes of section 551 (power of directors to allot shares etc: authorisation by company), they may be given power by the articles, or by a special resolution of the company, to allot equity securities pursuant to that authorisation as if section 561 (existing shareholders' right of pre-emption)-

    (a) did not apply to the allotment, or

    (b) applied to the allotment with such modifications as the directors may determine.

(2) Where the directors make an allotment under this section, the provisions of this Chapter have effect accordingly.

(3) The power conferred by this section ceases to have effect when the authorisation to which it relates-

    (a) is revoked, or

    (b) would (if not renewed) expire.

But if the authorisation is renewed the power may also be renewed, for a period not longer than that for which the authorisation is renewed, by a special resolution of the company.

(4) Notwithstanding that the power conferred by this section has expired, the directors may allot equity securities in pursuance of an offer or agreement previously made by the company if the power enabled the company to make an offer or agreement that would or might require equity securities to be allotted after it expired.

GENERAL NOTE

Under s.551 the directors may be empowered to allot securities by dint of a power given to them to do so in the company's articles. This section describes how the existing shareholders' right of pre-exemption in relation to an allotment of equity securities is disapplied in relation to companies with such a power in their articles.

Subsection (1)

This provision applies to all companies. Under s.552 the directors may be empowered to allot securities by dint of a power given to them to do so in the company's articles. Section 561, containing the existing shareholders' pre-emption rights, may not apply to companies with such a power contained in their articles. Thus, if the company's articles contain a power for the directors to allot shares, or if a special resolution of the company has been passed empowering the directors to allot shares, then s.561 will not apply, or will not apply to the extent specified by the articles or that special resolution as appropriate.

Subsection (2)

Where an allotment is made, the remaining provisions of Ch.3 of this Part of the Act will have effect as appropriate.

Subsection (3)

The power to allot securities under this section ceases when the authorisation on which it is predicated is either revoked or would expire (if not renewed). If the authorisation is renewed then the power to allot under this section may also be renewed. This formulation requires that the power to allot terminates automatically on the expiration of the authorisation and therefore must be renewed on each occasion that the authorisation is renewed by means of a special resolution of the company.

Subsection (4)

Further to subs.(3) the question arises as to what happens when the power to allot expires, and more precisely as to the effect of an agreement to allot equity securities which was made when the directors had a power to make such an allotment under the articles, but which cannot be performed because the power had expired before the securities were actually allotted. This subsection provides that the allotment may be made if the power permitted such an allotment to be made in these circumstances.

The position under the general law of contract is complicated here. The intended allottee would be entitled *prima facie* to sue for damages for any loss suffered by a breach of the agreement to allot securities under the general law of contract. The company may argue that it did not have the power to perform that contract because its power to do so had expired. However, ss.39-43 of the Companies Act 2006 would provide that the company may not rely on the contents of its articles of association to justify a breach of contract. A more difficult question arises in relation to specific performance. If the allottee wished to force the company to allot the shares to it then it may seek to rely on a specifically enforceable right to compel performance of the contract, or it may even seek to rely on the existence of a constructive trust over those shares (if they are identifiable as such) created by the contract requiring the allotment of shares to it. The contract may not be specifically enforceable, however, if the company through its directors has no power to allot shares in this fashion: a court of equity, exercising its discretion in relation to the equitable remedy of specific performance, may decide that the directors should not be compelled to carry out an act which is expressly prohibited by securities law for the protection of existing shareholders.

571.   Disapplication of pre-emption rights by special resolution

(1) Where the directors of a company are authorised for the purposes of section 551 (power of directors to allot shares etc: authorisation by company), whether generally or otherwise, the company may by special resolution resolve that section 561 (existing shareholders' right of pre-emption)-

    (a) does not apply to a specified allotment of equity securities to be made pursuant to that authorisation, or

    (b) applies to such an allotment with such modifications as may be specified in the resolution.

(2) Where such a resolution is passed the provisions of this Chapter have effect accordingly.

(3) A special resolution under this section ceases to have effect when the authorisation to which it relates-

    (a) is revoked, or

    (b) would (if not renewed) expire.

But if the authorisation is renewed the resolution may also be renewed, for a period not longer than that for which the authorisation is renewed, by a special resolution of the company.

(4) Notwithstanding that any such resolution has expired, the directors may allot equity securities in pursuance of an offer or agreement previously made by the company if the resolution enabled the company to make an offer or agreement that would or might require equity securities to be allotted after it expired.

(5) A special resolution under this section, or a special resolution to renew such a resolution, must not be proposed unless-

    (a) it is recommended by the directors, and

    (b) the directors have complied with the following provisions.

(6) Before such a resolution is proposed, the directors must make a written statement setting out-

    (a) their reasons for making the recommendation,

    (b) the amount to be paid to the company in respect of the equity securities to be allotted, and

    (c) the directors' justification of that amount.

(7) The directors' statement must-

    (a) if the resolution is proposed as a written resolution, be sent or submitted to every eligible member at or before the time at which the proposed resolution is sent or submitted to him;

    (b) if the resolution is proposed at a general meeting, be circulated to the members entitled to notice of the meeting with that notice.

GENERAL NOTE

It is a feature of ss.569-571, and of s.551 *et seq.*, that there is a modicum of repetition and of overlap between them. This provision enables a company to pass a special resolution to disapply the shareholders' right of pre-emption if the directors of a company are authorised for the purposes of s.551 to allot securities in relation to a specific allotment of securities. The same effect is discernible in the preceding section (under s.570(1)), further to which a special resolution could be passed to the same effect if the directors were generally empowered to allot securities. It is true that separating out essentially similar subject matter removes any potential confusions as to the scope, for example, of the powers of the company through special resolution, and that it also has the effect of reducing the length of statutory provisions. This provision, then, relates specifically to special resolutions to suspend the right of pre-emption over specific allotments of securities, whereas the preceding provision related to more general authorisations to suspend the right of pre-emption. The methodology for obtaining such a special resolution in this context is set out in subss.(5)-(7) below.

Subsection (1)

This provision applies to all companies. Under s.551 the directors may be empowered to allot securities by dint of a power given to them to do so in the company's articles. Section 561, containing the existing shareholders' pre-emption rights, may not apply to companies with such a power contained in their articles. Thus, if the company's articles contain a power for the directors to make a specific allotment of shares, then the company may resolve, by means of a special resolution, that s.561 does not apply to that specific allotment, or that it will only apply to the extent specified by that special resolution.

Subsection (2)

Where an allotment is made, the remaining provisions of Ch.3 of this Part of the Act will have effect as appropriate.

Subsection (3)

The power to allot securities under this section ceases when the special resolution on which it is predicated is either revoked or would expire (if not renewed). If the special resolution is renewed then the power to allot under this section may also be renewed. This formulation requires that the power to allot terminates automatically on the expiration of the special resolution and therefore must be renewed on each occasion that the authorisation is renewed by means of a special resolution of the company.

Subsection (4)

Further to subs.(3), the question arises as to what happens when the power to allot expires, and more precisely as to the effect of an agreement to allot equity securities which was made when the directors had a power to make such an allotment under the articles, but which cannot be performed because the power had expired before the securities were actually allotted. This subsection provides that the allotment may be made if the power permitted such an allotment to be made in these circumstances.

As to the position under the general law of contract, the reader is referred to the discussion of subs.(4) of the preceding provision.

Subsections (5), (6) and (7)

The methodology for obtaining such a special resolution in this context is set out in subss.(5)-(7). In short, these provisions place the onus on the directors to recommend and justify the special resolution to suspend the existing shareholders' right of pre-emption. The purpose behind this provision is to place the responsibility for any such suspension (in effect) of that right of pre-emption squarely on the directors' shareholders in the event that there is any harm caused to the rights of the existing shareholders by allotting shares to other people. There are two pre-requisites for the passage of a special resolution. First, the directors must recommend the special resolution. Secondly, the directors must make a written statement in the form specified in subss.(6) and (7). The written statement must give the directors' reasons for recommending the special resolution, it must state the amount of money which is to be paid to the company in relation to the equity securities which are to be allotted, and the written statement must also contain the directors' "justification" of that amount being (it is suggested) the workings which lead the directors to believe that that is the amount which will be paid to the company. That written statement must then be sent or submitted to "every eligible member" (a term which is undefined) if the resolution is proposed as a written resolution; or if the resolution is proposed at a general meeting then that written statement must be circulated to all members who are entitled to notice of the meeting with the notice of that meeting.

572. Liability for false statement in directors' statement

(1) This section applies in relation to a directors' statement under section 571 (special resolution disapplying pre-emption rights) that is sent, submitted or circulated under subsection (7) of that section.

(2) A person who knowingly or recklessly authorises or permits the inclusion of any matter that is misleading, false or deceptive in a material particular in such a statement commits an offence.

(3) A person guilty of an offence under this section is liable-
    (a) on conviction on indictment, to imprisonment for a term not exceeding two years or a fine (or both);
    (b) on summary conviction-
        (i) in England and Wales, to imprisonment for a term not exceeding twelve months or to a fine not exceeding the statutory maximum (or both);
        (ii) in Scotland or Northern Ireland, to imprisonment for a term not exceeding six months, or to a fine not exceeding the statutory maximum (or both).

GENERAL NOTE

    This section serves as a gloss to the preceding provision. The preceding provision provided for the possibility that a special resolution of the company could effectively suspend the existing shareholders' right of pre-emption in relation to a proposed allotment of equity securities. As part of the safeguards for shareholders' rights it was provided in that section that the directors must prepare a written statement in support of any such special resolution for that special resolution to be valid. This section deals with the result if there is any fraud in the preparation of that written statement.

Subsection (2)

    An offence is committed by any person who knowingly or recklessly authorises or permits the inclusion of any material in the directors' written statement which is "misleading, false or deceptive in a material particular".

    The concept of "knowingly" performing such an act is considered in *Archbold's Criminal Pleading, Evidence and Practice* (para.17-49) to connote the existence of "the doctrine of mens rea" in relation to an offence. Thus the prosecution is required to demonstrate that the defendant was consciously aware of all the elements of the offence. It is suggested that the weight of authority in criminal law is that one is only proved to have acted "knowingly" if one can be shown to have had "actual knowledge" of the requisite circumstances: see (*Westminster City Council v Croyalgrange Ltd* (1986) 83 Cr. App. Rep 155 at 164 *per* Lord Bridge. Hence the reference in the preceding sentence to the defendant needing to be "consciously" aware of all of the elements of the offence. However, there is authority which suggests something more akin to private law notions of knowledge. Thus in *Warner v Commissioner of Police of the Metropolis* [1969] 2 A.C. 256 at 279, Lord Reid suggested that in the criminal law an allegation of knowledge would be made out if one were "wilfully shutting one's eyes to the obvious".

    The concept of "recklessly" performing an act has been made clearer in the criminal law context by the House of Lords in *R. v G* [2004] 1 A.C. 1034, when there is a circumstance in which he is aware of a risk that that circumstance exists, and also that it is unreasonable for him to take that risk given that he is aware that the risk will come to fruition in the circumstances known to him. In effect this reinstates the subjective concept of recklessness originally set out in *R. v Cunningham* [1957] 2 Q.B. 396.

573. Disapplication of pre-emption rights: sale of treasury shares

(1) This section applies in relation to a sale of shares that is an allotment of equity securities by virtue of section 560(2)(b) (sale of shares held by company as treasury shares).

(2) The directors of a company may be given power by the articles, or by a special resolution of the company, to allot equity securities as if section 561 (existing shareholders' right of pre-emption)-
    (a) did not apply to the allotment, or

(b) applied to the allotment with such modifications as the directors may determine.

(3) The provisions of section 570(2) and (4) apply in that case as they apply to a case within subsection (1) of that section.

(4) The company may by special resolution resolve that section 561-
  (a) shall not apply to a specified allotment of securities, or
  (b) shall apply to the allotment with such modifications as may be specified in the resolution.

(5) The provisions of section 571(2) and (4) to (7) apply in that case as they apply to a case within subsection (1) of that section.

GENERAL NOTE

Sales of shares which are held by a company as treasury shares were considered in s.560(2)(b). It is possible, further to this section, for a company to give a power to its directors in its articles, or by means of a special resolution of the company, to allot equity securities which are held as treasury shares without the need to comply with the existing shareholders' right of pre-emption under s.561. The provisions of s.570(2) and (4) apply in relation to application and expiration of such authorisations. As with s.571, the company may pass a special resolution to disapply s.561 in relation to any specific allotment of equity securities held as treasury shares. In this context the provisions of s.571(2) and (4) apply in relation to the application and expiration of such authorisations.

Supplementary

574. References to holder of shares in relation to offer

(1) In this Chapter, in relation to an offer to allot securities required by-
  (a) section 561 (existing shareholders' right of pre-emption), or
  (b) any provision to which section 568 applies (articles conferring corresponding right),
a reference (however expressed) to the holder of shares of any description is to whoever was the holder of shares of that description at the close of business on a date to be specified in the offer.

(2) The specified date must fall within the period of 28 days immediately before the date of the offer.

GENERAL NOTE

There are two references to the "holder of shares", in s.561 and in s.568, the meaning of which term is explained, in part, by this provision to be a reference to the holder of any shares at the close of business at the date specified in the offer.

575. Saving for other restrictions on offer or allotment

(1) The provisions of this Chapter are without prejudice to any other enactment by virtue of which a company is prohibited (whether generally or in specified circumstances) from offering or allotting equity securities to any person.

(2) Where a company cannot by virtue of such an enactment offer or allot equity securities to a holder of ordinary shares of the company, those shares are disregarded for the purposes of section 561 (existing shareholders' right of pre-emption), so that-
  (a) the person is not treated as a person who holds ordinary shares, and
  (b) the shares are not treated as forming part of the ordinary share capital of the company.

GENERAL NOTE

Securities law in general may preclude or govern, as appropriate, the allotment, offer or sale of any securities to any person over and above the provisions in this Part of this Act. In particular the Prospectus Rules, the Disclosure Rules and the Transparency Rules implemented by the FSA, further to powers contained in the amended Financial Services and Markets Act 2000, place a large number of requirements on such dealings in securities.

Subsection (1)

Further to the point made in the General Note above, this subsection provides expressly that nothing in the allotment of equity securities provisions are to be taken to constitute a permission to allot securities or otherwise to deal with securities so as to disapply any other requirement of securities law.

Subsection (2)

Further to subs.(1), the question arises as to the manner in which the calculation of proportionate holdings of the company's total shareholding are to be carried out for the purposes of s.561 and the making of a pre-emptive offer to existing shareholders in the correct amount. That is, if an allotment has purportedly been made, but if that allotment is potentially void or voidable due to other aspects of securities law, should those securities be taken into account in carrying out the s.561 calculation? This subsection provides that any purported allotment of shares which is in breach of securities law generally shall be ignored in relation to that calculation for s.561 purposes.

576.   Saving for certain older pre-emption requirements

(1) In the case of a public company the provisions of this Chapter do not apply to an allotment of equity securities that are subject to a pre-emption requirement in relation to which section 96(1) of the Companies Act 1985 (c. 6) or Article 106(1) of the Companies (Northern Ireland) Order 1986 (S.I. 1986/1032 (N.I. 6)) applied immediately before the commencement of this Chapter.

(2) In the case of a private company a pre-emption requirement to which section 96(3) of the Companies Act 1985 or Article 106(3) of the Companies (Northern Ireland) Order 1986 applied immediately before the commencement of this Chapter shall have effect, so long as the company remains a private company, as if it were contained in the company's articles.

(3) A pre-emption requirement to which section 96(4) of the Companies Act 1985 or Article 106(4) of the Companies (Northern Ireland) Order 1986 applied immediately before the commencement of this section shall be treated for the purposes of this Chapter as if it were contained in the company's articles.

GENERAL NOTE

Possibly somewhat unsatisfactorily some provisions of the Companies Act 1985 in relation to allotment remain in effect in spite of the enactment of the Companies Act 2006. This section saves three particular provisions expressly. Each of the provisions which are saved relate to companies' pre-emption procedures which were operative before 1982. Thus the provisions of Ch.3 of this Part of this Act do not apply in the identified contexts.

577.   Provisions about pre-emption not applicable to shares taken on formation

The provisions of this Chapter have no application in relation to the taking of shares by the subscribers to the memorandum on the formation of the company.

GENERAL NOTE

As with s.559 in relation to Ch.2 of this Part of the Act, s.577 provides that nothing in Chapter of this Part of the Act applies to "the taking of shares by the subscribers to the memorandum on the formation of the company".

CHAPTER 4

PUBLIC COMPANIES: ALLOTMENT WHERE ISSUE NOT FULLY SUBSCRIBED

578.   Public companies: allotment where issue not fully subscribed

(1) No allotment shall be made of shares of a public company offered for subscription unless-
    (a) the issue is subscribed for in full, or
    (b) the offer is made on terms that the shares subscribed for may be allotted-
        (i) in any event, or

(ii) if specified conditions are met (and those conditions are met).

(2) If shares are prohibited from being allotted by subsection (1) and 40 days have elapsed after the first making of the offer, all money received from applicants for shares must be repaid to them forthwith, without interest.

(3) If any of the money is not repaid within 48 days after the first making of the offer, the directors of the company are jointly and severally liable to repay it, with interest at the rate for the time being specified under section 17 of the Judgments Act 1838 (c. 110) from the expiration of the 48th day.

A director is not so liable if he proves that the default in the repayment of the money was not due to any misconduct or negligence on his part.

(4) This section applies in the case of shares offered as wholly or partly payable otherwise than in cash as it applies in the case of shares offered for subscription.

(5) In that case-

    (a) the references in subsection (1) to subscription shall be construed accordingly;

    (b) references in subsections (2) and (3) to the repayment of money received from applicants for shares include-

        (i) the return of any other consideration so received (including, if the case so requires, the release of the applicant from any undertaking), or

        (ii) if it is not reasonably practicable to return the consideration, the payment of money equal to its value at the time it was so received;

    (c) references to interest apply accordingly.

(6) Any condition requiring or binding an applicant for shares to waive compliance with any requirement of this section is void.

GENERAL NOTE

Further to the policy underpinning Art.28 of the Second Company Law Directive (77/91/EEC) people who apply for shares are to be protected to the extent that the capital base of the company will not be increased if the issue is not fully subscribed or that it will only be increased if the terms of the issue envisaged an increase even if the issue was not fully subscribed. Thus, much turns on the precise terms of the proposed issue: it is only if the issue is to be made on terms that it may be carried out even if the issue has not been fully subscribed, or on some other terms contained in the issue, that that issue can indeed be so made.

579. Public companies: effect of irregular allotment where issue not fully subscribed

(1) An allotment made by a public company to an applicant in contravention of section 578 (public companies: allotment where issue not fully subscribed) is voidable at the instance of the applicant within one month after the date of the allotment, and not later.

(2) It is so voidable even if the company is in the course of being wound up.

(3) A director of a public company who knowingly contravenes, or permits or authorises the contravention of, any provision of section 578 with respect to allotment is liable to compensate the company and the allottee respectively for any loss, damages, costs or expenses that the company or allottee may have sustained or incurred by the contravention.

(4) Proceedings to recover any such loss, damages, costs or expenses may not be brought more than two years after the date of the allotment.

CHAPTER 5

PAYMENT FOR SHARES

GENERAL NOTE

An allotment made in contravention of the preceding section is voidable, and not automatically void. The applicant is the person who has the power to avoid the allotment within one month of the date of allotment. This provisions stands in the place of s.85 of the Companies Act 1985.

Subsection (3)

This provision is, broadly speaking, a parallel provision in relation to public companies to the provision in relation to liability for the making of false statements in relation to private companies in s.563(2) of this Act. The reader is referred to that discussion of s.563 in relation to the meaning of "knowingly" in this private law context, and in relation to the scope of the liability for "loss, damages, costs and expenses".

Subsection (4)

This provision is, broadly speaking, a parallel provision in relation to public companies to the provision in relation to liability for the making of false statements in relation to private companies in s.563(3) of this Act. The reader is referred to that discussion of s.563 in relation to the time limit for the bringing of proceedings.

General rules

580.   Shares not to be allotted at a discount

(1) A company's shares must not be allotted at a discount.

(2) If shares are allotted in contravention of this section, the allottee is liable to pay the company an amount equal to the amount of the discount, with interest at the appropriate rate.

GENERAL NOTE

This provision re-enacts s.100 of the Companies Act 1985. That provision is considered in detail in *Palmer's Company Law*, para.5.753 (at the time of writing). This prohibition was part of the common law, apparently, even before the Companies Act 1948: see *Walworth v Roper* [1892] A.C. 125 at 145 *per* Lord Macnaghten.

581.   Provision for different amounts to be paid on shares

A company, if so authorised by its articles, may-

(a) make arrangements on the issue of shares for a difference between the shareholders in the amounts and times of payment of calls on their shares;

(b) accept from any member the whole or part of the amount remaining unpaid on any shares held by him, although no part of that amount has been called up;

(c) pay a dividend in proportion to the amount paid up on each share where a larger amount is paid up on some shares than on others.

GENERAL NOTE

There was no direct equivalent of this provision in the Companies Act 1985. It retains the general approach taken in this Act, however, of stating a general principle in one provision (see the next provision) which is then capable of exclusion by means of an express provision in the company's articles.

582.   General rule as to means of payment

(1) Shares allotted by a company, and any premium on them, may be paid up in money or money's worth (including goodwill and know-how).

(2) This section does not prevent a company-

(a) from allotting bonus shares to its members, or

(b) from paying up, with sums available for the purpose, any amounts for the time being unpaid on any of its shares (whether on account of the nominal value of the shares or by way of premium).

(3) This section has effect subject to the following provisions of this Chapter (additional rules for public companies).

GENERAL NOTE

This provision replaces s.99 of the Companies Act 1985.

This provision replaces s.99(1) of the Companies Act 1985 in exactly the same words.

This provision replaces s.99(4) of the Companies Act 1985 in exactly the same words.

583. Meaning of payment in cash

(1) The following provisions have effect for the purposes of the Companies Acts.

(2) A share in a company is deemed paid up (as to its nominal value or any premium on it) in cash, or allotted for cash, if the consideration received for the allotment or payment up is a cash consideration.

(3) A "cash consideration" means-
   (a) cash received by the company,
   (b) a cheque received by the company in good faith that the directors have no reason for suspecting will not be paid,
   (c) a release of a liability of the company for a liquidated sum,
   (d) an undertaking to pay cash to the company at a future date, or
   (e) payment by any other means giving rise to a present or future entitlement (of the company or a person acting on the company's behalf) to a payment, or credit equivalent to payment, in cash.

(4) The Secretary of State may by order provide that particular means of payment specified in the order are to be regarded as falling within subsection (3)(e).

(5) In relation to the allotment or payment up of shares in a company-
   (a) the payment of cash to a person other than the company, or
   (b) an undertaking to pay cash to a person other than the company,
counts as consideration other than cash.
This does not apply for the purposes of Chapter 3 (allotment of equity securities: existing shareholders' right of pre-emption).

(6) For the purpose of determining whether a share is or is to be allotted for cash, or paid up in cash, "cash" includes foreign currency.

(7) An order under this section is subject to negative resolution procedure.

GENERAL NOTE
This provision had no equivalent in the Companies Act 1985.

Additional rules for public companies

584. Public companies: shares taken by subscribers of memorandum

Shares taken by a subscriber to the memorandum of a public company in pursuance of an undertaking of his in the memorandum, and any premium on the shares, must be paid up in cash.

GENERAL NOTE
This provision replaces s.106 of the Companies Act 1985. Subscribers to the memorandum are treated differently from other allottees of shares frequently in the allotment provisions of the 2006 Act, for example under s.577. Under this provision, a subscriber to the memorandum may only make payment for those shares in cash.

585. Public companies: must not accept undertaking to do work or perform services

(1) A public company must not accept at any time, in payment up of its shares or any premium on them, an undertaking given by any person that he or another should do work or perform services for the company or any other person.

(2) If a public company accepts such an undertaking in payment up of its shares or any premium on them, the holder of the shares when they or the premium are treated as paid up (in whole or in part) by the undertaking is liable-

    (a) to pay the company in respect of those shares an amount equal to their nominal value, together with the whole of any premium or, if the case so requires, such proportion of that amount as is treated as paid up by the undertaking; and

    (b) to pay interest at the appropriate rate on the amount payable under paragraph (a).

(3) The reference in subsection (2) to the holder of shares includes a person who has an unconditional right-

    (a) to be included in the company's register of members in respect of those shares, or

    (b) to have an instrument of transfer of them executed in his favour.

GENERAL NOTE

    This provision replaces s.99(2), (3) and (5) of the Companies Act 1985.

Subsection (1)

    This provision replaces s.99(2) of the Companies Act 1985 in exactly the same terms.

Subsection (2)

    This provision replaces s.99(3) of the Companies Act 1985 in exactly the same terms.

Subsection (3)

    This provision replaces s.99(5) of the Companies Act 1985 in exactly the same terms.

586.   Public companies: shares must be at least one-quarter paid up

(1) A public company must not allot a share except as paid up at least as to one-quarter of its nominal value and the whole of any premium on it.

(2) This does not apply to shares allotted in pursuance of an employees' share scheme.

(3) If a company allots a share in contravention of this section-

    (a) the share is to be treated as if one-quarter of its nominal value, together with the whole of any premium on it, had been received, and

    (b) the allottee is liable to pay the company the minimum amount which should have been received in respect of the share under subsection (1) (less the value of any consideration actually applied in payment up, to any extent, of the share and any premium on it), with interest at the appropriate rate.

(4) Subsection (3) does not apply to the allotment of bonus shares, unless the allottee knew or ought to have known the shares were allotted in contravention of this section.

GENERAL NOTE

    This provision effectively re-enacts s.101 of the Companies Act 1985 with a re-organisation of the subsections which contains effectively the same wording as s.101 with only changes of detail. The effect of that provision is considered in *Palmer's Company Law*, para.5.756 (at the time of writing).

587.   Public companies: payment by long-term undertaking

(1) A public company must not allot shares as fully or partly paid up (as to their nominal value or any premium on them) otherwise than in cash if the consideration for the allotment is or includes an undertaking which is to be, or may be, performed more than five years after the date of the allotment.

(2) If a company allots shares in contravention of subsection (1), the allottee is liable to pay the company an amount equal to the aggregate of their nominal value and the whole of any

premium (or, if the case so requires, so much of that aggregate as is treated as paid up by the undertaking), with interest at the appropriate rate.

(3) Where a contract for the allotment of shares does not contravene subsection (1), any variation of the contract that has the effect that the contract would have contravened the subsection, if the terms of the contract as varied had been its original terms, is void.

This applies also to the variation by a public company of the terms of a contract entered into before the company was re-registered as a public company.

(4) Where-

    (a) a public company allots shares for a consideration which consists of or includes (in accordance with subsection (1)) an undertaking that is to be performed within five years of the allotment, and

    (b) the undertaking is not performed within the period allowed by the contract for the allotment of the shares,

the allottee is liable to pay the company, at the end of the period so allowed, an amount equal to the aggregate of the nominal value of the shares and the whole of any premium (or, if the case so requires, so much of that aggregate as is treated as paid up by the undertaking), with interest at the appropriate rate.

(5) References in this section to a contract for the allotment of shares include an ancillary contract relating to payment in respect of them.

GENERAL NOTE

    This provision replaces s.102 of the Companies Act 1985.

Subsection (1)

    This provision is on almost exactly the same terms as s.102(1) of the Companies Act 1985 except that where in 1985 the company "shall not" allot shares, in the 2006 Act it is provided that the company "must not" allot shares.

Subsection (2)

    This provision replaces s.102(2) of the Companies Act 1985.

Subsection (3)

    This provision replaces both s.102(3) and (4) of the Companies Act 1985.

Subsection (4)

    This provision replaces both s.102(5) and (6) of the Companies Act 1985.

Subsection (5)

    This provision replaces s.102(7) of the Companies Act 1985.

Supplementary provisions

588. Liability of subsequent holders of shares

(1) If a person becomes a holder of shares in respect of which-

    (a) there has been a contravention of any provision of this Chapter, and

    (b) by virtue of that contravention another is liable to pay any amount under the provision contravened,

that person is also liable to pay that amount (jointly and severally with any other person so liable), subject as follows.

(2) A person otherwise liable under subsection (1) is exempted from that liability if either-

    (a) he is a purchaser for value and, at the time of the purchase, he did not have actual notice of the contravention concerned, or

    (b) he derived title to the shares (directly or indirectly) from a person who became a holder of them after the contravention and was not liable under subsection (1).

(3) References in this section to a holder, in relation to shares in a company, include any person who has an unconditional right-

    (a) to be included in the company's register of members in respect of those shares, or

    (b) to have an instrument of transfer of the shares executed in his favour.

(4) This section applies in relation to a failure to carry out a term of a contract as mentioned in section 587(4) (public companies: payment by long-term undertaking) as it applies in relation to a contravention of a provision of this Chapter.

GENERAL NOTE

    There are two purposes to this provision: first, to provide for joint and several liability for all people who become holders of shares passed in breach of this Chapter in subs.(1), and, secondly, to provide a defence of purchase good faith in subs.(2).

Subsection (2)

    This latter provision effectively translates to contracts for the allotment of shares the defence to a claim for recovery of property in relation to a bona fide purchaser for value without notice of the claimant's rights. Under English property law a purchaser, that is someone who has given consideration, of the common law title in property who has acted in good faith and who had no notice of the rights of a predecessor in title over that same property, has a good defence to the claimant's claim for recovery of that property: see, for example, *Westdeutsche Landesbank v Islington* [1996] A.C. 669. Importantly, however, the defence is available in this context provided that the defendant allottee did not have "actual notice" of the claimant's rights, as opposed to having the defence made unavailable by dint of the defendant having had constructive or imputed notice of the claimant's rights. As to the meaning of "actual notice" see, inter alia, *Eagle Trust v S.B.C. Securities* [1991] B.C.L.C. 438 at 447 *per* Vinelott J.; *Polly Peck International Plc v Nadir (No.2)* [1992] 4 All E.R. 769 at 782 *per* Scott L.J.

589.   Power of court to grant relief

(1) This section applies in relation to liability under-

    section 585(2) (liability of allottee in case of breach by public company of prohibition on accepting undertaking to do work or perform services),

    section 587(2) or (4) (liability of allottee in case of breach by public company of prohibition on payment by long-term undertaking), or

    section 588 (liability of subsequent holders of shares),

as it applies in relation to a contravention of those sections.

(2) A person who-

    (a) is subject to any such liability to a company in relation to payment in respect of shares in the company, or

    (b) is subject to any such liability to a company by virtue of an undertaking given to it in, or in connection with, payment for shares in the company,

may apply to the court to be exempted in whole or in part from the liability.

(3) In the case of a liability within subsection (2)(a), the court may exempt the applicant from the liability only if and to the extent that it appears to the court just and equitable to do so having regard to-

    (a) whether the applicant has paid, or is liable to pay, any amount in respect of-

        (i) any other liability arising in relation to those shares under any provision of this Chapter or Chapter 6, or

        (ii) any liability arising by virtue of any undertaking given in or in connection with payment for those shares;

    (b) whether any person other than the applicant has paid or is likely to pay, whether in pursuance of any order of the court or otherwise, any such amount;

    (c) whether the applicant or any other person-

     (i) has performed in whole or in part, or is likely so to perform any such undertaking, or

     (ii) has done or is likely to do any other thing in payment or part payment for the shares.

(4) In the case of a liability within subsection (2)(b), the court may exempt the applicant from the liability only if and to the extent that it appears to the court just and equitable to do so having regard to-

    (a) whether the applicant has paid or is liable to pay any amount in respect of liability arising in relation to the shares under any provision of this Chapter or Chapter 6;

    (b) whether any person other than the applicant has paid or is likely to pay, whether in pursuance of any order of the court or otherwise, any such amount.

(5) In determining whether it should exempt the applicant in whole or in part from any liability, the court must have regard to the following overriding principles-

    (a) a company that has allotted shares should receive money or money's worth at least equal in value to the aggregate of the nominal value of those shares and the whole of any premium or, if the case so requires, so much of that aggregate as is treated as paid up;

    (b) subject to that, where a company would, if the court did not grant the exemption, have more than one remedy against a particular person, it should be for the company to decide which remedy it should remain entitled to pursue.

(6) If a person brings proceedings against another ("the contributor") for a contribution in respect of liability to a company arising under any provision of this Chapter or Chapter 6 and it appears to the court that the contributor is liable to make such a contribution, the court may, if and to the extent that it appears to it just and equitable to do so having regard to the respective culpability (in respect of the liability to the company) of the contributor and the person bringing the proceedings-

    (a) exempt the contributor in whole or in part from his liability to make such a contribution, or

    (b) order the contributor to make a larger contribution than, but for this subsection, he would be liable to make.

GENERAL NOTE

The court has a power to grant relief to persons who would otherwise face liability under ss.585(2), 587(2) and 588 if it considers it just and equitable to do so. The defendant must apply to the court for relief.

590. Penalty for contravention of this Chapter

(1) If a company contravenes any of the provisions of this Chapter, an offence is committed by-
    (a) the company, and
    (b) every officer of the company who is in default.

(2) A person guilty of an offence under this section is liable-
    (a) on conviction on indictment, to a fine;
    (b) on summary conviction, to a fine not exceeding the statutory maximum.

GENERAL NOTE

For the purposes of this Chapter, this provision replaces s.114 of the Companies Act 1985.

591. Enforceability of undertakings to do work etc

(1) An undertaking given by any person, in or in connection with payment for shares in a company, to do work or perform services or to do any other thing, if it is enforceable by the company apart from this Chapter, is so enforceable notwithstanding that there has been a contravention in relation to it of a provision of this Chapter or Chapter 6.

(2) This is without prejudice to section 589 (power of court to grant relief etc in respect of liabilities).

GENERAL NOTE

This provision replaces s.115 of the Companies Act 1985, although with references in the 1985 Act to contravention of any part of the Act and so forth being replaced with references specifically to this Ch.5.

592. The appropriate rate of interest

(1) For the purposes of this Chapter the "appropriate rate" of interest is 5% per annum or such other rate as may be specified by order made by the Secretary of State.

(2) An order under this section is subject to negative resolution procedure.

GENERAL NOTE

This provision replaces s.107 of the Companies Act 1985 for the purposes of this Chapter.

CHAPTER 6

PUBLIC COMPANIES: INDEPENDENT VALUATION OF NON-CASH
CONSIDERATION

Non-cash consideration for shares

593. Public company: valuation of non-cash consideration for shares

(1) A public company must not allot shares as fully or partly paid up (as to their nominal value or any premium on them) otherwise than in cash unless-
   (a) the consideration for the allotment has been independently valued in accordance with the provisions of this Chapter,
   (b) the valuer's report has been made to the company during the six months immediately preceding the allotment of the shares, and
   (c) a copy of the report has been sent to the proposed allottee.

(2) For this purpose the application of an amount standing to the credit of-
   (a) any of a company's reserve accounts, or
   (b) its profit and loss account,
in paying up (to any extent) shares allotted to members of the company, or premiums on shares so allotted, does not count as consideration for the allotment.
Accordingly, subsection (1) does not apply in that case.

(3) If a company allots shares in contravention of subsection (1) and either-
   (a) the allottee has not received the valuer's report required to be sent to him, or
   (b) there has been some other contravention of the requirements of this section or section 596 that the allottee knew or ought to have known amounted to a contravention,
the allottee is liable to pay the company an amount equal to the aggregate of the nominal value of the shares and the whole of any premium (or, if the case so requires, so much of that aggregate as is treated as paid up by the consideration), with interest at the appropriate rate.

(4) This section has effect subject to-
   section 594 (exception to valuation requirement: arrangement with another company), and
   section 595 (exception to valuation requirement: merger).

Subsection (1)

This provision re-enacts the contents of s.103(1) of the Companies Act 1985.

Subsection (2)

This provision replaces s.103(2) of the Companies Act 1985 with minor amendments.

594. Exception to valuation requirement: arrangement with another company

(1) Section 593 (valuation of non-cash consideration) does not apply to the allotment of shares by a company ("company A") in connection with an arrangement to which this section applies.

(2) This section applies to an arrangement for the allotment of shares in company A on terms that the whole or part of the consideration for the shares allotted is to be provided by-

    (a) the transfer to that company, or

    (b) the cancellation,

of all or some of the shares, or of all or some of the shares of a particular class, in another company ("company B").

(3) It is immaterial whether the arrangement provides for the issue to company A of shares, or shares of any particular class, in company B.

(4) This section applies to an arrangement only if under the arrangement it is open to all the holders of the shares in company B (or, where the arrangement applies only to shares of a particular class, to all the holders of shares of that class) to take part in the arrangement.

(5) In determining whether that is the case, the following shall be disregarded-

    (a) shares held by or by a nominee of company A;

    (b) shares held by or by a nominee of a company which is-

        (i) the holding company, or a subsidiary, of company A, or

        (ii) a subsidiary of such a holding company;

    (c) shares held as treasury shares by company B.

(6) In this section-

    (a) "arrangement" means any agreement, scheme or arrangement (including an arrangement sanctioned in accordance with-

        (i) Part 26 (arrangements and reconstructions), or

        (ii) section 110 of the Insolvency Act 1986 (c. 45) or Article 96 of the Insolvency (Northern Ireland) Order 1989 (S.I. 1989/2405 (N.I. 19)) (liquidator in winding up accepting shares as consideration for sale of company property)), and

    (b) "company", except in reference to company A, includes any body corporate.

Subsections (1)-(3)

These provisions replace s.103(3) of the Companies Act 1985 with minor amendments.

Subsection (4)

This provision re-enacts the contents of s.103(4) of the Companies Act 1985.

595. Exception to valuation requirement: merger

(1) Section 593 (valuation of non-cash consideration) does not apply to the allotment of shares by a company in connection with a proposed merger with another company.

(2) A proposed merger is where one of the companies proposes to acquire all the assets and liabilities of the other in exchange for the issue of shares or other securities of that one to shareholders of the other, with or without any cash payment to shareholders.

(3) In this section "company", in reference to the other company, includes any body corporate.

GENERAL NOTE

Subsection (1)

This provision re-enacts the contents of s.103(5) of the Companies Act 1985.

596.   Non-cash consideration for shares: requirements as to valuation and report

(1) The provisions of sections 1150 to 1153 (general provisions as to independent valuation and report) apply to the valuation and report required by section 593 (public company: valuation of non-cash consideration for shares).

(2) The valuer's report must state-
   (a) the nominal value of the shares to be wholly or partly paid for by the consideration in question;
   (b) the amount of any premium payable on the shares;
   (c) the description of the consideration and, as respects so much of the consideration as he himself has valued, a description of that part of the consideration, the method used to value it and the date of the valuation;
   (d) the extent to which the nominal value of the shares and any premium are to be treated as paid up-
      (i) by the consideration;
      (ii) in cash.

(3) The valuer's report must contain or be accompanied by a note by him-
   (a) in the case of a valuation made by a person other than himself, that it appeared to himself reasonable to arrange for it to be so made or to accept a valuation so made,
   (b) whoever made the valuation, that the method of valuation was reasonable in all the circumstances,
   (c) that it appears to the valuer that there has been no material change in the value of the consideration in question since the valuation, and
   (d) that, on the basis of the valuation, the value of the consideration, together with any cash by which the nominal value of the shares or any premium payable on them is to be paid up, is not less than so much of the aggregate of the nominal value and the whole of any such premium as is treated as paid up by the consideration and any such cash.

(4) Where the consideration to be valued is accepted partly in payment up of the nominal value of the shares and any premium and partly for some other consideration given by the company, section 593 and the preceding provisions of this section apply as if references to the consideration accepted by the company included the proportion of that consideration that is properly attributable to the payment up of that value and any premium.

(5) In such a case-
   (a) the valuer must carry out, or arrange for, such other valuations as will enable him to determine that proportion, and
   (b) his report must state what valuations have been made under this subsection and also the reason for, and method and date of, any such valuation and any other matters which may be relevant to that determination.

GENERAL NOTE

This provision replaces s.108 of the Companies Act 1985 generally.

Subsection (2)

This provision re-enacts the contents of s.108(4) of the Companies Act 1985.

Subsection (3)

This provision re-enacts the contents of s.108(6) of the Companies Act 1985.

Subsection (4)

This provision re-enacts the contents of the introductory main clause in s.108(7) of the Companies Act 1985.

Subsection (5)

This provision re-enacts the contents of s.108(7)(a) and (b) of the Companies Act 1985.

597. Copy of report to be delivered to registrar

(1) A company to which a report is made under section 593 as to the value of any consideration for which, or partly for which, it proposes to allot shares must deliver a copy of the report to the registrar for registration.

(2) The copy must be delivered at the same time that the company files the return of the allotment of those shares under section 555 (return of allotment by limited company).

(3) If default is made in complying with subsection (1) or (2), an offence is committed by every officer of the company who is in default.

(4) A person guilty of an offence under this section is liable-

    (a) on conviction on indictment, to a fine;

    (b) on summary conviction, to a fine not exceeding the statutory maximum and, for continued contravention, a daily default fine not exceeding one-tenth of the statutory maximum.

(5) In the case of default in delivering to the registrar any document as required by this section, any person liable for the default may apply to the court for relief.

(6) The court, if satisfied-

    (a) that the omission to deliver the document was accidental or due to inadvertence, or

    (b) that it is just and equitable to grant relief,

may make an order extending the time for delivery of the document for such period as the court thinks proper.

GENERAL NOTE

This provision largely replaces the contents of s.111 of the Companies Act 1985, except for s.111(2). This provision requires a copy of the valuation report outlined in the preceding sections to be delivered to the registrar: failure to do so constitutes a criminal offence.

Subsection (1)

This provision re-enacts the contents of s.111(1) of the Companies Act 1985.

Subsection (3)

This provision effectively replaces the contents of s.111(3) and (4) of the Companies Act 1985.

Subsection (5)

This provision has no comparator in the Companies Act 1985.

Subsection (6)

This provision has no comparator in the Companies Act 1985.

Transfer of non-cash asset in initial period

598.   Public company: agreement for transfer of non-cash asset in initial period

(1) A public company formed as such must not enter into an agreement-
    (a) with a person who is a subscriber to the company's memorandum,
    (b) for the transfer by him to the company, or another, before the end of the company's initial period of one or more non-cash assets, and
    (c) under which the consideration for the transfer to be given by the company is at the time of the agreement equal in value to one-tenth or more of the company's issued share capital,
 unless the conditions referred to below have been complied with.
(2) The company's "initial period" means the period of two years beginning with the date of the company being issued with a certificate under section 761 (trading certificate).
(3) The conditions are those specified in-
    section 599 (requirement of independent valuation), and
    section 601 (requirement of approval by members).
(4) This section does not apply where-
    (a) it is part of the company's ordinary business to acquire, or arrange for other persons to acquire, assets of a particular description, and
    (b) the agreement is entered into by the company in the ordinary course of that business.
(5) This section does not apply to an agreement entered into by the company under the supervision of the court or of an officer authorised by the court for the purpose.

GENERAL NOTE

Subsection (1)
    Paragraphs (a) and (b) of this provision re-enacts the contents of s.104(1) of the Companies Act 1985, whereas para.(c) had no comparator in the 1985 Act.

Subsection (2)
    This provision re-enacts the contents of s.104(2) of the Companies Act 1985.

Subsection (4)
    This provision re-enacts the contents of s.104(4)(a) and (b) of the Companies Act 1985.

Subsection (5)
    This provision re-enacts the contents of s.104(6)(b) of the Companies Act 1985.

599.   Agreement for transfer of non-cash asset: requirement of independent valuation

(1) The following conditions must have been complied with-
    (a) the consideration to be received by the company, and any consideration other than cash to be given by the company, must have been independently valued in accordance with the provisions of this Chapter,
    (b) the valuer's report must have been made to the company during the six months immediately preceding the date of the agreement, and
    (c) a copy of the report must have been sent to the other party to the proposed agreement not later than the date on which copies have to be circulated to members under section 601(3).

(2) The reference in subsection (1)(a) to the consideration to be received by the company is to the asset to be transferred to it or, as the case may be, to the advantage to the company of the asset's transfer to another person.

(3) The reference in subsection (1)(c) to the other party to the proposed agreement is to the person referred to in section 598(1)(a).

If he has received a copy of the report under section 601 in his capacity as a member of the company, it is not necessary to send another copy under this section.

(4) This section does not affect any requirement to value any consideration for purposes of section 593 (valuation of non-cash consideration for shares).

GENERAL NOTE

This provision re-enacts the policy underpinning s.103 of the Companies Act 1985 by requiring that, as did s.103(1)(a) of the 1985 Act, any non-cash asset provided to the company be valued independently. The methodology for conducting such valuations was formerly set out in s.108 of the 1985 Act and is now set out variously across ss.600 and 601 of the 2006 Act.

600. Agreement for transfer of non-cash asset: requirements as to valuation and report

(1) The provisions of sections 1150 to 1153 (general provisions as to independent valuation and report) apply to the valuation and report required by section 599 (public company: transfer of non-cash asset).

(2) The valuer's report must state-
   (a) the consideration to be received by the company, describing the asset in question (specifying the amount to be received in cash) and the consideration to be given by the company (specifying the amount to be given in cash), and
   (b) the method and date of valuation.

(3) The valuer's report must contain or be accompanied by a note by him-
   (a) in the case of a valuation made by a person other than himself, that it appeared to himself reasonable to arrange for it to be so made or to accept a valuation so made,
   (b) whoever made the valuation, that the method of valuation was reasonable in all the circumstances,
   (c) that it appears to the valuer that there has been no material change in the value of the consideration in question since the valuation, and
   (d) that, on the basis of the valuation, the value of the consideration to be received by the company is not less than the value of the consideration to be given by it.

(4) Any reference in section 599 or this section to consideration given for the transfer of an asset includes consideration given partly for its transfer.

(5) In such a case-
   (a) the value of any consideration partly so given is to be taken as the proportion of the consideration properly attributable to its transfer,
   (b) the valuer must carry out or arrange for such valuations of anything else as will enable him to determine that proportion, and
   (c) his report must state what valuations have been made for that purpose and also the reason for and method and date of any such valuation and any other matters which may be relevant to that determination.

GENERAL NOTE

Section 109(2) of the Companies Act 1985 transposed the contents of s.108 of that Act into s.109. This provision copies parts of s.610 into this provision rather than incorporating them by reference.

Subsection (2)

This provision re-enacts the contents of s.109(2)(a) and (b) of the Companies Act 1985.

Paragraphs (a), (b) and (c) of this provision re-enacts the contents of s.108(6) of the Companies Act 1985. Paragraph (d) is new to the 2006 Act.

Subsection (5)

This provision re-enacts the contents of s.109(3) of the Companies Act 1985.

601. Agreement for transfer of non-cash asset: requirement of approval by members

(1) The following conditions must have been complied with-
    (a) the terms of the agreement must have been approved by an ordinary resolution of the company,
    (b) the requirements of this section must have been complied with as respects the circulation to members of copies of the valuer's report under section 599, and
    (c) a copy of the proposed resolution must have been sent to the other party to the proposed agreement.

(2) The reference in subsection (1)(c) to the other party to the proposed agreement is to the person referred to in section 598(1)(a).

(3) The requirements of this section as to circulation of copies of the valuer's report are as follows-
    (a) if the resolution is proposed as a written resolution, copies of the valuer's report must be sent or submitted to every eligible member at or before the time at which the proposed resolution is sent or submitted to him;
    (b) if the resolution is proposed at a general meeting, copies of the valuer's report must be circulated to the members entitled to notice of the meeting not later than the date on which notice of the meeting is given.

GENERAL NOTE

This provision has no comparator in the Companies Act 1985. There is now, in consequence, a requirement that the members of the company have approved the agreement to allot shares in consideration for the transfer of a non-cash asset and the valuation which underpins it, and also that the valuer's report has been circulated to the members.

602. Copy of resolution to be delivered to registrar

(1) A company that has passed a resolution under section 601 with respect to the transfer of an asset must, within 15 days of doing so, deliver to the registrar a copy of the resolution together with the valuer's report required by that section.

(2) If a company fails to comply with subsection (1), an offence is committed by-
    (a) the company, and
    (b) every officer of the company who is in default.

(3) A person guilty of an offence under this section is liable on summary conviction to a fine not exceeding level 3 on the standard scale and, for continued contravention, to a daily default fine not exceeding one-tenth of level 3 on the standard scale.

GENERAL NOTE

This provision replaces those provisions of s.111 of the Company Act 1985 which are not re-enacted by s.597 of this Act.

603. Adaptation of provisions in relation to company re-registering as public

The provisions of sections 598 to 602 (public companies: transfer of non-cash assets) apply with the following adaptations in relation to a company reregistered as a public company-

(a) the reference in section 598(1)(a) to a person who is a subscriber to the company's memorandum shall be read as a reference to a person who is a member of the company on the date of re-registration;

(b) the reference in section 598(2) to the date of the company being issued with a certificate under section 761 (trading certificate) shall be read as a reference to the date of re-registration.

GENERAL NOTE

The purpose of this provision is to ensure that the provisions of this Chapter correlate with the provisions dealing with the requirement of a private company to re-register as a public company, as described elsewhere in this Part and in particular in relation to s.761 below.

604. Agreement for transfer of non-cash asset: effect of contravention

(1) This section applies where a public company enters into an agreement in contravention of section 598 and either-

(a) the other party to the agreement has not received the valuer's report required to be sent to him, or

(b) there has been some other contravention of the requirements of this Chapter that the other party to the agreement knew or ought to have known amounted to a contravention.

(2) In those circumstances-

(a) the company is entitled to recover from that person any consideration given by it under the agreement, or an amount equal to the value of the consideration at the time of the agreement, and

(b) the agreement, so far as not carried out, is void.

(3) If the agreement is or includes an agreement for the allotment of shares in the company, then-

(a) whether or not the agreement also contravenes section 593 (valuation of non-cash consideration for shares), this section does not apply to it in so far as it is for the allotment of shares, and

(b) the allottee is liable to pay the company an amount equal to the aggregate of the nominal value of the shares and the whole of any premium (or, if the case so requires, so much of that aggregate as is treated as paid up by the consideration), with interest at the appropriate rate.

GENERAL NOTE

This section deals with agreements for transfer in consideration for a non-cash asset which have not complied with s.593. In the event of failure to comply with that section the company may recover any consideration which it has provided under the agreement. Furthermore any agreement between a public company and an allottee will be void "so far as not carried out". The allottee is then obliged to pay the company the nominal value of the shares, plus any premium, plus interest at the rate specified under s.609. The following provision describes the position of a person who becomes a holder of shares in breach of s.593.

Supplementary provisions

605. Liability of subsequent holders of shares

(1) If a person becomes a holder of shares in respect of which-

(a) there has been a contravention of section 593 (public company: valuation of non-cash consideration for shares), and

(b) by virtue of that contravention another is liable to pay any amount under the provision contravened,

that person is also liable to pay that amount (jointly and severally with any other person so liable), unless he is exempted from liability under subsection (3) below.

(2) If a company enters into an agreement in contravention of section 598 (public company: agreement for transfer of non-cash asset in initial period) and-

    (a) the agreement is or includes an agreement for the allotment of shares in the company,

    (b) a person becomes a holder of shares allotted under the agreement, and

    (c) by virtue of the agreement and allotment under it another person is liable to pay an amount under section 604,

the person who becomes the holder of the shares is also liable to pay that amount (jointly and severally with any other person so liable), unless he is exempted from liability under subsection (3) below. This applies whether or not the agreement also contravenes section 593.

(3) A person otherwise liable under subsection (1) or (2) is exempted from that liability if either-

    (a) he is a purchaser for value and, at the time of the purchase, he did not have actual notice of the contravention concerned, or

    (b) he derived title to the shares (directly or indirectly) from a person who became a holder of them after the contravention and was not liable under subsection (1) or (2).

(4) References in this section to a holder, in relation to shares in a company, include any person who has an unconditional right-

    (a) to be included in the company's register of members in respect of those shares, or

    (b) to have an instrument of transfer of the shares executed in his favour.

GENERAL NOTE

Whereas s.604 refers to the "allottee", this provision imposes liability to make payment further to s.604(3). Similarly to s.588 there are two purposes to this provision: first, to provide for joint and several liability for all people who become holders of shares passed in breach of this Chapter, and, secondly, to provide a defence of purchase in good faith.

606.   Power of court to grant relief

(1) A person who-

    (a) is liable to a company under any provision of this Chapter in relation to payment in respect of any shares in the company, or

    (b) is liable to a company by virtue of an undertaking given to it in, or in connection with, payment for any shares in the company,

may apply to the court to be exempted in whole or in part from the liability.

(2) In the case of a liability within subsection (1)(a), the court may exempt the applicant from the liability only if and to the extent that it appears to the court just and equitable to do so having regard to-

    (a) whether the applicant has paid, or is liable to pay, any amount in respect of-

        (i) any other liability arising in relation to those shares under any provision of this Chapter or Chapter 5, or

        (ii) any liability arising by virtue of any undertaking given in or in connection with payment for those shares;

    (b) whether any person other than the applicant has paid or is likely to pay, whether in pursuance of any order of the court or otherwise, any such amount;

    (c) whether the applicant or any other person-

        (i) has performed in whole or in part, or is likely so to perform any such undertaking, or

        (ii) has done or is likely to do any other thing in payment or part payment for the shares.

(3) In the case of a liability within subsection (1)(b), the court may exempt the applicant from the liability only if and to the extent that it appears to the court just and equitable to do so having regard to-

(a) whether the applicant has paid or is liable to pay any amount in respect of liability arising in relation to the shares under any provision of this Chapter or Chapter 5;

(b) whether any person other than the applicant has paid or is likely to pay, whether in pursuance of any order of the court or otherwise, any such amount.

(4) In determining whether it should exempt the applicant in whole or in part from any liability, the court must have regard to the following overriding principles-

(a) that a company that has allotted shares should receive money or money's worth at least equal in value to the aggregate of the nominal value of those shares and the whole of any premium or, if the case so requires, so much of that aggregate as is treated as paid up;

(b) subject to this, that where such a company would, if the court did not grant the exemption, have more than one remedy against a particular person, it should be for the company to decide which remedy it should remain entitled to pursue.

(5) If a person brings proceedings against another ("the contributor") for a contribution in respect of liability to a company arising under any provision of this Chapter or Chapter 5 and it appears to the court that the contributor is liable to make such a contribution, the court may, if and to the extent that it appears to it, just and equitable to do so having regard to the respective culpability (in respect of the liability to the company) of the contributor and the person bringing the proceedings-

(a) exempt the contributor in whole or in part from his liability to make such a contribution, or

(b) order the contributor to make a larger contribution than, but for this subsection, he would be liable to make.

(6) Where a person is liable to a company under section 604(2) (agreement for transfer of non-cash asset: effect of contravention), the court may, on application, exempt him in whole or in part from that liability if and to the extent that it appears to the court to be just and equitable to do so having regard to any benefit accruing to the company by virtue of anything done by him towards the carrying out of the agreement mentioned in that subsection.

GENERAL NOTE

This provision re-enacts the contents of s.113 of the Company Act 1985 with minor amendments.

607. Penalty for contravention of this Chapter

(1) This section applies where a company contravenes-
section 593 (public company allotting shares for non-cash consideration), or
section 598 (public company entering into agreement for transfer of noncash asset).

(2) An offence is committed by-
(a) the company, and
(b) every officer of the company who is in default.

(3) A person guilty of an offence under this section is liable-
(a) on conviction on indictment, to a fine;
(b) on summary conviction, to a fine not exceeding the statutory maximum.

GENERAL NOTE

This section provides for two offences in relation to s.593 and to s.598 as considered above.

608. Enforceability of undertakings to do work etc

(1) An undertaking given by any person, in or in connection with payment for shares in a company, to do work or perform services or to do any other thing, if it is enforceable by the company apart from this Chapter, is so enforceable notwithstanding that there has been a contravention in relation to it of a provision of this Chapter or Chapter 5.

(2) This is without prejudice to section 606 (power of court to grant relief etc in respect of liabilities).

GENERAL NOTE
   As considered in the General Note at the outset of Ch.2 of this Pt 17, the core of any agreement to allot shares or other securities is a contract. Whereas a number of provisions in this Part may lead to the invalidity of various agreements, this provision retains the enforceability of any undertaking to act on behalf of the company, in the same way that it would be ordinarily enforceable under contract law, regardless of any contravention of a provision of Ch.6. Thus, for example, in spite of the contravention of s.593 or s.598 in this Ch.6, the company may enforce any part of any otherwise valid agreement.

609. The appropriate rate of interest

(1) For the purposes of this Chapter the "appropriate rate" of interest is 5% per annum or such other rate as may be specified by order made by the Secretary of State.
(2) An order under this section is subject to negative resolution procedure.

GENERAL NOTE
   This provision replaces s.107 of the Companies Act 1985 for the purposes of Ch.6 of this Part of this Act.

CHAPTER 7

SHARE PREMIUMS

The share premium account

610. Application of share premiums

(1) If a company issues shares at a premium, whether for cash or otherwise, a sum equal to the aggregate amount or value of the premiums on those shares must be transferred to an account called "the share premium account".
(2) Where, on issuing shares, a company has transferred a sum to the share premium account, it may use that sum to write off-
   (a) the expenses of the issue of those shares;
   (b) any commission paid on the issue of those shares.
(3) The company may use the share premium account to pay up new shares to be allotted to members as fully paid bonus shares.
(4) Subject to subsections (2) and (3), the provisions of the Companies Acts relating to the reduction of a company's share capital apply as if the share premium account were part of its paid up share capital.
(5) This section has effect subject to-
   section 611 (group reconstruction relief);
   section 612 (merger relief);
   section 614 (power to make further provisions by regulations).
(6) In this Chapter "the issuing company" means the company issuing shares as mentioned in subsection (1) above.

GENERAL NOTE
   A consequence of the retention of the requirement for par value shares is that the concept of "share premiums" - subscription monies for shares in excess of their par value - remains part of the law. For the most part, share premiums are treated as if they were share capital and in particular they are subject to the rules on maintenance of capital. However, the share premium account may be applied for certain purposes for which share capital may not be used. Chapter 7 of Pt 17

contains the general rule that share premiums are to be treated in the same way as share capital and provides two reliefs from that general obligation.

This section restates s.130 of the Companies Act 1985, with some changes. It remains the case that the share premium account must be treated in the same way as share capital, save for certain limited purposes that are expressly authorised by the Act. The range of permitted purposes for which the share premium account can be used has been narrowed. This narrowing is broadly in line with CLR recommendations (*Company Formation and Capital Maintenance* (URN 99/1145) para.3.21).

Subsection (1)

The obligation to make a transfer to the share premium account which is imposed by this subsection is mandatory, subject to the reliefs provided by subsequent sections.

Subsection (2)

Share issuance expenses and commissions can be written off against sums transferred to the share premium account on the issue of those shares. The effect is that the share premium account and hence the overall undistributable reserves are increased by the net proceeds of the issue.

It is no longer permissible to use share premium account to write off initial expenses, commissions or discounts paid or allowed on the issue of other shares or debentures or any premium payable on the redemption of debentures.

Subsection (3)

Where share premiums are applied to pay up bonus shares this affects accounting entries but there is no overall reduction in the company's undistributable reserves.

Subsection (4)

This subsection makes it clear that the share premium account is subject to the rules on the maintenance and reduction of capital. For the application of the court-based reduction capital procedure to the share premium account see, e.g. *Ransomes Plc* [1999] 2 B.C.L.C. 591.

Subsection (5)

This subsection identifies other sections of the Companies Act 2006 to which the mandatory obligation to transfer sums to the share premium account is subject.

Subsection (6)

This subsection is derived from part of s.130(4) of the Companies Act 1985.

Relief from requirements as to share premiums

611. Group reconstruction relief

(1) This section applies where the issuing company-
    (a) is a wholly-owned subsidiary of another company ("the holding company"), and
    (b) allots shares-
        (i) to the holding company, or
        (ii) to another wholly-owned subsidiary of the holding company,
    in consideration for the transfer to the issuing company of non-cash assets of a company ("the transferor company") that is a member of the group of companies that comprises the holding company and all its wholly-owned subsidiaries.

(2) Where the shares in the issuing company allotted in consideration for the transfer are issued at a premium, the issuing company is not required by section 610 to transfer any amount in excess of the minimum premium value to the share premium account.

(3) The minimum premium value means the amount (if any) by which the base value of the consideration for the shares allotted exceeds the aggregate nominal value of the shares.

(4) The base value of the consideration for the shares allotted is the amount by which the base value of the assets transferred exceeds the base value of any liabilities of the transferor

company assumed by the issuing company as part of the consideration for the assets transferred.

(5) For the purposes of this section-

    (a) the base value of assets transferred is taken as-

        (i) the cost of those assets to the transferor company, or

        (ii) if less, the amount at which those assets are stated in the transferor company's accounting records immediately before the transfer;

    (b) the base value of the liabilities assumed is taken as the amount at which they are stated in the transferor company's accounting records immediately before the transfer.

GENERAL NOTE

    This section re-enacts most of s.132 of the Companies Act 1985, without substantive change and with only minor differences in the style of drafting. Certain savings for share issues that took place before December 1984 are not re-enacted as these have become redundant through lapse of time. The effect of the relief is to allow the issuing company to account for the premium on the basis of the cost or book value of the consideration received rather than its actual value. Group relief was first provided by the Companies Act 1981, as substituted by the Companies (Share Premiums) Regulations 1984 (SI 1984/2007) and later consolidated into the Companies Act 1985.

Subsections (1) and (2)

    These subsections set out the circumstances in which group relief from the obligation to make a transfer to the share premium account is available. The basic position is that where a wholly owned subsidiary issues shares to its parent company or to another wholly owned subsidiary in consideration of the transfer to it of non-cash assets of any company within the group, there is no obligation to form a share premium account in excess of the "minimum premium value" at which the shares are issued.

Subsections (3)-(5)

    These subsections explain how the "minimum premium value" is to be determined. They re-enact s.132(3)-(5) of the Companies Act 1985 with only minor drafting changes.

612.   Merger relief

(1) This section applies where the issuing company has secured at least a 90% equity holding in another company in pursuance of an arrangement providing for the allotment of equity shares in the issuing company on terms that the consideration for the shares allotted is to be provided-

    (a) by the issue or transfer to the issuing company of equity shares in the other company, or

    (b) by the cancellation of any such shares not held by the issuing company.

(2) If the equity shares in the issuing company allotted in pursuance of the arrangement in consideration for the acquisition or cancellation of equity shares in the other company are issued at a premium, section 610 does not apply to the premiums on those shares.

(3) Where the arrangement also provides for the allotment of any shares in the issuing company on terms that the consideration for those shares is to be provided-

    (a) by the issue or transfer to the issuing company of non-equity shares in the other company, or

    (b) by the cancellation of any such shares in that company not held by the issuing company,

relief under subsection (2) extends to any shares in the issuing company allotted on those terms in pursuance of the arrangement.

(4) This section does not apply in a case falling within section 611 (group reconstruction relief).

GENERAL NOTE

    This section re-enacts part of s.131 of the Companies Act 1985, without substantive change and with only minor differences in the style of drafting. The effect of the section is to displace the obligation to transfer an amount to the share premium account in circumstances where the issuing company has issued shares in order to acquire another company by means of a share for share exchange. This relief is subject to certain conditions. Merger relief was first made available by the Companies Act 1981, later consolidated into the Companies Act 1985 and thereafter amended by the Insolvency Act 1986, the Companies Act 1989, the Companies (Acquisition of Own Shares) (Treasury Shares) Regulations 2003 (SI 2003/1115).

Subsections (1)-(3)

These subsections re-state s.131(1)-(3) of the Companies Act 1985.

Subsection (4)

Merger relief is inapplicable in circumstances where group relief is available. This was also the position under the Companies Act 1985 (s.131(1) and s.131(8)) but the new drafting is clearer.

613. Merger relief: meaning of 90% equity holding

(1) The following provisions have effect to determine for the purposes of section 612 (merger relief) whether a company ("company A") has secured at least a 90% equity holding in another company ("company B") in pursuance of such an arrangement as is mentioned in subsection (1) of that section.

(2) Company A has secured at least a 90% equity holding in company B if in consequence of an acquisition or cancellation of equity shares in company B (in pursuance of that arrangement) it holds equity shares in company B of an aggregate amount equal to 90% or more of the nominal value of that company's equity share capital.

(3) For this purpose-

    (a) it is immaterial whether any of those shares were acquired in pursuance of the arrangement; and

    (b) shares in company B held by the company as treasury shares are excluded in determining the nominal value of company B's share capital.

(4) Where the equity share capital of company B is divided into different classes of shares, company A is not regarded as having secured at least a 90% equity holding in company B unless the requirements of subsection (2) are met in relation to each of those classes of shares taken separately.

(5) For the purposes of this section shares held by-

    (a) a company that is company A's holding company or subsidiary, or

    (b) a subsidiary of company A's holding company, or

    (c) its or their nominees,

are treated as held by company A.

GENERAL NOTE

This section re-enacts, with some changes in the style of drafting, s.131(4)-(6) of the Companies Act 1985. Its purpose is to amplify the meaning of the conditions that must be satisfied for merger relief to be available.

Subsection (1)

This subsection introduces a new style of drafting into the provisions on merger relief, which uses specific example companies ("Company A" and "Company B") in order to make it easier to understand which rules apply to which entities in what can be complex, multi-party transactions.

Subsections (2) and (3)

These subsections re-enact in clearer language s.131(4) of the Companies Act 1985.

Subsections (4) and (5)

These subsections re-enact in clearer language s.131(5)-(6) of the Companies Act 1985.

614. Power to make further provision by regulations

(1) The Secretary of State may by regulations make such provision as he thinks appropriate-

    (a) for relieving companies from the requirements of section 610 (application of share premiums) in relation to premiums other than cash premiums;

    (b) for restricting or otherwise modifying any relief from those requirements provided by this Chapter.

(2) Regulations under this section are subject to affirmative resolution procedure.

GENERAL NOTE

    This section, which re-states s.134 of the Companies Act 1985 without changes of substance, empowers the Secretary of State to add other cases to the relief from the obligation to form a share premium account, other than in relation to cash premiums, and also to restrict or modify the group relief or merger relief provided by the previous sections.

Subsection (2)

    Regulations made under this section are subject to the affirmative resolution procedure. The affirmative resolution procedure means that the regulations or orders must not be made unless a draft of the statutory instrument containing them has been laid before Parliament and approved by a resolution of each House of Parliament. See s.1290.

615. Relief may be reflected in company's balance sheet

An amount corresponding to the amount representing the premiums, or part of the premiums, on shares issued by a company that by virtue of any relief under this Chapter is not included in the company's share premium account may also be disregarded in determining the amount at which any shares or other consideration provided for the shares issued is to be included in the company's balance sheet.

GENERAL NOTE

    This section provides the complementary relief for the asset side of the balance sheet to the reliefs provided in respect of the capital side by s.611 (group reconstruction relief) and s.612 (merger relief). It re-enacts, without change of substance, s.133(1) of the Companies Act 1985.

Supplementary provisions

616. Interpretation of this Chapter

(1) In this Chapter-
    "arrangement" means any agreement, scheme or arrangement (including an arrangement sanctioned in accordance with-
        (a) Part 26 (arrangements and reconstructions), or
        (b) section 110 of the Insolvency Act 1986 (c. 45) or Article 96 of the Insolvency (Northern Ireland) Order 1989 (S.I. 1989/2405 (N.I. 19)) (liquidator in winding up accepting shares as consideration for sale of company property));

    "company", except in reference to the issuing company, includes any body corporate;
    "equity shares" means shares comprised in a company's equity share capital, and "non-equity shares" means shares (of any class) that are not so comprised;
    "the issuing company" has the meaning given by section 610(6).
(2) References in this Chapter (however expressed) to-
    (a) the acquisition by a company of shares in another company, and
    (b) the issue or allotment of shares to, or the transfer of shares to or by, a company,
include (respectively) the acquisition of shares by, and the issue or allotment or transfer of shares to or by, a nominee of that company. The reference in section 611 to the transferor company shall be read accordingly.
(3) References in this Chapter to the transfer of shares in a company include the transfer of a right to be included in the company's register of members in respect of those shares.

GENERAL NOTE
This definitional section brings together into one place explanations of terms used in Ch.7 of Pt 17. The definitions are a recast version of definitions previously found in s.130(7) ("arrangement", "equity shares" and "non-equity shares"), s.133(4) ("issuing company") and s.133(2)-(4) ("acquisition", "issue" or "allotment or "transfer" of shares, "company") of the 1985 Act.

Subsection (1)
The reference to Art.96 of the Insolvency (Northern Ireland) Order 1989 (SI 1989/2405) is new. The change is consequential upon the decision to extend the Companies Acts to Northern Ireland.

CHAPTER 8

ALTERATION OF SHARE CAPITAL

How share capital may be altered

617. Alteration of share capital of limited company

(1) A limited company having a share capital may not alter its share capital except in the following ways.

(2) The company may-

    (a) increase its share capital by allotting new shares in accordance with this Part, or

    (b) reduce its share capital in accordance with Chapter 10.

(3) The company may-

    (a) sub-divide or consolidate all or any of its share capital in accordance with section 618, or

    (b) reconvert stock into shares in accordance with section 620.

(4) The company may redenominate all or any of its shares in accordance with section 622, and may reduce its share capital in accordance with section 626 in connection with such a redenomination.

(5) Nothing in this section affects-

    (a) the power of a company to purchase its own shares, or to redeem shares, in accordance with Part 18;

    (b) the power of a company to purchase its own shares in pursuance of an order of the court under-

        (i) section 98 (application to court to cancel resolution for reregistration as a private company),

        (ii) section 721(6) (powers of court on objection to redemption or purchase of shares out of capital),

        (iii) section 759 (remedial order in case of breach of prohibition of public offers by private company), or

        (iv) Part 30 (protection of members against unfair prejudice);

    (c) the forfeiture of shares, or the acceptance of shares surrendered in lieu, in pursuance of the company's articles, for failure to pay any sum payable in respect of the shares;

    (d) the cancellation of shares under section 662 (duty to cancel shares held by or for a public company);

    (e) the power of a company-

        (i) to enter into a compromise or arrangement in accordance with Part 26 (arrangements and reconstructions), or

        (ii) to do anything required to comply with an order of the court on an application under that Part.

GENERAL NOTE

This section provides the framework for the alteration of share capital. Its starting point is prohibitory: a limited company having a share capital cannot alter its share capital except in accordance with specified statutory procedures. It then provides signposts to the various statutory procedures under which companies can alter their share capital. This list of permitted statutory procedures for alteration of share capital is intended to be exhaustive (Lord McKenzie, *Hansard*, HL col.GC518 (March 15, 2006)). Finally, the section makes it clear that the prohibition on alterations of share capital except in accordance with specified procedures does not affect the redemption or buyback of shares under Pt 18, share purchases in pursuance of a court order under various sections of the Act, the forfeiture of shares in accordance with articles of association, the cancellation of shares under s.662, and schemes of arrangement under Pt 26.

Subdivision or consolidation of shares

618.   Sub-division or consolidation of shares

(1) A limited company having a share capital may-

    (a) sub-divide its shares, or any of them, into shares of a smaller nominal amount than its existing shares, or

    (b) consolidate and divide all or any of its share capital into shares of a larger nominal amount than its existing shares.

(2) In any sub-division, consolidation or division of shares under this section, the proportion between the amount paid and the amount (if any) unpaid on each resulting share must be the same as it was in the case of the share from which that share is derived.

(3) A company may exercise a power conferred by this section only if its members have passed a resolution authorising it to do so.

(4) A resolution under subsection (3) may authorise a company-

    (a) to exercise more than one of the powers conferred by this section;

    (b) to exercise a power on more than one occasion;

    (c) to exercise a power at a specified time or in specified circumstances.

(5) The company's articles may exclude or restrict the exercise of any power conferred by this section.

GENERAL NOTE

This section restates part of s.121 of the Companies Act 1985, which permitted a company to alter its authorised share capital in certain ways. The need for certain of the old permissions has fallen away because of the abolition of authorised share capital. The new approach also diverges from the old by not making the alteration of share capital conditional upon authorisation in articles of association as well as a resolution of the members and in providing more flexibility with regard to the form and content of the members' resolution.

Subsection (1)

By sub-dividing its shares a company increases the number of shares that it has in issue. For example, a £10 share may be divided into ten £1 shares. By consolidating its shares a company reduces the number of shares that it has in issue. For example ten £1 shares may be consolidated into one £10 share.

Subsection (2)

This clarifies the effect of a sub-division, consolidation or division of partly paid shares. It is derived from s.121(3) of the Companies Act 1985, but is broader in scope because it applies to consolidations and divisions as well as to sub-divisions. As an example of its operation, if £2 is unpaid on a £10 share that is subdivided into ten £1 shares the amount unpaid on each of the £1 shares is 20p.

Subsection (3)

The default requirement is for an ordinary resolution of the members to authorise the alteration of share capital, but it would be possible for a company to impose more stringent requirements (for example a special resolution) in its articles of association (see subs.(5)).

Private companies are able to use the statutory written resolution procedure (see ss.288-300) to pass the authorising resolution. The statutory written resolution procedure is not available to public companies. However, public companies can make decisions by unanimous informal consent (the *Duomatic* principle). It was doubtful whether the *Duomatic* principle applied to s.121 of the Companies Act 1985 because that section referred specifically to the powers conferred by that section being exercised by the company in *general meeting*. The new wording omits the specific reference to a general meeting and therefore appears to relax the position for public companies but the point is likely to have only limited practical relevance because the *Duomatic* principle depends on unanimity which will be hard to achieve in all but very small companies.

Subsection (4)

This new subsection provides companies with the flexibility to pass resolutions that authorise more than one type of alteration or alterations on more than one occasion. In subs.(4)(c) it provides for conditional resolutions, which would enable shareholders to restrict the alteration of share capital where it is intended that this should occur only as part of a wider reorganisation of a company's share capital.

Subsection (5)

Companies can opt out of the statutory procedure for alteration of share capital or impose more restrictive requirements via provisions to that effect in their articles of association. This represents a reversal of the position under s.121 of the Companies Act 1985, which required companies to opt into the statutory permission to alter share capital via their articles.

619. Notice to registrar of sub-division or consolidation

(1) If a company exercises the power conferred by section 618 (sub-division or consolidation of shares) it must within one month after doing so give notice to the registrar, specifying the shares affected.

(2) The notice must be accompanied by a statement of capital.

(3) The statement of capital must state with respect to the company's share capital immediately following the exercise of the power-
   (a) the total number of shares of the company,
   (b) the aggregate nominal value of those shares,
   (c) for each class of shares-
      (i) prescribed particulars of the rights attached to the shares,
      (ii) the total number of shares of that class, and
      (iii) the aggregate nominal value of shares of that class, and
   (d) the amount paid up and the amount (if any) unpaid on each share (whether on account of the nominal value of the share or by way of premium).

(4) If default is made in complying with this section, an offence is committed by-
   (a) the company, and
   (b) every officer of the company who is in default.

(5) A person guilty of an offence under this section is liable on summary conviction to a fine not exceeding level 3 on the standard scale and, for continued contravention, a daily default fine not exceeding one-tenth of level 3 on the standard scale.

GENERAL NOTE

This section recasts the requirement previously in s.122 of the Companies Act 1985 to notify the registrar within one month of alteration of capital by way of sub-division or consolidation. There is a new requirement for a statement of capital to accompany the notice of the alteration. A statement of capital is a snapshot of a company's total share capital at a particular point in time. Other points in time when companies are required to file a statement of capital with the registrar are on formation (s.10), change of corporate status from unlimited to limited (s.108), the allotment of new shares (s.555), the re-conversion of stock into shares (s.621), the redenomination of share capital (ss.625 and 627), the reduction of capital (ss.644 and 649), the cancellation of shares (ss.663 and 708), the redemption of shares (ss.685 and 689), and in annual returns (s.856).

For public companies the requirement to file a statement of capital implements publicity obligations under the Second Company Law Directive (77/91/EEC), Art.2.

Subsection (3)

This subsection specifies the standard requirements for the contents of a statement of capital. See s.10.

Failure to comply with the requirements of this section constitutes an offence by the company and every officer who is in default. Corporate criminal liability is considered to be appropriate in circumstances where persons other than the company and its members could be adversely affected by the non-compliance.

Reconversion of stock into shares

620.   Reconversion of stock into shares

(1) A limited company that has converted paid-up shares into stock (before the repeal by this Act of the power to do so) may reconvert that stock into paid-up shares of any nominal value.

(2) A company may exercise the power conferred by this section only if its members have passed an ordinary resolution authorising it to do so.

(3) A resolution under subsection (2) may authorise a company to exercise the power conferred by this section-
   (a) on more than one occasion;
   (b) at a specified time or in specified circumstances.

GENERAL NOTE

This section preserves the right (previously in s.121(2)(c) of the Companies Act 1985) to re-convert stock into shares. Even though stock is largely a thing of the past, there could still be some companies that have it and the retention of this power is important for these cases.

Subsection (2)

A private company can pass the ordinary resolution under the statutory written resolution procedure (see ss.288-300). Where unanimity can be achieved, a public company should be able to make its decision informally under the *Duomatic* principle.

Subsection (3)

A conditional authorisation, as envisaged by (b), will be appropriate where the reconversion is intended to take place only as part of a broader reorganisation of a company's share capital.

621.   Notice to registrar of reconversion of stock into shares

(1) If a company exercises a power conferred by section 620 (reconversion of stock into shares) it must within one month after doing so give notice to the registrar, specifying the stock affected.

(2) The notice must be accompanied by a statement of capital.

(3) The statement of capital must state with respect to the company's share capital immediately following the exercise of the power-
   (a) the total number of shares of the company,
   (b) the aggregate nominal value of those shares,
   (c) for each class of shares-
      (i) prescribed particulars of the rights attached to the shares,
      (ii) the total number of shares of that class, and
      (iii) the aggregate nominal value of shares of that class, and
   (d) the amount paid up and the amount (if any) unpaid on each share (whether on account of the nominal value of the share or by way of premium).

(4) If default is made in complying with this section, an offence is committed by-
   (a) the company, and
   (b) every officer of the company who is in default.

(5) A person guilty of an offence under this section is liable on summary conviction to a fine not exceeding level 3 on the standard scale and, for continued contravention, a daily default fine not exceeding one-tenth of level 3 on the standard scale.

GENERAL NOTE

A general principle that runs through the provisions on capital is that the information on the public register must be up to date. Hence, this section makes provision for notification to the registrar of a reconversion of stock into shares (subs.(1)) and for an accompanying statement of capital (subs.(2)). On statements of capital see s.10.

Subsections (4) and (5)

Failure to comply with the requirements of this section constitutes an offence by the company and every officer who is in default. Corporate criminal liability is considered to be appropriate in circumstances where persons other than the company and its members could be adversely affected by the non-compliance.

Redenomination of share capital

622. Redenomination of share capital

(1) A limited company having a share capital may by resolution redenominate its share capital or any class of its share capital.
"Redenominate" means convert shares from having a fixed nominal value in one currency to having a fixed nominal value in another currency.
(2) The conversion must be made at an appropriate spot rate of exchange specified in the resolution.
(3) The rate must be either-
    (a) a rate prevailing on a day specified in the resolution, or
    (b) a rate determined by taking the average of rates prevailing on each consecutive day of a period specified in the resolution.
The day or period specified for the purposes of paragraph (a) or (b) must be within the period of 28 days ending on the day before the resolution is passed.
(4) A resolution under this section may specify conditions which must be met before the redenomination takes effect.
(5) Redenomination in accordance with a resolution under this section takes effect-
    (a) on the day on which the resolution is passed, or
    (b) on such later day as may be determined in accordance with the resolution.
(6) A resolution under this section lapses if the redenomination for which it provides has not taken effect at the end of the period of 28 days beginning on the date on which it is passed.
(7) A company's articles may prohibit or restrict the exercise of the power conferred by this section.
(8) Chapter 3 of Part 3 (resolutions affecting a company's constitution) applies to a resolution under this section.

GENERAL NOTE

The Act provides a new streamlined procedure for the redenomination of share capital from one currency to another. Previously, companies that wanted to redenominate their share capital had to go through a court-approved reduction of capital to cancel existing shares and replace them with shares denominated in a different currency or, in the case of private companies only, a buy-back or redemption of existing shares followed by an issue of new shares in the desired currency. In the March 2005 White Paper, the government described the existing position as cumbersome and unnecessary and said that it would introduce a simplified procedure (para.4.8).

The Second Company Law Directive (77/91/EEC), Art.6 requires that, in order that a company may be incorporated or obtain authorisation to commence business as a public company, it must have a minimum capital of not less than 25 000 ECU (expressed in euros or the domestic currency of the Member State). The United Kingdom has historically given effect to this provision of the Directive by requiring a newly incorporated public company to have a minimum capital of £50,000, expressed in sterling, when it applies for a trading certificate and by requiring a private company to satisfy a similar requirement when it re-registers as a public company. The Companies Act 2006 updates this requirement to the extent of permitting the authorised minimum to be £50,000 or its prescribed euro equivalent (see ss.763-766).

Once a public company has obtained its trading certificate or a private company has completed the process of re-registration as a public company, the Companies Act 2006 now permits it to redenominate all of its share capital. It used to be widely thought that the Second Directive, Art.6 might require a public company always to have at least its minimum capital denominated in a domestic currency, but the government has not accepted this view and has adopted a more purposive interpretation. Note, however, s.766 (Authorised minimum: application where shares denominated in different currencies etc).

The redenomination procedure applies only in relation to share capital. It is unnecessary to extend it to share premiums or other undistributable reserves because there is nothing in the companies legislation or the general law to prevent companies from redenominating these statutory reserves (Vera Baird MP, *Hansard* HC, Standing Committee D, cols 867-868 (July 20, 2006)).

Subsection (1)

The new procedure applies only to limited companies having a share capital. Unlimited companies are already free to redenominate their share capital as they think fit and the new procedure does not need to extend to them.

The power to redenominate share capital or any class of share capital by ordinary resolution can be overridden by a company's articles of association (see subs.(7)).

Subsections (2) and (3)

The conversion rate must be set out in the resolution. There is a choice of conversion rates, as indicated by subs.(3). The government thought it important to have reasonable proximity between the date on which a redenomination takes effect and the relevant rate of exchange on which it is based (Lord McKenzie, *Hansard*, HL col.GC36 (March 20, 2006)), hence the 28 day deadline in subs.(3) and a related deadline in subs.(5).

Subsection (4)

A conditional resolution is possible, but it will lapse if the conditions are not fulfilled within the time limits set by the section (see subs.(6)). This is designed to strike a balance between providing companies with the flexibility to pass such resolutions and the need to protect creditors and shareholders (Lord McKenzie, *Hansard* HL, col.GC36 (March 20, 2006)). Speaking for the government in the Parliamentary debate, Lord McKenzie emphasised the importance of the proximity of the effect of the resolution to when the spot rates were set for the redenomination. In particular, where there was more than one class of share capital proximity could be hugely important as not having it could unbalance the situation between the various shareholders (*Hansard*, cols GC36-37 (March 20, 2006)).

Subsection (6)

The government originally proposed a maximum period of 15 days for fulfilment of conditions. Opposition peers pressed for a period of 12 or three months, but the period of 28 days eventually emerged as a compromise (*Hansard*, HL Vol.682; HL cols 185-186 (May 16, 2006)).

Subsection (7)

A company can override the statutory permissive regime for redenomination of share capital by provision to that effect in its articles of association.

Subsection (8)

As a resolution under this section has constitutional implications it must be notified to the registrar. See further ss.29-30.

623. Calculation of new nominal values

For each class of share the new nominal value of each share is calculated as follows:

Step One

Take the aggregate of the old nominal values of all the shares of that class.

Step Two

Translate that amount into the new currency at the rate of exchange specified in the resolution.

Step Three

Divide that amount by the number of shares in the class.

GENERAL NOTE

This section explains how the new nominal value of a share that has been redenominated from one currency to another should be calculated. In the Parliamentary debate, the style of drafting adopted in this section was described as "rather splendid" and the draftsman was commended for having worked hard to make the procedure "clear and understandable" (Lord Hodgson, *Hansard*, col.GC38 (March 20, 2006)).

624.   Effect of redenomination

(1) The redenomination of shares does not affect any rights or obligations of members under the company's constitution, or any restrictions affecting members under the company's constitution.

In particular, it does not affect entitlement to dividends (including entitlement to dividends in a particular currency), voting rights or any liability in respect of amounts unpaid on shares.

(2) For this purpose the company's constitution includes the terms on which any shares of the company are allotted or held.

(3) Subject to subsection (1), references to the old nominal value of the shares in any agreement or statement, or in any deed, instrument or document, shall (unless the context otherwise requires) be read after the resolution takes effect as references to the new nominal value of the shares.

GENERAL NOTE

This section clarifies the effect of a redenomination of a company's share capital.

Subsection (1)

The redenomination process does not affect the currency in which dividends are to be paid. If a company and its shareholders wish to make provision for dividends to be paid in a particular currency post redenomination of the company's share capital, they are free to do so (Lord McKenzie, *Hansard*, col.GC41 (March 20, 2006)). This may require a change in the company's constitution.

Likewise, where a company has issued partly paid shares, the redenomination process does not affect the member's liability to the company which will remain in the currency in which the share was originally denominated (Lord McKenzie, *Hansard*, col.GC41 (March 20, 2006)).

Subsection (2)

This provision puts it beyond doubt that a company's constitution for this purpose includes the terms on which shares are allotted or held.

Subsection (3)

This provision seeks to override interpretative difficulties that could otherwise arise in relation to contractual and other documents that were drafted before the redenomination.

625.   Notice to registrar of redenomination

(1) If a limited company having a share capital redenominates any of its share capital, it must within one month after doing so give notice to the registrar, specifying the shares redenominated.

(2) The notice must—
(a) state the date on which the resolution was passed, and
(b) be accompanied by a statement of capital.

(3) The statement of capital must state with respect to the company's share capital as redenominated by the resolution—
(a) the total number of shares of the company,
(b) the aggregate nominal value of those shares,
(c) for each class of shares—

        (i) prescribed particulars of the rights attached to the shares,

        (ii) the total number of shares of that class, and

        (iii) the aggregate nominal value of shares of that class, and

    (d) the amount paid up and the amount (if any) unpaid on each share (whether on account of the nominal value of the share or by way of premium).

(4) If default is made in complying with this section, an offence is committed by-

    (a) the company, and

    (b) every officer of the company who is in default.

(5) A person guilty of an offence under this section is liable on summary conviction to a fine not exceeding level 3 on the standard scale and, for continued contravention, a daily default fine not exceeding one-tenth of level 3 on the standard scale.

GENERAL NOTE

This section gives effect in the context of redenominations to the general principle that actions relating to a company's capital are a matter of public record and must therefore be notified to the registrar. As is usual, the company is required to provide a statement of capital, which is a snapshot of its total capital at a particular point in time - in this case, after the redenomination.

Subsection (1)

The one month period runs from the date when the redenomination takes effect, which may be any time within the period of 28 days beginning on the date when the resolution is passed (Lord McKenzie, *Hansard*, col.GC38 (March 20, 2006)). A copy of the resolution itself must be forwarded to the registrar within 15 days after it is passed (see s.622(8) and s.30). There is no requirement to notify the registrar of the non-satisfaction of conditions as it will become evident from the absence of a filing under this section that a redenomination resolution has lapsed (Lord McKenzie, *Hansard*, col.GC38 (March 20, 2006)).

Subsection (3)

This subsection specifies the standard requirements for the contents of a statement of capital. See s.10.

Subsections (4) and (5)

Failure to comply with the requirements of this section constitutes an offence by the company and every officer who is in default. Corporate criminal liability is considered to be appropriate in circumstances where persons other than the company and its members could be adversely affected by the non-compliance.

626.   Reduction of capital in connection with redenomination

(1) A limited company that passes a resolution redenominating some or all of its shares may, for the purpose of adjusting the nominal values of the redenominated shares to obtain values that are, in the opinion of the company, more suitable, reduce its share capital under this section.

(2) A reduction of capital under this section requires a special resolution of the company.

(3) Any such resolution must be passed within three months of the resolution effecting the redenomination.

(4) The amount by which a company's share capital is reduced under this section must not exceed 10% of the nominal value of the company's allotted share capital immediately after the reduction.

(5) A reduction of capital under this section does not extinguish or reduce any liability in respect of share capital not paid up.

(6) Nothing in Chapter 10 applies to a reduction of capital under this section.

GENERAL NOTE

Shares denominated in awkward fractions of the new currency may result from a redenomination. Companies in this situation may wish to renominalise their share capital in order to achieve shares with nominal values that are in whole units of the new currency. It is possible to do so by increasing the nominal value of the shares, for which the company will need to have reserves available for capitalisation in this way. This section introduces an alternative new procedure whereby a company can reduce its share capital (but not its overall undistributable reserves) in order to round down the nominal value of redenominated shares to a whole number.

Subsections (2) and (6)

As is the case in the general reduction of capital procedure (see s.641), a special resolution of the members to reduce the share capital is required. However, unlike the general reduction of capital procedure, here there is no requirement for a directors' solvency statement or for court approval.

Subsection (3)

The three month time limit under this subsection runs from the date of the resolution effecting the redenomination and not from the possibly later date when the redenomination becomes effective. It is to be expected that companies will usually wish to act quickly to eliminate nominal values that are expressed in awkward fractions.

Subsection (4)

This limitation derives from the Second Company Law Directive (77/91/EEC), Art.33 which allows Member States not to apply the normal rule giving creditors the right to apply to court in a reduction of capital by a public company where the purpose of the reduction is to create a reserve that is capped at not more than ten per cent of the reduced share capital.

Subsection (5)

Where partly paid shares are redenominated and then reduced in accordance with this section, the holders remain liable to pay the balance of the original nominal amount, which remains denominated in the original currency (see s.624).

627. Notice to registrar of reduction of capital in connection with redenomination

(1) A company that passes a resolution under section 626 (reduction of capital in connection with redenomination) must within 15 days after the resolution is passed give notice to the registrar stating-
    (a) the date of the resolution, and
    (b) the date of the resolution under section 622 in connection with which it was passed.
  This is in addition to the copies of the resolutions themselves that are required to be delivered to the registrar under Chapter 3 of Part 3.

(2) The notice must be accompanied by a statement of capital.

(3) The statement of capital must state with respect to the company's share capital as reduced by the resolution-
    (a) the total number of shares of the company,
    (b) the aggregate nominal value of those shares,
    (c) for each class of shares-
        (i) prescribed particulars of the rights attached to the shares,
        (ii) the total number of shares of that class, and
        (iii) the aggregate nominal value of shares of that class, and
    (d) the amount paid up and the amount (if any) unpaid on each share (whether on account of the nominal value of the share or by way of premium).

(4) The registrar must register the notice and the statement on receipt.

(5) The reduction of capital is not effective until those documents are registered.

(6) The company must also deliver to the registrar, within 15 days after the resolution is passed, a statement by the directors confirming that the reduction in share capital is in accordance with section 626(4) (reduction of capital not to exceed 10% of nominal value of allotted shares immediately after reduction).

(7) If default is made in complying with this section, an offence is committed by-
    (a) the company, and
    (b) every officer of the company who is in default.

(8) A person guilty of an offence under this section is liable-
    (a) on conviction on indictment to a fine, and

(b) on summary conviction to a fine not exceeding the statutory maximum.

GENERAL NOTE

This section sets out the procedure for giving public notice of a reduction of capital in connection with the redenomination of share capital. Notice must be given to the registrar accompanied by a statement of capital, which must give details of the capital as it is immediately after the reduction of capital. This section also determines when a reduction of capital becomes effective.

Subsection (3)

This subsection specifies the standard requirements for the contents of a statement of capital. See s.10.

Subsections (4) and (5)

Failure to comply with the requirements of this section constitutes an offence by the company and every officer who is in default. Corporate criminal liability is considered to be appropriate in circumstances where persons other than the company and its members could be adversely affected by the non-compliance.

Subsection (6)

The directors must confirm that the reduction is within the ten per cent cap imposed by s.626(4). The registrar is not obliged to register the statement of the directors required by this subsection. The timing of the effectiveness of the reduction is not linked in any way to this delivery obligation.

Subsections (7) and (8)

Failure to comply with the requirements of this section constitutes an offence by the company and every officer who is in default. Corporate criminal liability is considered to be appropriate in circumstances where persons other than the company and its members could be adversely affected by the non-compliance.

Note also s.1112 whereby it is also a criminal offence knowingly or recklessly to deliver a document to the registrar that is misleading, false or deceptive in a material particular.

628.   Redenomination reserve

(1) The amount by which a company's share capital is reduced under section 626 (reduction of capital in connection with redenomination) must be transferred to a reserve, called "the redenomination reserve".
(2) The redenomination reserve may be applied by the company in paying up shares to be allotted to members as fully paid bonus shares.
(3) Subject to that, the provisions of the Companies Acts relating to the reduction of a company's share capital apply as if the redenomination reserve were paid-up share capital of the company.

GENERAL NOTE

A reduction of share capital in connection with the redenomination of shares gives rise to a new undistributable reserve. This section states what may be done with the redenomination reserve: it can be used to pay up fully paid bonus shares, but otherwise it is to be treated for the purposes of the rules on reduction of capital as if it were part of the share capital of the company.

Introductory

629. Classes of shares

(1) For the purposes of the Companies Acts shares are of one class if the rights attached to them are in all respects uniform.
(2) For this purpose the rights attached to shares are not regarded as different from those attached to other shares by reason only that they do not carry the same rights to dividends in the twelve months immediately following their allotment.

GENERAL NOTE

This Chapter replaces Ch.II of Pt V of the 1985 Act (ss.125-129) relating to the variation of class rights. Originally the Bill contained a number of clauses amending and expanding the 1985 Act sections. Those changes were subsumed into the full restatement of Ch.II of Pt V which is now contained in this Chapter.

This section restates s.128(2) of the 1985 Act as to what is to be regarded as a single class of shares not only for the purposes of the statutory rules on the variation of class rights, but also as a general definition for this Act. As such, it delineates what are separate classes for those purposes. In doing so it elevates what was a definition purely for the purposes of the former registration section, s.128, (see now ss.636 and 637), into one applicable to all aspects of the Act.

What amounts to a right attaching to a share is a matter for the articles, any shareholder agreements and the courts to decide: see *Cumbrian Newspaper Group Ltd v Cumberland and Westmorland Newspaper and Printing Co Ltd* [1987] Ch 1; *Harman v BML Group Ltd* [1994] 2 B.C.L.C. 674. This is a matter of some importance since a right, e.g. in the articles, which is deemed to be a class right can only be changed by at least a 75 per cent majority of the class concerned whereas any other right can be altered by a 75 per cent majority of all the members.

Variation of class rights

630. Variation of class rights: companies having a share capital

(1) This section is concerned with the variation of the rights attached to a class of shares in a company having a share capital.
(2) Rights attached to a class of a company's shares may only be varied-
   (a) in accordance with provision in the company's articles for the variation of those rights, or
   (b) where the company's articles contain no such provision, if the holders of shares of that class consent to the variation in accordance with this section.
(3) This is without prejudice to any other restrictions on the variation of the rights.
(4) The consent required for the purposes of this section on the part of the holders of a class of a company's shares is-
   (a) consent in writing from the holders of at least three-quarters in nominal value of the issued shares of that class (excluding any shares held as treasury shares), or
   (b) a special resolution passed at a separate general meeting of the holders of that class sanctioning the variation.
(5) Any amendment of a provision contained in a company's articles for the variation of the rights attached to a class of shares, or the insertion of any such provision into the articles, is itself to be treated as a variation of those rights.
(6) In this section, and (except where the context otherwise requires) in any provision in a company's articles for the variation of the rights attached to a class of shares, references to the variation of those rights include references to their abrogation.

GENERAL NOTE

This section replaces and simplifies s.125(1)-(5), (7) and (8) of the Companies Act 1985 as to the ways in which class rights may be varied. (Subsection (6) on the rules for the necessary meeting(s) is now in s.341 of this Act.) Any variation of such rights must be registered with the registrar under s.637.

Subsections (1)-(3)

These subsection provide for a variation procedure, by way of default, for a class right to be varied where the company has a share capital. The articles of the company may continue to provide the same or an alternative procedure.

Subsection (4)

This subsection restates both the default procedure and the majorities required for a variation as in the former s.125(2), with the substitution of a special resolution for an extraordinary resolution, since the latter has been discontinued under this Act. Such a variation is also subject to challenge under s.633.

Subsections (5) and (6)

These subsection restate s.125(7) and (8) of the 1985 Act.

631. Variation of class rights: companies without a share capital

(1) This section is concerned with the variation of the rights of a class of members of a company where the company does not have a share capital.

(2) Rights of a class of members may only be varied-
   (a) in accordance with provision in the company's articles for the variation of those rights, or
   (b) where the company's articles contain no such provision, if the members of that class consent to the variation in accordance with this section.

(3) This is without prejudice to any other restrictions on the variation of the rights.

(4) The consent required for the purposes of this section on the part of the members of a class is-
   (a) consent in writing from at least three-quarters of the members of the class, or
   (b) a special resolution passed at a separate general meeting of the members of that class sanctioning the variation.

(5) Any amendment of a provision contained in a company's articles for the variation of the rights of a class of members, or the insertion of any such provision into the articles, is itself to be treated as a variation of those rights.

(6) In this section, and (except where the context otherwise requires) in any provision in a company's articles for the variation of the rights of a class of members, references to the variation of those rights include references to their abrogation.

GENERAL NOTE

This new section mirrors s.630 in the context of the variation of class rights in companies which do not have a share capital. Any variation must be registered with the registrar under s.640.

The only differences from s.630 are, first, that both the procedure laid down in the articles (if any), and the default procedure, apply in relation to the rights of a class of members rather than to the holders of a class of shares. Secondly, that the written consent procedure requires a 75 per cent majority of the members of the class rather than holders of 75 per cent in value of the class of shares. A variation made under this section may be challenged under s.634. Otherwise, the note on the previous section applies equally to this section.

632. Variation of class rights: saving for court's powers under other provisions

Nothing in section 630 or 631 (variation of class rights) affects the power of the court under-
   section 98 (application to cancel resolution for public company to be reregistered as private),
   Part 26 (arrangements and reconstructions), or

Part 30 (protection of members against unfair prejudice).

GENERAL NOTE

This section replaces s.126 of the 1985 Act. As in that section, it preserves the ability of the court to prevent the privatisation of a company, sanction a scheme of arrangement or make an order subsequent on a finding of unfairly prejudicial conduct, without worrying about whether there is a variation of class rights within the purview of either of the preceding two sections.

The additional preservation in s.126 concerning the alteration of the objects clause in the memorandum is no longer needed.

633.   Right to object to variation: companies having a share capital

(1) This section applies where the rights attached to any class of shares in a company are varied under section 630 (variation of class rights: companies having a share capital).

(2) The holders of not less in the aggregate than 15% of the issued shares of the class in question (being persons who did not consent to or vote in favour of the resolution for the variation) may apply to the court to have the variation cancelled.

For this purpose any of the company's share capital held as treasury shares is disregarded.

(3) If such an application is made, the variation has no effect unless and until it is confirmed by the court.

(4) Application to the court-

    (a) must be made within 21 days after the date on which the consent was given or the resolution was passed (as the case may be), and

    (b) may be made on behalf of the shareholders entitled to make the application by such one or more of their number as they may appoint in writing for the purpose.

(5) The court, after hearing the applicant and any other persons who apply to the court to be heard and appear to the court to be interested in the application, may, if satisfied having regard to all the circumstances of the case that the variation would unfairly prejudice the shareholders of the class represented by the applicant, disallow the variation, and shall if not so satisfied confirm it.

The decision of the court on any such application is final.

(6) References in this section to the variation of the rights of holders of a class of shares include references to their abrogation.

GENERAL NOTE

This section restates s.127 of the 1985 Act, with the exception of subs.(5) of that section which is now restated in s.635. Apart from adapting the wording to the simplified variation procedure in s.630, there are no changes of substance.

The object of the section remains to protect a minority of a class of shares from being prejudiced by the majority who have other interests to protect (e.g. as holders of another class of shares). The minimum requirements for making an application to the court, the effect of such an application, the time limits involved and the powers of the court all remain as they were.

Any court order made under this section is subject to s.635.

634.   Right to object to variation: companies without a share capital

(1) This section applies where the rights of any class of members of a company are varied under section 631 (variation of class rights: companies without a share capital).

(2) Members amounting to not less than 15% of the members of the class in question (being persons who did not consent to or vote in favour of the resolution for the variation) may apply to the court to have the variation cancelled.

(3) If such an application is made, the variation has no effect unless and until it is confirmed by the court.

(4) Application to the court must be made within 21 days after the date on which the consent was given or the resolution was passed (as the case may be) and may be made on behalf of the members entitled to make the application by such one or more of their number as they may appoint in writing for the purpose.

(5) The court, after hearing the applicant and any other persons who apply to the court to be heard and appear to the court to be interested in the application, may, if satisfied having regard to all the circumstances of the case that the variation would unfairly prejudice the members of the class represented by the applicant, disallow the variation, and shall if not so satisfied confirm it.

The decision of the court on any such application is final.

(6) References in this section to the variation of the rights of a class of members include references to their abrogation.

GENERAL NOTE

    This section mirrors s.633 above as applied to applications to prevent the variation of the rights of members of a class of members of a company without a share capital made under s.631.

    The only difference is that the references are to members of a class rather than to the holders of a class of shares. Otherwise the note to the preceding section applies.

    Section 635 also applies to any order made by the court under this section.

635.   Copy of court order to be forwarded to the registrar

(1) The company must within 15 days after the making of an order by the court on an application under section 633 or 634 (objection to variation of class rights) forward a copy of the order to the registrar.

(2) If default is made in complying with this section an offence is committed by-
    (a) the company, and
    (b) every officer of the company who is in default.

(3) A person guilty of an offence under this section is liable on summary conviction to a fine not exceeding level 3 on the standard scale and, for continued contravention, a daily default fine not exceeding one-tenth of level 3 on the standard scale.

GENERAL NOTE

    This section restates s.127(6) of the 1985 Act and applies the obligation to register a court order to orders made under either ss.633 or 634. There is no alteration to the time limit. The sanctions for the offence in default are modified to comply with the general policy of offences in this Act (see Sch.3).

Matters to be notified to the registrar

636.   Notice of name or other designation of class of shares

(1) Where a company assigns a name or other designation, or a new name or other designation, to any class or description of its shares, it must within one month from doing so deliver to the registrar a notice giving particulars of the name or designation so assigned.

(2) If default is made in complying with this section, an offence is committed by-
    (a) the company, and
    (b) every officer of the company who is in default.

(3) A person guilty of an offence under this section is liable on summary conviction to a fine not exceeding level 3 on the standard scale and, for continued contravention, a daily default fine not exceeding one-tenth of level 3 on the standard scale.

GENERAL NOTE

Subsection (1)

This subsection restates s.128(4) of the 1985 Act, but applies the requirement to register a change of (or initial) name or designation of a class of shares to all such changes, however effected. The former exception to that, where the change was effected by an alteration of the memorandum or articles (which had to be registered as such) or by a resolution which would have had to have been registered under the 1985 Act, has been discontinued.

Note that the registration requirement on allotment of shares with class rights, formerly in s.128(1) of the 1985 Act, has been overtaken by the new requirements as to the registration of statements of capital under this Act.

Subsections (2) and (3)

The offence in default and sanction have been reworded from s.128(5) of the 1985 Act to comply with the treatment of offences under this Act (see Sch.3).

637. Notice of particulars of variation of rights attached to shares

(1) Where the rights attached to any shares of a company are varied, the company must within one month from the date on which the variation is made deliver to the registrar a notice giving particulars of the variation.

(2) If default is made in complying with this section, an offence is committed by-
    (a) the company, and
    (b) every officer of the company who is in default.

(3) A person guilty of an offence under this section is liable on summary conviction to a fine not exceeding level 3 on the standard scale and, for continued contravention, a daily default fine not exceeding one-tenth of level 3 on the standard scale.

GENERAL NOTE

Subsection (1)

This section restates the obligation, formerly in s.128(3) of the 1985 Act, to register particulars of a variation of rights attached to a class of shares. However, there is a major change in that this now applies to all variations. The former exception for cases where the fact of the variation would have been registered anyway (by reason of the alteration of the memorandum or articles or by a special or extraordinary resolution) has been discontinued.

Subsections (2) and (3)

The offence in default and sanction have been reworded from s.128(5) of the 1985 Act to comply with the treatment of offences under this Act (see Sch.3).

638. Notice of new class of members

(1) If a company not having a share capital creates a new class of members, the company must within one month from the date on which the new class is created deliver to the registrar a notice containing particulars of the rights attached to that class.

(2) If default is made in complying with this section, an offence is committed by-
    (a) the company, and
    (b) every officer of the company who is in default.

(3) A person guilty of an offence under this section is liable on summary conviction to a fine not exceeding level 3 on the standard scale and, for continued contravention, a daily default fine not exceeding one-tenth of level 3 on the standard scale.

GENERAL NOTE

Subsection (1)

This subsection restates the obligation, formerly in s.129(1) of the 1985 Act, for a company without a share capital to register particulars of the creation of a new class of member. However, there is a major change in that this now applies in all such cases. The former exception for cases where the creation would have been registered anyway (by being in the memorandum or articles or by an extraordinary or special resolution) has been discontinued.

This requirement was preserved (unlike former s.128(1)) because there is no equivalent of a statement of share capital for such companies.

Subsections (2) and (3)

The offence in default and sanction have been reworded from the former s.129(4) to comply with the treatment of offences under this Act (see Sch.3).

639.　Notice of name or other designation of class of members

(1) Where a company not having a share capital assigns a name or other designation, or a new name or other designation, to any class of its members, it must within one month from doing so deliver to the registrar a notice giving particulars of the name or designation so assigned.
(2) If default is made in complying with this section, an offence is committed by-
    (a)　the company, and
    (b)　every officer of the company who is in default.
(3) A person guilty of an offence under this section is liable on summary conviction to a fine not exceeding level 3 on the standard scale and, for continued contravention, a daily default fine not exceeding one-tenth of level 3 on the standard scale.

GENERAL NOTE

Subsection (1)

This subsection restates the obligation, formerly in s.129(3) of the 1985 Act, for a company without a share capital to register a change of (or initial) name of any class of members. However, there is a major change in that this now applies to all such cases. The former exception for cases where the change would have been registered anyway (by an alteration of the memorandum or articles or by an extraordinary or special resolution) has been discontinued.

Subsections (2) and (3)

The offence in default and sanction have been reworded from the former s.129(4) to comply with the treatment of offences under this Act (see Sch.3).

640.　Notice of particulars of variation of class rights

(1) If the rights of any class of members of a company not having a share capital are varied, the company must within one month from the date on which the variation is made deliver to the registrar a notice containing particulars of the variation.
(2) If default is made in complying with this section, an offence is committed by-
    (a)　the company, and
    (b)　every officer of the company who is in default.
(3) A person guilty of an offence under this section is liable on summary conviction to a fine not exceeding level 3 on the standard scale and, for continued contravention, a daily default fine not exceeding one-tenth of level 3 on the standard scale.

GENERAL NOTE

Subsection (1)

This subsection restates the obligation, formerly in s.129(2) of the 1985 Act, for a company without a share capital to register particulars of any variation of the rights of any class of member. However, there is a major change in that this obligation now applies to all such variations. The former exception for cases where the variation would have been registered anyway (by any alteration of the memorandum or articles or by an extraordinary or special resolution) has been discontinued.

Subsections (2) and (3)

The offence in default and sanction have been reworded from the former s.129(4) to comply with the treatment of offences under this Act (see Sch.3).

CHAPTER 10

REDUCTION OF SHARE CAPITAL

GENERAL NOTE

This chapter is concerned with the circumstances in which a limited company having a share capital may reduce its capital. It restates the law on the court-approved reductions of share capital that was previously contained in Ch.IV of Pt V of the Companies Act 1985. It also provides a new reduction of capital procedure for private companies, which requires the directors to make a solvency statement, but court approval is not required.

Introductory

641. Circumstances in which a company may reduce its share capital

(1) A limited company having a share capital may reduce its share capital-
   (a) in the case of a private company limited by shares, by special resolution supported by a solvency statement (see sections 642 to 644);
   (b) in any case, by special resolution confirmed by the court (see sections 645 to 651).
(2) A company may not reduce its capital under subsection (1)(a) if as a result of the reduction there would no longer be any member of the company holding shares other than redeemable shares.
(3) Subject to that, a company may reduce its share capital under this section in any way.
(4) In particular, a company may-
   (a) extinguish or reduce the liability on any of its shares in respect of share capital not paid up, or
   (b) either with or without extinguishing or reducing liability on any of its shares-
      (i) cancel any paid-up share capital that is lost or unrepresented by available assets, or
      (ii) repay any paid-up share capital in excess of the company's wants.
(5) A special resolution under this section may not provide for a reduction of share capital to take effect later than the date on which the resolution has effect in accordance with this Chapter.
(6) This Chapter (apart from subsection (5) above) has effect subject to any provision of the company's articles restricting or prohibiting the reduction of the company's share capital.

GENERAL NOTE

This section allows court-approved reductions of capital by public and private companies. To this extent it is based on s.135 of the Companies Act 1985. This section also provides a new procedure for private companies whereby a reduction of capital can be effected without court approval on the basis of a special resolution of the members and a directors' solvency statement for private companies, the new procedure sits alongside the court-approval procedure and does not replace it. The CLR's original suggestions had envisaged that the solvency statement procedure would replace the court approval procedure *Company Formation and Capital Maintenance* (URN 99/1145), para.3.27), but that suggestion did not command support and it was dropped (*Completing the Structure* (URN 00/1335) para.7.9).

The new procedure is not made available to public companies because of complications stemming from the United Kingdom's obligation to implement Community law. The 2nd Company Law Directive (77/91/EEC), Arts 30-34 regulate reductions of capital by public companies. Article 32 provides that creditors whose claims antedate the publication of the decision to reduce capital are entitled to have the right to obtain security for their claims. Furthermore, the reduction cannot proceed until the creditors have obtained satisfaction or a court has decided that their application should not be acceded to. Article 33 provides that Member States need not apply Art.32 to a reduction of capital that is to offset losses or to create an undistributable reserve of not more than ten per cent of the reduced capital. The Companies Act 1985 exceeded the requirements of the Second Directive by making all reductions of capital, by both public and private companies, subject to confirmation by the court.

The CLR's original proposals included that public companies be allowed to reduce their capital on the basis of a resolution of the members and a directors' solvency statement and without having to seek court approval (*Company Formation and Capital Maintenance* (URN 99/1145), paras 3.27-3.3.35). Compliance with the Second Directive would have been achieved by providing creditors with the opportunity, at their initiative, to challenge a reduction in court. Tracking Art.33 of the Second Directive, the right of creditors to apply to court would not have been extended to capital reductions to write off losses or to create undistributable reserves within the limits provided by that article.

Responses to the proposal to make the solvency statement procedure available to public companies were mixed. There were concerns that the safeguards that would need to be built into the procedure for public companies in order to meet Community obligations would mean that few public companies would use the procedure in practice. This led the government to decide against the introduction of the change for public companies (White Paper, March 2005 (Cm.6456) and Vera Baird MP, *Hansard*, Standing Committee D, col.854 (July 20, 2006)).

Directive 2006/68/EC of the European Parliament and of the Council of September 6, 2006 amending Council Directive 77/91/EEC as regards the formation of public limited liability companies and the maintenance of their capital revises Art.32 to limit the circumstances in which creditors can apply to court to object to a reduction of capital to where they can demonstrate that the reduction will prejudice the satisfaction of their claims and the company has provided no adequate safeguards. There are proposals for more far-reaching reform through the introduction on a pan-European basis on an alternative regime in which creditor protection is provided through requirements for solvency statements rather than capital maintenance obligations but these proposals are at a fairly early stage (European Commission, *Modernising Company Law and Enhancing Corporate Governance in the European Union - A Plan to Move Forward* (COM (2003) 284) (final) sec.3.2).

Subsection (1)

The requirement for a members' special resolution is common to the solvency statement procedure and the court approval procedure.

Subsection (2)

The underlying principle here is that a private company should not be able to reduce its capital to zero except with court approval. This provision mirrors a restriction on the power to issue redeemable shares (see s.684(4)) and the power to buy back shares (see s.690(2)). In the Parliamentary debate on the Bill it was claimed that as many as seven out of ten reductions of capital involve the momentary reduction of the existing share capital to zero before its immediate increase in a recapitalisation (Lord Hodgson, *Hansard*, col.GC4 (March 20, 2006)). This suggests that the practical utility of the new solvency statement procedure may be rather limited.

Subsections (3) and (4)

Subject to the restriction imposed by subs.(2) companies may reduce their share capital in any way. Subsection (4) provides a non-exhaustive list of examples. Subsection (4) is a re-enactment, without substantive change, of s.135(2) of the 1985 Act.

Subsection (5)

The date on which a reduction of capital by either procedure takes effect is set by the legislation (see s.644(4) and s.649.(3)) and this subsection makes it clear that it is not possible for companies to override this aspect of the procedure.

Subsection (6)

Companies can opt out of the statutory procedure for reduction of share capital or impose more restrictive requirements via provisions to that effect in their articles of association, save that the date on which a reduction takes effect cannot be overridden. The opt-out approach represents a reversal of the position under s.135 of the Companies Act 1985 whereby companies were required to opt into the statutory permission to reduce share capital via their articles.

Private companies: reduction of capital supported by solvency statement

642. Reduction of capital supported by solvency statement

(1) A resolution for reducing share capital of a private company limited by shares is supported by a solvency statement if-
  (a) the directors of the company make a statement of the solvency of the company in accordance with section 643 (a "solvency statement") not more than 15 days before the date on which the resolution is passed, and
  (b) the resolution and solvency statement are registered in accordance with section 644.

(2) Where the resolution is proposed as a written resolution, a copy of the solvency statement must be sent or submitted to every eligible member at or before the time at which the proposed resolution is sent or submitted to him.

(3) Where the resolution is proposed at a general meeting, a copy of the solvency statement must be made available for inspection by members of the company throughout that meeting.

(4) The validity of a resolution is not affected by a failure to comply with subsection (2) or (3).

GENERAL NOTE

This section sets out the procedural conditions that must be satisfied for a private company to reduce its share capital under the solvency statement procedure.

The directors' solvency statement must be made not more than 15 days before the date of the members' special resolution and the resolution and solvency statement must be registered within 15 days after the resolution is passed (see also s.644). The solvency statement must be made available to members when they vote on the resolution. The way in which the solvency statement is to be made available to members depends on the way in which the resolution is to be passed.

Subsection (2)

On eligible members to whom the solvency statement must be sent or submitted, see s.289.

Subsection (4)

Failure to observe the procedural requirements to make the solvency statement available to members will not invalidate the special resolution. The sanction is that defaulting officers of the company commit an offence if they deliver a solvency statement to the registrar that was not provided to the members (see s.644(7)). Furthermore if directors choose to propose a resolution for the reduction of capital without making the solvency statement available they run the risk of the resolution being vetoed by members. In the House of Lords debate, Lord Sainsbury, speaking on behalf of the government, expressed the view that this risk, together with the penalties on directors, should act as a sufficient deterrent (Lord Sainsbury, *Hansard*, col.GC12 (March 20, 2006)).

643. Solvency statement

(1) A solvency statement is a statement that each of the directors-
  (a) has formed the opinion, as regards the company's situation at the date of the statement, that there is no ground on which the company could then be found to be unable to pay (or otherwise discharge) its debts; and
  (b) has also formed the opinion-
    (i) if it is intended to commence the winding up of the company within twelve months of that date, that the company will be able to pay (or otherwise discharge) its debts in full within twelve months of the commencement of the winding up; or
    (ii) in any other case, that the company will be able to pay (or otherwise discharge) its debts as they fall due during the year immediately following that date.

(2) In forming those opinions, the directors must take into account all of the company's liabilities (including any contingent or prospective liabilities).

(3) The solvency statement must be in the prescribed form and must state-

      (a) the date on which it is made, and

      (b) the name of each director of the company.

(4) If the directors make a solvency statement without having reasonable grounds for the opinions expressed in it, and the statement is delivered to the registrar, an offence is committed by every director who is in default.

(5) A person guilty of an offence under subsection (4) is liable-

      (a) on conviction on indictment, to imprisonment for a term not exceeding two years or a fine (or both);

      (b) on summary conviction-

          (i) in England and Wales, to imprisonment for a term not exceeding twelve months or to a fine not exceeding the statutory maximum (or both);

          (ii) in Scotland or Northern Ireland, to imprisonment for a term not exceeding six months, or to a fine not exceeding the statutory maximum (or both).

GENERAL NOTE

The contents of the solvency statement required under this section are "almost identical" (Lord Sainsbury, *Hansard*, col GC14 (March 20, 2006)) to those of the statutory declaration or statement that used to be required of directors under the now repealed private company financial assistance "whitewash" procedure (s.155 of the Companies Act 1985). A noteworthy difference is that the directors' statement for a reduction of capital does not need to accompanied by a report from the company's auditors (the CLR initially supported a requirement for an auditors' report (*Company Formation and Capital Maintenance* (URN 99/1145), para.3.30) but that recommendation was later dropped (*Developing the Framework* (URN 00/656), para.7.26; *Completing the Structure* (URN 00/1335), para.7.9)). There are also close similarities with the statement required of directors in the procedure whereby private companies can repurchase their shares from capital, which was in ss.171-177 of the Companies Act 1985 and which is recast in ss.709-723 of the Companies Act 2006. The buy-back procedure has been revised to require directors to make statutory statements of solvency rather than statutory declarations (see s.714). The requirement for an auditors' report has been retained in the buy-back procedure (s.714).

Subsection (1)

A solvency statement must be made by all the directors of a company. A director who is unable or unwilling to join in the making of solvency statement would have to resign or be removed from office before that procedure can be used. In *In A Flap Envelope Co Ltd, Re* [2004] 1 B.C.L.C. 64, it was held that a statutory declaration for the purposes of s.155 of the Companies Act 1985 financial assistance whitewash procedure was not properly made where a director had resigned in order formally to distance himself from the procedure because the resignation was a sham and he remained as a de facto director of the company.

In *In A Flap Envelope Co Ltd, Re* it was said further that in order to satisfy the requirement for the formation of an opinion on the ability of the company to pay its debts, directors must make sufficient inquiries into the financial affairs of the company to satisfy themselves that the statement can be honestly made. The obligation on directors to make inquires is expressly stated in the procedure whereby private companies can use their capital to buy back shares (see s.714(3)).

The date of the statement is the point in time when the directors must form their position. In the Parliamentary debate on the clause, the government rejected an opposition amendment to change the key date to when the reduction became effective on the ground that it was more straightforward and sensible to use the date of the solvency statement, the timing of which the directors could control, rather than the date of the reduction becoming effective, the timing of which was dependent on matters not wholly within the directors' control (Lord Sainsbury, *Hansard*, cols GC14-17 (March 20, 2006)).

Subsection (2)

The directors are required to take account of prospective and contingent liabilities of the company. These are liabilities which the company will, or may, have to meet, but which have not accrued as at the relevant date (*MacPherson v European Strategic Bureau Ltd* [2000] 2 B.C.L.C. 683 at [39]).

Subsection (3)

The solvency statement must be *in* (not on) the prescribed form. In the Companies Acts, "prescribed" means prescribed (by order or by regulations) by the Secretary of State. See s.1167. In *Harlow v Loveday* [2005] 1 B.C.L.C. 41 and *SH & Co (Realisations) 1990 Ltd, Re* [1993] B.C.L.C. 1309, cases on the financial assistance whitewash procedure in the Companies Act 1985, statutory declarations were upheld despite containing errors because, when the declarations were considered as a whole, there was sufficient compliance. In both cases account was taken of the severe consequences of non-compliance.

Subsections (4) and (5)

Making a statutory statement without having reasonable grounds for the opinions expressed in it is a criminal offence for which the maximum punishment is imprisonment for up to two years.

This Act does not specify civil sanctions for making a false or inaccurate solvency statement. The CLR initially proposed that a reduction of capital contrary to statutory provisions, including where the directors' statement was made without reasonable grounds to believe in its truth, should result in any director or shareholder knowingly party to the default being liable at the suit of a creditor to pay up the capital reduced (*Company Formation and Capital Maintenance* (URN 99/1145), para.3.35). This recommendation was not adopted. Pre-Companies Act 2006 case law establishes that an unlawful return of capital is void (*MacPherson v European Strategic Bureau Ltd* [2000] 2 B.C.L.C. 683, CA; *Ridge Securities Ltd v Inland Revenue Commissioners* [1964] 1 All E.R. 275), that the responsible directors are in breach of their duties to the company (*Aveling Barford Ltd v Perion Ltd* [1989] B.C.L.C. 626) and that shareholders who receive capital unlawfully may be held liable to repay it (*Halt Garage (1964) Ltd, Re* [1982] 3 All E.R. 1016). These cases appear still to represent the law. A reduction of capital by paying off paid up share capital is not a distribution for the purposes of Pt 24 of the Companies Act 2006 (see s.829(2)(b)) and therefore s.847 (consequences of unlawful distribution) does not apply.

644. Registration of resolution and supporting documents

(1) Within 15 days after the resolution for reducing share capital is passed the company must deliver to the registrar-

    (a) a copy of the solvency statement, and

    (b) a statement of capital.

This is in addition to the copy of the resolution itself that is required to be delivered to the registrar under Chapter 3 of Part 3.

(2) The statement of capital must state with respect to the company's share capital as reduced by the resolution-

    (a) the total number of shares of the company,

    (b) the aggregate nominal value of those shares,

    (c) for each class of shares-

        (i) prescribed particulars of the rights attached to the shares,

        (ii) the total number of shares of that class, and

        (iii) the aggregate nominal value of shares of that class, and

    (d) the amount paid up and the amount (if any) unpaid on each share (whether on account of the nominal value of the share or by way of premium).

(3) The registrar must register the documents delivered to him under subsection (1) on receipt.

(4) The resolution does not take effect until those documents are registered.

(5) The company must also deliver to the registrar, within 15 days after the resolution is passed, a statement by the directors confirming that the solvency statement was-

    (a) made not more than 15 days before the date on which the resolution was passed, and

    (b) provided to members in accordance with section 642(2) or (3).

(6) The validity of a resolution is not affected by-

    (a) a failure to deliver the documents required to be delivered to the registrar under subsection (1) within the time specified in that subsection, or

    (b) a failure to comply with subsection (5).

(7) If the company delivers to the registrar a solvency statement that was not provided to members in accordance with section 642(2) or (3), an offence is committed by every officer of the company who is in default.

(8) If default is made in complying with this section, an offence is committed by-

    (a) the company, and

    (b) every officer of the company who is in default.

(9) A person guilty of an offence under subsection (7) or (8) is liable-

    (a) on conviction on indictment, to a fine;

    (b) on summary conviction, to a fine not exceeding the statutory maximum.

GENERAL NOTE

This is a mainly procedural section that is concerned with ensuring that there is a proper public record of reductions of capital made under the solvency statement procedure. Importantly this section also determines when a reduction of capital under this procedure takes effect.

Subsection (2)

In all circumstances where a company makes an alteration to its capital it is required to deliver a statement of capital to the registrar. On statements of capital see s.10.

Subsections (3) and (4)

The reduction of capital under the solvency statement procedure takes effect when the registrar registers the copy of the solvency statement, the statement of capital and the copy of the members' resolution. It is not possible for companies, in their articles or otherwise, to override this aspect of the procedure (see s.641(5)-(6)).

Subsection (5)

This additional statement from the directors must also be filed within 15 days after the resolution is passed but the registrar is not required to register it and its delivery does not affect the timing of the effectiveness of the reduction.

Subsection (6)

Failure to comply with filing requirements does not undermine the validity of the members' resolution.

Subsection (7)

This subsection provides the sanction for failure to make the solvency statement available to members as required by s.642(2) or (3).

Subsections (8) and (9)

Non-compliance with the requirements of this section can result in criminal sanctions against the company and defaulting officers. Corporate criminal liability is considered to be appropriate in circumstances where persons other than the company and its members could be adversely affected by non-compliance.

Reduction of capital confirmed by the court

645.   Application to court for order of confirmation

(1) Where a company has passed a resolution for reducing share capital, it may apply to the court for an order confirming the reduction.

(2) If the proposed reduction of capital involves either-

    (a) diminution of liability in respect of unpaid share capital, or

    (b) the payment to a shareholder of any paid-up share capital,

section 646 (creditors entitled to object to reduction) applies unless the court directs otherwise.

(3) The court may, if having regard to any special circumstances of the case it thinks proper to do so, direct that section 646 is not to apply as regards any class or classes of creditors.

(4) The court may direct that section 646 is to apply in any other case.

GENERAL NOTE

This section re-enacts part of s.136 of the Companies Act 1985. The substance is unchanged but the material has been re-ordered with a view to improving its accessibility.

Subsection (2)

This subsection is derived from s.136(2) of the Companies Act 1985 but differs from it to the extent that it relates only to reductions of capital involving either a diminution of shareholder liability or a repayment of capital to shareholders. Other types of reduction of capital are dealt with separately in subs.(4). As was the case previously, the statutory procedures whereby creditors can object to reductions *prima facie* apply to all reductions of capital of the type to which this subsection relates.

This subsection, derived from s.136(6), allows the court to dispense with the statutory creditor objection procedures in those types of reduction of capital to which they are *prima facie* applicable. A power of dispensation was first introduced by s.19(2) of the Companies Act 1928. It is standard modern practice for the courts to dispense with the statutory procedures because reductions of capital are typically structured so as to ensure that creditors' interests are not adversely affected. The existing case law on when the courts will grant dispensations will continue to apply: see, e.g. *New Duff House Sanatorium Ltd* 1931 S.L.T 337; *Lucania Temperance Billiard Halls Ltd, Re* [1966] Ch. 98.

Subsection (4)

This subsection, which is derived from s.136(2) of the 1985 Act, allows the court to apply the statutory creditor objection procedures to forms of reduction of capital that are not within the scope of subs.(2). For an example of circumstances where creditors failed to persuade the court that they should be allowed to object to a reduction of capital not involving a diminution of liability or a repayment of capital, see *Meux's Brewery Ltd, Re* [1919] 1 Ch. 28.

646. Creditors entitled to object to reduction

(1) Where this section applies (see section 645(2) and (4)), every creditor of the company who at the date fixed by the court is entitled to any debt or claim that, if that date were the commencement of the winding up of the company would be admissible in proof against the company, is entitled to object to the reduction of capital.

(2) The court shall settle a list of creditors entitled to object.

(3) For that purpose the court-
   (a) shall ascertain, as far as possible without requiring an application from any creditor, the names of those creditors and the nature and amount of their debts or claims, and
   (b) may publish notices fixing a day or days within which creditors not entered on the list are to claim to be so entered or are to be excluded from the right of objecting to the reduction of capital.

(4) If a creditor entered on the list whose debt or claim is not discharged or has not determined does not consent to the reduction, the court may, if it thinks fit, dispense with the consent of that creditor on the company securing payment of his debt or claim.

(5) For this purpose the debt or claim must be secured by appropriating (as the court may direct) the following amount-
   (a) if the company admits the full amount of the debt or claim or, though not admitting it, is willing to provide for it, the full amount of the debt or claim;
   (b) if the company does not admit, and is not willing to provide for, the full amount of the debt or claim, or if the amount is contingent or not ascertained, an amount fixed by the court after the like enquiry and adjudication as if the company were being wound up by the court.

GENERAL NOTE

This section re-states s.136(3)-(5) of the Companies Act 1985 without any changes of substance. It is concerned with the settling of a list of creditors entitled to object to a proposed reduction of capital.

647. Offences in connection with list of creditors

(1) If an officer of the company-
   (a) intentionally or recklessly-
      (i) conceals the name of a creditor entitled to object to the reduction of capital, or
      (ii) misrepresents the nature or amount of the debt or claim of a creditor, or
   (b) is knowingly concerned in any such concealment or misrepresentation,
he commits an offence.

(2) A person guilty of an offence under this section is liable-
   (a) on conviction on indictment, to a fine;

(b) on summary conviction, to a fine not exceeding the statutory maximum.

GENERAL NOTE

The statutory procedure for drawing up a list of creditors is underpinned by criminal sanctions provided by this section. This section is based on s.141 of the 1985 Act but the wording has been modernised in certain respects.

Subsection (1)

The standard of "intention" or "recklessness" replaces "wilfulness" as the mental state that an officer of the company must have had in order to be guilty of a concealment or misrepresentation offence. Being "knowingly concerned" in a concealment or misrepresentation is also an offence under this provision. This limb replaces the older offence of aiding, abetting or being privy to a concealment or misrepresentation.

648.   Court order confirming reduction

(1) The court may make an order confirming the reduction of capital on such terms and conditions as it thinks fit.

(2) The court must not confirm the reduction unless it is satisfied, with respect to every creditor of the company who is entitled to object to the reduction of capital that either-
    (a) his consent to the reduction has been obtained, or
    (b) his debt or claim has been discharged, or has determined or has been secured.

(3) Where the court confirms the reduction, it may order the company to publish (as the court directs) the reasons for reduction of capital, or such other information in regard to it as the court thinks expedient with a view to giving proper information to the public, and (if the court thinks fit) the causes that led to the reduction.

(4) The court may, if for any special reason it thinks proper to do so, make an order directing that the company must, during such period (commencing on or at any time after the date of the order) as is specified in the order, add to its name as its last words the words "and reduced".

If such an order is made, those words are, until the end of the period specified in the order, deemed to be part of the company's name.

GENERAL NOTE

This section re-states s.137 of the Companies Act 1985. There is some re-ordering of the material, but its substantive content is unchanged. This means that existing case law as to when the courts will approve a reduction of capital will continue to apply: see, e.g. *Ratners Group Plc* [1988] B.C.L.C. 685; *Thorn EMI Plc, Re* (1988) 4 B.C.C 698; *Ransomes Plc, Re* [1999] 1 B.C.L.C. 775 (affd [1999] 2 B.C.L.C. 591, CA); *Allied Domecq Plc, Re* [2000] 1 B.C.L.C. 134; *Hunting Plc, Re* [2005] 2 B.C.L.C. 211.

Subsection (1)

The court has a discretion whether to confirm a reduction of capital: *Prudential Assurance Co Ltd v Chatterley-Whitfield Collieries Co Ltd* [1949] A.C. 512.

Subsection (3)

This subsection preserves the power for the court to direct the publication of the reasons for the reduction. This power is only used occasionally.

Subsection (4)

The power for the court to require companies to add "and reduced" to their name is preserved by this section, even though in practice it has not been used for many years.

649. Registration of order and statement of capital

(1) The registrar, on production of an order of the court confirming the reduction of a company's share capital and the delivery of a copy of the order and of a statement of capital (approved by the court), shall register the order and statement.

This is subject to section 650 (public company reducing capital below authorised minimum).

(2) The statement of capital must state with respect to the company's share capital as altered by the order-

    (a) the total number of shares of the company,

    (b) the aggregate nominal value of those shares,

    (c) for each class of shares-

        (i) prescribed particulars of the rights attached to the shares,

        (ii) the total number of shares of that class, and

        (iii) the aggregate nominal value of shares of that class, and

    (d) the amount paid up and the amount (if any) unpaid on each share (whether on account of the nominal value of the share or by way of premium).

(3) The resolution for reducing share capital, as confirmed by the court's order, takes effect-

    (a) in the case of a reduction of share capital that forms part of a compromise or arrangement sanctioned by the court under Part 26 (arrangements and reconstructions)-

        (i) on delivery of the order and statement of capital to the registrar, or

        (ii) if the court so orders, on the registration of the order and statement of capital;

    (b) in any other case, on the registration of the order and statement of capital.

(4) Notice of the registration of the order and statement of capital must be published in such manner as the court may direct.

(5) The registrar must certify the registration of the order and statement of capital.

(6) The certificate-

    (a) must be signed by the registrar or authenticated by the registrar's official seal, and

    (b) is conclusive evidence-

        (i) that the requirements of this Act with respect to the reduction of share capital have been complied with, and

        (ii) that the company's share capital is as stated in the statement of capital.

GENERAL NOTE

This section is derived from s.138 of the Companies Act 1985. The changes are mainly to conform the publicity requirements for court-approved reductions of capital with the rest of the Companies Act 2006: i.e. the old requirement for the delivery of a minute (approved by the court) showing the details of the reduced share capital is replaced by a requirement for the delivery of a statement of capital (approved by the court) containing the prescribed information. Parts of s.138 of the 1985 Act that substituted the minute of reduction of capital into the company's memorandum are omitted because details of a company's capital are no longer a part of its memorandum (see s.8).

This section also determines when a court-approved reduction of capital takes effect.

Subsection (1)

This subsection requires the registrar to register the court order and the accompanying statement of capital (approved by the court).

Subsection (2)

On statements of capital see s.10.

Subsection (3)

As was the case under s.138(3) of the Companies Act 1985, a reduction of capital generally takes effect on registration: subs.(3)(b). Subsection (3)(a) is an entirely new provision which provides more flexibility on timing where a reduction forms part of a compromise or arrangement under Pt 26 of the 2006 Act. This change is in response to a finding by the CLR that the normal rule whereby the reduction takes effect on registration can cause difficulties in schemes, particularly for quoted companies, because it means that the timing is not within the company's control (*Final Report* ((URN 01/942), para.13.11(-

iv)). The provision for the reduction to take effect on delivery (by the company) of the order and statement of capital to the registrar addresses the problem.

Public company reducing capital below authorised minimum

650.   Public company reducing capital below authorised minimum

(1) This section applies where the court makes an order confirming a reduction of a public company's capital that has the effect of bringing the nominal value of its allotted share capital below the authorised minimum.

(2) The registrar must not register the order unless either-
    (a) the court so directs, or
    (b) the company is first re-registered as a private company.

(3) Section 651 provides an expedited procedure for re-registration in these circumstances.

GENERAL NOTE

This section, together with s.651, re-states s.139 of the 1985 Act, but without changes of substance. These sections are concerned with situations where the effect of a court-approved reduction of capital by a public company is to bring the nominal amount of its allotted capital below the authorised minimum (see s.763).

Subsection (2)

See *Allied Domecq Plc, Re* [2000] 1 B.C.L.C. 134 where an order was made requiring the court to register the order in circumstances where a reduction of capital, which was part of a larger re-organisation, had the effect of reducing the company's capital to below the authorised minimum for a public limited company.

651.   Expedited procedure for re-registration as a private company

(1) The court may authorise the company to be re-registered as a private company without its having passed the special resolution required by section 97.

(2) If it does so, the court must specify in the order the changes to the company's name and articles to be made in connection with the re-registration.

(3) The company may then be re-registered as a private company if an application to that effect is delivered to the registrar together with-
    (a) a copy of the court's order, and
    (b) notice of the company's name, and a copy of the company's articles, as altered by the court's order.

(4) On receipt of such an application the registrar must issue a certificate of incorporation altered to meet the circumstances of the case.

(5) The certificate must state that it is issued on re-registration and the date on which it is issued.

(6) On the issue of the certificate-
    (a) the company by virtue of the issue of the certificate becomes a private company, and
    (b) the changes in the company's name and articles take effect.

(7) The certificate is conclusive evidence that the requirements of this Act as to reregistration have been complied with.

GENERAL NOTE

This section provides a special procedure for re-registration of a company in connection with a court-approved reduction of capital.

Subsection (1)

Unless the court otherwise directs, the registrar must register a reduction of capital by a public company that has the effect of reducing its capital to below the authorised minimum only after the company has re-registered as a private company. The normal procedure for a public company to re-register as a private company is in ss.97-101 of the 2006 Act but this section provides an expedited procedure for re-registration on a reduction of capital, which is overseen by the court.

Effect of reduction of capital

652. Liability of members following reduction of capital

(1) Where a company's share capital is reduced a member of the company (past or present) is not liable in respect of any share to any call or contribution exceeding in amount the difference (if any) between-
   (a) the nominal amount of the share as notified to the registrar in the statement of capital delivered under section 644 or 649, and
   (b) the amount paid on the share or the reduced amount (if any) which is deemed to have been paid on it, as the case may be.

(2) This is subject to section 653 (liability to creditor in case of omission from list).

(3) Nothing in this section affects the rights of the contributories among themselves.

GENERAL NOTE

Sections 652 and 653 are derived from s.140 of the Companies Act 1985. The liability imposed by s.653 is a liability to contribute for the payment of the debt or claim of a creditor of the company and is not a liability owed directly by members to creditors.

653. Liability to creditor in case of omission from list of creditors

(1) This section applies where, in the case of a reduction of capital confirmed by the court-
   (a) a creditor entitled to object to the reduction of share capital is by reason of his ignorance-
      (i) of the proceedings for reduction of share capital, or
      (ii) of their nature and effect with respect to his debt or claim,
   not entered on the list of creditors, and
   (b) after the reduction of capital the company is unable to pay the amount of his debt or claim.

(2) Every person who was a member of the company at the date on which the resolution for reducing capital took effect under section 649(3) is liable to contribute for the payment of the debt or claim an amount not exceeding that which he would have been liable to contribute if the company had commenced to be wound up on the day before that date.

(3) If the company is wound up, the court on the application of the creditor in question, and proof of ignorance as mentioned in subsection (1)(a), may if it thinks fit-
   (a) settle accordingly a list of persons liable to contribute under this section, and
   (b) make and enforce calls and orders on them as if they were ordinary contributories in a winding up.

(4) The reference in subsection (1)(b) to a company being unable to pay the amount of a debt or claim has the same meaning as in section 123 of the Insolvency Act 1986 (c. 45) or Article 103 of the Insolvency (Northern Ireland) Order 1989 (S.I. 1989/ 2405 (N.I. 19)).

GENERAL NOTE

Subsection (1)

This section only applies to court-approved reductions of capital.

The reference to Northern Ireland is new and is a consequence of the decision to extend the Companies Acts to the province.

CHAPTER II

MISCELLANEOUS AND SUPPLEMENTARY PROVISIONS

654. Treatment of reserve arising from reduction of capital

(1) A reserve arising from the reduction of a company's share capital is not distributable, subject to any provision made by order under this section.

(2) The Secretary of State may by order specify cases in which-

    (a) the prohibition in subsection (1) does not apply, and

    (b) the reserve is to be treated for the purposes of Part 23 (distributions) as a realised profit.

(3) An order under this section is subject to affirmative resolution procedure.

GENERAL NOTE

The question whether the Act should specifically address the question whether a reserve arising from a reduction of capital should be regarded as distributable was not addressed in the original version of the Bill introduced in Parliament. It was raised in debate (see *Hansard*, cols GC6-8 (March 20, 2006)) and thereafter a provision was inserted into the legislation in the closing stages of the legislative process. The section is essentially a stop-gap measure because Parliamentary timetable pressure made it impossible to develop a workable response to the issues. A DTI memorandum submitted to the Select Committee on Delegated Powers and Regulatory Reform explained the thinking behind the section in these terms:

"25. This is a new power, which is intended to address an issue that has been drawn to our attention by the Law Society and the Institute of Chartered Accountants in England and Wales (ICAEW) as regards the circumstances in which a reserve created as a result of a reduction of capital may be applied. The issue is that it is unclear when such a reserve may be treated as a realised profit and, subject to other common law rules on distributions, therefore be distributable to a company's members. This uncertainty is exacerbated by the introduction of the new solvency statement procedure for capital reductions.

26. Currently, the extent of a company's profits which are available for distribution is determined in accordance with Pt 8 of the 1985 Act and generally speaking a company may only distribute an amount equal to its accumulated realised profits less its accumulated realised losses. The statutory rules are supplemented by authoritative guidance issued by the Institutes of Chartered Accountants because the law effectively leaves the issue of determining which profits are 'realised' to generally accepted accounting practice.

27. The ICAEW have stated that they have always viewed their guidance as no more than a 'stop gap' measure in this area as it does not readily fit with the framework of guidance on the accounting question of determining which profits are realised profits. The ICAEW and the Law Society consider it necessary, and we agree, that the Bill render clear the position on any reserve arising following a reduction of capital under the new solvency statement procedure in order that the intended benefits of that regime be realised (whilst at the same time placing their guidance on court approved reductions on a statutory footing).

28. The question of how a reserve arising from a reduction of capital should be treated should be put beyond doubt, as the position of creditors under the solvency statement procedure is not on all fours with the court-approved scheme. In particular: given that a company under the solvency regime is not required to provide security for its debts/claims at the time it makes a reduction (which the court will require before it will approve a reduction involving a return of capital to members) we do not consider, as a matter of policy, that the Bill should be amended to permit a private company to distribute any reserve arising from such a reduction of capital. We are not attracted to the various suggestions that the ICAEW have made to date regarding how this issue should be dealt with in the Bill as the suggestions in question do not appear to offer adequate protection to various categories of unsecured creditors who have no right to object to the reduction (as would be the case in court approved reductions of capital).

29.We consider that this raises difficult questions as to the circumstances in which a reserve arising from a non-court approved reduction should be treated as a realised profit and thereby feed into the distributions regime under new Part [Distributions] of the Bill. As this issue has arisen at a late stage in the passage of the Bill through Parliament, we are not confident that we can find a workable legislative solution which confers the same protection on the creditors of a company which utilises the solvency statement procedure to that which applies to creditors of a company which applies to court for a reduction of capital. In view of this we consider that it would be advisable for the Secretary of State to take a power to designate, by order, the circumstances in which the reserve arising on a reduction of capital may be treated as a realised profit for the purposes of new Part [Distributions]. We propose that this power should be exercisable in relation to both court- approved reductions and reductions pursuant to the solvency statement procedure and that the order may prescribe different circumstances applicable to either procedure undertaken by limited companies and also that it should apply in relation to reductions of capital undertaken by unlimited companies (which are not regulated under the Bill).

30.In view of the fact that the exercise of this power will affect the interests of shareholders and creditors it is considered that this power should be subject to affirmative resolution procedure."

This memorandum is included as Appendix 3 to the 26th Report of the Delegated Powers and Regulatory Reform Committee (November 2006).

Subsection (3)

The affirmative resolution procedure means that the regulations or orders must not be made unless a draft of the statutory instrument containing them has been laid before Parliament and approved by a resolution of each House of Parliament. See s.1290.

655. Shares no bar to damages against company

A person is not debarred from obtaining damages or other compensation from a company by reason only of his holding or having held shares in the company or any right to apply or subscribe for shares or to be included in the company's register of members in respect of shares.

GENERAL NOTE

This section re-enacts without any change (substantive or drafting) s.111A of the Companies Act 1985, which was inserted into the 1985 Act by the Companies Act 1989, s.131(1), as from April 1, 1990. It ensures that a person is not debarred from seeking damages from a company by reason only of the fact of holding shares or other rights relating to shares.

656. Public companies: duty of directors to call meeting on serious loss of capital

(1) Where the net assets of a public company are half or less of its called-up share capital, the directors must call a general meeting of the company to consider whether any, and if so what, steps should be taken to deal with the situation.

(2) They must do so not later than 28 days from the earliest day on which that fact is known to a director of the company.

(3) The meeting must be convened for a date not later than 56 days from that day.

(4) If there is a failure to convene a meeting as required by this section, each of the directors of the company who-

    (a) knowingly authorises or permits the failure, or

    (b) after the period during which the meeting should have been convened, knowingly authorises or permits the failure to continue,

commits an offence.

(5) A person guilty of an offence under this section is liable-

    (a) on conviction on indictment, to a fine;

    (b) on summary conviction, to a fine not exceeding the statutory maximum.

(6) Nothing in this section authorises the consideration at a meeting convened in pursuance of subsection (1) of any matter that could not have been considered at that meeting apart from this section.

GENERAL NOTE

This section re-states, with some drafting changes, s.142 of the 1985 Act. This section implements Second Company Law Directive (77/91/EEC), Art.17. It was first introduced into the companies legislation by the Companies Act 1980.

Subsection (1)

There is a statutory definition of "net assets" in s.677(2) (meaning of "financial assistance") and s.831(2) (net asset restriction by public companies): the aggregate of the company's assets less the aggregate of its liabilities. Technically, however, those definitions are only applicable in the particular contexts to which they relate.

Called-up share capital is defined generally for the Companies Acts by s.547.

Subsection (4)

The criminal sanctions that underpin the obligation imposed by this section no longer include as part of the offence a requirement that directors acted "willfully" as well as "knowingly".

657. General power to make further provision by regulations

(1) The Secretary of State may by regulations modify the following provisions of this Part-
     sections 552 and 553 (prohibited commissions, discounts and allowances),
     Chapter 5 (payment for shares),
     Chapter 6 (public companies: independent valuation of non-cash consideration),
     Chapter 7 (share premiums),
     sections 622 to 628 (redenomination of share capital),
     Chapter 10 (reduction of capital), and
     section 656 (public companies: duty of directors to call meeting on serious loss of capital).
(2) The regulations may-
     (a) amend or repeal any of those provisions, or
     (b) make such other provision as appears to the Secretary of State appropriate in place of any of those provisions.
(3) Regulations under this section may make consequential amendments or repeals in other provisions of this Act, or in other enactments.
(4) Regulations under this section are subject to affirmative resolution procedure.

GENERAL NOTE

The first version of the Bill that eventually became the Companies Act 2006 contained a Part that would have created a reform power for company law that could be used to amend primary legislation by secondary legislation passed in accordance with super-affirmative legislative procedures. The aim of this proposal was provide "flexibility for the future" by providing a fast-track procedure for "updating the law to reflect the changing business environment" (Lord Sainsbury, *Hansard*, HL Vol.677, col.187 (January 11, 2006)). However, there were concerns about the scope, process and proportionality of the new power and about its overlap with a more general reform power that was being proposed by the Legislative and Regulatory Reform Bill, which was also making its way through Parliament. The considerable overlap between the powers contained in the two Bills led eventually to a decision by the government not to proceed with the proposed reform power for company law in the Companies Bill (Lord Sainsbury, *Hansard*, cols GC405-406 (March 30, 2006)). However, in announcing that decision, Lord Sainsbury said that "The underlying need to provide some means of making changes over time in certain key areas remains" (*ibid.*). He identified capital maintenance as one of these key areas for the following reason:

> "those are rather technical rules where we are to some extent constrained by Europe, certainly as far as public companies are concerned. As and when Europe relaxes the rules for those companies, we may find ourselves wanting to make deregulatory changes for all companies in the United Kingdom. We cannot cater for that precisely in the Bill now. We do not know how far Europe will go. But it is important to business that as soon as we can relax the rules, we do so" (*ibid.*).

This section gives effect for capital maintenance purposes to the government's intention "to provide for specific powers to make provision by way of Regulations in a handful of areas" (Lord Sainsbury, *ibid.*).

The DTI's thinking behind this provision is explained in a memorandum that is reproduced as Appendix to the 26th Report of the Delegated Powers and Regulatory Reform Committee (November 2006). The DTI stated:

> "36. Whilst the Bill contains certain reforms in the area of capital maintenance (for example, the 1985 Act applied various of the provisions of the Second Directive to private companies, whereas

the remit of that Directive extends only to public companies and so the Bill has in certain areas deregulated the position for private companies) given the recently adopted amendments to the Second Directive (which will need to be implemented less than 18 months after the anticipated date for Royal Assent) and the possibility, in the medium term, of more fundamental reforms to the capital maintenance regime established by the Second Directive following the outcome of the feasibility study referred to above, it is considered desirable to take powers to modify the capital maintenance provisions of the Bill. In other words, the argument for taking these powers is that we cannot anticipate what the outcome of the discussions on the Second Directive will be, but that it is likely that the changes which it is wished to effect will go wider than could be made in pure implementation of any directive, in particular in relation to private companies. We also want to cover the possibility that no directive will be adopted.

37.Whilst it would have been possible to make further reforms to the law relating to private companies in the Bill, our present policy is not to make any further changes (other than those contained in the Bill) in respect of private companies nor to remove any provisions which go beyond the minimum required laid down by the Second Directive in respect of public companies, until the position in Europe becomes clearer. In particular, it would not make sense to make further changes to the law at this stage when there is a possibility that these changes may be overtaken by action at EU level.

38.Regulations under this section are subject to affirmative resolution procedure as they may make changes to provisions contained in primary legislation."

Subsections (2) and (3)

Regulations made under this section may amend or repeal the primary legislation mentioned in subs.(1) and make consequential amendments to other legislation. These powers, sometimes known as "Henry VIII powers" are controversial. In its Report the Delegated Powers and Regulatory Reform Committee 13 said that it considered that the approach the Minister set out in Grand Committee was the appropriate way to legislate on this subject (26th Report, November 2006, para.13). Parliament accepted that law relating to share capital was an appropriate case for the use of these powers because of the essentially technical nature of the subject and the clear, strong case for reform (*Hansard*, HL Vol.686, cols 441-445 (November 2, 2006); *Hansard*, HC Vol.451, cols 672-674 (November 6, 2006)).

Subsection (4)

The affirmative resolution procedure means that the regulations or orders must not be made unless a draft of the statutory instrument containing them has been laid before Parliament and approved by a resolution of each House of Parliament. See s.1290.

PART 18

ACQUISITION BY LIMITED COMPANY OF ITS OWN SHARES

CHAPTER I

GENERAL PROVISIONS

Introductory

658.   General rule against limited company acquiring its own shares

(1) A limited company must not acquire its own shares, whether by purchase, subscription or otherwise, except in accordance with the provisions of this Part.

(2) If a company purports to act in contravention of this section-
   (a) an offence is committed by-
      (i) the company, and
      (ii) every officer of the company who is in default, and
   (b) the purported acquisition is void.

(3) A person guilty of an offence under this section is liable-

    (a) on conviction on indictment, to imprisonment for a term not exceeding two years or a fine (or both);

    (b) on summary conviction-

        (i) in England and Wales, to imprisonment for a term not exceeding twelve months or a fine not exceeding the statutory maximum (or both);

        (ii) in Scotland or Northern Ireland, to imprisonment for a term not exceeding six months or a fine not exceeding the statutory maximum (or both).

GENERAL NOTE

This Part replaces Chs V, VI and VII of Pt V of the 1985 Act (ss.143-181). As such it covers the general rules governing companies holding their own shares (Ch.1), financial assistance by a company for the acquisition of its own shares (Ch.2), the power to issue and redeem redeemable shares (Ch.3), the power of companies to buy back their own shares (Ch.4), the ability of private companies to do either of those last two out of capital (Ch.5), the rules allowing certain listed companies to hold their own purchased shares as treasury shares (Ch.6) and certain consequential sections following on from Chs 3-5 (Ch.7).

Originally, following recommendations of the CLR, the Bill contained clauses amending the 1985 Act sections relating to financial assistance, redeemable shares and the power to buy back shares. As a result of the restatement exercise (see the General Note to the Act), those changes, together with those necessary to comply with the style and policy of the Act as a whole, were subsumed into these restated sections.

This section and the remainder of this Chapter (ss.658-676) replace ss.143-150 (and part of s.122) and Sch.2 to the 1985 Act with no changes of substance.

Subsection (1)

This subsection restates s.143(1) and 3(a) of the 1985 Act. As such it continues the codification of the basic common law rule prohibiting a company from acquiring its own shares as laid down in *Trevor v Whitworth* (1887) 12 A.C. 409; cf. *Acatos & Hutcheson Plc v Watson* [1995] 1 B.C.L.C. 218. All such acquisitions (unless excepted) are void and cannot be retrospectively validated: *R W Peak (Kings Lynn) Ltd, Re* [1998] 1 B.C.L.C. 193.

This prohibition is subject to a number of exceptions, however, two of which (the redemption of redeemable shares and the statutory buy back powers allowed for in this Part of the Act) are referred to here. The other exceptions are in s.659. For public companies, the consequences are set out in ss.662-669.

Subsections (2) and (3)

In addition to the civil consequences of a breach, the offence in default and sanctions, formerly in s.143(4) and (5), have been reworded to comply with the general treatment of offences under the Act (see Sch.3).

659. Exceptions to general rule

(1) A limited company may acquire any of its own fully paid shares otherwise than for valuable consideration.

(2) Section 658 does not prohibit-

    (a) the acquisition of shares in a reduction of capital duly made;

    (b) the purchase of shares in pursuance of an order of the court under-

        (i) section 98 (application to court to cancel resolution for reregistration as a private company),

        (ii) section 721(6) (powers of court on objection to redemption or purchase of shares out of capital),

        (iii) section 759 (remedial order in case of breach of prohibition of public offers by private company), or

        (iv) Part 30 (protection of members against unfair prejudice);

    (c) the forfeiture of shares, or the acceptance of shares surrendered in lieu, in pursuance of the company's articles, for failure to pay any sum payable in respect of the shares.

GENERAL NOTE

This section restates the remainder of s.143(3) of the 1985 Act, modified only in (ii) below, to take account of changes in other areas of the Act.

As such, it sets out the other exceptions to the prohibition in s.658(1). These are:

i   shares acquired otherwise than for a valuable consideration: see *Castiglione's WT, Re* [1958] All E.R. 480; cf. *Vision Express (UK) Ltd v Wilson (No.1)* [1995] 2 B.C.L.C. 419;

ii court orders made under ss.98, 721(6), 759 and Pt 30 of this Act; and

iii the forfeiture of shares or acceptance of any shares surrendered in lieu for failure to pay for them .

Shares held by company's nominee

660. Treatment of shares held by nominee

(1) This section applies where shares in a limited company-

    (a) are taken by a subscriber to the memorandum as nominee of the company,

    (b) are issued to a nominee of the company, or

    (c) are acquired by a nominee of the company, partly paid up, from a third person.

(2) For all purposes-

    (a) the shares are to be treated as held by the nominee on his own account, and

    (b) the company is to be regarded as having no beneficial interest in them.

(3) This section does not apply-

    (a) to shares acquired otherwise than by subscription by a nominee of a public company, where-

        (i) a person acquires shares in the company with financial assistance given to him, directly or indirectly, by the company for the purpose of or in connection with the acquisition, and

        (ii) the company has a beneficial interest in the shares;

    (b) to shares acquired by a nominee of the company when the company has no beneficial interest in the shares.

GENERAL NOTE

This section restates s.144(1) and 145(1)(a) of the 1985 Act. It should be read with s.661 and ss.671-676.

Subsections (1) and (2)

These subss, which restate s.144(1), are designed, subject to the exceptions in subs.(3), to prevent a company from circumventing the prohibition in s.658 by using a nominee to hold its own shares for it. The circumstances are as set out in subs.(1) where it is now made clear (as elsewhere in this Act) that it applies equally to a nominee taking shares automatically as a subscriber to the memorandum as it does to an issue of shares to a nominee.

The consequences are as set out in subs.(2). Theses are the same as in the previous sections - full ownership in the nominee and no interest for the company.

Subsection (3)

This subsection restates s.145(1) and 2(a) of the 1985 Act and provides for exceptions to subss.(1) and (2). These are: first, shares acquired with financial assistance from a public company (see the following Chapter) where the company has a beneficial interest in those shares (except for those acquired by subscription of the memorandum of a public company); and secondly, shares taken by, e.g. a trustee, as a nominee for the company but where the company has no beneficial interest in them. Section 145(2)(b) of the 1985 Act is spent and s.145(3) is now part of ss.671-676 of this Act.

For further details as to when the company is deemed to have a beneficial interest in such shares, see ss.671-676 of this Act.

661. Liability of others where nominee fails to make payment in respect of shares

(1) This section applies where shares in a limited company-
  (a) are taken by a subscriber to the memorandum as nominee of the company,
  (b) are issued to a nominee of the company, or
  (c) are acquired by a nominee of the company, partly paid up, from a third person.
(2) If the nominee, having been called on to pay any amount for the purposes of paying up, or paying any premium on, the shares, fails to pay that amount within 21 days from being called on to do so, then-
  (a) in the case of shares that he agreed to take as subscriber to the memorandum, the other subscribers to the memorandum, and
  (b) in any other case, the directors of the company when the shares were issued to or acquired by him,
are jointly and severally liable with him to pay that amount.
(3) If in proceedings for the recovery of an amount under subsection (2) it appears to the court that the subscriber or director-
  (a) has acted honestly and reasonably, and
  (b) having regard to all the circumstances of the case, ought fairly to be relieved from liability,
the court may relieve him, either wholly or in part, from his liability on such terms as the court thinks fit.
(4) If a subscriber to a company's memorandum or a director of a company has reason to apprehend that a claim will or might be made for the recovery of any such amount from him-
  (a) he may apply to the court for relief, and
  (b) the court has the same power to relieve him as it would have had in proceedings for recovery of that amount.
(5) This section does not apply to shares acquired by a nominee of the company when the company has no beneficial interest in the shares.

GENERAL NOTE

This section restates s.144(2)-(4) of the 1985 Act. Subject to subs.(5) (derived from s.145(2)(a)), it provides for the liability to pay any monies due on shares taken by a nominee for a company in the circumstances set out in subs.(1), which are identical to those in s.660(1). It is important to note, however, that there is no equivalent exception to this section as there is to that section in s.660(3)(a).

Subsections (2)-(4)

These subsections restate, with no changes of substance, the provision for the joint and several liability of others with the nominee for amounts due on the shares and the powers of the court to give relief from such liability.

Subsection (5)

For further details as to what amounts to a beneficial interest of the company see ss.671-676.

Shares held by or for public company

662. Duty to cancel shares in public company held by or for the company

(1) This section applies in the case of a public company-
  (a) where shares in the company are forfeited, or surrendered to the company in lieu of forfeiture, in pursuance of the articles, for failure to pay any sum payable in respect of the shares;
  (b) where shares in the company are surrendered to the company in pursuance of section 102C(1)(b) of the Building Societies Act 1986 (c. 53);

(c) where shares in the company are acquired by it (otherwise than in accordance with this Part or Part 30 (protection of members against unfair prejudice)) and the company has a beneficial interest in the shares;

(d) where a nominee of the company acquires shares in the company from a third party without financial assistance being given directly or indirectly by the company and the company has a beneficial interest in the shares; or

(e) where a person acquires shares in the company, with financial assistance given to him, directly or indirectly, by the company for the purpose of or in connection with the acquisition, and the company has a beneficial interest in the shares.

(2) Unless the shares or any interest of the company in them are previously disposed of, the company must-

    (a) cancel the shares and diminish the amount of the company's share capital by the nominal value of the shares cancelled, and

    (b) where the effect is that the nominal value of the company's allotted share capital is brought below the authorised minimum, apply for reregistration as a private company, stating the effect of the cancellation.

(3) It must do so no later than-

    (a) in a case within subsection (1)(a) or (b), three years from the date of the forfeiture or surrender;

    (b) in a case within subsection (1)(c) or (d), three years from the date of the acquisition;

    (c) in a case within subsection (1)(e), one year from the date of the acquisition.

(4) The directors of the company may take any steps necessary to enable the company to comply with this section, and may do so without complying with the provisions of Chapter 10 of Part 17 (reduction of capital).

See also section 664 (re-registration as private company in consequence of cancellation).

(5) Neither the company nor, in a case within subsection (1)(d) or (e), the nominee or other shareholder may exercise any voting rights in respect of the shares.

(6) Any purported exercise of those rights is void.

GENERAL NOTE

    This section restates ss.146 and 147(1) of the 1985 Act, with no changes of substance. It sets out the consequences in those circumstances where a public company takes advantage of the exceptions to the prohibition on acquiring its own shares in s.658 or using a nominee in s.660. It applies only to public companies because the second EC Directive (79/91/EEC), which imposed these rules, only required that (see Arts 20(2), (3) and 21). There are civil and criminal sanctions in default in ss.666 and 667.

    For further details as to what constitutes a beneficial interest ,see ss.671-676.

Subsections (1)-(3)

    These subsections restate the obligation in s.146(1)-(3) of the 1985 Act on a public company to dispose of or cancel the relevant shares. Note that the time limit is three years for shares acquired by way of gift, by forfeiture or surrender, and nominee acquisitions without financial assistance in which the company has a beneficial interest (e.g. gifts to a nominee). It is only one year, however, for shares acquired by a nominee with financial assistance from the company. Cancellation involves diminishing the amount of share capital, which may have further consequences (see s.664).

Subsection (4)

    This subsection restates s.147(1) of the 1985 Act. It allows the directors to reduce the share capital as a consequence of a cancellation of the shares without recourse to the reduction of capital procedures under this Act. (The remainder of s.147 is now in ss.664 and 665.)

Subsections (5) and (6)

    These subsections restate s.146(4) of the 1985 Act freezing any shares so acquired pending disposal or cancellation.

663. Notice of cancellation of shares

(1) Where a company cancels shares in order to comply with section 662, it must within one month after the shares are cancelled give notice to the registrar, specifying the shares cancelled.

(2) The notice must be accompanied by a statement of capital.

(3) The statement of capital must state with respect to the company's share capital immediately following the cancellation-

    (a) the total number of shares of the company,

    (b) the aggregate nominal value of those shares,

    (c) for each class of shares-

        (i) prescribed particulars of the rights attached to the shares,

        (ii) the total number of shares of that class, and

        (iii) the aggregate nominal value of shares of that class, and

    (d) the amount paid up and the amount (if any) unpaid on each share (whether on account of the nominal value of the share or by way of premium).

(4) If default is made in complying with this section, an offence is committed by-

    (a) the company, and

    (b) every officer of the company who is in default.

(5) A person guilty of an offence under this section is liable on summary conviction to a fine not exceeding level 3 on the standard scale and, for continued contravention, a daily default fine not exceeding one-tenth of level 3 on the standard scale.

GENERAL NOTE

    This section brings in the obligation to register a cancellation of shares consequent on s.675 which was formerly is s.122 of the 1985 Act. This obligation is now adapted to comply with the new statement of capital procedure introduced by this Act (see, e.g. s.10).

Subsection (1)

    This subsection restates s.122(1)(f) of the 1985 Act. There is no alteration to the time limit.

Subsections (2) and (3)

    These subsections incorporate the statement of capital regime introduced by this Act. As such it is the standard format under this Act.

Subsections (4) and (5)

    These subss, restating s.122(2) and (3) of the 1985 Act as to the default offence and sanction, have been reworded to comply with the general treatment of offences under this Act (see Sch.3).

664. Re-registration as private company in consequence of cancellation

(1) Where a company is obliged to re-register as a private company to comply with section 662, the directors may resolve that the company should be so reregistered.

Chapter 3 of Part 3 (resolutions affecting a company's constitution) applies to any such resolution.

(2) The resolution may make such changes-

    (a) in the company's name, and

    (b) in the company's articles,

 as are necessary in connection with its becoming a private company.

(3) The application for re-registration must contain a statement of the company's proposed name on re-registration.

(4) The application must be accompanied by-

(a) a copy of the resolution (unless a copy has already been forwarded under Chapter 3 of Part 3),

(b) a copy of the company's articles as amended by the resolution, and

(c) a statement of compliance.

(5) The statement of compliance required is a statement that the requirements of this section as to re-registration as a private company have been complied with.

(6) The registrar may accept the statement of compliance as sufficient evidence that the company is entitled to be re-registered as a private company.

GENERAL NOTE

This section, together with the following section, restates s.147(2)-(4). It applies where, as a consequence of a cancellation of shares under s.662, the company no longer has sufficient share capital to remain as a public company (see s.774) and so must re-register as a private company.

Subsections (1)-(3)

These subsections restate s.147(2) of the 1985 Act. There are no changes of substance (thus the directors may still pass the requisite resolution), but the wording is changed to reflect the downgrading of the memorandum and the fact that the articles need not specify the name of the company. The expanded concept of a company's constitution in Ch.3 of Pt 3 to this Act is also provided for.

Subsections (4)-(6)

These subsections restate the obligation, formerly in s.147(3) of the 1985 Act, as to the form of the application for re-registration. The wording has been amended to reflect the requirements for re-registration generally under this Act.

665. Issue of certificate of incorporation on re-registration

(1) If on an application under section 664 the registrar is satisfied that the company is entitled to be re-registered as a private company, the company shall be reregistered accordingly.

(2) The registrar must issue a certificate of incorporation altered to meet the circumstances of the case.

(3) The certificate must state that it is issued on re-registration and the date on which it is issued.

(4) On the issue of the certificate-

(a) the company by virtue of the issue of the certificate becomes a private company, and

(b) the changes in the company's name and articles take effect.

(5) The certificate is conclusive evidence that the requirements of this Act as to reregistration have been complied with.

GENERAL NOTE

This section restates s.147(4) of the 1985 Act with no changes of substance.

The consequences of the issue of a new certificate of incorporation are standard - the company becomes a fully-fledged private company with all changes in its constitution in force and its status as such cannot be challenged.

666. Effect of failure to re-register

(1) If a public company that is required by section 662 to apply to be re-registered as a private company fails to do so before the end of the period specified in subsection (3) of that section, Chapter 1 of Part 20 (prohibition of public offers by private company) applies to it as if it were a private company.

(2) Subject to that, the company continues to be treated as a public company until it is so re-registered.

GENERAL NOTE

This section restates s.149(1) of the 1985 Act as to the limited civil consequences of a public company failing to re-register as a private company consequent on its share capital falling below the authorised minimum (see s.774) as the result of the duty to cancel its shares under s.662. The only effect is a prohibition on the ability to make a public issue of shares.

The period specified for re-registration is either one or three years from the original acquisition (see s.662(3)).

There are criminal sanctions in s.667.

667.   Offence in case of failure to cancel shares or re-register

(1) This section applies where a company, when required to do by section 662-
    (a) fails to cancel any shares, or
    (b) fails to make an application for re-registration as a private company,
within the time specified in subsection (3) of that section.

(2) An offence is committed by-
    (a) the company, and
    (b) every officer of the company who is in default.

(3) A person guilty of an offence under this section is liable on summary conviction to a fine not exceeding level 3 on the standard scale and, for continued contravention, a daily default fine not exceeding one-tenth of level 3 on the standard scale.

GENERAL NOTE

This section restates s.149(2) as to the offence relating either to a failure to cancel shares consequent on s.662 and/or, if so required as a consequence, to re-register as a private company under s.664.

The period specified for both offences is either one or three years from the original acquisition (see s.662(3)).

The wording has been amended to comply with the general treatment of offences under this Act (see Sch.3).

668.   Application of provisions to company re-registering as public company

(1) This section applies where, after shares in a private company-
    (a) are forfeited in pursuance of the company's articles or are surrendered to the company in lieu of forfeiture,
    (b) are acquired by the company (otherwise than by any of the methods permitted by this Part or Part 30 (protection of members against unfair prejudice)), the company having a beneficial interest in the shares,
    (c) are acquired by a nominee of the company from a third party without financial assistance being given directly or indirectly by the company, the company having a beneficial interest in the shares, or
    (d) are acquired by a person with financial assistance given to him, directly or indirectly, by the company for the purpose of or in connection with the acquisition, the company having a beneficial interest in the shares,
the company is re-registered as a public company.

(2) In that case the provisions of sections 662 to 667 apply to the company as if it had been a public company at the time of the forfeiture, surrender or acquisition, subject to the following modification.

(3) The modification is that the period specified in section 662(3)(a), (b) or (c) (period for complying with obligations under that section) runs from the date of the re-registration of the company as a public company.

GENERAL NOTE

This section restates, without any changes of substance, s.148(1) and (2) of the 1985 Act. Section 148(4) which deals with an entirely separate matter is restated in s.682. (Section 148(3) as to what may constitute a beneficial interest is now subsumed into ss.671-676).

This section applies where a private company acquires its own shares (or uses a nominee to do so) in circumstances in which, had it been a public company, it would have been subject to s.662 (duty to cancel shares), and is then re-registered as a public company. In such a case ss.662-667 will apply to the company, but with the relevant time limits of either one or three years running from the date of re-registration rather than the acquisition of the shares.

669.   Transfer to reserve on acquisition of shares by public company or nominee

(1) Where-
    (a) a public company, or a nominee of a public company, acquires shares in the company, and
    (b) those shares are shown in a balance sheet of the company as an asset,

an amount equal to the value of the shares must be transferred out of profits available for dividend to a reserve fund and is not then available for distribution.

(2) Subsection (1) applies to an interest in shares as it applies to shares.

As it so applies the reference to the value of the shares shall be read as a reference to the value to the company of its interest in the shares.

GENERAL NOTE

This section restates s.148(4) of the 1985 Act with no changes of substance. Where a public company acquires its own shares (or uses a nominee to do so) and shows them as an asset in its balance sheet, a compensating non-distributable capital fund (reserve) must be created out of distributable profits.

Distributable profits - see s.736.

Charges of public company on own shares

670.   Public companies: general rule against lien or charge on own shares

(1) A lien or other charge of a public company on its own shares (whether taken expressly or otherwise) is void, except as permitted by this section.

(2) In the case of any description of company, a charge is permitted if the shares are not fully paid up and the charge is for an amount payable in respect of the shares.

(3) In the case of a company whose ordinary business-
    (a) includes the lending of money, or
    (b) consists of the provision of credit or the bailment (in Scotland, hiring) of goods under a hire-purchase agreement, or both,

a charge is permitted (whether the shares are fully paid or not) if it arises in connection with a transaction entered into by the company in the ordinary course of that business.

(4) In the case of a company that has been re-registered as a public company, a charge is permitted if it was in existence immediately before the application for re-registration.

GENERAL NOTE

This section restates s.150 of the 1985 Act with no changes of substance. It is derived from Art.23 of the Second EC Directive (79/91/EEC). In subs.(1) it prohibits public companies from taking liens or charges against their own shares.

There are three permitted exceptions: a lien for unpaid calls or instalments on those shares (subs.(2)); a lien of a lending or credit company arising in the ordinary course of business (subs.(3)); and a lien created by a private company prior to re-registration as a public company (subs.(4)).

Supplementary provisions

671.   Interests to be disregarded in determining whether company has beneficial interest

In determining for the purposes of this Chapter whether a company has a beneficial interest in shares, there shall be disregarded any such interest as is mentioned in-

> section 672 (residual interest under pension scheme or employees' share scheme),
> section 673 (employer's charges and other rights of recovery), or
> section 674 (rights as personal representative or trustee).

GENERAL NOTE

This section, together with ss.685-689, restates Sch.2 to the 1985 Act allowing certain interests of a company in its own shares to be treated other than as beneficial interests in those shares for the purposes of the restrictions and obligations of this Chapter (see ss.660-662 and 688-689).

The origin of these provisions (which are also further restated in relation to s.136 *et seq.* of this Act) was the Companies (Beneficial Interests) Act 1983. That Act was passed to avoid complications arising when corporate pension and employee share schemes invested in the shares of the employer company, usually through a subsidiary or trust deed. It was realised that certain residual interests for the company under such schemes could be regarded as beneficial interests (even though not in possession) and so render such purchases void, etc. unless they were excluded. This was effected by the 1983 Act both retrospectively and prospectively.

This section provides for the disregard of such interests as set out in the following three sections.

Pension schemes are defined in s.675 and *employee share schemes* in s.1166.

672.   Residual interest under pension scheme or employees' share scheme

(1) Where the shares are held on trust for the purposes of a pension scheme or employees' share scheme, there shall be disregarded any residual interest of the company that has not vested in possession.

(2) A "residual interest" means a right of the company to receive any of the trust property in the event of-
  (a) all the liabilities arising under the scheme having been satisfied or provided for, or
  (b) the company ceasing to participate in the scheme, or
  (c) the trust property at any time exceeding what is necessary for satisfying the liabilities arising or expected to arise under the scheme.

(3) In subsection (2)-
  (a) the reference to a right includes a right dependent on the exercise of a discretion vested by the scheme in the trustee or another person, and
  (b) the reference to liabilities arising under a scheme includes liabilities that have resulted, or may result, from the exercise of any such discretion.

(4) For the purposes of this section a residual interest vests in possession-
  (a) in a case within subsection (2)(a), on the occurrence of the event mentioned there (whether or not the amount of the property receivable pursuant to the right is ascertained);
  (b) in a case within subsection (2)(b) or (c), when the company becomes entitled to require the trustee to transfer to it any of the property receivable pursuant to that right.

(5) Where by virtue of this section shares are exempt from section 660 or 661 (shares held by company's nominee) at the time they are taken, issued or acquired but the residual interest in question vests in possession before they are disposed of or fully paid up, those sections apply to the shares as if they had been taken, issued or acquired on the date on which that interest vests in possession.

(6) Where by virtue of this section shares are exempt from sections 662 to 668 (shares held by or for public company) at the time they are acquired but the residual interest in question vests in

possession before they are disposed of, those sections apply to the shares as if they had been acquired on the date on which the interest vests in possession.

GENERAL NOTE

This section restates, with no changes of substance, para.1 (except for sub-para.(5) which is spent) and sub-paras 2(1), (3) and (4) of Sch.2 to the 1985 Act (sub-para.(2) is not relevant here). It details the three residual interests commonly found in trust deeds when they occur in an employee share scheme or a pension scheme and excludes them from being beneficial interests of the company so long as they have not vested in possession. When, and if, they vest in possession they cease to be so excluded and are dealt with by subss.(5) and (6).

For *employee* see also s.676.

Subsections (1)-(3)

These subsections restate sub-paras 1(1)-(3) of Sch.2 to the 1985 Act. The three residual interests set out in subs.(2) are all standard clauses in trust deeds.

Disregard is limited, however, to *employee share schemes* (defined in s.1166) and *pension schemes* (defined in s.675).

Subsection (4)

This subsection defines when an interest in subs.(2) vests in possession for the purposes of disregard. Note that in para.(b) the company must be entitled to require the trustee to require transfer of the property to it. (Some guidance on this can be found in *Crowe v Appleby* [1975] 3 All E.R. 529 in another context).

Subsections (5) and (6)

These subsections restate sub-paras 2(1), (3) and (4) of Sch.2 to the 1985 Act. If a residual interest does vest in possession then in the case of shares held by a nominee subject to ss.660 and 661, those sections will operate from the vesting in possession date rather then the date of acquisition of the interest. In the case of the duty to cancel shares and to re-register as a private company under s.662 *et seq.*, if applicable those sections will also operate as from the date of vesting in possession.

673. Employer's charges and other rights of recovery

(1) Where the shares are held on trust for the purposes of a pension scheme there shall be disregarded-

    (a) any charge or lien on, or set-off against, any benefit or other right or interest under the scheme for the purpose of enabling the employer or former employer of a member of the scheme to obtain the discharge of a monetary obligation due to him from the member;

    (b) any right to receive from the trustee of the scheme, or as trustee of the scheme to retain, an amount that can be recovered or retained-

        (i) under section 61 of the Pension Schemes Act 1993 (c. 48), or otherwise, as reimbursement or partial reimbursement for any contributions equivalent premium paid in connection with the scheme under Part 3 of that Act, or

        (ii) under section 57 of the Pension Schemes (Northern Ireland) Act 1993 (c. 49), or otherwise, as reimbursement or partial reimbursement for any contributions equivalent premium paid in connection with the scheme under Part 3 of that Act.

(2) Where the shares are held on trust for the purposes of an employees' share scheme, there shall be disregarded any charge or lien on, or set-off against, any benefit or other right or interest under the scheme for the purpose of enabling the employer or former employer of a member of the scheme to obtain the discharge of a monetary obligation due to him from the member.

GENERAL NOTE

This section restates, without any substantive changes, relevant parts of para.3 of Sch.2 to the 1985 Act as amended. As such it provides a disregard for this Chapter of certain rights of recovery for a company in a pension scheme (see s.675) or employee share scheme (see s.1166) holding, directly or indirectly, that company's shares. For "employee" see also s.676.

Subsections (1) (a) and (2)

These subsections apply the same criteria to both pension and employee share schemes. They provide a disregard for rights of recovery for debts owed by an employee to the company against the fund. Such rights may be against any benefit, right or other interest of the employee in the fund whatsoever.

Subsection (1) (b)

This subsection applies only to pension schemes. The right of recovery under s.61 of the Pension Schemes Act 1993 relates to the situation where an earner's service in contracted-out employment is terminated and he is entitled to a refund of benefits so that a "contributions equivalent premium" falls to be paid to any person in respect of him. The person by who the premium falls to be paid (in this case the employer company) is entitled on paying it to recover a certified amount from the pension fund.

The other rights, "or otherwise" in this sub-paragraph relate to the right of recovery of state scheme premiums.

674.   Rights as personal representative or trustee

Where the company is a personal representative or trustee, there shall be disregarded any rights that the company has in that capacity including, in particular-

> (a) any right to recover its expenses or be remunerated out of the estate or trust property, and
>
> (b) any right to be indemnified out of that property for any liability incurred by reason of any act or omission of the company in the performance of its duties as personal representative or trustee.

GENERAL NOTE

This section restates para.4(1) of Sch.2 to the 1985 Act. Unlike the previous sections it applies to all trusts. In effect it provides a disregard from being a beneficial interest for a corporate trustee's (or PR's) rights as such under the trust which holds that company's shares. These would include the standard trustee indemnity and charging clauses found in most trust deeds.

675.   Meaning of "pension scheme"

(1) In this Chapter "pension scheme" means a scheme for the provision of benefits consisting of or including relevant benefits for or in respect of employees or former employees.

(2) In subsection (1) "relevant benefits" means any pension, lump sum, gratuity or other like benefit given or to be given on retirement or on death or in anticipation of retirement or, in connection with past service, after retirement or death.

GENERAL NOTE

This section directly re-enacts sub-paras 5(1) and (2) of Sch.2 to the 1985 Act and defines a pension scheme for the purposes of ss.672 and 673. Employee share scheme is defined in s.1166 for the whole Act.

676.   Application of provisions to directors

For the purposes of this Chapter references to "employer" and "employee", in the context of a pension scheme or employees' share scheme, shall be read as if a director of a company were employed by it.

GENERAL NOTE

This section restates sub-para.5(3) of Sch.2 to the 1985 Act. For the purposes of ss.672 and 673, a director is always treated as an employee of the company, even if he has no service contract.

FINANCIAL ASSISTANCE FOR PURCHASE OF OWN SHARES

GENERAL NOTE

This chapter is derived from Ch.VI of Pt V of the Companies Act 1985. The most significant change is that the ban on the giving of financial assistance no longer applies to private companies. After some initial hesitation (*Company Formation and Capital Maintenance* (URN 99/1145), para.3.42) the CLR threw its weight behind the "radical" suggestion for outright repeal of the restrictions on financial assistance in relation to private companies (*Developing the Framework* (URN 00/656), para.7.25; *Completing the Structure* (URN 00/1335), para.7.12, *Final Report* ((URN 01/942), para.10.6). This recommendation was accepted by the government as part of its package of deregulation for private companies (White Paper (March 2005) p.41). The rules on maintenance of capital continue to apply to private companies. It is possible that some corporate actions that would have infringed the ban on financial assistance will remain unlawful notwithstanding its repeal for private companies because they are also contrary to the maintenance of capital regime. An attempt by the opposition to insert a provision into the legislation that would have provided a clear safe harbour from maintenance of capital concerns for financial assistance given a private company provided that any reduction in net assets was covered by distributable reserves or authorised as a reduction of capital was rejected by the government (*Hansard*, Standing Committee D, cols 864-865 (July 20, 2006)). An alternative proposed amendment that declared the giving of financial assistance by a private company to be lawful, which would have overridden maintenance of capital principles, also failed (*Hansard*, cols GC22-25 (March 20, 2006)). The concern underlying these proposed amendments was to ensure that actions that could have been entered into lawfully under the private company "whitewash" regime in s.155 of the 1985 Act would not be at risk of being held illegal under the common law maintenance of capital principle, a result that would have been at odds with the intended deregulatory purpose of abolishing the ban on financial assistance by private companies. Although not convinced that there was a problem with the common law, the government eventually agreed to make it clear in a saving provision under s.1296 (Power to make transitional provision and savings) that the removal of the prohibition on private companies giving financial assistance for a purchase of own shares would not prevent private companies entering into transactions which they could lawfully have entered into under the "whitewash" procedure (Lord Sainsbury, *Hansard*, HL Vol 686, cols 443-444 (November 2, 2006)).

Only modest refinements are made to the ban on the giving of financial assistance by public companies. Radical deregulation was not an option in relation to public companies because the Second Company Law Directive (77/91/EEC), Art.23 requires Member States to ban the giving of financial assistance by public companies. Directive 2006/68/EC of the European Parliament and of the Council of September 6, 2006 amending Council Directive 77/91/EEC, as regards the formation and public limited liability companies and the maintenance of their capital proposes revises Art.23 by inserting a new "gateway" procedure which will permit public companies to give financial assistance on certain conditions. When this gateway procedure was published in draft form the British Government's view was that the conditions subject to which financial assistance could be given were complex and onerous and were therefore unlikely to be utilised by companies (DTI, *Directive Proposals on Company Reporting, Capital Maintenance and Transfer of the Registered Office of a Company: A Consultative Document* (March 2005) para.3.4.2). The final version does not contain all of the conditions that were suggested in the original published draft but the gateway still remains subject to requirements that are likely to undermine its practical utility. These conditions include a requirement to obtain prior shareholder approval on a transaction-by-transaction basis, which in the view of the government, is unworkable in the context of most corporate transactions where financial assistance is an issue (ibid).

In 1996 and 1997, the DTI made proposals to improve the drafting of the sections on financial assistance, as follows (as summarised in *Company Formation and Capital Maintenance* (URN 99/1145) paras 3.42 and 3.43):

- reformulation of "principal purpose" exception to the ban on the giving of financial assistance;
- clarification that assistance by the foreign subsidiary of a British company is not caught;
- removal of unlimited companies from the scope of the prohibition (subject to certain safeguards);
- significant revision of the ban on post-acquisition assistance;
- removal of the sanction against the company for breach of the prohibition;
- express stipulation that transactions in breach of the prohibition should no longer be void for that reason alone;
- a new exception for payments of commissions, fees and indemnities and warranties for underwriting share issues;
- a new exception for financial assistance for a transaction which is itself the subject of an exception; and
- widening of the exception for financial assistance for the purpose of an employee share scheme.

These proposals were supported by the CLR. However, the opportunity was not taken to implement them fully in the Companies Act 2006. In the March 2005 White Paper the government said that it believed that it would be beneficial to introduce greater flexibility into the capital maintenance regime for public companies, but that in advance of significant amendments to the EU legislation it would not be possible to make major changes to United Kingdom capital maintenance regime. Furthermore, it said that while the CLR had recommended a number of technical changes to the rules on financial assistance by public companies, the government would instead seek to give priority to the CLR's overarching recommendation for fundamental reform of the capital maintenance regime through reform of the Second Company Law Directive (White Paper, pp.42-43). If the rather limited changes to the Second Directive made by Directive 2006/68/EC are anything to go by, it would be over-optimistic to expect radical change at the EU level in the short term. However, that Directive does give some hope to the proponents of fundamental reform by the inclusion of a recital to the effect that although modernisation and simplification of the Second Directive have first priority, this does not affect the need to proceed without delay to a general examination of the feasibility of alternatives to the capital maintenance regime which would adequately protect the interests of creditors and shareholders of a public limited liability company.

Introductory

677. Meaning of "financial assistance"

(1) In this Chapter "financial assistance" means-
    (a) financial assistance given by way of gift,
    (b) financial assistance given-
       (i) by way of guarantee, security or indemnity (other than an indemnity in respect of the indemnifier's own neglect or default), or
       (ii) by way of release or waiver,
    (c) financial assistance given-
       (i) by way of a loan or any other agreement under which any of the obligations of the person giving the assistance are to be fulfilled at a time when in accordance with the agreement any obligation of another party to the agreement remains unfulfilled, or
       (ii) by way of the novation of, or the assignment (in Scotland, assignation) of rights arising under, a loan or such other agreement, or
    (d) any other financial assistance given by a company where-
       (i) the net assets of the company are reduced to a material extent by the giving of the assistance, or
       (ii) the company has no net assets.
(2) "Net assets" here means the aggregate amount of the company's assets less the aggregate amount of its liabilities.
(3) For this purpose a company's liabilities include-
    (a) where the company draws up Companies Act individual accounts, any provision of a kind specified for the purposes of this subsection by regulations under section 396, and
    (b) where the company draws up IAS individual accounts, any provision made in those accounts.

GENERAL NOTE

    This section, together with s.683, provides the definition for the purposes of this chapter. There are no changes of substance between this section and those parts of s.152 of the Companies Act 1985 that it re-enacts.

    It remains the case that there is no definitive list of the forms of financial assistance that are prohibited because the statutory list, in this section, concludes with a catch-all provision covering "any other financial assistance". Cases on the need to examine the commercial substance of transactions to see whether they provide assistance that is financial in nature continue to apply: see, e.g. *Charterhouse v Tempest Diesels* [1986] B.C.L.C. 1; *Barclays Bank Plc v British & Commonwealth Holdings Plc* [1996] 1 B.C.L.C. 1, CA; *Chaston v SWP Group Plc* [2003] 1 B.C.L.C. 675, CA.

Subsection (1)

    The scope of the various forms of financial assistance listed in this subsection has been considered in a line of cases that continues to apply. The cases include: *Hill and Tyler Ltd (in administration); Harlow v Loveday, Re* [2005] 1 B.C.L.C. 41 (a charge to secure a loan which was on-lent to financially assist the acquisition of shares was a form of unlawful financial assistance (see subs.(1)(b)(i)); *Barclays Bank Plc v British & Commonwealth Holdings Plc* [1996] 1 B.C.L.C. 1, CA (the expression "indemnity" in this context carries its precise legal meaning of a contract by one party to keep the other harmless against loss (see subs.(1)(b)(i)); *Parlett v Guppys Bridport Ltd* [1996] 2 B.C.L.C. 34 (materiality in subs.(1)(d)(i) is a question of degree).

Subsection (3)

This subsection provides alternatives for determining liabilities depending on whether a company draws up its individual accounts in accordance with the requirements of the Companies Acts or in accordance with International Accounting Standards/International Financial Reporting Standards. The shift to IAS/IFRS (which are now mandatory for the consolidated accounts of companies that are admitted to trading on an EU regulated market) led to the companies legislation being amended by the Companies Act 1985 (International Accounting Standards and Other Accounting Amendments) Regulations 2004 (SI 2004/2947), as from November 12, 2004 in relation to companies' financial years which began on or after January 1, 2005.

Circumstances in which financial assistance prohibited

678. Assistance for acquisition of shares in public company

(1) Where a person is acquiring or proposing to acquire shares in a public company, it is not lawful for that company, or a company that is a subsidiary of that company, to give financial assistance directly or indirectly for the purpose of the acquisition before or at the same time as the acquisition takes place.

(2) Subsection (1) does not prohibit a company from giving financial assistance for the acquisition of shares in it or its holding company if-

    (a) the company's principal purpose in giving the assistance is not to give it for the purpose of any such acquisition, or

    (b) the giving of the assistance for that purpose is only an incidental part of some larger purpose of the company,

and the assistance is given in good faith in the interests of the company.

(3) Where-

    (a) a person has acquired shares in a company, and

    (b) a liability has been incurred (by that or another person) for the purpose of the acquisition,

it is not lawful for that company, or a company that is a subsidiary of that company, to give financial assistance directly or indirectly for the purpose of reducing or discharging the liability if, at the time the assistance is given, the company in which the shares were acquired is a public company.

(4) Subsection (3) does not prohibit a company from giving financial assistance if-

    (a) the company's principal purpose in giving the assistance is not to reduce or discharge any liability incurred by a person for the purpose of the acquisition of shares in the company or its holding company, or

    (b) the reduction or discharge of any such liability is only an incidental part of some larger purpose of the company,

and the assistance is given in good faith in the interests of the company.

(5) This section has effect subject to sections 681 and 682 (unconditional and conditional exceptions to prohibition).

GENERAL NOTE

This section is based on s.151 of the Companies Act 1985, but it applies only to the acquisition of shares of public companies. It also re-states the "principal" and "larger" purposes exemptions that were previously found in s.153(1)-(2); this is a presentational change rather than a change of substance.

Subsection (1)

This subsection is concerned with financial assistance for the purpose of a share acquisition that is proposed or which would be contemporaneous with the share acquisition.

In the Parliamentary debate on this provision Vera Baird MP, speaking on behalf of the government, said that, in its view, the references to "person" did not include the company itself (*Hansard*, Standing Committee D, cols 856-857 (July 20,

2006)). The judgment of Arden L.J. in *Chaston v. SWP Group plc* [2002] EWCA Civ 1999; [2003] 1 B.C.L.C. 675, CA, had appeared to contemplate that a company could provide assistance to itself, but the government did not accept that interpretation of the relevant passage in the judgment. Furthermore, the government suggested that to include the company within the scope of person to whom the company could not give financial assistance would be "at odds" with the Second Directive which envisages a person being a third party and not the company itself.

The ban on financially assisting the acquisition of own shares applies to public companies and also to their subsidiaries (whether public or private) provided that those subsidiaries are "companies". The proviso means that foreign subsidiaries are not within the scope of the ban because they are not "companies" as that term is defined by s.1 of the 2006 Act (Lord Sainsbury, *Hansard*, HL Vol.686, col.443 (November 2, 2006)). The effect of the proviso, which is new, is to codify the decision in *Arab Bank Plc v Merchantile Holdings Ltd* [1994] Ch. 71.

Subsection (2)

This subsection provides that subs.(1) does not apply where there is a "larger" or "principal" purpose alongside the purpose of giving financial assistance, provided that the assistance is given in good faith in the interests of the company. The decision of the House of Lords in *Brady v Brady* [1989] A.C. 755 continues to apply and this means that these exemptions have a very narrow scope.

The CLR had supported reformulation of the principal purpose exemption, which was an idea that had its origins in concerns that the House of Lords had interpreted the old exemption too narrowly in *Brady v Brady*. During the Parliamentary passage of the Companies Act 2006 Lord Sainsbury explained why the government had decided not to depart from the wording in the Companies Act 1985:

> "The concern is that the courts have interpreted the words "principal purpose" too narrowly and it is proposed that those words should be substituted by the words 'predominant reason' ... or 'dominant reason' ...
>
> WhileI recognise that the formulation of words used in the 1985 Act has been the subject of judicial analysis at the highest level, it is difficult to see why the proposed amendments would make any difference. In particular, the Government are not convinced that the suggested wording means anything other than that which is intended by the current wording. Notwithstanding that, it is accepted that the substitution of one set of words with another could signal that the Government intended a different interpretation. If that is, indeed, the effect of the proposed amendments, it may lead to undesirable results. What would be needed is not the substitution of one pair of words, which, on the face of it, mean the same as another pair of words, but a reworking of the provision so as to have the intended effect. I am afraid that I am not clear what effect that should be (Lord Sainsbury, *Hansard*, col.GC24, (March 20, 2006)).
>
> Wehave discussed this issue at some length ... but have not been persuaded that any transactions which companies might wish to enter into, and which would be compatible with the second directive, fall outside the current test but within the suggested reformulated exception.
>
> Ifwe are to take this matter forward, a clear indication is required of the intended effect of the suggested words rather than the substitution of one pair of words by another pair, which, on the face of it, mean the same. In other words, we cannot have a rational debate about this subject unless we can agree about the difference between 'principal purpose' and 'predominant reason'. Until we can agree that, we cannot debate whether things that we all might want to do would be allowed by the change.
>
> AsI commented in Grand Committee, this may point to a reworking of the provision so as to have the intended effect. Such a new provision could refer to concepts along the current lines or may be framed on an entirely different basis so long as it remained consistent with the implementation of Art.23 of the second company directive. In this connection I would remind noble Lords that the Government are proposing to take a power to make, by secondary legislation, provisions relating to capital maintenance and we believe that such a reworking would be more suitably addressed by use of that power than by piecemeal amendment to the existing sections" (Lord Sainsbury, *Hansard*, Vol.682, col.182 (May 16, 2006)).

Subsection (3)

This subsection relates to post-acquisition financial assistance. It makes it clear that the ban on post acquisition financial assistance applies only where the company whose shares have been acquired is a public company at the time when the assistance is given. This ensures that the ban on financial assistance does not affect refinancing activity relating to a public company that has been taken over so long as the acquired company is re-registered as a private company before the refinancing takes place. If a private company were to be acquired and then reregistered as a public company, this subsection would apply to any restructuring of the acquisition financing.

This subsection provides that subs.(3) does not apply where there is a "larger" or "principal" purpose alongside the purpose of giving financial assistance, provided that the assistance is given in good faith in the interests of the company. The decision of the House of Lords in *Brady v Brady* [1989] A.C. 755 makes it hard to identify clear circumstances in which either of these exemptions will apply.

679. Assistance by public company for acquisition of shares in its private holding company

(1) Where a person is acquiring or proposing to acquire shares in a private company, it is not lawful for a public company that is a subsidiary of that company to give financial assistance directly or indirectly for the purpose of the acquisition before or at the same time as the acquisition takes place.

(2) Subsection (1) does not prohibit a company from giving financial assistance for the acquisition of shares in its holding company if-

    (a) the company's principal purpose in giving the assistance is not to give it for the purpose of any such acquisition, or

    (b) the giving of the assistance for that purpose is only an incidental part of some larger purpose of the company,

and the assistance is given in good faith in the interests of the company.

(3) Where-

    (a) a person has acquired shares in a private company, and

    (b) a liability has been incurred (by that or another person) for the purpose of the acquisition,

it is not lawful for a public company that is a subsidiary of that company to give financial assistance directly or indirectly for the purpose of reducing or discharging the liability.

(4) Subsection (3) does not prohibit a company from giving financial assistance if-

    (a) the company's principal purpose in giving the assistance is not to reduce or discharge any liability incurred by a person for the purpose of the acquisition of shares in its holding company, or

    (b) the reduction or discharge of any such liability is only an incidental part of some larger purpose of the company,

and the assistance is given in good faith in the interests of the company.

(5) This section has effect subject to sections 681 and 682 (unconditional and conditional exceptions to prohibition).

GENERAL NOTE

This new section is consequential upon the repeal of the ban on the giving of financial assistance by private companies. It remains an offence, as this section makes clear, for a public company that is a subsidiary of a private company to give financial assistance for the acquisition of shares in its parent. The substantive contents of this section track those of s.678, save as noted.

Although the matter is not entirely free from doubt, it appears that it is at the time when the assistance is given that the parent company must be a private company. Any other interpretation would mean that where a public company is acquired and later reregistered as a private company (thus falling outside s.678(3))), any financial assistance given thereafter by a subsidiary that is a public company would fall outside the scope of the ban.

680. Prohibited financial assistance an offence

(1) If a company contravenes section 678(1) or (3) or section 679(1) or (3) (prohibited financial assistance) an offence is committed by-

    (a) the company, and

    (b) every officer of the company who is in default.

(2) A person guilty of an offence under this section is liable-

    (a) on conviction on indictment, to imprisonment for a term not exceeding two years or a fine (or both);

    (b) on summary conviction-

        (i) in England and Wales, to imprisonment for a term not exceeding twelve months or to a fine not exceeding the statutory maximum (or both);

        (ii) in Scotland or Northern Ireland, to imprisonment for a term not exceeding six months, or to a fine not exceeding the statutory maximum (or both).

GENERAL NOTE

The CLR considered decriminalising some offences, including the giving of financial assistance and giving greater emphasis to administrative penalties (*Completing the Structure* (URN 00/1335), para.13.42). Consultation elicited mixed views and in the end the CLR recommended retention of criminal sanctions for financial assistance because it was not convinced that an approach based on civil penalties and the market abuse provisions of the Financial Services and Market Act 2000 would work (*Final Report* (URN 01/942) para.15.18). According to the government spokesperson in the Parliamentary debate on the Companies Act 2006, it was appropriate to retain criminal sanctions for financial assistance because offences were less likely to be committed if they were backed up by criminal penalties (Vera Baird MP, *Hansard*, Standing Committee D, cols 858-860 (July 20, 2006)). In the government's view, criminal sanctions were appropriate, proportionate and essential for effective enforcement of breaches, but the underlying threat of prosecution enabled authorities to exercise a progressive approach to enforcement that secured compliance without prosecution (ibid).

In its general consideration of sanctions, the CLR suggested a presumption against liability on the company where both (i) the act was capable of seriously damaging the company, and (ii) making the responsible individuals criminally liable was likely to be a sufficient deterrent (Final Report ((URN 01/942) para.15.36). In the Explanatory Notes on the Act, the approach that the government eventually adopted is explained in the following terms:

> "1435. The general principle adopted as to whether a company should be liable for a breach of the requirements of Companies Acts is that where the only victims of the offence are the company or its members, the company should not be liable for the offence. On the other hand, where members or the company are potential victims, but not the only ones, then the company should be potentially liable for a breach.
>
> 1364.All the offences in the Companies Acts, both those in the Bill and those that remain in the 1985 Act, have been reviewed in the light of this principle."

The prohibition on the giving of financial assistance is intended to protect creditors as well as shareholders. It is therefore an example of conduct for which the corporate criminal liability is not ruled out under the general principle.

Subsection (2)

The rather odd fact that the maximum penalty on summary conviction for giving unlawful financial assistance is tougher in England and Wales than in Scotland and Northern Ireland is explained by the fact that criminal law sentencing is a devolved matter and Scotland and Northern Ireland have not followed the changes introduced by the Criminal Justice Act 2003, which increase the sentencing powers of magistrate courts in England and Wales from six to 12 months. The government saw no reason to limit sentencing powers on summary conviction in England and Wales (Lord Sainsbury, *Hansard*, col.GC20 (March 20, 2006); Margaret Hodge MP, *Hansard*, Standing Committee D, cols 863-864 (July 20, 2006)).

Exceptions from prohibition

681. Unconditional exceptions

(1) Neither section 678 nor section 679 prohibits a transaction to which this section applies.

(2) Those transactions are-

    (a) a distribution of the company's assets by way of-

        (i) dividend lawfully made, or

        (ii) distribution in the course of a company's winding up;

    (b) an allotment of bonus shares;

    (c) a reduction of capital under Chapter 10 of Part 17;

(d) a redemption of shares under Chapter 3 or a purchase of shares under Chapter 4 of this Part;

(e) anything done in pursuance of an order of the court under Part 26 (order sanctioning compromise or arrangement with members or creditors);

(f) anything done under an arrangement made in pursuance of section 110 of the Insolvency Act 1986 (c. 45) or Article 96 of the Insolvency (Northern Ireland) Order 1989 (S.I. 1989/2405 (N.I. 19)) (liquidator in winding up accepting shares as consideration for sale of company's property);

(g) anything done under an arrangement made between a company and its creditors that is binding on the creditors by virtue of Part 1 of the Insolvency Act 1986 or Part 2 of the Insolvency (Northern Ireland) Order 1989 (S.I. 1989/2405 (N.I. 19)).

GENERAL NOTE

This section re-enacts, with only minor drafting changes, the exceptions to the prohibition on the giving of financial assistance that were previously found in s.153(3) of the 1985 Act. The nine specific transactions are all otherwise permitted under company law.

Subsection (2)

The references to Northern Ireland in paras (f) and (g) are new and are consequential upon the decision to extend the Companies Acts to the province.

682. Conditional exceptions

(1) Neither section 678 nor section 679 prohibits a transaction to which this section applies-
  (a) if the company giving the assistance is a private company, or
  (b) if the company giving the assistance is a public company and-
    (i) the company has net assets that are not reduced by the giving of the assistance, or
    (ii) to the extent that those assets are so reduced, the assistance is provided out of distributable profits.

(2) The transactions to which this section applies are-
  (a) where the lending of money is part of the ordinary business of the company, the lending of money in the ordinary course of the company's business;
  (b) the provision by the company, in good faith in the interests of the company or its holding company, of financial assistance for the purposes of an employees' share scheme;
  (c) the provision of financial assistance by the company for the purposes of or in connection with anything done by the company (or another company in the same group) for the purpose of enabling or facilitating transactions in shares in the first-mentioned company or its holding company between, and involving the acquisition of beneficial ownership of those shares by-
    (i) bona fide employees or former employees of that company (or another company in the same group), or
    (ii) spouses or civil partners, widows, widowers or surviving civil partners, or minor children or step-children of any such employees or former employees;
  (d) the making by the company of loans to persons (other than directors) employed in good faith by the company with a view to enabling those persons to acquire fully paid shares in the company or its holding company to be held by them by way of beneficial ownership.

(3) The references in this section to "net assets" are to the amount by which the aggregate of the company's assets exceeds the aggregate of its liabilities.

(4) For this purpose-
  (a) the amount of both assets and liabilities shall be taken to be as stated in the company's accounting records immediately before the financial assistance is given, and

(b) "liabilities" includes any amount retained as reasonably necessary for the purpose of providing for a liability the nature of which is clearly defined and that is either likely to be incurred or certain to be incurred but uncertain as to amount or as to the date on which it will arise.

(5) For the purposes of subsection (2)(c) a company is in the same group as another company if it is a holding company or subsidiary of that company or a subsidiary of a holding company of that company.

GENERAL NOTE

This section contains the exceptions for loans as part of the ordinary course of business and employee share schemes that were previously found in s.153 of the 1985 Act. As was previously the case, these exceptions operate more restrictively in relation to public companies than in relation to private companies (which will only be affected by these provisions to the extent that financial assistance law continues to apply to private companies, that is for private companies within corporate groups that also include public companies).

Subsection (1)

Subsection 682(1)(b), which has the effect of restricting for public companies the exceptions provided by the section, is a re-enactment of s.154(1) of the Companies Act 1985. It gives effect to the Second Directive, Art.23.2, which provides that the giving of financial assistance in these circumstances is only permissible so long as it does not have the effect of reducing net assets below the amount of the subscribed capital and the undistributable reserves. This subsection has to be read with s.683, which defines "distributable profits" for the purposes of this Chapter.

Subsection (2)

This is a re-enactment of s.153(4) of the Companies Act 1985.

Subsections (3) and (4)

These subsections re-enact s.154(2) of the Companies Act 1985.

Subsection (5)

This subsection re-enacts s.153(5) of the Companies Act 1985.

Supplementary

683.　Definitions for this Chapter

(1) In this Chapter-

　　"distributable profits", in relation to the giving of any financial assistance-

　　　(a) means those profits out of which the company could lawfully make a distribution equal in value to that assistance, and

　　　(b) includes, in a case where the financial assistance consists of or includes, or is treated as arising in consequence of, the sale, transfer or other disposition of a non-cash asset, any profit that, if the company were to make a distribution of that character would be available for that purpose (see section 846); and

　　"distribution" has the same meaning as in Part 23 (distributions) (see section 829).

(2) In this Chapter-

　　　(a) a reference to a person incurring a liability includes his changing his financial position by making an agreement or arrangement (whether enforceable or unenforceable, and whether made on his own account or with any other person) or by any other means, and

　　　(b) a reference to a company giving financial assistance for the purposes of reducing or discharging a liability incurred by a person for the purpose of the acquisition of shares includes its giving such assistance for the purpose of wholly or partly restoring his financial position to what it was before the acquisition took place.

GENERAL NOTE

This is a definitional section that re-enacts, without substantive change, equivalent provisions of the Companies Act 1985.

Subsection (1)

These definitions of "distributable profits" and "distribution" are re-enactments of definitions previously contained in s.152(1)(b) and (c) of the Companies Act 1985.

Subsection (2)

These explanations were previously contained in s.152(3) of the Companies Act 1985.

CHAPTER 3

REDEEMABLE SHARES

684. Power of limited company to issue redeemable shares

(1) A limited company having a share capital may issue shares that are to be redeemed or are liable to be redeemed at the option of the company or the shareholder ("redeemable shares"), subject to the following provisions.

(2) The articles of a private limited company may exclude or restrict the issue of redeemable shares.

(3) A public limited company may only issue redeemable shares if it is authorised to do so by its articles.

(4) No redeemable shares may be issued at a time when there are no issued shares of the company that are not redeemable.

GENERAL NOTE

This Chapter replaces ss.159 and 160 of the 1985 Act as to the ability of companies generally to issue redeemable shares, originally introduced by the 1981 Act. (There was a limited power in the 1948 Act.) Unlike other Chapters in this Part, this replacement predated the restatement exercise (see the General Note to the Act) and was in the Bill before it reached the House of Commons. The restated sections therefore contain a number of amendments to the 1985 legislation based on recommendations of the CLR.

This section restates parts of s.159, but with substantive amendments, as to the basic power to issue of redeemable shares.

Subsection (1)

This subsection restates s.159(1) of the 1985 Act, subject to the changes in subss.(2) and (3) below. The power is still available to guarantee companies with a share capital which were formed prior to the 1980 Act. As before, redemption may be at the option of either the company or shareholder.

Subsections (2) and (3)

These new subsections limit the former prerequisite in s.159(1) of the 1985 Act of needing authority to issue redeemable shares in the articles to public companies. Private companies may, however, restrict or limit the authority in their articles.

Subsection (4)

This subsection restates s.159(2) of the 1985 Act - a company cannot redeem itself out of existence.

685. Terms and manner of redemption

(1) The directors of a limited company may determine the terms, conditions and manner of redemption of shares if they are authorised to do so-

    (a) by the company's articles, or

   (b) by a resolution of the company.

(2) A resolution under subsection (1)(b) may be an ordinary resolution, even though it amends the company's articles.

(3) Where the directors are authorised under subsection (1) to determine the terms, conditions and manner of redemption of shares-

   (a) they must do so before the shares are allotted, and

   (b) any obligation of the company to state in a statement of capital the rights attached to the shares extends to the terms, conditions and manner of redemption.

(4) Where the directors are not so authorised, the terms, conditions and manner of redemption of any redeemable shares must be stated in the company's articles.

GENERAL NOTE

    This new section follows a recommendation of the CLR (see *Final Report*, para.4.5) It replaces s.160(3) of the 1985 Act which provided that the terms and manner of redemption had to be fixed by the articles.

    Under this new section the directors of both public and private companies can determine the terms and manner of redemption if they are authorised to do so either under the articles or by an ordinary resolution. (Note subs.(2) which allows such a resolution to amend the articles if necessary, by way of exception to s.21). Only if the directors are not so authorised will the previous rule apply (subs.(4)).

Subsection (3)

    This subsection ensures both that the terms, etc. of redemption are defined before the shares are allotted and that the details of such terms, etc. will be on the register as part of the statement of capital which must be sent to the registrar when the shares are allotted under s.555 (see CLR *Final Report*, para.7.30).

686.   Payment for redeemable shares

(1) Redeemable shares in a limited company may not be redeemed unless they are fully paid.

(2) The terms of redemption of shares in a limited company may provide that the amount payable on redemption may, by agreement between the company and the holder of the shares, be paid on a date later than the redemption date.

(3) Unless redeemed in accordance with a provision authorised by subsection (2), the shares must be paid for on redemption.

GENERAL NOTE

    This section replaces s.159(3) of the 1985 Act with an amendment. It repeats, in subs.(1), the previous requirement that the shares must be fully paid before they can be redeemed.

    However, in subs.(2) it provides an exception to the other 1985 Act requirement that payment for the shares must take place on redemption; now restated in subs.(3). If there is agreement between the company and the shareholder, payment may now be postponed to a later date.

687.   Financing of redemption

(1) A private limited company may redeem redeemable shares out of capital in accordance with Chapter 5.

(2) Subject to that, redeemable shares in a limited company may only be redeemed out of-

   (a) distributable profits of the company, or

   (b) the proceeds of a fresh issue of shares made for the purposes of the redemption.

(3) Any premium payable on redemption of shares in a limited company must be paid out of distributable profits of the company, subject to the following provision.

(4) If the redeemable shares were issued at a premium, any premium payable on their redemption may be paid out of the proceeds of a fresh issue of shares made for the purposes of the redemption, up to an amount equal to-

    (a) the aggregate of the premiums received by the company on the issue of the shares redeemed, or

    (b) the current amount of the company's share premium account (including any sum transferred to that account in respect of premiums on the new shares),

whichever is the less.

(5) The amount of the company's share premium account is reduced by a sum corresponding (or by sums in the aggregate corresponding) to the amount of any payment made under subsection (4).

(6) This section is subject to section 735(4) (terms of redemption enforceable in a winding up).

GENERAL NOTE

    This section restates s.160(1) and (2) of the 1985 Act with no substantive changes. It sets out the funds available for redemption. As before, it is subject to the ability of private companies to use capital (under Ch.5 of this Part) and to s.735(4) if there is a subsequent winding up (subs.(6)).

Subsection (2)

    The ability to use the proceeds of a fresh issue of shares is qualified by subss.(3)-(5) restating s.159(2) of the 1985 Act.

Subsections (3)-(5)

    These subsections apply where the shares were originally issued at a premium. The proceeds of a fresh issue may only be used to fund the redemption of any such premium payable on redemption up to the amount of the original premiums received on the issue of the shares or the amount of the company's share premium account at the time of the redemption, whichever is smaller. The first balances the company's capital funds. The second is necessary if charges have been made on that account in the meantime. That account must be reduced by the amount used.

    Distributable profits - see s.736

688. Redeemed shares treated as cancelled

Where shares in a limited company are redeemed-

    (a) the shares are treated as cancelled, and

    (b) the amount of the company's issued share capital is diminished accordingly by the nominal value of the shares redeemed.

GENERAL NOTE

    This section restates s.160(4) of the 1985 Act. The only modification is that references to a company's authorised capital have been deleted following the discontinuance of that concept by this Act.

    The cancellation, etc. of such shares is obligatory. Redeemed shares, as distinct from redeemable shares, cannot be held as treasury shares under Ch.6 of this part.

689. Notice to registrar of redemption

(1) If a limited company redeems any redeemable shares it must within one month after doing so give notice to the registrar, specifying the shares redeemed.

(2) The notice must be accompanied by a statement of capital.

(3) The statement of capital must state with respect to the company's share capital immediately following the redemption-

    (a) the total number of shares of the company,

    (b) the aggregate nominal value of those shares,

    (c) for each class of shares-

        (i) prescribed particulars of the rights attached to the shares,

        (ii) the total number of shares of that class, and

        (iii) the aggregate nominal value of shares of that class, and

    (d) the amount paid up and the amount (if any) unpaid on each share (whether on account of the nominal value of the share or by way of premium).

(4) If default is made in complying with this section, an offence is committed by-
    (a) the company, and
    (b) every officer of the company who is in default.

(5) A person guilty of an offence under this section is liable on summary conviction to a fine not exceeding level 3 on the standard scale and, for continued contravention, a daily default fine not exceeding one-tenth of level 3 on the standard scale.

GENERAL NOTE

This section restates the obligation, formerly in s.122(1)(e) of the 1985 Act, to notify the registrar of a redemption (and cancellation) of redeemable shares.

The wording has been modified to comply with the practice elsewhere in this Act to require registration of a statement of capital on all changes to a company's issued shares.

The offence in default is also modified to comply with the general treatment of such offences under this Act (see Sch.3).

CHAPTER 4

PURCHASE OF OWN SHARES

General provisions

690.   Power of limited company to purchase own shares

(1) A limited company having a share capital may purchase its own shares (including any redeemable shares), subject to-
    (a) the following provisions of this Chapter, and
    (b) any restriction or prohibition in the company's articles.

(2) A limited company may not purchase its own shares if as a result of the purchase there would no longer be any issued shares of the company other than redeemable shares or shares held as treasury shares.

GENERAL NOTE

This Chapter (ss.690-708) replaces ss.162-169A of the 1985 Act as to the ability of companies to purchase their own shares, originally introduced by the 1981 Act. Additional funding for private companies is provided for in the following Chapter; the ability of some listed companies to retain such shares as treasury shares is in Ch.6; and some additional consequences are set out in Ch.7.

Originally the Bill contained clauses amending the 1985 Act sections, but these were subsumed into this Chapter as part of the restatement exercise (see the General Note to the Act).

Subsection (1)

This subsection restates s.162(1) and (3) of the 1985 Act but with one amendment. As before the power is available to all companies with a share capital (including guarantee companies with such a capital formed before they were prohibited by the 1980 Act) and covers redeemable shares (e.g. if the time for redemption has not been reached). Also, as before, nothing is said as to a company taking compulsory powers of acquisition which remains an area of doubt.

The one change is that authority to purchase in the articles is no longer a prerequisite for a purchase. Instead the articles may limit or prohibit the power. There are to be transitional provisions for existing companies.

Subsection (2)

This subsection restates s.162(3) of the 1985 Act and prevents a company from being able to redeem itself out of existence. As such it mirrors s.684(4).

691. Payment for purchase of own shares

(1) A limited company may not purchase its own shares unless they are fully paid.

(2) Where a limited company purchases its own shares, the shares must be paid for on purchase.

GENERAL NOTE

This section, together with the following section, adapts the rules for payment of redeemable shares in ss.686 and 687 to payment of shares acquired under s.690. As such they replace the rather oblique wording of s.162(2) of the 1985 Act (except for the obligation to cancel the shares which is now in s.706).

This section differs from the treatment of redeemable shares in that payment for the shares must be made on purchase - it cannot be delayed, even by agreement; otherwise, however, the terms of the purchase are not prescribed: see, e.g. *Peña v Dale* [2004] 2 B.C.L.C. 508, (cf. s.699(2)): see HC Comm D 21st sitting, col.867 (July 20, 2006)). However, like redeemable shares the shares must be fully paid up.

Distributable profits - see s.736.

692. Financing of purchase of own shares

(1) A private limited company may purchase its own shares out of capital in accordance with Chapter 5.

(2) Subject to that-
    (a) a limited company may only purchase its own shares out of-
        (i) distributable profits of the company, or
        (ii) the proceeds of a fresh issue of shares made for the purpose of financing the purchase, and
    (b) any premium payable on the purchase by a limited company of its own shares must be paid out of distributable profits of the company, subject to subsection (3).

(3) If the shares to be purchased were issued at a premium, any premium payable on their purchase by the company may be paid out of the proceeds of a fresh issue of shares made for the purpose of financing the purchase, up to an amount equal to-
    (a) the aggregate of the premiums received by the company on the issue of the shares purchased, or
    (b) the current amount of the company's share premium account (including any sum transferred to that account in respect of premiums on the new shares),
whichever is the less.

(4) The amount of the company's share premium account is reduced by a sum corresponding (or by sums in the aggregate corresponding) to the amount of any payment made under subsection (3).

(5) This section has effect subject to section 735(4) (terms of purchase enforceable in a winding up).

GENERAL NOTE

This section almost directly replicates s.687 of this Act on the financing of redeemable shares (with the curious exception that it has one subsection less (subss.(2) and (3) of s.687 being merged here). Both sections restate s.160(1) and (2) (applied to purchases by s.162(2)) of the 1985 Act with no substantive changes.

As before, these rules are subject to the ability of private companies to use capital (under Ch.5 of this Part) and to s.735(4) on a subsequent winding up. Where profits are used a capital redemption reserve must be created: see s.733.

Subsection (2)

The ability to use the proceeds of a fresh issue of shares in (a) is qualified by (b) and subss.(3) and (4) restating s.159(2) of the 1985 Act as applied by s.162(2) of that Act.

Subsections (3) and (4)

These subsections apply where the shares were originally issued at a premium. The proceeds of a fresh issue may only be used to fund the redemption of any such premium payable on redemption up to the amount of the original premiums received on the issue of the shares or the amount of the company's share premium account at the time of the redemption, whichever is smaller. The first balances the company's capital funds. The second is necessary if charges have been made on that account in the meantime. That account must be reduced by the amount used.

Distributable profits - see s.736.

Authority for purchase of own shares

693.   Authority for purchase of own shares

(1) A limited company may only purchase its own shares-
>   (a) by an off-market purchase, in pursuance of a contract approved in advance in accordance with section 694;
>   (b) by a market purchase, authorised in accordance with section 701.

(2) A purchase is "off-market" if the shares either-
>   (a) are purchased otherwise than on a recognised investment exchange, or
>   (b) are purchased on a recognised investment exchange but are not subject to a marketing arrangement on the exchange.

(3) For this purpose a company's shares are subject to a marketing arrangement on a recognised investment exchange if-
>   (a) they are listed under Part 6 of the Financial Services and Markets Act 2000 (c. 8), or
>   (b) the company has been afforded facilities for dealings in the shares to take place on the exchange-
>>   (i) without prior permission for individual transactions from the authority governing that investment exchange, and
>>   (ii) without limit as to the time during which those facilities are to be available.

(4) A purchase is a "market purchase" if it is made on a recognised investment exchange and is not an off-market purchase by virtue of subsection (2)(b).

(5) In this section "recognised investment exchange" means a recognised investment exchange (within the meaning of Part 18 of the Financial Services and Markets Act 2000) other than an overseas exchange (within the meaning of that Part).

GENERAL NOTE

This section restates, without any substantive changes, s.163 and part of s.164(1) of the 1985 Act. As such it continues the distinction between the procedures applicable to off-market and market purchases.

The major distinction is that an off-market purchase requires approval of a prior contract of purchase. A condition which would be impossible on a market purchase.

Subsection (2)

Recognised investment exchange is defined in subs.(5) and a marketing arrangement by subs.(3). In general, market purchases are limited to listed shares and those traded on the AIM.

Authority for off-market purchase

694.   Authority for off-market purchase

(1) A company may only make an off-market purchase of its own shares in pursuance of a contract approved prior to the purchase in accordance with this section.

(2) Either-

    (a) the terms of the contract must be authorised by a special resolution of the company before the contract is entered into, or

    (b) the contract must provide that no shares may be purchased in pursuance of the contract until its terms have been authorised by a special resolution of the company.

(3) The contract may be a contract, entered into by the company and relating to shares in the company, that does not amount to a contract to purchase the shares but under which the company may (subject to any conditions) become entitled or obliged to purchase the shares.

(4) The authority conferred by a resolution under this section may be varied, revoked or from time to time renewed by a special resolution of the company.

(5) In the case of a public company a resolution conferring, varying or renewing authority must specify a date on which the authority is to expire, which must not be later than 18 months after the date on which the resolution is passed.

(6) A resolution conferring, varying, revoking or renewing authority under this section is subject to-

    section 695 (exercise of voting rights), and

    section 696 (disclosure of details of contract).

GENERAL NOTE

    This section restates, with one substantive change, s.164(1), (3) and (4) and s.165 of the Companies Act 1985. As such it merges the sections on the similar approval procedure for what was referred to as a contingent purchase contract (s.165) and off-market purchases generally (s.164). The change of substance relates to allowing purchase contracts to be made without prior authorisation provided they cannot be activated without such authorisation. Although there is now no specific reference to a contingent purchase contract by name, its effect is preserved by subs.(3). The remaining parts of s.164 are restated in the following six sections.

Subsections (1) and (2)

    These subsections restate s.164(1) and (2) and s.165(2) of the 1985 Act. In that Act contingent purchase contracts were not specifically limited to off-market purchases. In practice, however, they were only possible in relation to such purchases because of the procedure involved. Now there is no theoretical power to enter into such contracts in respect of market purchases (see s.701).

Subsection (1)

    The merging of the sections on purchases generally and contingent purchase contracts has resulted in drafting changes. This subsection now provides for authorisation "prior to purchase" rather than "in advance".

Subsection (2)

    This subsection now provides for two types of contract: one (as in the previous Act) which requires authorisation of its terms prior to purchase; and a second which expressly provides that no purchases may be made under it without subsequent authorisation. The latter is a new provision.

    The authorisation procedure remains the same as before. See *R W Peak (Kings Lynn) Ltd* [1998] 1 B.C.L.C. 193. Further details are in ss.695 and 696.

Subsection (3)

    This subsection restates s.165(1) of the 1985 act with no substantive amendments but the term contingent purchase contract has been dropped.

Subsections (4) and (5)

    These subsections restate s.164(3) and (4) of the 1985 Act with no substantive amendments. There is a proposal to amend the 18-month time limit for public companies to approve the contract, imposed by the second EC Directive (79/91/EEC), to five years: see Com (2004) October 2004. Any consequential changes to this section will be made by regulation (see s.737). As to variations, see s.697.

695.   Resolution authorising off-market purchase: exercise of voting rights

(1) This section applies to a resolution to confer, vary, revoke or renew authority for the purposes of section 694 (authority for off-market purchase of own shares).

(2) Where the resolution is proposed as a written resolution, a member who holds shares to which the resolution relates is not an eligible member.

(3) Where the resolution is proposed at a meeting of the company, it is not effective if-
  (a) any member of the company holding shares to which the resolution relates exercises the voting rights carried by any of those shares in voting on the resolution, and
  (b) the resolution would not have been passed if he had not done so.

(4) For this purpose-
  (a) a member who holds shares to which the resolution relates is regarded as exercising the voting rights carried by those shares not only if he votes in respect of them on a poll on the question whether the resolution shall be passed, but also if he votes on the resolution otherwise than on a poll;
  (b) any member of the company may demand a poll on that question;
  (c) a vote and a demand for a poll by a person as proxy for a member are the same respectively as a vote and a demand by the member.

GENERAL NOTE

This section restates s.164(5) of the Companies Act 1985. There are no changes of substance, but the general theme of exclusion of the vendor from voting meaningfully on the required authorising resolution is applied by subs.(2) to the written resolution procedure as redrawn by this Act (see ss.288-300, especially s.289).

Except in relation to a written resolution, the vendor may vote with shares other than those subject to the purchase agreement (although questions of minority protection etc may then arise) and need only abstain in respect of the relevant shares - the vendor need not vote against the proposal. Note the right to demand a poll and the effect on a resolution to hold a poll in subs.(4). That right cannot be excluded by the articles: see s.321.

The members cannot waive these requirements: *Wright v Atlas Wright (Europe) Ltd* [1999] 2 B.C.L.C. 301 at 310-315.

696.   Resolution authorising off-market purchase: disclosure of details of contract

(1) This section applies in relation to a resolution to confer, vary, revoke or renew authority for the purposes of section 694 (authority for off-market purchase of own shares).

(2) A copy of the contract (if it is in writing) or a memorandum setting out its terms (if it is not) must be made available to members-
  (a) in the case of a written resolution, by being sent or submitted to every eligible member at or before the time at which the proposed resolution is sent or submitted to him;
  (b) in the case of a resolution at a meeting, by being made available for inspection by members of the company both-
    (i) at the company's registered office for not less than 15 days ending with the date of the meeting, and
    (ii) at the meeting itself.

(3) A memorandum of contract terms so made available must include the names of the members holding shares to which the contract relates.

(4) A copy of the contract so made available must have annexed to it a written memorandum specifying such of those names as do not appear in the contract itself.

(5) The resolution is not validly passed if the requirements of this section are not complied with

GENERAL NOTE

This section restates s.164(6) of the 1985 Act with no changes of substance except to apply its provisions to written resolutions as redrawn by this Act. It applies to the authorisation either of the contract itself or, if it is one which expressly requires authorisation to be activated, authorisation of such activation.

As such, the section provides for the availability of the contract or a memorandum of its terms for inspection at the company's office for 15 days ending with the date of the relevant meeting (to approve the contract or its activation, as appropriate) and at the meeting itself. For a written resolution it must be sent instead to each eligible member (see s.289) ahead of sending the resolution itself to those members. The names of all the proposed vendors whether on the face of the contract or not must be disclosed.

It has been held under the former section that the members themselves may agree to waive this requirement under the *Duomatic* principle: *BDG Roof-Bond v Douglas* [2000] 1 BCLC 401. The wording has been changed, however. In the former section it was stated that the resolution would not be effective if there was a breach. Now subs.(5) is more explicit ("not validly passed") and the question must be regarded as open.

697.   Variation of contract for off-market purchase

(1) A company may only agree to a variation of a contract authorised under section 694 (authority for off-market purchase) if the variation is approved in advance in accordance with this section.
(2) The terms of the variation must be authorised by a special resolution of the company before it is agreed to.
(3) That authority may be varied, revoked or from time to time renewed by a special resolution of the company.
(4) In the case of a public company a resolution conferring, varying or renewing authority must specify a date on which the authority is to expire, which must not be later than 18 months after the date on which the resolution is passed.
(5) A resolution conferring, varying, revoking or renewing authority under this section is subject to-
     section 698 (exercise of voting rights), and
     section 699 (disclosure of details of variation).

GENERAL NOTE

This section, together with the following two sections, replaces s.164(7) of the 1985 Act. In effect, together they apply all the procedural rules in ss.694-796, which apply to a resolution approving an off market purchase contract, to a resolution varying the terms of that contract, which is permitted under s.694(4). Under the 1985 Act this was achieved by a simple incorporation by reference.

This section mirrors subss.694(2) and (4)-(6) as to the basic requirement of prior approval of the variation by a special resolution. Note that the variation itself may be varied under the same procedure. See the notes to s.694(2) and (4)-(5).

698.   Resolution authorising variation: exercise of voting rights

(1) This section applies to a resolution to confer, vary, revoke or renew authority for the purposes of section 697 (variation of contract for off-market purchase of own shares).
(2) Where the resolution is proposed as a written resolution, a member who holds shares to which the resolution relates is not an eligible member.
(3) Where the resolution is proposed at a meeting of the company, it is not effective if-
     (a) any member of the company holding shares to which the resolution relates exercises the voting rights carried by any of those shares in voting on the resolution, and
     (b) the resolution would not have been passed if he had not done so.
(4) For this purpose-
     (a) a member who holds shares to which the resolution relates is regarded as exercising the voting rights carried by those shares not only if he votes in respect of them on a poll on the question whether the resolution shall be passed, but also if he votes on the resolution otherwise than on a poll;
     (b) any member of the company may demand a poll on that question;
     (c) a vote and a demand for a poll by a person as proxy for a member are the same respectively as a vote and a demand by the member.

GENERAL NOTE

This section, derived from s.164(7) of the 1985 Act, applies s.695 (voting on a resolution to approve a contract for an off-market purchase) to a resolution authorising a variation of such a contract. Formerly these provisions were incorporated by reference.

As such, this section restates s.164(5) of the 1985 Act. There are no changes of substance but the general theme of exclusion of the vendor from voting meaningfully on the required authorising resolution is applied by subs.(2) to the written resolution procedure as redrawn by this Act (see ss.288-300, especially s.289).

Except in relation to a written resolution, the vendor may vote with shares other than those subject to the purchase agreement (although questions of minority protection, etc. may then arise) and need only abstain in respect of the relevant shares - the vendor need not vote against the proposal. Note the general right to demand a poll and the effect on a resolution to hold a poll in subs.(4). The articles cannot exclude this right: see s.321.

The members cannot waive these requirements: *Wright v Atlas Wright (Europe) Ltd* [1999] 2 B.C.L.C. 301 at 310-315.

This section also applies to approval of a release from an off-market purchase under s.700.

699. Resolution authorising variation: disclosure of details of variation

(1) This section applies in relation to a resolution under section 697 (variation of contract for off-market purchase of own shares).

(2) A copy of the proposed variation (if it is in writing) or a written memorandum giving details of the proposed variation (if it is not) must be made available to members-

    (a) in the case of a written resolution, by being sent or submitted to every eligible member at or before the time at which the proposed resolution is sent or submitted to him;

    (b) in the case of a resolution at a meeting, by being made available for inspection by members of the company both-

        (i) at the company's registered office for not less than 15 days ending with the date of the meeting, and

        (ii) at the meeting itself.

(3) There must also be made available as mentioned in subsection (2) a copy of the original contract or, as the case may be, a memorandum of its terms, together with any variations previously made.

(4) A memorandum of the proposed variation so made available must include the names of the members holding shares to which the variation relates.

(5) A copy of the proposed variation so made available must have annexed to it a written memorandum specifying such of those names as do not appear in the variation itself.

(6) The resolution is not validly passed if the requirements of this section are not complied with.

GENERAL NOTE

This section, derived from s.164(7) of the 1985 Act, applies s.696 (disclosure of the details prior to a resolution to approve a contract for an off-market purchase) to a resolution authorising a variation of such a contract. Formerly these provisions were incorporated by reference, except for subs.(3) which was contained in s.164(7) itself.

As such, the section restates s.164(6) of the 1985 Act with no changes of substance, except to apply its provisions to written resolutions as redrawn by this Act. It provides for the availability of the variation or a memorandum of its terms for inspection at the company's office for 15 days ending with the date of the meeting and at the meeting itself. For a written resolution it must be sent instead to each eligible member (see s.289) ahead of sending the resolution itself to those members. The names of all the proposed vendors whether on the face of the contract or not must be disclosed.

Subsection (3) is an additional requirement to those in s.696. It was stated as such in s.164(7) of the 1985 Act.

It has been held under the former section that the members themselves may agree to waive this requirement under the *Duomatic* principle: *BDG Roof-Bond v Douglas* [2000] 1 B.C.L.C. 401. The wording has been changed, however. In the former section it was stated that the resolution would not be effective if there was a breach. Now subs.(6) is more explicit ("not validly passed") and the question must be regarded as open.

This section also applies to approval of a release from an off-market purchase under s.700.

700.   Release of company's rights under contract for off-market purchase

(1) An agreement by a company to release its rights under a contract approved under section 694 (authorisation of off-market purchase) is void unless the terms of the release agreement are approved in advance in accordance with this section.

(2) The terms of the proposed agreement must be authorised by a special resolution of the company before the agreement is entered into.

(3) That authority may be varied, revoked or from time to time renewed by a special resolution of the company.

(4) In the case of a public company a resolution conferring, varying or renewing authority must specify a date on which the authority is to expire, which must not be later than 18 months after the date on which the resolution is passed.

(5) The provisions of-
   section 698 (exercise of voting rights), and
   section 699 (disclosure of details of variation),
apply to a resolution authorising a proposed release agreement as they apply to a resolution authorising a proposed variation.

GENERAL NOTE

This section restates, without any changes of substance, s.167(2) of the 1985 Act in relation to an agreement by the company to release its rights under an off-market purchase or contingent purchase contract. (Section 167(1) is now in s.704).

As such, to avoid abuse by artificially agreeing to purchase shares and then paying off the vendor for the loss of the right to sell, the section requires any such agreement to be approved in advance by a special resolution passed in accordance with the requirements of ss.698 and 699.

The section now expressly states the provisions as to subsequent changes to the agreement and the time limit for public companies, formerly incorporated by reference into former s.167(2). See the note to s.694(4) and (5).

Authority for market purchase

701.   Authority for market purchase

(1) A company may only make a market purchase of its own shares if the purchase has first been authorised by a resolution of the company.

(2) That authority-
   (a) may be general or limited to the purchase of shares of a particular class or description, and
   (b) may be unconditional or subject to conditions.

(3) The authority must-
   (a) specify the maximum number of shares authorised to be acquired, and
   (b) determine both the maximum and minimum prices that may be paid for the shares.

(4) The authority may be varied, revoked or from time to time renewed by a resolution of the company.

(5) A resolution conferring, varying or renewing authority must specify a date on which it is to expire, which must not be later than 18 months after the date on which the resolution is passed.

(6) A company may make a purchase of its own shares after the expiry of the time limit specified if-
   (a) the contract of purchase was concluded before the authority expired, and
   (b) the terms of the authority permitted the company to make a contract of purchase that would or might be executed wholly or partly after its expiration.

(7) A resolution to confer or vary authority under this section may determine either or both the maximum and minimum price for purchase by-
   (a) specifying a particular sum, or

(b) providing a basis or formula for calculating the amount of the price (but without reference to any person's discretion or opinion).

(8) Chapter 3 of Part 3 (resolutions affecting a company's constitution) applies to a resolution under this section.

GENERAL NOTE

This section restates, in a slightly re-ordered way, s.166 of the 1985 Act, The obligation in s.166(7) has been modified in subs.(8).

As such the section provides the procedure for authorising a market purchase (as defined in s.693(4)) by a company of its own shares.

Subsections (1) and (2)

These subsections restate s.166(1) and (2) of the 1985 Act in permissive rather than negative language. As before, the need is for prior approval of a purchase rather than of any contract to purchase. The approving resolution need not be a special resolution, nor now need it be registered as such (subs.166(7) has been discontinued). However, the details of the purchase, etc. must be registered under ss.707 and 708.

Subsections (3)-(7)

These subsections restate s.166(3)-(6) of the 1985 Act. There is some re-ordering so that new subs.(5) derives from former subs.(3)(c) and the second part of former subs.(4). However, there are no changes of substance, continuing the permissive nature of the restrictions. Subsections (3) and (4) are the same (subject to the above) and subss.(6) and (7) correlate to former subss.(5) and (6). The time limit of 18 months for the duration of such authority for public companies, imposed by the Second EC Directive, is under review and could be amended later by regulations made under s.737.

Subsection (8)

This subsection adapts the obligation in former s.166(7) to send a copy of the resolution to the registrar to the concept of a company's constitution in Ch.3 of Pt 3 of this Act.

Supplementary provisions

702. Copy of contract or memorandum to be available for inspection

(1) This section applies where a company has entered into-
   (a) a contract approved under section 694 (authorisation of contract for offmarket purchase), or
   (b) a contract for a purchase authorised under section 701 (authorisation of market purchase).
(2) The company must keep available for inspection-
   (a) a copy of the contract, or
   (b) if the contract is not in writing, a written memorandum setting out its terms.
(3) The copy or memorandum must be kept available for inspection from the conclusion of the contract until the end of the period of ten years beginning with-
   (a) the date on which the purchase of all the shares in pursuance of the contract is completed, or
   (b) the date on which the contract otherwise determines.
(4) The copy or memorandum must be kept available for inspection-
   (a) at the company's registered office, or
   (b) at a place specified in regulations under section 1136.
(5) The company must give notice to the registrar-
   (a) of the place at which the copy or memorandum is kept available for inspection, and
   (b) of any change in that place,
unless it has at all times been kept at the company's registered office.
(6) Every copy or memorandum required to be kept under this section must be kept open to inspection without charge-

(a) by any member of the company, and

(b) in the case of a public company, by any other person.

(7) The provisions of this section apply to a variation of a contract as they apply to the original contract.

GENERAL NOTE

This section replaces s.169(4), (5) and (9) of the 1985 Act, with modifications. It restates the obligation of any company which enters into a contract (including a contingent purchase contract) for the purchase of its own shares, to keep, and make available for inspection, either at its registered office or at a place as specified in regulations to be made under s.1136, a copy of that contract or a memorandum of it. A private company need only allow members to do so; a public company must allow anyone such access; all free of charge. The same obligation applies to any variations to the contract approved under s.697. See the following section for the default offence and enforcement.

Subsection (3)

The ten year period is retained and in fact is now potentially longer, since it begins on making the contract (not necessarily the purchase) and ends ten years after the purchases under it are completed.

Subsection (4)

This subsection reflects the fact that the contract or memorandum may be kept elsewhere than the company's registered office.

703. Enforcement of right to inspect copy or memorandum

(1) If default is made in complying with section 702(2), (3) or (4) or default is made for 14 days in complying with section 702(5), or an inspection required under section 702(6) is refused, an offence is committed by-

(a) the company, and

(b) every officer of the company who is in default.

(2) A person guilty of an offence under this section is liable on summary conviction to a fine not exceeding level 3 on the standard scale and, for continued contravention, a daily default fine not exceeding one-tenth of level 3 on the standard scale.

(3) In the case of refusal of an inspection required under section 702(6) the court may by order compel an immediate inspection.

GENERAL NOTE

This section restates, with modifications, s.169(6)-(8) of the 1985 Act. It sets out the offence in default in relation to the keeping and inspection obligations imposed by the previous section and gives the court an enforcement power.

The wording of the sanction in subs.(2) has been amended to comply with the treatment of such offences generally under this Act (see Sch.3).

704. No assignment of company's right to purchase own shares

The rights of a company under a contract authorised under-

(a) section 694 (authority for off-market purchase), or

(b) section 701 (authority for market purchase)

are not capable of being assigned.

GENERAL NOTE

This section restates s.167(1) of the 1985 Act. It simply restates the rule that no company can assign its rights to purchase its own shares - it cannot trade against its own share price.

(Section 167(2) is now in s.700).

705. Payments apart from purchase price to be made out of distributable profits

(1) A payment made by a company in consideration of-

    (a) acquiring any right with respect to the purchase of its own shares in pursuance of a contingent purchase contract approved under section 694 (authorisation of off-market purchase),

    (b) the variation of any contract approved under that section, or

    (c) the release of any of the company's obligations with respect to the purchase of any of its own shares under a contract-

        (i) approved under section 694, or

        (ii) authorised under section 701 (authorisation of market purchase),

must be made out of the company's distributable profits.

(2) If this requirement is not met in relation to a contract, then-

    (a) in a case within subsection (1)(a), no purchase by the company of its own shares in pursuance of that contract may be made under this Chapter;

    (b) in a case within subsection (1)(b), no such purchase following the variation may be made under this Chapter;

    (c) in a case within subsection (1)(c), the purported release is void.

GENERAL NOTE

    This section restates s.168 of the 1985 Act with no changes of substance.

Subsection (1)

    This subsection requires that any payment made by a company under a purchase contract approved under s.694, a variation of any such purchase contract, and for a release from any of its obligations under purchase arrangements must be funded out of distributable profits. For purchases generally the sources of funding are wider: see s.692. Note that releases of market purchase obligations do not need prior approval: cf. s.700 for market purchases.

Subsection (2)

    In default any purchase contract or varied purchase contract may not be acted upon. Any release so obtained is void.
    Distributable profits - see s.736.

706. Treatment of shares purchased

Where a limited company makes a purchase of its own shares in accordance with this Chapter, then-

    (a) if section 724 (treasury shares) applies, the shares may be held and dealt with in accordance with Chapter 6;

    (b) if that section does not apply-

        (i) the shares are treated as cancelled, and

        (ii) the amount of the company's issued share capital is diminished accordingly by the nominal value of the shares cancelled.

GENERAL NOTE

    This section is derived from s.162(2) and (2B) of the 1985 Act. As such it repeats the pre-existing rules that unless the shares were capable of being held as treasury shares (see Ch.6 of this Part, ss.724-732), they must, like redeemed shares under s.688, be cancelled and the company's issued share capital diminished accordingly. These requirements are amplified by the following two sections.

707. Return to registrar of purchase of own shares

(1) Where a company purchases shares under this Chapter, it must deliver a return to the registrar within the period of 28 days beginning with the date on which the shares are delivered to it.

(2) The return must distinguish-

    (a) shares in relation to which section 724 (treasury shares) applies and shares in relation to which that section does not apply, and

    (b) shares in relation to which that section applies-

        (i) that are cancelled forthwith (under section 729 (cancellation of treasury shares)), and

        (ii) that are not so cancelled.

(3) The return must state, with respect to shares of each class purchased-

    (a) the number and nominal value of the shares, and

    (b) the date on which they were delivered to the company.

(4) In the case of a public company the return must also state-

    (a) the aggregate amount paid by the company for the shares, and

    (b) the maximum and minimum prices paid in respect of shares of each class purchased.

(5) Particulars of shares delivered to the company on different dates and under different contracts may be included in a single return.

In such a case the amount required to be stated under subsection (4)(a) is the aggregate amount paid by the company for all the shares to which the return relates.

(6) If default is made in complying with this section an offence is committed by every officer of the company who is in default.

(7) A person guilty of an offence under this section is liable-

    (a) on conviction on indictment, to a fine;

    (b) on summary conviction to a fine not exceeding the statutory maximum and, for continued contravention, a daily default fine not exceeding one-tenth of the statutory maximum.

GENERAL NOTE

    This section, together with the following section, is derived from s.169 of the 1985 Act.

Subsections (1) and (2)

    These subsections restate the obligation on all companies to register a return of all shares purchased under this Chapter within 28 days of delivery of the shares. It must specify whether they are potential treasury shares or not and, if they are whether they have been cancelled or retained in treasury.

Subsections (3)-(5)

    These subsections restate the particulars to be registered.

Subsections (6) and (7)

    These subsections retain the offence in default. The sanction has been reworded to comply with the general treatment of such offences under this Act.

708. Notice to registrar of cancellation of shares

(1) If on the purchase by a company of any of its own shares in accordance with this Part-

    (a) section 724 (treasury shares) does not apply (so that the shares are treated as cancelled), or

    (b) that section applies but the shares are cancelled forthwith (under section 729 (cancellation of treasury shares)), the company must give notice of cancellation to the registrar, within the period of 28 days beginning with the date on which the shares are delivered to it, specifying the shares cancelled.

(2) The notice must be accompanied by a statement of capital.

(3) The statement of capital must state with respect to the company's share capital immediately following the cancellation-

    (a) the total number of shares of the company,

    (b) the aggregate nominal value of those shares,

    (c) for each class of shares-

        (i) prescribed particulars of the rights attached to the shares,

        (ii) the total number of shares of that class, and

        (iii) the aggregate nominal value of shares of that class, and

    (d) the amount paid up and the amount (if any) unpaid on each share (whether on account of the nominal value of the share or by way of premium).

(4) If default is made in complying with this section, an offence is committed by-

    (a) the company, and

    (b) every officer of the company who is in default.

(5) A person guilty of an offence under this section is liable on summary conviction to a fine not exceeding level 3 on the standard scale and, for continued contravention, a daily default fine not exceeding one-tenth of level 3 on the standard scale.

GENERAL NOTE

This section is derived from s.169A of the 1985 Act, modified to comply with the statement of capital regime introduced by this Act. This is required whenever a company alters its share capital.

Subsection (1)

This subsection restates the pre-existing obligation to register the cancellation of shares purchased under this Chapter. This applies to all such purchases except of treasury shares which are to be retained under Ch.6 of this Part.

Subsections (2) and (3)

These new subsections dovetail this section into the general theme of this Act as to the need to file a statement of capital on formation and an amended statement on a change in that capital.

Subsections (4) and (5)

These subsections retain the offence in default, amended to comply with the general treatment of such offences in this Act (see Sch.3).

CHAPTER 5

REDEMPTION OR PURCHASE BY PRIVATE COMPANY OUT OF CAPITAL

Introductory

709. Power of private limited company to redeem or purchase own shares out of capital

(1) A private limited company may in accordance with this Chapter, but subject to any restriction or prohibition in the company's articles, make a payment in respect of the redemption or purchase of its own shares otherwise than out of distributable profits or the proceeds of a fresh issue of shares.

(2) References below in this Chapter to payment out of capital are to any payment so made, whether or not it would be regarded apart from this section as a payment out of capital.

GENERAL NOTE

This Chapter restates and amends ss.171-177 of the 1985 Act as to the ability of private companies to fund a redemption or purchase of its own shares out of capital where it has insufficient distributable profits or proceeds of a fresh issue, the permitted funds for all companies under ss.687 and 692.

The CLR and the 2002 White Paper proposed the repeal of these sections on the basis that the simplified reduction of capital procedure for private companies introduced by this Act (ss.642-644) would make them unnecessary. (The sections had been used by private companies in practice as a simplified reduction procedure.) At the last minute, however, they were reprieved on the basis that there would still be occasions when these sections would be available where the reduction procedure would not be.

An example was given in debate. This was where a company has no share premium or other capital reserves but wishes to purchase its shares at above their nominal value. The reduction procedure would not allow that (insufficient capital), but these sections might since they, unlike the reduction procedure, treat any revaluation reserve (unrealised profits) as being capital (see subs.(2) below). This would allow companies to continue to distribute surplus cash in circumstances where they have no distributable profits. (See *Hansard*, HL GC Day 10, cols 32-33).

Originally the Bill contained three clauses amending the 1985 Act sections. Two of these were subsumed as part of the restatement exercise. However one, only added at Report Stage in the HL, introducing a new s.177A into the 1985 Act, was dropped. It would have required a fresh statement of capital to be registered when capital was used for a redemption or purchase. This would have been in addition to the new statement of capital registered on the cancellation of the redeemed or purchased shares, which seemed to be overkill.

This section restates s.171(1) and (2) of the 1985 Act providing the general power for private companies to use capital for purchases and redemptions as permitted by the following sections. However, there is a change, consistent with those made to the powers of purchase and redemption for private companies, in that authority to do so in the articles is no longer a pre-requisite. Instead the articles may limit or negate the power. There will have to be consideration as to transitional provisions.

Subsection (2) reinforces the point made above about the width of these sections.

The permissible capital payment

710. The permissible capital payment

(1) The payment that may, in accordance with this Chapter, be made by a company out of capital in respect of the redemption or purchase of its own shares is such amount as, after applying for that purpose-
   (a) any available profits of the company, and
   (b) the proceeds of any fresh issue of shares made for the purposes of the redemption or purchase,
is required to meet the price of redemption or purchase.

(2) That is referred to below in this Chapter as "the permissible capital payment" for the shares.

GENERAL NOTE

This section restates s.171(3) of the 1985 Act with no changes of substance. It provides for the maximum amount of capital which may be used, referred to as the permissible capital payment ("PCP"). This is calculated by reference to the shortfall, if any, in the permitted funds (available distributable profits and proceeds of a fresh issue). Available profits must be used first. These are defined in the following two sections.

Distributable profits - see s.736.

711. Available profits

(1) For the purposes of this Chapter the available profits of the company, in relation to the redemption or purchase of any shares, are the profits of the company that are available for distribution (within the meaning of Part 23).

(2) But the question whether a company has any profits so available, and the amount of any such profits, shall be determined in accordance with section 712 instead of in accordance with sections 836 to 842 in that Part.

GENERAL NOTE

This section restates s.172(1) of the 1985 Act with no changes of substance. It defines available profits in calculating the PCP.

Subs (2) provides that they are all distributable profits available to the company as drawn up by reference to items in the following section as shown by accounts drawn up in accordance with that section. Under subs.(1), available profits are then those which would not contravene Pt 23 of this Act.

Distributable profits - see s.736.

712.   Determination of available profits

(1) The available profits of the company are determined as follows.

(2) First, determine the profits of the company by reference to the following items as stated in the relevant accounts-

    (a) profits, losses, assets and liabilities,

    (b) provisions of the following kinds-

        (i) where the relevant accounts are Companies Act accounts, provisions of a kind specified for the purposes of this subsection by regulations under section 396;

        (ii) where the relevant accounts are IAS accounts, provisions of any kind;

    (c) share capital and reserves (including undistributable reserves).

(3) Second, reduce the amount so determined by the amount of-

    (a) any distribution lawfully made by the company, and

    (b) any other relevant payment lawfully made by the company out of distributable profits,

after the date of the relevant accounts and before the end of the relevant period.

(4) For this purpose "other relevant payment lawfully made" includes-

    (a) financial assistance lawfully given out of distributable profits in accordance with Chapter 2,

    (b) payments lawfully made out of distributable profits in respect of the purchase by the company of any shares in the company, and

    (c) payments of any description specified in section 705 (payments other than purchase price to be made out of distributable profits) lawfully made by the company.

(5) The resulting figure is the amount of available profits.

(6) For the purposes of this section "the relevant accounts" are any accounts that-

    (a) are prepared as at a date within the relevant period, and

    (b) are such as to enable a reasonable judgment to be made as to the amounts of the items mentioned in subsection (2).

(7) In this section "the relevant period" means the period of three months ending with the date on which the directors' statement is made in accordance with section 714.

GENERAL NOTE

This section restates s.172(2)-(6) of the 1985 Act setting out the criteria for determining available profits for the previous section and thus in calculating the PCP.

Subsections (2) and (3)

These subsections restate s.172(2) and (4) of the 1985 Act. The items to be taken into account include undistributable reserves (see the General Note to s.709). The amounts to be deducted are distributions and other payments (see subs.(4) made between the date of the relevant accounts (see subs.(6)) and the three months ending with the statement made by the directors under s.714 (see subs.(7)). *Subsection (4)*

This subsection restates s.172(5) of the 1985 Act. It is limited to lawful payments since otherwise an unlawful payment would reduce the available profits and so increase the PCP

Requirements for payment out of capital

713. Requirements for payment out of capital

(1) A payment out of capital by a private company for the redemption or purchase of its own shares is not lawful unless the requirements of the following sections are met-

     section 714 (directors' statement and auditor's report);

     section 716 (approval by special resolution);

     section 719 (public notice of proposed payment);

     section 720 (directors' statement and auditor's report to be available for inspection).

(2) This is subject to any order of the court under section 721 (power of court to extend period for compliance on application by persons objecting to payment).

GENERAL NOTE

This section restates s.173(1) of the 1985 Act outlining the procedural steps necessary for a private company to use the PCP (s.710) to redeem or purchase its own shares. These are in addition to the procedure for actually redeeming or purchasing the shares. The basic procedure remains the same as before, but there are some amendments.

The following sections provide the various steps to be taken and have been re-ordered to provide a logical time progression.

714. Directors' statement and auditor's report

(1) The company's directors must make a statement in accordance with this section.

(2) The statement must specify the amount of the permissible capital payment for the shares in question.

(3) It must state that, having made full inquiry into the affairs and prospects of the company, the directors have formed the opinion-

     (a) as regards its initial situation immediately following the date on which the payment out of capital is proposed to be made, that there will be no grounds on which the company could then be found unable to pay its debts, and

     (b) as regards its prospects for the year immediately following that date, that having regard to-

         (i) their intentions with respect to the management of the company's business during that year, and

         (ii) the amount and character of the financial resources that will in their view be available to the company during that year,

     the company will be able to continue to carry on business as a going concern (and will accordingly be able to pay its debts as they fall due) throughout that year.

(4) In forming their opinion for the purposes of subsection (3)(a), the directors must take into account all of the company's liabilities (including any contingent or prospective liabilities).

(5) The directors' statement must be in the prescribed form and must contain such information with respect to the nature of the company's business as may be prescribed.

(6) It must in addition have annexed to it a report addressed to the directors by the company's auditor stating that-

     (a) he has inquired into the company's state of affairs,

     (b) the amount specified in the statement as the permissible capital payment for the shares in question is in his view properly determined in accordance with sections 710 to 712, and

     (c) he is not aware of anything to indicate that the opinion expressed by the directors in their statement as to any of the matters mentioned in subsection (3) above is unreasonable in all the circumstances.

GENERAL NOTE

This section restates s.173(3)-(5) of the 1985 Act, with amendments. The directors' statement and the annexed auditor's report are the first steps in the authorising procedure. The offence in default is now contained in the next section.

Subsections (1)-(3)

These subsections restate s.173(3) with one amendment. The former requirement that the directors make a statutory declaration has been replaced with the requirement to make a simple statement, in a form which will be prescribed under subs.(5). Such a statement does not need to be made before a solicitor or Commissioner of Oaths.

The directors are required, as before, to confirm both the current and prospective solvency of the company over the next year after taking into account the prospective use of the PCP. The criteria for this are set out in subs.(4).

Subsection (4)

This subsection restates s.173(4) of the 1985, Act but with a significant amendment. Under the previous section the directors were required to take into account the same liabilities (including contingent and prospective ones) as would be relevant in a compulsory winding up under s.122 of the Insolvency Act 1986. This has been changed to all liabilities, including contingent and prospective ones, whether or not relevant to s.122. This brings this subsection into line with the solvency statement required for the new reduction of capital procedure for private companies introduced by this Act (ss.642-644). The two procedures are seen as very closely linked.

Subsection (6)

This subsection restates s.173(5) relating to the auditor's report which must be annexed to the directors' statement. There are no changes of substance.

715.   Directors' statement: offence if no reasonable grounds for opinion

(1) If the directors make a statement under section 714 without having reasonable grounds for the opinion expressed in it, an offence is committed by every director who is in default.

(2) A person guilty of an offence under this section is liable-

    (a) on conviction on indictment, to imprisonment for a term not exceeding two years or a fine (or both);

    (b) on summary conviction-

        (i) in England and Wales, to imprisonment for a term not exceeding twelve months or a fine not exceeding the statutory maximum (or both);

        (ii) in Scotland or Northern Ireland, to imprisonment for a term not exceeding six months or a fine not exceeding the statutory maximum (or both).

GENERAL NOTE

This section restates s.173(6) and (7) of the 1985 Act. The wording of the offence has changed only to reflect that this relates to a statement and not a declaration. All directors in default remain liable.

Subsection (2) has been reworded to comply with the general treatment of such offences under this Act.

716.   Payment to be approved by special resolution

(1) The payment out of capital must be approved by a special resolution of the company.

(2) The resolution must be passed on, or within the week immediately following, the date on which the directors make the statement required by section 714.

(3) A resolution under this section is subject to-

    section 717 (exercise of voting rights), and

    section 718 (disclosure of directors' statement and auditors' report).

GENERAL NOTE

This section restates ss.173(2) and 174(1) of the Companies Act 1985. It provides for the second step in the procedure - the need for an authorising special resolution within a week following the making of the directors' statement under s.727. In general such a resolution requires 21 days-notice, but it is more likely that it will be effected by a written resolution under ss.288-300.

The control of voting rights on the resolution is the subject of the following section and other procedural requirements relating to the resolution are in s.718.

717. Resolution authorising payment: exercise of voting rights

(1) This section applies to a resolution under section 716 (authority for payment out of capital for redemption or purchase of own shares).

(2) Where the resolution is proposed as a written resolution, a member who holds shares to which the resolution relates is not an eligible member.

(3) Where the resolution is proposed at a meeting of the company, it is not effective if-

   (a) any member of the company holding shares to which the resolution relates exercises the voting rights carried by any of those shares in voting on the resolution, and

   (b) the resolution would not have been passed if he had not done so.

(4) For this purpose-

   (a) a member who holds shares to which the resolution relates is regarded as exercising the voting rights carried by those shares not only if he votes in respect of them on a poll on the question whether the resolution shall be passed, but also if he votes on the resolution otherwise than on a poll;

   (b) any member of the company may demand a poll on that question;

   (c) a vote and a demand for a poll by a person as proxy for a member are the same respectively as a vote and a demand by the member.

GENERAL NOTE

This section restates s.174(2), (3) and (5) of the Companies Act 1985. There are no changes of substance. The restrictions imposed on the vendor of the shares from voting are the same as those imposed in relation to the resolution authorising the purchase itself under s.695. There are no changes of substance but the general theme of exclusion of the vendor from voting meaningfully on the required authorising resolution is applied by subs.(2) to the written resolution procedure as redrawn by this Act (see ss.288-300, especially s.289).

Except in relation to a written resolution, the vendor may vote with shares other than those subject to the purchase agreement (although questions of minority protection etc may then arise) and need only abstain in respect of the relevant shares - the vendor need not vote against the proposal.

Note the general right to demand a poll and the effect on a resolution to hold a poll in subs.(4). This general right cannot be exclude by the articles: see s.321.

It is unlikely that the members can waive these requirements: *Wright v Atlas Wright (Europe) Ltd* [1999] 2 B.C.L.C. 301 at 310-315.

718. Resolution authorising payment: disclosure of directors' statement and auditor's report

(1) This section applies to a resolution under section 716 (resolution authorising payment out of capital for redemption or purchase of own shares).

(2) A copy of the directors' statement and auditor's report under section 714 must be made available to members-

   (a) in the case of a written resolution, by being sent or submitted to every eligible member at or before the time at which the proposed resolution is sent or submitted to him;

   (b) in the case of a resolution at a meeting, by being made available for inspection by members of the company at the meeting.

(3) The resolution is ineffective if this requirement is not complied with.

GENERAL NOTE

This section restates s.174(4) of the 1985 Act, amended by the addition of subs.(3), and to take into account the written resolution procedure under ss.285-307.

It is unclear whether the members themselves may agree to waive this, but not the other requirements, under the *Duomatic* principle on the basis that it is solely for the members' own protection. There is some authority to that effect by analogy with *BDG Roof-Bond v Douglas* [2000] 1 B.C.L.C. 401. However, subs.(3) is new and may suggest otherwise.

719. Public notice of proposed payment

(1) Within the week immediately following the date of the resolution under section 716 the company must cause to be published in the Gazette a notice-

   (a) stating that the company has approved a payment out of capital for the purpose of acquiring its own shares by redemption or purchase or both (as the case may be),

   (b) specifying-

      (i) the amount of the permissible capital payment for the shares in question, and

      (ii) the date of the resolution,

   (c) stating where the directors' statement and auditor's report required by section 714 are available for inspection, and

   (d) stating that any creditor of the company may at any time within the five weeks immediately following the date of the resolution apply to the court under section 721 for an order preventing the payment.

(2) Within the week immediately following the date of the resolution the company must also either-

   (a) cause a notice to the same effect as that required by subsection (1) to be published in an appropriate national newspaper, or

   (b) give notice in writing to that effect to each of its creditors.

(3) "An appropriate national newspaper" means a newspaper circulating throughout the part of the United Kingdom in which the company is registered.

(4) Not later than the day on which the company-

   (a) first publishes the notice required by subsection (1), or

   (b) if earlier, first publishes or gives the notice required by subsection (2),

the company must deliver to the registrar a copy of the directors' statement and auditor's report required by section 714.

GENERAL NOTE

This section restates, without any major changes of substance, s.175(1)-(5) of the Companies Act 1985. It provides the method of bringing the proposed payment to the attention of creditors, etc. who may have a vested interest in any such payment being made.

The section follows on from the passing of the resolution under s.716. It provides for publication within one week of that resolution of a notice in the appropriate Gazette (according to the jurisdiction of the company) and an "appropriate national newspaper". This is one circulating throughout the part of the United Kingdom in which the company is registered (subs.(3)) and not necessarily where it carries on business. There is an alternative to the newspaper route by writing to each of the company's creditors. The notice must now state where the directors' statement and auditor's report may be inspected. That may not necessarily be at its registered office (see s.720)

There is also a requirement to send the registrar a copy of the directors' statement and auditor's report on the first day that any of the above notices is published or given.

For applications to the court to cancel the resolution see s.721.

720. Directors' statement and auditor's report to be available for inspection

(1) The directors' statement and auditor's report must be kept available for inspection throughout the period-

   (a) beginning with the day on which the company-

      (i) first publishes the notice required by section 719(1), or

      (ii) if earlier, first publishes or gives the notice required by section 719(2), and

    (b) ending five weeks after the date of the resolution for payment out of capital.

(2) They must be kept available for inspection-

    (a) at the company's registered office, or

    (b) at a place specified in regulations under section 1136.

(3) The company must give notice to the registrar-

    (a) of the place at which the statement and report are kept available for inspection, and

    (b) of any change in that place,

unless they have at all times been kept at the company's registered office.

(4) They must be open to the inspection of any member or creditor of the company without charge.

(5) If default is made for 14 days in complying with subsection (3), or an inspection under subsection (4) is refused, an offence is committed by-

    (a) the company, and

    (b) every officer of the company who is in default.

(6) A person guilty of an offence under this section is liable on summary conviction to a fine not exceeding level 3 on the standard scale and, for continued contravention, a daily default fine not exceeding one-tenth of level 3 on the standard scale.

(7) In the case of a refusal of an inspection required by subsection (4), the court may by order compel an immediate inspection.

GENERAL NOTE

This section restates, with amendments, s.175(4), and (6)-(8). It provides, without any major changes of substance, the final procedural step in the authorisation process for the use of the PCP.

Subsections (1)-(4) require the company to keep and make available, free of charge, the directors' statement and auditor's report (made under s.714) from the date when the first notice under s.719 was published or given until five weeks from the date of the resolution. (That is the period within which any application to the court under s.721 must be brought.) Access is to be allowed to any member or creditor.

Modifications to the pre-existing law in subss.(2) and (3) provide that the documents must be kept available either at the company's registered office or such other place authorised by regulations made under s.1136. Further, the registrar must be notified of the location if the latter is the case (and of any change) so that it will be a matter of public record.

There are default offences in subs.(5) relating to a failure to notify the registrar as required above, and to a failure to allow inspection, with a sanction in subs.(6) reworded to comply with the general treatment of such offences in this Act. The court also has an enforcement power under subs.(7).

Objection to payment by members or creditors

721. Application to court to cancel resolution

(1) Where a private company passes a special resolution approving a payment out of capital for the redemption or purchase of any of its shares-

    (a) any member of the company (other than one who consented to or voted in favour of the resolution), and

    (b) any creditor of the company,

may apply to the court for the cancellation of the resolution.

(2) The application-

    (a) must be made within five weeks after the passing of the resolution, and

    (b) may be made on behalf of the persons entitled to make it by such one or more of their number as they may appoint in writing for the purpose.

(3) On an application under this section the court may if it thinks fit-

    (a) adjourn the proceedings in order that an arrangement may be made to the satisfaction of the court-

      (i) for the purchase of the interests of dissentient members, or

      (ii) for the protection of dissentient creditors, and

   (b) give such directions and make such orders as it thinks expedient for facilitating or carrying into effect any such arrangement.

(4) Subject to that, the court must make an order either cancelling or confirming the resolution, and may do so on such terms and conditions as it thinks fit.

(5) If the court confirms the resolution, it may by order alter or extend any date or period of time specified-

   (a) in the resolution, or

   (b) in any provision of this Chapter applying to the redemption or purchase to which the resolution relates.

(6) The court's order may, if the court thinks fit-

   (a) provide for the purchase by the company of the shares of any of its members and for the reduction accordingly of the company's capital, and

   (b) make any alteration in the company's articles that may be required in consequence of that provision.

(7) The court's order may, if the court thinks fit, require the company not to make any, or any specified, amendments of its articles without the leave of the court.

GENERAL NOTE

This section restates ss.176(1) and (2) and 177(1)-(4) of the 1985 Act. (Subsection 177(5) has not been continued as being redundant.) There are no changes of substance although there is some rewording. See also the following section.

Subsections (1) and (2) allow a single creditor or dissentient member to apply to the court to set the resolution aside. As before there is no financial minimum on creditors; the time limit is five weeks from the date of the resolution, although a creditor may only have four given that any notice altering them to the payment can be made up to a week later.

The powers of the court are set out in subss.(3)-(7). In particular it has interim powers, it can confirm or cancel the resolution on such terms and conditions as it thinks fit, including altering or putting an embargo on altering the articles of the company, and it can amend the procedural timetable.

722.   Notice to registrar of court application or order

(1) On making an application under section 721 (application to court to cancel resolution) the applicants, or the person making the application on their behalf, must immediately give notice to the registrar.

This is without prejudice to any provision of rules of court as to service of notice of the application.

(2) On being served with notice of any such application, the company must immediately give notice to the registrar.

(3) Within 15 days of the making of the court's order on the application, or such longer period as the court may at any time direct, the company must deliver to the registrar a copy of the order.

(4) If a company fails to comply with subsection (2) or (3) an offence is committed by-

   (a) the company, and

   (b) every officer of the company who is in default.

(5) A person guilty of an offence under this section is liable on summary conviction to a fine not exceeding level 3 on the standard scale and, for continued contravention, a daily default fine not exceeding one-tenth of level 3 on the standard scale.

GENERAL NOTE

This section restates, with some amendments, s.176(3)-(5) of the 1985 Act.

Where there is an application to the court under the preceding section, the applicant(s) must notify the company (new), which must then give notice to the registrar.

If the court makes an order under s.721, the company must send a copy of it to the registrar within 15 days, unless the court allows a longer period.

The default offence (which does not cover the applicant's duty) is retained, but the sanction has been reworded to comply with the treatment of such offences in this Act.

Supplementary provisions

723. When payment out of capital to be made

(1) The payment out of capital must be made-

    (a) no earlier than five weeks after the date on which the resolution under section 716 is passed, and

    (b) no more than seven weeks after that date.

(2) This is subject to any exercise of the court's powers under section 721(5) (power to alter or extend time where resolution confirmed after objection).

GENERAL NOTE

This section restates, without any substantive change, s.174(1) of the 1985 Act and finalises the procedural timetable under this Chapter. The window within which the power, if duly authorised, can be used is between five and seven weeks after the date of the resolution, unless the court orders otherwise.

CHAPTER 6

TREASURY SHARES

724. Treasury shares

(1) This section applies where-

    (a) a limited company makes a purchase of its own shares in accordance with Chapter 4,

    (b) the purchase is made out of distributable profits, and

    (c) the shares are qualifying shares.

(2) For this purpose "qualifying shares" means shares that-

    (a) are included in the official list in accordance with the provisions of Part 6 of the Financial Services and Markets Act 2000 (c. 8),

    (b) are traded on the market known as the Alternative Investment Market established under the rules of London Stock Exchange plc,

    (c) are officially listed in an EEA State, or

    (d) are traded on a regulated market.

In paragraph (a) "the official list" has the meaning given in section 103(1) of the Financial Services and Markets Act 2000.

(3) Where this section applies the company may-

    (a) hold the shares (or any of them), or

    (b) deal with any of them, at any time, in accordance with section 727 or 729.

(4) Where shares are held by the company, the company must be entered in its register of members as the member holding the shares.

(5) In the Companies Acts references to a company holding shares as treasury shares are to the company holding shares that-

    (a) were (or are treated as having been) purchased by it in circumstances in which this section applies, and

    (b) have been held by the company continuously since they were so purchased (or treated as purchased).

GENERAL NOTE

This Chapter restates, without any substantive amendments, the provisions on treasury shares, introduced by the Companies (Acquisition of Own Shares) (Treasury Shares) Regulations 2003 (SI 2003/1116) and the Companies (Acquisition of

Own Shares) (Treasury Shares) No.2 Regulations 2003 (SI 2003/3031). Those Regulations amended s.162 and introduced ss.162A-162G and 169A into the 1985 Act.

This section restates ss.162(2B) and 162A of the 1985 Act. It defines which of its own shares acquired by a company may qualify as treasury shares and what that means. As before, this has no effect on the acquisition process as such, as set out in the previous sections of this Act; it deals with the consequences.

Subsections (1) and (2)

These subsections restate, without any substantive changes, s.162(2B) and (4) added by the 2003 Regulations. They set out the criteria for shares purchased by a company to be regarded as treasury shares so that the options in subs.(3) become available. The purchase must be funded out of distributable profits (and the proceeds of a fresh issue) and the shares must either be listed or traded as set out in subs.(2). Thus all private company shares are excluded. The maximum number allowed of such shares is set out in the following section.

Regulated market is defined in s.1173.

Subsections (3)-(5)

These subsections restate s.162A of the 1985 Act, introduced by the 2003 Regulations, without any substantive changes. Instead of the immediate obligation to cancel the shares, treasury shares may be held (in treasury - see s.739), disposed of under s.727, or cancelled under s.729. If the shares are retained, the company must be shown as the registered holder. In many cases such shares (as defined in subs.(5)) are then discounted when a necessary percentage of the shares is required for some action under the Act.

Distributable profits - see s.736.

725. Treasury shares: maximum holdings

(1) Where a company has shares of only one class, the aggregate nominal value of shares held as treasury shares must not at any time exceed 10% of the nominal value of the issued share capital of the company at that time.

(2) Where the share capital of a company is divided into shares of different classes, the aggregate nominal value of the shares of any class held as treasury shares must not at any time exceed 10% of the nominal value of the issued share capital of the shares of that class at that time.

(3) If subsection (1) or (2) is contravened by a company, the company must dispose of or cancel the excess shares, in accordance with section 727 or 729, before the end of the period of twelve months beginning with the date on which that contravention occurs.

The "excess shares" means such number of the shares held by the company as treasury shares at the time in question as resulted in the limit being exceeded.

(4) Where a company purchases qualifying shares out of distributable profits in accordance with section 724, a contravention by the company of subsection (1) or (2) above does not render the acquisition void under section 658 (general rule against limited company acquiring its own shares).

GENERAL NOTE

This section restates, without any substantive changes, ss.162B and 143(2A) of the 1985 Act, introduced by the 2003 Regulations.

The ten per cent limit imposed by subss.(1) and (2) is the maximum allowed by Art.19.1b of the Second EC Directive (77/91/EEC). Under subs.(3), any shares in excess of that amount must be disposed of or cancelled under the procedures lad down in ss.740 and 742 within a year of the date of contravention.

Subsection (4)

This subsection restates s.143(2A) of the 1985 Act. Excess treasury share purchases are not void purchases under s.658.

726. Treasury shares: exercise of rights

(1) This section applies where shares are held by a company as treasury shares.

(2) The company must not exercise any right in respect of the treasury shares, and any purported exercise of such a right is void.

This applies, in particular, to any right to attend or vote at meetings.

(3) No dividend may be paid, and no other distribution (whether in cash or otherwise) of the company's assets (including any distribution of assets to members on a winding up) may be made to the company, in respect of the treasury shares.

(4) Nothing in this section prevents-

    (a) an allotment of shares as fully paid bonus shares in respect of the treasury shares, or

    (b) the payment of any amount payable on the redemption of the treasury shares (if they are redeemable shares).

(5) Shares allotted as fully paid bonus shares in respect of the treasury shares are treated as if purchased by the company, at the time they were allotted, in circumstances in which section 724(1) (treasury shares) applied.

GENERAL NOTE

This section restates, without any substantive changes, s.162C of the 1985 Act, introduced by the 2003 Regulations.

Subsections (1)-(3)

These subsections restate s.162C(1)-(4) of the 1985 Act. The complete embargo on the exercise of any rights in respect of shares held in treasury is wider than required by Art.22.1 of the Second Directive (71/91/EEC), which is limited to voting rights. The specific reference to meetings under a scheme of arrangement in s.162C(3) of the 1985 Act has been omitted in new subs.(2) - it was unnecessary anyway since without a right to vote the holder of such shares would not be included in calculating the necessary majority percentage.

Subsections (4) and (5)

These subsections restate s.162C(5) and (6) of the 1985 Act. They thus continue the exceptions to the rights embargo. Bonus shares issued in respect of existing treasury shares are allowed to be kept to prevent dilution of the holding. Such shares, however, become treasury shares on allotment and so subject to this Chapter. They will also have to be disclosed in the return of allotment under s.555.

Redeemable shares may be purchased as treasury shares and any subsequent obligation to redeem may be honoured.

727. Treasury shares: disposal

(1) Where shares are held as treasury shares, the company may at any time-

    (a) sell the shares (or any of them) for a cash consideration, or

    (b) transfer the shares (or any of them) for the purposes of or pursuant to an employees' share scheme.

(2) In subsection (1)(a) "cash consideration" means-

    (a) cash received by the company, or

    (b) a cheque received by the company in good faith that the directors have no reason for suspecting will not be paid, or

    (c) a release of a liability of the company for a liquidated sum, or

    (d) an undertaking to pay cash to the company on or before a date not more than 90 days after the date on which the company agrees to sell the shares, or

    (e) payment by any other means giving rise to a present or future entitlement (of the company or a person acting on the company's behalf) to a payment, or credit equivalent to payment, in cash.

For this purpose "cash" includes foreign currency.

(3) The Secretary of State may by order provide that particular means of payment specified in the order are to be regarded as falling within subsection (2)(e).

(4) If the company receives a notice under section 979 (takeover offers: right of offeror to buy out minority shareholders) that a person desires to acquire shares held by the company as treasury shares, the company must not sell or transfer the shares to which the notice relates except to that person.

(5) An order under this section is subject to negative resolution procedure.

GENERAL NOTE

This section restates s.162D(1)(a) and (b), (2) and (3) of the 1985 Act, with one addition set out in subss.2(e), (4) and (5).

Introduced by the 2003 Regulations, these provisions give a company the power to sell treasury shares for cash (as defined in subs.(2) - see also by analogy *System Controls plc v Munro Corporation Plc* [1990] B.C.C. 386) or to transfer them pursuant to an employees' share scheme (defined in s.1166), as an alternative to cancelling or holding onto them. The proceeds of sale must be dealt with according to s.731.

Subsection 2(e) was added to the definition of "cash" to provide for future rights to cash. The precise types of payment so caught are to be defined by an order made under the negative resolution procedure (subss.(4) and (5)).

This power is only subject to subs.(3). That provides that where a squeeze-out notice under s.979 of this Act has been served on the company following a successful takeover offer, the shares can only be transferred to the server of the notice.

728.   Treasury shares: notice of disposal

(1) Where shares held by a company as treasury shares-
  (a) are sold, or
  (b) are transferred for the purposes of an employees' share scheme,
the company must deliver a return to the registrar not later than 28 days after the shares are disposed of.

(2) The return must state with respect to shares of each class disposed of-
  (a) the number and nominal value of the shares, and
  (b) the date on which they were disposed of.

(3) Particulars of shares disposed of on different dates may be included in a single return.

(4) If default is made in complying with this section an offence is committed by every officer of the company who is in default.

(5) A person guilty of an offence under this section is liable-
  (a) on conviction on indictment, to a fine;
  (b) on summary conviction, to a fine not exceeding the statutory maximum and, for continued contravention, a daily default fine not exceeding one-tenth of the statutory maximum.

GENERAL NOTE

This section, together with s.730, restates, without any substantive changes, 169A of the 1985 Act, introduced by the 2003 Regulations. It sets out the registration requirement where treasury shares are disposed of under the previous section. (Section 730 restates the same obligation, but as amended, if the shares are instead cancelled.)

The 28-day period and the details with regard to the return are unaltered.

The sanction for the default offence (formerly in s.169A(5)) has been reworded to comply with the general treatment of such offences under this Act.

729.   Treasury shares: cancellation

(1) Where shares are held as treasury shares, the company may at any time cancel the shares (or any of them).

(2) If shares held as treasury shares cease to be qualifying shares, the company must forthwith cancel the shares.

(3) For this purpose shares are not to be regarded as ceasing to be qualifying shares by virtue only of-

(a) the suspension of their listing in accordance with the applicable rules in the EEA State in which the shares are officially listed, or

(b) the suspension of their trading in accordance with-

    (i) in the case of shares traded on the market known as the Alternative Investment Market, the rules of London Stock Exchange plc, and

    (ii) in any other case, the rules of the regulated market on which they are traded.

(4) If company cancels shares held as treasury shares, the amount of the company's share capital is reduced accordingly by the nominal amount of the shares cancelled.

(5) The directors may take any steps required to enable the company to cancel its shares under this section without complying with the provisions of Chapter 10 of Part 17 (reduction of share capital).

GENERAL NOTE

This section restates ss.162D(1)(c), (4) and (5) and 162E(1) and (2) of the 1985 Act, introduced by the 2003 Regulations. (Subsection 162E(3) is no longer required.) There are no substantive amendments.

Subsections (1)-(3)

These subsections restate s.162D(1)(c) and 162E(1) and (2). They provide for the cancellation of treasury shares both as an option (subs.(1)) and as a necessity (subs.(2)). Subsection (2) is qualified by subs.(3).

Regulated market is defined in s.1173.

Subsections (4) and (5)

These subsections restate s.162D(4) and (5) as to the internal consequences of cancellation with the omission of the reference to the now redundant concept of authorised capital. They are the same as in ss.688 and 706 on the cancellation of redeemed or purchased non treasury shares.

730. Treasury shares: notice of cancellation

(1) Where shares held by a company as treasury shares are cancelled, the company must deliver a return to the registrar not later than 28 days after the shares are cancelled.

This does not apply to shares that are cancelled forthwith on their acquisition by the company (see section 708).

(2) The return must state with respect to shares of each class cancelled-

    (a) the number and nominal value of the shares, and

    (b) the date on which they were cancelled.

(3) Particulars of shares cancelled on different dates may be included in a single return.

(4) The notice must be accompanied by a statement of capital.

(5) The statement of capital must state with respect to the company's share capital immediately following the cancellation-

    (a) the total number of shares of the company,

    (b) the aggregate nominal value of those shares,

    (c) for each class of shares-

        (i) prescribed particulars of the rights attached to the shares,

        (ii) the total number of shares of that class, and

        (iii) the aggregate nominal value of shares of that class, and

    (d) the amount paid up and the amount (if any) unpaid on each share (whether on account of the nominal value of the share or by way of premium).

(6) If default is made in complying with this section, an offence is committed by-

    (a) the company, and

    (b) every officer of the company who is in default.

(7) A person guilty of an offence under this section is liable on summary conviction to a fine not exceeding level 3 on the standard scale and, for continued contravention, a daily default fine not exceeding one-tenth of level 3 on the standard scale.

GENERAL NOTE

This section restates, with amendments, those parts of s.169A of the 1985 Act as are relevant to the registration of the cancellation of treasury shares.

Subsections (1)-(3)

These subsections restate s.169A(1)-(3) as to the requirement to notify the registrar of the cancellation of any treasury shares. The 28-day period and the details of registration are unaltered. Treasury shares cancelled on their acquisition never really become treasury shares and their cancellation will be registered under s.708.

Subsections (4) and (5)

These new subsections dovetail this section into the general theme of this Act as to the need to file a statement of capital on formation and an amended statement on a change in that capital.

Subsection (6) and (7)

These subsections retain the default offence in s.169A(4) and (5) amended to add the company as a potential defendant and to comply with the general treatment of such offences in this Act (see Sch.3).

731. Treasury shares: treatment of proceeds of sale

(1) Where shares held as treasury shares are sold, the proceeds of sale must be dealt with in accordance with this section.

(2) If the proceeds of sale are equal to or less than the purchase price paid by the company for the shares, the proceeds are treated for the purposes of Part 23 (distributions) as a realised profit of the company.

(3) If the proceeds of sale exceed the purchase price paid by the company-
(a) an amount equal to the purchase price paid is treated as a realised profit of the company for the purposes of that Part, and
(b) the excess must be transferred to the company's share premium account.

(4) For the purposes of this section-
(a) the purchase price paid by the company must be determined by the application of a weighted average price method, and
(b) if the shares were allotted to the company as fully paid bonus shares, the purchase price paid for them is treated as nil.

GENERAL NOTE

This section restates, with no substantive changes, s.162F of the 1985 Act, introduced by the 2003 Regulations, which sets out the rules for the treatment of the cash received on a sale of treasury shares under s.727 (no consideration in kind is allowed).

Subsections (1)-(3)

Restating s.162F(1)-(3), these subsections provide that if the proceeds of sale are equal to or less than the original purchase price (which must be funded out of distributable profits under s.724(1)) they can be regarded as distributable profits available for distribution since they are replacing like for like. Any excess over that price must, however, be regarded as capital with an equivalent amount being transferred to the share premium account.

Subsection (4)

Restating s.162F(4) and (5), these subsections provide that in determining whether the sale proceeds exceed the purchase price paid by the company or otherwise, the weighted average price method is to be used. That is by reference to the price and number of each acquisition parcel of shares.

Bonus treasury shares have a purchase price of zero.

732. Treasury shares: offences

(1) If a company contravenes any of the provisions of this Chapter (except section 730 (notice of cancellation)), an offence is committed by-
    (a) the company, and
    (b) every officer of the company who is in default.
(2) A person guilty of an offence under this section is liable-
    (a) on conviction on indictment, to a fine;
    (b) on summary conviction to a fine not exceeding the statutory maximum.

GENERAL NOTE

This section restates the general default offence in s.162G of the 1985 Act as introduced by the 2003 Regulations. The sanction in subs.(2) is required to comply with the general treatment of such offences in this Act.

CHAPTER 7

SUPPLEMENTARY PROVISIONS

733. The capital redemption reserve

(1) In the following circumstances a company must transfer amounts to a reserve, called the "capital redemption reserve".
(2) Where under this Part shares of a limited company are redeemed or purchased wholly out of the company's profits, the amount by which the company's issued share capital is diminished in accordance with-
    (a) section 688(b) (on the cancellation of shares redeemed), or
    (b) section 706(b)(ii) (on the cancellation of shares purchased),
must be transferred to the capital redemption reserve.
(3) If-
    (a) the shares are redeemed or purchased wholly or partly out of the proceeds of a fresh issue, and
    (b) the aggregate amount of the proceeds is less than the aggregate nominal value of the shares redeemed or purchased,
the amount of the difference must be transferred to the capital redemption reserve.
This does not apply in the case of a private company if, in addition to the proceeds of the fresh issue, the company applies a payment out of capital under Chapter 5 in making the redemption or purchase.
(4) The amount by which a company's share capital is diminished in accordance with section 729(4) (on the cancellation of shares held as treasury shares) must be transferred to the capital redemption reserve.
(5) The company may use the capital redemption reserve to pay up new shares to be allotted to members as fully paid bonus shares.
(6) Subject to that, the provisions of the Companies Acts relating to the reduction of a company's share capital apply as if the capital redemption reserve were part of its paid up share capital.

GENERAL NOTE

This section, together with the following section, restates s.170 of the 1985 Act as to the creation and operation of a capital redemption reserve consequent on a redemption or purchase by a company of its own shares. (Under the limited ability of companies to redeem shares prior to the 1981 Act there was a similar fund known as the capital redemption reserve fund.) There are no changes of substance.

Subsections (1)-(4)

These subsections restate s.170(1)-(3) of the 1985 Act as to the creation of the capital redemption reserve. Where a company uses distributable profits in whole or in part to fund a redemption or purchase of shares or a cancellation of treasury shares (or where the proceeds of a fresh issue alone are used but the amount is less than the aggregate nominal value of the relevant shares) a sum equivalent to the amount of profits used or shortfall must be transferred to a fund known as the capital redemption reserve. If, however, there is a payment out of capital involved (under Ch.5 of this Part), this section does not apply - the following section does.

Subsections (5) and (6)

These subsections restate s.170(4) as to the operation of the capital redemption reserve. It is a capital fund subject to all the rules on reduction of capital, etc. although it can be converted into bonus shares, which has no capital consequences.

Distributable profits - see s.736.

734. Accounting consequences of payment out of capital

(1) This section applies where a payment out of capital is made in accordance with Chapter 5 (redemption or purchase of own shares by private company out of capital).

(2) If the permissible capital payment is less than the nominal amount of the shares redeemed or purchased, the amount of the difference must be transferred to the company's capital redemption reserve.

(3) If the permissible capital payment is greater than the nominal amount of the shares redeemed or purchased-

    (a) the amount of any capital redemption reserve, share premium account or fully paid share capital of the company, and

    (b) any amount representing unrealised profits of the company for the time being standing to the credit of any revaluation reserve maintained by the company,

may be reduced by a sum not exceeding (or by sums not in total exceeding) the amount by which the permissible capital payment exceeds the nominal amount of the shares.

(4) Where the proceeds of a fresh issue are applied by the company in making a redemption or purchase of its own shares in addition to a payment out of capital under this Chapter, the references in subsections (2) and (3) to the permissible capital payment are to be read as referring to the aggregate of that payment and those proceeds.

GENERAL NOTE

This section restates s.171(4)-(6) of the 1985 Act with no changes of substance.

Subsection (2) mirrors the previous section on the need to create a capital redemption reserve consequent on a redemption or purchase by a company of its own shares, but this time where a payment out of capital by a private company under Ch.5 is involved. The reserve is needed where there is a shortfall in the capital used as against the aggregate nominal value of the shares so redeemed or purchased; e.g. where profits have also been used. Under subs.(4), where the proceeds of a fresh issue were also involved in the funding, then that amount is added onto the capital to calculate this shortfall.

Subsection (3) covers the converse case where the capital used exceeds the aggregate nominal value of the redeemed or purchased shares. In such a case the various capital reserves or the revaluation reserve may be reduced by the amount of the excess. Under subs.(4), where the proceeds of a fresh issue were also involved in the funding, then that amount is added onto the capital to calculate this excess.

735. Effect of company's failure to redeem or purchase

(1) This section applies where a company-

    (a) issues shares on terms that they are or are liable to be redeemed, or

    (b) agrees to purchase any of its shares.

(2) The company is not liable in damages in respect of any failure on its part to redeem or purchase any of the shares.

This is without prejudice to any right of the holder of the shares other than his right to sue the company for damages in respect of its failure.

(3) The court shall not grant an order for specific performance of the terms of redemption or purchase if the company shows that it is unable to meet the costs of redeeming or purchasing the shares in question out of distributable profits.

(4) If the company is wound up and at the commencement of the winding up any of the shares have not been redeemed or purchased, the terms of redemption or purchase may be enforced against the company.

When shares are redeemed or purchased under this subsection, they are treated as cancelled.

(5) Subsection (4) does not apply if-

    (a) the terms provided for the redemption or purchase to take place at a date later than that of the commencement of the winding up, or

    (b) during the period-

        (i) beginning with the date on which the redemption or purchase was to have taken place, and

        (ii) ending with the commencement of the winding up,

the company could not at any time have lawfully made a distribution equal in value to the price at which the shares were to have been redeemed or purchased.

(6) There shall be paid in priority to any amount that the company is liable under subsection (4) to pay in respect of any shares-

    (a) all other debts and liabilities of the company (other than any due to members in their character as such), and

    (b) if other shares carry rights (whether as to capital or as to income) that are preferred to the rights as to capital attaching to the first-mentioned shares, any amount due in satisfaction of those preferred rights.

Subject to that, any such amount shall be paid in priority to any amounts due to members in satisfaction of their rights (whether as to capital or income) as members.

GENERAL NOTE

This section restates s.178 of the 1985 Act on the consequences of a company's failure to redeem or purchase its own shares which thus could lead to an action for breach of contract against the company either before or during a winding up. If there were no restrictions, assets could be extracted from companies by artificially creating such claims. There are no substantive changes.

Subsections (2) and (3)

These subsections restate s.178(2) and part of (3) of the 1985 Act. They apply whilst the company is a going concern. The ban on an action for damages only relates to the actual failure by a company to redeem or purchase the shares and not, e.g. to an action for a breach of covenant by a third party consequent on such a failure: see *Barclays Bank Plc v British and Commonwealth Holdings Plc* [1996] 1 B.C.L.C. 1. It was also suggested in that case that it only applied to actions by the actual shareholder. Specific performance may be granted of it can be fulfilled out of distributable profits.

Subsections (4)-(6)

These subsections restate s.178(4)-(6) of the 1985 Act which apply to any action in a winding up where the winding up was after the due date for redemption or purchase. The shareholder may prove in the liquidation as a creditor for any loss suffered, but only if the company had distributable profits at any time between the due date and the commencement of the winding up. Such an applicant is a deferred creditor, however, not only as against other creditors, but also any shareholder with a prior right to return of capital, such as a preference share.

Distributable profits - see s.736

736. Meaning of "distributable profits"

In this Part (except in Chapter 2 (financial assistance): see section 683) "distributable profits", in relation to the making of any payment by a company, means profits out of which the company could lawfully make a distribution (within the meaning given by section 830) equal in value to the payment.

GENERAL NOTE

This section restates s.181(a) of the 1985 Act. It defines distributable profits for the purpose of all payments by companies under this Part, with the exception of Ch.2 on financial assistance.

737. General power to make further provision by regulations

(1) The Secretary of State may by regulations modify the provisions of this Part.
(2) The regulations may-
    (a) amend or repeal any of the provisions of this Part, or
    (b) make such other provision as appears to the Secretary of State appropriate in place of any of the provisions of this Part.
(3) Regulations under this section may make consequential amendments or repeals in other provisions of this Act, or in other enactments.
(4) Regulations under this section are subject to affirmative resolution procedure.

GENERAL NOTE

This new section allows for changes to this Part to be made by Regulations rather than by primary legislation. Introduced at a late stage, it was criticised as being part of a too wide delegation by the HL Select Committee on Delegated Powers and Regulatory Reform (26th Report of the 2005-6 Parliamentary Session; HL Paper 264). The subsequent Parliamentary consensus, however, was that this power should be retained. This is a largely technical area and it will enable a better response to be made to any future amendments to the Second EC Directive.

PART 19

DEBENTURES

GENERAL NOTE

This Part contains provisions relating to debentures generally, the register of debenture holders and certain ancillary matters. Some provisions are new, others are re-enacted versions of sections of the Companies Act 1985.

General provisions

738. Meaning of "debenture"

In the Companies Acts "debenture" includes debenture stock, bonds and any other securities of a company, whether or not constituting a charge on the assets of the company.

GENERAL NOTE

Apart from minor drafting differences, this definition is the same as that found previously in s.744 of the 1985 Act. The definitions in s.744 of the 1985 Act applied for the purposes of the Act *unless the contrary intention appears*. The definition in s.751 of the 2006 Act is not expressly qualified in this way. The statutory definition of debenture was first introduced into company law by the reforms of 1928-29.

739. Perpetual debentures

(1) A condition contained in debentures, or in a deed for securing debentures, is not invalid by reason only that the debentures are made-
    (a) irredeemable, or
    (b) redeemable only-
        (i) on the happening of a contingency (however remote), or
        (ii) on the expiration of a period (however long),
any rule of equity to the contrary notwithstanding.

(2) Subsection (1) applies to debentures whenever issued and to deeds whenever executed.

GENERAL NOTE

   This section re-enacts, without substantive change, s.193 of the Companies Act 1985. The effect of the section is to remove doubts as to the validity of debentures that are indefinite or which provide for prolonged postponement of the right of re-demption. A section overriding rules of equity that invalidate "clogs on the equity of redemption" was first enacted as s.14 of the Companies Act 1907.

740. Enforcement of contract to subscribe for debentures

A contract with a company to take up and pay for debentures of the company may be enforced by an order for specific performance.

GENERAL NOTE

   This section re-enacts, without change, s.195 of the Companies Act 1985. A provision allowing for a contract to subscribe for debentures to be enforced by an order for specific performance was first introduced in the Companies Act of 1908.

741. Registration of allotment of debentures

(1) A company must register an allotment of debentures as soon as practicable and in any event within two months after the date of the allotment.
(2) If a company fails to comply with this section, an offence is committed by-
    (a) the company, and
    (b) every officer of the company who is in default.
(3) A person guilty of an offence under this section is liable on summary conviction to a fine not exceeding level 3 on the standard scale and, for continued contravention, a daily default fine not exceeding one-tenth of level 3 on the standard scale.
(4) For the duties of the company as to the issue of the debentures, or certificates of debenture stock, see Part 21 (certification and transfer of securities)

GENERAL NOTE

   This section amends the law to require the registration of allotments of debentures. The requirements of this section mirror those of s.554 (Registration of allotment) relating to shares.

Subsection (1)

   Directors are required to effect registration as soon as practicable but in any event within two months of the date of allotment.

Subsection (2) and (3)

   Where a company fails to comply, the company and every officer of the company who is in default commits an offence. The penalty for this offence is set out in new subs.(3).

742. Debentures to bearer (Scotland)

Notwithstanding anything in the statute of the Scots Parliament of 1696, chapter 25, debentures to bearer issued in Scotland are valid and binding according to their terms.

GENERAL NOTE

   This re-enacts s.197 of the Companies Act 1985. The Act referred to is the Blank Bonds & Trusts Act 1696 (of the Scottish Parliament) which effectively prohibited the issue of bearer securities. The 1696 Act was itself repealed by the Requirements of Writing (Scotland) Act 1995.

Register of debenture holders

743.　Register of debenture holders

(1) Any register of debenture holders of a company that is kept by the company must be kept available for inspection-
　　(a) at the company's registered office, or
　　(b) at a place specified in regulations under section 1136.

(2) A company must give notice to the registrar of the place where any such register is kept available for inspection and of any change in that place.

(3) No such notice is required if the register has, at all times since it came into existence, been kept available for inspection at the company's registered office.

(4) If a company makes default for 14 days in complying with subsection (2), an offence is committed by-
　　(a) the company, and
　　(b) every officer of the company who is in default.

(5) A person guilty of an offence under this section is liable on summary conviction to a fine not exceeding level 3 on the standard scale and, for continued contravention, a daily default fine not exceeding one-tenth of level 3 on the standard scale.

(6) References in this section to a register of debenture holders include a duplicate-
　　(a) of a register of debenture holders that is kept outside the United Kingdom, or
　　(b) of any part of such a register.

GENERAL NOTE

This section replaces s.190 of the 1985 Act. It clarifies the requirements relating to the location at which the register of debenture holders (if there is one) is kept available for inspection. It broadly mirrors the requirements for the keeping of the company's register of members (see s.114). There is still no obligation to keep a register of debenture holders.

Subsection (1)

If a register of debenture holders is kept, it must be kept available for inspection either at the company's registered office or at another place specified in regulations under s.1136. Section 1136 authorises the Secretary of State to make provision by regulations specifying places other than a company's registered office at which mandatory company records may be so kept available for inspection. The regulations may specify a place by reference to the company's principal place of business, the part of the United Kingdom in which the company is registered, the place at which the company keeps any other records available for inspection or in any other way. The power for the Secretary of State to make these regulations is intended to meet the concern that, on the one hand, requirements relating to where records are kept should not impose unnecessary costs on business and, on the other hand, companies should not be able to make those wishing to inspect several company records which they have a statutory right to inspect to go to several different places. (DTI memorandum reproduced as Appendix 3 to the Twenty Sixth Report of the Delegated Powers and Regulatory Reform Committee (November 2006), para.69).

It is where the register is kept *available for inspection* that matters for this purpose, rather than where it is kept (which, in the case of an electronic register that may be updated from various locations, may be debatable).

Subsections (2) and (3)

The company must notify the registrar of the place where the register is kept available for inspection save that no notice is required where the register is, and has always been, kept at the company's registered office.

Subsections (4) and (5)

The obligations imposed by this section are underpinned by criminal sanctions.

Subsection (6)

The section applies to a duplicate of a register of debenture holders that is kept outside the United Kingdom or any part of such a register.

744. Register of debenture holders: right to inspect and require copy

(1) Every register of debenture holders of a company must, except when duly closed, be open to the inspection-
  (a) of the registered holder of any such debentures, or any holder of shares in the company, without charge, and
  (b) of any other person on payment of such fee as may be prescribed.

(2) Any person may require a copy of the register, or any part of it, on payment of such fee as may be prescribed.

(3) A person seeking to exercise either of the rights conferred by this section must make a request to the company to that effect.

(4) The request must contain the following information-
  (a) in the case of an individual, his name and address;
  (b) in the case of an organisation, the name and address of an individual responsible for making the request on behalf of the organisation;
  (c) the purpose for which the information is to be used; and
  (d) whether the information will be disclosed to any other person, and if so-
    (i) where that person is an individual, his name and address,
    (ii) where that person is an organisation, the name and address of an individual responsible for receiving the information on its behalf, and
    (iii) the purpose for which the information is to be used by that person.

(5) For the purposes of this section a register is "duly closed" if it is closed in accordance with provision contained-
  (a) in the articles or in the debentures,
  (b) in the case of debenture stock in the stock certificates, or
  (c) in the trust deed or other document securing the debentures or debenture stock.
The total period for which a register is closed in any year must not exceed 30 days.

(6) References in this section to a register of debenture holders include a duplicate-
  (a) of a register of debenture holders that is kept outside the United Kingdom, or
  (b) of any part of such a register.

GENERAL NOTE

This section is derived from part of s.191 of the Companies Act 1985. It modifies the right of public access to any register of debenture holders kept by a company by prescribing in more detail some aspects of the procedure. The changes broadly mirror similar requirements in Pt 8 relating to the register of members.

Unlike in relation to the register of members (see s.120), there is no requirement in this section, or elsewhere in the sections concerned with the register of debenture holders, for the company to advise those accessing the register of the date to which it has been made up. The regulation of the content of the register of debenture holders is less detailed than in relation to the register of members. In the Parliamentary debates on the Bill, Lord McKenzie, (*Hansard*, HL Vol.686, col.477 (November 2, 2006)) commented that "it would be anomalous for companies to be required to provide for the register of debenture holders the sort of information which they have to provide under Clause 119 [s.120] in relation to the register of members" ... and that "It would be excessively regulatory, and possibly wholly inappropriate, to impose an obligation for registers of debenture holders similar to Clause 119 [s.120] for registers of members."

Subsection (1)

This subsection re-enacts s.191(1) of the Companies Act 1985.

Subsection (2)

This subsection re-enacts s.191(2) of the Companies Act 1985.

Subsection (3) and (4)

These new provisions spell out procedural aspects of the exercise of the rights conferred by the section. Those seeking to inspect or to be provided with a copy of the register must provide their names and addresses, the purpose for which the information will be used, and, if the access is sought on behalf of others, similar information for them.

This subsection re-enacts s.191(6) of the Companies Act 1985.

745.   Register of debenture holders: response to request for inspection or copy

(1) Where a company receives a request under section 744 (register of debenture holders: right to inspect and require copy), it must within five working days either-
    (a) comply with the request, or
    (b) apply to the court.
(2) If it applies to the court it must notify the person making the request.
(3) If on an application under this section the court is satisfied that the inspection or copy is not sought for a proper purpose-
    (a) it shall direct the company not to comply with the request, and
    (b) it may further order that the company's costs (in Scotland, expenses) on the application be paid in whole or in part by the person who made the request, even if he is not a party to the application.
(4) If the court makes such a direction and it appears to the court that the company is or may be subject to other requests made for a similar purpose (whether made by the same person or different persons), it may direct that the company is not to comply with any such request.
The order must contain such provision as appears to the court appropriate to identify the requests to which it applies.
(5) If on an application under this section the court does not direct the company not to comply with the request, the company must comply with the request immediately upon the court giving its decision or, as the case may be, the proceedings being discontinued.

GENERAL NOTE

This section makes a significant change by providing a procedure for the company to refer the matter to the court if it considers the request is not for a proper purpose. There is an equivalent power for the company to apply to court where it receives a request relating to the register of members (see s.117). An underlying purpose of this change is to provide a mechanism for shielding investors in companies that are engaged in controversial business activities (such as drug companies that rely on animal testing) from extremist organisations.

Subsection (1)
The company has five working days either to comply with the request or to apply to the court.

Subsections (3)-(5)
These sub-sections apply if the company opts to apply to the court. Subsection (3) empowers the court to relieve the company of the obligation to meet the request if the court is satisfied that the access to the register of debenture holders is not sought for a proper purpose. "Proper purpose" is not defined. When this point was raised in the Parliamentary debate relating to the equivalent provision in Pt 8 on the register of members, Lord Sainsbury, speaking for the government, said that "A definition of either 'proper purpose' or 'improper purpose' could give rise to unintended loopholes or scams to get around the measure. We therefore consider that what is a proper purpose in this context is a matter best left to the courts to determine" (*Hansard*, col.GC150 (February 1, 2006)).

The court may require that the person who made the request pays the company's costs. Under subs.(4), the court may also relieve the company of the obligation to meet other requests for similar purposes. If the court does not make an order under subs.(3), or the proceedings are discontinued, then, under subs.(5), the company must immediately comply with the request.

746.   Register of debenture holders: refusal of inspection or default in providing copy

(1) If an inspection required under section 744 (register of debenture holders: right to inspect and require copy) is refused or default is made in providing a copy required under that section, otherwise than in accordance with an order of the court, an offence is committed by-
    (a) the company, and

(b) every officer of the company who is in default.

(2) A person guilty of an offence under this section is liable on summary conviction to a fine not exceeding level 3 on the standard scale and, for continued contravention, a daily default fine not exceeding one-tenth of level 3 on the standard scale.

(3) In the case of any such refusal or default the court may by order compel an immediate inspection or, as the case may be, direct that the copy required be sent to the person requesting it.

GENERAL NOTE

This section re-enacts part of s.191 of the 1985 Act. It provides criminal sanctions for failure to comply with requests. These sanctions do not apply where the court has relieved the company from the obligation to comply with a request.

Subsection (1)

Failure to comply, except where authorised by the court, is a criminal offence by the company and by every officer of the company who is in default. Corporate criminal liability is considered to be appropriate in circumstances where persons other than the company and its members could be adversely affected by the non-compliance.

747. Register of debenture holders: offences in connection with request for or disclosure of information

(1) It is an offence for a person knowingly or recklessly to make in a request under section 744 (register of debenture holders: right to inspect and require copy) a statement that is misleading, false or deceptive in a material particular.

(2) It is an offence for a person in possession of information obtained by exercise of either of the rights conferred by that section-

    (a) to do anything that results in the information being disclosed to another person, or

    (b) to fail to do anything with the result that the information is disclosed to another person,

knowing, or having reason to suspect, that person may use the information for a purpose that is not a proper purpose.

(3) A person guilty of an offence under this section is liable-

    (a) on conviction on indictment, to imprisonment for a term not exceeding two years or a fine (or both);

    (b) on summary conviction-

        (i) in England and Wales, to imprisonment for a term not exceeding twelve months or to a fine not exceeding the statutory maximum (or both);

        (ii) in Scotland or Northern Ireland, to imprisonment for a term not exceeding six months, or to a fine not exceeding the statutory maximum (or both).

GENERAL NOTE

This new section creates two new offences. The section mirrors an equivalent section in Pt 8 of the Act on the register of members (see s.119).

Subsection (1)

In relation to the new requirement in s.744 to provide information in a request for access, it is an offence knowingly or recklessly to make a statement that is misleading, false or deceptive in a material particular.

Subsection (2)

It is an offence for a person who has obtained information pursuant to an exercise of the rights in s.744 to do anything or fail to do anything which results in that information being disclosed to another person knowing or having reason to suspect that the other person may use the information for a purpose that is not a proper purpose. "Proper purpose" in this context is not defined. See further s.745.

748.   Time limit for claims arising from entry in register

(1) Liability incurred by a company-
    (a) from the making or deletion of an entry in the register of debenture holders, or
    (b) from a failure to make or delete any such entry,
is not enforceable more than ten years after the date on which the entry was made or deleted or, as the case may be, the failure first occurred.

(2) This is without prejudice to any lesser period of limitation (and, in Scotland, to any rule that the obligation giving rise to the liability prescribes before the expiry of that period).

GENERAL NOTE

   This clause replaces s.191(7) of the 1985 Act. The maximum time limit for claims arising from errors in the register is reduced from twenty years to ten years. This change mirrors equivalent provisions applicable to the register of members (see s.128).

Supplementary provisions

749.   Right of debenture holder to copy of deed

(1) Any holder of debentures of a company is entitled, on request and on payment of such fee as may be prescribed, to be provided with a copy of any trust deed for securing the debentures.

(2) If default is made in complying with this section, an offence is committed by every officer of the company who is in default.

(3) A person guilty of an offence under this section is liable on summary conviction to a fine not exceeding level 3 on the standard scale and, for continued contravention, a daily default fine not exceeding one-tenth of level 3 on the standard scale.

(4) In the case of any such default the court may direct that the copy required be sent to the person requiring it.

GENERAL NOTE

   This section re-enacts s.191(3) of the Companies Act 1985 and specifies the criminal sanctions for failure to comply with the obligation imposed by the section.

750.   Liability of trustees of debentures

(1) Any provision contained in-
    (a) a trust deed for securing an issue of debentures, or
    (b) any contract with the holders of debentures secured by a trust deed,
is void in so far as it would have the effect of exempting a trustee of the deed from, or indemnifying him against, liability for breach of trust where he fails to show the degree of care and diligence required of him as trustee, having regard to the provisions of the trust deed conferring on him any powers, authorities or discretions.

(2) Subsection (1) does not invalidate-
    (a) a release otherwise validly given in respect of anything done or omitted to be done by a trustee before the giving of the release;
    (b) any provision enabling such a release to be given-
        (i) on being agreed to by a majority of not less than 75% in value of the debenture holders present and voting in person or, where proxies are permitted, by proxy at a meeting summoned for the purpose, and
        (ii) either with respect to specific acts or omissions or on the trustee dying or ceasing to act.

(3) This section is subject to section 751 (saving for certain older provisions).

751. Liability of trustees of debentures: saving for certain older provisions

(1) Section 750 (liability of trustees of debentures) does not operate-
    (a) to invalidate any provision in force on the relevant date so long as any person-
        (i) then entitled to the benefit of the provision, or
        (ii) afterwards given the benefit of the provision under subsection (3) below,
    remains a trustee of the deed in question, or
    (b) to deprive any person of any exemption or right to be indemnified in respect of anything done or omitted to be done by him while any such provision was in force.
(2) The relevant date for this purpose is-
    (a) 1st July 1948 in a case where section 192 of the Companies Act 1985 (c. 6) applied immediately before the commencement of this section;
    (b) 1st July 1961 in a case where Article 201 of the Companies (Northern Ireland) Order 1986 (S.I. 1986/ 1032 (N.I. 6)) then applied.
(3) While any trustee of a trust deed remains entitled to the benefit of a provision saved by subsection (1) above the benefit of that provision may be given either-
    (a) to all trustees of the deed, present and future, or
    (b) to any named trustees or proposed trustees of it,
by a resolution passed by a majority of not less than 75% in value of the debenture holders present in person or, where proxies are permitted, by proxy at a meeting summoned for the purpose.
(4) A meeting for that purpose must be summoned in accordance with the provisions of the deed or, if the deed makes no provision for summoning meetings, in a manner approved by the court.

752. Power to re-issue redeemed debentures

(1) Where a company has redeemed debentures previously issued, then unless-
    (a) provision to the contrary (express or implied) is contained in the company's articles or in any contract made by the company, or
    (b) the company has, by passing a resolution to that effect or by some other act, manifested its intention that the debentures shall be cancelled,
the company may re-issue the debentures, either by re-issuing the same debentures or by issuing new debentures in their place.
This subsection is deemed always to have had effect.

(2) On a re-issue of redeemed debentures the person entitled to the debentures has (and is deemed always to have had) the same priorities as if the debentures had never been redeemed.

(3) The re-issue of a debenture or the issue of another debenture in its place under this section is treated as the issue of a new debenture for the purposes of stamp duty.

It is not so treated for the purposes of any provision limiting the amount or number of debentures to be issued.

(4) A person lending money on the security of a debenture re-issued under this section which appears to be duly stamped may give the debenture in evidence in any proceedings for enforcing his security without payment of the stamp duty or any penalty in respect of it, unless he had notice (or, but for his negligence, might have discovered) that the debenture was not duly stamped.

In that case the company is liable to pay the proper stamp duty and penalty.

GENERAL NOTE

This section re-enacts, without substantive change, most of s.194 of the 1985 Act. This section overrides a principle estab-lished by case law which was to the effect that a debenture once paid off was extinguished and could not be re-issued.

753. Deposit of debentures to secure advances

Where a company has deposited any of its debentures to secure advances from time to time on current account or otherwise, the debentures are not treated as redeemed by reason only of the company's account having ceased to be in debit while the debentures remained so deposited.

GENERAL NOTE

This section re-enacts, without substantive change, s.194(3) of the Companies Act 1985.

754. Priorities where debentures secured by floating charge

(1) This section applies where debentures of a company registered in England and Wales or Northern Ireland are secured by a charge that, as created, was a floating charge.

(2) If possession is taken, by or on behalf of the holders of the debentures, of any property comprised in or subject to the charge, and the company is not at that time in the course of being wound up, the company's preferential debts shall be paid out of assets coming to the hands of the persons taking possession in priority to any claims for principal or interest in respect of the debentures.

(3) "Preferential debts" means the categories of debts listed in Schedule 6 to the Insolvency Act 1986 (c. 45) or Schedule 4 to the Insolvency (Northern Ireland) Order 1989 (S.I. 1989/ 2405 (N.I. 19)).

For the purposes of those Schedules "the relevant date" is the date of possession being taken as mentioned in subsection (2).

(4) Payments under this section shall be recouped, as far as may be, out of the assets of the company available for payment of general creditors.

GENERAL NOTE

Save for the inclusion of new references to Northern Ireland, this section re-enacts, without substantive change, s.196 of the Companies Act 1985. Its purpose is to ensure that preferential debts are paid ahead of floating charge debenture holders.

PRIVATE AND PUBLIC COMPANIES

CHAPTER I

PROHIBITION OF PUBLIC OFFERS BY PRIVATE COMPANIES

755. Prohibition of public offers by private company

(1) A private company limited by shares or limited by guarantee and having a share capital must not-
- (a) offer to the public any securities of the company, or
- (b) allot or agree to allot any securities of the company with a view to their being offered to the public.

(2) Unless the contrary is proved, an allotment or agreement to allot securities is presumed to be made with a view to their being offered to the public if an offer of the securities (or any of them) to the public is made-
- (a) within six months after the allotment or agreement to allot, or
- (b) before the receipt by the company of the whole of the consideration to be received by it in respect of the securities.

(3) A company does not contravene this section if-
- (a) it acts in good faith in pursuance of arrangements under which it is to re-register as a public company before the securities are allotted, or
- (b) as part of the terms of the offer it undertakes to re-register as a public company within a specified period, and that undertaking is complied with.

(4) The specified period for the purposes of subsection (3)(b) must be a period ending not later than six months after the day on which the offer is made (or, in the case of an offer made on different days, first made).

(5) In this Chapter "securities" means shares or debentures.

GENERAL NOTE

This chapter refers to shares and debentures. It continues the prohibitions under ss.58(3), 81 and 742A of the Companies Act 1985 against private companies making offers of securities to the public.

Subsection (1)

This provision maintains the prohibition on private companies making offers of securities to the public which was previously contained in s.81(1) of the Companies Act 1985. The prohibition does not apply to companies limited by guarantee without a share capital nor to unlimited companies. It applies, therefore, only to private limited companies or to private companies limited by guarantee with a share capital.

Subsection (2)

Not only are private companies prohibited from making offers of securities from the public, but they are also prohibited from allotting their securities to other people with the intention that those securities be offered to the public by their allottee. This provision replaces s.58(3) of the 1985 Act.

Subsection (3)

Whereas a private company which offered its securities to the public would have committed an offence, the approach taken under the 2006 Act, broadly put, is to require that the company re-register as a public company, unless the court considers it impracticable or undesirable in the circumstances to do so. The company is not in breach of this requirement if it is acting in good faith in pursuance of the process of re-registering as a public company.

756.   Meaning of "offer to the public"

(1) This section explains what is meant in this Chapter by an offer of securities to the public.

(2) An offer to the public includes an offer to any section of the public, however selected.

(3) An offer is not regarded as an offer to the public if it can properly be regarded, in all the circumstances, as-

    (a) not being calculated to result, directly or indirectly, in securities of the company becoming available to persons other than those receiving the offer, or

    (b) otherwise being a private concern of the person receiving it and the person making it.

(4) An offer is to be regarded (unless the contrary is proved) as being a private concern of the person receiving it and the person making it if-

    (a) it is made to a person already connected with the company and, where it is made on terms allowing that person to renounce his rights, the rights may only be renounced in favour of another person already connected with the company; or

    (b) it is an offer to subscribe for securities to be held under an employees' share scheme and, where it is made on terms allowing that person to renounce his rights, the rights may only be renounced in favour of-

        (i) another person entitled to hold securities under the scheme, or

        (ii) a person already connected with the company.

(5) For the purposes of this section "person already connected with the company" means-

    (a) an existing member or employee of the company,

    (b) a member of the family of a person who is or was a member or employee of the company,

    (c) the widow or widower, or surviving civil partner, of a person who was a member or employee of the company,

    (d) an existing debenture holder of the company, or

    (e) a trustee (acting in his capacity as such) of a trust of which the principal beneficiary is a person within any of paragraphs (a) to (d).

(6) For the purposes of subsection (5)(b) the members of a person's family are the person's spouse or civil partner and children (including step-children) and their descendants.

GENERAL NOTE

This provision replaces s.742A of the Companies Act 1985. An offer to the public includes an offer to a section of the public.

Subsection (3)

Offers which are not to be regarded as being offers to the public are offers which, after consideration of all the appropriate circumstances, are "not calculated to result, directly or indirectly, in securities ... becoming available to persons other than those receiving the offer" or are "otherwise ... a private concern of the person receiving [the offer] and the person making it". The former exclusion is predicated on the notion that offers will be made to individual people or to very small groups of people, whereas if read literally that provision would nevertheless be satisfied if the offer were made to many thousands of people with no intention that any other people receive that offer. Equally, the latter exclusion could be satisfied literally if the same offer were made to many thousands of people with the intention that contractual relations be created between those thousands of offerees severally and the offeror. This latter provision is qualified in subs.(4). Nevertheless, to achieve its policy goals, this provision must therefore be read purposively.

Subsection (4)

For the purposes of subs.(3), a private concern arises in circumstances in which the offeree is already connected to the company or is an offer to subscribe under an employees' share scheme. Persons connected with the company are listed in subs.(5).

757. Enforcement of prohibition: order restraining proposed contravention

(1) If it appears to the court-
    (a) on an application under this section, or
    (b) in proceedings under Part 30 (protection of members against unfair prejudice),
that a company is proposing to act in contravention of section 755 (prohibition of public offers by private companies), the court shall make an order under this section.

(2) An order under this section is an order restraining the company from contravening that section.

(3) An application for an order under this section may be made by-
    (a) a member or creditor of the company, or
    (b) the Secretary of State.

GENERAL NOTE

This section empowers the court to make orders to prevent contravention of the unfair prejudice provisions contained in Pt 30 of the 2006 Act, whereas the next section grants the court power in the event that a contravention of the unfair prejudice provisions has already been committed. A member of the company, a creditor of the company or the Secretary of State may make an application under this section or in proceedings under the unfair prejudice provisions contained in Pt 30 of the 2006 Act for an order restraining the company from contravening the provisions of that Part (formerly s.459 of the Companies Act 1985).

758. Enforcement of prohibition: orders available to the court after contravention

(1) This section applies if it appears to the court-
    (a) on an application under this section, or
    (b) in proceedings under Part 30 (protection of members against unfair prejudice),
that a company has acted in contravention of section 755 (prohibition of public offers by private companies).

(2) The court must make an order requiring the company to re-register as a public company unless it appears to the court-
    (a) that the company does not meet the requirements for re-registration as a public company, and
    (b) that it is impractical or undesirable to require it to take steps to do so.

(3) If it does not make an order for re-registration, the court may make either or both of the following-
    (a) a remedial order (see section 759), or
    (b) an order for the compulsory winding up of the company.

(4) An application under this section may be made by-
    (a) a member of the company who-
        (i) was a member at the time the offer was made (or, if the offer was made over a period, at any time during that period), or
        (ii) became a member as a result of the offer,
    (b) a creditor of the company who was a creditor at the time the offer was made (or, if the offer was made over a period, at any time during that period), or
    (c) the Secretary of State.

GENERAL NOTE

In the event that a private company breaches s.755 by offering securities to the public, then the court may make one of two forms of order. First, an order requiring the company to re-register as a public company, unless it appears to the court both that the company does not meet the requirements for re-registration as a public company and that it is impractical or undesirable to require it to "take the steps to do so". Read more closely, the court "must" make such an order, but the compulsion to make that order may be overridden by the caveat of the unsuitability of re-registration for that company. Secondly, if an order for re-registration is not made, then the court may either make a remedial order (under the following section) or it may make an order for the compulsory winding up of the company, further to Ch.6 of Pt 4 of the Insolvency Act 1986.

759. Enforcement of prohibition: remedial order

(1) A "remedial order" is an order for the purpose of putting a person affected by anything done in contravention of section 755 (prohibition of public offers by private company) in the position he would have been in if it had not been done.
(2) The following provisions are without prejudice to the generality of the power to make such an order.
(3) Where a private company has-
    (a) allotted securities pursuant to an offer to the public, or
    (b) allotted or agreed to allot securities with a view to their being offered to the public,
a remedial order may require any person knowingly concerned in the contravention of section 755 to offer to purchase any of those securities at such price and on such other terms as the court thinks fit.
(4) A remedial order may be made-
    (a) against any person knowingly concerned in the contravention, whether or not an officer of the company;
    (b) notwithstanding anything in the company's constitution (which includes, for this purpose, the terms on which any securities of the company are allotted or held);
    (c) whether or not the holder of the securities subject to the order is the person to whom the company allotted or agreed to allot them.
(5) Where a remedial order is made against the company itself, the court may provide for the reduction of the company's capital accordingly.

GENERAL NOTE
    The court is empowered to make a remedial order under the preceding provision if a private company breaches s.755 by offering securities to the public. This section sets some perameters on the form of that order but without restricting the court's general discretion.

Subsection (1)
    The statutory purpose of such an order is compensate any person "affected by anything done in contravention of" the prohibition in s.755 to put that person "in the position he would have been in if it had not been done", although that statutory purpose is not to restrict the power to make the order under the preceding section.

Subsection (3)
    A remedial order may require any person who was "knowingly concerned" in the contravention of s.755 to "offer to purchase any of those securities at such price and on such terms as the court thinks fit". The requirement that a person "offer" to purchase securities should, it is suggested, be understood as compelling that person to enter into a contract to buy those securities on the terms fixed by the court; however, this provision should be read so that the holder of the securities has an implied power to retain those securities if he so chooses, just as the following section provides that an allotment of securities in breach of s.755 is not necessarily invalid. The concept "knowingly" is considered in detail in the note to s.563 in relation to civil law (and s.572 in relation to criminal law).

760. Validity of allotment etc not affected

Nothing in this Chapter affects the validity of any allotment or sale of securities or of any agreement to allot or sell securities.

GENERAL NOTE
    This provision replaces the provision formerly contained in s.81(3) of the Companies Act 1985. The allotment or sale of securities, or an agreement to allot or sell securities, will be valid despite being in contravention of this Ch.1. Thus for the purposes of the law of contract, the allottee or transferee of the shares is still entitled to enforce the contract and is entitled to the remedies available under the law of contract generally.

CHAPTER 2

MINIMUM SHARE CAPITAL REQUIREMENT FOR PUBLIC COMPANIES

761. Public company: requirement as to minimum share capital

(1) A company that is a public company (otherwise than by virtue of reregistration as a public company) must not do business or exercise any borrowing powers unless the registrar has issued it with a certificate under this section (a "trading certificate").

(2) The registrar shall issue a trading certificate if, on an application made in accordance with section 762, he is satisfied that the nominal value of the company's allotted share capital is not less than the authorised minimum.

(3) For this purpose a share allotted in pursuance of an employees' share scheme shall not be taken into account unless paid up as to-
(a) at least one-quarter of the nominal value of the share, and
(b) the whole of any premium on the share.

(4) A trading certificate has effect from the date on which it is issued and is conclusive evidence that the company is entitled to do business and exercise any borrowing powers.

GENERAL NOTE

Section 761 replaces, without substantive amendment, s.117(1), (2), (4) and (6) of the Companies Act 1985. As under that Act, a public company may not commence business or exercise borrowing powers unless and until the registrar of companies has issued it with a trading certificate (subs.(1)). A trading certificate is to be issued by the registrar on an application under s.762 (below) only if he is satisfied that the nominal value of the company's allotted share capital is not less than the authorised minimum (subs.(2)). In determining the nominal value of the company's allotted share capital, any share allotted under an employees' share scheme is only to be taken into account if it has been paid up as to at least one-quarter of the nominal value of the share and the whole of any premium on the share. (subs.(3)). Once a trading certificate is issued, it has effect from the issue date and is conclusive evidence that the company is entitled to do business an exercise borrowing powers (subs.(4)).

762. Procedure for obtaining certificate

(1) An application for a certificate under section 761 must-
(a) state that the nominal value of the company's allotted share capital is not less than the authorised minimum,
(b) specify the amount, or estimated amount, of the company's preliminary expenses,
(c) specify any amount or benefit paid or given, or intended to be paid or given, to any promoter of the company, and the consideration for the payment or benefit, and
(d) be accompanied by a statement of compliance.

(2) The statement of compliance is a statement that the company meets the requirements for the issue of a certificate under section 761.

(3) The registrar may accept the statement of compliance as sufficient evidence of the matters stated in it.

GENERAL NOTE

This section replaces s.117(3) of the Companies Act 1985 and prescribed the procedure for obtaining a trading certificate. An application must include a statement, which may be in paper or electronic form, that the company's allotted share capital is not less that the authorised minimum (as to which see below, at note to s.763) (subs.(1)(a)). The statement must also specific the actual or estimated amount of the company's preliminary expenses and any amount or benefit paid or given, intended to be paid or given, to any promoter of the company, along with the consideration for that payment of benefit (subss.(1)(b) and (c)). The application must also be accompanied by a statement of compliance to the effect that the company meets the requirements for the issue of a trading certificate under s.761 (subss.(1)(b) and (2)). The registrar may accept this statement as sufficient evidence of the matters stated in it (subs.(3)).

763. The authorised minimum

(1) "The authorised minimum", in relation to the nominal value of a public company's allotted share capital is-
   (a) £50,000, or
   (b) the prescribed euro equivalent.
(2) The Secretary of State may by order prescribe the amount in euros that is for the time being to be treated as equivalent to the sterling amount of the authorised minimum.
(3) This power may be exercised from time to time as appears to the Secretary of State to be appropriate.
(4) The amount prescribed shall be determined by applying an appropriate spot rate of exchange to the sterling amount and rounding to the nearest 100 euros.
(5) An order under this section is subject to negative resolution procedure.
(6) This section has effect subject to any exercise of the power conferred by section 764 (power to alter authorised minimum).

GENERAL NOTE

This provision replaces s.118 of the Companies Act 1985 and retains the authorised minimum capital for a public company, as required by Art.6 of the Second Company Law Directive (77/91/EEC) at £50,000 or the prescribed euro equivalent (subs.(1)). Subsection (2) enables the Secretary of State, by order (subject to the negative resolution procedure - subs.(5)) to prescribe the amount in euros that is to be treated as the equivalent sterling amount of the authorised minimum capital (the formula being specified in subs.(4)). Subsection (6) renders s.763 subject to the Secretary of State's power, in s.764 (below), to alter the authorised minimum capital.

764. Power to alter authorised minimum

(1) The Secretary of State may by order-
   (a) alter the sterling amount of the authorised minimum, and
   (b) make a corresponding alteration of the prescribed euro equivalent.
(2) The amount of the prescribed euro equivalent shall be determined by applying an appropriate spot rate of exchange to the sterling amount and rounding to the nearest 100 euros.
(3) An order under this section that increases the authorised minimum may-
   (a) require a public company having an allotted share capital of which the nominal value is less than the amount specified in the order to-
      (i) increase that value to not less than that amount, or
      (ii) re-register as a private company;
   (b) make provision in connection with any such requirement for any of the matters for which provision is made by this Act relating to-
      (i) a company's registration, re-registration or change of name,
      (ii) payment for shares comprised in a company's share capital, and
      (iii) offers to the public of shares in or debentures of a company,
   including provision as to the consequences (in criminal law or otherwise) of a failure to comply with any requirement of the order;
   (c) provide for any provision of the order to come into force on different days for different purposes.
(4) An order under this section is subject to affirmative resolution procedure.

GENERAL NOTE

This section retains from s.118 of the Companies Act 1985 the power of the Secretary of State, by order (subject to the affirmative resolution procedure (subs.(4)), to alter the sterling amount of the authorised minimum or its euro equivalent (to be calculated by reference to the formula in subs.(2)). It also retains the provision from s.118(2) that such an order may require any public company with an allotted capital the nominal value of which falls below the altered authorised minimum to increase that value to not less than the authorised minimum or to re-register as a private company (subs.(2)(a)). The order in question may also make provision in relation to the requirements of the Act concerned with the registration or re-registration of a company's name, the payment for its shares or offers to the public of its shares or debentures, including the consequences of a failure to comply with any of the order's requirements (subs.(3)(b)). Any order made under this section may have its provisions coming into force on different days for different purposes (subs.(3)(c)).

765. Authorised minimum: application of initial requirement

(1) The initial requirement for a public company to have allotted share capital of a nominal value not less than the authorised minimum, that is-
    (a) the requirement in section 761(2) for the issue of a trading certificate, or
    (b) the requirement in section 91(1)(a) for re-registration as a public company,
must be met either by reference to allotted share capital denominated in sterling or by reference to allotted share capital denominated in euros (but not partly in one and partly in the other).

(2) Whether the requirement is met is determined in the first case by reference to the sterling amount and in the second case by reference to the prescribed euro equivalent.

(3) No account is to be taken of any allotted share capital of the company denominated in a currency other than sterling or, as the case may be, euros.

(4) If the company could meet the requirement either by reference to share capital denominated in sterling or by reference to share capital denominated in euros, it must elect in its application for a trading certificate or, as the case may be, for re-registration as a public company which is to be the currency by reference to which the matter is determined.

GENERAL NOTE

This new section addresses the question of the denomination of the company's shares capital as regards the authorised minimum. The initial requirement in s.761(2) and in s.91(1)(a) (where a private company re-registers as a public company) is for the allotted share capital to be denominated in sterling or in euros (but not partly in one and partly in the other) - subs.(1). In order to determine whether or not the authorised minimum requirement of £50,000 is met in any given case reference is first made to the sterling amount and then to the prescribed euro equivalent (subs.(2)) and no account is taken of any allotted share capital denominated in other than sterling or in euros (subs.(3)). If the company can meet the requirement either by reference to share capital denominated in sterling or in euros, it must elect, in its application either for a trading certificate or for re-registration as the case may be, which currency is to apply for the purpose of determining whether the authorised minimum is met (subs.(4)).

766. Authorised minimum: application where shares denominated in different currencies etc

(1) The Secretary of State may make provision by regulations as to the application of the authorised minimum in relation to a public company that-
    (a) has shares denominated in more than one currency,
    (b) redenominates the whole or part of its allotted share capital, or
    (c) allots new shares.

(2) The regulations may make provision as to the currencies, exchange rates and dates by reference to which it is to be determined whether the nominal value of the company's allotted share capital is less than the authorised minimum.

(3) The regulations may provide that where-
    (a) a company has redenominated the whole or part of its allotted share capital, and
    (b) the effect of the redenomination is that the nominal value of the company's allotted share capital is less than the authorised minimum,
the company must re-register as a private company.

(4) Regulations under subsection (3) may make provision corresponding to any provision made by sections 664 to 667 (re-registration as private company in consequence of cancellation of shares).

(5) Any regulations under this section have effect subject to section 765 (authorised minimum: application of initial requirement).

(6) Regulations under this section are subject to negative resolution procedure.

GENERAL NOTE

This section enables the Secretary of State to make provision by regulations (subject to negative resolution procedure (subs.(6)) regarding the authorised minimum where a public company has shares denominated in more than one currency and redenominates all or part of its allotted capital or allots new shares (subs.(1)). The section is aimed at ensuring that, in such circumstances, the authorised minimum capital is met, and therefore the regulations may make provision in respect of currencies, exchange rates and dates by reference to which the question of whether the nominal value of the allotted share capital meets the authorised minimum is to be determined (subs.(2)). Where redenomination occurs and the effect is that the nominal value of the allotted share capital falls below the authorised minimum, the regulations may provide that the company must re-register as a private company (subs.(3)). Where this is the case, the regulations may also make provision corresponding to provision made by ss.664-667 (re-registration as a private company in consequence of cancellation of shares: see above.)

767. Consequences of doing business etc without a trading certificate

(1) If a company does business or exercises any borrowing powers in contravention of section 761, an offence is committed by-
    (a) the company, and
    (b) every officer of the company who is in default.

(2) A person guilty of an offence under subsection (1) is liable-
    (a) on conviction on indictment, to a fine;
    (b) on summary conviction, to a fine not exceeding the statutory maximum.

(3) A contravention of section 761 does not affect the validity of a transaction entered into by the company, but if a company-
    (a) enters into a transaction in contravention of that section, and
    (b) fails to comply with its obligations in connection with the transaction within 21 days from being called on to do so,
the directors of the company are jointly and severally liable to indemnify any other party to the transaction in respect of any loss or damage suffered by him by reason of the company's failure to comply with its obligations.

(4) The directors who are so liable are those who were directors at the time the company entered into the transaction.

GENERAL NOTE

This section replaces s.117(7) and (8) of the Companies Act 1985. It applies where a public company commences business or exercises borrowing powers without obtaining a trading certificate under s.761. The contravention of the requirements of that section constitutes a criminal offence committed by the company and every one of its officers in default (subs.(1)), the penalty for which is prescribed by subs.(2). Entry into a transaction without first obtaining a trading certificate does not affect the validity of the transaction, but where a company enters into such a transaction and does not, within 21 days of being called upon to comply with its obligations under s.761, obtain a trading certificate the directors of the company (being those at the time the transaction is entered into - subs.(4)) are jointly and severally liable to indemnify the counterparty to the transaction of any loss or damage suffered by him as a result of the company's failure to comply with its obligations (subs.(3)).

PART 21

CERTIFICATION AND TRANSFER OF SECURITIES

GENERAL NOTE

This Pt 21 contains provisions which underscore the differences between public companies and private companies by prohibiting the offer of securities in private companies to the public.

GENERAL NOTE

It is a cornerstone of securities law that offers of securities to the public may only be made by public companies which are expressly subject to the regulations - enforced in the United Kingdom by the Financial Services Authority ("FSA") - which are created under the applicable EC Directives relating to the form of prospectuses, the disclosure of information before any offer or any sale of securities is made to the public, and transparency once securities are in issue. The applicable principles are outlined in the General Note to Pt 43 of the 2006 Act in this Guide, and are considered in greater detail in Part 5 of *Palmer's Company Law* (26th edn, Sweet & Maxwell). Private companies are thus not permitted to make offers of securities to the public at large. This Ch.1 of Pt 21 of the 2006 Act is intended to restrain private companies from acting in that way.

Share certificates

768. Share certificate to be evidence of title

(1) In the case of a company registered in England and Wales or Northern Ireland, a certificate under the common seal of the company specifying any shares held by a member is prima facie evidence of his title to the shares.

(2) In the case of a company registered in Scotland-

    (a) a certificate under the common seal of the company specifying any shares held by a member, or

    (b) a certificate specifying any shares held by a member and subscribed by the company in accordance with the Requirements of Writing (Scotland) Act 1995 (c. 7),

is sufficient evidence, unless the contrary is shown, of his title to the shares.

GENERAL NOTE

This Chapter restates ss.182-189, part of Ch.VIII of Pt V of the 1985 Act and deals with the issues of ownership and transfer of shares and debentures in a more logical order. Most of those sections are restated with no substantive amendments, but there are amendments to the obligations of the directors of a company when presented with a request for a transfer (in former ss.183 and 185). Those amendments, which were originally in the Bill, were subsumed into the restatement exercise (see the General Note to the Act).

This section restates s.186 of the 1985 Act with no substantive amendments. It continues the rule that a share certificate is only *prima facie* (in Scotland sufficient) evidence of title; the register of members remains the title document. A share certificate is neither a document of title nor a negotiable instrument, although a full action for conversion may lie in respect of it: *MCC Proceeds Inc v Lehman Brothers International (Europe)* [1998] 2 B.C.L.C. 659. The alternative, a share warrant, is a negotiable instrument - see s.779 of this Act.

For the meaning of common seal in this context see s.50 of this Act.

Issue of certificates etc on allotment

769. Duty of company as to issue of certificates etc on allotment

(1) A company must, within two months after the allotment of any of its shares, debentures or debenture stock, complete and have ready for delivery-

    (a) the certificates of the shares allotted,

    (b) the debentures allotted, or

    (c) the certificates of the debenture stock allotted.

(2) Subsection (1) does not apply-

    (a) if the conditions of issue of the shares, debentures or debenture stock provide otherwise,

    (b) in the case of allotment to a financial institution (see section 778), or

(c) in the case of an allotment of shares if, following the allotment, the company has issued a share warrant in respect of the shares (see section 779).

(3) If default is made in complying with subsection (1) an offence is committed by every officer of the company who is in default.

(4) A person guilty of an offence under subsection (3) is liable on summary conviction to a fine not exceeding level 3 on the standard scale and, for continued contravention, a daily default fine not exceeding one-tenth of level 3 on the standard scale.

GENERAL NOTE

This section restates, with amendments, the parts of s.185, as amended, of the 1985 Act dealing with the issue of certificates, etc. on allotment. The other parts of that section, dealing with the issue of certificates on a transfer, are now in ss.776 and 778 of this Act.

This section includes amendments to take into account the fact that under s.122 of this Act companies may now issue share warrants direct (these are negotiable instruments - see s.779) without having to first issue the shares as registered shares with share certificates and then convert them.

Subsections (1) and (2)

These subsections restate the obligation on companies to have the appropriate certificate ready within two months of an allotment. The exceptions in paras (a) and (b) of subs.(2) are retained from the former section, but para.(c) is new. It is necessary because share warrants may now be issued directly on an allotment and need not be converted from registered shares. For shares allotted to a financial institution see s.778 of this Act.

Subsections (3) and (4)

These subsections restate the offence in default in s.185(5) of the 1985 Act. The sanction has been reworded to comply with the general treatment of such offences in this Act. There is also a civil remedy for a breach - see s.782 of this Act.

Transfer of securities

770. Registration of transfer

(1) A company may not register a transfer of shares in or debentures of the company unless-
    (a) a proper instrument of transfer has been delivered to it, or
    (b) the transfer-
        (i) is an exempt transfer within the Stock Transfer Act 1982 (c. 41), or
        (ii) is in accordance with regulations under Chapter 2 of this Part.

(2) Subsection (1) does not affect any power of the company to register as shareholder or debenture holder a person to whom the right to any shares in or debentures of the company has been transmitted by operation of law.

GENERAL NOTE

This section, the first dealing with the transfer process, restates s.183(1) and (2) of the 1985 Act, but with one drafting change.

Subsection (1)

This subsection repeats the requirement for a "proper instrument of transfer" to be lodged with the company. This has long been held to mean any document capable of being stamped: see, e.g. *Dempsey v Celtic Football and Athletic Co Ltd* [1993] B.C.C. 514; *Nisbet v Shepherd* [1994] 1 B.C.L.C. 300. The exceptions relate to electronic or paperless transfers.

Unlike the former section, however, there is no express provision to the effect that this requirement applies whatever the articles say, but the mandatory wording of the section makes that unnecessary.

Subsection (2)

This subsection restates s.185(2) of the 1985 Act. There is no need for a proper instrument if the transfer is occasioned by the transmission of securities (e.g. on a death). See s.773 of this Act.

771. Procedure on transfer being lodged

(1) When a transfer of shares in or debentures of a company has been lodged with the company, the company must either-

    (a) register the transfer, or

    (b) give the transferee notice of refusal to register the transfer, together with its reasons for the refusal,

as soon as practicable and in any event within two months after the date on which the transfer is lodged with it.

(2) If the company refuses to register the transfer, it must provide the transferee with such further information about the reasons for the refusal as the transferee may reasonably request.

This does not include copies of minutes of meetings of directors.

(3) If a company fails to comply with this section, an offence is committed by-

    (a) the company, and

    (b) every officer of the company who is in default.

(4) A person guilty of an offence under this section is liable on summary conviction to a fine not exceeding level 3 on the standard scale and, for continued contravention, a daily default fine not exceeding one-tenth of level 3 on the standard scale.

(5) This section does not apply-

    (a) in relation to a transfer of shares if the company has issued a share warrant in respect of the shares (see section 779);

    (b) in relation to the transmission of shares or debentures by operation of law.

GENERAL NOTE

This new section is based on recommendations of the CLR (see *Final Report* paras 7.44 and 7.45). It replaces s.183(5) and (6) of the 1985 Act. It imposes clearer and more stringent obligations on directors when presented with a request for a transfer. It does not apply where the transfer is of a share held as a share warrant (see s.789 of this Act) or on transmission of shares (see s.773 of this Act): subs.(6).

Subsections (1) and (2)

Directors must now either: register the transfer as soon as practicable and at the latest within two months of the transfer request (this was not made explicit before - see, e.g. *Swaledale Cleaners Ltd, Re* [1968] 1 W.L.R. 1710); or notify the transferee of their refusal to do so within that same time frame (as before, but the "soon as practicable" requirement is new). Powers of refusal must still be in the articles - there is no statutory power of refusal.

Notification of refusal must now also include the reasons for refusal (presumably even if the articles do not require them to be given - cf. *Berry and Stewart v Tottenham Hotspur Football Club Co Ltd* [1935] Ch. 718). Further, under new subs.(2), there is a statutory obligation to provide the transferee with such further information "as he may reasonably require" but that does not run to the minutes of board meetings. Quaere as to information in those minutes; e.g. as to how each director voted?

Subsections (3) and (4)

These subsections retain the default offence in s.183(6) of the 1985 Act. The sanction has been reworded to comply with the treatment of such offences under this Act.

772. Transfer of shares on application of transferor

On the application of the transferor of any share or interest in a company, the company shall enter in its register of members the name of the transferee in the same manner and subject to the same conditions as if the application for the entry were made by the transferee.

GENERAL NOTE

This section restates s.183(4) of the 1985 Act with no substantive changes. It enables the transferor as well as the transferee to enforce registration, etc. of the transfer, thus removing his or her name from the register and any obligations such as calls.

773.   Execution of share transfer by personal representative

An instrument of transfer of the share or other interest of a deceased member of a company-

(a) may be made by his personal representative although the personal representative is not himself a member of the company, and

(b) is as effective as if the personal representative had been such a member at the time of the execution of the instrument.

GENERAL NOTE

This section restates s.183(3) of the 1985 Act with no substantive changes. It enables personal representatives to transfer shares without themselves becoming registered members. See also ss.770(2) and 784 of this Act.

774.   Evidence of grant of probate etc

The production to a company of any document that is by law sufficient evidence of the grant of-

(a) probate of the will of a deceased person,

(b) letters of administration of the estate of a deceased person, or

(c) confirmation as executor of a deceased person,

shall be accepted by the company as sufficient evidence of the grant.

GENERAL NOTE

This section restates s.187 of the 1985 Act with one drafting change. It enables personal representatives to establish the right to be registered as shareholders if they so wish. This is not a transfer but a transmission of the shares (see s.770(2) of this Act) and registration is optional (see s.773). The phrase in the former section that this applies notwithstanding anything in the company's articles is not repeated, but the mandatory wording of the section makes it unnecessary.

775.   Certification of instrument of transfer

(1) The certification by a company of an instrument of transfer of any shares in, or debentures of, the company is to be taken as a representation by the company to any person acting on the faith of the certification that there have been produced to the company such documents as on their face show a prima facie title to the shares or debentures in the transferor named in the instrument.

(2) The certification is not to be taken as a representation that the transferor has any title to the shares or debentures.

(3) Where a person acts on the faith of a false certification by a company made negligently, the company is under the same liability to him as if the certification had been made fraudulently.

(4) For the purposes of this section-

(a) an instrument of transfer is certificated if it bears the words "certificate lodged" (or words to the like effect);

(b) the certification of an instrument of transfer is made by a company if-

(i) the person issuing the instrument is a person authorised to issue certificated instruments of transfer on the company's behalf, and

(ii) the certification is signed by a person authorised to certificate transfers on the company's behalf or by an officer or employee either of the company or of a body corporate so authorised;

(c) a certification is treated as signed by a person if-

(i) it purports to be authenticated by his signature or initials (whether handwritten or not), and

(ii) it is not shown that the signature or initials was or were placed there neither by himself nor by a person authorised to use the signature or initials for the purpose of certificating transfers on the company's behalf.

This section restates s.184 of the 1985 Act with no substantive changes. It is concerned with the legal consequences of a certification by a company of a transfer if it is effected as described in subs.(4).

The representation in subss.(1) and (2) accords with that given on the issue of a share certificate under s.768 of this Act. The protection given in subs.(3) is weakened by the requirement in subs.(4)(b) that the person making it is authorised to do so. In the absence of express authority it is not clear who exactly is included. This is balanced by the presumptions in subs.(4)(c).

Issue of certificates etc on transfer

776. Duty of company as to issue of certificates etc on transfer

(1) A company must, within two months after the date on which a transfer of any of its shares, debentures or debenture stock is lodged with the company, complete and have ready for delivery-

    (a) the certificates of the shares transferred,

    (b) the debentures transferred, or

    (c) the certificates of the debenture stock transferred.

(2) For this purpose a "transfer" means-

    (a) a transfer duly stamped and otherwise valid, or

    (b) an exempt transfer within the Stock Transfer Act 1982 (c. 41),

but does not include a transfer that the company is for any reason entitled to refuse to register and does not register.

(3) Subsection (1) does not apply-

    (a) if the conditions of issue of the shares, debentures or debenture stock provide otherwise,

    (b) in the case of a transfer to a financial institution (see section 778), or

    (c) in the case of a transfer of shares if, following the transfer, the company has issued a share warrant in respect of the shares (see section 779).

(4) Subsection (1) has effect subject to section 777 (cases where the Stock Transfer Act 1982 applies).

(5) If default is made in complying with subsection (1) an offence is committed by every officer of the company who is in default.

(6) A person guilty of an offence under this section is liable on summary conviction to a fine not exceeding level 3 on the standard scale and, for continued contravention, a daily default fine not exceeding one-tenth of level 3 on the standard scale.

This section restates, with one amendment, the parts of s.185, as amended, of the 1985 Act relating to the issue of certificates following the lodging of a transfer request. The other parts of s.185 are now in ss.769 and 778 of this Act.

The two-month obligation is retained in subs.(1), as is the definition of a transfer in subs.(2). Note that it does not apply where there is a valid refusal to register the transfer. The previous exceptions, now in subss.(3) and (4), are also retained: see also ss.777 and 778 of this Act.

Subsection (3)(c) is new and is needed since share warrants can now be issued directly to a member instead of being converted from registered shares

The default offence is retained in subs.(5) but the sanction in subs.(6) is reworded to comply with the general treatment of such offences under this Act. There is also a civil remedy in default - see s.782 of this Act.

777. Issue of certificates etc: cases within the Stock Transfer Act 1982

(1) Section 776(1) (duty of company as to issue of certificates etc on transfer) does not apply in the case of a transfer to a person where, by virtue of regulations under section 3 of the Stock

Transfer Act 1982, he is not entitled to a certificate or other document of or evidencing title in respect of the securities transferred.

(2) But if in such a case the transferee-

(a) subsequently becomes entitled to such a certificate or other document by virtue of any provision of those regulations, and

(b) gives notice in writing of that fact to the company,

section 776 (duty to company as to issue of certificates etc) has effect as if the reference in subsection (1) of that section to the date of the lodging of the transfer were a reference to the date of the notice.

GENERAL NOTE

This section restates s.185(3) of the 1985 Act with no substantive changes. It excludes any transfers subject to regulations made under s.3 of the Stock Transfer Act 1982 from the certificate requirements in the previous section and provides for the transition of such transfers back to the certificated system.

Issue of certificates etc on allotment or transfer to financial institution

778. Issue of certificates etc: allotment or transfer to financial institution

(1) A company-

(a) of which shares or debentures are allotted to a financial institution,

(b) of which debenture stock is allotted to a financial institution, or

(c) with which a transfer for transferring shares, debentures or debenture stock to a financial institution is lodged,

is not required in consequence of that allotment or transfer to comply with section 769(1) or 776(1) (duty of company as to issue of certificates etc).

(2) A "financial institution" means-

(a) a recognised clearing house acting in relation to a recognised investment exchange, or

(b) a nominee of-

(i) a recognised clearing house acting in that way, or

(ii) a recognised investment exchange,

designated for the purposes of this section in the rules of the recognised investment exchange in question.

(3) Expressions used in subsection (2) have the same meaning as in Part 18 of the Financial Services and Markets Act 2000 (c. 8).

GENERAL NOTE

This section restates, without substantive changes, s.185(4A)-(4D) of the 1985 Act, introduced in 2001 by SI 2001/3649. It continues the exclusion of shares, etc. allotted to, or being transferred to, a financial institution from the certificate requirements of ss.769 and 776 of this Act.

Financial institutions are defined for this purpose by subs.(2) by reference to the FSMA 2000.

Share warrants

779. Issue and effect of share warrant to bearer

(1) A company limited by shares may, if so authorised by its articles, issue with respect to any fully paid shares a warrant (a "share warrant") stating that the bearer of the warrant is entitled to the shares specified in it.

(2) A share warrant issued under the company's common seal or (in the case of a company registered in Scotland) subscribed in accordance with the Requirements of Writing (Scotland)

Act 1995 (c. 7) entitles the bearer to the shares specified in it and the shares may be transferred by delivery of the warrant.

(3) A company that issues a share warrant may, if so authorised by its articles, provide (by coupons or otherwise) for the payment of the future dividends on the shares included in the warrant.

GENERAL NOTE

This section restates s.188 of the 1985 Act with no substantive changes. It provides for the issue and effect of share warrants instead of share certificates. These may now be issued on an allotment or transfer of shares without the need for the shares first to be registered and have a share certificate (see s.122 of this Act). (For conversions the other way, see the following section.)

For *common seal* in this context see s.50 of this Act.

These are negotiable instruments by mercantile custom. As such they are more prone to abuse and therefore carry criminal penalties for forgery and personation under the Theft Act 1968. For Scotland there is a specific offence set out in s.781.

780. Duty of company as to issue of certificates on surrender of share warrant

(1) A company must, within two months of the surrender of a share warrant for cancellation, complete and have ready for delivery the certificates of the shares specified in the warrant.

(2) Subsection (1) does not apply if the company's articles provide otherwise.

(3) If default is made in complying with subsection (1) an offence is committed by every officer of the company who is in default.

(4) A person guilty of an offence under subsection (3) is liable on summary conviction to a fine not exceeding level 3 on the standard scale and, for continued contravention, a daily default fine not exceeding one-tenth of level 3 on the standard scale.

GENERAL NOTE

This new section tidies up the position where the member wishes, or is required, to convert a share warrant back into a share held in registered form. It provides that, subject to contrary intention in the articles, the share certificates must be ready within two months of the surrender of the warrant.

The offence in default and sanction are worded to comply with the general treatment of such offences under this Act. There is also a civil remedy for default - see s.782 of this Act.

781. Offences in connection with share warrants (Scotland)

(1) If in Scotland a person-
    (a) with intent to defraud, forges or alters, or offers, utters, disposes of, or puts off, knowing the same to be forged or altered, any share warrant or coupon, or any document purporting to be a share warrant or coupon issued in pursuance of this Act, or
    (b) by means of any such forged or altered share warrant, coupon or document-
        (i) demands or endeavours to obtain or receive any share or interest in a company under this Act, or
        (ii) demands or endeavours to receive any dividend or money payment in respect of any such share or interest,
knowing the warrant, coupon or document to be forged or altered,
he commits an offence.

(2) If in Scotland a person without lawful authority or excuse (of which proof lies on him)-
    (a) engraves or makes on any plate, wood, stone, or other material, any share warrant or coupon purporting to be-
        (i) a share warrant or coupon issued or made by any particular company in pursuance of this Act, or
        (ii) a blank share warrant or coupon so issued or made, or

      (iii) a part of such a share warrant or coupon, or
    (b) uses any such plate, wood, stone, or other material, for the making or printing of any such share warrant or coupon, or of any such blank share warrant or coupon or of any part of such a share warrant or coupon, or
    (c) knowingly has in his custody or possession any such plate, wood, stone, or other material,

he commits an offence.

(3) A person guilty of an offence under subsection (1) is liable on summary conviction to imprisonment for a term not exceeding six months or to a fine not exceeding level 5 on the standard scale (or both).

(4) A person guilty of an offence under subsection (2) is liable-
    (a) on conviction on indictment, to imprisonment for a term not exceeding seven years or a fine (or both);
    (b) on summary conviction, to imprisonment for a term not exceeding six months or a fine not exceeding the statutory maximum (or both).

GENERAL NOTE

    Section 781 re-enacts (with amended terminology) s.189 of the Companies Act 1985.

Subsection (1)

    This makes it a statutory offence to create or make use of a share warrant or coupon issued in pursuance of the Companies Act 2006, or by means of such a document to obtain or seek to obtain any share or interest in a company or any dividend or other payment in respect of any such share or interest knowing the document to be fraudulently forged or altered. "Share warrant" and "coupon" are defined in s.779.

Subsection (2)

    This makes it a criminal offence without proper authority to create or use the materials from which a share warrant or coupon may be made, or to possess such material.

Subsection (3)

    These specify the penalties which may be imposed on conviction of a criminal offence under subss.(1) or (2) respectively.

Supplementary provisions

782. Issue of certificates etc: court order to make good default

(1) If a company on which a notice has been served requiring it to make good any default in complying with-
    (a) section 769(1) (duty of company as to issue of certificates etc on allotment),
    (b) section 776(1) (duty of company as to issue of certificates etc on transfer), or
    (c) section 780(1) (duty of company as to issue of certificates etc on surrender of share warrant),

 fails to make good the default within ten days after service of the notice, the person entitled to have the certificates or the debentures delivered to him may apply to the court.

(2) The court may on such an application make an order directing the company and any officer of it to make good the default within such time as may be specified in the order.

(3) The order may provide that all costs (in Scotland, expenses) of and incidental to the application are to be borne by the company or by an officer of it responsible for the default.

GENERAL NOTE

    This section restates, with one addition, s.185(6) and (7) of the 1985 Act. It applies a civil remedy in addition to the offences connected with a failure to issue a certificate as required on an allotment under s.769, a transfer under s.776 or a surrender of a share warrant under s.780.

On service of a notice of default and after a ten day waiting period a person still aggrieved may ask the court for an order effectively of specific performance. Costs (or expenses) are to be met by the offending parties.

CHAPTER 2

EVIDENCING AND TRANSFER OF TITLE TO SECURITIES WITHOUT WRITTEN INSTRUMENT

GENERAL NOTE

Chapter 2 of Pt 21 contains provisions for the introduction of regulations relating to paperless systems for recording title to, and the transfer of, securities. With the notable exception of ss.786, 787, 789 and 790, the provisions re-enact the substance of s.207 of the Companies Act 1989. Section 207 permitted regulations to be made which enabled title to securities to be evidenced and transferred without a written instrument. The new provisions (see in particular s.786) permit regulations to be made whose effect will be to require title to securities to be so evidenced and transferred.

The regulations made under s.207 are preserved and continued by virtue of s.1297.

Introductory

783. Scope of this Chapter

In this Chapter-

   (a) "securities" means shares, debentures, debenture stock, loan stock, bonds, units of a collective investment scheme within the meaning of the Financial Services and Markets Act 2000 (c. 8) and other securities of any description;
   (b) references to title to securities include any legal or equitable interest in securities;
   (c) references to a transfer of title include a transfer by way of security;
   (d) references to transfer without a written instrument include, in relation to bearer securities, transfer without delivery.

GENERAL NOTE

This section provides the definitions for Ch.2 of Pt 21.

784. Power to make regulations

(1) The power to make regulations under this Chapter is exercisable by the Treasury and the Secretary of State, either jointly or concurrently.
(2) References in this Chapter to the authority having power to make regulations shall accordingly be read as references to both or either of them, as the case may require.
(3) Regulations under this Chapter are subject to affirmative resolution procedure.

GENERAL NOTE

Subsections (1) and (2)

These subsections confer the power to which Ch.2 relates on the Secretary of State and the Treasury, either jointly or concurrently. (Under s.207(1) of the Companies Act 1989, the power was initially conferred on the Secretary of State alone. Responsibility for the making of regulations under s.207 of the 1989 Act passed from the Department of Trade and Industry to HM Treasury by virtue of Art.2(1) of the Transfer of Functions (Financial Services) Order 1992 as part of a general transfer of responsibility for financial services matters.)

Subsection (3)

The regulations are subject to the affirmative resolution procedure for Parliamentary control. This was also the case under s.207(9) of the Companies Act 1989.

Powers exercisable

785.   Provision enabling procedures for evidencing and transferring title

(1) Provision may be made by regulations for enabling title to securities to be evidenced and transferred without a written instrument.

(2) The regulations may make provision-
    (a) for procedures for recording and transferring title to securities, and
    (b) for the regulation of those procedures and the persons responsible for or involved in their operation.

(3) The regulations must contain such safeguards as appear to the authority making the regulations appropriate for the protection of investors and for ensuring that competition is not restricted, distorted or prevented.

(4) The regulations may, for the purpose of enabling or facilitating the operation of the procedures provided for by the regulations, make provision with respect to the rights and obligations of persons in relation to securities dealt with under the procedures.

(5) The regulations may include provision for the purpose of giving effect to-
    (a) the transmission of title to securities by operation of law;
    (b) any restriction on the transfer of title to securities arising by virtue of the provisions of any enactment or instrument, court order or agreement;
    (c) any power conferred by any such provision on a person to deal with securities on behalf of the person entitled.

(6) The regulations may make provision with respect to the persons responsible for the operation of the procedures provided for by the regulations-
    (a) as to the consequences of their insolvency or incapacity, or
    (b) as to the transfer from them to other persons of their functions in relation to those procedures.

GENERAL NOTE

Subsection (1)

    This provision contains the main regulation-making power and delineates the scope of the regulations which may be made. The provision is a re-enactment of the first sentence of s.207(1) of the Companies Act 1989. Section 207(5) of the 1989 Act also enabled the regulations to include supplementary, incidental and transitional provisions. This power is now contained in s.1292.

Subsections (2) and (3)

    These subsections substantially re-enact s.207(2) and (3) of the Companies Act 1989.

Subsection (4)

    This provision substantially re-enacts the first sentence of s.207(4) of the Companies Act 1989. The second sentence of s.207(4), however, has been repealed. (That sentence read: "But the regulations shall be framed so as to secure that the rights and obligations in relation to securities dealt with under the new procedures correspond, so far as practicable, with those which would arise apart from any regulations under this section.")

Subsections (5) and (6)

    These subsections expressly expand the power to make regulations in relation to the matters stated. They substantially represent re-enactments of provisions which were contained in s.207 of the 1989 Act.

786.   Provision enabling or requiring arrangements to be adopted

(1) Regulations under this Chapter may make provision-

    (a) enabling the members of a company or of any designated class of companies to adopt, by ordinary resolution, arrangements under which title to securities is required to be evidenced or transferred (or both) without a written instrument; or

    (b) requiring companies, or any designated class of companies, to adopt such arrangements.

(2) The regulations may make such provision-

    (a) in respect of all securities issued by a company, or

    (b) in respect of all securities of a specified description.

(3) The arrangements provided for by regulations making such provision as is mentioned in subsection (1)-

    (a) must not be such that a person who but for the arrangements would be entitled to have his name entered in the company's register of members ceases to be so entitled, and

    (b) must be such that a person who but for the arrangements would be entitled to exercise any rights in respect of the securities continues to be able effectively to control the exercise of those rights.

(4) The regulations may-

    (a) prohibit the issue of any certificate by the company in respect of the issue or transfer of securities,

    (b) require the provision by the company to holders of securities of statements (at specified intervals or on specified occasions) of the securities held in their name, and

    (c) make provision as to the matters of which any such certificate or statement is, or is not, evidence.

(5) In this section-

    (a) references to a designated class of companies are to a class designated in the regulations or by order under section 787; and

    (b) "specified" means specified in the regulations.

GENERAL NOTE

    This section extends the existing power under s.207 of the 1989 Act with the introduction of a new power to make regulations under which the paperless system may be made compulsory. Pursuant to subs.(3) of s.784, the introduction of such regulations would be subject to the affirmative resolution procedure for Parliamentary control.

Subsection (1)

    Provision is made for regulations to enable companies generally, or any designated class of companies, to adopt a compulsory paperless system by ordinary resolution, as well as for regulations requiring companies, or any designated class of companies, to adopt a compulsory paperless system. The provision enables the regulations to be made in relation to either or both of the evidencing and transfer of securities without a written instrument.

Subsection (2)

    The provisions may be made applicable to all of a company's securities, or only to securities of a specified description. If the ordinary resolution mechanism is adopted, the possibility therefore arises of shareholders of a company passing a resolution which affects the mechanism by which securities other than shares may be held and/or transferred without a written instrument, thus empowering the members (albeit with the support of the regulations so made) to override the terms of the private contract between the company and the holders of the relevant security in so far as that contract addresses the means by which title may be evidenced and transferred.

Subsection (3)

    This subsection provides protection for holders of the affected security by ensuring that they cannot be deprived, by introduction of a compulsory paperless regime, of certain of their rights, including the right to have their name entered on the register. It would therefore appear that the compulsory paperless regime cannot oblige holders to hold their securities through nominees.

Subsection (4)

    This provision expands on the matters which may be addressed in any regulations made under this section.

787. Provision enabling or requiring arrangements to be adopted: order-making powers

(1) The authority having power to make regulations under this Chapter may by order-
  (a) designate classes of companies for the purposes of section 786 (provision enabling or requiring arrangements to be adopted);
  (b) provide that, in relation to securities of a specified description-
      (i) in a designated class of companies, or
      (ii) in a specified company or class of companies,
  specified provisions of regulations made under this Chapter by virtue of that section either do not apply or apply subject to specified modifications.

(2) In subsection (1) "specified" means specified in the order.

(3) An order under this section is subject to negative resolution procedure.

GENERAL NOTE

The section permits the authorities empowered to make regulations under this Chapter to designate classes of companies by order for the purpose of s.786, and to provide, also by order, that specified provisions of regulations made under s.786 either do not apply, or apply only in modified form, in relation to securities of a specified description. Orders made under this section are subject to the negative resolution procedure for Parliamentary control.

Supplementary

788. Provision that may be included in regulations

Regulations under this Chapter may-
  (a) modify or exclude any provision of any enactment or instrument, or any rule of law;
  (b) apply, with such modifications as may be appropriate, the provisions of any enactment or instrument (including provisions creating criminal offences);
  (c) require the payment of fees, or enable persons to require the payment of fees, of such amounts as may be specified in the regulations or determined in accordance with them;
  (d) empower the authority making the regulations to delegate to any person willing and able to discharge them any functions of the authority under the regulations.

GENERAL NOTE

This section re-enacts the so-called Henry VIII clause in s.207(7) of the Companies Act 1989.

789. Duty to consult

Before making-
  (a) regulations under this Chapter, or
  (b) any order under section 787,
the authority having power to make regulations under this Chapter must carry out such consultation as appears to it to be appropriate.

GENERAL NOTE

The authority making regulations or orders under this Chapter is required, before doing so, to carry out such consultation as appears to it to be appropriate.

790. Resolutions to be forwarded to registrar

Chapter 3 of Part 3 (resolutions affecting a company's constitution) applies to a resolution passed by virtue of regulations under this Chapter.

PART 22

INFORMATION ABOUT INTERESTS IN A COMPANY'S SHARES

Introductory

791. Companies to which this Part applies

This Part applies only to public companies.

792. Shares to which this Part applies

(1) References in this Part to a company's shares are to the company's issued shares of a class carrying rights to vote in all circumstances at general meetings of the company (including any shares held as treasury shares).

(2) The temporary suspension of voting rights in respect of any shares does not affect the application of this Part in relation to interests in those or any other shares.

Notice requiring information about interests in shares

793. Notice by company requiring information about interests in its shares

(1) A public company may give notice under this section to any person whom the company knows or has reasonable cause to believe-
  (a) to be interested in the company's shares, or
  (b) to have been so interested at any time during the three years immediately preceding the date on which the notice is issued.

(2) The notice may require the person-
  (a) to confirm that fact or (as the case may be) to state whether or not it is the case, and
  (b) if he holds, or has during that time held, any such interest, to give such further information as may be required in accordance with the following provisions of this section.

(3) The notice may require the person to whom it is addressed to give particulars of his own present or past interest in the company's shares (held by him at any time during the three year period mentioned in subsection (1)(b)).

(4) The notice may require the person to whom it is addressed, where-
  (a) his interest is a present interest and another interest in the shares subsists, or
  (b) another interest in the shares subsisted during that three year period at a time when his interest subsisted,

to give, so far as lies within his knowledge, such particulars with respect to that other interest as may be required by the notice.

(5) The particulars referred to in subsections (3) and (4) include-

    (a) the identity of persons interested in the shares in question, and

    (b) whether persons interested in the same shares are or were parties to-

        (i) an agreement to which section 824 applies (certain share acquisition agreements), or

        (ii) an agreement or arrangement relating to the exercise of any rights conferred by the holding of the shares.

(6) The notice may require the person to whom it is addressed, where his interest is a past interest, to give (so far as lies within his knowledge) particulars of the identity of the person who held that interest immediately upon his ceasing to hold it.

(7) The information required by the notice must be given within such reasonable time as may be specified in the notice.

GENERAL NOTE

    This section and the next three are concerned with the giving of notice requiring information about interests in shares. Under this section a company can give notice to any person who it knows or has reasonable cause to believe who is interested in the company's shares or to have been interested in them during the three years preceding the date on which the notice is issued (subs.(1)). The notice can require that person to confirm that fact or state whether or not it is the case and to give any further information as may be required (subs.(2)). Subsection (3) specifies that the notice may require the person to whom it is addressed to give particulars of his own present or past interest in the company's shares. Under subs.(4) the notice may require the person to whom it is addressed to give such particulars as may be required where his interest is a present interest and another interest in the shares subsists or another interest subsisted during that three year period at a time when his interest subsisted. The particulars referred to in the preceding subsections can include the identity of the person interested in the shares in question and whether persons interested in the same shares are or were parties to certain agreements (such as those under s.824) or an agreement or arrangement relating to the exercise of any rights conferred by the holding of the shares (subs.(5)). Under subs.(7) the information required under the notice must be given within such reasonable time as is specified in the notice.

794. Notice requiring information: order imposing restrictions on shares

(1) Where-

    (a) a notice under section 793 (notice requiring information about interests in company's shares) is served by a company on a person who is or was interested in shares in the company, and

    (b) that person fails to give the company the information required by the notice within the time specified in it,

the company may apply to the court for an order directing that the shares in question be subject to restrictions.

For the effect of such an order see section 797.

(2) If the court is satisfied that such an order may unfairly affect the rights of third parties in respect of the shares, the court may, for the purpose of protecting those rights and subject to such terms as it thinks fit, direct that such acts by such persons or descriptions of persons and for such purposes as may be set out in the order shall not constitute a breach of the restrictions.

(3) On an application under this section the court may make an interim order.

Any such order may be made unconditionally or on such terms as the court thinks fit.

(4) Sections 798 to 802 make further provision about orders under this section.

GENERAL NOTE

    This section applies where a notice has been given under the preceding section and that person fails to give the company the information required by the notice. Under subs.(1) the company can apply to the court for an order directing that the shares be subject to the restrictions laid down in Pt 15 of the Companies Act 1985. Pursuant to subs.(2) the court may, if it is satisfied that this may unfairly affect the rights of third parties in respect of the shares, direct that such acts shall not constitute a breach of the restrictions. The court may make an interim order, either unconditionally, or on such terms as the court thinks fit (subs.(3)).

795. Notice requiring information: offences

(1) A person who-
  (a) fails to comply with a notice under section 793 (notice requiring information about interests in company's shares), or
  (b) in purported compliance with such a notice-
    (i) makes a statement that he knows to be false in a material particular, or
    (ii) recklessly makes a statement that is false in a material particular,
commits an offence.
(2) A person does not commit an offence under subsection (1)(a) if he proves that the requirement to give information was frivolous or vexatious.
(3) A person guilty of an offence under this section is liable-
  (a) on conviction on indictment, to imprisonment for a term not exceeding two years or a fine (or both);
  (b) on summary conviction-
    (i) in England and Wales, to imprisonment for a term not exceeding twelve months or to a fine not exceeding the statutory maximum (or both);
    (ii) in Scotland or Northern Ireland, to imprisonment for a term not exceeding six months, or to a fine not exceeding the statutory maximum (or both).

GENERAL NOTE

This section sets out the offences for which a person may be liable where he has failed to comply with the preceding sections. Thus, under subs.(1) a person who fails to comply with a s.793 notice, or, in purported compliance with it makes a false or reckless statement in a material particular, commits an offence. There is not an offence if it is proved that the requirement go give information was frivolous or vexatious (subs.(2)). Subsection (3) sets out the consequences of being found guilty of an offence.

796. Notice requiring information: persons exempted from obligation to comply

(1) A person is not obliged to comply with a notice under section 793 (notice requiring information about interests in company's shares) if he is for the time being exempted by the Secretary of State from the operation of that section.
(2) The Secretary of State must not grant any such exemption unless-
  (a) he has consulted the Governor of the Bank of England, and
  (b) he (the Secretary of State) is satisfied that, having regard to any undertaking given by the person in question with respect to any interest held or to be held by him in any shares, there are special reasons why that person should not be subject to the obligations imposed by that section.

GENERAL NOTE

Under subs.(1) of this section of the Act a person is under no obligation to comply with a notice under s.793 if he is exempted from doing so by the Secretary of State. Subsection (2) specifies that the Secretary of State must have consulted the Governor of the Bank of England and be satisfied that there are special reasons why that person should not be subject to the obligations imposed by that section.

Orders imposing restrictions on shares

797. Consequences of order imposing restrictions

(1) The effect of an order under section 794 that shares are subject to restrictions is as follows-
    (a) any transfer of the shares is void;
    (b) no voting rights are exercisable in respect of the shares;
    (c) no further shares may be issued in right of the shares or in pursuance of an offer made to their holder;
    (d) except in a liquidation, no payment may be made of sums due from the company on the shares, whether in respect of capital or otherwise.

(2) Where shares are subject to the restriction in subsection (1)(a), an agreement to transfer the shares is void.

This does not apply to an agreement to transfer the shares on the making of an order under section 800 made by virtue of subsection (3)(b) (removal of restrictions in case of court-approved transfer).

(3) Where shares are subject to the restriction in subsection (1)(c) or (d), an agreement to transfer any right to be issued with other shares in right of those shares, or to receive any payment on them (otherwise than in a liquidation), is void.

This does not apply to an agreement to transfer any such right on the making of an order under section 800 made by virtue of subsection (3)(b) (removal of restrictions in case of court-approved transfer).

(4) The provisions of this section are subject-
    (a) to any directions under section 794(2) or section 799(3) (directions for protection of third parties), and
    (b) in the case of an interim order under section 794(3), to the terms of the order.

GENERAL NOTE

    This section is the first of several which is concerned with orders imposing restrictions on shares. Thus, subs.(1) spells out the effect of an order under s.794. Subsection (2) indicates that where any transfer of shares is made void under sub-s.(1)(a), any agreement to transfer them is void. This would not, however, apply to an agreement under s.800(3)(b). Subsection (3) concerns subs.(1)(c) and (d) and is to the effect that an agreement to transfer any right to be issued with other shares in right of those shares, or to receive any payment on them (otherwise than in a liquidation), is void. This does not apply to an agreement under s.800(3)(b). All the provisions of the section are expressed to be subject to ss.792(2), 799(3), and 794(3) (subs.(4)).

798. Penalty for attempted evasion of restrictions

(1) This section applies where shares are subject to restrictions by virtue of an order under section 794.

(2) A person commits an offence if he-
    (a) exercises or purports to exercise any right-
        (i) to dispose of shares that to his knowledge, are for the time being subject to restrictions, or
        (ii) to dispose of any right to be issued with any such shares, or
    (b) votes in respect of any such shares (whether as holder or proxy), or appoints a proxy to vote in respect of them, or
    (c) being the holder of any such shares, fails to notify of their being subject to those restrictions a person whom he does not know to be aware of that fact but does know to be entitled (apart from the restrictions) to vote in respect of those shares whether as holder or as proxy, or

(d) being the holder of any such shares, or being entitled to a right to be issued with other shares in right of them, or to receive any payment on them (otherwise than in a liquidation), enters into an agreement which is void under section 797(2) or (3).

(3) If shares in a company are issued in contravention of the restrictions, an offence is committed by-

   (a) the company, and

   (b) every officer of the company who is in default.

(4) A person guilty of an offence under this section is liable-

   (a) on conviction on indictment, to a fine;

   (b) on summary conviction, to a fine not exceeding the statutory maximum.

(5) The provisions of this section are subject-

   (a) to any directions under-

   section 794(2) (directions for protection of third parties), or

   section 799 or 800 (relaxation or removal of restrictions), and

   (b) in the case of an interim order under section 794(3), to the terms of the order.

GENERAL NOTE

This section applies when there is an attempted evasion of the restrictions imposed under s.794. The offences are specified in subs.(2). Subsection (3) provides that if shares are issued in contravention of any restrictions, an offence is committed by the company and also every officer of the company who is in default. The consequences are then spelt out in subs.(4). Finally, subs.(5) makes the section subject to directions under ss.794(2), 799, 800, and 794(3).

799. Relaxation of restrictions

(1) An application may be made to the court on the ground that an order directing that shares shall be subject to restrictions unfairly affects the rights of third parties in respect of the shares.

(2) An application for an order under this section may be made by the company or by any person aggrieved.

(3) If the court is satisfied that the application is well-founded, it may, for the purpose of protecting the rights of third parties in respect of the shares, and subject to such terms as it thinks fit, direct that such acts by such persons or descriptions of persons and for such purposes as may be set out in the order do not constitute a breach of the restrictions.

GENERAL NOTE

The restrictions imposed under this Part may be relaxed where these unfairly affect the rights of third parties in respect of the shares (subs.(1)). Application can be made by the company or any aggrieved person (subs.(2)) and, if the court is satisfied that the application is well-founded, it may, subject to such terms as it thinks fit, order that certain acts by such persons do not constitute a breach of the restrictions (subs.(3)).

800. Removal of restrictions

(1) An application may be made to the court for an order directing that the shares shall cease to be subject to restrictions.

(2) An application for an order under this section may be made by the company or by any person aggrieved.

(3) The court must not make an order under this section unless-

   (a) it is satisfied that the relevant facts about the shares have been disclosed to the company and no unfair advantage has accrued to any person as a result of the earlier failure to make that disclosure, or

   (b) the shares are to be transferred for valuable consideration and the court approves the transfer.

(4) An order under this section made by virtue of subsection (3)(b) may continue, in whole or in part, the restrictions mentioned in section 797(1)(c) and (d) (restrictions on issue of further shares or making of payments) so far as they relate to a right acquired or offer made before the transfer.

(5) Where any restrictions continue in force under subsection (4)-

   (a) an application may be made under this section for an order directing that the shares shall cease to be subject to those restrictions, and

   (b) subsection (3) does not apply in relation to the making of such an order.

GENERAL NOTE

Under this section it is possible for an application to be made to court for an order directing that the shares cease to be subject to any restrictions (subs.(1)). As was the case under s.799, an application under this section may be made by the company or by any aggrieved person (subs.(2)). The court must not make an order, however, unless the two criteria specified in subs.(3) are fulfilled. The first is that the court must not make an order unless it is satisfied that the relevant facts about the shares have been disclosed to the company and no unfair advantage has accrued to any person as a result of the earlier failure to make the disclosure. The second is that the court must not make an order unless the shares are to be transferred for valuable consideration and the court approves the transfer. Where an order is made in relation to the latter, subs.(4) specifies that an order may continue, in whole or part, the restrictions listed in s.797(1)(c) and (d) so far as they relate to a right acquired or offer made before the transfer. Where these restrictions continue in force an application may be made for an order directing that the shares are to cease to be subject to those restrictions and subs.(3) will not apply (subs.(5)).

801.   Order for sale of shares

(1) The court may order that the shares subject to restrictions be sold, subject to the court's approval as to the sale.

(2) An application for an order under subsection (1) may only be made by the company.

(3) Where the court has made an order under this section, it may make such further order relating to the sale or transfer of the shares as it thinks fit.

(4) An application for an order under subsection (3) may be made-

   (a) by the company,

   (b) by the person appointed by or in pursuance of the order to effect the sale, or

   (c) by any person interested in the shares.

(5) On making an order under subsection (1) or (3) the court may order that the applicant's costs (in Scotland, expenses) be paid out of the proceeds of sale.

GENERAL NOTE

Under this section the court has the power to order the shares which are subject to restrictions are sold, subject to the court's approval as to the sale (subs.(1)). An application may only be made by the company (subs.(2)). Where the court does make an order, it is empowered to make such further order relating to the sale or transfer of the shares as it thinks fit (subs.(3)). In relation to this, the application may be made by the company, by the person appointed to effect the sale, or by any person interested in the shares (subs.(4)). The court may also order that the costs be paid out of the proceeds of the sale (subs.(5)).

802.   Application of proceeds of sale under court order

(1) Where shares are sold in pursuance of an order of the court under section 801, the proceeds of the sale, less the costs of the sale, must be paid into court for the benefit of the persons who are beneficially interested in the shares.

(2) A person who is beneficially interested in the shares may apply to the court for the whole or part of those proceeds to be paid to him.

(3) On such an application the court shall order the payment to the applicant of-

   (a) the whole of the proceeds of sale together with any interest on them, or

(b) if another person had a beneficial interest in the shares at the time of their sale, such proportion of the proceeds and interest as the value of the applicant's interest in the shares bears to the total value of the shares.

This is subject to the following qualification.

(4) If the court has ordered under section 801(5) that the costs (in Scotland, expenses) of an applicant under that section are to be paid out of the proceeds of sale, the applicant is entitled to payment of his costs (or expenses) out of those proceeds before any person interested in the shares receives any part of those proceeds.

GENERAL NOTE

Where shares are sold under s.801, the proceeds, less the costs, are required to be paid into court for the benefit of those who are beneficially interested in the shares (subs.(1)). A person beneficially interested may apply to the court for the whole or part of the proceeds to be paid to him (subs.(2)). The court is then enjoined to order the payment to the applicant of the whole of the proceeds of sale together with any interest on them or, if some other person had a beneficial interest in them at the time of sale, such proportion of the proceeds and interest as the value of the applicant's interest in the shares bears to the total value of the shares (subs.(3)). However, where the court orders the costs to be paid out of the proceeds, the applicant is entitled to payment of his costs out of those proceeds before any person interested in the shares receives any part of them (subs.(4)).

Power of members to require company to act

803.   Power of members to require company to act

(1) The members of a company may require it to exercise its powers under section 793 (notice requiring information about interests in shares).

(2) A company is required to do so once it has received requests (to the same effect) from members of the company holding at least 10% of such of the paidup capital of the company as carries a right to vote at general meetings of the company (excluding any voting rights attached to any shares in the company held as treasury shares).

(3) A request-
  (a) may be in hard copy form or in electronic form,
  (b) must-
    (i) state that the company is requested to exercise its powers under section 793,
    (ii) specify the manner in which the company is requested to act, and
    (iii) give reasonable grounds for requiring the company to exercise those powers in the manner specified, and
  (c) must be authenticated by the person or persons making it.

GENERAL NOTE

This section empowers the members to require that the company should exercise its powers under s.793. Under subs.(2) the company can be required to do so where it has received requests from members holding at least ten per cent of the paid-up capital of the company which carries the right to vote at general meetings of the company, excluding voting rights attached to treasury shares. Under subs.(3) the request must be made in hard copy form or in electronic form and state that the company is requested to exercise its s.793 powers. It should also specify the manner in which the company is requested to act and give reasonable grounds for the request. Finally, it must be authenticated by those making it.

804.   Duty of company to comply with requirement

(1) A company that is required under section 803 to exercise its powers under section 793 (notice requiring information about interests in company's shares) must exercise those powers in the manner specified in the requests.

(2) If default is made in complying with subsection (1) an offence is committed by every officer of the company who is in default.

(3) A person guilty of an offence under this section is liable-
    (a) on conviction on indictment, to a fine;
    (b) on summary conviction, to a fine not exceeding the statutory maximum.

GENERAL NOTE

    If required to act under the preceding section, the company must exercise those powers in the manner specified (subs.(1)). Subsections (2) and (3) specify the penalties for default in doing so.

805. Report to members on outcome of investigation

(1) On the conclusion of an investigation carried out by a company in pursuance of a requirement under section 803 the company must cause a report of the information received in pursuance of the investigation to be prepared.
The report must be made available for inspection within a reasonable period (not more than 15 days) after the conclusion of the investigation.
(2) Where-
    (a) a company undertakes an investigation in pursuance of a requirement under section 803, and
    (b) the investigation is not concluded within three months after the date on which the company became subject to the requirement,
  the company must cause to be prepared in respect of that period, and in respect of each succeeding period of three months ending before the conclusion of the investigation, an interim report of the information received during that period in pursuance of the investigation.
(3) Each such report must be made available for inspection within a reasonable period (not more than 15 days) after the end of the period to which it relates.
(4) The reports must be retained by the company for at least six years from the date on which they are first made available for inspection and must be kept available for inspection during that time-
    (a) at the company's registered office, or
    (b) at a place specified in regulations under section 1136.
(5) The company must give notice to the registrar-
    (a) of the place at which the reports are kept available for inspection, and
    (b) of any change in that place,
  unless they have at all times been kept at the company's registered office.
(6) The company must within three days of making any report prepared under this section available for inspection, notify the members who made the requests under section 803 where the report is so available.
(7) For the purposes of this section an investigation carried out by a company in pursuance of a requirement under section 803 is concluded when-
    (a) the company has made all such inquiries as are necessary or expedient for the purposes of the requirement, and
    (b) in the case of each such inquiry-
        (i) a response has been received by the company, or
        (ii) the time allowed for a response has elapsed.

GENERAL NOTE

    After an investigation has been carried out, the company is required to produce a report of the information which has been received and this must be made available at the company's office not more than 15 days after the conclusion of the investigation (subs.(1)). If an investigation is ordered but not concluded within three months, subs.(2) specifies that a report of that period and each succeeding three month period before the conclusion of the investigation must be prepared. Each report has to be available for inspection within not more than 15 days after the end of the period to which it relates (subs.(3)). Reports are required to be retained by the company for a period of at least six years from the date when they were first made available and must be kept at the company's registered office or a place specified in regulations made pursuant to s.1136 (subs.(4)). The company is obliged to notify the registrar of the place where the reports are kept available for inspection and any change in that place, unless they have at all times been kept at the company's registered office (subs.(5)). Within three days of making a report, the company must notify the members who made the requests under s.803 where the report is available (subs.(6)). An investigation carried out under s.803 will be concluded when the company has made all such enquiries as are necessary or expedient for the purposes of the requirement and, in the case of each inquiry, that a response has been received by the company or the time allowed for a response has elapsed (subs.(7)).

806.   Report to members: offences

(1) If default is made for 14 days in complying with section 805(5) (notice to registrar of place at which reports made available for inspection) an offence is committed by-
    (a) the company, and
    (b) every officer of the company who is in default.
(2) A person guilty of an offence under subsection (1) is liable on summary conviction to a fine not exceeding level 3 on the standard scale and, for continued contravention, a daily default fine not exceeding one-tenth of level 3 on the standard scale.
(3) If default is made in complying with any other provision of section 805 (report to members on outcome of investigation), an offence is committed by every officer of the company who is in default.
(4) A person guilty of an offence under subsection (3) is liable-
    (a) on conviction on indictment, to a fine;
    (b) on summary conviction, to a fine not exceeding the statutory maximum.

GENERAL NOTE
   If there is a default for 14 days in complying with s.805(5), this is an offence and every officer in default is subject to the penalties set out in subs.(2). If there is a default in complying with any other provision of s.805, an offence is also committed by every officer of the company who is in default (subs.(3)) and the penalties are spelt out in subs.(4).

807.   Right to inspect and request copy of reports

(1) Any report prepared under section 805 must be open to inspection by any person without charge.
(2) Any person is entitled, on request and on payment of such fee as may be prescribed, to be provided with a copy of any such report or any part of it. The copy must be provided within ten days after the request is received by the company.
(3) If an inspection required under subsection (1) is refused, or default is made in complying with subsection (2), an offence is committed by-
    (a) the company, and
    (b) every officer of the company who is in default.
(4) A person guilty of an offence under this section is liable on summary conviction to a fine not exceeding level 3 on the standard scale and, for continued contravention, a daily default fine not exceeding one-tenth of level 3 on the standard scale.
(5) In the case of any such refusal or default the court may by order compel an immediate inspection or, as the case may be, direct that the copy required be sent to the person requiring it.

GENERAL NOTE
   A report prepared pursuant to s.805 must be open to inspection by any person without charge (subs.(1)). Under subs.(2) any person is entitled, on request and without charge, to a copy of any report or any part of it and this must be provided by the company within ten days after the request is received by the company. There are penalties for default in subss.(3) and (4). Under subs.(5) the court may, by order, compel an immediate inspection or direct that the copy be sent to the person who has asked for it.

Register of interests disclosed

808.   Register of interests disclosed

(1) The company must keep a register of information received by it in pursuance of a requirement imposed under section 793 (notice requiring information about interests in company's shares).
(2) A company which receives any such information must, within three days of the receipt, enter in the register-
  (a) the fact that the requirement was imposed and the date on which it was imposed, and
  (b) the information received in pursuance of the requirement.
(3) The information must be entered against the name of the present holder of the shares in question or, if there is no present holder or the present holder is not known, against the name of the person holding the interest.
(4) The register must be made up so that the entries against the names entered in it appear in chronological order.
(5) If default is made in complying with this section an offence is committed by-
  (a) the company, and
  (b) every officer of the company who is in default.
(6) A person guilty of an offence under this section is liable on summary conviction to a fine not exceeding level 3 on the standard scale and, for continued contravention, a daily default fine not exceeding one-tenth of level 3 on the standard scale.
(7) The company is not by virtue of anything done for the purposes of this section affected with notice of, or put upon inquiry as to, the rights of any person in relation to any shares.

GENERAL NOTE
  Under this section a company is obliged to keep a register of the information which it has received under a s.793 notice (subs.(1)). Under subs.(2) a company which receives the information must, within three days of receipt, enter in the register the fact that the information was imposed, the date on which it was imposed, and the information received in pursuance of the requirement. The record of this information must be entered against the name of the present holder of the shares in question or if there is no present holder (or he is unknown) against the name of the person holding the interest (subs.(3)). Subsection (4) specifies that the register must be made up so that the entries against the names appear in chronological order. Subsections (5) and (6) specify penalties for default. Finally, subs.(7) indicates that the company will not, by virtue of anything done for the purpose of the section, be affected with notice or put on enquiry as to the rights of any person in relation to any shares.

809.   Register to be kept available for inspection

(1) The register kept under section 808 (register of interests disclosed) must be kept available for inspection-
  (a) at the company's registered office, or
  (b) at a place specified in regulations under section 1136.
(2) A company must give notice to the registrar of companies of the place where the register is kept available for inspection and of any change in that place.
(3) No such notice is required if the register has at all times been kept available for inspection at the company's registered office.
(4) If default is made in complying with subsection (1), or a company makes default for 14 days in complying with subsection (2), an offence is committed by-
  (a) the company, and
  (b) every officer of the company who is in default.

(5) A person guilty of an offence under this section is liable on summary conviction to a fine not exceeding level 3 on the standard scale and, for continued contravention, a daily default fine not exceeding one-tenth of level 3 on the standard scale.

GENERAL NOTE

This section specifies that the register which is kept pursuant to s.808 has to be kept available for inspection at the company's registered office or at the place where the company's register of members is kept, as specified in regulations made pursuant to s.1136. Under subs.(2) a company must give notice to the registrar of companies of the place where the register is kept available for inspection and also of any change in that place. However, under subs.(3) no notice will be required if the register has, at all times, been kept available for inspection at the company's registered office. Subsections (4) and (5) specify the penalties prescribed for default.

810. Associated index

(1) Unless the register kept under section 808 (register of interests disclosed) is kept in such a form as itself to constitute an index, the company must keep an index of the names entered in it.

(2) The company must make any necessary entry or alteration in the index within ten days after the date on which any entry or alteration is made in the register.

(3) The index must contain, in respect of each name, a sufficient indication to enable the information entered against it to be readily found.

(4) The index must be at all times kept available for inspection at the same place as the register.

(5) If default is made in complying with this section, an offence is committed by-
   (a) the company, and
   (b) every officer of the company who is in default.

(6) A person guilty of an offence under this section is liable on summary conviction to a fine not exceeding level 3 on the standard scale and, for continued contravention, a daily default fine not exceeding one-tenth of level 3 on the standard scale.

GENERAL NOTE

Under this section, the company must keep an index of the names entered on the register, unless the register is itself in such a form as to constitute an index (subs.(1)). Under subs.(2) the company is required to make any necessary entry or alteration in the index within ten days after the date on which any entry or alteration is made in the register. As to the information required, subs.(3) specifies that the index must contain a sufficient indication to enable the information entered to be readily found. Under subs.(4) the index must be kept available for inspection at the same place as the register. Subsections (5) and (6) specify penalties for default.

811. Rights to inspect and require copy of entries

(1) The register required to be kept under section 808 (register of interests disclosed), and any associated index, must be open to inspection by any person without charge.

(2) Any person is entitled, on request and on payment of such fee as may be prescribed, to be provided with a copy of any entry in the register.

(3) A person seeking to exercise either of the rights conferred by this section must make a request to the company to that effect.

(4) The request must contain the following information-
   (a) in the case of an individual, his name and address;
   (b) in the case of an organisation, the name and address of an individual responsible for making the request on behalf of the organisation;
   (c) the purpose for which the information is to be used; and
   (d) whether the information will be disclosed to any other person, and if so-
      (i) where that person is an individual, his name and address,

(ii) where that person is an organisation, the name and address of an individual responsible for receiving the information on its behalf, and

(iii) the purpose for which the information is to be used by that person.

GENERAL NOTE

The section provides that the register which has to be kept under s.808 and associated index, must be kept open to inspection by any person without charge (subs.(1)). On payment of the prescribed fee, any person may request to be provided with a copy of any entry in the register (subs.(2)). A person who wishes to exercise either of the rights specified in the section must make a request to the company to that effect (subs.(3)). Subsection (4) lays down the information which the request must contain.

812.   Court supervision of purpose for which rights may be exercised

(1) Where a company receives a request under section 811 (register of interests disclosed: right to inspect and require copy), it must-
  (a) comply with the request if it is satisfied that it is made for a proper purpose, and
  (b) refuse the request if it is not so satisfied.
(2) If the company refuses the request, it must inform the person making the request, stating the reason why it is not satisfied.
(3) A person whose request is refused may apply to the court.
(4) If an application is made to the court-
  (a) the person who made the request must notify the company, and
  (b) the company must use its best endeavours to notify any persons whose details would be disclosed if the company were required to comply with the request.
(5) If the court is not satisfied that the inspection or copy is sought for a proper purpose, it shall direct the company not to comply with the request.
(6) If the court makes such a direction and it appears to the court that the company is or may be subject to other requests made for a similar purpose (whether made by the same person or different persons), it may direct that the company is not to comply with any such request.
The order must contain such provision as appears to the court appropriate to identify the requests to which it applies.
(7) If the court does not direct the company not to comply with the request, the company must comply with the request immediately upon the court giving its decision or, as the case may be, the proceedings being discontinued.

GENERAL NOTE

This section specifies that where a request is made under s.811, the company must comply if it is satisfied that the request is made for a proper purpose. Under subs.(2) the company, if refusing the request, must inform the person making the request, stating the reason why it is not satisfied. That person may apply to court (subs.(3)). If an application is thus made, the person must notify the company and the company must use its best endeavours to notify any person whose details would be disclosed if the company were required to comply with the request (subs.(4)). The court, if not satisfied that the inspection or copy is sought for a proper purpose, may direct that the company need not comply with the request (subs.(5)). If the court makes such a direction and it appears to it that the company may be subject to further requests, it may direct that the company need not comply (subs.(6)). If the court orders the company to comply, it must do so immediately on the court giving the decision or on the proceedings being discontinued (subs.(7)).

813.   Register of interests disclosed: refusal of inspection or default in providing copy

(1) If an inspection required under section 811 (register of interests disclosed: right to inspect and require copy) is refused or default is made in providing a copy required under that section, otherwise than in accordance with an order of the court, an offence is committed by-
  (a) the company, and
  (b) every officer of the company who is in default.

(2) A person guilty of an offence under this section is liable on summary conviction to a fine not exceeding level 3 on the standard scale and, for continued contravention, a daily default fine not exceeding one-tenth of level 3 on the standard scale.

(3) In the case of any such refusal or default the court may by order compel an immediate inspection or, as the case may be, direct that the copy required be sent to the person requesting it.

GENERAL NOTE

This section of the act provides for the imposition of penalties for default in the case of an inspection required under s.811 and where this is refused or default is made in providing a copy (subs.(1) and (2)). The court may by order compel an immediate inspection or direct that the copy required be sent to the person requesting it (subs.(3)).

814. Register of interests disclosed: offences in connection with request for or disclosure of information

(1) It is an offence for a person knowingly or recklessly to make in a request under section 811 (register of interests disclosed: right to inspect or require copy) a statement that is misleading, false or deceptive in a material particular.

(2) It is an offence for a person in possession of information obtained by exercise of either of the rights conferred by that section-
    (a) to do anything that results in the information being disclosed to another person, or
    (b) to fail to do anything with the result that the information is disclosed to another person,
 knowing, or having reason to suspect, that person may use the information for a purpose that is not a proper purpose.

(3) A person guilty of an offence under this section is liable-
    (a) on conviction on indictment, to imprisonment for a term not exceeding two years or a fine (or both);
    (b) on summary conviction-
        (i) in England and Wales, to imprisonment for a term not exceeding twelve months or to a fine not exceeding the statutory maximum (or both);
        (ii) in Scotland or Northern Ireland, to imprisonment for a term not exceeding six months, or to a fine not exceeding the statutory maximum (or both).

GENERAL NOTE

This section provides that it is an offence for a person knowingly or recklessly to make a statement that is misleading, false or deceptive in a material particular (subs.(1)). Subsection (2) provides that it is an offence for a person in possession of information obtained pursuant to s.811 to do anything which results in the information being disclosed to another person or failing to do anything, with the result that the information is disclosed to another person, and that person knows or has reason to suspect that person may use the information for an improper purpose. Subsection (3) lays down the penalties for breach under this section.

815. Entries not to be removed from register

(1) Entries in the register kept under section 808 (register of interests disclosed) must not be deleted except in accordance with-
    section 816 (old entries), or
    section 817 (incorrect entry relating to third party).

(2) If an entry is deleted in contravention of subsection (1), the company must restore it as soon as reasonably practicable.

(3) If default is made in complying with subsection (1) or (2), an offence is committed by-
    (a) the company, and
    (b) every officer of the company who is in default.

(4) A person guilty of an offence under this section is liable on summary conviction to a fine not exceeding level 3 on the standard scale and, for continued contravention of subsection (2), a daily default fine not exceeding one-tenth of level 3 on the standard scale.

GENERAL NOTE

This section provides that entries in the register kept under s.808 may not be deleted other than in accordance with ss.816 or 817. If the entry is deleted in contravention, then the company is obliged to restore it as soon as is reasonably practicable (subs.(2)). Subsections (3) and (4) lay down the penalties for default in complying with the section.

816. Removal of entries from register: old entries

A company may remove an entry from the register kept under section 808 (register of interests disclosed) if more than six years have elapsed since the entry was made.

GENERAL NOTE

This section provides that a company may remove an entry from the register kept under s.808 if more than six years has elapsed since the entry was made.

817. Removal of entries from register: incorrect entry relating to third party

(1) This section applies where in pursuance of an obligation imposed by a notice under section 793 (notice requiring information about interests in company's shares) a person gives to a company the name and address of another person as being interested in shares in the company.
(2) That other person may apply to the company for the removal of the entry from the register.
(3) If the company is satisfied that the information in pursuance of which the entry was made is incorrect, it shall remove the entry.
(4) If an application under subsection (3) is refused, the applicant may apply to the court for an order directing the company to remove the entry in question from the register.
The court may make such an order if it thinks fit.

GENERAL NOTE

This section makes provision for the situation where, pursuant to an obligation under s.793, a person gives the company the name and address of another person as being interested in the shares in the company. Under subs.(2) the other person may apply to the company for the removal of the entry from the register. The company, if satisfied that the information is incorrect, must remove the entry (subs.(3)). However, if the application is refused by the company, the applicant is entitled to apply to court for an order directing that the company remove the entry in question from the register. The court may make any such order as it thinks fit (subs.(4)).

818. Adjustment of entry relating to share acquisition agreement

(1) If a person who is identified in the register kept by a company under section 808 (register of interests disclosed) as being a party to an agreement to which section 824 applies (certain share acquisition agreements) ceases to be a party to the agreement, he may apply to the company for the inclusion of that information in the register.
(2) If the company is satisfied that he has ceased to be a party to the agreement, it shall record that information (if not already recorded) in every place where his name appears in the register as a party to the agreement.
(3) If an application under this section is refused (otherwise than on the ground that the information has already been recorded), the applicant may apply to the court for an order directing the company to include the information in question in the register.
The court may make such an order if it thinks fit.

GENERAL NOTE

Where a person is identified in the register as party to an agreement to which s.824 applies and ceases to be a part to the agreement, this section provides that he may apply to the company for the inclusion of that information in the register (subs.(1)). Where the company is satisfied that he has ceased to be a party to that agreement, it must record that information (if not already recorded) in every place where his name appears in the register as a party (subs.(2)). Where the application is refused, the applicant may apply to the court for an order directing the company to include that information in the register (subs.(3)). The court may make such an order as it thinks fit.

819. Duty of company ceasing to be public company

(1) If a company ceases to be a public company, it must continue to keep any register kept under section 808 (register of interests disclosed), and any associated index, until the end of the period of six years after it ceased to be such a company.

(2) If default is made in complying with this section, an offence is committed by-

    (a) the company, and

    (b) every officer of the company who is in default.

(3) A person guilty of an offence under this section is liable on summary conviction to a fine not exceeding level 3 on the standard scale and, for continued contravention, a daily default fine not exceeding one-tenth of level 3 on the standard scale.

GENERAL NOTE

Where the company ceases to be public company, this section provides that it must continue to keep any register as required under s.808 as well as any associated index, for a period of six years after it ceased to be such a company (subs.(1)). Failure to do so is an offence and subss.(2) and (3) specify the extent of the default and its consequences.

Meaning of interest in shares

820. Interest in shares: general

(1) This section applies to determine for the purposes of this Part whether a person has an interest in shares.

(2) In this Part-

    (a) a reference to an interest in shares includes an interest of any kind whatsoever in the shares, and

    (b) any restraints or restrictions to which the exercise of any right attached to the interest is or may be subject shall be disregarded.

(3) Where an interest in shares is comprised in property held on trust, every beneficiary of the trust is treated as having an interest in the shares.

(4) A person is treated as having an interest in shares if-

    (a) he enters into a contract to acquire them, or

    (b) not being the registered holder, he is entitled-

        (i) to exercise any right conferred by the holding of the shares, or

        (ii) to control the exercise of any such right.

(5) For the purposes of subsection (4)(b) a person is entitled to exercise or control the exercise of a right conferred by the holding of shares if he-

    (a) has a right (whether subject to conditions or not) the exercise of which would make him so entitled, or

    (b) is under an obligation (whether subject to conditions or not) the fulfilment of which would make him so entitled.

(6) A person is treated as having an interest in shares if-

    (a) he has a right to call for delivery of the shares to himself or to his order, or

    (b) he has a right to acquire an interest in shares or is under an obligation to take an interest in shares.

This applies whether the right or obligation is conditional or absolute.

(7) Persons having a joint interest are treated as each having that interest.

(8) It is immaterial that shares in which a person has an interest are unidentifiable.

GENERAL NOTE

   This part of the Act applies for the purpose of determining whether a person has an interest in shares (subs.(1)). This is defined in subs.(2) as an interest in any kind whatsoever and provides that any restraints or restrictions to which the exercise of the right may be subject are to be disregarded. Subsection (3) provides that where an interest arises from property held on trust, that every beneficiary under the trust is to be treated as having an interest in the shares. A person will be regarded as having an interest if he either enters into a contract for their acquisition or, not being the registered holder, is entitled to exercise any right conferred by the shares or to control the exercise of any such right (subs.(4)). For the purposes of the latter, subs.(5) elaborates when a person is entitled to exercise or control the exercise of a right conferred by the holding of shares. Subsection (6) provides that a person has an interest in shares if he has the right to call for their delivery to himself or to his order or he has a right to acquire an interest in shares or is under an obligation to take an interest in shares. Under subs.(7) persons who have a joint interest are treated as each having that interest. Subsection (8) provides that it is immaterial that shares in which a person has an interest are unidentifiable.

821.   Interest in shares: right to subscribe for shares

(1) Section 793 (notice by company requiring information about interests in its shares) applies in relation to a person who has, or previously had, or is or was entitled to acquire, a right to subscribe for shares in the company as it applies in relation to a person who is or was interested in shares in that company.

(2) References in that section to an interest in shares shall be read accordingly.

GENERAL NOTE

   This section relates back to s.793 and applies to a person who has, or previously had, or is or was entitled to acquire a right to subscribe for shares in the company as it applies in relation to a person who is or was interested in shares in that company (subs.(1)). References in s.793 to an interest in shares is intended to be read accordingly (subs.(2)).

822.   Interest in shares: family interests

(1) For the purposes of this Part a person is taken to be interested in shares in which-
   (a) his spouse or civil partner, or
   (b) any infant child or step-child of his,
is interested.

(2) In relation to Scotland "infant" means a person under the age of 18 years.

GENERAL NOTE

   This section confirms that a person will be taken to be interested in shares in which his spouse, civil partner, infant child, or step-child, is interested (subs.(1)). Subsection (2) provides that, for the purposes of Scots law, an infant means a person under the age of 18.

823. Interest in shares: corporate interests

(1) For the purposes of this Part a person is taken to be interested in shares if a body corporate is interested in them and-

    (a) the body or its directors are accustomed to act in accordance with his directions or instructions, or

    (b) he is entitled to exercise or control the exercise of one-third or more of the voting power at general meetings of the body.

(2) For the purposes of this section a person is treated as entitled to exercise or control the exercise of voting power if-

    (a) another body corporate is entitled to exercise or control the exercise of that voting power, and

    (b) he is entitled to exercise or control the exercise of one-third or more of the voting power at general meetings of that body corporate.

(3) For the purposes of this section a person is treated as entitled to exercise or control the exercise of voting power if-

    (a) he has a right (whether or not subject to conditions) the exercise of which would make him so entitled, or

    (b) he is under an obligation (whether or not subject to conditions) the fulfilment of which would make him so entitled.

GENERAL NOTE

A person will be taken to be interested in shares if a body corporate is interested in them and the body or its directors are accustomed to act in accordance with his directors or instructions or he is entitled to exercise or control the exercise of one-third or more of the voting power at general meetings (subs.(1)). A person will be treated as entitled to exercise or control the exercise of voting power if another body corporate is entitled to exercise or control the exercise of that voting power and is entitled to exercise or control the exercise of one-third or more of the voting power at general meetings (subs.(2)). A person is to be treated as entitled to exercise or control the exercise of voting power if he has a right the exercise of which would make him so entitled, or he is under an obligation, the fulfilment of which would make him so entitled (subs.(3)).

824. Interest in shares: agreement to acquire interests in a particular company

(1) For the purposes of this Part an interest in shares may arise from an agreement between two or more persons that includes provision for the acquisition by any one or more of them of interests in shares of a particular public company (the "target company" for that agreement).

(2) This section applies to such an agreement if-

    (a) the agreement includes provision imposing obligations or restrictions on any one or more of the parties to it with respect to their use, retention or disposal of their interests in the shares of the target company acquired in pursuance of the agreement (whether or not together with any other interests of theirs in the company's shares to which the agreement relates), and

    (b) an interest in the target company's shares is in fact acquired by any of the parties in pursuance of the agreement.

(3) The reference in subsection (2) to the use of interests in shares in the target company is to the exercise of any rights or of any control or influence arising from those interests (including the right to enter into an agreement for the exercise, or for control of the exercise, of any of those rights by another person).

(4) Once an interest in shares in the target company has been acquired in pursuance of the agreement, this section continues to apply to the agreement so long as the agreement continues to include provisions of any description mentioned in subsection (2).

This applies irrespective of-

    (a) whether or not any further acquisitions of interests in the company's shares take place in pursuance of the agreement;

(b) any change in the persons who are for the time being parties to it;

(c) any variation of the agreement.

References in this subsection to the agreement include any agreement having effect (whether directly or indirectly) in substitution for the original agreement.

(5) In this section-

    (a) "agreement" includes any agreement or arrangement, and

    (b) references to provisions of an agreement include-

        (i) undertakings, expectations or understandings operative under an arrangement, and

        (ii) any provision whether express or implied and whether absolute or not.

References elsewhere in this Part to an agreement to which this section applies have a corresponding meaning.

(6) This section does not apply-

    (a) to an agreement that is not legally binding unless it involves mutuality in the undertakings, expectations or understandings of the parties to it; or

    (b) to an agreement to underwrite or sub-underwrite an offer of shares in a company, provided the agreement is confined to that purpose and any matters incidental to it.

GENERAL NOTE

An interest in shares may arise from an agreement between two or more persons which includes provision for the acquisition by any one or more them of interests in shares of a particular public company (the target) (subs.(1)). The section will apply to such an agreement if the agreement includes provision imposing obligations or restrictions on any one or more of the parties to it with respect to their use, retention or disposal of their interests in the shares of the target company acquired in pursuance of the agreement and an interest in the target company's shares is in fact acquired by any of the parties in pursuance of the agreement (subs.(2)). Subsection (3) indicates that a reference to the use of interests in shares in the target company is to the exercise of any rights or of any control or influence arising from those interests, including the right to enter into an agreement for the exercise, or for control of the exercise, of any of those rights by another person. Subsection (4) indicates that once an interest in shares in the target company has been acquired in pursuance of the agreement, the section will continue to apply to it so long as it continues to include provisions of any description as is mentioned in subs.(2). This is stated to apply irrespective of whether or not any further acquisitions of interests in the company's shares take place in pursuance of the agreement; any change in the persons who are for the time being parties to it, or any variation of the agreement. Subsection (5) specifies how the term "agreement" is to be understood. Subsection (6) sets out those agreements to which the section will not apply.

825. Extent of obligation in case of share acquisition agreement

(1) For the purposes of this Part each party to an agreement to which section 824 applies is treated as interested in all shares in the target company in which any other party to the agreement is interested apart from the agreement (whether or not the interest of the other party was acquired, or includes any interest that was acquired, in pursuance of the agreement).

(2) For those purposes an interest of a party to such an agreement in shares in the target company is an interest apart from the agreement if he is interested in those shares otherwise than by virtue of the application of section 824 (and this section) in relation to the agreement.

(3) Accordingly, any such interest of the person (apart from the agreement) includes for those purposes any interest treated as his under section 822 or 823 (family or corporate interests) or by the application of section 824 (and this section) in relation to any other agreement with respect to shares in the target company to which he is a party.

(4) A notification with respect to his interest in shares in the target company made to the company under this Part by a person who is for the time being a party to an agreement to which section 824 applies must-

    (a) state that the person making the notification is a party to such an agreement,

    (b) include the names and (so far as known to him) the addresses of the other parties to the agreement, identifying them as such, and

    (c) state whether or not any of the shares to which the notification relates are shares in which he is interested by virtue of section 824 (and this section) and, if so, the number of those shares.

GENERAL NOTE

    This section indicates that for the purposes of the provisions in this Part each party to an agreement to which the preceding s.824 applies will be treated as interested in all shares in the target company in which any other party to the agreement is interested apart from the agreement (subs.(1)). Subsections (2) then elaborates further, to the effect that an interest of a party to such an agreement in shares in the target company is an interest apart from the agreement if he is interested in those shares otherwise than by virtue of the application of s.824. Any such interest of that person will include, for these purposes, any interest treated as his under s.822 or s.823 or by the application of s.824 and this section in relation to any other agreement with respect to shares in the target company to which he is a party (subs.(3)). Finally, subs.(4) specifies the form that the notification to the company must take.

Other supplementary provisions

826. Information protected from wider disclosure

(1) Information in respect of which a company is for the time being entitled to any exemption conferred by regulations under section 409(3) (information about related undertakings to be given in notes to accounts: exemption where disclosure harmful to company's business)-

    (a) must not be included in a report under section 805 (report to members on outcome of investigation), and

    (b) must not be made available under section 811 (right to inspect and request copy of entries).

(2) Where any such information is omitted from a report under section 805, that fact must be stated in the report.

GENERAL NOTE

    This section provides that information which would for the time being entitle the company to any exemption under the regulation made under s.409(3) must not be included in any report under s.805 and must not be available under s.811 (subs.(1)). Where any information is omitted from a report under s.805, then this fact must be stated in the report (subs.(2)).

827. Reckoning of periods for fulfilling obligations

Where the period allowed by any provision of this Part for fulfilling an obligation is expressed as a number of days, any day that is not a working day shall be disregarded in reckoning that period.

GENERAL NOTE

    This section simply provides that any day which is not a working day is to be disregarded for the purpose of reckoning the relevant period under this Part of the Act.

828. Power to make further provision by regulations

(1) The Secretary of State may by regulations amend-

    (a) the definition of shares to which this Part applies (section 792),

    (b) the provisions as to notice by a company requiring information about interests in its shares (section 793), and

    (c) the provisions as to what is taken to be an interest in shares (sections 820 and 821).

(2) The regulations may amend, repeal or replace those provisions and make such other consequential amendments or repeals of provisions of this Part as appear to the Secretary of State to be appropriate.

(3) Regulations under this section are subject to affirmative resolution procedure.

GENERAL NOTE

This section provides that the Secretary of State is empowered to make regulations amending the definition of shares to which this Part of the Act applies (s.792), the provisions as to notice by a company requiring information about interests in its shares (s.793), and the provisions as to what is taken to be an interest in shares (i.e. ss.820 and 821 above) (subs.(1)). The regulations in question may amend, repeal or replace those provisions and also make such other consequential amendments or repeals of provisions in this Part as appear to the Secretary of State to be appropriate (subs.(2)). The regulations so made are subject to the affirmative resolution procedure (subs.(3)).

PART 23

DISTRIBUTIONS

GENERAL NOTE

This Part of the Act was introduced into the legislation at a relatively late stage when it had been decided that it would replace the 1985 Act. As a result, the substance of Pt VIII of the 1985 Act has been restated in the new Pt 23, although the opportunity has been taken to reorder and reword the sections.

Where appropriate, reference should be made to recommendations made by the six major accountancy professional bodies in the United Kingdom and Ireland, who have published their joint advice via the Consultative Committee of Accountancy Bodies. Prior to the publication of the new Act, this was contained in three pronouncements: TECH 7/03, "Guidance on the Determination of Realised Profits and Losses in the Context of Distributions Under the Companies Act 1985" (www.icaew.co.uk/index.cfm?route=119579); TECH 21/05, "Distributable Profits: Implications of IFRS" (www.i-caew.co.uk/viewer/index.cfm?AUB=TB21.81950); and TECH 57/05, "Distributable Profits: Implications of IAS 10 and FRS 21 for Dividends" (www.icaew.co.uk/index.cfm?route=114384).

Originally a clause was tabled in the Bill that would have given the Secretary of State power to make further provisions by issuing regulations with respect to the rules covering distributions. Such regulations would have been subject to the affirmative resolution procedure (s.1290), and they would have been in addition to those recognised in the 1985 Act (e.g. extending the rules applying to "investment companies" to other companies (s.267(2)); and "financial assistance" given (ss.274(4) and 277(2))), but not now covered in the 2006 Act. In fact, it was only at the last minute that the clause was withdrawn, the government deciding when the Bill came before the House of Lords for the last time that it was inappropriate to give such powers to the Secretary of State (see *Hansard*, cols 441-444 (November 2, 2006): see www.publications.parliament.uk/pa/ld199900/ldhansrd/pdvn/lds06/text/61102-0005.htm). This was despite the fact that the clause had been tabled originally to help deal with the introduction of international accounting standards, which has made it difficult for a number of companies to pay dividends, even they were profitable under United Kingdom generally accepted accounting principles (United Kingdom GAAP).

The only provision empowering the Secretary of State to issue regulations in this Part of the Act is now given in s.835, dealing with the extension of provisions relating to investment companies.

Definitions

Various definitions are used in this Part, many of which can be identified in Schedule 8 (e.g. "accounting reference period", "called up share capital", "capital redemption reserve", "uncalled share capital"). However, the following definitions can be found in sections within this Part as follows: "capitalisation" s.853(3); "distribution" s.829; "investment company" s.833; "realised losses" ss.841(2) and 853(4)-(5); "realised profits" s.853(4)-(5); "revaluation provisions" s.841(3); and "undistributable reserves" s.831(4). Other expressions are defined in the sections where they are used.

CHAPTER I

RESTRICTIONS ON WHEN DISTRIBUTIONS MAY BE MADE

Introductory

829. Meaning of "distribution"

(1) In this Part "distribution" means every description of distribution of a company's assets to its members, whether in cash or otherwise, subject to the following exceptions.

(2) The following are not distributions for the purposes of this Part-
    (a) an issue of shares as fully or partly paid bonus shares;
    (b) the reduction of share capital-
        (i) by extinguishing or reducing the liability of any of the members on any of the company's shares in respect of share capital not paid up, or
        (ii) by repaying paid-up share capital;
    (c) the redemption or purchase of any of the company's own shares out of capital (including the proceeds of any fresh issue of shares) or out of unrealised profits in accordance with Chapter 3, 4 or 5 of Part 18;
    (d) a distribution of assets to members of the company on its winding up.

GENERAL NOTE

This section re-enacts, with certain re-arrangements of the text, subs.(2) of s.263 of the 1985 Act.

Subsections (1) and (2)

This subsection defines a distribution for the purpose of this Part of the Act. (*cf.* the definition for corporation tax purposes s.209 of ICTA 1988.) "Distribution" means every type of distribution of a company's assets to its members, whether in cash or otherwise, subject to the exemptions listed in subs.(2). These are: (i) a bonus issue of shares; (ii) a reduction in share capital; (iii) the redemption or purchase of the company's own shares out of capital or out of unrealised profits; and (iv) a distribution of assets to members on a winding up.

General rules

830. Distributions to be made only out of profits available for the purpose

(1) A company may only make a distribution out of profits available for the purpose.

(2) A company's profits available for distribution are its accumulated, realised profits, so far as not previously utilised by distribution or capitalisation, less its accumulated, realised losses, so far as not previously written off in a reduction or reorganisation of capital duly made.

(3) Subsection (2) has effect subject to sections 832 and 835 (investment companies etc: distributions out of accumulated revenue profits).

GENERAL NOTE

This section re-enacts, with certain re-arrangements of the text, subss.(1) and (3) of s.263 of the 1985 Act, and indicates that distributions are only to be made out of profits regarded as available for that purpose. For the consequences of a breach of this principle, see s.847, below.

Subsection (1)

This subsection restates subs.(1) of s.263 of the 1985 Act. While a company may only make a distribution out of profits available for the purpose, the company may impose further restrictions itself - see s.852 below.

Subsections (2) and (3)

These subsections restate subs.(3) of s.263 of the 1985 Act, indicating that the profits available for distribution by a company are its accumulated, realised profits, so far as not previously used, less its accumulated, realised losses, so far as not previously written off. Subsection (2) makes no distinction between capital and revenue profits and losses: see s.853(2) below. There must be accumulated realised profits, and past losses must be made good, so overruling the decisions in *Ammonia Soda Co Ltd v Chamberlain* [1918] 1 Ch. 266, CA and *Dimbula Valley (Ceylon) Tea Co Ltd v Laurie* [1961] Ch. 353 at 373.

Subs.(3) indicates that investment companies are subject to special provisions, outlined in ss.832 and 835.

831. Net asset restriction on distributions by public companies

(1) A public company may only make a distribution-
   (a) if the amount of its net assets is not less than the aggregate of its called-up share capital and undistributable reserves, and
   (b) if, and to the extent that, the distribution does not reduce the amount of those assets to less than that aggregate.
(2) For this purpose a company's "net assets" means the aggregate of the company's assets less the aggregate of its liabilities.
(3) "Liabilities" here includes-
   (a) where the relevant accounts are Companies Act accounts, provisions of a kind specified for the purposes of this subsection by regulations under section 396;
   (b) where the relevant accounts are IAS accounts, provisions of any kind.
(4) A company's undistributable reserves are-
   (a) its share premium account;
   (b) its capital redemption reserve;
   (c) the amount by which its accumulated, unrealised profits (so far as not previously utilised by capitalisation) exceed its accumulated, unrealised losses (so far as not previously written off in a reduction or reorganisation of capital duly made);
   (d) any other reserve that the company is prohibited from distributing-
      (i) by any enactment (other than one contained in this Part), or
      (ii) by its articles.

   The reference in paragraph (c) to capitalisation does not include a transfer of profits of the company to its capital redemption reserve.
(5) A public company must not include any uncalled share capital as an asset in any accounts relevant for purposes of this section.
(6) Subsection (1) has effect subject to sections 832 and 835 (investment companies etc: distributions out of accumulated revenue profits).

GENERAL NOTE
   This section re-enacts, with certain re-arrangements of the text, s.264 of the 1985 Act.

Subsection (1)

   This subsection restates subs.(1) of s.264 of the 1985 Act. It indicates that, in addition to the test under subss.(1)-(2) of s.830, a *public* company is not entitled to make a distribution if the result would be to reduce the value of the assets below that of the liabilities and capital. For the consequences of a breach of this rule, see s.847 below.

Subsections (2) and (3)

   These subsections restate subs.(2) of s.264 of the 1985 Act, as amended by Sch.1, para.22 of SI 2004/2947, "The Companies Act 1985 (International Accounting Standards and Other Accounting Amendments) Regulations 2004". In so doing, it indicates how the term "net assets" is to be interpreted, with "liabilities" including "provisions".

Subsection (4)

   This subsection restates subs.(3) of s.264 of the 1985 Act, indicating that a company's undistributable reserves are: (i) its share premium account; (ii) its capital redemption reserve; (iii) the amount by which its accumulated, unrealised profits (so far as not previously used) exceed its accumulated, unrealised losses (so far as not previously used); and (iv) any other reserve that the company is prohibited from distributing.

This subsection restates subs.(4) of s.264 of the 1985 Act, indicating that a public company must not include uncalled share capital as an asset in its accounts for the purpose of this section.

This subsection indicates that investment companies are subject to special provisions, outlined in ss.832 and 835, below.

Distributions by investment companies

832. Distributions by investment companies out of accumulated revenue profits

(1) An investment company may make a distribution out of its accumulated, realised revenue profits if the following conditions are met.

(2) It may make such a distribution only if, and to the extent that, its accumulated, realised revenue profits, so far as not previously utilised by a distribution or capitalisation, exceed its accumulated revenue losses (whether realised or unrealised), so far as not previously written off in a reduction or reorganisation of capital duly made.

(3) It may make such a distribution only-
   (a) if the amount of its assets is at least equal to one and a half times the aggregate of its liabilities to creditors, and
   (b) if, and to the extent that, the distribution does not reduce that amount to less than one and a half times that aggregate.

(4) For this purpose a company's liabilities to creditors include-
   (a) in the case of Companies Act accounts, provisions of a kind specified for the purposes of this subsection by regulations under section 396;
   (b) in the case of IAS accounts, provisions for liabilities to creditors.

(5) The following conditions must also be met-
   (a) the company's shares must be listed on a recognised UK investment exchange;
   (b) during the relevant period it must not have-
      (i) distributed any capital profits otherwise than by way of the redemption or purchase of any of the company's own shares in accordance with Chapter 3 or 4 of Part 18, or
      (ii) applied any unrealised profits or any capital profits (realised or unrealised) in paying up debentures or amounts unpaid on its issued shares;
   (c) it must have given notice to the registrar under section 833(1) (notice of intention to carry on business as an investment company)-
      (i) before the beginning of the relevant period, or
      (ii) as soon as reasonably practicable after the date of its incorporation.

(6) For the purposes of this section-
   (a) "recognised UK investment exchange" means a recognised investment exchange within the meaning of Part 18 of the Financial Services and Markets Act 2000 (c. 8), other than an overseas investment exchange within the meaning of that Part; and
   (b) the "relevant period" is the period beginning with-
      (i) the first day of the accounting reference period immediately preceding that in which the proposed distribution is to be made, or
      (ii) where the distribution is to be made in the company's first accounting reference period, the first day of that period,
   and ending with the date of the distribution.

(7) The company must not include any uncalled share capital as an asset in any accounts relevant for purposes of this section.

GENERAL NOTE

This section re-enacts, with certain re-arrangements of the text, s.265 of the 1985 Act. It provides for the application of the realised profits and net assets tests (ss.830 and 831) to investment companies, which are defined in s.833 below. If such a company has invested in shares that have fallen in value so that the net assets fall below cost, the company would be unable to comply with the net assets test in s.831. As an alternative, it may therefore apply the assets/liability test as described in this section. For the future extension of this section to other companies whose principal business is investing in securities, property, etc. see s.835 below.

Subsections (1)-(3)

These subsections, with revised wording, restate subs.(1) of s.265 of the 1985 Act. They state that an investment company may make a distribution out of its accumulated, realised profits (subs.(1)) if the following conditions are met: (i) its accumulated, realised profits, so far as not previously used, exceed its accumulated, realised losses, so far as not previously written off (subs.(2)); and (ii) its assets are at least equal to 1.5 times its liabilities, and the proposed distribution will not reduce the ratio below that level (subs.(3)).

Subsection (4)

This subsection restates subs.(2) of s.265 of the 1985 Act, as amended by Sch.1, para.23 of SI 2004/2947, "The Companies Act 1985 (International Accounting Standards and Other Accounting Amendments) Regulations 2004", defining the company's liabilities for the purpose of making the ratio calculation described in subs.(3).

Subsections (5) and (6)

These subsections, with revised wording, restate subss.(4), (4A), (5) and (6) of s.265 of the 1985 Act, as amended or substituted by The Financial Services Act 1986, Sch.16, para.19; SI 1999/2770, reg.2; and SI 2001/3649, Art.17. They set various conditions, namely: (i) the company's shares must be listed on a "recognised UK investment exchange" (defined in subs.(6)); (ii) during the "relevant period" (defined in subs.(6)) it must not have distributed capital profits other than for redeeming or purchasing its own shares, nor have applied unrealised profits or realised or unrealised capital profits in paying up debentures or amounts unpaid on its issued shares; and (iii) it must have given notice to the registrar under s.833(1) of its intention to carry on business as an "investment company".

Subsection (7)

This subsection restates subs.(3) of s.265 of the 1985 Act, indicating that uncalled share capital must not be included as an asset in its accounts for the purpose of this section.

833. Meaning of "investment company"

(1) In this Part an "investment company" means a public company that-
    (a) has given notice (which has not been revoked) to the registrar of its intention to carry on business as an investment company, and
    (b) since the date of that notice has complied with the following requirements.

(2) Those requirements are-
    (a) that the business of the company consists of investing its funds mainly in securities, with the aim of spreading investment risk and giving members of the company the benefit of the results of the management of its funds;
    (b) that the condition in section 834 is met as regards holdings in other companies;
    (c) that distribution of the company's capital profits is prohibited by its articles;
    (d) that the company has not retained, otherwise than in compliance with this Part, in respect of any accounting reference period more than 15% of the income it derives from securities.

(3) Subsection (2)(c) does not require an investment company to be prohibited by its articles from redeeming or purchasing its own shares in accordance with Chapter 3 or 4 of Part 18 out of its capital profits.

(4) Notice to the registrar under this section may be revoked at any time by the company on giving notice to the registrar that it no longer wishes to be an investment company within the meaning of this section.

(5) On giving such a notice, the company ceases to be such a company.

GENERAL NOTE

This section re-enacts, with certain re-arrangements of the text, s.266 of the 1985 Act. An investment company is defined by reference to the criteria in s.842 of ICTA 1988. For future extensions of this section, see s.835 below.

Subsection (1)

This subsection restates subs.(1) of s.266 of the 1985 Act. It indicates that the term "investment company" means a public company that has given notice to the registrar of its intention to carry on business as an investment company, and that since giving notice it has complied with the requirements set out in subss.(2) and (3).

For revocation of the notice, see subss.(4)-(5). (With respect to "notice", see s.832(5)(c).)

Subsection (2)

This subsection restates subs.(2)(a)(c)(d) of s.266 of the 1985 Act. It sets out the following requirements: (i) the company invests mainly in a portfolio of securities, thus spreading risk for the benefit of its members; (ii) the conditions with respect to holdings in other companies set out in s.834, below, are met; (iii) distribution of capital profits is prohibited by the company's articles (subject to subs.(3), below); and (iv) the company has not retained in any accounting period more than 15 per cent of the income derived from securities.

Subsection (3)

This subsection restates subs.(2A) of s.266 of the 1985 Act, as inserted by SI 1999/2770, reg.3. An investment company is not required by subs.(2) to prohibit by its articles the redemption or purchase of its own shares out of capital profits.

Subsections (4) and (5)

These subsections restate subs.(3) of s.266 of the 1985 Act, indicating that notice may be given to the registrar at any time indicating a company's wish no longer to operate as an investment company (subs.(4)), to come into effect immediately (subs.(5)).

834. Investment company: condition as to holdings in other companies

(1) The condition referred to in section 833(2)(b) (requirements to be complied with by investment company) is that none of the company's holdings in companies (other than those that are for the time being investment companies) represents more than 15% by value of the company's investments.

(2) For this purpose-
　(a) holdings in companies that-
　　(i) are members of a group (whether or not including the investing company), and
　　(ii) are not for the time being investment companies,
　are treated as holdings in a single company; and
　(b) where the investing company is a member of a group, money owed to it by another member of the group-
　　(i) is treated as a security of the latter held by the investing company, and
　　(ii) is accordingly treated as, or as part of, the holding of the investing company in the company owing the money.

(3) The condition does not apply-
　(a) to a holding in a company acquired before 6th April 1965 that on that date represented not more than 25% by value of the investing company's investments, or
　(b) to a holding in a company that, when it was acquired, represented not more than 15% by value of the investing company's investments,
so long as no addition is made to the holding.

(4) For the purposes of subsection (3)-
　(a) "holding" means the shares or securities (whether or one class or more than one class) held in any one company;
　(b) an addition is made to a holding whenever the investing company acquires shares or securities of that one company, otherwise than by being allotted shares or securities without becoming liable to give any consideration, and if an addition is made to a holding that holding is acquired when the addition or latest addition is made to the holding; and

(c) where in connection with a scheme of reconstruction a company issues shares or securities to persons holding shares or securities in a second company in respect of and in proportion to (or as nearly as may be in proportion to) their holdings in the second company, without those persons becoming liable to give any consideration, a holding of the shares or securities in the second company and a corresponding holding of the shares or securities so issued shall be regarded as the same holding.

(5) In this section-

"company" and "shares" shall be construed in accordance with sections 99 and 288 of the Taxation of Chargeable Gains Act 1992 (c. 12);

"group" means a company and all companies that are its 51% subsidiaries (within the meaning of section 838 of the Income and Corporation Taxes Act 1988 (c. 1)); and

"scheme of reconstruction" has the same meaning as in section 136 of the Taxation of Chargeable Gains Act 1992.

GENERAL NOTE

This section re-enacts and expands, with certain re-arrangements of the text, subss.(2)(b) and (4) of s.266 of the 1985 Act, the former being inserted by SI 1999/2770, reg.3, and the latter being substituted by s.117(3),(4) of the Finance Act 1988.

For the purposes of this section, the terms "company", "group", "scheme of reconstruction" and "shares" are defined in subs.(5)

Subsection (1)

This subsection restates subs.(2)(b) of s.266 of the 1985 Act, as amended by SI 1999/2770, reg.3. None of an investment company's holdings in other companies must represent more than 15 per cent of its investments.

Subsections (2)-(4)

These subsections elaborate subs.(4) of s.266 of the 1985 Act, as inserted, which indicated that subss.(1A)-(3) of s.842 of the Income and Corporation Taxes Act 1988 apply for the purpose of what is now subs.(1) of this section. Subsection (2) indicates that holdings in companies that are not investment companies, but which are members of a group, are to be treated as holdings in a single company. It also indicates how money owed to the investor company by another member of the group is to be treated. Subsection (3) deals with the situation where substantial holdings were acquired before 6 April 1965 or where holdings, when they were acquired, represented not more than 15 per cent of the investment company's investments. Subsection (4) defines, for the purpose of subs.(3), "holding", and indicates how additions in holdings and the impact of company reconstructions should be treated.

Subsection (5)

This subsection indicates that for the purpose of this section the definitions of "company", "shares", "group" and "scheme of reconstruction" should be those applied in various pieces of tax legislation.

835.   Power to extend provisions relating to investment companies

(1) The Secretary of State may by regulations extend the provisions of sections 832 to 834 (distributions by investment companies out of accumulated profits), with or without modifications, to other companies whose principal business consists of investing their funds in securities, land or other assets with the aim of spreading investment risk and giving their members the benefit of the results of the management of the assets.

(2) Regulations under this section are subject to affirmative resolution procedure.

GENERAL NOTE

This section re-enacts, with certain changes in wording, s.267 of the 1985 Act.

Subsection (1)

This subsection restates subs.(1) of s.267 of the 1985 Act, empowering the Secretary of State to issue regulations extending the provisions of ss.832-834 to apply to other companies whose principal business is investing funds on behalf of members in portfolios of securities, land or similar assets.

This subsection simplifies subs.(2) of s.267 of the 1985 Act, and indicates that any regulations issued under this section are subject to the affirmative resolution procedure (see s.1290).

CHAPTER 2

JUSTIFICATION OF DISTRIBUTION BY REFERENCE TO ACCOUNTS

Justification of distribution by reference to accounts

836. Justification of distribution by reference to relevant accounts

(1) Whether a distribution may be made by a company without contravening this Part is determined by reference to the following items as stated in the relevant accounts-
    (a) profits, losses, assets and liabilities;
    (b) provisions of the following kinds-
        (i) where the relevant accounts are Companies Act accounts, provisions of a kind specified for the purposes of this subsection by regulations under section 396;
        (ii) where the relevant accounts are IAS accounts, provisions of any kind;
    (c) share capital and reserves (including undistributable reserves).
(2) The relevant accounts are the company's last annual accounts, except that-
    (a) where the distribution would be found to contravene this Part by reference to the company's last annual accounts, it may be justified by reference to interim accounts, and
    (b) where the distribution is proposed to be declared during the company's first accounting reference period, or before any accounts have been circulated in respect of that period, it may be justified by reference to initial accounts.
(3) The requirements of-
    section 837 (as regards the company's last annual accounts),
    section 838 (as regards interim accounts), and
    section 839 (as regards initial accounts),
must be complied with, as and where applicable.
(4) If any applicable requirement of those sections is not complied with, the accounts may not be relied on for the purposes of this Part and the distribution is accordingly treated as contravening this Part.

GENERAL NOTE

This section re-enacts, with certain re-arrangements and changes in wording, s.270 of the 1985 Act. Together with ss.837-846 it provides the accounting requirements and definitions for ascertaining whether a company has distributed profits under the criteria set out in ss.829-832 above. In essence, the tests must be applied by reference to the specified items in the relevant accounts. These relevant accounts comprise, as appropriate, the annual accounts, interim accounts or initial accounts, and ss.837-839 respectively provide the requirements relating to each of these types of financial statement. Unless the accounts comply with the requirements of these sections, this is an automatic breach of ss.829-832: subs.(4).

Subsection (1)

This subsection restates subs.(2) of s.267 of the 1985 Act, as amended by Sch.1, para.26 of SI 2004/2947, "The Companies Act 1985 (International Accounting Standards and Other Accounting Amendments) Regulations 2004". It indicates that a distribution must be made by reference to various items stated in the "relevant accounts": namely, profits, losses, assets and liabilities; provisions; and share capital and reserves. For non-compliance, see subs.(4) below.

Subsection (2)

This subsection restates subs.(4) of s.267 of the 1985 Act and identifies the "relevant accounts" referred to in subs.(1). This will normally be the company's last annual accounts, but provision is made for the use of interim or initial accounts, where appropriate.

Subsection (3)

This subsection restates subss.(3) and (4) of s.267 of the 1985 Act, indicating that the requirements of the relevant sections dealing with annual accounts (s.837), interim accounts (s.838) and initial accounts (s.839) must be complied with.

Subsection (4)

This subsection restates subs.(5) of s.267 of the 1985 Act, indicating that failure to comply with the relevant requirements referred to in subs.(3) means that a distribution contravenes this Part of the Act.

Requirements applicable in relation to relevant accounts

837. Requirements where last annual accounts used

(1) The company's last annual accounts means the company's individual accounts-
    (a) that were last circulated to members in accordance with section 423 (duty to circulate copies of annual accounts and reports), or
    (b) if in accordance with section 426 the company provided a summary financial statement instead, that formed the basis of that statement.

(2) The accounts must have been properly prepared in accordance with this Act, or have been so prepared subject only to matters that are not material for determining (by reference to the items mentioned in section 836(1)) whether the distribution would contravene this Part.

(3) Unless the company is exempt from audit and the directors take advantage of that exemption, the auditor must have made his report on the accounts.

(4) If that report was qualified-
    (a) the auditor must have stated in writing (either at the time of his report or subsequently) whether in his opinion the matters in respect of which his report is qualified are material for determining whether a distribution would contravene this Part, and
    (b) a copy of that statement must-
        (i) in the case of a private company, have been circulated to members in accordance with section 423, or
        (ii) in the case of a public company, have been laid before the company in general meeting.

(5) An auditor's statement is sufficient for the purposes of a distribution if it relates to distributions of a description that includes the distribution in question, even if at the time of the statement it had not been proposed.

GENERAL NOTE

This section re-enacts, with certain re-arrangements and changes in wording, s.271 of the 1985 Act. It applies where the last annual accounts are the relevant accounts under s.836 and provides four requirements that must be observed to comply with that section.

Subsection (1)

This subsection elaborates subs.(1) of s.271 of the 1985 Act. It identifies a company's last annual accounts as those last circulated to shareholders or which formed the basis of a summary financial statement if that was circulated instead.

Subsection (2)

This subsection restates subs.(2) of s.271 of the 1985 Act, indicating that the accounts must have been properly prepared or only be defective in ways immaterial in determining whether the distribution is in breach of this Part of the Act.

Subsection (3)

This subsection restates subs.(3) of s.271 of the 1985 Act, indicating that the auditor must have reported on the accounts, unless the company is exempt from audit. [For exemptions from audit, see ss.477-481.]

Subsection (4)

This subsection restates subs.(4) of s.271 of the 1985 Act, indicating that if the auditor's report is qualified, he must state in writing whether in his view this affects the validity of the distribution. Moreover, such a statement must, in the case of a private company, have been properly circulated to members; or, in the case of a public company, have been laid before the company in general meeting. (Under s.495(4), an auditor's report must be either qualified or unqualified.)

Subsection (5)

This subsection restates subs.(5) of s.271 of the 1985 Act, indicating that the auditor's statement should be sufficient for the purpose of a distribution.

838. Requirements where interim accounts used

(1) Interim accounts must be accounts that enable a reasonable judgment to be made as to the amounts of the items mentioned in section 836(1).
(2) Where interim accounts are prepared for a proposed distribution by a public company, the following requirements apply.
(3) The accounts must have been properly prepared, or have been so prepared subject to matters that are not material for determining (by reference to the items mentioned in section 836(1)) whether the distribution would contravene this Part.
(4) "Properly prepared" means prepared in accordance with sections 395 to 397 (requirements for company individual accounts), applying those requirements with such modifications as are necessary because the accounts are prepared otherwise than in respect of an accounting reference period.
(5) The balance sheet comprised in the accounts must have been signed in accordance with section 414.
(6) A copy of the accounts must have been delivered to the registrar.
Any requirement of Part 35 of this Act as to the delivery of a certified translation into English of any document forming part of the accounts must also have been met.

GENERAL NOTE

This section re-enacts, with certain re-arrangements and changes in wording, s.272 of the 1985 Act. Subsections (1)-(3) restate subss.(1)-(2) of s.272 of the 1985 Act, subss.(4)-(5) subs.(3) of s.272 of the 1985 Act, and subs.(6) subss.(4)-(5) of s.272 of the 1985 Act.

Subsections (1)-(6)

The section applies where the interim accounts are the relevant accounts under s.836 (subs.(1)) and identifies three requirements if the company is a public company (subs.(2)), namely: (i) the accounts must have been "properly prepared" (defined in subs.(4)) so that the general principles applying to distributions with reference to accounts can be observed (subs.(3)); (ii) the balance sheet must have been properly signed (subs.(5)); and (iii) a copy of the interim accounts must have been delivered to the registrar of companies (subs.(6)).

839. Requirements where initial accounts used

(1) Initial accounts must be accounts that enable a reasonable judgment to be made as to the amounts of the items mentioned in section 836(1).
(2) Where initial accounts are prepared for a proposed distribution by a public company, the following requirements apply.
(3) The accounts must have been properly prepared, or have been so prepared subject to matters that are not material for determining (by reference to the items mentioned in section 836(1)) whether the distribution would contravene this Part.
(4) "Properly prepared" means prepared in accordance with sections 395 to 397 (requirements for company individual accounts), applying those requirements with such modifications as are

necessary because the accounts are prepared otherwise than in respect of an accounting reference period.

(5) The company's auditor must have made a report stating whether, in his opinion, the accounts have been properly prepared.

(6) If that report was qualified-

    (a) the auditor must have stated in writing (either at the time of his report or subsequently) whether in his opinion the matters in respect of which his report is qualified are material for determining whether a distribution would contravene this Part, and

    (b) a copy of that statement must-

        (i) in the case of a private company, have been circulated to members in accordance with section 423, or

        (ii) in the case of a public company, have been laid before the company in general meeting.

(7) A copy of the accounts, of the auditor's report and of any auditor's statement must have been delivered to the registrar.

Any requirement of Part 35 of this Act as to the delivery of a certified translation into English of any of those documents must also have been met.

GENERAL NOTE

    This section re-enacts, with certain re-arrangements and changes in wording, s.273 of the 1985 Act. Subsections (1)-(3) restate subss.(1)-(3) of s.273 of the 1985 Act, subs.(4) subs.(3) of s.273 of the 1985 Act, subs.(5) subs.(4) of s.273 of the 1985 Act, subs.(6) subs.(5) of s.273 of the 1985 Act, and subs.(7) subss.(6)-(7) of s.273 of the 1985 Act.

Subsections (1)-(7)

    The section applies where the initial accounts are the relevant accounts under s.836 (subs.(1)) and identifies five requirements if the company is a public company (subs.(2)), namely: (i) the accounts must have been "properly prepared" (defined in subs.(4)) so that the general principles applying to distributions with reference to accounts can be observed (subs.(3)); (ii) the company's auditor must have made a report stating that in his opinion the initial accounts have been properly prepared (subs.(5)); (iii) if the accounts are qualified, the auditor must have stated in writing whether such qualification is material in determining whether the proposed distribution would contravene the provisions of the Act (subs.(6)(a)); (iv) a copy of such a statement by the auditor must have been, in the case of a private company, circulated to members, or, in the case of a public company, have been laid before the company in general meeting (subs.(6)(b)); and (v) a copy of the initial accounts and the auditor's report, together with any auditor's statement, must have been delivered to the registrar of companies (subs.(7)).

Application of provisions to successive distributions etc

840.   Successive distributions etc by reference to the same accounts

(1) In determining whether a proposed distribution may be made by a company in a case where-

    (a) one or more previous distributions have been made in pursuance of a determination made by reference to the same relevant accounts, or

    (b) relevant financial assistance has been given, or other relevant payments have been made, since those accounts were prepared,

 the provisions of this Part apply as if the amount of the proposed distribution was increased by the amount of the previous distributions, financial assistance and other payments.

(2) The financial assistance and other payments that are relevant for this purpose are-

    (a) financial assistance lawfully given by the company out of its distributable profits;

    (b) financial assistance given by the company in contravention of section 678 or 679 (prohibited financial assistance) in a case where the giving of that assistance reduces the company's net assets or increases its net liabilities;

    (c) payments made by the company in respect of the purchase by it of shares in the company, except a payment lawfully made otherwise than out of distributable profits;

(d) payments of any description specified in section 705 (payments apart from purchase price of shares to be made out of distributable profits).

(3) In this section "financial assistance" has the same meaning as in Chapter 2 of Part 18 (see section 677).

(4) For the purpose of applying subsection (2)(b) in relation to any financial assistance-

(a) "net assets" means the amount by which the aggregate amount of the company's assets exceeds the aggregate amount of its liabilities, and

(b) "net liabilities" means the amount by which the aggregate amount of the company's liabilities exceeds the aggregate amount of its assets,

taking the amount of the assets and liabilities to be as stated in the company's accounting records immediately before the financial assistance is given.

(5) For this purpose a company's liabilities include any amount retained as reasonably necessary for the purposes of providing for any liability-

(a) the nature of which is clearly defined, and

(b) which is either likely to be incurred or certain to be incurred but uncertain as to amount or as to the date on which it will arise.

GENERAL NOTE

This section re-enacts, with certain re-arrangements and changes in wording, s.274 of the 1985 Act. It provides for the application of the relevant accounts under s.836 in determining whether the company has distributable profits under ss.829-832, where there are successive distributions by reference to the same accounts. These include the use of distributable profits by companies in giving financial assistance for the acquisition of its shares by another and in connection with the purchase or redemption by a company of its own shares.

Subsection (1)

This subsection restates subs.(1) of s.274 of the 1985 Act. It applies the general rule that all distributions made by reference to the same accounts are cumulative. Where financial assistance given by a company for the acquisition of its shares (defined in subs.(1) of s.677) involves either a reduction of its net assets or the use of distributable profits, or the purchase or redemption of its own shares by a company involves either the use of such profits or an unauthorised fund, such payments are to be regarded as distributions: i.e. as cumulative with other such distributions.

Subsection (2)

This subsection restates subs.(2) of s.274 of the 1985 Act. With respect to paras (a) (financial assistance lawfully given out of distributable profits) and (b) (prohibited financial assistance), s.678 deals with financial assistance for acquiring shares in a public company, and s.679 with financial assistance for acquiring shares in a private company. Both sections indicate what is prohibited and what is lawful. Paragraph (d) indicates that any funds lawfully used by a company to purchase its own shares (e.g. proceeds of a new issue of shares; or, for a private company, out of capital: s.692) are not regarded as a distribution for subs.(1) unless they are actually distributable profits. In para.(d), the payments referred to in s.705 must be made from distributable profits.

Subsections (3)-(5)

These subsections restate subs.(3) of s.274 of the 1985 Act, defining "financial assistance", "net assets", "net liabilities" and "liabilities".

CHAPTER 3

SUPPLEMENTARY PROVISIONS

Accounting matters

841. Realised losses and profits and revaluation of fixed assets

(1) The following provisions have effect for the purposes of this Part.

(2) The following are treated as realised losses-

    (a) in the case of Companies Act accounts, provisions of a kind specified for the purposes of this paragraph by regulations under section 396 (except revaluation provisions);

    (b) in the case of IAS accounts, provisions of any kind (except revaluation provisions).

(3) A "revaluation provision" means a provision in respect of a diminution in value of a fixed asset appearing on a revaluation of all the fixed assets of the company, or of all of its fixed assets other than goodwill.

(4) For the purpose of subsections (2) and (3) any consideration by the directors of the value at a particular time of a fixed asset is treated as a revaluation provided-

    (a) the directors are satisfied that the aggregate value at that time of the fixed assets of the company that have not actually been revalued is not less than the aggregate amount at which they are then stated in the company's accounts, and

    (b) it is stated in a note to the accounts-

        (i) that the directors have considered the value of some or all of the fixed assets of the company without actually revaluing them,

        (ii) that they are satisfied that the aggregate value of those assets at the time of their consideration was not less than the aggregate amount at which they were then stated in the company's accounts, and

        (iii) that accordingly, by virtue of this subsection, amounts are stated in the accounts on the basis that a revaluation of fixed assets of the company is treated as having taken place at that time.

(5) Where-

    (a) on the revaluation of a fixed asset, an unrealised profit is shown to have been made, and

    (b) on or after the revaluation, a sum is written off or retained for depreciation of that asset over a period,

an amount equal to the amount by which that sum exceeds the sum which would have been so written off or retained for the depreciation of that asset over that period, if that profit had not been made, is treated as a realised profit made over that period.

GENERAL NOTE

    This section re-enacts, with certain re-arrangements and changes in wording, s.275 of the 1985 Act. It provides guidelines for the calculation of realised profits and losses for the purpose of ss.829-832 above.

Subsections (1) and (2)

    These subsections restate subs.(1) of s.275 of the 1985 Act, as substituted by Sch.1, para.28 of SI 2004/ 2947, "The Companies Act 1985 (International Accounting Standards and Other Accounting Amendments) Regulations 2004". Subsection (1) is introductory. Subsection (2) indicates that all provisions, except "revaluation provisions" (defined in subs.(3) below), are to be treated as realised losses, which includes depreciation allowances.

Subsection (3)

    This subsection restates subs.(1A) of s.275 of the 1985 Act, as inserted by Sch.1, para.28 of SI 2004/ 2947, "The Companies Act 1985 (International Accounting Standards and Other Accounting Amendments) Regulations 2004". It indicates that a "revaluation provision" means a provision for diminution in value of a fixed asset that arises on a revaluation of all the fixed assets other than goodwill.

Subsections (4) and (5)

    These subsections restate the substance of subss.(4)-(6) of s.275 of the 1985 Act. They allow for a realised profit to be made where a depreciation allowance is lower than it would have been but for a revaluation (subs.(5)). In so doing, a wide meaning is given to the concept of a revaluation of an asset. However, a note to the accounts must state when the directors have considered the value of the company's assets without actually revaluing them, and they are satisfied that in aggregate their value is greater than the figure stated in the books (subs.(4)).

842.   Determination of profit or loss in respect of asset where records incomplete

In determining for the purposes of this Part whether a company has made a profit or loss in respect of an asset where-

(a) there is no record of the original cost of the asset, or

(b) a record cannot be obtained without unreasonable expense or delay,

its cost is taken to be the value ascribed to it in the earliest available record of its value made on or after its acquisition by the company.

GENERAL NOTE

This section re-enacts, with certain changes in wording, subs.(3) of s.275 of the 1985 Act. For the purpose of revaluing an asset if its original cost value is not recorded, its earliest known value after acquisition may be used.

843. Realised profits and losses of long-term insurance business

(1) The provisions of this section have effect for the purposes of this Part as it applies in relation to an authorised insurance company carrying on long-term business.

(2) An amount included in the relevant part of the company's balance sheet that-

(a) represents a surplus in the fund or funds maintained by it in respect of its long-term business, and

(b) has not been allocated to policy holders or, as the case may be, carried forward unappropriated in accordance with asset identification rules made under section 142(2) of the Financial Services and Markets Act 2000 (c. 8),

is treated as a realised profit.

(3) For the purposes of subsection (2)-

(a) the relevant part of the balance sheet is that part of the balance sheet that represents accumulated profit or loss;

(b) a surplus in the fund or funds maintained by the company in respect of its long-term business means an excess of the assets representing that fund or those funds over the liabilities of the company attributable to its long-term business, as shown by an actuarial investigation.

(4) A deficit in the fund or funds maintained by the company in respect of its longterm business is treated as a realised loss.

For this purpose a deficit in any such fund or funds means an excess of the liabilities of the company attributable to its long-term business over the assets representing that fund or those funds, as shown by an actuarial investigation.

(5) Subject to subsections (2) and (4), any profit or loss arising in the company's long-term business is to be left out of account.

(6) For the purposes of this section an "actuarial investigation" means an investigation made into the financial condition of an authorised insurance company in respect of its long-term business-

(a) carried out once in every period of twelve months in accordance with rules made under Part 10 of the Financial Services and Markets Act 2000, or

(b) carried out in accordance with a requirement imposed under section 166 of that Act,

by an actuary appointed as actuary to the company.

(7) In this section "long-term business" means business that consists of effecting or carrying out contracts of long-term insurance.

This definition must be read with section 22 of the Financial Services and Markets Act 2000, any relevant order under that section and Schedule 2 to that Act.

GENERAL NOTE

This section re-enacts, with certain re-arrangements and changes in wording, s.268 of the 1985 Act. It makes certain modifications to the general rules as to the profits available for distribution for insurance companies with long-term business. This is necessary because the annual profits of long-term insurance businesses are determined by referring to annual actuarial valuations, discounting future expected earning streams from investments and subtracting from them the discounted present value of expected future liabilities.

Subsection (1)

This subsection restates subs.(1) of s.268 of the 1985 Act, as amended by SI 2001/3649, Art.18, indicating that special rules apply to an authorised insurance company carrying on long term business.

Subsections (2)-(5)

These subsections restate subss.(2)-(3) of s.268 of the 1985 Act, as amended by SI 2001/3649, Art.18, and Sch.1, para.24 of SI 2004/2947, "The Companies Act 1985 (International Accounting Standards and Other Accounting Amendments) Regulations 2004". They indicate that the surplus or deficit on the funds maintained in respect of long-term business, as determined by an actuarial investigation, are to be treated respectively as realised profits or losses.

Subsection (6)

This subsection restates subs.(3) of s.268 of the 1985 Act, as inserted by SI 2001/3649, Art.18, and defines the meaning of "actuarial investigation".

Subsection (7)

This subsection restates subs.(4) of s.268 of the 1985 Act, as inserted by SI 2001/3649, Art.18, and defines "long term business".

844. Treatment of development costs

(1) Where development costs are shown or included as an asset in a company's accounts, any amount shown or included in respect of those costs is treated-

    (a) for the purposes of section 830 (distributions to be made out of profits available for the purpose) as a realised loss, and

    (b) for the purposes of section 832 (distributions by investment companies out of accumulated revenue profits) as a realised revenue loss.

This is subject to the following exceptions.

(2) Subsection (1) does not apply to any part of that amount representing an unrealised profit made on revaluation of those costs.

(3) Subsection (1) does not apply if-

    (a) there are special circumstances in the company's case justifying the directors in deciding that the amount there mentioned is not to be treated as required by subsection (1),

    (b) it is stated-

        (i) in the case of Companies Act accounts, in the note required by regulations under section 396 as to the reasons for showing development costs as an asset, or

        (ii) in the case of IAS accounts, in any note to the accounts,

   that the amount is not to be so treated, and

    (c) the note explains the circumstances relied upon to justify the decision of the directors to that effect.

GENERAL NOTE

This section re-enacts, with certain re-arrangements and changes in wording, s.269 of the 1985 Act. Where development costs are shown as an asset in the accounts, on the grounds that they give rise to future benefits, under subs.(1) they should nevertheless be written off for the purpose of determining profits available for distribution. However, under subs.(3) directors are given considerable discretion and may ignore subs.(1), provided that they explain the reasons for so doing in a note to the accounts.

Subsection (1)

This subsection restates subs.(1) of s.269 of the 1985 Act. It requires *prima facie* that all development costs should be written off in determining profits available for distribution.

Subsections (2) and (3)

This subsection restates subs.(1) of s.269 of the 1985 Act, as amended by Sch.1, para.25 of SI 2004/2947, "The Companies Act 1985 (International Accounting Standards and Other Accounting Amendments) Regulations 2004". Subsection (2) indicates that subs.(1) does not apply to any part of development costs that represents an unrealised profit on a revaluation of the asset. Subsection (3) permits directors to ignore subs.(1) if they believe their action is justified and they explain the circumstances in a note to the accounts.

Distributions in kind

GENERAL NOTE
Sections 845-846 elaborate the provisions of s.276 of the 1985 Act, as amended by Sch.10 of the 1989 Act and SI 1997/220. The purpose is to provide that where a company distributes an asset in kind that contains an element of unrealised profit, the amount of that profit is to be treated as though it were a realised profit for the purposes of ss.829-832. The provisions are in particular intended to facilitate the operation of demergers that involve the distribution of real property or shares out of a group (see ICTA 1988, ss.213-288). Section 851, below, deals with the effect of ss.845-846 on the rules of law restricting distributions or return of capital.

845. Distributions in kind: determination of amount

(1) This section applies for determining the amount of a distribution consisting of or including, or treated as arising in consequence of, the sale, transfer or other disposition by a company of a non-cash asset where-
  (a) at the time of the distribution the company has profits available for distribution, and
  (b) if the amount of the distribution were to be determined in accordance with this section, the company could make the distribution without contravening this Part.

(2) The amount of the distribution (or the relevant part of it) is taken to be-
  (a) in a case where the amount or value of the consideration for the disposition is not less than the book value of the asset, zero;
  (b) in any other case, the amount by which the book value of the asset exceeds the amount or value of any consideration for the disposition.

(3) For the purposes of subsection (1)(a) the company's profits available for distribution are treated as increased by the amount (if any) by which the amount or value of any consideration for the disposition exceeds the book value of the asset.

(4) In this section "book value", in relation to an asset, means-
  (a) the amount at which the asset is stated in the relevant accounts, or
  (b) where the asset is not stated in those accounts at any amount, zero.

(5) The provisions of Chapter 2 (justification of distribution by reference to accounts) have effect subject to this section.

GENERAL NOTE
This section is new and results from the Company Law Reform Committee's examination of the difficulties created by the decision in *Aveling Barford Ltd v Perion Ltd* [1989] B.C.L.C. 626. The Committee made a number of suggestions as to how these difficulties might be overcome, and what is now s.845 is intended to remove doubts raised by the decision in that case about when a transfer of an asset to a member amounts to a distribution. In particular, this concerns the impact of the decision on intra-group asset transfers conducted by reference to book value rather than the higher market value.

The *Aveling Barford* case concerned the sale of a property by a company (which had no distributable profits) at a considerable undervaluation to another company controlled by the company's ultimate sole beneficial shareholder. The transaction was held to be void as an unauthorised return of capital. It decided nothing about the situation where a company, which has distributable profits, makes an intra-group transfer of assets at book value, but concern was expressed after the case was decided that, as a transfer of an asset at book value may have an element of undervaluation, the transaction would constitute a distribution, thereby requiring the company to have distributable profits sufficient to cover the difference in value. The result was that companies were often required either to abandon a transfer or to structure it in a more complex way, for example, having the assets revalued and then sold (or distributed under s.846) so that the distributable reserves would be increased by the "realised profit" arising on the sale/distribution, followed by a capital contribution of the asset to the relevant group member.

Section 845 preserves the position in the *Aveling Barford* case inasmuch as, where a company which does not have distributable profits makes a distribution by way of a transfer of assets at an undervaluation, this will be an unlawful distribution contrary to the Act. However, it clarifies the position where a company does have distributable profits.

Subsection (1)

This subsection indicates that the provisions of the section apply where a non-cash asset is sold, transferred or otherwise disposed of where the company has profits that are available for distribution and if a distribution in kind were to be made the general rules with respect to distributions would not be contravened.

Subsection (2)

This states that where the value of consideration is greater than or equal to the book value of the asset concerned, the amount of consideration is taken to be zero. However, where book value exceeds the value of consideration, the difference is to be regarded as the distribution.

Subsection (3)

This states that that the profits available for distribution are to be treated as increased by the amount by which the value of consideration exceeds the book value of the asset.

Subsection (4)

This defines "book value".

Subsection (5)

This indicates that the provisions of Ch.2 (i.e. "Justification of Distribution by Reference to Accounts", ss.836-840 above) have effect, subject to this section.

846.   Distributions in kind: treatment of unrealised profits

(1) This section applies where-
    (a) a company makes a distribution consisting of or including, or treated as arising in consequence of, the sale, transfer or other disposition by the company of a non-cash asset, and
    (b) any part of the amount at which that asset is stated in the relevant accounts represents an unrealised profit.
(2) That profit is treated as a realised profit-
    (a) for the purpose of determining the lawfulness of the distribution in accordance with this Part (whether before or after the distribution takes place), and
    (b) for the purpose of the application, in relation to anything done with a view to or in connection with the making of the distribution, of any provision of regulations under section 396 under which only realised profits are to be included in or transferred to the profit and loss account.

GENERAL NOTE

This section is concerned with determining the treatment of unrealised profits in relation to distributions in kind. It re-enacts, with certain re-arrangements and changes in wording, s.276 of the 1985 Act.

Subsection (1)

This subsection indicates that the provisions of the section apply where a non-cash asset is sold, transferred or otherwise disposed of and any part of the amount at which the asset is stated in the relevant accounts represents an unrealised profit.

Subsection (2)

This provides that such an unrealised profit should be treated as a realised profit for determining the lawfulness of the distribution.

Consequences of unlawful distribution

847. Consequences of unlawful distribution

(1) This section applies where a distribution, or part of one, made by a company to one of its members is made in contravention of this Part.

(2) If at the time of the distribution the member knows or has reasonable grounds for believing that it is so made, he is liable-

    (a) to repay it (or that part of it, as the case may be) to the company, or

    (b) in the case of a distribution made otherwise than in cash, to pay the company a sum equal to the value of the distribution (or part) at that time.

(3) This is without prejudice to any obligation imposed apart from this section on a member of a company to repay a distribution unlawfully made to him.

(4) This section does not apply in relation to-

    (a) financial assistance given by a company in contravention of section 678 or 679, or

    (b) any payment made by a company in respect of the redemption or purchase by the company of shares in itself.

GENERAL NOTE

This section re-enacts, with certain re-arrangements and changes in wording, s.277 of the 1985 Act.

Subsections (1) and (2)

These subsections restate subs.(1) of s.277 of the 1985 Act. A liability is imposed on a shareholder who ought to have known of the breach to repay the money (or cash equivalent if the dividend has been paid in kind) to the company.

Subsections (3) and (4)

These subsections restate subss.(2)-(3) of s.277 of the 1985 Act. The general wording at the beginning of subs.(3) preserves the common law rules of liability. In subs.(4), the references to financial assistance and share purchases are designed to avoid a double penalty on the recipients of such payments. However, the phrase "in relation to" is ambiguous. Does it apply the exceptions only to the recipients of such payment, or does it protect the recipients of other dividends that prove to be unlawful because of the provision of financial assistance, share purchase or redemption money, which is deemed to be a distribution under s.840(2) above?

Other matters

848. Saving for certain older provisions in articles

(1) Where immediately before the relevant date a company was authorised by a provision of its articles to apply its unrealised profits in paying up in full or in part unissued shares to be allotted to members of the company as fully or partly paid bonus shares, that provision continues (subject to any alteration of the articles) as authority for those profits to be so applied after that date.

(2) For this purpose the relevant date is-

    (a) for companies registered in Great Britain, 22nd December 1980;

    (b) for companies registered in Northern Ireland, 1st July 1983.

GENERAL NOTE

This section re-enacts s.278 of the 1985 Act, but extends it to cover Northern Ireland as well as Great Britain. Effectively it preserves the power for companies registered in Great Britain to issue bonus shares applying unrealised profits if that power existed before the 1980 Companies Act came into force. Similar provisions exist with respect to the corresponding legislation in Northern Ireland (see subs.(2)(b)).

Subsection (1)

This subsection re-enacts s.278 of the 1985 Act.

Subsection (2)

This subsection accommodates companies in Northern Ireland as well as in Great Britain.

849.   Restriction on application of unrealised profits

A company must not apply an unrealised profit in paying up debentures or any amounts unpaid on its issued shares.

GENERAL NOTE

This section re-enacts subs.(4) of s.263 of the 1985 Act and prevents companies applying unrealised profits in paying up debentures or amounts unpaid on issued shares.

850.   Treatment of certain older profits or losses

(1) Where the directors of a company are, after making all reasonable enquiries, unable to determine whether a particular profit made before the relevant date is realised or unrealised, they may treat the profit as realised.

(2) Where the directors of a company, after making all reasonable enquiries, are unable to determine whether a particular loss made before the relevant date is realised or unrealised, they may treat the loss as unrealised.

(3) For the purposes of this section the relevant date is-
    (a) for companies registered in Great Britain, 22nd December 1980;
    (b) for companies registered in Northern Ireland, 1st July 1983.

GENERAL NOTE

This section re-enacts subs.(5) of s.263 of the 1985 Act, in so far as it related to Great Britain.

Subsections (1) and (2)

This permits all profits made before the relevant date at which legislation came into force to be treated as realised by companies if the directors are unable to determine whether they were realised or unrealised (subs.(1)). Similarly, all losses made before the relevant legislation came into force can be treated as unrealised by companies registered if the directors are unable to determine whether they were realised or unrealised (subs.(2)).

Subsection (3)

The relevant dates when legislation came into force are specified, that for Great Britain relating to the Companies Act 1980, and that for Northern Ireland being when the corresponding legislation came into force there on 1 July 1983.

851.   Application of rules of law restricting distributions

(1) Except as provided in this section, the provisions of this Part are without prejudice to any rule of law restricting the sums out of which, or the cases in which, a distribution may be made.

(2) For the purposes of any rule of law requiring distributions to be paid out of profits or restricting the return of capital to members-
    (a) section 845 (distributions in kind: determination of amount) applies to determine the amount of any distribution or return of capital consisting of or including, or treated as arising in consequence of the sale, transfer or other disposition by a company of a non-cash asset; and
    (b) section 846 (distributions in kind: treatment of unrealised profits) applies as it applies for the purposes of this Part.

(3) In this section references to distributions are to amounts regarded as distributions for the purposes of any such rule of law as is referred to in subsection (1).

GENERAL NOTE

This section is new and relates to ss.845 and 846 (distributions in kind). As explained in the General Note to s.845, the Company Law Reform Committee examined the difficulties created by the decision in *Aveling Barford Ltd v Perion Ltd* [1989] BCLC 626 and made a number of suggestions as to how these difficulties might be overcome. These included what is now s.851.

Subsections (1) and (2)

The existing common law rules on unlawful distributions continue to be an essential component in determining what constitutes an unlawful distribution (subs.(1)). However, they are subject to ss.845 and 846, which deal with distributions in kind, the former concerning the determination of the amount of such distributions and the latter the treatment of unrealised profits in such transactions (subs.(2)).

Subsection (3)

This subsection makes it clear that references to "distributions" in this section are to amounts regarded as distributions under common law rules.

852. Saving for other restrictions on distributions

The provisions of this Part are without prejudice to any enactment, or any provision of a company's articles, restricting the sums out of which, or the cases in which, a distribution may be made.

GENERAL NOTE

This section re-enacts s.281 of the 1985 Act, indicating that the provisions in this Part of the Act are subject to other legislation and provisions in a company's articles that restrict the sums out of which or the circumstances when a distribution may be made.

853. Minor definitions

(1) The following provisions apply for the purposes of this Part.
(2) References to profit or losses of any description-
    (a) are to profits or losses of that description made at any time, and
    (b) except where the context otherwise requires, are to profits or losses of a revenue or capital character.
(3) "Capitalisation", in relation to a company's profits, means any of the following operations (whenever carried out)-
    (a) applying the profits in wholly or partly paying up unissued shares in the company to be allotted to members of the company as fully or partly paid bonus shares, or
    (b) transferring the profits to capital redemption reserve.
(4) References to "realised profits" and "realised losses", in relation to a company's accounts, are to such profits or losses of the company as fall to be treated as realised in accordance with principles generally accepted at the time when the accounts are prepared, with respect to the determination for accounting purposes of realised profits or losses.
(5) Subsection (4) is without prejudice to-
    (a) the construction of any other expression (where appropriate) by reference to accepted accounting principles or practice, or
    (b) any specific provision for the treatment of profits or losses of any description as realised.
(6) "Fixed assets" means assets of a company which are intended for use on a continuing basis in the company's activities.

GENERAL NOTE

Subsections (1)-(3) are derived from s.280(1)-(3) of the 1985 Act; subss.(4)-(5) are derived from ss.262(3) and 742(2) of the 1985 Act; subs.(6) is new.

The section defines profits and losses to be of a revenue or capital character, except where the context otherwise requires; capitalisation; realised profits and realised losses; and fixed assets.

Subsections (1)-(3)

Subsection (1) is introductory. Subsection (2) restates the definitions given in subs.(3) of s.280 of the 1985 Act, indicating that profits and losses are of a revenue or capital character, except where the context otherwise requires. Subsection (3) restates the definitions given in subs.(2) of s.280 of the 1985 Act, indicating that capitalisation in relation to profits refers to the issue of bonus shares or transferring profits to capital redemption reserve.

Subsections (4) and (5)

These subsections restate the definitions given in subs.(3) of s.262 of the 1985 Act, indicating that realised profits and losses are those which are treated as realised applying generally accepted accounting principles at the time the accounts were prepared.

Subsection (6)

This subsection defines "fixed assets" for the purpose of this Part of the Act.

PART 24

A COMPANY'S ANNUAL RETURN

GENERAL NOTE

This Part replaces Ch.3 of Pt 11 of the 1985 Act. It applies to all companies (within the meaning of s.1), whether public or private, limited (whether by shares or by guarantee) or unlimited. It also applies to dormant companies (as defined by s.1169), but not, however, to overseas companies. It is wholly separate from any accounting exemptions or obligations.

It should perhaps be noted that in recent years Companies House has developed various systems to accommodate electronic filing. Thus annual returns and other documents can be submitted by email, although users must first register, and authentication is used in place of signatures. From 2005 Companies House has provided further security for its emailing system by introducing a PROOF (Protected Online Filing) service. It also offers a "monitor service" to Companies House Direct subscribers that alerts companies to unauthorised changes in their records. Fees can also be paid online (see www.companieshouse.gov.uk/toolsToHelp/efilingfaq.shtml).

The electronic filing system devised by Companies House is known as "WebFiling", and a user guide is accessible at www.companieshouse.gov.uk/infoAndGuide/faq/webFilingUserGuide.pdf. In the meantime, a number of computer based packages have been developed to help company secretaries meet their statutory obligations, including the preparation and filing of annual returns, and these are now widely used in practice.

In this Part of the Act, s.857 empowers the Secretary of State to issue regulations dealing with the information that is to be given in the annual return.

Definitions

Where definitions of particular terms are not given in sections where they are used, reference should be made to Sch.8, which provides an alphabetical "Index of defined expressions", giving cross references to sections where individual terms are defined.

854.   Duty to deliver annual returns

(1) Every company must deliver to the registrar successive annual returns each of which is made up to a date not later than the date that is from time to time the company's return date.
(2) The company's return date is-
    (a) the anniversary of the company's incorporation, or
    (b) if the company's last return delivered in accordance with this Part was made up to a different date, the anniversary of that date.
(3) Each return must-

(a) contain the information required by or under the following provisions of this Part, and

(b) be delivered to the registrar within 28 days after the date to which it is made up.

GENERAL NOTE

This section replaces subss.(1)-(2) of s.363 of the 1985 Act.

Subsection (1)

This retains the obligation for every company to file each year an annual return containing the required information made up to a date not later than the company's return date.

Subsection (2)

This states that the return date is to be the anniversary of a company's incorporation or - where a previous return was made up to a different date - the anniversary of that other date.

Subsection (3)

This subsection requires an annual return to be delivered to the registrar within 28 days after the date to which it is made up.

855. Contents of annual return: general

(1) Every annual return must state the date to which it is made up and contain the following information-

    (a) the address of the company's registered office;

    (b) the type of company it is and its principal business activities;

    (c) the prescribed particulars of-

        (i) the directors of the company, and

        (ii) in the case of a private company with a secretary or a public company, the secretary or joint secretaries;

    (d) if the register of members is not kept available for inspection at the company's registered office, the address of the place where it is kept available for inspection;

    (e) if any register of debenture holders (or a duplicate of any such register or a part of it) is not kept available for inspection at the company's registered office, the address of the place where it is kept available for inspection.

(2) The information as to the company's type must be given by reference to the classification scheme prescribed for the purposes of this section.

(3) The information as to the company's principal business activities may be given by reference to one or more categories of any prescribed system of classifying business activities.

GENERAL NOTE

This simplified section replaces s.364 of the 1985 Act, as substituted by the Companies Act 1989, s.139, and subsequently amended by reg.2 of SI 1999/2322.

Subsection (1)

This subsection specifies what information is to be contained in the annual return: namely, the address of the registered office; the type of company and its principal activities; prescribed particulars of the directors, any person appointed as an authorised signatory, and - in the case of a private company with a secretary or a public company - the secretary; the addresses at which the registers of members and (if applicable) debenture holders are held, if not the registered office.

The main difference from the 1985 Act is that, rather than specifying the information that must be given in relation to a company's directors and, as appropriate, company secretaries, this provision instead requires that "prescribed particulars" relating to them, as determined by the Secretary of State, should be disclosed.

The information on the company's type and its principal business activities has to be in accordance with prescribed classification systems.

Under SI 1996/1105, the Standard Industrial Classification of Activities 1992 was designated as the system for classifying activities for the purpose of completing the annual return and so comply with s.364(1)(b) of the Companies Act 1985.

856.   Contents of annual return: information about share capital and shareholders

(1) The annual return of a company having a share capital must also contain-
  (a) a statement of capital, and
  (b) the particulars required by subsections (3) to (6) about the members of the company.
(2) The statement of capital must state with respect to the company's share capital at the date to which the return is made up-
  (a) the total number of shares of the company,
  (b) the aggregate nominal value of those shares,
  (c) for each class of shares-
     (i) prescribed particulars of the rights attached to the shares,
     (ii) the total number of shares of that class, and
     (iii) the aggregate nominal value of shares of that class, and
  (d) the amount paid up and the amount (if any) unpaid on each share (whether on account of the nominal value of the share or by way of premium).
(3) The return must contain the prescribed particulars of every person who-
  (a) is a member of the company on the date to which the return is made up, or
  (b) has ceased to be a member of the company since the date to which the last return was made up (or, in the case of the first return, since the incorporation of the company).
The return must conform to such requirements as may be prescribed for the purpose of enabling the entries relating to any given person to be easily found.
(4) The return must also state-
  (a) the number of shares of each class held by each member of the company at the date to which the return is made up,
  (b) the number of shares of each class transferred-
     (i) since the date to which the last return was made up, or
     (ii) in the case of the first return, since the incorporation of the company,
   by each member or person who has ceased to be a member, and
  (c) the dates of registration of the transfers.
(5) If either of the two immediately preceding returns has given the full particulars required by subsections (3) and (4), the return need only give such particulars as relate-
  (a) to persons ceasing to be or becoming members since the date of the last return, and
  (b) to shares transferred since that date.
(6) Where the company has converted any of its shares into stock, the return must give the corresponding information in relation to that stock, stating the amount of stock instead of the number or nominal value of shares.

GENERAL NOTE

This section replaces s.364A of the 1985 Act, as inserted by s.139 of the Companies Act 1989. It recasts the provision in the style of the Act but without significant substantive change.

Subsection (1)

This requires companies with a share capital to give a statement of that capital and particulars of members as detailed in subss.(3)-(6).

Subsection (2)

This replaces and expands subss.(2)-(3) of s.364A of the 1985 Act, requiring companies to give details of the total number and aggregate nominal value of shares, as well as similar details for each class of shares and the rights attaching to each of them, together with amounts paid up and (if any) unpaid, indicating whether such amounts are on account of the nominal value or share premium.

Subsections (3)-(5)

These subsections detail the disclosures that must be made in prescribed form with regard to members of the company, including particulars of members at the return date and persons who have ceased to be members since the last return, and of the numbers of shares held and transferred during the period covered by the return. However, if either of the two preceding returns has given these details, it is only necessary to file details of persons ceasing to or becoming members and share transfers during the period covered by the return.

Subsection (6)

This restates s.364A(8), as inserted by the 1989 Act, dealing with the situation where a company has converted shares into stock.

857. Contents of annual return: power to make further provision by regulations

(1) The Secretary of State may by regulations make further provision as to the information to be given in a company's annual return.

(2) The regulations may-
   (a) amend or repeal the provisions of sections 855 and 856, and
   (b) provide for exceptions from the requirements of those sections as they have effect from time to time.

(3) Regulations under this section are subject to negative resolution procedure.

GENERAL NOTE

This section replaces s.365 of the 1985 Act, as inserted by s.139 of the Companies Act 1989.

Subsection (1)

This subsection confers power on the Secretary of State to make further provision as to the information to be provided in the annual return.

Subsection (2)

This provides a power to amend or repeal ss.855-856 (concerning the contents of the annual return) and to make exceptions to the requirements imposed by those sections.

Subsection (3)

This states that regulations made under this section are subject to the negative resolution procedure (see s.1289).

858. Failure to deliver annual return

(1) If a company fails to deliver an annual return before the end of the period of 28 days after a return date, an offence is committed by-
   (a) the company,
   (b) subject to subsection (4)-
       (i) every director of the company, and
       (ii) in the case of a private company with a secretary or a public company, every secretary of the company, and
   (c) every other officer of the company who is in default.

(2) A person guilty of an offence under subsection (1) is liable on summary conviction to a fine not exceeding level 5 on the standard scale and, for continued contravention, a daily default fine not exceeding one-tenth of level 5 on the standard scale.

(3) The contravention continues until such time as an annual return made up to that return date is delivered by the company to the registrar.

(4) It is a defence for a director or secretary charged with an offence under subsection (1)(b) to prove that he took all reasonable steps to avoid the commission or continuation of the offence.

(5) In the case of continued contravention, an offence is also committed by every officer of the company who did not commit an offence under subsection (1) in relation to the initial contravention but is in default in relation to the continued contravention.

A person guilty of an offence under this subsection is liable on summary conviction to a fine not exceeding one-tenth of level 5 on the standard scale for each day on which the contravention continues and he is in default.

GENERAL NOTE

This section replaces subss.(3)-(5) of s.363 of the 1985 Act.

Subsection (1)

This states that it is an offence not to file an annual return within the prescribed time. The offence is committed by the company (subs.(1)(a)). It is also committed by each director (subs.(1)(b)(i)), any other officer in default (subs.(1)(c)), and - in the case of a private company with a secretary or a public company - the secretary of the company (subs.(1)(b)(ii)).

Subsection (2)

This subsection indicates the penalty for not complying with subs.(1).

Subsection (3)

This subsection states that the offence continues after it is first committed until such time as the annual return is made.

Subsection (4)

It is a defence for directors, and for public company secretaries, in office at the time when the offence is first committed, to prove that they took all reasonable steps to avoid the commission or continuation of the offence. For all other officers, including those who take office after the offence is first committed, the standard "officer in default" regime of the Act applies (see s.1121).

However, it is no defence for an individual that he himself was not the person required to make the return if in fact he should have summoned the persons who were so required and he failed to do so: see Gibson v Barton, (1875) L.R. 10 Q.B. 329.

Subsection (5)

Where there is continued contravention, an offence is committed by every officer of the company, including those who did not commit an offence under subs.(1).

859. Application of provisions to shadow directors

For the purposes of this Part a shadow director is treated as a director.

GENERAL NOTE

This new section provides that a shadow director is to be treated as a director for the purposes of the annual return.

PART 25

COMPANY CHARGES

CHAPTER I

COMPANIES REGISTERED IN ENGLAND AND WALES OR IN NORTHERN IRELAND

GENERAL NOTE

In 2002, the DTI asked the Law Commission for England and Wales (and at the same time the Scottish Law Commission) to consider the case for reforming the law on company charges. This followed a recommendation in the CLR *Final Report* ((URN 01/942), paras 12.8-12.10. The CLR reported that it had received substantial criticism of the current system for registering charges and for deciding priority between them. However, because of lack of time for consultation, it was able itself to present only provisional conclusions in favour of reform. The Law Commission for England and Wales published a consultation paper in 2002 (Law Commission, *Registration of Security Interests: Company Charges and Property other than Land* (CP No.164, 2002)) and a more detailed consultative report in 2004 (Law Commission, *Company Security Interests, A Consultative Report* (CP No.176, 2004)). These papers outlined some radical ideas for an entirely new regulatory scheme for security interests created by companies. These proposals proved to be controversial and in its Report, published in August 2005, the Law Commission set out revised proposals, which were intended to remove some of the more unpalatable features of the provisional scheme (Law Commission, *Company Security Interests* (Report No.296, 2005). However, in July 2005 the DTI launched its own consultation seeking views on the economic impact of the recommendations of the Law Commission for England and Wales (and the Scottish Law Commission) in respect of company charges. This was followed by a Ministerial announcement in November 2005 that it was clear from the consultation that there was not a consensus of support for the Law Commissions' proposals and that therefore the new companies legislation would not include a specific power to implement charges measures, but that the Bill would include a new power to make company law reform orders and this would provide a mechanism for implementing certain changes in respect of company charges, on matters of company law (as against property law) if wished (*Hansard*, HL, col.WS27 (November 3, 2006)). The Government said it would continue to consider and to discuss with interested parties exactly what changes should be implemented (*ibid.*). The proposed new general power to make company law reform orders was dropped from the legislation during its passage through Parliament but there has been enacted a new power (see s.894) for the Secretary of State to amend Pt 25 by regulations.

In the Parliamentary debates on the Companies Bill, Lord Sainsbury, speaking for the government, described the approach adopted in Pt 25 in the following terms (*Hansard*, HL Vol.686, col.480 (November 2, 2006)):

> "These amendments restate provisions in the 1985 Act relating to the registration of company charges and provide three new regulation-making powers, meeting the commitment that I gave when we withdrew our proposals for a general reform power. The new clauses inserted by Amendments Nos. 675 to 707 restate Part XII of the 1985 Act, which provides a system for the registration of charges created by a company. As I have already explained in relation to other amendments that restate the 1985 Act, while there has been an element of restructuring, no substantive changes have been made other than to ensure compatibility with the Bill ... The approach to restatement of the existing provisions means that the new provisions retain the imperfections of the existing system."

Requirement to register company charges

860. Charges created by a company

(1) A company that creates a charge to which this section applies must deliver the prescribed particulars of the charge, together with the instrument (if any) by which the charge is created or evidenced, to the registrar for registration before the end of the period allowed for registration.

(2) Registration of a charge to which this section applies may instead be effected on the application of a person interested in it.

(3) Where registration is effected on the application of some person other than the company, that person is entitled to recover from the company the amount of any fees properly paid by him to the registrar on registration.

(4) If a company fails to comply with subsection (1), an offence is committed by-

    (a) the company, and

    (b) every officer of it who is in default.

(5) A person guilty of an offence under this section is liable-

    (a) on conviction on indictment, to a fine;

    (b) on summary conviction, to a fine not exceeding the statutory maximum.

(6) Subsection (4) does not apply if registration of the charge has been effected on the application of some other person.

(7) This section applies to the following charges-

    (a) a charge on land or any interest in land, other than a charge for any rent or other periodical sum issuing out of land,

    (b) a charge created or evidenced by an instrument which, if executed by an individual, would require registration as a bill of sale,

    (c) a charge for the purposes of securing any issue of debentures,

    (d) a charge on uncalled share capital of the company,

    (e) a charge on calls made but not paid,

    (f) a charge on book debts of the company,

    (g) a floating charge on the company's property or undertaking,

    (h) a charge on a ship or aircraft, or any share in a ship,

    (i) a charge on goodwill or on any intellectual property.

GENERAL NOTE

This section re-enacts, with no substantive changes, s.399 of the Companies Act 1985 and s.396(1) of the Companies Act 1985. It establishes the registration obligation and lists the types of charge to which the obligation relates.

The Law Commission for English and Wales has proposed that all charges created by companies would be registrable unless specifically exempted (Law Commission, *Company Security Interests* (Report No.296, 2005)). If adopted, this proposal would reverse the current position which is that the registration obligation applies only to the charges listed in s.860(7).

Subsections (1) and (2)

It remains the position that the duty to deliver prescribed particulars of a registrable charge created by as company falls on the company but any person who is interested in the charge may do so instead. Section 1167 defines "prescribed" as meaning "prescribed (by order or by regulations) by the Secretary of State".

Subsections (3)

Since March 1, 1999 a fee has been levied for registration.

Subsections (4) and (6)

If neither the company nor any person interested in the charge fulfils the registration obligation imposed by this section, the company and every officer who is in default is liable to a fine. Corporate criminal liability is appropriate in this instance because persons other than the company and its members would be adversely affected by non-compliance.

Subsection (7)

The list of registrable charges, found previously in s.396 of the 1985 Act, has been re-ordered, but not changed in substance (when read together with s.861 which amplifies the meaning of some of the terms used in this subsection). A charge which does not fall into any of the categories listed need not be registered. Existing cases on when the registration obligation applies continue to represent the law.

861.   Charges which have to be registered: supplementary

(1) The holding of debentures entitling the holder to a charge on land is not, for the purposes of section 860(7)(a), an interest in the land.

(2) It is immaterial for the purposes of this Chapter where land subject to a charge is situated.

(3) The deposit by way of security of a negotiable instrument given to secure the payment of book debts is not, for the purposes of section 860(7)(f), a charge on those book debts.

(4) For the purposes of section 860(7)(i), "intellectual property" means-

    (a) any patent, trade mark, registered design, copyright or design right;

    (b) any licence under or in respect of any such right.

(5) In this Chapter-

"charge" includes mortgage, and

"company" means a company registered in England and Wales or in Northern Ireland.

GENERAL NOTE

This section explains the meaning of certain terms used in s.860.

Subsection (1)

This subsection re-enacts s.396(3) of the Companies Act 1985.

Subsection (2)

This subsection is derived from s.396(1)(d) of the Companies Act 1985.

Subsection (3)

This subsection re-enacts s.396(2) of the Companies Act 1985.

Subsection (4)

This definition of intellectual property was found previously in s.396(3A) of the Companies Act 1985. It was inserted into the Companies Act 1985 by the Copyright, Designs and Patents Act 1988, as from August 1, 1999 and was amended by the Trade Marks Act 1994, as from October 31, 1994.

Subsection (5)

That the term "charge" in this context includes "mortgage" is a continuation of the position under s.396(4) of the Companies Act 1985.

The application of the requirements to companies registered in England and Wales is not new (see s.395(1) of the Companies Act 1985). The reference to companies registered in Northern Ireland is new and is consequential upon the decision to extend the legislation to the province.

862. Charges existing on property acquired

(1) This section applies where a company acquires property which is subject to a charge of a kind which would, if it had been created by the company after the acquisition of the property, have been required to be registered under this Chapter.

(2) The company must deliver the prescribed particulars of the charge, together with a certified copy of the instrument (if any) by which the charge is created or evidenced, to the registrar for registration.

(3) Subsection (2) must be complied with before the end of the period allowed for registration.

(4) If default is made in complying with this section, an offence is committed by-

    (a) the company, and

    (b) every officer of it who is in default.

(5) A person guilty of an offence under this section is liable-

    (a) on conviction on indictment, to a fine;

    (b) on summary conviction, to a fine not exceeding the statutory maximum.

GENERAL NOTE

This section re-enacts without changes of substance s.400 of the Companies Act 1985. It requires a company to register a charge to which property is subject when it is acquired by the company if the charge is of a kind that would be registrable if created by the company. As was previously the case, the only sanction for failure to comply with the obligation imposed by this section is a criminal one; the civil sanctions in s.874 do not apply.

Special rules about debentures

863.   Charge in series of debentures

(1) Where a series of debentures containing, or giving by reference to another instrument, any charge to the benefit of which debenture holders of that series are entitled *pari passu* is created by a company, it is for the purposes of section 860(1) sufficient if the required particulars, together with the deed containing the charge (or, if there is no such deed, one of the debentures of the series), are delivered to the registrar before the end of the period allowed for registration.

(2) The following are the required particulars-
   (a) the total amount secured by the whole series, and
   (b) the dates of the resolutions authorising the issue of the series and the date of the covering deed (if any) by which the series is created or defined, and
   (c) a general description of the property charged, and
   (d) the names of the trustees (if any) for the debenture holders.

(3) Particulars of the date and amount of each issue of debentures of a series of the kind mentioned in subsection (1) must be sent to the registrar for entry in the register of charges.

(4) Failure to comply with subsection (3) does not affect the validity of the debentures issued.

(5) Subsections (2) to (6) of section 860 apply for the purposes of this section as they apply for the purposes of that section, but as if references to the registration of a charge were references to the registration of a series of debentures.

GENERAL NOTE

This section re-enacts s.397(1) of the Companies Act 1985 but does not change its substance. It provides for an alternative mode of registration when a series of debentures, whose holders are entitled *pari passu* to the benefit of a charge, is issued.

864.   Additional registration requirement for commission etc in relation to debentures

(1) Where any commission, allowance or discount has been paid or made either directly or indirectly by a company to a person in consideration of his-
   (a) subscribing or agreeing to subscribe, whether absolutely or conditionally, for debentures in a company, or
   (b) procuring or agreeing to procure subscriptions, whether absolute or conditional, for such debentures,
the particulars required to be sent for registration under section 860 shall include particulars as to the amount or rate per cent. of the commission, discount or allowance so paid or made.

(2) The deposit of debentures as security for a debt of the company is not, for the purposes of this section, treated as the issue of debentures at a discount.

(3) Failure to comply with this section does not affect the validity of the debentures issued.

GENERAL NOTE

This section is a re-enactment of s.397(2)-(3) of the Companies Act 1985. When debentures are issued at a discount, this fact must be included in the particulars sent for registration but failure to do so does not affect the validity of the debentures. The deposit of debentures as a security for a debt of the company is not an issue of debentures at a discount for this purpose.

865.   Endorsement of certificate on debentures

(1) The company shall cause a copy of every certificate of registration given under section 869 to be endorsed on every debenture or certificate of debenture stock which is issued by the company, and the payment of which is secured by the charge so registered.

(2) But this does not require a company to cause a certificate of registration of any charge so given to be endorsed on any debenture or certificate of debenture stock issued by the company before the charge was created.

(3) If a person knowingly and wilfully authorises or permits the delivery of a debenture or certificate of debenture stock which under this section is required to have endorsed on it a copy of a certificate of registration, without the copy being so endorsed upon it, he commits an offence.

(4) A person guilty of an offence under this section is liable on summary conviction to a fine not exceeding level 3 on the standard scale.

GENERAL NOTE

This section, which re-enacts s.402 of the Companies Act 1985 almost word for word, requires that the certificate of registration of a charge must be endorsed on every debenture or certificate of debenture stock which is issued by the company after the charge is created and payment of which is secured by the charge.

Subsection (4)

This subsection makes a substantive amendment so as to provide that the penalty for the offence cannot exceed level 3 on the standard scale.

Charges in other jurisdictions

866. Charges created in, or over property in, jurisdictions outside the United Kingdom

(1) Where a charge is created outside the United Kingdom comprising property situated outside the United Kingdom, the delivery to the registrar of a verified copy of the instrument by which the charge is created or evidenced has the same effect for the purposes of this Chapter as the delivery of the instrument itself.

(2) Where a charge is created in the United Kingdom but comprises property outside the United Kingdom, the instrument creating or purporting to create the charge may be sent for registration under section 860 even if further proceedings may be necessary to make the charge valid or effectual according to the law of the country in which the property is situated.

GENERAL NOTE

This section re-enacts, without changes of substance, s.398(1) and (3) of the Companies Act 1985. Its effect is to make it clear that that the registration obligation applies even where a charge is created outside the United Kingdom or where a charge is created in the United Kingdom but comprises property outside the United Kingdom. The registration obligation applies irrespective of the proper law of the charge (*Weldtech Equipment, Re* [1991] 1 B.C.L.C. 393).

867. Charges created in, or over property in, another United Kingdom jurisdiction

(1) Subsection (2) applies where-
   (a) a charge comprises property situated in a part of the United Kingdom other than the part in which the company is registered, and
   (b) registration in that other part is necessary to make the charge valid or effectual under the law of that part of the United Kingdom.

(2) The delivery to the registrar of a verified copy of the instrument by which the charge is created or evidenced, together with a certificate stating that the charge was presented for registration in that other part of the United Kingdom on the date on which it was so presented has, for the purposes of this Chapter, the same effect as the delivery of the instrument itself.

GENERAL NOTE

This section is a slightly re-drafted version of s.398(4) of the Companies Act 1985. Its purpose is to clarify the operation of the registration requirements where a charge comprises property in a part of the United Kingdom other than the part in which the company itself is registered.

Orders charging land: Northern Ireland

868. Northern Ireland: registration of certain charges etc. affecting land

(1) Where a charge imposed by an order under Article 46 of the 1981 Order or notice of such a charge is registered in the Land Registry against registered land or any estate in registered land of a company, the Registrar of Titles shall as soon as may be cause two copies of the order made under Article 46 of that Order or of any notice under Article 48 of that Order to be delivered to the registrar.

(2) Where a charge imposed by an order under Article 46 of the 1981 Order is registered in the Registry of Deeds against any unregistered land or estate in land of a company, the Registrar of Deeds shall as soon as may be cause two copies of the order to be delivered to the registrar.

(3) On delivery of copies under this section, the registrar shall-

    (a) register one of them in accordance with section 869, and

    (b) not later than 7 days from that date of delivery, cause the other copy together with a certificate of registration under section 869(5) to be sent to the company against which judgment was given.

(4) Where a charge to which subsection (1) or (2) applies is vacated, the Registrar of Titles or, as the case may be, the Registrar of Deeds shall cause a certified copy of the certificate of satisfaction lodged under Article 132(1) of the 1981 Order to be delivered to the registrar for entry of a memorandum of satisfaction in accordance with section 872.

(5) In this section-

    "the 1981 Order" means the Judgments Enforcement (Northern Ireland) Order 1981 (S.I. 1981/226 (N.I. 6));

    "the Registrar of Deeds" means the registrar appointed under the Registration of Deeds Act (Northern Ireland) 1970 (c. 25);

    "Registry of Deeds" has the same meaning as in the Registration of Deeds Acts;

    "Registration of Deeds Acts" means the Registration of Deeds Act (Northern Ireland) 1970 and every statutory provision for the time being in force amending that Act or otherwise relating to the registry of deeds, or the registration of deeds, orders or other instruments or documents in such registry;

    "the Land Registry" and "the Registrar of Titles" are to be construed in accordance with section 1 of the Land Registration Act (Northern Ireland) 1970 (c. 18);

    "registered land" and "unregistered land" have the same meaning as in Part 3 of the Land Registration Act (Northern Ireland) 1970.

GENERAL NOTE

This is a new section which follows from the decision to extend the companies legislation to Northern Ireland.

Subsection (1)

The Judgments Enforcement (Northern Ireland) Order 1981 (SI 1981/226 (N.I. 6)), Art.46 provides for the making of orders imposing on land or estate in land a charge for securing the payment of the amount recoverable on a judgment or so much thereof as may be so specified. An order charging land may be made either absolutely or subject to such conditions as to notifying the debtor or as to the time when the charge is to become enforceable, or as to such other matters, as may be specified in the order. An order charging registered land does not have effect until the charge thereby imposed or, where applicable under provisions of the Land Registration Act (Northern Ireland) 1970, a notice of the order is registered by or on behalf of the creditor in the Land Registry.

Subsection (2)

An order charging unregistered land does not generally have effect until the order is registered by or on behalf of the creditor in the Registry of Deeds: Judgments Enforcement (Northern Ireland) Order 1981, Art.46(3).

Subsection (4)

The Judgments Enforcement (Northern Ireland) Order 1981, Art.132(1) provides that the lodgment in the Registry of Deeds or, subject to Land Registry Rules, in the Land Registry, as the case may require, of a certified copy (or, where the owner of the land is a company, two certified copies) of the certificate of satisfaction shall be effective to cancel the charge imposed by an order charging land or to cancel the notice of such an order.

The register of charges

869. Register of charges to be kept by registrar

(1) The registrar shall keep, with respect to each company, a register of all the charges requiring registration under this Chapter.

(2) In the case of a charge to the benefit of which holders of a series of debentures are entitled, the registrar shall enter in the register the required particulars specified in section 863(2).

(3) In the case of a charge imposed by the Enforcement of Judgments Office under Article 46 of the Judgments Enforcement (Northern Ireland) Order 1981, the registrar shall enter in the register the date on which the charge became effective.

(4) In the case of any other charge, the registrar shall enter in the register the following particulars-
   (a) if it is a charge created by a company, the date of its creation and, if it is a charge which was existing on property acquired by the company, the date of the acquisition,
   (b) the amount secured by the charge,
   (c) short particulars of the property charged, and
   (d) the persons entitled to the charge.

(5) The registrar shall give a certificate of the registration of any charge registered in pursuance of this Chapter, stating the amount secured by the charge.

(6) The certificate-
   (a) shall be signed by the registrar or authenticated by the registrar's official seal, and
   (b) is conclusive evidence that the requirements of this Chapter as to registration have been satisfied.

(7) The register kept in pursuance of this section shall be open to inspection by any person.

GENERAL NOTE

This section re-enacts s.401 of the 1985 Act with some minor changes and with one additional clause that is consequential on the decision to extend Great British company law to Northern Ireland. This section contains the important provision that the certificate of registration issued by the registrar is conclusive evidence of compliance with the registration requirements.

Subsection (1)

This subsection requires the registrar to keep with respect to each company a register of charges requiring registration. There is no longer any reference to the register being in a "prescribed form".

Subsection (2)

This subsection re-enacts s.401(1)(a) of the Companies Act 1985.

Subsection (3)

This is a new provision. Its inclusion is consequential upon the decision to include Northern Ireland within the scope of the legislation.

Subsection (4)

This subsection re-enacts without change the particulars of a charge, other than any charge within either of the two preceding sub-sections, that must be entered on the register. It implicitly states what are intended to be the prescribed particulars of which details must be delivered to the registrar (*Grove v Advantage Healthcare (T10) Ltd* [2000] 1 B.C.L.C. 661). It continues to be the case that the existence of a negative pledge in a floating charge is not included in the list of matters that the registrar is obliged to register.

Subsection (5)

It has been held that the holder of a charge is entitled to enforce the security for the full amount secured even though the certificate mistakenly states that a lesser amount is secured by the charge (*Mechanisations (Eaglescliffe) Ltd, Re* [1966] Ch. 20). This case continues to represent the law.

Subsection (6)

The cases that establish that the certificate of registration is conclusive even though the particulars delivered are incomplete or partially incorrect continue to represent the law (e.g. *CL Nye, Re* [1971] Ch. 442, CA; *Eric Holmes Ltd, Re* [1965] Ch. 1052; *National Provincial and Union Bank of England v Charnley* [1924] 1 K.B. 431; *Grove v Advantage Healthcare (T10) Ltd* [2000] 1 B.C.L.C. 661).

Subsection (7)

The register must be kept open for inspection.

870. The period allowed for registration

(1) The period allowed for registration of a charge created by a company is-
    (a) 21 days beginning with the day after the day on which the charge is created, or
    (b) if the charge is created outside the United Kingdom, 21 days beginning with the day after the day on which the instrument by which the charge is created or evidenced (or a copy of it) could, in due course of post (and if despatched with due diligence) have been received in the United Kingdom.
(2) The period allowed for registration of a charge to which property acquired by a company is subject is-
    (a) 21 days beginning with the day after the day on which the acquisition is completed, or
    (b) if the property is situated and the charge was created outside the United Kingdom, 21 days beginning with the day after the day on which the instrument by which the charge is created or evidenced (or a copy of it) could, in due course of post (and if despatched with due diligence) have been received in the United Kingdom.
(3) The period allowed for registration of particulars of a series of debentures as a result of section 863 is-
    (a) if there is a deed containing the charge mentioned in section 863(1), 21 days beginning with the day after the day on which that deed is executed, or
    (b) if there is no such deed, 21 days beginning with the day after the day on which the first debenture of the series is executed.

GENERAL NOTE

This section brings together in one place the requirements relating to the period for compliance with the registration requirements. The period is 21 days but the precise point from which time starts to run depends on a number of variables (whether the charge is created by the company or is on property acquired by the company; whether the charge is created outside the United Kingdom; the location of the property; and whether it is a charge relating to a series of debentures). There is a drafting change that helpfully spells out that the first day of the period is the day after the event which forms the trigger point.

Subsection (1)

(a) Is the "standard" requirement for registration within 21 days after the day on which a charge is created. It is derived from s.395(1) of the Companies Act 1985.

(b) Relates to charges created outside the United Kingdom. It is derived from s.398(1)-(2) of the Companies Act 1985. However, whereas s.398(1)-(2) applied where the charge was created outside the United Kingdom and comprised property situated outside the United Kingdom, this subsection does not make reference to the location of the property.

Subsection (2)

This subsection stipulates the period for registration of a charge on property acquired by a company. (a) (which is the "standard" requirement) is derived from s.400(2) of the Companies Act 1985. (b) (which applies where property is situated and the charge was created outside the United Kingdom) is derived from s.400(3) of the Companies Act 1985.

Subsection (3)

This subsection is concerned with the period for registration of particulars of a series of debentures. It is derived from s.397(1) of the Companies Act 1985.

871. Registration of enforcement of security

(1) If a person obtains an order for the appointment of a receiver or manager of a company's property, or appoints such a receiver or manager under powers contained in an instrument, he shall within 7 days of the order or of the appointment under those powers, give notice of the fact to the registrar.

(2) Where a person appointed receiver or manager of a company's property under powers contained in an instrument ceases to act as such receiver or manager, he shall, on so ceasing, give the registrar notice to that effect.

(3) The registrar must enter a fact of which he is given notice under this section in the register of charges.

(4) A person who makes default in complying with the requirements of this section commits an offence.

(5) A person guilty of an offence under this section is liable on summary conviction to a fine not exceeding level 3 on the standard scale and, for continued contravention, a daily default fine not exceeding one-tenth of level 3 on the standard scale.

GENERAL NOTE

This section imposes a registration obligation in respect of the appointment of a receiver or manager of the company's property. It re-enacts s.405 of the Companies Act 1985, but in a modest concession towards de-regulation does not continue the requirement for the notifications required by the section to be "in the prescribed form".

Subsection (3)

This subsection makes a new express reference to the level of the fines for non-compliance.

872. Entries of satisfaction and release

(1) Subsection (2) applies if a statement is delivered to the registrar verifying with respect to a registered charge-

    (a) that the debt for which the charge was given has been paid or satisfied in whole or in part, or

    (b) that part of the property or undertaking charged has been released from the charge or has ceased to form part of the company's property or undertaking.

(2) The registrar may enter on the register a memorandum of satisfaction in whole or in part, or of the fact part of the property or undertaking has been released from the charge or has ceased to form part of the company's property or undertaking (as the case may be).

(3) Where the registrar enters a memorandum of satisfaction in whole, the registrar shall if required send the company a copy of it.

GENERAL NOTE

This section re-enacts s.403 of the 1985 Act, which was amended by the Companies Act 1985 (Electronic Communications) Order 2000 (SI 2000/3373) to facilitate the use of electronic communications. It remains the position that there is no obligation on anyone to deliver a statement to the registrar and there is no obligation on the registrar to enter on the register any memorandum of satisfaction.

Subsection (1)

There are criminal sanctions for delivering a false statement to the registrar: see s.1112.

873.   Rectification of register of charges

(1) Subsection (2) applies if the court is satisfied-
   (a) that the failure to register a charge before the end of the period allowed for registration, or the omission or mis-statement of any particular with respect to any such charge or in a memorandum of satisfaction-
      (i) was accidental or due to inadvertence or to some other sufficient cause, or
      (ii) is not of a nature to prejudice the position of creditors or shareholders of the company, or
   (b) that on other grounds it is just and equitable to grant relief.

(2) The court may, on the application of the company or a person interested, and on such terms and conditions as seem to the court just and expedient, order that the period allowed for registration shall be extended or, as the case may be, that the omission or mis-statement shall be rectified.

GENERAL NOTE

This section re-enacts, with no significant change, s.404 of the 1985 Act. It empowers the court to order rectification of the register of charges in certain circumstances. Existing cases on the exercise of this power (such as *Victoria Housing Estates Ltd v Ashpurton Estates Ltd* [1983] Ch. 110; *Braemar Investments Ltd, Re* [1988] B.C.L.C. 556; and *Barrow Borough Transport Ltd, Re* [1990] Ch. 227) will continue to apply.

Subsection (2)

Cases on the wording of the order (such as *Joplin Brewery Co Ltd, Re* [1902] 1 Ch. 79; *LH Charles & Co, Re* [1935] W.N. 15; *IC Johnson & Co Ltd, Re* [1902] 2 Ch. 101; and *Fablehill Ltd, Re* [1991] B.C.L.C. 830) are still good law.

Avoidance of certain charges

874.   Consequence of failure to register charges created by a company

(1) If a company creates a charge to which section 860 applies, the charge is void (so far as any security on the company's property or undertaking is conferred by it) against-
   (a) a liquidator of the company,
   (b) an administrator of the company, and
   (c) a creditor of the company,
unless that section is complied with.

(2) Subsection (1) is subject to the provisions of this Chapter.

(3) Subsection (1) is without prejudice to any contract or obligation for repayment of the money secured by the charge; and when a charge becomes void under this section, the money secured by it immediately becomes payable.

GENERAL NOTE

With some drafting changes, this section re-enacts s.395 of the 1985 Act. The sanction for failure to register a registrable charge created by a company remains that the charge is void against a liquidator or administrator of the company (as interpreted in *Smith v Bridgend CBC* [2002] 1 A.C. 336) and against a creditor of the company. When a charge becomes void under the section the money secured by it immediately becomes repayable. Non-registration does not invalidate a charge against purchasers. Unless and until the company goes into liquidation or administration, unsecured creditors of the company have no right to object: *Ehrmann Bros Ltd, Re* [1906] 2 Ch. 697. Even when a company is in liquidation or administration, individual unsecured creditors do not have standing to complain and it is for the liquidator or administrator to bring the action: *Ayala Holdings Ltd, Re* [1993] B.C.L.C. 256.

Companies' records and registers

875. Companies to keep copies of instruments creating charges

(1) A company must keep available for inspection a copy of every instrument creating a charge requiring registration under this Chapter, including any document delivered to the company under section 868(3)(b) (Northern Ireland: orders imposing charges affecting land).

(2) In the case of a series of uniform debentures, a copy of one of the debentures of the series is sufficient.

GENERAL NOTE

This section is derived from s.406 of the 1985 Act.

Subsection (1)

The requirements relating to the location of the copies of instruments creating registrable charges that companies must keep available for inspection have been relaxed. See futher s.877.

The reference to an "order" or "notice" relates to a charge imposed by an order under the Judgments Enforcement (Northern Ireland) Order 1981, Art.46. See further s.868.

876. Company's register of charges

(1) Every limited company shall keep available for inspection a register of charges and enter in it-

    (a) all charges specifically affecting property of the company, and

    (b) all floating charges on the whole or part of the company's property or undertaking.

(2) The entry shall in each case give a short description of the property charged, the amount of the charge and, except in the cases of securities to bearer, the names of the persons entitled to it.

(3) If an officer of the company knowingly and wilfully authorises or permits the omission of an entry required to be made in pursuance of this section, he commits an offence.

(4) A person guilty of an offence under this section is liable-

    (a) on conviction on indictment, to a fine;

    (b) on summary conviction, to a fine not exceeding the statutory maximum.

GENERAL NOTE

This section re-enacts s.407 of the 1985 Act with little change.

Subsection (1)

The requirements relating to the location of the register that must be kept available for inspection have been relaxed. See further s.877.

Subsection (3) and (4)

As was also the case under the 1985 Act, non-compliance is an offence by defaulting officers, but not by the company itself. The penalty is spelt out in a way that follows the general approach to sanctions adopted throughout the Companies Act 2006.

877. Instruments creating charges and register of charges to be available for inspection

(1) This section applies to-
    (a) documents required to be kept available for inspection under section 875 (copies of instruments creating charges), and
    (b) a company's register of charges kept in pursuance of section 876.

(2) The documents and register must be kept available for inspection-
    (a) at the company's registered office, or
    (b) at a place specified in regulations under section 1136.

(3) The company must give notice to the registrar-
    (a) of the place at which the documents and register are kept available for inspection, and
    (b) of any change in that place,
unless they have at all times been kept at the company's registered office.

(4) The documents and register shall be open to the inspection-
    (a) of any creditor or member of the company without charge, and
    (b) of any other person on payment of such fee as may be prescribed.

(5) If default is made for 14 days in complying with subsection (3) or an inspection required under subsection (4) is refused, an offence is committed by-
    (a) the company, and
    (b) every officer of the company who is in default.

(6) A person guilty of an offence under this section is liable on summary conviction to a fine not exceeding level 3 on the standard scale and, for continued contravention, a daily default fine not exceeding one-tenth of level 3 on the standard scale.

(7) If an inspection required under subsection (4) is refused the court may by order compel an immediate inspection.

GENERAL NOTE

This section is derived from s.408 of the 1985 Act, but there are some changes. The key difference is that the documents and register to which the section relates need not necessarily be held at a company's registered office.

Subsection (1)

As was the case under the 1985 Act, copies of instruments creating charges requiring registration and the company own register of charges (including charges that are not registrable with the registrar) must be kept available for inspection.

Subsection (2)

The documents and register must be kept available for inspection either at the company's registered office or at another place specified in regulations under s.1136. Section 1136 authorises the Secretary of State to make provision by regulations specifying places other than a company's registered office at which mandatory company records may be so kept available for inspection. The regulations may specify a place by reference to the company's principal place of business, the part of the United Kingdom in which the company is registered, the place at which the company keeps any other records available for inspection or in any other way. The power for Secretary of State to make these regulations is intended to meet the concern that, on the one hand, requirements relating to where records are kept should not impose unnecessary costs on business and, on the other hand, companies should not be able to make those wishing to inspect several company records which they have a statutory right to inspect to go to several different places. (DTI memorandum reproduced as Appendix 3 to the Twenty-Sixth Report of the Delegated Powers and Regulatory Reform Committee (November 2006), para.69).

Subsection (3)

The company must notify the registrar of the place where the documents and register are kept available for inspection save that no notice is required where they are, and always have been, kept at the company's registered office.

Subsection (4)

The fee for inspection by persons others than creditors and members is to be prescribed. In the Companies Acts, "prescribed" means prescribed (by order or by regulations) by the Secretary of State. See s.1167. Previously, it was for the company to prescribe the inspection fee, but the fee could not exceed five pence.

Subsection (5)

There is a new offence that is consequential upon the introduction of the more relaxed regime for the location at which the documents and register to which this section applies are kept available for inspection: not informing the registrar of where this location is constitutes a criminal offence. The imposition of a criminal sanction for the failure to comply with the obligation to allow inspection is not fundamentally new. However, it is noteworthy that this offence (and also the notification offence) is committed by the company as well as by the defaulting officers. The 1985 Act did not impose corporate criminal liability in this context.

Subsection (6)

The penalties for non-compliance are drafted in conformity with the general approach to criminal sanctions adopted throughout the Companies Act 2006.

Subsection (7)

This is derived from s.408(3) of the Companies Act 1985.

CHAPTER 2

COMPANIES REGISTERED IN SCOTLAND

GENERAL NOTE

Chapter 2 of Pt 25 of the Companies Act 2006 re-states Ch.II of Pt XII of the 1985 Act in modified (and clearer) language. There are no substantive changes, except that s.424 of the 1985 Act is not re-enacted. Section 424 extended the provisions of Ch.II to require companies incorporated outside Great Britain which have a place of business in Scotland to register charges on property in Scotland which are created and charges on property in Scotland which is acquired. Section 879(2) defines "company" for the purposes of Ch.2 as "an incorporated company registered in Scotland" so that Ch.2 does not apply to an overseas company. It is understood, however, that regulations to be made under s.894 will apply (with appropriate modifications) Ch.2 of Pt 25 to overseas companies that are registered in Great Britain.

The provisions of this Chapter are incompatible with Pt 2 of the Bankruptcy and Diligence Etc (Scotland) Act 2006, which provides that a floating charge over property in Scotland is valid only upon its registration in the Register of Floating Charges created by that Act, without additional registration at Companies House. It is understood that the power granted to the Secretary of State by ss.893 and 894 will be used to amend Pt 25 so that registration in the Register of Floating Charges in Scotland will be sufficient publication without further registration at Companies House. It is also understood that these powers will be used to extend these arrangements to other public registers, such as the Register of Sasines and the Land Register of Scotland, when the appropriate electronic communication arrangements have been established.

It is assumed that Pt 25 will be extended to Limited Liability Partnerships and other entities to which Pt XII of the 1985 Act has been applied.

Charges requiring registration

878. Charges created by a company

(1) A company that creates a charge to which this section applies must deliver the prescribed particulars of the charge, together with a copy certified as a correct copy of the instrument (if any) by which the charge is created or evidenced, to the registrar for registration before the end of the period allowed for registration.

(2) Registration of a charge to which this section applies may instead be effected on the application of a person interested in it.

(3) Where registration is effected on the application of some person other than the company, that person is entitled to recover from the company the amount of any fees properly paid by him to the registrar on the registration.

(4) If a company fails to comply with subsection (1), an offence is committed by-

    (a) the company, and

    (b) every officer of the company who is in default.

(5) A person guilty of an offence under this section is liable-

    (a) on conviction on indictment, to a fine;

    (b) on summary conviction, to a fine not exceeding the statutory maximum.

(6) Subsection (4) does not apply if registration of the charge has been effected on the application of some other person.

(7) This section applies to the following charges-

    (a) a charge on land or any interest in such land, other than a charge for any rent or other periodical sum payable in respect of the land,

    (b) a security over incorporeal moveable property of any of the following categories-

        (i) goodwill,

        (ii) a patent or a licence under a patent,

        (iii) a trademark,

        (iv) a copyright or a licence under a copyright,

        (v) a registered design or a licence in respect of such a design,

        (vi) a design right or a licence under a design right,

        (vii) the book debts (whether book debts of the company or assigned to it), and

        (viii) uncalled share capital of the company or calls made but not paid,

    (c) a security over a ship or aircraft or any share in a ship,

    (d) a floating charge.

GENERAL NOTE

Subsection (1)

This continues the effect of s.410 (1) and (2) of the Companies Act 1985. A company to which s.878 applies must deliver prescribed particulars of the charge together with a certified copy of the instrument (if any) creating the charge to the Registrar of Companies in Scotland for registration, within the period allowed by s.886 (discussed below).

Subsections (2) and (3)

These continue the effect of s.415(1) (in part) and (2) of the 1985 Act. They allow a charge to be registered by a person (other than the company) having an interest in it, with right of recovery of any fee paid to the Registrar of Companies from the company granting the charge. In practice, charges are invariably registered by the person in whose favour the security is granted.

Subsections (4)-(6)

As with s.415(3) of the 1985 Act, if the company fails to deliver the documents required by subs.(1) it and every officer of the company who is in default commits an offence, and is liable to a fine. No offence is committed, however, if the charge is registered on the application of a person other than the company, which leaves open the possibility that the company has committed an offence if registration was to be effected by another person (such as the grantee) who failed to comply with the statutory provisions. This possibility also existed under the superseded provisions of s.415(3) of the 1985 Act.

Subsection (7)

This lists the charges whose particulars require to be delivered to the Registrar under subs.(1), namely, a security over land or an interest in land (but excluding a security over rent or other periodical sum payable in respect of land), a security over incorporeal moveable property specified in subs.(7)(b), a security over a ship or aircraft or any share in a ship and any floating charge. The list is in identical terms to that in s.410 (4) of the 1985 Act (as amended) save that:

● The provision that a charge on land includes a heritable security now appears as s.879(1); and

● "book debts" now includes debts that have been assigned to the company.

879. Charges which have to be registered: supplementary

(1) A charge on land, for the purposes of section 878(7)(a), includes a charge created by a heritable security within the meaning of section 9(8) of the Conveyancing and Feudal Reform (Scotland) Act 1970 (c. 35).

(2) The holding of debentures entitling the holder to a charge on land is not, for the purposes of section 878(7)(a), deemed to be an interest in land.

(3) It is immaterial for the purposes of this Chapter where land subject to a charge is situated.

(4) The deposit by way of security of a negotiable instrument given to secure the payment of book debts is not, for the purposes of section 878(7)(b)(vii), to be treated as a charge on those book debts.

(5) References in this Chapter to the date of the creation of a charge are-

    (a) in the case of a floating charge, the date on which the instrument creating the floating charge was executed by the company creating the charge, and

    (b) in any other case, the date on which the right of the person entitled to the benefit of the charge was constituted as a real right.

(6) In this Chapter "company" means an incorporated company registered in Scotland.

GENERAL NOTE

Subsection (1)

A registrable charge on land includes a heritable security within the meaning of the Conveyancing and Feudal Reform (Scotland) Act 1970. This includes (but is not limited to) a standard security under that Act.

Subsection (2)

This re-enacts s.413(1) of the 1985 Act. The holding of a debenture secured over land is not an interest in land for the purposes of s.878(7)(a). Charges created to secure debentures are dealt with in ss.882-883.

Subsection (3)

This continues the effect of s.410 (4)(a) of the 1985 Act and applies Ch.2 to a charge on land wherever situated.

Subsection (4)

This continues the effect of s.412 of the 1985 Act excluding from s.878(7)(b)(vii) the deposit of a negotiable instrument to secure book debts.

Subsection (5)

The definition of the "date of creation" of a charge re-enacts the equivalent part of s.410 (5) of the 1985 Act. A floating charge is "created" on the date it is executed by the company and a fixed security on the date it is constituted as a real right.

Subsection (6)

Section 410 (5) of the 1985 Act applied provisions equivalent to those of Pt 2 of Ch.25 only to a company registered in Scotland or (by virtue of s.424) to charges over property in Scotland by a company incorporated outside Great Britain which had a place of business in Scotland. As noted under the "General Note" above, Pt 2 of Ch.25 does not apply to overseas companies, but it is anticipated that regulations will be made to apply Ch.25 to overseas companies which have registered in Scotland.

The definition of the "Registrar of Companies" for the purposes of Ch.2 of Pt 25 as the Registrar of Companies in Scotland now appears as s.1060 of the 2006 Act.

880. Duty to register charges existing on property acquired

(1) Subsection (2) applies where a company acquires any property which is subject to a charge of any kind as would, if it had been created by the company after the acquisition of the property, have been required to be registered under this Chapter.

(2) The company must deliver the prescribed particulars of the charge, together with a copy (certified to be a correct copy) of the instrument (if any) by which the charge was created or is evidenced, to the registrar for registration before the end of the period allowed for registration.

(3) If default is made in complying with this section, an offence is committed by-

    (a) the company, and

    (b) every officer of it who is in default.

(4) A person guilty of an offence under this section is liable-

    (a) on conviction on indictment, to a fine;

    (b) on summary conviction, to a fine not exceeding the statutory maximum.

GENERAL NOTE

    Section 880 continues the effect of s.416 of the 1985 Act.

Subsections (1) and (2)

    If the company acquires property which is subject to an existing security which would have been registrable if it had been created by the company, the prescribed particulars and a certified copy of the charge in question must be delivered to the Registrar within the period permitted by s.886(2).

Subsections (3) and (4)

    Failure to comply with subss.(1) and (2) is an offence for which the company and any officer in default is liable to a fine.

881.   Charge by way of ex facie absolute disposition, etc

(1) For the avoidance of doubt, it is hereby declared that, in the case of a charge created by way of an *ex facie* absolute disposition or assignation qualified by a back letter or other agreement, or by a standard security qualified by an agreement, compliance with section 878(1) does not of itself render the charge unavailable as security for indebtedness incurred after the date of compliance.

(2) Where the amount secured by a charge so created is purported to be increased by a further back letter or agreement, a further charge is held to have been created by the *ex facie* absolute disposition or assignation or (as the case may be) by the standard security, as qualified by the further back letter or agreement.

(3) In that case, the provisions of this Chapter apply to the further charge as if-

    (a) references in this Chapter (other than in this section) to a charge were references to the further charge, and

    (b) references to the date of the creation of a charge were references to the date on which the further back letter or agreement was executed.

GENERAL NOTE

Subsection (1)

    This re-enacts s.414(1) of the Companies Act 1985, so that registration of a heritable security at Companies House does not, of itself, render that security unavailable for debts incurred after registration.

Subsections (2) and (3)

    This re-enacts with minor modification s.414(2) of the Companies Act 1985. If an agreement qualifying the effect of the original heritable security is amended so as to increase the amount secured, that is registrable as if it were a fresh security created on the date the modification to the qualifying agreement was executed.

Special rules about debentures

882. Charge in series of debentures

(1) Where a series of debentures containing, or giving by reference to any other instrument, any charge to the benefit of which the debenture-holders of that series are entitled *pari passu*, is created by a company, it is sufficient for purposes of section 878 if the required particulars, together with a copy of the deed containing the charge (or, if there is no such deed, of one of the debentures of the series) are delivered to the registrar before the end of the period allowed for registration.

(2) The following are the required particulars-
   (a) the total amount secured by the whole series,
   (b) the dates of the resolutions authorising the issue of the series and the date of the covering deed (if any) by which the security is created or defined,
   (c) a general description of the property charged,
   (d) the names of the trustees (if any) for the debenture-holders, and
   (e) in the case of a floating charge, a statement of any provisions of the charge and of any instrument relating to it which prohibit or restrict or regulate the power of the company to grant further securities ranking in priority to, or *pari passu* with, the floating charge, or which vary or otherwise regulate the order of ranking of the floating charge in relation to subsisting securities.

(3) Where more than one issue is made of debentures in the series, particulars of the date and amount of each issue of debentures of the series must be sent to the registrar for entry in the register of charges.

(4) Failure to comply with subsection (3) does not affect the validity of any of those debentures.

(5) Subsections (2) to (6) of section 878 apply for the purposes of this section as they apply for the purposes of that section but as if for the reference to the registration of the charge there was substituted a reference to the registration of the series of debentures.

GENERAL NOTE
   This section re-enacts in modified form s.413(1) and (2) of the 1985 Act.

Subsection (1)
   If the company issues a series of debentures whose holders are entitled to a separately constituted charge, s.878 is satisfied if together with the required particulars either a copy of the document containing the charge or, if there is no such document, of one of the debentures of the series is delivered to the Registrar within the required period.

Subsection (2)
   This sets out the particulars which are to be provided to the Registrar in the prescribed form pursuant to subs.(1) in identical terms to s.413(2) of the 1985 Act.

Subsections (3) and (4)
   If there are subsequent issues of debentures in the same series, particulars of the date and amount of each issue must be registered, but failure to do so does not affect the validity of any such debentures.

Subsection (5)
   The provisions of s.878 relating to registration by a person other than the company, and the offence of failure to deliver particulars, are applied to the issue of a series of debentures.

883. Additional registration requirement for commission etc in relation to debentures

(1) Where any commission, allowance or discount has been paid or made either directly or indirectly by a company to a person in consideration of his-
   (a) subscribing or agreeing to subscribe, whether absolutely or conditionally, for debentures in a company, or
   (b) procuring or agreeing to procure subscriptions, whether absolute or conditional, for such debentures,
the particulars required to be sent for registration under section 878 shall include particulars as to the amount or rate per cent. of the commission, discount or allowance so paid or made.
(2) The deposit of debentures as security for a debt of the company is not, for the purposes of this section, treated as the issue of debentures at a discount.
(3) Failure to comply with this section does not affect the validity of the debentures issued.

GENERAL NOTE

This section re-enacts with modification s.413(3) of the Companies Act 1985.

Subsection (1)

Particulars of any commission paid in connection with the issue of debentures are to be included in the particulars submitted to the Registrar.

Subsection (2)

Any deposit of debentures as security for a debt of the company is not to be treated as the issue of those debentures for the purposes of the provisions of s.883 regarding disclosure of commission.

Subsection (3)

Failure to comply with s.883 does not affect the validity of any debentures which have been issued.

Charges on property outside the United Kingdom

884.   Charges on property outside United Kingdom

Where a charge is created in the United Kingdom but comprises property outside the United Kingdom, the copy of the instrument creating or purporting to create the charge may be sent for registration under section 878 even if further proceedings may be necessary to make the charge valid or effectual according to the law of the country in which the property is situated.

GENERAL NOTE

This section continues the effect of s.411 of the Companies Act 1985. If a charge created in the United Kingdom includes property outside the United Kingdom, registration may still be effected pursuant to s.878 even if further procedure is required under the foreign jurisdiction to make the security legally effective.

The register of charges

885.   Register of charges to be kept by registrar

(1) The registrar shall keep, with respect to each company, a register of all the charges requiring registration under this Chapter.
(2) In the case of a charge to the benefit of which holders of a series of debentures are entitled, the registrar shall enter in the register the required particulars specified in section 882(2).
(3) In the case of any other charge, the registrar shall enter in the register the following particulars-
   (a) if it is a charge created by a company, the date of its creation and, if it is a charge which was existing on property acquired by the company, the date of the acquisition,
   (b) the amount secured by the charge,

(c) short particulars of the property charged,

(d) the persons entitled to the charge, and

(e) in the case of a floating charge, a statement of any of the provisions of the charge and of any instrument relating to it which prohibit or restrict or regulate the company's power to grant further securities ranking in priority to, or *pari passu* with, the floating charge, or which vary or otherwise regulate the order of ranking of the floating charge in relation to subsisting securities.

(4) The registrar shall give a certificate of the registration of any charge registered in pursuance of this Chapter, stating-

(a) the name of the company and the person first-named in the charge among those entitled to the benefit of the charge (or, in the case of a series of debentures, the name of the holder of the first such debenture issued), and

(b) the amount secured by the charge.

(5) The certificate-

(a) shall be signed by the registrar or authenticated by the registrar's official seal, and

(b) is conclusive evidence that the requirements of this Chapter as to registration have been satisfied.

(6) The register kept in pursuance of this section shall be open to inspection by any person.

GENERAL NOTE

This section re-enacts, with modification, ss.417 and 418 of the Companies Act 1985.

Subsections (1) and (6)

The Registrar of Companies must keep a Register of all Charges requiring registration, which is open for inspection by the public.

Subsections (2) and (3)

These specify the particulars to be registered, derived from the documents submitted to the Registrar pursuant to s.878 or s.882.

Subsections (4) and (5)

The Registrar is required to issue a Certificate of Registration in the form specified by the Act, (giving the company name, the first-named person entitled to the benefit of the charge and the amount secured) which is conclusive evidence that the requirements of Ch.2 of Pt 25 with respect to registration have been satisfied.

886. The period allowed for registration

(1) The period allowed for registration of a charge created by a company is-

(a) 21 days beginning with the day after the day on which the charge is created, or

(b) if the charge is created outside the United Kingdom, 21 days beginning with the day after the day on which a copy of the instrument by which the charge is created or evidenced could, in due course of post (and if despatched with due diligence) have been received in the United Kingdom.

(2) The period allowed for registration of a charge to which property acquired by a company is subject is-

(a) 21 days beginning with the day after the day on which the transaction is settled, or

(b) if the property is situated and the charge was created outside the United Kingdom, 21 days beginning with the day after the day on which a copy of the instrument by which the charge is created or evidenced could, in due course of post (and if despatched with due diligence) have been received in the United Kingdom.

(3) The period allowed for registration of particulars of a series of debentures as a result of section 882 is-

(a) if there is a deed containing the charge mentioned in section 882(1), 21 days beginning with the day after the day on which that deed is executed, or

(b) if there is no such deed, 21 days beginning with the day after the day on which the first debenture of the series is executed.

GENERAL NOTE

Section 886 re-enacts provisions found in several separate sections of the Companies Act 1985 specifying the period allowed for registration pursuant to this Chapter.

Subsection (1)

The fundamental obligation is to deliver particulars for registration within 21 days beginning with the day on which the charge is created (as defined in s.879(5)). However, if the charge is created outside the United Kingdom this period is extended to include the period required for a copy of the charge to reach the United Kingdom in due (diligent) course of post. This provision derives from ss.410(2) and 411(1) of the 1985 Act.

Subsection (2)

In the case of property acquired which is subject to a subsisting security, the period of 21 days is from the date the transaction by which the property was acquired was settled, with extension for postal delivery of a charge created outside the United Kingdom similar to subs.(1)(b). This provision derives from s.416(2) of the 1985 Act. The date a transaction is "settled" remains undefined.

Subsection (3)

In the case of a series of debentures registered pursuant to s.882, if there is a document containing a charge securing the debentures, it is registrable within 21 days beginning with the day after the date of execution of that document. If there is no such document, the 21 day period begins with the day after the date on which the first debenture of the series is executed. This provision derives from s.413(2) of the 1985 Act.

887. Entries of satisfaction and relief

(1) Subsection (2) applies if a statement is delivered to the registrar verifying with respect to any registered charge-
    (a) that the debt for which the charge was given has been paid or satisfied in whole or in part, or
    (b) that part of the property charged has been released from the charge or has ceased to form part of the company's property.
(2) If the charge is a floating charge, the statement must be accompanied by either-
    (a) a statement by the creditor entitled to the benefit of the charge, or a person authorised by him for the purpose, verifying that the statement mentioned in subsection (1) is correct, or
    (b) a direction obtained from the court, on the ground that the statement by the creditor mentioned in paragraph (a) could not be readily obtained, dispensing with the need for that statement.
(3) The registrar may enter on the register a memorandum of satisfaction (in whole or in part) regarding the fact contained in the statement mentioned in subsection (1).
(4) Where the registrar enters a memorandum of satisfaction in whole, he shall, if required, furnish the company with a copy of the memorandum.
(5) Nothing in this section requires the company to submit particulars with respect to the entry in the register of a memorandum of satisfaction where the company, having created a floating charge over all or any part of its property, disposes of part of the property subject to the floating charge.

GENERAL NOTE

As with the Companies Act 1985, this section makes provision for registration of the satisfaction in whole or in part of the obligation secured by a registered charge (a "Memorandum of Satisfaction") or the release of property from a registered charge either by agreement of the holder or upon the property being disposed of by the company (a "Memorandum of Release"). As with the 1985 Act, however, there is no obligation to register such an event, although this may be required by the purchaser of property from the company as confirmation that the security no longer attaches to it.

The Companies Act 1985 (Electronic Communications) Order 2000 (SI 2000/3373, Art.23) inserted provisions as s.419(1A), (1B) and (5A) allowing a Memorandum of Satisfaction or Release to be submitted electronically. Provisions allowing electronic submission of such documents now appear as ss.1068 to 1072 of the Act.

888. Rectification of register of charges

(1) Subsection (2) applies if the court is satisfied-
    (a) that the failure to register a charge before the end of the period allowed for registration, or the omission or mis-statement of any particular with respect to any such charge or in a memorandum of satisfaction-
        (i) was accidental or due to inadvertence or to some other sufficient cause, or
        (ii) is not of a nature to prejudice the position of creditors or shareholders of the company, or
    (b) that on other grounds it is just and equitable to grant relief.
(2) The court may, on the application of the company or a person interested, and on such terms and conditions as seem to the court just and expedient, order that the period allowed for registration shall be extended or, as the case may be, that the omission or mis-statement shall be rectified.

GENERAL NOTE
Section 888 re-enacts in modified terms s.420 of the Companies Act 1985.

Subsection (1)

The court requires to be satisfied that any failure to register within the prescribed time limit, or any error in the particulars registered, was accidental, inadvertent or due to some other cause that the court regards as being sufficient to grant relief, and does not prejudice creditors or shareholders, or the court is satisfied that it is just as equitable to grant relief.

Subsection (2)

This grants the court wide discretion of whether to grant relief and, if so, on what terms. Usually, the court order will allow late registration or the correction of an error in the particulars registered without prejudice to the rights of any creditor whose claim arose in the period prior to registration or correction pursuant to the court's order.

Avoidance of certain charges

889. Charges void unless registered

(1) If a company creates a charge to which section 878 applies, the charge is void (so far as any security on the company's property or any part of it is conferred by the charge) against-
    (a) the liquidator of the company,
    (b) an administrator of the company, and
    (c) any creditor of the company
unless that section is complied with.
(2) Subsection (1) is without prejudice to any contract or obligation for repayment of the money secured by the charge; and when a charge becomes void under this section the money secured by it immediately becomes payable.

GENERAL NOTE
Section 889 carves out from s.410 (2) of the 1985 Act the provision that a charge to which Ch.2 of Pt 25 applies is void in terms of s.889(1) unless timeously registered.

Subsection (1)

A charge not timeously registered is stated to be void in respect of any security thereby conferred against any liquidator, administrator or creditor of the company. It remains a valid right in security in a question with any other party. The sanction of avoidance applied by s.889 does not apply to any failure to register a charge on property acquired (pursuant to s.880) but it does apply to a failure to effect registration of a series of debentures pursuant to s.882(1). It does not apply, however, to a failure to register a further issue of such debentures (s.882(3) and (4)), nor to the omission of particulars relating to commission payable in respect of debentures pursuant to s.883. In the case of a heritable security ex facie absolute but qualified by agreement (as described in s.881(1)) any amendment of the agreement which increases the sum for which the security is available is deemed by s.881(2) and (3) to be a fresh registrable charge for which the heritable security will not be available unless appropriate particulars are delivered pursuant to s.878 as applied by s.881(3).

Subsection (2)

This re-enacts s.410 (3) of the 1985 Act. Failure to comply with the requirement to deliver particulars of a charge to the Registrar does not affect the obligation it was intended to secure and, in the case of a debt, the money becomes immediately repayable to the creditor.

Companies' records and registers

890.   Copies of instruments creating charges to be kept by company

(1) Every company shall cause a copy of every instrument creating a charge requiring registration under this Chapter to be kept available for inspection.

(2) In the case of a series of uniform debentures, a copy of one debenture of the series is sufficient.

GENERAL NOTE

This re-enacts s.421 of the Companies Act 1985.

Subsection (1)

The company is required to retain a copy of every instrument creating a charge which is registrable for inspection under s.892.

Subsection (2)

Where a series of uniform debentures has been created, a copy of one of the debentures is sufficient compliance with Subs.(1).

891.   Company's register of charges

(1) Every company shall keep available for inspection a register of charges and enter in it all charges specifically affecting property of the company, and all floating charges on any property of the company.

(2) There shall be given in each case a short description of the property charged, the amount of the charge and, except in the case of securities to bearer, the names of the persons entitled to it.

(3) If an officer of the company knowingly and wilfully authorises or permits the omission of an entry required to be made in pursuance of this section, he commits an offence.

(4) A person guilty of an offence under this section is liable-

    (a) on conviction on indictment, to a fine;

    (b) on summary conviction, to a fine not exceeding the statutory maximum.

GENERAL NOTE

Section 891 re-enacts in modified form s.422 of the Companies Act 1985.

Subsection (1)

Every company is required to maintain a Register of Charges with particulars of all fixed and floating charges on any of its property.

Subsection (2)

The Register must contain a short description of the property, the amount of the charge and (except for bearer securities) the persons entitled to it.

Subsections (3) and (4)

Any officer of the company responsible for the omission of any entry required by s.891 commits an offence and is liable to a fine.

892. Instruments creating charges and register of charges to be available for inspection

(1) This section applies to-
  (a) documents required to be kept available for inspection under section 890 (copies of instruments creating charges), and
  (b) a company's register of charges kept in pursuance of section 891.

(2) The documents and register must be kept available for inspection-
  (a) at the company's registered office, or
  (b) at a place specified in regulations under section 1136.

(3) The company must give notice to the registrar-
  (a) of the place at which the documents and register are kept available for inspection, and
  (b) of any change in that place,
unless they have at all times been kept at the company's registered office.

(4) The documents and register shall be open to the inspection-
  (a) of any creditor or member of the company without charge, and
  (b) of any other person on payment of such fee as may be prescribed.

(5) If default is made for 14 days in complying with subsection (3) or an inspection required under subsection (4) is refused, an offence is committed by-
  (a) the company, and
  (b) every officer of the company who is in default.

(6) A person guilty of an offence under this section is liable on summary conviction to a fine not exceeding level 3 on the standard scale and, for continued contravention, a daily default fine not exceeding one-tenth of level 3 on the standard scale.

(7) If an inspection required under subsection (4) is refused the court may by order compel an immediate inspection.

GENERAL NOTE

Section 892 re-enacts with modification s.423 of the Companies Act 1985.

Subsections (1)-(3)

The copies of charges to be retained by the company and its Register of Charges pursuant to ss.890 and 891 are to be kept available for inspection either at the registered office of the company or at another place specified in regulations made pursuant to s.1136 of the Act. If these documents are not kept at the registered office the company must give the Registrar of Companies due notice of where they may be inspected and of any change in that place.

Subsections (4)-(7)

Copies of registrable charges and the company's own Register of Charges must be available for inspection by any creditor or member of a company free of charge and by any other person on payment of a fee to be prescribed. If there is a delay of 14 days or more in making these documents available, the company and every officer who is responsible commits an offence and is liable to a fine. If inspection is refused, this may be ordered by the court.

CHAPTER 3

POWERS OF THE SECRETARY OF STATE

GENERAL NOTE

This new Part is inserted into the Act to confer two powers on the Secretary of State. Part 3 (ss.893 and 894) apply to England and Wales as well as to Scotland.

893. Power to make provision for effect of registration in special register

(1) In this section a "special register" means a register, other than the register of charges kept under this Part, in which a charge to which Chapter 1 or Chapter 2 applies is required or authorised to be registered.

(2) The Secretary of State may by order make provision for facilitating the making of information-sharing arrangements between the person responsible for maintaining a special register ("the responsible person") and the registrar that meet the requirement in subsection (4).

"Information-sharing arrangements" are arrangements to share and make use of information held by the registrar or by the responsible person.

(3) If the Secretary of State is satisfied that appropriate information-sharing arrangements have been made, he may by order provide that-

    (a) the registrar is authorised not to register a charge of a specified description under Chapter 1 or Chapter 2,

    (b) a charge of a specified description that is registered in the special register within a specified period is to be treated as if it had been registered (and certified by the registrar as registered) in accordance with the requirements of Chapter 1 or, as the case may be, Chapter 2, and

    (c) the other provisions of Chapter 1 or, as the case may be, Chapter 2 apply to a charge so treated with specified modifications.

(4) The information-sharing arrangements must ensure that persons inspecting the register of charges-

    (a) are made aware, in a manner appropriate to the inspection, of the existence of charges in the special register which are treated in accordance with provision so made, and

    (b) are able to obtain information from the special register about any such charge.

(5) An order under this section may-

    (a) modify any enactment or rule of law which would otherwise restrict or prevent the responsible person from entering into or giving effect to information-sharing arrangements,

    (b) authorise the responsible person to require information to be provided to him for the purposes of the arrangements,

    (c) make provision about-

        (i) the charging by the responsible person of fees in connection with the arrangements and the destination of such fees (including provision modifying any enactment which would otherwise apply in relation to fees payable to the responsible person), and

        (ii) the making of payments under the arrangements by the registrar to the responsible person,

    (d) require the registrar to make copies of the arrangements available to the public (in hard copy or electronic form).

(6) In this section "specified" means specified in an order under this section.

(7) A description of charge may be specified, in particular, by reference to one or more of the following-

    (a) the type of company by which it is created,

    (b) the form of charge which it is,

    (c) the description of assets over which it is granted,

    (d) the length of the period between the date of its registration in the special register and the date of its creation.

(8) Provision may be made under this section relating to registers maintained under the law of a country or territory outside the United Kingdom.

(9) An order under this section is subject to negative resolution procedure.

GENERAL NOTE

This provision is new. It empowers the Secretary of State to make provision for the introduction of a system whereby a charge registered at another register (a "special register") will be treated as if it had been registered with the registrar of companies. Where such a system is introduced it will remove the need for dual registration. The registration obligation under the 2006 Act operates in parallel with specialist registries for certain specific types of property, including land, aircraft, fishing vessels, ships trademarks, registered designs, patents and copyrights. In principle the new power could be exercised in any of the these cases, but, before doing so, the Secretary of State will be concerned to ensure that third parties will not be disadvantaged (DTI memorandum reproduced as Appendix 3 to the Twenty Sixth Report of the Delegated Powers and Regulatory Reform Committee (November 2006), paras 53 and 54). In the first instance, it is intended to use the new power needed to ensure the operability of the new registration system for floating charges in Scotland which is to be established under the Bankruptcy and Diligence etc. (Scotland) Act 2007 (see Lord Sainsbury, *Hansard*, HL Vol.686, col 481 (November 2, 2006) and DTI memorandum reproduced as Appendix 3 to the Twenty Sixth Report of the Delegated Powers and Regulatory Reform Committee (November 2006), paras 53 and 55).

Subsection (1)

This subsection defines a special register as a register, other than the register of charges kept by the registrar of companies, in which registrable charges are required or authorised to be registered.

Subsection (2)

This subsection empowers the Secretary of State with regard to "information-sharing arrangements".

The Secretary of State may by order make provision for facilitating the making of information-sharing arrangements between the keeper of the special register and the registrar of companies. "Information-sharing arrangements" are arrangements to share and make use of information held by the registrar or by the keeper of the special register. Additional features of an appropriate information-sharing arrangements are specified later in the section (see subs.(4)).

Subsection (3)

This subsection empowers the Secretary of State, once he is satisfied that appropriate information-sharing arrangements have been made, to make an order that a charge of a specified description that is registered in the special register within a specified period is to be treated as if it had been registered in accordance with the statutory requirements for the registration of charges. The Secretary of State may also order, in the same circumstances, that the registrar of companies is authorised not to register a charge of a specified description.

Subsection (4)

This subsection specifies additional features of an information-sharing arrangement. Although not mentioned in the Act, it seems likely that information-sharing arrangements will employ electronic links between the registers as a means of meeting these requirement.

Subsection (5)

This subsection clarifies the scope of the orders that may be made under the section.

Subsection (6) and (7)

These are definitional provisions.

Subsection (8)

This subsection makes it clear that orders made under the section may relate to non-United Kingdom registers.

Subsection (9)

The negative resolution procedure means that the statutory instrument containing the regulations or order is subject to annulment in pursuance of a resolution of either House of Parliament. See s.1289. The negative resolution procedure is appropriate in this instance as regulations or orders under this section will provide only for the change in the way that information for the public record is collected (DTI memorandum reproduced as Appendix 3 to the Twenty-Sixth Report of the Delegated Powers and Regulatory Reform Committee (November 2006), para.56).

894. General power to make amendments to this Part

(1) The Secretary of State may by regulations under this section-
    (a) amend this Part by altering, adding or repealing provisions,
    (b) make consequential amendments or repeals in this Act or any other enactment (whether passed or made before or after this Act).
(2) Regulations under this section are subject to affirmative resolution procedure.

GENERAL NOTE

    When the Bill that has become the Companies Act 2006 was originally presented to Parliament, it contained (Pt 31 of the Company Law Reform Bill 2005) a general power to restate and (subject to limitations) amend company law. This was explicitly intended to permit modification to what is now Pt 25 of the Companies Act 2006 in light of anticipated developments in the law and practice of the creation and registration of company charges or securities. The general power envisaged in the Bill was objected to on constitutional grounds and withdrawn, but the power to amend Pt 25 has been retained as s.894. Any regulations under this section are subject to affirmative procedure and the additional parliamentary scrutiny which that procedure entails.

PART 26

ARRANGEMENTS AND RECONSTRUCTIONS

Application of this Part

895. Application of this Part

(1) The provisions of this Part apply where a compromise or arrangement is proposed between a company and-
    (a) its creditors, or any class of them, or
    (b) its members, or any class of them.
(2) In this Part-
    "arrangement" includes a reorganisation of the company's share capital by the consolidation of shares of different classes or by the division of shares into shares of different classes, or by both of those methods; and
    "company"-
        (a) in section 900 (powers of court to facilitate reconstruction or amalgamation) means a company within the meaning of this Act, and
        (b) elsewhere in this Part means any company liable to be wound up under the Insolvency Act 1986 (c. 45) or the Insolvency (Northern Ireland) Order 1989 (S.I. 1989/2405 (N.I. 19)).

(3) The provisions of this Part have effect subject to Part 27 (mergers and divisions of public companies) where that Part applies (see sections 902 and 903).

GENERAL NOTE

    This Part of the Act restates, with minor amendments, ss.425-427 of the 1985 Act covering schemes of arrangement. It allows a company to alter the rights of either or both of its members or creditors so as to effect, e.g. an agreed merger, a takeover or a compromise with creditors. The sections have been re-ordered to provide a more logical progression through the three stages of a scheme (the initial application, the meetings and the sanction). One change of procedural substance is that under s.896 the court may now order the meetings (stage 1) on an application to that effect rather than on the application to sanction the scheme (now made at stage 3). Section 427A and Sch.15B to the 1985 Act (additional requirements for certain mergers and divisions of public companies) have been restated in the following Part of this Act.

This section sets out the scope of this Part, together with two definitions, one of which, as to the companies covered by the sections, is of particular importance.

Subsection (1)

This subsection repeats the opening words of s.425(1) of the 1985 Act and contains the well-known definition of a scheme of arrangement. The existing case law as to what constitutes a compromise or arrangement will thus continue to apply: see, e.g. *Savoy Hotel Ltd, Re* [1981] Ch. 351; *BTR Plc, Re* [2000] 1 B.C.L.C. 740.

Subsection (2)

This subsection re-enacts the existing definitions in ss.425(6) and 427(6) of the Companies Act 1985. With regard to the jurisdiction of the court to consider a scheme it is important to note the continuation of the distinction between the wide definition of a company for the purposes of the provisions applicable to the approval of a scheme and the narrower one for the specific provision addressed to the court actually effecting a merger under s.900. As to the former, see e.g. *Drax Holdings Ltd, Re* [2004] B.C.C. 334. The validity of such restrictions on jurisdiction involving other EC companies will have to be justified under EC law on public policy grounds: see *SEVIC Systems AG, Re* [2006] 2 B.C.L.C. 510.

A company within the meaning of this Act - see s.1.

Subsection (3)

This subsection makes it clear that for certain mergers and divisions of public companies effected by a scheme of arrangement the additional requirements of the following Part of this Act must also be complied with before the scheme can be sanctioned by the court.

Meeting of creditors or members

896. Court order for holding of meeting

(1) The court may, on an application under this section, order a meeting of the creditors or class of creditors, or of the members of the company or class of members (as the case may be), to be summoned in such manner as the court directs.

(2) An application under this section may be made by-

    (a) the company,

    (b) any creditor or member of the company, or

    (c) if the company is being wound up or an administration order is in force in relation to it, the liquidator or administrator.

GENERAL NOTE

This section re-enacts the power of the court to summon the appropriate meetings of creditors, members or any class thereof as appropriate (stage 1). However, unlike its predecessor section (s.425(1)), this can be done on an application to the court to summon the meetings rather than on an application for the sanctioning of the scheme. That subsequent application (stage 3) can now be made under s.899 after the scheme has been approved by the requisite majority(ies) at the relevant meetings (stage 2). That change is consequent on the requirement to identify any problems as to the constitution of the classes at this stage of a scheme (see Practice Statement [2002] 3 All ER 96).

The categories of applicant remain the same as in former s.425(1).

These meetings must approve the scheme by a 75 per cent majority before the court will sanction it (see s.899).

The existing case law as to what constitutes separate classes so as to require separate meetings, and the *prima facie* obligation on the applicant to identify them and any problems, at this stage, will continue to apply: see, e.g. *Hawk Insurance Co Ltd, Re* [2001] 2 B.C.L.C. 480; *Equitable Life Assurance Co, Re* [2002] 2 B.C.L.C. 510; *Telewest Communications Plc, Re* [2004] BCC 342.

897. Statement to be circulated or made available

(1) Where a meeting is summoned under section 896-
    (a) every notice summoning the meeting that is sent to a creditor or member must be accompanied by a statement complying with this section, and
    (b) every notice summoning the meeting that is given by advertisement must either-
        (i) include such a statement, or
        (ii) state where and how creditors or members entitled to attend the meeting may obtain copies of such a statement.

(2) The statement must-
    (a) explain the effect of the compromise or arrangement, and
    (b) in particular, state-
        (i) any material interests of the directors of the company (whether as directors or as members or as creditors of the company or otherwise), and
        (ii) the effect on those interests of the compromise or arrangement, in so far as it is different from the effect on the like interests of other persons.

(3) Where the compromise or arrangement affects the rights of debenture holders of the company, the statement must give the like explanation as respects the trustees of any deed for securing the issue of the debentures as it is required to give as respects the company's directors.

(4) Where a notice given by advertisement states that copies of an explanatory statement can be obtained by creditors or members entitled to attend the meeting, every such creditor or member is entitled, on making application in the manner indicated by the notice, to be provided by the company with a copy of the statement free of charge.

(5) If a company makes default in complying with any requirement of this section, an offence is committed by-
    (a) the company, and
    (b) every officer of the company who is in default.
This is subject to subsection (7) below.

(6) For this purpose the following are treated as officers of the company-
    (a) a liquidator or administrator of the company, and
    (b) a trustee of a deed for securing the issue of debentures of the company.

(7) A person is not guilty of an offence under this section if he shows that the default was due to the refusal of a director or trustee for debenture holders to supply the necessary particulars of his interests.

(8) A person guilty of an offence under this section is liable-
    (a) on conviction on indictment, to a fine;
    (b) on summary conviction, to a fine not exceeding the statutory maximum.

GENERAL NOTE

    This section in subss.(1)-(4) restates s.426(1)-(5) of the 1985 Act and sets out the requirement for an explanatory statement to be circulated or made available to those entitled to attend the meetings summoned under s.896. The only change is that the word "shall" has become the word "must".

Subsections (5)-(8)

    Subsection (5) restates the offence, formerly in s.426(6) of the 1985 Act, of failing to comply with this requirement. Subsections (6)-(8) replace the wording of s.426(6) as to who may be prosecuted, a possible defence and the sanction, so as to comply with the "house-style" of the Act on offences generally (see Sch.3). The defence should be read with s.898.

898. Duty of directors and trustees to provide information

(1) It is the duty of-
    (a) any director of the company, and

    (b) any trustee for its debenture holders,
 to give notice to the company of such matters relating to himself as may be necessary for the
purposes of section 897 (explanatory statement to be circulated or made available).

(2) Any person who makes default in complying with this section commits an offence.

(3) A person guilty of an offence under this section is liable on summary conviction to a fine not
    exceeding level 3 on the standard scale.

GENERAL NOTE

   This section restates s.426(7) of the 1985 Act with amendments as to the sanction in subs.(3). It requires directors and
trustees for debenture holders to provide information for the explanatory statement required under s.902. Failure to do so is
an offence and may be a defence for anyone charged under s.902(5).

Subsection (3)

   The criminal sanction was reworded to comply with the general approach to sanctions in this Act (see Sch.3).

Court sanction for compromise or arrangement

899.   Court sanction for compromise or arrangement

(1) If a majority in number representing 75% in value of the creditors or class of creditors or
    members or class of members (as the case may be), present and voting either in person or by
    proxy at the meeting summoned under section 896, agree a compromise or arrangement, the
    court may, on an application under this section, sanction the compromise or arrangement.

(2) An application under this section may be made by-
    (a) the company,
    (b) any creditor or member of the company, or
    (c) if the company is being wound up or an administration order is in force in relation it,
        the liquidator or administrator.

(3) A compromise or agreement sanctioned by the court is binding on-
    (a) all creditors or the class of creditors or on the members or class of members (as the
        case may be), and
    (b) the company or, in the case of a company in the course of being wound up, the
        liquidator and contributories of the company.

(4) The court's order has no effect until a copy of it has been delivered to the registrar.

GENERAL NOTE

   This section restates part of ss.425(1), 425(2) and the first part of 425(3) of the Companies Act 1985. It relates to the third
stage of a scheme, the sanction of the court following approval of the scheme by the meetings summoned under s.896. The
section now provides for the application to the court for its sanction to be made at this stage (after the meetings) rather than,
as formerly, at the initial stage of asking the court to summon the meetings. Those meetings are now to be summoned on
an application to the court for that purpose under s.896.

Subsection (1)

   There are no changes as to the required majorities for approval. The existing case law as to what factors the courts will
take into account in deciding whether to sanction a scheme will continue to apply: see, e.g. *Anglo-Continental Supply Co
Ltd, Re* [1922] 2 Ch 723 at 736; *Waste Recycling Group, Re* [2004] B.C.C. 328; *Telewest Communications Plc, Re* [2005]
B.C.C. 36; *BAT Industries Plc, Re*, September 3, 1998.

Subsection (2)

   The categories of applicant are the same as in s.425(1) of the 1985 Act and in s.896(2) of this Act.

Subsection (3)

   This subsection contains, unchanged, the rationale for using a scheme of arrangement - to bind dissenters.

This is one of two obligations relating to the court order. See also s.901.

Reconstructions and amalgamations

900. Powers of court to facilitate reconstruction or amalgamation

(1) This section applies where application is made to the court under section 899 to sanction a compromise or arrangement and it is shown that-

    (a) the compromise or arrangement is proposed for the purposes of, or in connection with, a scheme for the reconstruction of any company or companies, or the amalgamation of any two or more companies, and

    (b) under the scheme the whole or any part of the undertaking or the property of any company concerned in the scheme ("a transferor company") is to be transferred to another company ("the transferee company").

(2) The court may, either by the order sanctioning the compromise or arrangement or by a subsequent order, make provision for all or any of the following matters-

    (a) the transfer to the transferee company of the whole or any part of the undertaking and of the property or liabilities of any transferor company;

    (b) the allotting or appropriation by the transferee company of any shares, debentures, policies or other like interests in that company which under the compromise or arrangement are to be allotted or appropriated by that company to or for any person;

    (c) the continuation by or against the transferee company of any legal proceedings pending by or against any transferor company;

    (d) the dissolution, without winding up, of any transferor company;

    (e) the provision to be made for any persons who, within such time and in such manner as the court directs, dissent from the compromise or arrangement;

    (f) such incidental, consequential and supplemental matters as are necessary to secure that the reconstruction or amalgamation is fully and effectively carried out.

(3) If an order under this section provides for the transfer of property or liabilities-

    (a) the property is by virtue of the order transferred to, and vests in, the transferee company, and

    (b) the liabilities are, by virtue of the order, transferred to and become liabilities of that company.

(4) The property (if the order so directs) vests freed from any charge that is by virtue of the compromise or arrangement to cease to have effect.

(5) In this section-

    "property" includes property, rights and powers of every description; and

    "liabilities" includes duties.

(6) Every company in relation to which an order is made under this section must cause a copy of the order to be delivered to the registrar within seven days after its making.

(7) If default is made in complying with subsection (6) an offence is committed by-

    (a) the company, and

    (b) every officer of the company who is in default.

(8) A person guilty of an offence under subsection (7) is liable on summary conviction to a fine not exceeding level 3 on the standard scale and, for continued contravention, a daily default fine not exceeding one-tenth of level 3 on the standard scale.

GENERAL NOTE

    This section restates s.427(1)-(5) and part of (6) of the 1985 Act. It provides for additional wide powers for the court to effect the scheme if it is either one for the reconstruction of one or more companies or the amalgamation of two or more companies. Note the more restrictive definition of a company for this purpose (see s.895(2)). So far as schemes involving companies from other EC States are concerned this restrictive definition will have to be justified under EC law on public policy grounds: see *SEVIC Systems AG, Re* [2006] 2 B.C.L.C. 510. The best justification will be on the grounds of practicability.

There are no changes of any substance to the former wording so that the existing case law will continue to be relevant. There is some doubt as to the meaning of a reconstruction in this context: see *Mytravel Plc, Re* [2004] EWHC 2741, Ch.

Subsection (6) restates the requirement in s.427(5) of the Companies Act 1985 to deliver a copy of the order to the registrar. The default offence in subss.(7) and (8) was reworded to comply with the general policy on offences under this Act (see Sch.3).

Obligations of company with respect to articles etc

901. Obligations of company with respect to articles etc

(1) This section applies-
- (a) to any order under section 899 (order sanctioning compromise or arrangement), and
- (b) to any order under section 900 (order facilitating reconstruction or amalgamation) that alters the company's constitution.

(2) If the order amends-
- (a) the company's articles, or
- (b) any resolution or agreement to which Chapter 3 of Part 3 applies (resolution or agreement affecting a company's constitution),

the copy of the order delivered to the registrar by the company under section 899(4) or section 900(6) must be accompanied by a copy of the company's articles, or the resolution or agreement in question, as amended.

(3) Every copy of the company's articles issued by the company after the order is made must be accompanied by a copy of the order, unless the effect of the order has been incorporated into the articles by amendment.

(4) In this section-
- (a) references to the effect of the order include the effect of the compromise or arrangement to which the order relates; and
- (b) in the case of a company not having articles, references to its articles shall be read as references to the instrument constituting the company or defining its constitution.

(5) If a company makes default in complying with this section an offence is committed by-
- (a) the company, and
- (b) every officer of the company who is in default.

(6) A person guilty of an offence under this section is liable on summary conviction to a fine not exceeding level 3 on the standard scale.

GENERAL NOTE

This section, derived from ss.425(3) and 427(5) of the 1985 Act, expands the former requirements when a court order either sanctioning a scheme under s.899 or facilitating the merger under s.900, amends the company's articles or constitution (as defined in Pt 3).

In such a case a copy of the order must either be attached to the articles (see subs.(4)(b)) on all subsequent issues or the effect of the order (see subs.(4)(a)) must have been incorporated into them.

There is a default offence set out in accordance with the scheme of the Act (see Sch.3).

PART 27

MERGERS AND DIVISIONS OF PUBLIC COMPANIES

CHAPTER I

INTRODUCTORY

902.   Application of this Part

(1) This Part applies where-
   (a) a compromise or arrangement is proposed between a public company and-
      (i)   its creditors or any class of them, or
      (ii) its members or any class of them,
   for the purposes of, or in connection with, a scheme for the reconstruction of any company or companies or the amalgamation of any two or more companies,
   (b) the scheme involves-
      (i)   a merger (as defined in section 904), or
      (ii) a division (as defined in section 919), and
   (c) the consideration for the transfer (or each of the transfers) envisaged is to be shares in the transferee company (or one or more of the transferee companies) receivable by members of the transferor company (or transferor companies), with or without any cash payment to members.
(2) In this Part-
   (a) a "new company" means a company formed for the purposes of, or in connection with, the scheme, and
   (b) an "existing company" means a company other than one formed for the purposes of, or in connection with, the scheme.
(3) This Part does not apply where the company in respect of which the compromise or arrangement is proposed is being wound up.

GENERAL NOTE

This Part of the Act restates s.427A and Sch.15B to the 1985 Act with no changes of substance apart from a new independence requirement for the expert or valuer. It provides for additional requirements for the implementation of a scheme of arrangement under the previous Part of this Act where the purpose of the scheme is to effect certain types of merger or division of public companies. These provisions originate from the Third EC directive on Mergers (Dir 78/855/EEC, July 25, 1978), and the Sixth EC directive on Divisions (Dir 82/891/EEC, December 17, 1982), of public companies.

Section 427A and Sch.15B were originally introduced into the 1985 Act by the Companies (Mergers and Divisions) Regulations 1987 (SI 1987/1991). In restating these provisions in this Act, one section and 15 paragraphs of a Schedule have been transformed into no less than 40 sections. This is largely due to the fact that many of the additional requirements and exceptions applicable to mergers and divisions are now dealt with separately, even though most of those requirements apply in identical fashion to both.

In the two cases of mergers specified in s.904, and a division as specified in s.919, the court cannot sanction a scheme unless no fewer than eight additional requirements are satisfied (with two more for divisions). There are, however, seven exemptions from some or all of these requirements in different circumstances. There are also knock-on exemptions from aspects of the previous Part.

Sections 902, 903 and 935-941 apply to both mergers and divisions; ss.904-918 to mergers; and ss.919-934 to divisions.

This section restates s.427A(1) and (4) of the 1985 Act with some additional drafting inserts.

Subsection (1)

This subsection restates subs.427A(1) of the 1985 Act and provides for the scope of this Part. It defines that scope partly by reference to the two types of merger and a division as specified now in ss.904 and 919, and partly itself in para.(c) by limiting such mergers and divisions to those involving a share exchange between the transferor and transferee companies.

Subsection (2)

This subsection is new in the sense that it has taken the wording formerly used to delineate companies in the definition of a relevant merger or division and given those companies a new short title of "new" or "existing" company. That shorthand is now used in the subsequent sections, including the definition sections, ss.904 and 919.

Subsection (3)

This subsection restates s.427A(4) of the 1985 Act and so excludes voluntary reconstructions under s.110 of the Insolvency Act 1986 from these requirements.

903. Relationship of this Part to Part 26

(1) The court must not sanction the compromise or arrangement under Part 26 (arrangements and reconstructions) unless the relevant requirements of this Part have been complied with.

(2) The requirements applicable to a merger are specified in sections 905 to 914.

Certain of those requirements, and certain general requirements of Part 26, are modified or excluded by the provisions of sections 915 to 918.

(3) The requirements applicable to a division are specified in sections 920 to 930.

Certain of those requirements, and certain general requirements of Part 26, are modified or excluded by the provisions of sections 931 to 934.

GENERAL NOTE

This section imposes the additional restrictions etc of this Part on the relevant schemes of arrangement under s.902. As such it restates the obligations imposed by s.427A(1) and Sch.15B to the 1985 Act.

Subsections (2) and (3) are new drafting provisions and confirm the separation of most of the provisions providing for the imposing of the restrictions etc as between mergers and divisions, which were formerly treated together.

CHAPTER 2

MERGER

Introductory

904. Mergers and merging companies

(1) The scheme involves a merger where under the scheme-
   (a) the undertaking, property and liabilities of one or more public companies, including the company in respect of which the compromise or arrangement is proposed, are to be transferred to another existing public company (a "merger by absorption"), or
   (b) the undertaking, property and liabilities of two or more public companies, including the company in respect of which the compromise or arrangement is proposed, are to be transferred to a new company, whether or not a public company, (a "merger by formation of a new company").

(2) References in this Part to "the merging companies" are-
   (a) in relation to a merger by absorption, to the transferor and transferee companies;
   (b) in relation to a merger by formation of a new company, to the transferor companies.

GENERAL NOTE

Subsection (1)

Subsection (1) restates the first two parts of s.427A(2) of the 1985 Act. It provides for the two types of merger subject to the additional requirements. These were formerly known as Case 1 and Case 2 in the 1985 Act. There are no changes of substance. Note that in the case of a merger by formation, the new company does not have to be a public company.

These definitions must be read in conjunction with s.902(1)(c). For the terms "new" and "existing" company see s.902(2).

Property and liabilities - see s.941.

Subsection (2)

Subsection (2) is a drafting addition. Part (a) is somewhat unsurprising since there are no other companies directly involved. Part (b) makes it clear that the additional requirements do not apply to the new company.

Requirements applicable to merger

905. Draft terms of scheme (merger)

(1) A draft of the proposed terms of the scheme must be drawn up and adopted by the directors of the merging companies.

(2) The draft terms must give particulars of at least the following matters-

   (a) in respect of each transferor company and the transferee company-

      (i) its name,

      (ii) the address of its registered office, and

      (iii) whether it is a company limited by shares or a company limited by guarantee and having a share capital;

   (b) the number of shares in the transferee company to be allotted to members of a transferor company for a given number of their shares (the "share exchange ratio") and the amount of any cash payment;

   (c) the terms relating to the allotment of shares in the transferee company;

   (d) the date from which the holding of shares in the transferee company will entitle the holders to participate in profits, and any special conditions affecting that entitlement;

   (e) the date from which the transactions of a transferor company are to be treated for accounting purposes as being those of the transferee company;

   (f) any rights or restrictions attaching to shares or other securities in the transferee company to be allotted under the scheme to the holders of shares or other securities in a transferor company to which any special rights or restrictions attach, or the measures proposed concerning them;

   (g) any amount of benefit paid or given or intended to be paid or given-

      (i) to any of the experts referred to in section 909 (expert's report), or

      (ii) to any director of a merging company,

   and the consideration for the payment of benefit.

(3) The requirements in subsection (2)(b), (c) and (d) are subject to section 915 (circumstances in which certain particulars not required).

GENERAL NOTE

This section restates paras 2(1)(a), 2(2) and 12(2) of Sch.15B to the 1985 Act in so far as they applied to mergers. There are no changes of substance, so that the obligation on the directors of all the merging companies (as defined in s.904(2)) to adopt draft terms of the merger and the minimum content of such a draft remain the same.

There are still seven areas to be included in the draft terms, three of which may be waived if s.915 applies.

906. Publication of draft terms (merger)

(1) The directors of each of the merging companies must deliver a copy of the draft terms to the registrar.

(2) The registrar must publish in the Gazette notice of receipt by him from that company of a copy of the draft terms.

(3) That notice must be published at least one month before the date of any meeting of that company summoned for the purpose of approving the scheme.

GENERAL NOTE

This section restates paras 2(1)(b) and 2(1)(c) of Sch.15B to the 1985 Act in so far as they applied to mergers. There are no changes of substance, so that the obligation to deliver a copy of the draft terms to the registrar and their publication by him in the relevant Gazette (depending on the jurisdiction of the approving court) at least one month before any meetings held under s.896 remain.

The one exception to this requirement only applies in the case of a division.

907. Approval of members of merging companies

(1) The scheme must be approved by a majority in number, representing 75% in value, of each class of members of each of the merging companies, present and voting either in person or by proxy at a meeting.

(2) This requirement is subject to sections 916, 917 and 918 (circumstances in which meetings of members not required).

GENERAL NOTE

This section restates para.1 of Sch.15B to the 1985 Act as it applied to mergers. There are no changes of substance, so that meetings of all relevant classes of shareholders and the 75 per cent majority approval requirement imposed by s.904 on the transferor company(ies) are also imposed on the transferee company(ies).

The exceptions to this requirement, now in ss.916-918, have also been continued.

908. Directors' explanatory report (merger)

(1) The directors of each of the merging companies must draw up and adopt a report.

(2) The report must consist of-

    (a) the statement required by section 897 (statement explaining effect of compromise or arrangement), and

    (b) insofar as that statement does not deal with the following matters, a further statement-

        (i) setting out the legal and economic grounds for the draft terms, and in particular for the share exchange ratio, and

        (ii) specifying any special valuation difficulties.

(3) The requirement in this section is subject to section 915 (circumstances in which reports not required).

GENERAL NOTE

This section restates paras 3(a) and 4(1) of Sch.15B to the 1985 Act in so far as they applied to mergers. There are no changes of substance, so that the obligation on the directors of all the merging companies (see s.904(2)) to draw up and adopt an explanatory report and its minimum content remain the same. Note that this incorporates the explanatory statement required for all schemes of arrangement under s.897 of this Act.

The exceptions to this requirement now in s.915 are also continued.

909.   Expert's report (merger)

(1) An expert's report must be drawn up on behalf of each of the merging companies.
(2) The report required is a written report on the draft terms to the members of the company.
(3) The court may on the joint application of all the merging companies approve the appointment of a joint expert to draw up a single report on behalf of all those companies.
If no such appointment is made, there must be a separate expert's report to the members of each merging company drawn up by a separate expert appointed on behalf of that company.
(4) The expert must be a person who-
    (a) is eligible for appointment as a statutory auditor (see section 1212), and
    (b) meets the independence requirement in section 936.
(5) The expert's report must-
    (a) indicate the method or methods used to arrive at the share exchange ratio;
    (b) give an opinion as to whether the method or methods used are reasonable in all the circumstances of the case, indicate the values arrived at using each such method and (if there is more than one method) give an opinion on the relative importance attributed to such methods in arriving at the value decided on;
    (c) describe any special valuation difficulties that have arisen;
    (d) state whether in the expert's opinion the share exchange ratio is reasonable; and
    (e) in the case of a valuation made by a person other than himself (see section 935), state that it appeared to him reasonable to arrange for it to be so made or to accept a valuation so made.
(6) The expert (or each of them) has-
    (a) the right of access to all such documents of all the merging companies, and
    (b) the right to require from the companies' officers all such information,
as he thinks necessary for the purposes of making his report.
(7) The requirement in this section is subject to section 915 (circumstances in which reports not required).

GENERAL NOTE

This section restates paras 3(d) and 5(1)-(3), (7) and (8) of Sch.15B to the 1985 Act in so far as they applied to mergers. There are no changes of substance, so that the obligation to produce a separate expert's report on the draft terms of the merger (see s.905) by each of the merging companies, unless the court allows a joint report, remains: subss.(1)-(3). So too do the requirements as to the contents of the report (subs.(5)) and the powers of the expert(s) to access documents and information (subs.(6)).

The exception to this requirement, now in s.915, is also continued.

The minimum qualifications for an expert in subs.(4) have been amended to take into account the introduction of the concept of a statutory auditor in Pt 42 of this Act and to take on board the concepts of independence in that Part, now formulated for both mergers and divisions in ss.936 and 937.

The other parts of para.5 of Sch.15B allowing an expert to obtain a valuation from a more suitably qualified person are now in s.935, which also applies to both mergers and divisions.

910.   Supplementary accounting statement (merger)

(1) If the last annual accounts of any of the merging companies relate to a financial year ending more than seven months before the first meeting of the company summoned for the purposes of approving the scheme, the directors of that company must prepare a supplementary accounting statement.
(2) That statement must consist of-
    (a) a balance sheet dealing with the state of affairs of the company as at a date not more than three months before the draft terms were adopted by the directors, and
    (b) where the company would be required under section 399 to prepare group accounts if that date were the last day of a financial year, a consolidated balance sheet dealing with

the state of affairs of the company and the undertakings that would be included in such a consolidation.

(3) The requirements of this Act (and where relevant Article 4 of the IAS Regulation) as to the balance sheet forming part of a company's annual accounts, and the matters to be included in notes to it, apply to the balance sheet required for an accounting statement under this section, with such modifications as are necessary by reason of its being prepared otherwise than as at the last day of a financial year.

(4) The provisions of section 414 as to the approval and signing of accounts apply to the balance sheet required for an accounting statement under this section.

GENERAL NOTE

This section restates paras 6(1)(e) and (2)-(4) of Sch.15B to the 1985 Act in so far as they applied to mergers. There are minor amendments to take into account changes in this Act to the formation and approval of accounts but no changes of substance.

Therefore the obligation to produce a supplementary accounting statement if the accounts of any of the merging companies (see s.904(2)) are more than seven months old, the nature of that statement, its requirement to comply with accounting standards and its approval, all remain.

Subsections (3) and (4) contain modified wording to reflect the changes to those standards and approval.

911. Inspection of documents (merger)

(1) The members of each of the merging companies must be able, during the period specified below-
    (a) to inspect at the registered office of that company copies of the documents listed below relating to that company and every other merging company, and
    (b) to obtain copies of those documents or any part of them on request free of charge.

(2) The period referred to above is the period-
    (a) beginning one month before, and
    (b) ending on the date of,
the first meeting of the members, or any class of members, of the company for the purposes of approving the scheme.

(3) The documents referred to above are-
    (a) the draft terms;
    (b) the directors' explanatory report;
    (c) the expert's report;
    (d) the company's annual accounts and reports for the last three financial years ending on or before the first meeting of the members, or any class of members, of the company summoned for the purposes of approving the scheme; and
    (e) any supplementary accounting statement required by section 910.

(4) The requirements of subsection (3)(b) and (c) are subject to section 915 (circumstances in which reports not required).

GENERAL NOTE

This section restates paras 3(e) and 6(1) of Sch.15B to the 1985 Act in so far as they applied to mergers. There are no changes of substance, so that the obligation to allow inspection of and the obtaining of copies of the various additional documents required under the previous sections of this Part by the members of the merging companies (see s.904(2)) remains. So too does the minimum time to be allowed for such inspection, etc.

The exception to this obligation, now in s.915, also remains. This is where there is no obligation to produce some or all of the documents.

912.   Approval of articles of new transferee company (merger)

In the case of a merger by formation of a new company, the articles of the transferee company, or a draft of them, must be approved by ordinary resolution of the transferor company or, as the case may be, each of the transferor companies.

GENERAL NOTE

   This section restates para.3(f) of Sch.15B to the 1985 Act in so far as it applied to mergers. There are no changes of substance but the wording has been modified to take into account the diminished role of the memorandum under this Act. The obligation on the members of the transferor companies in a merger by formation (see s.904(1)) to approve the constitution of the new transferee company is thus limited to the latter's articles.

913.   Protection of holders of securities to which special rights attached (merger)

(1) The scheme must provide that where any securities of a transferor company (other than shares) to which special rights are attached are held by a person otherwise than as a member or creditor of the company, that person is to receive rights in the transferee company of equivalent value.
(2) Subsection (1) does not apply if-
    (a) the holder has agreed otherwise, or
    (b) the holder is, or under the scheme is to be, entitled to have the securities purchased by the transferee company on terms that the court considers reasonable.

GENERAL NOTE

   This section restates para.8 of Sch.15B to the 1985 Act in so far as it applied to mergers. There are no changes of substance so that the obligation to continue on a merger any special rights attached to securities of a transferor company does not apply to shares. The exceptions in subs.(2) remain the same.

914.   No allotment of shares to transferor company or its nominee (merger)

The scheme must not provide for shares in the transferee company to be allotted to a transferor company (or its nominee) in respect of shares in the transferor company held by it (or its nominee).

GENERAL NOTE

   This section restates para.7 of Sch.15B to the 1985 Act. There are no changes of substance, only of drafting, so that the prohibition lies against the scheme and not the court order. The section applies where the transferor company holds its own shares (treasury shares - see s.724 of this Act). In such cases no shares in the transferee company may be allotted to it in respect of those shares.

Exceptions where shares of transferor company held by transferee company

915.   Circumstances in which certain particulars and reports not required (merger)

(1) This section applies in the case of a merger by absorption where all of the relevant securities of the transferor company (or, if there is more than one transferor company, of each of them) are held by or on behalf of the transferee company.
(2) The draft terms of the scheme need not give the particulars mentioned in section 905(2)(b), (c) or (d) (particulars relating to allotment of shares to members of transferor company).
(3) Section 897 (explanatory statement to be circulated or made available) does not apply.
(4) The requirements of the following sections do not apply-
       section 908 (directors' explanatory report),
       section 909 (expert's report).

(5) The requirements of section 911 (inspection of documents) so far as relating to any document required to be drawn up under the provisions mentioned in subsection (3) above do not apply.

(6) In this section "relevant securities", in relation to a company, means shares or other securities carrying the right to vote at general meetings of the company.

GENERAL NOTE

This section restates paras 12(1)-(3) of Sch.15B to the 1985 Act in so far as they applied to mergers. There are no changes of substance, so the stated exceptions will continue to apply where, in the case of a merger by absorption, the transferor company(ies) is or are wholly owned subsidiaries (in terms of voting securities - see subs.(6)) of the transferee company.

The exceptions thus allowed are that there is no need to include details of any shares to be allotted by the transferee company, to publish an explanatory statement under s.897 of this Act, or to produce or allow the inspection etc of either a directors' explanatory statement or an expert's report. Inspection of any of those documents is also not required.

916. Circumstances in which meeting of members of transferee company not required (merger)

(1) This section applies in the case of a merger by absorption where 90% or more (but not all) of the relevant securities of the transferor company (or, if there is more than one transferor company, of each of them) are held by or on behalf of the transferee company.

(2) It is not necessary for the scheme to be approved at a meeting of the members, or any class of members, of the transferee company if the court is satisfied that the following conditions have been complied with.

(3) The first condition is that publication of notice of receipt of the draft terms by the registrar took place in respect of the transferee company at least one month before the date of the first meeting of members, or any class of members, of the transferor company summoned for the purpose of agreeing to the scheme.

(4) The second condition is that the members of the transferee company were able during the period beginning one month before, and ending on, that date-

    (a) to inspect at the registered office of the transferee company copies of the documents listed in section 911(3)(a), (d) and (e) relating to that company and the transferor company (or, if there is more than one transferor company, each of them), and

    (b) to obtain copies of those documents or any part of them on request free of charge.

(5) The third condition is that-

    (a) one or more members of the transferee company, who together held not less than 5% of the paid-up capital of the company which carried the right to vote at general meetings of the company (excluding any shares in the company held as treasury shares) would have been able, during that period, to require a meeting of each class of members to be called for the purpose of deciding whether or not to agree to the scheme, and

    (b) no such requirement was made.

(6) In this section "relevant securities", in relation to a company, means shares or other securities carrying the right to vote at general meetings of the company.

GENERAL NOTE

This section restates para.14 of Sch.15B to the 1985 Act in so far as it applies to mergers. There are no changes of substance but the former wording which incorporated the conditions in para.10(2) of Sch.15B by reference, has been replaced by setting out the conditions in full in subss.(3)-(5).

The section applies where in a merger by absorption, the transferee company holds at least 90 per cent but less than 100 per cent of the voting securities (see subs.(6)) of a transferor company. In such cases no meetings of the transferee company are required if the three conditions now set out in full are complied with. (For the position with regard to 100 per cent subsidiaries see the next section)

The first two conditions are compliance with both the publication of notice of receipt of the draft terms in the Gazette and the requirements as to inspection and copying of documents. The third condition is that 5 per cent or more of the holders of paid up voting capital of the transferee company (excluding treasury shares - see s.724) could have required meetings to be called and did not do so. Note that that requirement differs from the definition of voting securities used elsewhere in the section.

See also the following section and s.938.

917.   Circumstances in which no meetings required (merger)

(1) This section applies in the case of a merger by absorption where all of the relevant securities of the transferor company (or, if there is more than one transferor company, of each of them) are held by or on behalf of the transferee company.

(2) It is not necessary for the scheme to be approved at a meeting of the members, or any class of members, of any of the merging companies if the court is satisfied that the following conditions have been complied with.

(3) The first condition is that publication of notice of receipt of the draft terms by the registrar took place in respect of all the merging companies at least one month before the date of the court's order.

(4) The second condition is that the members of the transferee company were able during the period beginning one month before, and ending on, that date-

    (a) to inspect at the registered office of that company copies of the documents listed in section 911(3) relating to that company and the transferor company (or, if there is more than one transferor company, each of them), and

    (b) to obtain copies of those documents or any part of them on request free of charge.

(5) The third condition is that-

    (a) one or more members of the transferee company, who together held not less than 5% of the paid-up capital of the company which carried the right to vote at general meetings of the company (excluding any shares in the company held as treasury shares) would have been able, during that period, to require a meeting of each class of members to be called for the purpose of deciding whether or not to agree to the scheme, and

    (b) no such requirement was made.

(6) In this section "relevant securities", in relation to a company, means shares or other securities carrying the right to vote at general meetings of the company.

GENERAL NOTE

This section restates paras 12(1), (4) and (5) of Sch.15B to the 1985 Act. There are no changes of substance, so that it still applies where the transferor company in a merger by absorption (see s.904) is a wholly owned subsidiary of the transferee company (in terms of voting securities - see subs.(6)).

In such cases, no meetings of any of the merging companies (see s.904(2)) need be held, provided the three conditions set out in subss.(3)-(5) have been met. These conditions are: publication of the notice of the draft terms in the appropriate Gazette at least one month prior to the date of the court order sanctioning the scheme; compliance with the inspection and copying of documents provisions; and the right of 5 per cent or more of the holders of voting paid up capital (excluding treasury shares - see s.724) to require a meeting which has not been exercised. (Note the difference between that concept and that in subs.6.)

See also the following section and s.938.

Other exceptions

918.   Other circumstances in which meeting of members of transferee company not required (merger)

(1) In the case of any merger by absorption, it is not necessary for the scheme to be approved by the members of the transferee company if the court is satisfied that the following conditions have been complied with.

(2) The first condition is that publication of notice of receipt of the draft terms by the registrar took place in respect of that company at least one month before the date of the first meeting of

members, or any class of members, of the transferor company (or, if there is more than one transferor company, any of them) summoned for the purposes of agreeing to the scheme.

(3) The second condition is that the members of that company were able during the period beginning one month before, and ending on, the date of any such meeting-

    (a) to inspect at the registered office of that company copies of the documents specified in section 911(3) relating to that company and the transferor company (or, if there is more than one transferor company, each of them), and

    (b) to obtain copies of those documents or any part of them on request free of charge.

(4) The third condition is that-

    (a) one or more members of that company, who together held not less than 5% of the paid-up capital of the company which carried the right to vote at general meetings of the company (excluding any shares in the company held as treasury shares) would have been able, during that period, to require a meeting of each class of members to be called for the purpose of deciding whether or not to agree to the scheme, and

    (b) no such requirement was made.

GENERAL NOTE

This section restates para.10 of Sch.15B to the 1985 Act in so far as it applies to mergers. There are no changes of substance, so that there remains a general exception to the need to call meetings of the transferee company in the case of a merger by absorption.

There are the same three pre-conditions for this exemption: that notice of the receipt of the draft terms has been published in the appropriate Gazette; that the provisions as to inspection and copying of documents have been complied with; and that the holders of 5 per cent of the voting paid up capital (excluding treasury shares - see s.724 of this Act) had the right to request a meeting and have not done so.

See also the preceding two sections and s.938.

CHAPTER 3

DIVISION

Introductory

919. Divisions and companies involved in a division

(1) The scheme involves a division where under the scheme the undertaking, property and liabilities of the company in respect of which the compromise or arrangement is proposed are to be divided among and transferred to two or more companies each of which is either-

    (a) an existing public company, or

    (b) a new company (whether or not a public company).

(2) References in this Part to the companies involved in the division are to the transferor company and any existing transferee companies.

GENERAL NOTE

This section restates the third part of s.427A(2) of the 1985 Act. It sets out, with minor drafting changes, the definition of a division so as to fall within this Part. This was formerly known as Case 3.

This definition must be read in conjunction with s.895(1)(c). For the terms "new" and "existing" company see s.895(2). Note that a new transferee company need not be a public company.

Property and liabilities - see s.941.

Subs (2) is a drafting addition. It refers to the definitions in s.904(2).

Requirements to be complied with in case of division

920.   Draft terms of scheme (division)

(1) A draft of the proposed terms of the scheme must be drawn up and adopted by the directors
     of each of the companies involved in the division.
(2) The draft terms must give particulars of at least the following matters-
     (a) in respect of the transferor company and each transferee company-
          (i)   its name,
          (ii) the address of its registered office, and
          (iii) whether it is a company limited by shares or a company limited by guarantee and
                having a share capital;
     (b) the number of shares in a transferee company to be allotted to members of the
          transferor company for a given number of their shares (the "share exchange ratio") and
          the amount of any cash payment;
     (c) the terms relating to the allotment of shares in a transferee company;
     (d) the date from which the holding of shares in a transferee company will entitle the
          holders to participate in profits, and any special conditions affecting that entitlement;
     (e) the date from which the transactions of the transferor company are to be treated for
          accounting purposes as being those of a transferee company;
     (f) any rights or restrictions attaching to shares or other securities in a transferee company
          to be allotted under the scheme to the holders of shares or other securities in the
          transferor company to which any special rights or restrictions attach, or the measures
          proposed concerning them;
     (g) any amount of benefit paid or given or intended to be paid or given-
          (i)   to any of the experts referred to in section 924 (expert's report), or
          (ii) to any director of a company involved in the division,
     and the consideration for the payment of benefit.
(3) The draft terms must also-
     (a) give particulars of the property and liabilities to be transferred (to the extent that these
          are known to the transferor company) and their allocation among the transferee
          companies;
     (b) make provision for the allocation among and transfer to the transferee companies of
          any other property and liabilities that the transferor company has acquired or may subse-
          quently acquire; and
     (c) specify the allocation to members of the transferor company of shares in the transferee
          companies and the criteria upon which that allocation is based.

GENERAL NOTE
   This section restates paras 2(1)(a), (2) and (3) of Sch.15B to the 1985 Act in so far as they applied to divisions. There are
no changes of substance, so that the obligation on the directors of *all* the merging companies (as defined in s.904(2)) to adopt
draft terms of the merger and the minimum content of such a draft remain the same. There are still ten areas to be included;
subs.(3) provides for the three additional areas not required in the case of a merger. Unlike mergers there are no exceptions
to the required contents.
   Property and liabilities - see s.941

921.   Publication of draft terms (division)

(1) The directors of each company involved in the division must deliver a copy of the draft terms
     to the registrar.

(2) The registrar must publish in the Gazette notice of receipt by him from that company of a copy of the draft terms.

(3) That notice must be published at least one month before the date of any meeting of that company summoned for the purposes of approving the scheme.

(4) The requirements in this section are subject to section 934 (power of court to exclude certain requirements).

GENERAL NOTE

This section restates paras 2(1)(b) and 2(1)(c) of Sch.15B to the 1985 Act in so far as they applied to divisions. There are no changes of substance, so that the obligation to deliver a copy of the draft terms to the registrar and their publication by him in the relevant Gazette (depending on the jurisdiction of the approving court) at least one month before any meetings held under s.896 remain.

The one exception to this requirement applies only to divisions and allows the court to exempt any transferor or pre-existing transferee company from these obligations.

922. Approval of members of companies involved in the division

(1) The compromise or arrangement must be approved by a majority in number, representing 75% in value, of each class of members of each of the companies involved in the division, present and voting either in person or by proxy at a meeting.

(2) This requirement is subject to sections 931 and 932 (circumstances in which meeting of members not required).

GENERAL NOTE

This section restates para.1 of Sch.15B to the 1985 Act as it applied to divisions. There are no changes of substance, so that meetings of all relevant classes of shareholders and the 75 per cent majority approval requirement imposed by s.896 on the transferor company(ies) are also imposed on the transferee company(ies).

The exceptions to this requirement, now in ss.931-934, have also been continued.

923. Directors' explanatory report (division)

(1) The directors of the transferor and each existing transferee company must draw up and adopt a report.

(2) The report must consist of-
  (a) the statement required by section 897 (statement explaining effect of compromise or arrangement), and
  (b) insofar as that statement does not deal with the following matters, a further statement-
      (i) setting out the legal and economic grounds for the draft terms, and in particular for the share exchange ratio and for the criteria on which the allocation to the members of the transferor company of shares in the transferee companies was based, and
      (ii) specifying any special valuation difficulties.

(3) The report must also state-
  (a) whether a report has been made to any transferee company under section 593 (valuation of non-cash consideration for shares), and
  (b) if so, whether that report has been delivered to the registrar of companies.

(4) The requirement in this section is subject to section 933 (agreement to dispense with reports etc).

GENERAL NOTE

This section restates paras 3(a) and 4(1) and (2) of Sch.15B to the 1985 Act in so far as they applied to divisions. There are no changes of substance, so that the obligation on the directors of all the pre-existing companies involved in the division (see 919(2)) to draw up and adopt an explanatory report and its minimum content remain the same. Note that this incorporates the explanatory statement required for all schemes of arrangement under s.897 of this Act. Subsection (3) imposes additional requirements which do not apply to mergers.

The exceptions to this requirement, now in s.933, are also continued.

924.   Expert's report (division)

(1) An expert's report must be drawn up on behalf of each company involved in the division.

(2) The report required is a written report on the draft terms to the members of the company.

(3) The court may on the joint application of the companies involved in the division approve the appointment of a joint expert to draw up a single report on behalf of all those companies.

If no such appointment is made, there must be a separate expert's report to the members of each company involved in the division drawn up by a separate expert appointed on behalf of that company.

(4) The expert must be a person who-
- (a) is eligible for appointment as a statutory auditor (see section 1212), and
- (b) meets the independence requirement in section 936.

(5) The expert's report must-
- (a) indicate the method or methods used to arrive at the share exchange ratio;
- (b) give an opinion as to whether the method or methods used are reasonable in all the circumstances of the case, indicate the values arrived at using each such method and (if there is more than one method) give an opinion on the relative importance attributed to such methods in arriving at the value decided on;
- (c) describe any special valuation difficulties that have arisen;
- (d) state whether in the expert's opinion the share exchange ratio is reasonable; and
- (e) in the case of a valuation made by a person other than himself (see section 935), state that it appeared to him reasonable to arrange for it to be so made or to accept a valuation so made.

(6) The expert (or each of them) has-
- (a) the right of access to all such documents of the companies involved in the division, and
- (b) the right to require from the companies' officers all such information,

as he thinks necessary for the purposes of making his report.

(7) The requirement in this section is subject to section 933 (agreement to dispense with reports etc).

GENERAL NOTE

This section restates paras 3(d) and 5(1)-(3), (7) and (8) of Sch.15B to the 1985 Act in so far as they applied to divisions. There are no changes of substance, so that the obligation to produce a separate expert's report on the draft terms of the division (see s.923) by *each* of the companies involved in the division, unless the court allows a joint report, remains: subss.(1)-(3). So too do the requirements as to the contents of the report (subs.5) and the powers of the expert(s) to access documents and information (subs.(6)).

The exception to this requirement, now in s.933, is also continued.

The minimum qualifications for an expert in subs.(4) have been amended to take into account the introduction of the concept of a statutory auditor in Pt 42 of this Act and to take on board the concepts of independence in that Part, now formulated for both mergers and divisions in ss.936 and 937.

The other parts of para.5 of Sch.15B allowing an expert to obtain a valuation from a more suitably qualified person are now in s.935, which also applies to both mergers and divisions.

925.   Supplementary accounting statement (division)

(1) If the last annual accounts of a company involved in the division relate to a financial year ending more than seven months before the first meeting of the company summoned for the purposes of approving the scheme, the directors of that company must prepare a supplementary accounting statement.

(2) That statement must consist of-

    (a) a balance sheet dealing with the state of affairs of the company as at a date not more than three months before the draft terms were adopted by the directors, and

    (b) where the company would be required under section 399 to prepare group accounts if that date were the last day of a financial year, a consolidated balance sheet dealing with the state of affairs of the company and the undertakings that would be included in such a consolidation.

(3) The requirements of this Act (and where relevant Article 4 of the IAS Regulation) as to the balance sheet forming part of a company's annual accounts, and the matters to be included in notes to it, apply to the balance sheet required for an accounting statement under this section, with such modifications as are necessary by reason of its being prepared otherwise than as at the last day of a financial year.

(4) The provisions of section 414 as to the approval and signing of accounts apply to the balance sheet required for an accounting statement under this section.

(5) The requirement in this section is subject to section 933 (agreement to dispense with reports etc).

GENERAL NOTE

    This section restates paras 6(1)(e) and (2)-(4) of Sch.15B to the 1985 Act in so far as they applied to divisions. There are minor amendments to take into account changes in this Act in the formation and approval of accounts but no changes of substance.

    Therefore the obligation to produce a supplementary accounting statement if the accounts of any of the companies involved in the division (see s.919(2)) are more than seven months old, the nature of that statement, the requirement to comply with accounting standards and its approval all remain. Subsections (3) and (4) contain modified wording to reflect the changes to those standards and approval.

    There is an exception in s.933 where all the shareholders of all the companies involved in the division agree. There is no equivalent exception in the case of a merger.

926. Inspection of documents (division)

(1) The members of each company involved in the division must be able, during the period specified below-

    (a) to inspect at the registered office of that company copies of the documents listed below relating to that company and every other company involved in the division, and

    (b) to obtain copies of those documents or any part of them on request free of charge.

(2) The period referred to above is the period-

    (a) beginning one month before, and

    (b) ending on the date of,

the first meeting of the members, or any class of members, of the company for the purposes of approving the scheme.

(3) The documents referred to above are-

    (a) the draft terms;

    (b) the directors' explanatory report;

    (c) the expert's report;

    (d) the company's annual accounts and reports for the last three financial years ending on or before the first meeting of the members, or any class of members, of the company summoned for the purposes of approving the scheme; and

    (e) any supplementary accounting statement required by section 925.

(4) The requirements in subsection (3)(b), (c) and (e) are subject to section 933 (agreement to dispense with reports etc) and section 934 (power of court to exclude certain requirements).

GENERAL NOTE

    This section restates paras 3(e) and 6(1) of Sch.15B to the 1985 Act in so far as they applied to divisions. There are no changes of substance, so that the obligation to allow inspection of, and the obtaining of copies of, the various additional documents required under the previous sections of this Part by the members of the merging companies (see s.904(2)) remains. So too does the minimum time to be allowed for such inspection, etc.

The exceptions to this obligation, now in ss.933 and 934, also remain. These are either where there is no obligation to produce some or all of the documents or there is unanimous consent by the members of all the companies involved in the division.

927.   Report on material changes of assets of transferor company (division)

(1) The directors of the transferor company must report-
    (a) to every meeting of the members, or any class of members, of that company summoned for the purpose of agreeing to the scheme, and
    (b) to the directors of each existing transferee company,
any material changes in the property and liabilities of the transferor company between the date when the draft terms were adopted and the date of the meeting in question.

(2) The directors of each existing transferee company must in turn-
    (a) report those matters to every meeting of the members, or any class of members, of that company summoned for the purpose of agreeing to the scheme, or
    (b) send a report of those matters to every member entitled to receive notice of such a meeting.

(3) The requirement in this section is subject to section 933 (agreement to dispense with reports etc).

GENERAL NOTE

This section restates paras 3(b) and (c) of Sch.15B to the 1985 Act. There are no changes of substance and the obligation on the directors of the transferor companies to notify their members and the directors of any pre-existing transferee company of any material changes to the value of their company's property and liabilities between the adoption of the draft terms and the meetings, remains. There is also a consequential duty on the transferee directors to notify their members.

For property and liabilities, see s.941.

This obligation has only ever applied to divisions and is subject to s.933 where the obligation may be waived by unanimous agreement.

928.   Approval of articles of new transferee company (division)

The articles of every new transferee company, or a draft of them, must be approved by ordinary resolution of the transferor company.

GENERAL NOTE

This section restates para.3(f) of Sch.15B to the 1985 Act in so far as it applied to divisions. There are no changes of substance, but the wording has been modified to take into account the diminished role of the memorandum under this Act. The obligation on the members of the transferor companies in a division (see s.919(1)) to approve the constitution of a new transferee company is thus limited to the latter's articles.

929.   Protection of holders of securities to which special rights attached (division)

(1) The scheme must provide that where any securities of the transferor company (other than shares) to which special rights are attached are held by a person otherwise than as a member or creditor of the company, that person is to receive rights in a transferee company of equivalent value.

(2) Subsection (1) does not apply if-
    (a) the holder has agreed otherwise, or
    (b) the holder is, or under the scheme is to be, entitled to have the securities purchased by a transferee company on terms that the court considers reasonable.

GENERAL NOTE

This section restates para.8 of Sch.15B to the 1985 Act in so far as it applied to divisions. There are no changes of substance, so that the obligation to continue on a merger any special rights attached to securities of a transferor company does not apply to shares.

The exceptions in subs.(2) remain the same.

930. No allotment of shares to transferor company or its nominee (division)

The scheme must not provide for shares in a transferee company to be allotted to the transferor company (or its nominee) in respect of shares in the transferor company held by it (or its nominee).

GENERAL NOTE

This section restates para.7 of Sch.15B to the 1985 Act in so far as it applied to divisions. There are no changes of substance, only of drafting, so that the prohibition lies against the scheme and not the court order. The section applies where the transferor company holds its own shares (treasury shares - see s.724). In such cases no shares in the transferee company may be allotted to it in respect of those shares.

Exceptions where shares of transferor company held by transferee company

931. Circumstances in which meeting of members of transferor company not required (division)

(1) This section applies in the case of a division where all of the shares or other securities of the transferor company carrying the right to vote at general meetings of the company are held by or on behalf of one or more existing transferee companies.

(2) It is not necessary for the scheme to be approved by a meeting of the members, or any class of members, of the transferor company if the court is satisfied that the following conditions have been complied with.

(3) The first condition is that publication of notice of receipt of the draft terms by the registrar took place in respect of all the companies involved in the division at least one month before the date of the court's order.

(4) The second condition is that the members of every company involved in the division were able during the period beginning one month before, and ending on, that date-

    (a) to inspect at the registered office of their company copies of the documents listed in section 926(3) relating to every company involved in the division, and

    (b) to obtain copies of those documents or any part of them on request free of charge.

(5) The third condition is that-

    (a) one or more members of the transferor company, who together held not less than 5% of the paid-up capital of the company (excluding any shares in the company held as treasury shares) would have been able, during that period, to require a meeting of each class of members to be called for the purpose of deciding whether or not to agree to the scheme, and

    (b) no such requirement was made.

(6) The fourth condition is that the directors of the transferor company have sent-

    (a) to every member who would have been entitled to receive notice of a meeting to agree to the scheme (had any such meeting been called), and

    (b) to the directors of every existing transferee company,

a report of any material change in the property and liabilities of the transferor company between the date when the terms were adopted by the directors and the date one month before the date of the court's order.

GENERAL NOTE

This section restates para.13 of Sch.15B to the 1985 Act which only applied to divisions. There are only drafting changes so that meetings of a transferor company (which would be otherwise be required not only by s.922 but also by s.896) may still be dispensed with if all the voting securities of that company are already owned by one or more of the pre-existing transferee companies.

There are four conditions for this waiver. There must be compliance with the three obligations as to the draft terms of the division in ss.921, 925 and 926 and there must be the right for holders of 5 per cent of the paid up capital of the transferor company (excluding treasury shares - see s.724) to require a meeting to be held which has not been exercised. Note that the requirement differs from the concept of voting shares and securities used elsewhere in the section.

See also the following section and s.938.

Other exceptions

932.　Circumstances in which meeting of members of transferee company not required (division)

(1)　In the case of a division, it is not necessary for the scheme to be approved by the members of a transferee company if the court is satisfied that the following conditions have been complied with in relation to that company.

(2)　The first condition is that publication of notice of receipt of the draft terms by the registrar took place in respect of that company at least one month before the date of the first meeting of members of the transferor company summoned for the purposes of agreeing to the scheme.

(3)　The second condition is that the members of that company were able during the period beginning one month before, and ending on, that date-

　　(a)　to inspect at the registered office of that company copies of the documents specified in section 926(3) relating to that company and every other company involved in the division, and

　　(b)　to obtain copies of those documents or any part of them on request free of charge.

(4)　The third condition is that-

　　(a)　one or more members of that company, who together held not less than 5% of the paid-up capital of the company which carried the right to vote at general meetings of the company (excluding any shares in the company held as treasury shares) would have been able, during that period, to require a meeting of each class of members to be called for the purpose of deciding whether or not to agree to the scheme, and

　　(b)　no such requirement was made.

(5)　The first and second conditions above are subject to section 934 (power of court to exclude certain requirements).

GENERAL NOTE

This section restates para.10 of Sch.15B to the 1985 Act in so far as it applied to divisions. There are no changes of sub-stance, so that there remains a general exception to the need to call meetings of the transferee company under s.922 if three conditions are satisfied.

These conditions are: that notice of the receipt of the draft terms has been published in the appropriate Gazette; that the provisions as to inspection and copying of documents have been complied with; and that the holders of 5 per cent of the voting paid up capital (excluding treasury shares - see s.724 of this Act) had the right to request a meeting and have not done so.

See also the preceding section and ss.934 and 938.

933.　Agreement to dispense with reports etc (division)

(1)　If all members holding shares in, and all persons holding other securities of, the companies involved in the division, being shares or securities that carry a right to vote in general meetings of the company in question, so agree, the following requirements do not apply.

(2)　The requirements that may be dispensed with under this section are-

    (a) the requirements of-
        (i) section 923 (directors' explanatory report),
        (ii) section 924 (expert's report),
        (iii) section 925 (supplementary accounting statement), and
        (iv) section 927 (report on material changes in assets of transferor company); and
    (b) the requirements of section 926 (inspection of documents) so far as relating to any document required to be drawn up under the provisions mentioned in paragraph (a)(i), (ii) or (iii) above.
(3) For the purposes of this section-
    (a) the members, or holders of other securities, of a company, and
    (b) whether shares or other securities carry a right to vote in general meetings of the company,
are determined as at the date of the application to the court under section 896.

GENERAL NOTE

    This section restates paras 11(1) and (2) of Sch.15B to the 1985 Act which only applied to divisions. There are no changes of substance and all the voting members (see subs.(1)) of the companies involved in a division (see s.919(2)), acting unanimously, may continue to waive a number of the additional requirements imposed by this Part.

    Under subs.(3) the voting members concerned are those as at the date of the initial application to the court to summon meetings under the scheme (s.896).

    The obligations which may be so waived are those in ss.923, 924, 925 and 927. See also the following section.

934. Power of court to exclude certain requirements (division)

(1) In the case of a division, the court may by order direct that-
    (a) in relation to any company involved in the division, the requirements of-
        (i) section 921 (publication of draft terms), and
        (ii) section 926 (inspection of documents),
    do not apply, and
    (b) in relation to an existing transferee company, section 932 (circumstances in which meeting of members of transferee company not required) has effect with the omission of the first and second conditions specified in that section,
if the court is satisfied that the following conditions will be fulfilled in relation to that company.
(2) The first condition is that the members of that company will have received, or will have been able to obtain free of charge, copies of the documents listed in section 926-
    (a) in time to examine them before the date of the first meeting of the members, or any class of members, of that company summoned for the purposes of agreeing to the scheme, or
    (b) in the case of an existing transferee company where in the circumstances described in section 932 no meeting is held, in time to require a meeting as mentioned in subsection (4) of that section.
(3) The second condition is that the creditors of that company will have received or will have been able to obtain free of charge copies of the draft terms in time to examine them-
    (a) before the date of the first meeting of the members, or any class of members, of the company summoned for the purposes of agreeing to the scheme, or
    (b) in the circumstances mentioned in subsection (2)(b) above, at the same time as the members of the company.
(4) The third condition is that no prejudice would be caused to the members or creditors of the transferor company or any transferee company by making the order in question.

GENERAL NOTE

    This section restates paras 11(3) and (4) of Sch.15B to the 1985 Act which only applied to divisions. There are no changes of substance and the court may continue to order that certain requirements imposed by this Part do not apply if specified conditions have been met.

Subsection (1)

The obligations which can be so disapplied are those under ss.921 and 926 as to publication and inspection of the draft terns and documents. There is also the power to disapply those requirements from the list of pre-conditions for a transferee company to dispense with meetings under s.932.

Subsection (2)

The conditions require first that the relevant members and creditors have received or can receive free of charge copies of the documents which can be inspected under s.926 (draft terms, expert's report, explanatory statement, accounts for the last three years and supplementary accounting statement). This must either be before the meeting summoned under s.922, or, if there is to be no meeting, in time to exercise the right to ask for one under s.932(4). The second condition is the absence of prejudice to any member or creditor of any transferor or transferee company.

CHAPTER 4

SUPPLEMENTARY PROVISIONS

Expert's report and related matters

935.　Expert's report: valuation by another person

(1) Where it appears to an expert-
　　(a) that a valuation is reasonably necessary to enable him to draw up his report, and
　　(b) that it is reasonable for that valuation, or part of it, to be made by (or for him to accept a valuation made by) another person who-
　　　　(i) appears to him to have the requisite knowledge and experience to make the valuation or that part of it, and
　　　　(ii) meets the independence requirement in section 936,
he may arrange for or accept such a valuation, together with a report which will enable him to make his own report under section 909 or 924.

(2) Where any valuation is made by a person other than the expert himself, the latter's report must state that fact and must also-
　　(a) state the former's name and what knowledge and experience he has to carry out the valuation, and
　　(b) describe so much of the undertaking, property and liabilities as was valued by the other person, and the method used to value them, and specify the date of the valuation.

GENERAL NOTE

This section restates paras 5(4) and (6) modified to take into account the incorporation of the new criteria on the independence of experts and valuers, applied in Pt 42 of this Act, in the following two sections. The section applies to expert's reports for both mergers (s.909) and divisions (s.924).

The section allows an expert to appoint a valuer to assist him in making his report. There are requirements as to the competence and independence of the valuer and as to the inclusion of the valuer's report in the expert's report.

Property and liabilities - see, s.941.

936.　Experts and valuers: independence requirement

(1) A person meets the independence requirement for the purposes of section 909 or 924 (expert's report) or section 935 (valuation by another person) only if-
　　(a) he is not-
　　　　(i) an officer or employee of any of the companies concerned in the scheme, or
　　　　(ii) a partner or employee of such a person, or a partnership of which such a person is a partner;

(b) he is not-
    (i) an officer or employee of an associated undertaking of any of the companies concerned in the scheme, or
    (ii) a partner or employee of such a person, or a partnership of which such a person is a partner; and
(c) there does not exist between-
    (i) the person or an associate of his, and
    (ii) any of the companies concerned in the scheme or an associated undertaking of such a company,

a connection of any such description as may be specified by regulations made by the Secretary of State.

(2) An auditor of a company is not regarded as an officer or employee of the company for this purpose.

(3) For the purposes of this section-
    (a) the "companies concerned in the scheme" means every transferor and existing transferee company;
    (b) "associated undertaking", in relation to a company, means-
        (i) a parent undertaking or subsidiary undertaking of the company, or
        (ii) a subsidiary undertaking of a parent undertaking of the company; and
    (c) "associate" has the meaning given by section 937.

(4) Regulations under this section are subject to negative resolution procedure.

GENERAL NOTE

This section is new and replaces para.5(3) of Sch.15B to the 1985 Act. It is modelled on s.1214 of this Act which applies to statutory auditors.

Subsections (1)-(3)

This subsection sets out the three restrictions so as to create the independence requirement of experts and valuers appointed under ss.909, 924 and 935. The expert or valuer cannot be an officer (but see subs.(2)) or employee of any company involved in the merger or division (see ss.904 and 919) or of an associated undertaking (see subs.(3)). Nor can he be a partner or employee of any such officer or employee.

Further there must not exist a connection (to be specified in regulations under subs.(4)) between the person or an associate (see the next section) and any of the companies concerned in the scheme (see subs.(3)) or associated undertakings (see subs.(3)).

Subsection (4)

For the negative resolution procedure see s.1289.

937. Experts and valuers: meaning of "associate"

(1) This section defines "associate" for the purposes of section 936 (experts and valuers: independence requirement).

(2) In relation to an individual, "associate" means-
    (a) that individual's spouse or civil partner or minor child or step-child,
    (b) any body corporate of which that individual is a director, and
    (c) any employee or partner of that individual.

(3) In relation to a body corporate, "associate" means-
    (a) any body corporate of which that body is a director,
    (b) any body corporate in the same group as that body, and
    (c) any employee or partner of that body or of any body corporate in the same group.

(4) In relation to a partnership that is a legal person under the law by which it is governed, "associate" means-
    (a) any body corporate of which that partnership is a director,
    (b) any employee of or partner in that partnership, and

(c) any person who is an associate of a partner in that partnership.

(5) In relation to a partnership that is not a legal person under the law by which it is governed, "associate" means any person who is an associate of any of the partners.

(6) In this section, in relation to a limited liability partnership, for "director" read "member".

GENERAL NOTE

This new section defines the concept of an associate for the purposes of establishing the independence requirement of experts and valuers under the previous section. It is modelled on s.1260 of this Act which relates to statutory auditors.

There are four different provisions depending upon the legal status of the principal involved. These are: individuals; bodies corporate (companies and LLPs - see subs.(6)); partnerships with legal personality (which would include Scottish and many continental partnerships); and partnerships without such personality (e.g. English, Northern Irish and Irish partnerships).

Each of these has its own list of associates. It does not appear that the definition of a group, applied by s.1261 to s.1260, has been applied to this section.

Powers of the court

938. Power of court to summon meeting of members or creditors of existing transferee company

(1) The court may order a meeting of-
    (a) the members of an existing transferee company, or any class of them, or
    (b) the creditors of an existing transferee company, or any class of them,
to be summoned in such manner as the court directs.

(2) An application for such an order may be made by-
    (a) the company concerned,
    (b) a member or creditor of the company, or
    (c) if an administration order is in force in relation to the company, the administrator.

GENERAL NOTE

This section restates s.427A(3) of the 1985 Act. There are no changes of substance and the power of the court to summon a meeting of the members or creditors of an existing transferee company is preserved.

This power is necessary since such meetings are required for schemes under this Part, ss.907 (mergers) and 922 (divisions), but the court only has the power to summon meetings of transferor companies under s.896. This section mirrors the powers of the court under s.900 and the possible applicants under s.899 (with the omission of a liquidator which is not relevant to schemes under this Part).

939. Court to fix date for transfer of undertaking etc of transferor company

(1) Where the court sanctions the compromise or arrangement, it must-
    (a) in the order sanctioning the compromise or arrangement, or
    (b) in a subsequent order under section 900 (powers of court to facilitate reconstruction or amalgamation),
fix a date on which the transfer (or transfers) to the transferee company (or transferee companies) of the undertaking, property and liabilities of the transferor company is (or are) to take place.

(2) Any such order that provides for the dissolution of the transferor company must fix the same date for the dissolution.

(3) If it is necessary for the transferor company to take steps to ensure that the undertaking, property and liabilities are fully transferred, the court must fix a date, not later than six months after the date fixed under subsection (1), by which such steps must be taken.

(4) In that case, the court may postpone the dissolution of the transferor company until that date.

(5) The court may postpone or further postpone the date fixed under subsection (3) if it is satisfied that the steps mentioned cannot be completed by the date (or latest date) fixed under that subsection.

GENERAL NOTE

This section restates para.9 of Sch.15B to the 1985 Act and applies to both mergers and divisions.

Subsections (1) and (2)

There are no changes of substance so that the court when sanctioning a scheme subject to this Part (under either ss.899 or 903) must fix a date on which the relevant transfer from the transferor to the transferee company and any dissolution of the transferor company (which is envisaged in this Part) is to take place.

Property and liabilities - see s.941.

Subsections (3)-(5)

That date may be postponed initially for up to six months to allow for the transfer and dissolution to take effect. Further postponements may also be applied for.

Liability of transferee companies

940.   Liability of transferee companies for each other's defaults

(1) In the case of a division, each transferee company is jointly and severally liable for any liability transferred to any other transferee company under the scheme to the extent that the other company has made default in satisfying that liability. This is subject to the following provisions.
(2) If a majority in number representing 75% in value of the creditors or any class of creditors of the transferor company, present and voting either in person or by proxy at a meeting summoned for the purposes of agreeing to the scheme, so agree, subsection (1) does not apply in relation to the liabilities owed to the creditors or that class of creditors.
(3) A transferee company is not liable under this section for an amount greater than the net value transferred to it under the scheme.

The "net value transferred" is the value at the time of the transfer of the property transferred to it under the scheme less the amount at that date of the liabilities so transferred.

GENERAL NOTE

This section restates para.15 of Sch.15B to the 1985 Act which only applied to divisions. There are no changes of substance and the liability of each transferee company for liabilities of the transferor transferred to any of the transferee companies remains. The liability is joint and several but it is limited to the net value transferred to the particular transferee company.

Net value transferred is defined at the end of subs.(3).

Property and liabilities - see s.941.

Subsection (2) allows a 75 per cent majority in value of the creditors (or any class) of the transferor company to waive the rights under this section at a scheme meeting.

Interpretation

941.   Meaning of "liabilities" and "property"

In this Part-
>   "liabilities" includes duties;
>   "property" includes property, rights and powers of every description.

GENERAL NOTE

   This section, restating ss.426(6) and 427A(8) of the 1985 Act provides definitions for the concepts of liabilities and property. They are exactly the same as are provided by s.900(5) for all schemes of arrangement.

PART 28

TAKEOVERS ETC

CHAPTER I

THE TAKEOVER PANEL

The Panel and its rules

942.   The Panel

(1) The body known as the Panel on Takeovers and Mergers ("the Panel") is to have the functions conferred on it by or under this Chapter.

(2) The Panel may do anything that it considers necessary or expedient for the purposes of, or in connection with, its functions.

(3) The Panel may make arrangements for any of its functions to be discharged by-
>   (a) a committee or sub-committee of the Panel, or
>   (b) an officer or member of staff of the Panel, or a person acting as such.

This is subject to section 943(4) and (5).

GENERAL NOTE

   Section 492 gives the Takeover Panel the statutory authority to regulate all takeovers, not merely those subject to the Takeovers Directive (Directive 2004/25/EC) ("the Directive"). Prior to the implementation of the Takeovers Directive on May 20, 2006, the Takeover Panel was an independent, self regulating body set up by the main institutions and organisations with an involvement in public company takeovers. The Panel was founded in 1968. Its main functions were and continue to be the issue and administration of the City Code on Takeovers and Mergers ("the Code") and the supervision and regulation of public company takeovers. Its central objective is to ensure fair treatment for all shareholders in takeover bids. The members of the Panel include the main representatives of the major investing institutions, the Confederation of British Industry, the Chartered Accountants' Institute and the London Investment Banking Association. In addition there is a Chairman and there are up to two Deputy Chairmen and up to 20 other members, all appointed by the Panel.

   Although it had no statutory power until May 20, 2006, the authority of the Panel derived from the fact that its membership represented the main parties with a material interest in takeovers. Failure to comply with the Code or Panel rulings carried a number of potential sanctions, including public or private criticism and a requirement on the institutions represented on the Panel to withdraw the facilities of the securities markets from the offender. The power of these sanctions were demonstrated by the fact that defiance of Panel rulings was almost unheard of. Subsequently, the sanctions available to the Panel were bolstered by regulations made under the Financial Services Act 1986, under which the Financial Services Authority could require its members to "cold shoulder" parties who refused to comply with Panel rulings.

   The adoption by the European Union of the Takeovers Directive resulted in the requirement for these non-statutory arrangements to be replaced by regulation by a body with statutory powers. The United Kingdom Government was keen to preserve the Takeover Panel as the supervisory authority for takeovers. This is reflected in para.7 of the Preamble to the Directive and Art.4.1 of the Directive which specifically permits the supervisory authority to be a private body.

As it would have to have statutory powers to regulate takeovers covered by the Takeover Directive, which only applied to listed companies, it would have been possible to leave the Panel's status as non-statutory in relation to the other public companies regulated by the Panel. However, for consistency, the government decided that all of the Panel's powers should be put on a statutory basis. Initially, it was intended that the granting of statutory powers to the Panel would be done through the Companies Act 2006 but as the timetable for this slipped, it was decided to grant the statutory powers through regulations made under the European Companies Act 1972. Accordingly, the Takeovers Directive (Interim Implementation) Regulations 2006 (2006/1183) came into force on May 20, 2006. Because these regulations were made under the European Communities Act, they could only apply in so far as required to give effect to the Directive. Accordingly, the regulations only applied to companies covered by the Directive and other companies, such as companies traded on the Alternative Investment Market, were still regulated under the traditional, self-regulatory system. The Interim Implementation Regulations were promulgated on fairly short notice and did barely more than the minimum necessary to comply with the obligation to implement the Directive. Sections 942-964 and 992 are far more detailed, although in practice they do not make any material change beyond the extension of the statutory powers of the Panel described above.

With effect from May 20, 2006 the Panel promulgated a new edition of the Code which, for the first time, had statutory force (at least as regards companies and transactions covered by the Directive). This statutory force derived from the Interim Implementation Regulations. That edition of the Code, with such changes as the Panel decides, will derive its entire authority from s.942, and the temporary dual jurisdiction which has existed since May 20, 2006 will come to an end.

Subsection (2)

This gives the Panel the widest possible power to carry out its functions.

Subsection (3)

The Panel operates through a number of bodies and individuals. The most significant is the executive, which is a full time body which deals with the day to day business of the Panel. In addition, there is a Hearings Committee which deals with appeals and references from the executive, and the Takeover Appeal Board which deals with appeals against rulings of the Hearings Committee. The Code Committee is responsible for promulgating the Code and amendments. (City Code on Takeovers and Mergers, May 2006 edition, Introduction).

943. Rules

(1) The Panel must make rules giving effect to Articles 3.1, 4.2, 5, 6.1 to 6.3, 7 to 9 and 13 of the Takeovers Directive.

(2) Rules made by the Panel may also make other provision-
    (a) for or in connection with the regulation of-
        (i) takeover bids,
        (ii) merger transactions, and
        (iii) transactions (not falling within sub-paragraph (i) or (ii)) that have or may have, directly or indirectly, an effect on the ownership or control of companies;
    (b) for or in connection with the regulation of things done in consequence of, or otherwise in relation to, any such bid or transaction;
    (c) about cases where-
        (i) any such bid or transaction is, or has been, contemplated or apprehended, or
        (ii) an announcement is made denying that any such bid or transaction is intended.

(3) The provision that may be made under subsection (2) includes, in particular, provision for a matter that is, or is similar to, a matter provided for by the Panel in the City Code on Takeovers and Mergers as it had effect immediately before the passing of this Act.

(4) In relation to rules made by virtue of section 957 (fees and charges), functions under this section may be discharged either by the Panel itself or by a committee of the Panel (but not otherwise).

(5) In relation to rules of any other description, the Panel must discharge its functions under this section by a committee of the Panel.

(6) Section 1 (meaning of "company") does not apply for the purposes of this section.

(7) In this section "takeover bid" includes a takeover bid within the meaning of the Takeovers Directive.

(8) In this Chapter "the Takeovers Directive" means Directive 2004/25/EC of the European Parliament and of the Council.

(9) A reference to rules in the following provisions of this Chapter is to rules under this section.

GENERAL NOTE

Subsection (1)

This requires the Panel to make rules which give effect to General Principles set out in Art.3.1 of the Directive. The Panel has already complied with this requirement in the edition of the Code which came into effect on May 20, 2006, although it is possible that the widening of its statutory powers to govern all takeovers of public companies may result in certain consequential changes. These General Principles in the Code are those set out in Art.3.1 of the Directive, replacing the previous General Principles, although the differences are not of any substance. In addition, the Panel is required to make rules concerning the companies and transactions subject to the Code, (Art.4.2 of the Directive), the provision of information (Arts 6.1-6.3 of the Directive), timing (Art.7 of the Directive), publication of information about takeovers (Art.8 of the Directive), the obligations of the board of the offeree company (Art.9 of the Directive) and the lapsing of bids, competing bids, disclosure of results of bids and irrevocability of bids and conditions permitted (Art.13 of the Directive). As with the General Principles, these requirements are already reflected in the Code.

Subsection (2)

This gives the Panel additional powers beyond those required for the implementation of the Directive to make rules not required by the Directive and rules governing companies other than those required to be covered by the Directive.

Subsection (5)

This makes it clear that a separate committee of the Panel (currently the Code Committee) is responsible for promulgating rules (other than those relating to fees and charges which may also be promulgated by the Panel itself). This is to ensure that the body promulgating the rules is not the body which interprets them. The Code Committee was formed several years ago precisely to ensure this separation.

944.　Further provisions about rules

(1) Rules may-
  (a) make different provision for different purposes;
  (b) make provision subject to exceptions or exemptions;
  (c) contain incidental, supplemental, consequential or transitional provision;
  (d) authorise the Panel to dispense with or modify the application of rules in particular cases and by reference to any circumstances.

Rules made by virtue of paragraph (d) must require the Panel to give reasons for acting as mentioned in that paragraph.

(2) Rules must be made by an instrument in writing.

(3) Immediately after an instrument containing rules is made, the text must be made available to the public, with or without payment, in whatever way the Panel thinks appropriate.

(4) A person is not to be taken to have contravened a rule if he shows that at the time of the alleged contravention the text of the rule had not been made available as required by subsection (3).

(5) The production of a printed copy of an instrument purporting to be made by the Panel on which is endorsed a certificate signed by an officer of the Panel authorised by it for that purpose and stating-
  (a) that the instrument was made by the Panel,
  (b) that the copy is a true copy of the instrument, and
  (c) that on a specified date the text of the instrument was made available to the public as required by subsection (3),

is evidence (or in Scotland sufficient evidence) of the facts stated in the certificate.

(6) A certificate purporting to be signed as mentioned in subsection (5) is to be treated as having been properly signed unless the contrary is shown.

(7) A person who wishes in any legal proceedings to rely on an instrument by which rules are made may require the Panel to endorse a copy of the instrument with a certificate of the kind mentioned in subsection (5).

GENERAL NOTE

One of the key features of the Panel's jurisdiction, and one which the United Kingdom regarded as essential to be preserved when the Directive was adopted, was and is flexibility. This flexibility is contained in para.(6) of the Preamble to the Directive and in Art.4.5 of the Directive. This provides that provision may be made for derogation from rules and for the supervisory authority (the Panel) to have power to waive rules to take account of circumstances, in which case a reasoned decision must be given.

Subsection (1)

This embodies the provisions of the Directive relating to flexibility. The Panel has the power to make specific provision in its rules for exceptions and exemptions, and, provided that a reasoned decision is given, the Panel has a great deal of flexibility to dispense with of modify the application of rules in order to deal with specific circumstances coming before it.

945. Rulings

(1) The Panel may give rulings on the interpretation, application or effect of rules.

(2) To the extent and in the circumstances specified in rules, and subject to any review or appeal, a ruling has binding effect.

GENERAL NOTE

This provides that Panel rulings are effectively legally binding. This has been the case since May 20, 2006 for the companies covered by the Directive, and will now be the case for all companies and transactions regulated by the Panel even if these are not covered by the Directive.

946. Directions

Rules may contain provision conferring power on the Panel to give any direction that appears to the Panel to be necessary in order-

    (a) to restrain a person from acting (or continuing to act) in breach of rules;

    (b) to restrain a person from doing (or continuing to do) a particular thing, pending determination of whether that or any other conduct of his is or would be a breach of rules;

    (c) otherwise to secure compliance with rules.

GENERAL NOTE

This gives the Panel power to issue directions to restrain a person from certain conduct or otherwise to secure compliance with the Code. Failing to comply with such a direction could lead to the sanctions described in ss.495(2)-495(5).

Information

947. Power to require documents and information

(1) The Panel may by notice in writing require a person-

    (a) to produce any documents that are specified or described in the notice;

    (b) to provide, in the form and manner specified in the notice, such information as may be specified or described in the notice.

(2) A requirement under subsection (1) must be complied with-

    (a) at a place specified in the notice, and

    (b) before the end of such reasonable period as may be so specified.

(3) This section applies only to documents and information reasonably required in connection with the exercise by the Panel of its functions.

(4) The Panel may require-

    (a) any document produced to be authenticated, or

    (b) any information provided (whether in a document or otherwise) to be verified,

in such manner as it may reasonably require.

(5) The Panel may authorise a person to exercise any of its powers under this section.

(6) A person exercising a power by virtue of subsection (5) must, if required to do so, produce evidence of his authority to exercise the power.

(7) The production of a document in pursuance of this section does not affect any lien that a person has on the document.

(8) The Panel may take copies of or extracts from a document produced in pursuance of this section.

(9) A reference in this section to the production of a document includes a reference to the production of-

    (a) a hard copy of information recorded otherwise than in hard copy form, or

    (b) information in a form from which a hard copy can be readily obtained.

(10) A person is not required by this section to disclose documents or information in respect of which a claim to legal professional privilege (in Scotland, to confidentiality of communications) could be maintained in legal proceedings.

GENERAL NOTE

The Panel has the right to require the provision of documents and information. Failure to comply with such a requirement could result in sanctions under s.952.

Subsection (10)

There is no requirement to disclose documents or information covered by legal professional privilege.

948. Restrictions on disclosure

(1) This section applies to information (in whatever form)-

    (a) relating to the private affairs of an individual, or

    (b) relating to any particular business,

that is provided to the Panel in connection with the exercise of its functions.

(2) No such information may, during the lifetime of the individual or so long as the business continues to be carried on, be disclosed without the consent of that individual or (as the case may be) the person for the time being carrying on that business.

(3) Subsection (2) does not apply to any disclosure of information that-

    (a) is made for the purpose of facilitating the carrying out by the Panel of any of its functions,

    (b) is made to a person specified in Part 1 of Schedule 2,

    (c) is of a description specified in Part 2 of that Schedule, or

    (d) is made in accordance with Part 3 of that Schedule.

(4) The Secretary of State may amend Schedule 2 by order subject to negative resolution procedure.

(5) An order under subsection (4) must not-

    (a) amend Part 1 of Schedule 2 by specifying a person unless the person exercises functions of a public nature (whether or not he exercises any other function);

    (b) amend Part 2 of Schedule 2 by adding or modifying a description of disclosure unless the purpose for which the disclosure is permitted is likely to facilitate the exercise of a function of a public nature;

(c) amend Part 3 of Schedule 2 so as to have the effect of permitting disclosures to be made to a body other than one that exercises functions of a public nature in a country or territory outside the United Kingdom.

(6) Subsection (2) does not apply to-

  (a) the disclosure by an authority within subsection (7) of information disclosed to it by the Panel in reliance on subsection (3);

  (b) the disclosure of such information by anyone who has obtained it directly or indirectly from an authority within subsection (7).

(7) The authorities within this subsection are-

  (a) the Financial Services Authority;

  (b) an authority designated as a supervisory authority for the purposes of Article 4.1 of the Takeovers Directive;

  (c) any other person or body that exercises functions of a public nature, under legislation in an EEA State other than the United Kingdom, that are similar to the Panel's functions or those of the Financial Services Authority.

(8) This section does not prohibit the disclosure of information if the information is or has been available to the public from any other source.

(9) Nothing in this section authorises the making of a disclosure in contravention of the Data Protection Act 1998 (c. 29).

GENERAL NOTE

Confidential information provided to the Panel may not be disclosed without the consent of the person to whom it relates other than for the purpose of carrying out the Panel's functions. In addition, disclosure may be made to persons specified in Pts 1, 2 and 3 of Sch.2. Part 1 of Sch.2 sets out the specified persons, who include the Secretary of State, the Treasury, the Bank of England, the Financial Services Authority, the HM Revenue & Customs and any constable. Part 2 sets out the purposes for which disclosure may be made, which include investigations under the Financial Services and Markets Act 2000, for enabling the Commissioners of the Revenue and Customs to exercise their functions and for the purpose of enabling or assisting the Office of Fair Trading to exercise its functions. A total of 70 types of disclosure are specified in Pt 2 of Sch.2. In addition, disclosure may be made in accordance with Pt 3 of Sch.2 to certain overseas regulatory bodies whose functions are similar to those of the Panel or of the Financial Services Authority.

This is consistent with Art.4 para.4 of the Directive which provides for co-operation amongst regulators.

949. Offence of disclosure in contravention of section 948

(1) A person who discloses information in contravention of section 948 is guilty of an offence, unless-

  (a) he did not know, and had no reason to suspect, that the information had been provided as mentioned in section 948(1), or

  (b) he took all reasonable steps and exercised all due diligence to avoid the commission of the offence.

(2) A person guilty of an offence under this section is liable-

  (a) on conviction on indictment, to imprisonment for a term not exceeding two years or a fine (or both);

  (b) on summary conviction-

    (i) in England and Wales, to imprisonment for a term not exceeding twelve months or to a fine not exceeding the statutory maximum (or both);

    (ii) in Scotland or Northern Ireland, to imprisonment for a term not exceeding six months, or to a fine not exceeding the statutory maximum (or both).

(3) Where a company or other body corporate commits an offence under this section, an offence is also committed by every officer of the company or other body corporate who is in default.

GENERAL NOTE

The obligation of confidentiality in s.948 is backed by criminal sanctions.

Co-operation

950. Panel's duty of co-operation

(1) The Panel must take such steps as it considers appropriate to co-operate with-
    (a) the Financial Services Authority;
    (b) an authority designated as a supervisory authority for the purposes of Article 4.1 of the Takeovers Directive;
    (c) any other person or body that exercises functions of a public nature, under legislation in any country or territory outside the United Kingdom, that appear to the Panel to be similar to its own functions or those of the Financial Services Authority.
(2) Co-operation may include the sharing of information that the Panel is not prevented from disclosing.

GENERAL NOTE

The Panel's duty of co-operation with other regulators is derived from on Art.4.4 of the Directive.

Hearings and appeals

951. Hearings and appeals

(1) Rules must provide for a decision of the Panel to be subject to review by a committee of the Panel (the "Hearings Committee") at the instance of such persons affected by the decision as are specified in the rules.
(2) Rules may also confer other functions on the Hearings Committee.
(3) Rules must provide for there to be a right of appeal against a decision of the Hearings Committee to an independent tribunal (the "Takeover Appeal Board") in such circumstances and subject to such conditions as are specified in the rules.
(4) Rules may contain-
    (a) provision as to matters of procedure in relation to proceedings before the Hearings Committee (including provision imposing time limits);
    (b) provision about evidence in such proceedings;
    (c) provision as to the powers of the Hearings Committee dealing with a matter referred to it;
    (d) provision about enforcement of decisions of the Hearings Committee and the Takeover Appeal Board.
(5) Rules must contain provision-
    (a) requiring the Panel, when acting in relation to any proceedings before the Hearings Committee or the Takeover Appeal Board, to do so by an officer or member of staff of the Panel (or a person acting as such);
    (b) preventing a person who is or has been a member of the committee mentioned in section 943(5) from being a member of the Hearings Committee or the Takeover Appeal Board;
    (c) preventing a person who is a member of the committee mentioned in section 943(5), of the Hearings Committee or of the Takeover Appeal Board from acting as mentioned in paragraph (a).

GENERAL NOTE

The Takeover Panel has always had an appeal procedure. The Hearings Committee (formerly known as the full Panel) has been in operation since the Directive came into force on May 20, 2006. The Takeover Appeal Board has also been in existence since the Directive came into force. The functions of these bodies are set out in the Introduction to the Code. The

Takeover Appeal Board has the power to hear appeals on wider grounds than those applicable to the Appeals Committee (the final appeal body of the Panel before May 20, 2006) and it will be interesting to see if this results in a greater number of appeals from the Hearings Committee than from the old full Panel.

Contravention of rules etc

952. Sanctions

(1) Rules may contain provision conferring power on the Panel to impose sanctions on a person who has-
    (a) acted in breach of rules, or
    (b) failed to comply with a direction given by virtue of section 946.

(2) Subsection (3) applies where rules made by virtue of subsection (1) confer power on the Panel to impose a sanction of a kind not provided for by the City Code on Takeovers and Mergers as it had effect immediately before the passing of this Act.

(3) The Panel must prepare a statement (a "policy statement") of its policy with respect to-
    (a) the imposition of the sanction in question, and
    (b) where the sanction is in the nature of a financial penalty, the amount of the penalty that may be imposed.

An element of the policy must be that, in making a decision about any such matter, the Panel has regard to the factors mentioned in subsection (4).

(4) The factors are-
    (a) the seriousness of the breach or failure in question in relation to the nature of the rule or direction contravened;
    (b) the extent to which the breach or failure was deliberate or reckless;
    (c) whether the person on whom the sanction is to be imposed is an individual.

(5) The Panel may at any time revise a policy statement.

(6) The Panel must prepare a draft of any proposed policy statement (or revised policy statement) and consult such persons about the draft as the Panel considers appropriate.

(7) The Panel must publish, in whatever way it considers appropriate, any policy statement (or revised policy statement) that it prepares.

(8) In exercising, or deciding whether to exercise, its power to impose a sanction within subsection (2) in the case of any particular breach or failure, the Panel must have regard to any relevant policy statement published and in force at the time when the breach or failure occurred.

GENERAL NOTE

   This section gives authority for the imposition of sanctions by the Panel, which can include financial penalties. It is for the Panel to publish its policy statement on sanctions, and it must have regard to that policy statement when deciding on the imposition of sanctions.

953. Failure to comply with rules about bid documentation

(1) This section applies where a takeover bid is made for a company that has securities carrying voting rights admitted to trading on a regulated market in the United Kingdom.

(2) Where an offer document published in respect of the bid does not comply with offer document rules, an offence is committed by-
    (a) the person making the bid, and
    (b) where the person making the bid is a body of persons, any director, officer or member of that body who caused the document to be published.

(3) A person commits an offence under subsection (2) only if-

(a) he knew that the offer document did not comply, or was reckless as to whether it complied, and

(b) he failed to take all reasonable steps to secure that it did comply.

(4) Where a response document published in respect of the bid does not comply with response document rules, an offence is committed by any director or other officer of the company referred to in subsection (1) who-

(a) knew that the response document did not comply, or was reckless as to whether it complied, and

(b) failed to take all reasonable steps to secure that it did comply.

(5) Where an offence is committed under subsection (2)(b) or (4) by a company or other body corporate ("the relevant body")-

(a) subsection (2)(b) has effect as if the reference to a director, officer or member of the person making the bid included a reference to a director, officer or member of the relevant body;

(b) subsection (4) has effect as if the reference to a director or other officer of the company referred to in subsection (1) included a reference to a director, officer or member of the relevant body.

(6) A person guilty of an offence under this section is liable-

(a) on conviction on indictment, to a fine;

(b) on summary conviction, to a fine not exceeding the statutory maximum.

(7) Nothing in this section affects any power of the Panel in relation to the enforcement of its rules.

(8) Section 1 (meaning of "company") does not apply for the purposes of this section.

(9) In this section-

"designated" means designated in rules;

"offer document" means a document required to be published by rules giving effect to Article 6.2 of the Takeovers Directive;

"offer document rules" means rules designated as rules that give effect to Article 6.3 of that Directive;

"response document" means a document required to be published by rules giving effect to Article 9.5 of that Directive;

"response document rules" means rules designated as rules that give effect to the first sentence of Article 9.5 of that Directive;

"securities" means shares or debentures;

"takeover bid" has the same meaning as in that Directive;

"voting rights" means rights to vote at general meetings of the company in question, including rights that arise only in certain circumstances.

GENERAL NOTE

The Government, somewhat controversially, decided that the Directive required it to provide for criminal sanctions to underpin rule relating to the contents of the offer document and of the document from the target board responding to the offer (see Art.17 of the Directive).

These sanctions apply to a takeover bid for any company (whether or not incorporated in the United Kingdom) (s.953(8)) provided that the company has voting securities admitted to trading on a regulated market in the United Kingdom (currently the only regulated market is the Official List of the London Stock Exchange). Offer and response documents relating to other public companies are not subject to criminal sanctions, and in this respect (as in the case of s.966) the rules applying to companies covered by the Directive differ from those relating to other public companies.

The criminal sanctions only apply to the offer document and the response document, which in subs.(9) are respectively described as the document required to be published pursuant to Art.6.2 of the Directive (the document which contains the offer) and that required to be published pursuant to Art.9.5 of the Directive (the response to the offer from the target board. It would therefore appear that any documents which the offeror or offeree company choose to publish but which are not so required to be published are not subject to criminal sanctions even if their contents fail to comply with the Takeover Code.

Subsection 2 provides that the offence in relation to the offer document is committed by the person making the bid. This does not distinguish between a person making a bid as agent and as principal. Accordingly, it is unlikely that an investment bank will wish to make the bid as agent for the offeror because in doing so it potentially renders itself liable to criminal sanctions. The offence would also be committed by any director or officer of the bidder who caused the document to be published, but only if he knew of or was reckless as to the defect and failed to take all reasonable steps to ensure the document did comply with the Code.

In the case of the response document, the offence would be committed by any director or officer of the target who caused the document to be published, but only if he knew of or was reckless as to the defect and failed to take all reasonable steps to ensure the document did comply with the Code.

It should be noted that the rules relating to the contents of the offer document and the response document are those in the Code and that the Panel can vary these rules and grant dispensations and derogations from time to time.

954. Compensation

(1) Rules may confer power on the Panel to order a person to pay such compensation as it thinks just and reasonable if he is in breach of a rule the effect of which is to require the payment of money.

(2) Rules made by virtue of this section may include provision for the payment of interest (including compound interest).

GENERAL NOTE

This section gives statutory authority to the Panel to create rules requiring a person to pay compensation. In 1989, under its self regulatory jurisdiction, the Panel required Guinness Plc to pay compensation of around £85 million to former shareholders of The Distillers Company for breaches of the Code in failing to make a cash alternative available to them at the level required by the Code. Guinness complied fully with this ruling. The ruling itself is set out in Panel Statement 1989/13.

955. Enforcement by the court

(1) If, on the application of the Panel, the court is satisfied-
　　(a) that there is a reasonable likelihood that a person will contravene a rule-based requirement, or
　　(b) that a person has contravened a rule-based requirement or a disclosure requirement,
the court may make any order it thinks fit to secure compliance with the requirement.

(2) In subsection (1) "the court" means the High Court or, in Scotland, the Court of Session.

(3) Except as provided by subsection (1), no person-
　　(a) has a right to seek an injunction, or
　　(b) in Scotland, has title or interest to seek an interdict or an order for specific performance,
to prevent a person from contravening (or continuing to contravene) a rule-based requirement or a disclosure requirement.

(4) In this section-
　　"contravene" includes fail to comply;
　　"disclosure requirement" means a requirement imposed under section 947;
　　"rule-based requirement" means a requirement imposed by or under rules.

GENERAL NOTE

The Panel can apply to court for an injunction to prevent a person from contravening a rule of the Code, or for an order requiring compliance with the Code. This was not a power available to the Panel under the old self-regulatory system.

956. No action for breach of statutory duty etc

(1) Contravention of a rule-based requirement or a disclosure requirement does not give rise to any right of action for breach of statutory duty.

(2) Contravention of a rule-based requirement does not make any transaction void or unenforceable or (subject to any provision made by rules) affect the validity of any other thing.

(3) In this section-
  (a) "contravention" includes failure to comply;
  (b) "disclosure requirement" and "rule-based requirement" have the same meaning as in section 955.

GENERAL NOTE

One of the concerns of the government was to minimise the possibility of takeover litigation as a result of the implementation of the Directive. This was because it was considered important that takeovers should be decided on their substantive merits, and that the outcome should as far as possible not depend on tactical litigation. In the United Kingdom (unlike certain other jurisdictions) there is a clear timetable for a takeover bid, and the delays caused by tactical litigation could effectively cause a bid to fail without the shareholders having had the chance to decide for themselves. Section 956 takes away the right which might otherwise arise for one party to a bid to sue another for breach of statutory duty as a result of contravention of the Takeover Code and also provides that contravention of the Takeover Code does not make a transaction void or unenforceable.

Funding

957. Fees and charges

(1) Rules may provide for fees or charges to be payable to the Panel for the purpose of meeting any part of its expenses.

(2) A reference in this section or section 958 to expenses of the Panel is to any expenses that have been or are to be incurred by the Panel in, or in connection with, the discharge of its functions, including in particular-
  (a) payments in respect of the expenses of the Takeover Appeal Board;
  (b) the cost of repaying the principal of, and of paying any interest on, any money borrowed by the Panel;
  (c) the cost of maintaining adequate reserves.

958. Levy

(1) For the purpose of meeting any part of the expenses of the Panel, the Secretary of State may by regulations provide for a levy to be payable to the Panel-
  (a) by specified persons or bodies, or persons or bodies of a specified description, or
  (b) on transactions, of a specified description, in securities on specified markets.
  In this subsection "specified" means specified in the regulations.

(2) The power to specify (or to specify descriptions of) persons or bodies must be exercised in such a way that the levy is payable only by persons or bodies that appear to the Secretary of State-
  (a) to be capable of being directly affected by the exercise of any of the functions of the Panel, or
  (b) otherwise to have a substantial interest in the exercise of any of those functions.

(3) Regulations under this section may in particular-
  (a) specify the rate of the levy and the period in respect of which it is payable at that rate;
  (b) make provision as to the times when, and the manner in which, payments are to be made in respect of the levy.

(4) In determining the rate of the levy payable in respect of a particular period, the Secretary of State-
  (a) must take into account any other income received or expected by the Panel in respect of that period;
  (b) may take into account estimated as well as actual expenses of the Panel in respect of that period.

(5) The Panel must-
    (a) keep proper accounts in respect of any amounts of levy received by virtue of this section;
    (b) prepare, in relation to each period in respect of which any such amounts are received, a statement of account relating to those amounts in such form and manner as is specified in the regulations.

Those accounts must be audited, and the statement certified, by persons appointed by the Secretary of State.

(6) Regulations under this section-
    (a) are subject to affirmative resolution procedure if subsection (7) applies to them;
    (b) otherwise, are subject to negative resolution procedure.

(7) This subsection applies to-
    (a) the first regulations under this section;
    (b) any other regulations under this section that would result in a change in the persons or bodies by whom, or the transactions on which, the levy is payable.

(8) If a draft of an instrument containing regulations under this section would, apart from this subsection, be treated for the purposes of the Standing Orders of either House of Parliament as a hybrid instrument, it is to proceed in that House as if it were not such an instrument.

959. Recovery of fees, charges or levy

An amount payable by any person or body by virtue of section 957 or 958 is a debt due from that person or body to the Panel, and is recoverable accordingly.

GENERAL NOTE

    The Takeover Panel is self-financing through the charging of fees on offer documents and circulars seeking waivers from the mandatory obligation, and levies on certain financial market transactions. Sections 957-959 put this on a statutory basis.

Miscellaneous and supplementary

960. Panel as party to proceedings

The Panel is capable (despite being an unincorporated body) of-
    (a) bringing proceedings under this Chapter in its own name;
    (b) bringing or defending any other proceedings in its own name.

961. Exemption from liability in damages

(1) Neither the Panel, nor any person within subsection (2), is to be liable in damages for anything done (or omitted to be done) in, or in connection with, the discharge or purported discharge of the Panel's functions.

(2) A person is within this subsection if-
    (a) he is (or is acting as) a member, officer or member of staff of the Panel, or
    (b) he is a person authorised under section 947(5).

(3) Subsection (1) does not apply-
    (a) if the act or omission is shown to have been in bad faith, or
    (b) so as to prevent an award of damages in respect of the act or omission on the ground that it was unlawful as a result of section 6(1) of the Human Rights Act 1998 (c. 42) (acts of public authorities incompatible with Convention rights).

GENERAL NOTE

    The Panel and its personnel are exempt from liability in damages. In the absence of such a provision, the amounts of money which turn on a Panel decision are so large that the risk of potential liability could be a deterrent to anyone working for the Panel. However, this immunity does not apply in the case of an act or omission in bad faith, or to the extent of an act or omission which is unlawful as a result of s.6(1) of the Human Rights Act 1998 (act of public authority incompatible with rights under the European Convention on Human Rights). The Panel has been subject to the Human Rights Act since that Act came into force, and the exception in s.961 maintains that position.

962.   Privilege against self-incrimination

(1) A statement made by a person in response to-
    (a) a requirement under section 947(1), or
    (b) an order made by the court under section 955 to secure compliance with such a require-
        ment,
 may not be used against him in criminal proceedings in which he is charged with an offence to which this subsection applies.
(2) Subsection (1) applies to any offence other than an offence under one of the following provisions (which concern false statements made otherwise than on oath)-
    (a) section 5 of the Perjury Act 1911 (c. 6);
    (b) section 44(2) of the Criminal Law (Consolidation) (Scotland) Act 1995 (c. 39);
    (c) Article 10 of the Perjury (Northern Ireland) Order 1979 (S.I. 1979/ 1714 (N.I. 19)).

GENERAL NOTE
    If a person makes a response to the Panel when required to do so, then such statement cannot be used against that person in criminal proceedings (other than for perjury). However there is no privilege against self-incrimination in respect of a "civil offence" such as a breach of the Code of Market Conduct. So it would appear that a person who, when required to do so by the Panel, discloses facts which show he has been guilty of insider dealing, that statement cannot be used in a prosecution for insider dealing under the Criminal Justice Act 1993, but may perhaps be used in proceedings by the Financial Services Authority in respect of the Code of Market Conduct.

963.   Annual reports

(1) After the end of each financial year the Panel must publish a report.
(2) The report must-
    (a) set out how the Panel's functions were discharged in the year in question;
    (b) include the Panel's accounts for that year;
    (c) mention any matters the Panel considers to be of relevance to the discharge of its
        functions.

964.   Amendments to Financial Services and Markets Act 2000

(1) The Financial Services and Markets Act 2000 (c. 8) is amended as follows.
(2) Section 143 (power to make rules endorsing the City Code on Takeovers and Mergers etc) is repealed.
(3) In section 144 (power to make price stabilising rules), for subsection (7) substitute-
    "(7) "Consultation procedures" means procedures designed to provide an opportunity for
        persons likely to be affected by alterations to those provisions to make representations
        about proposed alterations to any of those provisions.".
(4) In section 349 (exceptions from restrictions on disclosure of confidential information), after subsection (3) insert-
    "(3A) Section 348 does not apply to-
        (a) the disclosure by a recipient to which subsection (3B) applies of confidential infor-
            mation disclosed to it by the Authority in reliance on subsection (1);
        (b) the disclosure of such information by a person obtaining it directly or indirectly
            from a recipient to which subsection (3B) applies.
    (3B) This subsection applies to-

    (a) the Panel on Takeovers and Mergers;

    (b) an authority designated as a supervisory authority for the purposes of Article 4.1 of the Takeovers Directive;

    (c) any other person or body that exercises public functions, under legislation in an EEA State other than the United Kingdom, that are similar to the Authority's functions or those of the Panel on Takeovers and Mergers.".

(5) In section 354 (Financial Services Authority's duty to co-operate with others), after subsection (1) insert-

    "(1A) The Authority must take such steps as it considers appropriate to cooperate with-

        (a) the Panel on Takeovers and Mergers;

        (b) an authority designated as a supervisory authority for the purposes of Article 4.1 of the Takeovers Directive;

        (c) any other person or body that exercises functions of a public nature, under legislation in any country or territory outside the United Kingdom, that appear to the Authority to be similar to those of the Panel on Takeovers and Mergers.".

(6) In section 417(1) (definitions), insert at the appropriate place-

    ""Takeovers Directive" means Directive 2004/25/EC of the European Parliament and of the Council;".

965. Power to extend to Isle of Man and Channel Islands

Her Majesty may by Order in Council direct that any of the provisions of this Chapter extend, with such modifications as may be specified in the Order, to the Isle of Man or any of the Channel Islands.

CHAPTER 2

IMPEDIMENTS TO TAKEOVERS

Opting in and opting out

966. Opting in and opting out

(1) A company may by special resolution (an "opting-in resolution") opt in for the purposes of this Chapter if the following three conditions are met in relation to the company.

(2) The first condition is that the company has voting shares admitted to trading on a regulated market.

(3) The second condition is that-

    (a) the company's articles of association-

        (i) do not contain any such restrictions as are mentioned in Article 11 of the Takeovers Directive, or

        (ii) if they do contain any such restrictions, provide for the restrictions not to apply at a time when, or in circumstances in which, they would be disapplied by that Article,

    and

    (b) those articles do not contain any other provision which would be incompatible with that Article.

(4) The third condition is that-

    (a) no shares conferring special rights in the company are held by-

        (i) a minister,

        (ii) a nominee of, or any other person acting on behalf of, a minister, or

        (iii) a company directly or indirectly controlled by a minister,

    and

    (b) no such rights are exercisable by or on behalf of a minister under any enactment.

(5) A company may revoke an opting-in resolution by a further special resolution (an "opting-out resolution").

(6) For the purposes of subsection (3), a reference in Article 11 of the Takeovers Directive to Article 7.1 or 9 of that Directive is to be read as referring to rules under section 943(1) giving effect to the relevant Article.

(7) In subsection (4) "minister" means-

    (a) the holder of an office in Her Majesty's Government in the United Kingdom;

    (b) the Scottish Ministers;

    (c) a Minister within the meaning given by section 7(3) of the Northern Ireland Act 1998 (c. 47);

and for the purposes of that subsection "minister" also includes the Treasury, the Board of Trade, the Defence Council and the National Assembly for Wales.

(8) The Secretary of State may by order subject to negative resolution procedure provide that subsection (4) applies in relation to a specified person or body that exercises functions of a public nature as it applies in relation to a minister.

"Specified" means specified in the order.

967.   Further provision about opting-in and opting-out resolutions

(1) An opting-in resolution or an opting-out resolution must specify the date from which it is to have effect (the "effective date").

(2) The effective date of an opting-in resolution may not be earlier than the date on which the resolution is passed.

(3) The second and third conditions in section 966 must be met at the time when an opting-in resolution is passed, but the first one does not need to be met until the effective date.

(4) An opting-in resolution passed before the time when voting shares of the company are admitted to trading on a regulated market complies with the requirement in subsection (1) if, instead of specifying a particular date, it provides for the resolution to have effect from that time.

(5) An opting-in resolution passed before the commencement of this section complies with the requirement in subsection (1) if, instead of specifying a particular date, it provides for the resolution to have effect from that commencement.

(6) The effective date of an opting-out resolution may not be earlier than the first anniversary of the date on which a copy of the opting-in resolution was forwarded to the registrar.

(7) Where a company has passed an opting-in resolution, any alteration of its articles of association that would prevent the second condition in section 966 from being met is of no effect until the effective date of an opting-out resolution passed by the company.

GENERAL NOTE

Sections 966-973 replace and reenact Pt 3 of the Interim Implementation Regulations, which themselves implemented Art.11 of the Directive. Article 11 limits the use of contracts which restrict the transfer of shares to the offeror in certain circumstances, or which limit the free vote of shareholders on certain matters which could frustrate the bid or the offeror's ability to take control once it has obtained 75 per cent or more of the voting rights of a company. The practical issues associated with Art.11 and the potential overriding of contractual rights mean that in common with other European Union Member States, the United Kingdom has opted out of Art.11 save for the mandatory requirement to allow individual companies to opt in to that Article.

Section 968 allows a company to pass an opting-in resolution. To do so, the company must have voting shares admitted to trading on a regulated market. The only regulated market in the United Kingdom is the Official List of the London Stock Exchange, so these sections only apply to fully listed companies, not to other companies subject to the Code. The resolution has the effect set out below on an agreement to which s.968 applies. Such an agreement is invalid in so far as it places any restriction on:

- the transfer of shares in the company to the offeror during the offer period;
- the transfer to any person of shares in the company at a time in the offer period when the offeror holds at least 75 per cent in value (presumably nominal value) of all the voting shares in the company;
- rights to vote at a general meeting that decides to take any action that might frustrate a bid;

- rights to vote at a general meeting that is:
- the first such meeting after the end of the offer period; and
- is held at a time when the offeror holds shares amounting to not less than 75 per cent in value of the voting shares in the company.

Section 968 only applies to an agreement if it was entered into between two shareholders on or after April 21, 2006 or it was entered into between the company and a shareholder at any time. The offer period is the period during which the offer can be accepted (this is different from the definition in the Code, where the offer period is the period from the first public announcement of an offer or possible offer until the offer lapses is withdrawn or becomes unconditional as to acceptances).

Under s.968(3), such a resolution applies to a contract even if that contract is governed by the law of another country, which may give rise to some interesting issues on conflict of laws.

Section 968(6) provides that where a person suffers loss as a result of anything which would be a breach of contract but for these provisions of the Regulations, the court is given power to order "just and equitable" compensation to that person from the person who would be liable for committing or inducing the breach. It seems to follow from this that, say, if a shareholder accepts an offer in contravention of a contract, he is not in breach of contract (because the opting out resolution will have rendered the contract invalid for this purpose), but may still have to pay "just and equitable" compensation to the other party to the contract. So in reality it may be prudent to comply to comply with contractual terms even though they are invalid. One may then question what purpose was served by rendering them invalid in the first place.

An opting-in resolution may be revoked (by an "opting-out" resolution) effective not earlier than 12 months after the opting-in resolution was sent to the Registrar of Companies.

The difficulties associated with these sections mean that it in practice it is unlikely that any company will choose to pass an opting-in resolution.

Consequences of opting in

968. Effect on contractual restrictions

(1) The following provisions have effect where a takeover bid is made for an opted-in company.

(2) An agreement to which this section applies is invalid in so far as it places any restriction-

    (a) on the transfer to the offeror, or at his direction to another person, of shares in the company during the offer period;

    (b) on the transfer to any person of shares in the company at a time during the offer period when the offeror holds shares amounting to not less than 75% in value of all the voting shares in the company;

    (c) on rights to vote at a general meeting of the company that decides whether to take any action which might result in the frustration of the bid;

    (d) on rights to vote at a general meeting of the company that-

        (i) is the first such meeting to be held after the end of the offer period, and

        (ii) is held at a time when the offeror holds shares amounting to not less than 75% in value of all the voting shares in the company.

(3) This section applies to an agreement-

    (a) entered into between a person holding shares in the company and another such person on or after 21st April 2004, or

    (b) entered into at any time between such a person and the company,

and it applies to such an agreement even if the law applicable to the agreement (apart from this section) is not the law of a part of the United Kingdom.

(4) The reference in subsection (2)(c) to rights to vote at a general meeting of the company that decides whether to take any action which might result in the frustration of the bid includes a reference to rights to vote on a written resolution concerned with that question.

(5) For the purposes of subsection (2)(c), action which might result in the frustration of a bid is any action of that kind specified in rules under section 943(1) giving effect to Article 9 of the Takeovers Directive.

(6) If a person suffers loss as a result of any act or omission that would (but for this section) be a breach of an agreement to which this section applies, he is entitled to compensation, of such

amount as the court considers just and equitable, from any person who would (but for this section) be liable to him for committing or inducing the breach.

(7) In subsection (6) "the court" means the High Court or, in Scotland, the Court of Session.

(8) A reference in this section to voting shares in the company does not include-
   (a) debentures, or
   (b) shares that, under the company's articles of association, do not normally carry rights to vote at its general meetings (for example, shares carrying rights to vote that, under those articles, arise only where specified pecuniary advantages are not provided).

969. Power of offeror to require general meeting to be called

(1) Where a takeover bid is made for an opted-in company, the offeror may by making a request to the directors of the company require them to call a general meeting of the company if, at the date at which the request is made, he holds shares amounting to not less than 75% in value of all the voting shares in the company.

(2) The reference in subsection (1) to voting shares in the company does not include-
   (a) debentures, or
   (b) shares that, under the company's articles of association, do not normally carry rights to vote at its general meetings (for example, shares carrying rights to vote that, under those articles, arise only where specified pecuniary advantages are not provided).

(3) Sections 303 to 305 (members' power to require general meetings to be called) apply as they would do if subsection (1) above were substituted for subsections (1) to (3) of section 303, and with any other necessary modifications.

Supplementary

970. Communication of decisions

(1) A company that has passed an opting-in resolution or an opting-out resolution must notify-
   (a) the Panel, and
   (b) where the company-
      (i) has voting shares admitted to trading on a regulated market in an EEA State other than the United Kingdom, or
      (ii) has requested such admission,
   the authority designated by that state as the supervisory authority for the purposes of Article 4.1 of the Takeovers Directive.

(2) Notification must be given within 15 days after the resolution is passed and, if any admission or request such as is mentioned in subsection (1)(b) occurs at a later time, within 15 days after that time.

(3) If a company fails to comply with this section, an offence is committed by-
   (a) the company, and
   (b) every officer of it who is in default.

(4) A person guilty of an offence under this section is liable on summary conviction to a fine not exceeding level 3 on the standard scale and, for continued contravention, a daily default fine not exceeding one-tenth of level 3 on the standard scale.

971. Interpretation of this Chapter

(1) In this Chapter-
   "offeror" and "takeover bid" have the same meaning as in the Takeovers Directive;
   "offer period", in relation to a takeover bid, means the time allowed for acceptance of the bid by-
      (a) rules under section 943(1) giving effect to Article 7.1 of the Takeovers Directive, or

(b) where the rules giving effect to that Article which apply to the bid are those of an EEA State other than the United Kingdom, those rules;

"opted-in company" means a company in relation to which-
    (a) an opting-in resolution has effect, and
    (b) the conditions in section 966(2) and (4) continue to be met;

"opting-in resolution" has the meaning given by section 966(1);
"opting-out resolution" has the meaning given by section 966(5);
"the Takeovers Directive" means Directive 2004/25/EC of the European Parliament and of the Council;
"voting rights" means rights to vote at general meetings of the company in question, including rights that arise only in certain circumstances;
"voting shares" means shares carrying voting rights.

(2) For the purposes of this Chapter-
    (a) securities of a company are treated as shares in the company if they are convertible into or entitle the holder to subscribe for such shares;
    (b) debentures issued by a company are treated as shares in the company if they carry voting rights.

972. Transitory provision

(1) Where a takeover bid is made for an opted-in company, section 368 of the Companies Act 1985 (c. 6) (extraordinary general meeting on members' requisition) and section 378 of that Act (extraordinary and special resolutions) have effect as follows until their repeal by this Act.

(2) Section 368 has effect as if a members' requisition included a requisition of a person who-
    (a) is the offeror in relation to the takeover bid, and
    (b) holds at the date of the deposit of the requisition shares amounting to not less than 75% in value of all the voting shares in the company.

(3) In relation to a general meeting of the company that-
    (a) is the first such meeting to be held after the end of the offer period, and
    (b) is held at a time when the offeror holds shares amounting to not less than 75% in value of all the voting shares in the company,

section 378(2) (meaning of "special resolution") has effect as if "4 days' notice" were substituted for "21 days' notice".

(4) A reference in this section to voting shares in the company does not include-
    (a) debentures, or
    (b) shares that, under the company's articles of association, do not normally carry rights to vote at its general meetings (for example, shares carrying rights to vote that, under those articles, arise only where specified pecuniary advantages are not provided).

973. Power to extend to Isle of Man and Channel Islands

Her Majesty may by Order in Council direct that any of the provisions of this Chapter extend, with such modifications as may be specified in the Order, to the Isle of Man or any of the Channel Islands.

CHAPTER 3

"SQUEEZE-OUT" AND "SELL-OUT"

Takeover offers

974.   Meaning of "takeover offer"

(1) For the purposes of this Chapter an offer to acquire shares in a company is a "takeover offer" if the following two conditions are satisfied in relation to the offer.

(2) The first condition is that it is an offer to acquire-
    (a) all the shares in a company, or
    (b) where there is more than one class of shares in a company, all the shares of one or more classes,
other than shares that at the date of the offer are already held by the offeror. Section 975 contains provision supplementing this subsection.

(3) The second condition is that the terms of the offer are the same-
    (a) in relation to all the shares to which the offer relates, or
    (b) where the shares to which the offer relates include shares of different classes, in relation to all the shares of each class.
Section 976 contains provision treating this condition as satisfied in certain circumstances.

(4) In subsections (1) to (3) "shares" means shares, other than relevant treasury shares, that have been allotted on the date of the offer (but see subsection (5)).

(5) A takeover offer may include among the shares to which it relates-
    (a) all or any shares that are allotted after the date of the offer but before a specified date;
    (b) all or any relevant treasury shares that cease to be held as treasury shares before a specified date;
    (c) all or any other relevant treasury shares.

(6) In this section-
    "relevant treasury shares" means shares that-
        (a) are held by the company as treasury shares on the date of the offer, or
        (b) become shares held by the company as treasury shares after that date but before a specified date;

    "specified date" means a date specified in or determined in accordance with the terms of the offer.

(7) Where the terms of an offer make provision for their revision and for acceptances on the previous terms to be treated as acceptances on the revised terms, then, if the terms of the offer are revised in accordance with that provision-
    (a) the revision is not to be regarded for the purposes of this Chapter as the making of a fresh offer, and
    (b) references in this Chapter to the date of the offer are accordingly to be read as references to the date of the original offer.

GENERAL NOTE

This Chapter replaces ss.428-430F of the 1985 Act (derived in turn from the 1948 Act, as substantially amended by the FSA 1986) setting out the squeeze-out and sell-out provisions. These enable an offeror, who has 90 per cent or more acceptances of a takeover offer, to acquire the shares of the dissenting minority (squeeze-out). They also allow the dissenting minority in such a situation to require the offeror to buy them out (sell-out). In addition to restating the majority of the 1985 Act provisions, these revised sections incorporate changes required to implement both Arts 15 and 16 of the Takeovers Directive (Dir 2004/25/EC; OJ L 142 12) and recommendations of the Company Law Review (*Modern Company Law: Final Report*, paras 13.19 et seq.).

For offers for target companies listed on the Official List, virtually all of these changes were made with effect from 20/5/06 by virtue of the Takeovers Directive (Interim Implementation) Regulations 2006 (SI 2006/1183). Once this Chapter is brought into effect, those Regulations will cease to apply. Unlike the Regulations, however, this Chapter applies to offers for all target companies.

This section, together with the following four sections, defines what is meant by a takeover offer. This is solely for the purpose of this Chapter (see per Browne-Wilkinson J. in *Chez Nico Restaurants Ltd, Re* [1991] B.C.C. 736). In itself it contains no changes of substance from the former sections.

Subsections (1)-(3)

These subsections are derived from s.428(1) of the 1985 Act. The two stated conditions are applied both to offers for all the shares of a target company and those for all of a class of shares. Which shares are then so included is amplified by ss.975 and 976. As to what can amount to the same terms of an offer, see s.976. Problems associated with the communication and acceptance of the offer are covered by s.978.

Subsections (4)-(6)

These subsections are direct replacements for s.428(2) and (2A) of the 1985 Act. They relate to treasury shares and shares allotted after the date of the offer for the purposes of calculating the relevant thresholds. If treasury shares are excluded from the offer they play no part in the squeeze-out process, but still have a limited role in the sell-out calculations - see s.983(5).

Subsection (7)

This subsection replaces s.428(7) of the 1985 Act relating to revised offers, with only drafting amendments (see *Chez Nico Restaurants Ltd, Re* [1991] B.C.C. 736).

975. Shares already held by the offeror etc

(1) The reference in section 974(2) to shares already held by the offeror includes a reference to shares that he has contracted to acquire, whether unconditionally or subject to conditions being met.

This is subject to subsection (2).

(2) The reference in section 974(2) to shares already held by the offeror does not include a reference to shares that are the subject of a contract-

   (a) intended to secure that the holder of the shares will accept the offer when it is made, and

   (b) entered into-

      (i) by deed and for no consideration,

      (ii) for consideration of negligible value, or

      (iii) for consideration consisting of a promise by the offeror to make the offer.

(3) In relation to Scotland, this section applies as if the words "by deed and" in subsection (2)(b)(i) were omitted.

(4) The condition in section 974(2) is treated as satisfied where-

   (a) the offer does not extend to shares that associates of the offeror hold or have contracted to acquire (whether unconditionally or subject to conditions being met), and

   (b) the condition would be satisfied if the offer did extend to those shares.

(For further provision about such shares, see section 977(2)).

GENERAL NOTE

This section deals with the position of shares already held by the offeror. It repeats s.428(5) and (6) of the 1948 Act in excluding such shares from the offer (and, so, from the squeeze-out threshold), but with modifications suggested by the CLR. It also incorporates the equivalent modified provision in s.430E of the 1985 Act in relation to shares held by associates of the offeror. It should be read together with s.977.

Subsections (1)-(3)

Shares excluded from the offer now include all shares which the offeror has already contracted to acquire whether unconditionally (see s.991(2)) or conditionally. However, as before, this does not apply to irrevocable commitments to accept the offer where there is no consideration and they are made under seal (except in Scotland), or they are made for negligible consideration (new), or where, as is usual, the consideration is the promise to make the offer. Note that in such cases all that is needed for a commitment to be irrevocable is that the giver intends to secure that the legal holder will accept the offer when it is made.

Subsection (4)

   Associate is defined in s.988.

976.   Cases where offer treated as being on same terms

(1) The condition in section 974(3) (terms of offer to be the same for all shares or all shares of
    particular classes) is treated as satisfied where subsection (2) or (3) below applies.

(2) This subsection applies where-
   (a) shares carry an entitlement to a particular dividend which other shares of the same
       class, by reason of being allotted later, do not carry,
   (b) there is a difference in the value of consideration offered for the shares allotted earlier
       as against that offered for those allotted later,
   (c) that difference merely reflects the difference in entitlement to the dividend, and
   (d) the condition in section 974(3) would be satisfied but for that difference.

(3) This subsection applies where-
   (a) the law of a country or territory outside the United Kingdom-
       (i) precludes an offer of consideration in the form, or any of the forms, specified in
           the terms of the offer ("the specified form"), or
       (ii) precludes it except after compliance by the offeror with conditions with which he
            is unable to comply or which he regards as unduly onerous,
   (b) the persons to whom an offer of consideration in the specified form is precluded are
       able to receive consideration in another form that is of substantially equivalent value,
       and
   (c) the condition in section 974(3) would be satisfied but for the fact that an offer of consid-
       eration in the specified form to those persons is precluded.

GENERAL NOTE

   This section introduces a recommendation of the CLR as to differences in the offer price arising from variations in the
dividend rights attached to the target shares. It also restates s.428(4) of the 1985 Act as to differences in the consideration
being offered arising from compliance with the domestic laws of the offerees.

Subsection (2)

   Where some target shares carry a particular dividend requirement and others do not (e.g. because of different issue
dates), any difference in the offer price which reflects that difference is not a different term for the purposes of s.974.

Subsection (3)

   This subsection is a direct replacement for s.428(5) of the 1985 Act covering problems, e.g. offering shares as consideration for the offer, under the domestic law of the offeree.

977.   Shares to which an offer relates

(1) Where a takeover offer is made and, during the period beginning with the date of the offer
    and ending when the offer can no longer be accepted, the offeror-
   (a) acquires or unconditionally contracts to acquire any of the shares to which the offer
       relates, but
   (b) does not do so by virtue of acceptances of the offer,
 those shares are treated for the purposes of this Chapter as excluded from those to which the
offer relates.

(2) For the purposes of this Chapter shares that an associate of the offeror holds or has
    contracted to acquire, whether at the date of the offer or subsequently, are not treated as shares
    to which the offer relates, even if the offer extends to such shares.
In this subsection "contracted" means contracted unconditionally or subject to conditions being
met.

(3) This section is subject to section 979(8) and (9).

GENERAL NOTE

Subsection (1)

This subsection replaces part of s.429(9) of the 1985 Act and provides that acquisitions or *unconditional contracts to acquire* (see s.991(2)) target shares by the *offeror* (see s.958(1)) made otherwise than by acceptance of the offer do not count as shares to which the offer relates under s.941. Thus they cannot be counted towards the squeeze-out threshold. However, this restriction is subject to s.979(8) and (9), which replace the other parts of s.429(9), and allow for such purchases, etc. to count if either they are made on or below the offer price or the offer price is raised to meet the higher purchase price (which is required anyway if the offer is subject to the City Code). Conditional contracts to acquire the shares are not excluded by this section if they are taken by the offeror.

Subsection (2)

This subsection applies a similar rule to shares acquired by associates (see s.988) formerly in s.430E(1) of the 1985 Act. However, there is a modification, recommended by the CLR, in that in such cases even conditional contracts to acquire target shares if made outside the offer do not count. Again, however, this is subject to s.979(8) and (9).

978. Effect of impossibility etc of communicating or accepting offer

(1) Where there are holders of shares in a company to whom an offer to acquire shares in the company is not communicated, that does not prevent the offer from being a takeover offer for the purposes of this Chapter if-
   (a) those shareholders have no registered address in the United Kingdom,
   (b) the offer was not communicated to those shareholders in order not to contravene the law of a country or territory outside the United Kingdom, and
   (c) either-
      (i) the offer is published in the Gazette, or
      (ii) the offer can be inspected, or a copy of it obtained, at a place in an EEA State or on a website, and a notice is published in the Gazette specifying the address of that place or website.
(2) Where an offer is made to acquire shares in a company and there are persons for whom, by reason of the law of a country or territory outside the United Kingdom, it is impossible to accept the offer, or more difficult to do so, that does not prevent the offer from being a takeover offer for the purposes of this Chapter.
(3) It is not to be inferred-
   (a) that an offer which is not communicated to every holder of shares in the company cannot be a takeover offer for the purposes of this Chapter unless the requirements of paragraphs (a) to (c) of subsection (1) are met, or
   (b) that an offer which is impossible, or more difficult, for certain persons to accept cannot be a takeover offer for those purposes unless the reason for the impossibility or difficulty is the one mentioned in subsection (2).

GENERAL NOTE

This is a new section derived from a recommendation of the CLR (*Final Report*, para.13.45). It relates to problems of communicating or accepting the offer. The issue was whether the strict contractual rules of offer and acceptance should be applied to establish whether a takeover offer had indeed been made (see *Joseph Holt Plc, Re* [2001] 2 BCLC 604).

This section partially clarifies the situation. Non-communication to a target shareholder will not affect the status of the offer if the three conditions in subs.(1) are met. Publication in the appropriate Gazette according to the domicile of the target company was selected ahead of a national newspaper (as had been the previous practice in such cases). Subsection (2) makes it clear that an inability to accept an offer under local law does not affect the offer's status as such.

But subs.(3) makes it clear that even in circumstances outside subss.(1) and (2) an inability to receive or accept an offer does not automatically mean that there is no takeover offer under s.974. This will therefore still be a matter for the courts to decide.

"Squeeze-out"

979. Right of offeror to buy out minority shareholder

(1) Subsection (2) applies in a case where a takeover offer does not relate to shares of different classes.

(2) If the offeror has, by virtue of acceptances of the offer, acquired or unconditionally contracted to acquire-

(a) not less than 90% in value of the shares to which the offer relates, and

(b) in a case where the shares to which the offer relates are voting shares, not less than 90% of the voting rights carried by those shares,

he may give notice to the holder of any shares to which the offer relates which the offeror has not acquired or unconditionally contracted to acquire that he desires to acquire those shares.

(3) Subsection (4) applies in a case where a takeover offer relates to shares of different classes.

(4) If the offeror has, by virtue of acceptances of the offer, acquired or unconditionally contracted to acquire-

(a) not less than 90% in value of the shares of any class to which the offer relates, and

(b) in a case where the shares of that class are voting shares, not less than 90% of the voting rights carried by those shares,

he may give notice to the holder of any shares of that class to which the offer relates which the offeror has not acquired or unconditionally contracted to acquire that he desires to acquire those shares.

(5) In the case of a takeover offer which includes among the shares to which it relates-

(a) shares that are allotted after the date of the offer, or

(b) relevant treasury shares (within the meaning of section 974) that cease to be held as treasury shares after the date of the offer,

the offeror's entitlement to give a notice under subsection (2) or (4) on any particular date shall be determined as if the shares to which the offer relates did not include any allotted, or ceasing to be held as treasury shares, on or after that date.

(6) Subsection (7) applies where-

(a) the requirements for the giving of a notice under subsection (2) or (4) are satisfied, and

(b) there are shares in the company which the offeror, or an associate of his, has contracted to acquire subject to conditions being met, and in relation to which the contract has not become unconditional.

(7) The offeror's entitlement to give a notice under subsection (2) or (4) shall be determined as if-

(a) the shares to which the offer relates included shares falling within paragraph (b) of subsection (6), and

(b) in relation to shares falling within that paragraph, the words "by virtue of acceptances of the offer" in subsection (2) or (4) were omitted.

(8) Where-

(a) a takeover offer is made,

(b) during the period beginning with the date of the offer and ending when the offer can no longer be accepted, the offeror-

(i) acquires or unconditionally contracts to acquire any of the shares to which the offer relates, but

(ii) does not do so by virtue of acceptances of the offer, and

(c) subsection (10) applies,

then for the purposes of this section those shares are not excluded by section 977(1) from those to which the offer relates, and the offeror is treated as having acquired or contracted to acquire them by virtue of acceptances of the offer.

(9) Where-

    (a) a takeover offer is made,

    (b) during the period beginning with the date of the offer and ending when the offer can no longer be accepted, an associate of the offeror acquires or unconditionally contracts to acquire any of the shares to which the offer relates, and

    (c) subsection (10) applies,

then for the purposes of this section those shares are not excluded by section 977(2) from those to which the offer relates.

(10) This subsection applies if-

    (a) at the time the shares are acquired or contracted to be acquired as mentioned in subsection (8) or (9) (as the case may be), the value of the consideration for which they are acquired or contracted to be acquired ("the acquisition consideration") does not exceed the value of the consideration specified in the terms of the offer, or

    (b) those terms are subsequently revised so that when the revision is announced the value of the acquisition consideration, at the time mentioned in paragraph (a), no longer exceeds the value of the consideration specified in those terms.

GENERAL NOTE

This section, together with ss.980-982, replaces ss.429 and 430 of the 1985 Act, with modifications arising from both the Takeovers Directive and the recommendations of the CLR. These are concerned with the right to serve a squeeze-out notice on a minority shareholder and so acquire those shares, together with the mechanics etc of such acquisitions.

This section sets out when the right to serve a notice arises. Section 980 is concerned with the timing and form of the notice and ss.981 and 982 with the legal effect of such a notice. This right is subject to an application to the court under s.986 and there are modifications in the case of joint offerors under s.987.

Subsections (1)-(4)

These subsections replace s.429(1) and (2) of the 1948 Act. They retain the basic threshold requirement of 90 per cent acceptances in value of the shares (or a class of shares) to which the offer relates. (This therefore excludes both those shares excluded by s.942 and treasury shares unless included in the offer - see s.974(4) and (5)). The acceptances must be by virtue of the offer (see s.977 and subss.(8)-(10)). However, following art 15 of the Takeovers Directive (2004/25/EC), in the case of voting shares, the acceptances must also now amount to shares holding not less than 90 per cent of the voting rights of the shares or class.

Unconditionally acquired, offeror, voting shares and *voting rights* are defined in s.991.

Subsection (5)

This subsection follows a recommendation of the CLR and allows for the situation where the offer under s.974 applies to shares allotted after the *date of the offer* (see s.991) or to shares ceasing to be treasury shares after that date. The solution is that, at any given time, the squeeze-out threshold is calculated by shares actually in issue. Further subsequent issues of shares will not invalidate notices already served, but any subsequent notice must take those new shares into account.

Subsections (6) and (7)

These are new provisions which are consequent on the restriction is s.983(6) and (7) on a minority shareholder's ability to exercise his or her sell-out right. This arises where the sell-out threshold has been achieved only by including conditional contracts to acquire shares which have not yet become unconditional. There is in effect a wait-and-see period imposed. These subsections provide that the minority shareholder cannot be squeezed-out whilst that period is in operation.

Subsections (8)-(10)

These subsections replace most of s.429(9) and 430E(2) and allow for shares acquired or *unconditionally contracted to be acquired* (see s.958) by the *offeror* or an associate (see s.988), otherwise than by acceptances of the offer, to be counted towards the squeeze-out threshold under this section if the conditions in subs.(10) are complied with (as they will be under the City Code).

See also the note on s.977 and the position of conditional contracts to acquire the shares taken by the offeror (but not by an associate) which are not excluded by s.977.

980. Further provision about notices given under section 979

(1) A notice under section 979 must be given in the prescribed manner.

(2) No notice may be given under section 979(2) or (4) after the end of-

    (a) the period of three months beginning with the day after the last day on which the offer can be accepted, or

    (b) the period of six months beginning with the date of the offer, where that period ends earlier and the offer is one to which subsection (3) below applies.

(3) This subsection applies to an offer if the time allowed for acceptance of the offer is not governed by rules under section 943(1) that give effect to Article 7 of the Takeovers Directive.

In this subsection "the Takeovers Directive" has the same meaning as in section 943.

(4) At the time when the offeror first gives a notice under section 979 in relation to an offer, he must send to the company-

    (a) a copy of the notice, and

    (b) a statutory declaration by him in the prescribed form, stating that the conditions for the giving of the notice are satisfied.

(5) Where the offeror is a company (whether or not a company within the meaning of this Act) the statutory declaration must be signed by a director.

(6) A person commits an offence if-

    (a) he fails to send a copy of a notice or a statutory declaration as required by subsection (4), or

    (b) he makes such a declaration for the purposes of that subsection knowing it to be false or without having reasonable grounds for believing it to be true.

(7) It is a defence for a person charged with an offence for failing to send a copy of a notice as required by subsection (4) to prove that he took reasonable steps for securing compliance with that subsection.

(8) A person guilty of an offence under this section is liable-

    (a) on conviction on indictment, to imprisonment for a term not exceeding two years or a fine (or both);

    (b) on summary conviction-

        (i) in England and Wales, to imprisonment for a term not exceeding twelve months or to a fine not exceeding the statutory maximum (or both) and, for continued contravention, a daily default fine not exceeding one-fiftieth of the statutory maximum;

        (ii) in Scotland or Northern Ireland, to imprisonment for a term not exceeding six months, or to a fine not exceeding the statutory maximum (or both) and, for continued contravention, a daily default fine not exceeding one-fiftieth of the statutory maximum.

GENERAL NOTE

This section replaces s.429(4)-(7) with modifications required by the Takeovers Directive (2004/25/EC) as to the time within which a s.979 notice must be served.

Subsection (1)

This subsection directly replaces part of s.429(4).

Subsections (2) and (3)

These subsections introduce new provisions required by the Directive. No notice can be served unless the necessary threshold has been acquired within three months after the last day on which the offer could be accepted (usually 60 days maximum for offers subject to the City Code). If the offer is not subject to the Code (rules under s.943 etc.), so that there is no legal restriction on the offer period, there is a maximum time limit of six months from the *date of the offer* (see s.991).

Subsections (4)-(8)
These subsections replace parts of s.429(4) and s.429(5)-(7) imposing the requirements on the offeror to send a copy of the notice and a statutory declaration to the target company, with criminal sanctions in the event of a default. Those sanctions are reworded to comply with the general rules for sanctions in the Act (see Sch.3).

981. Effect of notice under section 979

(1) Subject to section 986 (applications to the court), this section applies where the offeror gives a shareholder a notice under section 979.

(2) The offeror is entitled and bound to acquire the shares to which the notice relates on the terms of the offer.

(3) Where the terms of an offer are such as to give the shareholder a choice of consideration, the notice must give particulars of the choice and state-

    (a) that the shareholder may, within six weeks from the date of the notice, indicate his choice by a written communication sent to the offeror at an address specified in the notice, and

    (b) which consideration specified in the offer will apply if he does not indicate a choice.

The reference in subsection (2) to the terms of the offer is to be read accordingly.

(4) Subsection (3) applies whether or not any time-limit or other conditions applicable to the choice under the terms of the offer can still be complied with.

(5) If the consideration offered to or (as the case may be) chosen by the shareholder-

    (a) is not cash and the offeror is no longer able to provide it, or

    (b) was to have been provided by a third party who is no longer bound or able to provide it,

the consideration is to be taken to consist of an amount of cash, payable by the offeror, which at the date of the notice is equivalent to the consideration offered or (as the case may be) chosen.

(6) At the end of six weeks from the date of the notice the offeror must immediately-

    (a) send a copy of the notice to the company, and

    (b) pay or transfer to the company the consideration for the shares to which the notice relates.

Where the consideration consists of shares or securities to be allotted by the offeror, the reference in paragraph (b) to the transfer of the consideration is to be read as a reference to the allotment of the shares or securities to the company.

(7) If the shares to which the notice relates are registered, the copy of the notice sent to the company under subsection (6)(a) must be accompanied by an instrument of transfer executed on behalf of the holder of the shares by a person appointed by the offeror.

On receipt of that instrument the company must register the offeror as the holder of those shares.

(8) If the shares to which the notice relates are transferable by the delivery of warrants or other instruments, the copy of the notice sent to the company under subsection (6)(a) must be accompanied by a statement to that effect.

On receipt of that statement the company must issue the offeror with warrants or other instruments in respect of the shares, and those already in issue in respect of the shares become void.

(9) The company must hold any money or other consideration received by it under subsection (6)(b) on trust for the person who, before the offeror acquired them, was entitled to the shares in respect of which the money or other consideration was received.

Section 982 contains further provision about how the company should deal with such money or other consideration.

GENERAL NOTE

This section replaces s.430(1)-(9) of the 1985 Act, with minor clarifications in subss.(4) and (5) to the situation where it is no longer possible to provide the same consideration in kind for the acquisition as was available under the offer.

Subsection (2)

This subsection directly re-enacts s.430(2) of the 1985 Act. See comments in *Greythorn Ltd, Re* [2002] 1 BCLC 437 at 450.

Subsections (3)-(5)

These subsections provide for the situation where the offer provides for a choice of consideration. A similar choice must always be given to the dissenters, with a default choice, who must exercise it within six weeks of the date of the notice. The position is then clarified so that if the offer is in whole or in part in kind and that is no longer available, the choice must still be offered and the cash equivalent of that consideration in kind, if chosen, must be paid.

Subsections (6)-(9)

These subsections replace s.430(5)-(9) of the 1985 Act without any changes of substance. They provide for the mechanics of an acquisition following a s.979 notice. After a six-week moratorium from the date of the notice (to allow for applications to the court under s.986), the target company transfers the shares to the offeror on receipt of the consideration which it holds on trust for the shareholders on terms provided by s.982.

982.   Further provision about consideration held on trust under section 981(9)

(1) This section applies where an offeror pays or transfers consideration to the company under section 981(6).

(2) The company must pay into a separate bank account that complies with subsection (3)-
　　(a) any money it receives under paragraph (b) of section 981(6), and
　　(b) any dividend or other sum accruing from any other consideration it receives under that paragraph.

(3) A bank account complies with this subsection if the balance on the account-
　　(a) bears interest at an appropriate rate, and
　　(b) can be withdrawn by such notice (if any) as is appropriate.

(4) If-
　　(a) the person entitled to the consideration held on trust by virtue of section 981(9) cannot be found, and
　　(b) subsection (5) applies,
the consideration (together with any interest, dividend or other benefit that has accrued from it) must be paid into court.

(5) This subsection applies where-
　　(a) reasonable enquiries have been made at reasonable intervals to find the person, and
　　(b) twelve years have elapsed since the consideration was received, or the company is wound up.

(6) In relation to a company registered in Scotland, subsections (7) and (8) apply instead of subsection (4).

(7) If the person entitled to the consideration held on trust by virtue of section 981(9) cannot be found and subsection (5) applies-
　　(a) the trust terminates,
　　(b) the company or (if the company is wound up) the liquidator must sell any consideration other than cash and any benefit other than cash that has accrued from the consideration, and
　　(c) a sum representing-
　　　　(i) the consideration so far as it is cash,
　　　　(ii) the proceeds of any sale under paragraph (b), and
　　　　(iii) any interest, dividend or other benefit that has accrued from the consideration,
　　must be deposited in the name of the Accountant of Court in a separate bank account complying with subsection (3) and the receipt for the deposit must be transmitted to the Accountant of Court.

(8) Section 58 of the Bankruptcy (Scotland) Act 1985 (c. 66) (so far as consistent with this Act) applies (with any necessary modifications) to sums deposited under subsection (7) as it applies to sums deposited under section 57(1)(a) of that Act.

(9) The expenses of any such enquiries as are mentioned in subsection (5) may be paid out of the money or other property held on trust for the person to whom the enquiry relates.

GENERAL NOTE

This section replaces s.430(10)-(15) of the 1985 Act without any changes of substance.

Subsections (2)-(5) and (9)

These subsections establish the parameters for the holding of the trust fund established under s.981(9) and provide for the eventuality that the non-acceptors cannot be found after reasonable enquiries (paid for out of the fund) have been made over a 12-year period (or earlier if the target company is wound up). The fund is then to be paid into court. Subsection (4) does not apply to Scotland.

Subsections (6)-(8)

These subsections apply to Scotland in place of subs.(4).

"Sell-out"

983. Right of minority shareholder to be bought out by offeror

(1) Subsections (2) and (3) apply in a case where a takeover offer relates to all the shares in a company.

For this purpose a takeover offer relates to all the shares in a company if it is an offer to acquire all the shares in the company within the meaning of section 974.

(2) The holder of any voting shares to which the offer relates who has not accepted the offer may require the offeror to acquire those shares if, at any time before the end of the period within which the offer can be accepted-

    (a) the offeror has by virtue of acceptances of the offer acquired or unconditionally contracted to acquire some (but not all) of the shares to which the offer relates, and

    (b) those shares, with or without any other shares in the company which he has acquired or contracted to acquire (whether unconditionally or subject to conditions being met)-

        (i) amount to not less than 90% in value of all the voting shares in the company (or would do so but for section 990(1)), and

        (ii) carry not less than 90% of the voting rights in the company (or would do so but for section 990(1)).

(3) The holder of any non-voting shares to which the offer relates who has not accepted the offer may require the offeror to acquire those shares if, at any time before the end of the period within which the offer can be accepted-

    (a) the offeror has by virtue of acceptances of the offer acquired or unconditionally contracted to acquire some (but not all) of the shares to which the offer relates, and

    (b) those shares, with or without any other shares in the company which he has acquired or contracted to acquire (whether unconditionally or subject to conditions being met), amount to not less than 90% in value of all the shares in the company (or would do so but for section 990(1)).

(4) If a takeover offer relates to shares of one or more classes and at any time before the end of the period within which the offer can be accepted-

    (a) the offeror has by virtue of acceptances of the offer acquired or unconditionally contracted to acquire some (but not all) of the shares of any class to which the offer relates, and

    (b) those shares, with or without any other shares of that class which he has acquired or contracted to acquire (whether unconditionally or subject to conditions being met)-

        (i) amount to not less than 90% in value of all the shares of that class, and

(ii) in a case where the shares of that class are voting shares, carry not less than 90% of the voting rights carried by the shares of that class,

the holder of any shares of that class to which the offer relates who has not accepted the offer may require the offeror to acquire those shares.

(5) For the purposes of subsections (2) to (4), in calculating 90% of the value of any shares, shares held by the company as treasury shares are to be treated as having been acquired by the offeror.

(6) Subsection (7) applies where-

    (a) a shareholder exercises rights conferred on him by subsection (2), (3) or (4),

    (b) at the time when he does so, there are shares in the company which the offeror has contracted to acquire subject to conditions being met, and in relation to which the contract has not become unconditional, and

    (c) the requirement imposed by subsection (2)(b), (3)(b) or (4)(b) (as the case may be) would not be satisfied if those shares were not taken into account.

(7) The shareholder is treated for the purposes of section 985 as not having exercised his rights under this section unless the requirement imposed by paragraph (b) of subsection (2), (3) or (4) (as the case may be) would be satisfied if-

    (a) the reference in that paragraph to other shares in the company which the offeror has contracted to acquire unconditionally or subject to conditions being met were a reference to such shares which he has unconditionally contracted to acquire, and

    (b) the reference in that subsection to the period within which the offer can be accepted were a reference to the period referred to in section 984(2).

(8) A reference in subsection (2)(b), (3)(b), (4)(b), (6) or (7) to shares which the offeror has acquired or contracted to acquire includes a reference to shares which an associate of his has acquired or contracted to acquire.

GENERAL NOTE

This section, together with sections 984 and 985, replaces ss.430A and 430B of the 1985 Act, so as to provide for the exercise of the right of sell-out by a minority shareholder of a target company. There are modifications to take into account Art.16 of the Takeovers Directive (2004/25/EC) and the recommendations of the CLR. This sell-out right is subject to an application to the court under s.986 and modified to allow for joint offerors by s.987.

Subsections (1)-(4)

These subsections replace s.430A(1) and (2) of the 1985 Act. There are substantive changes involving the threshold required for exercise of the right. The threshold, as required by the Directive, is that the offeror (or an associate - see s.988) has achieved 90 per cent in value, and if the shares are voting shares, 90 per cent of the voting rights, of all the shares or all of the class of shares as appropriate.

This threshold is calculated by adding together (i) all the shares to which the offer relates (see ss.975 and 977), whether acquired or unconditionally contracted to be acquired by the offeror or an associate, and (ii) all other target shares (or class) which the offeror has acquired or contracted to acquire, whether conditionally or unconditionally (new clarification). In the case of a holder of non-voting shares, the threshold is 90 per cent in value of all the shares (or class).

Note this is a different threshold to that required for a squeeze-out since it includes, e.g. shares held by the offeror at the date of the offer and all contractual acquisitions, whether or not for a consideration.

Unconditionally contracted to acquire, offeror, voting rights, voting shares and *non voting shares* are defined in s.991.

Subsection (5)

This subsection re-enacts s.430A(2A) and preserves the rule that treasury shares count against the offeror for sell-out even if they are excluded from the offer.

Subsections (6) and (7)

Since conditionally acquired shares can be included in calculating the sell-out threshold, the relevant target may be reached only by including such shares. If in fact those conditions subsequently remain unfulfilled, the offeror may have to buy out the dissenter without actually ever owning 90 per cent of the relevant shares. Accordingly, these subsections provide that in such a situation, the obligation to buy will only arise if the target is reached without including such conditional contracts within the period allowed for the exercise of the sell-our right under s.984(2). In such a case there is a corresponding temporary freeze on the offeror's right of squeeze-out in s.979(6) and (7).

Subsection (8)
This subsection replaces s.430E(3). For *associate* see s.988.

984. Further provision about rights conferred by section 983

(1) Rights conferred on a shareholder by subsection (2), (3) or (4) of section 983 are exercisable by a written communication addressed to the offeror.

(2) Rights conferred on a shareholder by subsection (2), (3) or (4) of that section are not exercisable after the end of the period of three months from-

    (a) the end of the period within which the offer can be accepted, or

    (b) if later, the date of the notice that must be given under subsection (3) below.

(3) Within one month of the time specified in subsection (2), (3) or (4) (as the case may be) of that section, the offeror must give any shareholder who has not accepted the offer notice in the prescribed manner of-

    (a) the rights that are exercisable by the shareholder under that subsection, and

    (b) the period within which the rights are exercisable.

If the notice is given before the end of the period within which the offer can be accepted, it must state that the offer is still open for acceptance.

(4) Subsection (3) does not apply if the offeror has given the shareholder a notice in respect of the shares in question under section 979.

(5) An offeror who fails to comply with subsection (3) commits an offence.

If the offeror is a company, every officer of that company who is in default or to whose neglect the failure is attributable also commits an offence.

(6) If an offeror other than a company is charged with an offence for failing to comply with subsection (3), it is a defence for him to prove that he took all reasonable steps for securing compliance with that subsection.

(7) A person guilty of an offence under this section is liable-

    (a) on conviction on indictment, to a fine;

    (b) on summary conviction, to a fine not exceeding the statutory maximum and, for continued contravention, a daily default fine not exceeding one-fiftieth of the statutory maximum.

GENERAL NOTE

This section imposes new time limits on the exercise of the right of sell-out as required by the Directive and otherwise re-enacts s.430A(5)-(7) of the 1985 Act as to the giving of the notice.

Subsections (1)-(4)

These subsections now provide that any sell-out right must be exercised either within three months of the offer period (whether the offer is subject to the City Code or otherwise) or, if later, within three months from the date of the notice of entitlement. The offeror is obliged to send such a notice to the dissenters under subs.(3) within one month of the sell-out threshold being achieved under s.950. There is no such obligation (just as before in s.430A(4) of the 1985 Act) if a squeeze-out notice has already been issued under s.979.

Subsections (5)-(7)

These subsections re-enact s.430A(6) and (7) of the 1985 Act imposing a criminal offence in default, with modifications to the sanctions in line with the Act as a whole (see Sch.3).

985. Effect of requirement under section 983

(1) Subject to section 986, this section applies where a shareholder exercises his rights under section 983 in respect of any shares held by him.

(2) The offeror is entitled and bound to acquire those shares on the terms of the offer or on such other terms as may be agreed.

(3) Where the terms of an offer are such as to give the shareholder a choice of consideration-

    (a) the shareholder may indicate his choice when requiring the offeror to acquire the shares, and

    (b) the notice given to the shareholder under section 984(3)-

        (i) must give particulars of the choice and of the rights conferred by this subsection, and

        (ii) may state which consideration specified in the offer will apply if he does not indicate a choice.

The reference in subsection (2) to the terms of the offer is to be read accordingly.

(4) Subsection (3) applies whether or not any time-limit or other conditions applicable to the choice under the terms of the offer can still be complied with.

(5) If the consideration offered to or (as the case may be) chosen by the shareholder-

    (a) is not cash and the offeror is no longer able to provide it, or

    (b) was to have been provided by a third party who is no longer bound or able to provide it,

the consideration is to be taken to consist of an amount of cash, payable by the offeror, which at the date when the shareholder requires the offeror to acquire the shares is equivalent to the consideration offered or (as the case may be) chosen.

GENERAL NOTE

    This section re-enacts s.430B of the 1985 Act, with some clarifications in the case of offers with a choice of consideration as recommended by the CLR, mirroring those in s.981.

Subsection (2)

    This subsection directly reproduces s.430B(2) of the 1985 Act.

Subsections (3)-(5)

    Any notice served by the offeror must in the case of a choice of consideration provide for the same choice, and default choice, irrespective of any limits in the original offer. Consideration in kind, even if no longer available, must be offered and the cash equivalent at the date of the sell-out request must be paid.

Supplementary

986. Applications to the court

(1) Where a notice is given under section 979 to a shareholder the court may, on an application made by him, order-

    (a) that the offeror is not entitled and bound to acquire the shares to which the notice relates, or

    (b) that the terms on which the offeror is entitled and bound to acquire the shares shall be such as the court thinks fit.

(2) An application under subsection (1) must be made within six weeks from the date on which the notice referred to in that subsection was given. If an application to the court under subsection (1) is pending at the end of that period, section 981(6) does not have effect until the application has been disposed of.

(3) Where a shareholder exercises his rights under section 983 in respect of any shares held by him, the court may, on an application made by him or the offeror, order that the terms on which the offeror is entitled and bound to acquire the shares shall be such as the court thinks fit.

(4) On an application under subsection (1) or (3)-

    (a) the court may not require consideration of a higher value than that specified in the terms of the offer ("the offer value") to be given for the shares to which the application relates unless the holder of the shares shows that the offer value would be unfair;

    (b) the court may not require consideration of a lower value than the offer value to be given for the shares.

(5) No order for costs or expenses may be made against a shareholder making an application under subsection (1) or (3) unless the court considers that-

    (a) the application was unnecessary, improper or vexatious,

    (b) there has been unreasonable delay in making the application, or

    (c) there has been unreasonable conduct on the shareholder's part in conducting the proceedings on the application.

(6) A shareholder who has made an application under subsection (1) or (3) must give notice of the application to the offeror.

(7) An offeror who is given notice of an application under subsection (1) or (3) must give a copy of the notice to-

    (a) any person (other than the applicant) to whom a notice has been given under section 979;

    (b) any person who has exercised his rights under section 983.

(8) An offeror who makes an application under subsection (3) must give notice of the application to-

    (a) any person to whom a notice has been given under section 979;

    (b) any person who has exercised his rights under section 983.

(9) Where a takeover offer has not been accepted to the extent necessary for entitling the offeror to give notices under subsection (2) or (4) of section 979 the court may, on an application made by him, make an order authorising him to give notices under that subsection if it is satisfied that-

    (a) the offeror has after reasonable enquiry been unable to trace one or more of the persons holding shares to which the offer relates,

    (b) the requirements of that subsection would have been met if the person, or all the persons, mentioned in paragraph (a) above had accepted the offer, and

    (c) the consideration offered is fair and reasonable.

This is subject to subsection (10).

(10) The court may not make an order under subsection (9) unless it considers that it is just and equitable to do so having regard, in particular, to the number of shareholders who have been traced but who have not accepted the offer.

GENERAL NOTE

This section re-enacts s.430C of the 1985 Act in relation to applications to the court in respect of either squeeze-out or sell-out procedures with two substantive modifications in subss.(4) and (6)-(8).

Subsections (1)-(3) and (5)

These subsections re-enact s.430C(1)-(4) allowing for applications to the court by anyone subject to a squeeze-out notice, or by either party in a sell-out situation. Thus the existing jurisprudence on such applications will continue to apply, subject only to the new restrictions imposed by subs.(4): see, e.g. *Britoil, Re* [1990] B.C.C. 70; *Trafalgar House Plc, Re*, July 22 1996; *Lifecare International Plc, Re* [1990] B.C.L.C. 222; *Greythorn Ltd, Re* [2002] 1 B.C.L.C. 437; *Joseph Holt Plc, Re* [2001] 2 B.C.L.C. 604; *Evertite Locknuts, Re* [1945] Ch. 22; *Grierson, Oldham and Adams Ltd, Re* [1967] 1 W.L.R. 385; *Bugle Press, Re* [1961] Ch. 270; *Fiske Nominees Ltd v Dwyka Diamonds Ltd* [2002] 2 B.C.L.C. 123.

Subsection (4)

This new provision was introduced as a result of the Takeovers Directive (2004/25/EC). The court cannot vary the terms of the acquisition so as to reduce the consideration payable below the value of the offer. Conversely, it may not increase the consideration payable above that amount unless the applicant can show that that is unfair.

Subsections (6)-(8)

These new subsections enact a recommendation of the CLR. Any shareholder applying to the court, whether on a squeeze-out or sell-out, must promptly notify the offeror. In turn the offeror must then in turn notify anyone else, not being a party to the proceedings, who is either subject to a squeeze-out notice or is exercising a sell-out notice of the application.

If an offeror applies in relation to a sell-out, it must also notify anyone who is either subject to a squeeze-out notice or is exercising a sell-out right.

Subsections (9) and (10)

These subsections re-enact s.430C(5) in relation to applications by offerors to lower the squeeze-out threshold where the shortfall is due entirely to untraceable shareholders.

987. Joint offers

(1) In the case of a takeover offer made by two or more persons jointly, this Chapter has effect as follows.

(2) The conditions for the exercise of the rights conferred by section 979 are satisfied-

    (a) in the case of acquisitions by virtue of acceptances of the offer, by the joint offerors acquiring or unconditionally contracting to acquire the necessary shares jointly;

    (b) in other cases, by the joint offerors acquiring or unconditionally contracting to acquire the necessary shares either jointly or separately.

(3) The conditions for the exercise of the rights conferred by section 983 are satisfied-

    (a) in the case of acquisitions by virtue of acceptances of the offer, by the joint offerors acquiring or unconditionally contracting to acquire the necessary shares jointly;

    (b) in other cases, by the joint offerors acquiring or contracting (whether unconditionally or subject to conditions being met) to acquire the necessary shares either jointly or separately.

(4) Subject to the following provisions, the rights and obligations of the offeror under sections 979 to 985 are respectively joint rights and joint and several obligations of the joint offerors.

(5) A provision of sections 979 to 986 that requires or authorises a notice or other document to be given or sent by or to the joint offerors is complied with if the notice or document is given or sent by or to any of them (but see subsection (6)).

(6) The statutory declaration required by section 980(4) must be made by all of the joint offerors and, where one or more of them is a company, signed by a director of that company.

(7) In sections 974 to 977, 979(9), 981(6), 983(8) and 988 references to the offeror are to be read as references to the joint offerors or any of them.

(8) In section 981(7) and (8) references to the offeror are to be read as references to the joint offerors or such of them as they may determine.

(9) In sections 981(5)(a) and 985(5)(a) references to the offeror being no longer able to provide the relevant consideration are to be read as references to none of the joint offerors being able to do so.

(10) In section 986 references to the offeror are to be read as references to the joint offerors, except that-

    (a) an application under subsection (3) or (9) may be made by any of them, and

    (b) the reference in subsection (9)(a) to the offeror having been unable to trace one or more of the persons holding shares is to be read as a reference to none of the offerors having been able to do so.

GENERAL NOTE

This section re-enacts s.430D of the 1985 Act, with minor modifications, so as to apply the squeeze-out and sell-out procedures to the situation where there are joint offerors.

Subsections (2) and (4)

These subsections are a modified replacement for s.430D(2). For both the squeeze-out and sell-out thresholds all shares acquired by joint offerors by virtue of acceptances of the offer jointly are to be added together. In the case of squeeze-out, all other acquisitions by joint offerors will be counted if they were acquired or *unconditionally contracted to be acquired* (see s.991(2)) either jointly or separately. In the case of sell-out, such other acquisitions will also count even if they were conditionally contracted to be acquired. That difference mirrors the differences in the two rights. As before, for joint offerors, all rights under this Chapter are joint rights but the obligations are joint and several.

These subsections re-enact s.430D(3)-(7) modifying various provisions of the sections in this chapter to provide for joint offerors. There are no substantive changes.

Interpretation

988. Associates

(1) In this Chapter "associate", in relation to an offeror, means-
    (a) a nominee of the offeror,
    (b) a holding company, subsidiary or fellow subsidiary of the offeror or a nominee of such a holding company, subsidiary or fellow subsidiary,
    (c) a body corporate in which the offeror is substantially interested,
    (d) a person who is, or is a nominee of, a party to a share acquisition agreement with the offeror, or
    (e) (where the offeror is an individual) his spouse or civil partner and any minor child or step-child of his.

(2) For the purposes of subsection (1)(b) a company is a fellow subsidiary of another body corporate if both are subsidiaries of the same body corporate but neither is a subsidiary of the other.

(3) For the purposes of subsection (1)(c) an offeror has a substantial interest in a body corporate if-
    (a) the body or its directors are accustomed to act in accordance with his directions or instructions, or
    (b) he is entitled to exercise or control the exercise of one-third or more of the voting power at general meetings of the body.

Subsections (2) and (3) of section 823 (which contain provision about when a person is treated as entitled to exercise or control the exercise of voting power) apply for the purposes of this subsection as they apply for the purposes of that section.

(4) For the purposes of subsection (1)(d) an agreement is a share acquisition agreement if-
    (a) it is an agreement for the acquisition of, or of an interest in, shares to which the offer relates,
    (b) it includes provisions imposing obligations or restrictions on any one or more of the parties to it with respect to their use, retention or disposal of such shares, or their interests in such shares, acquired in pursuance of the agreement (whether or not together with any other shares to which the offer relates or any other interests of theirs in such shares), and
    (c) it is not an excluded agreement (see subsection (5)).

(5) An agreement is an "excluded agreement"-
    (a) if it is not legally binding, unless it involves mutuality in the undertakings, expectations or understandings of the parties to it, or
    (b) if it is an agreement to underwrite or sub-underwrite an offer of shares in a company, provided the agreement is confined to that purpose and any matters incidental to it.

(6) The reference in subsection (4)(b) to the use of interests in shares is to the exercise of any rights or of any control or influence arising from those interests (including the right to enter into an agreement for the exercise, or for control of the exercise, of any of those rights by another person).

(7) In this section-
    (a) "agreement" includes any agreement or arrangement;
    (b) references to provisions of an agreement include-
        (i) undertakings, expectations or understandings operative under an arrangement, and
        (ii) any provision whether express or implied and whether absolute or not.

GENERAL NOTE

This section defines who is an associate for the purposes of including their acquisitions in calculating the various thresholds under ss.979 and 983. As such it re-enacts, without any changes of substance, s.430E(4)-(8) of the 1985 Act. Former sub-ss.430E(1)-(3) have been integrated within the substantive squeeze-out and sell-out sections.

989.   Convertible securities

(1) For the purposes of this Chapter securities of a company are treated as shares in the company if they are convertible into or entitle the holder to subscribe for such shares. References to the holder of shares or a shareholder are to be read accordingly.

(2) Subsection (1) is not to be read as requiring any securities to be treated-
  (a) as shares of the same class as those into which they are convertible or for which the holder is entitled to subscribe, or
  (b) as shares of the same class as other securities by reason only that the shares into which they are convertible or for which the holder is entitled to subscribe are of the same class.

GENERAL NOTE

This section restates s.430F of the 1985 Act and provides for convertible securities to be treated as a separate class of shares for the purposes of this Chapter.; thus avoiding the problems of *Simo Securities Trust, Re* [1971] 1 WLR 1455.

990.   Debentures carrying voting rights

(1) For the purposes of this Chapter debentures issued by a company to which subsection (2) applies are treated as shares in the company if they carry voting rights.

(2) This subsection applies to a company that has voting shares, or debentures carrying voting rights, which are admitted to trading on a regulated market.

(3) In this Chapter, in relation to debentures treated as shares by virtue of subsection (1)-
  (a) references to the holder of shares or a shareholder are to be read accordingly;
  (b) references to shares being allotted are to be read as references to debentures being issued.

GENERAL NOTE

This new section provides that debentures in the target company carrying voting rights which are listed on the Official List (or if the target company is so listed) are treated as a class of shares for the purposes of this Chapter. Thus the issue of such debentures is an allotment of shares and the holders of such debentures are holders of shares.

Regulated market - see Art.1(13) of Directive 93/22/EEC.

991.   Interpretation

(1) In this Chapter-
  "the company" means the company whose shares are the subject of a takeover offer;
  "date of the offer" means-
      (a) where the offer is published, the date of publication;
      (b) where the offer is not published, or where any notices of the offer are given before the date of publication, the date when notices of the offer (or the first such notices) are given;
    and references to the date of the offer are to be read in accordance with section 974(7) (revision of offer terms) where that applies;
  "non-voting shares" means shares that are not voting shares;
  "offeror" means (subject to section 987) the person making a takeover offer;
  "voting rights" means rights to vote at general meetings of the company, including rights that arise only in certain circumstances;

"voting shares" means shares carrying voting rights.

(2) For the purposes of this Chapter a person contracts unconditionally to acquire shares if his entitlement under the contract to acquire them is not (or is no longer) subject to conditions or if all conditions to which it was subject have been met.

A reference to a contract becoming unconditional is to be read accordingly.

GENERAL NOTE

This section provides a number of definitions pertinent to this Chapter. Note that voting rights include rights to vote only on specific occasions.

The only possible problem relates to the definition of *the date of an offer* where it is not published. It is not entirely clear what is meant by a *notice of the offer*. This must be more than notification of an intention to make an offer, but less than the formal offer document. The date of the offer is also subject to revision under s.974(7).

CHAPTER 4

AMENDMENTS TO PART 7 OF THE COMPANIES ACT 1985

992. Matters to be dealt with in directors' report

(1) Part 7 of the Companies Act 1985 (c. 6) (accounts and audit) is amended as follows.

(2) In Schedule 7 (matters to be dealt with in directors' report), after Part 6 insert-

PART 7

"DISCLOSURE REQUIRED BY CERTAIN PUBLICLY-TRADED COMPANIES

13.

(1) This Part of this Schedule applies to the directors' report for a financial year if the company had securities carrying voting rights admitted to trading on a regulated market at the end of that year.

(2) The report shall contain detailed information, by reference to the end of that year, on the following matters-

    (a) the structure of the company's capital, including in particular-

        (i) the rights and obligations attaching to the shares or, as the case may be, to each class of shares in the company, and

        (ii) where there are two or more such classes, the percentage of the total share capital represented by each class;

    (b) any restrictions on the transfer of securities in the company, including in particular-

        (i) limitations on the holding of securities, and

        (ii) requirements to obtain the approval of the company, or of other holders of securities in the company, for a transfer of securities;

    (c) in the case of each person with a significant direct or indirect holding of securities in the company, such details as are known to the company of-

        (i) the identity of the person,

        (ii) the size of the holding, and

        (iii) the nature of the holding;

    (d) in the case of each person who holds securities carrying special rights with regard to control of the company-

        (i) the identity of the person, and

        (ii) the nature of the rights;

    (e) where-

> (i) the company has an employees' share scheme, and
> (ii) shares to which the scheme relates have rights with regard to control of the company that are not exercisable directly by the employees,
>
> how those rights are exercisable;
>
> (f) any restrictions on voting rights, including in particular-
>> (i) limitations on voting rights of holders of a given percentage or number of votes,
>> (ii) deadlines for exercising voting rights, and
>> (iii) arrangements by which, with the company's cooperation, financial rights carried by securities are held by a person other than the holder of the securities;
>
> (g) any agreements between holders of securities that are known to the company and may result in restrictions on the transfer of securities or on voting rights;
> (h) any rules that the company has about-
>> (i) appointment and replacement of directors, or
>> (ii) amendment of the company's articles of association;
>
> (i) the powers of the company's directors, including in particular any powers in relation to the issuing or buying back by the company of its shares;
> (j) any significant agreements to which the company is a party that take effect, alter or terminate upon a change of control of the company following a takeover bid, and the effects of any such agreements;
> (k) any agreements between the company and its directors or employees providing for compensation for loss of office or employment (whether through resignation, purported redundancy or otherwise) that occurs because of a takeover bid.
>
> (3) For the purposes of sub-paragraph (2)(a) a company's capital includes any securities in the company that are not admitted to trading on a regulated market.
> (4) For the purposes of sub-paragraph (2)(c) a person has an indirect holding of securities if-
>> (a) they are held on his behalf, or
>> (b) he is able to secure that rights carried by the securities are exercised in accordance with his wishes.
>
> (5) Sub-paragraph (2)(j) does not apply to an agreement if-
>> (a) disclosure of the agreement would be seriously prejudicial to the company, and
>> (b) the company is not under any other obligation to disclose it.
>
> (6) In this paragraph-
>> "securities" means shares or debentures;
>> "takeover bid" has the same meaning as in the Takeovers Directive;
>> "the Takeovers Directive" means Directive 2004/25/EC of the European Parliament and of the Council;
>> "voting rights" means rights to vote at general meetings of the company in question, including rights that arise only in certain circumstances.".

(3) In section 234ZZA (requirements of directors' reports), at the end of subsection (4) (contents of Schedule 7) insert-

> "Part 7 specifies information to be disclosed by certain publicly-traded companies.".

(4) After that subsection insert-

> "(5) A directors' report shall also contain any necessary explanatory material with regard to information that is required to be included in the report by Part 7 of Schedule 7.".

(5) In section 251 (summary financial statements), after subsection (2ZA) insert-

> "(2ZB) A company that sends to an entitled person a summary financial statement instead of a copy of its directors' report shall-
>> (a) include in the statement the explanatory material required to be included in the directors' report by section 234ZZA(5), or
>> (b) send that material to the entitled person at the same time as it sends the statement.

For the purposes of paragraph (b), subsections (2A) to (2E) apply in relation to the material referred to in that paragraph as they apply in relation to a summary financial statement.".

(6) The amendments made by this section apply in relation to directors' reports for financial years beginning on or after 20th May 2006.

GENERAL NOTE

This section requires information regarding share capital in particular information which is relevant to control of the company, to be disclosed in the Directors' report for a financial year. However, this does not apply to all companies subject to the Takeover Code, only those which have securities carrying voting rights admitted to trading on a regulated market at the end of the year. The disclosure requirements, however, apply if such a company has securities which are not admitted to trading on a regulated market (such as a separate class of shares). This requirement is included in compliance with Art.10 of the Directive.

Certain of the information required may not be in the knowledge of the company, for example agreements between holders of securities which may result in restrictions on transfers or on voting rights (subs.(2)(g)). There is a question as to whether an uncompleted sale agreement could fall within the category of restrictions on transfer, although this is probably not the case in the absence of unusual features. More significantly, subs.(2)(j), which requires information on agreements take effect, alter or terminate on a change of control of the company, and the effects of such provisions, may result in sensitive information having to be disclosed. Such agreements are not uncommon, and are often of considerable significance to the company. The requirement in subs.(2) is to disclose "detailed information". It is not clear how far this will require companies to disclose previously confidential information.

PART 29

FRAUDULENT TRADING

993. Offence of fraudulent trading

(1) If any business of a company is carried on with intent to defraud creditors of the company or creditors of any other person, or for any fraudulent purpose, every person who is knowingly a party to the carrying on of the business in that manner commits an offence.

(2) This applies whether or not the company has been, or is in the course of being, wound up.

(3) A person guilty of an offence under this section is liable-

    (a) on conviction on indictment, to imprisonment for a term not exceeding ten years or a fine (or both);

    (b) on summary conviction-

        (i) in England and Wales, to imprisonment for a term not exceeding twelve months or a fine not exceeding the statutory maximum (or both);

        (ii) in Scotland or Northern Ireland, to imprisonment for a term not exceeding six months or a fine not exceeding the statutory maximum (or both).

GENERAL NOTE

This section replaces s.458 of the Companies Act 1985, where the business of a company is carried on with the intention of defrauding creditors of the company or of any other person, or where the business has been carried on for a fraudulent purpose, every party knowingly a party to that action commits an offence. It makes no difference, for the purpose of this section, whether the company has been or is in the course of being wound up (subs.(2), and *cf.* s.213 of the Insolvency Act 1986, where a liquidator of a company can apply to the court for an order that any party knowingly a party to fraudulent trading should make a contribution to the assets of the company). The penalty for the offence is prescribed in subs.(3). A person convicted on indictment may be imprisoned for a term not exceeding ten years or fined, or both, and a person on a summary conviction may be imprisoned for not more than 12 months (in England and Wales) or six months (in Scotland or Northern Ireland). In England and Wales or Scotland and Northern Ireland a person, on a summary conviction, may also be subject to a fine not exceeding the statutory maximum.

PROTECTION OF MEMBERS AGAINST UNFAIR PREJUDICE

GENERAL NOTE

Part 30 of the Act is one of the parts introduced at a late stage in the Parliamentary process in order to make the 2006 Act a fuller restatement of company law and to reduce the need for reliance on the 1985 Act in the future. Its aim therefore is to restate, rather than to amend in any significant way, what was previously Pt XVII of the 1985 Act on protection against unfair prejudice. In spite of the practical importance of this part of the Act it is not intended to provide detailed annotation of its provisions, since in the main they replicate what was in the 1985 Act. One can note the different style of drafting, which has produced rather longer, but easier to read, sections. One can note that Pt 30 of the 2006 Act contains six sections as against three in Pt XVII of the former Act. This is the result of the introduction of three sections (ss.997-999) headed 'supplementary provisions'. These sections spell out material previously contained within the substantive sections. Section 999 is particularly notable in this respect. It spells out matters previously contained in s.461(4) of the 1985 Act, i.e. the consequences of an alteration made to the company's articles by the court as a result of a successful unfair prejudice petition. But it also goes further than that by embracing changes to any aspect of the company's constitution, which is the concept used by the 2006 Act in place of the 'memorandum and articles' which lay at the core of the 1985 Act. See Ch.3 of Pt 3 of the 2006 Act and especially, for these purposes, s.29 - resolution or agreement affecting a company's constitution.

Main provisions

994.   Petition by company member

(1) A member of a company may apply to the court by petition for an order under this Part on the ground-
    (a) that the company's affairs are being or have been conducted in a manner that is unfairly prejudicial to the interests of members generally or of some part of its members (including at least himself), or
    (b) that an actual or proposed act or omission of the company (including an act or omission on its behalf) is or would be so prejudicial.
(2) The provisions of this Part apply to a person who is not a member of a company but to whom shares in the company have been transferred or transmitted by operation of law as they apply to a member of a company.
(3) In this section, and so far as applicable for the purposes of this section in the other provisions of this Part, "company" means-
    (a) a company within the meaning of this Act, or
    (b) a company that is not such a company but is a statutory water company within the meaning of the Statutory Water Companies Act 1991 (c. 58).

995.   Petition by Secretary of State

(1) This section applies to a company in respect of which-
    (a) the Secretary of State has received a report under section 437 of the Companies Act 1985 (c. 6) (inspector's report);
    (b) the Secretary of State has exercised his powers under section 447 or 448 of that Act (powers to require documents and information or to enter and search premises);
    (c) the Secretary of State or the Financial Services Authority has exercised his or its powers under Part 11 of the Financial Services and Markets Act 2000 (c. 8) (information gathering and investigations); or
    (d) the Secretary of State has received a report from an investigator appointed by him or the Financial Services Authority under that Part.
(2) If it appears to the Secretary of State that in the case of such a company-

    (a) the company's affairs are being or have been conducted in a manner that is unfairly pre-judicial to the interests of members generally or of some part of its members, or

    (b) an actual or proposed act or omission of the company (including an act or omission on its behalf) is or would be so prejudicial,

he may apply to the court by petition for an order under this Part.

(3) The Secretary of State may do this in addition to, or instead of, presenting a petition for the winding up of the company.

(4) In this section, and so far as applicable for the purposes of this section in the other provisions of this Part, "company" means any body corporate that is liable to be wound up under the Insolvency Act 1986 (c. 45) or the Insolvency (Northern Ireland) Order 1989 (S.I. 1989/2405 (N.I. 19)).

996.   Powers of the court under this Part

(1) If the court is satisfied that a petition under this Part is well founded, it may make such order as it thinks fit for giving relief in respect of the matters complained of.

(2) Without prejudice to the generality of subsection (1), the court's order may-

    (a) regulate the conduct of the company's affairs in the future;

    (b) require the company-

        (i) to refrain from doing or continuing an act complained of, or

       (ii) to do an act that the petitioner has complained it has omitted to do;

    (c) authorise civil proceedings to be brought in the name and on behalf of the company by such person or persons and on such terms as the court may direct;

    (d) require the company not to make any, or any specified, alterations in its articles without the leave of the court;

    (e) provide for the purchase of the shares of any members of the company by other members or by the company itself and, in the case of a purchase by the company itself, the reduction of the company's capital accordingly.

Supplementary provisions

997.   Application of general rule-making powers

  The power to make rules under section 411 of the Insolvency Act 1986 (c. 45) or Article 359 of the Insolvency (Northern Ireland) Order 1989 (S.I. 1989/2405 (N.I. 19)), so far as relating to a winding-up petition, applies for the purposes of a petition under this Part.

998.   Copy of order affecting company's constitution to be delivered to registrar

(1) Where an order of the court under this Part-

    (a) alters the company's constitution, or

    (b) gives leave for the company to make any, or any specified, alterations to its constitution,

the company must deliver a copy of the order to the registrar.

(2) It must do so within 14 days from the making of the order or such longer period as the court may allow.

(3) If a company makes default in complying with this section, an offence is committed by-

    (a) the company, and

    (b) every officer of the company who is in default.

(4) A person guilty of an offence under this section is liable on summary conviction to a fine not exceeding level 3 on the standard scale and, for continued contravention, a daily default fine not exceeding one-tenth of level 3 on the standard scale.

999.   Supplementary provisions where company's constitution altered

(1) This section applies where an order under this Part alters a company's constitution.

(2) If the order amends-

    (a) a company's articles, or

    (b) any resolution or agreement to which Chapter 3 of Part 3 applies (resolution or agreement affecting a company's constitution),

the copy of the order delivered to the registrar by the company under section 998 must be accompanied by a copy of the company's articles, or the resolution or agreement in question, as amended.

(3) Every copy of a company's articles issued by the company after the order is made must be accompanied by a copy of the order, unless the effect of the order has been incorporated into the articles by amendment.

(4) If a company makes default in complying with this section an offence is committed by-

    (a) the company, and

    (b) every officer of the company who is in default.

(5) A person guilty of an offence under this section is liable on summary conviction to a fine not exceeding level 3 on the standard scale.

PART 31

DISSOLUTION AND RESTORATION TO THE REGISTER

GENERAL NOTE

Part 31 comprises three Chapters. Chapter 1 deals with the striking off of a company by the registrar, and Ch.2 with the company's property on dissolution. Chapter 3 covers restoration to the register of a company previously struck off. It substantially re-enacts provisions of the Companies Act 1985 but makes certain amendments to their application.

CHAPTER I

STRIKING OFF

Registrar's power to strike off defunct company

1000. Power to strike off company not carrying on business or in operation

(1) If the registrar has reasonable cause to believe that a company is not carrying on business or in operation, the registrar may send to the company by post a letter inquiring whether the company is carrying on business or in operation.

(2) If the registrar does not within one month of sending the letter receive any answer to it, the registrar must within 14 days after the expiration of that month send to the company by post a registered letter referring to the first letter, and stating-

    (a) that no answer to it has been received, and

    (b) that if an answer is not received to the second letter within one month from its date, a notice will be published in the Gazette with a view to striking the company's name off the register.

(3) If the registrar-

    (a) receives an answer to the effect that the company is not carrying on business or in operation, or

    (b) does not within one month after sending the second letter receive any answer,

the registrar may publish in the Gazette, and send to the company by post, a notice that at the expiration of three months from the date of the notice the name of the company mentioned in it will, unless cause is shown to the contrary, be struck off the register and the company will be dissolved.

(4) At the expiration of the time mentioned in the notice the registrar may, unless cause to the contrary is previously shown by the company, strike its name off the register.

(5) The registrar must publish notice in the Gazette of the company's name having been struck off the register.

(6) On the publication of the notice in the Gazette the company is dissolved.

(7) However-

    (a) the liability (if any) of every director, managing officer and member of the company continues and may be enforced as if the company had not been dissolved, and

    (b) nothing in this section affects the power of the court to wind up a company the name of which has been struck off the register.

GENERAL NOTE

This section replaces, without substantial amendment, s.652 of the Companies Act 1985. It provides for the registrar of companies, where he has reasonable cause to believe that a company is not carrying on business or in operation, to enquire in writing whether this is the case (subs.(1)). If no response is made to this initial enquiry within one month, the registrar must, within 14 days after the expiration of that month, send a registered letter to the company referring to the first letter and stating that he has not received an answer to it and that, if no answer to the second letter is received within one month from its date, he will publish a notice in the Gazette with a view to striking the company's name off the register (subs.(2)). If the registrar receives an answer to the effect that the company is not in operation or carrying on business, or receives no answer within one month of sending the second letter, he may publish in the Gazette a notice (which he may send to the company by post) that, at the expiration if a period of three months from the date of the notice, the company's name will be struck off the register and the company dissolved unless cause to the contrary is shown (subs.(3)). On the expiration of the three month period mentioned in the notice, the registrar may strike the company's name off the register unless the company shows cause to the contrary (subs.(4)) and must then publish a second notice in the Gazette stating that the company's name has been struck off the register (subs.(5)). The publication of this notice has the effect of dissolving the company (subs.(6)), but this does not effect any liability of any director, managing officer or member of the company which continues and may be enforced as though the company had not been dissolved, nor does it affect the power of the court to wind the company up (subs.(7)).

1001. Duty to act in case of company being wound up

(1) If, in a case where a company is being wound up-

    (a) the registrar has reasonable cause to believe-

        (i) that no liquidator is acting, or

        (ii) that the affairs of the company are fully wound up, and

    (b) the returns required to be made by the liquidator have not been made for a period of six consecutive months,

the registrar must publish in the Gazette and send to the company or the liquidator (if any) a notice that at the expiration of three months from the date of the notice the name of the company mentioned in it will, unless cause is shown to the contrary, be struck off the register and the company will be dissolved.

(2) At the expiration of the time mentioned in the notice the registrar may, unless cause to the contrary is previously shown by the company, strike its name off the register.

(3) The registrar must publish notice in the Gazette of the company's name having been struck off the register.

(4) On the publication of the notice in the Gazette the company is dissolved.

(5) However-

    (a) the liability (if any) of every director, managing officer and member of the company continues and may be enforced as if the company had not been dissolved, and

    (b) nothing in this section affects the power of the court to wind up a company the name of which has been struck off the register.

This section replaces s.652(4) of the Companies Act 1985. It applies where a company is being wound up and the registrar has cause the believe that no liquidator is acting or that the affairs of the company are fully wound up, or where liquidator's returns have not been made for a period of six consecutive months. In such a case the registrar must public in the Gazette a notice (to be sent to the company or any liquidator) that the name of the company will, unless cause to the contrary is shown, be struck off the register and the company will be dissolved (subs.(1)). On the expiration of the three-month period mentioned in the notice the registrar may strike the company's name off the register unless the company shows cause to the contrary (subs.(2)) and must then publish a second notice in the Gazette stating that the company's name has been struck off the register (subs.(3)). The publication of this notice has the effect of dissolving the company (subs.(4)), but this does not affect any liability of any director, managing officer or member of the company which continues and may be enforced as though the company had not been dissolved, nor does it affect the power of the court to wind the company up (subs.(5)).

1002. Supplementary provisions as to service of letter or notice

(1) A letter or notice to be sent under section 1000 or 1001 to a company may be addressed to the company at its registered office or, if no office has been registered, to the care of some officer of the company.

(2) If there is no officer of the company whose name and address are known to the registrar, the letter or notice may be sent to each of the persons who subscribed the memorandum (if their addresses are known to the registrar).

(3) A notice to be sent to a liquidator under section 1001 may be addressed to him at his last known place of business.

GENERAL NOTE
This section re-enacts s.652(7) of the Companies Act 1985 and makes provision as to the service of a letter or a notice under ss.1000 or 1001. In the case of service on the company, it may be effected by sending the letter or notice to the company's registered office or, where no office has been registered, to the care of some officer of the company (subs.(1)). Where the registrar does not know the names or addresses of the company's officers, service may be effected by sending the letter or notice to the subscribers to the memorandum, if their addresses are known to the registrar (subs.(2)). A notice sent to the liquidator under s.1001 may be addressed to him at his last known place of business (subs.(3)).

Voluntary striking off

1003. Striking off on application by company

(1) On application by a company, the registrar of companies may strike the company's name off the register.

(2) The application-
    (a) must be made on the company's behalf by its directors or by a majority of them, and
    (b) must contain the prescribed information.

(3) The registrar may not strike a company off under this section until after the expiration of three months from the publication by the registrar in the Gazette of a notice-
    (a) stating that the registrar may exercise the power under this section in relation to the company, and
    (b) inviting any person to show cause why that should not be done.

(4) The registrar must publish notice in the Gazette of the company's name having been struck off.

(5) On the publication of the notice in the Gazette the company is dissolved.

(6) However-
    (a) the liability (if any) of every director, managing officer and member of the company continues and may be enforced as if the company had not been dissolved, and

(b) nothing in this section affects the power of the court to wind up a company the name of which has been struck off the register.

GENERAL NOTE

This section re-enacts s.652A of the Companies Act 1985 and extends its application to public companies. It provides for a company itself to apply to the registrar for the striking off of its name from the register (subs.(1)). The application must be made by the directors or a majority of them and must contain the prescribed information (subs.(2)). On receiving an application, the registrar must publish a notice in the Gazette stating that he may exercise his power under s.1003 and inviting any person to show cause why that should not be done, and he may not strike off a company until three months after the date of publication of that notice (subs.(3)). If no such cause is shown the registrar may strike the company's name off the register and must then publish a second notice in the Gazette stating that the company's name has been struck off the register (subs.(4)). The publication of this notice has the effect of dissolving the company (subs.(5)), but this does not effect any liability of any director, managing officer or member of the company which continues and may be enforced as though the company had not been dissolved, nor does it affect the power of the court to wind the company up (subs.(6)).

1004. Circumstances in which application not to be made: activities of company

(1) An application under section 1003 (application for voluntary striking off) on behalf of a company must not be made if, at any time in the previous three months, the company has-
    (a) changed its name,
    (b) traded or otherwise carried on business,
    (c) made a disposal for value of property or rights that, immediately before ceasing to trade or otherwise carry on business, it held for the purpose of disposal for gain in the normal course of trading or otherwise carrying on business, or
    (d) engaged in any other activity, except one which is-
        (i) necessary or expedient for the purpose of making an application under that section, or deciding whether to do so,
        (ii) necessary or expedient for the purpose of concluding the affairs of the company,
        (iii) necessary or expedient for the purpose of complying with any statutory requirement, or
        (iv) specified by the Secretary of State by order for the purposes of this subparagraph.
(2) For the purposes of this section, a company is not to be treated as trading or otherwise carrying on business by virtue only of the fact that it makes a payment in respect of a liability incurred in the course of trading or otherwise carrying on business.
(3) The Secretary of State may by order amend subsection (1) for the purpose of altering the period in relation to which the doing of the things mentioned in paragraphs (a) to (d) of that subsection is relevant.
(4) An order under this section is subject to negative resolution procedure.
(5) It is an offence for a person to make an application in contravention of this section.
(6) In proceedings for such an offence it is a defence for the accused to prove that he did not know, and could not reasonably have known, of the existence of the facts that led to the contravention.
(7) A person guilty of an offence under this section is liable-
    (a) on conviction on indictment, to a fine;
    (b) on summary conviction, to a fine not exceeding the statutory maximum.

GENERAL NOTE

This section replaces s.652B(1), (2) and (9) of the Companies Act 1985 and prohibits the making of an application on behalf of the company to have it struck off the register where it has, in the past three months changed its name (subs.(1)(a)), traded or carried on business (subs.(1)(b)), disposed of property or rights for value which were held for that purpose in the normal course of trading (subs.(1)(c)) or engaged in any activity other than those necessary for the purposes of applying under s.1003, for concluding the affairs of the company, for complying with any statutory requirement or otherwise specified by the Secretary of State for the purposes of s.1004(1) (subs.(1)(d)). The making of a payment in respect of an existing trading liability is not to be treated as "trading" or "carrying on business" for the purpose of subs.(1)(b) (subs.(2)), and the Secretary of State may by order (subject to negative resolution procedure - subs.(4)), amend the period of three months mentioned in subs.(1)). Any person making an application in contravention of this section commits an offence (subs.(5)), and in proceedings for that offence it is for the defendant to prove that he did not know or could not reasonably have known of the existence of facts leading to the contravention (i.e. of any of the circumstances listed in subs.(1)) (subs.(6)). The penalty for the offence is prescribed in subs.(7).

1005. Circumstances in which application not to be made: other proceedings not concluded

(1) An application under section 1003 (application for voluntary striking off) on behalf of a company must not be made at a time when-
    (a) an application to the court under Part 26 has been made on behalf of the company for the sanctioning of a compromise or arrangement and the matter has not been finally concluded;
    (b) a voluntary arrangement in relation to the company has been proposed under Part 1 of the Insolvency Act 1986 (c. 45) or Part 2 of the Insolvency (Northern Ireland) Order 1989 (S.I. 1989/2405 (N.I. 19)) and the matter has not been finally concluded;
    (c) the company is in administration under Part 2 of that Act or Part 3 of that Order;
    (d) paragraph 44 of Schedule B1 to that Act or paragraph 45 of Schedule B1 to that Order applies (interim moratorium on proceedings where application to the court for an administration order has been made or notice of intention to appoint administrator has been filed);
    (e) the company is being wound up under Part 4 of that Act or Part 5 of that Order, whether voluntarily or by the court, or a petition under that Part for winding up of the company by the court has been presented and not finally dealt with or withdrawn;
    (f) there is a receiver or manager of the company's property;
    (g) the company's estate is being administered by a judicial factor.
(2) For the purposes of subsection (1)(a), the matter is finally concluded if-
    (a) the application has been withdrawn,
    (b) the application has been finally dealt with without a compromise or arrangement being sanctioned by the court, or
    (c) a compromise or arrangement has been sanctioned by the court and has, together with anything required to be done under any provision made in relation to the matter by order of the court, been fully carried out.
(3) For the purposes of subsection (1)(b), the matter is finally concluded if-
    (a) no meetings are to be summoned under section 3 of the Insolvency Act 1986 (c. 45) or Article 16 of the Insolvency (Northern Ireland) Order 1989,
    (b) meetings summoned under that section or Article fail to approve the arrangement with no, or the same, modifications,
    (c) an arrangement approved by meetings summoned under that section, or in consequence of a direction under section 6(4)(b) of that Act or Article 19(4)(b) of that Order, has been fully implemented, or
    (d) the court makes an order under section 6(5) of that Act or Article 19(5) of that Order revoking approval given at previous meetings and, if the court gives any directions under section 6(6) of that Act or Article 19(6) of that Order, the company has done whatever it is required to do under those directions.
(4) It is an offence for a person to make an application in contravention of this section.
(5) In proceedings for such an offence it is a defence for the accused to prove that he did not know, and could not reasonably have known, of the existence of the facts that led to the contravention.
(6) A person guilty of an offence under this section is liable-
    (a) on conviction on indictment, to a fine;

(b) on summary conviction, to a fine not exceeding the statutory maximum.

1006. Copy of application to be given to members, employees, etc

(1) A person who makes an application under section 1003 (application for voluntary striking off) on behalf of a company must secure that, within seven days from the day on which the application is made, a copy of it is given to every person who at any time on that day is-
    (a) a member of the company,
    (b) an employee of the company,
    (c) a creditor of the company,
    (d) a director of the company,
    (e) a manager or trustee of any pension fund established for the benefit of employees of the company, or
    (f) a person of a description specified for the purposes of this paragraph by regulations made by the Secretary of State.
Regulations under paragraph (f) are subject to negative resolution procedure.
(2) Subsection (1) does not require a copy of the application to be given to a director who is a party to the application.
(3) The duty imposed by this section ceases to apply if the application is withdrawn before the end of the period for giving the copy application.
(4) A person who fails to perform the duty imposed on him by this section commits an offence.
If he does so with the intention of concealing the making of the application from the person concerned, he commits an aggravated offence.
(5) In proceedings for an offence under this section it is a defence for the accused to prove that he took all reasonable steps to perform the duty.
(6) A person guilty of an offence under this section (other than an aggravated offence) is liable-
    (a) on conviction on indictment, to a fine;
    (b) on summary conviction, to a fine not exceeding the statutory maximum.
(7) A person guilty of an aggravated offence under this section is liable-
    (a) on conviction on indictment, to imprisonment for a term not exceeding seven years or a fine (or both);
    (b) on summary conviction-
        (i) in England and Wales, to imprisonment for a term not exceeding twelve months or to a fine not exceeding the statutory maximum (or both);
        (ii) in Scotland or Northern Ireland, to imprisonment for a term not exceeding six months, or to a fine not exceeding the statutory maximum (or both).

GENERAL NOTE

This section replaces s.652B(6), (7) and (8) and, in part, s.652E of the Companies Act 1985. It requires a copy of any application made under s.1003 to be sent, within seven days of the making of the application, to members, employees, creditors and directors of the company (unless the director is a party to the application (subs.(2)), to the managers or trustees of any employee pension fund and to any person of a description specified by the Secretary of State in regulations made by the Secretary of State (subs.(1)). Such regulations are subject to negative resolution procedure. This duty ceases to apply on withdrawal of the application if that takes place before the end of the seven days prescribed in subs.(1). Non-compliance with this section constitutes an offence, and if a person fails to comply with the intention of concealing the application from any person concerned he commits an aggravated offence (subs.(4)). It is a defence to prove that the defendant took all reasonable steps to perform the duty imposed by the section (subs.(5)), the penalties for which are prescribed in subss.(6) and (7)).

1007. Copy of application to be given to new members, employees, etc

(1) This section applies in relation to any time after the day on which a company makes an application under section 1003 (application for voluntary striking off) and before the day on which the application is finally dealt with or withdrawn.

(2) A person who is a director of the company at the end of a day on which a person (other than himself) becomes-
   (a) a member of the company,
   (b) an employee of the company,
   (c) a creditor of the company,
   (d) a director of the company,
   (e) a manager or trustee of any pension fund established for the benefit of employees of the company, or
   (f) a person of a description specified for the purposes of this paragraph by regulations made by the Secretary of State,
 must secure that a copy of the application is given to that person within seven days from that day.
Regulations under paragraph (f) are subject to negative resolution procedure.
(3) The duty imposed by this section ceases to apply if the application is finally dealt with or withdrawn before the end of the period for giving the copy application.
(4) A person who fails to perform the duty imposed on him by this section commits an offence.
If he does so with the intention of concealing the making of the application from the person concerned, he commits an aggravated offence.
(5) In proceedings for an offence under this section it is a defence for the accused to prove-
   (a) that at the time of the failure he was not aware of the fact that the company had made an application under section 1003, or
   (b) that he took all reasonable steps to perform the duty.
(6) A person guilty of an offence under this section (other than an aggravated offence) is liable-
   (a) on conviction on indictment, to a fine;
   (b) on summary conviction, to a fine not exceeding the statutory maximum.
(7) A person guilty of an aggravated offence under this section is liable-
   (a) on conviction on indictment, to imprisonment for a term not exceeding seven years or a fine (or both);
   (b) on summary conviction-
      (i) in England and Wales, to imprisonment for a term not exceeding twelve months or to a fine not exceeding the statutory maximum (or both);
      (ii) in Scotland or Northern Ireland, to imprisonment for a term not exceeding six months, or to a fine not exceeding the statutory maximum (or both).

GENERAL NOTE
   This section replaces s.652C(1), (2) and (3) and, in part, s.652E of the Companies Act 1985 and extends the duty to send a copy of an application under s.1003 to new members, employees, creditors, directors and managers or trustees of employee pension funds, and to any other person of a description specified by the Secretary of State in regulations. It applies in the same way as s.1006 (above) to the period between the making of the application and before the day when it is finally dealt with or withdrawn, and to any person falling into any of the categories stated within that period (subss.(1) and (2)).

1008. Copy of application: provisions as to service of documents

(1) The following provisions have effect for the purposes of-
   section 1006 (copy of application to be given to members, employees, etc), and
   section 1007 (copy of application to be given to new members, employees, etc).
(2) A document is treated as given to a person if it is-
   (a) delivered to him, or
   (b) left at his proper address, or
   (c) sent by post to him at that address.
(3) For the purposes of subsection (2) and section 7 of the Interpretation Act 1978 (c. 30) (service of documents by post) as it applies in relation to that subsection, the proper address of a person is-

(a) in the case of a firm incorporated or formed in the United Kingdom, its registered or principal office;

(b) in the case of a firm incorporated or formed outside the United Kingdom-

    (i) if it has a place of business in the United Kingdom, its principal office in the United Kingdom, or

    (ii) if it does not have a place of business in the United Kingdom, its registered or principal office;

(c) in the case of an individual, his last known address.

(4) In the case of a creditor of the company a document is treated as given to him if it is left or sent by post to him-

(a) at the place of business of his with which the company has had dealings by virtue of which he is a creditor of the company, or

(b) if there is more than one such place of business, at each of them.

GENERAL NOTE

This section replaces s.652D(1), (2), (3) and (4) of the Companies Act 1985 and deals with the question of service of documents under ss.1006 and 1007 (above). Documents are treated as given to a person if they are delivered to him, left at his proper address or sent to that address by post (subs.(2)). The proper address of a firm incorporated or formed in the United Kingdom is its registered principal office, and for a firm incorporated or formed outside the United Kingdom its registered principal office inside the United Kingdom or, if it does not have a place of business there, its registered principal office (subss.(3)(a) and (b)). The proper address of an individual is his last known address (subs.(3)(c)). As far as creditors are concerned, a document is treated as given to a creditor if it is left or sent by post to him at the place of business of his at which the company had dealings with him in his capacity as its creditor or, if there is more than one such place, at each of them (subs.(4)).

1009. Circumstances in which application to be withdrawn

(1) This section applies where, at any time on or after the day on which a company makes an application under section 1003 (application for voluntary striking off) and before the day on which the application is finally dealt with or withdrawn-

(a) the company-

    (i) changes its name,

    (ii) trades or otherwise carries on business,

    (iii) makes a disposal for value of any property or rights other than those which it was necessary or expedient for it to hold for the purpose of making, or proceeding with, an application under that section, or

    (iv) engages in any activity, except one to which subsection (4) applies;

(b) an application is made to the court under Part 26 on behalf of the company for the sanctioning of a compromise or arrangement;

(c) a voluntary arrangement in relation to the company is proposed under Part 1 of the Insolvency Act 1986 (c. 45) or Part 2 of the Insolvency (Northern Ireland) Order 1989 (S.I. 1989/2405 (N.I. 19));

(d) an application to the court for an administration order in respect of the company is made under paragraph 12 of Schedule B1 to that Act or paragraph 13 of Schedule B1 to that Order;

(e) an administrator is appointed in respect of the company under paragraph 14 or 22 of Schedule B1 to that Act or paragraph 15 or 23 of Schedule B1 to that Order, or a copy of notice of intention to appoint an administrator of the company under any of those provisions is filed with the court;

(f) there arise any of the circumstances in which, under section 84(1) of that Act or Article 70 of that Order, the company may be voluntarily wound up;

(g) a petition is presented for the winding up of the company by the court under Part 4 of that Act or Part 5 of that Order;

(h) a receiver or manager of the company's property is appointed; or

      (i) a judicial factor is appointed to administer the company's estate.

(2) A person who, at the end of a day on which any of the events mentioned in subsection (1) occurs, is a director of the company must secure that the company's application is withdrawn forthwith.

(3) For the purposes of subsection (1)(a), a company is not treated as trading or otherwise carrying on business by virtue only of the fact that it makes a payment in respect of a liability incurred in the course of trading or otherwise carrying on business.

(4) The excepted activities referred to in subsection (1)(a)(iv) are-

    (a) any activity necessary or expedient for the purposes of-

        (i) making, or proceeding with, an application under section 1003 (application for voluntary striking off),

       (ii) concluding affairs of the company that are outstanding because of what has been necessary or expedient for the purpose of making, or proceeding with, such an application, or

      (iii) complying with any statutory requirement;

    (b) any activity specified by the Secretary of State by order for the purposes of this subsection.

An order under paragraph (b) is subject to negative resolution procedure.

(5) A person who fails to perform the duty imposed on him by this section commits an offence.

(6) In proceedings for an offence under this section it is a defence for the accused to prove-

    (a) that at the time of the failure he was not aware of the fact that the company had made an application under section 1003, or

    (b) that he took all reasonable steps to perform the duty.

(7) A person guilty of an offence under this section is liable-

    (a) on conviction on indictment, to a fine;

    (b) on summary conviction, to a fine not exceeding the statutory maximum.

GENERAL NOTE

    This section makes provision for circumstance where a director of a company which has made an application under s.1003 must take steps to secure that that application is withdrawn. The circumstances are those found in s.1004(1) (i.e. that the company has changed its name, traded or carried on business, disposed of property or rights for value other than for the purpose of the application or engaged in any activity other than that to which subs.(4) applies - subs.(1)(a)). These are supplemented by a series of circumstances to which s.652B of the Companies Act 1985 applied, that section providing that an application for striking off could not be made in any of the circumstance listed. This section now provides that such an application must be withdrawn if the company enters insolvency proceedings (which include a voluntary arrangement, administration, receivership or the appointment of a judicial factor) or if circumstances arise under which the company could be voluntarily wound up under s.84 of the Insolvency Act 1986, or if a petition for the winding up of the company is presented or if a scheme of arrangement or compromise is sanctioned under Pt 26 of the Act (subss.(1)(b)-(i)). A director who fails to perform this duty commits an offence (subs.(5)), to which it is a defence to prove that he was not aware that the application had been made or that he took all reasonable steps to perform the duty (subs.(6)). The penalty for the offence is prescribed by subs.(7).

1010. Withdrawal of application

An application under section 1003 is withdrawn by notice to the registrar.

GENERAL NOTE

    This section replaces s.652D(6) of the Companies Act 1985.

1011. Meaning of "creditor"

In this Chapter "creditor" includes a contingent or prospective creditor.

GENERAL NOTE

    This section replaces s.652D(8) of the Companies Act 1985.

Chapter 2

Property of Dissolved Company

Property vesting as bona vacantia

1012. Property of dissolved company to be bona vacantia

(1) When a company is dissolved, all property and rights whatsoever vested in or held on trust for the company immediately before its dissolution (including leasehold property, but not including property held by the company on trust for another person) are deemed to be bona vacantia and-

    (a) accordingly belong to the Crown, or to the Duchy of Lancaster or to the Duke of Cornwall for the time being (as the case may be), and

    (b) vest and may be dealt with in the same manner as other bona vacantia accruing to the Crown, to the Duchy of Lancaster or to the Duke of Cornwall.

(2) Subsection (1) has effect subject to the possible restoration of the company to the register under Chapter 3 (see section 1034).

GENERAL NOTE

This section replaces s.654(1) of the Companies Act 1985 and re-enacts the rule that, on dissolution, any property or rights held by or on trust for the company immediately before dissolution (except for property held by the company on trust for another person, are deemed to be *bona vacantia* and thereafter belong to the Crown - subs.(1)). This subsection is subject to the possibility that the company may be restored to the register under Ch.3 (see below).

1013. Crown disclaimer of property vesting as bona vacantia

(1) Where property vests in the Crown under section 1012, the Crown's title to it under that section may be disclaimed by a notice signed by the Crown representative, that is to say the Treasury Solicitor, or, in relation to property in Scotland, the Queen's and Lord Treasurer's Remembrancer.

(2) The right to execute a notice of disclaimer under this section may be waived by or on behalf of the Crown either expressly or by taking possession.

(3) A notice of disclaimer must be executed within three years after-

    (a) the date on which the fact that the property may have vested in the Crown under section 1012 first comes to the notice of the Crown representative, or

    (b) if ownership of the property is not established at that date, the end of the period reasonably necessary for the Crown representative to establish the ownership of the property.

(4) If an application in writing is made to the Crown representative by a person interested in the property requiring him to decide whether he will or will not disclaim, any notice of disclaimer must be executed within twelve months after the making of the application or such further period as may be allowed by the court.

(5) A notice of disclaimer under this section is of no effect if it is shown to have been executed after the end of the period specified by subsection (3) or (4).

(6) A notice of disclaimer under this section must be delivered to the registrar and retained and registered by him.

(7) Copies of it must be published in the Gazette and sent to any persons who have given the Crown representative notice that they claim to be interested in the property.

(8) This section applies to property vested in the Duchy of Lancaster or the Duke of Cornwall under section 1012 as if for references to the Crown and the Crown representative there were respectively substituted references to the Duchy of Lancaster and to the Solicitor to that

Duchy, or to the Duke of Cornwall and to the Solicitor to the Duchy of Cornwall, as the case may be.

GENERAL NOTE

This section replaces s.656 of the Companies Act 1985 and amends the time periods within which the Crown may disclaim property vesting in it as bona vacantia. Disclaimer may take place by notice signed by the Crown representative (the Treasury Solicitor or the Queen's and Lord Treasurer's Remembrancer for property in Scotland) (subs.(1)). The notice of disclaimer must be executed within three years after the date of vesting under s.1012 first comes to the attention of the Crown representative (subs.(3)(a), increasing the period under s.656 from 12 months) or, if ownership of the property is not established at that date, at the end of a period reasonably necessary for the Crown representative to establish the ownership of that property (subs.(3)(b)). Where the Crown representative receives an application in writing from a person interested in any property vesting in the Crown and requiring him to decide whether or not he will disclaim it, the Crown representative has a further 12 months to execute the notice of disclaimer (increased from three months under s.656 of the Companies Act 1985) or such further period as is allowed by the court (subs.(4)). Any notice of disclaimer issued outside of these time limits is of no effect (subs.(5)) and the notice must be delivered to the registrar of companies, who must retain and register it (subs.(6)). Copies of the notice must be published in the Gazette and sent to any persons who have given the Crown representative notice that they claim to be interested in the property (subs.(7)).

1014.   Effect of Crown disclaimer

(1) Where notice of disclaimer is executed under section 1013 as respects any property, that property is deemed not to have vested in the Crown under section 1012.

(2) The following sections contain provisions as to the effect of the Crown disclaimer-
  sections 1015 to 1019 apply in relation to property in England and Wales or Northern Ireland;
  sections 1020 to 1022 apply in relation to property in Scotland.

GENERAL NOTE

This section replaces s.657(1) and (2) of the Companies Act 1985.

Effect of Crown disclaimer: England and Wales and Northern Ireland

1015.   General effect of disclaimer

(1) The Crown's disclaimer operates so as to terminate, as from the date of the disclaimer, the rights, interests and liabilities of the company in or in respect of the property disclaimed.

(2) It does not, except so far as is necessary for the purpose of releasing the company from any liability, affect the rights or liabilities of any other person.

GENERAL NOTE

This section replaces s.657(2) of the Companies Act 1985, which makes reference to ss.178(4), and 179-182 of the Insolvency Act 1986. It deals with the general effect of the Crown's disclaimer, which is to terminate, as from its date, any interests rights and liabilities of the company in or in respect of the disclaimed property (subs.(1), with reference to the application s.178(4) of the Insolvency Act 1986). The rights or liabilities of any other person are not affected, except so far as necessary to release the company from liability (subs.(2)).

1016.   Disclaimer of leaseholds

(1) The disclaimer of any property of a leasehold character does not take effect unless a copy of the disclaimer has been served (so far as the Crown representative is aware of their addresses) on every person claiming under the company as underlessee or mortgagee, and either-
> (a) no application under section 1017 (power of court to make vesting order) is made with respect to that property before the end of the period of 14 days beginning with the day on which the last notice under this paragraph was served, or
> (b) where such an application has been made, the court directs that the disclaimer shall take effect.

(2) Where the court gives a direction under subsection (1)(b) it may also, instead of or in addition to any order it makes under section 1017, make such order as it thinks fit with respect to fixtures, tenant's improvements and other matters arising out of the lease.

(3) In this section the "Crown representative" means-
> (a) in relation to property vested in the Duchy of Lancaster, the Solicitor to that Duchy;
> (b) in relation to property vested in the Duke of Cornwall, the Solicitor to the Duchy of Cornwall;
> (c) in relation to property in Scotland, the Queen's and Lord Treasurer's Remembrancer;
> (d) in relation to other property, the Treasury Solicitor.

GENERAL NOTE

This section replaces s.657(2) of the Companies Act 1985 in so far as it refers to the s.179 of the Insolvency Act 1986. It deals with the effect of the Crown's disclaimer under s.1013 of any leasehold property. Such disclaimer does not take effect until a copy of the disclaimer is served on persons claiming under the company as underlessee or mortgagee unless no application has been made to the court under s.1017 (see below) or the court, on such application, has directed that the disclaimer shall take effect (subs.(1)).

1017.   Power of court to make vesting order

(1) The court may on application by a person who-
> (a) claims an interest in the disclaimed property, or
> (b) is under a liability in respect of the disclaimed property that is not discharged by the disclaimer,

make an order under this section in respect of the property.

(2) An order under this section is an order for the vesting of the disclaimed property in, or its delivery to-
> (a) a person entitled to it (or a trustee for such a person), or
> (b) a person subject to such a liability as is mentioned in subsection (1)(b) (or a trustee for such a person).

(3) An order under subsection (2)(b) may only be made where it appears to the court that it would be just to do so for the purpose of compensating the person subject to the liability in respect of the disclaimer.

(4) An order under this section may be made on such terms as the court thinks fit.

(5) On a vesting order being made under this section, the property comprised in it vests in the person named in that behalf in the order without conveyance, assignment or transfer.

GENERAL NOTE

This section inserts the provisions of s.181 of the Insolvency Act 1986 in so far as they apply to the Crown's disclaimer of property under s.657(2) of the Companies Act 1985. A person may make an application to court claiming an interest in property disclaimed by the Crown or an application in respect of a liability in relation to such property which is not discharged by the disclaimer and the court is empowered to make an order under this section (subs.(1)). The order is one for vesting the disclaimed property in or delivering it to a person entitled to it (or his trustee) or a person subject to a liability in relation to it (subs.(2)), but only, in the latter case, where it would be just to do so for the purpose of compensating the person subject to the liability in respect of the disclaimer (subs.(3)). The order may be on such terms as the court thinks fit (subs.(5)) and has the effect of vesting the property comprised in it in the person named in it without conveyance, assignment or transfer (subs.(5)).

1018.   Protection of persons holding under a lease

(1) The court must not make an order under section 1017 vesting property of a leasehold nature in a person claiming under the company as underlessee or mortgagee except on terms making that person-
   - (a) subject to the same liabilities and obligations as those to which the company was subject under the lease, or
   - (b) if the court thinks fit, subject to the same liabilities and obligations as if the lease had been assigned to him.

(2) Where the order relates to only part of the property comprised in the lease, subsection (1) applies as if the lease had comprised only the property comprised in the vesting order.

(3) A person claiming under the company as underlessee or mortgagee who declines to accept a vesting order on such terms is excluded from all interest in the property.

(4) If there is no person claiming under the company who is willing to accept an order on such terms, the court has power to vest the company's estate and interest in the property in any person who is liable (whether personally or in a representative character, and whether alone or jointly with the company) to perform the lessee's covenants in the lease.

(5) The court may vest that estate and interest in such a person freed and discharged from all estates, incumbrances and interests created by the company.

GENERAL NOTE

This section inserts the provisions of s.182 of the Insolvency Act 1986 in so far as they apply to the Crown's disclaimer of leasehold property under s.657(2) of the Companies Act 1985. On an application under s.1017 (above), no order vesting leasehold property in an underlessee or mortgagee of the company may be made except on terms subjecting that person to the same liabilities and obligations as those to which the company was subject under the lease or subject to the same liabilities and obligations as if the lease had been assigned to him (subs.(1)). A vesting order under this section may relate to only part of the leasehold property, and in such a case subs.(1) applies as if the lease had comprised only the property comprised in the vesting order (subs.(2)). Should an underlessee or mortgagee decline to accept, a vesting order of the court on these terms is excluded from all interest in the property comprised in it (subs.(3)). If there is no person claiming under the company who is willing to accept an order on such terms, the court may vest the company's estate and interest in the property in any person who is liable to perform the lessee's covenants under the lease, and may do so on terms that that person is freed and discharged from all estates, incumbrances and interests created by the company (subss.(4), (5)).

1019.   Land subject to rentcharge

Where in consequence of the disclaimer land that is subject to a rentcharge vests in any person, neither he nor his successors in title are subject to any personal liability in respect of sums becoming due under the rentcharge, except sums becoming due after he, or some person claiming under or through him, has taken possession or control of the land or has entered into occupation of it.

GENERAL NOTE

This section replaces s.658 of the Companies Act 1985 and applies the provisions of s.180 of the Insolvency Act 1986 to the disclaimer of land subject to a rentcharge. Liability for sums due in respect of the rentcharge is restricted to sums becoming due after the person in whom the land vests, or some person claiming through or under him takes possession or control of the land or enters into occupation of it. This protection extends to successors in title of that person.

Effect of Crown disclaimer: Scotland

1020. General effect of disclaimer

(1) The Crown's disclaimer operates to determine, as from the date of the disclaimer, the rights, interests and liabilities of the company, and the property of the company, in or in respect of the property disclaimed.

(2) It does not (except so far as is necessary for the purpose of releasing the company and its property from liability) affect the rights or liabilities of any other person.

GENERAL NOTE

Sections 1020 to 1022 apply to Scotland only. Sections 1020 and 1021 re-enact (with modifications) s.657(3)-(6) of the Companies Act 1985, and provide for the effect of a disclaimer by the Crown of property of a dissolved company which has vested in it as bona vacantia pursuant to ss.1012-1013 of the Act. Such a disclaimer is regularly granted where the Crown is satisfied that a person other than the company is entitled to that property. Section 1022 (relating to disclaimed leases) re-enacts in modified form Pt II of Sch.20 of the 1985 Act (referred to in s.657(7)).

Section 1020 re-enacts s.657(4) of the 1985 Act.

Subsection (1)

Crown disclaimer terminates any claim the company may have in respect of that property.

Subsection (2)

Disclaimer does not affect the rights or liabilities of any persons other than the company except so far as necessary to release the company and its property from liability to the Crown.

1021. Power of court to make vesting order

(1) The court may-
   (a) on application by a person who either claims an interest in disclaimed property or is under a liability not discharged by this Act in respect of disclaimed property, and
   (b) on hearing such persons as it thinks fit,
make an order for the vesting of the property in or its delivery to any persons entitled to it, or to whom it may seem just that the property should be delivered by way of compensation for such liability, or a trustee for him.

(2) The order may be made on such terms as the court thinks fit.

(3) On a vesting order being made under this section, the property comprised in it vests accordingly in the person named in that behalf in the order, without conveyance or assignation for that purpose.

GENERAL NOTE

This re-enacts (with modifications) s.657(5) and (6) of the 1985 Act.

Subsections (1) and (2)

Any person who claims property which the Crown has disclaimed or who is under a liability which has not been discharged in respect of that property may apply to the court for an order vesting the property or compensating for that liability either in his or her favour or in favour of a trustee for him. The procedure is governed by rules of court in Scotland and allows for objections by other parties claiming an interest.

Subsection (3)

A vesting order granted by the court automatically vests the property in the person named in the order without further procedure. However, that person may complete his title to the property in question in the manner appropriate to the nature of the property, e.g. by recording or registering a notice of title in the property registers or intimating his acquisition of an incorporeal moveable right to the debtor under that obligation.

1022. Protection of persons holding under a lease

(1) Where the property disclaimed is held under a lease the court must not make a vesting order in favour of a person claiming under the company, whether-
    (a) as sub-lessee, or
    (b) as creditor in a duly registered or (as the case may be) recorded heritable security over a lease,
except on the following terms.

(2) The person must by the order be made subject-
    (a) to the same liabilities and obligations as those to which the company was subject under the lease in respect of the property, or
    (b) if the court thinks fit, only to the same liabilities and obligations as if the lease had been assigned to him.
In either event (if the case so requires) the liabilities and obligations must be as if the lease had comprised only the property comprised in the vesting order.

(3) A sub-lessee or creditor declining to accept a vesting order on such terms is excluded from all interest in and security over the property.

(4) If there is no person claiming under the company who is willing to accept an order on such terms, the court has power to vest the company's estate and interest in the property in any person liable (either personally or in a representative character, and either alone or jointly with the company) to perform the lessee's obligations under the lease.

(5) The court may vest that estate and interest in such a person freed and discharged from all interests, rights and obligations created by the company in the lease or in relation to the lease.

(6) For the purposes of this section a heritable security-
    (a) is duly recorded if it is recorded in the Register of Sasines, and
    (b) is duly registered if registered in accordance with the Land Registration (Scotland) Act 1979 (c. 33).

GENERAL NOTE

    This section is designed to protect a person whose interest as lessor or creditor derives from a lease held by the company which has been the subject of Crown disclaimer.

Subsections (1) and (2)

    If the property disclaimed is a lease held by the company and an application for a vesting order is made by a person claiming as sub-tenant or as creditor in a heritable security over that lease, the court must order that person to accept the same liabilities and obligations as those of the company or (if the court thinks fit) as if the lease had been assigned to him

Subsection (3)

    If the applicant declines to accept a vesting order on those terms, he forfeits all interest in and security over the lease.

Subsections (4) and (5)

    If no sub-tenant or creditor is willing to accept a vesting order on the terms required, the court may make such an order on the same terms in favour of any other person who is liable jointly with the company to perform the lessee's obligations under the lease. Moreover, the court may release the person in whom the lease is vested from all interests, rights and obligations created by the company.

Subsection (6)

    This defines a heritable security for the purposes of s.1022 as one which has been duly recorded or registered in the appropriate property register.

Supplementary provisions

1023.   Liability for rentcharge on company's land after dissolution

(1) This section applies where on the dissolution of a company land in England and Wales or Northern Ireland that is subject to a rentcharge vests by operation of law in the Crown or any other person ("the proprietor").

(2) Neither the proprietor nor his successors in title are subject to any personal liability in respect of sums becoming due under the rentcharge, except sums becoming due after the proprietor, or some person claiming under or through him, has taken possession or control of the land or has entered into occupation of it.

(3) In this section "company" includes any body corporate.

GENERAL NOTE

This section applies the rule stated in s.1019 to circumstance where the dissolution of a company vests land by operation of law in the Crown or any other person (referred to as "the proprietor").

CHAPTER 3

RESTORATION TO THE REGISTER

GENERAL NOTE

This Chapter implements the recommendations of the Company Law Review (Final Report, pp.227-229) that the mechanisms in ss.651 and 653 of the Companies Act 1985 for restoring a company to the register by court order once it has been struck off be replaced in certain circumstances by an administrative restoration procedure.

Administrative restoration to the register

1024.   Application for administrative restoration to the register

(1) An application may be made to the registrar to restore to the register a company that has been struck off the register under section 1000 or 1001 (power of registrar to strike off defunct company).

(2) An application under this section may be made whether or not the company has in consequence been dissolved.

(3) An application under this section may only be made by a former director or former member of the company.

(4) An application under this section may not be made after the end of the period of six years from the date of the dissolution of the company.

For this purpose an application is made when it is received by the registrar.

GENERAL NOTE

This new provision provides for an application to be made to the registrar of companies to restore to the register a company that has been struck off under ss.1000 or 1001 (subs.(1)). This is to be the case whether or not the company has been dissolved (subs.(2)), but the application under this section may only be made by a former director or member of the company (subs.(3)) and within six years of the date of the company's dissolution (subs.(4)).

1025.   Requirements for administrative restoration

(1) On an application under section 1024 the registrar shall restore the company to the register if, and only if, the following conditions are met.

(2) The first condition is that the company was carrying on business or in operation at the time of its striking off.

(3) The second condition is that, if any property or right previously vested in or held on trust for the company has vested as *bona vacantia*, the Crown representative has signified to the registrar in writing consent to the company's restoration to the register.

(4) It is the applicant's responsibility to obtain that consent and to pay any costs (in Scotland, expenses) of the Crown representative-

    (a) in dealing with the property during the period of dissolution, or

    (b) in connection with the proceedings on the application,

that may be demanded as a condition of giving consent.

(5) The third condition is that the applicant has-

    (a) delivered to the registrar such documents relating to the company as are necessary to bring up to date the records kept by the registrar, and

    (b) paid any penalties under section 453 or corresponding earlier provisions (civil penalty for failure to deliver accounts) that were outstanding at the date of dissolution or striking off.

(6) In this section the "Crown representative" means-

    (a) in relation to property vested in the Duchy of Lancaster, the Solicitor to that Duchy;

    (b) in relation to property vested in the Duke of Cornwall, the Solicitor to the Duchy of Cornwall;

    (c) in relation to property in Scotland, the Queen's and Lord Treasurer's Remembrancer;

    (d) in relation to other property, the Treasury Solicitor.

GENERAL NOTE

   This new provision prescribes the conditions to be fulfilled if the registrar is to restore the company to the register following an application under s.1024. These are that the company was carrying on business or in operation at the time it was struck off (subs.(2)) and that where property has vested in the Crown as bona vacantia the Crown representative (as defined in subs.(6)) consents in writing to the registrar to the company's restoration to the register (subs.(3)). The applicant must obtain the consent of the Crown representative and must pay any costs or expenses of the Crown representative incurred in dealing with the property during the dissolution period or that are connected with the application and demanded as a condition of consent (subs.(4)). A further condition in subs.(5) is that the applicant has delivered any documents relating to the company necessary to update the registrar's records and paid any penalties under s.453 (or corresponding earlier provisions) outstanding at the date of dissolution or striking off. These penalties are the civil penalties for failure to deliver accounts.

1026.   Application to be accompanied by statement of compliance

(1) An application under section 1024 (application for administrative restoration to the register) must be accompanied by a statement of compliance.

(2) The statement of compliance required is a statement-

    (a) that the person making the application has standing to apply (see subsection (3) of that section), and

    (b) that the requirements for administrative restoration (see section 1025) are met.

(3) The registrar may accept the statement of compliance as sufficient evidence of those matters.

GENERAL NOTE

   An application under s.24 must be accompanied by a statement of compliance to the effect that the applicant has standing to apply (i.e. is a former director or member of the company - s.1024(3)) and that the requirements for administrative restoration under s.1025 have been met (subs.(2)). This statement may be accepted by the registrar as sufficient evidence of these matters (subs.(3)).

1027. Registrar's decision on application for administrative restoration

(1) The registrar must give notice to the applicant of the decision on an application under section 1024 (application for administrative restoration to the register).
(2) If the decision is that the company should be restored to the register, the restoration takes effect as from the date that notice is sent.
(3) In the case of such a decision, the registrar must-
    (a) enter on the register a note of the date as from which the company's restoration to the register takes effect, and
    (b) cause notice of the restoration to be published in the Gazette.
(4) The notice under subsection (3)(b) must state-
    (a) the name of the company or, if the company is restored to the register under a different name (see section 1033), that name and its former name,
    (b) the company's registered number, and
    (c) the date as from which the restoration of the company to the register takes effect.

GENERAL NOTE

This new section requires the registrar to give notice to the applicant under s.1024 of his decision (subs.(1)) and if that decision is to restore the company to the register, the restoration takes effect from the date such notice is sent (subs.(2)). If a decision to restore the company to the register is made, the registrar must enter on the register a note of the date of restoration and cause a notice of restoration to be published in the Gazette (subs.(3)), which must state the name of the company (or if restoration is under a new name in accordance with s.1033, both the former and new names), the company's registered number and the date as from which restoration takes effect (subs.(4)).

1028. Effect of administrative restoration

(1) The general effect of administrative restoration to the register is that the company is deemed to have continued in existence as if it had not been dissolved or struck off the register.
(2) The company is not liable to a penalty under section 453 or any corresponding earlier provision (civil penalty for failure to deliver accounts) for a financial year in relation to which the period for filing accounts and reports ended-
    (a) after the date of dissolution or striking off, and
    (b) before the restoration of the company to the register.
(3) The court may give such directions and make such provision as seems just for placing the company and all other persons in the same position (as nearly as may be) as if the company had not been dissolved or struck off the register.
(4) An application to the court for such directions or provision may be made any time within three years after the date of restoration of the company to the register.

GENERAL NOTE

This new provision prescribes the effect of restoration to the register which, in general, is that the company is deemed to have continued in existence as though it had not been dissolved or struck off (subs.(1)). Any penalty for failure to deliver accounts (under s.453 (see above)) will not be levied against the company for the time between dissolution or striking off and restoration (subs.(2)). The court is empowered to give any directions or make any provisions as seems just for restoring the position of the company and all other persons in the same position to what it would have been had the company not been dissolved or struck off (subs.(3)), and an application for such directions or provision may be made at any time within three years after the date of restoration (subs.(4)).

Restoration to the register by the court

1029.   Application to court for restoration to the register

(1) An application may be made to the court to restore to the register a company-

    (a) that has been dissolved under Chapter 9 of Part 4 of the Insolvency Act 1986 (c. 45) or Chapter 9 of Part 5 of the Insolvency (Northern Ireland) Order 1989 (S.I. 1989/2405 (N.I. 19)) (dissolution of company after winding up),

    (b) that is deemed to have been dissolved under paragraph 84(6) of Schedule B1 to that Act or paragraph 85(6) of Schedule B1 to that Order (dissolution of company following administration), or

    (c) that has been struck off the register-

        (i) under section 1000 or 1001 (power of registrar to strike off defunct company), or

        (ii) under section 1003 (voluntary striking off),

    whether or not the company has in consequence been dissolved.

(2) An application under this section may be made by-

    (a) the Secretary of State,

    (b) any former director of the company,

    (c) any person having an interest in land in which the company had a superior or derivative interest,

    (d) any person having an interest in land or other property-

        (i) that was subject to rights vested in the company, or

        (ii) that was benefited by obligations owed by the company,

    (e) any person who but for the company's dissolution would have been in a contractual relationship with it,

    (f) any person with a potential legal claim against the company,

    (g) any manager or trustee of a pension fund established for the benefit of employees of the company,

    (h) any former member of the company (or the personal representatives of such a person),

    (i) any person who was a creditor of the company at the time of its striking off or dissolution,

    (j) any former liquidator of the company,

    (k) where the company was struck off the register under section 1003 (voluntary striking off), any person of a description specified by regulations under section 1006(1)(f) or 1007(2)(f) (persons entitled to notice of application for voluntary striking off),

or by any other person appearing to the court to have an interest in the matter.

GENERAL NOTE

    This provision replaces ss.651 and 653 of the Companies Act 1985 and prescribes a new procedure whereby the court may order the restoration of a company to the register in accordance with the recommendations of the Company Law Review *Final Report* (pp.227-229). This procedure is largely based on the procedure in s.653 of the Companies Act 1985. Subsection (2) lists all those parties with standing to make an application to the court to restore to the register a company which has been dissolved after winding up or administration, or which has been struck off the register (whether it has been dissolved or not) under ss, 1000, 1001 or 1003 (see above). The parties with standing are: the Secretary of State, a former director of the company, any person with an interest in land in which the company had a superior or derivative interest (e.g. the company's tenant or its landlord) or with an interest in land or other property subject to rights vested in the company or benefited by obligations owed by it, a party who would have been in a contractual relationship with the company but for its dissolution, a person with a potential legal claim against the company, the manager or trustee of an employee pension fund of the company, a former member of the company (or his personal representative), a creditor of the company at the time of striking off or dissolution, or any person entitled to notice of an application for the voluntary striking off of the company under s.1003 (see ss.1006(1)(f) and 1007(2)(f) above). Finally, an application may be made by any other person appearing to the court to have an interest in the matter.

1030.   When application to the court may be made

(1) An application to the court for restoration of a company to the register may be made at any time for the purpose of bringing proceedings against the company for damages for personal injury.

(2) No order shall be made on such an application if it appears to the court that the proceedings would fail by virtue of any enactment as to the time within which proceedings must be brought.

(3) In making that decision the court must have regard to its power under section 1032(3) (power to give consequential directions etc) to direct that the period between the dissolution (or striking off) of the company and the making of the order is not to count for the purposes of any such enactment.

(4) In any other case an application to the court for restoration of a company to the register may not be made after the end of the period of six years from the date of the dissolution of the company, subject as follows.

(5) In a case where-

    (a) the company has been struck off the register under section 1000 or 1001 (power of registrar to strike off defunct company),

    (b) an application to the registrar has been made under section 1024 (application for administrative restoration to the register) within the time allowed for making such an application, and

    (c) the registrar has refused the application,

an application to the court under this section may be made within 28 days of notice of the registrar's decision being issued by the registrar, even if the period of six years mentioned in subsection (4) above has expired.

(6) For the purposes of this section-

    (a) "personal injury" includes any disease and any impairment of a person's physical or mental condition; and

    (b) references to damages for personal injury include-

        (i) any sum claimed by virtue of section 1(2)(c) of the Law Reform (Miscellaneous Provisions) Act 1934 (c. 41) or section 14(2)(c) of the Law Reform (Miscellaneous Provisions) Act (Northern Ireland) 1937 (1937 c. 9 (N.I.)) (funeral expenses)), and

        (ii) damages under the Fatal Accidents Act 1976 (c. 30), the Damages (Scotland) Act 1976 (c. 13) or the Fatal Accidents (Northern Ireland) Order 1977 (S.I. 1977/ 1251 (N.I. 18)).

GENERAL NOTE

Under s.651(4) of the Companies Act 1985 an application to court to declare the dissolution of a company void must be made within two years of the date of dissolution. Under s.653(2) of the Companies Act a person may object to a company being struck off the register within 20 years of a notice of striking off appearing in the Gazette. This new section provides that an application for restoration made for the purposes of bringing proceedings for damages or personal injury (as defined in subs.(6)) against the company may be made at any time (subs.(1)), but that on such an application the court must not make an order if it appears that those proceedings would fail by virtue of any enactment (e.g. a Limitations statute) (subs.(2)). The court must have regard to its power under s.1032(3) to direct that the period between the dissolution (or striking off) of the company and the making of the order is not to count for the purposes of any such enactment (subs.(3)). An application for any other purpose than that mentioned in subs.(1) may not be made more than six years from the date of the dissolution of the company (subs.(4)). Subsection 4 is subject to subs.(5), which states that where striking off from the register occurred under ss.1001 or 1002, and the registrar refused to restore the company to the register on an application under s.1024, an application to the court under this section may be made within 28 days of notice of the registrar's decision being issued by the registrar, even if the period of six years mentioned in subs.(4) above has expired.

1031.   Decision on application for restoration by the court

(1) On an application under section 1029 the court may order the restoration of the company to the register-
   (a) if the company was struck off the register under section 1000 or 1001 (power of registrar to strike off defunct companies) and the company was, at the time of the striking off, carrying on business or in operation;
   (b) if the company was struck off the register under section 1003 (voluntary striking off) and any of the requirements of sections 1004 to 1009 was not complied with;
   (c) if in any other case the court considers it just to do so.
(2) If the court orders restoration of the company to the register, the restoration takes effect on a copy of the court's order being delivered to the registrar.
(3) The registrar must cause to be published in the Gazette notice of the restoration of the company to the register.
(4) The notice must state-
   (a) the name of the company or, if the company is restored to the register under a different name (see section 1033), that name and its former name,
   (b) the company's registered number, and
   (c) the date on which the restoration took effect.

GENERAL NOTE

   This section replaces s.651(2) and states the circumstances in which the court may order the restoration of the company to the register. If the company was struck off under ss.1001 or 1002 and the court is satisfied that it was carrying on business or in operation at that time it may order its restoration to the register (subs.(1)(a)). If the company was struck off the register under s.1003 and any of the requirements in ss.1004-1009 were not complied with the court may order the restoration of the company to the register (subs.(1)(b)). Finally, the court may order a company restored to the register where it considers it just to do so (subs.(1)(c)). Restoration takes effect when a copy of the court's order is delivered to the registrar (subs.(2)), who must cause a notice of restoration to be published in the Gazette (subs.(3)). The notice must state the name of the company (if the company is restored to the register under a different name in accordance with s.1033 below, the former and new name must be stated), the company's registered number and the date on which restoration took effect (subs.(4)).

1032.   Effect of court order for restoration to the register

(1) The general effect of an order by the court for restoration to the register is that the company is deemed to have continued in existence as if it had not been dissolved or struck off the register.
(2) The company is not liable to a penalty under section 453 or any corresponding earlier provision (civil penalty for failure to deliver accounts) for a financial year in relation to which the period for filing accounts and reports ended-
   (a) after the date of dissolution or striking off, and
   (b) before the restoration of the company to the register.
(3) The court may give such directions and make such provision as seems just for placing the company and all other persons in the same position (as nearly as may be) as if the company had not been dissolved or struck off the register.
(4) The court may also give directions as to-
   (a) the delivery to the registrar of such documents relating to the company as are necessary to bring up to date the records kept by the registrar,
   (b) the payment of the costs (in Scotland, expenses) of the registrar in connection with the proceedings for the restoration of the company to the register,
   (c) where any property or right previously vested in or held on trust for the company has vested as *bona vacantia*, the payment of the costs (in Scotland, expenses) of the Crown representative-
      (i) in dealing with the property during the period of dissolution, or

(ii) in connection with the proceedings on the application.

(5) In this section the "Crown representative" means-

    (a) in relation to property vested in the Duchy of Lancaster, the Solicitor to that Duchy;

    (b) in relation to property vested in the Duke of Cornwall, the Solicitor to the Duchy of Cornwall;

    (c) in relation to property in Scotland, the Queen's and Lord Treasurer's Remembrancer;

    (d) in relation to other property, the Treasury Solicitor.

GENERAL NOTE

This section describes the effect of a court order for restoration to the register. In general terms, the company is deemed to have continued in existence as though it had not been dissolved or struck off (subs.(1)). Any penalty for failure to deliver accounts (under s.453 (see above)) will not be levied against the company for the time between dissolution or striking off and restoration (subs.(2)). The court is empowered to give any directions or make any provisions as seems just for restoring the position of the company an all other persons in the same position to what it would have been had the company not been dissolved or struck off (subs.(3)). The court may also give directions as to the delivery of documents to the registrar to enable him to bring his records up to date, as to the payment of costs and expenses in connection with the proceedings for restoration and as to the payment of the Crown representative's expenses incurred in connection with rights or property which vested in the Crown as *bona vacantia* (subs.(4)).

Supplementary provisions

1033. Company's name on restoration

(1) A company is restored to the register with the name it had before it was dissolved or struck off the register, subject to the following provisions.

(2) If at the date of restoration the company could not be registered under its former name without contravening section 66 (name not to be the same as another in the registrar's index of company names), it must be restored to the register-

    (a) under another name specified-

        (i) in the case of administrative restoration, in the application to the registrar, or

        (ii) in the case of restoration under a court order, in the court's order, or

    (b) as if its registered number was also its name.

References to a company's being registered in a name, and to registration in that context, shall be read as including the company's being restored to the register.

(3) If a company is restored to the register under a name specified in the application to the registrar, the provisions of-

    section 80 (change of name: registration and issue of new certificate of incorporation), and

    section 81 (change of name: effect),

apply as if the application to the registrar were notice of a change of name.

(4) If a company is restored to the register under a name specified in the court's order, the provisions of-

    section 80 (change of name: registration and issue of new certificate of incorporation), and

    section 81 (change of name: effect),

apply as if the copy of the court order delivered to the registrar were notice of a change a name.

(5) If the company is restored to the register as if its registered number was also its name-

    (a) the company must change its name within 14 days after the date of the restoration,

    (b) the change may be made by resolution of the directors (without prejudice to any other method of changing the company's name),

    (c) the company must give notice to the registrar of the change, and

    (d) sections 80 and 81 apply as regards the registration and effect of the change.

(6) If the company fails to comply with subsection (5)(a) or (c) an offence is committed by-

    (a) the company, and

    (b) every officer of the company who is in default.

(7) A person guilty of an offence under subsection (6) is liable on summary conviction to a fine not exceeding level 5 on the standard scale and, for continued contravention, a daily default fine not exceeding one-tenth of level 5 on the standard scale.

GENERAL NOTE

    In the usual case, a company restored to the register will have the same name as it had at the time of striking off (subs.(1)), but it may be the case that restoration under that name would contravene s.66 (see below) in that in the interim another company may have been registered with the same name. This section makes provision for this possibility by providing that restoration will take place under a name specified by the registrar or the court (depending up whether the restoration takes place under s.1027 or s.1031), or as if the company's registered number was also its name (subs.(2)). If restoration takes place under a name specified by either the registrar or the court, ss.80 and 81 (above) apply as if the application to the registrar or the court order delivered to the registrar were notice of a change of name (subss.(3) and (4)). If the company is restored to the register as if its registered number were its name it must change its name within 14 days after restoration and may do so by a resolution of the directors (subs.(5)(a)(b)). The registrar must be given notice of the change of name, to which ss.80 and 81 (above) apply (subs.(5)(c)(d)). Failure to comply with subs.5(a) or (c) constitutes an offence committed by the company and every officer in default (subs.(6), the penalty for which is prescribed in subs.(7)).

1034.   Effect of restoration to the register where property has vested as bona vacantia

(1) The person in whom any property or right is vested by section 1012 (property of dissolved company to be *bona vacantia*) may dispose of, or of an interest in, that property or right despite the fact that the company may be restored to the register under this Chapter.

(2) If the company is restored to the register-

    (a) the restoration does not affect the disposition (but without prejudice to its effect in relation to any other property or right previously vested in or held on trust for the company), and

    (b) the Crown or, as the case may be, the Duke of Cornwall shall pay to the company an amount equal to-

        (i) the amount of any consideration received for the property or right or, as the case may be, the interest in it, or

        (ii) the value of any such consideration at the time of the disposition,

    or, if no consideration was received an amount equal to the value of the property, right or interest disposed of, as at the date of the disposition.

(3) There may be deducted from the amount payable under subsection (2)(b) the reasonable costs of the Crown representative in connection with the disposition (to the extent that they have not been paid as a condition of administrative restoration or pursuant to a court order for restoration).

(4) Where a liability accrues under subsection (2) in respect of any property or right which before the restoration of the company to the register had accrued as *bona vacantia* to the Duchy of Lancaster, the Attorney General of that Duchy shall represent Her Majesty in any proceedings arising in connection with that liability.

(5) Where a liability accrues under subsection (2) in respect of any property or right which before the restoration of the company to the register had accrued as *bona vacantia* to the Duchy of Cornwall, such persons as the Duke of Cornwall (or other possessor for the time being of the Duchy) may appoint shall represent the Duke (or other possessor) in any proceedings arising out of that liability.

(6) In this section the "Crown representative" means-

    (a) in relation to property vested in the Duchy of Lancaster, the Solicitor to that Duchy;

    (b) in relation to property vested in the Duke of Cornwall, the Solicitor to the Duchy of Cornwall;

    (c) in relation to property in Scotland, the Queen's and Lord Treasurer's Remembrancer;

    (d) in relation to other property, the Treasury Solicitor.

GENERAL NOTE

This section replaces s.655 of the Companies Act 1985 and makes provision for the effect of restoration to the register where the company's property has vested as bona vacantia under s.1012. Such property may be disposed of notwithstanding the fact that the company may be restored to the registrar (subs.(1)). If restoration tales place, it does not affect the disposition, but the Crown is required to pay to the company any consideration it received for the property, or the value of such consideration or, if no consideration was received, an amount equal to the value of the property at the date of the disposition (subs.(2)). The Crown may deduct from this amount its reasonable costs in connection with the disposition, unless they have been paid as a condition of restoration or pursuant to a court order (subs.(3)).

PART 32

COMPANY INVESTIGATIONS: AMENDMENTS

GENERAL NOTE

This section and the four that follow it provide for the insertion into the Companies Act 1985 of certain sections. All the sections provide for modifications to the existing regime for company investigations, as earlier amended by the Companies (Audit, Investigations, and Community Enterprise) Act 2004.

1035. Powers of Secretary of State to give directions to inspectors

(1) In Part 14 of the Companies Act 1985 (c. 6) (investigation of companies and their affairs), after section 446 insert-

"Powers of Secretary of State to give directions to inspectors

446A   General powers to give directions

(1) In exercising his functions an inspector shall comply with any direction given to him by the Secretary of State under this section.
(2) The Secretary of State may give an inspector appointed under section 431, 432(2) or 442(1) a direction-
  (a) as to the subject matter of his investigation (whether by reference to a specified area of a company's operation, a specified transaction, a period of time or otherwise), or
  (b) which requires the inspector to take or not to take a specified step in his investigation.
(3) The Secretary of State may give an inspector appointed under any provision of this Part a direction requiring him to secure that a specified report under section 437-
  (a) includes the inspector's views on a specified matter,
  (b) does not include any reference to a specified matter,
  (c) is made in a specified form or manner, or
  (d) is made by a specified date.
(4) A direction under this section-
  (a) may be given on an inspector's appointment,
  (b) may vary or revoke a direction previously given, and
  (c) may be given at the request of an inspector.
(5) In this section-
  (a) a reference to an inspector's investigation includes any investigation he undertakes, or could undertake, under section 433(1) (power to investigate affairs of holding company or subsidiary);
  (b) "specified" means specified in a direction under this section.

446B   Direction to terminate investigation

(1) The Secretary of State may direct an inspector to take no further steps in his investigation.

(2) The Secretary of State may give a direction under this section to an inspector appointed under section 432(1) or 442(3) only on the grounds that it appears to him that-

    (a) matters have come to light in the course of the inspector's investigation which suggest that a criminal offence has been committed, and

    (b) those matters have been referred to the appropriate prosecuting authority.

(3) Where the Secretary of State gives a direction under this section, any direction already given to the inspector under section 437(1) to produce an interim report, and any direction given to him under section 446A(3) in relation to such a report, shall cease to have effect.

(4) Where the Secretary of State gives a direction under this section, the inspector shall not make a final report to the Secretary of State unless-

    (a) the direction was made on the grounds mentioned in subsection (2) and the Secretary of State directs the inspector to make a final report to him, or

    (b) the inspector was appointed under section 432(1) (appointment in pursuance of order of the court).

(5) An inspector shall comply with any direction given to him under this section.

(6) In this section, a reference to an inspector's investigation includes any investigation he undertakes, or could undertake, under section 433(1) (power to investigate affairs of holding company or subsidiary).".

GENERAL NOTE

Subsection (1)

Subsection (1) provides for the insertion of two new sections after Companies Act 1985, s.446. These will be known as s.446A and 446B. The first of these two new sections sets out general powers to give directions. Thus, s.446A provides that the Secretary of State may gave an inspector who is appointed under ss.431, 432(2) or 442(1) a direction as to the subject matter of his investigation or one which requires the inspector to take or not to take a specified step in his investigation. He may also, pursuant to subs.(2), require the inspector to specify in a report under s.437 of the Companies Act 1985, what his own views are on a specific matter, which does not include any reference to a specified matter, which is made in a specified form or manner, or which is made by a specified date. By subs.(4) the direction may be made at the time of the inspector's appointment. The direction may also vary or revoke a direction previously given and may be given at the request of an inspector. For the purposes of the subsection, any reference to an investigation is stated to include the power to investigate the affairs of a holding company or subsidiary under s.433(1) of the Companies Act 1985.

The new s.446B of the 1985 Act is concerned with the Secretary of State's powers to terminate an investigation. He may do so, in relation to inspectors appointed under ss.432(1) or 442(3), only on the grounds that matters have come to light in the course of the investigation which suggest that a criminal offence has been committed and these matters have been referred to the appropriate prosecuting authority. Where directions are given under this section, previous directions given under s.446A will cease to have effect. No final report is required to be made to the Secretary of State unless the latter directs the inspector to make a final report to him or where the inspector was appointed in pursuance of an order of the court (Companies Act 1985, s.432(1)). The inspector is obliged to comply with any direction which is given to him under this section.

Subsections (2)-(5)

These subsections make a number of house-keeping alterations: to ss.431, 432, 437 and 442 of the Companies Act 1985.

(2) In section 431 of that Act (inspectors' powers during investigation) in subsection (1) for "report on them in such manner as he may direct" substitute "report the result of their investigations to him".

(3) In section 432 of that Act (other company investigations) in subsection (1) for "report on them in such manner as he directs" substitute "report the result of their investigations to him".

(4) In section 437 of that Act (inspectors' reports)-
   (a) in subsection (1) omit the second sentence, and
   (b) subsections (1B) and (1C) shall cease to have effect.
(5) In section 442 of that Act (power to investigate company ownership), omit subsection (2).

1036. Resignation, removal and replacement of inspectors

After section 446B of the Companies Act 1985 (c. 6) (inserted by section 1035 above) insert-

"Resignation, removal and replacement of inspectors

446C   Resignation and revocation of appointment

(1) An inspector may resign by notice in writing to the Secretary of State.
(2) The Secretary of State may revoke the appointment of an inspector by notice in writing to the inspector.

446D   Appointment of replacement inspectors

(1) Where-
   (a) an inspector resigns,
   (b) an inspector's appointment is revoked, or
   (c) an inspector dies,
   the Secretary of State may appoint one or more competent inspectors to continue the investigation.
(2) An appointment under subsection (1) shall be treated for the purposes of this Part (apart from this section) as an appointment under the provision of this Part under which the former inspector was appointed.
(3) The Secretary of State must exercise his power under subsection (1) so as to secure that at least one inspector continues the investigation.
(4) Subsection (3) does not apply if-
   (a) the Secretary of State could give any replacement inspector a direction under section 446B (termination of investigation), and
   (b) such a direction would (under subsection (4) of that section) result in a final report not being made.
(5) In this section, references to an investigation include any investigation the former inspector conducted under section 433(1) (power to investigate affairs of holding company or subsidiary).".

GENERAL NOTE

   This section inserts two new sections in the Companies Act 1985, viz. s.446C and 446D. The new s.446C permits an inspector to resign by notice in writing to the Secretary of State and also provides that the Secretary of State may revoke the appointment of an inspector by notice in writing to him. The new s.446D provides for the appointment of replacement inspectors. Thus, where an inspector resigns, or his appointment is revoked, or he dies, the Secretary of State may appoint one or more competent inspectors to continue the investigation and such an appointment will be treated as an appointment under which the former inspector was appointed. Subsection (3) of the new s.446D provides that the Secretary of State must exercise his power such that at least one inspector continues the investigation. Subsections (4) and (5) provide for qualifications to these provisions.

1037.   Power to obtain information from former inspectors etc

(1) After section 446D of the Companies Act 1985 (c. 6) (inserted by section 1036 above) insert-

> *"Power to obtain information from former inspectors etc*

446E   Obtaining information from former inspectors etc

(1) This section applies to a person who was appointed as an inspector under this Part-
>   (a) who has resigned, or
>   (b) whose appointment has been revoked.

(2) This section also applies to an inspector to whom the Secretary of State has given a direction under section 446B (termination of investigation).

(3) The Secretary of State may direct a person to whom this section applies to produce documents obtained or generated by that person during the course of his investigation to-
>   (a) the Secretary of State, or
>   (b) an inspector appointed under this Part.

(4) The power under subsection (3) to require production of a document includes power, in the case of a document not in hard copy form, to require the production of a copy of the document-
>   (a) in hard copy form, or
>   (b) in a form from which a hard copy can be readily obtained.

(5) The Secretary of State may take copies of or extracts from a document produced in pursuance of this section.

(6) The Secretary of State may direct a person to whom this section applies to inform him of any matters that came to that person's knowledge as a result of his investigation.

(7) A person shall comply with any direction given to him under this section.

(8) In this section-
>   (a) references to the investigation of a former inspector or inspector include any investigation he conducted under section 433(1) (power to investigate affairs of holding company or subsidiary), and
>   (b) "document" includes information recorded in any form.".

(2) In section 451A of that Act (disclosure of information by Secretary of State or inspector), in subsection (1)(a) for "446" substitute "446E".

(3) In section 452(1) of that Act (privileged information) for "446" substitute "446E".

GENERAL NOTE

Subsection (1)

This subsection provides for the insertion of a new s.446E into the Companies Act 1985. Its principal purpose is concerned with obtaining information from former inspectors. Thus, the section is stated to apply to a person who was appointed as an inspector and has resigned or has had his appointment revoked. It will also apply to an inspector to whom the Secretary of State has given directions under the new s.446B. Under this section, the Secretary of State can direct such a former inspector to produce documents obtained or generated during the course of his investigation to the Secretary of State or to an inspector appointed. The power, in the case of documents, can, in the case of a document which is not in hard copy form, be to require it in hard copy or in a form from which a hard copy can be readily obtained. Once received, the Secretary of State is entitled to take copies of or extracts from such a document. Further, the Secretary of State may direct a person to whom the section applies to inform him of any matters that come to that person's knowledge as a result of his investigation. A person to whom this section applies is required to comply with any direction which is given to him.

Subsections (2) and (3)

These subsections make minor housekeeping changes to s.451A and s.452(1) of the 1985 Act.

1038. Power to require production of documents

(1) In section 434 of the Companies Act 1985 (c. 6) (production of documents and evidence to inspectors), for subsection (6) substitute-

"(6) In this section "document" includes information recorded in any form.

(7) The power under this section to require production of a document includes power, in the case of a document not in hard copy form, to require the production of a copy of the document-

    (a) in hard copy form, or

    (b) in a form from which a hard copy can be readily obtained.

(8) An inspector may take copies of or extracts from a document produced in pursuance of this section.".

(2) In section 447 of the Companies Act 1985 (power of Secretary of State to require documents and information), for subsection (9) substitute-

"(9) The power under this section to require production of a document includes power, in the case of a document not in hard copy form, to require the production of a copy of the document-

    (a) in hard copy form, or

    (b) in a form from which a hard copy can be readily obtained.".

GENERAL NOTE

Subsection (1)

This subsection substitutes a new s.434(6) in the Companies Act 1985. The new subs.(6) provides that a document for the purposes of s.434 includes information which is recorded in any form, including the production of a document not in hard copy form, to be produced in hard copy form or in a form from which a hard copy can be readily obtained. An inspector is empowered to take copies of or extracts from a document which is so produced.

Subsection (2)

This subsection substitutes a new s.447(9) in the Companies Act 1985. It provides that any document which has to be produced under that section which is not in hard copy form can be required to be produced in hard copy form or in a form from which a hard copy can be readily obtained.

1039. Disqualification orders: consequential amendments

In section 8(1A)(b)(i) of the Company Directors Disqualification Act 1986 (c. 46) (disqualification after investigation of company: meaning of "investigative material")-

    (a) after "section" insert "437, 446E,", and

    (b) after "448" insert ", 451A".

GENERAL NOTE

This section makes a number of consequential amendments to the s.8(1A)(b)(i) of the Company Directors Disqualification Act 1986.

PART 33

UK COMPANIES NOT FORMED UNDER COMPANIES LEGISLATION

GENERAL NOTE

Part 33 is concerned with United Kingdom companies not formed under companies legislation. It has two Chapters. Chapter 1 deals with companies not formed under companies legislation but authorised to register. Chapter 2 deals with unregistered companies.

COMPANIES NOT FORMED UNDER COMPANIES LEGISLATION BUT
AUTHORISED TO REGISTER

1040. Companies authorised to register under this Act

(1) This section applies to-
    (a) any company that was in existence on 2nd November 1862 (including any company registered under the Joint Stock Companies Acts), and
    (b) any company formed after that date (whether before or after the commencement of this Act)-
        (i) in pursuance of an Act of Parliament other than this Act or any of the former Companies Acts,
        (ii) in pursuance of letters patent, or
        (iii) that is otherwise duly constituted according to law.

(2) Any such company may on making application register under this Act.

(3) Subject to the following provisions, it may register as an unlimited company, as a company limited by shares or as a company limited by guarantee.

(4) A company having the liability of its members limited by Act of Parliament or letters patent-
    (a) may not register under this section unless it is a joint stock company, and
    (b) may not register under this section as an unlimited company or a company limited by guarantee.

(5) A company that is not a joint stock company may not register under this section as a company limited by shares.

(6) The registration of a company under this section is not invalid by reason that it has taken place with a view to the company's being wound up.

GENERAL NOTE

    This section replaces s.680 of the 1985 Act. Certain companies (listed in s.1040(1)) that are incorporated within the United Kingdom, but not formed under the Companies Acts (or certain earlier companies legislation), may apply to register under the 2006 Act.

Subsection (1)

    This lists the type of companies that can take advantage of this provision. It effectively reproduces the list that appeared in s.680 (1) of the 1985 Act.

Subsection (2)

    This states that the companies in subs.(1) can apply to register under the 2006 Act. This statement was previously contained in s.680(1) of the 1985 Act, along with the list of companies.

Subsection (3)

    The companies in subs.(1) may apply to register as a company limited by shares, a company limited by guarantee or as an unlimited company (see s.3 of the 2006 Act). Subsections (4) and (5) impose restrictions on this choice.

Subsection (4)

    A company with limited liability (by reason of an Act of Parliament) may not register under this section unless it is a joint stock company. It may not register as an unlimited company or as a company limited by guarantee (see s.3 of the 2006 Act). Section 1041 of the 2006 Act provides a definition of "joint stock company" for the purpose of this section.

Subsection (5)

    This imposes a further restriction on the choice of companies registering under this section: a company that is not a joint stock company may not register under this section as a company limited by shares. When read with s.1041 of the 2006 Act the purpose of this provision is clear: only a company with share capital may register as a company limited by shares.

A company may wish to apply to register under the 2006 Act in order to take advantage of legislation applying to companies registered under the Companies Acts. Subsection (6) makes it clear that a company may register even if it is in order to take advantage of certain provisions of the Insolvency Act 1986 that are unavailable to unregistered companies (eg, s.221(4) of the Insolvency Act 1986).

1041.   Definition of "joint stock company"

(1) For the purposes of section 1040 (companies authorised to register under this Act) "joint stock company" means a company-
   (a) having a permanent paid-up or nominal share capital of fixed amount divided into shares, also of fixed amount, or held and transferable as stock, or divided and held partly in one way and partly in the other, and
   (b) formed on the principle of having for its members the holders of those shares or that stock, and no other persons.
(2) Such a company when registered with limited liability under this Act is deemed a company limited by shares.

GENERAL NOTE

Subsection (1)

This provides a definition of "joint stock company" for the purpose of s.1040 of the 2006 Act. This definition is the same as that contained in s.683 of the 1985 Act.

Subsection (2)

This states that when a joint stock company is registered with limited liability under s.1040 it is deemed to be a company limited by shares.

1042.   Power to make provision by regulations

(1) The Secretary of State may make provision by regulations-
   (a) for and in connection with registration under section 1040 (companies authorised to register under this Act), and
   (b) as to the application to companies so registered of the provisions of the Companies Acts.
(2) Without prejudice to the generality of that power, regulations under this section may make provision corresponding to any provision formerly made by Chapter 2 of Part 22 of the Companies Act 1985 (c. 6).
(3) Regulations under this section are subject to negative resolution procedure.

GENERAL NOTE

This section confers a new power on the Secretary of State to make regulations in connection with the registration of a company following an application under s.1040 of the 2006 Act. Regulations made under this clause will replace the provisions made by ss.681-682, 684-690 of and Sch.21 to the 1985 Act. The regulations are intended to cover a number of matters including the procedural requirements for registration, the conditions to be satisfied before registration can take place and the consequences of registration. The regulations are subject to the negative resolution procedure (subs.(3)).

CHAPTER 2

UNREGISTERED COMPANIES

1043. Unregistered companies

(1) This section applies to bodies corporate incorporated in and having a principal place of business in the United Kingdom, other than-
  (a) bodies incorporated by, or registered under, a public general Act of Parliament;
  (b) bodies not formed for the purpose of carrying on a business that has for its object the acquisition of gain by the body or its individual members;
  (c) bodies for the time being exempted from this section by direction of the Secretary of State;
  (d) open-ended investment companies.
(2) The Secretary of State may make provision by regulations applying specified provisions of the Companies Acts to all, or any specified description of, the bodies to which this section applies.
(3) The regulations may provide that the specified provisions of the Companies Acts apply subject to any specified limitations and to such adaptations and modifications (if any) as may be specified.
(4) This section does not-
  (a) repeal or revoke in whole or in part any enactment, royal charter or other instrument constituting or regulating any body in relation to which provisions of the Companies Acts are applied by regulations under this section, or
  (b) restrict the power of Her Majesty to grant a charter in lieu or supplementary to any such charter.
 But in relation to any such body the operation of any such enactment, charter or instrument is suspended in so far as it is inconsistent with any of those provisions as they apply for the time being to that body.
(5) In this section "specified" means specified in the regulations.
(6) Regulations under this section are subject to negative resolution procedure.

GENERAL NOTE
  The Company Law Review (CLR) considered the position of unregistered companies in Ch.9 of *Completing the Structure* and presented their recommendations in paras 11.34-11.38 of the *Final Report*. The CLR noted that although some of the provisions of the 1985 Act applied to unregistered companies formed for the acquisition of gain, there were a number of significant provisions which did not apply to any unregistered companies. These included the rules on directors' conflicts of interests; company names, including the requirement for the name to end with "public limited company" or "limited"; disclosure of interests in shares; appointment and removal of directors; distribution of profits and assets; registration of charges; arrangements and reconstructions; takeover offers; protection of members against unfair prejudice; keeping the register of members; and meetings and resolutions. The CLR noted that the position of unregistered companies was anomalous, especially for those companies whose object is the acquisition of gain, which offer shares to the public and which are listed on the stock exchange. The CLR therefore recommended that the significant provisions listed above should apply to unregistered companies formed for the acquisition of gain "as far as practicable" (*Final Report*, para.11.37). The provisions in this Chapter are the Government's response to that recommendation.
  Section 1043 of the 2006 Act replaces s.718 of the 1985 Act and confers a power on the Secretary of State to apply provisions of the Companies Acts to certain unregistered companies. These are companies incorporated in the United Kingdom and having their principal business in the United Kingdom, but not formed or registered under the Companies Acts or any other public general Act of Parliament, e.g. a company formed by private Act of Parliament. Subsection (1) exempts certain other companies from regulations made under this section including those exempted by direction of the Secretary of State (subs.(1)(c)). This list repeats the list at s.718(2) of the 1985 Act.
  Regulations made under this section will replace the provisions made by schedule 22 of the 1985 Act. The regulations may apply specified provisions of the Companies Acts to all unregistered companies, or to certain specified unregistered companies (subs.(2)). The regulations may make limitations, adaptations and modifications to the application of the Companies Acts to unregistered companies (subs.(3)). The word "specified" is defined for the purposes of this section in subs.(5).

The regulations are subject to the negative resolution procedure (subs.(6)). Only once these regulations are in place will it be possible to ascertain how far the recommendations of the CLR have been fulfilled in this regard.

PART 34

OVERSEAS COMPANIES

GENERAL NOTE

Part 34 is concerned with overseas companies (which were referred to as "oversea companies" in the 1985 Act). This Part, together with the regulations made under it by the Secretary of State, replace the provisions made by Pt 23 and Sch.21 A-D of the 1985 Act. Part 23 of the 1985 Act applied to companies outside Great Britain that established a place of business in Great Britain. Subsequently the Eleventh Company Law Directive (89/666/EC) imposed a different set of disclosure requirements on those overseas companies with branches in the United Kingdom. The branch disclosure requirements also differed according to whether or not the overseas company was incorporated within another EEA state.

As a result, prior to the 2006 Act two parallel regimes applied to overseas companies, with slightly different definitions of the connecting factor with Great Britain, different disclosure requirements, etc. The Company Law Review (CLR) criticised the complexity and lack of clarity in this area of the law and recommended a simplification of the regime (see *Strategic Framework*, ch 5.6 and their consultation paper *Reforming the law concerning overseas companies* (October 1999)). The CLR's final conclusions were presented in paras 11.21-11.33 of their *Final Report*. In particular, the CLR recommended that the dual regime be replaced with a single regime, based on the concept of "place of business" and the requirements of the Eleventh Directive (*Final Report*, para.11.26), which would apply to all businesses. This Part is the Government's response to those recommendations. It creates a single regime, and that regime is one based on the requirements of the Eleventh Directive. It confers powers on the Secretary of State to make various regulations in respect to this area. The 2006 Act is silent on the issue of the relevant connection with the United Kingdom that will trigger the various disclosure and other obligations in this Part. It is intended that the regulations made under this Part will be able to specify this connection.

Introductory

1044. Overseas companies

In the Companies Acts an "overseas company" means a company incorporated outside the United Kingdom.

GENERAL NOTE

This section provides a definition of an "overseas company", stating that it is a company incorporated outside the United Kingdom. This definition replaces the definition of an "oversea company" in s.744 of the 1985 Act. It is wider than the definition found in s.744, which referred merely to companies incorporated outside Great Britain that established a place of business in Great Britain. In part this change is necessary to remove Northern Ireland companies from the definition of overseas companies, since the 2006 Act creates a single company law regime for the whole of the United Kingdom (see Pt 45 of the 2006 Act).

The other change here is that while s.744 of the 1985 Act specified the connection giving rise to the various disclosure obligations (the establishment of a place of business in Great Britain) this section is silent on this point. The CLR had recommended that the Act specify the connection as being the establishment of a place of business in the United Kingdom by an overseas company (*Final Report*, para.11.26). It is intended that the Regulations made under s.1046 of the 2006 Act will be able to specify the connection with the United Kingdom that will give rise to the various disclosure obligations imposed under this Part. Until these regulations are made it will remain unclear whether the CLR's recommendations have been fully implemented.

1045. Company contracts and execution of documents by companies

(1) The Secretary of State may make provision by regulations applying sections 43 to 52 (formalities of doing business and other matters) to overseas companies, subject to such exceptions, adaptations or modifications as may be specified in the regulations.

(2) Regulations under this section are subject to negative resolution procedure.

GENERAL NOTE

This section allows the Secretary of State to make regulations applying ss.43-52 of the 2006 Act, which deal with the formalities of doing business and other matters, to overseas companies. This is subject to whatever exceptions or modifications of ss.43-52 are specified in the regulations. These regulations will be subject to the negative resolution procedure (subs.(2)).

Registration of particulars

1046.   Duty to register particulars

(1) The Secretary of State may make provision by regulations requiring an overseas company-
    (a) to deliver to the registrar for registration a return containing specified particulars, and
    (b) to deliver to the registrar with the return specified documents.

(2) The regulations-
    (a) must, in the case of a company other than a Gibraltar company, require the company to register particulars if the company opens a branch in the United Kingdom, and
    (b) may, in the case of a Gibraltar company, require the company to register particulars if the company opens a branch in the United Kingdom, and
    (c) may, in any case, require the registration of particulars in such other circumstances as may be specified.

(3) In subsection (2)-
    "branch" means a branch within the meaning of the Eleventh Company Law Directive (89/666/EEC);
    "Gibraltar company" means a company incorporated in Gibraltar.

(4) The regulations may provide that where a company has registered particulars under this section and any alteration is made-
    (a) in the specified particulars, or
    (b) in any document delivered with the return,
the company must deliver to the registrar for registration a return containing specified particulars of the alteration.

(5) The regulations may make provision-
    (a) requiring the return under this section to be delivered for registration to the registrar for a specified part of the United Kingdom, and
    (b) requiring it to be so delivered before the end of a specified period.

(6) The regulations may make different provision according to-
    (a) the place where the company is incorporated, and
    (b) the activities carried on (or proposed to be carried on) by it.
This is without prejudice to the general power to make different provision for different cases.

(7) In this section "specified" means specified in the regulations.

(8) Regulations under this section are subject to affirmative resolution procedure.

GENERAL NOTE

Subsection (1)

This confers on the Secretary of State a new power to make regulations to require overseas companies to register with the registrar of companies. The regulations may require particular information to be included in the registration, e.g. an address for the company or details of its directors. The regulations may also require particular documents to be sent to the registrar, such as a copy of the company's constitution.

Subsection (2)

This ensures that the regulations implement the requirements of the Eleventh Company Law Directive under which an overseas company must register if the company opens a branch in the United Kingdom. Prior to this Act companies registered in Northern Ireland and Gibraltar were not eligible to register under the branch regime, but were required to register under the place of business regime. Obviously due the changes implemented by Pt 45 of the 2006 Act, and the new definition of "overseas companies" in s.1044, Northern Ireland companies are no longer regarded as overseas companies.

However, the position regarding companies registered in Gibraltar still needed to be regularised. While the regulations "must" require an overseas company other than a Gibraltar company to register particulars if it opens a branch office, they "may" require a Gibraltar company to do so.

Subsection (3)

This provides definitions of a "branch" and a "Gibraltar company" for the purposes of subs.(2). The definition of a branch is the same as that adopted in the 1985 Act, and refers back to the Eleventh Directive. Unfortunately, there is no definition of a branch within the Eleventh Directive. Some assistance as to the meaning of "branch" has in the past been derived from Directive 89/117/EEC, a companion Directive to the Eleventh Directive, which provides a definition of a bank branch (and see s.1050 of the 2006 Act in this regard). That definition refers to a place of business that "conducts directly all or some of the operations inherent in the business" (s.699A(3) of the 1985 Act, s.1050(2) of the 2006 Act). The definition of a branch adopted by the European Court of Justice for the purposes of the Brussels convention is similar: a branch has the appearance of permanency and is physically equipped to negotiate business with third parties directly (Case 33/78, *Sofamer v Saar-Ferngas* [1978] ECR 2183). This would suggest that purely ancillary activities will not constitute the establishment of a branch.

Subsection (4)

Regulations may require the overseas company to inform the registrar of companies of any changes in the details or documents it has registered.

Subsection (5)

The regulations may set deadlines for sending information to the registrar of companies. They may also determine whether the overseas company should register with the registrar for England and Wales, the registrar for Scotland or the registrar for Northern Ireland.

Subsection (6)

The Eleventh Company Law Directive imposes different disclosure requirements depending on where the overseas company setting up the branch is incorporated. Different reporting requirements are imposed on credit and financial institutions. Therefore regulations under this section may make different provision according to the place where the company is incorporated and the activities carried on by it.

Subsection (7)

This provides a definition of "specified" for the purposes of this section.

Subsection (8)

Regulations under this section are subject to the affirmative resolution procedure.

1047. Registered name of overseas company

(1) Regulations under section 1046 (duty to register particulars) must require an overseas company that is required to register particulars to register its name.
(2) This may be-
    (a) the company's corporate name (that is, its name under the law of the country or territory in which it is incorporated) or
    (b) an alternative name specified in accordance with section 1048.
(3) Subject only to subsection (5), an EEA company may always register its corporate name.
(4) In any other case, the following provisions of Part 5 (a company's name) apply in relation to the registration of the name of an overseas company-
    (a) section 53 (prohibited names);
    (b) sections 54 to 56 (sensitive words and expressions);
    (c) section 65 (inappropriate use of indications of company type or legal form);
    (d) sections 66 to 74 (similarity to other names);
    (e) section 75 (provision of misleading information etc);
    (f) section 76 (misleading indication of activities).
(5) The provisions of section 57 (permitted characters etc) apply in every case.

(6) Any reference in the provisions mentioned in subsection (4) or (5) to a change of name shall be read as a reference to registration of a different name under section 1048.

GENERAL NOTE

This section, together with s.1048, replaces s.694 of the 1985 Act. Broadly, this section applies the rules which apply to United Kingdom companies in relation to names to the names under which overseas companies trade in the United Kingdom, with some small changes. The Eleventh Directive does not require the application of controls on the choice of name to overseas companies, and so the imposition of these requirements could be said potentially to infringe EC companies' rights to freedom of establishment in the United Kingdom. However, these controls are capable of justification on the basis that they protect third parties dealing with the company, as long as the burdens being placed on overseas companies here are not disproportionate to the benefits obtained by third parties.

Subsection (1)

This section applies to overseas companies required to register with the registrar of companies by regulations made under s.1046. Overseas companies registered under that section must register their name. The name will be entered on the index of company names.

Subsection (2)

The company may register its corporate name, that is its registered or legal name in its place of incorporation, or another name (an "alternative name") under s.1048. All companies are free to choose whether to register a corporate name or an alternative name, subject to the restrictions imposed by subss.(4) and (5).

Subsection (3)

An EEA company (see s.1170 of the 2006 Act) may always be registered under its corporate name, subject to subs.(5). Therefore an overseas company incorporated in an EEA state may always register its company name, even if it does not comply with the requirements imposed on names of companies formed under the Act (see Chs 1-4 of Pt 5 of the 2006 Act) i.e. subs.(4) does not apply to EEA companies. There is one exception to this rule: the requirement relating to permitted characters (see s.57 of the 2006 Act) does continue to apply to EEA companies (subs.(5)).

Subsection (4)

An alternative name can only be registered if it complies with the requirements imposed on the names of companies formed and registered under the 2006 Act. Likewise, unless the overseas company is incorporated in an EEA state, its corporate name can only be registered if it complies with these requirements.

Subsection (5)

All companies registering a name under this section must take account of the requirement relating to permitted characters (see s.57 of the 2006 Act). Therefore, although an EEA company can register its corporate name without regard to most of the provisions regarding companies' names imposed by the Act, it must nevertheless still comply with this requirement.

Subsection (6)

This clarifies that any reference to a change of name under subss.(4) and (5) should be treated as registration of a different name under s.1048.

1048.   Registration under alternative name

(1) An overseas company that is required to register particulars under section 1046 may at any time deliver to the registrar for registration a statement specifying a name, other than its corporate name, under which it proposes to carry on business in the United Kingdom.
(2) An overseas company that has registered an alternative name may at any time deliver to the registrar of companies for registration a statement specifying a different name under which it proposes to carry on business in the United Kingdom (which may be its corporate name or a further alternative) in substitution for the name previously registered.
(3) The alternative name for the time being registered under this section is treated for all purposes of the law applying in the United Kingdom as the company's corporate name.
(4) This does not-

(a) affect the references in this section or section 1047 to the company's corporate name,

(b) affect any rights or obligation of the company, or

(c) render defective any legal proceedings by or against the company.

(5) Any legal proceedings that might have been continued or commenced against the company by its corporate name, or any name previously registered under this section, may be continued or commenced against it by its name for the time being so registered.

GENERAL NOTE

This section enables an overseas company to be registered under an alternative name (subs.(1)) and enables an overseas company to change the name by which it is registered (subs.(2)). To do so it must deliver a statement to the registrar of companies with its proposed new name for registration. As long as the proposed name complies with the requirements for registration (see s.1047 of the 2006 Act) the registrar will enter it on the index of company names. This section also clarifies that whatever the name under which the overseas company is registered, whether its corporate name or an alternative, that name is treated as being its corporate name for the purposes of the law in the United Kingdom (subs.(3)). The change of name will not affect any legal proceedings that are continued or commenced against the company (subs.(4) and (5)).

Other requirements

1049. Accounts and reports: general

(1) The Secretary of State may make provision by regulations requiring an overseas company that is required to register particulars under section 1046-

(a) to prepare the like accounts and directors' report, and

(b) to cause to be prepared such an auditor's report,

as would be required if the company were formed and registered under this Act.

(2) The regulations may for this purpose apply, with or without modifications, all or any of the provisions of-

Part 15 (accounts and reports), and

Part 16 (audit).

(3) The Secretary of State may make provision by regulations requiring an overseas company to deliver to the registrar copies of-

(a) the accounts and reports prepared in accordance with the regulations, or

(b) the accounts and reports that it is required to prepare and have audited under the law of the country in which it is incorporated.

(4) Regulations under this section are subject to negative resolution procedure.

GENERAL NOTE

This section confers on the Secretary of State a power to make regulations requiring overseas companies to prepare accounts and directors' reports and to obtain an auditor's report. The requirements must be like those imposed on companies formed and registered under this Act (subs.(1)). The accounts, directors' report and auditor's report requirements applying to companies formed and registered under this Act appear in Pt 15 and Pt 16 of the 2006 Act (subs.(2)). Regulations made under this section may modify those requirements in their application to overseas companies (subs.(2)). Subsection (3) clarifies what the regulations may require the overseas company to deliver to the registrar of companies by way of accounts and reports. Regulations made under this section replace ss.699AA-703 and Sch.21D of the 1985 Act and are subject to the negative resolution procedure (subs.(4)).

1050. Accounts and reports: credit or financial institutions

(1) This section applies to a credit or financial institution-

(a) that is incorporated or otherwise formed outside the United Kingdom and Gibraltar,

(b) whose head office is outside the United Kingdom and Gibraltar, and

(c) that has a branch in the United Kingdom.

(2) In subsection (1) "branch" means a place of business that forms a legally dependent part of the institution and conducts directly all or some of the operations inherent in its business.

(3) The Secretary of State may make provision by regulations requiring an institution to which this section applies-

    (a) to prepare the like accounts and directors' report, and

    (b) to cause to be prepared such an auditor's report,

as would be required if the institution were a company formed and registered under this Act.

(4) The regulations may for this purpose apply, with or without modifications, all or any of the provisions of-

    Part 15 (accounts and reports), and

    Part 16 (audit).

(5) The Secretary of State may make provision by regulations requiring an institution to which this section applies to deliver to the registrar copies of-

    (a) accounts and reports prepared in accordance with the regulations, or

    (b) accounts and reports that it is required to prepare and have audited under the law of the country in which the institution has its head office.

(6) Regulations under this section are subject to negative resolution procedure.

GENERAL NOTE

    The regulations made under this section replace s.699A and Sch.21C of the 1985 Act. This section applies only to credit and financial institutions incorporated or formed outside the United Kingdom and Gibraltar, with their head office outside the United Kingdom and Gibraltar, but which have a branch in the United Kingdom (subs.(1)). This section confers on the Secretary of State a power to make regulations specifically in respect of accounts and directors' reports of these institutions. Regulations under this section implement requirements of the Bank Branches Directive 89/117/EC of the Council of 13 February 1989. The definition of "branch" introduced in subs.(2) is based on Art.1(3) of Directive 2000/12/EC of the European Parliament and of the Council of 20 March 2000 relating to the taking up and pursuit of the business of credit institutions.

1051. Trading disclosures

(1) The Secretary of State may by regulations make provision requiring overseas companies carrying on business in the United Kingdom-

    (a) to display specified information in specified locations,

    (b) to state specified information in specified descriptions of document or communication, and

    (c) to provide specified information on request to those they deal with in the course of their business.

(2) The regulations-

    (a) shall in every case require a company that has registered particulars under section 1046 to disclose the name registered by it under section 1047, and

    (b) may make provision as to the manner in which any specified information is to be displayed, stated or provided.

(3) The regulations may make provision corresponding to that made by-

    section 83 (civil consequences of failure to make required disclosure), and

    section 84 (criminal consequences of failure to make required disclosure).

(4) In this section "specified" means specified in the regulations.

(5) Regulations under this section are subject to affirmative resolution procedure.

GENERAL NOTE

    This section confers a power on the Secretary of State to make regulations as to the information that overseas companies must display in specified locations (e.g. a sign with its name outside every branch), include in specified documents or communications (e.g. its names and country of incorporation on every invoice), or provide to those who make a request in the course of business (subs.(1)). It complements a similar power under s.82 of the 2006 Act to make regulations imposing trading disclosure obligations on companies formed and registered under the Companies Acts. Regulations made under this section, like those under s.82, are subject to the affirmative resolution procedure (see subs.(5) in both instances).

The Regulations may also make provision, corresponding to that made by ss.83 and 84 of the 2006 Act, in respect of a failure by a company to comply with the trading disclosure requirements imposed on them. The regulations made under this section replace s.693 of the 1985 Act.

1052. Company charges

(1) The Secretary of State may by regulations make provision about the registration of specified charges over property in the United Kingdom of a registered overseas company.

(2) The power in subsection (1) includes power to make provision about-
    (a) a registered overseas company that-
        (i) has particulars registered in more than one part of the United Kingdom;
        (ii) has property in more than one part of the United Kingdom;
    (b) the circumstances in which property is to be regarded, for the purposes of the regulations, as being, or not being, in the United Kingdom or in a particular part of the United Kingdom;
    (c) the keeping by a registered overseas company of records and registers about specified charges and their inspection;
    (d) the consequences of a failure to register a charge in accordance with the regulations;
    (e) the circumstances in which a registered overseas company ceases to be subject to the regulations.

(3) The regulations may for this purpose apply, with or without modifications, any of the provisions of Part 25 (company charges).

(4) The regulations may modify any reference in an enactment to Part 25, or to a particular provision of that Part, so as to include a reference to the regulations or to a specified provision of the regulations.

(5) Regulations under this section are subject to negative resolution procedure.

(6) In this section-
    "registered overseas company" means an overseas company that has registered particulars under section 1046(1), and
    "specified" means specified in the regulations.

GENERAL NOTE

This section was introduced quite late in the drafting process, and did not appear in the final version of the Bill, published in July 2006. This section enables the Secretary of State to make regulations to require the registration of specified charges over property in the United Kingdom of overseas companies which have registered their particulars under s.1046 of the 2006 Act. Subsection (2) provides further details about the scope of the regulations. The regulations under this section may apply the provisions of Pt 25 of the 2006 Act, concerning company charges, with or without modifications (subs.(3)).

1053. Other returns etc

(1) This section applies to overseas companies that are required to register particulars under section 1046.

(2) The Secretary of State may make provision by regulations requiring the delivery to the registrar of returns-
    (a) by a company to which this section applies that-
        (i) is being wound up, or
        (ii) becomes or ceases to be subject to insolvency proceedings, or an arrangement or composition or any analogous proceedings;
    (b) by the liquidator of a company to which this section applies.

(3) The regulations may specify-
    (a) the circumstances in which a return is to be made,

    (b) the particulars to be given in it, and

    (c) the period within which it is to be made.

(4) The Secretary of State may make provision by regulations requiring notice to be given to the registrar of the appointment in relation to a company to which this section applies of a judicial factor (in Scotland).

(5) The regulations may include provision corresponding to any provision made by section 1154 of this Act (duty to notify registrar of certain appointments).

(6) Regulations under this section are subject to affirmative resolution procedure.

GENERAL NOTE

    This section applies to overseas companies that are required to register particulars under s.1046. It confers on the Secretary of State a power to make regulations requiring those companies to deliver returns to the registrar if they are being wound up or subjected to insolvency proceedings (subs.(2)). The regulations may also require the liquidator of such a company to deliver returns to the registrar. The regulations may specify the information to be included in the return and set deadlines for sending it to the registrar (subs.(3)). The regulations may require notice to be given to the registrar of the appointment of a judicial factor in Scotland (subs.(4)) and may to that end include any provision corresponding to the equivalent obligation placed on companies incorporated in the United Kingdom by s.1154 of the 2006 Act (subs.(5)). The regulations replace ss.703P and 703Q of the 1985 Act.

Supplementary

1054. Offences

(1) Regulations under this Part may specify the person or persons responsible for complying with any specified requirement of the regulations.

(2) Regulations under this Part may make provision for offences, including provision as to-

    (a) the person or persons liable in the case of any specified contravention of the regulations, and

    (b) circumstances that are, or are not, to be a defence on a charge of such an offence.

(3) The regulations must not provide-

    (a) for imprisonment, or

    (b) for the imposition on summary conviction of a fine exceeding level 5 on the standard scale and, for continued contravention, a daily default fine not exceeding one-tenth of level 5 on the standard scale.

(4) In this section "specified" means specified in the regulations.

GENERAL NOTE

    This section ensures that the regulations under this Part will be able to specify the person(s) who will be responsible for complying with any specified requirement of the regulations. It allows regulations made under this Part to provide for offences, including who will be liable in the event of any contravention and what might be considered a defence should a charge be brought. The maximum level of penalty permissible under the regulations on indictment is set out in subs.(3).

1055. Disclosure of individual's residential address: protection from disclosure

Where regulations under section 1046 (overseas companies: duty to register particulars) require an overseas company to register particulars of an individual's usual residential address, they must contain provision corresponding to that made by Chapter 8 of Part 10 (directors' residential addresses: protection from disclosure).

GENERAL NOTE

    If the regulations under s.1046 of the 2006 Act require an overseas company to register an individual's usual residential address then the regulations must also provide for its protection on the same basis as is provided for the directors' residential addresses in Ch.8 of Pt 10 of the 2006 Act.

1056.   Requirement to identify persons authorised to accept service of documents

Regulations under section 1046 (overseas companies: duty to register particulars) must require an overseas company to register-

(a) particulars identifying every person resident in the United Kingdom authorised to accept service of documents on behalf of the company, or

(b) a statement that there is no such person.

GENERAL NOTE

This section replaces the provision made by s.691(1)(b)(ii) and para.3(e) of Sch.21A to the 1985 Act. Every overseas company required by the regulations under s.1046 to register with the registrar of companies must register particulars identifying every person resident in the United Kingdom who is authorised to accept service of documents on the company's behalf, or make a statement that there is no such person.

1057.   Registrar to whom returns, notices etc to be delivered

(1) This section applies to an overseas company that is required to register or has registered particulars under section 1046 in more than one part of the United Kingdom.

(2) The Secretary of State may provide by regulations that, in the case of such a company, anything authorised or required to be delivered to the registrar under this Part is to be delivered-

(a) to the registrar for each part of the United Kingdom in which the company is required to register or has registered particulars, or

(b) to the registrar for such part or parts of the United Kingdom as may be specified in or determined in accordance with the regulations.

(3) Regulations under this section are subject to negative resolution procedure.

GENERAL NOTE

This section makes provision for regulations in respect of overseas companies that are required to register, or have registered, particulars under s.1046 in more than one part of the United Kingdom.

1058.   Duty to give notice of ceasing to have registrable presence

(1) The Secretary of State may make provision by regulations requiring an overseas company-

(a) if it has registered particulars following the opening of a branch, in accordance with regulations under section 1046(2)(a) or (b), to give notice to the registrar if it closes that branch;

(b) if it has registered particulars in other circumstances, in accordance with regulations under section 1046(2)(c), to give notice to the registrar if the circumstances that gave rise to the obligation to register particulars cease to obtain.

(2) The regulations must provide for the notice to be given to the registrar for the part of the United Kingdom to which the original return of particulars was delivered.

(3) The regulations may specify the period within which notice must be given.

(4) Regulations under this section are subject to negative resolution procedure.

GENERAL NOTE

Where an overseas company has registered particulars with the registrar following the opening of a branch in the United Kingdom, this section enables regulations to require the overseas company to give notice to the registrar if it subsequently loses that branch. In addition, an overseas company that has registered particulars in other circumstances specified by the regulation under s.1046 may be required by regulations to give notice to the registrar if those circumstances "cease to obtain".

1059.   Application of provisions in case of relocation of branch

For the purposes of this Part-
    (a) the relocation of a branch from one part of the United Kingdom to another counts as the closing of one branch and the opening of another;
    (b) the relocation of a branch within the same part of the United Kingdom does not.

GENERAL NOTE

This section provides that the relocation of a branch from one part of the United Kingdom to another is to be treated as the closing of one branch and the opening of another. This section replaces the provision made by s.695A(4) of the 1985 Act.

PART 35

THE REGISTRAR OF COMPANIES

GENERAL NOTE

This Part of the Act replaces Pt 24 of the Companies Act 1985 and is concerned with the function of the registrar of companies. As observed in the explanatory notes, these functions are currently carried out by Companies House in England and Wales and in Scotland, and by the equivalent registry in Northern Ireland. Certain recommendations of the Company Law Review are implemented in new provisions in this Part. The underlying object of this Part is to ensure that the registrar is able to keep, and, in many cases, make available to the public, records concerning companies on a central register, and many of the new provisions are designed to achieve that objective.

The registrar

1060.   The registrar

(1) There shall continue to be-
    (a) a registrar of companies for England and Wales,
    (b) a registrar of companies for Scotland, and
    (c) a registrar of companies for Northern Ireland.
(2) The registrars shall be appointed by the Secretary of State.
(3) In the Companies Acts "the registrar of companies" and "the registrar" mean the registrar of companies for England and Wales, Scotland or Northern Ireland, as the case may require.
(4) References in the Companies Acts to registration in a particular part of the United Kingdom are to registration by the registrar for that part of the United Kingdom.

GENERAL NOTE

This section maintains the approach of s.704 of the Companies Act 1985. The office of registrar of companies for England and Wales, for Scotland and for Northern Ireland is continued, with the registrars being appointed by the Secretary of State.

1061.   The registrar's functions

(1) The registrar shall continue-
    (a) to perform the functions conferred on the registrar-
        (i) under the Companies Acts, and
        (ii) under the enactments listed in subsection (2), and
    (b) to perform such functions on behalf of the Secretary of State, in relation to the registration of companies or other matters, as the Secretary of State may from time to time direct.

(2) The enactments are-

the Joint Stock Companies Acts;

the Newspaper Libel and Registration Act 1881 (c. 60);

the Limited Partnerships Act 1907 (c. 24);

section 53 of the Industrial and Provident Societies Act 1965 (c. 12) or, for Northern Ireland, section 62 of the Industrial and Provident Societies Act (Northern Ireland) 1969 (c. 24 (N.I.));

the Insolvency Act 1986 (c. 45) or, for Northern Ireland, the Insolvency (Northern Ireland) Order 1989 (S.I. 1989/2405 (N.I. 19));

section 12 of the Statutory Water Companies Act 1991 (c. 58);

sections 3, 4, 6, 63 and 64 of, and Schedule 1 to, the Housing Act 1996 (c. 52) or, for Northern Ireland, Articles 3 and 16 to 32 of the Housing (Northern Ireland) Order 1992 (S.I. 1992/1725 (N.I. 15));

sections 2, 4 and 26 of the Commonwealth Development Corporation Act 1999 (c. 20);

Part 6 and section 366 of the Financial Services and Markets Act 2000 (c. 8);

the Limited Liability Partnerships Act 2000 (c. 12);

section 14 of the Insolvency Act 2000 (c. 39) or, for Northern Ireland, Article 11 of the Insolvency (Northern Ireland) Order 2002 (S.I. 2002/3152 (N.I. 6));

section 121 of the Land Registration Act 2002 (c. 9);

section 1248 of this Act.

(3) References in this Act to the functions of the registrar are to functions within subsection (1)(a) or (b).

GENERAL NOTE

This section defines the functions of the registrar as those conferred on the registrar by the Companies Acts, by any other enactment listed in subs.(2) and those functions on behalf of the Secretary of State, in relation to the registration of companies or other matters, as the Secretary of State may from time to time direct.

1062.   The registrar's official seal

The registrar shall have an official seal for the authentication of documents in connection with the performance of the registrar's functions.

GENERAL NOTE

This section replaces s.704(4) of the Companies Act 1985 and is self-explanatory.

1063.   Fees payable to registrar

(1) The Secretary of State may make provision by regulations requiring the payment to the registrar of fees in respect of-

    (a) the performance of any of the registrar's functions, or

    (b) the provision by the registrar of services or facilities for purposes incidental to, or otherwise connected with, the performance of any of the registrar's functions.

(2) The matters for which fees may be charged include-

    (a) the performance of a duty imposed on the registrar or the Secretary of State,

    (b) the receipt of documents delivered to the registrar, and

    (c) the inspection, or provision of copies, of documents kept by the registrar.

(3) The regulations may-

    (a) provide for the amount of the fees to be fixed by or determined under the regulations;

    (b) provide for different fees to be payable in respect of the same matter in different circumstances;

    (c) specify the person by whom any fee payable under the regulations is to be paid;

    (d) specify when and how fees are to be paid.

(4) Regulations under this section are subject to negative resolution procedure.

(5) In respect of the performance of functions or the provision of services or facilities-

    (a) for which fees are not provided for by regulations, or

    (b) in circumstances other than those for which fees are provided for by regulations,

the registrar may determine from time to time what fees (if any) are chargeable.

(6) Fees received by the registrar are to be paid into the Consolidated Fund.

(7) The Limited Partnerships Act 1907 (c. 24) is amended as follows-

    (a) in section 16(1) (inspection of statements registered)-

        (i) omit the words ", and there shall be paid for such inspection such fees as may be appointed by the Board of Trade, not exceeding 5p for each inspection", and

        (ii) omit the words from "and there shall be paid for such certificate" to the end;

    (b) in section 17 (power to make rules)-

        (i) omit the words "(but as to fees with the concurrence of the Treasury)", and

        (ii) omit paragraph (a).

GENERAL NOTE

This section replaces s.708 of the Companies Act 1985 and provides non-exhaustive information of the contents of regulations made by the Secretary of State under s.1063. The regulations, which are subject to negative resolution procedure (subs.(4)), may require the payment of fees to the registrar in respect of the performance of any of his functions and the provision by the registrar of services or facilities for purposes incidental to, or otherwise connected with, the performance of any of the registrar's functions (subs.(1)). By subs.(2), fees may be charged for the performance of a duty imposed on the registrar or the Secretary of State, the receipt of documents delivered to the registrar, and the inspection, or provision of copies, of documents kept by the registrar. The regulations may also provide for the level of fees to be determined by them, or for different fees to be payable in respect of the same matter in different circumstances, and may specify who is responsible for paying the fees and how and when they are to be paid (subs.(3)). Subsection (5) retains the power of the registrar, as previously contained in s.708(5) of the Companies Act 1985, to determine fees in respect of the performance of functions or the provision of services or facilities where these are not provided for in the regulations. With the imminent introduction of electronic formation, it is not unlikely that regulations will not make provision for every eventuality, and it will fall to the registrar to determine appropriate fees where none are prescribed. Any fees received by the registrar are to be paid into the Consolidated Fund (subs.(6)).

Certificates of incorporation

1064.　Public notice of issue of certificate of incorporation

(1) The registrar must cause to be published-

    (a) in the Gazette, or

    (b) in accordance with section 1116 (alternative means of giving public notice),

notice of the issue by the registrar of any certificate of incorporation of a company.

(2) The notice must state the name and registered number of the company and the date of issue of the certificate.

(3) This section applies to a certificate of incorporation issued under-

    (a) section 80 (change of name),

    (b) section 88 (Welsh companies), or

    (c) any provision of Part 7 (re-registration),

as well as to the certificate issued on a company's formation.

GENERAL NOTE

This section replaces s.711(1)(a) of the Companies Act 1985 and requires the registrar to cause to be published in the Gazette or in accordance with s.1116 (below, which deals with alternative methods of giving public notice) a notice that he has issued a certificate of incorporation of a company (subs.(1)). The notice must state the name and registered number of the company and the date of the issue of the certificate (subs.(2)), and this requirement applies also to any certificate issued on a change of name under s.80, under s.88 or whenever an amended certificate is issued on re-registration under Pt 7 of the Act (subs.(3)).

1065. Right to certificate of incorporation

Any person may require the registrar to provide him with a copy of any certificate of incorporation of a company, signed by the registrar or authenticated by the registrar's seal.

GENERAL NOTE

This section replaces s.710 Companies Act and re-enacts the rule that any person may require the registrar to provide him with a copy of any certificate of incorporation of a company, signed by the registrar or authenticated by his seal.

Registered numbers

1066. Company's registered numbers

(1) The registrar shall allocate to every company a number, which shall be known as the company's registered number.

(2) Companies' registered numbers shall be in such form, consisting of one or more sequences of figures or letters, as the registrar may determine.

(3) The registrar may on adopting a new form of registered number make such changes of existing registered numbers as appear necessary.

(4) A change of a company's registered number has effect from the date on which the company is notified by the registrar of the change.

(5) For a period of three years beginning with that date any requirement to disclose the company's registered number imposed by regulations under section 82 or section 1051 (trading disclosures) is satisfied by the use of either the old number or the new.

(6) In this section "company" includes an overseas company whose particulars have been registered under section 1046, other than a company that appears to the registrar not to be required to register particulars under that section.

GENERAL NOTE

This section replaces s.705 of the Companies Act 1985 without substantive change and requires the registrar to allocate a number (the registered number) to every company. The form of the number is dealt with in subs.(2), and if the registrar adopts a new form he may make any necessary changes to existing registered numbers (subs.(3)), this change taking effect from the date that the registrar notifies the company of the change (subs.(4)). For a period of three years after that date, any requirement to disclose the registered number under s.82 regulations or s.1051 is satisfied by using either the old or the new number (subs.(5)).

1067. Registered numbers of branches of overseas company

(1) The registrar shall allocate to every branch of an overseas company whose particulars are registered under section 1046 a number, which shall be known as the branch's registered number.

(2) Branches' registered numbers shall be in such form, consisting of one or more sequences of figures or letters, as the registrar may determine.

(3) The registrar may on adopting a new form of registered number make such changes of existing registered numbers as appear necessary.

(4) A change of a branch's registered number has effect from the date on which the company is notified by the registrar of the change.

(5) For a period of three years beginning with that date any requirement to disclose the branch's registered number imposed by regulations under section 1051 (trading disclosures) is satisfied by the use of either the old number or the new.

Under s.1046 of the Companies Act 2006 an overseas company may be required to register particulars of its branches. Where such branches are registered, the registrar is required by this section to allocate to that branch a registered number (subs.(1)). The provisions of s.1066(2)-(5) (above) apply in an identical manner to branch registered numbers.

Delivery of documents to the registrar

1068.   Registrar's requirements as to form, authentication and manner of delivery

(1) The registrar may impose requirements as to the form, authentication and manner of delivery of documents required or authorised to be delivered to the registrar under any enactment.

(2) As regards the form of the document, the registrar may-
    (a) require the contents of the document to be in a standard form;
    (b) impose requirements for the purpose of enabling the document to be scanned or copied.

(3) As regards authentication, the registrar may-
    (a) require the document to be authenticated by a particular person or a person of a particular description;
    (b) specify the means of authentication;
    (c) require the document to contain or be accompanied by the name or registered number of the company to which it relates (or both).

(4) As regards the manner of delivery, the registrar may specify requirements as to-
    (a) the physical form of the document (for example, hard copy or electronic form);
    (b) the means to be used for delivering the document (for example, by post or electronic means);
    (c) the address to which the document is to be sent;
    (d) in the case of a document to be delivered by electronic means, the hardware and software to be used, and technical specifications (for example, matters relating to protocol, security, anti-virus protection or encryption).

(5) The registrar must secure that as from 1st January 2007 all documents subject to the Directive disclosure requirements (see section 1078) may be delivered to the registrar by electronic means.

(6) The power conferred by this section does not authorise the registrar to require documents to be delivered by electronic means (see section 1069).

(7) Requirements imposed under this section must not be inconsistent with requirements imposed by any enactment with respect to the form, authentication or manner of delivery of the document concerned.

GENERAL NOTE
This section empowers the registrar of companies to prescribe the form in which documents are required to be delivered to him, how they are to be authenticated and the method of delivery (subs.(1)). It amplifies upon the requirements the registrar may impose as the the form of the document (subs.(2) - the registrar may require the contents to be in standard form or to be copiable or scannable)), the authentication of the document (subs.(3) - the registrar may require authentication by a specific means or a specific person, or that it is accompanied by the name and/or registered number of the company to which it relates), and the method of delivery (i.e. a hard copy or electronic copy, by post or electronically, and the address to which it must be sent - subs.(4)). Subsection (5) is important in that it requires the registrar to ensure that as from January 1, 2007 all documents subject to s.1078 (see below) may be delivered by electronic means, although this section does not empower the registrar to require delivery by that method (subs.(6), and see s.1069, below). The registrar may not impose requirements that are inconsistent with those in any other enactment (subs.(7)).

1069.   Power to require delivery by electronic means

(1) The Secretary of State may make regulations requiring documents that are authorised or required to be delivered to the registrar to be delivered by electronic means.

(2) Any such requirement to deliver documents by electronic means is effective only if registrar's rules have been published with respect to the detailed requirements for such delivery.

(3) Regulations under this section are subject to affirmative resolution procedure.

GENERAL NOTE

This new section empowers the Secretary of State (but not the registrar - see s.1068(6) above) to make regulations (subject to affirmative resolution procedure (subs.(3)) requiring documents authorised or required to be delivered to the registrar to be delivered by electronic means (subs.(1)). Any such requirement will only be effective if the registrar's rules as to the detailed requirements of such delivery have been published.

1070.   Agreement for delivery by electronic means

(1) The registrar may agree with a company that documents relating to the company that are required or authorised to be delivered to the registrar-

    (a) will be delivered by electronic means, except as provided for in the agreement, and

    (b) will conform to such requirements as may be specified in the agreement or specified by the registrar in accordance with the agreement.

(2) An agreement under this section may relate to all or any description of documents to be delivered to the registrar.

(3) Documents in relation to which an agreement is in force under this section must be delivered in accordance with the agreement.

GENERAL NOTE

Whilst the registrar cannot *require* documents to be delivered electronically, this new section allows the registrar to reach an agreement with a company that documents relating to it shall be so delivered (subs.(1)). The agreement may relate to all documents to be delivered or just to some of them (which may depend upon whether there exists a facility for electronic delivery) (subs.(2)). The agreement may be in standard form, and, according to the explanatory notes, it is envisaged that it will contain detailed provisions for communication in this way, including the possible use of codes and encryption.

1071.   Document not delivered until received

(1) A document is not delivered to the registrar until it is received by the registrar.

(2) Provision may be made by registrar's rules as to when a document is to be regarded as received.

GENERAL NOTE

This section makes it clear that delivery of a document requires it to have been received by the registrar (so that posting the document does not amount to delivery of it) (subs.(1)). The registrar's rules may make more detailed provision as to when a document is to be regarded as received (subs.(2)).

Requirements for proper delivery

1072.   Requirements for proper delivery

(1) A document delivered to the registrar is not properly delivered unless all the following requirements are met-

    (a) the requirements of the provision under which the document is to be delivered to the registrar as regards-
        (i) the contents of the document, and
       (ii) form, authentication and manner of delivery;
    (b) any applicable requirements under-
        section 1068 (registrar's requirements as to form, authentication and manner of delivery),
        section 1069 (power to require delivery by electronic means), or
        section 1070 (agreement for delivery by electronic means);
    (c) any requirements of this Part as to the language in which the document is drawn up and delivered or as to its being accompanied on delivery by a certified translation into English;
    (d) in so far as it consists of or includes names and addresses, any requirements of this Part as to permitted characters, letters or symbols or as to its being accompanied on delivery by a certificate as to the transliteration of any element;
    (e) any applicable requirements under section 1111 (registrar's requirements as to certification or verification);
    (f) any requirement of regulations under section 1082 (use of unique identifiers);
    (g) any requirements as regards payment of a fee in respect of its receipt by the registrar.
(2) A document that is not properly delivered is treated for the purposes of the provision requiring or authorising it to be delivered as not having been delivered, subject to the provisions of section 1073 (power to accept documents not meeting requirements for proper delivery).

GENERAL NOTE
   This section deals with the requirements for proper delivery of documents to the registrar. A document is not properly delivered unless requirements as to the contents, form, authentication and manner of delivery are fulfilled and unless any applicable requirements under ss.1068, 1069 and 1070 (see above) are fulfilled (subs.(1)(a)(b)). For a document to be properly delivered it must also meet any language requirement or requirement for a certified translation (subs.(1)(c)), any requirement as regards permitted characters letters or symbols (subs.(1)(d)) and any requirements under ss.1111 and 1082 (see below), as well as as to fees (subss.(1)(e), (f) and (g)). If a document is not properly delivered it is treated as not having been delivered unless the provisions of s.1073 (below) are applicable (subs.(2)).

1073.   Power to accept documents not meeting requirements for proper delivery

(1) The registrar may accept (and register) a document that does not comply with the requirements for proper delivery.
(2) A document accepted by the registrar under this section is treated as received by the registrar for the purposes of section 1077 (public notice of receipt of certain documents).
(3) No objection may be taken to the legal consequences of a document's being accepted (or registered) by the registrar under this section on the ground that the requirements for proper delivery were not met.
(4) The acceptance of a document by the registrar under this section does not affect-
    (a) the continuing obligation to comply with the requirements for proper delivery, or
    (b) subject as follows, any liability for failure to comply with those requirements.
(5) For the purposes of-
    (a) section 453 (civil penalty for failure to file accounts and reports), and
    (b) any enactment imposing a daily default fine for failure to deliver the document,
 the period after the document is accepted does not count as a period during which there is default in complying with the requirements for proper delivery.
(6) But if, subsequently-
    (a) the registrar issues a notice under section 1094(4) in respect of the document (notice of administrative removal from the register), and

(b) the requirements for proper delivery are not complied with before the end of the period of 14 days after the issue of that notice,

any subsequent period of default does count for the purposes of those provisions.

GENERAL NOTE

Where a document is not properly delivered under s.1072 it may satisfy some of the requirements for proper delivery but not others. This section empowers the registrar to accept and register such a document (subs.(1)), which is then treated as received by the registrar for the purposes of s.1077 (see below). Whilst no objection may be made to the effect that proper delivery of a document accepted by the registrar was not made (subs.(3)), that acceptance has no effect on the continuing obligation of the company to make proper delivery of the document, or on any liability for failure to comply with require-ment of proper delivery (subs.(4)). This is subject to subs.(5), so that for the purposes of the s.453 obligation to file accounts and reports, and for any enactment imposing a daily fine for failure to deliver a document, any period after the document is accepted is not taken into account for the purpose of determining whether there has been default as regards the proper delivery requirement. If, subsequently, the registrar issues a notice under s.1094 (below) the company has 14 days to comply with the requirement for proper delivery, after which any period of default does count for those purposes (subs.(6)).

1074. Documents containing unnecessary material

(1) This section applies where a document delivered to the registrar contains unnecessary material.
(2) "Unnecessary material" means material that-
    (a) is not necessary in order to comply with an obligation under any enactment, and
    (b) is not specifically authorised to be delivered to the registrar.
(3) For this purpose an obligation to deliver a document of a particular description, or conforming to certain requirements, is regarded as not extending to anything that is not needed for a document of that description or, as the case may be, conforming to those require-ments.
(4) If the unnecessary material cannot readily be separated from the rest of the document, the document is treated as not meeting the requirements for proper delivery.
(5) If the unnecessary material can readily be separated from the rest of the document, the registrar may register the document either-
    (a) with the omission of the unnecessary material, or
    (b) as delivered.

GENERAL NOTE

Documents may be defectively delivered in a case where they contain unnecessary material, which is defined in subs.(2) as material not necessary to comply with an obligation under an enactment and which is not specifically authorised for de-livery the registrar (subss.(1) and (2)). If any unnecessary material cannot be readily separated from the rest of the docu-ment, that document does not meet the requirements for proper delivery (subs.(4)). If separation of the unnecessary material can take place the registrar may register the document and omit the unnecessary material or register it as delivered (subs.(5)).

1075. Informal correction of document

(1) A document delivered to the registrar may be corrected by the registrar if it appears to the registrar to be incomplete or internally inconsistent.
(2) This power is exercisable only-
    (a) on instructions, and
    (b) if the company has given (and has not withdrawn) its consent to instructions being given under this section.
(3) The following requirements must be met as regards the instructions-
    (a) the instructions must be given in response to an enquiry by the registrar;

     (b) the registrar must be satisfied that the person giving the instructions is authorised to do so-

          (i) by the person by whom the document was delivered, or

         (ii) by the company to which the document relates;

     (c) the instructions must meet any requirements of registrar's rules as to-

          (i) the form and manner in which they are given, and

         (ii) authentication.

(4) The company's consent to instructions being given under this section (and any withdrawal of such consent)-

     (a) may be in hard copy or electronic form, and

     (b) must be notified to the registrar.

(5) This section applies in relation to documents delivered under Part 25 (company charges) by a person other than the company as if the references to the company were to the company or the person by whom the document was delivered.

(6) A document that is corrected under this section is treated, for the purposes of any enactment relating to its delivery, as having been delivered when the correction is made.

(7) The power conferred by this section is not exercisable if the document has been registered under section 1073 (power to accept documents not meeting requirements for proper delivery).

GENERAL NOTE

   This new section gives the registrar power, in narrowly prescribed circumstances, to correct documents which appear to be incomplete or internally inconsistent. This correction could take place, according to the explanatory notes, by taking amendments or additions through telephone communications with the company. An electronically submitted standard form might, for example, have an "empty" section, and it would be convenient for the registrar to remedy the omission. The registrar may only make corrections through instructions in circumstances where the company has given (and not withdrawn) consent to those instructions being given (subs.(2)). The instructions in subs.(2) must be given in response to the registrar's enquiry and the registrar must be satisfied that the person giving them is authorised to do so (subs.(3)). The company's consent may be given by hard copy or electronically and must be notified to the registrar (subs.(4)), and the section applies equally to a person other than the company delivering documents under Pt 25 (i.e. documents relating to company charges, which may be registered by persons other than the company) (subs.(5)). Where a document is corrected under s.1075 it is treated as properly delivered (subs.(6)), but documents accepted and registered under s.1073 (above) may not be corrected under this section (subs.(7)).

1076.   Replacement of document not meeting requirements for proper delivery

(1) The registrar may accept a replacement for a document previously delivered that-

     (a) did not comply with the requirements for proper delivery, or

     (b) contained unnecessary material (within the meaning of section 1074).

(2) A replacement document must not be accepted unless the registrar is satisfied that it is delivered by-

     (a) the person by whom the original document was delivered, or

     (b) the company to which the original document relates, and that it complies with the requirements for proper delivery.

(3) The power of the registrar to impose requirements as to the form and manner of delivery includes power to impose requirements as to the identification of the original document and the delivery of the replacement in a form and manner enabling it to be associated with the original.

(4) This section does not apply where the original document was delivered under Part 25 (company charges) (but see sections 873 and 888 (rectification of register of charges)).

GENERAL NOTE

   This section empowers the registrar to accept a replacement document where a previously delivered equivalent was not properly delivered or contained unnecessary material (as defined in s.1074) (subs.(1)). In order to exercise this power the registrar must be satisfied that the replacement is delivered by the person who originally delivered the defective document or by the company to which it related and that the replacement is properly delivered (subs.(2)). The registrar may also impose requirements to ensure that the replacement document can be associated with the original (subs.(3)). The power to accept replacement documents does not apply to the delivery of documents relating to company charges under Pt 25, but rectification of the register may occur under ss.873 and 888 in such circumstances (subs.(4)).

Public notice of receipt of certain documents

1077. Public notice of receipt of certain documents

(1) The registrar must cause to be published-
    (a) in the Gazette, or
    (b) in accordance with section 1116 (alternative means of giving public notice),
 notice of the receipt by the registrar of any document that, on receipt, is subject to the Directive disclosure requirements (see section 1078).

(2) The notice must state the name and registered number of the company, the description of document and the date of receipt.

(3) The registrar is not required to cause notice of the receipt of a document to be published before the date of incorporation of the company to which the document relates.

GENERAL NOTE

This section replaces the requirement in s.711 of the Companies Act 1985 for the registrar to cause the be published in the Gazette or by alternative means under s.1116 (below) notice of his receipt of any document subject to the Directive disclosure requirements (the documents in question are listed in s.1078, below). The notice must state the name and registered number of the company and the date of receipt (subs.(2)), but publication of the notice need not take place before the date of incorporation of the company to which it relates (subs.(3)).

1078. Documents subject to Directive disclosure requirements

(1) The documents subject to the "Directive disclosure requirements" are as follows.
The requirements referred to are those of Article 3 of the First Company Law Directive (68/151/EEC), as amended, extended and applied.

(2) In the case of every company-
Constitutional documents
    1. The company's memorandum and articles.
    2. Any amendment of the company's articles (including every resolution or agreement required to be embodied in or annexed to copies of the company's articles issued by the company).
    3. After any amendment of the company's articles, the text of the articles as amended.
    4. Any notice of a change of the company's name.
Directors
    1. The statement of proposed officers required on formation of the company.
    2. Notification of any change among the company's directors.
    3. Notification of any change in the particulars of directors required to be delivered to the registrar.
Accounts, reports and returns
    1. All documents required to be delivered to the registrar under section 441 (annual accounts and reports).
    2. The company's annual return.
Registered office
    Notification of any change of the company's registered office.

Winding up
  1. Copy of any winding-up order in respect of the company.
  2. Notice of the appointment of liquidators.
  3. Order for the dissolution of a company on a winding up.
  4. Return by a liquidator of the final meeting of a company on a winding up.

(3) In the case of a public company-
  Share capital
  1. Any statement of capital and initial shareholdings.
  2. Any return of allotment and the statement of capital accompanying it.
  3. Copy of any resolution under section 570 or 571 (disapplication of preemption rights).
  4. Copy of any report under section 593 or 599 as to the value of a non-cash asset.
  5. Statement of capital accompanying notice given under section 625 (notice by company of redenomination of shares).
  6. Statement of capital accompanying notice given under section 627 (notice by company of reduction of capital in connection with redenomination of shares).
  7. Notice delivered under section 636 (notice of new name of class of shares) or 637 (notice of variation of rights attached to shares).
  8. Statement of capital accompanying order delivered under section 649 (order of court confirming reduction of capital).
  9. Notification (under section 689) of the redemption of shares and the statement of capital accompanying it.
  10. Statement of capital accompanying return delivered under section 708 (notice of cancellation of shares on purchase of own shares) or 730 (notice of cancellation of shares held as treasury shares).
  11. Any statement of compliance delivered under section 762 (statement that company meets conditions for issue of trading certificate).
  Mergers and divisions
  1. Copy of any draft of the terms of a scheme required to be delivered to the registrar under section 906 or 921.
  2. Copy of any order under section 899 or 900 in respect of a compromise or arrangement to which Part 27 (mergers and divisions of public companies) applies.

(4) Where a private company re-registers as a public company (see section 96)-
  (a) the last statement of capital relating to the company received by the registrar under any provision of the Companies Acts becomes subject to the Directive disclosure requirements, and
  (b) section 1077 (public notice of receipt of certain documents) applies as if the statement had been received by the registrar when the reregistration takes effect.
(5) In the case of an overseas company, such particulars, returns and other documents required to be delivered under Part 34 as may be specified by the Secretary of State by regulations.
(6) Regulations under subsection (5) are subject to negative resolution procedure.

GENERAL NOTE
  This section replaces s.711 of the Companies Act 1985 and lists all documents to which s.1077 applies, so that the registrar has to publish a notice of receipt of them. All are documents to which Art.3 of the First Company Law Directive (68/151/EEC), as amended, and are listed in the section under various headings.

1079. Effect of failure to give public notice

(1) A company is not entitled to rely against other persons on the happening of any event to which this section applies unless-

    (a) the event has been officially notified at the material time, or

    (b) the company shows that the person concerned knew of the event at the material time.

(2) The events to which this section applies are-

    (a) an amendment of the company's articles,

    (b) a change among the company's directors,

    (c) (as regards service of any document on the company) a change of the company's registered office,

    (d) the making of a winding-up order in respect of the company, or

    (e) the appointment of a liquidator in a voluntary winding up of the company.

(3) If the material time falls-

    (a) on or before the 15th day after the date of official notification, or

    (b) where the 15th day was not a working day, on or before the next day that was,

the company is not entitled to rely on the happening of the event as against a person who shows that he was unavoidably prevented from knowing of the event at that time.

(4) "Official notification" means-

    (a) in relation to an amendment of the company's articles, notification in accordance with section 1077 (public notice of receipt by registrar of certain documents) of the amendment and the amended text of the articles;

    (b) in relation to anything else stated in a document subject to the Directive disclosure requirements, notification of that document in accordance with that section;

    (c) in relation to the appointment of a liquidator in a voluntary winding up, notification of that event in accordance with section 109 of the Insolvency Act 1986 (c. 45) or Article 95 of the Insolvency (Northern Ireland) Order 1989 (S.I.1989/2405 (N.I. 19)).

GENERAL NOTE

This section replaces s.42 of the Companies Act 1985 and re-enacts the basic rule that a company may not rely on the consequences of certain events as against third parties unless notice of that event has been officially notified or that the third party in question knew about the event at the material time (subs.(1)). The events in question are listed in subs.(2) as an amendment to the company's articles, a change of its directors or registered address, the making of a winding up order in respect of it or the appointment of a liquidator in its voluntary winding up. Thus, where a company changes, say, its registered address it cannot claim a document sent to its old address is not validly served on it before notice of the change has been published unless the sender knew of the change. The meaning of "officially notified" is set out in subs.(4).

The register

1080. The register

(1) The registrar shall continue to keep records of-

    (a) the information contained in documents delivered to the registrar under any enactment,

    (b) certificates of incorporation issued by the registrar, and

    (c) certificates issued by the registrar under section 869(5) or 885(4) (certificates of registration of charge).

(2) The records relating to companies are referred to collectively in the Companies Acts as "the register".

(3) Information deriving from documents subject to the Directive disclosure requirements (see section 1078) that are delivered to the registrar on or after 1st January 2007 must be kept by the registrar in electronic form.

(4) Subject to that, information contained in documents delivered to the registrar may be recorded and kept in any form the registrar thinks fit, provided it is possible to inspect it and produce a copy of it.

This is sufficient compliance with any duty of the registrar to keep, file or register the document or to record the information contained in it.

(5) The records kept by the registrar must be such that information relating to a company is associated with that company, in such manner as the registrar may determine, so as to enable all the information relating to the company to be retrieved.

GENERAL NOTE

This section requires the registrar to keep records of information delivered to him under any enactment and all certificates of incorporation or registration of charges issued by him (subs.(1)), these records being referred to collectively as "the register" in the Companies Acts (subs.(2)). By subs.(3), any information from documents subject to the Directive disclosure requirements delivered to the registrar on or after January 1, 2007 must be kept in electronic form (for a list of such information see s.1078 (above)). Subject to this the registrar may record information and keep it in any form he thinks fit so long as it is possible to inspect it and produce a copy of it (subs.(4)). The registrar is under a duty to ensure that any records kept by him are kept in such a way as to enable him to associate any information in the records with the company to which it refers (subs.(5)).

1081.   Annotation of the register

(1) The registrar must place a note in the register recording-
  (a) the date on which a document is delivered to the registrar;
  (b) if a document is corrected under section 1075, the nature and date of the correction;
  (c) if a document is replaced (whether or not material derived from it is removed), the fact that it has been replaced and the date of delivery of the replacement;
  (d) if material is removed-
      (i) what was removed (giving a general description of its contents),
      (ii) under what power, and
      (iii) the date on which that was done.
(2) The Secretary of State may make provision by regulations-
  (a) authorising or requiring the registrar to annotate the register in such other circumstances as may be specified in the regulations, and
  (b) as to the contents of any such annotation.
(3) No annotation is required in the case of a document that by virtue of section 1072(2) (documents not meeting requirements for proper delivery) is treated as not having been delivered.
(4) A note may be removed if it no longer serves any useful purpose.
(5) Any duty or power of the registrar with respect to annotation of the register is subject to the court's power under section 1097 (powers of court on ordering removal of material from the register) to direct-
  (a) that a note be removed from the register, or
  (b) that no note shall be made of the removal of material that is the subject of the court's order.
(6) Notes placed in the register in accordance with subsection (1), or in pursuance of regulations under subsection (2), are part of the register for all purposes of the Companies Acts.
(7) Regulations under this section are subject to negative resolution procedure.

GENERAL NOTE

The register is intended to provide an accurate source of information for those who view it and, with this in mind, this section requires the registrar to add annotations to it in certain circumstances. These are set out in subs.(2) as the date of delivery of any document, the nature and date of any correction to any document under s.1075, the fact that a document has been replaced and the date of delivery of the replacement and, where material is removed, a general description of the removed content, under what power it was removed and the date of removal (subs.(1)). The Secretary of State may by regulations (subject to negative resolution procedure - subs.(7)) prescribe further circumstances in which annotations must be made and the content of any annotations (subs.(2)). The registrar need not make an annotation where a document is treated as not having been delivered under s.1072(2) (subs.(3)), and annotations that no longer serve a useful purpose may be removed under subs.(4). The registrar's duty and power in this respect is subject to the court's power under s.1097 to order the removal of noted from the register (subs.(5)). All notes placed on the register under this section are part of the register for the purposes of the Companies Act (subs.(6)).

1082. Allocation of unique identifiers

(1) The Secretary of State may make provision for the use, in connection with the register, of reference numbers ("unique identifiers") to identify each person who-

    (a) is a director of a company,

    (b) is secretary (or a joint secretary) of a company, or

    (c) in the case of an overseas company whose particulars are registered under section 1046, holds any such position as may be specified for the purposes of this section by regulations under that section.

(2) The regulations may-

    (a) provide that a unique identifier may be in such form, consisting of one or more sequences of letters or numbers, as the registrar may from time to time determine;

    (b) make provision for the allocation of unique identifiers by the registrar;

    (c) require there to be included, in any specified description of documents delivered to the registrar, as well as a statement of the person's name-

        (i) a statement of the person's unique identifier, or

        (ii) a statement that the person has not been allocated a unique identifier;

    (d) enable the registrar to take steps where a person appears to have more than one unique identifier to discontinue the use of all but one of them.

(3) The regulations may contain provision for the application of the scheme in relation to persons appointed, and documents registered, before the commencement of this Act.

(4) The regulations may make different provision for different descriptions of person and different descriptions of document.

(5) Regulations under this section are subject to affirmative resolution procedure.

GENERAL NOTE

This new section empowers the Secretary of State to make provision for the use of reference numbers, known as "unique identifiers" to identify directors, secretaries and any person holding a position specified by regulations under s.1046 in relation to overseas companies. Any regulations (which are subject to affirmative resolution procedure - subs.(5)) may prescribe the form of a unique identifier, provide for their allocation by the registrar and require them to be referred to in specified documents delivered to the registrar (subs.(2)). The regulations may provide for unique identifiers to be allocated to persons appointed and documents registered before the commencement of the 2006 Act and may make different provision for different descriptions of person and different descriptions of document (subs.(3) and (4)).

1083. Preservation of original documents

(1) The originals of documents delivered to the registrar in hard copy form must be kept for three years after they are received by the registrar, after which they may be destroyed provided the information contained in them has been recorded in the register.

This is subject to section 1087(3) (extent of obligation to retain material not available for public inspection).

(2) The registrar is under no obligation to keep the originals of documents delivered in electronic form, provided the information contained in them has been recorded in the register.

(3) This section applies to documents held by the registrar when this section comes into force as well as to documents subsequently received.

GENERAL NOTE

This section replaces s.707A of the Companies Act 1985 and reduces the period for which the registrar has to keep in hard copy form the originals of documents delivered to him from ten years to three years. After that period the originals may be destroyed as long as the information contained in them has been recorded on the register (subs.(l), which is subject to s.1087(3) (below)). Where documents are delivered in electronic form, there is no obligation to keep the originals provided that the information contained in them has been recorded on the register (subs.(2)). The section applies to documents held by the registrar when it comes into force, as well as to those received subsequently (subs.(3)).

1084.   Records relating to companies that have been dissolved etc

(1) This section applies where-
    (a) a company is dissolved,
    (b) an overseas company ceases to have any connection with the United Kingdom by virtue of which it is required to register particulars under section 1046, or
    (c) a credit or financial institution ceases to be within section 1050 (overseas institutions required to file accounts with the registrar).
(2) At any time after two years from the date on which it appears to the registrar that-
    (a) the company has been dissolved,
    (b) the overseas company has ceased to have any connection with the United Kingdom by virtue of which it is required to register particulars under section 1046, or
    (c) the credit or financial institution has ceased to be within section 1050 (overseas institutions required to file accounts with the registrar),
the registrar may direct that records relating to the company or institution may be removed to the Public Record Office or, as the case may be, the Public Record Office of Northern Ireland.
(3) Records in respect of which such a direction is given shall be disposed of under the enactments relating to that Office and the rules made under them.
(4) In subsection (1)(a) "company" includes a company provisionally or completely registered under the Joint Stock Companies Act 1844 (c. 110).
(5) This section does not extend to Scotland.

GENERAL NOTE
    This section replaces s.707(3) and (4) of the Companies Act 1985 and applies where a company (including a company registered under the Joint Stock Companies Act 1844 (subs.(4)) has been dissolved, an overseas company ceases to have any connection with the United Kingdom or a credit or financial institution ceases to be within s.1050 (overseas institutions required to file accounts with the registrar) (subs.(1)). It provides that at any time after two years of these events occurring the registrar may direct that records relating to the company or institution may be removed to the Public Records Office (subs.(2)), and may be disposed of according to enactments relating to that Office and rules made under them (subs.(3)). This section does not extend to Scotland (subs.(5)).

Inspection etc of the register

1085.   Inspection of the register

(1) Any person may inspect the register.
(2) The right of inspection extends to the originals of documents delivered to the registrar in hard copy form if, and only if, the record kept by the registrar of the contents of the document is illegible or unavailable.
The period for which such originals are to be kept is limited by section 1083(1).
(3) This section has effect subject to section 1087 (material not available for public inspection).

GENERAL NOTE
    This section replaces the rule in s.709 of the Companies Act 1985 that any person has a right to inspect the register, subject to s.1087 (below), which restricts the public availability of certain material on the register. The right extends to the originals of documents delivered in hard copy form only if the record of the information in them kept by the registrar is illegible or unavailable.

1086.   Right to copy of material on the register

(1) Any person may require a copy of any material on the register.

(2) The fee for any such copy of material derived from a document subject to the Directive disclosure requirements (see section 1078), whether in hard copy or electronic form, must not exceed the administrative cost of providing it.

(3) This section has effect subject to section 1087 (material not available for public inspection).

GENERAL NOTE

This section replaces s.709(1)(a) of the Companies Act 1985 and retains the right of any person to require a copy of any material on the register (subs.(1)). Fees may be charged in this regard, but where the material required is derived from a document subject to the Directive disclosure requirements (as to which see s.1078) that fee must not exceed the administrative cost of providing it (subs.(2)). As with s.1086 (above), this section is subject to s.1087 (below) (subs.(3)).

1087.   Material not available for public inspection

(1) The following material must not be made available by the registrar for public inspection-

    (a) the contents of any document sent to the registrar containing views expressed pursuant to section 56 (comments on proposal by company to use certain words or expressions in company name);

    (b) protected information within section 242(1) (directors' residential addresses: restriction on disclosure by registrar) or any corresponding provision of regulations under section 1046 (overseas companies);

    (c) any application to the registrar under section 1024 (application for administrative restoration to the register) that has not yet been determined or was not successful;

    (d) any document received by the registrar in connection with the giving or withdrawal of consent under section 1075 (informal correction of documents);

    (e) any application or other document delivered to the registrar under section 1088 (application to make address unavailable for public inspection) and any address in respect of which such an application is successful;

    (f) any application or other document delivered to the registrar under section 1095 (application for rectification of register);

    (g) any court order under section 1096 (rectification of the register under court order) that the court has directed under section 1097 (powers of court on ordering removal of material from the register) is not to be made available for public inspection;

    (h) the contents of-

        (i) any instrument creating or evidencing a charge and delivered to the registrar under section 860 (registration of company charges: England and Wales or Northern Ireland), or

        (ii) any certified copy of an instrument creating or evidencing a charge and delivered to the registrar under section 878 (registration of company charges: Scotland);

    (i) any e-mail address, identification code or password deriving from a document delivered for the purpose of authorising or facilitating electronic filing procedures or providing information by telephone;

    (j) the contents of any documents held by the registrar pending a decision of the Regulator of Community Interest Companies under section 36 or 38 of the Companies (Audit, Investigations and Community Enterprise) Act 2004 (c. 27) (decision on eligibility for registration as community interest company) and that the registrar is not later required to record;

    (k) any other material excluded from public inspection by or under any other enactment.

(2) A restriction applying by reference to material deriving from a particular description of document does not affect the availability for public inspection of the same information

contained in material derived from another description of document in relation to which no such restriction applies.

(3) Material to which this section applies need not be retained by the registrar for longer than appears to the registrar reasonably necessary for the purposes for which the material was delivered to the registrar.

GENERAL NOTE

This section circumscribes the general right to inspect the register and to require a copy of material on it in respect of all the material specified in subs.(1). However, where such material is available for public inspection from a source other than the register it can be accessed via that means (subs.(2)). The registrar need not retain material to which subs.(1) applies longer than appears to him to be reasonably necessary for the purposes for which it was delivered to him (subs.(3)).

1088.   Application to registrar to make address unavailable for public inspection

(1) The Secretary of State may make provision by regulations requiring the registrar, on application, to make an address on the register unavailable for public inspection.

(2) The regulations may make provision as to-
   (a) who may make an application,
   (b) the grounds on which an application may be made,
   (c) the information to be included in and documents to accompany an application,
   (d) the notice to be given of an application and of its outcome, and
   (e) how an application is to be determined.

(3) Provision under subsection (2)(e) may in particular-
   (a) confer a discretion on the registrar;
   (b) provide for a question to be referred to a person other than the registrar for the purposes of determining the application.

(4) An application must specify the address to be removed from the register and indicate where on the register it is.

(5) The regulations may provide-
   (a) that an address is not to be made unavailable for public inspection under this section unless replaced by a service address, and
   (b) that in such a case the application must specify a service address.

(6) Regulations under this section are subject to affirmative resolution procedure.

GENERAL NOTE

This is a new provision, which empowers the Secretary of State to make provision by regulations (subject to affirmative resolution procedure - subs.(6)) requiring the registrar, on application, to make an address on the register unavailable for public inspection. Any regulations under this section may prescribe rules as to who may make an application, and on what grounds, what information should be included in an application, how its outcome is to be notified and how it is to be determined (subs.(2)). In this final respect, subs.(3) expressly contemplates that discretion may be conferred upon the registrar or that a question be referred to a person other than the registrar. Subsection (5) provides that the regulations may prescribe that an address cannot be made unavailable unless it is replaced by a service address.

1089.   Form of application for inspection or copy

(1) The registrar may specify the form and manner in which application is to be made for-
   (a) inspection under section 1085, or
   (b) a copy under section 1086.

(2) As from 1st January 2007, applications in respect of documents subject to the Directive disclosure requirements may be submitted to the registrar in hard copy or electronic form, as the applicant chooses.

This does not affect the registrar's power under subsection (1) above to impose requirements in respect of other matters.

GENERAL NOTE

GENERAL NOTE

Where an application to inspect the register is made under s.1085 or a copy of material on the register required under s.1086, the registrar may specify the form and manner in which the application is to be made (subs.(1)). However, where the application relates to documents to which the Directive disclosure requirements apply the applicant may choose to submit his application in hard copy or electronic form (subs.(2)).

1090. Form and manner in which copies to be provided

(1) The following provisions apply as regards the form and manner in which copies are to be provided under section 1086.

(2) As from 1st January 2007, copies of documents subject to the Directive disclosure requirements must be provided in hard copy or electronic form, as the applicant chooses.

This is subject to the following proviso.

(3) The registrar is not obliged by subsection (2) to provide copies in electronic form of a document that was delivered to the registrar in hard copy form if-

 (a) the document was delivered to the registrar on or before 31st December 1996, or

 (b) the document was delivered to the registrar on or before 31st December 2006 and ten years or more elapsed between the date of delivery and the date of receipt of the first application for a copy on or after 1st January 2007.

(4) Subject to the preceding provisions of this section, the registrar may determine the form and manner in which copies are to be provided.

GENERAL NOTE

Section 1086 provides that an applicant may require a copy of documents on the register, and this section prescribes the form and manner in which such copies are to be provided. Where the document in question is subject to the Directive disclosure requirements the applicant may, as from January 1, 2007, require a hard copy or a copy in electronic form as he chooses (subs.(2)). Subsection (3) provides exceptions to this rule where the document was delivered on or before December 31, 1996 or the document was delivered to the registrar on or before December 31, 2006 and ten years or more elapsed between the date of delivery and the date of receipt of the first application for a copy on or after January 1, 2007. In respect of documents other than those subject to the Directive disclosure requirements, the registrar has discretion as to the form and manner in which copies are to be provided.

1091. Certification of copies as accurate

(1) Copies provided under section 1086 in hard copy form must be certified as true copies unless the applicant dispenses with such certification.

(2) Copies so provided in electronic form must not be certified as true copies unless the applicant expressly requests such certification.

(3) A copy provided under section 1086, certified by the registrar (whose official position it is unnecessary to prove) to be an accurate record of the contents of the original document, is in all legal proceedings admissible in evidence-

 (a) as of equal validity with the original document, and

 (b) as evidence (in Scotland, sufficient evidence) of any fact stated in the original document of which direct oral evidence would be admissible.

(4) The Secretary of State may make provision by regulations as to the manner in which such a certificate is to be provided in a case where the copy is provided in electronic form.

(5) Except in the case of documents that are subject to the Directive disclosure requirements (see section 1078), copies provided by the registrar may, instead of being certified in writing to be an accurate record, be sealed with the registrar's official seal.

GENERAL NOTE

This section also responds to the requirements of the amended First Company Law Directive. It provides that any copies of documents provided under s.1086 must be certified as true copies, although the applicant may choose to dispense with certification (subs.(1)). This requirement does not apply where the copy is provided in electronic form, unless the applicant requests certification (subs.(2)). Where a certified copy of a document is provided under s.1086 it is admissible in legal proceedings as evidence of equal validity to that of the original document (subs.(3)). Where a copy of a document is provide in electronic form, the Secretary of State may make provision by regulations as to the manner of certification (subs.(4)), and copies provided by the registrar may, instead of being certified as an accurate record, be sealed with the registrar's official seal (subs.(5), although this does not apply to copies of documents subject to the Directive disclosure requirements under s.1078).

1092.   Issue of process for production of records kept by the registrar

(1) No process for compelling the production of a record kept by the registrar shall issue from any court except with the permission of the court.
(2) Any such process shall bear on it a statement that it is issued with the permission of the court.

GENERAL NOTE

This section reproduces the effect of s.709(5) of the Companies Act 1985 that no person can proceed against the registrar for the production of records unless the court has given permission.

Correction or removal of material on the register

1093.   Registrar's notice to resolve inconsistency on the register

(1) Where it appears to the registrar that the information contained in a document delivered to the registrar is inconsistent with other information on the register, the registrar may give notice to the company to which the document relates-
    (a) stating in what respects the information contained in it appears to be inconsistent with other information on the register, and
    (b) requiring the company to take steps to resolve the inconsistency.
(2) The notice must-
    (a) state the date on which it is issued, and
    (b) require the delivery to the registrar, within 14 days after that date, of such replacement or additional documents as may be required to resolve the inconsistency.
(3) If the necessary documents are not delivered within the period specified, an offence is committed by-
    (a) the company, and
    (b) every officer of the company who is in default.
(4) A person guilty of an offence under subsection (3) is liable on summary conviction to a fine not exceeding level 5 on the standard scale and, for continued contravention, a daily default fine not exceeding one-tenth of level 5 on the standard scale.

GENERAL NOTE

This section is directed towards maintaining the accuracy of the register, and empowers the registrar, where it appears to him that information contained in any document delivered to him is inconsistent with other information on the register to notify to company of the inaccuracy and requiring it to take steps to resolve it (subs.(1)). The Explanatory Notes give the example of delivery of a document notifying the registrar that a director has been removed when there is no corresponding record of his appointment. A notice under this section must state the date in which it was issued and require delivery to the registrar within 14 days of that date any replacement or additional documents necessary to resolve the inconsistency (subs.(2)). Failure to comply with this requirement constitutes, under subs.(3), an offence committed by the company and every officer in default, the penalty for which is prescribed in subs.(4).

1094.   Administrative removal of material from the register

(1) The registrar may remove from the register anything that there was power, but no duty, to include.

(2) This power is exercisable, in particular, so as to remove-

(a) unnecessary material within the meaning of section 1074, and

(b) material derived from a document that has been replaced under-

section 1076 (replacement of document not meeting requirements for proper delivery), or

section 1093 (notice to remedy inconsistency on the register).

(3) This section does not authorise the removal from the register of-

(a) anything whose registration has had legal consequences in relation to the company as regards-

(i)   its formation,

(ii)   a change of name,

(iii) its re-registration,

(iv)   its becoming or ceasing to be a community interest company,

(v)   a reduction of capital,

(vi)   a change of registered office,

(vii) the registration of a charge, or

(viii) its dissolution;

(b) an address that is a person's registered address for the purposes of section 1140 (service of documents on directors, secretaries and others).

(4) On or before removing any material under this section (otherwise than at the request of the company) the registrar must give notice-

(a) to the person by whom the material was delivered (if the identity, and name and address of that person are known), or

(b) to the company to which the material relates (if notice cannot be given under paragraph (a) and the identity of that company is known).

(5) The notice must-

(a) state what material the registrar proposes to remove, or has removed, and on what grounds, and

(b) state the date on which it is issued.

GENERAL NOTE

This section empowers the registrar to remove from the registrar anything he has a power, but no duty to enter (subs.(1)) Without prejudice to the generality of the power, subs.(2) specifies the registrar's power to remove unnecessary material (s.1074, above), and material derived from a document that has been replaced under s.1076 or s.1093. The registrar may not, however, remove from the register anything whose registration has legal consequences as regards the formation of the company, a change of it name, its re-registration, it becoming or ceasing to be a community interest company, a reduction of its capital, a change to its registered office, the registration of a charge or its dissolution (subs.(3)(a)) or any address that is a person's registered address for the purpose of service of documents under s.1140 (subs.(3)(b)). The registrar must notify the person who delivered the material (if their identity and address is known) or, if notifying that person is not possible, the company to which the material relates before removing any material (subs.(4)) and this notice must state the material proposed to be removed and on what grounds, and the date on which the notice was issued (subs.(5)).

1095.   Rectification of register on application to registrar

(1) The Secretary of State may make provision by regulations requiring the registrar, on application, to remove from the register material of a description specified in the regulations that-

(a) derives from anything invalid or ineffective or that was done without the authority of the company, or

    (b) is factually inaccurate, or is derived from something that is factually inaccurate or forged.

(2) The regulations may make provision as to-

    (a) who may make an application,

    (b) the information to be included in and documents to accompany an application,

    (c) the notice to be given of an application and of its outcome,

    (d) a period in which objections to an application may be made, and

    (e) how an application is to be determined.

(3) An application must-

    (a) specify what is to be removed from the register and indicate where on the register it is, and

    (b) be accompanied by a statement that the material specified in the application complies with this section and the regulations.

(4) If no objections are made to the application, the registrar may accept the statement as sufficient evidence that the material specified in the application should be removed from the register.

(5) Where anything is removed from the register under this section the registration of which had legal consequences as mentioned in section 1094(3), any person appearing to the court to have a sufficient interest may apply to the court for such consequential orders as appear just with respect to the legal effect (if any) to be accorded to the material by virtue of its having appeared on the register.

(6) Regulations under this section are subject to affirmative resolution procedure.

GENERAL NOTE

   This section also attempts to ensure the accuracy of the register by empowering the Secretary of State to make provision by regulations (subject to affirmative resolution procedure) requiring the registrar, on application, to remove from the register material deriving from anything that was invalid, defective or done without authority or is inaccurate or derives from anything that was inaccurate or forged (subs.(1)). The regulations may make provision as to who may apply and how, how the outcome of the application will be notified, when objections may be made to the application and how it will be determined (subs.(2)). Any such application must specify what is to be removed from the register and from where and be accompanied by a statement of compliance with the section and the regulations (subs.(3)), and if no objection is made to the application this statement may be accepted by the registrar as sufficient evidence that the material specified should be removed (subs.(4)).

1096.   Rectification of the register under court order

(1) The registrar shall remove from the register any material-

    (a) that derives from anything that the court has declared to be invalid or ineffective, or to have been done without the authority of the company, or

    (b) that a court declares to be factually inaccurate, or to be derived from something that is factually inaccurate, or forged,

 and that the court directs should be removed from the register.

(2) The court order must specify what is to be removed from the register and indicate where on the register it is.

(3) The court must not make an order for the removal from the register of anything the registration of which had legal consequences as mentioned in section 1094(3) unless satisfied-

    (a) that the presence of the material on the register has caused, or may cause, damage to the company, and

    (b) that the company's interest in removing the material outweighs any interest of other persons in the material continuing to appear on the register.

(4) Where in such a case the court does make an order for removal, it may make such consequential orders as appear just with respect to the legal effect (if any) to be accorded to the material by virtue of its having appeared on the register.

(5) A copy of the court's order must be sent to the registrar for registration.

(6) This section does not apply where the court has other, specific, powers to deal with the matter, for example under-

    (a) the provisions of Part 15 relating to the revision of defective accounts and reports, or

    (b) section 873 or 888 (rectification of the register of charges).

GENERAL NOTE

    This section makes provision for rectification of the register by court order. The court's power in this respect operates in the same circumstance as would the registrar's under regulations made according to s.1095(1)(a)(b) (above). The court's power is wider than that of the registrar, however, as there is no limit on the type of document covered, so that the court may order the removal from the register of anything the registration of which had legal consequences as mentioned in s.1094(3) if it is satisfied that its presence has caused or may cause damage to the company and the company's interest in removing the material outweighs any interest of other persons in the material continuing to appear on the register (subs.(3)). A copy of any order made by the court must be sent to the registrar for registration (subs.(5)), but where the court has other powers to order rectification of the register then this section does not apply (subs.(6)).

1097. Powers of court on ordering removal of material from the register

(1) Where the court makes an order for the removal of anything from the register under section 1096 (rectification of the register), it may give directions under this section.

(2) It may direct that any note on the register that is related to the material that is the subject of the court's order shall be removed from the register.

(3) It may direct that its order shall not be available for public inspection as part of the register.

(4) It may direct-

    (a) that no note shall be made on the register as a result of its order, or

    (b) that any such note shall be restricted to such matters as may be specified by the court.

(5) The court shall not give any direction under this section unless it is satisfied-

    (a) that-

        (i) the presence on the register of the note or, as the case may be, of an unrestricted note, or

        (ii) the availability for public inspection of the court's order,

    may cause damage to the company, and

    (b) that the company's interest in non-disclosure outweighs any interest of other persons in disclosure.

GENERAL NOTE

    This section supplements s.1096 (above). It empowers the court, on making an order under that section, to give further directions (subs.(1)) which may be to the effect that any note on the register relating to the material that is to be removed shall also be removed (subs.(2)). The court may also direct that its order shall nto be made available for public inspection (subs.(3)) and that no note, or only a restricted note, shall be made on the register as a result of its order (subs.(4)). Any direction under this section may only be made where the court is satisfied that the presence of the register of any note (or restricted note) or the availability of its order for public inspection may damage the company and that the company's interest in non-disclosure outweighs any interest of other persons in disclosure (subs.(5)).

1098. Public notice of removal of certain material from the register

(1) The registrar must cause to be published-

    (a) in the Gazette, or

    (b) in accordance with section 1116 (alternative means of giving public notice),

notice of the removal from the register of any document subject to the Directive disclosure requirements (see section 1078) or of any material derived from such a document.

(2) The notice must state the name and registered number of the company, the description of document and the date of receipt.

GENERAL NOTE

This section applies where any document subject to the Directive Disclosure requirements is removed from the register. The registrar must cause to be published in the Gazette, or give public notice in accordance with s.1116 (below), a notice of that removal, and the notice must state the name and registered number of the company, a description of the document and the date of receipt.

The registrar's index of company names

1099. The registrar's index of company names

(1) The registrar of companies must keep an index of the names of the companies and other bodies to which this section applies.

This is "the registrar's index of company names".

(2) This section applies to-
    (a) UK-registered companies;
    (b) any body to which any provision of the Companies Acts applies by virtue of regulations under section 1043 (unregistered companies); and
    (c) overseas companies that have registered particulars with the registrar under section 1046, other than companies that appear to the registrar not to be required to do so.

(3) This section also applies to-
    (a) limited partnerships registered in the United Kingdom;
    (b) limited liability partnerships incorporated in the United Kingdom;
    (c) European Economic Interest Groupings registered in the United Kingdom;
    (d) open-ended investment companies authorised in the United Kingdom;
    (e) societies registered under the Industrial and Provident Societies Act 1965 (c. 12) or the Industrial and Provident Societies Act (Northern Ireland) 1969 (c. 24 (N.I.)).

(4) The Secretary of State may by order amend subsection (3)-
    (a) by the addition of any description of body;
    (b) by the deletion of any description of body.

(5) Any such order is subject to negative resolution procedure.

GENERAL NOTE

Section 1099 replaces s.714 of the Companies Act 1985 and maintains the requirement that the registrar keep an index of the names of companies and any other bodies to which the section applies. Subsections (2) and (3) specify which bodies must be included in this register, which is known as is "the registrar's index of company names" (subs.(1)). The Secretary of State may, by order subject to negative resolution procedure (subs.(5)), amend subs.(3) by addition or deletion of any of the bodies mentioned therein (subs.(4)).

1100. Right to inspect index

Any person may inspect the registrar's index of company names.

GENERAL NOTE

The registrar's index of company names may be inspected by any person.

1101. Power to amend enactments relating to bodies other than companies

(1) The Secretary of State may by regulations amend the enactments relating to any description of body for the time being within section 1099(3) (bodies other than companies whose names are to be entered in the registrar's index), so as to-

(a) require the registrar to be provided with information as to the names of bodies registered, incorporated, authorised or otherwise regulated under those enactments, and

(b) make provision in relation to such bodies corresponding to that made by-

section 66 (company name not to be the same as another in the index), and

sections 67 and 68 (power to direct change of company name in case of similarity to existing name).

(2) Regulations under this section are subject to affirmative resolution procedure.

GENERAL NOTE

Section 1099(3) makes provisions for bodies other than companies to be included on the registrar's index of company names. This section empowers the Secretary of State to amend by regulations (subject to affirmative resolution procedure - subs.(2)) enactments relating to those bodies so as to require the provision to the registrar of information as to the names of bodies registered, incorporated, authorised or otherwise regulated under those enactments (subs.(1)(a)). The regulations may also make provisions for those bodies corresponding to those in ss.66, 67 and 68. Thus, where the name of, say, a limited liability partnership is the same or similar to one already on the register, the regulations may provide that it should be changed.

Language requirements: translation

1102. Application of language requirements

(1) The provisions listed below apply to all documents required to be delivered to the registrar under any provision of-

(a) the Companies Acts, or

(b) the Insolvency Act 1986 (c. 45) or the Insolvency (Northern Ireland) Order 1989 (S.I. 1989/2405 (N.I. 19)).

(2) The Secretary of State may make provision by regulations applying all or any of the listed provisions, with or without modifications, in relation to documents delivered to the registrar under any other enactment.

(3) The provisions are-

section 1103 (documents to be drawn up and delivered in English),

section 1104 (documents relating to Welsh companies),

section 1105 (documents that may be drawn up and delivered in other languages),

section 1107 (certified translations).

(4) Regulations under this section are subject to negative resolution procedure.

GENERAL NOTE

This section is preliminary to the following sections relating to language requirements for documents delivered to the registrar. These provisions apply to all such documents required to be delivered under the Companies Acts, the Insolvency Act 1986 and the Insolvency (Northern Ireland) Order 1989 (subs.(1)). Subsection (2) empowers the Secretary of State to make provision by regulations (subject to the negative resolution procedure - subs.(4)) applying the provisions listed in subs.(3), with or without modification, in relation to documents delivered to the registrar under any other enactment.

1103. Documents to be drawn up and delivered in English

(1) The general rule is that all documents required to be delivered to the registrar must be drawn up and delivered in English.

(2) This is subject to-

section 1104 (documents relating to Welsh companies) and

section 1105 (documents that may be drawn up and delivered in other languages).

GENERAL NOTE

This section provides the basic rule that all documents required to be delivered to the registrar must be drawn up and delivered in English. It is subject to ss.1104 and 1105 (below).

1104. Documents relating to Welsh companies

(1) Documents relating to a Welsh company may be drawn up and delivered to the registrar in Welsh.

(2) On delivery to the registrar any such document must be accompanied by a certified translation into English, unless it is-

(a) of a description excepted from that requirement by regulations made by the Secretary of State, or

(b) in a form prescribed in Welsh (or partly in Welsh and partly in English) by virtue of section 26 of the Welsh Language Act 1993 (c. 38).

(3) Where a document is properly delivered to the registrar in Welsh without a certified translation into English, the registrar must obtain such a translation if the document is to be available for public inspection.

The translation is treated as if delivered to the registrar in accordance with the same provision as the original.

(4) A Welsh company may deliver to the registrar a certified translation into Welsh of any document in English that relates to the company and is or has been delivered to the registrar.

(5) Section 1105 (which requires certified translations into English of documents delivered to the registrar in another language) does not apply to a document relating to a Welsh company that is drawn up and delivered in Welsh.

GENERAL NOTE

This section replaces, without substantive change, s.710B Companies Act 1985 and provides that documents relating to a Welsh company may be drawn up and delivered to the registrar in Welsh (subs.(1)). Such documents must be accompanied by a certified translation into English unless they are of a kind exempted from this requirement by regulations made by the Secretary of State or in a form prescribed in Welsh by virtue of s.26 of the Welsh Language Act 1993 (subs.(2)). Where a document is properly delivered without a certified translation the registrar is required to obtain such a translation if the document is to made available for public inspection (subs.(3)) and a Welsh company may deliver a certified translation *into* Welsh of any document in English that relates to the company and has been delivered to the registrar (subs.(4)). Section 1105 (below) does not apply to documents of Welsh companies drawn uo and delivered in Welsh (subs.(5)).

1105. Documents that may be drawn up and delivered in other languages

(1) Documents to which this section applies may be drawn up and delivered to the registrar in a language other than English, but when delivered to the registrar they must be accompanied by a certified translation into English.

(2) This section applies to-

(a) agreements required to be forwarded to the registrar under Chapter 3 of Part 3 (agreements affecting the company's constitution);

(b) documents required to be delivered under section 400(2)(e) or section 401(2)(f) (company included in accounts of larger group: required to deliver copy of group accounts);

(c) instruments or copy instruments required to be delivered under Part 25 (company charges);

(d) documents of any other description specified in regulations made by the Secretary of State.

(3) Regulations under this section are subject to negative resolution procedure.

GENERAL NOTE

GENERAL NOTE

This section specifies which documents may be drawn up and delivered to the registrar in a language other than English, but which must be accompanied by a certified translation into English. The documents, as provided in subs.(2), are any agreements required to be forwarded to the registrar under Ch.3 of Pt 3 of the Act (agreements affecting the company's constitution), documents relating to the delivery of group accounts, documents relating to company charges and any other documents as specified in regulations made by the Secretary of State (which will be subject to negative resolution procedure - subs.(3)). The rationale behind this provision is that the documents in question may originate in another jurisdiction with a different language.

1106. Voluntary filing of translations

(1) A company may deliver to the registrar one or more certified translations of any document relating to the company that is or has been delivered to the registrar.

(2) The Secretary of State may by regulations specify-

    (a) the languages, and

    (b) the descriptions of document,

in relation to which this facility is available.

(3) The regulations must provide that it is available as from 1st January 2007-

    (a) in relation to all the official languages of the European Union, and

    (b) in relation to all documents subject to the Directive disclosure requirements (see section 1078).

(4) The power of the registrar to impose requirements as to the form and manner of delivery includes power to impose requirements as to the identification of the original document and the delivery of the translation in a form and manner enabling it to be associated with the original.

(5) Regulations under this section are subject to negative resolution procedure.

(6) This section does not apply where the original document was delivered to the registrar before this section came into force.

GENERAL NOTE

This new section is aimed at implementing certain requirements of the amended First Company Law Directive, and enables companies to send to the registrar certified translations of any document relating to the company that has been delivered to the registrar. The Secretary of State may specify by regulations (subject to negative resolution procedure - subs.(5)) the languages and the types of document to which this facility applies, but any regulations must make the facility available, as from January 1, 2007, in relation to all the official languages within the European Union and all documents subject to the Directive disclosure requirements (subs.(3)). The registrar may impose requirements as to the identification of the original document and the delivery of the translation so as to allow the translation to be associated with the original (subs.(4)). Where the original document was delivered to the registrar prior to the coming into force of this section, then it does not apply (subs.(6)).

1107. Certified translations

(1) In this Part a "certified translation" means a translation certified to be a correct translation.

(2) In the case of any discrepancy between the original language version of a document and a certified translation-

    (a) the company may not rely on the translation as against a third party, but

    (b) a third party may rely on the translation unless the company shows that the third party had knowledge of the original.

(3) A "third party" means a person other than the company or the registrar.

GENERAL NOTE

This section defines "certified translation" as a translation certified to be a correct translation (subs.(1)). Where there is any discrepancy between the original language document and the certified translation of it the company may not, as against a third party, rely on the translation, although the third party, unless he is shown by the company to have knowledge of the original document, may rely on it (subs.(2)). A third party for the purposes of this section is a person other than the company or the registrar (subs.(3)).

Language requirements: transliteration

1108.   Transliteration of names and addresses: permitted characters

(1) Names and addresses in a document delivered to the registrar must contain only letters, characters and symbols (including accents and other diacritical marks) that are permitted.
(2) The Secretary of State may make provision by regulations-
    (a) as to the letters, characters and symbols (including accents and other diacritical marks) that are permitted, and
    (b) permitting or requiring the delivery of documents in which names and addresses have not been transliterated into a permitted form.
(3) Regulations under this section are subject to negative resolution procedure.

GENERAL NOTE

This new section addresses the question of the letters, characters and symbols in which names and addresses in documents delivered to the registrar are to be permitted (subs.(1)) and is largely concerned with possibility that documents containing names and addresses may be delivered to the registrar with those names and addresses expressed in characters from an alphabet different to the Roman alphabet. It empowers the Secretary of State to make provision by regulations (subject to negative resolution procedure - subs.(3)) as to which letters characters and symbols are permitted, but also to permit or require the delivery of documents in which names or addresses have not been transliterated into a permitted form (subs.(2)). To transliterate means to translate from one alphabet into another.

1109.   Transliteration of names and addresses: voluntary transliteration into Roman characters

(1) Where a name or address is or has been delivered to the registrar in a permitted form using other than Roman characters, the company may deliver to the registrar a transliteration into Roman characters.
(2) The power of the registrar to impose requirements as to the form and manner of delivery includes power to impose requirements as to the identification of the original document and the delivery of the transliteration in a form and manner enabling it to be associated with the original.

GENERAL NOTE

This new section allows a company to deliver to the registrar a transliteration into Roman characters of a name and address submitted in a permitted form other than Roman characters (subs.(1)). The registrar may impose such requirements as to the form and delivery of such a transliteration as are necessary to enable the original document to be associated with the transliteration (subs.(2)).

1110.   Transliteration of names and addresses: certification

(1) The Secretary of State may make provision by regulations requiring the certification of transliterations and prescribing the form of certification.
(2) Different provision may be made for compulsory and voluntary transliterations.
(3) Regulations under this section are subject to negative resolution procedure.

This new section allows the Secretary of State to make provision by regulations (subject to negative resolution procedure - subs.(3)) requiring the certification on transliterations under ss.1108 and 1109 (subs.(1)), and explicitly envisages the possibility that different provision may be made for transliteration certification under the two different sections (subs.(2)).

Supplementary provisions

1111. Registrar's requirements as to certification or verification

(1) Where a document required or authorised to be delivered to the registrar under any enactment is required-
  (a) to be certified as an accurate translation or transliteration, or
  (b) to be certified as a correct copy or verified,
the registrar may impose requirements as to the person, or description of person, by whom the certificate or verification is to be given.

(2) The power conferred by section 1068 (registrar's requirements as to form, authentication and manner of delivery) is exercisable in relation to the certificate or verification as if it were a separate document.

(3) Requirements imposed under this section must not be inconsistent with requirements imposed by any enactment with respect to the certification or verification of the document concerned.

GENERAL NOTE

This section concerns the situation where documents required or authorised to be delivered to the registrar under any enactment are required to be certified either as an accurate translation or transliteration or to be verified. In such circumstances the registrar may impose requirements as to the person, or description of persons by whom the certificate or verification is to be given. Such requirements may be, for example, as to qualification or membership of a professional body (subs.(1)). The power of the registrar to impose requirements as to the form, authentication and manner of delivery of a document under s.1068 may be exercised in relation to a certificate or verification under this section as though it were a separate document (subs.(2)). Any requirements imposed by the registrar must, however, be consistent with requirements imposed by any enactment concerned with certification or verification of the document in question (subs.(3)).

1112. General false statement offence

(1) It is an offence for a person knowingly or recklessly-
  (a) to deliver or cause to be delivered to the registrar, for any purpose of the Companies Acts, a document, or
  (b) to make to the registrar, for any such purpose, a statement,
that is misleading, false or deceptive in a material particular.

(2) A person guilty of an offence under this section is liable-
  (a) on conviction on indictment, to imprisonment for a term not exceeding two years or a fine (or both);
  (b) on summary conviction-
    (i) in England and Wales, to imprisonment for a term not exceeding twelve months or to a fine not exceeding the statutory maximum (or both);
    (ii) in Scotland or Northern Ireland, to imprisonment for a term not exceeding six months, or to a fine not exceeding the statutory maximum (or both).

GENERAL NOTE

This section provides for a new offence of delivering or causing to be delivered to the registrar a document that is misleading, false or deceptive in a material particular or making to the registrar a statement that is misleading, false or deceptive in a material particular. The offence may be committed knowingly or recklessly and the penalty for the offence is prescribed in subs.(2). This is a general offence, and its inclusion implements the recommendation of the Company Law Review (*Final*

Report, para.11.48) that specific offences regarding the making of false statements or the provision of false information should be replaced by an overarching offence.

1113. Enforcement of company's filing obligations

(1) This section applies where a company has made default in complying with any obligation under the Companies Acts-
    (a) to deliver a document to the registrar, or
    (b) to give notice to the registrar of any matter.

(2) The registrar, or any member or creditor of the company, may give notice to the company requiring it to comply with the obligation.

(3) If the company fails to make good the default within 14 days after service of the notice, the registrar, or any member or creditor of the company, may apply to the court for an order directing the company, and any specified officer of it, to make good the default within a specified time.

(4) The court's order may provide that all costs (in Scotland, expenses) of or incidental to the application are to be borne by the company or by any officers of it responsible for the default.

(5) This section does not affect the operation of any enactment making it an offence, or imposing a civil penalty, for the default.

GENERAL NOTE

This section replaces s.713 of the Companies Act 1985 and re-enacts its provisions as to circumstance in which the company fails to comply with any obligation to make delivery of a document or give notice of a matter to the registrar (subs.(1)). In such circumstance, the registrar, or any member or creditor of the company, may serve a notice on the company requiring it to remedy the default (subs.(2)), and if the company fails to do so within 14 days of the notice the registrar, member or creditor may apply to court for an order requiring the company and any specified office to remedy the default within a specific time (subs.(3)). Subsection (4) enables the court to provide in its order that direct and incidental costs of any such application are born by the company or those of its officers responsible for the default. The provisions of this section are additional to any provision in any enactment imposing criminal or civil liability for the same default (subs.(5)).

1114. Application of provisions about documents and delivery

(1) In this Part-
    (a) "document" means information recorded in any form, and
    (b) references to delivering a document include forwarding, lodging, registering, sending, producing or submitting it or (in the case of a notice) giving it.

(2) Except as otherwise provided, this Part applies in relation to the supply to the registrar of information otherwise than in documentary form as it applies in relation to the delivery of a document.

GENERAL NOTE

This section replaces s.715A of the Companies Act 1985. It defines "document" as information recorded in any form and provides that references to 'delivering' include forwarding lodging, registering, sending, producing, submitting or giving the document (subs.(1)). Subsection (2) makes clear that Pt 35 applies, unless otherwise provided, to information supplied in other than documentary form (the explanatory notes giving the example, tentatively, of information sent by a website).

1115. Supplementary provisions relating to electronic communications

(1) Registrar's rules may require a company to give any necessary consents to the use of electronic means for communications by the registrar to the company as a condition of making use of any facility to deliver material to the registrar by electronic means.

(2) A document that is required to be signed by the registrar or authenticated by the registrar's seal shall, if sent by electronic means, be authenticated in such manner as may be specified by registrar's rules.

GENERAL NOTE

This section replaces s.710A of the Companies Act 1985 and enables the registrar to require a company which has chosen to submit information and documents electronically to consent to communications from the registrar to be provided electronically (subs.(1)). Where the registrar is required to sign or authenticate a document with his seal, such a document sent electronically may be authenticated or signed in any way specified by the registrar's rules (subs.(2)).

1116. Alternative to publication in the Gazette

(1) Notices that would otherwise need to be published by the registrar in the Gazette may instead be published by such means as may from time to time be approved by the registrar in accordance with regulations made by the Secretary of State.

(2) The Secretary of State may make provision by regulations as to what alternative means may be approved.

(3) The regulations may, in particular-
    (a) require the use of electronic means;
    (b) require the same means to be used-
        (i) for all notices or for all notices of specified descriptions, and
        (ii) whether the company is registered in England and Wales, Scotland or Northern Ireland;
    (c) impose conditions as to the manner in which access to the notices is to be made available.

(4) Regulations under this section are subject to negative resolution procedure.

(5) Before starting to publish notices by means approved under this section the registrar must publish at least one notice to that effect in the Gazette.

(6) Nothing in this section prevents the registrar from giving public notice both in the Gazette and by means approved under this section.
In that case, the requirement of public notice is met when notice is first given by either means.

GENERAL NOTE

This new section implements a recommendation of the Company Law Review (*Final Report*, para.11.48) that alternative methods of publications required of the registrar should be made available. At present required publications are made in the London or Edinburgh Gazettes (as appropriate), but the Review noted that increasingly sophisticated methods of communication, and specifically electronic methods, could be made use of in this respect. Therefore, this section provides that notices that the registrar must cause to be published in either of the Gazettes may, instead, by published by such other means as are approved by the registrar in accordance with regulations (subject to negative resolution procedure - subs.(4)) made by the Secretary of State (subs.(1)). Such regulations may specify the alternative methods of giving notice that may be approved (subs.(2)) and may, in particular, require the use of electronic methods or require the same method to be used for all notices or all notices of specified descriptions, wherever the company is registered (subs.(3)). Before the registrar may adopt alternative means of making notification he must publish at least one notice to the effect that he will be doing so in the Gazette (subs.(5)), and it remains open to the registrar to give public notice by both methods. If the registrar does so, his obligation to give public notice is satisfied when it is first given by either method (subs.(6)).

1117. Registrar's rules

(1) Where any provision of this Part enables the registrar to make provision, or impose requirements, as to any matter, the registrar may make such provision or impose such requirements by means of rules under this section. This is without prejudice to the making of such provision or the imposing of such requirements by other means.

(2) Registrar's rules-

    (a) may make different provision for different cases, and

    (b) may allow the registrar to disapply or modify any of the rules.

(3) The registrar must-

    (a) publicise the rules in a manner appropriate to bring them to the notice of persons affected by them, and

    (b) make copies of the rules available to the public (in hard copy or electronic form).

GENERAL NOTE

    This Part of the Act enables the registrar to impose requirements as to various matters, including, for example, the form or method of delivery of documents. This section provides that any such requirements should be made by rules under this section (subs.(1)). The content of the rules is at the discretion of the registrar (subs.(2)), but he must publicise those rules in a way that will ensure those affected by them can be aware of them (subs.(3)(a)). Hard or electronic copies of the rules must be made available to the public (subs.(3)(b)).

1118.   Payments into the Consolidated Fund

Nothing in the Companies Acts or any other enactment as to the payment of receipts into the Consolidated Fund shall be read as affecting the operation in relation to the registrar of section 3(1) of the Government Trading Funds Act 1973 (c. 63).

GENERAL NOTE

    This section provides that nothing in this Act or any other enactment regarding payments of receipts into the Consolidated Fund affects the operation of s.3(1) of the Government Trading Funds Act 1973 as far as the registrar is concerned.

1119.   Contracting out of registrar's functions

(1) Where by virtue of an order made under section 69 of the Deregulation and Contracting Out Act 1994 (c. 40) a person is authorised by the registrar to accept delivery of any class of documents that are under any enactment to be delivered to the registrar, the registrar may direct that documents of that class shall be delivered to a specified address of the authorised person.

Any such direction must be printed and made available to the public (with or without payment).

(2) A document of that class that is delivered to an address other than the specified address is treated as not having been delivered.

(3) Registrar's rules are not subordinate legislation for the purposes of section 71 of the Deregulation and Contracting Out Act 1994 (functions excluded from contracting out).

GENERAL NOTE

    This section replaces, and substantially restates s.704(3) and (4) of the Companies Act 1985. The registrar, under s.69 of the Deregulation and Contracting Out Act 1994, is authorised to "delegate" (or to contract out) certain of his functions to another person. Subsection (1) allows the registrar to direct that classes of documents falling within delegated functions are to be delivered to the specified address of that person, with such a direction being printed and made available to the public. Any document subject to such a direction that is delivered to an address different to that specified by the registrar is treated as not having been delivered (subs.(2)).

1120.   Application of this Part to overseas companies

Unless the context otherwise requires, the provisions of this Part apply to an overseas company as they apply to a company as defined in section 1.

GENERAL NOTE

    This section provides that Pt 35 applies, unless the context requires otherwise, to overseas companies.

OFFENCES UNDER THE COMPANIES ACTS

GENERAL NOTE

The Company Law Review *Final Report* considered that any new Companies Act should be "underpinned by an efficient and effective sanctions regime which enhances investor and creditor confidence, protects those involved with companies and encourages a culture of compliance, without endangering competitiveness" (para.15.1: see also Ch.13 of *Completing the Structure*). It made particular recommendations as to the definition of an "officer in default" and in relation to circumstances in which the company itself should be criminally liable. As regards this latter question, a general principle was adopted whereby criminal liability should only be imposed where the 'victims' of the default were outsiders (i.e. not the company or its members). A review of all the offences in the Companies Acts was conducted in the light of this general principle and the following provisions are guided by it.

Liability of officer in default

1121.   Liability of officer in default

(1) This section has effect for the purposes of any provision of the Companies Acts to the effect that, in the event of contravention of an enactment in relation to a company, an offence is committed by every officer of the company who is in default.

(2) For this purpose "officer" includes-

(a) any director, manager or secretary, and

(b) any person who is to be treated as an officer of the company for the purposes of the provision in question.

(3) An officer is "in default" for the purposes of the provision if he authorises or permits, participates in, or fails to take all reasonable steps to prevent, the contravention.

GENERAL NOTE

This section seeks to define, for the purposes of liability under the Companies Acts, who may be an "officer of the company" and when that officer will be "in default" (subs.(1)). Subsection (2) defines an "officer" as including any director, manager or secretary of the company, but also any other person who is to be treated as an officer for the purposes of any particular provision. As an example, several sections of the Companies Act 2006 explicitly provide that a "shadow director", or "a liquidator" may be treated as an officer of the company for the purposes of liability. An officer is "in default" for the purposes of any provision is he authorises or permits, participates in, or fails to take all reasonable steps to prevent, the contravention attracting liability (subs.(3)).

1122.   Liability of company as officer in default

(1) Where a company is an officer of another company, it does not commit an offence as an officer in default unless one of its officers is in default.

(2) Where any such offence is committed by a company the officer in question also commits the offence and is liable to be proceeded against and punished accordingly.

(3) In this section "officer" and "in default" have the meanings given by section 1121.

GENERAL NOTE

A company may be the officer of another company, and default may be made in relation to one of the provisions of the Act by that other company. This section makes it clear that the company which is an officer of the company in default is only itself in default if one of its own officers is in default (subs.(1)). The defaulting officer of the first company also commits the offence in question (subs.(2)).

1123.   Application to bodies other than companies

(1) Section 1121 (liability of officers in default) applies to a body other than a company as it applies to a company.

(2) As it applies in relation to a body corporate other than a company-

   (a) the reference to a director of the company shall be read as referring-

      (i) where the body's affairs are managed by its members, to a member of the body,

      (ii) in any other case, to any corresponding officer of the body, and

   (b) the reference to a manager or secretary of the company shall be read as referring to any manager, secretary or similar officer of the body.

(3) As it applies in relation to a partnership-

   (a) the reference to a director of the company shall be read as referring to a member of the partnership, and

   (b) the reference to a manager or secretary of the company shall be read as referring to any manager, secretary or similar officer of the partnership.

(4) As it applies in relation to an unincorporated body other than a partnership-

   (a) the reference to a director of the company shall be read as referring-

      (i) where the body's affairs are managed by its members, to a member of the body,

      (ii) in any other case, to a member of the governing body, and

   (b) the reference to a manager or secretary of the company shall be read as referring to any manager, secretary or similar officer of the body.

GENERAL NOTE

   This section applies the provisions of s.1121 as to the meaning of 'officer in default' to bodies that are not companies as though they were companies. Thus, the reference to "director" in s.1121 is to be read as referring to a corresponding officer of a body that is not a company, or, where that body's affairs are managed by its members, to a member of that body (sub-s.(2)(a)). The reference to a manager or secretary in s.1121 is to be read as a reference to any manager, secretary or similar officer of that body (subs.(2)(b)). A member of a partnership is treated as a director for the purposes of s.1121, as is a manager, secretary or similar officer of a partnership (subs.(3)). Subsection (4) makes similar provision in relation to unincorporated bodies.

Offences under the Companies Act 1985

1124.   Amendments of the Companies Act 1985

Schedule 3 contains amendments of the Companies Act 1985 (c. 6) relating to offences.

GENERAL NOTE

   This section identifies Sch.3 as containing amendments to the Companies Act 1985 relating to offences.

General provisions

1125.   Meaning of "daily default fine"

(1) This section defines what is meant in the Companies Acts where it is provided that a person guilty of an offence is liable on summary conviction to a fine not exceeding a specified amount "and, for continued contravention, a daily default fine" not exceeding a specified amount.

(2) This means that the person is liable on a second or subsequent summary conviction of the offence to a fine not exceeding the latter amount for each day on which the contravention is continued (instead of being liable to a fine not exceeding the former amount).

GENERAL NOTE

Many of the offences under the Companies Acts impose liability to a fine and, where the contravention continues, to a daily default fine. This section replaces s.730(4) of the Companies Act 1985 and subs.(2) explains that under such provisions the person in question is liable on a second or subsequent summary conviction of the offence to a fine not exceeding the latter amount for each day on which the contravention is continued (instead of being liable to a fine not exceeding the former amount).

1126. Consents required for certain prosecutions

(1) This section applies to proceedings for an offence under any of the following provisions-
    section 458, 460 or 949 of this Act (offences of unauthorised disclosure of information);
    section 953 of this Act (failure to comply with rules about takeover bid documents);
    section 448, 449, 450, 451 or 453A of the Companies Act 1985 (c. 6) (offences in connection with company investigations);
    section 798 of this Act or section 455 of the Companies Act 1985 (offence of attempting to evade restrictions on shares).

(2) No such proceedings are to be brought in England and Wales except by or with the consent of-
    (a) in the case of an offence under-
        (i) section 458, 460 or 949 of this Act,
        (ii) section 953 of this Act, or
        (iii) section 448, 449, 450, 451 or 453A of the Companies Act 1985,
   the Secretary of State or the Director of Public Prosecutions;
    (b) in the case of an offence under section 798 of this Act or section 455 of the Companies Act 1985, the Secretary of State.

(3) No such proceedings are to be brought in Northern Ireland except by or with the consent of-
    (a) in the case of an offence under-
        (i) section 458, 460 or 949 of this Act,
        (ii) section 953 of this Act, or
        (iii) section 448, 449, 450, 451 or 453A of the Companies Act 1985,
   the Secretary of State or the Director of Public Prosecutions for Northern Ireland;
    (b) in the case of an offence under section 798 of this Act or section 455 of the Companies Act 1985, the Secretary of State.

GENERAL NOTE

This section replaces s.731(1) and (2) of the Companies Act 1985. It specifies those offences under the Companies Acts for which the consent to the bringing of proceedings of a particular person (usually the Secretary of State or the Director of Public Prosecutions) is required.

1127. Summary proceedings: venue

(1) Summary proceedings for any offence under the Companies Acts may be taken-
    (a) against a body corporate, at any place at which the body has a place of business, and
    (b) against any other person, at any place at which he is for the time being.

(2) This is without prejudice to any jurisdiction exercisable apart from this section.

GENERAL NOTE

This section replaces s.731(1) of the Companies Act 1985. If provides that summary proceedings under the Companies Acts may be taken against a company anywhere that that company has a place of business and against a person at any place at which he is for the time being.

1128.   Summary proceedings: time limit for proceedings

(1) An information relating to an offence under the Companies Acts that is triable by a magistrates' court in England and Wales may be so tried if it is laid-

    (a) at any time within three years after the commission of the offence, and

    (b) within twelve months after the date on which evidence sufficient in the opinion of the Director of Public Prosecutions or the Secretary of State (as the case may be) to justify the proceedings comes to his knowledge.

(2) Summary proceedings in Scotland for an offence under the Companies Acts-

    (a) must not be commenced after the expiration of three years from the commission of the offence;

    (b) subject to that, may be commenced at any time-

        (i) within twelve months after the date on which evidence sufficient in the Lord Advocate's opinion to justify the proceedings came to his knowledge, or

        (ii) where such evidence was reported to him by the Secretary of State, within twelve months after the date on which it came to the knowledge of the latter.

  Section 136(3) of the Criminal Procedure (Scotland) Act 1995 (c. 46) (date when proceedings deemed to be commenced) applies for the purposes of this subsection as for the purposes of that section.

(3) A magistrates' court in Northern Ireland has jurisdiction to hear and determine a complaint charging the commission of a summary offence under the Companies Acts provided that the complaint is made-

    (a) within three years from the time when the offence was committed, and

    (b) within twelve months from the date on which evidence sufficient in the opinion of the Director of Public Prosecutions for Northern Ireland or the Secretary of State (as the case may be) to justify the proceedings comes to his knowledge.

(4) For the purposes of this section a certificate of the Director of Public Prosecutions, the Lord Advocate, the Director of Public Prosecutions for Northern Ireland or the Secretary of State (as the case may be) as to the date on which such evidence as is referred to above came to his notice is conclusive evidence.

GENERAL NOTE

  This section replaces s.731(2), (3) and (4) of the Companies Act 1985 and prescribes the time limits within which proceedings for offences under the Companies Acts must be brought. In relation to summary proceedings, these must be brought within three years of the commission of the offence and within twelve months after evidence comes to the knowledge of the Director of Public Prosecutions or the Secretary of State (as the case may be) which, in his opinion, is sufficient to justify the proceedings (subs.(1)). These time limits apply in England and Wales, in Scotland and in Northern Ireland (subss.(1), (2) and (3)).

1129.   Legal professional privilege

In proceedings against a person for an offence under the Companies Acts, nothing in those Acts is to be taken to require any person to disclose any information that he is entitled to refuse to disclose on grounds of legal professional privilege (in Scotland, confidentiality of communications).

GENERAL NOTE

  This section replaces s.732(3) of the Companies Act 1985 and re-enacts the general principle that, as regards offences under the Companies Act, nothing in any of those Acts requires a person to disclose information that he is entitled to refuse to disclose on grounds of legal professional privilege.

1130.   Proceedings against unincorporated bodies

(1) Proceedings for an offence under the Companies Acts alleged to have been committed by an unincorporated body must be brought in the name of the body (and not in that of any of its members).

(2) For the purposes of such proceedings-

   (a) any rules of court relating to the service of documents have effect as if the body were a body corporate, and

   (b) the following provisions apply as they apply in relation to a body corporate-

      (i) in England and Wales, section 33 of the Criminal Justice Act 1925 (c. 86) and Schedule 3 to the Magistrates' Courts Act 1980 (c. 43),

      (ii) in Scotland, sections 70 and 143 of the Criminal Procedure (Scotland) Act 1995 (c. 46),

      (iii) in Northern Ireland, section 18 of the Criminal Justice Act (Northern Ireland) 1945 (c. 15 (N.I.)) and Article 166 of and Schedule 4 to the Magistrates' Courts (Northern Ireland) Order 1981 (S.I. 1981/1675 (N.I. 26)).

(3) A fine imposed on an unincorporated body on its conviction of an offence under the Companies Acts must be paid out of the funds of the body.

GENERAL NOTE

This section re-enacts s.734(1)-(4) of the Companies Act 1985 and continues to provide for proceedings for offences under the Companies Acts to be brought against an unincorporated body (as opposed to any of its members) (subs.(1)). Subsection (2) provides that, for the purposes of any rules of court concerning service of documents, an unincorporated body is treated as though it were a body corporate, and that certain statutory provisions concerning criminal procedure (e.g. s.25 of the Criminal Justice Act 1925) apply to unincorporated bodies as they do to bodies corporate. Where a fine is imposed on an unincorporated body by virtue of its conviction of an offence under the Companies Acts that fine must be paid out if its funds (subs.(3)).

1131.   Imprisonment on summary conviction in England and Wales: transitory provision

(1) This section applies to any provision of the Companies Acts that provides that a person guilty of an offence is liable on summary conviction in England and Wales to imprisonment for a term not exceeding twelve months.

(2) In relation to an offence committed before the commencement of section 154(1) of the Criminal Justice Act 2003 (c. 44), for "twelve months" substitute "six months".

GENERAL NOTE

Section 154(1) of the Criminal Justice Act 2003 makes new provision as to the powers of magistrates' courts in England and Wales to impose prison sentences on a summary conviction. This section is a transitory provision in relation to any of the provisions of the Companies Acts which state that a person guilty of an offence on a summary conviction is liable to imprisonment for a term not exceeding 12 months. This section applies to any offence committed before the commencement of the 1993 Act and substitutes for such an offence a maximum term of six months.

Production and inspection of documents

1132.   Production and inspection of documents where offence suspected

(1) An application under this section may be made-

   (a) in England and Wales, to a judge of the High Court by the Director of Public Prosecutions, the Secretary of State or a chief officer of police;

   (b) in Scotland, to one of the Lords Commissioners of Justiciary by the Lord Advocate;

(c) in Northern Ireland, to the High Court by the Director of Public Prosecutions for Northern Ireland, the Department of Enterprise, Trade and Investment or a chief super-intendent of the Police Service of Northern Ireland.

(2) If on an application under this section there is shown to be reasonable cause to believe-

    (a) that any person has, while an officer of a company, committed an offence in connection with the management of the company's affairs, and

    (b) that evidence of the commission of the offence is to be found in any documents in the possession or control of the company,

an order under this section may be made.

(3) The order may-

    (a) authorise any person named in it to inspect the documents in question, or any of them, for the purpose of investigating and obtaining evidence of the offence, or

    (b) require the secretary of the company, or such other officer of it as may be named in the order, to produce the documents (or any of them) to a person named in the order at a place so named.

(4) This section applies also in relation to documents in the possession or control of a person carrying on the business of banking, so far as they relate to the company's affairs, as it applies to documents in the possession or control of the company, except that no such order as is referred to in subsection (3)(b) may be made by virtue of this subsection.

(5) The decision under this section of a judge of the High Court, any of the Lords Commissioners of Justiciary or the High Court is not appealable.

(6) In this section "document" includes information recorded in any form.

GENERAL NOTE

    This section applies where there is reasonable cause to believe that a person committed an offence in connection with the management of a company's affairs whilst an officer of the company and the documents in the possession or control of the company may contain evidence relating to that offence (subs.(2)). In such circumstances an application may be made to the officials identified in subs.(1) by any of the officials also identified in that section for an order authorising the persons named in it to inspect the documents for the purpose of investigating and obtaining evidence in connection with the offence (subs.(3)(a)). The order may also require the company's secretary or any other officer of the company named in it to produce any such documents to a person named in it (subs.(3)(b)). This section applies also to documents relating to the company's affairs that are in the possession or control of a person carrying on a banking business, although an order of the kind referred to in subs.(3)(b) cannot be made under it.

Supplementary

1133. Transitional provision

The provisions of this Part except section 1132 do not apply to offences committed before the commencement of the relevant provision.

GENERAL NOTE

    This section makes it clear that none of the provisions of Pt 36, except for s.1132 (above) apply to offences committed before the commencement of the provision in question.

COMPANIES: SUPPLEMENTARY PROVISIONS

GENERAL NOTE

The provisions falling within this Part are entirely new and must be read alongside Schs 4 and 5.

Company records

1134. Meaning of "company records"

In this Part "company records" means-
- (a) any register, index, accounting records, agreement, memorandum, minutes or other document required by the Companies Acts to be kept by a company, and
- (b) any register kept by a company of its debenture holders.

GENERAL NOTE

This section provides for definitions relevant to this Part. Thus, "company records" means any register, index, accounting records, agreement, memorandum, minutes or other document required to be kept by the company. It also includes any register which is kept by a company of its debenture holders.

1135. Form of company records

(1) Company records-
- (a) may be kept in hard copy or electronic form, and
- (b) may be arranged in such manner as the directors of the company think fit,

provided the information in question is adequately recorded for future reference.

(2) Where the records are kept in electronic form, they must be capable of being reproduced in hard copy form.

(3) If a company fails to comply with this section, an offence is committed by every officer of the company who is in default.

(4) A person guilty of an offence under this section is liable on summary conviction to a fine not exceeding level 3 on the standard scale and, for continued contravention, a daily default fine not exceeding one-tenth of level 3 on the standard scale.

(5) Any provision of an instrument made by a company before 12th February 1979 that requires a register of holders of the company's debentures to be kept in hard copy form is to be read as requiring it to be kept in hard copy or electronic form.

GENERAL NOTE

Under subs.(1) of this new section company records may be kept in hard copy or in electronic form and may be arranged in such a manner as the directors of the company see fit, subject to them being adequately recorded for future reference. If the records are kept in electronic form, they must be capable of being reproduced in hard copy form (subs.(2)). It is an offence if the company fails to comply with this section and an offence is committed by every officer of the company who is in default (subs.(3)). The extent of the consequences are specified in subs.(4). Finally, subs.(5) provides that any provision of an instrument made before February 12, 1979 requiring a register of holders of debentures to be kept in hard copy form is now to be read as requiring it to be kept in hard copy or electronic form.

1136. Regulations about where certain company records to be kept available for inspection

(1) The Secretary of State may make provision by regulations specifying places other than a company's registered office at which company records required to be kept available for inspection under a relevant provision may be so kept in compliance with that provision.

(2) The "relevant provisions" are-

section 114 (register of members);

section 162 (register of directors);

section 228 (directors' service contracts);

section 237 (directors' indemnities);

section 275 (register of secretaries);

section 358 (records of resolutions etc);

section 702 (contracts relating to purchase of own shares);

section 720 (documents relating to redemption or purchase of own shares out of capital by private company);

section 743 (register of debenture holders);

section 805 (report to members of outcome of investigation by public company into interests in its shares);

section 809 (register of interests in shares disclosed to public company);

section 877 (instruments creating charges and register of charges: England and Wales);

section 892 (instruments creating charges and register of charges: Scotland).

(3) The regulations may specify a place by reference to the company's principal place of business, the part of the United Kingdom in which the company is registered, the place at which the company keeps any other records available for inspection or in any other way.

(4) The regulations may provide that a company does not comply with a relevant provision by keeping company records available for inspection at a place specified in the regulations unless conditions specified in the regulations are met.

(5) The regulations-

(a) need not specify a place in relation to each relevant provision;

(b) may specify more than one place in relation to a relevant provision.

(6) A requirement under a relevant provision to keep company records available for inspection is not complied with by keeping them available for inspection at a place specified in the regulations unless all the company's records subject to the requirement are kept there.

(7) Regulations under this section are subject to negative resolution procedure.

GENERAL NOTE

This section of the Act permits the Secretary of State to make provision, by regulations, specifying those places other than a company's registered office, at which company records are required to be kept available for inspection. Subsection (2) lists the relevant provisions, and includes s.114 (register of members) and s.743 (register of debenture holders). Under subs.(3) the regulations may specify a place by reference to the company's principal place of business, the part of the United Kingdom in which the company is registered, the place at which the company keeps any other records available for inspection, or in any other way. By subs.(4) the regulations may provide that a company does not comply with a relevant provision by keeping company records available for inspection at a place specified in the regulations unless the conditions specified are met. However, under subs.(5), it is provided that the regulations do not need to specify a place in relation to each relevant provision and may specify more than one place in relation to a relevant provision. The requirements will not be fulfilled unless all the company's records are kept there (subs.(6)). Regulations made under this provision of the Act are subject to the negative resolution procedure (subs.(7)).

1137. Regulations about inspection of records and provision of copies

(1) The Secretary of State may make provision by regulations as to the obligations of a company that is required by any provision of the Companies Acts-

(a) to keep available for inspection any company records, or

(b) to provide copies of any company records.

(2) A company that fails to comply with the regulations is treated as having refused inspection or, as the case may be, having failed to provide a copy.

(3) The regulations may-

    (a) make provision as to the time, duration and manner of inspection, including the circum-
stances in which and extent to which the copying of information is permitted in the
course of inspection, and

    (b) define what may be required of the company as regards the nature, extent and manner
of extracting or presenting any information for the purposes of inspection or the
provision of copies.

(4) Where there is power to charge a fee, the regulations may make provision as to the amount
of the fee and the basis of its calculation.

(5) Nothing in any provision of this Act or in the regulations shall be read as preventing a
company-

    (a) from affording more extensive facilities than are required by the regulations, or

    (b) where a fee may be charged, from charging a lesser fee than that prescribed or none at
all.

(6) Regulations under this section are subject to negative resolution procedure.

GENERAL NOTE

    This section empowers the Secretary of State to make further regulations as to those obligations of a company required
by any provision of the Companies Acts to be kept available for inspection any company records or to provide copies of
any company records (subs.(1)). A company which fails to comply will be treated as having refused inspection or having
failed to provide a copy (subs.(2)). Additionally, the regulations may make provision as to the time, duration and the manner
of inspection, including those circumstances in which and extent to which the copying of information is permitted in the
course of inspection. The regulations may also define what is required of the company concerning the nature, extent and
manner of extracting or presenting any information for the purposes of inspection or the provision of copies (subs.(3)). In
the case where there is a power to charge a fee, the regulations may make provision as to the amount of such fee and also the
basis of its calculation (subs.(4)). The section makes it clear, however, that nothing in the Act or such Regulations should
be read as preventing a company from affording more extensive facilities than required by the regulations or from charging
a lesser fee than that prescribed or none at all (subs.(5)). Finally, regulations made pursuant to this section are expressed
to be subject to the negative resolution procedure (subs.(6)).

1138. Duty to take precautions against falsification

(1) Where company records are kept otherwise than in bound books, adequate precautions must
be taken-

    (a) to guard against falsification, and

    (b) to facilitate the discovery of falsification.

(2) If a company fails to comply with this section, an offence is committed by every officer of
the company who is in default.

(3) A person guilty of an offence under this section is liable on summary conviction to a fine not
exceeding level 3 on the standard scale and, for continued contravention, a daily default fine
not exceeding one-tenth of level 3 on the standard scale.

(4) This section does not apply to the documents required to be kept under-

    (a) section 228 (copy of director's service contract or memorandum of its terms); or

    (b) section 237 (qualifying indemnity provision).

GENERAL NOTE

    This section is concerned with the possibility of falsifications and the duty to take precautions to ensure that such falsifi-
cations cannot occur. Thus, subs.(1) specifies that where company records are kept otherwise than in bound books, adequate
precautions must be taken to guard against falsification and to facilitate the discovery of falsification. It is an offence if
the company fails to comply and an offence is committed by every officer of the company who is in default (subs.(2)). Subsection (3) sets out the level of penalty involved in the event of a breach. Two exclusions are identified in subs.(4), viz. in
the case of a copy of a director's service contract or memorandum of its terms (s.228), and in the case of a qualifying indemnity provision (s.237).

Service addresses

1139.   Service of documents on company

(1) A document may be served on a company registered under this Act by leaving it at, or sending it by post to, the company's registered office.

(2) A document may be served on an overseas company whose particulars are registered under section 1046-

    (a) by leaving it at, or sending it by post to, the registered address of any person resident in the United Kingdom who is authorised to accept service of documents on the company's behalf, or

    (b) if there is no such person, or if any such person refuses service or service cannot for any other reason be effected, by leaving it at or sending by post to any place of business of the company in the United Kingdom.

(3) For the purposes of this section a person's "registered address" means any address for the time being shown as a current address in relation to that person in the part of the register available for public inspection.

(4) Where a company registered in Scotland or Northern Ireland carries on business in England and Wales, the process of any court in England and Wales may be served on the company by leaving it at, or sending it by post to, the company's principal place of business in England and Wales, addressed to the manager or other head officer in England and Wales of the company.

Where process is served on a company under this subsection, the person issuing out the process must send a copy of it by post to the company's registered office.

(5) Further provision as to service and other matters is made in the company communications provisions (see section 1143).

GENERAL NOTE

   This section is the first of four sections which is concerned with service addresses. Subsection (1) provides that a document may be served on a registered company by leaving it at, or sending it by post to, the company's registered office. In the case of an overseas company, subs.(2) provides that a document may be served by leaving it at, or sending it by post to, the registered address of any person resident in the United Kingdom who is authorised to accept service of documents on the company's behalf. If there is no such person or if a person refuses service it may be left at or sent by post to any place of business of the company in the United Kingdom. By subs.(3) it is specified that "registered address" is that which is stated in the part of the register available for public inspection. In the case of a company registered in Scotland or Northern Ireland carrying on business in England and Wales, process of an English court is served by leaving it at, or sending it by post to, the company's principal place of business in England and Wales. The person issuing process is required to send a copy of it by post to the company's registered office (subs.(4)).

1140.   Service of documents on directors, secretaries and others

(1) A document may be served on a person to whom this section applies by leaving it at, or sending it by post to, the person's registered address.

(2) This section applies to-

    (a) a director or secretary of a company;

    (b) in the case of an overseas company whose particulars are registered under section 1046, a person holding any such position as may be specified for the purposes of this section by regulations under that section;

    (c) a person appointed in relation to a company as-

        (i) a judicial factor (in Scotland),

        (ii) a receiver and manager appointed under section 18 of the Charities Act 1993 (c. 10), or

(iii) a manager appointed under section 47 of the Companies (Audit, Investigations and Community Enterprise) Act 2004 (c. 27).

(3) This section applies whatever the purpose of the document in question.

It is not restricted to service for purposes arising out of or in connection with the appointment or position mentioned in subsection (2) or in connection with the company concerned.

(4) For the purposes of this section a person's "registered address" means any address for the time being shown as a current address in relation to that person in the part of the register available for public inspection.

(5) If notice of a change of that address is given to the registrar, a person may validly serve a document at the address previously registered until the end of the period of 14 days beginning with the date on which notice of the change is registered.

(6) Service may not be effected by virtue of this section at an address-

    (a) if notice has been registered of the termination of the appointment in relation to which the address was registered and the address is not a registered address of the person concerned in relation to any other appointment;

    (b) in the case of a person holding any such position as is mentioned in subsection (2)(b), if the overseas company has ceased to have any connection with the United Kingdom by virtue of which it is required to register particulars under section 1046.

(7) Further provision as to service and other matters is made in the company communications provisions (see section 1143).

(8) Nothing in this section shall be read as affecting any enactment or rule of law under which permission is required for service out of the jurisdiction.

GENERAL NOTE

This section is concerned with the service of documents on directors, secretaries and others and applies whatever the purpose of the document in question (subs.(3)). Subsection (1) provides that a document may be served on such a person by leaving it at, or sending it by post to, the person's registered address. Subsection (2) elaborates those persons to whom the section applies and these include: a director or secretary of a company, a person holding any position as may be specified in regulations relating to overseas companies, and a person appointed in relation to a company as a judicial factor (in Scotland), as a receiver or manager under the Charities Act 1993, and a manager appointed under the Companies (Audit, Investigations and Community Enterprise) Act 2004. For the purposes of the section "registered address" is a reference to the current address shown in relation to that person in the part of the register which is available for public inspection (subs.(4)). Where a notice of change of address is notified to the registrar, it is provided that a person may validly serve a document at the previous address up to 14 days beginning with the date on which the notice of the change is registered (subs.(5)). On the other hand, service may not be effected if notice has been registered of the termination of the appointment in relation to which the address was registered and the address is not a registered address of the person concerned in relation to any other appointment (subs.(6)).

1141. Service addresses

(1) In the Companies Acts a "service address", in relation to a person, means an address at which documents may be effectively served on that person.

(2) The Secretary of State may by regulations specify conditions with which a service address must comply.

(3) Regulations under this section are subject to negative resolution procedure.

GENERAL NOTE

This section is concerned with service addresses, defined, in relation to a person, as an address at which documents may be effectively served on that person (subs.(1)). The Secretary of State is permitted to make regulations specifying conditions with which a service address must comply (subs.(2)) and such regulations are subject to the negative resolution procedure (subs.(3)).

1142. Requirement to give service address

Any obligation under the Companies Acts to give a person's address is, unless otherwise expressly provided, to give a service address for that person.

GENERAL NOTE

This section specifies that any obligation under the Acts to give an address is to a service address, unless otherwise expressly provided.

Sending or supplying documents or information

1143. The company communications provisions

(1) The provisions of sections 1144 to 1148 and Schedules 4 and 5 ("the company communications provisions") have effect for the purposes of any provision of the Companies Acts that authorises or requires documents or information to be sent or supplied by or to a company.

(2) The company communications provisions have effect subject to any requirements imposed, or contrary provision made, by or under any enactment.

(3) In particular, in their application in relation to documents or information to be sent or supplied to the registrar, they have effect subject to the provisions of Part 35.

(4) For the purposes of subsection (2), provision is not to be regarded as contrary to the company communications provisions by reason only of the fact that it expressly authorises a document or information to be sent or supplied in hard copy form, in electronic form or by means of a website.

GENERAL NOTE

This section and the next six sections are concerned with the sending or supplying of documents or information and must be read together with the provisions of Schs 4 and 5 of the Act. Subsection (1) provides that all these provisions have effect for the purposes of any provision of the Acts which authorises or requires documents or information to be sent or supplied by or to a company. Subsection (2) specifies that these provisions are to have effect subject to any requirements which are imposed, or contrary provisions made, by or under any enactment and, in particular, they are to have effect subject to Pt 35 of the Act (subs.(3)). Finally, subs.(4) confirms that provision is not to be regarded as contrary to the company communications provisions merely because it expressly authorises a document or information to be sent or supplied in hard copy form, in electronic form, or by means of a website.

1144. Sending or supplying documents or information

(1) Documents or information to be sent or supplied to a company must be sent or supplied in accordance with the provisions of Schedule 4.

(2) Documents or information to be sent or supplied by a company must be sent or supplied in accordance with the provisions of Schedule 5.

(3) The provisions referred to in subsection (2) apply (and those referred to in subsection (1) do not apply) in relation to documents or information that are to be sent or supplied by one company to another.

GENERAL NOTE

Subsection (1) provides that where information has to be sent or supplied to a company then this must be done in compliance with Sch.4. Documents or information supplied by a company must be done in compliance with Sch.5 (subs.(2)). Schedule 5 will also apply in relation to documents or information sent or supplied by one company to another (subs.(3)).

1145.   Right to hard copy version

(1) Where a member of a company or a holder of a company's debentures has received a document or information from the company otherwise than in hard copy form, he is entitled to require the company to send him a version of the document or information in hard copy form.

(2) The company must send the document or information in hard copy form within 21 days of receipt of the request from the member or debenture holder.

(3) The company may not make a charge for providing the document or information in that form.

(4) If a company fails to comply with this section, an offence is committed by the company and every officer of it who is in default.

(5) A person guilty of an offence under this section is liable on summary conviction to a fine not exceeding level 3 on the standard scale and, for continued contravention, a daily default fine not exceeding one-tenth of level 3 on the standard scale.

GENERAL NOTE

It is possible for a member of a company or a holder of its debentures to require that he is sent a version of the document or information in hard copy form (subs.(1)). Where so requested, the company is required to send the document or information in this form within 21 days of receipt of the request from the member or debenture holder (subs.(2)). The company may not make a charge for doing so (subs.(3)). It is an offence for the company not to comply and every officer of it in default also commits an offence (subs.(4)). Subsection (5) sets out the applicable penalties which will apply.

1146.   Requirement of authentication

(1) This section applies in relation to the authentication of a document or information sent or supplied by a person to a company.

(2) A document or information sent or supplied in hard copy form is sufficiently authenticated if it is signed by the person sending or supplying it.

(3) A document or information sent or supplied in electronic form is sufficiently authenticated-
    (a) if the identity of the sender is confirmed in a manner specified by the company, or
    (b) where no such manner has been specified by the company, if the communication contains or is accompanied by a statement of the identity of the sender and the company has no reason to doubt the truth of that statement.

(4) Where a document or information is sent or supplied by one person on behalf of another, nothing in this section affects any provision of the company's articles under which the company may require reasonable evidence of the authority of the former to act on behalf of the latter.

GENERAL NOTE

This section will apply in relation to the authentication of a document or information sent or supplied by a person to a company (subs.(1)). Subsection (2) provides that a document or information sent or supplied in hard copy form is sufficiently authenticated if it is signed by the person sending or supplying it. Subsection (3) then deals with the position of information which is sent in electronic form. This will be sufficiently authenticated if the identity of the sender is confirmed in a manner specified by the company, or where no such information is specified, if the communication contains or is accompanied by a statement of the identity of the sender and the company has no reason to doubt the truth of the statement. If the document or information is sent or supplied by one person on behalf of another, this section does not affect any provision of the articles by which the company specifies that it requires reasonable evidence of the authority of the former to act on behalf of the latter (subs.(4)).

1147.   Deemed delivery of documents and information

(1) This section applies in relation to documents and information sent or supplied by a company.

(2) Where-

    (a) the document or information is sent by post (whether in hard copy or electronic form) to an address in the United Kingdom, and

    (b) the company is able to show that it was properly addressed, prepaid and posted,

it is deemed to have been received by the intended recipient 48 hours after it was posted.

(3) Where-

    (a) the document or information is sent or supplied by electronic means, and

    (b) the company is able to show that it was properly addressed,

it is deemed to have been received by the intended recipient 48 hours after it was sent.

(4) Where the document or information is sent or supplied by means of a website, it is deemed to have been received by the intended recipient-

    (a) when the material was first made available on the website, or

    (b) if later, when the recipient received (or is deemed to have received) notice of the fact that the material was available on the website.

(5) In calculating a period of hours for the purposes of this section, no account shall be taken of any part of a day that is not a working day.

(6) This section has effect subject to-

    (a) in its application to documents or information sent or supplied by a company to its members, any contrary provision of the company's articles;

    (b) in its application to documents or information sent or supplied by a company to its debentures holders, any contrary provision in the instrument constituting the debentures;

    (c) in its application to documents or information sent or supplied by a company to a person otherwise than in his capacity as a member or debenture holder, any contrary provision in an agreement between the company and that person.

GENERAL NOTE

In certain circumstances information in documents and information sent or supplied by a company will be deemed to have been delivered. Subsection (2) specifies that a document or information will be deemed to have been delivered where the document or information is sent by post to an address in the United Kingdom and the company can show that it was properly addressed, prepaid and posted. In the case of an electronic document, this will be deemed to have been received by the recipient 48 hours after it was sent where the company is able to show that it was properly addressed (subs.(3)). In the case of the document or information being supplied by website, this will be deemed to have been received by the intended recipient when the material was first made available on the website or, if later, when the recipient received (or is deemed to have received) notice of the fact that the material was available on the website (subs.(4)). For the purpose of calculating any period of hours, no account is stated to be taken of any part of a day which is not a working day (subs.(5)). Subsection (6) lays down a number of caveats. Thus, the section is subject to any contrary provision of the company's articles, any contrary provisions in the instrument constituting debentures, or any contrary provision in an agreement between the company and a person.

1148.   Interpretation of company communications provisions

(1) In the company communications provisions-

    "address" includes a number or address used for the purposes of sending or receiving documents or information by electronic means;

    "company" includes any body corporate;

    "document" includes summons, notice, order or other legal process and registers.

(2) References in the company communications provisions to provisions of the Companies Acts authorising or requiring a document or information to be sent or supplied include all such

provisions, whatever expression is used, and references to documents or information being sent or supplied shall be construed accordingly.

(3) References in the company communications provisions to documents or information being sent or supplied by or to a company include references to documents or information being sent or supplied by or to the directors of a company acting on behalf of the company.

GENERAL NOTE

Subsection (1) sets out various definitions of words using in the company communications provisions. Subsection (2) provides that references to provisions of the Acts authorising or requiring a document or information to be sent or supplied, is to include all such provisions, whatever expression is used. Subsection (3) specifies that this will also include documents or information being sent or supplied by or to the directors of a company acting on its behalf.

Requirements as to independent valuation

1149. Application of valuation requirements

The provisions of sections 1150 to 1153 apply to the valuation and report required by-
    section 93 (re-registration as public company: recent allotment of shares for non-cash consideration);
    section 593 (allotment of shares of public company in consideration of non-cash asset);
    section 599 (transfer of non-cash asset to public company).

GENERAL NOTE

This section and those which follow it are concerned with requirements for an independent valuation. This section merely indicates that the provisions which follow apply to the valuation and report required under three specified sections of the Act, namely those dealing with re-registration of a public company and the recent allotment of shares of a non-cash consideration (s.93), the allotment of shares in a public company by consideration of a non-cash asset (s.593), and the transfer of a non-cash asset to a public company (s.599).

1150. Valuation by qualified independent person

(1) The valuation and report must be made by a person ("the valuer") who-
    (a) is eligible for appointment as a statutory auditor (see section 1212), and
    (b) meets the independence requirement in section 1151.
(2) However, where it appears to the valuer to be reasonable for the valuation of the consideration, or part of it, to be made by (or for him to accept a valuation made by) another person who-
    (a) appears to him to have the requisite knowledge and experience to value the consideration or that part of it, and
    (b) is not an officer or employee of-
        (i) the company, or
        (ii) any other body corporate that is that company's subsidiary or holding company or a subsidiary of that company's holding company,
    or a partner of or employed by any such officer or employee,
he may arrange for or accept such a valuation, together with a report which will enable him to make his own report under this section.
(3) The references in subsection (2)(b) to an officer or employee do not include an auditor.
(4) Where the consideration or part of it is valued by a person other than the valuer himself, the latter's report must state that fact and shall also-
    (a) state the former's name and what knowledge and experience he has to carry out the valuation, and
    (b) describe so much of the consideration as was valued by the other person, and the method used to value it, and specify the date of that valuation.

GENERAL NOTE

Pursuant to subs.(1) a valuation and report has to be made by a valuer who is eligible for appointment as a statutory auditor (s.1212) and meets the requisite independence requirement specified in the next section (s.1151). Subsection (2) provides for a valuation by another person who has the requisite knowledge and experience to value the consideration or that part of it and is not an officer or employee of the company or any other body corporate. Such other person may be used where it appears to the valuer to be reasonable and, if acceptable, the valuer may arrange for or accept such a valuation, together with a report which will enable him to make his own report. Where the valuation is carried out by another person, the valuer's report must state this as well as providing the name of the person and the knowledge and experience that he has to carry out the valuation. The report must also describe so much of the consideration valued by the other person, the method used to value it, and the date of that valuation (subs.(4)). The references to officer or employee in the above subsection do not include an auditor (subs.(3)).

1151.   The independence requirement

(1)   A person meets the independence requirement for the purposes of section 1150 only if-
    (a)   he is not-
        (i)   an officer or employee of the company, or
        (ii)   a partner or employee of such a person, or a partnership of which such a person is a partner;
    (b)   he is not-
        (i)   an officer or employee of an associated undertaking of the company, or
        (ii)   a partner or employee of such a person, or a partnership of which such a person is a partner; and
    (c)   there does not exist between-
        (i)   the person or an associate of his, and
        (ii)   the company or an associated undertaking of the company,
    a connection of any such description as may be specified by regulations made by the Secretary of State.
(2)   An auditor of the company is not regarded as an officer or employee of the company for this purpose.
(3)   In this section-
    "associated undertaking" means-
        (a)   a parent undertaking or subsidiary undertaking of the company, or
        (b)   a subsidiary undertaking of a parent undertaking of the company; and

    "associate" has the meaning given by section 1152.
(4)   Regulations under this section are subject to negative resolution procedure.

GENERAL NOTE

This section elaborates further as to the independence requirement. Thus, a person will meet the independence requirement for the purpose of the previous section only if he is not an officer or employee of the company or a partner or employee of such a person, or a partnership of which such a person is a partner. Similarly, he should not be an officer or employee of an associated undertaking or be connected in such a way as may be specified in regulations made by the Secretary of State (subs.(1)). As in the previous section, it is specified here that an auditor of a company is not to be regarded as an officer or employee of the company for this purpose (subs.(2)). Associated undertaking and associate are defined in subs.(3), and the latter receives closer attention in the next section (s.1152). Any regulations made under this section are, like many others in this Part and elsewhere in the Act, subject to the negative resolution procedure (subs.(4)).

1152. Meaning of "associate"

(1) This section defines "associate" for the purposes of section 1151 (valuation: independence requirement).

(2) In relation to an individual, "associate" means-

    (a) that individual's spouse or civil partner or minor child or step-child,

    (b) any body corporate of which that individual is a director, and

    (c) any employee or partner of that individual.

(3) In relation to a body corporate, "associate" means-

    (a) any body corporate of which that body is a director,

    (b) any body corporate in the same group as that body, and

    (c) any employee or partner of that body or of any body corporate in the same group.

(4) In relation to a partnership that is a legal person under the law by which it is governed, "associate" means-

    (a) any body corporate of which that partnership is a director,

    (b) any employee of or partner in that partnership, and

    (c) any person who is an associate of a partner in that partnership.

(5) In relation to a partnership that is not a legal person under the law by which it is governed, "associate" means any person who is an associate of any of the partners.

(6) In this section, in relation to a limited liability partnership, for "director" read "member".

GENERAL NOTE

For the purposes of this section an associate is regarded as an individual's spouse or civil partner or minor child or step-child, any body corporate of which that individual is a director (member in the case of an LLP - see subs.(6)) - and any employee or partner of that person (subs.(2)). As applied to a body corporate, an associate means any body corporate of which that body is a director, any body corporate in the same group as that body, and any employee or partner of that body or of any body corporate in the same group (subs.(3)). This is extended also to partnerships in subs.(4). However, subs.(5) provides that in the case of a partnership which is not a legal person, associate is to mean any person who is an associate of any of the partners.

1153. Valuer entitled to full disclosure

(1) A person carrying out a valuation or making a report with respect to any consideration proposed to be accepted or given by a company, is entitled to require from the officers of the company such information and explanation as he thinks necessary to enable him to-

    (a) carry out the valuation or make the report, and

    (b) provide any note required by section 596(3) or 600(3) (note required where valuation carried out by another person).

(2) A person who knowingly or recklessly makes a statement to which this subsection applies that is misleading, false or deceptive in a material particular commits an offence.

(3) Subsection (2) applies to a statement-

    (a) made (whether orally or in writing) to a person carrying out a valuation or making a report, and

    (b) conveying or purporting to convey any information or explanation which that person requires, or is entitled to require, under subsection (1).

(4) A person guilty of an offence under subsection (2) is liable-

    (a) on conviction on indictment, to imprisonment for a term not exceeding two years or a fine (or both);

    (b) on summary conviction-

        (i) in England and Wales, to imprisonment for a term not exceeding twelve months or to a fine not exceeding the statutory maximum (or both);

        (ii) in Scotland or Northern Ireland, to imprisonment for a term not exceeding six months, or to a fine not exceeding the statutory maximum (or both).

GENERAL NOTE

This section specifies the type of disclosure as may be required by a person carrying out a valuation or making a report with respect to any consideration proposed to be accepted or given by a company. Thus, pursuant to subs.(1), the person carrying out such a valuation is entitled to require from the officers of the company such information and explanation as is necessary for him to carry out the valuation or make the report and provide any note, where this is required (e.g. under s.596(3) or s.600(3)). A person who knowingly or recklessly makes a statement which is misleading, false, or deceptive in a material particular is held to have committed an offence (subs.(2)). The consequences following from such a deception are spelled out in subs.(3).

Notice of appointment of certain officers

1154.   Duty to notify registrar of certain appointments etc

(1) Notice must be given to the registrar of the appointment in relation to a company of-
    (a) a judicial factor (in Scotland),
    (b) a receiver and manager appointed under section 18 of the Charities Act 1993 (c. 10), or
    (c) a manager appointed under section 47 of the Companies (Audit, Investigations and Community Enterprise) Act 2004 (c. 27).
(2) The notice must be given-
    (a) in the case of appointment of a judicial factor, by the judicial factor;
    (b) in the case of appointment of a receiver and manager under section 18 of the Charities Act 1993 (c. 10), by the Charity Commission;
    (c) in the case of appointment of a manager under section 47 of the Companies (Audit, Investigations and Community Enterprise) Act 2004, by the Regulator of Community Interest Companies.
(3) The notice must specify an address at which service of documents (including legal process) may be effected on the person appointed. Notice of a change in the address for service may be given to the registrar by the person appointed.
(4) Where notice has been given under this section of the appointment of a person, notice must also be given to the registrar of the termination of the appointment.
This notice must be given by the person specified in subsection (2).

GENERAL NOTE

This section is concerned with information which must be given to the registrar on the occurrence of certain appointments. Thus, notice has to be given of the appointment, in relation to a company, of a judicial factor (in Scotland), of a receiver or manager under the Charities Act, or a manager appointed under the Companies (Audit, Investigations and Community Enterprise) Act (subs.(1)). Subsection (2) specifies who has to give the notice, while subs.(3) requires that the notice specify an address at which service of documents (including legal process) may be effected on the person appointed. Notice also has to be given to the registrar on termination of an appointment, by the person specified in subs.(2) (subs.(4)).

1155.   Offence of failure to give notice

(1) If a judicial factor fails to give notice of his appointment in accordance with section 1154 within the period of 14 days after the appointment he commits an offence.
(2) A person guilty of an offence under this section is liable on summary conviction to a fine not exceeding level 5 on the standard scale and, for continued contravention, a daily default fine not exceeding one-tenth of level 5 on the standard scale.

GENERAL NOTE

A judicial factor who fails to give notice within 14 days commits an offence (subs.(1)). Subsection (2) sets out the level at which the offence is punishable.

Courts and legal proceedings

1156. Meaning of "the court"

(1) Except as otherwise provided, in the Companies Acts "the court" means-
    (a) in England and Wales, the High Court or (subject to subsection (3)) a county court;
    (b) in Scotland, the Court of Session or the sheriff court;
    (c) in Northern Ireland, the High Court.

(2) The provisions of the Companies Acts conferring jurisdiction on "the court" as defined above have effect subject to any enactment or rule of law relating to the allocation of jurisdiction or distribution of business between courts in any part of the United Kingdom.

(3) The Lord Chancellor may, with the concurrence of the Lord Chief Justice, by order-
    (a) exclude a county court from having jurisdiction under the Companies Acts, and
    (b) for the purposes of that jurisdiction attach that court's district, or any part of it, to another county court.

(4) The Lord Chief Justice may nominate a judicial office holder (as defined in section 109(4) of the Constitutional Reform Act 2005 (c. 4)) to exercise his functions under subsection (3).

GENERAL NOTE

    The final two sections in this Part are concerned with courts and legal proceedings. This first section is concerned with the meaning of court: the High Court in the case of England and Wales, the Court of Session or Sheriff Court, in the case of Scotland, and the High Court in Northern Ireland (subs.(1)). Where jurisdiction is conferred on such a court by the Companies Acts, this is to have effect subject to any enactment or rule of law relating to the allocation of jurisdiction or distribution of business between courts in any part of the United Kingdom (subs.(2)). By subs.(3), the Lord Chancellor, with the concurrence of the Lord Chief Justice, may exclude a county court from having jurisdiction and, for the purposes of that jurisdiction, attach that court's district, or any part of it, to another county court (subs.(3)). The Lord Chancellor's functions may be delegated to a judicial office holder, as defined in the Constitutional Reform Act 2005 (subs.(4)).

1157. Power of court to grant relief in certain cases

(1) If in proceedings for negligence, default, breach of duty or breach of trust against-
    (a) an officer of a company, or
    (b) a person employed by a company as auditor (whether he is or is not an officer of the company),
it appears to the court hearing the case that the officer or person is or may be liable but that he acted honestly and reasonably, and that having regard to all the circumstances of the case (including those connected with his appointment) he ought fairly to be excused, the court may relieve him, either wholly or in part, from his liability on such terms as it thinks fit.

(2) If any such officer or person has reason to apprehend that a claim will or might be made against him in respect of negligence, default, breach of duty or breach of trust-
    (a) he may apply to the court for relief, and
    (b) the court has the same power to relieve him as it would have had if it had been a court before which proceedings against him for negligence, default, breach of duty or breach of trust had been brought.

(3) Where a case to which subsection (1) applies is being tried by a judge with a jury, the judge, after hearing the evidence, may, if he is satisfied that the defendant (in Scotland, the defender) ought in pursuance of that subsection to be relieved either in whole or in part from the liability sought to be enforced against him, withdraw the case from the jury and forthwith direct judgment to be entered for the defendant (in Scotland, grant decree of absolvitor) on such terms as to costs (in Scotland, expenses) or otherwise as the judge may think proper.

GENERAL NOTE

   This section is concerned with those instances where the court is permitted to grant relief. Subsection (1) provides that in the case of proceedings for negligence, default, breach of duty, or breach of trust, against an officer of a company, or a person employed by a company as auditor, it appears that that person has acted honestly and reasonably and ought fairly to be excused, the court may relieve him, either wholly or in part from his liability - and on such terms as it thinks fit. An officer referred to in subs.(1) may apply to court for relief (subs.(2). In the case of a trial with a jury, the judge may, after hearing the evidence, withdraw the case from the jury and direct judgment to be entered for the defendant on such terms as to costs as is thought proper (subs.(3)).

PART 38

COMPANIES: INTERPRETATION

Meaning of "UK-registered company"

1158.   Meaning of "UK-registered company"

In the Companies Acts "UK-registered company" means a company registered under this Act. The expression does not include an overseas company that has registered particulars under section 1046.

GENERAL NOTE

   This section introduces a new definition of a "UK-registered company". No such definition was included in the 1985 Act. This definition acknowledges the changes introduced by Pt 45 of the 2006 Act, namely the extension of the Companies Acts to the whole of the United Kingdom, including Northern Ireland (see s.1284 of the 2006 Act).

Meaning of "subsidiary" and related expressions

1159.   Meaning of "subsidiary" etc

(1) A company is a "subsidiary" of another company, its "holding company", if that other company-
   (a) holds a majority of the voting rights in it, or
   (b) is a member of it and has the right to appoint or remove a majority of its board of directors, or
   (c) is a member of it and controls alone, pursuant to an agreement with other members, a majority of the voting rights in it,
 or if it is a subsidiary of a company that is itself a subsidiary of that other company.
(2) A company is a "wholly-owned subsidiary" of another company if it has no members except that other and that other's wholly-owned subsidiaries or persons acting on behalf of that other or its wholly-owned subsidiaries.
(3) Schedule 6 contains provisions explaining expressions used in this section and otherwise supplementing this section.
(4) In this section and that Schedule "company" includes any body corporate.

GENERAL NOTE

   This section, together with s.1160 of and Sch.6 to the 2006 Act, was introduced as part of the restatement exercise carried out in the summer of 2006. These provisions restate ss.736, 736A and 736B of the 1985 Act (as amended by the 1989 Act) and deal with the meaning of the expressions "subsidiary", "wholly-owned subsidiary" and "holding company" for the purposes of the Companies Acts. No amendments of substance are made to the 1985 Act provisions, but the material has been re-ordered, with much of the material that previously existed in the body of the 1985 Act being moved to Sch.6 to the 2006 Act.

Subsection (1)

This subsection restates and replaces s.736(1) of the 1985 Act, and provides definitions of the terms "subsidiary" and "holding company". The subsection retains the same three connecting factors for establishing the holding-subsidiary relationship as are found in s.736(1), namely "voting control", "director control" and "contract control" (subs.(1) (a), (b) and (c) respectively). Definitions of some of the terms used in this subsection are found in Sch.6 of the 2006 Act, e.g. "right to appoint or remove a majority of its board of its directors" (para.3 of Sch.6 to the 2006 Act) and "voting rights" (para.2 of Sch.6 to the 2006 Act).

Subsection (2)

This subsection replaces s.736(2) of the 1985 Act. It provides a definition of the term "wholly-owned subsidiary", repeating the definition found in s.736(2) in identical terms.

Subsection (3)

This subsection is new. It provides that provisions explaining expressions used in s.1159 can be found in Sch.6 of the 2006 Act. The content of Sch.6 effectively repeats the provisions previously found in s.736A of the 1985 Act, but the drafters of the 2006 Act decided to reorganise this material by moving it to Sch.6 rather than leaving it in the body of the Act.

Subsection (4)

This subsection repeats s.736(3) of the 1985 Act, but includes reference to Sch.6, as required by the reorganisation of this material in the 2006 Act (see subs.(3)).

1160. Meaning of "subsidiary" etc: power to amend

(1) The Secretary of State may by regulations amend the provisions of section 1159 (meaning of "subsidiary" etc) and Schedule 6 (meaning of "subsidiary" etc: supplementary provisions) so as to alter the meaning of the expressions "subsidiary", "holding company" or "wholly-owned subsidiary".

(2) Regulations under this section are subject to negative resolution procedure.

(3) Any amendment made by regulations under this section does not apply for the purposes of enactments outside the Companies Acts unless the regulations so provide.

(4) So much of section 23(3) of the Interpretation Act 1978 (c. 30) as applies section 17(2)(a) of that Act (effect of repeal and re-enactment) to deeds, instruments and documents other than enactments does not apply in relation to any repeal and re-enactment effected by regulations under this section.

GENERAL NOTE

This section restates s.736B of the 1985 Act and allows the Secretary of State to amend s.1159 and Sch.6 by regulations subject to the negative resolution procedure. This enables the Secretary of State to amend the definitions of "subsidiary company", "holding company" and "wholly-owned subsidiary".

Subsection (1)

This subsection repeats s.736B(1) of the 1985 Act and states that the Secretary of State may amend s.1159 and Sch.6 by regulations.

Subsections (2)-(4)

These subsections restate s.736B(3)-(5) with minor changes to the wording of those sections. Subsection 736B(2) of the 1985 Act, which stated that "The regulations may make different provision for different classes of case and may contain such incidental and supplementary provisions as the Secretary of State thinks fit" is not repeated in the 2006 Act.

Meaning of "undertaking" and related expressions

1161.   Meaning of "undertaking" and related expressions

(1) In the Companies Acts "undertaking" means-
  (a) a body corporate or partnership, or
  (b) an unincorporated association carrying on a trade or business, with or without a view to profit.
(2) In the Companies Acts references to shares-
  (a) in relation to an undertaking with capital but no share capital, are to rights to share in the capital of the undertaking; and
  (b) in relation to an undertaking without capital, are to interests-
    (i) conferring any right to share in the profits or liability to contribute to the losses of the undertaking, or
    (ii) giving rise to an obligation to contribute to the debts or expenses of the undertaking in the event of a winding up.
(3) Other expressions appropriate to companies shall be construed, in relation to an undertaking which is not a company, as references to the corresponding persons, officers, documents or organs, as the case may be, appropriate to undertakings of that description.
This is subject to provision in any specific context providing for the translation of such expressions.
(4) References in the Companies Acts to "fellow subsidiary undertakings" are to undertakings which are subsidiary undertakings of the same parent undertaking but are not parent undertakings or subsidiary undertakings of each other.
(5) In the Companies Acts "group undertaking", in relation to an undertaking, means an undertaking which is-
  (a) a parent undertaking or subsidiary undertaking of that undertaking, or
  (b) a subsidiary undertaking of any parent undertaking of that undertaking.

GENERAL NOTE
  This section replaces, and largely restates, s.259 of the 1985 Act, although s.259(2)(a) is not reproduced in the 2006 Act.

1162.   Parent and subsidiary undertakings

(1) This section (together with Schedule 7) defines "parent undertaking" and "subsidiary undertaking" for the purposes of the Companies Acts.
(2) An undertaking is a parent undertaking in relation to another undertaking, a subsidiary undertaking, if-
  (a) it holds a majority of the voting rights in the undertaking, or
  (b) it is a member of the undertaking and has the right to appoint or remove a majority of its board of directors, or
  (c) it has the right to exercise a dominant influence over the undertaking-
    (i) by virtue of provisions contained in the undertaking's articles, or
    (ii) by virtue of a control contract, or
  (d) it is a member of the undertaking and controls alone, pursuant to an agreement with other shareholders or members, a majority of the voting rights in the undertaking.
(3) For the purposes of subsection (2) an undertaking shall be treated as a member of another undertaking-
  (a) if any of its subsidiary undertakings is a member of that undertaking, or

(b) if any shares in that other undertaking are held by a person acting on behalf of the undertaking or any of its subsidiary undertakings.

(4) An undertaking is also a parent undertaking in relation to another undertaking, a subsidiary undertaking, if-

(a) it has the power to exercise, or actually exercises, dominant influence or control over it, or

(b) it and the subsidiary undertaking are managed on a unified basis.

(5) A parent undertaking shall be treated as the parent undertaking of undertakings in relation to which any of its subsidiary undertakings are, or are to be treated as, parent undertakings; and references to its subsidiary undertakings shall be construed accordingly.

(6) Schedule 7 contains provisions explaining expressions used in this section and otherwise supplementing this section.

(7) In this section and that Schedule references to shares, in relation to an undertaking, are to allotted shares.

GENERAL NOTE

This section needs to be read together with Sch.7 of the 2006 Act. Together these provisions, replace and largely restate s.258 and Sch.10A to the 1985 Act. Together, they define the expressions "parent undertaking" and "subsidiary undertaking" which are used for the purposes of the accounting provisions of the Companies Act and which derive from the Seventh Company Law Directive 83/349/EEC. One modification which they make to the 1985 provisions is to amend para.4(3) of Sch.10A to the Companies Act 1985 to reflect changes to the definition of subsidiary undertaking for accounting purposes which were made in 2004 when the Accounts Modernisation Directive (2003/51/EEC) was implemented (see para.4(3) of Sch.8 to the 2006 Act). A new subsection, s.1162(7), is also introduced, which clarifies that for these purposes references to shares, in relation to an undertaking, are to allotted shares.

Other definitions

1163. "Non-cash asset"

(1) In the Companies Acts "non-cash asset" means any property or interest in property, other than cash.

For this purpose "cash" includes foreign currency.

(2) A reference to the transfer or acquisition of a non-cash asset includes-

(a) the creation or extinction of an estate or interest in, or a right over, any property, and

(b) the discharge of a liability of any person, other than a liability for a liquidated sum.

GENERAL NOTE

This section provides a definition of the term "non-cash asset". It replaces and restates s.739 of the 1985 Act without alteration to the substance of that test.

1164. Meaning of "banking company" and "banking group"

(1) This section defines "banking company" and "banking group" for the purposes of the Companies Acts.

(2) "Banking company" means a person who has permission under Part 4 of the Financial Services and Markets Act 2000 (c. 8) to accept deposits, other than-

(a) a person who is not a company, and

(b) a person who has such permission only for the purpose of carrying on another regulated activity in accordance with permission under that Part.

(3) The definition in subsection (2) must be read with section 22 of that Act, any relevant order under that section and Schedule 2 to that Act.

(4) References to a banking group are to a group where the parent company is a banking company or where-

    (a) the parent company's principal subsidiary undertakings are wholly or mainly credit institutions, and

    (b) the parent company does not itself carry on any material business apart from the acquisition, management and disposal of interests in subsidiary undertakings.

"Group" here means a parent undertaking and its subsidiary undertakings.

(5) For the purposes of subsection (4)-

    (a) a parent company's principal subsidiary undertakings are the subsidiary undertakings of the company whose results or financial position would principally affect the figures shown in the group accounts, and

    (b) the management of interests in subsidiary undertakings includes the provision of services to such undertakings.

GENERAL NOTE

    This section restates the definition of "banking company" previously found in s.742B of the 1985 Act, and adds a new definition of "banking group".

Subsection (2)

    This subsection provides a definition of a "banking company". It restates s.742B(1) and (2) of the 1985 Act, in a slightly different form, although no changes of substance seem to be intended.

Subsection (3)

    This subsection restates s.742B(3) of the 1985 Act.

Subsection (4)

    This subsection provides a definition of a "banking group" for the purposes of the Companies Acts. This is a new provision. It explains that a banking group is a group where a parent company is a banking company, as defined by subs.(2), or the parent company's principal subsidiary undertakings are wholly or mainly credit institutions (defined by s.1173 of the 2006 Act) and the parent company doesn't carry on any material business other than the acquisition, management or disposal of interests in its subsidiary undertakings. A group for these purposes means a parent undertaking and its subsidiary undertakings.

Subsection (5)

    This is a new subsection. It provides definitions of a "parent company's principal subsidiary undertakings" and "the management of interests in subsidiary undertakings" for the purposes of subs.(4).

1165. Meaning of "insurance company" and related expressions

(1) This section defines "insurance company", "authorised insurance company", "insurance group" and "insurance market activity" for the purposes of the Companies Acts.

(2) An "authorised insurance company" means a person (whether incorporated or not) who has permission under Part 4 of the Financial Services and Markets Act 2000 (c. 8) to effect or carry out contracts of insurance.

(3) An "insurance company" means-

    (a) an authorised insurance company, or

    (b) any other person (whether incorporated or not) who-

        (i) carries on insurance market activity, or

        (ii) may effect or carry out contracts of insurance under which the benefits provided by that person are exclusively or primarily benefits in kind in the event of accident to or breakdown of a vehicle.

(4) Neither expression includes a friendly society within the meaning of the Friendly Societies Act 1992 (c. 40).

(5) References to an insurance group are to a group where the parent company is an insurance company or where-

(a) the parent company's principal subsidiary undertakings are wholly or mainly insurance companies, and

(b) the parent company does not itself carry on any material business apart from the acquisition, management and disposal of interests in subsidiary undertakings.

"Group" here means a parent undertaking and its subsidiary undertakings.

(6) For the purposes of subsection (5)-

(a) a parent company's principal subsidiary undertakings are the subsidiary undertakings of the company whose results or financial position would principally affect the figures shown in the group accounts, and

(b) the management of interests in subsidiary undertakings includes the provision of services to such undertakings.

(7) "Insurance market activity" has the meaning given in section 316(3) of the Financial Services and Markets Act 2000.

(8) References in this section to contracts of insurance and to the effecting or carrying out of such contracts must be read with section 22 of that Act, any relevant order under that section and Schedule 2 to that Act.

GENERAL NOTE

This section restates the definitions of "insurance company" and "authorised insurance company" previously found in s.742C of the 1985 Act. Although these definitions have been reorganised in the 2006 Act, no change of substance seems to be intended. In addition, this section creates a new definition of "insurance group" and confirms that the definition of "insurance market activity" of the Companies Acts is identical to that currently found in the Financial Services and Markets Act 2000.

Subsection (2)

This subsection provides a definition of an "authorised insurance company", restating the definition that was previously found at ss.742C(4) and 742C(2)(a) of the 1985 Act.

Subsection (3)

This subsection provides a definition of an "insurance company", restating the definition previously found at s.742C(2) of the 1985 Act.

Subsection (4)

This subsection restates s.742C(3) of the 1985 Act.

Subsection (5)

This subsection creates a new definition of an "insurance group". It mirrors the definition of a "banking group" found at s.1164(4) of the 2006 Act.

Subsection (6)

This subsection creates definitions for a "parent company's principal subsidiary undertakings" and "the management of interests in subsidiary undertakings" for the purposes of subs.(5). These definitions are identical to those found in s.1164(5) of the 2006 Act regarding banking groups.

Subsection (7)

This subsection confirms that for the purposes of the Companies Acts "insurance market activity" has the same definition as given by s.316(3) of the Financial Services and Markets Act 2000.

Subsection (8)

This subsection restates s.742C(5) of the 1985 Act.

1166. "Employees' share scheme"

For the purposes of the Companies Acts an employees' share scheme is a scheme for encouraging or facilitating the holding of shares in or debentures of a company by or for the benefit of-

(a) the bona fide employees or former employees of-

      (i) the company,

      (ii) any subsidiary of the company, or

      (iii) the company's holding company or any subsidiary of the company's holding company, or

  (b) the spouses, civil partners, surviving spouses, surviving civil partners, or minor children or step-children of such employees or former employees.

GENERAL NOTE

    This section provides a definition of "employees' share scheme". It restates s.743 of the 1985 Act, albeit in a slightly different form. Changes have been made to the list of relatives who may benefit from the scheme (at (b)). This list is updated to include reference to "civil partners" and "former civil partners" following the Civil Partnership Act 2004. A small wording change also sees "children or step-children under the age of 18" becoming "minor children or step-children".

1167.　Meaning of "prescribed"

In the Companies Acts "prescribed" means prescribed (by order or by regulations) by the Secretary of State.

GENERAL NOTE

    This section provides a definition of "prescribed" for the purpose of the Companies Acts and replaces the definition previously found in s.744 of the 1985 Act. This section removes part (a) of the previous definition and restates part (b) of the previous definition.

1168.　Hard copy and electronic form and related expressions

(1)　The following provisions apply for the purposes of the Companies Acts.

(2)　A document or information is sent or supplied in hard copy form if it is sent or supplied in a paper copy or similar form capable of being read. References to hard copy have a corresponding meaning.

(3)　A document or information is sent or supplied in electronic form if it is sent or supplied-

    (a) by electronic means (for example, by e-mail or fax), or

    (b) by any other means while in an electronic form (for example, sending a disk by post).

References to electronic copy have a corresponding meaning.

(4)　A document or information is sent or supplied by electronic means if it is-

    (a) sent initially and received at its destination by means of electronic equipment for the processing (which expression includes digital compression) or storage of data, and

    (b) entirely transmitted, conveyed and received by wire, by radio, by optical means or by other electromagnetic means.

References to electronic means have a corresponding meaning.

(5)　A document or information authorised or required to be sent or supplied in electronic form must be sent or supplied in a form, and by a means, that the sender or supplier reasonably considers will enable the recipient-

    (a) to read it, and

    (b) to retain a copy of it.

(6)　For the purposes of this section, a document or information can be read only if-

    (a) it can be read with the naked eye, or

    (b) to the extent that it consists of images (for example photographs, pictures, maps, plans or drawings), it can be seen with the naked eye.

(7)　The provisions of this section apply whether the provision of the Companies Acts in question uses the words "sent" or "supplied" or uses other words (such as "deliver", "provide", "produce" or, in the case of a notice, "give") to refer to the sending or supplying of a document or information.

GENERAL NOTE
This section is a new provision. It creates definitions of the terms "hard copy", "electronic form" and related expressions for the purposes of the Companies Acts. Subsection (5) requires that "electronic form" documents or information be sent in a form that is capable of being read and retained for future reference (see subs.(2) for a similar requirement in relation to "hard copy form" documents). As a result subs.(6) makes it clear that a document can be "read" for these purposes even if it consists of images.

1169. Dormant companies

(1) For the purposes of the Companies Acts a company is "dormant" during any period in which it has no significant accounting transaction.

(2) A "significant accounting transaction" means a transaction that is required by section 386 to be entered in the company's accounting records.

(3) In determining whether or when a company is dormant, there shall be disregarded-

    (a) any transaction arising from the taking of shares in the company by a subscriber to the memorandum as a result of an undertaking of his in connection with the formation of the company;

    (b) any transaction consisting of the payment of-

        (i) a fee to the registrar on a change of the company's name,

        (ii) a fee to the registrar on the re-registration of the company,

        (iii) a penalty under section 453 (penalty for failure to file accounts), or

        (iv) a fee to the registrar for the registration of an annual return.

(4) Any reference in the Companies Acts to a body corporate other than a company being dormant has a corresponding meaning.

GENERAL NOTE
This section provides a definition of "dormant companies", restating the definition of a dormant company in s.249AA(4)-(7) of the 1985 Act. Subsection (4) applies the definition to a body corporate other than a company. Subject to certain exceptions, a dormant company is exempt from having its accounts audited (see ss.480-481 of the 2006 Act).

1170. Meaning of "EEA State" and related expressions

In the Companies Acts-

    "EEA State" means a state which is a Contracting Party to the Agreement on the European Economic Area signed at Oporto on 2nd May 1992 (as it has effect from time to time);

    "EEA company" and "EEA undertaking" mean a company or undertaking governed by the law of an EEA State.

GENERAL NOTE
This section provides a definition of "EEA State" which reproduces the definition in s.744 of the 1985 Act without change of substance. New definitions of "EEA company" and "EEA undertaking" are also provided.

1171. The former Companies Acts

In the Companies Acts-

    "the former Companies Acts" means-

        (a) the Joint Stock Companies Acts, the Companies Act 1862 (c. 89), the Companies (Consolidation) Act 1908 (c. 69), the Companies Act 1929 (c. 23), the Companies Act (Northern Ireland) 1932 (c. 7 (N.I.)), the Companies Acts 1948 to 1983, the Companies Act (Northern Ireland) 1960 (c. 22 (N.I.)), the Companies (Northern Ireland) Order 1986 (S.I. 1986/1032 (N.I. 6)) and the Companies Consolidation (Consequential Provisions) (Northern Ireland) Order 1986 (S.I. 1986/1035 (N.I. 9)), and

(b) the provisions of the Companies Act 1985 (c. 6) and the Companies Consolidation (Consequential Provisions) Act 1985 (c. 9) that are no longer in force;

"the Joint Stock Companies Acts" means the Joint Stock Companies Act 1856 (c. 47), the Joint Stock Companies Acts 1856, 1857 (20 & 21 Vict. c. 14), the Joint Stock Banking Companies Act 1857 (c. 49), and the Act to enable Joint Stock Banking Companies to be formed on the principle of limited liability (1858 c. 91), but does not include the Joint Stock Companies Act 1844 (c. 110).

GENERAL NOTE

This section defines "former Companies Acts" by listing those pieces of companies legislation (that are no longer in force) that are included within the term. The list expands upon the equivalent provision in the 1985 Act (s.735) to take account of equivalent provisions for Northern Ireland. This is necessary to take account of the fact that the new Companies Act provides a single regime for the whole of the United Kingdom (see Pt 45 of the 2006 Act).

General

1172. References to requirements of this Act

References in the company law provisions of this Act to the requirements of this Act include the requirements of regulations and orders made under it.

GENERAL NOTE

This section is an interpretative provision. It provides that requirements to be imposed under the Act (by regulations or orders made under a power contained in the Act) are also caught by references in the company law provisions in the Act to "the requirements of this Act".

1173. Minor definitions: general

(1) In the Companies Acts-
"body corporate" and "corporation" include a body incorporated outside the United Kingdom, but do not include-
    (a) a corporation sole, or
    (b) a partnership that, whether or not a legal person, is not regarded as a body corporate under the law by which it is governed;

"credit institution" means a credit institution as defined in Article 4.1(a) of Directive 2006/ 48/ EC of the European Parliament and of the Council relating to the taking up and pursuit of the business of credit institutions;
"financial institution" means a financial institution within the meaning of Article 1.1 of the Council Directive on the obligations of branches established in a Member State of credit and financial institutions having their head offices outside that Member State regarding the publication of annual accounting documents (the Bank Branches Directive, 89/ 117/ EEC);
"firm" means any entity, whether or not a legal person, that is not an individual and includes a body corporate, a corporation sole and a partnership or other unincorporated association;
"the Gazette" means-
    (a) as respects companies registered in England and Wales, the London Gazette,
    (b) as respects companies registered in Scotland, the Edinburgh Gazette, and
    (c) as respects companies registered in Northern Ireland, the Belfast Gazette;

"hire-purchase agreement" has the same meaning as in the Consumer Credit Act 1974 (c. 39);

"officer", in relation to a body corporate, includes a director, manager or secretary;

"parent company" means a company that is a parent undertaking (see section 1162 and Schedule 7);

"regulated activity" has the meaning given in section 22 of the Financial Services and Markets Act 2000 (c. 8);

"regulated market" has the same meaning as in Directive 2004/39/EC of the European Parliament and of the Council on markets in financial instruments (see Article 4.1(14));

"working day", in relation to a company, means a day that is not a Saturday or Sunday, Christmas Day, Good Friday or any day that is a bank holiday under the Banking and Financial Dealings Act 1971 (c. 80) in the part of the United Kingdom where the company is registered.

(2) In relation to an EEA State that has not implemented Directive 2004/39/EC of the European Parliament and of the Council on markets in financial instruments, the following definition of "regulated market" has effect in place of that in subsection (1)-

"regulated market" has the same meaning as it has in Council Directive 93/22/EEC on investment services in the securities field.

GENERAL NOTE

This section provides definitions of a number of terms used in the Act.

1174. Index of defined expressions

Schedule 8 contains an index of provisions defining or otherwise explaining expressions used in the Companies Acts.

GENERAL NOTE

This section introduces Sch.8 to the 2006 Act which provides an index setting out where the definitions of terms used in the Companies Acts are to be found.

PART 39

COMPANIES: MINOR AMENDMENTS

1175. Removal of special provisions about accounts and audit of charitable companies

(1) Part 7 of the Companies Act 1985 (c. 6) and Part 8 of the Companies (Northern Ireland) Order 1986 (accounts and audit) are amended in accordance with Schedule 9 to this Act so as to remove the special provisions about companies that are charities.

(2) In that Schedule-

Part 1 contains repeals and consequential amendments of provisions of the Companies Act 1985;

Part 2 contains repeals and consequential amendments of provisions of the Companies (Northern Ireland) Order 1986.

GENERAL NOTE

This section introduces Sch.9 to the Act.

When the new legislation was first drafted, it was proposed to replace the reporting accountant with an independent examiner as the person who reports on the accounts of small charitable companies in lieu of audit. However, the clauses that would have implemented this change were removed from the Bill at a late stage and the role of the reporting accountant instead dealt with in the Charities Bill. Consequently, the special treatment of small charitable companies with respect to the audit of their accounts is now dealt with in ss.32-33 of the Charities Act 2006 (see www.opsi.gov.uk/acts/acts2006/20060050.htm#aofs).

Schedule 9 was a late insertion into the Companies Bill that removes the special provisions relating to the accounts and audit of charitable companies. It does this by amending the text of various sections in the 1985 Act (Pt 1) and the corresponding legislation for Northern Ireland (Pt 2).

Subsections (1) and (2)

Subsection (1) introduces Sch.9, while subs.(2) indicates that Pt 1 of that Schedule amends provisions in various sections in the 1985 Act and Pt 2 the corresponding legislation for Northern Ireland.

1176.　Power of Secretary of State to bring civil proceedings on company's behalf

(1) Section 438 of the Companies Act 1985 (power of Secretary of State to bring civil proceedings on company's behalf) shall cease to have effect.

(2) In section 439 of that Act (expenses of investigating company's affairs)-
- (a) in subsection (2) omit ", or is ordered to pay the whole or any part of the costs of proceedings brought under section 438,";
- (b) omit subsections (3) and (7) (which relate to section 438);
- (c) in subsection (8)-
    - (i) for "subsections (2) and (3)" substitute "subsection (2)", and
    - (ii) omit "; and any such liability imposed by subsection (2) is (subject as mentioned above) a liability also to indemnify all persons against liability under subsection (3)".

(3) In section 453(1A) of that Act (investigation of overseas companies: provisions not applicable), omit paragraph (b) (which relates to section 438).

(4) Nothing in this section affects proceedings brought under section 438 before the commencement of this section.

GENERAL NOTE

This section repeals s.438 of the Companies Act 1985, consequent on the responses received by the DTI to its consultation paper: *Company Investigations: Powers for the 21st Century*, July 2001. That section allowed the Secretary of State to bring civil proceedings on the company's behalf following a DTI investigation under Pt XIV of the 1985 Act. That Part of the 1985 Act was not consolidated into this Act. There are consequential amendments to ss.439 and 453 of the 1985 Act. The repeal has no effect on proceedings brought before this section comes into effect.

1177.　Repeal of certain provisions about company directors

The following provisions of Part 10 of the Companies Act 1985 shall cease to have effect-
　　section 311 (prohibition on tax-free payments to directors);
　　sections 323 and 327 (prohibition on directors dealing in share options);
　　sections 324 to 326 and 328 to 329, and Parts 2 to 4 of Schedule 13 (register of directors' interests);
　　sections 343 and 344 (special procedure for disclosure by banks).

GENERAL NOTE

This section repeals a number of provisions formerly in Pt X of the Companies Act 1985 (statutory limitations on the powers of directors). The remainder of that Part has been re-enacted in modified form in Pt 10 of this Act, so this section in effect details the 1985 Act provisions which have been discontinued.

Section 311 of the 1985 Act (company cannot pay a director free of tax) is repealed. This was recommended by the Law Commissions in their Report on *Company Directors: Regulating Conflicts of Interests and Formulating a Statement of Duties* (Law Com.261, Scot Law Com.173, September 1999), para.7.99. The reasons are that such non deduction of tax would be an emolument of a director under tax law anyway and disclosure is required in the annual accounts.

Sections 323 and 327 of the 1985 Act (prohibition on directors and their families from taking options on their company's securities) has also been repealed after a recommendation by the Law Commissions (see the Report above, paras 11.7 and 11.14).

Sections 324-326, 328-329 and Sch.13 to the 1985 Act (notification of shareholdings) are repealed although that was not recommended by the Law Commissions (see the Report above). Such matters are dealt with in the Model Code on Corporate Governance.

Sections 343 and 344 of the 1985 Act (special disclosure rules for loans, etc. to directors by credit institutions) have been repealed because they are now covered by s.413 of this Act.

1178. Repeal of requirement that certain companies publish periodical statement

The following provisions shall cease to have effect-

section 720 of the Companies Act 1985 (c. 6) (certain companies to publish periodical statement), and

Schedule 23 to that Act (form of statement under section 720).

GENERAL NOTE

This section repeals s.720 and Sch.23 to the 1985 Act (periodical statement by insurers, deposit, provident or benevolent societies). Those provisions had been overtaken by the FSMA 2000 for all United Kingdom companies. Nor did they apply to EEA companies carrying on business in the United Kingdom which comply with their equivalent home rules.

1179. Repeal of requirement that Secretary of State prepare annual report

Section 729 of the Companies Act 1985 (annual report to Parliament by Secretary of State on matters within the Companies Acts) shall cease to have effect.

GENERAL NOTE

This section repeals s.729 of the 1985 Act requiring the Secretary of State to prepare an Annual Report on matters within the Companies Acts for both Houses of Parliament. This was canvassed in Annex C to the 2005 White Paper (Cm.6456). There were few sales in practice of this Report since there are now annual reports prepared by both Companies House and the Insolvency Service.

1180. Repeal of certain provisions about company charges

Part 4 of the Companies Act 1989 (c. 40) (registration of company charges), which has not been brought into force, is repealed.

GENERAL NOTE

This section repeals Pt 4 of the Companies Act 1989 relating to company charges which were never brought into force. This difficult area remains under discussion with the rejection of the Law Commission's Report on *Company Security Interests* (Law Com.296, July 2005).

1181. Access to constitutional documents of RTE and RTM companies

(1) The Secretary of State may by order-
   (a) amend Chapter 1 of Part 1 of the Leasehold Reform, Housing and Urban Development Act 1993 (c. 28) for the purpose of facilitating access to the provisions of the articles or any other constitutional document of RTE companies;
   (b) amend Chapter 1 of Part 2 of the Commonhold and Leasehold Reform Act 2002 (c. 15) (leasehold reform) for the purpose of facilitating access to the provisions of the articles or any other constitutional document of RTM companies.

(2) References in subsection (1) to provisions of a company's articles or any other constitutional document include any provisions included in those documents by virtue of any enactment.

(3) An order under this section is subject to negative resolution procedure.

(4) In this section-
   "RTE companies" has the same meaning as in Chapter 1 of Part 1 of the Leasehold Reform, Housing and Urban Development Act 1993;
   "RTM companies" has the same meaning as in Chapter 1 of Part 2 of the Commonhold and Leasehold Reform Act 2002.

GENERAL NOTE

This section gives a new power to the Secretary of State to amend certain provisions of the Commonhold and Leasehold Reform Act 2002 and the Leasehold Reform, Housing and Urban Development Act 1993 (which the former amended) by order under the negative resolution procedure.

These sections relate to the constitutional documents of RTM (Right to Manage) and RTE (Right to Enfranchise) companies subject to those Acts. The point is that there are prescribed model constitutions for such companies which take precedence if different to any constitution the company may have created and been registered with at Companies House. There is at present nothing on that register to indicate that certain provisions of the constitution may be so invalidated by the model forms. There will also be a need to modernise the constitutional documents of such companies, e.g. to reflect the future status of the memorandum.

PART 40

COMPANY DIRECTORS: FOREIGN DISQUALIFICATION ETC

Introductory

1182. Persons subject to foreign restrictions

(1) This section defines what is meant by references in this Part to a person being subject to foreign restrictions.

(2) A person is subject to foreign restrictions if under the law of a country or territory outside the United Kingdom-

    (a) he is, by reason of misconduct or unfitness, disqualified to any extent from acting in connection with the affairs of a company,

    (b) he is, by reason of misconduct or unfitness, required-

        (i) to obtain permission from a court or other authority, or

        (ii) to meet any other condition,

  before acting in connection with the affairs of a company, or

    (c) he has, by reason of misconduct or unfitness, given undertakings to a court or other authority of a country or territory outside the United Kingdom-

        (i) not to act in connection with the affairs of a company, or

        (ii) restricting the extent to which, or the way in which, he may do so.

(3) The references in subsection (2) to acting in connection with the affairs of a company are to doing any of the following-

    (a) being a director of a company,

    (b) acting as receiver of a company's property, or

    (c) being concerned or taking part in the promotion, formation or management of a company.

(4) In this section-

    (a) "company" means a company incorporated or formed under the law of the country or territory in question, and

    (b) in relation to such a company-

        "director" means the holder of an office corresponding to that of director of a UK company; and

        "receiver" includes any corresponding officer under the law of that country or territory.

GENERAL NOTE

This section defines what is meant by a person being subject to foreign restrictions (i.e. restrictions under the law of a country or territory outside the United Kingdom) in relation to acting in connection with the affairs of a company (see subss.(2) and (3)).

1183. Meaning of "the court" and "UK company"

In this Part-
  "the court" means-
    (a) in England and Wales, the High Court or a county court;
    (b) in Scotland, the Court of Session or the sheriff court;
    (c) in Northern Ireland, the High Court;

  "UK company" means a company registered under this Act.

GENERAL NOTE

  This section defines "court" and "UK company" for the purposes of this Part.

Power to disqualify

1184. Disqualification of persons subject to foreign restrictions

(1) The Secretary of State may make provision by regulations disqualifying a person subject to foreign restrictions from-
    (a) being a director of a UK company,
    (b) acting as receiver of a UK company's property, or
    (c) in any way, whether directly or indirectly, being concerned or taking part in the promotion, formation or management of a UK company.
(2) The regulations may provide that a person subject to foreign restrictions-
    (a) is disqualified automatically by virtue of the regulations, or
    (b) may be disqualified by order of the court on the application of the Secretary of State.
(3) The regulations may provide that the Secretary of State may accept an undertaking (a "disqualification undertaking") from a person subject to foreign restrictions that he will not do anything which would be in breach of a disqualification under subsection (1).
(4) In this Part-
    (a) a "person disqualified under this Part" is a person-
      (i) disqualified as mentioned in subsection (2)(a) or (b), or
      (ii) who has given and is subject to a disqualification undertaking;
    (b) references to a breach of a disqualification include a breach of a disqualification undertaking.
(5) The regulations may provide for applications to the court by persons disqualified under this Part for permission to act in a way which would otherwise be in breach of the disqualification.
(6) The regulations must provide that a person ceases to be disqualified under this Part on his ceasing to be subject to foreign restrictions.
(7) Regulations under this section are subject to affirmative resolution procedure.

GENERAL NOTE

  This section permits the Secretary of State to make provision by regulations to disqualify, either automatically or by order of the court, those who are subject to foreign restrictions (s.1182). The disqualification would prevent them from being a director or receiver or being directly or indirectly concerned in the promotion, formation or management of a United Kingdom company.

Subsection (5)

  The regulations may allow applications for permission to act in a way which would otherwise be in breach of the disqualification.

Note that the regulations must provide that a person ceases to be disqualified under Pt 40 on his ceasing to be subject to foreign restrictions.

1185.   Disqualification regulations: supplementary

(1) Regulations under section 1184 may make different provision for different cases and may in particular distinguish between cases by reference to-
   (a) the conduct on the basis of which the person became subject to foreign restrictions;
   (b) the nature of the foreign restrictions;
   (c) the country or territory under whose law the foreign restrictions were imposed.
(2) Regulations under section 1184(2)(b) or (5) (provision for applications to the court)-
   (a) must specify the grounds on which an application may be made;
   (b) may specify factors to which the court shall have regard in determining an application.
(3) The regulations may, in particular, require the court to have regard to the following factors-
   (a) whether the conduct on the basis of which the person became subject to foreign restrictions would, if done in relation to a UK company, have led a court to make a disqualification order on an application under the Company Directors Disqualification Act 1986 (c. 46) or the Company Directors Disqualification (Northern Ireland) Order 2002 (S.I. 2002/ 3150 (N.I. 4));
   (b) in a case in which the conduct on the basis of which the person became subject to foreign restrictions would not be unlawful if done in relation to a UK company, the fact that the person acted unlawfully under foreign law;
   (c) whether the person's activities in relation to UK companies began after he became subject to foreign restrictions;
   (d) whether the person's activities (or proposed activities) in relation to UK companies are undertaken (or are proposed to be undertaken) outside the United Kingdom.
(4) Regulations under section 1184(3) (provision as to undertakings given to the Secretary of State) may include provision allowing the Secretary of State, in determining whether to accept an undertaking, to take into account matters other than criminal convictions notwithstanding that the person may be criminally liable in respect of those matters.
(5) Regulations under section 1184(5) (provision for application to court for permission to act) may include provision-
   (a) entitling the Secretary of State to be represented at the hearing of the application, and
   (b) as to the giving of evidence or the calling of witnesses by the Secretary of State at the hearing of the application.

GENERAL NOTE
This section describes the compulsory and permitted content of regulations under s.1184.

1186.   Offence of breach of disqualification

(1) Regulations under section 1184 may provide that a person disqualified under this Part who acts in breach of the disqualification commits an offence.
(2) The regulations may provide that a person guilty of such an offence is liable-
   (a) on conviction on indictment, to imprisonment for a term not exceeding two years or a fine (or both);
   (b) on summary conviction-
      (i) in England and Wales, to imprisonment for a term not exceeding twelve months or to a fine not exceeding the statutory maximum (or both);
      (ii) in Scotland or Northern Ireland, to imprisonment for a term not exceeding six months, or to a fine not exceeding the statutory maximum (or both).

(3) In relation to an offence committed before the commencement of section 154(1) of the Criminal Justice Act 2003 (c. 44), for "twelve months" in subsection (2)(b)(i) substitute "six months".

GENERAL NOTE

This section indicates that regulations under s.1184 may provide that a person disqualified under this Part who acts in breach of the disqualification commits an offence.

Power to make persons liable for company's debts

1187. Personal liability for debts of company

(1) The Secretary of State may provide by regulations that a person who, at a time when he is subject to foreign restrictions-
    (a) is a director of a UK company, or
    (b) is involved in the management of a UK company,
is personally responsible for all debts and other liabilities of the company incurred during that time.

(2) A person who is personally responsible by virtue of this section for debts and other liabilities of a company is jointly and severally liable in respect of those debts and liabilities with-
    (a) the company, and
    (b) any other person who (whether by virtue of this section or otherwise) is so liable.

(3) For the purposes of this section a person is involved in the management of a company if he is concerned, whether directly or indirectly, or takes part, in the management of the company.

(4) The regulations may make different provision for different cases and may in particular distinguish between cases by reference to-
    (a) the conduct on the basis of which the person became subject to foreign restrictions;
    (b) the nature of the foreign restrictions;
    (c) the country or territory under whose law the foreign restrictions were imposed.

(5) Regulations under this section are subject to affirmative resolution procedure.

GENERAL NOTE

This section indicates that the Secretary of State may provide by regulation that a person who is a director or is involved in the management of a United Kingdom company at a time when he is subject to foreign restrictions is personally responsible for all the debts and other liabilities of the company incurred during that time. This liability will be joint and several with the company and any others who are also liable.

Power to require statements to be sent to the registrar of companies

1188. Statements from persons subject to foreign restrictions

(1) The Secretary of State may make provision by regulations requiring a person who-
    (a) is subject to foreign restrictions, and
    (b) is not disqualified under this Part,
to send a statement to the registrar if he does anything that, if done by a person disqualified under this Part, would be in breach of the disqualification.

(2) The statement must include such information as may be specified in the regulations relating to-
    (a) the person's activities in relation to UK companies, and
    (b) the foreign restrictions to which the person is subject.

(3) The statement must be sent to the registrar within such period as may be specified in the regulations.

(4) The regulations may make different provision for different cases and may in particular distinguish between cases by reference to-

    (a) the conduct on the basis of which the person became subject to foreign restrictions;

    (b) the nature of the foreign restrictions;

    (c) the country or territory under whose law the foreign restrictions were imposed.

(5) Regulations under this section are subject to affirmative resolution procedure.

GENERAL NOTE

    This section allows the Secretary of State to make regulations requiring a person who is subject to foreign restrictions but not disqualified under this Part, to send a statement to the registrar if he does anything that, if done by a person disqualified under this Part, would be in breach of the disqualification.

1189.   Statements from persons disqualified

(1) The Secretary of State may make provision by regulations requiring a statement or notice sent to the registrar of companies under any of the provisions listed below that relates (wholly or partly) to a person who-

    (a) is a person disqualified under this Part, or

    (b) is subject to a disqualification order or disqualification undertaking under the Company Directors Disqualification Act 1986 (c. 46) or the Company Directors Disqualification (Northern Ireland) Order 2002 (S.I. 2002/ 3150 (N.I. 4)),

to be accompanied by an additional statement.

(2) The provisions referred to above are-

    (a) section 12 (statement of a company's proposed officers),

    (b) section 167(2) (notice of person having become director), and

    (c) section 276 (notice of a person having become secretary or one of joint secretaries).

(3) The additional statement is a statement that the person has obtained permission from a court, on an application under section 1184(5) or (as the case may be) for the purposes of section 1(1)(a) of the Company Directors Disqualification Act 1986 (c. 46) or Article 3(1) of the Company Directors Disqualification (Northern Ireland) Order 2002 (S.I. 2002/ 3150 (N.I. 4)), to act in the capacity in question.

(4) Regulations under this section are subject to affirmative resolution procedure.

GENERAL NOTE

    This section allows the Secretary of State to make regulations requiring a person who is subject to foreign restrictions, and who is disqualified under this Part or under the Company Directors Disqualification Act 1986, to make an additional statement to the registrar of companies indicating that the person has obtained appropriate permission (see subs.(3)) to act in the capacity in question.

1190.   Statements: whether to be made public

(1) Regulations under section 1188 or 1189 (statements required to be sent to registrar) may provide that a statement sent to the registrar of companies under the regulations is to be treated as a record relating to a company for the purposes of section 1080 (the companies register).

(2) The regulations may make provision as to the circumstances in which such a statement is to be, or may be-

    (a) withheld from public inspection, or

    (b) removed from the register.

(3) The regulations may, in particular, provide that a statement is not to be withheld from public inspection or removed from the register unless the person to whom it relates provides such information, and satisfies such other conditions, as may be specified.

(4) The regulations may provide that section 1081 (note of removal of material from the register) does not apply, or applies with such modifications as may be specified, in the case of material removed from the register under the regulations.

(5) In this section "specified" means specified in the regulations.

GENERAL NOTE

This section notes that the regulations referred to in ss.1188 and 1189 may provide that the statement should be public, and under what terms.

1191. Offences

(1) Regulations under section 1188 or 1189 may provide that it is an offence for a person-
    (a) to fail to comply with a requirement under the regulations to send a statement to the registrar;
    (b) knowingly or recklessly to send a statement under the regulations to the registrar that is misleading, false or deceptive in a material particular.

(2) The regulations may provide that a person guilty of such an offence is liable-
    (a) on conviction on indictment, to imprisonment for a term not exceeding two years or a fine (or both);
    (b) on summary conviction-
        (i) in England and Wales, to imprisonment for a term not exceeding twelve months or to a fine not exceeding the statutory maximum (or both);
        (ii) in Scotland or Northern Ireland, to imprisonment for a term not exceeding six months, or to a fine not exceeding the statutory maximum (or both).

(3) In relation to an offence committed before the commencement of section 154(1) of the Criminal Justice Act 2003 (c. 44), for "twelve months" in subsection (2)(b)(i) substitute "six months".

GENERAL NOTE

This section notes that the regulations referred to in ss.1188 and 1189 may create offences.

PART 41

BUSINESS NAMES

CHAPTER I

RESTRICTED OR PROHIBITED NAMES

GENERAL NOTE

The provisions of this Part replace those of the Business Names Act 1985. It contains three Chapters, the first relating to restricted or prohibited names, the second to what disclosure is required of an individual or partnership and the third containing supplementary provisions. This Part is concerned, as was the Business Names Act, with the regulation of names under which a person can carry on business in order generally to protect the public.

Introductory

1192. Application of this Chapter

(1) This Chapter applies to any person carrying on business in the United Kingdom.

(2) The provisions of this Chapter do not prevent-

    (a) an individual carrying on business under a name consisting of his surname without any addition other than a permitted addition, or

    (b) individuals carrying on business in partnership under a name consisting of the surnames of all the partners without any addition other than a permitted addition.

(3) The following are the permitted additions-

    (a) in the case of an individual, his forename or initial;

    (b) in the case of a partnership-

        (i) the forenames of individual partners or the initials of those forenames, or

        (ii) where two or more individual partners have the same surname, the addition of "s" at the end of that surname;

    (c) in either case, an addition merely indicating that the business is carried on in succession to a former owner of the business.

GENERAL NOTE

    This section replaces s.1 of the Business Names Act 1985. It provides that whilst the Chapter applies to any person carrying on business in the United Kingdom (subs.(1)), nothing in it prevents an individual carrying on business under a name consisting of his surname and a permitted addition or individuals from carrying on a business in partnership under a name consisting of the surnames of all the partners and any permitted additions (subs.(2)). Permitted additions are defined in subs.(3). For an individual a permitted addition is his forename or initial , and for a partnership the forenames of the individual partners or the initials of those forenames, and where two or more partners have the same surname, the addition of the letter "s" at the end of that surname is a permitted addition. Finally an addition is a permitted addition if it indicates that the business is carried on in succession to a former owner of the business.

Sensitive words or expressions

1193. Name suggesting connection with government or public authority

(1) A person must not, without the approval of the Secretary of State, carry on business in the United Kingdom under a name that would be likely to give the impression that the business is connected with-

    (a) Her Majesty's Government, any part of the Scottish administration or Her Majesty's Government in Northern Ireland,

    (b) any local authority, or

    (c) any public authority specified for the purposes of this section by regulations made by the Secretary of State.

(2) For the purposes of this section-

    "local authority" means-

        (a) a local authority within the meaning of the Local Government Act 1972 (c. 70), the Common Council of the City of London or the Council of the Isles of Scilly,

        (b) a council constituted under section 2 of the Local Government etc. (Scotland) Act 1994 (c. 39), or

        (c) a district council in Northern Ireland;

    "public authority" includes any person or body having functions of a public nature.

(3) Regulations under this section are subject to affirmative resolution procedure.

(4) A person who contravenes this section commits an offence.

(5) Where an offence under this section is committed by a body corporate, an offence is also committed by every officer of the body who is in default.

(6) A person guilty of an offence under this section is liable on summary conviction to a fine not exceeding level 3 on the standard scale and, for continued contravention, a daily default fine not exceeding one-tenth of level 3 on the standard scale.

GENERAL NOTE
This section replaces s.2(1)(a) of the Business Names Act 1985 and is roughly equivalent to s.54 in Ch.5 of the Companies Act 2006 (see above) as that section applies to the registered names of companies. It provides that the approval of the Secretary of State is required for the carrying on of a business in the United Kingdom with a name that would be likely to give the impression that the business is connected with local or national government, whether in England and Wales, Scotland or Northern Ireland, any local authority or any public authority specified by regulations (subject to affirmative resolution procedure - subs.(3)) made by the Secretary of State. "Local authority" is defined in subs.(2) as a local authority within the meaning of Local Government Act 1972, the Common Council of the City of London or the Council of the Isles of Scilly, a council constituted under s.2 of the Local Government etc. (Scotland) Act 1994 or a district council in Northern Ireland. "Public authority" is defined in the same subsection as including any person or body having functions of a public nature. Contravention of this section constitutes an offence which can be committed by an individual (subs.(4)) or, where committed by a body corporate, also by every officer of that body corporate who is in default (subs.(5)). The penalty for the offence is prescribed in subs.(6).

1194. Other sensitive words or expressions

(1) A person must not, without the approval of the Secretary of State, carry on business in the United Kingdom under a name that includes a word or expression for the time being specified in regulations made by the Secretary of State under this section.

(2) Regulations under this section are subject to approval after being made.

(3) A person who contravenes this section commits an offence.

(4) Where an offence under this section is committed by a body corporate, an offence is also committed by every officer of the body who is in default.

(5) A person guilty of an offence under this section is liable on summary conviction to a fine not exceeding level 3 on the standard scale and, for continued contravention, a daily default fine not exceeding one-tenth of level 3 on the standard scale.

GENERAL NOTE
This section replaces s.2(1)(b) of the Business Names Act 1985 and is roughly equivalent to s.55 in Ch.5 of the 2006 Act as that section applied to a company's registered name. This section provides that the approval of the Secretary of State is required for the carrying on of a business with a name that includes a word or expression specified by the Secretary of State in regulations made under the section (subs.(1)). Regulations made under this section are subject to approval after being made (subs.(2)). Regulations currently specifying words or expressions include the Company and Business Names Regulations 1981 (SI 1981/ 1685). Some of the words and expressions listed therein in are association, benevolent, charitable, duke, her majesty, king, midwife, patent and royal. Contravention of this section constitutes an offence which can be committed by an individual (subs.(3)) or, where committed by a body corporate, also by every officer of that body corporate who is in default (subs.(4)). The penalty for the offence is prescribed in subs.(5).

1195. Requirement to seek comments of government department or other relevant body

(1) The Secretary of State may by regulations under-
    (a) section 1193 (name suggesting connection with government or public authority), or
    (b) section 1194 (other sensitive words or expressions),
require that, in connection with an application for the approval of the Secretary of State under that section, the applicant must seek the view of a specified Government department or other body.

(2) Where such a requirement applies, the applicant must request the specified department or other body (in writing) to indicate whether (and if so why) it has any objections to the proposed name.

(3) He must submit to the Secretary of State a statement that such a request has been made and a copy of any response received from the specified body.

(4) If these requirements are not complied with, the Secretary of State may refuse to consider the application for approval.

(5) In this section "specified" means specified in the regulations.

GENERAL NOTE

This section replaces s.3 of the Business Names Act 1985 and is roughly equivalent in its application to business names to s.56 in Ch.5 of the 2006 Act as that applies to the registered names of companies. Where the Secretary of State makes regulations under ss.1193 or 1194 he may by regulations, on an application for approval of a name suggesting a connection with government or containing a sensitive word or expression, require the applicant to seek the view of a specified government department or other body (subs.(1)). Examples contained in the Company and Business Names Regulations 1981 (SI 1981/ 1685) include the Home Office or Scottish Ministers in connection with the use of the terms "her majesty" or "royal" and the Charity Commission or the Scottish Ministers in connection with the use of the term "charitable".

Subsections (2)-(4)

In circumstance where the section applies, the applicant must write to the specified department or body requesting an indication as to whether and, if so, why it objects to the proposed name. He must then submit to the Secretary of State a statement that he has made the required request and include a copy of any response received. The Secretary of State may refuse to consider any application for approval of a proposed business name if the requirements of this section are not complied with.

1196. Withdrawal of Secretary of State's approval

(1) This section applies to approval given for the purposes of-
    section 1193 (name suggesting connection with government or public authority), or
    section 1194 (other sensitive words or expressions).
(2) If it appears to the Secretary of State that there are overriding considerations of public policy that require such approval to be withdrawn, the approval may be withdrawn by notice in writing given to the person concerned.
(3) The notice must state the date as from which approval is withdrawn.

GENERAL NOTE

This section applies to any approval given by the Secretary of State under ss.1193 and 1194 (above) and empowers the Secretary of State to withdraw the approval by giving written notice (stating the date from which the approval is withdrawn - subs.(3)) to the person concerned (subs.(2)). The Secretary of State must believe that there are overriding considerations of public policy that require such approval to be withdrawn in order to withdraw approval under this section (subs.(2)).

Misleading names

1197. Name containing inappropriate indication of company type or legal form

(1) The Secretary of State may make provision by regulations prohibiting a person from carrying on business in the United Kingdom under a name consisting of or containing specified words, expressions or other indications-
    (a) that are associated with a particular type of company or form of organisation, or
    (b) that are similar to words, expressions or other indications associated with a particular type of company or form of organisation.
(2) The regulations may prohibit the use of words, expressions or other indications-
    (a) in a specified part, or otherwise than in a specified part, of a name;
    (b) in conjunction with, or otherwise than in conjunction with, such other words, expressions or indications as may be specified.
(3) In this section "specified" means specified in the regulations.
(4) Regulations under this section are subject to negative resolution procedure.
(5) A person who uses a name in contravention of regulations under this section commits an offence.
(6) Where an offence under this section is committed by a body corporate, an offence is also committed by every officer of the body who is in default.

(7) A person guilty of an offence under this section is liable on summary conviction to a fine not exceeding level 3 on the standard scale and, for continued contravention, a daily default fine not exceeding one-tenth of level 3 on the standard scale.

GENERAL NOTE

This section replaces ss.33, 34 and 34A of the Companies Act 1985 and is directed at preventing the use of any words, terms or expressions that may give the impression that a business is a company or of some other legal form when in fact it is not. Subsection (1) empowers the Secretary of State to make provision by regulations (subject to negative resolution procedure - subs.(4)) prohibiting the carrying on of business in the United Kingdom under a name containing any specified words, expressions or other indications similar to those that would be associated with or similar to a particular type of company or form of organisation.

These regulations may prohibit the use of use of such words, etc. in a specified part of a business name (or otherwise than in a specified part or in conjunction or otherwise than in conjunction with other specified words, expressions or indications (subs.(2)). Contravention of these regulations constitutes an offence which, if committed by a company, is also committed by any of its officers who are in default (subss.(5) and (6)). The penalty for this offence is prescribed in subs.(7).

1198.   Name giving misleading indication of activities

(1) A person must not carry on business in the United Kingdom under a name that gives so misleading an indication of the nature of the activities of the business as to be likely to cause harm to the public.
(2) A person who uses a name in contravention of this section commits an offence.
(3) Where an offence under this section is committed by a body corporate, an offence is also committed by every officer of the body who is in default.
(4) A person guilty of an offence under this section is liable on summary conviction to a fine not exceeding level 3 on the standard scale and, for continued contravention, a daily default fine not exceeding one-tenth of level 3 on the standard scale.

GENERAL NOTE

This is a new provision with has an effect roughly equivalent to that of s.76 of the Companies Act 2006. it prohibits the carrying on of a business in the United Kingdom under a name that gives so misleading an indication of the nature of its activities that harm to the public is likely to be caused (subs.(1)). Contravention of this section constitutes an offence (subs.(2)) which, if committed by a company, is also committed by any of its officers who are in default (subs.(3)). The penalty for this offence is prescribed in subs.(4).

Supplementary

1199.   Savings for existing lawful business names

(1) This section has effect in relation to-
  sections 1192 to 1196 (sensitive words or expressions), and
  section 1197 (inappropriate indication of company type or legal form).
(2) Those sections do not apply to the carrying on of a business by a person who-
  (a) carried on the business immediately before the date on which this Chapter came into force, and
  (b) continues to carry it on under the name that immediately before that date was its lawful business name.
(3) Where-
  (a) a business is transferred to a person on or after the date on which this Chapter came into force, and
  (b) that person carries on the business under the name that was its lawful business name immediately before the transfer,

those sections do not apply in relation to the carrying on of the business under that name during the period of twelve months beginning with the date of the transfer.

(4) In this section "lawful business name", in relation to a business, means a name under which the business was carried on without contravening-

    (a) section 2(1) of the Business Names Act 1985 (c. 7) or Article 4(1) of the Business Names (Northern Ireland) Order 1986 (S.I. 1986/ 1033 N.I. 7)), or

    (b) after this Chapter has come into force, the provisions of this Chapter.

GENERAL NOTE

    This section is a savings provision and applies in relation to ss.1192-1197 (above). Any person carrying on a business under a name that was lawful prior to the coming into force of those sections is exempted from their effect (subs.(2)), as is a person to whom that business is transferred on or after that date, but only for a period of twelve months beginning with the date of the transfer (subs.(3)). Subsection (4) defines "lawful business name" as a name that did not contravene s.2(1) of the Business Names Act 1985 or Art.4(1) of the Business Names (Northern Ireland) Order 1986 (S.I. 1986/ 1033 N.I. 7)).

CHAPTER 2

DISCLOSURE REQUIRED IN CASE OF INDIVIDUAL OR PARTNERSHIP

Introductory

1200. Application of this Chapter

(1) This Chapter applies to an individual or partnership carrying on business in the United Kingdom under a business name.

References in this Chapter to "a person to whom this Chapter applies" are to such an individual or partnership.

(2) For the purposes of this Chapter a "business name" means a name other than-

    (a) in the case of an individual, his surname without any addition other than a permitted addition;

    (b) in the case of a partnership-

        (i) the surnames of all partners who are individuals, and

        (ii) the corporate names of all partners who are bodies corporate,

    without any addition other than a permitted addition.

(3) The following are the permitted additions-

    (a) in the case of an individual, his forename or initial;

    (b) in the case of a partnership-

        (i) the forenames of individual partners or the initials of those forenames, or

        (ii) where two or more individual partners have the same surname, the addition of "s" at the end of that surname;

    (c) in either case, an addition merely indicating that the business is carried on in succession to a former owner of the business.

GENERAL NOTE

    This section prescribes the application of Ch.2 of this Part, which is to an individual or partnership carrying on business in the United Kingdom under a business name (subs.(1)). The term "business name" is defined in subs.(2) as any name other than those mentioned in s.1192(2) and (3). The Chapter is concerned with the information which a person or partnership to which it applies must disclose.

1201. Information required to be disclosed

The "information required by this Chapter" is-

    (a) in the case of an individual, his name;

    (b) in the case of a partnership, the name of each member of the partnership;

This section replaces s.4(1)(a)(i), (ii) and (iv) of the Business Names Act 1985. Any person or partnership to which this Chapter applies is required to disclose, in the case of an individual, his name, and in the case of a partnership the names of each of its members, and in relation to each named person a United Kingdom address at which effective service of any document relating to the business may be made.

Disclosure requirements

1202. Disclosure required: business documents etc

(1) A person to whom this Chapter applies must state the information required by this Chapter, in legible characters, on all-
    (a) business letters,
    (b) written orders for goods or services to be supplied to the business,
    (c) invoices and receipts issued in the course of the business, and
    (d) written demands for payment of debts arising in the course of the business.
This subsection has effect subject to section 1203 (exemption for large partnerships if certain conditions met).

(2) A person to whom this Chapter applies must secure that the information required by this Chapter is immediately given, by written notice, to any person with whom anything is done or discussed in the course of the business and who asks for that information.

(3) The Secretary of State may by regulations require that such notices be given in a specified form.

(4) Regulations under this section are subject to negative resolution procedure.

GENERAL NOTE
This section replaces s.4(1)(a) of the Business names Act 1985 and requires a person to whom this Chapter applies to state the information required by it, in legible characters on all of the documents mentioned in subs.(1). These are business letters, written orders for goods or services to be supplied to the business, invoices and receipts issued in the course of the business and written demands for payment of debts arising in the course of the business. Where any person who has done or discussed anything in the course of the business asks for this information the person to whom the request is made, providing that he is a person to whom the Chapter applies, must provide the information immediately by written notice (subs.(2)). The Secretary of State may, by regulations subject to negative resolution procedure (subs.(4)), prescribe the form in which such notice must be given (subs.(3)).

1203. Exemption for large partnerships if certain conditions met

(1) Section 1202(1) (disclosure required in business documents) does not apply in relation to a document issued by a partnership of more than 20 persons if the following conditions are met.

(2) The conditions are that-
    (a) the partnership maintains at its principal place of business a list of the names of all the partners,
    (b) no partner's name appears in the document, except in the text or as a signatory, and
    (c) the document states in legible characters the address of the partnership's principal place of business and that the list of the partners' names is open to inspection there.

(3) Where a partnership maintains a list of the partners' names for the purposes of this section, any person may inspect the list during office hours.

(4) Where an inspection required by a person in accordance with this section is refused, an offence is committed by any member of the partnership concerned who without reasonable excuse refused the inspection or permitted it to be refused.

(5) A person guilty of an offence under subsection (4) is liable on summary conviction to a fine not exceeding level 3 on the standard scale and, for continued contravention, a daily default fine not exceeding one-tenth of level 3 on the standard scale.

GENERAL NOTE

This section reproduces the exemption from the application of s.1202(1) to large partnerships in s.4(3)-(4A) of the Business Names Act 1985. Thus, a partnership of more than 20 persons need not make the disclosures required by s.1202(1) if certain conditions are met (subs.(1)). The conditions are that the partnership keeps a list of all the partners' names at its principal place of business, that no partner's name appears in the document other than in the text or as signatory and that the document states in legible letters the address of the principal place of business and the fact that the list of partners' names is open to inspection at that place (subs.(2)). Where such a list is kept any person may inspect it during office hours (subs.(3)), and where a the right of inspection is refused an offence is committed by any member of the partnership who refused the request, or permitted its refusal, with reasonable excuse (subs.(4)). The penalty for the offence is prescribed in subs.(5)).

1204.   Disclosure required: business premises

(1) A person to whom this Chapter applies must, in any premises-
    (a) where the business is carried on, and
    (b) to which customers of the business or suppliers of goods or services to the business have access,
display in a prominent position, so that it may easily be read by such customers or suppliers, a notice containing the information required by this Chapter.
(2) The Secretary of State may by regulations require that such notices be displayed in a specified form.
(3) Regulations under this section are subject to negative resolution procedure.

GENERAL NOTE

This section replaces s.4(1)(c) Business names Act 1985 and requires any person to whom Ch.2 of Pt 41 applies and who carries on a business in premises to which customers and suppliers have access to prominently display so that it may easily be read a notice containing the information required by Ch.2 of Pt 41 (subs.(1)). Thus, customers and suppliers will be able to discover the name and the service address of such a person. The Secretary of State may make regulations (subject to negative resolution procedure - subs.(3)) requiring any such notice to be displayed in a specified form.

Consequences of failure to make required disclosure

1205.   Criminal consequences of failure to make required disclosure

(1) A person who without reasonable excuse fails to comply with the requirements of-
    section 1202 (disclosure required: business documents etc), or
    section 1204 (disclosure required: business premises), commits an offence.
(2) Where an offence under this section is committed by a body corporate, an offence is also committed by every officer of the body who is in default.
(3) A person guilty of an offence under this section is liable on summary conviction to a fine not exceeding level 3 on the standard scale and, for continued contravention, a daily default fine not exceeding one-tenth of level 3 on the standard scale.
(4) References in this section to the requirements of section 1202 or 1204 include the requirements of regulations under that section.

GENERAL NOTE

This section replaces s.7 of the Business Names Act 1985 and retains the existing offences of failing to comply with the requirement to disclose on business documents and on business premises under ss.1202 and 1204, including any regulations made under them (subs.(4)), of the 2006 Act (subs.(1)). Offences under this section committed by bodies corporate are also committed by any officer of such a body in default (subs.(2)). The penalty for the offence is prescribed in subs.(3).

1206. Civil consequences of failure to make required disclosure

(1) This section applies to any legal proceedings brought by a person to whom this Chapter applies to enforce a right arising out of a contract made in the course of a business in respect of which he was, at the time the contract was made, in breach of section 1202(1) or (2) (disclosure in business documents etc) or section 1204(1) (disclosure at business premises).

(2) The proceedings shall be dismissed if the defendant (in Scotland, the defender) to the proceedings shows-

    (a) that he has a claim against the claimant (pursuer) arising out of the contract that he has been unable to pursue by reason of the latter's breach of the requirements of this Chapter, or

    (b) that he has suffered some financial loss in connection with the contract by reason of the claimant's (pursuer's) breach of those requirements,

unless the court before which the proceedings are brought is satisfied that it is just and equitable to permit the proceedings to continue.

(3) References in this section to the requirements of this Chapter include the requirements of regulations under this Chapter.

(4) This section does not affect the right of any person to enforce such rights as he may have against another person in any proceedings brought by that person.

GENERAL NOTE

This section replaces, without substantive amendment, s.5 Business Names Act 1985. Where a person to whom Ch.2 applies is in breach of the requirements of ss.1202(1) and (2) or 1204 and brings legal proceedings against another party to enforce a contractual right, those proceedings are to be dismissed where the defendant can show that he has a contractual claim against the claimant which he cannot pursue because of the breach or that he has suffered financial loss in connection with the contract by reason of the claimant's breach (subs.(2)). This is subject to the courts discretion to allow the proceedings to continue if it is satisfied that it would be just and equitable to do so.

CHAPTER 3

SUPPLEMENTARY

1207. Application of general provisions about offences

The provisions of sections 1121 to 1123 (liability of officer in default) and 1125 to 1131 (general provisions about offences) apply in relation to offences under this Part as in relation to offences under the Companies Acts.

GENERAL NOTE

The provisions of ss.1121-1123 and 1125-1131 apply to offences under this Part of the Act.

1208. Interpretation

In this Part-

    "business" includes a profession;

    "initial" includes any recognised abbreviation of a name;

    "partnership" means-

        (a) a partnership within the Partnership Act 1890 (c. 39), or

        (b) a limited partnership registered under the Limited Partnerships Act 1907 (c. 24),

    or a firm or entity of a similar character formed under the law of a country or territory outside the United Kingdom;

    "surname", in relation to a peer or person usually known by a British title different from his surname, means the title by which he is known.

GENERAL NOTE

This section replaces s.8 of the Business Names Act 1985.

PART 42

STATUTORY AUDITORS

GENERAL NOTE

This Part of the Act: (1) replaces Pt 2 of the 1989 Act and equivalent Northern Ireland provisions, by restating those provisions with some modifications; (2) extends the category of auditors that are subject to regulation and makes provision for the registration and regulation of auditors (whether based in the United Kingdom or not) who audit companies that are incorporated outside the European Union but listed in the United Kingdom; and (3) provides that the Comptroller and Auditor General and the regional Auditors General are eligible to be appointed to perform statutory audits, and it provides a mechanism for the regulation and supervision of their functions as statutory auditor.

Many of the provisions in this Part of the Act implement requirements in the European Union's Eight Company Law Directive on Audit (adopted and published in *The Official Journal of the European Communities* on June 9, 2006, its provisions coming into force from June 29, 2006: see [2006] O.J. L157/87, http://eur-lex.europa.eu/LexUriServ/site/en/oj/2006/L157/L15720060609en00870107.pdf).

The provisions relating to Auditors General implement many of the recommendations made in "Holding to Account, The Review of Audit and Accountability for Central Government", a report by Lord Sharman of Redlynch. This was published in February 2001 (see www.iia.org.uk/cms/IIA/uploads/2c9103-ea9f7e9fbe–7e1c/SharmanReport.pdf), and was warmly endorsed by the government, its response being released in March 2002 (see www.hm-treasury.gov.uk/media/AF8/90/CM5456.Sharmans1.pdf).

The government has to decide how to implement the various audit provisions required by the EU's Eighth Directive, which has a deadline of June 29, 2008 and will therefore need to be brought in earlier than the October 2008 backstop date for the Act as a whole. Part 42 is a relatively "stand alone" part of the Act, and it seems likely that it will be brought into force before the end of June 2008. However, it is possible that the provisions relating to the independent oversight of the Auditors General will be carved out for later implementation as these are not required by the Directive.

This Part of the Act gives considerable powers to the Secretary of State via delegated legislation. He can issue regulations under the following sections:

- s.1214: Independence requirement;
- s.1239: The register of auditors;
- s.1240: Information to be made available to public;
- s.1246: Removal of third country auditors from the register of auditors;
- s.1251: Fees;
- s.1261: Minor definitions; and
- s.1263 Power to make provision in consequence of changes affecting accountancy bodies.

The Secretary of State is also empowered to issue orders under the following sections:

- s.1210: Meaning of "statutory auditor" etc.;
- s.1228: Appointment of the Independent Supervisor;
- s.1241: Meaning of "third country auditor", "registered third country auditor", etc.; and
- s.1252: Delegation of the Secretary of State's functions.

Five Schedules relate to this Part of the Act:

- s.1217: Supervisory bodies, Sch.10: Recognised supervisory bodiess;
- s.1220: Qualifying bodies and recognised professional qualifications, Sch.11: Recognised professional qualifications;
- s.1242: Duties of registered third country auditors, Sch.12: Arrangements in which third country auditors are required to participate;
- s.1252: Delegation of Secretary of State's functions, Sch.13: Supplementary provisions with respect to delegation orders; and
- s.1264: Consequential amendments, Sch.14: Statutory auditors: consequential amendments.

The meaning of "associate" in this Part of the Act is dealt with in s.1260. Definitions of the terms "address", "company", "director", "firm", "group", "holding company", "subsidiary", "officer", "parent undertaking", and "subsidiary undertaking" used in this Part of the Act are given in s.1261. Further, an index to defined terms used in this Part of the Act is given in tabular form in s.1262.

Schedule 8 provides an alphabetical "Index of defined expressions", giving cross references to sections where individual terms are defined.

CHAPTER I

INTRODUCTORY

1209. Main purposes of Part

The main purposes of this Part are-

    (a) to secure that only persons who are properly supervised and appropriately qualified are appointed as statutory auditors, and

    (b) to secure that audits by persons so appointed are carried out properly, with integrity and with a proper degree of independence.

GENERAL NOTE

This section replaces s.24(1) of the 1989 Act and identifies the main purposes of this Part of the Act: namely, to ensure that only properly supervised and qualified persons are appointed as statutory auditors of companies; and that audits are carried out with integrity and a proper degree of independence.

1210. Meaning of "statutory auditor" etc

(1) In this Part "statutory auditor" means-

    (a) a person appointed as auditor under Part 16 of this Act,

    (b) a person appointed as auditor under section 77 of or Schedule 11 to the Building Societies Act 1986 (c. 53),

    (c) a person appointed as auditor of an insurer that is a friendly society under section 72 of or Schedule 14 to the Friendly Societies Act 1992 (c. 40),

    (d) a person appointed as auditor of an insurer that is an industrial and provident society under section 4 of the Friendly and Industrial and Provident Societies Act 1968 (c. 55) or under section 38 of the Industrial and Provident Societies Act (Northern Ireland) 1969 (c. 24 (N.I.)),

    (e) a person appointed as auditor for the purposes of regulation 3 of the Insurance Accounts Directive (Lloyd's Syndicate and Aggregate Accounts) Regulations 2004 (S.I. 2004/3219) or appointed to report on the "aggregate accounts" within the meaning of those Regulations,

    (f) a person appointed as auditor of an insurer for the purposes of regulation 3 of the Insurance Accounts Directive (Miscellaneous Insurance Undertakings) Regulations 1993 (S.I. 1993/3245),

    (g) a person appointed as auditor of a bank for the purposes of regulation 4 of the Bank Accounts Directive (Miscellaneous Banks) Regulations 1991 (S.I. 1991/2704), and

    (h) a person appointed as auditor of a prescribed person under a prescribed enactment authorising or requiring the appointment;

and the expressions "statutory audit" and "statutory audit work" are to be construed accordingly.

(2) In this Part "audited person" means the person in respect of whom a statutory audit is conducted.

(3) In subsection (1)-

"bank" means a person who-

    (a) is a credit institution within the meaning given by Article 4.1(a) of Directive 2006/48/EC of the European Parliament and of the Council relating to the taking up and pursuit of the business of credit institutions, and

    (b) is a company or a firm as defined in Article 48 of the Treaty establishing the European Community;

"friendly society" means a friendly society within the meaning of the Friendly Societies Act 1992 (c. 40);

"industrial and provident society" means-

    (a) a society registered under the Industrial and Provident Societies Act 1965 (c. 12) or a society deemed by virtue of section 4 of that Act to be so registered, or

    (b) a society registered under the Industrial and Provident Societies Act (Northern Ireland) 1969 or a society deemed by virtue of section 4 of that Act to be so registered;

"insurer" means a person who is an insurance undertaking within the meaning given by Article 2.1 of Council Directive 1991/674/EEC on the annual accounts and consolidated accounts of insurance undertakings;

"prescribed" means prescribed, or of a description prescribed, by order made by the Secretary of State for the purposes of subsection (1)(h).

(4) An order under this section is subject to negative resolution procedure.

GENERAL NOTE

    This section replaces s.24(2) of the 1989 Act and is primarily concerned with defining the meaning of various terms used in this Part.

    In order to achieve greater consistency with respect to the regulation of auditors, the existing regulatory regime for "company auditors" has been extended to cover auditors of building societies, banks and insurance undertakings (including those that are industrial and provident societies or friendly societies), all of which will now register as "statutory auditors".

Subsection (1)

    This subsection defines the meaning of statutory auditor more broadly than previously in s.24 of the Companies Act 1989, which only related to the statutory auditors of companies. Persons now regarded as "statutory auditors" are listed in paras (a)-(g). This list includes those persons who audit companies (as required under Pt 16 of the Act) and those who audit building societies, banks, insurers that are friendly societies, and insurance undertakings. In addition, under para.(h) the Secretary of State has power to add auditors of other persons to this list.

Subsection (2)

    This subsection defines the meaning of "audited person" for this Part of the Act.

Subsection (3)

    This subsection defines, for the purpose of subs.(1), the meaning of "bank", "friendly society", "industrial and provident society", "insurer" and "prescribed".

Subsection (4)

    This indicates that an order under this section is subject to the negative resolution procedure (see s.1289).

1211.   Eligibility for appointment as a statutory auditor: overview

A person is eligible for appointment as a statutory auditor only if the person is so eligible-

    (a) by virtue of Chapter 2 (individuals and firms), or

    (b) by virtue of Chapter 3 (Comptroller and Auditor General, etc).

GENERAL NOTE

    This new section cross-refers the eligibility for appointment as a statutory auditor to the requirements contained in Ch.2 or Ch.3 of this Part of the Act.

INDIVIDUALS AND FIRMS

GENERAL NOTE

Some minor changes have been made with respect to the eligibility and independence requirements relating to auditors. Consequently audit firms may need to carry out new checks to ensure that they are in compliance.

Eligibility for appointment

GENERAL NOTE

Sections 1212 and 1213 are restatements of ss.25 and 28 of the 1989 Act, adapted so as to apply in relation to statutory auditors. The sections provide that for a person or firm (defined in s.1261) to be eligible for appointment as a statutory auditor, the person must be a member of a recognised supervisory body and be eligible for appointment under the rules of that body.

1212. Individuals and firms: eligibility for appointment as a statutory auditor

(1) An individual or firm is eligible for appointment as a statutory auditor if the individual or firm-
   (a) is a member of a recognised supervisory body, and
   (b) is eligible for appointment under the rules of that body.
(2) In the cases to which section 1222 applies (individuals retaining only 1967 Act authorisation) a person's eligibility for appointment as a statutory auditor is restricted as mentioned in that section.

GENERAL NOTE

This section replaces s.25 of the 1989 Act and deals with the eligibility of individual persons and of firms as statutory auditors.

Subsection (1)

This indicates that only individuals or firms can be appointed as company statutory auditors if they are members of a recognised supervisory body and are eligible for appointment under the rules of that body.

Subsection (2)

This clarifies that references to members of a recognised supervisory body include references to persons who are not members but who are subject to the body's rules (s.1222). (Section 1217 and Sch.10 deal with the recognition of supervisory bodies, and specify the requirements they must meet to be recognised.)

1213. Effect of ineligibility

(1) No person may act as statutory auditor of an audited person if he is ineligible for appointment as a statutory auditor.
(2) If at any time during his term of office a statutory auditor becomes ineligible for appointment as a statutory auditor, he must immediately-
   (a) resign his office (with immediate effect), and
   (b) give notice in writing to the audited person that he has resigned by reason of his becoming ineligible for appointment.
(3) A person is guilty of an offence if-
   (a) he acts as a statutory auditor in contravention of subsection (1), or
   (b) he fails to give the notice mentioned in paragraph (b) of subsection (2) in accordance with that subsection.

(4) A person guilty of an offence under subsection (3) is liable-
    (a) on conviction on indictment, to a fine;
    (b) on summary conviction, to a fine not exceeding the statutory maximum.

(5) A person is guilty of an offence if-
    (a) he has been convicted of an offence under subsection (3)(a) or this subsection, and
    (b) he continues to act as a statutory auditor in contravention of subsection (1) after the conviction.

(6) A person is guilty of an offence if-
    (a) he has been convicted of an offence under subsection (3)(b) or this subsection, and
    (b) he continues, after the conviction, to fail to give the notice mentioned in subsection (2)(b).

(7) A person guilty of an offence under subsection (5) or (6) is liable-
    (a) on conviction on indictment, to a fine;
    (b) on summary conviction, to a fine not exceeding one-tenth of the statutory maximum for each day on which the act or the failure continues.

(8) In proceedings against a person for an offence under this section it is a defence for him to show that he did not know and had no reason to believe that he was, or had become, ineligible for appointment as a statutory auditor.

GENERAL NOTE

This section replaces part of s.28 of the 1989 Act and sets out the consequences of the prohibition from acting as a statutory auditor on grounds of ineligibility. In this context, a person may either be ineligible or become ineligible. In the latter case, he should vacate office and give notice in writing to the company that he has resigned because of ineligibility.

Subsection (1)

This indicates that no person may act as a statutory auditor if he is ineligible.

Subsection (2)

This subsection further requires that, on becoming ineligible, the auditor must resign his office and give notice in writing.

Subsections (3) and (4)

Failure to comply with the requirements of subs.(1) or subs.(2)(b) is an offence and conviction can result in a fine.

Subsections (5)-(7)

This indicates that if the auditor continues to act as a statutory auditor after conviction (subs.(5)), or continues to fail to give notice that he is ineligible for appointment as a statutory auditor (subs.(6)), he commits a further offence for which a daily fine may be imposed after conviction (subs.(7)).

Subsection (8)

This provides a defence if the person did not know or had no reason to believe that he was, or had become, ineligible.

Independence requirement

1214.   Independence requirement

(1) A person may not act as statutory auditor of an audited person if one or more of subsections (2), (3) and (4) apply to him.

(2) This subsection applies if the person is-
    (a) an officer or employee of the audited person, or
    (b) a partner or employee of such a person, or a partnership of which such a person is a partner.

(3) This subsection applies if the person is-
    (a) an officer or employee of an associated undertaking of the audited person, or

    (b) a partner or employee of such a person, or a partnership of which such a person is a partner.

(4) This subsection applies if there exists, between-

    (a) the person or an associate of his, and

    (b) the audited person or an associated undertaking of the audited person,

a connection of any such description as may be specified by regulations made by the Secretary of State.

(5) An auditor of an audited person is not to be regarded as an officer or employee of the person for the purposes of subsections (2) and (3).

(6) In this section "associated undertaking", in relation to an audited person, means-

    (a) a parent undertaking or subsidiary undertaking of the audited person, or

    (b) a subsidiary undertaking of a parent undertaking of the audited person.

(7) Regulations under subsection (4) are subject to negative resolution procedure.

GENERAL NOTE

This section restates s.27 of the 1989 Act and indicates circumstances where a person may not act as a statutory auditor on grounds of lack of independence.

The Auditing Practices Board ("APB"), which is part of the Financial Reporting Council (FRC), has issued a series of Ethical Standards that deal with independence and related matters. These can be accessed at www.frc.org.uk/apb/publications/ethical.cfm. These Ethical Standards comply with the European Commission's recommendation on this matter, "Statutory Auditors' Independence in the EU: a Set of Fundamental Principles", and further guidance can be obtained in section 1.2 of the Members' Handbook of the Institute of Chartered Accountants in England and Wales, which deals with Professional Ethics. The text of this can be accessed at www.icaew.co.uk/membershandbook/index.cfm.

The Financial Reporting Council monitors the work of statutory auditors through the Audit Inspection Unit (AIU), which reports annually on its findings.

Subsection (1)

This indicates that a person cannot act as a statutory auditor if he or an associated person is an officer or employee of the company being audited itself or an associated undertaking (i.e. a parent or subsidiary: see subs.(6)) of the audited entity.

Subsection (2)

This indicates that individuals who may not act include persons who are officers or employees of the audited entity, or the partner or employee of such a body.

Subsection (3)

This subsection indicates that individuals who may not act include a person who is an officer or employee of an associated undertaking (i.e. a parent or subsidiary: see subs.(6)) of the audited entity.

Subsection (4)

This subsection allows the Secretary of State to make regulations regarding other connections between the audited entity or an associated undertaking (i.e. a parent or subsidiary: see subs.(6)) and the statutory auditor by virtue of which a person will be regarded as lacking independence. Such regulations are subject to the negative resolution procedure (see subs.(7) below).

Subsection (5)

This subsection indicates that the auditor of a company is not to be regarded as an officer or employee of the company for the purposes of subss.(2)-(3).

Subsection (6)

This subsection defines, for the purpose of this section, "associated undertaking" as meaning a parent or subsidiary undertaking of the company being audited or a fellow subsidiary within a group.

Subsection (7)

This subsection states that regulations issued under subs.(4) are subject to the negative resolution procedure: see s.1289.

1215. Effect of lack of independence

(1) If at any time during his term of office a statutory auditor becomes prohibited from acting by section 1214(1), he must immediately-
    (a) resign his office (with immediate effect), and
    (b) give notice in writing to the audited person that he has resigned by reason of his lack of independence.

(2) A person is guilty of an offence if-
    (a) he acts as a statutory auditor in contravention of section 1214(1), or
    (b) he fails to give the notice mentioned in paragraph (b) of subsection (1) in accordance with that subsection.

(3) A person guilty of an offence under subsection (2) is liable-
    (a) on conviction on indictment, to a fine;
    (b) on summary conviction, to a fine not exceeding the statutory maximum.

(4) A person is guilty of an offence if-
    (a) he has been convicted of an offence under subsection (2)(a) or this subsection, and
    (b) he continues to act as a statutory auditor in contravention of section 1214(1) after the conviction.

(5) A person is guilty of an offence if-
    (a) he has been convicted of an offence under subsection (2)(b) or this subsection, and
    (b) after the conviction, he continues to fail to give the notice mentioned in subsection (1)(b).

(6) A person guilty of an offence under subsection (4) or (5) is liable-
    (a) on conviction on indictment, to a fine;
    (b) on summary conviction, to a fine not exceeding one-tenth of the statutory maximum for each day on which the act or the failure continues.

(7) In proceedings against a person for an offence under this section it is a defence for him to show that he did not know and had no reason to believe that he was, or had become, prohibited from acting as statutory auditor of the audited person by section 1214(1).

GENERAL NOTE

    This section replaces part of s.28 of the 1989 Act and sets out the consequences of the prohibition from acting as a statutory auditor on grounds of lack of independence, as defined in s.1214.

Subsection (1)

    This indicates that a person who during his term of office becomes ineligible to act as a statutory auditor through lack of independence under s.1214(1) must resign immediately and give written notice to the company of the reason for his resignation.

Subsections (2) and (3)

    Failure to comply with the requirements of subs.(1) is an offence and conviction can result in a fine.

Subsections (4)-(6)

    This indicates that if the auditor continues to act as a statutory auditor after conviction (subs.(4)), or continues to fail to give notice that he is ineligible to act as a statutory auditor (subs.(5)), he commits a further offence for which a daily fine may be imposed after conviction (subs.(6)).

Subsection (7)

    This provides a defence if the person did not know or had no reason to believe that he was, or had become, ineligible.

Effect of appointment of a partnership

1216. Effect of appointment of a partnership

(1) This section applies where a partnership constituted under the law of-
- (a) England and Wales,
- (b) Northern Ireland, or
- (c) any other country or territory in which a partnership is not a legal person,

is by virtue of this Chapter appointed as statutory auditor of an audited person.

(2) Unless a contrary intention appears, the appointment is an appointment of the partnership as such and not of the partners.

(3) Where the partnership ceases, the appointment is to be treated as extending to-
- (a) any appropriate partnership which succeeds to the practice of that partnership, or
- (b) any other appropriate person who succeeds to that practice having previously carried it on in partnership.

(4) For the purposes of subsection (3)-
- (a) a partnership is to be regarded as succeeding to the practice of another partnership only if the members of the successor partnership are substantially the same as those of the former partnership, and
- (b) a partnership or other person is to be regarded as succeeding to the practice of a partnership only if it or he succeeds to the whole or substantially the whole of the business of the former partnership.

(5) Where the partnership ceases and the appointment is not treated under subsection (3) as extending to any partnership or other person, the appointment may with the consent of the audited person be treated as extending to an appropriate partnership, or other appropriate person, who succeeds to-
- (a) the business of the former partnership, or
- (b) such part of it as is agreed by the audited person is to be treated as comprising the appointment.

(6) For the purposes of this section, a partnership or other person is "appropriate" if it or he-
- (a) is eligible for appointment as a statutory auditor by virtue of this Chapter, and
- (b) is not prohibited by section 1214(1) from acting as statutory auditor of the audited person.

GENERAL NOTE

This section is a restatement of s.26 of the 1989 Act. The effect of the section is to ensure that when a partnership constituted in England and Wales, Northern Ireland, or any other country or territory in which a partnership is not a legal person, is appointed as a statutory auditor under this Part, the appointment may continue even if a partner leaves the partnership. For a partnership or other person to be considered as appropriate for the appointment to continue, they must be eligible for appointment as a statutory auditor and not prohibited from so acting (as indicated in s.1214(1)). Without this provision, the appointment would cease every time the membership of the partnership changed.

Subsection (1)

This states that s.1216 applies where a partnership constituted in England and Wales, Northern Ireland, or any other country or territory in which a partnership is not a legal person, is appointed as a statutory auditor.

Subsection (2)

This states that unless a contrary intention appears, the appointment is of a partnership rather than individual partners.

Subsections (3) and (4)

When a partnership ceases, the appointment to act as statutory auditor is to be treated as extending to a successor practice (subs.(3)), but only where the members of the successor practice and the business are substantially the same (subs.(4)).

Subsection (5)

Where a partnership ceases, but there is no automatic extension to a successor practice under subss.(3)-(4) above, the appointment may nevertheless be treated as extending to an appropriate partnership if the company subject to audit agrees.

Subsection (6)

This subsection defines, for the purpose of this section, the meaning of "appropriate" with respect to being appointed as a statutory auditor.

Supervisory bodies

1217.　Supervisory bodies

(1) In this Part a "supervisory body" means a body established in the United Kingdom (whether a body corporate or an unincorporated association) which maintains and enforces rules as to-

    (a) the eligibility of persons for appointment as a statutory auditor, and

    (b) the conduct of statutory audit work,

which are binding on persons seeking appointment or acting as a statutory auditor either because they are members of that body or because they are otherwise subject to its control.

(2) In this Part references to the members of a supervisory body are to the persons who, whether or not members of the body, are subject to its rules in seeking appointment or acting as a statutory auditor.

(3) In this Part references to the rules of a supervisory body are to the rules (whether or not laid down by the body itself) which the body has power to enforce and which are relevant for the purposes of this Part.

This includes rules relating to the admission or expulsion of members of the body, so far as relevant for the purposes of this Part.

(4) Schedule 10 has effect with respect to the recognition of supervisory bodies for the purposes of this Part.

GENERAL NOTE

This section restates s.30 of the 1989 Act. This section and the following sections should be read in conjunction with Sch.10, "Recognised supervisory bodies". The main recognised supervisory bodies are currently the Institute of Chartered Accountants in England and Wales; the Institute of Chartered Accountants of Scotland; the Institute of Chartered Accountants in Ireland; and the Association of Chartered Certified Accountants.

Subsections (1)-(3)

These subsections define for this Part of the Act a "supervisory body" as a body established in the United Kingdom that maintains and enforces rules regarding the eligibility of persons (its "members") appointed as statutory auditors and the conduct of statutory audit work. The rules of the supervisory body referred to here must be relevant to the purposes of this Part of the Act and relate to persons who are seeking appointment or acting as a statutory auditor, whether or not they are a member of the supervisory body.

Subsection (4)

This subsection introduces Sch.10, which specifies both the requirements that supervisory bodies must meet in order to be recognised, and the process for doing so.

1218. Exemption from liability for damages

(1) No person within subsection (2) is to be liable in damages for anything done or omitted in the discharge or purported discharge of functions to which this subsection applies.

(2) The persons within this subsection are-
- (a) any recognised supervisory body,
- (b) any officer or employee of a recognised supervisory body, and
- (c) any member of the governing body of a recognised supervisory body.

(3) Subsection (1) applies to the functions of a recognised supervisory body so far as relating to, or to matters arising out of, any of the following-
- (a) rules, practices, powers and arrangements of the body to which the requirements of Part 2 of Schedule 10 apply;
- (b) the obligations with which paragraph 20 of that Schedule requires the body to comply;
- (c) any guidance issued by the body;
- (d) the obligations imposed on the body by or by virtue of this Part.

(4) The reference in subsection (3)(c) to guidance issued by a recognised supervisory body is a reference to any guidance or recommendation which is-
- (a) issued or made by it to all or any class of its members or persons seeking to become members, and
- (b) relevant for the purposes of this Part,

including any guidance or recommendation relating to the admission or expulsion of members of the body, so far as relevant for the purposes of this Part.

(5) Subsection (1) does not apply-
- (a) if the act or omission is shown to have been in bad faith, or
- (b) so as to prevent an award of damages in respect of the act or omission on the ground that it was unlawful as a result of section 6(1) of the Human Rights Act 1998 (c. 42) (acts of public authorities incompatible with Convention rights).

GENERAL NOTE

This section is a restatement of s.48 of the 1989 Act, as modified by Sch.8, para.1 of the Companies (Audit, Investigations and Community Enterprise) Act 2004 (which repealed s.48(3)).

Subsections (1)-(4)

These subsections set out those bodies and individuals (subs.(2)) that are exempt from liability for damages arising from the discharge or claimed discharge of supervisory functions as specified in this Part of the Act (subs.(1)).

The supervisory functions that might give rise to potential actions for damages include matters arising from applying the rules, practices, powers and arrangements of the body (subs.(3)), as well as any guidance it may have issued to members or persons seeking to become members (subs.(4)). It applies to recognised supervisory bodies (see s.1217 and Sch.10) and their officers, employees and members of their governing bodies (subs.(2)). The rules, practices, powers and arrangements of the supervisory body will concern the granting of professional qualifications and the means of assuring that members are fit and proper persons to be auditors, as well as dealing with such matters as professional integrity and independence; technical standards; procedures for maintaining competence; monitoring and enforcing compliance with rules; independent monitoring of audits of listed companies and other major bodies; procedures relating to the admission, discipline and expulsion of members; the investigation of complaints; independent investigation for disciplinary purposes of public interest cases; meeting claims arising out of audit work; the keeping of a register of auditors open to public scrutiny (see s.1239); taking account of costs of compliance; and the promotion and maintenance of standards.

Subsection (5)

The exemption under subs.(1) does not apply if the bodies and individuals concerned have acted in bad faith, or if it would prevent an award of damages because the act was unlawful under the Human Rights Act.

Professional qualifications

1219.　Appropriate qualifications

(1)　A person holds an appropriate qualification for the purposes of this Chapter if and only if-
  (a)　he holds a recognised professional qualification obtained in the United Kingdom,
  (b)　immediately before the commencement of this Chapter, he-
    (i)　held an appropriate qualification for the purposes of Part 2 of the Companies Act 1989 (c. 40) (eligibility for appointment as company auditor) by virtue of section 31(1)(a) or (c) of that Act, or
    (ii)　was treated as holding an appropriate qualification for those purposes by virtue of section 31(2), (3) or (4) of that Act,
  (c)　immediately before the commencement of this Chapter, he-
    (i)　held an appropriate qualification for the purposes of Part III of the Companies (Northern Ireland) Order 1990 (S.I. 1990/593 (N.I. 5)) by virtue of Article 34(1)(a) or (c) of that Order, or
    (ii)　was treated as holding an appropriate qualification for those purposes by virtue of Article 34(2), (3) or (4) of that Order,
  (d)　he is within subsection (2),
  (e)　he has been authorised to practise the profession of statutory auditor pursuant to the European Communities (Recognition of Professional Qualifications) (First General System) Regulations 2005 (S.I. 2005/18) and has fulfilled any requirements imposed pursuant to regulation 6 of those Regulations, or
  (f)　subject to any direction under section 1221(5), he is regarded for the purposes of this Chapter as holding an approved overseas qualification.
(2)　A person is within this subsection if-
  (a)　before 1st January 1990, he began a course of study or practical training leading to a professional qualification in accountancy offered by a body established in the United Kingdom,
  (b)　he obtained that qualification on or after 1st January 1990 and before 1st January 1996, and
  (c)　the Secretary of State approves his qualification as an appropriate qualification for the purposes of this Chapter.
(3)　The Secretary of State may approve a qualification under subsection (2)(c) only if he is satisfied that, at the time the qualification was awarded, the body concerned had adequate arrangements to ensure that the qualification was awarded only to persons educated and trained to a standard equivalent to that required, at that time, in the case of a recognised professional qualification under Part 2 of the Companies Act 1989 (c. 40) (eligibility for appointment as company auditor).

GENERAL NOTE
This section restates s.31 of the 1989 Act.

Subsection (1)
This provides that a person has an appropriate audit qualification if he holds a professional qualification obtained in the United Kingdom that is recognised in accordance with s.1220 and Sch.11 (sub.(1)(a)-(b)). Qualifications recognised under Pt 2 of the 1989 Act or the Companies (Northern Ireland) Order 1990 (SI 1990/53) will continue to be recognised (sub.(1)(c)). Persons whose qualifications from other EU Member States are recognised under the European Communities (Recognition of Professional Qualifications) (First General System) Regulations 2005 (SI 2005/18) to practise as statutory auditors are also considered to hold an appropriate qualification (subs.(1)(e)). So too are overseas qualifications from non-EU countries if approved under s.1221 (subs.(1)(f)).

This subsection restates a transitional provision from the 1989 Act for those persons who have begun a course of study in accountancy before January 1, 1990 and obtained a qualification between January 1, 1990 and January 1, 1996, enabling them to apply to the Secretary of State for approval of their qualification (subs.(2)). The Secretary of State may only approve such a qualification if he is satisfied that the body awarding it had adequate arrangements at the time to ensure that equivalent educational and training standards were applied as by United Kingdom recognised supervisory bodies (subs.(3)).

The transitional provisions contained in subss.(2) and (3) of s.31 of the 1989 Act have not been restated.

1220.   Qualifying bodies and recognised professional qualifications

(1) In this Part a "qualifying body" means a body established in the United Kingdom (whether a body corporate or an unincorporated association) which offers a professional qualification in accountancy.

(2) In this Part references to the rules of a qualifying body are to the rules (whether or not laid down by the body itself) which the body has power to enforce and which are relevant for the purposes of this Part.

This includes, so far as so relevant, rules relating to-

    (a) admission to or expulsion from a course of study leading to a qualification,

    (b) the award or deprivation of a qualification, or

    (c) the approval of a person for the purposes of giving practical training or the withdrawal of such approval.

(3) Schedule 11 has effect with respect to the recognition for the purposes of this Part of a professional qualification offered by a qualifying body.

GENERAL NOTE

This section is a restatement of s.32 of the 1989 Act. This section and the following sections should be read in conjunction with Sch.11, "Recognised professional qualifications". Examples of qualifying bodies are the Institute of Chartered Accountants in England and Wales; the Institute of Chartered Accountants of Scotland; the Institute of Chartered Accountants in Ireland; and the Association of Chartered Certified Accountants.

Subsection (1)

This defines the term "qualifying body" as a body that offers a professional qualification in accountancy.

Subsection (2)

This identifies that references to rules of a qualifying body in this Part of the Act are to its rules on admission or expulsion from a course of study leading to a professional qualification; the award or revocation of a qualification; or the approval or withdrawal of approval of a person authorised to provide practical training.

Subsection (3)

This subsection introduces Sch.11, which sets out the requirements that qualifying bodies must impose. Only a qualification recognised in accordance with these provisions can be considered a recognised professional qualification within the meaning of s.1219(1)(a).

1221.   Approval of overseas qualifications

(1) The Secretary of State may declare that the following are to be regarded for the purposes of this Chapter as holding an approved overseas qualification-

    (a) persons who are qualified to audit accounts under the law of a specified foreign country, or

    (b) persons who hold a specified professional qualification in accountancy obtained in a specified foreign country.

(2) A declaration under subsection (1)(b) may be expressed to be subject to the satisfaction of any specified requirement or requirements.

(3) The Secretary of State may make a declaration under subsection (1) only if he is satisfied that-

    (a) in the case of a declaration under subsection (1)(a), the fact that the persons in question are qualified to audit accounts under the law of the specified foreign country, or

    (b) in the case of a declaration under subsection (1)(b), the specified professional qualification taken with any requirement or requirements to be specified under subsection (2),

affords an assurance of professional competence equivalent to that afforded by a recognised professional qualification.

(4) The Secretary of State may make a declaration under subsection (1) only if he is satisfied that the treatment that the persons who are the subject of the declaration will receive as a result of it is comparable to the treatment which is, or is likely to be, afforded in the specified foreign country or a part of it to-

    (a) in the case of a declaration under subsection (1)(a), some or all persons who are eligible to be appointed as a statutory auditor, and

    (b) in the case of a declaration under subsection (1)(b), some or all persons who hold a corresponding recognised professional qualification.

(5) The Secretary of State may direct that persons holding an approved overseas qualification are not to be treated as holding an appropriate qualification for the purposes of this Chapter unless they hold such additional educational qualifications as the Secretary of State may specify for the purpose of ensuring that such persons have an adequate knowledge of the law and practice in the United Kingdom relevant to the audit of accounts.

(6) The Secretary of State may give different directions in relation to different approved overseas qualifications.

(7) The Secretary of State may, if he thinks fit, having regard to the considerations mentioned in subsections (3) and (4), withdraw a declaration under subsection (1) in relation to-

    (a) persons becoming qualified to audit accounts under the law of the specified foreign country after such date as he may specify, or

    (b) persons obtaining the specified professional qualification after such date as he may specify.

(8) The Secretary of State may, if he thinks fit, having regard to the considerations mentioned in subsections (3) and (4), vary or revoke a requirement specified under subsection (2) from such date as he may specify.

(9) In this section "foreign country", in relation to any time, means a country or territory that, at that time, is not a "relevant State" within the meaning of the European Communities (Recognition of Professional Qualifications) (First General System) Regulations 2005 (S.I. 2005/18) or part of such a State.

GENERAL NOTE

This section restates s.33 of the 1989 Act as regards the approval of overseas qualifications from non-EU countries. It therefore sets out the conditions that will need to be satisfied, relating to the assurance of professional competence, to enable someone from overseas to act as a statutory auditor in the United Kingdom.

Subsections (1)-(3)

These subsections provide for approval of all those in a specified country who are qualified to audit accounts (subs.(1)(a)), or only those who hold specified qualifications in that country (subs.(1)(b)). In the case of the latter, the Secretary of State may specify any additional requirements that need to be satisfied (subs.(2)).

Subsections (3) and (4)

In order to make a declaration under subs.(1), the Secretary of State must be satisfied that the persons concerned should have equivalent professional competence to United Kingdom qualified auditors. The Secretary of State is also required to ensure that there is reciprocity before recognising an overseas qualification: i.e. there must be comparable treatment for United Kingdom qualified auditors operating in the country in question.

The Secretary of State may require additional qualifications to ensure an overseas auditor has an adequate knowledge of law and practice in the United Kingdom relevant to the audit of accounts (subs.(5)). He may also give different directions in relation to different approved overseas qualifications (subs.(6)).

Subsections (7) and (8)

The Secretary of State may also withdraw recognition of an overseas qualification after a specified date if he is no longer satisfied that there is equivalent competence or there are inadequate reciprocal arrangements.

Subsection (9)

This subsection defines "foreign country" as one not being a "relevant state" within the meaning of the European Communities (Recognition of Professional Qualifications) (First General System) Regulations 2005 (SI 2005/18).

1222.   Eligibility of individuals retaining only 1967 Act authorisation

(1) A person whose only appropriate qualification is based on his retention of an authorisation originally granted by the Board of Trade or the Secretary of State under section 13(1) of the Companies Act 1967 (c. 81) is eligible only for appointment as auditor of an unquoted company.

(2) A company is "unquoted" if, at the time of the person's appointment, neither the company, nor any parent undertaking of which it is a subsidiary undertaking, is a quoted company within the meaning of section 385(2).

(3) References to a person eligible for appointment as a statutory auditor by virtue of this Part in enactments relating to eligibility for appointment as auditor of a person other than a company do not include a person to whom this section applies.

GENERAL NOTE

This section restates s.34 of the 1989 Act.

Prior to 1967, auditors of an unquoted company were exempt from the statutory qualification requirements placed on other company auditors. The Companies Act 1967 abolished this exemption, but allowed an auditor with sufficient practical experience to apply to the Secretary of State for authorisation to practise.

Subsection (1)

Past authorisations will continue to be valid by virtue of the transitional provision in s.1219(1)(b), but an authorised person is only eligible for appointment as an auditor of an unquoted company (as defined in subss.(2)-(3) of s.385).

Subsection (2)

This defines an "unquoted" company if, at the time of the authorised person's appointment, neither it nor any parent undertaking is a quoted company within the meaning of s.385(2).

Subsection (3)

This subsection provides that auditors authorised under the 1967 Act may not be treated as statutory auditors for any purpose other than to perform the statutory audit of an unquoted company.

Information

1223.   Matters to be notified to the Secretary of State

(1) The Secretary of State may require a recognised supervisory body or a recognised qualifying body-

> (a) to notify him immediately of the occurrence of such events as he may specify in writing and to give him such information in respect of those events as is so specified;
>
> (b) to give him, at such times or in respect of such periods as he may specify in writing, such information as is so specified.

(2) The notices and information required to be given must be such as the Secretary of State may reasonably require for the exercise of his functions under this Part.

(3) The Secretary of State may require information given under this section to be given in a specified form or verified in a specified manner.

(4) Any notice or information required to be given under this section must be given in writing unless the Secretary of State specifies or approves some other manner.

GENERAL NOTE

This section is a restatement of s.37 of the 1989 Act.

Subsection (1)

This subsection enables the Secretary of State to require recognised supervisory and qualifying bodies to notify him in writing of certain specified events, if they occur.

Subsections (2) and (4)

The information required must be such as is reasonably required for the Secretary of State to carry out his functions - e.g. it might include annual reports, or notification of rule or bye-law changes (subs.(2)). The information may be required to be given in a specified form or be verified in some way (subs.(3)), and either be submitted in writing or in some other specified manner (subs.(4)). The information so required might relate to specific time periods or specific occurrences.

1224.   The Secretary of State's power to call for information

(1) The Secretary of State may by notice in writing require a person within subsection (2) to give him such information as he may reasonably require for the exercise of his functions under this Part.

(2) The persons within this subsection are-

> (a) any recognised supervisory body,
>
> (b) any recognised qualifying body, and
>
> (c) any person eligible for appointment as a statutory auditor by virtue of this Chapter.

(3) The Secretary of State may require that any information which he requires under this section is to be given within such reasonable time and verified in such manner as he may specify.

GENERAL NOTE

This section restates s.38 of the 1989 Act.

Subsections (1) and (2)

The section enables the Secretary of State to require, by giving notice in writing, information (subs.(1)) from a recognised supervisory body, a recognised qualifying body or an individual statutory auditor (subs.(2)). (For instance, as a result of a report provided under s.1223, the Secretary of State may request further information on a specific point to clarify if a recognised supervisory body is complying with the requirements in Sch.10.)

Subsection (3)

The Secretary of State can specify the time period in which this information has to be provided and also that it should be verified in some specified manner.

Enforcement

1225. Compliance orders

(1) If at any time it appears to the Secretary of State-
 (a) in the case of a recognised supervisory body, that any requirement of Schedule 10 is not satisfied,
 (b) in the case of a recognised professional qualification, that any requirement of Schedule 11 is not satisfied, or
 (c) that a recognised supervisory body or a recognised qualifying body has failed to comply with an obligation to which it is subject under or by virtue of this Part,
  he may, instead of revoking the relevant recognition order, make an application to the court under this section.

(2) If on an application under this section the court decides that the requirement in question is not satisfied or, as the case may be, that the body has failed to comply with the obligation in question, it may order the body to take such steps as the court directs for securing that the requirement is satisfied or that the obligation is complied with.

(3) In this section "the court" means the High Court or, in Scotland, the Court of Session.

GENERAL NOTE
  This section is a restatement of s.39 of the 1989 Act.

Subsection (1)
  If a recognised supervisory or qualifying body fails to meet the requirements in Schs 10 or 11, or it fails to comply with another requirement contained in this Part of the Act, then the Secretary of State may apply to the court for an order to make the body comply.

Subsection (2)
  The court is empowered to order the body concerned to take such steps as necessary to ensure compliance, with the ultimate sanction for non-compliance being revocation of its status as a recognised body under Schs 10 or 11.

Subsection (3)
  This subsection defines the term "the court" to mean the High Court or, in Scotland, the Court of Session.

Chapter 3

Auditors General

GENERAL NOTE
  As explained in the General Note to this Part of the Act, Ch.3 dealing with Auditors General is new legislation.

Eligibility for appointment

1226. Auditors General: eligibility for appointment as a statutory auditor

(1) In this Part "Auditor General" means-
 (a) the Comptroller and Auditor General,
 (b) the Auditor General for Scotland,
 (c) the Auditor General for Wales, or

(d) the Comptroller and Auditor General for Northern Ireland.

(2) An Auditor General is eligible for appointment as a statutory auditor.

(3) Subsection (2) is subject to any suspension notice having effect under section 1234 (notices suspending eligibility for appointment as a statutory auditor).

GENERAL NOTE

This section deals with the eligibility of Auditors General as statutory auditors.

Subsection (1)

This subsection defines an "Auditor General" for the purposes of this Part of the Act as the Comptroller and Auditor General, the Auditor General for Scotland, the Auditor General for Wales, and the Comptroller and Auditor General for Northern Ireland.

Subsections (2) and (3)

These subsections explain that an Auditor General is eligible for appointment as a statutory auditor (subs.(2)), unless his eligibility has been suspended by the Independent Supervisor under s.1234, below (subs.(3)).

Conduct of audits

1227. Individuals responsible for audit work on behalf of Auditors General

An Auditor General must secure that each individual responsible for statutory audit work on behalf of that Auditor General is eligible for appointment as a statutory auditor by virtue of Chapter 2.

GENERAL NOTE

This section requires an Auditor General to ensure that the individuals within his charge, who are carrying out statutory audits on his behalf, are, in their own right, eligible for appointment as a statutory auditor by virtue of the qualifications and requirements that are set out in Ch.2 of this Part of the Act.

The Independent Supervisor

1228. Appointment of the Independent Supervisor

(1) The Secretary of State must appoint a body ("the Independent Supervisor") to discharge the function mentioned in section 1229(1) ("the supervision function").

(2) An appointment under this section must be made by order.

(3) The order has the effect of making the body appointed under subsection (1) designated under section 5 of the Freedom of Information Act 2000 (c. 36) (further powers to designate public authorities).

(4) A body may be appointed under this section only if it is a body corporate or an unincorporated association which appears to the Secretary of State-

    (a) to be willing and able to discharge the supervision function, and

    (b) to have arrangements in place relating to the discharge of that function which are such as to be likely to ensure that the conditions in subsection (5) are met.

(5) The conditions are-

    (a) that the supervision function will be exercised effectively, and

    (b) where the order is to contain any requirements or other provisions specified under subsection (6), that that function will be exercised in accordance with any such requirements or provisions.

(6) An order under this section may contain such requirements or other provisions relating to the exercise of the supervision function by the Independent Supervisor as appear to the Secretary of State to be appropriate.

(7) An order under this section is subject to negative resolution procedure.

GENERAL NOTE

This section deals with the appointment of a body as the Independent Supervisor of Auditors General.

A House of Commons amendment to drop subs.(3) was overruled by the House of Lords, although it was widely understood that it would be removed when the Bill finally returned to the Commons. However, it was not, apparently due to procedural or timetabling concerns rather than for policy reasons. Subsection (3) has legal and practical implications for oversight of the Auditors General. The problem is basically that designation as a delegated body under the Freedom of Information Act means that all reports and related material will have to be available for anyone to access, although there are exemptions (e.g. for commercially sensitive information).

Subsections (1) and (2)

These subsections require the Secretary of State to appoint by order (subs.(2)) a body as "the Independent Supervisor" of Auditors General in respect of the exercise of statutory audit functions referred to in s.1229(1), below (subs.(1)). The appointed Independent Supervisor must perform its function on a United Kingdom-wide basis for all four Auditors General in accordance with s.1229(1).

Subsection (3)

The delegation order has the effect of making the nominated body subject to s.5 of the Freedom of Information Act 2000.

Subsections (4)-(6)

The body appointed has to be willing and suitable to discharge the supervisory function (subs.(4)), and it must have arrangements in place that will ensure the supervision is carried out effectively, and that it will exercise such functions and requirements as may be laid down in the Secretary of State's order appointing it (subss.(5)-(6)).

Subsection (7)

An order made under this section is subject to the negative resolution procedure: see s.1289.

Supervision of Auditors General

1229. Supervision of Auditors General by the Independent Supervisor

(1) The Independent Supervisor must supervise the performance by each Auditor General of his functions as a statutory auditor.

(2) The Independent Supervisor must discharge that duty by-

(a) entering into supervision arrangements with one or more bodies, and

(b) overseeing the effective operation of any supervision arrangements entered into by it.

(3) For this purpose "supervision arrangements" are arrangements entered into by the Independent Supervisor with a body, for the purposes of this section, in accordance with which the body does one or more of the following-

(a) determines standards relating to professional integrity and independence which must be applied by an Auditor General in statutory audit work;

(b) determines technical standards which must be applied by an Auditor General in statutory audit work and the manner in which those standards are to be applied in practice;

(c) monitors the performance of statutory audits carried out by an Auditor General;

(d) investigates any matter arising from the performance by an Auditor General of a statutory audit;

(e) holds disciplinary hearings in respect of an Auditor General which appear to be desirable following the conclusion of such investigations;

(f) decides whether (and, if so, what) disciplinary action should be taken against an Auditor General to whom such a hearing related.

(4) The Independent Supervisor may enter into supervision arrangements with a body despite any relationship that may exist between the Independent Supervisor and that body.

(5) The Independent Supervisor must notify each Auditor General in writing of any supervision arrangements that it enters into under this section.

(6) Supervision arrangements within subsection (3)(f) may, in particular, provide for the payment by an Auditor General of a fine to any person.

(7) Any fine received by the Independent Supervisor under supervision arrangements is to be paid into the Consolidated Fund.

GENERAL NOTE

This section sets the framework for the supervision arrangements to be carried out by the Independent Supervisor.

Subsection (1)

This provides that the Independent Supervisor must supervise the performance of each Auditor General carrying out his functions as a statutory auditor.

Subsection (2)

This subsection requires the Independent Supervisor to establish arrangements with one or more third parties to carry out aspects of the supervisory function.

Subsection (3)

The arrangements with a third party cover standards on professional integrity and independence, as well as the technical standards for statutory audit work; monitoring performance; investigating matters arising from that performance; and as necessary holding disciplinary hearings and deciding whether any disciplinary action should be taken.

Subsections (4) and (5)

The Independent Supervisor is not prevented from entering into supervision arrangements with a body where there is already a relationship between the two (subs.(4)), but the Independent Supervisor is required to inform each Auditor General of the supervision arrangements entered into under s.1229.

Subsections (6) and (7)

These subsections make provisions relating to the payment of fines under the disciplinary arrangements.

1230. Duties of Auditors General in relation to supervision arrangements

(1) Each Auditor General must-
  (a) comply with any standards of the kind mentioned in subsection (3)(a) or (b) of section 1229 determined under the supervision arrangements,
  (b) take such steps as may be reasonably required of that Auditor General to enable his performance of statutory audits to be monitored by means of inspections carried out under the supervision arrangements, and
  (c) comply with any decision of the kind mentioned in subsection (3)(f) of that section made under the supervision arrangements.

(2) Each Auditor General must pay to the body or bodies with which the Independent Supervisor enters into the supervision arrangements such proportion of the costs incurred by the body or bodies for the purposes of the arrangements as the Independent Supervisor may notify to him in writing.

(3) Expenditure under subsection (2) is-
  (a) in the case of expenditure of the Comptroller and Auditor General, to be regarded as expenditure of the National Audit Office for the purposes of section 4(1) of the National Audit Act 1983 (c. 44);
  (b) in the case of expenditure of the Comptroller and Auditor General for Northern Ireland, to be regarded as expenditure of the Northern Ireland Audit Office for the

purposes of Article 6(1) of the Audit (Northern Ireland) Order 1987 (S.I. 1987/460 (N.I. 5)).

(4) In this section "the supervision arrangements" means the arrangements entered into under section 1229.

GENERAL NOTE

This section outlines the duties of Auditors General with respect to their supervision arrangements.

Subsection (1)

Under this subsection, each Auditor General has a duty to comply with the standards set under the independent supervision arrangements, as well as submitting to the monitoring procedures and observing decisions made as part of those arrangements.

Subsection (2)

Each Auditor General has to pay the proportion of the costs of the independent supervisory arrangements that may be notified to him in writing.

Subsection (3)

The payment of such costs is to be regarded as expenditure of the National Audit Office in the case of the Comptroller and Auditor General, and as expenditure of the Northern Ireland Audit Office in the case of the Comptroller and Auditor General for Northern Ireland. (In the case of the Auditor General for Scotland, under s.13 of the Public Finance and Accountability (Scotland) Act 2000 (asp 1) the expenses of the Auditor General are to be paid by Audit Scotland. In the case of the Auditor General for Wales, under s.93 of the Government of Wales Act 1998 the expenses of the Auditor General are to be met by the Assembly.)

Subsection (4)

This subsection defines the meaning of "the supervision arrangements" referred to in this section as relating to arrangements entered into under s.1229.

Reporting requirement

1231. Reports by the Independent Supervisor

(1) The Independent Supervisor must, at least once in each calendar year, prepare a report on the discharge of its functions.

(2) The Independent Supervisor must give a copy of each report prepared under subsection (1) to-
    (a) the Secretary of State;
    (b) the First Minister in Scotland;
    (c) the First Minister and the deputy First Minister in Northern Ireland;
    (d) the Assembly First Secretary in Wales.

(3) The Secretary of State must lay before each House of Parliament a copy of each report received by him under subsection (2)(a).

(4) In relation to a calendar year during which an appointment of a body as the Independent Supervisor is made or revoked by an order under section 1228, this section applies with such modifications as may be specified in the order.

GENERAL NOTE

This section indicates how often and to whom the Independent Supervisor should submit reports.

Subsection (1)

The Independent Supervisor must provide at least one report each calendar year.

Subsection (2)
Subsection (2)

Copies of this report must be given to the Secretary of State and to the First Minister in Scotland, the First Minister and the Deputy First Minister in Northern Ireland and the Assembly First Minister in Wales.

Subsection (3)

The Secretary of State must then lay the report before each House of Parliament.

Subsection (4)

This subsection modifies the above requirements where the Independent Supervisor's appointment is for less than a full calendar year.

Information

1232.   Matters to be notified to the Independent Supervisor

(1) The Independent Supervisor may require an Auditor General-
  (a) to notify the Independent Supervisor immediately of the occurrence of such events as it may specify in writing and to give it such information in respect of those events as is so specified;
  (b) to give the Independent Supervisor, at such times or in respect of such periods as it may specify in writing, such information as is so specified.
(2) The notices and information required to be given must be such as the Independent Supervisor may reasonably require for the exercise of the functions conferred on it by or by virtue of this Part.
(3) The Independent Supervisor may require information given under this section to be given in a specified form or verified in a specified manner.
(4) Any notice or information required to be given under this section must be given in writing unless the Independent Supervisor specifies or approves some other manner.

GENERAL NOTE

This section deals with the notices and information required to be given by Auditors General to the Independent Supervisor.

Subsections (1) and (2)

An Auditor General may be required by the body acting as the Independent Supervisor to notify it of specified events for particular periods (subs.(1)) in a manner which is consistent with the requirement for other statutory auditors as contained in s.1223 (subs.(2)).

Subsection (3)

The Independent Supervisor may require this information to be given within a reasonable time and to be verified in a specified manner.

Subsection (4)

Notice given and information supplied should normally be in writing.

1233.   The Independent Supervisor's power to call for information

(1) The Independent Supervisor may by notice in writing require an Auditor General to give it such information as it may reasonably require for the exercise of the functions conferred on it by or by virtue of this Part.
(2) The Independent Supervisor may require that any information which it requires under this section is to be given within such reasonable time and verified in such manner as it may specify.

GENERAL NOTE

This section specifies the Independent Supervisor's power to call for information and is consistent with the requirement for other statutory auditors as contained in s.1224.

Subsection (1)

The Independent Supervisor may require an Auditor General to provide him with particular information.

Subsection (2)

In so doing, he may specify the period within which the information must be provided and how the information must be verified.

Enforcement

1234. Suspension notices

(1) The Independent Supervisor may issue-

    (a) a notice (a "suspension notice") suspending an Auditor General's eligibility for appointment as a statutory auditor in relation to all persons, or any specified person or persons, indefinitely or until a date specified in the notice;

    (b) a notice amending or revoking a suspension notice previously issued to an Auditor General.

(2) In determining whether it is appropriate to issue a notice under subsection (1), the Independent Supervisor must have regard to-

    (a) the Auditor General's performance of the obligations imposed on him by or by virtue of this Part, and

    (b) the Auditor General's performance of his functions as a statutory auditor.

(3) A notice under subsection (1) must-

    (a) be in writing, and

    (b) state the date on which it takes effect (which must be after the period of three months beginning with the date on which it is issued).

(4) Before issuing a notice under subsection (1), the Independent Supervisor must-

    (a) give written notice of its intention to do so to the Auditor General, and

    (b) publish the notice mentioned in paragraph (a) in such manner as it thinks appropriate for bringing it to the attention of any other persons who are likely to be affected.

(5) A notice under subsection (4) must-

    (a) state the reasons for which the Independent Supervisor proposes to act, and

    (b) give particulars of the rights conferred by subsection (6).

(6) A person within subsection (7) may, within the period of three months beginning with the date of service or publication of the notice under subsection (4) or such longer period as the Independent Supervisor may allow, make written representations to the Independent Supervisor and, if desired, oral representations to a person appointed for that purpose by the Independent Supervisor.

(7) The persons within this subsection are-

    (a) the Auditor General, and

    (b) any other person who appears to the Independent Supervisor to be affected.

(8) The Independent Supervisor must have regard to any representations made in accordance with subsection (6) in determining-

    (a) whether to issue a notice under subsection (1), and

    (b) the terms of any such notice.

(9) If in any case the Independent Supervisor considers it appropriate to do so in the public interest it may issue a notice under subsection (1), without regard to the restriction in subsection (3)(b), even if-

    (a) no notice has been given or published under subsection (4), or

(b) the period of time for making representations in pursuance of such a notice has not expired.

(10) On issuing a notice under subsection (1), the Independent Supervisor must-

(a) give a copy of the notice to the Auditor General, and

(b) publish the notice in such manner as it thinks appropriate for bringing it to the attention of persons likely to be affected.

(11) In this section "specified" means specified in, or of a description specified in, the suspension notice in question.

GENERAL NOTE

This section deals with notices being given by the Independent Supervisor to an Auditor General suspending his eligibility to act as a statutory auditor.

Subsection (1)

The Independent Supervisor may issue a notice (a "suspension notice") suspending an Auditor General's eligibility for appointment as a statutory auditor if, for instance, he falls short of the standards laid down for performance of statutory audit work. Such a notice can subsequently be amended or revoked.

Subsections (2)-(9)

These subsections set out the provisions as to how the suspension will be effected, the considerations pertaining to the decision to suspend, the reasons for such a decision and so on. In deciding whether to issue a "suspension notice", the Independent Supervisor must have regard to the Auditor General's performance of his obligations and his functions as a statutory auditor (subs.(2)). The notice must be in writing and state the date on which it takes effect, which must be after a period of three months (subs.(3)), unless there are overriding considerations of public interest (subs.(9)). However, before it is issued the Independent Supervisor must give notice of his intention to do so to the Auditor General and other interested parties (subs.(4)), stating the reasons for issuing the notice (subs.(5)). The Auditor General or other interested party (subs.(7)) may, normally within three months, make written and, as appropriate, oral representations (subs.(6)), which have to be considered by the Independent Supervisor (subs.(8)).

Subsection (10)

The Independent Supervisor must give a copy of a "suspension notice" issued under subs.(1) to the Auditor General and publish it in such a way to bring it to the attention of potentially interested parties.

Subseciton (11)

This subsection defines the meaning of "specified" in this section.

1235.   Effect of suspension notices

(1) An Auditor General must not act as a statutory auditor at any time when a suspension notice issued to him in respect of the audited person has effect.

(2) If at any time during an Auditor General's term of office as a statutory auditor a suspension notice issued to him in respect of the audited person takes effect, he must immediately-

(a) resign his office (with immediate effect), and

(b) give notice in writing to the audited person that he has resigned by reason of his becoming ineligible for appointment.

(3) A suspension notice does not make an Auditor General ineligible for appointment as a statutory auditor for the purposes of section 1213 (effect of ineligibility: criminal offences).

GENERAL NOTE

This section outlines the effect of the Independent Supervisor issuing a suspension notice.

Subsection (1)

An Auditor General must not act as a statutory auditor of a particular entity if he is suspended in relation to that entity.

If the suspension starts during his term of office, the Auditor General must resign as a statutory auditor immediately and inform in writing the audited entity that he has resigned.

Subsection (3)

This makes it clear that the criminal offences identified in s.1213 (effect of ineligibility for appointment as a statutory auditor) do not apply to an Auditor General who is ineligible by virtue of a suspension notice.

1236. Compliance orders

(1) If at any time it appears to the Independent Supervisor that an Auditor General has failed to comply with an obligation imposed on him by or by virtue of this Part, the Independent Supervisor may make an application to the court under this section.
(2) If on an application under this section the court decides that the Auditor General has failed to comply with the obligation in question, it may order the Auditor General to take such steps as the court directs for securing that the obligation is complied with.
(3) In this section "the court" means the High Court or, in Scotland, the Court of Session.

GENERAL NOTE

This section deals with the issue of a court order requiring an Auditor General to comply with obligations imposed on him by the Independent Supervisor.

Subsection (1)

This subsection enables the Independent Supervisor to take an Auditor General to court if he fails to comply with any obligation imposed by or by virtue of this Part of the Act

Subsection (2)

The court may direct the Auditor General to take such steps as it thinks fit to ensure compliance.

Subsection (3)

This subsection defines the term "the court" to mean the High Court or, in Scotland, the Court of Session.

Proceedings

1237. Proceedings involving the Independent Supervisor

(1) If the Independent Supervisor is an unincorporated association, any relevant proceedings may be brought by or against it in the name of any body corporate whose constitution provides for the establishment of the body.
(2) For this purpose "relevant proceedings" means proceedings brought in or in connection with the exercise of any function by the body as the Independent Supervisor.
(3) Where an appointment under section 1228 is revoked, the revoking order may make such provision as the Secretary of State thinks fit with respect to pending proceedings.

GENERAL NOTE

This section provides that where the Independent Supervisor is an unincorporated association, it may initiate proceedings in the name of the body corporate under which it is constituted.

Subsection (1)

Where the Independent Supervisor is an unincorporated association, it may take "relevant proceedings" in the name of the body corporate under which it is constituted.

Subsection (2)

This subsection defines "relevant proceedings".

Subsection (3)

This subsection deals with the situation where an appointment under s.1228 is revoked, indicating that the revoking order may make provision as the Secretary of State sees fit with respect to pending proceedings.

Grants

1238. Grants to the Independent Supervisor

In section 16 of the Companies (Audit, Investigations and Community Enterprise) Act 2004 (c. 27) (grants to bodies concerned with accounting standards etc), after subsection (2)(k) insert-

    "(ka) exercising functions of the Independent Supervisor appointed under Chapter 3 of Part 42 of the Companies Act 2006;".

GENERAL NOTE

This section amends s.16(2) of the Companies (Audit, Investigations and Community Enterprise) Act 2004. The effect of the amendment is that the body that carries out the functions of the Independent Supervisor is eligible for grants from the Secretary of State under s.16 of that Act to meet the expenditure of the body and any subsidiary undertaking. It also means that the body may be exempt from liability in damages under s.18 of the Act.

CHAPTER 4

THE REGISTER OF AUDITORS ETC

1239. The register of auditors

(1) The Secretary of State must make regulations requiring the keeping of a register of-
    (a) the persons eligible for appointment as a statutory auditor, and
    (b) third country auditors (see Chapter 5) who apply to be registered in the specified manner and in relation to whom specified requirements are met.

(2) The regulations must require each person's entry in the register to contain-
    (a) his name and address,
    (b) in the case of an individual eligible for appointment as a statutory auditor, the specified information relating to any firm on whose behalf he is responsible for statutory audit work,
    (c) in the case of a firm eligible for appointment as a statutory auditor, the specified information relating to the individuals responsible for statutory audit work on its behalf,
    (d) in the case of an individual or firm eligible for appointment as a statutory auditor by virtue of Chapter 2, the name of the relevant supervisory body, and
    (e) in the case of a firm eligible for appointment as a statutory auditor by virtue of Chapter 2 or a third country auditor, the information mentioned in subsection (3),

and may require each person's entry to contain other specified information.

(3) The information referred to in subsection (2)(e) is-
    (a) in relation to a body corporate, except where paragraph (b) applies, the name and address of each person who is a director of the body or holds any shares in it;
    (b) in relation to a limited liability partnership, the name and address of each member of the partnership;
    (c) in relation to a corporation sole, the name and address of the individual for the time being holding the office by the name of which he is the corporation sole;
    (d) in relation to a partnership, the name and address of each partner.

(4) The regulations may provide that different parts of the register are to be kept by different persons.

(5) The regulations may impose such obligations as the Secretary of State thinks fit on-
  (a) recognised supervisory bodies,
  (b) any body designated by order under section 1252 (delegation of Secretary of State's functions),
  (c) persons eligible for appointment as a statutory auditor,
  (d) third country auditors,
  (e) any person with whom arrangements are made by one or more recognised supervisory bodies, or by any body designated by order under section 1252, with respect to the keeping of the register, or
  (f) the Independent Supervisor appointed under section 1228.

(6) The regulations may include-
  (a) provision requiring that specified entries in the register be open to inspection at times and places specified or determined in accordance with the regulations;
  (b) provision enabling a person to require a certified copy of specified entries in the register;
  (c) provision authorising the charging of fees for inspection, or the provision of copies, of such reasonable amount as may be specified or determined in accordance with the regulations.

(7) The Secretary of State may direct in writing that the requirements imposed by the regulations in accordance with subsections (2)(e) and (3), or such of those requirements as are specified in the direction, are not to apply, in whole or in part, in relation to a particular registered third country auditor or class of registered third country auditors.

(8) The obligations imposed by regulations under this section on such persons as are mentioned in subsection (5)(b) or (e) are enforceable on the application of the Secretary of State by injunction or, in Scotland, by an order under section 45 of the Court of Session Act 1988 (c. 36).

(9) In this section "specified" means specified by regulations under this section.

(10) Regulations under this section are subject to negative resolution procedure.

GENERAL NOTE

This section restates s.35 of the 1989 Act, but extends the provision to cover other statutory auditors (as defined in s.1210) and third country auditors (as defined in s.1241).

Subsection (1)

This requires the Secretary of State to make regulations that require the keeping of a register of those persons eligible to be a statutory auditor and registered third country auditors.

Subsection (2)

This subsection sets out the information that must be included on the register with respect to each person. This includes their name and address and the name of the relevant supervisory body. If an individual statutory auditor works for a firm that is a statutory auditor, both must be entered separately on the register and cross-referenced.

Subsection (3)

This requires additional information (namely, the name and address of directors, members or partners) to be disclosed in the register by bodies corporate (including limited liability partnerships), corporations sole, and partnerships.

Subsection (4)

This subsection allows for certain parts of the register to be kept by different persons: for instance, an oversight body may keep the information regarding third country auditors, whilst the recognised supervisory bodies may keep information regarding other statutory auditors.

Subsection (5)

Subsection (5)

The Secretary of State is empowered to impose obligations under the regulations as he sees fit on recognised supervisory bodies, any body delegated under s.1252 to carry out the Secretary of State's functions, persons eligible for appointment as statutory auditors, third country auditors, any person with whom arrangements have been made to keep the register, or the Independent Supervisor.

Subsection (6)

This confers a power to provide that information in the register, or a certified copy of it, should be made available to the public upon request, either by inspection or by obtaining certified copies. A reasonable charge for access to this information is permitted.

Subsection (7)

This subsection permits the Secretary of State to disapply some or all of the requirements of subss.(2)(e) and (3) in relation to third country auditors (for instance, if they are already subject to equivalent supervision in their home country).

Subsection (8)

The obligations imposed are enforceable by injunction or (in Scotland) by an order under s.45 of the Court of Session Act 1988.

Subsection (9)

This subsection defines the meaning of "specified" under this section.

Subsection (10)

This indicates that regulations under this section are subject to the negative resolution procedure: see s.1289.

1240.   Information to be made available to public

(1) The Secretary of State may make regulations requiring a person eligible for appointment as a statutory auditor, or a member of a specified class of such persons, to keep and make available to the public specified information, including information regarding-
    (a) the person's ownership and governance,
    (b) the person's internal controls with respect to the quality and independence of its audit work,
    (c) the person's turnover, and
    (d) the audited persons of whom the person has acted as statutory auditor.
(2) Regulations under this section may-
    (a) impose such obligations as the Secretary of State thinks fit on persons eligible for appointment as a statutory auditor;
    (b) require the information to be made available to the public in a specified manner.
(3) In this section "specified" means specified by regulations under this section.
(4) Regulations under this section are subject to negative resolution procedure.

GENERAL NOTE

This is a new provision that gives the Secretary of State power to make regulations placing an obligation on statutory auditors to make information available to the public regarding the ownership and governance of their firms, as well as the internal controls that exist relating to quality and independence of audit work, turnover, and the names of entities for which the person has acted as statutory auditor. Any such obligations are additional to those referred to in s.1239.

Subsection (1)

The Secretary of State is authorised to make regulations requiring a person eligible for appointment as a statutory auditor, or a member of a particular class of persons, to keep and make available to the public specified information regarding the ownership and governance of their firms, internal controls with respect to the quality and independence of audit work, turnover, and the entities for which they have acted as statutory auditor.

Subsection (2)

Regulations issued under this section may impose such obligations as the Secretary of State deems fit on persons eligible for appointment as a statutory auditor, and they may also determine the information to be disclosed in a specified manner.

Subsection (9)

This subsection defines the meaning of "specified" under this section.

Subsection (10)

This indicates that regulations under this section are subject to the negative resolution procedure: see s.1289.

CHAPTER 5

REGISTERED THIRD COUNTRY AUDITORS

Introductory

1241. Meaning of "third country auditor", "registered third country auditor" etc

(1) In this Part-

"third country auditor" means the auditor of the accounts of a traded non-Community company, and the expressions "third country audit" and "third country audit work" are to be construed accordingly;

"registered third country auditor" means a third country auditor who is entered in the register kept in accordance with regulations under section 1239(1).

(2) In subsection (1) "traded non-Community company" means a body corporate-

(a) which is incorporated or formed under the law of a country or territory which is not a member State or part of a member State,

(b) whose transferable securities are admitted to trading on a regulated market situated or operating in the United Kingdom, and

(c) which has not been excluded, or is not of a description of bodies corporate which has been excluded, from this definition by an order made by the Secretary of State.

(3) For this purpose-

"regulated market" has the meaning given by Article 4.1(14) of Directive 2004/39/EC of the European Parliament and of the Council on markets in financial instruments;

"transferable securities" has the meaning given by Article 4.1(18) of that Directive.

(4) An order under this section is subject to negative resolution procedure.

GENERAL NOTE

This is a new provision that sets out the definition of a third country auditor and a registered third country auditor.

Subsection (1)

This subsection provides that a "third country auditor" is an auditor (whether based in the United Kingdom or not) of the accounts of a "traded non-Community company". A "registered third country auditor" means a "third country auditor" who is entered in the register (see s.1239(1)).

Subsection (2)

This defines a "traded non-Community company" as one incorporated or formed in a non-EU country, whose shares are admitted for trading on a United Kingdom "regulated market", such as the London Stock Exchange.

Subsection (3)

This defines terms used in subs.(2), namely "regulated market" and "transferable securities".

Subsection (4)

This indicates that an order under this section is subject to the negative resolution procedure: see s.1289.

Duties

1242.   Duties of registered third country auditors

(1) A registered third country auditor must participate in-
    (a) arrangements within paragraph 1 of Schedule 12 (arrangements for independent monitoring of audits of traded non-Community companies), and
    (b) arrangements within paragraph 2 of that Schedule (arrangements for independent investigation for disciplinary purposes of public interest cases).
(2) A registered third country auditor must-
    (a) take such steps as may be reasonably required of it to enable its performance of third country audits to be monitored by means of inspections carried out under the arrangements mentioned in subsection (1)(a), and
    (b) comply with any decision as to disciplinary action to be taken against it made under the arrangements mentioned in subsection (1)(b).
(3) Schedule 12 makes further provision with respect to the arrangements in which registered third country auditors are required to participate.
(4) The Secretary of State may direct in writing that subsections (1) to (3) are not to apply, in whole or in part, in relation to a particular registered third country auditor or class of registered third country auditors.

GENERAL NOTE
    This section outlines the supervision arrangements relating to registered third country auditors.

Subsections (1)-(3)
    These subsections require registered third country auditors to be subject to systems of independent monitoring and discipline in the United Kingdom in accordance with Sch.12 (subs.(1)). These provisions are similar to supervision arrangements for statutory auditors contained in s.1212(1) (membership of a Recognised Supervisory Body) and s.1217 (Supervisory Bodies) and Sch.10: e.g. with respect to monitoring via inspections and compliance with disciplinary decisions (subs.(2)). Schedule 12 makes additional provisions with respect to arrangements affecting third country auditors (subs.(3)).

Subsection (4)
    This subsection empowers the Secretary of State to disapply the requirements, in whole or in part, in subss.(1)-(3) to a particular third country auditor or to a class of third country auditors. For instance, he may disapply the requirements if satisfied that the third country auditor is already subject to equivalent supervision arrangements in his home country.

Information

GENERAL NOTE
    These sections replicate for registered third country auditors the requirements in ss.1223 and 1224 for the notification of information to the Secretary of State. Third country auditors may be required to provide any information that might reasonably be required for the Secretary of State to carry out his functions.

1243.   Matters to be notified to the Secretary of State

(1) The Secretary of State may require a registered third country auditor-
    (a) to notify him immediately of the occurrence of such events as he may specify in writing and to give him such information in respect of those events as is so specified;
    (b) to give him, at such times or in respect of such periods as he may specify in writing, such information as is so specified.

(2) The notices and information required to be given must be such as the Secretary of State may reasonably require for the exercise of his functions under this Part.

(3) The Secretary of State may require information given under this section to be given in a specified form or verified in a specified manner.

(4) Any notice or information required to be given under this section must be given in writing unless the Secretary of State specifies or approves some other manner.

GENERAL NOTE

This section details the powers of the Secretary of State in respect of his requiring registered third country auditors to provide him with certain specified information.

Subsection (1)

This subsection enables the Secretary of State to require a registered third country auditor to notify him in writing of certain specified events, if they should occur.

Subsections (2)-(4)

The information required must be such as is reasonably required for the Secretary of State to carry out his functions - e.g. it might include annual reports, or notification of rule or bye-law changes (subs.(2)). The information may be required to be given in a specified form or be verified in some way (subs.(3)), and either be submitted in writing or in some other specified manner (subs.(4)). The information so required might relate to specific time periods or specific occurrences.

1244. The Secretary of State's power to call for information

(1) The Secretary of State may by notice in writing require a registered third country auditor to give him such information as he may reasonably require for the exercise of his functions under this Part.

(2) The Secretary of State may require that any information which he requires under this section is to be given within such reasonable time and verified in such manner as he may specify.

GENERAL NOTE

This section gives the Secretary of State power to require information to be supplied to him by a registered third country auditor.

Subsection (1)

This subsection enables the Secretary of State to require, by giving notice in writing, information from a registered third country auditor. (For instance, as a result of a report provided under s.1243, the Secretary of State may request further information on a specific point to clarify if a third country auditor is complying with the requirements in Sch.12.)

Subsection (2)

The Secretary of State can specify the time period in which this information has to be provided and also that it should be verified in some specified manner.

Enforcement

1245. Compliance orders

(1) If at any time it appears to the Secretary of State that a registered third country auditor has failed to comply with an obligation imposed on him by or by virtue of this Part, the Secretary of State may make an application to the court under this section.

(2) If on an application under this section the court decides that the auditor has failed to comply with the obligation in question, it may order the auditor to take such steps as the court directs for securing that the obligation is complied with.

(3) In this section "the court" means the High Court or, in Scotland, the Court of Session.

GENERAL NOTE

This section empowers the Secretary of State to apply for a court order if a registered third country auditor fails to comply with an obligation imposed upon him.

Subsection (1)

This subsection states that the Secretary of State may apply to the court for an order to make a registered third country auditor comply with his obligations under this Part of the Act.

Subsection (2)

The court may direct the registered third country auditor to take such steps as it thinks fit to ensure compliance.

Subsection (3)

This subsection defines the term "the court" to mean the High Court or, in Scotland, the Court of Session.

1246. Removal of third country auditors from the register of auditors

(1) The Secretary of State may, by regulations, confer on the person keeping the register in accordance with regulations under section 1239(1) power to remove a third country auditor from the register.

(2) Regulations under this section must require the person keeping the register, in determining whether to remove a third country auditor from the register, to have regard to the auditor's compliance with obligations imposed on him by or by virtue of this Part.

(3) Where provision is made under section 1239(4) (different parts of the register to be kept by different persons), references in this section to the person keeping the register are to the person keeping that part of the register which relates to third country auditors.

(4) Regulations under this section are subject to negative resolution procedure.

GENERAL NOTE

This section deals with the powers to remove a third country auditor from the register of auditors.

Subsection (1)

The provisions in this section empower the Secretary of State to make provision as to the removal of the third country auditors from the register of auditors in certain circumstances.

Subsection (2)

In doing so, regard must be had to whether the third country auditor has complied with his obligations under this Part of the Act.

Subsection (3)

This subsection deals with the situation where different parts of the register are kept by different persons under s.1239(4).

Subsection (4)

This indicates that regulations under this section are subject to the negative resolution procedure: see s.1289.

1247. Grants to bodies concerned with arrangements under Schedule 12

In section 16 of the Companies (Audit, Investigations and Community Enterprise) Act 2004 (c. 27) (grants to bodies concerned with accounting standards etc), after subsection (2)(ka) (inserted by section 1238) insert-

> "(kb) establishing, maintaining or carrying out arrangements within paragraph 1 or 2 of Schedule 12 to the Companies Act 2006;".

GENERAL NOTE

GENERAL NOTE

This section amends s.16(2) of the Companies (Audit, Investigations and Community Enterprise) Act 2004. The effect of the amendment is that the body that under s.1252 carries out the delegated functions of the Secretary of State in relation to third country auditors is eligible for grants from the Secretary of State under s.16 of that Act. It also means that the body may be exempt from liability in damages under s.18 of the Act.

CHAPTER 6

SUPPLEMENTARY AND GENERAL

GENERAL NOTE

Sections 1248-1249 restate s.29 of the 1989 Act, empowering the Secretary of State to require a second audit of a company in circumstances where the person appointed as statutory auditor was not eligible for appointment or was not independent of the company audited.

Power to require second company audit

1248. Secretary of State's power to require second audit of a company

(1) This section applies where a person appointed as statutory auditor of a company was not an appropriate person for any part of the period during which the audit was conducted.

(2) The Secretary of State may direct the company concerned to retain an appropriate person-

    (a) to conduct a second audit of the relevant accounts, or

    (b) to review the first audit and to report (giving his reasons) whether a second audit is needed.

(3) For the purposes of subsections (1) and (2) a person is "appropriate" if he-

    (a) is eligible for appointment as a statutory auditor or, if the person is an Auditor General, for appointment as statutory auditor of the company, and

    (b) is not prohibited by section 1214(1) (independence requirement) from acting as statutory auditor of the company.

(4) The Secretary of State must send a copy of a direction under subsection (2) to the registrar of companies.

(5) The company is guilty of an offence if-

    (a) it fails to comply with a direction under subsection (2) within the period of 21 days beginning with the date on which it is given, or

    (b) it has been convicted of a previous offence under this subsection and the failure to comply with the direction which led to the conviction continues after the conviction.

(6) The company must-

    (a) send a copy of a report under subsection (2)(b) to the registrar of companies, and

    (b) if the report states that a second audit is needed, take such steps as are necessary for the carrying out of that audit.

(7) The company is guilty of an offence if-

    (a) it fails to send a copy of a report under subsection (2)(b) to the registrar within the period of 21 days beginning with the date on which it receives it,

    (b) in a case within subsection (6)(b), it fails to take the steps mentioned immediately it receives the report, or

    (c) it has been convicted of a previous offence under this subsection and the failure to send a copy of the report, or take the steps, which led to the conviction continues after the conviction.

(8) A company guilty of an offence under this section is liable on summary conviction-

    (a) in a case within subsection (5)(a) or (7)(a) or (b), to a fine not exceeding level 5 on the standard scale, and

(b) in a case within subsection (5)(b) or (7)(c), to a fine not exceeding one-tenth of level 5 on the standard scale for each day on which the failure continues.

(9) In this section "registrar of companies" has the meaning given by section 1060.

GENERAL NOTE

This section deals with the Secretary of State's power to require a second audit where the person appointed as statutory auditor was not an "appropriate" person.

Subsection (1)

This subsection replaces subss.(1), (2), (3) and (5) of s.29 of the 1989 Act and identifies that the section applies where the person appointed as statutory auditor was not an "appropriate" person for part of the period covered by the audit.

Subsection (2)

The Secretary of State is permitted to direct that an appropriate person should undertake a second audit or review the first audit, reporting (with reasons) whether a second audit is required.

Subsection (3)

A person is "inappropriate" to act as a statutory auditor if he is ineligible or is prohibited by s.1214(1) from acting through lack of independence.

Subsection (4)

The Secretary of State is required to send a copy of a direction issued under subs.(2) to the registrar of companies.

Subsection (5)

This sets out the nature of the offence committed by a company if it fails to comply with a direction issued under subs.(2).

Subsection (6)

The company is required to send a copy of the report received under subs.(2) as part of the review of a first audit to the registrar of companies and make arrangements for the conduct of a second audit.

Subsection (7)

The company is guilty of an offence if it fails to comply with the requirements laid out in subss.(2) and (6).

Subsection (8)

This subsection outlines the penalties for not complying with the various requirements in this section relating to a second audit.

Subsection (9)

This defines "registrar of companies" as being the meaning given in s.1060.

1249. Supplementary provision about second audits

(1) If a person accepts an appointment, or continues to act, as statutory auditor of a company at a time when he knows he is not an appropriate person, the company may recover from him any costs incurred by it in complying with the requirements of section 1248.

For this purpose "appropriate" is to be construed in accordance with subsection (3) of that section.

(2) Where a second audit is carried out under section 1248, any statutory or other provision applying in relation to the first audit applies also, in so far as practicable, in relation to the second audit.

(3) A direction under section 1248(2) is, on the application of the Secretary of State, enforceable by injunction or, in Scotland, by an order under section 45 of the Court of Session Act 1988 (c. 36).

GENERAL NOTE

GENERAL NOTE

This section replaces subss.(4), (6), and (7) of s.29 of the 1989 Act and makes further provisions with respect to a second audit.

Subsection (1)

This subsection allows the audited person to recover the costs of the second audit from the first auditor, if the first auditor knew when he acted that he was not eligible or not independent.

Subsection (2)

Any statutory or other provision applying in relation to a first audit equally applies to a second audit.

Subsection (3)

A direction issued under subs.(2) of s.1248 can be enforced, on application by the Secretary of State, by injunction or, in Scotland, by an order under s.45 of the Court of Session Act 1988.

False and misleading statements

1250. Misleading, false and deceptive statements

(1) A person is guilty of an offence if-
    (a) for the purposes of or in connection with any application under this Part, or
    (b) in purported compliance with any requirement imposed on him by or by virtue of this Part,

he knowingly or recklessly furnishes information which is misleading, false or deceptive in a material particular.

(2) It is an offence for a person whose name does not appear on the register of auditors kept under regulations under section 1239 in an entry made under subsection (1)(a) of that section to describe himself as a registered auditor or so to hold himself out as to indicate, or be reasonably understood to indicate, that he is a registered auditor.

(3) It is an offence for a person whose name does not appear on the register of auditors kept under regulations under that section in an entry made under subsection (1)(b) of that section to describe himself as a registered third country auditor or so to hold himself out as to indicate, or be reasonably understood to indicate, that he is a registered third country auditor.

(4) It is an offence for a body which is not a recognised supervisory body or a recognised qualifying body to describe itself as so recognised or so to describe itself or hold itself out as to indicate, or be reasonably understood to indicate, that it is so recognised.

(5) A person guilty of an offence under subsection (1) is liable-
    (a) on conviction on indictment, to imprisonment for a term not exceeding two years or to a fine (or both);
    (b) on summary conviction-
        (i) in England and Wales, to imprisonment for a term not exceeding twelve months or to a fine not exceeding the statutory maximum (or both),
        (ii) in Scotland or Northern Ireland, to imprisonment for a term not exceeding six months or to a fine not exceeding the statutory maximum (or both).

In relation to an offence committed before the commencement of section 154(1) of the Criminal Justice Act 2003 (c. 44), for "twelve months" in paragraph (b)(i) substitute "six months".

(6) Subject to subsection (7), a person guilty of an offence under subsection (2), (3) or (4) is liable on summary conviction-
    (a) in England and Wales, to imprisonment for a term not exceeding 51 weeks or to a fine not exceeding level 5 on the standard scale (or both),
    (b) in Scotland or Northern Ireland, to imprisonment for a term not exceeding six months or to a fine not exceeding level 5 on the standard scale (or both).

In relation to an offence committed before the commencement of section 281(5) of the Criminal Justice Act 2003, for "51 weeks" in paragraph (a) substitute "six months".

(7) Where a contravention of subsection (2), (3) or (4) involves a public display of the offending description, the maximum fine that may be imposed is an amount equal to level 5 on the standard scale multiplied by the number of days for which the display has continued.

(8) It is a defence for a person charged with an offence under subsection (2), (3) or (4) to show that he took all reasonable precautions and exercised all due diligence to avoid the commission of the offence.

GENERAL NOTE

This section is a restatement of the offences in s.41 of the 1989 Act, but it also extends these offences to third country auditors.

Subsection (1)

This sets out offences in respect of persons who provide information that they know to be misleading, false or deceptive.

Subsections (2) and (3)

Subsection (2) makes it an offence for a person to hold himself out as a registered auditor when he is not registered as such in accordance with s.1239. Subsection (3) makes a similar provision for third country auditors.

Subsection (4)

It is an offence for either a supervisory or qualifying body to hold itself out as recognised when it is not so recognised.

Subsections (5)-(7)

These subsections indicate the penalties for being guilty of offences under subs.(1) (subs.(5)) and subss.(2)-(4) (subs.(6)), the latter being qualified in subs.(7) if the offence involves a person or body publicly holding themselves out as registered or recognised.

Subsection (8)

This subsection provides a defence with respect to offences under subss.(2)-(4) if the person took all reasonable precautions and exercised due diligence to avoid committing the offence.

Fees

1251. Fees

(1) An applicant for a recognition order under this Part must pay such fee in respect of his application as the Secretary of State may by regulations prescribe; and no application is to be regarded as duly made unless this subsection is complied with.

(2) The Secretary of State may by regulations prescribe periodical fees to be paid by-
    (a) every recognised supervisory body,
    (b) every recognised qualifying body,
    (c) every Auditor General, and
    (d) every registered third country auditor.

(3) Fees received by the Secretary of State by virtue of this Part are to be paid into the Consolidated Fund.

(4) Regulations under this section are subject to negative resolution procedure.

GENERAL NOTE

This section is based on s.45 of the 1989 Act.

Subsection (1)
This subsection provides for the payment of fees by applicants for recognition, as set out in regulations issued by the Secretary of State.

Subsection (2)
The periodical fees are payable, not only by recognised supervisory and qualifying bodies as previously, but also now by the Auditors General and registered third country auditors.

Subsection (3)
The fees are to be paid into the Consolidated Fund.

Subsection (4)
This indicates that regulations under this section are subject to the negative resolution procedure: see s.1289.

Delegation of Secretary of State's functions

GENERAL NOTE

Sections 1252-1253 replace ss.46 and 46A of the 1989 Act, as amended by para.(2)(2) of Sch.2 to the Competition Act 1998 and Other Enactments (Amendment) Regulations (SI 2004/1261) and ss.3-5 of the Companies (Audit, Investigations and Community Enterprise) Act 2004. Under these sections, the Secretary of State is empowered to establish a body, or to appoint an existing body, to exercise his functions relating to statutory auditors and the recognition of bodies that supervise auditors and/or provide professional qualifications.

The power to exercise the Secretary of State's functions under s.46 of the 1989 Act have currently been delegated under SI 2005/2337 to the Professional Oversight Board for Accountancy of the Financial Reporting Council (FRC) (see www.opsi.gov.uk/si/si2005/20052337.htm)

1252. Delegation of the Secretary of State's functions

(1) The Secretary of State may make an order under this section (a "delegation order") for the purpose of enabling functions of the Secretary of State under this Part to be exercised by a body designated by the order.

(2) The body designated by a delegation order may be either-
   (a) a body corporate which is established by the order, or
   (b) subject to section 1253, a body (whether a body corporate or an unincorporated association) which is already in existence ("an existing body").

(3) A delegation order has the effect of making the body designated by the order designated under section 5 of the Freedom of Information Act 2000 (c. 36) (further powers to designate public authorities).

(4) A delegation order has the effect of transferring to the body designated by it all functions of the Secretary of State under this Part-
   (a) subject to such exceptions and reservations as may be specified in the order, and
   (b) except-
      (i) his functions in relation to the body itself, and
      (ii) his functions under section 1228 (appointment of Independent Supervisor).

(5) A delegation order may confer on the body designated by it such other functions supplementary or incidental to those transferred as appear to the Secretary of State to be appropriate.

(6) Any transfer of functions under the following provisions must be subject to the reservation that the functions remain exercisable concurrently by the Secretary of State-
   (a) section 1224 (power to call for information from recognised bodies etc);
   (b) section 1244 (power to call for information from registered third country auditors);
   (c) section 1254 (directions to comply with international obligations).

(7) Any transfer of-

    (a) the function of refusing to make a declaration under section 1221(1) (approval of overseas qualifications) on the grounds referred to in section 1221(4) (lack of comparable treatment), or

    (b) the function of withdrawing such a declaration under section 1221(7) on those grounds,

must be subject to the reservation that the function is exercisable only with the consent of the Secretary of State.

(8) A delegation order may be amended or, if it appears to the Secretary of State that it is no longer in the public interest that the order should remain in force, revoked by a further order under this section.

(9) Where functions are transferred or resumed, the Secretary of State may by order confer or, as the case may be, take away such other functions supplementary or incidental to those transferred or resumed as appear to him to be appropriate.

(10) Where a delegation order is made, Schedule 13 has effect with respect to-

    (a) the status of the body designated by the order in exercising functions of the Secretary of State under this Part,

    (b) the constitution and proceedings of the body where it is established by the order,

    (c) the exercise by the body of certain functions transferred to it, and

    (d) other supplementary matters.

(11) An order under this section which has the effect of transferring or resuming any functions is subject to affirmative resolution procedure.

(12) Any other order under this section is subject to negative resolution procedure.

GENERAL NOTE

This section derives from s.46 of the 1989 Act and deals with the Secretary of State's power to delegate his functions under this Part of the Act to a specified body.

A House of Commons amendment to drop subs.(3) was overruled by the House of Lords, although it was widely understood that it would be removed when the Bill finally returned to the Commons. However, it was not, apparently due to procedural or timetabling concerns rather than for policy reasons. Subsection (3) has legal and practical implications for oversight of the auditing profession by the Public Oversight Board ("POB") and - even though it is not technically carrying out delegated functions on behalf of the Secretary of State - the FRC's Audit Inspection Unit ("AIU") reporting on individual firms. The problem is basically that designation as a delegated body under the Freedom of Information Act means that all reports and related material will have to be available for anyone to access, although there are exemptions (e.g. for commercially sensitive information).

Subsection (1)

The Secretary of State is empowered to make a "delegation order" to enable his functions under this Part of the Act to be exercised by a designated body.

Subsection (2)

The designated body may either be established specifically for the purpose or be an existing body.

Subsection (3)

The delegation order has the effect of making the nominated body subject to s.5 of the Freedom of Information Act 2000.

Subsections (4)-(7)

The delegation order will transfer to the body all the functions of the Secretary of State under this Part of the Act, apart from his powers with respect to the designated body and to appoint an Independent Supervisor under s.1228 (subs.(4)). Other functions may be conferred on the designated body (subs.(5)), but the Secretary of State will still be able to exercise powers concurrently with respect to the provisions of ss.1224 and 1244 on the power to call for information and s.1254 concerning the power to issue directions to comply with international obligations (subs.(6)). Furthermore, delegated functions under s.1221(1) and 1221(7), concerning overseas qualifications, can only be exercised with the consent of the Secretary of State (subs.(7)).

A delegation order can be amended or be revoked (subs.(8)), and the Secretary of State may by order confer or take away supplementary or incidental functions as he sees fit (subs.(9)).

Subsection (10)

Where a delegation order is made, the provisions of Sch.13, "Supplementary provisions with respect to delegation order", have effect.

Subsections (11) and (12)

The delegation order itself is subject to the affirmative resolution procedure (see s.1290) (subs.11)), and other orders made under s.1252 to the negative resolution procedure (see s.1289) (subs.(12)).

1253.   Delegation of functions to an existing body

(1) The Secretary of State's power to make a delegation order under section 1252 which designates an existing body is exercisable in accordance with this section.

(2) The Secretary of State may make such a delegation order if it appears to him that-
    (a) the body is able and willing to exercise the functions that would be transferred by the order, and
    (b) the body has arrangements in place relating to the exercise of those functions which are such as to be likely to ensure that the conditions in subsection (3) are met.

(3) The conditions are-
    (a) that the functions in question will be exercised effectively, and
    (b) where the delegation order is to contain any requirements or other provisions specified under subsection (4), that those functions will be exercised in accordance with any such requirements or provisions.

(4) The delegation order may contain such requirements or other provision relating to the exercise of the functions by the designated body as appear to the Secretary of State to be appropriate.

(5) An existing body-
    (a) may be designated by a delegation order under section 1252, and
    (b) may accordingly exercise functions of the Secretary of State in pursuance of the order,
despite any involvement of the body in the exercise of any functions under arrangements within paragraph 21, 22, 23(1) or 24(1) of Schedule 10 or paragraph 1 or 2 of Schedule 12.

GENERAL NOTE

This section derives from s.46A of the 1989 Act, as inserted, and empowers the Secretary of State to delegate his functions to an existing body, where it is willing and able to act.

Subsections (1) and (2)

The Secretary of State can make a delegation order to an existing body if it appears to him to be appropriate and certain necessary conditions are met.

Subsections (3) and (4)

The conditions are that the Secretary of State should be satisfied that the functions will be exercised effectively (subs.(3)) and other duties delegated to such a body under subs.(4) will be carried out properly.

Subsection (5)

This subsection ensures that an existing body is not precluded from exercising any delegated function on the basis of its involvement with the monitoring, investigation or disciplinary arrangements that are set out in Schs 10 and 12.

International obligations

1254.   Directions to comply with international obligations

(1) If it appears to the Secretary of State-

    (a) that any action proposed to be taken by a recognised supervisory body or a recognised qualifying body, or a body designated by order under section 1252, would be incompatible with Community obligations or any other international obligations of the United Kingdom, or

    (b) that any action which that body has power to take is required for the purpose of implementing any such obligations,

he may direct the body not to take or, as the case may be, to take the action in question.

(2) A direction may include such supplementary or incidental requirements as the Secretary of State thinks necessary or expedient.

(3) A direction under this section given to a body designated by order under section 1252 is enforceable on the application of the Secretary of State by injunction or, in Scotland, by an order under section 45 of the Court of Session Act 1988 (c. 36).

GENERAL NOTE

    This section restates s.40 of the 1989 Act, as modified by para.3(a) of Sch.2 to the Companies (Audit, Investigations and Community Enterprise) Act 2004.

Subsection (1)

    The Secretary of State may direct recognised supervisory or qualifying bodies, or any body delegated under s.1252, to comply with Community or other international obligations.

Subsection (2)

    A direction may include supplementary or incidental requirements as appropriate.

Subsection (3)

    If the body fails to comply with a direction, the Secretary of State can apply to the court for his direction to be enforced by injunction or, in Scotland, by an order under s.45 of the Court of Session Act 1988.

General provision relating to offences

1255.   Offences by bodies corporate, partnerships and unincorporated associations

(1) Where an offence under this Part committed by a body corporate is proved to have been committed with the consent or connivance of, or to be attributable to any neglect on the part of, an officer of the body, or a person purporting to act in any such capacity, he as well as the body corporate is guilty of the offence and liable to be proceeded against and punished accordingly.

(2) Where an offence under this Part committed by a partnership is proved to have been committed with the consent or connivance of, or to be attributable to any neglect on the part of, a partner, he as well as the partnership is guilty of the offence and liable to be proceeded against and punished accordingly.

(3) Where an offence under this Part committed by an unincorporated association (other than a partnership) is proved to have been committed with the consent or connivance of, or to be attributable to any neglect on the part of, any officer of the association or any member of its governing body, he as well as the association is guilty of the offence and liable to be proceeded against and punished accordingly.

GENERAL NOTE

This section restates s.42 of the 1989 Act and deals with offences committed by bodies corporate, partnerships and other unincorporated associations.

Subsections (1)-(3)

Where an offence committed by a body corporate is committed with the consent or connivance of, or is attributable to the neglect of, an officer (in the case of a body corporate) (subs.(1)), a partner (in the case of a partnership) (subs.2)) or an officer or member (in the case of an unincorporated association) (subs.(3)), that officer, partner or member is also guilty of the offence.

1256.   Time limits for prosecution of offences

(1) An information relating to an offence under this Part which is triable by a magistrates' court in England and Wales may be so tried if it is laid at any time within the period of twelve months beginning with the date on which evidence sufficient in the opinion of the Director of Public Prosecutions or the Secretary of State to justify the proceedings comes to his knowledge.

(2) Proceedings in Scotland for an offence under this Part may be commenced at any time within the period of twelve months beginning with the date on which evidence sufficient in the Lord Advocate's opinion to justify proceedings came to his knowledge or, where such evidence was reported to him by the Secretary of State, within the period of twelve months beginning with the date on which it came to the knowledge of the Secretary of State.

(3) For the purposes of subsection (2) proceedings are to be deemed to be commenced on the date on which a warrant to apprehend or cite the accused is granted, if the warrant is executed without undue delay.

(4) A complaint charging an offence under this Part which is triable by a magistrates' court in Northern Ireland may be so tried if it is made at any time within the period of twelve months beginning with the date on which evidence sufficient in the opinion of the Director of Public Prosecutions for Northern Ireland or the Secretary of State to justify the proceedings comes to his knowledge.

(5) This section does not authorise-
   (a) in the case of proceedings in England and Wales, the trial of an information laid,
   (b) in the case of proceedings in Scotland, the commencement of proceedings, or
   (c) in the case of proceedings in Northern Ireland, the trial of a complaint made,
more than three years after the commission of the offence.

(6) For the purposes of this section a certificate of the Director of Public Prosecutions, the Lord Advocate, the Director of Public Prosecutions for Northern Ireland or the Secretary of State as to the date on which such evidence as is referred to above came to his knowledge is conclusive evidence.

(7) Nothing in this section affects proceedings within the time limits prescribed by section 127(1) of the Magistrates' Courts Act 1980 (c. 43), section 331 of the Criminal Procedure (Scotland) Act 1975 or Article 19 of the Magistrates' Courts (Northern Ireland) Order 1981 (S.I. 1981/1675 (N.I. 26)) (the usual time limits for criminal proceedings).

GENERAL NOTE

This section restates s.43 of the 1989 Act and sets a twelve-month time limit for the prosecution of offences within each of the jurisdictions.

Subsections (1)-(4)

These provisions identify that the date on which knowledge of sufficient evidence of the offence becomes known to the Secretary of State or Director of Public Prosecutions (for England and Wales) (subs.(1)), the Lord Advocate (for Scotland) (subss.(2)-(3)) or Director of Public Prosecutions for Northern Ireland (subs.(4)) is taken as the date from which the twelve month time limit commences.

Subsection (5)

In any event, the prosecution may not be commenced if three years have passed since the date on which the offence was committed.

Subsection (6)

A certificate from the relevant prosecuting authority as to the date on which evidence came to his knowledge is to be regarded as conclusive evidence.

Subsection (7)

Nothing in s.1256 affects proceedings within the normal time limits in magistrates courts.

1257. Jurisdiction and procedure in respect of offences

(1) Summary proceedings for an offence under this Part may, without prejudice to any jurisdiction exercisable apart from this section, be taken-
   (a) against a body corporate or unincorporated association at any place at which it has a place of business, and
   (b) against an individual at any place where he is for the time being.
(2) Proceedings for an offence alleged to have been committed under this Part by an unincorporated association must be brought in the name of the association (and not in that of any of its members), and for the purposes of any such proceedings any rules of court relating to the service of documents apply as in relation to a body corporate.
(3) Section 33 of the Criminal Justice Act 1925 (c. 86) and Schedule 3 to the Magistrates' Courts Act 1980 (c. 43) (procedure on charge of offence against a corporation) apply in a case in which an unincorporated association is charged in England and Wales with an offence under this Part as they apply in the case of a corporation.
(4) Section 18 of the Criminal Justice Act (Northern Ireland) 1945 (c. 15 (N.I.)) and Article 166 and Schedule 4 to the Magistrates' Courts (Northern Ireland) Order 1981 (S.I. 1981/1675 (N.I. 26)) (procedure on charge of offence against a corporation) apply in a case in which an unincorporated association is charged in Northern Ireland with an offence under this Part as they apply in the case of a corporation.
(5) In relation to proceedings on indictment in Scotland for an offence alleged to have been committed under this Part by an unincorporated association, section 70 of the Criminal Procedure (Scotland) Act 1995 (proceedings on indictment against bodies corporate) applies as if the association were a body corporate.
(6) A fine imposed on an unincorporated association on its conviction of such an offence must be paid out of the funds of the association.

GENERAL NOTE

This section restates s.44 of the 1989 Act and deals with the jurisdiction and procedure in respect of offences.

Subsection (1)

This specifies that the appropriate jurisdiction is that in which a body corporate or unincorporated association has its place of business or, in the case of an individual, where he is located.

Subsection (2)

This subsection provides that an unincorporated association is to be treated in the same way as a body corporate, with proceedings being brought in its name rather than in the name of any of its members.

Subsections (3)-(5)

These subsections indicate the legislation under which proceedings can be brought in England and Wales (subs.(3)), Northern Ireland (subs.(4)) and Scotland (subs.(5)).

Subsection (6)

A fine on an unincorporated association must be paid out of its funds.

Notices etc

1258. Service of notices

(1) This section has effect in relation to any notice, direction or other document required or authorised by or by virtue of this Part to be given to or served on any person other than the Secretary of State.

(2) Any such document may be given to or served on the person in question-
    (a) by delivering it to him,
    (b) by leaving it at his proper address, or
    (c) by sending it by post to him at that address.

(3) Any such document may-
    (a) in the case of a body corporate, be given to or served on an officer of that body;
    (b) in the case of a partnership, be given to or served on any partner;
    (c) in the case of an unincorporated association other than a partnership, be given to or served on any member of the governing body of that association.

(4) For the purposes of this section and section 7 of the Interpretation Act 1978 (c. 30) (service of documents by post) in its application to this section, the proper address of any person is his last known address (whether of his residence or of a place where he carries on business or is employed) and also-
    (a) in the case of a person who is eligible under the rules of a recognised supervisory body for appointment as a statutory auditor and who does not have a place of business in the United Kingdom, the address of that body;
    (b) in the case of a body corporate or an officer of that body, the address of the registered or principal office of that body in the United Kingdom;
    (c) in the case of an unincorporated association other than a partnership or a member of its governing body, its principal office in the United Kingdom.

GENERAL NOTE

This section restates s.49 of the 1989 Act.

Subsections (1) and (2)

Subsection (1) relates to notices and other documents that may be served under this Part of the Act on any person other than the Secretary of State. The three permitted methods of service are: delivery to the person, leaving the document at the person's address, or sending it by post to the person's address (subs.(2)).

Subsection (3)

A document may be served on an officer of a body corporate, a partner in a partnership, or on a member of the governing body of an unincorporated body other than a partnership.

Subsection (4)

For the purpose of serving a document, the proper address of a person is his last known address or, in the case of a body, its registered address or principal office in the United Kingdom.

1259. Documents in electronic form

(1) This section applies where-
    (a) section 1258 authorises the giving or sending of a notice, direction or other document by its delivery to a particular person ("the recipient"), and

    (b) the notice, direction or other document is transmitted to the recipient-
        (i) by means of an electronic communications network, or
        (ii) by other means but in a form that requires the use of apparatus by the recipient to render it intelligible.

(2) The transmission has effect for the purposes of this Part as a delivery of the notice, direction or other document to the recipient, but only if the recipient has indicated to the person making the transmission his willingness to receive the notice, direction or other document in the form and manner used.

(3) An indication to a person for the purposes of subsection (2)-
    (a) must be given to the person in such manner as he may require,
    (b) may be a general indication or an indication that is limited to notices, directions or other documents of a particular description,
    (c) must state the address to be used,
    (d) must be accompanied by such other information as the person requires for the making of the transmission, and
    (e) may be modified or withdrawn at any time by a notice given to the person in such manner as he may require.

(4) In this section "electronic communications network" has the same meaning as in the Communications Act 2003 (c. 21).

GENERAL NOTE

This is a new provision to allow delivery of notices, directions or other documents in electronic form.

Subsections (1)-(3)

The use of e-communications is permitted where s.1258 authorises the giving or sending of a notice or document (subs.(1)). Such means can be used where provisions in this Part of the Act impose requirements on the giving or sending of notices, directions or other documents, provided the recipient indicates he is prepared to accept this form of delivery (subs.(2)). The requirements for the recipient to indicate that he is prepared to accept this form of delivery are detailed in subs.(3).

Subsection (4)

This subsection defines the term "electronic communications network" for the purposes of this section as having the same meaning as in the Communications Act 2003.

Interpretation

1260.   Meaning of "associate"

(1) In this Part "associate", in relation to a person, is to be construed as follows.

(2) In relation to an individual, "associate" means-
    (a) that individual's spouse, civil partner or minor child or step-child,
    (b) any body corporate of which that individual is a director, and
    (c) any employee or partner of that individual.

(3) In relation to a body corporate, "associate" means-
    (a) any body corporate of which that body is a director,
    (b) any body corporate in the same group as that body, and
    (c) any employee or partner of that body or of any body corporate in the same group.

(4) In relation to a partnership constituted under the law of Scotland, or any other country or territory in which a partnership is a legal person, "associate" means-
    (a) any body corporate of which that partnership is a director,
    (b) any employee of or partner in that partnership, and
    (c) any person who is an associate of a partner in that partnership.

(5) In relation to a partnership constituted under the law of England and Wales or Northern Ireland, or the law of any other country or territory in which a partnership is not a legal person, "associate" means any person who is an associate of any of the partners.

(6) In subsections (2)(b), (3)(a) and (4)(a), in the case of a body corporate which is a limited liability partnership, "director" is to be read as "member".

GENERAL NOTE

This section restates s.52 of the 1989 Act.

Subsections (1)-(5)

These subsections define the meaning of "associate" (subs.(1)) in relation to an individual (subs.(2)), a body corporate (subs.(3)), a partnership where that is a separate legal person (e.g. in Scotland) (subs.(4)), and a partnership that is not a separate legal person (e.g. in England and Wales or in Northern Ireland) (subs.(5)). This definition is particularly relevant for the independence requirement for statutory auditors set out in s.1214.

Subsection (6)

In the case of a body corporate that is a limited liability partnership, the reference to "director" in various subsections is to be read as "member".

1261. Minor definitions

(1) In this Part, unless a contrary intention appears-
"address" means-
  (a) in relation to an individual, his usual residential or business address;
  (b) in relation to a firm, its registered or principal office in the United Kingdom;

"company" means any company or other body the accounts of which must be audited in accordance with Part 16;
"director", in relation to a body corporate, includes any person occupying in relation to it the position of a director (by whatever name called) and any person in accordance with whose directions or instructions (not being advice given in a professional capacity) the directors of the body are accustomed to act;
"firm" means any entity, whether or not a legal person, which is not an individual and includes a body corporate, a corporation sole and a partnership or other unincorporated association;
"group", in relation to a body corporate, means the body corporate, any other body corporate which is its holding company or subsidiary and any other body corporate which is a subsidiary of that holding company;
"holding company" and "subsidiary" are to be read in accordance with section 1159 and Schedule 6;
"officer", in relation to a body corporate, includes a director, a manager, a secretary or, where the affairs of the body are managed by its members, a member;
"parent undertaking" and "subsidiary undertaking" are to be read in accordance with section 1162 and Schedule 7.

(2) For the purposes of this Part a body is to be regarded as "established in the United Kingdom" if and only if-
  (a) it is incorporated or formed under the law of the United Kingdom or a part of the United Kingdom, or
  (b) its central management and control are exercised in the United Kingdom;
and any reference to a qualification "obtained in the United Kingdom" is to a qualification obtained from such a body.

(3) The Secretary of State may by regulations make such modifications of this Part as appear to him to be necessary or appropriate for the purposes of its application in relation to any firm, or description of firm, which is not a body corporate or a partnership.

(4) Regulations under subsection (3) are subject to negative resolution procedure.

GENERAL NOTE

This section is a restatement of s.53 of the 1989 Act, with a number of additional definitions.

Subsection (1)

This lists alphabetically various terms that appear in this Part of the Act, namely: "address", "company", "director", "firm", "group", "holding company", "subsidiary", "officer", "parent undertaking" and "subsidiary undertaking".

Subsection (2)

This indicates that for this Part of the Act a body is to be regarded as "established in the UK" only if it incorporated under the law of the United Kingdom or its central management and control are exercised in the United Kingdom. Likewise, a qualification "obtained in the UK" refers to a qualification obtained from such a body.

Subsection (3)

The Secretary of State may by regulations make appropriate amendments that are needed in relation to the application of this Part of the Act to a "firm" (as defined by subs.(1)) which is not a partnership or body corporate.

Subsection (4)

Regulations under subs.(3) are subject to the negative resolution procedure (see s.1289.)

1262.   Index of defined expressions

The following Table shows provisions defining or otherwise explaining expressions used in this Part (other than provisions defining or explaining an expression used only in the same section)-

Expression	*Provision*
address	section 1261(1)
appropriate qualification	section 1219
associate	section 1260
audited person	section 1210(2)
Auditor General	section 1226(1)
company	section 1261(1)
delegation order	section 1252(1)
director (of a body corporate)	section 1261(1)
enactment	section 1293
established in the United Kingdom	section 1261(2)
firm	section 1261(1)
group (in relation to a body corporate)	section 1261(1)
holding company	section 1261(1)
main purposes of this Part	section 1209
member (of a supervisory body)	section 1217(2)
obtained in the United Kingdom	section 1261(2)
officer	section 1261(1)
parent undertaking	section 1261(1)

Expression	Provision
qualifying body	section 1220(1)
recognised, in relation to a professional qualification	section 1220(3) and Schedule 11
recognised, in relation to a qualifying body	paragraph 1(2) of Schedule 11
recognised, in relation to a supervisory body	section 1217(4) and Schedule 10
registered third country auditor	section 1241(1)
rules of a qualifying body	section 1220(2)
rules of a supervisory body	section 1217(3)
statutory auditor, statutory audit and statutory audit work	section 1210(1)
subsidiary	section 1261(1)
supervisory body	section 1217(1)
subsidiary undertaking	section 1261(1)
third country auditor, third country audit and third country audit work	section 1241(1)

GENERAL NOTE

This provision, which replaces. Section 54 of the 1989 Act, contains an index, set out in tabular form, to the defined terms used in this Part of the Act.

Miscellaneous and general

1263. Power to make provision in consequence of changes affecting accountancy bodies

(1) The Secretary of State may by regulations make such amendments of enactments as appear to him to be necessary or expedient in consequence of any change of name, merger or transfer of engagements affecting-

    (a) a recognised supervisory body or recognised qualifying body, or

    (b) a body of accountants referred to in, or approved, authorised or otherwise recognised for the purposes of, any other enactment.

(2) Regulations under this section are subject to negative resolution procedure.

GENERAL NOTE

This section restates s.51 of the 1989 Act.

Subsection (1)

The Secretary of State is empowered to amend by regulation legislation (including this Act) that refers to recognised supervisory and qualifying bodies and to accountancy bodies in the event of a name change, merger or transfer of engagements affecting such bodies.

Subsection (2)

Regulations issued under subs.(1) are subject to the negative resolution procedure (see s.1289.)

1264. Consequential amendments

Schedule 14 contains consequential amendments relating to this Part.

This new section introduces Sch.14, which contains amendments consequential on this Part of the Act to the Companies (Audit, Investigations and Community Enterprise) Act 2004.

PART 43

TRANSPARENCY OBLIGATIONS AND RELATED MATTERS

GENERAL NOTE

Introduction to Transparency Obligations

Part 43 is a new introduction to United Kingdom company law; or more specifically to United Kingdom securities law. United Kingdom securities law is comprised of a number of different sources: EC directives which have been implemented by means of Act of Parliament (principally the Financial Services and Markets Act 2000, as amended); statutory instruments and Financial Services Authority ("FSA") regulation (as part of the FSA Rulebook); other statutory enactments of the United Kingdom Parliament; and case law appropriate to the jurisdiction in which the issue arises (i.e. Scots law, or English common law and equity). The "transparency obligations" referred to in this Pt 43 are the principles established by the EC Transparency Obligations Directive (2004/109/EC) which was to be implemented into United Kingdom securities law before the end of January 2007. Part 43 of the Companies Act 2006 came into force on the day that the Act received the Royal Assent - that is, on November 8, 2006 - before the remainder of this Act, as is provided by s.1300 of this Act. Implementation of the directive is thus achieved by means of Pt 43 of the Companies Act 2006 and, in time, by the introduction of "Transparency Rules" as part of the FSA Rulebook to give effect to the more detailed provisions both of the directive and of the EC Commission's technical regulation relating to the directive.

A word on nomenclature. In the literature before these provisions were added to the Company Law Reform Bill (which in turn became the Companies Act 2006), this directive was known colloquially as the "Transparency Directive", although the Bill introduced a reference to the "Transparency Obligations Directive": the latter is the name which will be used here. At the time of writing, the Transparency Obligations Directive is discussed in detail in *Palmer's Company Law* at paras 5.307 *et seq.*

Briefly put, transparency obligations impose continuing obligations on the issuers of securities traded on regulated markets to provide certain types of information to investors about those securities once those securities have been issued. Obligations are also imposed on the professional advisors and directors of those issuers. Thus, the "transparency" referred to is the provision of all required information so that it is available to all potential investors. Thus, it is expected, the affairs of the issuing entity will become transparent to the investing community. By contrast, the prospectus requirements on issuers of securities, which were included by addition to the Financial Services and Markets Act 2000 by means of the Prospectus Regulations 2005, imposed obligations on issuers and their advisors relating to securities which were being issued for the first time, whereas the transparency obligations (broadly put) create continuing obligations once those securities have been issued. The detail of these various sets of provisions and the FSA regulations to which they have given rise are considered in detail in *Palmer's Company Law* at para.5.300 et seq.

The implementation structure for the provisions of the Transparency Obligations Directive mirrors that used for the implementation of the preceding EC securities directive: the Prospectus Directive. That directive was implemented by means of the introduction of additional provisions to the Financial Services and Markets Act 2000, by means of the Prospectus Regulations, and also by means of the creation of the Prospectus Rules by the FSA. For this purpose, a statutory instrument was also required to effect those additions. The terms of the Transparency Obligations Directive and of the EC Commission's technical regulation relating to the directive have thus been implemented by means of the Companies Act 2006 introducing new provisions to the Financial Services and Markets Act 2000 and by means of the FSA's Transparency Rules. In the Act are high-level, framework principles and provisions which facilitate and delegate the power for the FSA to implement more detailed provisions by means of its own regulations. The implementation procedure which had been used previously was for some duplication between the Financial Services and Markets Act 2000, statutory instruments implemented further to that Act, and amendment of FSA regulation.

The FSA is acting as the competent authority for the purposes of EC securities law in its role as the United Kingdom Listing Authority ("UKLA").

The EC legislative process in relation to securities law

The process for the creation of EC legislation in this field is as follows. (A more detailed analysis of this procedure is presented in *Palmer's Company Law*, paras 5.300 *et seq.*) The 1957 Treaty of Rome (as amended) which created the principle of free movement of capital within the European Community. However, that principle was not in itself sufficient to spark the creation of an effective single market in financial services. The 1966 Segre Report (Report by a Group of Experts Appointed by the EEC Commission, *The Development of a European Capital Market* (1966)) highlighted shortcomings in the provision of financial services markets across the Community, typified by the different regulatory regimes dealing with securities markets and the provision of investment services between Member States. The next staging-post in the attempt to develop a pan-European securities law was the 1977 Commission recommendation for a European Code of Conduct relating to Transferable Securities (Recommendation 77/534/EEC ([1977] O.J. L212/37)). However, this initiative also failed to trigger the development of a viable, pan-European securities market. The problem remained that securities markets were regulated differently in different Member States, that a security admitted to trading in one jurisdiction would not necessarily qualify to be traded in another jurisdiction, and so forth.

The policy focus therefore shifted towards the mutual recognition principle under which an issue of securities which was approved in one Member State would receive a "passport" whereby it would automatically be authorised for offers to the public in all Member States. The other long-standing policy goal is that of harmonisation, whereby the securities laws of each Member State would become effectively the same. However, recent EC securities directives have expressly permitted national competent authorities to implement these directives in their municipal laws in ways which are more stringent than the minimum requirements of the directive, provided that there is no greater requirement imposed on issues authorised in another Member State than on issues authorised in the jurisdiction enforcing that more stringent municipal law. Thus harmonisation has moved, effectively, to the back-burner, now that it is recognised that not all securities laws within the European Union will be identical; and so Member States are now permitted to "gold-plate" their own securities law by making them more stringent than the minima established in the directive.

The beginnings of the legislative movement towards the harmonisation and passporting of instruments within the European Union can be identified in the Investment Services Directive of 1993 (93/22/EEC); nevertheless, it required the Financial Services Action Plan ("FSAP") of 1999 (COM(1999)232) to reinvigorate the legislative agenda. (Consequently the Investment Services Directive is to be replaced by the Markets in Financial Instruments Directives ("MiFID", 2004/39/EC), which is supposed to be implemented in the United Kingdom by November 2007.) The principal concern was that the lethargy in the production of adequate, harmonised securities regulation across the European Union was due in the part to the slowness with which directives were produced compared to the pace of change and of development in securities markets. In the wake of the FSAP, the so-called "Committee of Wise Men" produced the Lamfalussy Report in 2000 which, inter alia, suggested a new methodology for the creation of EC Directives in this field. This methodology has led to passporting but not true, full harmonisation. Thus authorisations will be recognised across the European Union (a passport) but securities laws will not be identical across the European Union.

The new methodology is comprised of four levels of legislation. The first level identifies framework principles which are to be provided in the directives. Article 249 EC states that:

"A directive shall be binding, as to the result to be achieved, upon each Member State to which it is addressed, but shall leave to the national authorities the choice of form and methods."

Thus the United Kingdom can decide in which form to give effect to the terms of any Directive.

The second level leaves it to the Commission to create rules relating to more technical issues. This division in competence means that the principal legislation in the form of directives need only establish underlying principles without the need to deal with the technical detail which might otherwise delay the legislative process. This second level takes the form of lengthy technical regulations generated by the Commission which, in the United Kingdom, have been transposed into FSA regulation. The third level encapsulates guidance from the Committee of European Securities Regulators ("CESR") which seeks to ensure uniform implementation of the framework principles and the technical material by the competent authorities of each Member State. The fourth level is an enforcement mechanism via the Commission.

There are five directives which are of significance at the time of writing: first, the Consolidated Admission and Reporting Directive of 2001 (2001/34/EC); secondly, the Prospectus Directive (2003/71/EC); thirdly, the Transparency Directive (2004/109/EC) ; fourthly, the Market Abuse Directive; and fifthly, the International Accounting Standards Directive. These directives are discussed in *Palmer's Company Law* at paras 5.300 *et seq.*

The mechanism used by Pt 43 of the Companies Act 2006

To introduce the transparency obligations to United Kingdom securities law what Pt 43 does in large part is to add new ss.89A-89O, 90A, 90B and s.100A to Pt 6 of the Financial Services and Markets Act 2000. Part 6 of the Financial Services and Markets Act 2000 is the part dealing with "Official Listing of Securities". (The rest of that Pt 6 of the 2000 Act receives a full analysis in Part 5 of *Palmer's Company Law*.) The remainder of Pt 43 is comprised of consequential provisions relating to the introduction of those new provisions to the 2000 Act.

The reference to "UK securities law"

English lawyers are used to talking of "English law" and Scots lawyers are used to talking of "Scots law", and Northern Ireland has ordinarily functioned primarily on delegated legislation from the United Kingdom Parliament. One effect of the Companies Act 2006 has been to create a single company law for the entire United Kingdom for the first time. Securities law has been United Kingdom securities law ever since the EC securities directives began to impose minimum requirements on all Member States and the Financial Services and Markets Act 2000 created a new base for statutory securities law across the United Kingdom. Therefore, references in this part are to "UK securities law", although English case law and Scots case law will also be important in practice. On this see Part 5 of *Palmer's Company Law* and A.S. Hudson, *Securities Law* (Sweet & Maxwell, upcoming 2007). The Financial Services and Markets Act 2000 is referred to hereafter as "FSMA 2000"; whereas the Companies Act 2006 will be referred to as "the 2006 Act".

The FSA Transparency Rules and Corporate Governance Rules

The transparency obligation provisions of the 2006 Act will be supported by the FSA's Transparency Rules and Corporate Governance Rules in time. Those rules were not publicly available at the time of writing. They will be accessible on the FSA website www.fsa.gov.uk in time. At the time of writing all that is available is the text of the "near final" rules contained in the Appendices to the FSA Policy Statement 06/11 "Implementation of the Transparency Directive", which was published in the wake of FSA Consultation Paper 06/4. The full implementation of the terms of the Transparency Obligations Directive will require the implementation of these FSA principles. Those rules will be considered in full in *Palmer's Company Law*, paras 5.300 *et seq.*, once they are published.

The general approach of the "transparency rules" in the Companies Act 2006

The tone adopted in the Act in this context is entirely permissive. The provisions read "the regulations may" provide for such-and-such, as opposed to obliging the FSA to provide rigidly for any given thing. The FSA in turn has conducted a consultation process on the precise form of the "Transparency Rules" (capitalised for this purpose) which will form part of the FSA Rulebook. Thus the precise, final form of the regulations is unknown at the time of writing. (A full analysis of those rules will however be made available in *Palmer's Company Law* as soon as is practicable.) Consequently, the "transparency rules", in lower case in this Act (s.1266, which introduces s.89A(6) FSMA 2000), suggest items for inclusion in FSA regulation. The larger context of securities law is that the EC Transparency Obligations Directive requires the United Kingdom to implement its provisions into domestic law, as required by Art.249 of the EC Treaty. Therefore, for all the permissive wording of the 2006 Act which is intended to leave the FSA room for manoeuvre as to how stringent to make the detail of the regulations, the underlying directive makes mandatory the implementation of a minimum level of regulation in UK securities law. The tendency is for FSA regulations in recent years to reproduce large amounts of the precise language contained the English translation of the appropriate EC directives as a result.

"Voting rights"

The transparency obligations provisions deal primarily with the obligations of people who control voting rights in relation to securities, as opposed simply to imposing obligations on people who are the registered owners of shares. This is because "transparency", in securities law terms, requires that investors know who controls the company in which they are considering investing, as opposed to knowing only who appears to own shares on their face. Clearly, a person could acquire shares through a number of human agents, or controlled companies, or by means of a trust so that his control of the voting and other rights attaching to those shares is hidden. The purpose of many of the provisions to follow, particularly new ss.89B-89E to be inserted into FSMA 2000 (under s.1266 of the 2006 Act below), is to treat all voting rights under common control as constituting a single block of voting rights. As defined in s.89F(4) below (introduced by s.1266 of the 2006 Act), voting rights, in general terms, are rights attaching to a share which permit the shareholder to vote at company meetings (provided that the shares at issue have been admitted to trading on a regulated market). Thus the transparency obligations provisions are concerned to enable investors to know who holds and who ultimately controls such rights, as well as to make transparent financial information about the company and so forth.

Introductory

1265.   The transparency obligations directive

In Part 6 of the Financial Services and Markets Act 2000 (c. 8) (which makes provision about official listing, prospectus requirements for transferable securities, etc), in section 103(1) (interpretation), at the appropriate place insert-

> ""the transparency obligations directive" means Directive 2004/109/EC of the European Parliament and of the Council relating to the harmonisation of transparency requirements in relation to information about issuers whose securities are admitted to trading on a regulated market;".

GENERAL NOTE

This provision adds a reference to the "transparency obligations directive" to Pt 6 of the Financial Services and Markets Act 2000 so that a clear reference to that directive is included in the interpretation provisions of Pt 6 of FSMA 2000, as referred in the following provisions.

Transparency obligations

1266. Transparency rules

(1) After section 89 of the Financial Services and Markets Act 2000 insert-

"Transparency obligations

89A Transparency rules

(1) The competent authority may make rules for the purposes of the transparency obligations directive.

(2) The rules may include provision for dealing with any matters arising out of or related to any provision of the transparency obligations directive.

(3) The competent authority may also make rules-

    (a) for the purpose of ensuring that voteholder information in respect of voting shares traded on a UK market other than a regulated market is made public or notified to the competent authority;

    (b) providing for persons who hold comparable instruments (see section 89F(1)(c)) in respect of voting shares to be treated, in the circumstances specified in the rules, as holding some or all of the voting rights in respect of those shares.

(4) Rules under this section may, in particular, make provision-

    (a) specifying how the proportion of-

       (i) the total voting rights in respect of shares in an issuer, or

       (ii) the total voting rights in respect of a particular class of shares in an issuer,

    held by a person is to be determined;

    (b) specifying the circumstances in which, for the purposes of any determination of the voting rights held by a person ("P") in respect of voting shares in an issuer, any voting rights held, or treated by virtue of subsection (3)(b) as held, by another person in respect of voting shares in the issuer are to be regarded as held by P;

    (c) specifying the nature of the information which must be included in any notification;

    (d) about the form of any notification;

    (e) requiring any notification to be given within a specified period;

    (f) specifying the manner in which any information is to be made public and the period within which it must be made public;

    (g) specifying circumstances in which any of the requirements imposed by rules under this section does not apply.

(5) Rules under this section are referred to in this Part as "transparency rules".

(6) Nothing in sections 89B to 89G affects the generality of the power to make rules under this section.

89B Provision of voteholder information

(1) Transparency rules may make provision for voteholder information in respect of voting shares to be notified, in circumstances specified in the rules-

    (a) to the issuer, or

    (b) to the public,

or to both.

(2) Transparency rules may make provision for voteholder information notified to the issuer to be notified at the same time to the competent authority.

(3) In this Part "voteholder information" in respect of voting shares means information relating to the proportion of voting rights held by a person in respect of the shares.

(4) Transparency rules may require notification of voteholder information relating to a person-

    (a) initially, not later than such date as may be specified in the rules for the purposes of the first indent of Article 30.2 of the transparency obligations directive, and

    (b) subsequently, in accordance with the following provisions.

(5) Transparency rules under subsection (4)(b) may require notification of voteholder information relating to a person only where there is a notifiable change in the proportion of-

    (a) the total voting rights in respect of shares in the issuer, or

    (b) the total voting rights in respect of a particular class of share in the issuer,

held by the person.

(6) For this purpose there is a "notifiable change" in the proportion of voting rights held by a person when the proportion changes-

    (a) from being a proportion less than a designated proportion to a proportion equal to or greater than that designated proportion,

    (b) from being a proportion equal to a designated proportion to a proportion greater or less than that designated proportion, or

    (c) from being a proportion greater than a designated proportion to a proportion equal to or less than that designated proportion.

(7) In subsection (6) "designated" means designated by the rules.

89C   Provision of information by issuers of transferable securities

(1) Transparency rules may make provision requiring the issuer of transferable securities, in circumstances specified in the rules-

    (a) to make public information to which this section applies, or

    (b) to notify to the competent authority information to which this section applies,

or to do both.

(2) In the case of every issuer, this section applies to-

    (a) information required by Article 4 of the transparency obligations directive;

    (b) information relating to the rights attached to the transferable securities, including information about the terms and conditions of those securities which could indirectly affect those rights; and

    (c) information about new loan issues and about any guarantee or security in connection with any such issue.

(3) In the case of an issuer of debt securities, this section also applies to information required by Article 5 of the transparency obligations directive.

(4) In the case of an issuer of shares, this section also applies to-

    (a) information required by Article 5 of the transparency obligations directive;

    (b) information required by Article 6 of that directive;

    (c) voteholder information-

        (i) notified to the issuer, or

        (ii) relating to the proportion of voting rights held by the issuer in respect of shares in the issuer;

    (d) information relating to the issuer's capital; and

    (e) information relating to the total number of voting rights in respect of shares or shares of a particular class.

89D   Notification of voting rights held by issuer

(1) Transparency rules may require notification of voteholder information relating to the proportion of voting rights held by an issuer in respect of voting shares in the issuer-

(a) initially, not later than such date as may be specified in the rules for the purposes of the second indent of Article 30.2 of the transparency obligations directive, and

(b) subsequently, in accordance with the following provisions.

(2) Transparency rules under subsection (1)(b) may require notification of voteholder information relating to the proportion of voting rights held by an issuer in respect of voting shares in the issuer only where there is a notifiable change in the proportion of-

(a) the total voting rights in respect of shares in the issuer, or

(b) the total voting rights in respect of a particular class of share in the issuer,

held by the issuer.

(3) For this purpose there is a "notifiable change" in the proportion of voting rights held by a person when the proportion changes-

(a) from being a proportion less than a designated proportion to a proportion equal to or greater than that designated proportion,

(b) from being a proportion equal to a designated proportion to a proportion greater or less than that designated proportion, or

(c) from being a proportion greater than a designated proportion to a proportion equal to or less than that designated proportion.

(4) In subsection (3) "designated" means designated by the rules.

89E   Notification of proposed amendment of issuer's constitution

Transparency rules may make provision requiring an issuer of transferable securities that are admitted to trading on a regulated market to notify a proposed amendment to its constitution-

(a) to the competent authority, and

(b) to the market on which the issuer's securities are admitted,

at times and in circumstances specified in the rules.

89F   Transparency rules: interpretation etc

(1) For the purposes of sections 89A to 89G-

(a) the voting rights in respect of any voting shares are the voting rights attached to those shares,

(b) a person is to be regarded as holding the voting rights in respect of the shares-

(i) if, by virtue of those shares, he is a shareholder within the meaning of Article 2.1(e) of the transparency obligations directive;

(ii) if, and to the extent that, he is entitled to acquire, dispose of or exercise those voting rights in one or more of the cases mentioned in Article 10(a) to (h) of the transparency obligations directive;

(iii) if he holds, directly or indirectly, a financial instrument which results in an entitlement to acquire the shares and is an Article 13 instrument, and

(c) a person holds a "comparable instrument" in respect of voting shares if he holds, directly or indirectly, a financial instrument in relation to the shares which has similar economic effects to an Article 13 instrument (whether or not the financial instrument results in an entitlement to acquire the shares).

(2) Transparency rules under section 89A(3)(b) may make different provision for different descriptions of comparable instrument.

(3) For the purposes of sections 89A to 89G two or more persons may, at the same time, each be regarded as holding the same voting rights.

(4) In those sections-

"Article 13 instrument" means a financial instrument of a type determined by the European Commission under Article 13.2 of the transparency obligations directive;

"UK market" means a market that is situated or operating in the United Kingdom;

"voting shares" means shares of an issuer to which voting rights are attached.

89G   Transparency rules: other supplementary provisions

(1) Transparency rules may impose the same obligations on a person who has applied for the admission of transferable securities to trading on a regulated market without the issuer's consent as they impose on an issuer of transferable securities.

(2) Transparency rules that require a person to make information public may include provision authorising the competent authority to make the information public in the event that the person fails to do so.

(3) The competent authority may make public any information notified to the authority in accordance with transparency rules.

(4) Transparency rules may make provision by reference to any provision of any rules made by the Panel on Takeovers and Mergers under Part 28 of the Companies Act 2006.

(5) Sections 89A to 89F and this section are without prejudice to any other power conferred by this Part to make Part 6 rules.".

(2) The effectiveness for the purposes of section 155 of the Financial Services and Markets Act 2000 (c. 8) (consultation on proposed rules) of things done by the Financial Services Authority before this section comes into force with a view to making transparency rules (as defined in the provisions to be inserted in that Act by subsection (1) above) is not affected by the fact that those provisions were not then in force.

GENERAL NOTE

This section introduces five new sections to Pt 6 of the Financial Services and Markets Act 2000 ("FSMA 2000") immediately following the existing s.89 of that Act. (Section 89 itself has no significance for present purposes relating to transparency obligations, rather it simply happens to be the previous section. Section 89 refers to the different issue of the public censure of sponsors.) These five new sections set out the basic principles on which the transparency obligations will function.

(1) The FSA acts as the United Kingdom Listing Authority ("UKLA") and for these purposes is the "competent authority" as required by the Transparency Obligations Directive and other EC securities directives.

New s.89A FSMA 2000

This provision grants general authorisation for the FSA to create transparency rules relating, in relation to the new clauses to be added to FSMA 2000 which are grouped together under s.1266 of the Act, to obligations on the part of shareholders, the issuer, and others to make public notifications of their holdings of voting rights in the company at issue.

New s.89A (1) FSMA 2000

The FSA is thus empowered to create the Transparency Rules which will form part of the FSA Rulebook dealing with listing of securities, in common with the existing Prospectus Rules and Disclosure Rules, and the new Corporate Governance Rules which are introduced by dint of s.1269 of the 2006 Act below.

New s.89A (2) FSMA 2000

The Transparency Rules implement the Transparency Obligations Directive but, on the terms of that directive and as suggested by the wording of this subsection, the FSA is able to impose more stringent obligations than are contained in the directive provided that they apply to all issuers equally. Thus UK securities law can be more demanding (but not less demanding) than the requirements of the directive, provided that there is no disadvantage to issuers in other jurisdictions seeking listing in the United Kingdom.

New s.89A (3) (a) FSMA 2000

Whereas the Transparency Obligations Directive is restricted to securities issued on "regulated markets", this provision empowers the FSA to make these requirements apply by means of the FSA Rulebook to issues of securities whether on regulated markets or not. Those rules, however, would need to make it clear whether or not this would be limited to issues to the public in the same manner as the Transparency Obligations Directive - a point which is not made clear at this point in the Act. The term "regulated market" is defined by reference to s.1273(6) of the 2006 Act below.

New s.89A (3) (b) FSMA 2000

Of interest here is the expression "persons who hold comparable instruments": that phrase being qualified by s.89F(1)(c) (considered below) which refers to an "article 13 instrument". This requires a little explanation. There is a code relating to people who hold financial instruments which, although not vote-carrying shares, grant rights equivalent to such shares which is set out principally in new ss.89B-89E of FSMA 2000, as considered in detail below. Article 13(1) of the Transparency Obligations Directive defines such an instrument to be one which provides a person with "an entitlement to acquire, on such holder's own initiative alone, under a formal agreement, shares to which voting rights are attached, already issued, of an issuer whose shares are admitted to trading on a regulated market". These instruments are further defined by Commission technical regulation in similar terms.

Two issues arise from this definition. First, this category of instrument seems to cover bonds which are convertible into voting shares and options to acquire shares (so-called "call options"). (The call option in this context would need to be one that is physically-settled, that is one which delivers ownership of the shares at issue; whereas most call options are cash-settled in off-exchange derivatives markets, meaning that no shares are delivered but rather only an amount of money equalling the profit which the option holder would have made had she actually owned the shares. (On the legal treatment of derivatives like options, see A.S. Hudson, *The Law on Financial Derivatives* (4th edn, Sweet & Maxwell, 2006) generally, and paras *2-30 et seq.* in particular.)) In this context the option which is meant must be a call option because a put option (one which is imposed on the buyer of the option by the seller of that option) would not be exercisable on the holder's own initiative. This would be so unless one were to take a strained interpretation of "one's own initiative" so as to say that entering into the put option contract in the first place was an act of initiative so that being forced to buy the share with the voting rights was the result of that initiative. By contrast, a call option is exercised at the holder's initiative because the holder of that option must choose to exercise it.

This leads to the second issue: there are, however, some call options which are automatically exercised without the holder of the option choosing consciously to call for the shares. Here, it is suggested, that it would be more natural to accept that the holder of the call option was acting on his or her own initiative when receiving shares under an automatically-exercisable, physically-settled call option because he had chosen to receive those shares once those shares reached a given market value: under ordinary option pricing models this would require the holder of the option to be receiving those shares at a price which is advantageous to the holder (either because it shows a profit or otherwise provides shares at a price acceptable to the holder of the option.)

Section 89F(2) provides that the transparency rules may create a different definition of instruments comparable to shares carrying voting rights from the definition which is provided in Art.13 of the Transparency Obligations Directive. The effect of Art.13 is considered in detail below in relation to s.89B(3).

New s.89A (4) (a) FSMA 2000

FSA regulation may be required to specify how one calculates the appropriate proportion of votes held by any given person.

New s.89A (4) (b) FSMA 2000

FSA regulation may also specify those circumstances in which voting rights shall be deemed to be owned by any given person. This would refer, inter alia, to circumstances in which voting shares are held on trust for a person, are held on discretionary trust or subject to a power of appointment where such a person is a potential object of that power, or are directly or indirectly under the control of that person whether through the agency of some other person or not.

New s.89A (5) FSMA 2000

In this discussion the rules intended to be introduced by the FSA are referred to as the Transparency Rules, and the statute refers to the rules in s.89A as being "transparency rules".

New s.89A (6) FSMA 2000

This provision was introduced to the bill in its final stages to ensure that there would be nothing which would inhibit the FSA's ability to make regulations relating to transparency obligations.

New s.89B FSMA 2000

The principal focus of this new provision is to provide authorisation for FSA Transparency Rules to make provision in turn for significant changes in the shareholding of any given person. A person whose proportionate holding of voting rights in the issuer's share capital crosses some identified threshold of the total shareholding is required to make a notification of that fact in the manner considered below. Thus, "transparency" in its securities law sense involves, in part, the notification of the identity of those people who control giving proportions of the voting control of companies to the company itself and to the FSA. As will emerge from the discussion to follow, the regulations will deal with voting rights which a person controls (for example, by means of contract, trust, agency or otherwise) and not simply with direct, absolute ownership of shares.

New s.89B(1) FSMA 2000

The keynote of the transparency rules is the provision of information on a continuing basis both to the investing public and to the regulator, the FSA acting as United Kingdom Listing Authority ("UKLA") and so in turn as competent authority. The FSA is empowered to make the necessary transparency rules to put into effect the provisions Transparency Obligations Directive, including an implied power to reach beyond the requirements of that directive (on which see the discussion of s.89B(5) below). It is a matter for the transparency rules whether the obligation to make a notification is to be made to the issuer of the shares only or whether it is also to be made to the public at large (or, potentially, only to the public at large without necessarily involving an obligation to notify the issuer specifically).

New s.89B(2) FSMA 2000

It is a matter for the FSA's transparency rules whether notification of this information relating to voteholders (as considered in relation to the next subsection) is also to be made to the FSA itself as well as to issuer. On this requirement see *Palmer's Company Law*, paras 5.300 *et seq.*

New s.89B(3) FSMA 2000

The reference to "voteholder information" is a reference to any information relating to the proportion of voting rights which are held by a person in relation to those shares. This should be read in tandem with s.89A(4) of FSMA 2000 as to the context in which people can be deemed to be the owners of shares. As considered next in relation to s.89B(4)(a), the provisions of the Transparency Obligations Directive identify a number of situations in which voting rights are controlled, as opposed necessarily to being owned, by the person required to make some notification.

New s.89B(4) FSMA 2000

The FSA is empowered to make transparency rules which take the following form. Importantly, as expressed in the statute, there is no obligation to make such a notification: rather notification "may" be made. The precise detail as to whether or not notifications need to be made, as set out in the following paragraphs of the section, require cross-reference with the appropriate EC directives and FSA Transparency Rules, as is considered next.

(a) Such a notification can be made "initially". The reference to "the first indent of Article 30.2 of the transparency obligations directive" is to a date (as identified in that provision) at the latest two months after January 20, 2007 by which time "a shareholder shall notify the issuer ... of the proportion of voting rights and capital it holds ... unless it has already made a notification before that date". There is a cross-reference from this provision to Arts 9, 10 and 13 of the directive which relates to "Information about major shareholdings". Thus, the obligation to make notifications falls only on shareholders identified in Arts 9, 10 and 13 as holding major shareholdings carrying voting rights.

Article 9 requires notification on crossing thresholds of 5 per cent, 10 per cent, 15 per cent, 20 per cent, 25 per cent, 30 per cent, 50 per cent and 75 per cent in relation to shares which are "admitted to trading on a regulated market and to which voting rights are attached". Notification is also required in relation to "events changing the breakdown of voting rights", such as the issue of new shares or the cancellation of shares.

Market makers are not required to make such notifications when they cross the 5 per cent threshold, provided it is authorised so to act under MiFID (the EC "Markets in Financial Instruments Directive", 2004/39/EC) and neither "intervenes in the management of the issuer concerned nor exerts any influence on the issuer to buy back such shares or back the share price" (Art.9(5)).

Article 10 deals with eight different situations in which shares are either acquired or disposed of, and requires that the notification requirements of Art.9 shall apply to any of these eight situations. Those situations relate to the "ownership" of the voting rights, as opposed necessarily to any outright assignment of the shares to which those voting rights attach. This encompasses the situation in which, for example further to a contract, there is no transfer of the shares but further to some other arrangement the voting rights are exercised in accordance with the legally binding instructions of some third party. They are, in summary form, as follows (retaining the numbering from Art.10): (a) a situation in which two parties act in concert in relation to their several voting rights by means of an "agreement", by which it is suggested there must be an enforceable contract or possibly an arrangement from which both parties could be prevented or estopped from resiling; (b) voting rights held further to an agreement (as before) which provides for a temporary transfer of those voting rights (as opposed to the shares more generally) in return for some valuable consideration; (c) voting rights which are lodged "as collateral", ordinarily understood as being security in a financial transaction further to the EC Collateral Directive (as to which see A.S. Hudson, *The Law on Financial Derivatives* (4th end, Sweet & Maxwell, 2006), pp.537 *et seq.* and especially p.548), so as to transfer control of the voting rights; (d) voting rights attached to shares in which the person has the life interest under a settlement; (e) or more generally voting rights the exercise of which further to categories (a)-(d) above is controlled by some undertaking; (f) voting rights attaching to shares which have been deposited with a person such that that person has a discretion as to how those voting rights are exercised; (g) voting rights held by a third party on behalf of that person, for example on bare trust; or (h) voting rights which are exercised by that person as a proxy and in relation to which that person may exercise his unfettered discretion without instruction from his principal.

Article 13 extends the notification provisions of Art.9 to situations in which the persons obliged to make notification of their shareholding actually hold "financial instruments", such as a physically-settled call option, which entitle them to acquire shares carrying voting rights. This instrument must be in the form of a formal agreement. Oddly, it must also carry the entitlement to acquire shares "on such holder's initiative alone" - however, it is usual for such call options to be exercisable once they are "in the money", that is once the value of the underlying share crosses an identified threshold: something which would seem to abnegate the requirement that the holder exercise some initiative, unless that initiative is deemed to have been exercised at the time the agreement was created. (See the discussion of this point in relation to s.89A(3)(b) above.) In relation to a convertible bond which is exercisable only on the holder's demand, there would also be an obligation to make notification. The range of instruments to which this provision applies is to be the subject of a technical regulation from the Commission.

(b) The effect of further provisions having an effect is considered below.

New s.89B(5) FSMA 2000

Transparency rules effected by the FSA under s.89B(3)(b) "may" require notification only where there is a "notifiable change" (as defined in s.89B(5) below) in a person's total voting rights either in the issuer's shares or in a particular class of the issuer's shares. Thus, instead of simply effecting the detailed provisions of the Transparency Obligations Directive as considered in relation to s.89B(3), the FSA may take a different tack in its transparency rules, providing always that it complies at least with the minima set out in the directive.

New s.89B(6) FSMA 2000

A "notifiable change" is a change in the proportion of a person's voting rights across some specified threshold of the issuer's shares, whether by means of an increase or a decrease in the proportionate shareholding.

New s.89B(6) FSMA 2000

The thresholds in relation to a "notifiable change" are to be set out in the transparency rules.

New s.89C FSMA 2000

The issuer may be obliged by the FSA Transparency Rules to make notification of certain matters either publicly or directly to the FSA. (We shall continue to use the lower case "transparency rules" here as that term is used in the 2006 Act.) It is worth noting that s.89C was altered significantly during the final stages of the passage of the bill through Parliament, and that s.89D and 89E following, dealing with related matters, were new introductions to the bill in its final stages. The title of s.89C changed from "Provision of information by issuers" to the more specific "Provision of information by issuers of transferable securities". Principally the effect of the change has been to have s.89C(2) focus primarily on matters in Art.4 (where Art.4 deals with annual financial reports) and to have s.89C(4) focus primarily on matters in Arts 5 and 6 of the Transparency Obligations Directive separately from one another (where Art.5 deals with half-yearly financial reports and Art.6 with interim management standards). Notification of voteholder information and of proposed amendments to the issuer's constitution have been separated out into s.89D and 89E respectively. Consequently, whereas five matters were dealt with under s.89C(2) previously, there are now only three.

New s.89C(1) FSMA 2000

The obligation to make notification of the information provided in the transparency rules may be an obligation to make that information public or an obligation to make notification to the FSA as competent authority only, or to do both (whereby the obligation formally to notify the FSA specifically imposes an obligation over and above one to make information generally known).

New s.89C(2) FSMA 2000

There are three categories of information which must be notified under this provision, with differing levels of specificity. During the passage of the bill there had originally been five categories of information, but they have now been whittled down to three. As will emerge in the discussion to follow, many of the matters described in this provision are potentially very broad indeed. This is to be expected because these provisions are to be thought of as enabling legislation which gives powers to the FSA to create transparency rules to deal with the matters considered below. At the time of writing, as explained in the General Note to this Pt 43, no final rules are publicly available. Therefore, it will be for the transparency rules to answer the many questions as to the meaning of statutory expressions which are raised below when they are introduced by the FSA.

(a) Article 4 of the Transparency Obligations Directive deals with "periodic information" dealing with the issuer's financial position which the issuer is required to make public in the form of annual financial reports. Under Art.4, the annual financial report is to be made public not more than four months from the end of the financial year and it must remain publicly available for five years thereafter. It shall comprise the audited financial statements, the management report and statements by the persons responsible for the financial statements to the effect that they give a "true and fair view" of the issuer's financial position as required by the appropriate EC directive.

(b) The expression "information relating to the rights attached to the shares or other securities" could potentially encompass a very broad range of material. In relation to the ordinary share capital, and assuming no overlap to matters considered in relation to s.89C(4)(d) below, it could relate to decisions of company meetings to alter the company's constitutional documents as to shareholder rights, decisions to exercise any right in the company's constitution as to enlarging the rights of some identified shareholders or limiting the rights of a minority, or similar matters. In relation to preference shares, it could relate to an alteration in the scope or nature of the rights attached to them as to voting or dividends. In relation to other share capital, such as the company's ordinary bonds it could relate to an alteration in the coupon to be paid to investors or to the performance of some covenant in the bond documentation. In relation to convertible shares, the information might relate to the convertibility of those shares, or to some condition precedent to their conversion, or to the rights attaching to such bonds should they be converted.

(c) This provision relates to the loan capital of the issuer, and any connected security device which the issuer is required to provide, such as a guarantee, or a collateral agreement, or a charge, or a mortgage, or a trust, or a pledge, or a lien, or otherwise.

New s.89C(3) FSMA 2000

This provision extends the preceding provisions to cover debt securities also.

New s.89C(4) FSMA 2000

For the purposes of this provision it is important to cross-refer with Arts 5 and 6 of the Transparency Obligations Directive. Article 5 of the Transparency Obligations Directive deals with "periodic information" which the issuer is required to make public in the form of half-yearly financial reports.

(a) Under Art.5, half-yearly financial reports are to be made public by the issuer of shares and issuer of debt securities. Otherwise, this statement is in similar, if shortened form, to the annual financial report.

(b) Article 6 of the Transparency Obligations Directive deals with "periodic information" which the issuer is required to make public in the form of interim management statements. Interim management statements, further to Art.6, are to be made in relation to each six month period in the financial year giving an explanation of "material events and transactions" which have taken place during the period to which the statement relates, and "a general description of the financial position and performance of the issuer and its controlled undertakings" during the period covered by the statement.

(c) There must be notification of "voteholder information", which is a reference to any information relating to the proportion of voting rights which are held by a person in relation to those shares. This should be read in tandem with s.89A(5)(b) of FSMA 2000 as to the context in which people can be deemed to be the owners of shares. The two forms of voteholder information are information which has been notified to the issuer and information as to the proportion of the total voting rights in the issuer's share capital held by any given person. The voteholder information which is to be notified to the issuer, or which is to be made publicly available, and the obligations of persons to make notification of holdings or control of given proportions of the total shareholding, were described in s.89B above.

(d) The expression "information relating to the issuer's capital" is potentially extraordinarily broad. At its absolute broadest, the expenditure of any money or the disposal of any asset at all would have some trifling effect on the issuer's capital. In this context, it could be interpreted so as to be limited only to matters which have an effect the issuer's share capital - such as the acquisition or disposal of shares in the issuer, as well as decisions to issue new shares or redeem existing shares. It could be interpreted so that any change in the company's shareholding which would cross the thresholds identified in s.89B(3)(a) would be the only information which would be notifiable. Alternatively, it could be limited so that only information which was notifiable to the issuer or to the FSA would be notifiable by the FSA, beyond more general obligations in the listing rules and elsewhere on the issuer to make notification to the FSA as competent authority of matters affecting the issuer and the value of its shares.

New s.89D FSMA 2000

This provision was introduced to the bill in its final stages. Its effect is part of the process, referred to in relation to the previous section, of breaking up a long provision for ease of reference and to divide more clearly between the various categories of information which may be required by FSA transparency rules.

New s.89D(1) FSMA 2000

In relation to s.89B(4)(a) above, there is an obligation on certain persons to make notification of their shareholding in the issuer in the manner to be specified in the transparency rules. In relation to that provision, we have considered the scope of the Transparency Obligations Directive in this regard. Briefly put, with a cross-reference to that earlier discussion in relation to s.89B(4)(a) as to the effect of the directive, the issuer may be required by the transparency rules to make a notification of the shareholding held by the issuer in the issuer itself. Instead of simply effecting the detailed provisions of the Transparency Obligations Directive as considered in relation to s.89B(4)(a), the FSA may create more stringent transparency rules further to s.89C(4)(b) and (5), providing always that it complies at least with the minima set out in the directive. *New s.89D(2) FSMA 2000*

This provision grants authorisation to the transparency rules to make provision in turn for the issuer to make a notification of its holding in its own voting shares.

New s.89D(3) FSMA 2000

A change which requires notification is a "notifiable change" and relates to some alteration across a threshold identified in the transparency rules, either by means of an increase or a decrease, in the issuer's proportionate holding of the total number of shares carrying voting rights in the issuer.

New s.89D(4) FSMA 2000

The thresholds referred to immediately above will be designated by the transparency rules, and may therefore differ from those in Art.9 of the Transparency Obligations Directive, as considered above.

New s.89E FSMA 2000

This provision was introduced to the bill in its final stages. It was not previously identified in the Act. Its purpose is to make clear than one item of information which must be notified both the FSA and to the market on which securities are traded is any proposed amendment to the constitution of an issuer of transferable securities.

New s.89F FSMA 2000

This provision is the interpretation clause for the preceding provisions in Pt 43 of the Act. The overall purpose of the provision is to extend notification obligations beyond simply the owners of shares to people who, more specifically, hold shares with voting rights or who are able to control the use of voting rights in relation to shares. By exposing the voting control in a company, the regulations will be able to enhance the transparency of that company's affairs.

New s.89F(1) (a) FSMA 2000

As considered above, Pt 43 of the Act is concerned with control of voting rights as opposed to ownership of shares per se.

(b) A person holds voting rights in a company in the following circumstances:

(i) if they are a shareholder: the reference to Art.2.1e of the Transparency Obligations Directive is to a definitions provision which defines a "shareholder" to be "any natural person or legal entity governed by private or public law, who holds, directly or indirectly (where the numbering in this list represents that reproduced in the directive):

(i) shares of the issuer in its own name and on its own account;

(ii) shares of the issuer in its own name, but on behalf of another natural person or legal entity;

(iii) depositary receipts, in which case the holder of the depositary receipt shall be considered as the shareholder of the underlying shares represented by the depositary receipts."

(ii) a person who is entitled to deal with those voting rights in one of the following circumstances, as listed in Art.10 of the Transparency Obligations Directive (these alternatives were analysed in greater detail above in relation to s.89B(3)) (where the numbering (a)-(h) in this list is as reproduced in that directive):

(a) further to an "agreement", the situation in which two parties act in concert in relation to their several voting rights;

(b) voting rights held further to an agreement which provides for a temporary transfer of those voting rights in return for some valuable consideration;

(c) voting rights which are lodged "as collateral", (on which see A.S. Hudson, *The Law on Financial Derivatives* (4th edn, Sweet & Maxwell, 2006), pp.537 *et seq.*), so as to transfer control of the voting rights;

(d) voting rights attached to shares in which the person has the life interest under a settlement;

(e) or more generally voting rights the exercise of which further to categories (a)-(d) above is controlled by some undertaking;

(f) voting rights attaching to shares which have been deposited with a person such that that person has a discretion as to how those voting rights are exercised;

(g) voting rights held by a third party on behalf of that person; or

(h) voting rights which are exercised by that person as a proxy and in relation to which that person may exercise his or her discretion without instruction from his principal.

(iii) a person who holds a financial instrument directly or indirectly (that is, perhaps it is held on trust for him of her or by an agent acting on his or her behalf) further to Art.13 of the Transparency Obligations Directive which deals with instruments which entitle the instrument holder to acquire voting rights in the issuer (for example further to a convertible bond or a physically-settled call option to acquire shares): this provision was analysed in detail above in relation to s.89B(3).

New s.89F(2) FSMA 2000

This provision was considered above in relation to s.89A(4).

New s.89F(3) FSMA 2000

It is not explained on what basis people are to be treated as owning the same voting rights simultaneously. There are two significant contexts: either generally whether or not a person is to be treated as the owner of voting rights, or specifically in relation to calculating whether or not that person's total holding of voting rights has crossed a threshold.

As to the first, general situation, it is not clear whether or not such persons are to be treated as being tenants in common at common law of those voting rights, or whether one is holding those rights on trust for another person such that one will be the owner of the legal title in those rights as trustee and the other as the owner of the equitable interest in those rights, or otherwise. Rather, the purpose of this provision is not to allocate ownership per se, but rather to facilitate a fiction whereby someone who is de facto in control of the exercise of voting rights cannot elude regulatory oversight by virtue of some legal device which suggests that he has no formal ownership of a given portion of voting rights: for example, if someone tries to conceal their ownership of voting rights by having them held on trust for him or by having them held by some company which is indirectly under his or her control.

This brings us to the second question: at what stage will such a de facto controller of voting rights be required to make a notification of such a holding? That question is answered by ss.89B-89E, as considered above. What is not explained by those provisions, however, is whether or not all of the people who are treated by this provision as holding voting rights simultaneously are all required to make notification of their ownership of voting rights, or if only the person who is deemed to control the voting rights is required to make that notification.

New s.89F(4) FSMA 2000

Most significantly in this provision, the reference to "voting shares" is a reference to voting rights attaching to a share which permit the shareholder to vote at company meetings. Importantly, a reference in an earlier version of the bill to a further requirement that the shares at issue have been admitted to trading on a regulated market has been removed.

New s.89G FSMA 2000

The purpose of this provision is to make further enabling powers for the creation of FSA transparency rules.

New s.89G(1) FSMA 2000

This provision was a new addition to the bill in its final stages. It makes plain that transparency obligations are imposed on anyone who seeks to admit securities to listing, even if that person does not have the authorisation of the issuer so to do.

New s.89G(2) FSMA 2000

As considered above, the transparency rules may require that information be made public or that it be communicated specifically to the FSA or both: in the event that someone has failed to make public some information which he was obliged to have made public, then the FSA as competent authority may make that information public itself.

New s.89G(3) FSMA 2000

The transparency rules will provide for the manner in which the FSA, acting as competent authority, will make prescribed information public one it has been notified to the FSA further to the provisions considered above.

New s.89G(4) FSMA 2000

There is a potential overlap, clearly, between notification obligations in this Part of the Act and obligations in relation to takeovers, as set out in Pt 28 of the Act.

New s.89G(5) FSMA 2000

This provision makes it plain that nothing in the preceding provisions 89A through 89F is intended to limit the powers of the FSA to make rules.

(2) This general subs.(2) qualifies the entire s.1266 of the 2006 Act, as opposed to the new provisions which are to be interpolated into FSMA 2000. It is a saving provision in relation to any rules introduced by the FSA before the coming into force of these new provisions of FSMA 2000.

1267. Competent authority's power to call for information

In Part 6 of the Financial Services and Markets Act 2000 after the sections inserted by section 1266 above insert-

"Power of competent authority to call for information"

89H   Competent authority's power to call for information

(1) The competent authority may by notice in writing given to a person to whom this section applies require him-

    (a) to provide specified information or information of a specified description, or

    (b) to produce specified documents or documents of a specified description.

(2) This section applies to-

    (a) an issuer in respect of whom transparency rules have effect;

    (b) a voteholder;

    (c) an auditor of-

        (i) an issuer to whom this section applies, or

        (ii) a voteholder;

    (d) a person who controls a voteholder;

    (e) a person controlled by a voteholder;

    (f) a director or other similar officer of an issuer to whom this section applies;

    (g) a director or other similar officer of a voteholder or, where the affairs of a voteholder are managed by its members, a member of the voteholder.

(3) This section applies only to information and documents reasonably required in connection with the exercise by the competent authority of functions conferred on it by or under sections 89A to 89G (transparency rules).

(4) Information or documents required under this section must be provided or produced-

    (a) before the end of such reasonable period as may be specified, and

    (b) at such place as may be specified.

(5) If a person claims a lien on a document, its production under this section does not affect the lien.

89I   Requirements in connection with call for information

(1) The competent authority may require any information provided under section 89H to be provided in such form as it may reasonably require.

(2) The competent authority may require-

    (a) any information provided, whether in a document or otherwise, to be verified in such manner as it may reasonably require;

    (b) any document produced to be authenticated in such manner as it may reasonably require.

(3) If a document is produced in response to a requirement imposed under section 89H, the competent authority may-

    (a) take copies of or extracts from the document; or

    (b) require the person producing the document, or any relevant person, to provide an explanation of the document.

(4) In subsection (3)(b) "relevant person", in relation to a person who is required to produce a document, means a person who-

    (a) has been or is a director or controller of that person;

    (b) has been or is an auditor of that person;

    (c) has been or is an actuary, accountant or lawyer appointed or instructed by that person; or

    (d) has been or is an employee of that person.

(5) If a person who is required under section 89H to produce a document fails to do so, the competent authority may require him to state, to the best of his knowledge and belief, where the document is.

89J   Power to call for information: supplementary provisions

(1) The competent authority may require an issuer to make public any information provided to the authority under section 89H.

(2) If the issuer fails to comply with a requirement under subsection (1), the competent authority may, after seeking representations from the issuer, make the information public.

(3) In sections 89H and 89I (power of competent authority to call for information)-
  "control" and "controlled" have the meaning given by subsection (4) below;
  "specified" means specified in the notice;
  "voteholder" means a person who-
> (a) holds voting rights in respect of any voting shares for the purposes of sections 89A to 89G (transparency rules), or
> (b) is treated as holding such rights by virtue of rules under section 89A(3)(b).

(4) For the purposes of those sections a person ("A") controls another person ("B") if-
> (a) A holds a majority of the voting rights in B,
> (b) A is a member of B and has the right to appoint or remove a majority of the members of the board of directors (or, if there is no such board, the equivalent management body) of B,
> (c) A is a member of B and controls alone, pursuant to an agreement with other share-holders or members, a majority of the voting rights in B, or
> (d) A has the right to exercise, or actually exercises, dominant influence or control over B.

(5) For the purposes of subsection (4)(b)-
> (a) any rights of a person controlled by A, and
> (b) any rights of a person acting on behalf of A or a person controlled by A,

are treated as held by A.".

GENERAL NOTE

The new sections introduced to the Financial Services and Markets Act 2000 ("FSMA 2000") by this section refer to the power of the FSA (acting the United Kingdom Listing Authority ("UKLA")) to call for information from the issuers of securities. Briefly put, the FSA, acting as competent authority (or "UKLA" in this context), is entitled to demand information from a variety of people in connection with issues of securities, provided always that that information is specified clearly and that it is reasonably required by the FSA in connection with its functions as competent authority in relation to s.89A through 89G (considered immediately above).

New s.89H FSMA 2000

The purpose of this section is to empower UKLA to require further information from the issuer of securities and others to maintain the "transparency" of the issue. In effect, this mirrors the powers of UKLA to demand that information about an upcoming issue of securities (relating to the securities themselves, or to the issuer, or to some related matter), although instead of being a pre-requisite to an issue of securities it relates to securities which have already been issued and in relation to which UKLA requires further information to be given. Significantly, the right to require the provision of information is limited to information necessary for the proper provision of information required by those sections introduced to FSMA 2000 by s.1230 of the Companies Act as described immediately above.

New s.89H(1) FSMA 2000

The power of UKLA, as the competent authority, is thus to require the provision both of information or of specific documents for the furtherance of the transparency obligations of people identified in s.1230 above (on which see s.89H(3) below).

New s.89H(2) FSMA 2000

In common with the preceding provisions relating to transparency, it is not only the issuer who is required to provide information. Rather, much of transparency is concerned with information as to the holders of securities, specifically as to the identity of "voteholders" (as defined in s.89J(1) below) who consequently have, inter alia, some power to control the company which has issued the securities. Equally the inclusion of the issuer's auditor and of a voteholder's auditor within the list of persons who may be called upon to provide information enlarges the scope of persons who will be able to provide information about the control of the issuing entity. The concept "control" is this context is defined in s.89J(2) of FSMA 2000.

New s.89H(3) FSMA 2000

Sections 89B and 89C require the provision of voteholder information and of information by issuers respectively (as described above). It is information relating to these types of information which UKLA can demand from those categories of people identified in s.89H(2). Furthermore, those documents must be "reasonably required" for those purposes.

New s.89H(4) FSMA 2000

UKLA is empowered to specify a "reasonable period" for the provision of information or documents, and may also specify the place at which that information or those documents may reasonably be required to be produced. Thus, it is suggested, a recipient of such a demand could protest on the basis of public law categories of unreasonableness, or on the basis of unreasonableness within the compass of this Act and of its transparency obligations.

New s.89H(5) FSMA 2000

Documents may be held subject to a lien, for example, by a banker taking possession of mortgage documents or by solicitor further to their lien. There are a number of circumstances in which professionals and others who are simply owed money may claim rights of lien over documentation which entitles them to retain that document to secure payment of money by the common law owner of that document. In any such circumstance, the lien-holder will be reluctant to give up possession of the document because to do so would rob them of the force of the lien as a form of security which is dependent on the possession of the debtor's property. The lien-holder may therefore seek to resist an instruction from UKLA to deliver up the document. This subs.(5) provides that "production" of the document does not affect the lien. The lien-holder might prefer the provision to read that "transfer of possession of the document" to UKLA because mere "production" of the document might not be interpreted as being equivalent to leaving possession of the document with UKLA for some weeks or months. The lien-holder might be nervous about being deemed to have surrendered or waived possession permanently if the document were left with UKLA and no active steps taken to recover it quickly. No provision is provided to deal, for example, with the event that the document should inadvertently come back into the possession of the debtor. It is suggested that this provision is intended to leave the lien undisturbed and therefore that it ought to be understood as leaving the lien in full force and effect so that, in effect, UKLA is holding the property as an agent of the lien-holder until it is returned.

New s.89I FSMA 2000

It is suggested that this provision must be read as providing a gloss to s.89H, because that is a natural reading of what would otherwise be entirely free-standing references to the provision of information, although there is no express mention of this cross-reference. The general purpose of this provision is to permit the FSA to require the manner in which information or documentation is provided, including a power to require explanations of documentation from specified categories of people. What is not clear is how the FSA can act if such people refuse to provide explanations or if such people claim to be unable to do so in full.

New s.89I(1) FSMA 2000

Where it is information which is to be provided, the form in which information, as identified in s.89H preceding, may be required to be produced may be specified by UKLA provided that that form is reasonable.

New s.89I(2) FSMA 2000

Where it is documentation or information which is to be provided, there may be issues as to the authenticity of documentation or information - whether purportedly audited financial statements or other information in another language from another Member State of the European Union - such that the authenticity of that documentation may require verification. UKLA may make a stipulation as to the authentification of documentation or as to the verification of information as it reasonably requires.

New s.89I(3) FSMA 2000

Documentation may require explanation before it is able to achieve the purpose identified in the transparency obligation provisions of s.89A-89J of FSMA 2000. Thus, for example, where voteholding rights are held further to an agreement between two or more people as to control of a company, the purpose and terms of that agreement may require elucidation. This provision empowers UKLA to require such an explanation either from "the person producing the document" or "any relevant person", as defined in s.89I(4). The term "control" in this context is defined in s.89J(4) FSMA 2000.

New s.89I(4) FSMA 2000

As considered in relation to s.89I(3)(b) above, "any relevant person" may be required to explain documentation required by UKLA from a person further to the transparency obligations of FSMA 2000. Whereas explanations may, ideally, be wanted from many people who may have been involved in the drafting of the document, nevertheless s.89I(4) limits the forms of "relevant person" to only four categories who can be so compelled: (a) directors, former directors and controllers of the person who provides the document; (b) a current or former auditor of the person providing the document; (c) current or former actuaries, accountants or lawyers "appointed or instructed" by that person (whether or not they actually give advice or agree to act, it would seem), but presumably subject to matters of professional privilege; (d) a current or former employee of the person providing the document. What is not made clear in this provision is whether or not such a person is entitled to decline to provide information (perhaps out of fear of incriminating himself or of opening himself to some private law action for damages), and if someone does refuse what action the FSA is entitled to take.

New s.89I(5) FSMA 2000

Further to the last point made in relation to s.89I(4), it is only in relation to the location of documents that s.89I(5) permits the FSA to "require" that person provide that limited information in the event that that person otherwise fails to provide documentation.

New s.89J(1) FSMA 2000

s.89J(1) With reference to the definition of "voteholder", the discussion of what is meant by a "voteholder" is considered in detail above in the appropriate provisions of s.89A and so forth.

New s.89J(2) FSMA 2000

The concept of "control" is important in relation to the transparency obligations because much of the concern about transparency within the provisions of FSMA 2000 (as opposed to the general transparency rules to be introduced by the FSA) is with identifying the people who control the issuer either directly by holding securities which carry or which might come to carry votes over that company's affairs, or with identifying people who control other people with such voting rights. Hence the reference to people who hold a majority of voting rights in others, or who have the right to alter the composition of another person's board of directors, or who controls the voting rights in another person perhaps by virtue of some shareholders' agreement, or who either has a legal right to exercise a dominant influence over another person or who "actually exercises" a dominant influence over that other person. What is not clear is what is meant by "actually exercises": it could mean that that person has actual control by virtue of the use of some legal right or that that person has actual control by virtue of some non-legal ability to influence the behaviour of others in relation to the affairs of a company. Thus, in relation to a family company, for example, a family patriarch may be able to command the obedience of others by virtue of force of personality even though he has no legally enforceable right to command that obedience. This could be identified as being "dominant influence". Alternatively, the expression "dominant influence" could be limited so as to refer to relationships, including contracts between shareholders to vote in concert or contracts such as convertible bonds which entitle the bondholder to acquire voting shares in return for disposal of the bond rights, and might not refer to mere personal, non-legal influence.

1268. Powers exercisable in case of infringement of transparency obligation

In Part 6 of the Financial Services and Markets Act 2000 (c. 8), after the sections inserted by section 1267 above insert-

"Powers exercisable in case of infringement of transparency obligation

89K   Public censure of issuer

(1) If the competent authority finds that an issuer of securities admitted to trading on a regulated market is failing or has failed to comply with an applicable transparency obligation, it may publish a statement to that effect.

(2) If the competent authority proposes to publish a statement, it must give the issuer a warning notice setting out the terms of the proposed statement.

(3) If, after considering any representations made in response to the warning notice, the competent authority decides to make the proposed statement, it must give the issuer a decision notice setting out the terms of the statement.

(4) A notice under this section must inform the issuer of his right to refer the matter to the Tribunal (see section 89N) and give an indication of the procedure on such a reference.

(5) In this section "transparency obligation" means an obligation under-

    (a) a provision of transparency rules, or

    (b) any other provision made in accordance with the transparency obligations directive.

(6) In relation to an issuer whose home State is a member State other than the United Kingdom, any reference to an applicable transparency obligation must be read subject to section 100A(2).

89L Power to suspend or prohibit trading of securities

(1) This section applies to securities admitted to trading on a regulated market.

(2) If the competent authority has reasonable grounds for suspecting that an applicable transparency obligation has been infringed by an issuer, it may-

    (a) suspend trading in the securities for a period not exceeding 10 days,

    (b) prohibit trading in the securities, or

    (c) make a request to the operator of the market on which the issuer's securities are traded-

        (i) to suspend trading in the securities for a period not exceeding 10 days, or

        (ii) to prohibit trading in the securities.

(3) If the competent authority has reasonable grounds for suspecting that a provision required by the transparency obligations directive has been infringed by a voteholder of an issuer, it may-

    (a) prohibit trading in the securities, or

    (b) make a request to the operator of the market on which the issuer's securities are traded to prohibit trading in the securities.

(4) If the competent authority finds that an applicable transparency obligation has been infringed, it may require the market operator to prohibit trading in the securities.

(5) In this section "transparency obligation" means an obligation under-

    (a) a provision contained in transparency rules, or

    (b) any other provision made in accordance with the transparency obligations directive.

(6) In relation to an issuer whose home State is a member State other than the United Kingdom, any reference to an applicable transparency obligation must be read subject to section 100A(2).

89M Procedure under section 89L

(1) A requirement under section 89L takes effect-

    (a) immediately, if the notice under subsection (2) states that that is the case;

    (b) in any other case, on such date as may be specified in the notice.

(2) If the competent authority-

    (a) proposes to exercise the powers in section 89L in relation to a person, or

    (b) exercises any of those powers in relation to a person with immediate effect,

it must give that person written notice.

(3) The notice must-

    (a) give details of the competent authority's action or proposed action;

    (b) state the competent authority's reasons for taking the action in question and choosing the date on which it took effect or takes effect;

    (c) inform the recipient that he may make representations to the competent authority within such period as may be specified by the notice (whether or not he had referred the matter to the Tribunal);

(d) inform him of the date on which the action took effect or takes effect;

(e) inform him of his right to refer the matter to the Tribunal (see section 89N) and give an indication of the procedure on such a reference.

(4) The competent authority may extend the period within which representations may be made to it.

(5) If, having considered any representations made to it, the competent authority decides to maintain, vary or revoke its earlier decision, it must give written notice to that effect to the person mentioned in subsection (2).

89N   Right to refer matters to the Tribunal

A person-

(a) to whom a decision notice is given under section 89K (public censure), or

(b) to whom a notice is given under section 89M (procedure in connection with suspension or prohibition of trading),

may refer the matter to the Tribunal.".

GENERAL NOTE

The penalties for breach of any of the requirements of the preceding provisions are limited to the public censure of the issuer of the securities or to the power to suspend or prohibit trading in securities. Appeal from either of these penalties may be referred by the respondent to Tribunal created by FSMA 2000 to hear such matters under that Act generally.

New s.89K FSMA 2000

The order of proceedings in relation to the public censure of the issuer of securities is as follows (that order being somewhat obscured by the order of provisions in s.89K). First, the FSA must give a warning notice to the issuer that it intends to publish such a censure: presumably that warning notice, although the Act does not make this clear, must specify that the FSA considers that the issuer has failed to comply with a transparency obligation which specifies the obligation in question, the securities in question and the purported breach (as opposed generally to making a warning that a publication of censure will be made). A transparency obligation in this context refers to any obligation under this Part of FSMA 2000, or under the FSA's transparency rules, or in relation to the implementation of the transparency obligations directive more generally. As with transparency obligations in this fascicule of obligations more generally, s.89K applies only to securities which are traded on a regulated market in the United Kingdom. This initial communication must make the respondent aware of its right of appeal to the Tribunal under s.89N of FSMA 2000. Secondly, the issuer has an opportunity to make representations in response to the notice. Thirdly, the FSA may publish the censure of the issuer, if it is not swayed by the issuer's representations.

New s.89K(6) FSMA 2000

The effect of the cross-reference to s.100A(2) here is that, in relation to an issuer whose home state is a member state other than the United Kingdom, the FSA is only permitted to act by means of public censure if the issuer has infringed some provision of the EC transparency obligations directive. Therefore, it is suggested, that it would not seem to encompass the breach of provisions included in the FSA's transparency rules which were not included in the EC directive. Counter-intuitively and possibly unlawfully under EU law, if this analysis were correct, only issuers for which the United Kingdom was the home member state could be subject to public censure for breach of FSA transparency rules (if those rules were not also part of the EC directive): thus United Kingdom home issuers would be treated less favourably under FSA regulation than issuers with different home member states.

New s.89L FSMA 2000

This provision was changed markedly in the final stages of the bill's passage through Parliament. Previously it had read so as to discriminate between issuers within and without the United Kingdom. This may have breached principles of EU law. Now most of the references to that jurisdiction have been removed. Now, as with transparency obligations in this fascicule of obligations more generally, this provision applies only to securities which are traded on a regulated market. This provision grants FSA the power, through its regulations, to prohibit or to suspend trading in securities where there has been a breach of a relevant transparency obligation. As is set out in s.89M(1), such a suspension or prohibition may take effect either immediately or from a date specified in the FSA's notice of suspension or prohibition. If the power to suspend or prohibit trading is to be exercised immediately, then the FSA must furnish the person at issue with a written notice of the fact.

New s.89L(2) FSMA 2000

The UKLA must have "reasonable grounds" for believing that there has been an infringement of a transparency obligation by an issuer. There are then three possible courses of action open to UKLA. First, UKLA may (but is not required to) order the operator of the appropriate regulated market to suspend trading in the securities for a period not exceeding ten days. Secondly, UKLA may prohibit trading in those securities. Thirdly, UKLA may "make a request" to the operator of the market on which those securities are traded to suspend trading for a period not exceeding ten days or to prohibit trading in those securities.

New s.89L(3) FSMA 2000

The UKLA must have "reasonable grounds" for believing that there has been an infringement of a transparency obligation by a voteholder. There are then two possible courses of action open to UKLA. First, UKLA may prohibit trading in those securities; or, secondly, UKLA may "make a request" to the operator of the market on which those securities are traded to prohibit trading in those securities.

New s.89L(4) FSMA 2000

By contrast with s.89L(2) and (3), in s.89L(4) there is a power to prohibit trading in securities in general. While the statute does not make this clear, the particular transparency obligation which needs to have been breached may need to be stipulated as such in the transparency rules. Therefore, it is in the FSA transparency obligations that we shall see a division between suspension or prohibition of trading with a time period and discontinuances without such a limit.

New s.89L(6) FSMA 2000

A similar issue arises in relation to discontinuance as with public censure in s.89K(6) immediately above, in that the effect of the cross-reference to s.100A(2) here is that, in relation to an issuer whose home state is a member state other than the United Kingdom, the FSA is only permitted to act by means of suspension or prohibition of listing if the issuer has infringed some provision of the EC transparency obligations directive.

New s.89M FSMA 2000

This provision supplements s.89L, and many of its provisions have already been discussed in that context. The principal requirement is the need to provide a person who is to be the subject of an action under s.89L with a notice of that fact, further to s.89L(2).

New s.89M(3) FSMA 2000

The required terms of the notice are more than is required in relation to public censure under s.89K. Importantly, the respondent is required to be given information which could furnish it with grounds for challenging the FSA's decision, including details of the proposed action, importantly a statement of the FSA's reasons for taking the action in question and for choosing the date on which such action should begin, and informing the respondent of his right of appeal to the FSA Tribunal (as considered in relation to the next section).

New s.89N FSMA 2000

The Financial Services and Markets Tribunal ("the Tribunal") was established by s.132 and related provisions of the Financial Services and Markets Act 2000 ("FSMA 2000"). The detailed provisions relating to the Tribunal are provided in Sch13 to the FSMA 2000. The purpose of the Tribunal is to hear appeals from decisions of the FSA, to save on the expensive formality (in the first place at least) of litigation against the FSA under public law in its role as a public body.

Other matters

1269. Corporate governance rules

In Part 6 of the Financial Services and Markets Act 2000 (c. 8), after the sections inserted by section 1268 above insert-

"Corporate governance

89O Corporate governance rules

(1) The competent authority may make rules ("corporate governance rules")-

(a) for the purpose of implementing, enabling the implementation of or dealing with matters arising out of or related to, any Community obligation relating to the corporate governance of issuers who have requested or approved admission of their securities to trading on a regulated market;

(b) about corporate governance in relation to such issuers for the purpose of implementing, or dealing with matters arising out of or related to, any Community obligation.

(2) "Corporate governance", in relation to an issuer, includes-

(a) the nature, constitution or functions of the organs of the issuer;

(b) the manner in which organs of the issuer conduct themselves;

(c) the requirements imposed on organs of the issuer;

(d) the relationship between the different organs of the issuer;

(e) the relationship between the organs of the issuer and the members of the issuer or holders of the issuer's securities.

(3) The burdens and restrictions imposed by rules under this section on foreign-traded issuers must not be greater than the burdens and restrictions imposed on UK-traded issuers by-

(a) rules under this section, and

(b) listing rules.

(4) For this purpose-

"foreign-traded issuer" means an issuer who has requested or approved admission of the issuer's securities to trading on a regulated market situated or operating outside the United Kingdom;

"UK-traded issuer" means an issuer who has requested or approved admission of the issuer's securities to trading on a regulated market situated or operating in the United Kingdom.

(5) This section is without prejudice to any other power conferred by this Part to make Part 6 rules.".

GENERAL NOTE

New s.89O FSMA 2000

As part of the FSA's transparency rules, there will be a subset of "corporate governance rules". The Listing Rules, most recently created by the FSA under authority from FSMA 2000, have long included a statement of "the Model Code" of corporate governance obligations with which listed companies are expected to comply. The transparency obligations require that companies whose securities are traded on regulated markets provide a range of information, either to the public or to UKLA specifically. The underlying policy behind these obligations is to ensure that the investors continue to be able to make informed decisions about their investment once the Prospectus Rules have been complied with at the time when the securities are originally offered to the public. Corporate governance rules are concerned with the manner in which a company conducts its internal business, mainly focusing at this level on the inter-action of the various organs of the complex corporate entities which issue securities on such regulated markets and their debt and equity investors (dealing specifically in this instance with the nature, constitution or functions of the issuer's organs; the manner in which the organs of the issuer conduct themselves; the requirements imposed on organs of the issuer; the relationship between different organs of the issuer; and the relationship between those different organs and members of the issuer or holders of the issuer's securities). At the time of writing, no such corporate governance rules are publicly available.

New s.89O(3) FSMA 2000

The "burdens and restrictions" which are to be imposed by listing rules and corporate governance rules on foreign-traded issuers must not be more burdensome than those imposed on United Kingdom-traded issuers. Thus, the ability of national regulators to "gold-plate" their domestic regulations must not result, in the United Kingdom context, in uneven obligations on securities traded within the United Kingdom and those traded outwith the United Kingdom.

1270. Liability for false or misleading statements in certain publications

In Part 6 of the Financial Services and Markets Act 2000 (c. 8), after section 90 insert-

90A "Compensation for statements in certain publications

(1) The publications to which this section applies are-

    (a) any reports and statements published in response to a requirement imposed by a provision implementing Article 4, 5 or 6 of the transparency obligations directive, and

    (b) any preliminary statement made in advance of a report or statement to be published in response to a requirement imposed by a provision implementing Article 4 of that directive, to the extent that it contains information that it is intended-

        (i) will appear in the report or statement, and

        (ii) will be presented in the report or statement in substantially the same form as that in which it is presented in the preliminary statement.

(2) The securities to which this section applies are-

    (a) securities that are traded on a regulated market situated or operating in the United Kingdom, and

    (b) securities that-

        (i) are traded on a regulated market situated or operating outside the United Kingdom, and

        (ii) are issued by an issuer for which the United Kingdom is the home Member State within the meaning of Article 2.1(i) of the transparency obligations directive.

(3) The issuer of securities to which this section applies is liable to pay compensation to a person who has-

    (a) acquired such securities issued by it, and

    (b) suffered loss in respect of them as a result of-

        (i) any untrue or misleading statement in a publication to which this section applies, or

        (ii) the omission from any such publication of any matter required to be included in it.

(4) The issuer is so liable only if a person discharging managerial responsibilities within the issuer in relation to the publication-

    (a) knew the statement to be untrue or misleading or was reckless as to whether it was untrue or misleading, or

    (b) knew the omission to be dishonest concealment of a material fact.

(5) A loss is not regarded as suffered as a result of the statement or omission in the publication unless the person suffering it acquired the relevant securities-

    (a) in reliance on the information in the publication, and

    (b) at a time when, and in circumstances in which, it was reasonable for him to rely on that information.

(6) Except as mentioned in subsection (8)-

    (a) the issuer is not subject to any other liability than that provided for by this section in respect of loss suffered as a result of reliance by any person on-

        (i) an untrue or misleading statement in a publication to which this section applies, or

        (ii) the omission from any such publication of any matter required to be included in it, and

    (b) a person other than the issuer is not subject to any liability, other than to the issuer, in respect of any such loss.

(7) Any reference in subsection (6) to a person being subject to a liability includes a reference to another person being entitled as against him to be granted any civil remedy or to rescind or repudiate an agreement.

(8) This section does not affect-

(a) the powers conferred by section 382 and 384 (powers of the court to make a restitution order and of the Authority to require restitution);

(b) liability for a civil penalty;

(c) liability for a criminal offence.

(9) For the purposes of this section-

  (a) the following are persons "discharging managerial responsibilities" in relation to a publication-

    (i) any director of the issuer (or person occupying the position of director, by whatever name called),

    (ii) in the case of an issuer whose affairs are managed by its members, any member of the issuer,

    (iii) in the case of an issuer that has no persons within subparagraph (i) or (ii), any senior executive of the issuer having responsibilities in relation to the publication;

  (b) references to the acquisition by a person of securities include his contracting to acquire them or any interest in them.

90B   Power to make further provision about liability for published information

(1) The Treasury may by regulations make provision about the liability of issuers of securities traded on a regulated market, and other persons, in respect of information published to holders of securities, to the market or to the public generally.

(2) Regulations under this section may amend any primary or subordinate legislation, including any provision of, or made under, this Act.".

GENERAL NOTE

New s.90A FSMA 2000

Section 90 FSMA 2000 provides that "[a]ny person responsible for listing particulars [or a prospectus] is liable to pay compensation" to anyone who has acquired securities and suffered loss as a result due to untrue or misleading statements in the prospectus or as a result of an omission from that prospectus. This provision interacts with the general obligation of full disclosure in listing particulars and prospectuses under s.80 of FSMA 2000. The new s.90A of FSMA 2000, introduced by this provision, provides for compensation to be paid in relation to untrue or misleading statements contained in, or in relation to omissions from, the annual financial reports, the half-yearly financial reports, or interim management statements which are required to be published by Arts 4, 5 and 6 of the Transparency Obligations Directive respectively. Thus s.90A in effect extends the effect of s.90 to the new dimension which is added to securities regulation by the Transparency Obligations Directive. Whereas s.90 relates specifically to prospectuses prepared relating to the offer of securities to the public, the purpose of s.90A is to ensure the application of the same liability to the activities of people responsible for the continuing transparency obligations thereafter. Subsection (2), introduced to the bill in its final stages, makes clear that the Act relates only to securities traded on regulated markets.

New s.90A (4) FSMA 2000

What is unclear is what is meant by the term "knowledge" in this context. "Knowledge" could relate to matters (as set out in *Baden Delvaux v. Societe Generale* [1992] 4 All E.R. 161; [1993] 1 W.L.R. 509) which the defendant actually knew, or to matters of which the defendant would have had knowledge but for failing to make the inquiries which an honest and reasonable person would have made, or to matters of which the defendant would have had knowledge but for shutting his eyes to the obvious (whether or not any of these three things were done wilfully or not, see *Montagu's Settlements, Re* [1987] Ch. 264), or to matters which an objectively reasonable person could be deemed to have had knowledge or appreciation in the defendant's circumstances; or they could be limited to matters which an honest person would have known provided that the defendant understood that such a person would have had knowledge of them (see, for example, *Twinsectra Ltd v Yardley* [2002] 2 All E.R. 377 at 387 *per* Lord Hutton). It is suggested that "recklessly" would have the meaning set out in *Derry v Peek* (1889) L.R. 14 App. Cas. 337 at 369 *per* Lord Herschell, or in *Joliffe v Baker* (1883) 11 Q.B.D. 255 at 275 *per* Smith J. to the effect that a person makes a statement recklessly if it is made "not caring whether it was true or false".

New s.90A(6) FSMA 2000

The meaning of this provision is unclear, even when read with s.90A(7) and s.90A(8). At first blush, it is not clear is whether it is all obligations, including obligations at common law or in equity relating to loss, which are to be excluded; or whether it is only obligations under FSMA 2000 which are excluded. However, s.90A(7) suggests that it is all civil remedies which are to be excluded, unless they are "civil penalties" which are saved by s.90A(8): as discussed below. What is unclear then, is which civil actions may be saved and which excluded by s.90A of FSMA 2000. Under the general law (i.e. the law outside FSMA 2000), there could not be double recovery for the same loss (whether by means of common law damages for breach of contract or in tort, or for equitable compensation), but in many circumstances a range of claims might be brought at once so that the claimant could identify during the litigation which claim had the best likelihood of success. Therefore, this provision s.90A(6) could be read either as precluding the bringing of any claim outside s.90A whatsoever (even as an alternative claim should the s.90A fail for some reason which would not prejudice a claim under the general law) or as simply providing that there may not be double recovery if the whole of the claimant's loss were met by a claim under s.90A. The remit of this subsection is qualified by the next two subsections.

New s.90A(7) FSMA 2000

This provision puts a gloss on s.90A(6) to the effect that a claim for "any civil remedy" or to rescind or repudiate an agreement may not be brought where a claim stands under s.90A(6). However, "recession and repudiation" of agreements are equitable remedies and therefore might not be read as falling under the term "any civil remedy". If, as here, the provision is apparently drafted with the intention of distinguishing between "civil remedies" on the one hand and "recession and repudiation" on the other. If they do not fall within the term "any civil remedy" then the term "any civil remedy" must have another meaning than "all remedies which may be brought under civil or private law": that meaning is unclear. Furthermore, s.90A(8) makes this less clear.

New s.90A(8) FSMA 2000

The exclusion of other liabilities rendered in s.90A(6) does not include restitution orders under s.382 and s.384 of FSMA 2000, nor "liability for a civil penalty", nor "liability for a criminal offence". Now, if "liability for a civil penalty" is not excluded by s.90A(6), then to what extent is a claim for "any civil remedy" actually excluded? What is the distinction here between a civil "penalty" and a civil "remedy"? This distinction is not defined in the 2006 Act.

New s.90B FSMA 2000

Two important matters emerge from this provision. First, the Treasury may make regulations to deal with the extent of the liability of issuers of securities on regulated markets - in itself a very broad term of reference indeed. Secondly, those regulations may overrule the terms of the 2006 Act: thus Treasury regulation may be of greater force and effect than provisions of an Act of Parliament. The term "regulated market" is defined in Pt 6 of the Financial Services and Markets Act 2000, as amended by para.11 of Sch.15 to the 2006 Act so as to incorporate by reference the definition of that term used in the Transparency Directive, Art.4(14), in the following terms:

> "'Regulated market' means a multilateral system operated and/or managed by a market operator, which brings together or facilitates the bringing together of multiple third party buying and selling interests in financial instruments - in the system and in accordance with non discretionary rules - in a way that results in a contract in accordance with the provisions of Title II [of the Prospectus Directive]."

1271. Exercise of powers where UK is host member State

In Part 6 of the Financial Services and Markets Act 2000 (c. 8), after section 100 insert-

100A "Exercise of powers where UK is host member state

(1) This section applies to the exercise by the competent authority of any power under this Part exercisable in case of infringement of-
  (a) a provision of prospectus rules or any other provision made in accordance with the prospectus directive, or
  (b) a provision of transparency rules or any other provision made in accordance with the transparency obligations directive,
  in relation to an issuer whose home State is a member State other than the United Kingdom.
(2) The competent authority may act in such a case only in respect of the infringement of a provision required by the relevant directive. Any reference to an applicable provision or applicable transparency obligation shall be read accordingly.

(3) If the authority finds that there has been such an infringement, it must give a notice to that effect to the competent authority of the person's home State requesting it-

    (a) to take all appropriate measures for the purpose of ensuring that the person remedies the situation that has given rise to the notice, and

    (b) to inform the authority of the measures it proposes to take or has taken or the reasons for not taking such measures.

(4) The authority may not act further unless satisfied-

    (a) that the competent authority of the person's home State has failed or refused to take measures for the purpose mentioned in subsection (3)(a), or

    (b) that the measures taken by that authority have proved inadequate for that purpose.

This does not affect exercise of the powers under section 87K(2), 87L(2) or (3) or 89L(2) or (3) (powers to protect market).

(5) If the authority is so satisfied, it must, after informing the competent authority of the person's home State, take all appropriate measures to protect investors.

(6) In such a case the authority must inform the Commission of the measures at the earliest opportunity.".

GENERAL NOTE

New s.100A FSMA 2000

Part of the policy underpinning the EC Transparency Obligations Directive is to enable issues of securities in one Member State to be traded across the European Union once the issue has been approved by the issue's "host state". Similarly, the issuer will have a "home state" in which it is organised and registered, although it may seek to issue its securities, for whatever reason, in another member state. As part of the process of issuing securities in another state, the issuer may seek to have the issue approved in a state other than its home state (and indeed may not seek to have the securities traded in its home state at all). The state in which the approval of the issue is sought is known as the "host state". Trading in those securities may then be conducted in the host state and other Member States, by dint of being passported once there has been approval in that host state. Thus a Maltese entity may seek a listing in London because it considers that the market will look favourably on an issue which has complied with London's stringent listing requirements, and may not seek to have those securities traded in Malta at all, but rather only in London, Paris and Frankfurt. Thus, an approval by UKLA would permit passporting to France and to Germany, making the United Kingdom the host state, even though Malta is the home state. Section 100A is a part of providing for the powers of the FSA where the United Kingdom is the host Member State of an issue of securities.

The competent authority in the issuer's home state retains regulatory oversight, unless that regulator fails to act. Only in that case can the FSA act.

New s.100A(1) FSMA 2000

The "prospectus rules" are those regulations introduced by the FSA acting as UKLA further to the Prospectus Regulations 2005, which in turn introduced inter alia ss.84-87R of the Financial Services and Markets Act 2000, which came into effect on July 1, 2005. The "transparency rules" are the comparator regulations which the FSA will bring into force in the wake of the powers granted to it by the Companies Act 2006 further to the Transparency Obligations Directive. (For a summary discussion of this EC legislation and of its United Kingdom enabling legislation, see the General Note at the beginning of the notes to this Pt 43 of the Companies Act 2006.)

New s.100A(3) FSMA 2000

Notice of any infringement of the transparency obligations in Pt 43 being made by the FSA, where the United Kingdom is the host state, is to be given to the competent authority of the applicable home state with a "request" that that home state competent authority takes the appropriate regulatory measures in accordance with the Transparency Obligations Directive, including informing the FSA of the measures which it will be taking.

New s.100A(4) FSMA 2000

Further to the duty to notify the competent authority of a home state set out in s.100A(3) (considered immediately above), the FSA is thus prevented from taking regulatory action itself (because that is a matter for the person's home state) unless the provisions of this subsection apply. In effect, if the competent authority in the home state fails to act or has taken inadequate action can the FSA act instead. Alternatively, powers in relation to s.87K(2), 87L(2) or (3), or 89L(2) or (3) (as considered severally above where appropriate) are not affected by this prohibition on the FSA taking action in s.100A(3) and (4).

The actions which the FSA is empowered to take, further to s.100A(4), are "all appropriate measures to protect investors". This expression, as considered in the General Note to Pt 43 above, is one of the key regulatory principles expressed in the Transparency Obligations Directive.

1272. Transparency obligations and related matters: minor and consequential amendments

(1) Schedule 15 to this Act makes minor and consequential amendments in connection with the provision made by this Part.

(2) In that Schedule-
Part 1 contains amendments of the Financial Services and Markets Act 2000 (c. 8);
Part 2 contains amendments of the Companies (Audit, Investigations and Community Enterprise) Act 2004 (c. 27).

GENERAL NOTE

The effect of Sch.15 is considered separately.

1273. Corporate governance regulations

(1) The Secretary of State may make regulations-
  (a) for the purpose of implementing, enabling the implementation of or dealing with matters arising out of or related to, any Community obligation relating to the corporate governance of issuers who have requested or approved admission of their securities to trading on a regulated market;
  (b) about corporate governance in relation to such issuers for the purpose of implementing, or dealing with matters arising out of or related to, any Community obligation.

(2) "Corporate governance", in relation to an issuer, includes-
  (a) the nature, constitution or functions of the organs of the issuer;
  (b) the manner in which organs of the issuer conduct themselves;
  (c) the requirements imposed on organs of the issuer;
  (d) the relationship between different organs of the issuer;
  (e) the relationship between the organs of the issuer and the members of the issuer or holders of the issuer's securities.

(3) The regulations may-
  (a) make provision by reference to any specified code on corporate governance that may be issued from time to time by a specified body;
  (b) create new criminal offences (subject to subsection (4));
  (c) make provision excluding liability in damages in respect of things done or omitted for the purposes of, or in connection with, the carrying on, or purported carrying on, of any specified activities.
  "Specified" here means specified in the regulations.

(4) The regulations may not create a criminal offence punishable by a greater penalty than-
  (a) on indictment, a fine;
  (b) on summary conviction, a fine not exceeding the statutory maximum or (if calculated on a daily basis) £100 a day.

(5) Regulations under this section are subject to negative resolution procedure.

(6) In this section "issuer", "securities" and "regulated market" have the same meaning as in Part 6 of the Financial Services and Markets Act 2000 (c. 8).

GENERAL NOTE

In common with s.89O of FSMA 2000 (which grants powers to the FSA), considered above, the powers granted to the Secretary of State in this s.1273 of the Companies Act 2006 relate to the need for clear corporate governance principles which ensure compliance with EC securities regulation. What is meant by "corporate governance" is that same matters considered in relation to s.89O, namely: the nature, constitution or functions of the issuer's organs; the manner in which the organs of the issuer conduct themselves; the requirements imposed on organs of the issuer; the relationship between different organs of the issuer; and the relationship between those different organs and members of the issuer or holders of the issuer's securities. The Secretary of State is empowered to cross-refer with any existing code of governance issued by another body, to create new criminal offences in relation to corporate governance, and to provide for the extent to which any person's liability in damages may be excluded in relation to matters concerning corporate governance.

PART 44

MISCELLANEOUS PROVISIONS

GENERAL NOTE

Sections 1274-1276 amend ss.16 and 17, and are also relevant to s.18, of the Companies (Audit, Investigations and Community Enterprise) Act 2004 (hereafter referred to as the "C(AICE) Act").

Sections 16-18 of the C(AICE) Act 2004 have three principal functions, namely:

1   to permit the Secretary of State to make a grant to any body whose activities include oversight of accountancy and the auditors' profession;
2   to allow the Secretary of State to impose a levy on certain other bodies and persons payable to the body undertaking the oversight role for the purpose of meeting any part of its expenses; and
3   to provide the oversight body with a statutory immunity from liability in damages in respect of its oversight activities.

These clauses represent the first step in implementing the central recommendation of Sir Derek Morris's Review of the Actuarial Profession, the final version of which was published in March 2005. The Review's key proposal was that the Financial Reporting Council (the "FRC") should take on a similar role in relation to the oversight of the actuarial profession to the one it currently exercises with respect to the accountancy and audit profession.

The government warmly welcomed the recommendations of the so-called Morris Review

    (see www.hm-treasury.gov.uk/media/CA0/9C/morris.final.pdf)

and responded positively to its main proposals

    (see www.hm-treasury.gov.uk/media/ABE/E4/morris.govtresponse.pdf).

Subsequently it was announced in the 2005 budget statement that it was the government's intention to legislate in due course to put the oversight regime onto a full statutory footing. However, as details of such a regime had yet to be developed, such proposals could not be included in the Act. In the meantime, the FRC and the Institute and Faculty of Actuaries have agreed that, pending the introduction of a full statutory regime, the former body will begin voluntary oversight of the actuarial profession at the earliest possible opportunity. In fact, the FRC assumed responsibility for actuarial standards and oversight of the profession in April 2006.

The aim of ss.1274-1276 is to provide the minimum necessary statutory underpinning to facilitate a voluntary regime. They achieve this by making amendments to the C(AICE) Act 2004 in two ways. First, they extend the statutory immunity conferred on the FRC and its companion bodies so that it covers acts or omissions relating to oversight of the actuarial profession. Secondly, they allow the Secretary of State, if necessary, to make regulations to require beneficiaries of the actuarial oversight process to contribute towards the funding costs of the proposed regime. This is intended to be a reserve power. It is proposed, as is currently the case with the accountancy and audit profession, to fund this activity on a non-statutory basis by agreement with the insurance and pensions industries and the actuarial profession. The FRC published its final funding proposals in March 2006

    (see www.frc.org.uk/images/uploaded/documents/Actuarial%20standards%20and%20regul
    ation%20-%20FRC%20final%20funding%20proposals%20.1%20March..pdf).

The amendments to the C(AICE) Act 2004 made by the provisions in the Act apply to Scotland only in so far as they relate to matters for which provision would be outside the legislative competence of the Scottish Parliament. However, the amendments do extend to Northern Ireland.

By virtue of subs.(1)(b) of s.1300, ss.1274 and 1276 obtain early commencement, taking effect immediately upon Royal Assent.

Regulation of actuaries etc

1274. Grants to bodies concerned with actuarial standards etc

(1) Section 16 of the Companies (Audit, Investigations and Community Enterprise) Act 2004 (c. 27) (grants to bodies concerned with accounting standards etc) is amended as follows.

(2) In subsection (2) (matters carried on by bodies eligible for grants) for paragraph (l) substitute-

"(l) issuing standards to be applied in actuarial work;

(m) issuing standards in respect of matters to be contained in reports or other communications required to be produced or made by actuaries or in accordance with standards within paragraph (l);

(n) investigating departures from standards within paragraph (l) or (m);

(o) taking steps to secure compliance with standards within paragraph (l) or (m);

(p) carrying out investigations into public interest cases arising in connection with the performance of actuarial functions by members of professional actuarial bodies;

(q) holding disciplinary hearings relating to members of professional actuarial bodies following the conclusion of investigations within paragraph (p);

(r) deciding whether (and, if so, what) disciplinary action should be taken against members of professional actuarial bodies to whom hearings within paragraph (q) related;

(s) supervising the exercise by professional actuarial bodies of regulatory functions in relation to their members;

(t) overseeing or directing any of the matters mentioned above.".

(3) In subsection (5) (definitions) at the appropriate places insert-

""professional actuarial body" means-

(a) the Institute of Actuaries, or

(b) the Faculty of Actuaries in Scotland,

and the "members" of a professional actuarial body include persons who, although not members of the body, are subject to its rules in performing actuarial functions;"

""regulatory functions", in relation to professional actuarial bodies, means any of the following-

(a) investigatory or disciplinary functions exercised by such bodies in relation to the performance by their members of actuarial functions,

(b) the setting by such bodies of standards in relation to the performance by their members of actuarial functions, and

(c) the determining by such bodies of requirements in relation to the education and training of their members;".

GENERAL NOTE

This section deals with the award of grants to bodies concerned with setting actuarial standards and monitoring those who apply them.

Subsection (1)

This recognises that s.1274 amends s.16 of the C(AICE) Act 2004.

Subsection (2)

This subsection amends subs.(2) of s.16 by inserting, into the pre-existing list of matters carried on by bodies eligible for grants, a list of matters relating to activities concerned with the setting of actuarial standards, compliance with those standards, oversight of the actuarial profession and associated matters.

This amends subs.(5) of s.16 so that it includes definitions of "professional actuarial body", "members" of such a body, and "regulatory functions". These amendments are consequential on the amendments to subs.(2) of s.16.

1275.   Levy to pay expenses of bodies concerned with actuarial standards etc

(1) Section 17 of the Companies (Audit, Investigations and Community Enterprise) Act 2004 (c. 27) (levy to pay expenses of bodies concerned with accounting standards etc) is amended in accordance with subsections (2) to (5).

(2) In subsection (3)(a) after "to which" insert ", or persons within subsection (3A) to whom,".

(3) After subsection (3) insert-

"(3A) The following persons are within this subsection-

     (a) the administrators of a public service pension scheme (within the meaning of section 1 of the Pension Schemes Act 1993);

     (b) the trustees or managers of an occupational or personal pension scheme (within the meaning of that section).".

(4) After subsection (4)(b) insert-

"(c) make different provision for different cases.".

(5) After subsection (12) insert-

"(13) If a draft of any regulations to which subsection (10) applies would, apart from this subsection, be treated for the purposes of the standing orders of either House of Parliament as a hybrid instrument, it is to proceed in that House as if it were not such an instrument.".

(6) The above amendments have effect in relation to any exercise of the power to make regulations under section 17 of the Companies (Audit, Investigations and Community Enterprise) Act 2004 after this section comes into force, regardless of when the expenses to be met by the levy in respect of which the regulations are made were incurred.

(7) In Schedule 3 to the Pensions Act 2004 (c. 35) (disclosure of information held by the Pensions Regulator), in the entry relating to the Secretary of State, in the second column, for "or" at the end of paragraph (g) substitute-

     "(ga) Section 17 of the Companies (Audit, Investigations and Community Enterprise) Act 2004 (levy to pay expenses of bodies concerned with accounting standards, actuarial standards etc), or".

GENERAL NOTE

This section indicates how funds are to be raised by a levy to pay the expenses of bodies concerned with setting actuarial standards and monitoring those who apply them.

Subsection (1)

This recognises that s.1275 amends s.17 of the C(AICE) Act 2004.

Subsection (2)

This subsection amends subs.(3)(a) of s.17 so that it includes, amongst those by whom a levy may be payable under this provision, certain persons (as defined in the following subsection), as well as bodies.

Subsection (3)

This subsection inserts a new subsection 3A into s.17, which defines persons for the purposes of subs.(3)(a) of s.17 as the administrators of a public service pension scheme and the trustees and managers of an occupational or personal pension scheme (within the meaning of the Pension Schemes Act 1993). The amendments in subss.(2)-(3) thus enable the Secretary of State to specify such persons as being liable to pay a levy if he considers that the operations of the FRC are substantially relevant to their activities.

This subsection inserts into subs.(4) of s.17 a provision enabling regulations under s.17 to make different provisions where appropriate: e.g. different rates of levy should be payable by various types of bodies or persons.

Subsection (5)
This subsection inserts after subs.(12) a new subsection, (13), the effect of which is to prevent the first regulations made under s.17 - and indeed any other regulations issued under that section that would result in any change in the bodies or persons by whom the levy is payable - from being treated as hybrid instruments for the purposes of the standing orders of either House of Parliament. The effect of such regulations not being treated as hybrid instruments for these purposes is that they would not be subject to the special procedures in the House of Lords that apply to such instruments.

Subsection (6)
This subsection ensures that the amendments made by the previous subsections in s.1275 have effect in relation to any regulations made under s.17 of the C(AICE) Act 2004 after this section comes into force, even if those regulations impose a levy to meet expenditure incurred previously.

Subsection (7)
This amends Sch.3 to the Pensions Act 2004, enabling the Pensions Regulator to disclose restricted information to the Secretary of State to enable or assist him in the exercise of his functions under s.17 of the C(AICE) Act 2004.

1276. Application of provisions to Scotland and Northern Ireland

(1) Section 16 of the Companies (Audit, Investigations and Community Enterprise) Act 2004 (grants to bodies concerned with accounting standards etc) is amended as follows.

(2) For subsection (6) (application of section to Scotland) substitute-

"(6) In their application to Scotland, subsection (2)(a) to (t) are to be read as referring only to matters provision relating to which would be outside the legislative competence of the Scottish Parliament.".

(3) In subsection (2) in paragraph (c), after "1985 (c. 6)" insert "or the 1986 Order".

(4) In subsection (5)-

  (a) in the definition of "company" after "1985 (c. 6)" insert "or the 1986 Order",

  (b) in the definition of "subsidiary" after "1985" insert "or Article 4 of the 1986 Order", and

  (c) after that definition insert-

    ""the 1986 Order" means the Companies (Northern Ireland) Order 1986 (S.I. 1986/1032 (N.I. 6)).".

(5) In section 66 of that Act (extent), in subsection (2) (provisions extending to Northern Ireland, as well as England and Wales and Scotland) for "17" substitute "16 to 18".

GENERAL NOTE
This section deals with the application to Scotland and Northern Ireland of the provisions concerning the setting and monitoring of actuarial standards.

Subsection (1)
In addition to the provisions of s.1275, s.1276 further amends s.16 of the C(AICE) Act 2004 as indicated in the following subsections.

Subsection (2)
This substitutes a new subs.(6) into s.16 of the C(AICE) Act 2004, which provides that paras (a)-(t) of subs.(2) of s.16 (which list matters carried on by bodies eligible for grants) only apply to Scotland in so far as they relate to matters for which provision would be outside the legislative competence of the Scottish Parliament. This is necessary because, while s.16 of the C(AICE) Act 2004 and ss.1274 and 1276 extend to Scotland, some of the matters listed in paras (a)-(t) are not reserved matters for the purposes of s.30 of and Sch.5 to the Scotland Act 1998 and, as such, would otherwise cover areas within the legislative competence of the Scottish Parliament.

Subsection (3)

This makes a minor amendment to s.16(2)(c) of the C(AICE) Act 2004.

Subsection (4)

This makes three minor amendments to s.16(5) of the C(AICE) Act 2004.

Subsection (5)

This amends s.66(2) of the C(AICE) Act 2004 to the effect that ss.16 and 18, as well as s.17, extend to Northern Ireland.

Information as to exercise of voting rights by institutional investors

1277.   Power to require information about exercise of voting rights

(1) The Treasury or the Secretary of State may make provision by regulations requiring institutions to which this section applies to provide information about the exercise of voting rights attached to shares to which this section applies.

(2) This power is exercisable in accordance with-
    section 1278 (institutions to which information provisions apply),
    section 1279 (shares to which information provisions apply), and
    section 1280 (obligations with respect to provision of information).

(3) In this section and the sections mentioned above-
    (a) references to a person acting on behalf of an institution include-
        (i) any person to whom authority has been delegated by the institution to take decisions as to any matter relevant to the subject matter of the regulations, and
        (ii) such other persons as may be specified; and
    (b) "specified" means specified in the regulations.

(4) The obligation imposed by regulations under this section is enforceable by civil proceedings brought by-
    (a) any person to whom the information should have been provided, or
    (b) a specified regulatory authority.

(5) Regulations under this section may make different provision for different descriptions of institution, different descriptions of shares and for other different circumstances.

(6) Regulations under this section are subject to affirmative resolution procedure.

GENERAL NOTE

The group of sections from 1277-1280 (inclusive) provides for regulatory powers for either the Treasury or the Secretary of State to create regulations governing those situations in which information must be provided about the exercise of voting rights attaching to shares. The underlying purpose of this group of provisions is to make it clear how many shares in various companies each of these institutions holds at any given time.

Part 43 of the Companies Act 2006 implemented the Transparency Obligations Directive (on which see the General Note to Pt 43 above). That directive is concerned with the provision of information relating to securities which are already in issue. In turn the Financial Services Authority ("FSA") will introduce transparency rules and corporate governance implementing that directive and the Commission's technical regulation in detail as part of United Kingdom law. One of the key provisions in the transparency obligations code relates to information which is to be provided about the control of voting rights in companies. Institutional investors of the types identified in s.1278(1) are some of the principal investors in the United Kingdom equities markets and, therefore, if one is to make known which entities own what proportion of any given company, then the best place to start such a survey is with those institutional investors. That is the goal of the following three sections.

1278.   Institutions to which information provisions apply

(1) The institutions to which section 1277 applies are-
    (a) unit trust schemes within the meaning of the Financial Services and Markets Act 2000 (c. 8) in respect of which an order is in force under section 243 of that Act;

(b) open-ended investment companies incorporated by virtue of regulations under section 262 of that Act;

(c) companies approved for the purposes of section 842 of the Income and Corporation Taxes Act 1988 (c. 1) (investment trusts);

(d) pension schemes as defined in section 1(5) of the Pension Schemes Act 1993 (c. 48) or the Pension Schemes (Northern Ireland) Act 1993 (c. 49);

(e) undertakings authorised under the Financial Services and Markets Act 2000 to carry on long-term insurance business (that is, the activity of effecting or carrying out contracts of long-term insurance within the meaning of the Financial Services and Markets (Regulated Activities) Order 2001 (S.I. 2001/544);

(f) collective investment schemes that are recognised by virtue of section 270 of that Act (schemes authorised in designated countries or territories).

(2) Regulations under that section may-

(a) provide that the section applies to other descriptions of institution;

(b) provide that the section does not apply to a specified description of institution.

(3) The regulations must specify by whom, in the case of any description of institution, the duty imposed by the regulations is to be fulfilled.

GENERAL NOTE

This provision identifies which forms of institution may be subject to the regulations for the provision of information: they are (briefly put) unit trusts, oeics, investment trusts, pension schemes, entities carrying on long-term insurance business, and collective investment schemes, which are authorised in designated countries or territories. The regulations may extend this provision to other forms of institution or alternatively limit the application of this provision.

Subsection (3)

Importantly, the regulations must specify who is to perform the obligation of providing the information from within any such institution. This is particularly so given that many of them have a number of fiduciary officers of different sorts. For example, unit trusts have a scheme manager and a trustee, both of whom owe fiduciary obligations to the unit trust's participants. Consequently, it will be important to identify which fiduciary entity will bear the burden of providing that information, and possibly who within those entities will bear the particular responsibility of providing the information.

1279. Shares to which information provisions apply

(1) The shares to which section 1277 applies are shares-

(a) of a description traded on a specified market, and

(b) in which the institution has, or is taken to have, an interest.

Regulations under that section may provide that the section does not apply to shares of a specified description.

(2) For this purpose an institution has an interest in shares if the shares, or a depositary certificate in respect of them, are held by it, or on its behalf.

A "depositary certificate" means an instrument conferring rights (other than options)-

(a) in respect of shares held by another person, and

(b) the transfer of which may be effected without the consent of that person.

(3) Where an institution has an interest-

(a) in a specified description of collective investment scheme (within the meaning of the Financial Services and Markets Act 2000 (c. 8)), or

(b) in any other specified description of scheme or collective investment vehicle,

it is taken to have an interest in any shares in which that scheme or vehicle has or is taken to have an interest.

(4) For this purpose a scheme or vehicle is taken to have an interest in shares if it would be regarded as having such an interest in accordance with subsection (2) if it was an institution to which section 1277 applied.

GENERAL NOTE

Having identified which forms of institution must supply this information, it is then important to identify the sorts of shares in relation to which information must be supplied. The regulations will specify the markets on which those shares are to be traded. In turn, an institution is required to make a declaration of information if it has an interest in any shares traded on those specified markets. An institution is taken to have an interest in shares under subs.(2) if it holds a depositary certificate in relation to such a share or under subs.(3) if the institution has an interest in a specified form of collective investment scheme which in turn has an interest in specified shares.

1280. Obligations with respect to provision of information

(1) Regulations under section 1277 may require the provision of specified information about-
    (a) the exercise or non-exercise of voting rights by the institution or any person acting on its behalf,
    (b) any instructions given by the institution or any person acting on its behalf as to the exercise or non-exercise of voting rights, and
    (c) any delegation by the institution or any person acting on its behalf of any functions in relation to the exercise or non-exercise of voting rights or the giving of such instructions.

(2) The regulations may require information to be provided in respect of specified occasions or specified periods.

(3) Where instructions are given to act on the recommendations or advice of another person, the regulations may require the provision of information about what recommendations or advice were given.

(4) The regulations may require information to be provided-
    (a) in such manner as may be specified, and
    (b) to such persons as may be specified, or to the public, or both.

(5) The regulations may provide-
    (a) that an institution may discharge its obligations under the regulations by referring to information disclosed by a person acting on its behalf, and
    (b) that in such a case it is sufficient, where that other person acts on behalf of more than one institution, that the reference is to information given in aggregated form, that is-
        (i) relating to the exercise or non-exercise by that person of voting rights on behalf of more than one institution, or
        (ii) relating to the instructions given by that person in respect of the exercise or non-exercise of voting rights on behalf of more than one institution, or
        (iii) relating to the delegation by that person of functions in relation to the exercise or non-exercise of voting rights, or the giving of instructions in respect of the exercise or non-exercise of voting rights, on behalf of more than one institution.

(6) References in this section to instructions are to instructions of any description, whether general or specific, whether binding or not and whether or not acted upon.

GENERAL NOTE

The sorts of information which are to be provided may extend beyond simply bald information about ownership of certain types of shares. Information may be required by regulation in relation to the manner in which voting rights are exercised, any exercise of voting rights by an institution's agent, any instructions given by an institution to its agents as to the exercise of voting rights, and any delegation of voting rights by an institution. The extension of such categories of information would be in line with the transparency obligations in ss.89B-89E of the FSMA 2000 and the Transparency Obligations Directive generally, which require information not only about ownership of shares, but rather information in greater detail concerning the control of voting rights in relation both to publicly issued securities and entities offering securities to the public. The regulations may require information to be given about advice or recommendations which were given by identified categories of people as to dealings in certain types of security. The manner of the provision of such information and whether or not that information will be published are matters which will be provided by regulation.

Disclosure of information under the Enterprise Act 2002

1281. Disclosure of information under the Enterprise Act 2002

In Part 9 of the Enterprise Act 2002 (c. 40) (information), after section 241 insert-

241A "Civil proceedings

(1) A public authority which holds prescribed information to which section 237 applies may disclose that information to any person-

   (a) for the purposes of, or in connection with, prescribed civil proceedings (including prospective proceedings) in the United Kingdom or elsewhere, or

   (b) for the purposes of obtaining legal advice in relation to such proceedings, or

   (c) otherwise for the purposes of establishing, enforcing or defending legal rights that are or may be the subject of such proceedings.

(2) Subsection (1) does not apply to-

   (a) information which comes to a public authority in connection with an investigation under Part 4, 5 or 6 of the 1973 Act or under section 11 of the Competition Act 1980;

   (b) competition information within the meaning of section 351 of the Financial Services and Markets Act 2000;

   (c) information which comes to a public authority in connection with an investigation under Part 3 or 4 or section 174 of this Act;

   (d) information which comes to a public authority in connection with an investigation under the Competition Act 1998 (c. 41).

(3) In subsection (1) "prescribed" means prescribed by order of the Secretary of State.

(4) An order under this section-

   (a) may prescribe information, or civil proceedings, for the purposes of this section by reference to such factors as appear to the Secretary of State to be appropriate;

   (b) may prescribe for the purposes of this section all information, or civil proceedings, or all information or civil proceedings not falling within one or more specified exceptions;

   (c) must be made by statutory instrument subject to annulment in pursuance of a resolution of either House of Parliament.

(5) Information disclosed under this section must not be used by the person to whom it is disclosed for any purpose other than those specified in subsection (1).".

GENERAL NOTE

  This section inserts into Pt 9 of the Enterprise Act 2002 a new section (s.241A) so that a public authorities can, in certain circumstances, disclose prescribed information which it holds, for the use in civil proceedings or otherwise for the purpose of establishing, enforcing or defending legal rights (subs.(1)). Subsection (2) excepts from disclosure information under a series of provisions in various enactments. "Prescribed" means prescribed by order of the Secretary of State (subs.(3)).

Expenses of winding up

1282. Payment of expenses of winding up

(1) In Chapter 8 of Part 4 of the Insolvency Act 1986 (c. 45) (winding up of companies: provisions of general application), before section 176A (under the heading *"Property subject to floating charge"*) insert-

176ZA   "Payment of expenses of winding up (England and Wales)

(1) The expenses of winding up in England and Wales, so far as the assets of the company available for payment of general creditors are insufficient to meet them, have priority over any claims to property comprised in or subject to any floating charge created by the company and shall be paid out of any such property accordingly.

(2) In subsection (1)-
    (a) the reference to assets of the company available for payment of general creditors does not include any amount made available under section 176A(2)(a);
    (b) the reference to claims to property comprised in or subject to a floating charge is to the claims of-
        (i) the holders of debentures secured by, or holders of, the floating charge, and
        (ii) any preferential creditors entitled to be paid out of that property in priority to them.

(3) Provision may be made by rules restricting the application of subsection (1), in such circumstances as may be prescribed, to expenses authorised or approved-
    (a) by the holders of debentures secured by, or holders of, the floating charge and by any preferential creditors entitled to be paid in priority to them, or
    (b) by the court.

(4) References in this section to the expenses of the winding up are to all expenses properly incurred in the winding up, including the remuneration of the liquidator.".

(2) In Chapter 8 of Part 5 of the Insolvency (Northern Ireland) Order 1989 (S.I. 1989/2405 (N.I. 19)) (winding up of companies: provisions of general application), before Article 150A (under the heading "*Property subject to floating charge*") insert-

Payment of expenses of winding up

"**150ZA**—(1) The expenses of winding up, so far as the assets of the company available for payment of general creditors are insufficient to meet them, have priority over any claims to property comprised in or subject to any floating charge created by the company and shall be paid out of any such property accordingly.

(2) In paragraph (1)-
    (a) the reference to assets of the company available for payment of general creditors does not include any amount made available under Article 150A(2)(a);
    (b) the reference to claims to property comprised in or subject to a floating charge is to the claims of-
        (i) the holders of debentures secured by, or holders of, the floating charge, and
        (ii) any preferential creditors entitled to be paid out of that property in priority to them.

(3) Provision may be made by rules restricting the application of paragraph (1), in such circumstances as may be prescribed, to expenses authorised or approved-
    (a) by the holders of debentures secured by, or holders of, the floating charge and by any preferential creditors entitled to be paid in priority to them, or
    (b) by the Court.

(4) References in this Article to the expenses of the winding up are to all expenses properly incurred in the winding up, including the remuneration of the liquidator.".

GENERAL NOTE

This is a new section which amends the Insolvency Act 1986 so as to reverse the effect of the decision of the House of Lords in *Buchler v Talbot* [2004] UKHL 9. That decision was to the effect that liquidation expenses, whilst taking priority over the claims of preferential and unsecured creditors, did not enjoy the same priority over the claims of floating charge holders. The decision is reversed by the insertion, after s.176A Insolvency Act 1986 of a new section, s.176ZA. It provides that the expenses of the winding up, in so far as the free assets of the company are insufficient to meet them, shall be met out of the proceeds of assets subject to a floating charge in priority to the claims of the floating charge holder (s.176ZA(1)). However, by s.176ZA(3), the general application of subs.(1) may be restricted by rules to expenses authorised or approved by the floating charge holder and any preferential creditors or by the court. Subsection (2) of s.1282 makes similar provision for Northern Ireland.

Commonhold associations

1283. Amendment of memorandum or articles of commonhold association

In paragraph 3(1) of Schedule 3 to the Commonhold and Leasehold Reform Act 2002 (c. 15) (alteration of memorandum or articles by commonhold association to be of no effect until altered version registered with Land Registry) for "An alteration of the memorandum or articles of association" substitute "Where a commonhold association alters its memorandum or articles at a time when the land specified in its memorandum is commonhold land, the alteration".

GENERAL NOTE

This section amends para.3(1) of Sch.3 to the Commonhold and Leasehold Reform Act 2002. That Act established a new form of company, the commonhold association. Commonhold associations are companies limited by guarantee. Commonhold associations must register their memoranda and articles of association with Companies House (on formation) and with HM Land Registry (on registration of the commonhold). Commonhold associations may, to some extent, alter the provisions of their articles and memoranda. Prior to the 2006 Act, para.3 of Sch.3 to the Commonhold and Leasehold Reform Act 2002 provided that any alteration of a commonhold association's memorandum or articles of association which was not registered with the Land Registry was of no effect. The purpose of that provision was to ensure that the version of those documents held by the Land Registry was up to date. However, an unintended consequence was effectively to prohibit any change to the memoranda or articles before they were registered at the Land Registry, i.e. before the registration of the commonhold. This section amends para.3(1) of Sch.3 to the Commonhold and Leasehold Reform Act 2002 so as to remove this difficulty. It creates an exception to the general rule that alterations to the articles or memoranda of commonhold associations must be registered at the Land Registry for commonhold associations during the pre-commonhold period.

PART 45

NORTHERN IRELAND

GENERAL NOTE

Since 1929, Companies Acts have extended to Great Britain only. However, Northern Ireland companies legislation has closely followed changes in GB companies legislation. Prior to the 2006 Act, the principal piece of companies legislation in Northern Ireland was the Companies (Northern Ireland) Order 1986, which was effectively a copy of the 1985 Act, with some very minor modifications. A public consultation, initiated by Northern Ireland ministers, proposed that the new Companies Act, and future legislation under it, should extend directly to Northern Ireland. This was accepted by the Government and this Part of the 2006 Act implements that proposal. However, company law remains in formal terms a transferred matter, and a future Northern Ireland Assembly could, for example, decide to enact separate Northern Ireland companies legislation if it so wished.

1284. Extension of Companies Acts to Northern Ireland

(1) The Companies Acts as defined by this Act (see section 2) extend to Northern Ireland.

(2) The Companies (Northern Ireland) Order 1986 (S.I. 1986/1032 (N.I. 6)), the Companies Consolidation (Consequential Provisions) (Northern Ireland) Order 1986 (S.I. 1986/1035 (N.I. 9)) and Part 3 of the Companies (Audit, Investigations and Community Enterprise) Order 2005 (S.I. 2005/1967 (N.I. 17)) shall cease to have effect accordingly.

GENERAL NOTE

This section provides that the Companies Acts will extend to the whole of the United Kingdom, including Northern Ireland (subs.(1)). This section also repeals the principal pieces of separate Northern Ireland legislation (subs.(2)).

1285.   Extension of GB enactments relating to SEs

(1) The enactments in force in Great Britain relating to SEs extend to Northern Ireland.

(2) The following enactments shall cease to have effect accordingly-
- (a) the European Public Limited-Liability Company Regulations (Northern Ireland) 2004 (SR 2004/ 417), and
- (b) the European Public Limited-Liability Company (Fees) Regulations (Northern Ireland) 2004 (SR 2004/ 418).

(3) In this section "SE" means a European Public Limited-Liability Company (or Societas Europaea) within the meaning of Council Regulation 2157/ 2001/ EC of 8 October 2001 on the Statute for a European Company.

GENERAL NOTE

This section extends GB legislation in relation to European Public Limited Liability Companies (SEs) to Northern Ireland (subs.(1)) and repeals the separate Northern Ireland legislation in this area (subs.(2)).

1286.   Extension of GB enactments relating to certain other forms of business organisation

(1) The enactments in force in Great Britain relating to-
- (a) limited liability partnerships,
- (b) limited partnerships,
- (c) open-ended investment companies, and
- (d) European Economic Interest Groupings,

extend to Northern Ireland.

(2) The following enactments shall cease to have effect accordingly-
- (a) the Limited Liability Partnerships Act (Northern Ireland) 2002 (c. 12 (N. I.));
- (b) the Limited Partnerships Act 1907 (c. 24) as it formerly had effect in Northern Ireland;
- (c) the Open-Ended Investment Companies Act (Northern Ireland) 2002 (c. 13 (N.I.));
- (d) the European Economic Interest Groupings Regulations (Northern Ireland) 1989 (SR 1989/ 216).

GENERAL NOTE

This section extends to Northern Ireland GB legislation relating to several other forms of business organisation, namely limited liability partnerships, limited partnerships, open-ended investment companies, and European Economic Interest Groups (subs.(1)). It also repeals the separate Northern Ireland legislation in these areas (subs.(2)).

1287.   Extension of enactments relating to business names

(1) The provisions of Part 41 of this Act (business names) extend to Northern Ireland.

(2) The Business Names (Northern Ireland) Order 1986 (S.I. 1986/ 1033 (N.I. 7)) shall cease to have effect accordingly.

GENERAL NOTE

This section extends GB legislation on business names to Northern Ireland (subs.(1)) and repeals the separate Northern Ireland legislation on this issue (subs.(2)).

GENERAL SUPPLEMENTARY PROVISIONS

Regulations and orders

1288. Regulations and orders: statutory instrument

Except as otherwise provided, regulations and orders under this Act shall be made by statutory instrument.

GENERAL NOTE

There are numerous powers in the Act for the appropriate body to make regulations and orders, including areas previously regulated only by primary legislation. Most of these powers are given to the Secretary of State and in those cases the section provides that they are to be made by statutory instrument under one of the three procedures set out in the following sections, unless provided otherwise. There are other occasions, as in previous companies legislation, where the Secretary of State is merely required to prescribe various particulars in relation to disclosure requirements without any Parliamentary scrutiny.

Other bodies given rule-making powers by the Act are the Registrar of Companies, the Takeover Panel and the FSA - they do not need to use statutory instruments.

These delegated powers were initially considered by the HL Delegated Powers and Regulatory Reform Committee in its 9th Report of the 2005-6 Parliamentary session (HL Paper 86). In the Bill as originally introduced, there was to be a general power created which would have allowed any aspect of company law to be amended by delegated legislation under a new special Parliamentary procedure. This was severely criticised by the HL Committee in their Report and it was not proceeded with. Otherwise, in general, the various powers were approved, although the procedure to be adopted for implementation was sometimes criticised. In all such cases the procedure was duly changed.

Delegated powers introduced in the various changes to the Bill up to the end of the Committee stage in the HC were approved by the HL Committee in its 19th Report of the 2005-6 session (HL Paper 176). Those introduced even later, relating to general powers to amend the sections on share capital, purchase and redemption of shares and distributions were criticised as being too wide, if taken together, in the Committee's 26th Report of the 2005/6 Session (HL Paper 264). In the event there was a Parliamentary consensus which involved dropping the power on distributions, but retaining the other two.

1289. Regulations and orders: negative resolution procedure

Where regulations or orders under this Act are subject to "negative resolution procedure" the statutory instrument containing the regulations or order shall be subject to annulment in pursuance of a resolution of either House of Parliament.

GENERAL NOTE

Under this procedure, the SI or Order is laid before both Houses of Parliament (usually at least 21 days before it is due to come into force), and will be revoked if either House passes a resolution to that effect within 40 days.

The HL Committee on Delegated Powers and Regulatory Reform in its Report (HL Paper 86) approved the, relatively few, cases where this procedure was specified in the Act, with one exception (see s.1294 below).

1290. Regulations and orders: affirmative resolution procedure

Where regulations or orders under this Act are subject to "affirmative resolution procedure" the regulations or order must not be made unless a draft of the statutory instrument containing them has been laid before Parliament and approved by a resolution of each House of Parliament.

GENERAL NOTE

Under this procedure, the most widely used, the SI or Order will only come into effect when it has been approved by a resolution of both Houses of Parliament. In practice many such SIs, etc. are first issued in draft form for consultation purposes before the Parliamentary debates.

1291.   Regulations and orders: approval after being made

(1) Regulations or orders under this Act that are subject to "approval after being made"-
    (a) must be laid before Parliament after being made, and
    (b) cease to have effect at the end of 28 days beginning with the day on which they were made unless during that period they are approved by resolution of each House.

(2) In reckoning the period of 28 days no account shall be taken of any time during which Parliament is dissolved or prorogued or during which both Houses are adjourned for more than four days.

(3) The regulations or order ceasing to have effect does not affect-
    (a) anything previously done under them or it, or
    (b) the making of new regulations or a new order.

GENERAL NOTE

 This procedure is a variation on the affirmative resolution procedure of the previous section. Under it, the SI or Order is made and comes into effect immediately. It is then laid before each House and will cease to have effect after 28 Parliamentary days unless it is approved by a resolution of each House. If it does so lapse, anything done under it in the interim is valid.

1292.   Regulations and orders: supplementary

(1) Regulations or orders under this Act may-
    (a) make different provision for different cases or circumstances,
    (b) include supplementary, incidental and consequential provision, and
    (c) make transitional provision and savings.

(2) Any provision that may be made by regulations under this Act may be made by order; and any provision that may be made by order under this Act may be made by regulations.

(3) Any provision that may be made by regulations or order under this Act for which no Parliamentary procedure is prescribed may be made by regulations or order subject to negative or affirmative resolution procedure.

(4) Any provision that may be made by regulations or order under this Act subject to negative resolution procedure may be made by regulations or order subject to affirmative resolution procedure.

GENERAL NOTE

 This section sets out the width of the delegated powers under the Act; provides that the use of regulations or an order are interchangeable; and that where a procedure for enacting an SI or Order is set out, a more stringent procedure may be used. These allow for a combination of powers to be exercised in a single instrument.

Meaning of "enactment"

1293.   Meaning of "enactment"

In this Act, unless the context otherwise requires, "enactment" includes-
    (a) an enactment contained in subordinate legislation within the meaning of the Interpretation Act 1978 (c. 30),
    (b) an enactment contained in, or in an instrument made under, an Act of the Scottish Parliament, and
    (c) an enactment contained in, or in an instrument made under, Northern Ireland legislation within the meaning of the Interpretation Act 1978.

This section provides that, subject to contrary intention, an "enactment" as referred to in the Act includes all subordinated legislation in the United Kingdom, as defined in s.21 of the Interpretation Act 1978, and all primary and subordinate legislation of the Scottish Parliament.

Consequential and transitional provisions

1294. Power to make consequential amendments etc

(1) The Secretary of State or the Treasury may by order make such provision amending, repealing or revoking any enactment to which this section applies as they consider necessary or expedient in consequence of any provision made by or under this Act.

(2) This section applies to-
    (a) any enactment passed or made before the passing of this Act,
    (b) any enactment contained in this Act or in subordinate legislation made under it, and
    (c) any enactment passed or made before the end of the session after that in which this Act is passed.

(3) Without prejudice to the generality of the power conferred by subsection (1), orders under this section may-
    (a) make provision extending to other forms of organisation any provision made by or under this Act in relation to companies, or
    (b) make provision corresponding to that made by or under this Act in relation to companies,

in either case with such adaptations or other modifications as appear to the Secretary of State or the Treasury to be necessary or expedient.

(4) The references in subsection (3) to provision made by this Act include provision conferring power to make provision by regulations, orders or other subordinate legislation.

(5) Amendments and repeals made under this section are additional, and without prejudice, to those made by or under any other provision of this Act.

(6) Orders under this section are subject to affirmative resolution procedure.

This section gives the Secretary of State power to make orders additional to those already provided for in the Act. These orders are to be consequential on the changes made by the Act. The power allows for the amendment or repeal of any other prior "enactment" (see the previous section), any "enactment" contained in this Act, or any "enactment" passed before the end of the next Parliamentary session. As such it is a standard provision.

Originally subject to the negative resolution procedure in the Bill, this power is subject to the affirmative resolution procedure following criticism by the HL Committee on Delegated Powers and Regulatory Reform (HL Paper 86).

Subsection (3)
This is an important use of this order making power. It will, for example, allow the DTI to amend the legislation applicable to LLPs to bring it into line with this Act.

1295. Repeals

The enactments specified in Schedule 16, which include enactments that are no longer of practical utility, are repealed to the extent specified.

This section is a standard one introducing Sch.16 to the Act which sets out the various parts and/or sections of other Acts which are repealed by this Act (including most of the Companies Acts 1985 and 1989). To some extent there is an element of duplication since some of those repeals are set out in the body of the Act. This conforms with standard practice whereby only a repeal which presages a substantial change in the law it is set out in the body of the Act. All repeals are set out in the final Schedule to the Act.

1296.   Power to make transitional provision and savings

(1) The Secretary of State or the Treasury may by order make such transitional provision and savings as they consider necessary or expedient in connection with the commencement of any provision made by or under this Act.

(2) An order may, in particular, make such adaptations of provisions brought into force as appear to be necessary or expedient in consequence of other provisions of this Act not yet having come into force.

(3) Transitional provision and savings made under this section are additional, and without prejudice, to those made by or under any other provision of this Act.

(4) Orders under this section are subject to negative resolution procedure.

GENERAL NOTE

This section provides for the necessary power to provide for transitional arrangements as a result of changes made on the implementation of the Act (see s.1300 below). These will include such matters as the status of the memorandum of association of existing companies and the role of pre-existing private company secretaries. The necessary SIs are to be widely consulted on. They are subject to the negative resolution procedure. See also the following section for the situation where there is no change to the pre-existing law, but a re-enactment of it.

1297.   Continuity of the law

(1) This section applies where any provision of this Act re-enacts (with or without modification) an enactment repealed by this Act.

(2) The repeal and re-enactment does not affect the continuity of the law.

(3) Anything done (including subordinate legislation made), or having effect as if done, under or for the purposes of the repealed provision that could have been done under or for the purposes of the corresponding provision of this Act, if in force or effective immediately before the commencement of that corresponding provision, has effect thereafter as if done under or for the purposes of that corresponding provision.

(4) Any reference (express or implied) in this Act or any other enactment, instrument or document to a provision of this Act shall be construed (so far as the context permits) as including, as respects times, circumstances or purposes in relation to which the corresponding repealed provision had effect, a reference to that corresponding provision.

(5) Any reference (express or implied) in any enactment, instrument or document to a repealed provision shall be construed (so far as the context permits), as respects times, circumstances and purposes in relation to which the corresponding provision of this Act has effect, as being or (according to the context) including a reference to the corresponding provision of this Act.

(6) This section has effect subject to any specific transitional provision or saving contained in this Act.

(7) References in this section to this Act include subordinate legislation made under this Act.

(8) In this section "subordinate legislation" has the same meaning as in the Interpretation Act 1978 (c. 30).

GENERAL NOTE

Where there is no change to the law, but there is a re-enactment of previous legislation, this section provides that the former provisions will continue to be legally effective, thus avoiding the need for a myriad of transitional SIs under the previous section.

This will be useful for extant company documents such as the articles, resolutions and contracts, which refer to the former statutory or subordinate legislative provisions (e.g. Table A). If there is a simple re-enactment, such references will be automatically up-dated by this section and their legal effect preserved. It is thus not fully comprehensive, but will save considerable amounts of paper.

PART 47

FINAL PROVISIONS

1298. Short title

The short title of this Act is the Companies Act 2006.

GENERAL NOTE

The change of short title of the Act from the Company Law Reform Act to the Companies Act, was brought about by a cross party vote in favour (see the HC Committee D, col.493). It reflects the fact that although the majority of the Act's provisions do make amendments and innovations to the previous law, substantial parts of it (both as originally drafted and by later additions) are simply re-enactments of former sections of the 1985 and 1989 Acts - thus making it both a reforming and consolidating Act at the same time.

The move to include a substantial consolidation exercise emerged as an agreed strategy during the Parliamentary progress of the Act. Somewhat unusually, most of the re-enacted sections were scrutinised by the Law Society over the summer recess (between the HC Committee and Report stages) rather than by any Parliamentary process. Cynical commentators, comparing the original impetus for the CLRC with the bill as first drafted, have suggested that the original short title was misleading in any event.

1299. Extent

Except as otherwise provided (or the context otherwise requires), the provisions of this Act extend to the whole of the United Kingdom.

GENERAL NOTE

This section reflects the fact that the Act will (unlike its predecessors) apply throughout the United Kingdom, thus including Northern Ireland for the first time. That expansion is considered in more detail in the notes to Pt 45 of the Act.

Company law is a reserved matter for the United Kingdom Parliament under Sch.5 to the Scotland Act 1998 and has not been delegated to the Scottish Parliament.

1300. Commencement

(1) The following provisions come into force on the day this Act is passed-
    (a) Part 43 (transparency obligations and related matters), except the amendment in paragraph 11(2) of Schedule 15 of the definition of "regulated market" in Part 6 of the Financial Services and Markets Act 2000 (c. 8),
    (b) in Part 44 (miscellaneous provisions)-
        section 1274 (grants to bodies concerned with actuarial standards etc), and
        section 1276 (application of provisions to Scotland and Northern Ireland),
    (c) Part 46 (general supplementary provisions), except section 1295 and Schedule 16 (repeals), and
    (d) this Part.
(2) The other provisions of this Act come into force on such day as may be appointed by order of the Secretary of State or the Treasury.

SCHEDULES

SCHEDULE 1   Sections 254 and 255

CONNECTED PERSONS: REFERENCES TO AN INTEREST IN SHARES OR DEBENTURES

Introduction

1. (1) The provisions of this Schedule have effect for the interpretation of references in sections 254 and 255 (directors connected with or controlling a body corporate) to an interest in shares or debentures.

(2) The provisions are expressed in relation to shares but apply to debentures as they apply to shares.

General provisions

2. (1) A reference to an interest in shares includes any interest of any kind whatsoever in shares.

(2) Any restraints or restrictions to which the exercise of any right attached to the interest is or may be subject shall be disregarded.

(3) It is immaterial that the shares in which a person has an interest are not identifiable.

(4) Persons having a joint interest in shares are deemed each of them to have that interest.

Rights to acquire shares

3. (1) A person is taken to have an interest in shares if he enters into a contract to acquire them.

(2) A person is taken to have an interest in shares if-

    (a) he has a right to call for delivery of the shares to himself or to his order, or

    (b) he has a right to acquire an interest in shares or is under an obligation to take an interest in shares,

whether the right or obligation is conditional or absolute.

(3) Rights or obligations to subscribe for shares are not to be taken for the purposes of sub-paragraph (2) to be rights to acquire or obligations to take an interest in shares.

(4) A person ceases to have an interest in shares by virtue of this paragraph-

    (a) on the shares being delivered to another person at his order-

        (i) in fulfilment of a contract for their acquisition by him, or

        (ii) in satisfaction of a right of his to call for their delivery;

    (b) on a failure to deliver the shares in accordance with the terms of such a contract or on which such a right falls to be satisfied;

    (c) on the lapse of his right to call for the delivery of shares.

Right to exercise or control exercise of rights

4. (1) A person is taken to have an interest in shares if, not being the registered holder, he is entitled-

    (a) to exercise any right conferred by the holding of the shares, or

    (b) to control the exercise of any such right.

(2) For this purpose a person is taken to be entitled to exercise or control the exercise of a right conferred by the holding of shares if he-

    (a) has a right (whether subject to conditions or not) the exercise of which would make him so entitled, or

    (b) is under an obligation (whether or not so subject) the fulfilment of which would make him so entitled.

(3) A person is not by virtue of this paragraph taken to be interested in shares by reason only that-

    (a) he has been appointed a proxy to exercise any of the rights attached to the shares, or

    (b) he has been appointed by a body corporate to act as its representative at any meeting of a company or of any class of its members.

Bodies corporate

5. (1) A person is taken to be interested in shares if a body corporate is interested in them and-

    (a) the body corporate or its directors are accustomed to act in accordance with his directions or instructions, or

    (b) he is entitled to exercise or control the exercise of more than one-half of the voting power at general meetings of the body corporate.

(2) For the purposes of sub-paragraph (1)(b) where-

    (a) a person is entitled to exercise or control the exercise of more than one-half of the voting power at general meetings of a body corporate, and

    (b) that body corporate is entitled to exercise or control the exercise of any of the voting power at general meetings of another body corporate,

the voting power mentioned in paragraph (b) above is taken to be exercisable by that person.

Trusts

6. (1) Where an interest in shares is comprised in property held on trust, every beneficiary of the trust is taken to have an interest in shares, subject as follows.

(2) So long as a person is entitled to receive, during the lifetime of himself or another, income from trust property comprising shares, an interest in the shares in reversion or remainder or (as regards Scotland) in fee shall be disregarded.

(3) A person is treated as not interested in shares if and so long as he holds them-

    (a) under the law in force in any part of the United Kingdom, as a bare trustee or as a custodian trustee, or

    (b) under the law in force in Scotland, as a simple trustee.

(4) There shall be disregarded any interest of a person subsisting by virtue of-

    (a) an authorised unit trust scheme (within the meaning of section 237 of the Financial Services and Markets Act 2000 (c. 8));

    (b) a scheme made under section 22 or 22A of the Charities Act 1960 (c. 58), section 25 of the Charities Act (Northern Ireland) 1964 (c. 33 (N.I.)) or section 24 or 25 of the Charities Act 1993 (c. 10), section 11 of the Trustee Investments Act 1961 (c. 62) or section 42 of the Administration of Justice Act 1982 (c. 53); or

    (c) the scheme set out in the Schedule to the Church Funds Investment Measure 1958 (1958 No. 1).

(5) There shall be disregarded any interest-

    (a) of the Church of Scotland General Trustees or of the Church of Scotland Trust in shares held by them;

    (b) of any other person in shares held by those Trustees or that Trust otherwise than as simple trustees.

"The Church of Scotland General Trustees" are the body incorporated by the order confirmed by the Church of Scotland (General Trustees) Order Confirmation Act 1921 (1921 c. xxv), and "the Church of Scotland Trust" is the body incorporated by the order confirmed by the Church of Scotland Trust Order Confirmation Act 1932 (1932 c. xxi).

GENERAL NOTE

This schedule replaces Pt 1 of Sch.13 to the 1985 Act.

Paragraph 1

This is a new paragraph. Sub-paragraph (1) states that the schedule assists with the interpretation of ss.254 and 255, and sub-para.(2) states that although the provisions are expressed in relation to shares they apply equally to debentures.

Paragraph 2

This paragraph replaces paras 1, 7 and 8 of Sch.13 to the 1985 Act without substantive change.

Paragraph 3

This paragraph replaces paras 3(1)(a), 6 and 13 of Sch.13 to the 1985 Act without substantive change.

Paragraph 4

This paragraph replaces paras 3(1)(b), (2) and (3) of Sch.13 to the 1985 Act without significant change. The only change is that the statement in sub-para.(3)(a) that 'persons are not by virtue of para.4 to be taken to be interested in shares by reason only that he has been appointed a proxy to vote at a specified meeting' has been extended to so as to apply to the exercise of any rights attached to the shares, not only voting rights at specific meetings.

Paragraph 5

This paragraph replaces paras 4 and 5 of Sch.13 to the 1985 Act without substantive change.

Paragraph 6

This paragraph replaces paras 2 and 9-12 of Sch.13 to the 1985 Act without substantive change.

SPECIFIED PERSONS, DESCRIPTIONS OF DISCLOSURES ETC FOR THE PURPOSES OF SECTION 948

PART 1

SPECIFIED PERSONS

1. The Secretary of State.

2. The Department of Enterprise, Trade and Investment for Northern Ireland.

3. The Treasury.

4. The Bank of England.

5. The Financial Services Authority.

6. The Commissioners for Her Majesty's Revenue and Customs.

7. The Lord Advocate.

8. The Director of Public Prosecutions.

9. The Director of Public Prosecutions for Northern Ireland.

10. A constable.

11. A procurator fiscal.

12. The Scottish Ministers.

PART 2

SPECIFIED DESCRIPTIONS OF DISCLOSURES

13. A disclosure for the purpose of enabling or assisting a person authorised under section 457 of this Act (persons authorised to apply to court) to exercise his functions.
Until the coming into force of section 457, the reference to that section is to be read as a reference to section 245C of the Companies Act 1985 (c. 6).

14. A disclosure for the purpose of enabling or assisting an inspector appointed under Part 14 of the Companies Act 1985 (investigation of companies and their affairs, etc) to exercise his functions.

15. A disclosure for the purpose of enabling or assisting a person authorised under section 447 of the Companies Act 1985 (power to require production of documents) or section 84 of the Companies Act 1989 (c. 40) (exercise of powers by officer etc) to exercise his functions.

16. A disclosure for the purpose of enabling or assisting a person appointed under section 167 of the Financial Services and Markets Act 2000 (c. 8) (general investigations) to conduct an investigation to exercise his functions.

17. A disclosure for the purpose of enabling or assisting a person appointed under section 168 of the Financial Services and Markets Act 2000 (investigations in particular cases) to conduct an investigation to exercise his functions.

18. A disclosure for the purpose of enabling or assisting a person appointed under section 169(1)(b) of the Financial Services and Markets Act 2000 (investigation in support of overseas regulator) to conduct an investigation to exercise his functions.

19. A disclosure for the purpose of enabling or assisting the body corporate responsible for administering the scheme referred to in section 225 of the Financial Services and Markets Act 2000 (the ombudsman scheme) to exercise its functions.

20. A disclosure for the purpose of enabling or assisting a person appointed under paragraph 4 (the panel of ombudsmen) or 5 (the Chief Ombudsman) of Schedule 17 to the Financial Services and Markets Act 2000 to exercise his functions.

21. A disclosure for the purpose of enabling or assisting a person appointed under regulations made under section 262(1) and (2)(k) of the Financial Services and Markets Act 2000 (investigations into open-ended investment companies) to conduct an investigation to exercise his functions.

22. A disclosure for the purpose of enabling or assisting a person appointed under section 284 of the Financial Services and Markets Act 2000 (investigations into affairs of certain collective investment schemes) to conduct an investigation to exercise his functions.

23. A disclosure for the purpose of enabling or assisting the investigator appointed under paragraph 7 of Schedule 1 to the Financial Services and Markets Act 2000 (arrangements for investigation of complaints) to exercise his functions.

24. A disclosure for the purpose of enabling or assisting a person appointed by the Treasury to hold an inquiry into matters relating to financial services (including an inquiry under section 15 of the Financial Services and Markets Act 2000 (c. 8)) to exercise his functions.

25. A disclosure for the purpose of enabling or assisting the Secretary of State or the Treasury to exercise any of their functions under any of the following-
    (a) the Companies Acts;
    (b) Part 5 of the Criminal Justice Act 1993 (c. 36) (insider dealing);
    (c) the Insolvency Act 1986 (c. 45);
    (d) the Company Directors Disqualification Act 1986 (c. 46);
    (e) Part 42 of this Act (statutory auditors);
    (f) Part 3 (investigations and powers to obtain information) or 7 (financial markets and insolvency) of the Companies Act 1989 (c. 40);
    (g) the Financial Services and Markets Act 2000.
Until the coming into force of Part 42 of this Act, the reference to it in paragraph (e) is to be read as a reference to Part 2 of the Companies Act 1989.

26. A disclosure for the purpose of enabling or assisting the Scottish Ministers to exercise their functions under the enactments relating to insolvency.

27. A disclosure for the purpose of enabling or assisting the Department of Enterprise, Trade and Investment for Northern Ireland to exercise any powers conferred on it by the enactments relating to companies or insolvency.

28. A disclosure for the purpose of enabling or assisting a person appointed or authorised by the Department of Enterprise, Trade and Investment for Northern Ireland under the enactments relating to companies or insolvency to exercise his functions.

29. A disclosure for the purpose of enabling or assisting the Pensions Regulator to exercise the functions conferred on it by or by virtue of any of the following-
    (a) the Pension Schemes Act 1993 (c. 48);
    (b) the Pensions Act 1995 (c. 26);
    (c) the Welfare Reform and Pensions Act 1999 (c. 30);
    (d) the Pensions Act 2004 (c. 35);
    (e) any enactment in force in Northern Ireland corresponding to any of those enactments.

30. A disclosure for the purpose of enabling or assisting the Board of the Pension Protection Fund to exercise the functions conferred on it by or by virtue of Part 2 of the Pensions Act 2004 or any enactment in force in Northern Ireland corresponding to that Part.

31. A disclosure for the purpose of enabling or assisting-
    (a) the Bank of England,
    (b) the European Central Bank, or
    (c) the central bank of any country or territory outside the United Kingdom,
to exercise its functions.

32. A disclosure for the purpose of enabling or assisting the Commissioners for Her Majesty's Revenue and Customs to exercise their functions.

33. A disclosure for the purpose of enabling or assisting organs of the Society of Lloyd's (being organs constituted by or under the Lloyd's Act 1982 (c. xiv)) to exercise their functions under or by virtue of the Lloyd's Acts 1871 to 1982.

34. A disclosure for the purpose of enabling or assisting the Office of Fair Trading to exercise its functions under any of the following-
    (a) the Fair Trading Act 1973 (c. 41);
    (b) the Consumer Credit Act 1974 (c. 39);
    (c) the Estate Agents Act 1979 (c. 38);

　　(d) the Competition Act 1980 (c. 21);

　　(e) the Competition Act 1998 (c. 41);

　　(f) the Financial Services and Markets Act 2000 (c. 8);

　　(g) the Enterprise Act 2002 (c. 40);

　　(h) the Control of Misleading Advertisements Regulations 1988 (S.I. 1988/915);

　　(i) the Unfair Terms in Consumer Contracts Regulations 1999 (S.I. 1999/2083).

35. A disclosure for the purpose of enabling or assisting the Competition Commission to exercise its functions under any of the following-

　　(a) the Fair Trading Act 1973;

　　(b) the Competition Act 1980;

　　(c) the Competition Act 1998;

　　(d) the Enterprise Act 2002.

36. A disclosure with a view to the institution of, or otherwise for the purposes of, proceedings before the Competition Appeal Tribunal.

37. A disclosure for the purpose of enabling or assisting an enforcer under Part 8 of the Enterprise Act 2002 (enforcement of consumer legislation) to exercise its functions under that Part.

38. A disclosure for the purpose of enabling or assisting the Charity Commission to exercise its functions.

39. A disclosure for the purpose of enabling or assisting the Attorney General to exercise his functions in connection with charities.

40. A disclosure for the purpose of enabling or assisting the National Lottery Commission to exercise its functions under sections 5 to 10 (licensing) and 15 (power of Secretary of State to require information) of the National Lottery etc. Act 1993 (c. 39).

41. A disclosure by the National Lottery Commission to the National Audit Office for the purpose of enabling or assisting the Comptroller and Auditor General to carry out an examination under Part 2 of the National Audit Act 1983 (c. 44) into the economy, effectiveness and efficiency with which the National Lottery Commission has used its resources in discharging its functions under sections 5 to 10 of the National Lottery etc. Act 1993.

42. A disclosure for the purpose of enabling or assisting a qualifying body under the Unfair Terms in Consumer Contracts Regulations 1999 (S.I. 1999/ 2083) to exercise its functions under those Regulations.

43. A disclosure for the purpose of enabling or assisting an enforcement authority under the Consumer Protection (Distance Selling) Regulations 2000 (S.I. 2000/2334) to exercise its functions under those Regulations.

44. A disclosure for the purpose of enabling or assisting an enforcement authority under the Financial Services (Distance Marketing) Regulations 2004 (S.I. 2004/2095) to exercise its functions under those Regulations.

45. A disclosure for the purpose of enabling or assisting a local weights and measures authority in England and Wales to exercise its functions under section 230(2) of the Enterprise Act 2002 (c. 40) (notice of intention to prosecute, etc).

46. A disclosure for the purpose of enabling or assisting the Financial Services Authority to exercise its functions under any of the following-

　　(a) the legislation relating to friendly societies or to industrial and provident societies;

　　(b) the Building Societies Act 1986 (c. 53);

　　(c) Part 7 of the Companies Act 1989 (c. 40) (financial markets and insolvency);

　　(d) the Financial Services and Markets Act 2000 (c. 8).

47. A disclosure for the purpose of enabling or assisting the competent authority for the purposes of Part 6 of the Financial Services and Markets Act 2000 (official listing) to exercise its functions under that Part.

48. A disclosure for the purpose of enabling or assisting a body corporate established in accordance with section 212(1) of the Financial Services and Markets Act 2000 (compensation scheme manager) to exercise its functions.

49. A disclosure for the purpose of enabling or assisting a recognised investment exchange or a recognised clearing house to exercise its functions as such.

"Recognised investment exchange" and "recognised clearing house" have the same meaning as in section 285 of the Financial Services and Markets Act 2000.

50. A disclosure for the purpose of enabling or assisting a person approved under the Uncertificated Securities Regulations 2001 (S.I. 2001/3755) as an operator of a relevant system (within the meaning of those regulations) to exercise his functions.

51. A disclosure for the purpose of enabling or assisting a body designated under section 326(1) of the Financial Services and Markets Act 2000 (designated professional bodies) to exercise its functions in its capacity as a body designated under that section.

52. A disclosure with a view to the institution of, or otherwise for the purposes of, civil proceedings arising under or by virtue of the Financial Services and Markets Act 2000.

53. A disclosure for the purpose of enabling or assisting a body designated by order under section 1252 of this Act (delegation of functions of Secretary of State) to exercise its functions under Part 42 of this Act (statutory auditors).
Until the coming into force of that Part, the references to section 1252 and Part 42 are to be read as references to section 46 of the Companies Act 1989 (c. 40) and Part 2 of that Act respectively.

54. A disclosure for the purpose of enabling or assisting a recognised supervisory or qualifying body, within the meaning of Part 42 of this Act, to exercise its functions as such.
Until the coming into force of that Part, the reference to it is to be read as a reference to Part 2 of the Companies Act 1989.

55. A disclosure for the purpose of enabling or assisting an official receiver (including the Accountant in Bankruptcy in Scotland and the Official Assignee in Northern Ireland) to exercise his functions under the enactments relating to insolvency.

56. A disclosure for the purpose of enabling or assisting the Insolvency Practitioners Tribunal to exercise its functions under the Insolvency Act 1986 (c. 45).

57. A disclosure for the purpose of enabling or assisting a body that is for the time being a recognised professional body for the purposes of section 391 of the Insolvency Act 1986 (recognised professional bodies) to exercise its functions as such.

58. A disclosure for the purpose of enabling or assisting an overseas regulatory authority to exercise its regulatory functions.
"Overseas regulatory authority" and "regulatory functions" have the same meaning as in section 82 of the Companies Act 1989.

59. A disclosure for the purpose of enabling or assisting the Regulator of Community Interest Companies to exercise functions under the Companies (Audit, Investigations and Community Enterprise) Act 2004 (c. 27).

60. A disclosure with a view to the institution of, or otherwise for the purposes of, criminal proceedings.

61. A disclosure for the purpose of enabling or assisting a person authorised by the Secretary of State under Part 2, 3 or 4 of the Proceeds of Crime Act 2002 (c. 29) to exercise his functions.

62. A disclosure with a view to the institution of, or otherwise for the purposes of, proceedings on an application under section 6, 7 or 8 of the Company Directors Disqualification Act 1986 (c. 46) (disqualification for unfitness).

63. A disclosure with a view to the institution of, or otherwise for the purposes of, proceedings before the Financial Services and Markets Tribunal.

64. A disclosure for the purposes of proceedings before the Financial Services Tribunal by virtue of the Financial Services and Markets Act 2000 (Transitional Provisions) (Partly Completed Procedures) Order 2001 (S.I. 2001/3592).

65. A disclosure for the purposes of proceedings before the Pensions Regulator Tribunal.

66. A disclosure for the purpose of enabling or assisting a body appointed under section 14 of the Companies (Audit, Investigations and Community Enterprise) Act 2004 (supervision of periodic accounts and reports of issuers of listed securities) to exercise functions mentioned in subsection (2) of that section.

67. A disclosure with a view to the institution of, or otherwise for the purposes of, disciplinary proceedings relating to the performance by a solicitor, barrister, advocate, foreign lawyer, auditor, accountant, valuer or actuary of his professional duties.
"Foreign lawyer" has the meaning given by section 89(9) of the Courts and Legal Services Act 1990 (c. 41).

68. A disclosure with a view to the institution of, or otherwise for the purposes of, disciplinary proceedings relating to the performance by a public servant of his duties.
"Public servant" means an officer or employee of the Crown or of any public or other authority for the time being designated for the purposes of this paragraph by the Secretary of State by order subject to negative resolution procedure.

69. A disclosure for the purpose of the provision of a summary or collection of information framed in such a way as not to enable the identity of any person to whom the information relates to be ascertained.

70. A disclosure in pursuance of any Community obligation.

PART 3

OVERSEAS REGULATORY BODIES

71. A disclosure is made in accordance with this Part of this Schedule if-
    (a) it is made to a person or body within paragraph 72, and
    (b) it is made for the purpose of enabling or assisting that person or body to exercise the functions mentioned in that paragraph.

72. The persons or bodies that are within this paragraph are those exercising functions of a public nature, under legislation in any country or territory outside the United Kingdom, that appear to the Panel to be similar to its own functions or those of the Financial Services Authority.

73. In determining whether to disclose information to a person or body in accordance with this Part of this Schedule, the Panel must have regard to the following considerations-
    (a) whether the use that the person or body is likely to make of the information is sufficiently important to justify making the disclosure;
    (b) whether the person or body has adequate arrangements to prevent the information from being used or further disclosed otherwise than for the purposes of carrying out the functions mentioned in paragraph 72 or any other purposes substantially similar to those for which information disclosed to the Panel could be used or further disclosed.

GENERAL NOTE
See discussion above under s.948.

SCHEDULE 3   Section 1124

AMENDMENTS OF REMAINING PROVISIONS OF THE COMPANIES ACT 1985 RELATING TO OFFENCES

Failure to give information about interests in shares etc

1. (1) In subsection (3) of section 444 of the Companies Act 1985 (c. 6) (failure to give information requested by Secretary of State relating to interests in shares etc) for "is liable to imprisonment or a fine, or both" substitute "commits an offence".
(2) At the end of that section add-
    "(4) A person guilty of an offence under this section is liable-
        (a) on conviction on indictment, to imprisonment for a term not exceeding two years or a fine (or both);
        (b) on summary conviction-
            (i) in England and Wales, to imprisonment for a term not exceeding twelve months or to a fine not exceeding the statutory maximum (or both) and, for continued contravention, a daily default fine not exceeding onefiftieth of the statutory maximum;
            (ii) in Scotland or Northern Ireland, to imprisonment for a term not exceeding six months, or to a fine not exceeding the statutory maximum (or both) and, for continued contravention, a daily default fine not exceeding one-fiftieth of the statutory maximum.".

Obstruction of rights conferred by a warrant or failure to comply with requirement under section 448

2. (1) In section 448(7) of the Companies Act 1985 (obstruction of rights conferred by or by virtue of warrant for entry and search of premises) omit the words "and liable to a fine." to the end.
(2) After that provision insert-
    "(7A) A person guilty of an offence under this section is liable-
        (a) on conviction on indictment, to a fine;
        (b) on summary conviction, to a fine not exceeding the statutory maximum.".

Wrongful disclosure of information to which section 449 applies

3. (1) Section 449 of the Companies Act 1985 (wrongful disclosure of information obtained in course of company investigation) is amended as follows.
(2) For subsection (6)(a) and (b) substitute "is guilty of an offence."

(3) After subsection (6) insert-
"(6A) A person guilty of an offence under this section is liable-
    (a) on conviction on indictment, to imprisonment for a term not exceeding two years or a fine (or both);
    (b) on summary conviction-
        (i) in England and Wales, to imprisonment for a term not exceeding twelve months or to a fine not exceeding the statutory maximum (or both);
        (ii) in Scotland or Northern Ireland, to imprisonment for a term not exceeding six months, or to a fine not exceeding the statutory maximum (or both).".

(4) Omit subsection (7).

Destruction, mutilation etc of company documents

4. (1) For subsection (3) of section 450 of the Companies Act 1985 (offence of destroying, etc company documents) substitute-
"(3) A person guilty of an offence under this section is liable-
    (a) on conviction on indictment, to imprisonment for a term not exceeding seven years or a fine (or both);
    (b) on summary conviction-
        (i) in England and Wales, to imprisonment for a term not exceeding twelve months or to a fine not exceeding the statutory maximum (or both);
        (ii) in Scotland or Northern Ireland, to imprisonment for a term not exceeding six months, or to a fine not exceeding the statutory maximum (or both).".

(2) Omit subsection (4) of that section.

Provision of false information in purported compliance with section 447

5. (1) For subsection (2) of section 451 of the Companies Act 1985 (c. 6) (provision of false information in response to requirement under section 447) substitute-
"(2) A person guilty of an offence under this section is liable-
    (a) on conviction on indictment, to imprisonment for a term not exceeding two years or a fine (or both);
    (b) on summary conviction-
        (i) in England and Wales, to imprisonment for a term not exceeding twelve months or to a fine not exceeding the statutory maximum (or both);
        (ii) in Scotland or Northern Ireland, to imprisonment for a term not exceeding six months, or to a fine not exceeding the statutory maximum (or both).".

(2) Omit subsection (3) of that section.

Obstruction of inspector, etc exercising power to enter and remain on premises

6. (1) Section 453A of the Companies Act 1985 (obstruction of inspector etc exercising power to enter and remain on premises) is amended as follows.

(2) For subsection (5)(a) and (b) substitute "is guilty of an offence."

(3) After subsection (5) insert-
"(5A) A person guilty of an offence under this section is liable-
    (a) on conviction on indictment, to a fine;
    (b) on summary conviction, to a fine not exceeding the statutory maximum.".

(4) Omit subsection (6).

Attempted evasion of restrictions under Part 15

7. (1) In subsection (1) of section 455 of the Companies Act 1985 (attempted evasion of restrictions under Part 15) for "is liable to a fine if he" substitute "commits an offence if he".

(2) In subsection (2) of that section for the words "the company" to the end substitute
"an offence is committed by-
    (a) the company, and
    (b) every officer of the company who is in default."

(3) After that subsection insert-
"(2A) A person guilty of an offence under this section is liable-
    (a) on conviction on indictment, to a fine;
    (b) on summary conviction, to a fine not exceeding the statutory maximum.".

GENERAL NOTE
This Schedule contains amendments to any remaining provisions of the Companies Act 1985 concerned with offences. It contains seven paragraphs, each dealing with a separate provision of that Act.

Failure to give information about interests in shares etc
This paragraph amends s.444(3) of the Companies Act 1985. It also adds a new subs.(4) to that section which provides that the penalty for an offence under it is, in England and Wales, a term of imprisonment not exceeding twelve months or a

fine not exceeding the statutory maximum (or both and, for continued contravention, a daily default fine not exceeding one fiftieth of the statutory maximum). In Scotland or Northern Ireland the maximum term of imprisonment is six months.

Obstruction of rights conferred by a warrant or failure to comply with requirement under s.448

This paragraph amends s.448(7) of the Companies Act 1985 and adds a new subs.(7A) prescribing the penalty for an offence under the section.

Wrongful disclosure of information to which s.449 applies

This paragraph amends s.449 of the Companies Act 1985 so as to omit subs.(7) of that section and to insert a new subs.(6A) which prescribes the penalty for an offence under s.449.

Destruction, mutilation etc of company documents

This section amends s.450(3) of the Companies Act 1985 to prescribe the penalty for an offence under that section on conviction on indictment as a term of imprisonment not exceeding seven months or a fine (or both). On summary conviction the penalty in England and Wales is imprisonment for a term not exceeding twelve months or to a fine not exceeding the statutory maximum (or both) and in Scotland or Northern Ireland, to imprisonment for a term not exceeding six months, or to a fine not exceeding the statutory maximum (or both). Section 450(4) is omitted.

Provision of false information in purported compliance with s.447

This paragraph amends s.451(2) of the Companies Act 1985 to prescribe the penalties for an offence committed under the section, and omits subs.(3) of that section.

Obstruction of inspector, etc. exercising power to enter and remain on premises

This paragraph amends s.453A of the Companies Act 1985. The penalty for an offence under that section is prescribed in a new subs.(5A) and subs.(6) is omitted.

Attempted evasion of restrictions under Pt 15

This paragraph amends s.455 of the Companies Act 1985. It inserts a new subs.(3A) to prescribe the penalties for an offence committed under the section.

SCHEDULE 4   Section 1144(1)

DOCUMENTS AND INFORMATION SENT OR SUPPLIED TO A COMPANY

PART 1

INTRODUCTION

Application of Schedule

1. (1) This Schedule applies to documents or information sent or supplied to a company.

(2) It does not apply to documents or information sent or supplied by another company (see section 1144(3) and Schedule 5).

PART 2

COMMUNICATIONS IN HARD COPY FORM

Introduction

2. A document or information is validly sent or supplied to a company if it is sent or supplied in hard copy form in accordance with this Part of this Schedule.

948

Method of communication in hard copy form

3. (1) A document or information in hard copy form may be sent or supplied by hand or by post to an address (in accordance with paragraph 4).

(2) For the purposes of this Schedule, a person sends a document or information by post if he posts a prepaid envelope containing the document or information.

Address for communications in hard copy form

4. A document or information in hard copy form may be sent or supplied-

    (a) to an address specified by the company for the purpose;

    (b) to the company's registered office;

    (c) to an address to which any provision of the Companies Acts authorises the document or information to be sent or supplied.

PART 3

COMMUNICATIONS IN ELECTRONIC FORM

Introduction

5. A document or information is validly sent or supplied to a company if it is sent or supplied in electronic form in accordance with this Part of this Schedule.

Conditions for use of communications in electronic form

6. A document or information may only be sent or supplied to a company in electronic form if-

    (a) the company has agreed (generally or specifically) that the document or information may be sent or supplied in that form (and has not revoked that agreement), or

    (b) the company is deemed to have so agreed by a provision in the Companies Acts.

Address for communications in electronic form

7. (1) Where the document or information is sent or supplied by electronic means, it may only be sent or supplied to an address-

    (a) specified for the purpose by the company (generally or specifically), or

    (b) deemed by a provision in the Companies Acts to have been so specified.

(2) Where the document or information is sent or supplied in electronic form by hand or by post, it must be sent or supplied to an address to which it could be validly sent if it were in hard copy form.

PART 4

OTHER AGREED FORMS OF COMMUNICATION

8. A document or information that is sent or supplied to a company otherwise than in hard copy form or electronic form is validly sent or supplied if it is sent or supplied in a form or manner that has been agreed by the company.

GENERAL NOTE

Part 1: Introduction

    This Schedule is intended to apply where documents or information is sent or supplied to a company (para.(1)).

Part 2: Communications in Hard Copy Form

    This Part specifies that a document is validly sent or supplied to a company if this is effected in accordance with this Part of the Schedule (para.(2)). Such a document or information in hard copy form may be sent or supplied by hand or by post to an address and such is sent by post if it is posted in a prepaid envelope (para.(3)). Pursuant to para.(4), a document or information in hard copy form may be sent or supplied to an address specified by the company, to the registered office, or to an address which is authorised by the Companies Acts.

Part 3: Communications in electronic form

    This Part of the Schedule is concerned with communications in electronic form and this may only be effected if the company has agreed, whether generally or specifically, that the document or information may be sent or supplied in that form or the company is deemed to have agreed to do so (para.(6)). The address for such electronic communications is one which is specified for the purpose by the company, either generally or specifically, or is deemed by a relevant provision of the Companies Acts to have been so specified. In the case of the document or information being sent or supplied in electronic form by hand or by post, then it must be sent or supplied to an address to which it could be validly sent if it were in hard copy form (para.(7)).

Part 4: Other agreed forms of communication

This provision simply provides that a document or information which is sent or supplied to the company other than in electronic form will be validly sent or supplied if it is done in a form or manner agreed by the company (para.(8)).

SCHEDULE 5   Section 1144(2)

COMMUNICATIONS BY A COMPANY

PART 1

INTRODUCTION

Application of this Schedule

1. This Schedule applies to documents or information sent or supplied by a company.

PART 2

COMMUNICATIONS IN HARD COPY FORM

Introduction

2. A document or information is validly sent or supplied by a company if it is sent or supplied in hard copy form in accordance with this Part of this Schedule.

Method of communication in hard copy form

3. (1) A document or information in hard copy form must be-
  (a) handed to the intended recipient, or
  (b) sent or supplied by hand or by post to an address (in accordance with paragraph 4).
(2) For the purposes of this Schedule, a person sends a document or information by post if he posts a prepaid envelope containing the document or information.

Address for communications in hard copy form

4. (1) A document or information in hard copy form may be sent or supplied by the company-
  (a) to an address specified for the purpose by the intended recipient;
  (b) to a company at its registered office;
  (c) to a person in his capacity as a member of the company at his address as shown in the company's register of members;
  (d) to a person in his capacity as a director of the company at his address as shown in the company's register of directors;
  (e) to an address to which any provision of the Companies Acts authorises the document or information to be sent or supplied.
(2) Where the company is unable to obtain an address falling within sub-paragraph (1), the document or information may be sent or supplied to the intended recipient's last address known to the company.

5. COMMUNICATIONS IN ELECTRONIC FORM

Introduction

5. A document or information is validly sent or supplied by a company if it is sent in electronic form in accordance with this Part of this Schedule.

Agreement to communications in electronic form

6. A document or information may only be sent or supplied by a company in electronic form-

    (a) to a person who has agreed (generally or specifically) that the document or information may be sent or supplied in that form (and has not revoked that agreement), or

    (b) to a company that is deemed to have so agreed by a provision in the Companies Acts.

Address for communications in electronic form

7. (1) Where the document or information is sent or supplied by electronic means, it may only be sent or supplied to an address-

    (a) specified for the purpose by the intended recipient (generally or specifically), or

    (b) where the intended recipient is a company, deemed by a provision of the Companies Acts to have been so specified.

(2) Where the document or information is sent or supplied in electronic form by hand or by post, it must be-

    (a) handed to the intended recipient, or

    (b) sent or supplied to an address to which it could be validly sent if it were in hard copy form.

PART 4

COMMUNICATIONS BY MEANS OF A WEBSITE

Use of website

8. A document or information is validly sent or supplied by a company if it is made available on a website in accordance with this Part of this Schedule.

Agreement to use of website

9. A document or information may only be sent or supplied by the company to a person by being made available on a website if the person-

    (a) has agreed (generally or specifically) that the document or information may be sent or supplied to him in that manner, or

    (b) is taken to have so agreed under-

        (i) paragraph 10 (members of the company etc), or

        (ii) paragraph 11 (debenture holders),

and has not revoked that agreement.

Deemed agreement of members of company etc to use of website

10. (1) This paragraph applies to a document or information to be sent or supplied to a person-

    (a) as a member of the company, or

    (b) as a person nominated by a member in accordance with the company's articles to enjoy or exercise all or any specified rights of the member in relation to the company, or

    (c) as a person nominated by a member under section 146 to enjoy information rights.

(2) To the extent that-

    (a) the members of the company have resolved that the company may send or supply documents or information to members by making them available on a website, or

    (b) the company's articles contain provision to that effect,

a person in relation to whom the following conditions are met is taken to have agreed that the company may send or supply documents or information to him in that manner.

(3) The conditions are that-

    (a) the person has been asked individually by the company to agree that the company may send or supply documents or information generally, or the documents or information in question, to him by means of a website, and

    (b) the company has not received a response within the period of 28 days beginning with the date on which the company's request was sent.

(4) A person is not taken to have so agreed if the company's request-

    (a) did not state clearly what the effect of a failure to respond would be, or

    (b) was sent less than twelve months after a previous request made to him for the purposes of this paragraph in respect of the same or a similar class of documents or information.

(5) Chapter 3 of Part 3 (resolutions affecting a company's constitution) applies to a resolution under this paragraph.

Deemed agreement of debenture holders to use of website

11. (1) This paragraph applies to a document or information to be sent or supplied to a person as holder of a company's debentures.

(2) To the extent that-

    (a) the relevant debenture holders have duly resolved that the company may send or supply documents or information to them by making them available on a website, or

    (b) the instrument creating the debenture in question contains provision to that effect,

a debenture holder in relation to whom the following conditions are met is taken to have agreed that the company may send or supply documents or information to him in that manner.

(3) The conditions are that-

    (a) the debenture holder has been asked individually by the company to agree that the company may send or supply documents or information generally, or the documents or information in question, to him by means of a website, and

    (b) the company has not received a response within the period of 28 days beginning with the date on which the company's request was sent.

(4) A person is not taken to have so agreed if the company's request-

    (a) did not state clearly what the effect of a failure to respond would be, or

    (b) was sent less than twelve months after a previous request made to him for the purposes of this paragraph in respect of the same or a similar class of documents or information.

(5) For the purposes of this paragraph-

    (a) the relevant debenture holders are the holders of debentures of the company ranking *pari passu for all purposes with the intended recipient, and*

    (b) a resolution of the relevant debenture holders is duly passed if they agree in accordance with the provisions of the instruments creating the debentures.

Availability of document or information

12. (1) A document or information authorised or required to be sent or supplied by means of a website must be made available in a form, and by a means, that the company reasonably considers will enable the recipient-

    (a) to read it, and

    (b) to retain a copy of it.

(2) For this purpose a document or information can be read only if-

    (a) it can be read with the naked eye, or

    (b) to the extent that it consists of images (for example photographs, pictures, maps, plans or drawings), it can be seen with the naked eye.

Notification of availability

13. (1) The company must notify the intended recipient of-

    (a) the presence of the document or information on the website,

    (b) the address of the website,

    (c) the place on the website where it may be accessed, and

    (d) how to access the document or information.

(2) The document or information is taken to be sent-

    (a) on the date on which the notification required by this paragraph is sent, or

    (b) if later, the date on which the document or information first appears on the website after that notification is sent.

Period of availability on website

14. (1) The company must make the document or information available on the website throughout-

    (a) the period specified by any applicable provision of the Companies Acts, or

    (b) if no such period is specified, the period of 28 days beginning with the date on which the notification required under paragraph 13 is sent to the person in question.

(2) For the purposes of this paragraph, a failure to make a document or information available on a website throughout the period mentioned in sub-paragraph (1) shall be disregarded if-

    (a) it is made available on the website for part of that period, and

    (b) the failure to make it available throughout that period is wholly attributable to circumstances that it would not be reasonable to have expected the company to prevent or avoid.

PART 5

OTHER AGREED FORMS OF COMMUNICATION

15. A document or information that is sent or supplied otherwise than in hard copy or electronic form or by means of a website is validly sent or supplied if it is sent or supplied in a form or manner that has been agreed by the intended recipient.

PART 6

SUPPLEMENTARY PROVISIONS

Joint holders of shares or debentures

16. (1) This paragraph applies in relation to documents or information to be sent or supplied to joint holders of shares or debentures of a company.

(2) Anything to be agreed or specified by the holder must be agreed or specified by all the joint holders.

(3) Anything authorised or required to be sent or supplied to the holder may be sent or supplied either-

     (a) to each of the joint holders, or

     (b) to the holder whose name appears first in the register of members or the relevant register of debenture holders.

(4) This paragraph has effect subject to anything in the company's articles.

Death or bankruptcy of holder of shares

17. (1) This paragraph has effect in the case of the death or bankruptcy of a holder of a company's shares.

(2) Documents or information required or authorised to be sent or supplied to the member may be sent or supplied to the persons claiming to be entitled to the shares in consequence of the death or bankruptcy-

     (a) by name, or

     (b) by the title of representatives of the deceased, or trustee of the bankrupt, or by any like description,

at the address in the United Kingdom supplied for the purpose by those so claiming.

(3) Until such an address has been so supplied, a document or information may be sent or supplied in any manner in which it might have been sent or supplied if the death or bankruptcy had not occurred.

(4) This paragraph has effect subject to anything in the company's articles.

(5) References in this paragraph to the bankruptcy of a person include-

     (a) the sequestration of the estate of a person;

     (b) a person's estate being the subject of a protected trust deed (within the meaning of the Bankruptcy (Scotland) Act 1985 (c. 66)).

In such a case the reference in sub-paragraph (2)(b) to the trustee of the bankrupt is to be read as the permanent or interim trustee (within the meaning of that Act) on the sequestrated estate or, as the case may be, the trustee under the protected deed.

GENERAL NOTE

Part 1: Introduction

     This Schedule is concerned with documents or information which is sent or supplied by a company (para.(1)).

Part 2: Communications in hard copy form

     Documents or information may be validly sent or supplied by a company in hard copy form (para.(2)) but must be handed to the intended recipient or sent or supplied by hand or by post to an address. For these purposes, posting an item involves posting the item in a prepaid envelope (para.(3)). The address for communications in hard copy form may be one which is specified for the purpose by the intended recipient, a company's registered office, a person's address as shown in a company's register, a person's address as shown in a company's register of directors, and an address to which any provision of the Companies Acts authorizes the document or information to be sent or supplied. If no address is obtainable, the documentation or information to be sent or supplied may be sent to the intended recipient's last known address (para.(4)).

Part 3: Communications in electronic form

     This Part of the Schedule is concerned with communications in electronic form and documents or information may be so sent, if this is done in accordance with this Part (para.(5)). Thus, electronic forms are permissible where a person has agreed, generally or specifically, that the document or information may be sent or supplied in that form or the company is deemed to have so agreed by a provision in the Companies Acts (para.(6)). However, such a document or information may only be sent to an address specified for the purpose by the intended recipient, either generally or specifically, or where the intended recipient is a company, as deemed by a provision of the Companies Acts to have been specified in this way. Finally, where the document or information is sent or supplied in electronic form by hand or by post, it has to be handed to the intended recipient or sent or supplied to an address to which it could be validly sent if it were in hard copy form (para.(7)).

Part 4 Communications by means of a website

    This Part of Schedule, which relates to communications by means of a website, is also the most detailed. A document or information may only be sent or supplied on a website if the person has agreed that the document or information may be sent or supplied in this manner or where he has taken to have so agreed and has not revoked his agreement (para.(9)). Paragraph (10) sets out the circumstances in which a member of a company may be deemed to have agreed to the use of a website. Thus, to the extent that the members of the company have passed a resolution to this effect or the company's articles contains provisions to this effect, a person will be said to have agreed that the company may send or supply documents or information to him in this manner. However the conditions which must be met include the person being asked individually by the company to agree to the supply by means of a website and the company not having had a response within 28 days. A person will not be taken to have so agreed if the request by the company did not clearly state what the effect of a failure to respond would be or if it was sent less than twelve months after a previous request made to him in respect of the same or a similar class of documents or information. Similar requirements are set out in para.(11) for the holders of debentures. Paragraph (12) requires that the information or document placed on a website must be in a form and by a means which will enable the recipient to read it and to retain a copy of it. This means that the document must be capable of being read with the naked eye or, to the extent that images are used, that these can also be seen with the naked eye. Under para.(13), the company is required to take steps to notify the intended recipient of the availability of the document or information on the website, the address of the website, the place on the website where the information may be accessed, and also the means of accessing the document or information. Such document or information is taken to be sent on the date on which the notification required is sent or, if later, the date on which the document or information first appears on the website after the sending of the notification. Paragraph (14) requires the company to make the information available on the website for the period specified in the Companies Acts or, where not specified, 28 days beginning with the date on which the notification is sent to the person in question. For these purposes, a failure to make a document or information available will be disregarded if it is made available on the website for part of that period and the failure to make it available throughout is wholly attributable to circumstances that it would not be reasonable to have expected the company to prevent or avoid.

Part 5 Other agreed forms of communication

    This Part provides that a document or information sent otherwise than in hard copy, or electronic form, or by a website, is validly sent or supplied if it is sent or supplied in a manner that has been agreed by the intended recipient.

Part 6 Supplementary provisions

    There are two regulations in this Part. Para (16) is concerned with joint holders of shares or debentures. Thus, anything to be agreed or specified by the holder must be agreed or specified by all the joint holders while anything authorised or required to be sent or supplied to the holder may be sent or supplied either to each of the joint holders or to the holder whose name appears first in the register of members or the register of debenture holders. Para (17) is concerned with the death or bankruptcy of a holder of shares.

SCHEDULE 6   Section 1159

MEANING OF "SUBSIDIARY" ETC: SUPPLEMENTARY PROVISIONS

Introduction

1 The provisions of this Part of this Schedule explain expressions used in section 1159 (meaning of "subsidiary" etc) and otherwise supplement that section.

Voting rights in a company

  2 In section 1159(1)(a) and (c) the references to the voting rights in a company are to the rights conferred on shareholders in respect of their shares or, in the case of a company not having a share capital, on members, to vote at general meetings of the company on all, or substantially all, matters.

Right to appoint or remove a majority of the directors

3 (1) In section 1159(1)(b) the reference to the right to appoint or remove a majority of the board of directors is to the right to appoint or remove directors holding a majority of the voting rights at meetings of the board on all, or substantially all, matters.

(2) A company shall be treated as having the right to appoint to a directorship if-

    (a) a person's appointment to it follows necessarily from his appointment as director of the company, or

    (b) the directorship is held by the company itself.

(3) A right to appoint or remove which is exercisable only with the consent or concurrence of another person shall be left out of account unless no other person has a right to appoint or, as the case may be, remove in relation to that directorship.

Rights exercisable only in certain circumstances or temporarily incapable of exercise

4 (1) Rights which are exercisable only in certain circumstances shall be taken into account only-

    (a) when the circumstances have arisen, and for so long as they continue to obtain, or

    (b) when the circumstances are within the control of the person having the rights.

(2) Rights which are normally exercisable but are temporarily incapable of exercise shall continue to be taken into account.

Rights held by one person on behalf of another

5 Rights held by a person in a fiduciary capacity shall be treated as not held by him.

6. (1) Rights held by a person as nominee for another shall be treated as held by the other.

(2) Rights shall be regarded as held as nominee for another if they are exercisable only on his instructions or with his consent or concurrence.

Rights attached to shares held by way of security

7 Rights attached to shares held by way of security shall be treated as held by the person providing the security-

    (a) where apart from the right to exercise them for the purpose of preserving the value of the security, or of realising it, the rights are exercisable only in accordance with his instructions, and

    (b) where the shares are held in connection with the granting of loans as part of normal business activities and apart from the right to exercise them for the purpose of preserving the value of the security, or of realising it, the rights are exercisable only in his interests.

Rights attributed to holding company

8 (1) Rights shall be treated as held by a holding company if they are held by any of its subsidiary companies.

(2) Nothing in paragraph 6 or 7 shall be construed as requiring rights held by a holding company to be treated as held by any of its subsidiaries.

(3) For the purposes of paragraph 7 rights shall be treated as being exercisable in accordance with the instructions or in the interests of a company if they are exercisable in accordance with the instructions of or, as the case may be, in the interests of-

    (a) any subsidiary or holding company of that company, or

    (b) any subsidiary of a holding company of that company.

Disregard of certain rights

9 The voting rights in a company shall be reduced by any rights held by the company itself.

Supplementary

10 References in any provision of paragraphs 5 to 9 to rights held by a person include rights falling to be treated as held by him by virtue of any other provision of those paragraphs but not rights which by virtue of any such provision are to be treated as not held by him.

GENERAL NOTE

This schedule, together with ss.1159 and 1160 of the 2006 Act, were introduced as part of the restatement exercise carried out in the summer of 2006. These provisions together restate ss.736, 736A and 736B of the 1985 Act (as amended by the 1989 Act) and deal with the meaning of the expressions "subsidiary", "wholly-owned subsidiary" and "holding company" for the purposes of the Act. No amendments of substance are made to the 1985 Act provisions, but the material has been re-ordered, with much of the material that previously existed in the body of the 1985 Act being moved to this Schedule instead. Paragraph 1 is an introductory provision. Then paras 2, 3, 4, 5, 6 and 7 repeat ss.736A(2), (3), (4), (5), (6) and (7) of the 1985 Act respectively. Paragraph 8 repeats and combines the provisions in s.736A(8) and (9) of the 1985 Act. Paragraphs 9 and 10 restate s.736A(10) and (11) of the 1986 Act respectively. Section 736A(12) of the 1985 Act is not restated in this Schedule as it appears at s.1159(4) of the 2006 Act.

Parent and Subsidiary Undertakings: Supplementary Provisions

Introduction

1 The provisions of this Schedule explain expressions used in section 1162 (parent and subsidiary undertakings) and otherwise supplement that section.

Voting rights in an undertaking

2 (1) In section 1162(2)(a) and (d) the references to the voting rights in an undertaking are to the rights conferred on shareholders in respect of their shares or, in the case of an undertaking not having a share capital, on members, to vote at general meetings of the undertaking on all, or substantially all, matters.

(2) In relation to an undertaking which does not have general meetings at which matters are decided by the exercise of voting rights the references to holding a majority of the voting rights in the undertaking shall be construed as references to having the right under the constitution of the undertaking to direct the overall policy of the undertaking or to alter the terms of its constitution.

Right to appoint or remove a majority of the directors

3 (1) In section 1162(2)(b) the reference to the right to appoint or remove a majority of the board of directors is to the right to appoint or remove directors holding a majority of the voting rights at meetings of the board on all, or substantially all, matters.

(2) An undertaking shall be treated as having the right to appoint to a directorship if-

(a) a person's appointment to it follows necessarily from his appointment as director of the undertaking, or

(b) the directorship is held by the undertaking itself.

(3) A right to appoint or remove which is exercisable only with the consent or concurrence of another person shall be left out of account unless no other person has a right to appoint or, as the case may be, remove in relation to that directorship.

Right to exercise dominant influence

4 (1) For the purposes of section 1162(2)(c) an undertaking shall not be regarded as having the right to exercise a dominant influence over another undertaking unless it has a right to give directions with respect to the operating and financial policies of that other undertaking which its directors are obliged to comply with whether or not they are for the benefit of that other undertaking.

(2) A "control contract" means a contract in writing conferring such a right which-

(a) is of a kind authorised by the articles of the undertaking in relation to which the right is exercisable, and

(b) is permitted by the law under which that undertaking is established.

(3) This paragraph shall not be read as affecting the construction of section 1162(4)(a).

Rights exercisable only in certain circumstances or temporarily incapable of exercise

5 (1) Rights which are exercisable only in certain circumstances shall be taken into account only-

(a) when the circumstances have arisen, and for so long as they continue to obtain, or

(b) when the circumstances are within the control of the person having the rights.

(2) Rights which are normally exercisable but are temporarily incapable of exercise shall continue to be taken into account.

Rights held by one person on behalf of another

6 Rights held by a person in a fiduciary capacity shall be treated as not held by him.

7. (1) Rights held by a person as nominee for another shall be treated as held by the other.

(2) Rights shall be regarded as held as nominee for another if they are exercisable only on his instructions or with his consent or concurrence.

Rights attached to shares held by way of security

8 Rights attached to shares held by way of security shall be treated as held by the person providing the security-

(a) where apart from the right to exercise them for the purpose of preserving the value of the security, or of realising it, the rights are exercisable only in accordance with his instructions, and

(b) where the shares are held in connection with the granting of loans as part of normal business activities and apart from the right to exercise them for the purpose of preserving the value of the security, or of realising it, the rights are exercisable only in his interests.

Rights attributed to parent undertaking

9 (1) Rights shall be treated as held by a parent undertaking if they are held by any of its subsidiary undertakings.

(2) Nothing in paragraph 7 or 8 shall be construed as requiring rights held by a parent undertaking to be treated as held by any of its subsidiary undertakings.

(3) For the purposes of paragraph 8 rights shall be treated as being exercisable in accordance with the instructions or in the interests of an undertaking if they are exercisable in accordance with the instructions of or, as the case may be, in the interests of any group undertaking.

Disregard of certain rights

10 The voting rights in an undertaking shall be reduced by any rights held by the undertaking itself.

Supplementary

11 References in any provision of paragraphs 6 to 10 to rights held by a person include rights falling to be treated as held by him by virtue of any other provision of those paragraphs but not rights which by virtue of any such provision are to be treated as not held by him.

GENERAL NOTE

This schedule explains expressions used in s.1162 of the Act regarding the definition of parent and subsidiary undertakings and otherwise supplements that section. This Schedule repeats Sch.10A of the 1985 Act, which it replaces, without change of substance.

SCHEDULE 8   Section 1174

INDEX OF DEFINED EXPRESSIONS

arrangement	
- in Chapter 7 of Part 17	section 616(1)
- in Part 26	section 895(2)
articles	section 18
associate (in Chapter 3 of Part 28)	section 988
associated bodies corporate and associated company (in Part 10)	section 256
authenticated, in relation to a document or information sent or supplied to a company	section 1146
authorised group, of members of a company (in Part 14)	section 370(3)
authorised insurance company	section 1165(2)
authorised minimum (in relation to share capital of public company)	section 763
available profits (in Chapter 5 of Part 18)	sections 711 and 712
banking company and banking group	section 1164
body corporate	section 1173(1)
called-up share capital	section 547
capital redemption reserve	section 733
capitalisation in relation to a company's profits (in Part 23)	section 853(3)
cash (in relation to paying up or allotting shares)	section 583
cause of action, in relation to derivative proceedings (in Chapter 2 of Part 11)	section 265(7)
certified translation (in Part 35)	section 1107
charge (in Chapter 1 of Part 25)	section 861(5)
circulation date, in relation to a written resolution (in Part 13)	section 290
class of shares	section 629
the Companies Acts	section 2
Companies Act accounts	sections 395(1)(a) and 403(2)(a)
Companies Act group accounts	section 403(2)(a)
Companies Act individual accounts	section 395(1)(a)
companies involved in the division (in Part 27)	section 919(2)
company	
- generally in the Companies Acts	section 1
- in Chapter 7 of Part 17	section 616(1)
- in Chapter 1 of Part 25	section 861(5)
- in Chapter 2 of Part 25	section 879(6)
- in Part 26	section 895(2)
- in Chapter 3 of Part 28	section 991(1)
- in the company communications provisions	section 1148(1)
the company communications provisions	section 1143
the company law provisions of this Act	section 2(2)
company records (in Part 37)	section 1134
connected with, in relation to a director (in Part 10)	sections 252 to 254

investment company (in Part 23)	section 833
ISD investment firm	
- in Part 15	section 474(1)
- in Part 16	section 539
issued share capital and issued shares	section 546(1)(a) and (2)
the issuing company (in Chapter 7 of Part 17)	section 610(6)
the Joint Stock Companies Acts	section 1171
liabilities (in Part 27)	section 941
liability, references to incurring, reducing or discharging (in Chapter 2 of Part 18)	section 683(2)
limited by guarantee	section 3(3)
limited by shares	section 3(2)
limited company	section 3
the main register (of members) (in Chapter 3 of Part 8)	section 131(1)
major audit (in sections 522 and 525)	section 525(2)
market purchase, by a company of its own shares (in Chapter 4 of Part 18)	section 693(4)
member, of a company	
- generally in the Companies Acts	section 112
- in Chapter 1 of Part 11	section 260(5)
- in Chapter 2 of Part 11	section 265(7)
memorandum of association	section 8
merger (in Part 27)	section 904
merging companies (in Part 27)	section 904(2)
merger by absorption (in Part 27)	section 904(1)(a)
merger by formation of a new company (in Part 27)	section 904(1)(b)
negative resolution procedure, in relation to regulations and orders	section 1289
net assets (in Part 7)	section 92
new company (in Part 27)	section 902(2)
non-cash asset	section 1163
non-voting shares (in Chapter 3 of Part 28)	section 991(1)
number, in relation to shares	section 540(4)(b)
off-market purchase, by a company of its own shares (in Chapter 4 of Part 18)	section 693(2)
offer period (in Chapter 2 of Part 28)	section 971(1)
offer to the public (in Chapter 1 of Part 20)	section 756
offeror	
- in Chapter 2 of Part 28	section 971(1)
- in Chapter 3 of Part 28	section 991(1)
officer, in relation to a body corporate	section 1173(1)
officer in default	section 1121

voting rights

voting shares

GENERAL NOTE

This schedule provides an index of defined expressions and should be read in conjunction with s.1174 of the 2006 Act.

SCHEDULE 9   Section 1175

REMOVAL OF SPECIAL PROVISIONS ABOUT ACCOUNTS AND AUDIT OF CHARITABLE COMPANIES

PART I

THE COMPANIES ACT 1985 (C. 6)

1. In section 240 (requirements in connection with publication of accounts)-
    (a) in subsection (1) omit from "or, as the case may be," to "section 249A(2)";
    (b) in subsection (3)(c) omit from "and, if no such report" to "any financial year";
    (c) after subsection (3)(c) insert ", and";
    (d) omit subsection (3)(e) and the ", and" preceding it;
    (e) in the closing words of subsection (3) omit from "or any report" to "section 249A(2)".

2. In section 245 (voluntary revision of annual accounts or directors' report), in subsection (4)(b) omit "or reporting accountant".

3. In section 249A (exemptions from audit)-
    (a) omit subsections (2), (3A) and (4);
    (b) in subsection (6) for "figures for turnover or gross income" substitute "figure for turnover";
    (c) in subsection (6A) omit "or (2)";
    (d) in subsection (7) omit the definition of "gross income" and the ", and" preceding it.

4. In section 249B (cases where exemptions not available)-
    (a) in the opening words of subsection (1) omit "or (2)";
    (b) in subsection (1C)(b) omit from "where the company referred to" to "is not a charity";
    (c) in subsection (3) omit "or (2)";
    (d) in subsection (4), in the opening words and in paragraph (a), omit "or (2)".

5. Omit section 249C (report required for purposes of section 249A(2)).

6. Omit section 249D (the reporting accountant).

7. In section 249E (effect of exemptions) omit subsection (2).

8. In section 262A (index of defined expressions) omit the entry for "reporting accountant".

PART 2

THE COMPANIES (NORTHERN IRELAND) ORDER 1986 (S.I. 1986/1032 (N.I. 6)

9. In Article 248 (requirements in connection with publication of accounts)-
    (a) in paragraph (1) omit from "or, as the case may be," to "Article 257A(2)";
    (b) in paragraph (3)(c) omit from "and, if no such report" to "any such financial year";
    (c) after paragraph (3)(c) insert ", and";
    (d) omit paragraph (3)(e) and the word ", and" preceding it;
    (e) in the closing words of paragraph (3) omit from "or any report" to "Article 257A(2)".

10. In Article 253 (voluntary revision of annual accounts or directors' report), in paragraph (4)(b) omit "or reporting accountant".

11. In Article 257A (exemptions from audit)-
    (a) omit paragraphs (2), (3A) and (4);
    (b) in paragraph (6) for "figures for turnover or gross income" substitute "figure for turnover";
    (c) in paragraph (6A) omit "or (2)";
    (d) in paragraph (7) omit the definition of "gross income" and the ", and" preceding it.

12. In Article 257B (cases where exemptions not available)-
    (a) in the opening words of paragraph (1) omit "or (2)";
    (b) in paragraph (1C)(b) omit from "where the company referred to" to "is not a charity";
    (c) in paragraph (3) omit "or (2)";
    (d) in paragraph (4), in the opening words and in sub-paragraph (a), omit "or (2)".

13. Omit Article 257C (report required for purposes of Article 257A(2).

14. Omit Article 257D (the reporting accountant).

15. In Article 257E (effect of exemptions) omit paragraph (2).

16. In Article 270A (index of defined expressions) omit the entry for "reporting accountant".

GENERAL NOTE

When the new legislation was first drafted, it was proposed to replace the reporting accountant with an independent examiner as the person who reports on the accounts of small charitable companies in lieu of audit. However, the clauses that would have implemented this change were removed from the Bill at a late stage and the role of the reporting accountant instead dealt with in the Charities Bill. Consequently, the special treatment of small charitable companies with respect to the audit of their accounts is now dealt with in ss.32-33 of the Charities Act 2006 (see www.opsi.gov.uk/acts/acts2006/20060050.htm#aofs).

Schedule 9 was a late insertion into the Companies Bill that removes the special provisions relating to the accounts and audit of charitable companies. It does this by amending the text of various sections in the 1985 Act (Pt 1) and the corresponding legislation for Northern Ireland (Pt 2).

The sections amended in the 1985 Act are: s.240 (requirements in connection with publication of accounts), s.245 (voluntary revision of annual accounts or directors' report), s.249A (exemptions from audit), s.249B (cases where exemptions are not available), s.249C (report required for the purpose of s.249A(2) [i.e. the report by the "reporting accountant", identified in s.249D]), s.249D (the reporting accountant), s.249E (effect of audit exemptions) and s.262A (index of defined expressions).

RECOGNISED SUPERVISORY BODIES

Application for recognition of supervisory body

1. (1) A supervisory body may apply to the Secretary of State for an order declaring it to be a recognised supervisory body for the purposes of this Part of this Act ("a recognition order").

(2) Any such application must be-

    (a) made in such manner as the Secretary of State may direct, and

    (b) accompanied by such information as the Secretary of State may reasonably require for the purpose of determining the application.

(3) At any time after receiving an application and before determining it the Secretary of State may require the applicant to furnish additional information.

(4) The directions and requirements given or imposed under sub-paragraphs (2) and (3) may differ as between different applications.

(5) The Secretary of State may require any information to be furnished under this paragraph to be in such form or verified in such manner as he may specify.

(6) Every application must be accompanied by-

    (a) a copy of the applicant's rules, and

    (b) a copy of any guidance issued by the applicant in writing.

(7) The reference in sub-paragraph (6)(b) to guidance issued by the applicant is a reference to any guidance or recommendation-

    (a) issued or made by it to all or any class of its members or persons seeking to become members,

    (b) relevant for the purposes of this Part, and

    (c) intended to have continuing effect,

including any guidance or recommendation relating to the admission or expulsion of members of the body, so far as relevant for the purposes of this Part.

Grant and refusal of recognition

2. (1) The Secretary of State may, on an application duly made in accordance with paragraph 1 and after being furnished with all such information as he may require under that paragraph, make or refuse to make a recognition order in respect of the applicant.

(2) The Secretary of State may make a recognition order only if it appears to him, from the information furnished by the body and having regard to any other information in his possession, that the requirements of Part 2 of this Schedule are satisfied in the case of that body.

(3) The Secretary of State may refuse to make a recognition order in respect of a body if he considers that its recognition is unnecessary having regard to the existence of one or more other bodies which-

    (a) maintain and enforce rules as to the appointment and conduct of statutory auditors, and

    (b) have been or are likely to be recognised.

(4) Where the Secretary of State refuses an application for a recognition order he must give the applicant a written notice to that effect-

    (a) specifying which requirements, in the opinion of the Secretary of State, are not satisfied, or

    (b) stating that the application is refused on the ground mentioned in sub-paragraph (3).

(5) A recognition order must state the date on which it takes effect.

Revocation of recognition

3. (1) A recognition order may be revoked by a further order made by the Secretary of State if at any time it appears to him-

    (a) that any requirement of Part 2 of this Schedule is not satisfied in the case of the body to which the recognition order relates ("the recognised body"),

    (b) that the body has failed to comply with any obligation imposed on it by or by virtue of this Part of this Act, or

    (c) that the continued recognition of the body is undesirable having regard to the existence of one or more other bodies which have been or are to be recognised.

(2) An order revoking a recognition order must state the date on which it takes effect, which must be after the period of three months beginning with the date on which the revocation order is made.

(3) Before revoking a recognition order the Secretary of State must-

    (a) give written notice of his intention to do so to the recognised body,

    (b) take such steps as he considers reasonably practicable for bringing the notice to the attention of the members of the body, and

    (c) publish the notice in such manner as he thinks appropriate for bringing it to the attention of any other persons who are in his opinion likely to be affected.

(4) A notice under sub-paragraph (3) must-

    (a) state the reasons for which the Secretary of State proposes to act, and

    (b) give particulars of the rights conferred by sub-paragraph (5).

(5) A person within sub-paragraph (6) may, within the period of three months beginning with the date of service or publication of the notice under sub-paragraph (3) or such longer period as the Secretary of State may allow, make written representations to the Secretary of State and, if desired, oral representations to a person appointed for that purpose by the Secretary of State.

(6) The persons within this sub-paragraph are-

    (a) the recognised body on which a notice is served under sub-paragraph (3),

    (b) any member of the body, and

    (c) any other person who appears to the Secretary of State to be affected.

(7) The Secretary of State must have regard to any representations made in accordance with sub-paragraph (5) in determining whether to revoke the recognition order.

(8) If in any case the Secretary of State considers it essential to do so in the public interest he may revoke a recognition order without regard to the restriction imposed by sub-paragraph (2), even if-

    (a) no notice has been given or published under sub-paragraph (3), or

    (b) the period of time for making representations in pursuance of such a notice has not expired.

(9) An order revoking a recognition order may contain such transitional provision as the Secretary of State thinks necessary or expedient.

(10) A recognition order may be revoked at the request or with the consent of the recognised body and any such revocation is not subject to-

    (a) the restrictions imposed by sub-paragraphs (1) and (2), or

    (b) the requirements of sub-paragraphs (3) to (5) and (7).

(11) On making an order revoking a recognition order in respect of a body the Secretary of State must-

    (a) give written notice of the making of the order to the body,

    (b) take such steps as he considers reasonably practicable for bringing the making of the order to the attention of the members of the body, and

    (c) publish a notice of the making of the order in such manner as he thinks appropriate for bringing it to the attention of any other persons who are in his opinion likely to be affected.

Transitional provision

4. A recognition order made and not revoked under-

    (a) paragraph 2(1) of Schedule 11 to the Companies Act 1989 (c. 40), or

    (b) paragraph 2(1) of Schedule 11 to the Companies (Northern Ireland) Order 1990 (S.I. 1990/593 (N.I. 5)),

before the commencement of this Chapter of this Part of this Act is to have effect after the commencement of this Chapter as a recognition order made under paragraph 2(1) of this Schedule.

Orders not statutory instruments

5. Orders under this Part of this Schedule shall not be made by statutory instrument.

PART 2

REQUIREMENTS FOR RECOGNITION OF A SUPERVISORY BODY

Holding of appropriate qualification

6 (1) The body must have rules to the effect that a person is not eligible for appointment as a statutory auditor unless-

    (a) in the case of an individual, he holds an appropriate qualification,

    (b) in the case of a firm-

        (i) each individual responsible for statutory audit work on behalf of the firm is eligible for appointment as a statutory auditor, and

        (ii) the firm is controlled by qualified persons (see paragraph 7 below).

(2) Sub-paragraph (1) does not prevent the body from imposing more stringent requirements.

(3) A firm which has ceased to comply with the conditions mentioned in sub-paragraph (1)(b) may be permitted to remain eligible for appointment as a statutory auditor for a period of not more than three months.

7. (1) This paragraph explains what is meant in paragraph 6(1)(b) by a firm being "controlled by qualified persons".

(2) In this paragraph references to a person being qualified are-

    (a) in relation to an individual, to his holding-

(i) an appropriate qualification, or

(ii) a corresponding qualification to audit accounts under the law of a member State, or part of a member State, other than the United Kingdom;

(b) in relation to a firm, to its-

(i) being eligible for appointment as a statutory auditor, or

(ii) being eligible for a corresponding appointment as an auditor under the law of a member State, or part of a member State, other than the United Kingdom.

(3) A firm is to be treated as controlled by qualified persons if, and only if-

(a) a majority of the members of the firm are qualified persons, and

(b) where the firm's affairs are managed by a board of directors, committee or other management body, a majority of that body are qualified persons or, if the body consists of two persons only, at least one of them is a qualified person.

(4) A majority of the members of a firm means-

(a) where under the firm's constitution matters are decided upon by the exercise of voting rights, members holding a majority of the rights to vote on all, or substantially all, matters;

(b) in any other case, members having such rights under the constitution of the firm as enable them to direct its overall policy or alter its constitution.

(5) A majority of the members of the management body of a firm means-

(a) where matters are decided at meetings of the management body by the exercise of voting rights, members holding a majority of the rights to vote on all, or substantially all, matters at such meetings;

(b) in any other case, members having such rights under the constitution of the firm as enable them to direct its overall policy or alter its constitution.

(6) Paragraphs 5 to 11 of Schedule 7 to this Act (rights to be taken into account and attribution of rights) apply for the purposes of this paragraph.

Auditors to be fit and proper persons

8 (1) The body must have adequate rules and practices designed to ensure that the persons eligible under its rules for appointment as a statutory auditor are fit and proper persons to be so appointed.

(2) The matters which the body may take into account for this purpose in relation to a person must include-

(a) any matter relating to any person who is or will be employed by or associated with him for the purposes of or in connection with statutory audit work;

(b) in the case of a body corporate, any matter relating to-

(i) any director or controller of the body,

(ii) any other body corporate in the same group, or

(iii) any director or controller of any such other body; and

(c) in the case of a partnership, any matter relating to-

(i) any of the partners,

(ii) any director or controller of any of the partners,

(iii) any body corporate in the same group as any of the partners,

or

(iv) any director or controller of any such other body.

(3) Where the person is a limited liability partnership, in sub-paragraph (2)(b) "director" is to be read as "member".

(4) In sub-paragraph (2)(b) and (c) "controller", in relation to a body corporate, means a person who either alone or with an associate or associates is entitled to exercise or control the exercise of 15% or more of the rights to vote on all, or substantially all, matters at general meetings of the body or another body corporate of which it is a subsidiary.

Professional integrity and independence

9 (1) The body must have adequate rules and practices designed to ensure that-

(a) statutory audit work is conducted properly and with integrity, and

(b) persons are not appointed as statutory auditors in circumstances in which they have an interest likely to conflict with the proper conduct of the audit.

(2) The body must participate in arrangements within paragraph 21, and the rules and practices mentioned in sub-paragraph (1) must include provision requiring compliance with any standards for the time being determined under such arrangements.

(3) The body must also have adequate rules and practices designed to ensure that no firm is eligible under its rules for appointment as a statutory auditor unless the firm has arrangements to prevent a person to whom sub-paragraph (4) applies from being able to exert any influence over the way in which a statutory audit is conducted in circumstances in which that influence would be likely to affect the independence or integrity of the audit.

(4) This sub-paragraph applies to-

(a) any individual who is not a qualified person within the meaning of paragraph 7, and

(b) any person who is not a member of the firm.

Technical standards

10 (1) The body must have rules and practices as to-

(a) the technical standards to be applied in statutory audit work, and

(b) the manner in which those standards are to be applied in practice.

(2) The body must participate in arrangements within paragraph 22, and the rules and practices mentioned in sub-paragraph (1) must include provision requiring compliance with any standards for the time being determined under such arrangements.

Procedures for maintaining competence

11 The body must have rules and practices designed to ensure that persons eligible under its rules for appointment as a statutory auditor continue to maintain an appropriate level of competence in the conduct of statutory audits.

Monitoring and enforcement

12 (1) The body must have adequate arrangements and resources for the effective monitoring and enforcement of compliance with its rules.

(2) The arrangements for monitoring may make provision for that function to be performed on behalf of the body (and without affecting its responsibility) by any other body or person who is able and willing to perform it.

Independent monitoring of audits of listed companies and other major bodies

13 (1) The body must-
    (a) participate in arrangements within paragraph 23(1), and
    (b) have rules designed to ensure that members of the body who perform any statutory audit functions in respect of major audits take such steps as may be reasonably required of them to enable their performance of any such functions to be monitored by means of inspections carried out under the arrangements.

(2) Any monitoring of such persons under the arrangements is to be regarded (so far as their performance of statutory audit functions in respect of major audits is concerned) as monitoring of compliance with the body's rules for the purposes of paragraph 12(1).

(3) In this paragraph-
    "major audit" means a statutory audit conducted in respect of-
        (a) a company any of whose securities have been admitted to the official list (within the meaning of Part 6 of the Financial Services and Markets Act 2000 (c. 8)), or
        (b) any other person in whose financial condition there is a major public interest;

    "statutory audit function" means any function performed as a statutory auditor.

Membership, eligibility and discipline

14 The rules and practices of the body relating to-
    (a) the admission and expulsion of members,
    (b) the grant and withdrawal of eligibility for appointment as a statutory auditor, and
    (c) the discipline it exercises over its members,
must be fair and reasonable and include adequate provision for appeals.

Investigation of complaints

15 (1) The body must have effective arrangements for the investigation of complaints against-
    (a) persons who are eligible under its rules for appointment as a statutory auditor, and
    (b) the body in respect of matters arising out of its functions as a supervisory body.

(2) The arrangements mentioned in sub-paragraph (1) may make provision for the whole or part of that function to be performed by and to be the responsibility of a body or person independent of the body itself.

Independent investigation for disciplinary purposes of public interest cases

16 (1) The body must-
    (a) participate in arrangements within paragraph 24(1), and
    (b) have rules and practices designed to ensure that, where the designated persons have decided that any particular disciplinary action should be taken against a member of the body following the conclusion of an investigation under such arrangements, that decision is to be treated as if it were a decision made by the body in disciplinary proceedings against the member.

(2) In sub-paragraph (1) "the designated persons" means the persons who, under the arrangements, have the function of deciding whether (and if so, what) disciplinary action should be taken against a member of the body in the light of an investigation carried out under the arrangements.

Meeting of claims arising out of audit work

17 (1) The body must have adequate rules or arrangements designed to ensure that persons eligible under its rules for appointment as a statutory auditor take such steps as may reasonably be expected of them to secure that they are able to meet claims against them arising out of statutory audit work.

(2) This may be achieved by professional indemnity insurance or other appropriate arrangements.

Register of auditors and other information to be made available

18 The body must have rules requiring persons eligible under its rules for appointment as a statutory auditor to comply with any obligations imposed on them by-

    (a) requirements under section 1224 (Secretary of State's power to call for information);

    (b) regulations under section 1239 (the register of auditors);

    (c) regulations under section 1240 (information to be made available to the public).

Taking account of costs of compliance

19 The body must have satisfactory arrangements for taking account, in framing its rules, of the cost to those to whom the rules would apply of complying with those rules and any other controls to which they are subject.

Promotion and maintenance of standards

20 The body must be able and willing-

    (a) to promote and maintain high standards of integrity in the conduct of statutory audit work, and

    (b) to co-operate, by the sharing of information and otherwise, with the Secretary of State and any other authority, body or person having responsibility in the United Kingdom for the qualification, supervision or regulation of auditors.

PART 3

ARRANGEMENTS IN WHICH RECOGNISED SUPERVISORY BODIES ARE REQUIRED TO PARTICIPATE

Arrangements for setting standards relating to professional integrity and independence

21. The arrangements referred to in paragraph 9(2) are appropriate arrangements-

    (a) for the determining of standards for the purposes of the rules and practices mentioned in paragraph 9(1), and

    (b) for ensuring that the determination of those standards is done independently of the body.

Arrangements for setting technical standards

22. The arrangements referred to in paragraph 10(2) are appropriate arrangements-

    (a) for the determining of standards for the purposes of the rules and practices mentioned in paragraph 10(1), and

    (b) for ensuring that the determination of those standards is done independently of the body.

Arrangements for independent monitoring of audits of listed companies and other major bodies

23. (1) The arrangements referred to in paragraph 13(1) are appropriate arrangements-

    (a) for enabling the performance by members of the body of statutory audit functions in respect of major audits to be monitored by means of inspections carried out under the arrangements, and

    (b) for ensuring that the carrying out of such monitoring and inspections is done independently of the body.

(2) In this paragraph "major audit" and "statutory audit function" have the same meaning as in paragraph 13.

Arrangements for independent investigation for disciplinary purposes of public interest cases

24. (1) The arrangements referred to in paragraph 16(1) are appropriate arrangements-

    (a) for the carrying out of investigations into public interest cases arising in connection with the performance of statutory audit functions by members of the body,

    (b) for the holding of disciplinary hearings relating to members of the body which appear to be desirable following the conclusion of such investigations,

    (c) for requiring such hearings to be held in public except where the interests of justice otherwise require,

    (d) for the persons before whom such hearings have taken place to decide whether (and, if so, what) disciplinary action should be taken against the members to whom the hearings related, and

    (e) for ensuring that the carrying out of those investigations, the holding of those hearings and the taking of those decisions are done independently of the body.

(2) In this paragraph-

"public interest cases" means matters which raise or appear to raise important issues affecting the public interest;

"statutory audit function" means any function performed as a statutory auditor.

Supplementary: arrangements to operate independently of body

25. (1) This paragraph applies for the purposes of-

    (a) paragraph 21(b),

    (b) paragraph 22(b),

    (c) paragraph 23(1)(b), or

    (d) paragraph 24(1)(e).

(2) Arrangements are not to be regarded as appropriate for the purpose of ensuring that a thing is done independently of the body unless they are designed to ensure that the body-

    (a) will have no involvement in the appointment or selection of any of the persons who are to be responsible for doing that thing, and

    (b) will not otherwise be involved in the doing of that thing.

(3) Sub-paragraph (2) imposes a minimum requirement and does not preclude the possibility that additional criteria may need to be satisfied in order for the arrangements to be regarded as appropriate for the purpose in question.

Supplementary: funding of arrangements

26. The body must pay any of the costs of maintaining any arrangements within paragraph 21, 22, 23 or 24 which the arrangements provide are to be paid by it.

Supplementary: scope of arrangement

27. Arrangements may qualify as arrangements within any of paragraphs 21, 22, 23 and 24 even though the matters for which they provide are more extensive in any respect than those mentioned in the applicable paragraph.

GENERAL NOTE

This schedule relates to the provisions of s.1217, which refer to the recognition of "supervisory bodies", and it replaces and extends the provisions of Sch.11 to the 1989 Act. Many of the changes arise from the need to implement requirements in the EU's Eight Company Law Directive on Audit (adopted and published in *The Official Journal of the European Communities* on June 9, 2006, its provisions coming into force from June 29, 2006: see [2006] O.J. L157/ 87, http:/ /eur-lex.europa.eu/ LexUriServ/ site/ en/ oj/ 2006/ L157/ L15720060609en00870107.pdf).

Professional bodies (such as the Institutes of Chartered Accountants) can only secure recognition if they have adequate rules and arrangements to ensure that only eligible members will undertake company audits.

Part 1: Grant and revocation of recognition of a supervisory body

This part of the schedule restates, with some rewording and modifications, provisions in paras 1-3 in Pt 1 of Sch.11 to the 1989 Act. The new paragraphs deal with transitional arrangements (para.4) and the use of orders (para.5).

Paragraph 1 identifies the steps a body is required to take to become recognised by the Secretary of State.

Paragraph 2 deals with the grant and refusal of recognition.

Paragraph 3 sets out the procedure the Secretary of State is required to follow if the recognition of the body is revoked.

Paragraph 4 outlines transitional arrangements that allow bodies recognised under the 1989 Act or the Companies (Northern Ireland) Order 1990 to continue to be recognised.

Paragraph 5 states that recognition and revocation orders shall not be made by statutory instruments.

Part 2: Requirements for recognition of a supervisory body

This part of the schedule restates, with some rewording and modifications, provisions in paras 4-16 in Pt 2 of Sch.11 to the 1989 Act. The new paragraphs deal with independent monitoring of audits of listed companies and other major bodies (para.13) and independent investigation for disciplinary purposes of public interest cases (para.16).

Paragraphs 6 and 7 require a recognised supervisory body to ensure that persons eligible for appointment as a statutory auditor hold appropriate qualifications (as defined in s.1219). They require a firm that is a statutory auditor to be controlled by qualified persons.

Paragraphs 8-11 require the bodies to have rules and practices which ensure that auditors are fit and proper persons, that professional integrity and independence is maintained, that technical standards for audits are assured and that there are procedures for maintaining appropriate levels of competence.

Paragraphs 12-16 specify the requirements for monitoring, enforcement, discipline and investigation of complaints.

Paragraphs 17-20 indicate that a supervisory body must have rules dealing with funding compensation claims (e.g. through professional indemnity insurance), keeping a register of auditors, information to be made available to the Secretary of State and to the public, arrangements for taking account of compliance costs, and promoting and maintaining standards of integrity.

Part 3: Arrangements in which recognised supervisory bodies are required to participate

This part of the schedule is new, and its provisions to some extent deal with obligations set out in the EU's 8th Company Law Directive on Audit.

Paragrahs 21-27 specify the arrangements with independent bodies that recognised supervisory bodies must enter into in order to meet the requirements of this schedule described above. These include arrangements for setting standards relating to professional integrity and independence, for setting technical standards, for independent monitoring of audits of listed companies and other major bodies, for independent investigation for disciplinary purposes of public interest cases, and for funding.

Recognised Professional Qualifications

Part i

Grant and Revocation of Recognition of a Professional Qualification

Application for recognition of professional qualification

1. (1) A qualifying body may apply to the Secretary of State for an order declaring a qualification offered by it to be a recognised professional qualification for the purposes of this Part of this Act ("a recognition order").

(2) In this Part of this Act "a recognised qualifying body" means a qualifying body offering a recognised professional qualification.

(3) Any application must be-

    (a) made in such manner as the Secretary of State may direct, and

    (b) accompanied by such information as the Secretary of State may reasonably require for the purpose of determining the application.

(4) At any time after receiving an application and before determining it the Secretary of State may require the applicant to furnish additional information.

(5) The directions and requirements given or imposed under sub-paragraphs (3) and (4) may differ as between different applications.

(6) The Secretary of State may require any information to be furnished under this paragraph to be in such form or verified in such manner as he may specify.

(7) In the case of examination standards, the verification required may include independent moderation of the examinations over such a period as the Secretary of State considers necessary.

(8) Every application must be accompanied by-

    (a) a copy of the applicant's rules, and

    (b) a copy of any guidance issued by the applicant in writing.

(9) The reference in sub-paragraph (8)(b) to guidance issued by the applicant is a reference to any guidance or recommendation-

    (a) issued or made by it to all or any class of persons holding or seeking to hold a qualification, or approved or seeking to be approved by the body for the purposes of giving practical training,

    (b) relevant for the purposes of this Part of this Act, and

    (c) intended to have continuing effect,

including any guidance or recommendation relating to a matter within sub-paragraph (10).

(10) The matters within this sub-paragraph are-

    (a) admission to or expulsion from a course of study leading to a qualification,

    (b) the award or deprivation of a qualification, and

    (c) the approval of a person for the purposes of giving practical training or the withdrawal of such an approval,

so far as relevant for the purposes of this Part of this Act.

Grant and refusal of recognition

2. (1) The Secretary of State may, on an application duly made in accordance with paragraph 1 and after being furnished with all such information as he may require under that paragraph, make or refuse to make a recognition order in respect of the qualification in relation to which the application was made.

(2) The Secretary of State may make a recognition order only if it appears to him, from the information furnished by the applicant and having regard to any other information in his possession, that the requirements of Part 2 of this Schedule are satisfied in relation to the qualification.

(3) Where the Secretary of State refuses an application for a recognition order he must give the applicant a written notice to that effect specifying which requirements, in his opinion, are not satisfied.

(4) A recognition order must state the date on which it takes effect.

Revocation of recognition

3. (1) A recognition order may be revoked by a further order made by the Secretary of State if at any time it appears to him-

    (a) that any requirement of Part 2 of this Schedule is not satisfied in relation to the qualification to which the recognition order relates, or

(b) that the qualifying body has failed to comply with any obligation imposed on it by or by virtue of this Part of this Act.

(2) An order revoking a recognition order must state the date on which it takes effect, which must be after the period of three months beginning with the date on which the revocation order is made.

(3) Before revoking a recognition order the Secretary of State must-

    (a) give written notice of his intention to do so to the qualifying body,

    (b) take such steps as he considers reasonably practicable for bringing the notice to the attention of persons holding the qualification or in the course of studying for it, and

    (c) publish the notice in such manner as he thinks appropriate for bringing it to the attention of any other persons who are in his opinion likely to be affected.

(4) A notice under sub-paragraph (3) must-

    (a) state the reasons for which the Secretary of State proposes to act, and

    (b) give particulars of the rights conferred by sub-paragraph (5).

(5) A person within sub-paragraph (6) may, within the period of three months beginning with the date of service or publication or such longer period as the Secretary of State may allow, make written representations to the Secretary of State and, if desired, oral representations to a person appointed for that purpose by the Secretary of State.

(6) The persons within this sub-paragraph are-

    (a) the qualifying body on which a notice is served under sub-paragraph (3),

    (b) any person holding the qualification or in the course of studying for it, and

    (c) any other person who appears to the Secretary of State to be affected.

(7) The Secretary of State must have regard to any representations made in accordance with sub-paragraph (5) in determining whether to revoke the recognition order.

(8) If in any case the Secretary of State considers it essential to do so in the public interest he may revoke a recognition order without regard to the restriction imposed by sub-paragraph (2), even if-

    (a) no notice has been given or published under sub-paragraph (3), or

    (b) the period of time for making representations in pursuance of such a notice has not expired.

(9) An order revoking a recognition order may contain such transitional provision as the Secretary of State thinks necessary or expedient.

(10) A recognition order may be revoked at the request or with the consent of the qualifying body and any such revocation is not subject to-

    (a) the restrictions imposed by sub-paragraphs (1) and (2), or

    (b) the requirements of sub-paragraphs (3) to (5) and (7).

(11) On making an order revoking a recognition order the Secretary of State must-

    (a) give written notice of the making of the order to the qualifying body,

    (b) take such steps as he considers reasonably practicable for bringing the making of the order to the attention of persons holding the qualification or in the course of studying for it, and

    (c) publish a notice of the making of the order in such manner as he thinks appropriate for bringing it to the attention of any other persons who are in his opinion likely to be affected.

Transitional provision

4. A recognition order made and not revoked under-

    (a) paragraph 2(1) of Schedule 12 to the Companies Act 1989 (c. 40), or

    (b) paragraph 2(1) of Schedule 12 to the Companies (Northern Ireland) Order 1990 (S.I. 1990/593 (N.I. 5)),

before the commencement of this Chapter of this Part of this Act is to have effect after the commencement of this Chapter as a recognition order made under paragraph 2(1) of this Schedule.

Orders not statutory instruments

5. Orders under this Part of this Schedule shall not be made by statutory instrument.

PART 2

REQUIREMENTS FOR RECOGNITION OF A PROFESSIONAL QUALIFICATION

Entry requirements

6. (1) The qualification must only be open to persons who-

    (a) have attained university entrance level, or

    (b) have a sufficient period of professional experience.

(2) In relation to a person who has not been admitted to a university or other similar establishment in the United Kingdom, "attaining university entrance level" means-

    (a) being educated to such a standard as would entitle him to be considered for such admission on the basis of-

        (i) academic or professional qualifications obtained in the United Kingdom and recognised by the Secretary of State to be of an appropriate standard, or

(ii) academic or professional qualifications obtained outside the United Kingdom which the Secretary of State considers to be of an equivalent standard, or

(b) being assessed, on the basis of written tests of a kind appearing to the Secretary of State to be adequate for the purpose (with or without oral examination), as of such a standard of ability as would entitle him to be considered for such admission.

(3) The assessment, tests and oral examination referred to in sub-paragraph (2)(b) may be conducted by-

(a) the qualifying body, or

(b) some other body approved by the Secretary of State.

(4) The reference in sub-paragraph (1)(b) to "a sufficient period of professional experience" is to not less than seven years' experience in a professional capacity in the fields of finance, law and accountancy.

Requirement for theoretical instruction or professional experience

7. (1) The qualification must be restricted to persons who-

(a) have completed a course of theoretical instruction in the subjects prescribed for the purposes of paragraph 8, or

(b) have a sufficient period of professional experience.

(2) The reference in sub-paragraph (1)(b) to "a sufficient period of professional experience" is to not less than seven years' experience in a professional capacity in the fields of finance, law and accountancy.

Examination

8. (1) The qualification must be restricted to persons who have passed an examination (at least part of which is in writing) testing-

(a) theoretical knowledge of the subjects prescribed for the purposes of this paragraph by regulations made by the Secretary of State, and

(b) ability to apply that knowledge in practice,

and requiring a standard of attainment at least equivalent to that required to obtain a degree from a university or similar establishment in the United Kingdom.

(2) The qualification may be awarded to a person without his theoretical knowledge of a subject being tested by examination if he has passed a university or other examination of equivalent standard in that subject or holds a university degree or equivalent qualification in it.

(3) The qualification may be awarded to a person without his ability to apply his theoretical knowledge of a subject in practice being tested by examination if he has received practical training in that subject which is attested by an examination or diploma recognised by the Secretary of State for the purposes of this paragraph.

(4) Regulations under this paragraph are subject to negative resolution procedure.

Practical training

9. (1) The qualification must be restricted to persons who have completed at least three years' practical training of which-

(a) part was spent being trained in statutory audit work, and

(b) a substantial part was spent being trained in statutory audit work or other audit work of a description approved by the Secretary of State as being similar to statutory audit work.

(2) For the purpose of sub-paragraph (1) "statutory audit work" includes the work of a person appointed as the auditor of a person under the law of a country or territory outside the United Kingdom where it appears to the Secretary of State that the law and practice with respect to the audit of accounts is similar to that in the United Kingdom.

(3) The training must be given by persons approved by the body offering the qualification as persons whom the body is satisfied, in the light of undertakings given by them and the supervision to which they are subject (whether by the body itself or some other body or organisation), will provide adequate training.

(4) At least two-thirds of the training must be given by a person-

(a) eligible for appointment as a statutory auditor, or

(b) eligible for a corresponding appointment as an auditor under the law of a member State, or part of a member State, other than the United Kingdom.

Supplementary provision with respect to a sufficient period of professional experience

10. (1) Periods of theoretical instruction in the fields of finance, law and accountancy may be deducted from the required period of professional experience, provided the instruction-

(a) lasted at least one year, and

(b) is attested by an examination recognised by the Secretary of State for the purposes of this paragraph;

but the period of professional experience may not be so reduced by more than four years.

(2) The period of professional experience together with the practical training required in the case of persons satisfying the requirement in paragraph 7 by virtue of having a sufficient period of professional experience must not be shorter than the course of theoretical instruction referred to in that paragraph and the practical training required in the case of persons satisfying the requirement of that paragraph by virtue of having completed such a course.

The body offering the qualification

11. (1) The body offering the qualification must have-
    (a) rules and arrangements adequate to ensure compliance with the requirements of paragraphs 6 to 10, and
    (b) adequate arrangements for the effective monitoring of its continued compliance with those requirements.
(2) The arrangements must include arrangements for monitoring-
    (a) the standard of the body's examinations, and
    (b) the adequacy of the practical training given by the persons approved by it for that purpose.

GENERAL NOTE

This schedule relates to the provisions of s.1220, which refer to the recognition of professional qualifications, and it replaces and extends the provisions of Sch.12 to the 1989 Act. Many of the changes arise from the need to implement requirements in the EU's 8th Company Law Directive on Audit (adopted and published in *The Official Journal of the European Communities* on June 9, 2006, its provisions coming into force from June 29, 2006: see [2006] O.J. L157/ 87, http://eur-lex.-europa.eu/LexUriServ/site/en/oj/2006/L157/L15720060609en00870107.pdf).

Part 1: Grant and revocation of recognition of a professional qualification

This part of the schedule restates, with some rewording and modifications, provisions in paras 1-3 in Pt 1 of Sch.12 to the 1989 Act. The new paragraphs deal with transitional arrangements (para.4) and the use of orders (para.5).

Paragraph 1 identifies the steps a body is required to take for a qualification it offers to be recognised by the Secretary of State.

Paragraph 2 deals with the grant and refusal of recognition.

Paragraph 3 specifies the steps that the Secretary of State is required to take if the recognition is revoked.

Paragraph 4 outlines transitional arrangements that allow bodies recognised under the 1989 Act or the Companies (Northern Ireland) Order 1990 to continue to be recognised.

Paragraph 5 indicates that recognition and revocation orders are not to be statutory instruments.

Part 2: Requirements for recognition of a professional qualification

This part of the schedule restates, with some rewording and modifications, provisions in paras 4-9 in Pt 2 of Sch.12 to the 1989 Act. A new paragraph sets out supplementary provision with respect to a sufficient period of professional experience (para.10).

Paragraph 6 sets the minimum academic standards that a person must have attained before he can attempt the professional qualification.

Paragraph 7 replaces paras 5 and 6 of Sch.12 to the 1989 Act, which respectively dealt with "Course of theoretical instruction" and "Sufficient period of professional experience". Para.7 requires that the qualification is restricted to persons who have either completed a relevant academic course or have seven years' professional experience.

Paragraph 8 requires that an examination must be passed (part of which has to be in writing) for the person to achieve the qualification. This examination must be in subjects of theoretical knowledge prescribed by the Secretary of State; or a university or equivalent level examination; or by practical demonstration of knowledge to examination or diploma level that is recognised by the Secretary of State.

Paragraph 9 requires persons to carry out at least three years' practical training.

Paragraph 10 sets out the supplementary provision with respect to a sufficient period of professional experience, dealing with the interaction between theoretical instruction and professional experience.

Paragraph 11 replaces para.9 of Sch.12 to the 1989 Act, dealing with the body offering the qualification.

SCHEDULE 12   Section 1242

ARRANGEMENTS IN WHICH REGISTERED THIRD COUNTRY AUDITORS ARE REQUIRED TO PARTICIPATE

Arrangements for independent monitoring of audits of traded non-Community companies

1. (1) The arrangements referred to in section 1242(1)(a) are appropriate arrangements-
    (a) for enabling the performance by the registered third country auditor of third country audit functions to be monitored by means of inspections carried out under the arrangements, and
    (b) for ensuring that the carrying out of such monitoring and inspections is done independently of the registered third country auditor.
(2) In this paragraph "third country audit function" means any function performed as a third country auditor.

Arrangements for independent investigations for disciplinary purposes

2. (1) The arrangements referred to in section 1242(1)(b) are appropriate arrangements-

    (a) for the carrying out of investigations into matters arising in connection with the performance of third country audit functions by the registered third country auditor,

    (b) for the holding of disciplinary hearings relating to the registered third country auditor which appear to be desirable following the conclusion of such investigations,

    (c) for requiring such hearings to be held in public except where the interests of justice otherwise require,

    (d) for the persons before whom such hearings have taken place to decide whether (and, if so, what) disciplinary action should be taken against the registered third country auditor, and

    (e) for ensuring that the carrying out of those investigations, the holding of those hearings and the taking of those decisions are done independently of the registered third country auditor.

(2) In this paragraph-

"disciplinary action" includes the imposition of a fine; and

"third country audit function" means any function performed as a third country auditor.

Supplementary: arrangements to operate independently of third country auditor

3. (1) This paragraph applies for the purposes of-

    (a) paragraph 1(1)(b), or

    (b) paragraph 2(1)(e).

(2) Arrangements are not to be regarded as appropriate for the purpose of ensuring that a thing is done independently of the registered third country auditor unless they are designed to ensure that the registered third country auditor-

    (a) will have no involvement in the appointment or selection of any of the persons who are to be responsible for doing that thing, and

    (b) will not otherwise be involved in the doing of that thing.

(3) Sub-paragraph (2) imposes a minimum requirement and does not preclude the possibility that additional criteria may need to be satisfied in order for the arrangements to be regarded as appropriate for the purpose in question.

Supplementary: funding of arrangements

4. (1) The registered third country auditor must pay any of the costs of maintaining any relevant arrangements which the arrangements provide are to be paid by it.

(2) For this purpose "relevant arrangements" are arrangements within paragraph 1 or 2 in which the registered third country auditor is obliged to participate.

Supplementary: scope of arrangements

5. Arrangements may qualify as arrangements within either of paragraphs 1 and 2 even though the matters for which they provide are more extensive in any respect than those mentioned in the applicable paragraph.

Specification of particular arrangements by the Secretary of State

6. (1) If there exist two or more sets of arrangements within paragraph 1 or within paragraph 2, the obligation of a registered third country auditor under section 1242(1)(a) or (b), as the case may be, is to participate in such set of arrangements as the Secretary of State may by order specify.

(2) An order under sub-paragraph (1) is subject to negative resolution procedure.

GENERAL NOTE

    Chapter 5 of Pt 42 of the Act on "Statutory Auditors" is new and deals with "Registered Third Country Auditors". The provisions of this new schedule, which relates to s.1242, describe the independent monitoring and investigation arrangements to which third country auditors are subject.

    Paragraph 1 deals with the arrangements for independent monitoring of audits of traded non-Community companies.

    Paragraph 2 is concerned with arrangements for independent investigations for disciplinary purposes.

    Paragraphs 3-5 deal with specific arrangements with respect to third country auditors concerning the independence of monitoring and investigating for disciplinary purposes their activities; funding the special arrangements; and identifying the scope of such special arrangements.

    Paragraph 6 deals with the power of the Secretary of State to specify the special arrangements.

SUPPLEMENTARY PROVISIONS WITH RESPECT TO DELEGATION ORDER

Operation of this Schedule

1 (1) This Schedule has effect in relation to a body designated by a delegation order under section 1252 as follows-

    (a) paragraphs 2 to 12 have effect in relation to the body where it is established by the order;

    (b) paragraphs 2 and 6 to 11 have effect in relation to the body where it is an existing body;

    (c) paragraph 13 has effect in relation to the body where it is an existing body that is an unincorporated association.

(2) In their operation in accordance with sub-paragraph (1)(b), paragraphs 2 and 6 apply only in relation to-

    (a) things done by or in relation to the body in or in connection with the exercise of functions transferred to it by the delegation order, and

    (b) functions of the body which are functions so transferred.

(3) Any power conferred by this Schedule to make provision by order is a power to make provision by an order under section 1252.

Status

2 The body is not to be regarded as acting on behalf of the Crown and its members, officers and employees are not to be regarded as Crown servants.

Name, members and chairman

3 (1) The body is to be known by such name as may be specified in the delegation order.

(2) The body is to consist of such persons (not being less than eight) as the Secretary of State may appoint after such consultation as he thinks appropriate.

(3) The chairman of the body is to be such person as the Secretary of State may appoint from among its members.

(4) The Secretary of State may make provision by order as to-

    (a) the terms on which the members of the body are to hold and vacate office;

    (b) the terms on which a person appointed as chairman is to hold and vacate the office of chairman.

Financial provisions

4 (1) The body must pay to its chairman and members such remuneration, and such allowances in respect of expenses properly incurred by them in the performance of their duties, as the Secretary of State may determine.

(2) As regards any chairman or member in whose case the Secretary of State so determines, the body must pay or make provision for the payment of-

    (a) such pension, allowance or gratuity to or in respect of that person on his retirement or death, or

    (b) such contributions or other payment towards the provision of such a pension, allowance or gratuity,

as the Secretary of State may determine.

(3) Where-

    (a) a person ceases to be a member of the body otherwise than on the expiry of his term of office, and

    (b) it appears to the Secretary of State that there are special circumstances which make it right for that person to receive compensation,

the body must make a payment to him by way of compensation of such amount as the Secretary of State may determine.

Proceedings

5 (1) The delegation order may contain such provision as the Secretary of State considers appropriate with respect to the proceedings of the body.

(2) The delegation order may, in particular-

    (a) authorise the body to discharge any functions by means of committees consisting wholly or partly of members of the body;

    (b) provide that the validity of proceedings of the body, or of any such committee, is not affected by any vacancy among the members or any defect in the appointment of any member.

Fees

6 (1) The body may retain fees payable to it.

(2) The fees must be applied for-

    (a) meeting the expenses of the body in discharging its functions, and

    (b) any purposes incidental to those functions.

(3) Those expenses include any expenses incurred by the body on such staff, accommodation, services and other facilities as appear to it to be necessary or expedient for the proper performance of its functions.

(4) In prescribing the amount of fees in the exercise of the functions transferred to it the body must prescribe such fees as appear to it sufficient to defray those expenses, taking one year with another.

(5) Any exercise by the body of the power to prescribe fees requires the approval of the Secretary of State.

(6) The Secretary of State may, after consultation with the body, by order vary or revoke any regulations prescribing fees made by the body.

Legislative functions

7 (1) Regulations or an order made by the body in the exercise of the functions transferred to it must be made by instrument in writing, but not by statutory instrument.

(2) The instrument must specify the provision of this Part of this Act under which it is made.

(3) The Secretary of State may by order impose such requirements as he thinks necessary or expedient as to the circumstances and manner in which the body must consult on any regulations or order it proposes to make.

(4) Nothing in this Part applies to make regulations or an order made by the body subject to negative resolution procedure or affirmative resolution procedure.

8. (1) Immediately after an instrument is made it must be printed and made available to the public with or without payment.

(2) A person is not to be taken to have contravened any regulation or order if he shows that at the time of the alleged contravention the instrument containing the regulation or order had not been made available as required by this paragraph.

9. (1) The production of a printed copy of an instrument purporting to be made by the body on which is endorsed a certificate signed by an officer of the body authorised by it for the purpose and stating-

    (a) that the instrument was made by the body,

    (b) that the copy is a true copy of the instrument, and

    (c) that on a specified date the instrument was made available to the public as required by paragraph 8,

is evidence (or, in Scotland, sufficient evidence) of the facts stated in the certificate.

(2) A certificate purporting to be signed as mentioned in sub-paragraph (1) is to be deemed to have been duly signed unless the contrary is shown.

(3) Any person wishing in any legal proceedings to cite an instrument made by the body may require the body to cause a copy of it to be endorsed with such a certificate as is mentioned in this paragraph.

Report and accounts

10 (1) The body must, at least once in each calendar year for which the delegation order is in force, make a report to the Secretary of State on-

    (a) the discharge of the functions transferred to it, and

    (b) such other matters as the Secretary of State may by order require.

(2) The delegation order may modify sub-paragraph (1) as it has effect in relation to the calendar year in which the order comes into force or is revoked.

(3) The Secretary of State must lay before Parliament copies of each report received by him under this paragraph.

(4) The following provisions of this paragraph apply as follows-

    (a) sub-paragraphs (5) and (6) apply only where the body is established by the order, and

    (b) sub-paragraphs (7) and (8) apply only where the body is an existing body.

(5) The Secretary of State may, with the consent of the Treasury, give directions to the body with respect to its accounts and the audit of its accounts.

(6) A person may only be appointed as auditor of the body if he is eligible for appointment as a statutory auditor.

(7) Unless the body is a company to which section 394 (duty to prepare individual company accounts) applies, the Secretary of State may, with the consent of the Treasury, give directions to the body with respect to its accounts and the audit of its accounts.

(8) Whether or not the body is a company to which section 394 applies, the Secretary of State may direct that any provisions of this Act specified in the directions are to apply to the body, with or without any modifications so specified.

Other supplementary provisions

11 (1) The transfer of a function to a body designated by a delegation order does not affect anything previously done in the exercise of the function transferred; and the resumption of a function so transferred does not affect anything previously done in exercise of the function resumed.

(2) The Secretary of State may by order make such transitional and other supplementary provision as he thinks necessary or expedient in relation to the transfer or resumption of a function.

(3) The provision that may be made in connection with the transfer of a function includes, in particular, provision-

    (a) for modifying or excluding any provision of this Part of this Act in its application to the function transferred;

    (b) for applying to the body designated by the delegation order, in connection with the function transferred, any provision applying to the Secretary of State which is contained in or made under any other enactment;

    (c) for the transfer of any property, rights or liabilities from the Secretary of State to that body;

    (d) for the carrying on and completion by that body of anything in the process of being done by the Secretary of State when the order takes effect;

    (e) for the substitution of that body for the Secretary of State in any instrument, contract or legal proceedings.

(4) The provision that may be made in connection with the resumption of a function includes, in particular, provision-

    (a) for the transfer of any property, rights or liabilities from that body to the Secretary of State;

    (b) for the carrying on and completion by the Secretary of State of anything in the process of being done by that body when the order takes effect;

    (c) for the substitution of the Secretary of State for that body in any instrument, contract or legal proceedings.

12. Where a delegation order is revoked, the Secretary of State may by order make provision-

    (a) for the payment of compensation to persons ceasing to be employed by the body established by the delegation order;

    (b) as to the winding up and dissolution of the body.

13. (1) This paragraph applies where the body is an unincorporated association.

(2) Any relevant proceedings may be brought by or against the body in the name of any body corporate whose constitution provides for the establishment of the body.

(3) In sub-paragraph (2) "relevant proceedings" means proceedings brought in or in connection with the exercise of any transferred function.

(4) In relation to proceedings brought as mentioned in sub-paragraph (2), any reference in paragraph 11(3)(e) or (4)(c) to the body replacing or being replaced by the Secretary of State in any legal proceedings is to be read with the appropriate modifications.

GENERAL NOTE

This schedule relates to the provisions of s.1252 and restates the provisions of Sch.13 to the 1989 Act, as amended by s.5 of the Companies (Audit, Investigations and Community Enterprise) Act 2004 (colloquially referred to as the C(AICE) Act).

The schedule refers to a delegated body that can exercise the Secretary of State's powers as set out in Pt 42 of the Act concerning statutory auditors.

Paragraph 1 deals with the operation of the schedule.

Paragraph 2 deals with the status of the delegated body and provides that it is not to be regarded as acting on behalf of the Crown.

Paragraph 3 is concerned with the name of the delegated body and its chairman and members.

Paragraphs 4-6 are concerned with financial provisions relating to the delegated body, its proceedings and the use of fee income that it generates.

Paragraphs 7-9 provide for the delegated body to exercise any legislative functions by instrument in writing and not by statutory instrument. Instruments must be made available to the public, and the Secretary of State may require the body to consult prior to the making of regulations.

Paragraph 10 requires the delegated body to submit an annual report (including audited accounts) to the Secretary of State dealing with the performance of its functions.

Paragraphs 11-13 deal with various supplementary matters, including the transfer of powers and assets and liabilities, transitional arrangements, revocation of the delegation order, and proceedings against the delegated body when it is an unincorporated association

SCHEDULE 14   Section 1264

STATUTORY AUDITORS: CONSEQUENTIAL AMENDMENTS

Companies (Audit, Investigations and Community Enterprise) Act 2004 (c. 27)

1. (1) Section 16 of the Companies (Audit, Investigations and Community Enterprise) Act 2004 (c. 27) (grants to bodies concerned with accounting standards etc) is amended as follows.

(2) In subsection (2)-

    (a) in paragraph (f) for "paragraph 17" to the end substitute "paragraph 21, 22, 23(1) or 24(1) of Schedule 10 to the Companies Act 2006;",

    (b) in paragraph (g) for "Part 2 of that Act" substitute "Part 42 of that Act".

(3) In subsection (5), in the definition of "professional accountancy body"-

    (a) in paragraph (a) for "Part 2 of the Companies Act 1989 (c. 40)" substitute "Part 42 of the Companies Act 2006", and

    (b) in paragraph (b) for "section 32" substitute "section 1220".

GENERAL NOTE

This is a new Schedule, referred to in s.1264, that makes minor consequential amendments to s.16 of the Companies (Audit, Investigations and Community Enterprise) Act 2004 (colloquially referred to as the C(AICE) Act). The section deals with grants to bodies concerned with accounting, auditing and actuarial standards, and the amendments change the references to provisions in previous legislation to the corresponding material in the new Act.

SCHEDULE 15   Section 1272

Transparency Obligations and Related Matters: Minor and Consequential Amendments

Part i

Amendments of the Financial Services and Markets Act 2000

1. Part 6 of the Financial Services and Markets Act 2000 (listing and other matters) is amended as follows.

2. In sectioan 73 (general duty of competent authority), after subsection (1) insert-

    "(1A) To the extent that those general functions are functions under or relating to transparency rules, subsection (1)(c) and (f) have effect as if the references to a regulated market were references to a market."

3. In section 73A (Part 6 Rules), after subsection (5) insert-

    "(6) Transparency rules and corporate governance rules are not listing rules, disclosure rules or prospectus rules, but are Part 6 rules."

4. For the cross-heading before section 90 substitute "Compensation for false or misleading statements etc".

5. For the heading to section 90 substitute "**Compensation for statements in listing particulars or prospectus**".

6. (1) Section 91 (penalties for breach of Part 6 rules) is amended as follows.

(2) For subsection (1) substitute-

    "(1) If the competent authority considers that-

        (a) an issuer of listed securities, or

        (b) an applicant for listing,

has contravened any provision of listing rules, it may impose on him a penalty of such amount as it considers appropriate.

    (1ZA) If the competent authority considers that-

        (a) an issuer who has requested or approved the admission of a financial instrument to trading on a regulated market,

        (b) a person discharging managerial responsibilities within such an issuer, or

        (c) a person connected with such a person discharging managerial responsibilities,

has contravened any provision of disclosure rules, it may impose on him a penalty of such amount as it considers appropriate.".

(3) After subsection (1A) insert-

    "(1B) If the competent authority considers-

        (a) that a person has contravened-

            (i) a provision of transparency rules or a provision otherwise made in accordance with the transparency obligations directive, or

            (ii) a provision of corporate governance rules, or

        (b) that a person on whom a requirement has been imposed under section 89L (power to suspend or prohibit trading of securities in case of infringement of applicable transparency obligation), has contravened that requirement,

it may impose on the person a penalty of such amount as it considers appropriate.".

(4) In subsection (2) for "(1)(a), (1)(b)(i) or (1A)" substitute "(1), (1ZA)(a), (1A) or (1B)".

7. In section 96B (persons discharging managerial responsibilities and connected persons)-

    (a) for the heading substitute "**Disclosure rules: persons responsible for compliance**".

    (b) in subsection (1) for "For the purposes of this Part" substitute "for the purposes of the provisions of this Part relating to disclosure rules".

8. In section 97(1) (appointment by the competent authority of persons to carry out investigations), for paragraphs (a) and (b) substitute-

    "(a) there may have been a contravention of-

        (i) a provision of this Part or of Part 6 rules, or

        (ii) a provision otherwise made in accordance with the prospectus directive or the transparency obligations directive;

    (b) a person who was at the material time a director of a person mentioned in section 91(1), (1ZA)(a), (1A) or (1B) has been knowingly concerned in a contravention by that person of-

        (i) a provision of this Part or of Part 6 rules, or

        (ii) a provision otherwise made in accordance with the prospectus directive or the transparency obligations directive;".

9. In section 99 (fees) after subsection (1B) insert-

    "(1C) Transparency rules may require the payment of fees to the competent authority in respect of the continued admission of financial instruments to trading on a regulated market.".

10. (1) Section 102A (meaning of "securities" etc) is amended as follows.

(2) After subsection (3) insert-

    "(3A) "Debt securities" has the meaning given in Article 2.1(b) of the transparency obligations directive.".

(3) In subsection (3) (meaning of "transferable securities") for "the investment services directive" substitute "Directive 2004/39/EC of the European Parliament and of the Council on markets in financial instruments".

(4) In subsection (6) (meaning of "issuer"), after paragraph (a) insert-

    "(aa) in relation to transparency rules, means a legal person whose securities are admitted to trading on a regulated market or whose voting shares are admitted to trading on a UK market other than a regulated market, and in the case of depository receipts representing securities, the issuer is the issuer of the securities represented;".

11. (1) Section 103(1) (interpretation of Part 6) is amended as follows.

(2) In the definition of "regulated market" for "Article 1.13 of the investment services directive" substitute "Article 4.1(14) of Directive 2004/39/EC of the European Parliament and of the Council on markets in financial instruments".

(3) At the appropriate place insert-

    ""transparency rules" has the meaning given by section 89A(5);

    "voteholder information" has the meaning given by section 89B(3);".

12. In section 429(2) (Parliamentary control of statutory instruments: affirmative procedure) of the Financial Services and Markets Act 2000 (c. 8) after "section" insert "90B or".

PART 2

AMENDMENTS OF THE COMPANIES (AUDIT, INVESTIGATIONS AND COMMUNITY ENTERPRISE)
ACT 2004

13. Chapter 2 of Part 1 of the Companies (Audit, Investigations and Community Enterprise) Act 2004 (accounts and reports) is amended as follows.

14. (1) Section 14 (supervision of periodic accounts and reports of issuers of listed securities) is amended as follows.

(2) In subsection (2)(a)-

    (a) for "listed" substitute "transferable";

    (b) for "listing" substitute "Part 6".

(3) In subsection (3)(a)-

    (a) for "listed" substitute "transferable";

    (b) for "listing" substitute "Part 6".

(4) In subsection (7)(b) for "listed" substitute "transferable".

(5) In subsection (12)-

    (a) for ""listed securities" and "listing rules" have" substitute ""Part 6 rules" has";

    (b) for the definition of "issuer" substitute-

        ""issuer" has the meaning given by section 102A(6) of that Act;";

    (c) in the definition of "periodic" for "listing" substitute "Part 6";

    (d) at the end add-

        ""transferable securities" has the meaning given by section 102A(3) of that Act.".

15. (1) Section 15 (application of certain company law provisions to bodies appointed under section 14) is amended as follows.

(2) In subsection (5)(a)-

    (a) for "listed" substitute "transferable";

    (b) for "listing" substitute "Part 6".

(3) In subsection (5B)(a)-
- (a) for "liste" substitute "transferable";
- (b) for "listing" substitute "Part 6".

(4) In subsection (6)(b) for ""listing rules" and "security"" substitute ""Part 6 rules" and "transferable securities"".

GENERAL NOTE

Schedule 15 is concerned only to make minor amendments to the Financial Services and Markets Act 2000 ("FSMA 2000") so that the transparency obligations provisions which are contained in Pt 43 of the Companies Act 2006 can be smoothly incorporated into Pt VI of FSMA 2000 which deals with the listing of securities and the offer of securities to the public. Part 43 of the Companies Act 2006 implemented the Transparency Obligations Directive (on which see the General Note to Pt 43 above). That directive is concerned with the provision of information relating to securities which are already in issue. In turn the Financial Services Authority ("FSA") will introduce transparency rules implementing that directive and the Commission's technical regulation in detail as part of United Kingdom law. There are two recent EC securities directives which are of significance: the Prospectus Directive and the Transparency Directive. The Prospectus Directive has already been incorporated into FSMA 2000 and has already been implemented by the FSA in the form of the "Prospectus Rules" and the "Disclosure Rules", which are in turn part of the "Listing Rules" in the FSA Rulebook more generally. References in Sch.15 to these "rules" are to those two additions to the FSA Rulebook. The Transparency Directive will be implemented by means of the provisions set out in Pt 43 of the 2006 Act and by means of "transparency rules" and "corporate governance rules", both of which are referred to in Pt 43, which are to be brought into being by the FSA as further additions to the FSA Rulebook. Consequently, in the provisions of Sch.15 there are references to FSMA 2000, to subordinate legislation effected under FSMA 2000, and the FSA rulebooks. With those cross-references, Sch.15 does not make any substantive provision which has not already been considered in relation to the notes on Pt 43 of the 2006 Act.

SCHEDULE 16   Section 1295

REPEALS

Company law repeals
(Great Britain)

Short title and chapter	Extent of repeal
Companies Act 1985 (c. 6)	Sections 1 to 430F.
	In section 437-
	(a) in subsection (1), the second sentence, and
	(b) subsections (1B) and (1C).
	Section 438.
	In section 439-
	(a) in subsection (2), ", or is ordered to pay the whole or any part of the costs of proceedings brought under section 438",
	(b) subsections (3) and (7), and
	(c) in subsection (8), "; and any such liability imposed by subsection (2) is (subject as mentioned above) a liability also to indemnify all persons against liability under subsection (3)".
	Section 442(2).
	Section 446.
	In section 448(7), the words "and liable to a fine." to the end.
	Section 449(7).
	Section 450(4).
	Section 451(3).
	In section 453(1A)-
	(a) paragraph (b), and
	(b) paragraph (d) and the word "and" preceding it.
	Section 453A(6).
	Sections 458 to 461.
	Sections 651 to 746.
	Schedules 1 to 15B.
	Schedules 20 to 25.
Insolvency Act 1985 (c. 65)	Schedule 6.

Short title and chapter	Extent of repeal
Insolvency Act 1986 (c. 45)	In Schedule 13, in Part 1, the entries relating to the following provisions of the Companies Act 1985- (a) section 13(4), (b) section 44(7), (c) section 103(7), (d) section 131(7), (e) section 140(2), (f) section 156(3), (g) section 173(4), (h) section 196, (i) section 380(4), (j) section 461(6), (k) section 462(5), (l) section 463(2), (m) section 463(3), (n) section 464(6), (o) section 657(2), (p) section 658(1), and (q) section 711(2).
Building Societies Act 1986 (c. 53)	Section 102C(5).
Finance Act 1988 (c. 39)	In section 117(3), from the beginning to "that section";". In section 117(4), the words "and (3)".
Water Act 1989 (c. 15)	In Schedule 25, paragraph 71(3).
Companies Act 1989 (c. 40)	Sections 1 to 22. Section 56(5). Sections 57 and 58. Section 64(2). Section 66(3). Section 71. Sections 92 to 110. Sections 113 to 138. Section 139(1) to (3). Sections 141 to 143. Section 144(1) to (3) and (6). Section 207. Schedules 1 to 9. In Schedule 10, paragraphs 1 to 24. Schedules 15 to 17. In Schedule 18, paragraphs 32 to 38. In Schedule 19, paragraphs 1 to 9 and 11 to 21.
Age of Legal Capacity (Scotland) Act 1991 (c. 50)	In Schedule 1, paragraph 39.
Water Consolidation (Consequential Provisions) Act 1991 (c. 60)	In Schedule 1, paragraph 40(2).
Charities Act 1992 (c. 41)	In Schedule 6, paragraph 11.
Charities Act 1993 (c. 10)	In Schedule 6, paragraph 20.
Criminal Justice Act 1993 (c. 36)	In Schedule 5, paragraph 4.
Welsh Language Act 1993 (c. 38)	Section 30.
Pension Schemes Act 1993 (c. 48)	In Schedule 8, paragraph 16.
Trade Marks Act 1994 (c. 26)	In Schedule 4, in paragraph 1(2), the reference to the Companies Act 1985.
Deregulation and Contracting Out Act 1994 (c. 40)	Section 13(1). Schedule 5. In Schedule 16, paragraphs 8 to 10. In Schedule 4, paragraphs 51 to 56.

Short title and chapter	Extent of repeal
Requirements of Writing (Scotland) Act 1995 (c. 7)	
Criminal Procedure (Consequential Provisions) (Scotland) Act 1995 (c. 40)	In Schedule 4, paragraph 56(3) and (4).
Disability Discrimination Act 1995 (c. 50)	In Schedule 6, paragraph 4.
Financial Services and Markets Act 2000 (c. 8)	Section 143. Section 263.
Limited Liability Partnerships Act 2000 (c. 12)	In the Schedule, paragraph 1.
Political Parties, Elections and Referendums Act 2000 (c. 41)	Sections 139 and 140. Schedule 19. In Schedule 23, paragraphs 12 and 13.
Criminal Justice and Police Act 2001 (c. 16)	Section 45. In Schedule 2, paragraph 17.
Enterprise Act 2002 (c. 40)	In Schedule 17, paragraphs 3 to 8.
Companies (Audit, Investigations and Community Enterprise) Act 2004 (c. 27)	Sections 7 to 10. Section 11(1). Sections 12 and 13. Sections 19 and 20. Schedule 1. In Schedule 2, paragraphs 5 to 10, 22 to 24 and 26. In Schedule 6, paragraphs 1 to 9.
Civil Partnership Act 2004 (c. 33)	In Schedule 27, paragraphs 99 to 105.
Constitutional Reform Act 2005 (c. 4)	In Schedule 11, in paragraph 4(3), the reference to the Companies Act 1985.

Repeals and revocations
relating to Northern Ireland

Short title and chapter	Extent of repeal or revocation
Companies (Northern Ireland) Order 1986 (S.I. 1986/1032 (N.I. 6))	The whole Order.
Companies Consolidation (Consequential Provisions) (Northern Ireland) Order 1986 (S.I. 1986/1035 (N.I. 9))	The whole Order.
Business Names (Northern Ireland) Order 1986 (S.I. 1986/1033 (N.I. 7))	The whole Order.
Industrial Relations (Northern Ireland) Order 1987 (S.I. 1987/936 N.I. 9))	Article 3.
Finance Act 1988 (c. 39)	In section 117(3), the words from "and for" to the end.
Companies (Northern Ireland) Order 1989 (S.I. 1989/2404 (N.I. 18))	The whole Order.
Insolvency (Northern Ireland) Order 1989 (S.I. 1989/2405 (N.I. 19))	In Schedule 7, in the entry relating to Article 166(4), the word "office". In Schedule 9, Part I.
European Economic Interest Groupings Regulations (Northern Ireland) 1989 (S.R. 1989/216)	The whole Regulations.
Companies (Northern Ireland) Order 1990 (S.I. 1990/593 (N.I. 5))	The whole Order.
Companies (No. 2) (Northern Ireland) Order 1990 (S.I. 1990/1504 (N.I. 10))	Parts II to IV. Part VI.

Short title and chapter	Extent of repeal or revocation
	Schedules 1 to 6.
Criminal Justice Act 1993 (c. 36)	In Schedule 5, Part 2.
	Schedule 6.
Financial Provisions (Northern Ireland) Order 1993 (S.I. 1993/1252 (N.I. 5))	Article 15.
Deregulation and Contracting Out Act 1994 (c. 40)	Section 13(2).
	Schedule 6.
Pensions (Northern Ireland) Order 1995 (S.I. 1995/3213 (N.I. 22))	In Schedule 3, paragraph 7.
Deregulation and Contracting Out (Northern Ireland) Order 1996 (S.I. 1996/1632 (N.I. 11))	Article 11.
	Schedule 2.
	In Schedule 5, paragraph 4.
Youth Justice and Criminal Evidence Act 1999 (c. 23)	In Schedule 4, paragraph 18.
Limited Liability Partnerships Act (Northern Ireland) 2002 (c. 12 (N.I.))	The whole Act.
Open-Ended Investment Companies Act (Northern Ireland) 2002 (c. 13)	The whole Act.
Company Directors Disqualification (Northern Ireland) Order 2002 (S.I. 2002/3150 (N.I. 4))	In Schedule 3, paragraphs 3 to 5.
Companies (Audit, Investigations and Community Enterprise) Act 2004 (c. 27)	Section 11(2).
	In Schedule 2, paragraphs 11 to 15.
Law Reform (Miscellaneous Provisions) (Northern Ireland) Order 2005 (S.I. 2005/1452 (N.I. 7))	Article 4(2).
Companies (Audit, Investigations and Community Enterprise) (Northern Ireland) Order 2005 (S.I. 2005/1967 (N.I. 17))	The whole Order.

Other repeals

Short title and chapter	Extent of repeal or revocation
Limited Partnerships Act 1907 (c. 24)	In section 16(1)-
	(a) the words ", and there shall be paid for such inspection such fees as may be appointed by the Board of Trade, not exceeding 5p for each inspection", and
	(b) the words from "and there shall be paid for such certificate" to the end.
	In section 17-
	(a) the words "(but as to fees with the concurrence of the Treasury)", and
	(b) paragraph (a).
Business Names Act 1985 (c. 7)	The whole Act.
Companies Act 1989 (c. 40)	Sections 24 to 54.
	Schedules 11 to 13.
Criminal Procedure (Consequential Provisions) (Scotland) Act 1995 (c. 40)	In Schedule 4, paragraph 74(2).
Companies (Audit, Investigations and Community Enterprise) Act 2004 (c. 27)	Sections 1 to 6.
	In Schedule 2, Part 1.
Civil Partnership Act 2004 (c. 33)	In Schedule 27, paragraph 128.

GENERAL NOTE

Introduced by s.1295, this Schedule contains a list of all the repeals made by this Act, whether or not they are also contained in the body of the Act. They include not only repeals consequent on the reform and consolidation brought about by this Act, but also of matters which are no longer of any practical use.

APPENDIX I

BANKRUPTCY AND DILIGENCE ETC. (SCOTLAND) ACT 2007

(2007 asp 3)

PART 2

FLOATING CHARGES

GENERAL NOTE

The Bankruptcy and Diligence etc. (Scotland) Act 2007 of the Scottish Parliament amends Scots law on personal bankruptcy and diligence against a debtor's assets. Part 2 (ss.37-49) (which follows the Scottish Law Commission's Report on Registration of Rights in Security by Companies, Scot.Law Com. No.197 of September 2004) ("the SLC Report") and amends the law on the creation and registration of floating charges granted by a company in relation to property situated in Scotland, the events which cause such a charge to "crystallise", and related matters. Only Pt 2 is considered in this commentary.

In this Appendix references to "the Scottish Act" are, unless otherwise stated, to the Bankruptcy and Diligence etc. (Scotland) Act 2007, references to "the 2006 Act" are to the Companies Act 2006 and references to "the 1985 Act" are to the Companies Act 1985. Subject to savings and transitional arrangements, Pt XVIII (Floating Charges: Scotland) of the 1985 Act (so far as not previously repealed) is repealed and replaced by the provisions of the Scottish Act.

Part 2 of the Scottish Act cannot come into force without amendment to (*inter alia*) Ch.2 of Pt 25 ("Company Charges") of the 2006 Act (ss.878-892), in particular by removing from those sections the requirement to register a floating charge granted by a Scottish company with the Registrar of Companies within twenty one days of its creation. In addition, arrangements will require to be made so that a search against a company which is registered at Companies House in any part of the United Kingdom will automatically generate a report in respect of that company from the Register of Floating Charges created by the Scottish Act and from Companies House. Consultation on the necessary statutory instruments and practical arrangements are expected to delay implementation of both Pt 2 of the Scottish Act and Pt 25 of the 2006 Act. Pending commencement of these Acts the existing legislation relating to floating charges in Scotland, principally Ch.II of Pt XII and Pt XVIII (so far as not previously repealed) of the 1985 Act will continue to govern the matters dealt with in the Scottish Act.

Background and General Effect of the Scottish Act

Prior to the Companies (Floating Charges) (Scotland) Act 1961 ("the 1961 Act"), Scots law did not recognise a floating charge as effective security over assets located in Scotland. Section 1 of the 1961 Act provided for the recognition by Scots law of a floating charge granted by an incorporated company in terms now found as s.462(1) of the 1985 Act (which is repealed by the Scottish Act). Until the Companies (Floating Charges and Receivers) (Scotland) Act 1972 ("the 1972 Act"), the holder of a floating charge granted by a company incorporated in Scotland could only enforce his security by petitioning the court for a winding up order. In addition to the grounds for granting such an order available to creditors generally, the court could grant a winding up order if it was satisfied that the security of the creditor entitled to the benefit of the floating charge was in jeopardy; this remedy remains available under the Insolvency Act 1986, s.122(2). The 1972 Act introduced into Scots law the power of the holder of a floating charge to appoint a receiver in respect of the property subject to the charge (or to apply to the court for such an appointment). The Enterprise Act 2002, s.250 restricted this power in respect of floating charges granted after the commencement date of that section (September 13, 2003) if the receiver would be an "administrative receiver" but extended the power of the holder of a floating charge to appoint an administrator (or to apply to the court for such an appointment). The provisions relating to receivers are now found in Chs II-IV of Pt III of the Insolvency Act 1986 (ss.50-72H). The provisions relating to receivers in Scots law are not affected by either the 2006 Act or the Scottish Act.

The 1961 Act referred to above also introduced into Scots law the requirement (now Pt XII Ch.II of the 1985 Act) that prescribed particulars and a certified copy of any floating charge or fixed security over heritable property and certain other forms of fixed security created by a company incorporated in Scotland had to be presented to the Registrar of Companies for Scotland for registration within 21 days of the date of creation (or such longer period as the court might allow). In the absence of such presentation for registration, the charge is said to be "void against the liquidator or administrator and any creditor of a company", although contractual obligations undertaken by the parties would subsist and any sum secured by it becomes payable. These provisions (in amended form) now appear as Ch.2 of Pt 25 of the 2006 Act. As noted above, upon the Scottish Act being commenced the requirement to register a floating charge by a Scottish company will cease but (subject to any other amendments to the 2006 Act) the provisions with respect to registration at Companies House will continue to apply to fixed securities granted by a company incorporated in Scotland.

The 1961 Act provided that, on commencement of the winding up of the company which granted the charge, a floating charge would attach to the property then comprised in the company's property and undertaking (so far as affected by the charge) subject to (a) effectually executed diligence (b) any prior ranking fixed security and (c) any prior ranking floating charge. This event is commonly referred to as the "crystallisation" of the charge. This provision is currently found as s.463 of the Insolvency Act 1986. Crystallisation also occurs on the appointment of a receiver (Insolvency Act 1986, ss.53(7) and 54(6)) and upon the registration of a notice by an administrator that the company had insufficient funds to distribute to unsecured creditors other than the "prescribed part" (Insolvency Act 1986, Sch.B1, paras 115(2) and (3)). Section 45 of the Scottish Act in substance retains these provisions but also provides for crystallisation upon the opening of insolvency proceedings in another Member State pursuant to the European Community Regulation on Insolvency Proceedings.

The Scottish Act provides (s.38) that a floating charge created by any company after the commencement of the Act is only effective against assets located in Scotland if the charge has been registered in the new Register of Floating Charges created pursuant to the Act. Accordingly, it will not be sufficient to create an effective floating charge security over Scottish assets owned by a company incorporated in England and Wales, Northern Ireland or elsewhere outwith Scotland to comply with the registration requirements of that jurisdiction; the charge must also be registered in the Scottish Register of Floating Charges.

The Scottish Act does not in terms apply to limited liability partnerships incorporated in Scotland and other entities whose floating charges are recognised in Scots law, but it is anticipated that it will be extended by statutory instrument to such entities on the same basis as for companies.

Registration and creation etc

37. Register of Floating Charges

(1) The Keeper of the Registers of Scotland (in this Part, the "Keeper") must establish and maintain a register to be known as the Register of Floating Charges.

(2) The Keeper must accept an application for registration of-

    (a) any document delivered to the Keeper in pursuance of section 38, 41, 42, 43 or 44 of this Act; and

    (b) any notice delivered to the Keeper in pursuance of section 39 or 45(2) of this Act,

provided that the application is accompanied by such information as the Keeper may require for the purposes of the registration.

(3) On receipt of such an application, the Keeper must note the date of receipt of the application; and, where the application is accepted by the Keeper, that date is to be treated for the purposes of this Part as the date of registration of the document or notice to which the application relates.

(4) The Keeper must, after accepting such an application, complete registration by registering in the Register of Floating Charges the document or notice to which the application relates.

(5) The Keeper must-

    (a) make the Register of Floating Charges available for public inspection at all reasonable times;

    (b) provide facilities for members of the public to obtain copies of the documents in the Register; and

    (c) supply an extract of a document in the Register, certified as a true copy of the original, to any person requesting it.

(6) An extract certified as mentioned in subsection (5)(c) above is sufficient evidence of the original.

(7) The Keeper may charge such fees-

    (a) for registering a document or notice in the Register of Floating Charges; or

    (b) in relation to anything done under subsection (5) above,

as the Scottish Ministers may by regulations prescribe.

(8) The Scottish Ministers may by regulations make provision as to-
   (a) the form and manner in which the Register of Floating Charges is to be maintained;
   (b) the form of documents (including notices as mentioned in sections 39(1) and 45(2) of this Act) for registration in that Register, the particulars they are to contain and the manner in which they are to be delivered to the Keeper.
(9) Provision under subsection (8) above may, in particular, facilitate the use-
   (a) of electronic communication;
   (b) of documents in electronic form (and of certified electronic signatures in documents).

GENERAL NOTE

Section 37 establishes a new Register of Floating Charges to be maintained by the Keeper of the Registers of Scotland (whose existing responsibilities include maintaining the Scottish Property Registers). Floating charges intended to affect assets located in Scotland and other documents relating to such charges referred to in the Act are to be submitted to the Keeper for registration along with an application in a form to be prescribed by subordinate regulation (which may include provision for electronic filing). The original of the documents submitted will be retained and they will be available for public inspection and copying. The Keeper will also provide an official certified copy on request, which will be sufficient evidence of the original document. The date of receipt by the Keeper is to be noted and, if registration follows, that (subject to s.39 (Advance Notice)) will be the date of registration. Details of the content of the Register are to be prescribed. Unless otherwise stated, references in this Appendix to registration or the Register are to registration pursuant to the Scottish Act and to the Register of Floating Charges.

38. Creation of floating charges

(1) It continues to be competent, for the purpose of securing any obligation to which this subsection applies, for a company to grant in favour of the creditor in the obligation a charge (known as a "floating charge") over all or any part of the property which may from time to time be comprised in the company's property and undertaking.
(2) Subsection (1) above applies to any debt or other obligation incurred or to be incurred by, or binding upon, the company or any other person.
(3) From the coming into force of this section, a floating charge is (subject to section 39 of this Act) created only when a document-
   (a) granting a floating charge; and
   (b) subscribed by the company granting the charge,
is registered in the Register of Floating Charges.
(4) References in this Part to a document which grants a floating charge are to a document by means of which a floating charge is granted.

GENERAL NOTE

Section 38(1) and (2) provides that Scots law will continue to recognise a (duly registered) floating charge by a company (as defined in s.47) over all or any part of the property which may from time to time be comprised in its property and undertaking. A floating charge may be granted to secure any debt or other obligation incurred or to be incurred by or binding upon the company or any other person.

Section 38(1) and (2) re-enact s.462 (1) of the 1985 Act with the omission of references to "cautionary obligations" (guarantees) and "uncalled capital". This was recommended by the SLC Report) on the basis that these are included in the terms "any obligation" and "property and undertaking".

Section 38(3) provides that, subject to s.39 (Advance Notice) a floating charge is created only when a document granting a floating charge is subscribed by the company and is duly registered. This replaces the provisions of s.402(5) of the 1985 Act and s.879(5)(a) of the 2006 Act under which a floating charge is created when it is executed by the company. The manner of execution is prescribed in s.48(1) (discussed below).

Section 38(4) (replacing s.462(4) of the 1985 Act) provides that references to a document which grants a floating charge are to a document by means of which such a charge is granted. The word "grants" is not essential; the document is a floating charge if its effect is within the description contained in s.38(1).

Section 462(5) of the 1985 Act, which states that a floating charge which relates to heritable property does not require to be recorded or registered in the Scottish property registers, is not re-enacted. The SLC Report (p.49) pointed out that it is unnecessary under the terms of the Scottish Act.

39.   Advance notice of floating charges

(1) Where a company proposes to grant a floating charge, the company and the person in whose favour the charge is to be granted may apply to have joint notice of the proposed charge registered in the Register of Floating Charges.

(2) Subsection (3) below applies where-

    (a) a notice under subsection (1) above is registered in the Register of Floating Charges; and

    (b) within 21 days of the notice being so registered, a document-

        (i) granting a floating charge conforming with the particulars contained in the notice; and

        (ii) subscribed by the company granting the charge,

    is registered in the Register of Floating Charges.

(3) Where this subsection applies, the floating charge so created is to be treated as having been created when the notice under subsection (1) above was so registered.

GENERAL NOTE

    Section 39 introduces a facility not previously available in Scots law which permits the registration of an advance notice jointly by the company and the person in whose favour a floating charge is to be granted. The form and content of such a notice are to be prescribed under s.37(8) and (9). If a floating charge conforming to the particulars contained in the notice is registered within twenty-one days of the date of registration of the notice, the effective date of creation of the floating charge is the date of registration of the advance notice.

40.   Ranking of floating charges

(1) Subject to subsections (4) and (5) below, a floating charge-

    (a) created on or after the coming into force of this section; and

    (b) which has attached to all or any part of the property of a company,

ranks as described in subsection (2) below.

(2) The floating charge referred to in subsection (1) above-

    (a) ranks with-

        (i) any other floating charge which has attached to that property or any part of it; or

        (ii) any fixed security over that property or any part of it,

    according to date of creation; and

    (b) ranks equally with any floating charge or fixed security referred to in paragraph (a) above which was created on the same date as the floating charge referred to in subsection (1) above.

(3) For the purposes of subsection (2) above-

    (a) the date of creation of a fixed security is the date on which the right to the security was constituted as a real right; and

    (b) the date of creation of a floating charge subsisting before the coming into force of this section is the date on which the instrument creating the charge was executed by the company granting the charge.

(4) Where all or any part of the property of a company is subject to both-

    (a) a floating charge; and

    (b) a fixed security arising by operation of law,

the fixed security has priority over the floating charge.

(5) Where the holder of a floating charge over all or any part of the property of a company has received intimation in writing of the subsequent creation of-

    (a) another floating charge over the same property or any part of it; or

    (b) a fixed security over the same property or any part of it,

the priority of ranking of the first-mentioned charge is restricted to security for the matters referred to in subsection (6) below.

(6) Those matters are-

    (a) the present debt incurred (whenever payable);

    (b) any future debt which, under the contract to which the charge relates, the holder is required to allow the debtor to incur;

    (c) any interest due or to become due on the debts referred to in paragraphs (a) and (b) above;

    (d) any expenses or outlays which may be reasonably incurred by the holder; and

    (e) in the case of a floating charge to secure a contingent liability (other than a liability arising under any further debts incurred from time to time), the maximum sum to which the contingent liability is capable of amounting, whether or not it is contractually limited.

(7) Subsections (1) to (6) above, and any provision made under section 41(1) of this Act, are subject to sections 175 and 176A (provision for preferential debts and share of assets) of the Insolvency Act 1986 (c.45).

GENERAL NOTE

Section 40(1), (2), (3) and (4) restates, with modifications, the rules in s.464(2) and (4) of the 1985 Act on the ranking of floating charges where the parties have not agreed to their variation.

Subject to any such agreed variation, floating charges and fixed securities rank on the property affected according to their respective dates of creation, and floating charges or fixed securities created on the same date rank equally. A floating charge subsisting before s.40 came into force is created for this purpose when it was executed by the company (as under the superseded provisions of s.402(5)(a) of the 1985 Act and s.879(5)(a) of the 2006 Act). A fixed security which arises by operation of law, however, has priority over any floating charge.

Section 462(1)(a) and (1A) of the 1985 Act under which a floating charge may prohibit the creation of any subsequent or *pari passu* security (a "negative pledge") is not re-enacted since the ranking provisions of the Scottish Act apply to a floating charge created on or after s.40 comes into force, unless all interested parties agree to their variation pursuant to s.41 (discussed below).

Section 40(5) and (6) (re-enacting with modifications s.464(5) of the 1985 Act) provides that where the holder of a floating charge receives intimation that a subsequent floating charge or fixed security has been created over the property affected or any part of it the ranking of his floating charge is restricted to the debt for which it was granted (including any future debt which he is required to allow the company debtor to incur), interest and expenses; where the debt secured is a contingent liability (other than such future debts) the security is restricted to the maximum amount which the contingent liability is capable of attaining.

Neither the statutory ranking provisions nor any agreement to vary them affect the Insolvency Act 1986, ss.175 (Preferential Debts) or 176A (the "Prescribed Part").

41. Ranking clauses

(1) The document granting a floating charge over all or any part of the property of a company may make provision regulating the order in which the charge ranks with any other floating charge or any fixed security (including a future floating charge or fixed security) over that property or any part of it.

(2) Provision under subsection (1) above-

    (a) may displace in whole or part-

        (i) subsections (1) and (2) of section 40 of this Act;

        (ii) subsections (5) and (6) of that section;

    (b) may not affect the operation of subsection (4) of that section (whether as against subsections (1) and (2) of that section or other provision under subsection (1) above).

(3) Accordingly, subsections (1), (2), (5) and (6) of that section have effect subject to any provision made under subsection (1) above.

(4) Provision under subsection (1) above is not valid unless it is made with the consent of the holder of any subsisting floating charge, or any subsisting fixed security, which would be adversely affected by the provision.

(5) A document of consent for the purpose of subsection (4) above may be registered in the Register of Floating Charges.

GENERAL NOTE

Section 41 (replacing s.464(1)(b) and (3) of the 1985 Act) provides that ranking provisions to vary the statutory scheme may be contained in the floating charge with the consent of the holder of any subsisting floating charge or fixed security which would be adversely affected by such provisions. Section 43 (discussed below) permits the subsequent alteration of such a provision. A variation of the statutory ranking scheme may extend to the effect of the intimation of a subsequent security (s.42(5) and (6)), but cannot affect either the priority of a fixed security arising by operation of law (s.42(4)) or the statutory definition of the date of creation of a right in security (s.42(3)). As noted above in connection with s.40, the provisions of ss.175 and 176A of the Insolvency Act 1986 cannot be varied by agreement. Any necessary consents by the holders of other charges or fixed securities do not require to be given in writing but a written document of consent may nevertheless be registered.

42.   Assignation of floating charges

(1) A floating charge may be assigned (and the rights under it vested in the assignee) by the registration in the Register of Floating Charges of a document of assignation subscribed by the holder of the charge.

(2) An assignation under subsection (1) above may be in whole or to such extent as may be specified in the document of assignation.

(3) This section is without prejudice to any other enactment, or any rule of law, by virtue of which a floating charge may be assigned.

GENERAL NOTE

Section 42 permits the assignation of the creditor's rights (in whole or in part) under a floating charge in the form of a document subscribed by the holder of the charge and registered in the Register of Floating Charges. Under the superseded provisions of the 1985 Act, although in principle the charge-holder's interest could be assigned, there was no facility for this to be published by registration at Companies House. Section 42 is without prejudice to any other enactment or rule of law permitting assignation of a floating charge.

Section 42(1) provides that a duly registered assignation vests the rights assigned in the assignee without the necessity of intimation to the company. It is not made clear in the Scottish Act (as it surely should have been) that the assignor and assignee ought to intimate the assignation to the debtor company (a) to ensure that the company makes any payment due to the correct party and (b) to enable the company to fulfil its obligation (to which criminal sanctions are attached) under s.422(2) of the 1985 Act and s.891(2) of the 2006 Act to show on its own register the names of the persons entitled to the charge.

43.   Alteration of floating charges

(1) A document of alteration may alter (whether by addition, deletion or substitution of text or otherwise) the terms of a document granting a floating charge.

(2) If (and in so far as) an alteration to the terms of a document granting a floating charge concerns-
  (a) the ranking of the charge with any other floating charge or any fixed security; or
  (b) the specification of-
      (i) the property that is subject to the charge; or
      (ii) the obligations that are secured by the charge,
  the alteration is not valid unless subsection (3) below is satisfied.

(3) This subsection is satisfied if the alteration is made by a document of alteration which is-
  (a) subscribed by-
      (i) the company which granted the charge;
      (ii) the holder of the charge; and
      (iii) the holder of any other subsisting floating charge, or any subsisting fixed security, which would be adversely affected by the alteration; and

    (b) registered in the Register of Floating Charges.

  (4) But paragraph (a)(i) of subsection (3) above does not apply in respect of an alteration which-

    (a) relates only to the ranking of the floating charge first-mentioned in that subsection with any other floating charge or any fixed security; and

    (b) does not adversely affect the interests of the company which granted the charge.

  (5) The granting, by the holder of a floating charge, of consent to the release from the scope of the charge of any particular property, or class of property, which is subject to the charge is to be treated as constituting an alteration-

    (a) to the terms of the document granting the charge; and

    (b) as to the specification of the property that is subject to the charge.

  (6) For the purpose of subsection (5) above, property is not to be regarded as released from the scope of a floating charge by reason only of its ceasing to be the property of the company which granted the charge.

GENERAL NOTE

Section 43 provides for the alteration of a floating charge (replacing s.466 of the 1985 Act). Section 43(1) permits any provision of a floating charge to be amended by a "document of alteration". Under s.43(2) if (but only if) the document concerns (a) the ranking of the floating charge with any other security or (b) the specification of the property subject to the charge or the obligations secured by it, the alteration is not valid unless s.43(3) is satisfied. Section 43(3) requires that (subject to s.43(4) such a document of alteration must be subscribed by the company, the holder and the holder of any floating charge or fixed security adversely affected, and that it is registered in the Register of Floating Charges. Section 43(4) provides, however, that the company need not be a party if the document only alters ranking and the company is not adversely affected.

Prima facie, s.43(2) and (3) require the holder's agreement to reduce the obligations secured to be executed by the relevant parties and registered, on pain of invalidity. This, however, must be incorrect as the holder and any receiver or administrator appointed by him would in any event be barred from enforcing rights he has agreed to abandon.

Under s.466(4) and (5) the 1985 Act there was no requirement to register an alteration unless it increased the sum secured or the property to which the floating charge applied.

Under s.419(1)(b) of the 1985 Act (s.887(1)(b) of the 2006 Act), although a memorandum could be registered when property was released from the scope of the floating charge (other than on its disposal by the company), registration was not mandatory. Under s.43(5) of the Scottish Act, however, if the holder consents to release any particular property or class of property from the scope of the charge, this is to be treated as an alteration with respect to the specification of the property subject to the charge and, to be effective, requires to be in the form of a document of alteration executed and registered according to s.43(2) and (3).

Section 43(6) provides that if the company disposes of property subject to a floating charge that is not an "alteration" which requires to be registered.

It is not clear what would be the effect of a failure to register the consent of the holder to the release of property from the scope of a floating charge. As with a failure to register the holder's agreement to reduce the obligations secured, the holder and any receiver or administrator appointed by him must be barred from insisting that the charge still affected that property.

44. Discharge of floating charges

  (1) A floating charge may be discharged by the registration in the Register of Floating Charges of a document of discharge subscribed by the holder of the charge.

  (2) A discharge under subsection (1) above may be in whole or to such extent as may be specified in the document of discharge.

  (3) This section is without prejudice to any other means by which a floating charge may be discharged or extinguished.

GENERAL NOTE

Section 44 provides that a floating charge may be discharged (in whole or in part) by the registration of a document of discharge subscribed by the holder. As with the similar provisions of s.419(1)(a) of the 1985 Act (s.887(1)(a) of the 2006 Act), registration of a discharge is not mandatory and is without prejudice to other methods by which a floating charge may be discharged or extinguished.

45. Effect of floating charges on winding up

(1) Where a company goes into liquidation, a floating charge created over property of the company attaches to the property to which it relates.

(2) But, in a case mentioned in subsection (7)(a) below, there is no attachment under subsection (1) above until such time as a notice of attachment is registered in the Register of Floating Charges on the application of the holder of the charge.

(3) The attachment of a floating charge to property under subsection (1) above is subject to the rights of any person who-

   (a) has effectually executed diligence on the property to which the charge relates or any part of it;

   (b) holds over that property or any part of it a fixed security ranking in priority to the floating charge; or

   (c) holds over that property or any part of it another floating charge so ranking.

(4) Interest accrues in respect of a floating charge which has attached to property until payment is made of any sum due under the charge.

(5) Part IV, except section 185, of the Insolvency Act 1986 has (subject to subsection (1) above) effect in relation to a floating charge as if the charge were a fixed security over the property to which it has attached in respect of the principal of the debt or obligation to which it relates and any interest due or to become due on it.

(6) Subsections (1) to (5) above do not affect the operation of-

   (a) sections 53(7) and 54(6) (attachment of floating charge on appointment of receiver) of the Insolvency Act 1986;

   (b) sections 175 and 176A of that Act; or

   (c) paragraph 115(3) of Schedule B1 (attachment of floating charge on delivery of a notice by an administrator) to that Act.

(7) For the purposes of this section, reference to a company going into liquidation-

   (a) in a case where a court of a member State has under the EC Regulation jurisdiction as respects the company which granted the relevant floating charge, means the opening of insolvency proceedings in that State;

   (b) in any other case, is to be construed in accordance with section 247(2) and (3) of the Insolvency Act 1986 (c.45).

(8) In subsection (7)(a) above-

   "the EC Regulation" is the Regulation of the Council of the European Union published as Council Regulation (EC) No 1346/ 2000 on insolvency proceedings;

   "court" is to be construed in accordance with Article 2(d) of that Regulation;

   "insolvency proceedings" is to be construed in accordance with Article 2(a) of that Regulation;

   "member State" means a member State of the European Union apart from the United Kingdom.

GENERAL NOTE

Section 45 restates, with amendments, the pre-existing law on the circumstances upon which the floating charge will attach to the property to which it relates - "crystallisation". Crystallisation will occur only on one of the following events:

1   Where the company goes into liquidation as defined in s.247(2) and (3) of the Insolvency Act 1986 and as provided in s.45(7)(a) of the Scottish Act;

2   Where the holder of the charge (but not any other floating charge) appoints a receiver pursuant to ss.53(7) or 54(6) of the Insolvency Act 1986 (which provisions are saved by s.45(6)(a));

3   Where an administrator delivers a notice to the Registrar of Companies pursuant to para.115 (2) and (3) of Sch.B1 to the Insolvency Act 1986 to the effect that he considers the company has insufficient property to enable a distribution to be made to unsecured creditors other than the "prescribed part" (see s.45(6)(c));

By virtue of s.45(7)(a) and (8) "Liquidation" includes the opening of insolvency proceedings in another Member State pursuant to the EC Regulation on Insolvency Proceedings but (under s.45(2)) crystallisation occurs only when a notice of attachment in a form to be prescribed has been registered by the holder in the Register of Floating Charges.

Crystallisation is subject to the rights of any person who holds effectually executed diligence against the property to which the charge relates or holds a prior ranking fixed security or floating charge over that property. In the case of liquidation this is provided in s.45(3) itself; in relation to receivership this is provided in the Insolvency Act 1986, s.60; in the case of administration para.43 of Sch.B1 to the 1986 Act provides that diligence may not be executed or continued while a company is in administration without the consent of the court or the administrator and any diligence which had not become "effectual" when the company went into administration would therefore be invalid.

When a charge has crystallised, under s.45(4) interest continues to accrue at the rate specified in the floating charge.

If the charge crystallises on liquidation, the liquidation process will continue subject to the floating charge being treated as if it were a fixed security over the property to which it has attached. The Insolvency Act 1986, s.185 (which relates to the treatment of diligence in the liquidation process), s.175 (Preferential Debts) and s.176A (the "Prescribed Part") are not affected (s.45(5) and (6)(b)).

46. Repeals, savings and transitional arrangements

(1) Part XVIII (floating charges: Scotland) of the Companies Act 1985 (c.6) is repealed.

(2) Nothing in this Part (except sections 40 and 41 so far as they concern the ranking of floating charges subsisting immediately before the coming into force of this section) affects the validity or operation of floating charges subsisting before the coming into force of this section.

(3) So, despite the repeal of Chapters I and III of Part XVIII of that Act by subsection (1) above, the provisions of those Chapters are to be treated as having effect for the purposes of floating charges subsisting immediately before the coming into force of this section.

(4) In particular-

   (a) floating charges subsisting immediately before the coming into force of this section rank with each other as they ranked with each other in accordance with section 464 of the Companies Act 1985 immediately before that section was repealed by subsection (1) above; and

   (b) a floating charge subsisting immediately before the coming into force of this section ranks with a fixed security so subsisting as it ranked with the security in accordance with section 464 of the Companies Act 1985 immediately before that section was repealed by subsection (1) above.

(5) Section 140 (floating charges (Scotland)) of the Companies Act 1989 (c.40) is repealed (but, despite being repealed, is to be treated as having effect for the purposes of subsections (3) and (4) above).

GENERAL NOTE

Section 46 repeals Pt XVIII of the 1985 Act (so far as not previously repealed) and s.140 of the Companies Act 1989 (which amended Pt XVIII). These provisions, however, remain effective in relation to floating charges subsisting immediately before the Scottish Act came into force.

47. Interpretation

In this Part-

   "company" means an incorporated company (whether or not a company within the meaning of the Companies Act 1985 (c.6));

   "fixed security", in relation to any property of a company, means any security (other than a floating charge or a charge having the character of a floating charge) which on the winding up of the company in Scotland would be treated as an effective security over that property including, in particular, a heritable security (within the meaning of section 9(8) of the Conveyancing and Feudal Reform (Scotland) Act 1970 (c.35)).

Section 47 repeals the relevant provisions of s.486 of the 1985 Act. It defines "company" as "an incorporated company (whether or not a company within the meaning of the Companies Act 1985)".

"Fixed Security" is defined as any security which would be an effective security over any property of the company on its winding up (other than a floating charge).

Related further provision

48.   Formalities as to documents

(1) In section 6 (registration of documents) of the Requirements of Writing (Scotland) Act 1995 (c.7), after subsection (1)(a), insert-

"(aa) to register a document in the Register of Floating Charges;".

(2) In section 46 (extract decree of reduction to be recorded) of the Conveyancing (Scotland) Act 1924 (c.27)-

(a) in subsection (2), for the words "This section" substitute "Subsection (1) above"; and

(b) after subsection (2), insert-

"(3) This section shall apply in relation to a document registered in the Register of Floating Charges as it applies in relation to a deed or other document pertaining to a heritable security which is recorded in the Register of Sasines (and the references to recording are to be read accordingly).".

(3) In section 8 (rectification of defectively expressed documents) of the Law Reform (Miscellaneous Provisions) (Scotland) Act 1985 (c.73), after subsection (5), insert-

"(5A) Subsection (5) above applies in relation to document registered in the Register of Floating Charges as it applies in relation to a document recorded in the Register of Sasines (and the references to recording are to be read accordingly).".

GENERAL NOTE

Section 48(1) (Formalities as to Documents) provides that a floating charge or any other document to be registered in the Register of Floating Charges must be executed in the manner prescribed by s.6(1) of the Requirements of Writing (Scotland) Act 1995. If the granter is an individual a witness is necessary. If it is a company it must be either (a) subscribed by a director, or by its secretary, or by a person bearing to have been authorised to subscribe the document on its behalf, in each case, together with a witness, or (b) be signed by two directors of the company, one director and its secretary or two persons bearing to have been authorised to subscribe the document on behalf of the company. These formalities (which are only summarised in these comments) apply to any document which is intended to affect Scottish property, regardless of the domicile or place of registration of the granter.

Section 48 also makes consequential amendments to the Conveyancing (Scotland) Act 1924 and the Law Reform (Miscellaneous Provisions) (Scotland) Act 1985 in relation to the execution and rectification of documents to which these provisions apply.

49.   Industrial and provident societies

(1) For section 3 (application to registered societies of provisions relating to floating charges) of the Industrial and Provident Societies Act 1967 (c.48) substitute-

3.   "Application to registered societies of provisions relating to floating charges

(1) The provisions of Part 2 of the Bankruptcy and Diligence etc. (Scotland) Act 2007 (asp 3) (in this section referred to as the "relevant provisions") shall apply to a registered society as they apply to an incorporated company.

(2) Where, in the case of a registered society-

(a) there are in existence-

(i) a floating charge created under the relevant provisions (as applied by this section), and

(ii) an agricultural charge created under Part II of the Agricultural Credits (Scotland) Act 1929 (c.13), and

(b) any assets of the society are subject to both charges,

sections 40(1) to (3) (including as subject to section 41(1) to (4)) and 45(3)(c) of the Bankruptcy and Diligence etc. (Scotland) Act 2007 shall have effect for the purposes of determining the ranking with one another of those charges as if the agricultural charge were a floating charge created under the relevant provisions on the date of creation of the agricultural charge.".

(2) Section 4 (filing of information relating to charges) of that Act is repealed.

(3) In section 5 (supplemental provisions) of that Act-

(a) for paragraph (b) of subsection (1) substitute-

"(b) any security, except a floating charge, granted by a registered society over any of its assets,"

; and

(b) the references to section 4 of that Act are to be treated as references to that section as it had effect immediately before its repeal by subsection (2) above.

GENERAL NOTE

Section 49 applies the Scottish Act to a registered industrial or provident society.

APPENDIX II

SURVIVING PROVISIONS: COMPANIES ACTS 1985 AND 1989, AND COMPANIES (AUDIT, INVESTIGATIONS AND COMMUNITY ENTERPRISE) ACT 2004

The Companies Act 2006 when fully implemented and in force will not totally repeal (and re-enact with or without amendment) all the existing provisions of the Companies Act 1985, the Companies Act 1989 or the Companies (Audit, Investigations and Community Enterprise) Act 2004. Certain provisions (mainly on investigations, financial markets and insolvency, certain accounting regulatory bodies and assistance of overseas regulators) will remain as they are regarded by the Department of Trade and Industry (DTI) as being outside mainstream company law. The measures in the 2004 Act on community interest companies will continue as they are regarded by the DTI as forming a complete code which sits alongside company law but does not form a part of it.

The great majority of the Companies Act 1985 will be repealed by the Companies Act 2006 and the only substantive Part that will remain is Pt XIV (together with Sch.15C and 15D) on company investigations (subject to certain repeals and amendments but note also the insertion of new ss.446A-446E into the 1985 Act by ss.1035-1037 of the 2006 Act). The DTI considers that investigations can go beyond companies to cover other types of organisation and so do not have a place in the new Companies Act. The Companies Act 2006 also does not repeal Pt XV (ss.454-457) of the 1985 Act (orders imposing restrictions on shares). The 2006 Act does not repeal the remaining provisions of Pt XVIII of the Companies Act 1985 (i.e. ss.462-466, 486 and 487) on floating charges in Scotland as these are to be repealed by s.46 of the Bankruptcy and Diligence etc. (Scotland) Act 2007.

Similarly the Companies Act 1989 will be largely repealed by the Companies Act 2006 but provisions in Pt III of the 1989 Act (investigations and powers to obtain information) will remain in force. (These mainly amended the investigations provisions in Pt XIV of the Companies Act 1985 above.) As will the remaining measures in Pt VII on financial markets and insolvency. Provisions on investigations in the Companies (Audit, Investigations and Community Enterprise) Act 2004 will also remain, as will the self-standing provisions on community interest companies in that Act and measures on the Financial Reporting Council and the Financial Reporting Review Panel.

The repeals by the Companies Act 2006 are mainly provided by s.1295 and Sch.16, although some of these repeals have a "belt and braces" effect to repeal provisions which have ceased to have effect by virtue of measures elsewhere in the body of the 2006 Act. For example in Pt 39, although ss.1176-1179 cause ss.311, 323-329, 343, 344, 438, 720, 729 of, and Sch.13, Pt 2-4 and Sch.23 to the Companies Act 1985 to cease to have effect, and s.1180 causes Pt 4 of the Companies Act 1989 to cease to have effect, these provisions are all repealed by Sch.16 to the 2006 Act.

The continuing existing provisions of the above statutes not repealed by the Companies Act 2006 or other legislation are listed below with the relevant subject matter indicated.

Companies Act 1985

Sections

Company investigations

431-437 (1), (1A), (2), (3)

439(1), (2), (4)-(6), (8)-(10)

441-442(1), (3)-(4)

443-445

446A-446E (to be inserted by the Companies Act 2006, ss.1035-1037)

447-450(1)-(3), (5)

451-453A(1)-(5), (7), (8)

453B-453C

Orders imposing restrictions on shares

454-457

Schedules

15C (Specified persons - disclosure of information provided to Secretary of State in investigation)

15D (Disclosures - of information provided to Secretary of State in investigation)

Companies Act 1989

Sections

23 (together with Sch.10, paras 25-39) (consequential amendment re companies' accounts)

Investigations - amendments of Companies Act 1985

55, 56(1)-(4), (6)

59-62

64(1)

66(1), (2), (4)

68-70

Investigations amendment of Building Societies Act 1986

80

Powers exercisable to assist overseas regulatory authorities

82-91

Charitable companies (Scotland)

112

Amendment of Company Directors Disqualification Act 1986

139(4)

Consequential amendments and regulation-making powers re subsidiaries etc.

144(4), (5)

Minor amendments to Companies Act 1985

145 (together with Sch.19, para.10)

21-24 (Investigations)

25 (Minor and consequential amendments)

26-63 (Community interest companies)

64-67 (Supplementary)

Schedules

2, paras 16-21, 25, 27-31 (Amendments relating to investigations)

3 (Regulator of Community Interest Companies)

4 (Appeal Officer for Community Interest Companies)

5 (Official Property Holder for Community Interest Companies)

6, para.10 (Amendment of Limited Liability Partnerships Act 2002 re community interest companies' names)

7 (Community interest companies: investigations)

8 (Repeals and revocations)

APPENDIX III

COMPANIES ACT 2006 TABLE OF DERIVATIONS

The table below shows the derivation of the provisions of the Companies Act 2006 by reference to the enactments in force on November 8, 2006, when the Act received Royal Assent. The table does not provide the source of any amendments to the originating legislation made before that date. The derivation of a provision of the Companies Act 2006 from the Companies (Northern Ireland) Order 1986 (SI 1986/1032 (NI 6)) is only acknowledged where it makes significantly different provision in relation to Northern Ireland than in relation to England and Wales or Great Britain.

The word "drafting" after an entry indicates a new provision of a mechanical or editorial nature (e.g. a provision defining an expression to avoid repetition or indicating where other relevant provisions are to be found).

The word "(changed)" following an entry means that the provision referred to has been re-enacted with one or more primary, and not just consequential, changes. The table does not show changes in the maximum penalties for offences.

The word "new" indicates a provision which has no predecessor in the repealed legislation or which is fundamentally different from its predecessor.

The entries in the table should only be taken as a guide. The table has no official status and has been adapted from a table prepared by the Department of Trade and Industry which has been considerably amended and extended.

The following abbreviations are used in the table:
"1985" means the Companies Act 1985 (c.6);
"BNA 1985" means the Business Names Act 1985 (c.7);
"CA 1989" means the Companies Act 1989 (c.40);
"C(AICE)A 2004" means the Companies (Audit, Investigations and Community Enterprise) Act 2004 (c.27);
"IA 1986" means the Insolvency Act 1986 (c.45); and
"1986 Order" means the Companies (Northern Ireland) Order 1986 (SI 1986/1032 (NI 6)).

Section of 2006 Act	*Derivation*
PART 1 GENERAL INTRODUCTORY PROVISIONS	
1(1)	1985 s.735(1)(a), (b)
(2), (3)	drafting
2(1)	1985 s.744 (changed)
(2)	new
3(1)	1985 s.1(2)
(2)	1985 s.1(2)(a)
(3)	1985 s.1(2)(b)
(4)	1985 s.1(2)(c)
4(1)	1985 s.1(3)
(2)	1985 s.1(3)(a), (b)
(3)	1985 s.1(3)(b), 1986 Order art.12(3)
(4)	drafting
5(1)	1985 s.1(4)
(2)	1984 s.1(4), 1986 Order art.12(4)
(3)	1985 s.15(2)
6(1), (2)	drafting
PART 2 COMPANY FORMATION	
7(1), (2)	1985 s.1(1) (changed)

Section of 2006 Act	Derivation
8(1)	1985 ss.1(1), 2(5)(b) (changed)
(2)	1985 s.3(1)
9(1)	1985 s.10(1) (changed)
(2)	1985 ss.1(3)(a), 2(1)(a), (b), (2), (3) (changed)
(3)	1985 s.10(4)
(4)	1985 ss.2(4), (5), 10(2) (changed)
(5)	1985 ss.7(1), 10(1)(a), (6)
(6)	1985 s.10(1)(a), (b)
10(1)	new
(2)	1985, s.2(5)(a)
(3)	new
(4)	1985, s.2(5)(c)
(5)	new
11(1)	drafting
(2)	new
(3)	1985 s.2(4) (changed)
12(1)	1985 s.10(2) (changed)
(2)	1985 s.10(2) (changed)
(3)	1985 s.10(3)
13(1)	1985 s.12(2) (changed)
(2)	1985 s.12(3), (3A) (changed)
14	1985 s.12(1), (2)
15(1)	1985 s.13(1)
(2)	1985 s.13(6) (changed)
(3)	1985 s.13(2)
(4)	1985 s.13(7)(a)
16(1)	drafting
(2)	1985 s.13(3) (changed)
(3)	1985 s.13(4)
(4), (5)	new
(6)	1985 s.13(5)

PART 3 A COMPANY'S CONSTITUTION

Chapter 1 Introductory

17	new

Section of 2006 Act	**Derivation**
Chapter 2 Articles of association	
18(1)	1985 s.7(1) (changed)
(2)	1985 s.7(1) (changed)
(3)	1985 s.7(3) (changed)
(4)	1985 s.744
19(1)	1985 s.8(1) (changed)
(2)	1985 s.8(4) (changed)
(3)	1985 s.8(1) (changed)
(4)	1985, s.8(3) (changed)
(5)	1985 s.8(5)
20(1)	1985 s.8(2) (changed)
(2)	1985 s.8(1), (4) (changed)
21(1)	1985 s.9(1)
(2), (3)	drafting (see 1985 s.17(2)(b) (changed))
22(1)-(3)	new
23(1), (2)	new
24(1)-(4)	new
25(1)	1985 s.16(1)
(2)	1985 s.16(2)
26(1)	1985 s.18(2) (changed)
(2)	new
(3)	1985 s.18(3)
(4)	1985 s.18(3), Sch.24
27(1)-(5)	new
28(1)-(3)	new
Chapter 3 Resolutions and agreements affecting a company's constitution	
29(1)	1985 s.380(4) (changed)
(2)	1985 s.380(4A)
30(1)	1985 s.380(1)
(2)	1985 s.380(5), (6)
(3)	1985 s.380(5), (6), Sch.24
(4)	1985 s.380(7)
Chapter 4 Miscellaneous and supplementary provisions	
31(1)	1985 ss.2(1)(c), 3A (changed)

Section of 2006 Act	Derivation
(2)	1985 s.6(1) (changed)
(3)-(5)	new
32(1)	1985 s.19(1) (changed)
(2)	new
(3)	1985 s.19(2) (changed)
(4)	1985 s.19(2) Sch.24 (changed)
33(1)	1985 s.14(1) (changed)
(2)	1985 s.14(2) (changed)
34(1)	1985 s.18(1) (changed)
(2)	1985 s.18(1) (changed)
(3)	1985 s.18(2) (changed)
(4)	new
(5)	1985 s.18(3) (changed)
(6)	1985 s.18(3), Sch.24 (changed)
35(1)-(5)	new
36(1)	1985 s.380(2) (changed)
(2)	new
(3)	1985 s.380(6) (changed)
(4)	1985 s.380(6), Sch.24 (changed)
(5)	1985 s.380(7)
37	1985 s.15(1)
38	See 1985 s.1(3A) and Companies (Single Member Private Limited Companies) Regulations 1992 (SI 1992/ 1699) (changed)

PART 4 A COMPANY'S CAPACITY AND RELATED MATTERS

39(1)	1985 s.35(1) (changed)
(2)	1985 s.35(4)
40(1)	1985 s.35A(1)
(2)	1985 ss.35A(2), 35B
(3)	1985 s.35A(3)
(4)	1985 s.35A(4)
(5)	1985 s.35A(5)
(6)	1985 s.35A(6)
41(1)	1985 s.322A(1), (4)
(2)	1985 s.322A(1), (2)

Section of 2006 Act	*Derivation*
(3)	1985 s.322A(3)
(4)	1985 s.322A(5)
(5)	1985 s.322A(6)
(6)	1985 s.322A(7)
(7)	1985 s.322A(8)
42(1)	Charities Act 1993 s.65(1)
(2)	Charities Act 1993 s.65(2)
(3)	Charities Act 1993 s.65(3)
(4)	Charities Act 1993 s.65(4)
(5)	drafting
43(1), (2)	1985 s.36
44(1)	1985 s.36A(1)-(3)
(2)(a), (3), (4)	1985 s.36A(4)
(2)(b)	new
(5)	1985 s.36A(6) (changed)
(6)	1985 s.36A(4A)
(7)	1985 s.36A(8)
(8)	1985 s.36A(7)
45(1)	1985 s.36A(3)
(2)	1985 s.350(1)
(3)	1985 s.350(1) (changed)
(4), (5)	1985 s.350(2), Sch.24
(6)	drafting
46(1)	1985 s.36AA(1)
(2)	1985 s.36AA(2)
47(1)	1985 s.38(1) (changed), (3)
(2)	1985 s.38(2) (changed)
48(1)	Requirements of Writing (Scotland) Act 1995 (c.7) s.15(3)
(2)	1985 s.36B(1)
(3)	1985 s.36B(2)
49(1)	1985 s.39(1) (changed)
(2)	1985 s.39(1)
(3)	1985 s.39(2), (2A)
(4)	1985 s.39(3)

Section of 2006 Act	Derivation
(5)	1985 s.39(4)
(6)	1985 s.39(5)
50(1), (2)	1985 s.40(1)
51(1)	1985 s.36C(1)
(2)	1985 s.36C(2)
52	1985 s.37

PART 5 A COMPANY'S NAME

Chapter 1 General requirements

53	1985 s.26(1)(d), (e)
54(1)-(3)	1985 s.26(2)(a), second sentence (changed)
55(1)	1985 ss.26(2)(b), 29(1)(a)
(2)	1985 s.29(6)
56(1)	1985 s.29(1)(b) (changed)
(2)	1985 s.29(2)
(3), (4)	1985 s.29(3) (changed)
(5)	drafting
57(1)-(5)	new

Chapter 2 Indications of company type or legal form

58(1)	1985 ss.25(1), 27(4)(b)
(2)	1985 ss.25(1), 27(4)(d)
(3)	drafting
59(1)	1985 ss.25(2) (opening words), 27(4)(a)
(2)	1985 ss.25(2)(b), 27(4)(c)
(3)	1985 s.25(2)(a)
(4)	drafting
60(1)(a), (b)	new
(1)(c)	drafting
(2)	1985 s.30(5B)
(3)	1985 s.30(4)
(4)	new
61(1)	1985 s.30(2), 1986 Order art.40(2)
(2)-(4)	1985 s.30(2), (3) (changed)
62(1)-(3)	1985 s.30(2), (3) (changed)
63(1)	1985 s.31(1)

Section of 2006 Act	Derivation
(2), (3)	1985 s.31(5), Sch.24
(4), (5)	new
64(1)-(3)	1985 s.31(2) first sentence
(4)	1985 s.31(2) second sentence (changed)
(5), (6)	1985 s.31(6), Sch.24
(7)	1985 s.31(3)
65(1)-(5)	1985 s.26(1)(a), (b), (bb), (bbb) (changed)

Chapter 3 Similarity to other names

66(1)	1985 s.26(1)(c)
(2), (3)	1985 s.26(3) (changed)
(4)-(6)	new
67(1)	1985 s.28(2)
(2)-(6)	new
68(1)	drafting
(2)	1985 s.28(2)
(3)	1985 s.28(4)
(4)	1985 s.28(2), (4)
(5), (6)	1985 s.28(5), Sch.24
69(1)-(7)	new
70(1)-(6)	new
71(1)-(4)	new
72(1), (2)	new
73(1)-(6)	new
74(1)-(5)	new

Chapter 4 Other powers of the Secretary of State

75(1), (2)	1985 s.28(3)
(3)	1985 s.28(4)
(4)	1985 s.28(3)
(5), (6)	1985 s.28(5), Sch.24
76(1)	1985 s.32(1)
(2)	new
(3)	1985 s.32(2)
(4), (5)	1985 s.32(3)
(6), (7)	1985 s.32(4) (changed), Sch.24

Section of 2006 Act	Derivation
Chapter 5 Change of name	
77(1)(a)	1985 s.28(1)
(1)(b)	new
(2)	drafting
78(1)-(3)	new
79(1), (2)	new
80(1), (2)	1985 ss.28(6), 32(5) (changed)
(3)	1985 ss.28(6), 32(5)
81(1)	1985 ss.28(6), 32(5)
(2), (3)	1985 ss.28(7), 32(6)
Chapter 6 Trading disclosures	
82(1), (2)	1985 ss.348(1), 349(1), 351(1), (2), BNA 1985 s.4(1) (changed)
(3)-(5)	new
83(1), (2)	BNA 1985 s.5(1)
(3)	BNA 1985 s.5(2)
84(1), (2)	1985 ss.348(2), 349(2), (3), 351(5), BNA 1985 s.7 (changed)
(3)	new
85(1), (2)	new
PART 6 A COMPANY'S REGISTERED OFFICE	
86	1985 s.287(1)
87(1)	1985 s.287(3)
(2)	1985 s.287(4)
(3)	1985 s.287(5)
(4)	1985 s.287(6)
88(1)	drafting
(2)	1985 s.2(2)
(3), (4)	new
PART 7 RE-REGISTRATION AS A MEANS OF ALTERING A COMPANY'S STATUS	
89	drafting
90(1)	1985 s.43(1) (changed)
(2)	1985 s.43(1); drafting
(3)	1985 s.43(2)
(4)	1985 s.48(1), (2)

Section of 2006 Act	Derivation
91(1)	1985 s.45(1)-(4)
(2)	1985 s.45(5), 1986 Order art.55(5)
(3)	1985 s.45(6)
(4)	1985 s.45(7)
(5)	1985 s.47(3) (changed)
92(1)	1985 s.43(3)(b), (c), (4)
(2)	1985 s.43(e)(ii)
(3), (4)	1985 s.46(2), (3)
(5), (6)	1985 s.46(4)
93(1)	1985 s.44(1)
(2)	1985 s.44(2), drafting
(3)-(5)	1985 s.44(4), (5)
(6)	1985 s.44(6), (7)(b)
(7)	1985 s.44(2), (7)(a)
94(1)	new
(2)	1985 s.43(3)(a)-(d)
(3)	1985 s.43(e)(i)
(4)	1984 s.47(2)
95(1)-(3)	new
96(1), (2)	1985 s.47(1)
(3)	new
(4), (5)	1985 s.47(4), (5)
97(1)	1985 s.53(1) (changed)
(2)	new
(3)	1985 s.53(2)
98(1)	1985 s.54(1), (2)
(2)	1985 s.54(3)
(3), (4)	1985 s.54(5)
(5)	1985 s.54(6)
(6)	1985 s.54(8)
99(1), (2)	1985 s.54(4) (changed)
(3)	1985 s.54(7)
(4), (5)	1985 s.54(10), Sch.24
100(1)	new

Section of 2006 Act	Derivation
(2)	1985 s.53(1)(b) (changed)
(3), (4)	new
101(1), (2)	1985 s.55(1)
(3)	new
(4), (5)	1985 s.55(2), (3)
102(1)	1985 s.49(1), (4), (8)(a) (changed)
(2)	1985 s.49(2)
(3)	1985 s.49(5)-(7) (changed)
(4)	1985 s.49(9)
(5)	new
103(1)	new
(2)	1985 s.49(8)(a), (c), (d)
(3), (4)	1985 s.49(8)(b), (8A) (changed)
(5)	new
104(1), (2)	1985 s.50(1)(b)
(3)	new
(4), (5)	1985 s.50(2), (3)
105(1)	1985 s.51(1) (changed)
(2)	1985 s.51(2)
(3), (4)	1985 s.51(3)
106(1)	new
(2)	1985 s.51(5) (changed)
(3)-(5)	new
107(1), (2)	1985 s.52(1)
(3)	new
(4), (5)	1985 s.52(2), (3)
108(1)-(5)	new
109(1)-(5)	new
110(1)-(5)	new
111(1)-(5)	new

PART 8 A COMPANY'S MEMBERS

Chapter 1 The members of a company

112(1)	1985 s.22(1) (changed)
(2)	1985 s.22(2)

Section of 2006 Act	Derivation
Chapter 2 Register of members	
113(1), (2)	1985 s.352(1), (2)
(3), (4)	1985 s.352(3)
(5)	new
(6)	1985 s.352(4)
(7), (8)	1985 s.352(5), Sch.24
114(1)	1985 s.353(1) (changed)
(2)	1985 s.353(2)
(3)	1985 s.353(3)
(4)	1985 s.353(3), 1986 Order art.361(3)
(5), (6)	1985 s.353(4), Sch.24
115(1), (2)	1985 s.354(1)
(3)	1985 s.354(2)
(4)	1985 s.354(3) (changed)
(5), (6)	1985 s.354(4), Sch.24
116(1)	1985 s.356(1) (changed)
(2)	1985 s.356(3) first branch
(3), (4)	new
117(1)-(5)	new
118(1), (2)	1985 s.356(5), Sch.24 (changed)
(3)	1985 s.356(6)
119(1)-(3)	new
120(1)-(4)	new
121	1985 s.352(6) (changed)
122(1)	1985 s.355(1) (changed)
(2)	1985 s.355(4)
(3)	1985 s.355(5)
(4), (5)	1985 s.355(2), (3)
(6)	1985 s.355(4)
123(1)	new
(2), (3)	1985 s.352A(1), (2) (changed)
(4), (5)	1985 s.352A(3), Sch.24
124(1), (2)	1985 s.352(3A)
125(1)-(4)	1985 s.359(1)-(4)

Section of 2006 Act	Derivation
126	1985 s.360
127	1985 s.361
128(1), (2)	1985 s.352(7)

Chapter 3 Overseas branch registers

129(1)	1985 s.362(1), (2) opening words
(2)	1985 Sch.14 Pt 1
(3), (4)	new
(5)	1985 s.362(2)(b), (c)
130(1)	1985 s.362(3), Sch.14 Pt 2 para.1(1), (2)
(2), (3)	1985 s.362(3), Sch.14 Pt 2 para.1(3), Sch.24
131(1)	1985 s.362(3), Sch.14 Pt 2 para.2(1)
(2), (3)	new
(4)	1985 s.362(3), Sch.14 Pt 2 para.7
132(1), (2)	1985 s.362(3), Sch.14 Pt 2 para.4(1) (changed)
(3), (4)	1985 s.362(3), Sch.14 Pt 2 para.4(2), Sch.24
133(1), (2)	1985 s.362(3), Sch.14 Pt 2 para.5
(3)	1985 s.362(3), Sch.14 Pt 2 para.8
134(1), (2)	1985 s.362(3), Sch.14 Pt 2 para.3(1) (changed)
(3)	1985 s.362(3), Sch.14 Pt 2 para.3(2)
135(1), (2)	1985 s.362(3), Sch.14 Pt 2 para.6
(3)	1985 s.362(3), Sch.14 Pt 2 para.1(1), (2)
(4), (5)	1985 s.362(3), Sch.14 Pt 2 para.1(3), Sch.24

Chapter 4 Prohibition on subsidiary being member of its holding company

136(1)	1985 s.23(1)
(2)	drafting
137(1)	1985 s.23(4), (5)
(2)	1985 s.23(4), 1986 Order art.33(4)
(3), (4)	1985 s.23(6)
138(1), (2)	1985 s.23(2), Sch.2 para.4(1), (2); drafting
139(1)-(4)	1985 Sch.2 para.1(1)-(4)
(5)	1985 Sch.2 para.5(2)
(6)	1985 Sch.2 para.5(2), (3)
140(1), (2)	1985 Sch.2 para.3(1), (2)
(3), (4)	1985 Sch.2 para.5(2), (3)

Section of 2006 Act	Derivation
141(1), (2)	1985 s.23(3)
141(3), (4)	1985 s.23(3A), (3B)
(5)	1985 s.23(3BA)
142(1), (2)	1985 s.23(3C)
143	1985 s.23(8)
144	1985 s.23(7)

PART 9 EXERCISE OF MEMBERS' RIGHTS

145(1)-(4)	new
146(1)-(5)	new
147(1)-(6)	new
148(1)-(8)	new
149(1)-(3)	new
150(1)-(7)	new
151(1)-(3)	new
152(1)-(4)	new
153(1), (2)	new

PART 10 A COMPANY'S DIRECTORS

Chapter 1 Appointment and removal of directors

154(1)	1985 s.282(3)
(2)	1985 s.282(1) (changed)
155(1), (2)	new
156(1)-(7)	new
157(1)-(6)	new
158(1)-(5)	new
159(1)-(4)	new
160(1)-(4)	1985 s.292(1)-(4)
161(1), (2)	1985 s.285 (changed)
162(1)-(3)	1985 s.288(1) (changed)
(4)	new
(5)	1985 s.288(3)
(6)	1985 s.288(4), (6)
(7)	1985 s.288(4), Sch.24
(8)	1985 s.288(5)
163(1)	1985 s.289(1)(a) (changed)

Section of 2006 Act	Derivation
(2)	1985 s.289(2)(a)
(3)	new
(4)	1985 s.289(2)(b) (changed)
(5)	new
164	1985 s.289(1)(b) (changed)
165(1)-(6)	new
166(1), (2)	new
167(1), (2)	1985 s.288(2) (changed)
(3)	new
(4)	1985 s.288(4), (6)
(5)	1985 s.288(4), Sch.24
168(1)	1985 s.303(1) (changed)
(2)-(5)	1985 s.303(2)-(5)
169(1), (2)	1985 s.304(1)
(3), (4)	1985 s.304(2), (3)
(5)	1985 s.304(4) (changed)
(6)	1985 s.304(5)

Chapter 2 General duties of directors

170(1)-(5)	new
171	new
172(1)	1985 s.309(1) (changed)
(2), (3)	new
173(1), (2)	new
174(1), (2)	new
175(1)-(7)	new
176(1)-(5)	new
177(1)-(6)	new
178(1), (2)	new
179	new
180(1)-(5)	new
181(1)-(5)	new

Chapter 3 Declaration of interest in existing transaction or arrangement

182(1)	1985 s.317(1), (5) (changed)
(2)	1985 s.317(2) (changed)

Section of 2006 Act	Derivation
(3)-(6)	new
183(1)	1985 s.317(7)
(2)	1985 s.317(7), Sch.24
184(1)-(5)	new
185(1), (2)	1985 s.317(3) (changed)
(3)	new
(4)	1985 s.317(4)
186(1), (2)	new
187(1)-(4)	1985 s.317(8) (changed)

Chapter 4 Transactions with directors requiring approval of members

188(1)	1985 s.319(1) (changed)
(2)	1985 s.319(3) (changed)
(3)	1985 s.319(1) (changed)
(4)	1985 s.319(2) (changed)
(5)	1985 s.319(5), Sch.15A para.7 (changed)
(6)	1985 s.319(4)
(7)	1985 s.319(7)(a)
189	1985 s.319(6)
190(1), (2)	1985 s.320(1) (changed)
(3)	new
(4)	1985 s.321(1)
(5), (6)	new
191(1)-(5)	1985 s.320(2) (changed)
192	1985 s.321(2)(a), (3) (changed)
193(1), (2)	1985 s.321(2)(b) (changed)
194(1), (2)	1985 s.321(4)
195(1)	1985 s.322(1), (3)
(2)	1985 s.322(1), (2)(a), (b)
(3)	1985 s.322(3), (4)
(4)	1985 s.322(3)
(5)	1985 s.322(4)
(6)	1985 s.322(5)
(7)	1985 s.322(6)
(8)	1985 s.322(4)

Section of 2006 Act	Derivation
196	1985 s.322(2)(c)
197(1)	1985 s.330(2) (changed)
(2)-(5)	new
198(1)	1985 ss.330(3), 331(6)
(2)	1985 s.330(3)(a), (c) (changed)
(3)-(6)	new
199(1)	1985 s.331(3)
(2), (3)	1985 s.331(4)
200(1)	1985 ss.330(3), 331(6)
(2)	1985 s.330(3)(b), (c) (changed)
(3)-(6)	new
201(1)	1985 ss.330(4), 331(6)
(2)	1985 s.330(4) (changed)
(3)-(6)	new
202(1)	1985 s.331(7)
(2)	1985 s.331(9)(b)
(3)	1985 s.331(8), (10)
203(1)	1985 s.330(6), (7) (changed)
(2)-(5)	new
(6)	1985 s.330(6)
204(1)	1985 s.337(1), (2) (changed)
(2)	1985 ss.337(3), 339(1), (2) (changed)
205(1)	1985 s.337A(1), (3) (changed)
(2)	1985 s.337A(4)
(3)	1985 s.337A(5)
(4)	1985 s.337A(6)
(5)	1985 s.337A(2)
206	new
207(1)	1985 ss.334, 339(1), (2) (changed)
(2)	1985 ss.335(1), 339(1), (2) (changed)
(3)	1985 s.335(2)
208(1)	1985 ss.333, 336(a) (changed)
(2)	1985 s.336(b) (changed)
209(1)	1985 s.338(1), (3)

Section of 2006 Act	Derivation
(2)	1985 s.338(2)
(3), (4)	1985 s.338(6) (changed)
210(1)	1985 s.339(1)
(2)	1985 s.339(2)
(3)	1985 s.339(2), (3)
(4)	1985 s.339(2), (3)
(5)	1985 s.339(5)
211(1)	1985 ss.339(6), 340(1)
(2)	1985 s.340(2)
(3)	1985 s.340(3)
(4)	1985 s.340(6)
(5)	1985 s.340(4)
(6)	1985 s.340(5)
(7)	1985 s.340(7) (changed)
212	1985 s.331(9)(a)-(d)
213(1), (2)	1985 s.341(1)
(3), (4)	1985 s.341(2)
(5)	1985 s.341(3)
(6)	1985 s.341(4)
(7)	1985 s.341(5)
(8)	1985 s.341(3)
214	new
215(1)	1985 ss.312, 313(1), 314(1) (changed)
(2)-(4)	new
216(1), (2)	1985 s.316(2) (changed)
217(1)	1985 s.312
(2)	new
(3)	1985 s.312 (changed)
(4)	new
218(1)	1985 s.313(1)
(2)	new
(3)	1985 s.313(1) (changed)
(4)	new
(5)	1985 s.316(1)

Section of 2006 Act	Derivation
219(1)	1985 ss.314(1), 315(1)(b) (changed)
(2)	1985 s.315(1)(b)
(3), (4)	new
(5)	1985 s.315(3)
(6)	new
(7)	1985 s.316(1)
220(1)	1985 s.316(3) (changed)
(2)-(5)	new
221(1)-(4)	new
222(1)	new
(2)	1985 s.313(2)
(3)	1985 s.315(1)
(4), (5)	new
223(1)	1985, ss.319(6), 320(3), 330(5)
(2)	new
224(1), (2)	new
225(1)-(3)	new
226	new

Chapter 5 Directors' service contracts

227	new
228(1)	1985 s.318(1)
(2)	1985 s.318(2), (3) (changed)
(3)	new
(4)	1985 s.318(4)
(5)	1985 s.318(8) (changed)
(6)	1985 s.318(8), Sch.24
(7)	1985 s.318(10)
229(1)	1985 s.318(7)
(2)	new
(3)	1985 s.318(8) (changed)
(4)	1985 s.318(8), Sch.24
(5)	1985 s.318(9) (changed)
230	1985 s.318(6)

Section of 2006 Act	Derivation
Chapter 6 Contracts with sole members who are directors	
231(1)	1985 s.322B(1), (2) (changed)
(2)	1985 s.322B(1)
(3)	1985 s.322B(4) (changed)
(4)	1985 s.322B(4), Sch.24
(5)	1985 s.322B(3)
(6)	1985 s.322B(6)
(7)	1985 s.322B(5)
Chapter 7 Directors' liabilities	
232(1)	1985 s.309A(1), (2)
(2)	1985 s.309A(1), (3) (changed)
(3)	1985 s.309A(6)
(4)	new
233	1985 s.309A(5)
234(1)	1985 s.309A(4)
(2)	1985 s.309B(1), (2)
(3)	1985 s.309B(3), (4)
(4)	1985 s.309B(5)
(5)	1985 s.309B(6), (7)
(6)	1985 s.309B(4)(c)
235(1)-(6)	new
236(1)	1985 s.309C(1) (changed)
(2), (3)	1985 s.309C(2)
(4), (5)	1985 s.309C(3)
237(1)	1985 s.309C(4), (5)
(2)	1985 ss.309C(5), 318(1)
(3)	1985 ss.309C(5), 318(2), (3) (changed)
(4)	new
(5)	1985 ss.309C(5), 318(4)
(6)	1985 ss.309C(5), 318(8) (changed)
(7)	1985 ss.309C(5), 318(8), Sch.24
(8)	1985 ss.309C(5), 318(10)
(9)	new
238(1)	1985 ss.309C(5), 318(7)

Section of 2006 Act	Derivation
(2)	new
(3)	1985 ss.309C(5), 318(8) (changed)
(4)	1985 ss.309C(5), 318(8), Sch.24
(5)	1985 ss.309C(5), 318(9) (changed)
239(1)-(7)	new

Chapter 8 Directors' residential addresses: protection from disclosure

240(1)-(3)	new
241(1), (2)	new
242(1)-(3)	new
243(1)-(8)	new
244(1)-(4)	new
245(1)-(6)	new
246(1)-(7)	new

Chapter 9 Supplementary provisions

247(1)	1985 s.719(1)
(2)	1985 s.719(2) (changed)
(3)	new
(4)	1985 s.719(3)
(5)	1985 s.719(3) (changed)
(6)	1985 s.719(3)
(7)	1985 s.719(4) (changed)
248(1)	1985 s.382(1)
(2)	new
(3)	1985 s.382(5) (changed)
(4)	1985 s.382(5), Sch.24
249(1)	1985 s.382(2)
(2)	1985 s.382(4)
250	1985 s.741(1)
251(1), (2)	1985 s.741(2)
(3)	1985 s.741(3)
252(1)	1985 s.346(1)
(2)	1985 s.346(2), (3) (changed)
(3)	1985 s.346(2)
253(1)	drafting

Section of 2006 Act	Derivation
(2)	1985 s.346(2), (3) (changed)
(3)	new
254(1)	1985 s.346(1)
(2)	1985 s.346(4)
(3)	1985 s.346(7)
(4)	1985 s.346(8)
(5)	1985 s.346(4)
(6)	1985 s.346(6)
255(1)	1985 s.346(1)
(2)	1985 s.346(5)
(3)	1985 s.346(7)
(4)	1985 s.346(8)
(5)	1985 s.346(5)
(6)	1985 s.346(6)
256	new
257(1), (2)	new
258(1)	1985 s.345(1)
(2)	1985 s.345(2)
(3)	1985 s.345(3)
259	1985 s.347

PART 11 DERIVATIVE CLAIMS AND PROCEEDINGS BY MEMBERS

Chapter 1 Derivative claims in England and Wales or Northern Ireland

260(1)-(5)	new
261(1)-(4)	new
262(1)-(5)	new
263(1)-(7)	new
264(1)-(5)	new

Chapter 2 Derivative proceedings in Scotland

265(1)-(7)	new
266(1)-(5)	new
267(1)-(5)	new
268(1)-(6)	new
269(1)-(5)	new

Section of 2006 Act	*Derivation*
PART 12 COMPANY SECRETARIES	
270(1), (2)	new
(3)	1985 s.283(3) (changed)
271	1985 s.283(1) (changed)
272(1)-(7)	new
273(1), (2)	1985 s.286(1) (changed)
(3)	1985 s.286(2)
274	1985 s.283(3) (changed)
275(1)-(3)	1985 s.288(1) (changed)
(4)	new
(5)	1985 s.288(3)
(6)	1985 s.288(4), (6)
(7)	1985 s.288(4), Sch.24
(8)	1985 s.288(5)
276(1), (2)	1985 s.288(2)
(3)	1985 s.288(4), (6) (changed)
(4)	1985 s.288(4), Sch.24
277(1)	1985 s.290(1)(a) (changed)
(2)	1985 ss.289(2)(a), 290(3)
(3)	new
(4)	1985 ss.289(2)(b), 290(3) (changed)
(5)	new
278(1)	1985 s.290(1)(b) (changed)
(2)	1985 s.290(2)
279(1), (2)	new
280	1985 s.284
PART 13 RESOLUTIONS AND MEETINGS	
Chapter 1 General provisions about resolutions	
281(1)-(4)	new
282(1)-(5)	new
283(1)	1985 s.378(1), (2) (changed)
(2), (3)	new
(4)	1985 s.378(1), (2) (changed)
(5)	1985 s.378(1), (2), (5) (changed)

Section of 2006 Act	Derivation
(6)	1985 s.378(2) (changed)
284(1)	1985 s.370(6)
(2)	Table A, para.54 (changed)
(3)	1985 s.370(6), Table A, para.54 (changed)
(4)	1985 s.370(1), Table A, para.54
285(1)-(3)	new
286(1)-(3)	Table A, para.55
287	new

Chapter 2 Written resolutions

288(1)	new
(2)	1985 s.381A(7), Sch.15A, para.1
(3)	new
(4)	1985 s.381A(1) (changed)
(5)	1985 s.381A(4)
289(1)	1985 s.381A(1) (changed)
(2)	new
290	new
291(1)-(7)	new
292(1)-(6)	new
293(1)-(7)	new
294(1), (2)	new
295(1), (2)	new
296(1)	1985 s.381A(2) (changed)
(2)-(4)	new
297(1), (2)	new
298(1), (2)	new
299(1), (2)	new
300	1985 s.381C(1)

Chapter 3 Resolutions at meetings

301	1985 s.378(6) (changed)
302	Table A, para.37
303(1)	1985 s.368(1)
(2)	1985 s.368(1), (2), (2A)
(3)	1985 s.368(2) (changed)

Section of 2006 Act	Derivation
(4)	1985 s.368(3) (changed)
(5)	new
(6)	1985 s.368(3) (changed)
304(1)	1985 s.368(4), (8)
(2), (3)	new
(4)	1985 s.368(7)
305(1)	1985 s.368(4)
(2)	new
(3)	1985 s.368(4)
(4)	1985 s.368(5)
(5)	new
(6), (7)	1985 s.368(6)
306(1), (2)	1985 s.371(1)
(3), (4)	1985 s.371(2)
(5)	1985 s.371(3)
307(1)	new
(2)	1985 s.369(1), (2) (changed)
(3)	1985 s.369(1), (2)
(4)	1985 s.369(3) (changed)
(5), (6)	1985 s.369(4) (changed)
(7)	drafting
308	1985 s.369(4A), (4B) (changed)
309(1)	1985 s.369(4B)
(2)	1985 s.369(4C) (changed)
(3)	1985 s.369(4B)(d)
310(1)	1985 s.370(2), Table A, para.38 (changed)
(2)	Table A, para.38 (changed)
(3)	new
(4)	1985 s.370(1), Table A para.38
311(1), (2)	Table A, para.38
312(1)	1985 s.379(1)
(2)	1985 s.379(2)
(3)	1985 s.379(2) (changed)
(4)	1985 s.379(3)

Section of 2006 Act	Derivation
313(1), (2)	1985 Table A, para.39 (changed)
314(1)	1985 s.376(1)(b)
(2), (3)	1985 s.376(2) (changed)
(4)	1985 ss.376(1), 377(1)(a) (changed)
315(1)	1985 s.376(3), (5)
(2)	1985 s.376(1)
(3)	1985 s.376(7)
(4)	1985 s.376(7), Sch.24
316(1)	new
(2)	1985 ss.376(1), 377(1)(b) (changed)
317(1)	1985 s.377(3) (changed)
(2)	1985 s.377(3)
318(1)	1985 s.370A
(2)	1985 s.370(1), (4) (changed)
(3)	1985 s.370A (changed)
319(1)	1985 s.370(5)
(2)	1985 s.370(1)
320(1)	1985 s.378(4), Table A, para.47
(2)	Table A, para.47
(3)	1985 s.378(4), Table A, paras 47, 48 (changed)
321(1)	1985 s.373(1)(a)
(2)	1985 s.373(1)(b) (changed)
322	1985 s.374
323(1)	1985 s.375(1)(a)
(2), (3)	1985 s.375(2) (changed)
(4)	new
324(1)	1985 s.372(1) (changed)
(2)	1985 s.372(2)(b) (changed)
325(1)	1985 s.372(3) (changed)
(2)	new
(3)	1985 s.372(4)
(4)	1985 s.372(4), Sch.24
326(1), (2)	1985 s.372(6)
(3)	1985 s.372(6) (changed)

Section of 2006 Act	Derivation
(4)	1985 s.372(6), Sch.24
327(1)	1985 s.372(5)
(2)	1985 s.372(5) (changed)
(3)	new
328(1), (2)	new
329(1)	1985 s.373(2)
(2)	1985 s.373(2) (changed)
330(1)-(7)	Table A, para.63 (changed)
331	new
332	1985 s.381
333(1)-(4)	new
334(1)-(3)	1985 s.125(6) (changed)
(4)	1985 s.125(6)(a)
(5)	new
(6)	1985 s.125(6)(b)
(7)	1985 s.125(7), (8)
335(1)-(6)	new

Chapter 4 Public companies: additional requirements for AGMs

Section of 2006 Act	Derivation
336(1)	1985 s.366(1) (changed)
(2)	new
(3)	1985 s.366(4) (changed)
(4)	1985 s.366(4), Sch.24
337(1)	1985 s.366(1)
(2)	1985 s.369(3)(a)
338(1)	1985 s.376(1)(b)
(2)	new
(3)	1985 s.376(2) (changed)
(4)	1985 ss.376(1), 377(1)(a), (2) (changed)
339(1)	1985 s.376(3), (5)
(2)	1985 s.376(1)
(3)	1985 s.376(6)
(4)	1985 s.376(7)
(5)	1985 s.376(7), Sch.24
340(1)	new

Section of 2006 Act	Derivation
(2)	1985 ss.376(1), 377(1)(b) (changed)

Chapter 5 Additional requirements for quoted companies

341(1)-(6)	new
342(1)-(4)	new
343(1)-(6)	new
344(1)-(4)	new
345(1)-(6)	new
346(1)-(5)	new
347(1)-(4)	new
348(1)-(4)	new
349(1)-(5)	new
350(1)-(5)	new
351(1)-(5)	new
352(1), (2)	new
353(1)-(5)	new
354(1)-(4)	new

Chapter 6 Records of resolutions and meetings

355(1)	1985 s.382(1), s.382A(1) (changed)
(2)	new
(3)	1985 s.382(5) (changed)
(4)	1985 s.382(5), Sch.24
356(1)	drafting
(2), (3)	1985 s.382A(2)
(4)	1985 s.382(2)
(5)	1985 s.382(4)
357(1), (2)	1985 s.382B(1)
(3)	1985 s.382B(2)
(4)	1985 s.382B(2), Sch.24
(5)	1985 s.382B(3)
358(1)	1985 s.383(1) (changed)
(2)	new
(3)	1985 s.383(1)
(4)	1985 s.383(3) (changed)
(5)	1985 s.383(4) (changed)

Section of 2006 Act	*Derivation*
(6)	1985 s.383(4), Sch.24
(7)	1985 s.383(5)
359	new

Chapter 7 Supplementary provisions

360(1), (2)	new
361	new

PART 14 CONTROL OF POLITICAL DONATIONS AND EXPENDITURE

362	1985 s.347A(1) (changed)
363(1)	1985 s.347A(6), (7)(a), (9)
(2)	1985 s.347A(6)(b), (7)(b), (c) (changed)
(3)	new
(4)	drafting
364(1)	drafting
(2)	1985 s.347A(4)
(3)	new
(4)	new
365(1)	1985 s.347A(5) (changed)
(2)	new
366(1)	1985 s.347C(1) (changed)
(2)	1985 ss.347C(1), 347D(1), (2), (3) (changed)
(3)	1985 s.347D(3) (changed)
(4)	new
(5)	1985 ss.347A(10), 347C(1), 347D(2), (3)
(6)	1985 ss.347C(6), 347D(9)
367(1), (2)	new
(3)	1985 ss.347C(2), 347D(4) (changed)
(4)	new
(5)	1985 ss.347C(4), 347D(6)
(6)	1985 ss.347C(2), 347D(4) (changed)
(7)	new
368(1)	1985 ss.347C(3)(b), 347D(5)
(2)	1985 ss.347C(3), 347D(5)
369(1)	1985 s.347F(1)
(2)	1985 s.347F(2), (3), (4)

Section of 2006 Act	Derivation
(3)	1985 s.347F(2), (6) (changed)
(4)	new
(5)	1985 s.347F(3)
(6)	1985 s.347F(5)
370(1)	1985 s.347I(1) (changed)
(2)	1985 s.347I(1)
(3)	1985 s.54(2), s.347I(2) (changed)
(4)	1985 s.347I(3)
(5)	new
371(1)	1985 s.347I(3)
(2)	1985 s.347I(4), (5)
(3)	1985 s.347I(6)
(4)	1985 s.347I(7)
(5)	1985 s.347I(8)
372(1)	1985 s.347J(1)
(2)	1985 s.347J(2)
(3)	1985 s.347J(3)
(4)	1985 s.347J(4), (5)
(5)	1985 s.347J(6)
373(1)	1985 s.347K(1)
(2)	1985 s.347K(2)
374(1)-(3)	new
375(1)	1985 s.347B(1)
(2)	1985 s.347B(2) (changed)
376(1), (2)	1985 s.347B(3)
377(1)	1985 s.347B(8)
(2)	1985 s.347B(10)
(3)	1985 s.347B(9)
(4)	1985 s.347B(11)
378(1)	1985 s.347B(4), (6), (7) (changed)
(2)	new
(3)	1985 s.347B(5)
379(1)	1985 s.347A(3), (8)
(2)	1985 s.347A(10)

Section of 2006 Act	Derivation

PART 15 ACCOUNTS AND REPORTS

Chapter 1 Introduction

380(1)-(4)	drafting
381	drafting
382(1)	1985 s.247(1)(a)
(2)	1985 s.247(1)(b), (2)
(3), (4)	1985 s.247(3), (4)
(5)	1985 s.247(5) (changed)
(6)	1985 s.247(6), Sch.4 para.56(2), (3)
(7)	drafting
383(1)	1985 s.247A(3)
(2)	1985 s.249(1)(a)
(3)	1985 s.249(1)(b), (2)
(4)	1985 s.249(3)
(5), (6)	1985 s.249(4)
(7)	1985 s.249(5), (6)
384(1)	1985 s.247A(1)-(1B)
(2)	1985 s.247A(2) (changed)
(3)	1985 s.247A(2A)
385(1)	new
(2)	1985 s.262(1) "quoted company"
(3)	drafting
(4)-(6)	new

Chapter 2 Accounting records

386(1), (2)	1985 s.221(1)
(3)-(5)	1985 s.221(2)-(4)
387(1), (2)	1985 s.221(5)
(3)	1985 s.221(6), Sch.24
388(1)-(3)	1985 s.222(1)-(3)
(4), (5)	1985 s.222(5)
389(1), (2)	1985 s.222(4)
(3)	1985 s.222(6)
(4)	1985 s.222(4), (6), Sch.24

Section of 2006 Act	**Derivation**
Chapter 3 A company's financial year	
390(1)-(5)	1985 s.223(1)-(5)
391(1)	1985 s.224(1)
(2)	1985 s.224(2), (3)
(3)	1986 Order art. 232(2), (3)
(4)	1985 s.224(3A), 1986 Order art.232(3A)
(5)-(7)	1985 s.224(4)-(6)
392(1)	1985 s.225(1)
(2)-(6)	1985 s.225(3)-(7)
Chapter 4 Annual accounts	
393(1), (2)	new
394	1985 s.226(1)
395(1)-(5)	1985 s.226(2)-(6)
396(1), (2)	1985 s.226A(1), (2)
(3)	1985 s.226A(3) (changed)
(4)	1985 s.226A(4)
(5)	1985 s.226A(5), (6)
397	1985 s.226B
398	1985 ss.227(8), 248(1) (changed)
399(1), (2)	1985 ss.227(1), (8), 248(1), (2) (changed)
(3)	1985 s.227(8)
(4)	new
400(1), (2)	1985 s.228(1), (2)
(3)	1985 s.228(5)
(4)	1985 s.228(3)
(5)	1985 s.228(4)
(6)	1985 s.228(6)
401(1), (2)	1985 s.228A(1), (2)
(3)	1985 s.228A(5)
(4)	1985 s.228A(3)
(5)	1985 s.228A(4)
(6)	1985 s.228A(6)
402	1985 s.229(5)
403(1)-(6)	1985 s.227(2)-(7)

Section of 2006 Act	Derivation
404(1), (2)	1985 s.227A(1), (2)
(3)	1985 s.227A(3) (changed)
(4)	1985 s.227A(4)
(5)	1985 s.227A(5), (6)
405(1), (2)	1985 s.229(1), (2)
(3), (4)	1985 s.229(3)
406	1985 s.227B
407(1)-(5)	1985 s.227C(1)-(5)
408(1)	1985 s.230(1) (changed)
(2)	1985 s.230(2) (changed)
(3), (4)	1985 s.230(3), (4)
409(1), (2)	1985 s.231(1), (2) (changed)
(3), (4)	1985 s.231(3) (changed)
(5)	1985 s.231(4)
410(1), (2)	1985 s.231(5)
(3)	1985 s.231(6)
(4), (5)	1985 s.231(7), Sch.24
411(1)	1985 ss.231A(1), 246(3)(b)(ai)
(2)	1985 s.231A(5)
(3)-(5)	1985 s.231A(2)-(4)
(6)	1985 s.231A(7), Sch.4 para.94(1), (2)
(7)	1985 s.231A(6)
412(1)-(4)	new
(5)	1985 s.232(3)
(6)	1985 s.232(4), Sch.24
413(1)-(8)	new
414(1), (2)	1985 s.233(1), (2)
(3)	1985 s.246(8)
(4), (5)	1985 s.233(5) (changed), Sch.24

Chapter 5 Directors' report

415(1)	1985 s.234(1)
(2), (3)	1985 s.234(2), (3)
(4), (5)	1985 s.234(5), Sch.24
416(1)	1985 s.234ZZA(1)(a), (b)

Section of 2006 Act	Derivation
(2)	1985 s.234ZZA(2)
(3)	1985 ss.234ZZA(1)(c), 246(4)(a)
(4)	1985 s.234ZZA(3), (4) (changed)
417(1)	1985 ss.234(1)(a), 246(4)(a)
(2)	new
(3), (4)	1985 s.234ZZB(1), (2)
(5)	new
(6)	1985 s.234ZZB(3), (5)
(7)	1985 s.246A(2A)
(8)	1985 s.234ZZB(4)
(9)	1985 s.234ZZB(6)
(10), (11)	new
418(1)	1985 s.234ZA(1)
(2)	1985 ss.234(1)(b), 234ZA(2)
(3), (4)	1985 s.234ZA(3), (4)
(5), (6)	1985 s.234ZA(6), Sch.24
419(1)	1985 s.234A(1)
(2)	1985 s.246(8)(b)
(3), (4)	1985 ss.234(5), 234A(4) (changed), Sch.24

Chapter 6 Quoted companies: directors' remuneration report

420(1)	1985 s.421(1)
(2)	1985 s.234B(3), (4) (changed)
(3)	1985 s.234B(3), Sch.24
421(1), (2)	1985 s.234B(1), (2) (changed)
(3)	1985 s.234B(5), (6)
(4)	1985 s.234B(6), Sch.24
422(1)	1985 s.234C(1)
(2), (3)	1985 s.234C(4) (changed), Sch.24

Chapter 7 Publication of accounts and reports

423(1)	1985 s.238(1), (1A)
(2), (3)	new
(4)	1985 s.238(3)
(5)	1985 s.238(6)
(6)	drafting

Section of 2006 Act	Derivation
424(1)-(3)	1985 s.238(1) (changed)
(4)	1985 s.238(4) (changed)
(5)	new
(6)	drafting
425(1), (2)	1985 s.238(5), Sch.24
426(1)	1985 s.251(1)
(2), (3)	1985 s.251(2)
(4)	drafting
(5)	new
(6)	1985 s.251(5)
427(1)	1985 s.251(1) "summary financial statement"
(2)	1985 s.251(3)
(3)	1985 s.251(3A)
(4)	1985 s.251(4)
(5)	new
(6)	1985 s.251(5)
428(1)	1985 s.251(1) "summary financial statement"
(2)	1985 s.251(3)
(3)	1985 s.251(3A)
(4)	1985 s.251(4)
(5)	new
(6)	1985 s.251(5)
429(1), (2)	1985 s.251(6), Sch.24
430(1)-(7)	new
431(1), (2)	1985 s.239(1), (2)
(3), (4)	1985 s.239(3), Sch.24
432(1), (2)	1985 s.239(1), (2)
(3), (4)	1985 s.239(3), Sch.24
433(1)-(3)	1985 ss.233(3), 234A(2), 234C(2)
(4), (5)	1985 ss.233(6)(a), 234A(4)(a), 234C(4)(a), Sch.24
434(1)	1985 s.240(1) (changed)
(2)	1985 s.240(2) (changed)
(3)	1985 s.240(5)
(4), (5)	1985 s.240(6), Sch.24

Section of 2006 Act	Derivation
(6)	1985 s.251(7)
435(1), (2)	1985 s.240(3) (changed)
(3)	1985 s.240(5) (changed)
(4)	new
(5), (6)	1985 s.240(6), Sch.24
(7)	1985 s.251(7)
436(1), (2)	1985 ss.233(3), 234A(2), 234C(2), 240(4) (changed)

Chapter 8 Public companies: laying of accounts and reports before general meeting

437(1)	1985 s.241(1) (changed)
(2)	1985 s.241(2)
(3)	drafting
438(1)-(3)	1985 s.241(2)-(4)
(4)	1985 s.241(2), Sch.24

Chapter 9 Quoted companies: members' approval of directors' remuneration report

439(1)	1985 s.241A(1), (3)
(2)	1985 s.241A(4)
(3)	1985 s.241A(5), (7)
(4)	1985 s.241A(6)
(5)	1985 s.241A(8)
(6)	1985 s.241A(2), (12)
440(1)	1985 s.241A(9)
(2), (3)	1985 s.241A(10), (11)
(4)	1985 s.241A(9), (10), Sch.24
(5)	1985 s.241A(2), (12)

Chapter 10 Filing of accounts and reports

441(1)	1985 s.242(1)
(2)	drafting
442(1)	drafting
(2), (3)	1985 s.244(1), (2) (changed)
(4), (5)	1985 s.244(4), (5)
(6)	new
(7)	1985 s.244(6)
443(1)-(5)	new
444(1)	1985 ss.242(1)(a), (b), 246(5)

Section of 2006 Act	Derivation
(2)	1985 ss.242(1)(d), 249E(1)(b) (changed)
(3)	1985 s.246(5), (6) (changed)
(4)	1985 s.247B(2)
(5)	1985 s.246(8)
(6)	1985 ss.233(4), 234A(3), 246(7)
(7)	1985 s.236(3)
445(1)	1985 ss.242(1)(a), (b), 246A(1)
(2)	1985 ss.242(1)(d), 249E(1)(b) (changed)
(3)	1985 s.246A(2), (3) (changed)
(4)	1985 s.247B(2)
(5)	1985 ss.233(4), 234A(3) (changed)
(6)	new
(7)	drafting
446(1)	1985 s.242(1)(a), (b)
(2)	1985 ss.242(1)(d), 249E(1)(b)
(3)	1985 ss.233(4), 234A(3) (changed)
(4)	new
(5)	drafting
447(1)	1985 s.242(1)(a), (b), (c)
(2)	1985 ss.242(1)(d)
(3)	1985 ss.233(4), 234A(3), 234C(3) (changed)
(4)	new
448(1)-(3)	1985 s.254(1)-(3)
(4)	1985 s.254(4)
(5)	1985 s.244(6)
449(1)-(5)	1985 s.247B(1)-(5)
450(1), (2)	1985 ss.233(1), (2), 246(7)
(3)	1985 s.246(8), 246A(4)
(4), (5)	1985 s.233(5), Sch.24
451(1)	1985 s.242(2)
(2), (3)	1985 s.242(4), (5)
(4)	1985 s.242(2), Sch.24
452(1), (2)	1985 s.242(3)
453(1)	1985 s.242A(1)

Section of 2006 Act	Derivation
(2)	1985 s.242A(2) (changed)
(3), (4)	1985 s.242A(3), (4)
(5)	new

Chapter 11 Revision of defective accounts and reports

454(1)-(3)	1985 s.245(1)-(3)
(4)	1985 s.245(4) (changed)
(5)	1985 s.245(5)
455(1), (2)	1985 s.245A(1)
(3)-(5)	1985 s.245A(2)-(4)
456(1)-(3)	1985 s.245B(1)-(3)
(4)	1985 s.245B(3A)
(5)-(8)	1985 s.245B(4)-(7)
457(1)	1985 s.245C(1)
(2), (3)	1985 s.245C(2), (3)
(4)	1985 s.245C(4B)
(5)	1985 s.245C(1A), (4A)
(6)	1985 s.245C(5)
(7)	1985 s.245C(4)
458(1)	1985 s.245D(1), (3)
(2)	1985 s.245D(2)
(3)	1985 s.245E(1), (2)
(4)	1985 s.245E(3), (4) (changed)
(5)	1985 s.245E(3), Sch.24
459(1)-(8)	1985 s.245F(1)-(8)
460(1), (2)	1985 s.245G(1), (2)
(3)	drafting; 1985 s.245G(3), (10)
(4)	1985 s.245G(7)(a), (8)
(5)	1985 s.245G(7)(b), Sch.24
461(1)	1985 s.245G(3)
(2)	1985 s.245G(3)(a)
(3)	1985 s.245G(3)(b), Sch.7B Pt 1
(4)	1985 s.245G(3)(c), Sch.7B Pt 2
(5), (6)	1985 s.245G(3)(d), Sch.7B Pt 3
(7)	1985 s.245G(11)

Section of 2006 Act	Derivation
462(1)-(3)	1985 s.245G(4)-(6)

Chapter 12 Supplementary provisions

463(1)-(6)	new
464(1), (2)	1985 s.256(1), (2)
(3)	1985 s.256(4)
465(1)	1985 s.247(1)(a)
(2)	1985 s.247(1)(b), (2)
(3), (4)	1985 s.247(3), (4)
(5)	1985 s.247(5) (changed)
(6)	1985 s.247(6), Sch.4 para.56(2), (3)
(7)	drafting
466(1)	1985 s.247A(3)
(2)	1985 s.249(1)(a)
(3)	1985 s.249(1)(b), (2)
(4)	1985 s.249(3)
(5), (6)	1985 s.249(4)
(7)	1985 s.249(5), (6)
467(1)	1985 s.247A(1)-(1B)
(2)	1985 s.247A(2)
(3)	1985 s.247A(2A)
468(1)-(5)	new
469(1)-(4)	1985 s.242B(1)-(4) (changed)
470(1)	1985 s.255D(1)
(2)	1985 s.255D(2), (2A)
(3)	1985 s.255D(5)
(4)	1985 s.255D(4)
471(1)	1985 s.262(1) "annual accounts"
(2), (3)	1985 s.238(1A); drafting
472(1), (2)	1985 s.261(1), (2)
473(1)-(4)	1985 s.257(2), (3) (changed)
474(1)	1985 ss.262(1), 744 "regulated activity"
(2)	1985 s.262(2)

Section of 2006 Act	**Derivation**
PART 16 AUDIT	
Chapter 1 Requirement for audited accounts	
475(1)	1985 s.235(1) (changed)
(2), (3)	1985 s.249B(4)
(4)	1985 s.249B(5)
476(1)-(3)	1985 s.249B(2)
477(1)	1985 s.249A(1)
(2)	1985 s.249A(3)
(3)	1985 s.249A(6)
(4)	1985 s.249A(3)(a), (7)
(5)	drafting
478	1985 s.249B(1)(a)-(e)
479(1)-(3)	1985 s.249B(1)(f), (1A)-(1C)
(4)	drafting
(5), (6)	1985 s.249B(1C)
480(1), (2)	1985 s.249AA(1), (2)
(3)	drafting
481	1985 s.249AA(3)
482(1)-(4)	new
483(1)-(5)	new
484(1)	1985 s.257(1)
484(2)	1985 s.257(4)(c)
484(3)	1985 s.257 (2)(b), (d)
484(4)	1985 s.257 (3)
Chapter 2 Appointment of auditors	
485(1)	1985 s.384(1)
(2)-(5)	new
486(1), (2)	1985 s.387(1), (2)
(3), (4)	1985 s.387(2), Sch.24
487(1)-(4)	new
488(1)-(3)	new
489(1)	1985 s.384(1) (changed)
(2)	1985 ss.384(2), 385(2)
(3)	1985 ss.385(3), 388(1) (changed)

Section of 2006 Act	Derivation
(4)	1985 s.385(2), (4) (changed)
(5)	drafting
490(1), (2)	1985 s.387(1), (2)
(3), (4)	1985 s.387(2), Sch.24
491(1)	1985 s.385(2) (changed)
(2)	drafting
492(1)	1985 s.390A(1)
(2), (3)	1985 s.390A(2)
(4), (5)	1985 s.390A(4), (5)
493(1)-(4)	new
494(1)	1985 s.390B(1), (8)
(2)-(4)	1985 s.390B(2)-(4)
(5)	1985 s.390B(5)(a)
(6)	1985 s.390B(9)

Chapter 3 Functions of auditor

495(1)	1985 s.235(1); drafting
(2)	1985 s.235(1A)
(3)	1985 s.235(1B), (2)
(4)	1985 s.235(2A)
496	1985 s.235(3)
497(1), (2)	1985 s.235(4), (5)
498(1)-(4)	1985 s.237(1)-(4)
(5)	1985 s.237(4A)
499(1), (2)	1985 s.389A(1), (2)
(3)	1985 s.389A(6)
(4)	1985 s.389A(7)
500(1)-(3)	1985 s.389A(3)-(5)
(4)	1985 s.389A(6)
(5)	1985 s.389A(7)
501(1)	1985 s.389B(1)
(2)	1985 s.389B(1), Sch.24
(3)	1985 s.389B(2), (3) (changed)
(4)	1985 s.389B(4)
(5)	1985 s.389B(4), Sch.24

Section of 2006 Act	Derivation
(6)	1985 s.389B(5)
502(1)	1985 s.390(2)
(2)	1985 s.390(1)
(3)	1985 s.390(3)
503(1), (2)	1985 s.236(1)
(3)	new
504(1)-(4)	new
505(1), (2)	1985 s.236(2) (changed)
(3), (4)	1985 s.236(4), Sch.24
506(1), (2)	new
507(1)-(4)	new
508(1)-(4)	new
509(1)-(4)	new

Chapter 4 Removal, resignation, etc of auditors

Section of 2006 Act	Derivation
510(1), (2)	1985 s.391(1); drafting
(3)	1985 s.391(3)
(4)	drafting
511(1)	1985 s.391A(1)(a)
(2)-(6)	1985 s.391A(2)-(6)
512(1)	1985 s.391(2)
(2), (3)	1985 s.391(2), Sch.24
513(1), (2)	1985 s.391(4)
514(1)-(8)	new
515(1)	1985 s.391A(1)(b)
(2)	1985 s.391A(1) opening words (changed)
(3)-(7)	1985 s.391A(2)-(6)
516(1), (2)	1985 s.392(1)
(3)	1985 s.392(2)
517(1)	1985 s.392(3)
(2), (3)	1985 s.392(3), Sch.24
518(1)-(4)	1985 s.392A(1)-(4)
(5)	1985 s.392A(5)
(6), (7)	1985 s.392(5), Sch.24
(8)-(10)	1985 s.392A(6)-(8)

Section of 2006 Act	Derivation
519(1)-(3)	1985 s.394(1) (changed)
(4)	1985 s.394(2) (changed)
(5), (6)	1985 s.394A(1), (2)
(7)	1985 s.394(1), Sch.24
520(1)	drafting
(2), (3)	1985 s.394(3), (4)
(4)	1985 s.394(6)
(5)	1985 s.394(7) (changed)
(6)	1985 s.394A(4)
(7)	new
(8)	1985 s.394A(4), Sch.24 (changed)
521(1)	1985 s.394(5)
(2)	1985 s.394(7)
(3), (4)	1985 s.394A(1), (2)
(5)	1985 s.394A(1), Sch.24
522(1)-(8)	new
523(1)-(6)	new
524(1)-(4)	new
525(1)-(3)	new
526	1985 s.388(2)

Chapter 5 Quoted companies: right of members to raise audit concerns at accounts meeting

527(1)-(6)	new
528(1)-(5)	new
529(1)-(4)	new
530(1), (2)	new
531(1), (2)	new

Chapter 6 Auditors' liability

532(1)	1985 s.310(1) (changed)
(2)	1985 s.310(2), drafting
(3)	1985 s.310(1)
(4)	new
533	1985 s.310(3)(b)
534(1)-(3)	new
535(1)-(5)	new

Section of 2006 Act	Derivation
536(1)-(5)	new
537(1)-(3)	new
538(1)-(3)	new

Chapter 7 Supplementary provisions

539	1985 s.262(1)

PART 17 A COMPANY'S SHARE CAPITAL

Chapter 1 Shares and share capital of a company

540(1)	1985 s.744 ("share")
(2), (3)	new
(4)	1985 s.744 ("share"), drafting
541	1985 s.182(1)(a)
542(1)-(5)	new
543(1), (2)	1985 s.182(2)
544(1), (2)	1985 s.182(1)(b)
(3)	drafting
545	new
546(1), (2)	new
547	1985 s.737(1), (2)
548	1985 s.744 ("equity share capital")

Chapter 2 Allotment of shares: general provisions

549(1)	1985 s.80(1), (2) (changed)
(2), (3)	1985 s.80(2)
(4)	1985 s.80(9)
(5)	1985 s.80(9), Sch.24
(6)	1985 s.80(10) (changed)
550	new
551(1)	1985 s.80(1), (2)
(2)	1985 s.80(3)
(3)	1985 s.80(4)
(4)	1985 s.80(4), (5)
(5)	1985 s.80(5)
(6)	1985 s.80(6)
(7)	1985 s.80(7)
(8)	1985 s.80(8)

Section of 2006 Act	Derivation
(9)	drafting
552(1)	1985 s.98(1)
(2)	1985 s.98(2)
(3)	1985 s.98(3)
553(1)	1985 s.97(1)
(2)	1985 s.97(2)(a)
(3)	1985 s.98(4)
554(1)-(5)	new
555(1)	1985 s.88(1)
(2)	1985 s.88(2) (changed)
(3), (4)	new
556(1)	1985 s.128(1), (2) (changed)
(2), (3)	1985 s.128(1)
(4)	1985 s.128(2)
557(1)	1985 ss.88(5), 128(5) (changed)
(2)	1985 ss.88(5), 128(5), Sch.24
(3)	1985 s.88(6) (changed)
558	1985 s.738(1)
559	1985 s.80(2)(a)

Chapter 3 Allotment of equity securities: existing shareholders' right of pre-emption

560(1)	1985 s.94(2), (5)
(2)	1985 s.94(3), (3A)
561(1)	1985 s.89(1)
(2)	1985 s.89(4)
(3)	1985 s.94(3)
(4)	1985 s.89(6)
(5)	drafting
562(1)	1985 s.90(1)
(2)	new
(3)	1985 s.90(5) (changed)
(4)	1985 s.90(6)
(5)	1985 s.90(6) (changed)
(6), (7)	new
563(1), (2)	1985 s.92(1)

Section of 2006 Act	Derivation
(3)	1985 s.92(2)
564	1985 s.94(2)
565	1985 s.89(4)
566	1985 s.89(5)
567(1), (2)	1985 s.91(1)
(3), (4)	1985 s.91(2)
568(1)	1985 s.89(2), (3)
(2)	1985 s.89(3)
(3)	1985 s.90(1)
(4)	1985 s.92(1)
(5)	1985 s.92(2)
569(1), (2)	new
570(1), (2)	1985 s.95(1)
(3)	1985 s.95(3)
(4)	1985 s.95(4)
571(1), (2)	1985 s.95(2)
(3)	1985 s.95(3)
(4)	1985 s.95(4)
(5), (6)	1985 s.95(5)
(7)	1985 s.95(5), Sch.15A para.3(1), (2)
572(1), (2)	1985 s.95(6)
(3)	1985 s.95(6), Sch.24
573(1)	1985 s.95(2A)
(2)	1985 s.95(1), (2A)
(3)	1985 s.95(1), (2A), (4)
(4)	1985 s.95(2), (2A)
(5)	1985 s.95(1), (2A), (4), (5), Sch.15A para.3(1), (2)
574(1), (2)	1985 s.94(7)
575(1)	1985 s.93(1)
(2)	1985 s.93(2)
576(1)	1985 s.96(1), (2)
(2)	1985 s.96(3)
(3)	1985 s.96(4)
577	1985 s.94(2)

Section of 2006 Act	Derivation
Chapter 4 Public companies: allotment where issue not fully subscribed	
578(1)	1985 s.84(1)
(2)	1985 s.84(2)
(3)	1985 s.84(3) (changed)
(4)	1985 s.84(4)
(5)	1985 s.84(4), (5)
(6)	1985 s.84(6)
579(1), (2)	1985 s.85(1)
(3)	1985 s.85(2)
(4)	1985 s.85(3)
Chapter 5 Payment for shares	
580(1)	1985 s.100(1)
(2)	1985 s.100(2)
581	1985 s.119
582(1)	1985 s.99(1)
(2)	1985 s.99(4)
(3)	1985 s.99(1)
583(1)	drafting
(2)-(3)(d)	1985 s.738(2)
(3)(e), (4)	new
(4)	new
(5)	1985 s.738(3)
(6)	1985 s.738(4)
(7)	new
584	1985 s.106
585(1)	1985 s.99(2)
(2)	1985 s.99(3)
(3)	1985 s.99(5)
586(1)	1985 s.101(1)
(2)	1985 s.101(2)
(3)	1985 s.101(3), (4)
(4)	1985 s.101(5)
587(1)	1985 s.102(1)
(2)	1985 s.102(2)

Section of 2006 Act	Derivation
(3)	1985 s.102(3), (4)
(4)	1985 s.102(5), (6)
(5)	1985 s.102(7)
588(1)	1985 s.112(1), (5)(a)
(2)	1985 s.112(3)
(3)	1985 s.112(4)
(4)	1985 s.112(5)(b)
589(1), (2)	1985 s.113(1)
(3)	1985 s.113(2), (3) (changed)
(4)	1985 s.113(4)
(5)	1985 s.113(5)
(6)	1985 s.113(6), (7)
590(1)	1985 s.114
(2)	1985 s.114. Sch.24
591(1), (2)	1985 s.115(1)
592(1), (2)	1985 s.107

Chapter 6 Public companies: independent valuation of non-cash consideration

593(1)	1985 s.103(1)
(2)	1985 s.103(2)
(3)	1985 s.103(6)
(4)	drafting
594(1)-(3)	1985 s.103(3)
(4), (5)	1985 s.103(4)
(6)	1985 s.103(7)
595(1), (2)	1985 s.103(5)
(3)	1985 s.103(7)(b)
596(1)	drafting
(2)	1985 s.108(4)
(3)	1985 s.108(6)
(4), (5)	1985 s.108(7)
597(1), (2)	1985 s.111(1)
(3), (4)	1985 s.111(3), Sch.24
(5), (6)	1985 ss.88(6), 111(3)
598(1)	1985 s.104(1)

Section of 2006 Act	Derivation
(2)	1985 s.104(2)
(3)	drafting
(4)	1985 s.104(6)(a)
(5)	1985 s.104(6)(b)
599(1)	1985 s.104(4)(a), (b), (d)
(2)	1985 s.104(5)(a)
(3)	1985 s.104(4)(d)
(4)	1985 s.104(5)(b)
600(1)	drafting
(2)	1985 s.109(2)(a), (b)
(3)	1985 ss.108(6)(a), (b), (c), 109(2)(c), (d)
(4), (5)	1985 s.109(3)
601(1), (2)	1985 s.104(4)(c), (d)
(3)	1985 s.104(4)(c) (changed)
602(1)	1985 s.111(2)
(2), (3)	1984 s.111(4), Sch.24
603	1985 s.104(3)
604(1)	1985 s.105(1)
(2)	1985 s.105(2)
(3)	1985 s.105(3)
605(1)	1985 s.112(1)
(2)	1985 s.112(2)
(3)	1985 s.112(3)
(4)	1985 s.112(4)
606(1)	1985 s.113(1)
(2)	1985 s.113(2), (3) (changed)
(3)	1985 s.113(4)
(4)	1985 s.113(5)
(5)	1985 s.113(6), (7)
(6)	1985 s.113(8)
607(1)	drafting
(2)	1985 s.114
(3)	1985 s.114, Sch.24
608(1), (2)	1985 s.115(1)

Section of 2006 Act	Derivation
609(1), (2)	1985 s.107
Chapter 7 Share premiums	
610(1)	1985 s.130(1)
(2), (3)	1985 s.130(2) (changed)
(4)	1985 s.130(3)
(5), (6)	1985 s.130(4)
611(1)	1985 s.132(1)
(2)	1985 s.132(2)
(3)	1985 s.132(3)
(4)	1985 s.132(4)
(5)	1985 s.132(5)
612(1)	1985 s.131(1)
(2)	1985 s.131(2)
(3)	1985 s.131(3)
(4)	1985 ss.131(1), 132(8)
613(1)	drafting
(2), (3)	1985 s.131(4)
(4)	1985 s.131(5)
(5)	1985 s.131(6)
614(1)	1985 s.134(1)
(2)	1985 s.134(3)
615	1985 s.133(1)
616(1)	1985 ss.131(7), 133(4)
(2)	1985 s.133(2)
(3)	1985 s.133(3)
Chapter 8 Alteration of share capital	
617(1)	1985 s.121(1) (changed)
(2)	1985 s.121(2)(a) (changed)
(3)	1985 s.121(2)(b), (c), (d) (changed)
(4), (5)	new
618(1)	1985 s.121(2)(b), (d)
(2)	1985 s.121(3) (changed)
(3)	1985 s.121(4) (changed)
(4), (5)	new

Section of 2006 Act	**Derivation**
619(1)	1985 s.122(1)(a), (d)
(2), (3)	1985 s.122(1) (changed)
(4)	1985 s.122(2)
(5)	1985 s.122(2), Sch.24
620(1)	1985 s.121(2)(c) (changed)
(2)	1985 s.121(4) (changed)
(3)	new
621(1)	1985 s.122(1)(c)
(2), (3)	new
(4)	1985 s.122(2)
(5)	1985 s.122(2), Sch.24
622(1)-(8)	new
623	new
624(1)-(3)	new
625(1)-(5)	new
626(1)-(6)	new
627(1)-(8)	new
628(1)-(3)	new

Chapter 9 Classes of share and class rights

629(1)	new
(2)	1985 s.128(2)
630(1)	1985 s.125(1)
(2)-(4)	1985 s.125(2) (changed)
(5)	1985 s.125(7)
(6)	1985 s.125(8)
631(1)-(6)	new
632	1985 s.126 (changed)
633(1)	1985 s.127(1)(b)
(2)	1985 s.127(2), (2A)
(3)	1985 s.127(2)
(4)	1985 s.127(3)
(5)	1985 s.127(4)
(6)	1985 s.127(6)
634(1)-(6)	new

Section of 2006 Act	Derivation
635(1)-(3)	1985 s.127(5)
636(1)	1985 s.128(4) (changed)
(2)	1985 s.128(5)
(3)	1985 s.128(5), Sch.24
637(1)	1985 s.128(3) (changed)
(2)	1985 s.128(5)
(3)	1985 s.128(5), Sch.24
638(1)	1985 s.129(1) (changed)
(2)	1985 s.129(4)
(3)	1985 s.129(4), Sch.24
639(1)	1985 s.129(3) (changed)
(2)	1985 s.129(4)
(3)	1985 s.129(4), Sch.24
640(1)	1985 s.129(2) (changed)
(2)	1985 s.129(4)
(3)	1985 s.129(4), Sch.24

Chapter 10 Reduction of share capital

641(1)-(3)	1985 s.135(1) (changed)
(4)	1985 s.135(2)
(5), (6)	new
642(1)-(4)	new
643(1)-(5)	new
644(1)-(9)	new
645(1)	1985 s.136(1)
(2)	1985 s.136(2), (6)
(3)	1985 s.136(6)
(4)	1985 s.136(2)
646(1)	1985 s.136(3)
(2), (3)	1985 s.136(4)
(4), (5)	1985 s.136(5)
647(1)	1985 s.141 (changed)
(2)	1985 s.141, Sch.24
648(1), (2)	1985 s.137(1)
(3)	1985 s.137(2)(b)

Section of 2006 Act	Derivation
(4)	1985 s.137(2)(a), (3)
649(1)	1985 s.138(1) (changed)
(2)	new
(3)	1985 s.138(2) (changed)
(4)	1985 s.138(3) (changed)
(5)	1985 s.138(4) (changed)
(6)	1985 s.138(4)
650(1)	1985 s.139(1)
(2)	1985 s.139(2)
(3)	drafting
651(1), (2)	1985 s.139(3)
(3)	1985 s.139(4) (changed)
(4)	1985 s.139(5)
(5)	new
(6)	1985 s.139(5)(a)
(7)	1985 s.139(5)(b)
652(1)	1985 s.140(1) (changed)
(2)	drafting
(3)	1985 s.140(5)
653(1)	1985 s.140(2)
(2)	1985 s.140(3)
(3)	1985 s.140(4)
(4)	drafting

Chapter 11 Miscellaneous and supplementary provisions

654(1)-(3)	new
655	1985 s.111A
656(1)-(3)	1985 s.142(1)
(4)	1985 s.142(2) (changed)
(5)	1985 s.142(2), Sch.24
(6)	1985 s.142(3)
657(1)-(4)	new

PART 18 ACQUISITION BY LIMITED COMPANY OF ITS OWN SHARES

Chapter 1 General provisions

658(1)	1985 s.143(1)

Section of 2006 Act	Derivation
(2)	1985 s.143(2)
(3)	1985 s.143(2), Sch.24
659(1), (2)	1985 s.143(3)
660(1), (2)	1985 s.144(1) (changed)
(3)	1985 s.145(1), (2)(a)
661(1), (2)	1985 s.144(2) (changed)
(3)	1985 s.144(3)
(4)	1985 s.144(4)
(5)	1985 s.145(2)(a)
662(1)	1985 s.146(1)
(2)	1985 s.146(2)
(3)	1985 s.146(2), (3)
(4)	1985 s.147(1)
(5), (6)	1985 s.146(4)
663(1)	1985 s.122(1)(f)
(2), (3)	new
(4)	1985 s.122(2)
(5)	1985 s.122(2), Sch.24
664(1), (2)	1985 s.147(2) (changed)
(3)	new
(4)	1985 s.147(3) (changed)
(5), (6)	new
665(1), (2)	1985 s.147(4)
(3)	new
(4)	1985 s.147(4)(a) (changed)
(5)	1985 s.147(4)(b)
666(1), (2)	1985 s.149(1)
667(1), (2)	1985 s.149(2)
(3)	1985 s.149(2), Sch.24
668(1), (2)	1985 s.148(1)
(3)	1985 s.148(2)
669(1), (2)	1985 s.148(4)
670(1)	1985 s.150(1)
(2)	1985 s.150(2)

Section of 2006 Act	Derivation
(3)	1985 s.150(3)
(4)	1985 s.150(4)
671	1985 ss.145(3), 146(1), 148(3)
672(1)	1985 Sch.2 para.1(1)
(2)	1985 Sch.2 para.1(2)
(3)	1985 Sch.2 para.1(3)
(4)	1985 Sch.2 para.1(4)
(5)	1985 Sch.2 para.2(3)
(6)	1985 Sch.2 para.2(4)
673(1)	1985 Sch.2 para.3(1)(a), (2)
(2)	1985 Sch.2 para.3(1)(b), (2)(a)
674	1985 Sch.2 para.4(1), (3)
675(1), (2)	1985 Sch.2 para.5(1), (2)
676	1985 Sch.2 para.5(1), (3)

Chapter 2 Financial assistance for purchase of own shares

Section of 2006 Act	Derivation
677(1)	1985 s.152(1)(a)
(2), (3)	1985 s.152(2)
678(1)	1985 s.151(1) (changed)
(2)	1985 s.153(1)
(3)	1985 s.151(2) (changed)
(4)	1985 s.153(2)
(5)	drafting
679(1)	1985 s.151(1) (changed)
(2)	1985 s.153(1) (changed)
(3)	1985 s.151(2) (changed)
(4)	1985 s.153(2) (changed)
(5)	drafting
680(1)	1985 s.151(3)
(2)	1985 s.151(3), Sch.24
681(1), (2)	1985 s.153(3)
682(1)	1985 ss.153(4), 154(1)
(2)	1985 s.153(4)
(3), (4)	1985 s.154(2)
(5)	1985 s.153(5)

Section of 2006 Act	Derivation
683(1)	1985 s.152(1)(b), (c)
(2)	1985 s.152(3)

Chapter 3 Redeemable shares

684(1)	1985 s.159(1) (changed)
(2)	new
(3)	1985 s.159(1) (changed)
(4)	1985 s.159(2)
685(1)-(4)	new
686(1)-(3)	1985 s.159(3) (changed)
687(1)-(3)	1985 s.160(1)
(4), (5)	1985 s.160(2)
(6)	1985 s.160(1)
688	1985 s.160(4) (changed)
689(1)	1985 s.122(1)(e)
(2), (3)	new
(4)	1985 s.122(2)
(5)	1985 s.122(2), Sch.24

Chapter 4 Purchase of own shares

690(1)	1985 s.162(1) (changed)
(2)	1985 s.162(3)
691(1), (2)	1985 ss.159(3), 162(2)
692(1), (2)	1985 ss.160(1), 162(2)
(3), (4)	1985 ss.160(2), 162(2)
(5)	1985 ss.160(1), 162(2)
693(1)	1985 ss.164(1), 166(1)
(2)	1985 s.163(1)
(3)	1985 s.163(2)
(4)	1985 s.163(3)
(5)	1985 s.163(4), (5)
694(1)	1985 s.164(1)
(2)	1985 ss.164(2), 165(2) (changed)
(3)	1985 s.165(1)
(4)	1985 ss.164(3), 165(2)
(5)	1985 ss.164(4), 165(2)

Section of 2006 Act	Derivation
(6)	drafting
695(1)	1985 ss.164(5), 165(2)
(2)	1985 Sch.15A para.5(1), (2)
(3), (4)	1985 ss.164(5), 165(2)
696(1)	1985 ss.164(6), 165(2)
(2)	1985 ss.164(6), 165(2), Sch.15A, para.5(3), (4)
(3)-(5)	1985 s.164(6), s.165(2)
697(1), (2)	1985 s.164(7)
(3)	1985 s.164(3), (7)
(4)	1985 s.164(4), (7)
(5)	drafting
698(1)	1985 s.164(5), (7)
(2)	1985 Sch.15A, para.5(1), (2)
(3), (4)	1985 s.164(5), (7)
699(1)	1985 s.164(6), (7)
(2)	1985 s.164(6), (7), Sch.15A para.5(3)
(3)-(6)	1985 s.164(6), (7)
700(1), (2)	1985 s.167(2)
(3)	1985 ss.164(3), (7), 167(2)
(4)	1985 ss.164(4), (7), 167(2)
(5)	1985 ss.164(5), (6), (7), 167(2)
701(1)	1985 s.166(1)
(2)	1985 s.166(2)
(3)	1985 s.166(3)(a), (b)
(4)	1985 s.166(4)
(5)	1985 s.166(3)(c), (4)
(6)	1985 s.166(5)
(7)	1985 s.166(6)
(8)	1985 s.166(7)
702(1)-(4)	1985 s.169(4) (changed)
(5)	new
(6)	1985 s.169(5)
(7)	1985 s.169(9)
703(1)	1985 s.169(7) (changed)

Section of 2006 Act	Derivation
(2)	1985 s.169(7), Sch.24
(3)	1985 s.169(8)
704	1985 s.167(1)
705(1)	1985 s.168(1)
(2)	1985 s.168(2)
706	1985 ss.160(4), 162(2), (2B)
707(1)-(3)	1985 s.169(1), (1A), (1B) (changed)
(4)	1985 s.169(2)
(5)	1985 s.169(3)
(6)	1985 s.169(6)
(7)	1985 s.169(6), Sch.24
708(1)	1985 s.169(1), (1A), (1B) (changed)
(2), (3)	new
(4)	1985 s.169(6)
(5)	1985 s.169(6), Sch.24

Chapter 5 Redemption or purchase by private company out of capital

Section of 2006 Act	Derivation
709(1)	1985 s.171(1) (changed)
(2)	1985 s.171(2)
710(1), (2)	1985 s.171(3)
711(1), (2)	1985 s.172(1)
712(1)	drafting
(2)	1985 s.172(2)
(3)	1985 s.172(4)
(4)	1985 s.172(5)
(5)	drafting
(6)	1985 s.172(3)
(7)	1985 s.172(6)
713(1), (2)	1985 s.173(1)
714(1)-(3)	1985 s.173(3) (changed)
(4)	1985 s.173(4) (changed)
(5), (6)	1985 s.173(5) (changed)
715(1)	1985 s.173(6)
(2)	1985 s.173(6), Sch.24
716(1)	1985 s.173(2)

Section of 2006 Act	Derivation
(2)	1985 s.174(1)
(3)	drafting
717(1)	drafting
(2)	1985 Sch.15A para.6(1), (2)
(3)	1985 s.174(2)
(4)	1985 s.174(3), (5)
718(1)	drafting
(2)	1985 s.174(4), Sch.15A para.6(1), (3)
(3)	1985 s.174(4)
719(1)	1985 s.175(1)
(2)	1985 s.175(2)
(3)	1985 s.175(3)
(4)	1985 s.175(4), (5)
720(1)	1985 s.175(4), (6)(a)
(2)	1985 s.175(6)(a) (changed)
(3)	new
(4)	1985 s.175(6)(b)
(5)	1985 s.175(7) (changed)
(6)	1985 s.175(7), Sch.24
(7)	1985 s.175(8)
721(1)	1985 s.176(1)
(2)	1985 s.176(1), (2)
(3)	1985 s.177(1)
(4), (5)	1985 s.177(2)
(6)	1985 s.177(3)
(7)	1985 s.177(4)
722(1)	new
(2)	1985 s.176(3)(a)
(3)	1985 s.176(3)(b)
(4)	1985 s.176(4)
(5)	1985 s.176(4), Sch.24
723(1)	1985 s.174(1)
(2)	drafting

Section of 2006 Act	Derivation
Chapter 6 Treasury shares	
724(1)	1985 s.162(2B)
(2)	1985 s.162(4)
(3)	1985 s.162A(1)
(4)	1985 s.162A(2)
(5)	1985 s.162A(3)
725(1)	1985 s.162B(1)
(2)	1985 s.162B(2)
(3)	1985 s.162B(3)
(4)	1985 s.143(2A)
726(1)	1985 s.162C(1)
(2)	1985 s.162C(2), (3)
(3)	1985 s.162C(4)
(4)	1985 s.162C(5)
(5)	1985 s.162C(6)
727(1)	1985 s.162D(1)(a), (b)
(2)	1985 s.162D(2) (changed)
(3)	1985 s.162D(3)
(4), (5)	new
728(1)	1985 s.169A(1)(b)(ii), (2)
(2)	1985 s.169A(2)
(3)	1985 s.169A(3)
(4)	1985 s.169A(4)
(5)	1985 s.169A(4), Sch.24
729(1)	1985 s.162D(1)(c)
(2)	1985 s.162E(1)
(3)	1985 s.162E(2)
(4)	1985 s.162D(4)
(5)	1985 s.162D(5)
730(1)	1985 s.169A(1)(b)(i), (2)
(2)	1985 s.169A(2)
(3)	1985 s.169A(3)
(4), (5)	new
(6)	1985 s.169A(4)

Section of 2006 Act	Derivation
(7)	1985 s.169A(4), Sch.24
731(1)	1985 s.162F(1)
(2)	1985 s.162F(2)
(3)	1985 s.162F(3)
(4)	1985 s.162F(4), (5)
732(1)	1985 s.162G (changed)
(2)	1985 s.162G

Chapter 7 Supplementary provisions

733(1), (2)	1985 s.170(1)
(3)	1985 s.170(2), (3)
(4)	1985 s.170(1)
(5), (6)	1985 s.170(4)
734(1)	drafting
(2)	1985 s.171(4)
(3)	1985 s.171(5)
(4)	1985 s.171(6)
735(1)	1985 s.178(1)
(2)	1985 s.178(2), (3)
(3)	1985 s.178(3)
(4)	1985 s.178(4)
(5)	1985 s.178(5)
(6)	1985 s.178(6)
736	1985 s.181(a)
737(1)	1985 s.179(1) (changed)
(2)	1985 s.179(3)
(3)	1985 s.179(3)
(4)	1985 s.179(4) (changed)

PART 19 DEBENTURES

738	1985 s.744 ("debenture")
739(1), (2)	1985 s.193
740	1985 s.195
741(1)-(4)	new
742	1985 s.197
743(1)	new

Section of 2006 Act	Derivation
(2)	1985 s.190(5) (changed)
(3)	1985 s.190(6)
(4), (5)	new
(6)	1985 s.190(1), (5)
744(1)	1985 s.191(1)
(2)	1985 s.191(2)
(3), (4)	new
(5)	1985 s.191(6)
(6)	new
745(1)-(5)	new
746(1)	1985 s.191(4) (changed)
(2)	1985 s.191(4), Sch.24
(3)	1985 s.191(5)
747(1)-(3)	new
748(1)	1985 s.191(7) (changed)
(2)	1985 s.191(7)
749(1)	1985 s.191(3)
(2)	1985 s.191(4)
(3)	1985 s.191(4), Sch.24
(4)	1985 s.191(5)
750(1)	1985 s.192(1)
(2)	1985 s.192(2)
(3)	1985 s.192(1)
751(1)	1985 s.192(3)
(2)	1985 s.192(3), 1986 Order art.201(3)
(3), (4)	1985 s.192(4)
752(1)	1985 s.194(1)
(2)	1985 s.194(2)
(3)	1985 s.194(4)
(4)	1985 s.194(5)
753	1985 s.194(3)
754(1)	1985 s.196(1)
(2)	1985 s.196(2)
(3)	1985 s.196(3)

Section of 2006 Act	Derivation
(4)	1985 s.196(4)

PART 20 PUBLIC AND PRIVATE COMPANIES

Chapter 1 Prohibition of public offers by private companies

755(1)	1985 s.81(1) (changed)
(2)	1985 s.58(3)
(3), (4)	new
(5)	drafting
756(1), (2)	1985 s.742A(1)
(3)	1985 s.742A(2)
(4)	1985 s.742A(3), (4), (5)
(5)	1985 s.742A(3)(a), (6)(b) (changed)
(6)	1985 s.742A(6)(a)
757(1)-(3)	new
758(1)-(4)	new
759(1)-(5)	new
760	1985 s.81(3)

Chapter 2 Minimum share capital requirement for public companies

761(1)	1985 s.117(1)
(2)	1985 s.117(2) (changed)
(3)	1985 s.117(4)
(4)	1985 s.117(6) (changed)
762(1)	1985 s.117(3) (changed)
(2)	new
(3)	1985 s.117(5)
763(1)	1985 s.118(1) (changed)
(2)-(6)	new
764(1)	1985 s.118(1) (changed)
(2)	new
(3)	1985 s.118(2)
(4)	1985 s.118(3)
765(1)-(4)	new
766(1)-(6)	new
767(1)	1985 s.117(7)
(2)	1985 s.117(7), Sch.24

Section of 2006 Act	Derivation
(3)	1985 s.117(8)
(4)	new

PART 21 CERTIFICATION AND TRANSFER OF SECURITIES

Chapter 1 Certification and transfer of securities: general

768(1)	1985 s.186(1)(a)
(2)	1985 s.186(1)(b), (2)
769(1)	1985 s.185(1)(a)
(2)	1985 s.185(1), (4)(a), (b)
(3)	1985 s.185(5)
(4)	1985 s.185(5), Sch.24
770(1)	1985 s.183(1)
(2)	1985 s.183(2)
771(1)-(6)	new
772	1985 s.183(4)
773	1985 s.183(3)
774	1985 s.187
775(1), (2)	1985 s.184(1)
(3)	1985 s.184(2)
(4)	1985 s.184(3)
776(1)	1985 s.185(1)(b)
(2)	1985 s.185(2)
(3)	1985 s.185(1), (4)(c)
(4)	drafting
(5)	1985 s.185(5)
(6)	1985 s.185(5), Sch.24
777(1), (2)	1985 s.185(3)
778(1)	1985 s.185(4), (4A)
(2)	1985 s.185(4B), (4C)
(3)	1985 s.185(4D)
779(1)	1985 s.188(1)
(2)	1985 s.188(2)
(3)	1985 s.188(3)
780(1)-(4)	new
781(1)	1985 s.189(1)

Section of 2006 Act	Derivation
(2)	1985 s.189(2)
(3)	1985 s.189(1), Sch.24
(4)	1985 s.189(2), Sch.24
782(1)	1985 s.185(6)
(2), (3)	1985 s.185(7)

Chapter 2 Evidencing and transfer of title to securities without written instrument

783	CA 1989 s.207(1), (10)
784(1), (2)	new
(3)	CA 1989 s.207(9)
785(1)	CA 1989 s.207(1)
(2)	CA 1989 s.207(2)
(3)	CA 1989 s.207(3)
(4)	CA 1989 s.207(4)
(5)	CA 1989 s.207(5)
(6)	CA 1989 s.207(6)
786(1)-(5)	new
787(1)-(3)	new
788	CA 1989 s.207(7)
789	new
790	new

PART 22 INFORMATION ABOUT INTERESTS IN A COMPANY'S SHARES

791	new
792(1)	1985 s.198(2) (changed)
(2)	1985 s.198(2)(b)
793(1), (2)	1985 s.212(1) (changed)
(3)	1985 s.212(2)(a)
(4)	1985 s.212(2)(b)
(5)	1985 s.212(3)
(6)	1985 s.212(2)(c)
(7)	1985 s.212(4)
794(1)	1985 s.216(1)
(2)	1985 s.216(1B)
(3)	1985 s.216(1A)
(4)	drafting

Section of 2006 Act	Derivation
795(1)	1985 s.216(3)
(2)	1985 s.216(4)
(3)	1985 s.216(3), Sch.24
796(1), (2)	1985 s.216(5)
797(1)	1985 s.454(1)
(2)	1985 s.454(2)
(3)	1985 s.454(3)
(4)	1985 s.454(2), (3)
798(1), (2)	1985 s.455(1)
(3)	1985 s.455(2)
(4)	1985 s.455(2), Sch.24
(5)	1985 s.455(1), (2)
799(1)	1985 s.456(1A)
(2)	1985 s.456(2)
(3)	1985 s.456(1A)
800(1)	1985 s.456(1)
(2)	1985 s.456(2)
(3)	1985 s.456(3)
(4)	1985 s.456(6)
(5)	1985 s.456(7)
801(1), (2)	1985 s.456(4)
(3), (4)	1985 s.456(5)
(5)	1985 s.457(3)
802(1), (2)	1985 s.457(1)
(3)	1985 s.457(2)
(4)	1985 s.457(3)
803(1), (2)	1985 s.214(1) (changed)
(3)	1985 s.214(2) (changed)
804(1)	1985 s.214(4)
(2)	1985 s.214(5) (changed)
(3)	1985 s.214(5), Sch.24
805(1)	1985 s.215(1), (3)
(2)	1985 s.215(2)
(3)	1985 s.215(2), (3)

Section of 2006 Act	Derivation
(4)	1985 s.215(7) (changed)
(5)	new
(6)	1985 s.215(5)
(7)	1985 s.215(6)
806(1), (2)	new
(3)	1985 s.215(8) (changed)
(4)	1985 s.215(8), Sch.24
807(1)	1985 ss.215(7)(b), 219(1)
(2)	1985 ss.215(7)(b), 219(2)
(3)	1985 ss.215(7)(b), 219(3)
(4)	1985 ss.215(7)(b), 219(3), Sch.24
(5)	1985 ss.215(7)(b), 219(4)
808(1)	1985 s.213(1)
(2)	1985 ss.211(3), 213(1), (3)
(3)	1985 s.213(1) (changed)
(4)	1985 ss.211(5), 213(3)
(5)	1985 ss.211(10), 213(3)
(6)	1985 ss.211(10), 213(3), Sch.24
(7)	1985 ss.211(4), 213(3)
809(1)	1985 ss.211(8), 213(3) (changed)
(2), (3)	1985 ss.211(8), 213(3), 325(5), Sch.13, para.27
(4), (5)	new
810(1)-(3)	1985 ss.211(6), 213(3)
(4)	1985 ss.211(8), 213(3)
(5), (6)	new
811(1)	1985 ss.211(8)(b), 213(3), 219(1)
(2)	1985 ss.211(8)(b), 213(3), 219(2) (changed)
(3)	new
(4)	new
812(1)-(7)	new
813(1)	1985 ss.211(8)(b), 213(3), 219(3) (changed)
(2)	1985 ss.211(8)(b), 213(3), 219(3), Sch.24
(3)	1985 ss.211(8)(b), 213(3), 219(4)
814(1)-(3)	new

Section of 2006 Act	Derivation
815(1)	1985 s.218(1)
(2)	1985 s.218(2)
(3)	1985 s.218(3)
(4)	1985 s.218(3), Sch.24
816	1985 s.217(1) (changed)
817(1)	1985 s.217(2) (changed)
(2), (3)	1985 s.217(3)
(4)	1985 s.217(5)
818(1), (2)	1985 s.217(4)
(3)	1985 s.217(5)
819(1)	1985 ss.211(7), 213(3)
(2)	1985 ss.211(10), 213(3)
(3)	1985 ss.211(10), 213(3), Sch.24
820(1)	1985 ss.208(1), 212(5)
(2)	1985 ss.208(2), 212(5)
(3)	1985 s.208(3), s.212(5)
(4)	1985 ss.208(4), 212(5)
(5)	1985 ss.208(6), 212(5)
(6)	1985 ss.208(5), 212(5)
(7)	1985 ss.208(7), 212(5)
(8)	1985 ss.208(8), 212(5)
821(1), (2)	1985 s.212(6)
822(1), (2)	1985 ss.203(1), 212(5)
823(1)	1985 ss.203(2), 212(5)
(2)	1985 ss.203(3), 212(5)
(3)	1985 ss.203(4), 212(5)
824(1)	1985 ss.204(1), (2), 212(5)
(2)	1985 ss.204(2), 212(5)
(3)	1985 ss.204(3), 212(5)
(4)	1985 ss.204(4), 212(5)
(5)	1985 ss.204(5), 212(5)
(6)	1985 ss.204(6), 212(5)
825(1)	1985 ss.205(1), 212(5)
(2)	1985 ss.205(2), 212(5)

Section of 2006 Act	Derivation
(3)	1985 ss.205(3), 212(5)
(4)	1985 ss.205(4), 212(5)
826(1)	1985 ss.211(9), 213(3), 215(4)
(2)	1985 s.215(4)
827	1985 s.220(2) (changed)
828(1), (2)	1985 s.210A(1)
(3)	1985 s.210A(5)

PART 23 DISTRIBUTIONS

Chapter 1 Restrictions on when distributions may be made

829(1), (2)	1985 s.263(2)
830(1)	1985 s.263(1)
(2), (3)	1985 s.263(3)
831(1)	1985 s.264(1)
(2), (3)	1985 s.264(2)
(4)	1985 s.264(3)
(5)	1985 s.264(4)
(6)	1985 s.264(1)
832(1)-(3)	1985 s.265(1)
(4)	1985 s.265(2)
(5)	1985 s.265(4), (6)
(6)	1985 s.265(4A), (5)
(7)	1985 s.265(3)
833(1)	1985 s.266(1)
(2)	1985 s.266(2)
(3)	1985 s.266(2A)
(4), (5)	1985 s.266(3)
834(1)	1985 s.266(2)(b)
(2)	1985 s.266(4), Income and Corporation Taxes Act 1988 s.842(1A)
(3)	1985 s.266(4), Income and Corporation Taxes Act 1988 s.842(2)
(4)	1985 s.266(4), Income and Corporation Taxes Act 1988 s.842(3)
(5)	1985 s.266(4), Income and Corporation Taxes Act 1988 ss.838, 842(1A), (4)
835(1)	1985 s.267(1)

Section of 2006 Act	**Derivation**
(2)	1985 s.267(2)(b)

Chapter 2 Justification of distribution by reference to accounts

836(1)	1985 s.270(1), (2)
(2)	1985 s.270(3), (4)
(3), (4)	1985 s.270(5)
837(1)	1985 s.270(3)
(2)	1985 s.271(2)
(3)	1985 s.271(3)
(4)	1985 s.271(3), (4)
(5)	1985 s.271(5)
838(1)	1985 s.270(4)
(2)	1985 s.272(1)
(3)	1985 s.272(2)
(4), (5)	1985 s.272(3)
(6)	1985 s.272(4), (5)
839(1)	1985 s.270(4)
(2)	1985 s.273(1)
(3)	1985 s.273(2)
(4)	1985 ss.272(3), 273(3)
(5)	1985 s.273(4)
(6)	1985 s.273(4), (5)
(7)	1985 s.273(6), (7)
840(1)	1985 s.274(1), (2)
(2)	1985 s.274(2)
(3)	1985 s.274(3) ("financial assistance")
(4)	1985 ss.154(2)(a), 274(3) ("net assets", "net liabilities")
(5)	1985 ss.154(2)(b), 274(3) ("net liabilities")

Chapter 3 Supplementary provisions

841(1), (2)	1985 s.275(1)
(3)	1985 s.275(1A)
(4)	1985 s.275(4), (5), (6)
(5)	1985 s.275(2)
842	1985 s.275(3)
843(1)	1985 s.268(1)

Section of 2006 Act	Derivation
(2)	1985 s.268(1)(a)
(3)	1985 s.268(2)(aa), (a)
(4)	1985 s.268(1)(b), (2)(b)
(5)	1985 s.268(1)
(6)	1985 s.268(3)(a)
(7)	1985 s.268(3)(b), (4)
844(1)	1985 s.269(1)
(2), (3)	1985 s.269(2)
845(1)-(5)	new
846(1), (2)	1985 s.276 (changed)
847(1), (2)	1985 s.277(1)
(3), (4)	1985 s.277(2)
848(1)	1985 s.278
(2)	1985 s.278, 1986 Order art.286
849	1985 s.263(4)
850(1), (2)	1985 s.263(5)
(3)	1985 s.263(5), 1986 Order art.271(5)
851(1)	1985 s.281 (changed)
(2), (3)	new
852	1985 s.281
853(1)	1985 s.280(1)
(2)	1985 s.280(3)
(3)	1985 s.280(2)
(4), (5)	1985 ss.262(3), 742(2)
(6)	1985 ss.262(1), 742(1)

PART 24 A COMPANY'S ANNUAL RETURN

854(1), (2)	1985 s.363(1)
(3)	1985 s.363(2) (changed)
855(1)	1985 s.364(1) (changed)
(2)	1985 s.364(2)
(3)	1985 s.364(3)
856(1)	1985 s.364A(1)
(2)	1985 s.364A(2), (3) (changed)
(3)	1985 s.364A(4) (changed)

Section of 2006 Act	Derivation
(4)	1985 s.364A(5)
(5)	1985 s.364A(6)
(6)	1985 s.364A(8)
857(1), (2)	1985 s.365(1)
(3)	1985 s.365(2)
858(1)	1985 s.363(3), (4) (changed)
(2)	1985 s.363(3), (4), Sch.24
(3)	1985 s.363(3)
(4)	1985 s.363(4)
(5)	new
859	1985 s.365(3)

PART 25 COMPANY CHARGES

Chapter 1 Companies registered in England and Wales or in Northern Ireland

Section of 2006 Act	Derivation
860(1)	1985 ss.395(1), 399(1)
(2)	1985 s.399(1)
(3)	1985 s.399(2)
(4)-(6)	1985 s.399(3), Sch.24 (changed)
(7)	1985 s.396(1)
861(1)	1985 s.396(3)
(2)	1985 s.396(1)(d)
(3)	1985 s.396(2)
(4)	1985 s.396(3A)
(5)	1985 ss.395(1) ("company"), 396(4) ("charge"), 400(1) ("company")
862(1)	1985 s.400(1)
(2), (3)	1985 s.400(2)
(4), (5)	1985 s.400(4), Sch.24 (changed)
863(1)-(4)	1985 s.397(1)
(5)	1985 s.399(1)-(3)
864(1)	1985 s.397(2)
(2)	1985 s.397(3)
(3)	1985 s.397(2)
865(1)	1985 s.402(1)
(2)	1985 s.402(2)
(3), (4)	1985 s.402(3), Sch.24

Section of 2006 Act	Derivation
866(1)	1985 s.398(1)
(2)	1985 s.398(3)
867(1), (2)	1985 s.398(4)
868(1), (2)	1986 Order art.408(1)
(3)	1986 Order art.408(2)
(4)	1986 Order art.408(3)
(5)	drafting
869(1)	1985 s.401(1) (opening words)
(2)	1985 s.401(1)(a)
(3)	1986 Order art.409(2)(b)
(4)	1985 s.401(1)(b)
(5), (6)	1985 s.401(2)
(7)	1985 s.401(3)
870(1)	1985 ss.395(1), 398(2)
(2)	1985 s.400(2), (3)
(3)	1985 s.397(1)
871(1)	1985 s.405(1)
(2)	1985 s.405(2)
(3)	1985 s.405(1), (2)
(4), (5)	1985 s.405(4), Sch.24
872(1), (2)	1985 s.403(1) (changed)
(3)	1985 s.403(2)
873(1)	1985 s.404(1)
(2)	1985 s.404(2)
874(1), (2)	1985 s.395(1)
(3)	1985 s.395(2)
875(1)	1985 s.406(1), 1986 Order art.414(1)
(2)	1985 s.406(2)
876(1)	1985 s.407(1)
(2)	1985 s.407(2)
(3), (4)	1985 s.407(3), Sch.24
877(1)	1985 s.408(1)
(2)	1985 ss.406(1), 407(1), 408(1) (changed)
(3)	new

Section of 2006 Act	Derivation
(4)	1985 s.408(1), (2) (changed)
(5), (6)	1985 s.408(3), Sch.24 (changed)
(7)	1985 s.408(4)

Chapter 2 Companies registered in Scotland

878(1)	1985 ss.410(2), 415(1)
(2)	1985 s.415(1)
(3)	1985 s.415(2)
(4)-(6)	1985 s.415(3), Sch.24 (changed)
(7)	1985 s.410(4)
879(1)	1985 s.410(4)(a)
(2)	1985 s.413(1)
(3)	1985 s.410(4)(a)
(4)	1985 s.412
(5)	1985 s.410(5)
(6)	1985 s.410(5) ("company")
880(1), (2)	1985 s.416(1)
(3), (4)	1985 s.416(3), Sch.24 (changed)
881(1)	1985 s.414(1)
(2), (3)	1985 s.414(2)
882(1)-(4)	1985 s.413(2)
(5)	1985 s.415(1)-(3)
883(1)-(3)	1985 s.413(3)
884	1985 s.411(2)
885(1)	1985 s.417(1)
(2)	1985 s.417(2)
(3)	1985 s.417(3)
(4)	1985 s.418(1), (2)(b)
(5)	1985 s.418(2)(a), (c)
(6)	1985 s.417(4)
886(1)	1985 ss.410(2), 411(1)
(2)	1985 s.416(1), (2)
(3)	1985 s.413(2)
887(1)	1985 s.419(1) (changed)
(2)	1985 s.419(1B)(a), (c), (3) (changed)

Section of 2006 Act	Derivation
(3)	1985 s.419(1)
(4)	1985 s.419(2)
(5)	1985 s.419(4)
888(1), (2)	1985 s.420
889(1)	1985 s.410(2)
(2)	1985 s.410(3)
890(1)	1985 s.421(1)
(2)	1985 s.421(2)
891(1)	1985 s.422(1)
(2)	1985 s.422(2)
(3), (4)	1985 s.422(3), Sch.24
892(1)	1985 s.423(1)
(2)	1985 ss.421(1), 422(1), 423(1) (changed)
(3)	new
(4)	1985 s.423(1), (2) (changed)
(5), (6)	1985 s.423(3), Sch.24 (changed)
(7)	1985 s.423(4)

Chapter 3 Powers of the Secretary of State

893(1)-(9)	new
894(1), (2)	new

PART 26 ARRANGEMENTS AND RECONSTRUCTIONS

895(1)	1985 s.425(1)
(2)	1985 ss.425(6), 427(6)
(3)	drafting
896(1), (2)	1985 s.425(1)
897(1)	1985 s.426(1), (2), (3)
(2)	1985 s.426(2)
(3)	1985 s.426(4)
(4)	1985 s.426(5)
(5)-(8)	1985 s.426(6), Sch.24
898(1)-(3)	1985 s.426(7), Sch.24
899(1)	1985 s.425(2)
(2)	new
(3)	1985 s.425(2)

Section of 2006 Act	Derivation
(4)	1985 s.425(3)
900(1)	1985 s.427(1), (2)
(2)	1985 s.427(2), (3)
(3), (4)	1985 s.427(4)
(5)	1985 s.427(6)
(6)-(8)	1985 s.427(5), Sch.24
901(1), (2)	new
(3), (4)	1985 s.425(3) (changed)
(5), (6)	1985 s.425(4), Sch.24

PART 27 MERGERS AND DIVISIONS OF PUBLIC COMPANIES

Chapter 1 Introductory

902(1)	1985 s.427A(1)
(2)	drafting
(3)	1985 s.427A(4)
903(1)	1985 s.427A(1)
(2), (3)	drafting

Chapter 2 Merger

904(1)	1985 s.427A(2) Cases 1, 2
(2)	drafting
905(1)	1985 Sch.15B para.2(1)(a)
(2), (3)	1985 Sch.15B para.2(2)
906(1), (2)	1985 Sch.15B para.2(1)(b)
(3)	1985 Sch.15B para.2(1)(c)
907(1)	1985 s.425(2), Sch.15B para.1
(2)	1985 s.427A(1) closing words, Sch.15B para.1 opening words
908(1)	1985 Sch.15B para.3(a)
(2)	1985 Sch.15B para.4(1)
(3)	1985 Sch.15B para.3 opening words
909(1)	1985 Sch.15B para.3(d)
(2)	1985 Sch.15B para.5(1)
(3)	1985 Sch.15B para.5(1), (2)
(4)	1985 Sch.15B para.5(3)
(5)	1985 Sch.15B para.5(7)
(6)	1985 Sch.15B para.5(8)

Section of 2006 Act	Derivation
(7)	1985 Sch.15B para.3 opening words
910(1)	1985 Sch.15B para.6(1)(e)
(2)	1985 Sch.15B para.6(2)
(3)	1985 Sch.15B para.6(3) (changed)
(4)	1985 Sch.15B para.6(4)
911(1), (2)	1985 Sch.15B para.3(e)
(3)	1985 Sch.15B para.6(1)
(4)	1985 Sch.15B para.3 opening words
912	1985 Sch.15B para.3(f)
913(1)	1985 Sch.15B para.8(1)
(2)	1985 Sch.15B para.8(2)
914	1985 Sch.15B para.7
915(1)	1985 Sch.15B para.12(1)
(2)	1985 Sch.15B para.12(2)
(3)-(5)	1985 Sch.15B para.12(3)
(6)	1985 Sch.15B para.12(1)(a), (b)
916(1)	1985 Sch.15B para.14(1)
(2)	1985 Sch.15B para.14(2)
(3)-(5)	1985 Sch.15B paras 10(2), 14(3)
(6)	1985 Sch.15B para 14(1)(a), (b)
917(1)	1985 Sch.15B para.12(1)
(2)	1985 Sch.15B para.12(4)
(3)-(5)	1985 Sch.15B para.12(5)
(6)	1985 Sch.15B para.12(1)(a), (b)
918(1)	1985 Sch.15B para.10(1)
(2)-(4)	1985 Sch.15B para.10(2)
Chapter 3 Division	
919(1)	1985 s.427A(2) Case 3
(2)	drafting
920(1)	1985 Sch.15B para.2(1)(a)
(2)	1985 Sch.15B para.2(2)
(3)	1985 Sch.15B para.2(3)
921(1), (2)	1985 Sch.15B para.2(1)(b)
(3)	1985 Sch.15B para.2(1)(c)

Section of 2006 Act	Derivation
(4)	1985 Sch.15B para.2(1)(b), (c) opening words
922(1)	1985 s.425(2), Sch.15B para.1
(2)	1985 s.427A(1) closing words, Sch.15B para.1 opening words
923(1)	1985 Sch.15B para.3(a)
(2)	1985 Sch.15B para.4(1)
(3)	1985 Sch.15B para.4(2)
(4)	1985 Sch.15B para.3 opening words
924(1)	1985 Sch.15B para.3(d)
(2)	1985 Sch.15B para.5(1)
(3)	1985 Sch.15B para.5(1), (2)
(4)	1985 Sch.15B para.5(3)
(5)	1985 Sch.15B para.5(7)
(6)	1985 Sch.15B para.5(8)
(7)	1985 Sch.15B para.3 opening words
925(1)	1985 Sch.15B para.6(1)(e)
(2)	1985 Sch.15B para.6(2)
(3)	1985 Sch.15B para.6(3) (changed)
(4)	1985 Sch.15B para.6(4)
(5)	1985 Sch.15B para.3 opening words
926(1), (2)	1985 Sch.15B para.3(e)
(3)	1985 Sch.15B para.6(1)
(4)	1985 Sch.15B para.3 opening words
927(1)	1985 Sch.15B para.3(b)
(2)	1985 Sch.15B para.3(c)
(3)	1985 Sch.15B para.3 opening words
928	1985 Sch.15B para.3(f)
929(1)	1985 Sch.15B para.8(1)
(2)	1985 Sch.15B para.8(2)
930	1985 Sch.15B para.7
931(1)	1985 Sch.15B para.13(1)
(2)	1985 Sch.15B para.13(2)
(3)	1985 Sch.15B paras 12(5)(a), 13(3)(a)
(4)	1985 Sch.15B para.13(3)(b)
(5)	1985 Sch.15B paras 12(5)(c), 13(3)(a)

Section of 2006 Act	Derivation
(6)	1985 Sch.15B para.13(3)(c)
932(1)	1985 Sch.15B para.10(1)
(2)-(4)	1985 Sch.15B para.10(2)
(5)	1985 Sch.15B para.10(2) opening words
933(1)-(3)	1985 Sch.15B para.11(1), (2)
934(1)	1985 Sch.15B para.11(1), (3)
(2)	1985 Sch.15B para.11(4)(a), (b)
(3)	1985 Sch.15B para.11(4)(c)
(4)	1985 Sch.15B para.11(4)(d)

Chapter 4 Supplementary provisions

935(1)	1985 Sch.15B para.5(4) (changed)
(2)	1985 Sch.15B para.5(6)
936(1)-(4)	new
937(1)-(6)	new
938(1), (2)	1985 s.427A(3)
939(1)	1985 Sch.15B para.9(1), (2)
(2)	1985 Sch.15B para.9(2)
(3), (4)	1985 Sch.15B para.9(3)
(5)	1985 Sch.15B para.9(4)
940(1)	1985 Sch.15B para.15(1)
(2)	1985 Sch.15B para.15(2)
(3)	1985 Sch.15B para.15(1)
941	1985 ss.427(6), 427A(8)

PART 28 TAKEOVERS ETC

Chapter 1 The Takeover Panel

942(1)-(3)	new
943(1)-(9)	new
944(1)-(7)	new
945(1), (2)	new
946	new
947(1)-(10)	new
948(1)-(9)	new
949(1)-(3)	new
950(1), (2)	new

Section of 2006 Act	Derivation
951(1)-(5)	new
952(1)-(8)	new
953(1)-(9)	new
954(1), (2)	new
955(1)-(4)	new
956(1)-(3)	new
957(1), (2)	new
958(1)-(8)	new
959	new
960	new
961(1)-(3)	new
962(1), (2)	new
963(1), (2)	new
964(1)-(6)	new
965	new

Chapter 2 Impediments to takeovers

966(1)-(8)	new
967(1)-(7)	new
968(1)-(8)	new
969(1)-(3)	new
970(1)-(4)	new
971(1), (2)	new
972(1)-(4)	new
973	new

Chapter 3 "Squeeze-out" and "sell-out"

974(1)-(3)	1985 s.428(1), drafting
(4), (5)	1985 s.428(2)
(6)	1985 s.428(2A)
(7)	1985 s.428(7)
975(1), (2)	1985 s.428(5) (changed)
(3)	1985 s.428(6) (changed)
(4)	1985 s.430E(1)
976(1)	1985 s.428(3)
(2)	new

Section of 2006 Act	Derivation
(3)	1985 s.428(4)
977(1)	1985 s.429(8) (changed)
(2)	1985 s.430E(1) (changed)
(3)	drafting
978(1)-(3)	new
979(1), (2)	1985 s.429(1) (changed)
(3), (4)	1985 s.429(2) (changed)
(5)-(7)	new
(8)	1985 s.429(8) (changed)
(9)	1985 ss.429(8), 430E(2) (changed)
(10)	1985 s.429(8) (changed)
980(1)	1985 s.429(4)
(2)	1985 s.429(3) (changed)
(3)	new
(4)	1985 s.429(4)
(5)	1985 s.429(5)
(6)	1985 s.429(6)
(7)	1985 s.429(7)
(8)	1985 s.429(6), Sch.24
981(1)	1985 s.430(1)
(2)	1985 s.430(2)
(3)	1985 s.430(3)
(4)	1985 s.430(4)
(5)	1985 s.430(4) (changed)
(6)	1985 s.430(5), (8)
(7)	1985 s.430(6)
(8)	1985 s.430(7)
(9)	1985 s.430(9), drafting
982(1)	drafting
(2), (3)	1985 s.430(10)
(4), (5)	1985 s.430(11)
(6)	1985 s.430(12)
(7)	1985 s.430(13)
(8)	1985 s.430(14)

Section of 2006 Act	Derivation
(9)	1985 s.430(15)
983(1)	1985 s.430A(1), (1A)
(2), (3)	1985 s.430A(1) (changed)
(4)	1985 s.430A(2) (changed)
(5)	1985 s.430A(2A)
(6), (7)	new
(8)	1985 s.430E(3)
984(1)	1985 s.430A(1)
(2)	1985 s.430A(4) (changed)
(3)	1985 s.430A(3)
(4)	1985 s.430A(5)
(5)	1985 s.430A(6)
(6)	1985 s.430A(7)
(7)	1985 s.430A(6), Sch.24
985(1)	1985 s.430B(1)
(2)	1985 s.430B(2)
(3)	1985 s.430B(3)
(4)	1985 s.430B(4)
(5)	1985 s.430B(4) (changed)
986(1)	1985 s.430C(1)
(2)	1985 s.430C(1), (2)
(3)	1985 s.430C(3)
(4)	new
(5)	1985 s.430C(4)
(6)-(8)	new
(9), (10)	1985 s.430C(5)
987(1)	1985 s.430D(1)
(2), (3)	1985 s.430D(2) (changed)
(4)	1985 s.430D(4) (changed)
(5), (6)	1985 s.430D(3)
(7)	1985 s.430D(4)
(8)	1985 s.430D(5)
(9)	1985 s.430D(6)
(10)	1985 s.430D(7)

Section of 2006 Act	Derivation
988(1)	1985 s.430E(4), (8)
(2)	1985 s.430E(5)
(3)	1985 s.430E(6), (7)
(4)	1985 ss.204(2)(a), 430E(4)(d)
(5)	1985 ss.204(6), 430E(7)
(6)	1985 s.204(3)
(7)	1985 ss.204(5), 430E(7)
989(1)	1985 s.430F(1)
(2)	1985 s.430F(2)
990(1)-(3)	new
991(1)	1985 s.428(8) ("the company", "the offeror"), new ("date of the offer", "non-voting shares", "voting rights", "voting shares")
(2)	new

Chapter 4 Amendments to Part 7 of the Companies Act 1985

992(1)-(6)	new (amends 1985 Pt 7)

PART 29 FRAUDULENT TRADING

993(1)-(3)	1985 s.458, Sch.24

PART 30 PROTECTION OF MEMBERS AGAINST UNFAIR PREJUDICE

994(1)	1985 s.459(1)
(2)	1985 s.459(2)
(3)	1985 s.459(3)
995(1)	1985 s.460(1A)
(2), (3)	1985 s.460(1)
(4)	1985 s.460(2)
996(1)	1985 s.461(1)
(2)	1985 s.461(2), (3)
997	1985 s.461(6)
998(1)-(4)	1985 s.461(5)
999(1)-(5)	new

PART 31 DISSOLUTION AND RESTORATION TO THE REGISTER

Chapter 1 Striking off

1000(1)	1985 s.652(1)
(2)	1985 s.652(2)
(3)	1985 s.652(3)

Section of 2006 Act	**Derivation**
(4)-(6)	1985 s.652(5)
(7)	1985 s.652(6)
1001(1)	1985 s.652(4)
(2)-(4)	1985 s.652(5)
(5)	1985 s.652(6)
1002(1)-(3)	1985 s.652(7)
1003(1)	1985 s.652A(1) (changed)
(2)	1985 s.652A(2) (changed)
(3)	1985 s.652A(3)
(4)	1985 s.652A(4)
(5)	1985 s.652A(5)
(6)	1985 s.652A(6), (7)
1004(1)	1985 s.652B(1)
(2)	1985 s.652B(2)
(3)	1985 s.652B(9)
(4)	1985 ss.652D(5)(c)
(5)	1985 s.652E(1)
(6)	1985 s.652E(3)
(7)	1985 s.652E(1), Sch.24
1005(1)	1985 s.652B(3)
(2)	1985 s.652B(4)
(3)	1985 s.652B(5)
(4)	1985 s.652E(1)
(5)	1985 s.652E(3)
(6)	1985 s.652E(1), Sch.24
1006(1)	1985 ss.652B(6), 652D(5)(c)
(2)	1985 s.652B(7)
(3)	1985 s.652B(8)
(4)	1985 s.652E(1), (2)
(5)	1985 s.652E(4)
(6)	1985 s.652E(1), Sch.24
(7)	1985 s.652E(2), Sch.24
1007(1)	1985 s.652C(1)
(2)	1985 ss.652C(2), 652D(5)(c)

Section of 2006 Act	Derivation
(3)	1985 s.652C(3)
(4)	1985 s.652E(1), (2)
(5)	1985 s.652E(5)
(6)	1985 s.652E(1), Sch.24
(7)	1985 s.652E(2), Sch.24
1008(1), (2)	1985 s.652D(1)
(3)	1985 s.652D(2), (3)
(4)	1985 s.652D(4)
1009(1)	1985 s.652C(4)
(2)	1985 s.652C(5)
(3)	1985 s.652C(7)
(4)	1985 ss.652C(6), 652D(5)(c)
(5)	1985 s.652E(1)
(6)	1985 s.652E(5)
(7)	1985 s.652E(1), Sch.24
1010	1985 s.652D(6)
1011	1985 s.652D(8)

Chapter 2 Property of dissolved company

1012(1)	1985 s.654(1)
(2)	1985 s.654(2)
1013(1)	1985 s.656(1)
(2)	1985 s.656(2) (changed)
(3)-(5)	1985 s.656(3) (changed)
(6), (7)	1985 s.656(5)
(8)	1985 s.656(6)
1014(1)	1985 s.657(1)
(2)	drafting
1015(1), (2)	1985 s.657(2), IA 1986 s.178(4)
1016(1)	1985 s.657(2), IA 1986 s.179(1)
(2)	1985 s.657(2), IA 1986 s.179(2)
(3)	drafting
1017(1)	1985 s.657(2), 1A 1986 s.181(2), (3)
(2)	1985 s.657(2), 1A 1986 s.181(3)
(3)	1985 s.657(2), 1A 1986 s.181(4)

Section of 2006 Act	Derivation
(4)	1985 s.657(2), 1A 1986 s.181(3)
(5)	1985 s.657(2), 1A 1986 s.181(6)
1018(1)	1985 s.657(2), 1A 1986 s.182(1)
(2)	1985 s.657(2), 1A 1986 s.182(2)
(3)	1985 s.657(2), 1A 1986 s.182(4)
(4), (5)	1985 s.657(2), 1A 1986 s.182(3)
1019	1985 s.657(2), 1A 1986 s.180(1), (2)
1020(1), (2)	1985 s.657(4)
1021(1), (2)	1985 s.657(5)
(3)	1985 s.657(6)
1022(1)	1985 Sch.20 para.5
(2)	1985 Sch.20 para.6
(3)	1985 Sch.20 para.7
(4), (5)	1985 Sch.20 para.8
(6)	1985 Sch.20 para.9
1023(1)	1985 s.658(1), IA s.180(1)
(2)	1985 s.658(1), IA s.180(2)
(3)	1985 s.658(2)

Chapter 3 Restoration to the register

1024(1)-(4)	new
1025(1)-(6)	new
1026(1)-(3)	new
1027(1)-(4)	new
1028(1)-(4)	new
1029(1), (2)	new
1030(1)-(6)	new
1031(1)-(4)	new
1032(1)-(5)	new
1033(1)-(7)	new
1034(1)	1985 s.655(1)
(2)	1985 s.655(2)
(3)	new
(4)	1985 s.655(3)
(5)	1985 s.655(4)

Section of 2006 Act	Derivation
(6)	drafting

PART 32 COMPANY INVESTIGATIONS: AMENDMENTS

1035(1)-(5)	new (inserts 1985 ss.446A, 446B; amends 1985 ss.431, 432, 437, 442)
1036	new (inserts 1985 ss.446C, 446D)
1037(1)-(3)	new (inserts 1985 s.446E; amends 1985 ss.451A, 452)
1038(1), (2)	new (amends 1985 ss.434, 447)
1039	new (amends Company Directors Disqualification Act 1986 s.8)

PART 33 UK COMPANIES NOT FORMED UNDER THE COMPANIES LEGISLATION

Chapter 1 Companies not formed under companies legislation but authorised to register

1040(1)	1985 s.680(1)(a), (b), (1A), (2)
(2), (3)	1985 s.680(1) (closing words)
(4)	1985 s.680(3), (4)
(5)	1985 s.680(5)
(6)	1985 s.680(1) (closing words)
1041(1)	1985 s.683(1)
(2)	1985 s.683(2)
1042(1)-(3)	new

Chapter 2 Unregistered companies

1043(1)	1985 s.718(1), (2)
(2)	1985 s.718(3) (changed)
(3)	1985 s.718(1) (changed)
(4)	1985 s.718(5)
(5)	1985 s.718(1), (3)
(6)	1985 s.718(6)

PART 34 OVERSEAS COMPANIES

1044	1985 s.744 ("overseas company") (changed)
1045(1), (2)	CA 1989 s.130(6)
1046(1)-(8)	new
1047(1)-(6)	new
1048(1), (2)	1985 s.694(4) (changed)
(3)-(5)	1985 s.694(5)
1049(1)-(4)	new

Section of 2006 Act	Derivation
1050(1)-(6)	new
1051(1)-(5)	new
1052(1)-(6)	new
1053(1)-(6)	new
1054(1)-(4)	new
1055	new
1056	new
1057(1)-(3)	new
1058(1)-(4)	new
1059	1985 s.695A(4)

PART 35 THE REGISTRAR OF COMPANIES

Section of 2006 Act	Derivation
1060(1), (2)	1985 s.704(2)
(3)	1985 s.744 ("the registrar of companies", "the registrar")
(4)	drafting
1061(1)-(3)	drafting
1062	1985 s.704(4) (changed)
1063(1)-(3)	1985 s.708(1) (changed)
(4)	1985 s.708(2), (3) (changed)
(5)	1985 s.708(5) (changed)
(6)	1985 s.708(4)
(7)	new
1064(1)-(3)	1985 s.711(1)(a) (changed)
1065	1985 s.710
1066(1)-(3)	1985 s.705(1)-(3)
(4), (5)	1985 s.705(4)
(6)	1985 s.705(5)(za)
1067(1)	1985 s.705A(1), (2) (changed)
(2)	1985 s.705A(3)
(3)	1985 s.705A(4)
(4), (5)	1985 s.705A(5)
1068(1)-(7)	new
1069(1)-(3)	new
1070(1)-(3)	new
1071(1), (2)	new

Section of 2006 Act	Derivation
1072(1), (2)	new
1073(1)-(6)	new
1074(1)-(5)	new
1075(1)-(7)	new
1076(1)-(4)	new
1077(1)	1985 s.711(1) opening words
(2), (3)	new
1078(1)	drafting
(2), (3)	1985 s.711(1) (changed)
(4)	new
(5), (6)	new
1079(1)-(3)	1985 s.42(1)
(4)	1985 s.711(2) (changed)
1080(1), (2)	drafting
(3)	new
(4)	1985 s.707A(1)
(5)	new
1081(1)-(7)	new
1082(1)-(5)	new
1083(1)	1985 s.707A(2) (changed)
(2), (3)	new
1084(1)-(3)	1985 s.707A(3) (changed)
(4)	1985 s.707A(4)
(5)	1985 s.707A(3)
1085(1)	1985 s.709(1)
(2)	1985 s.709(2) (changed)
(3)	drafting
1086(1)	1985 s.709(1)(a), (b)
(2)	new
(3)	drafting
1087(1)-(3)	new
1088(1)-(6)	new
1089(1), (2)	new
1090(1)-(4)	new

Section of 2006 Act	Derivation
1091(1), (2)	new
(3)	1985 s.709(3)
(4)	new
(5)	1985 s.709(4)
1092(1), (2)	1985 s.709(5)
1093(1)-(4)	new
1094(1)-(5)	new
1095(1)-(6)	new
1096(1)-(6)	new
1097(1)-(5)	new
1098(1), (2)	new
1099(1)-(3)	1985 s.714(1) (changed)
(4), (5)	1985 s.714(2)
1100	1985 s.709(1)
1101(1), (2)	new
1102(1)-(4)	new
1103(1), (2)	new
1104(1), (2)	1985 s.710B(1)-(3)
(3)	1985 s.710B(4)
(4)	1985 s.710B(5)
(5)	drafting
1105(1)-(3)	new
1106(1)-(6)	new
1107(1)	drafting
1107(2), (3)	new
1108(1)-(3)	new
1109(1), (2)	new
1110(1)-(3)	new
1111(1)-(3)	new
1112(1), (2)	new
1113(1)-(3)	1985 s.713(1)
(4), (5)	1985 s.713(2), (3)
1114(1)	1985 s.715A(1) "document", (2)
(2)	new

Section of 2006 Act	Derivation
1115(1)	new
(2)	1985 s.710A(2)
1116(1)-(6)	new
1117(1)-(3)	new
1118	drafting
1119(1), (2)	1985 s.704(7), (8)
(3)	new
1120	new

PART 36 OFFENCES UNDER THE COMPANIES ACTS

1121(1)	1985 s.730(5)
(2)	1985 s.744 "officer"
(3)	1985 s.730(5) (changed)
1122(1)-(3)	new
1123(1)-(4)	new
1124, Sch.3	new (amend 1985 Act)
1125(1)	drafting
(2)	1985 s.730(4)
1126(1)	1985 s.732(1)
(2)	1985 s.732(2) (changed)
(3)	1986 Order art.680(2) (changed)
1127(1), (2)	1985 s.731(1)
1128(1)	1985 s.731(2)
(2)	1985 s.731(3)
(3)	1986 Order art.679(2)
(4)	1985 s.731(4), 1986 Order art.679(3)
1129	1985 s.732(3) (changed)
1130(1)	1985 s.734(1) (changed)
(2)	1985 s.734(1), (3), (4)
(3)	1985 s.734(2)
1131(1), (2)	new
1132(1), (2)	1985 s.721(1)
(3)	1985 s.721(2)
(4)	1985 s.721(3)
(5)	1985 s.721(4)

Section of 2006 Act	Derivation
(6)	drafting
1133	new

PART 37 COMPANIES: SUPPLEMENTARY PROVISIONS

Section of 2006 Act	Derivation
1134	1985 s.722(1) (changed)
1135(1)	1985 ss.722(1), 723(1) (changed)
(2)	new
(3), (4)	new
(5)	1985 s.723(2)
1136(1)-(7)	new
1137(1), (2)	1985 s.723A(1)
(3)	1985 s.723A(2), (3)
(4)	1985 s.723A(4)
(5), (6)	1985 s.723A(6), (7)
1138(1)	1985 s.722(2)
(2), (3)	1985 s.722(3), Sch.24
(4)	new
1139(1)	1985 s.725(1)
(2)	1985 s.695(1), (2) (changed)
(3)	new
(4)	1985 s.725(2), (3)
(5)	drafting
1140(1)-(8)	new
1141(1)	drafting
(2), (3)	new
1142	new
1143(1)-(4), Schs 4, 5	new
1144(1)-(3)	new
1145(1)-(5)	new
1146(1)-(4)	new
1147(1)-(6)	new
1148(1)-(3)	new
1149	drafting
1150(1)	1985 s.108(1) (changed)
(2), (3)	1985 s.108(2), (3)

Section of 2006 Act	Derivation
(4)	1985 s.108(5)
1151(1)-(4)	new
1152(1)-(6)	new
1153(1)	1985 s.110(1)
(2), (3)	1985 s.110(2), (3)
(4)	1985 s.110(2), Sch.24
1154(1)-(4)	new
1155(1), (2)	new
1156(1)-(3)	1985 s.744 "the court", IA 1986 s.117 (changed)
1157(1)-(3)	1985 s.727(1)-(3)
	(3), (4)

PART 38 COMPANIES: INTERPRETATION

1158	drafting
1159(1), (2)	1985 s.736(1), (2)
(3), Sch.6	1985 s.736A(1)-(11)
(4)	1985 ss.736(3), 736A(12)
1160(1)	1985 s.736B(1)
(2)-(4)	1985 s.736B(3)-(5)
1161(1)-(5)	1985 s.259(1)-(5)
1162(1)-(5)	1985 s.258(1)-(5)
(6), Sch.7	1985 s.258(6), Sch.10A
1163(1), (2)	1985 s.739(1), (2)
1164(1)-(3)	1985 s.742B(1)-(3)
(4)	1985 s.255A(4)
(5)	1985 s.255A(5A)
1165(1)	drafting
(2)-(4)	1985 s.742C(1)-(4)
(5)	1985 s.255A(5)
(6)	1985 s.255A(5A)
(7)	1985 s.744 "insurance market activity"
(8)	1985 s.742C(5)
1166	1985 s.743
1167	1985 s.744 "prescribed"
1168(1)-(7)	new

Section of 2006 Act	Derivation
1169(1)	1985 s.249AA(4)
(2), (3)	1985 s.249AA(5)-(7)
(4)	drafting
1170	1985 s.744 "EEA State", drafting
1171 "the former Companies Acts"	1985 s.735(1)(c) (changed)
"the Joint Stock Companies Acts"	1985 s.735(3)
1172	drafting
1173(1) "body corporate", "corporation"	new
"credit institution"	1985 s.262 "credit institution" (changed)
"financial institution"	1985 s.699A(3) "financial institution"
"firm"	new
"the Gazette"	1985 s.744 "the Gazette"
"hire-purchase agreement"	1985 s.744 "hire purchase agreement"
"officer"	1985 s.744 "officer"
"parent company"	1985 ss.258(1), 742(1)
"regulated activity"	1985 s.744 "regulated activity"
"regulated market"	1985 (throughout) (changed)
"working day"	drafting
(2)	drafting
1174, Sch.8	drafting

PART 39 COMPANIES: MINOR AMENDMENTS

1175(1), (2), Sch.9	new (amend 1985 Pt 7, 1986 Order Pt 8)
1176(1)-(3)	new (repeals 1985 s.438, amends 1985 ss.439, 453)
1177	new (repeals 1985 ss.311, 323-329, Pts 2-4 of Sch.13, ss.343, 344)
1178	new (repeals 1985 s.720, Sch.23)
1179	new (repeals 1985 s.729)
1180	new (repeals 1985 Pt 4)
1181(1)-(4)	new (power to amend)

PART 40 COMPANY DIRECTORS: FOREIGN DISQUALIFICATION ETC

1182	new
1183	new
1184	new
1185	new

Section of 2006 Act	Derivation
1186	new
1187	new
1188	new
1189	new
1190	new
1191	new

PART 41 BUSINESS NAMES

Chapter 1 Restricted or prohibited names

1192(1), (2)	BNA 1985 s.1(1) (changed)
(3)	BNA 1985 s.1(2) (changed)
1193(1)	BNA 1985 s.2(1) (changed)
(2)	BNA 1985 s.8(1) (changed)
(3)	BNA 1985 s.6(2) (changed)
(4)	BNA 1985 ss.2(4), 7(2) (changed)
(5)	BNA 1985 s.7(4) (changed)
(6)	BNA 1985 s.7(1), (2), (3) (changed)
1194(1)	BNA 1985 s.2(1) (changed)
(2)	BNA 1985 s.6(2) (changed)
(3)	BNA 1985 ss.2(4), 7(2) (changed)
(4)	BNA 1985 s.7(4) (changed)
(5)	BNA 1985 s.7(1), (2), (3) (changed)
1195(1)	BNA 1985 s.3(2) (changed)
(2)	BNA 1985 s.3(2)(a) (changed)
(3)	BNA 1985 s.3(2)(b) (changed)
(4), (5)	new
1196	new
1197(1)-(3)	1985 s.33, 34, 34A (changed)
(4)	BNA 1985 s.6(2) (changed)
(5)	1985 s.33(2), 34, 34A(1), (2) (changed)
(6)	1985 s.33(3), 34A(5), BNA 1985, s.7(4) (changed)
(7)	1985 s.33(3), 34A(5), BNA 1985, s.7(1), (2), (3) (changed)
1198	new
1199	new

Section of 2006 Act	Derivation
Chapter 2 Disclosure required in case of individual or partnership	
1200(1), (2)	BNA 1985 s.1(1) (changed)
1200(3)	BNA 1985 s.1(2) (changed)
1201	BNA 1985 s.4(1)(a) (changed)
1202(1)	BNA 1985 s.4(1)(a) (changed)
(2)	BNA 1985 s.4(2) (changed)
(3)	BNA 1985 s.4(5)
(4)	BNA 1985 s.6(3) (changed)
1203(1), (2)	BNA 1985 s.4(3)
(3)	BNA 1985 s.4(4)
(4), (5)	BNA 1985 s.4(7) (changed)
1204(1)	BNA 1985 s.4(1)(b) (changed)
(2)	BNA 1985 s.4(5)
(3)	BNA 1985 s.6(3) (changed)
1205(1)	BNA 1985 s.7 (changed)
(2)	BNA 1985 s.7(4) (changed)
(3)	BNA 1985 s.7(2), changed)
(4)	new
1206(1), (2)	BNA 1985 s.5(1)
(3)	new
(4)	BNA 1985 s.5(2)
Chapter 3 Supplementary	
1207	BNA 1985, s.7(6) (changed)
1208	BNA 1985, s.8(1) (changed)
PART 42 STATUTORY AUDITORS	
Chapter 1 Introductory	
1209	CA 1989 s.24(1) (changed)
1210(1)	CA 1989 s.24(2) (changed)
(2)-(4)	new
1211	new
Chapter 2 Individuals and firms	
1212(1)	CA 1989 s.25(1), (2) (changed)
(2)	CA 1989 s.25(3)
1213(1)	CA 1989 s.28(1)

Section of 2006 Act	Derivation
(2)	CA 1989 s.28(2)
(3), (4)	CA 1989 s.28(3)
(5)-(7)	CA 1989 s.28(4)
(8)	CA 1989 s.28(5)
1214(1)-(3), (5)	CA 1989 s.27(1)
(4)	CA 1989 s.27(2)
(6)	CA 1989 s.27(3)
(7)	CA 1989 s.27(4)
1215(1)	CA 1989 s.28(2)
(2), (3)	CA 1989 s.28(3)
(4)-(6)	CA 1989 s,28(4)
(7)	CA 1989 s,28(5)
1216(1)	CA 1989 s.26(1)
(2)	CA 1989 s.26(2)
(3)	CA 1989 s.26(3)
(4)	CA 1989 s.26(4)
(5)	CA 1989 s.26(5)
(6)	new
1217(1)	CA 1989 s.30(1)
(2)	CA 1989 s.30(2)
(3)	CA 1989 s.30(3)
(4)	CA 1989 s.30(5)
1218(1), (2)	CA 1989 s.48(1)
(3)	CA 1989 s.48(2)
(4)	CA 1989 s.30(4)
(5)	CA 1989 s.48(1)
1219(1)	CA 1989 s.31(1), (6)
(2)	CA 1989 s.31(4)
(3)	CA 1989 s.31(5)
1220(1)	CA 1989 s.32(1)
(2)	CA 1989 s.32(2)
(3)	CA 1989 s.32(4)
1221(1)	CA 1989 s.33(1)
(2)	CA 1989 s.33(1A)

Section of 2006 Act	Derivation
(3)	CA 1989 s.33(2)
(4)	CA 1989 s.33(3)
(5)	CA 1989 s.33(4)
(6)	CA 1989 s.33(5)
(7), (8)	CA 1989 s.33(6)
(9)	new
1222(1)	CA 1989 s.34(1)
(2)	CA 1989 s.34(2)
(3)	CA 1989 s.34(4)
1223(1)	CA 1989 s.37(1)
(2)	CA 1989 s.37(2)
(3)	CA 1989 s.37(3)
(4)	CA 1989 s.37(4)
1224(1), (2)	CA 1989 s.38(1)
(3)	CA 1989 s.38(2)
1225(1)	CA 1989 s.39(1)
(2)	CA 1989 s.39(2)
(3)	CA 1989 s.39(3)

Chapter 3 Auditors General

1226	new
1227	new
1228	new
1229	new
1230	new
1231	new
1232	new
1233	new
1234	new
1235	new
1236	new
1237	new
1238	new

Chapter 4 The register of auditors etc

1239(1)	CA 1989 s.35(1) (changed)

Section of 2006 Act	Derivation
(2)	CA 1989 s.35(2) (changed)
(3), (4)	new
(5)	CA 1989 s.35(3) (changed)
(6)	CA 1989 s.35(4)(changed)
(7)	new
(8)	CA 1989 s.35(6)
(9)	new
(10)	CA 1989 s.35(5)
1240	new

Chapter 5 Registered third country auditors

1241	new
1242	new
1243	new
1244	new
1245	new
1246	new
1247	new

Chapter 6 Supplementary and general

1248(1), (2)	CA 1989 s.29(1) (changed)
(3)	
(4)	CA 1989 s.29(1) (changed)
(5)	CA 1989 s.29(5) (changed)
(6)	CA 1989 s.29(3) (changed)
(7), (8)	CA 1989 s.29(5) (changed)
1249(1)	CA 1989 s.29(7) (changed)
(2)	CA 1989 s.29(4) (changed)
(3)	CA 1989 s.29(6) (changed)
1250(1)	CA 1989 s.41(1) (changed)
(2)	CA 1989 s.41(2) (changed)
(3)	new
(4)	CA 1989 s.41(3) (changed)
(5)	CA 1989 s.41(4) (changed)
(6), (7)	CA 1989 s.41(5) (changed)
(8)	CA 1989 s.41(6) (changed)

Section of 2006 Act	Derivation
1251(1)	CA 1989 s.45(1), (3) (changed)
(2)	CA 1989 s.45(2) (changed)
(3)	CA 1989 s.45(5) (changed)
(4)	CA 1989 s.45(4) (changed)
1252(1)	CA 1989 s.46(1)
(2)	CA 1989 s.46(1A) (changed)
(3)	CA 1989 s.46(2) (changed)
(4)	CA 1989 s.46(3) (changed)
(5)	CA 1989 s.46(2) (changed)
(6), (7)	CA 1989 s.46(3) (changed)
(8)	CA 1989 s.46(4) (changed)
(9)	CA 1989 s.46(5)
(10)	CA 1989 s.46(6)
(11), (12)	CA 1989 s.46(8) (changed)
1253(1)	CA 1989 s.46A(1)
(2)	CA 1989 s.46A(2)
(3)	CA 1989 s.46A(3)
(4)	CA 1989 s.46A(4)
(5)	CA 1989 s.46A(5) (changed)
1254(1)	CA 1989 s.40(1)
(2)	CA 1989 s.40(2)
(3)	CA 1989 s.40(3)
1255(1)	CA 1989 s.42(1) (changed)
(2)	CA 1989 s.42(3)
(3)	CA 1989 s.42(4)
1256(1)	CA 1989 s.43(1)
(2), (3)	CA 1989 s.43(2)
(4)	new
(5)	CA 1989 s.43(3) (changed)
(6)	CA 1989 s.43(4) (changed)
(7)	CA 1989 s.43(5) (changed)
1257(1)	CA 1989 s.44(1)
(2)	CA 1989 s.44(2)
(3)	CA 1989 s.44(3)

Section of 2006 Act	Derivation
(4)	new
(5)	CA 1989 s.44(4)
(6)	CA 1989 s.44(5)
1258(1)	CA 1989 s.49(1)
(2)	CA 1989 s.49(2)
(3)	CA 1989 s.49(3) (changed)
(4)	CA 1989 s.49(4) (changed)
1259	new
1260(1)	CA 1989 s.52(1)
(2)	CA 1989 s.52(2)
(3)	CA 1989 s.52(3)
(4)	CA 1989 s.52(4)
(5)	CA 1989 s.52(5)
(6)	new
1261(1)	CA 1989 s.53(1) (changed)
(2)	CA 1989 s.53(2)
(3)	new
(4)	new
1262	CA 1989 s.54 (changed)
1263(1)	CA 1989 s.51(1) (changed)
(2)	CA 1989 s.51(2) (changed)
1264	new (See 1985 s.50 (changed))

PART 43 TRANSPARENCY OBLIGATIONS AND RELATED MATTERS

1265	new
1266	new
1267	new
1268	new
1269	new
1270	new
1271	new
1272	new
1273	new

PART 44 MISCELLANEOUS PROVISIONS

1274	new (see C(AICE)A 2004, s.l6(2), (5) (changed))

Section of 2006 Act	Derivation
1275	new (see C(AICE)A 2004, s.17(3), (4), (12), Pensions Act 2004, Sch.3 (changed))
1276	new (see C(AICE)A 2004, s.16(2), (5), (6), 66 (changed))
1277	new
1278	new
1279	new
1280	new
1281	new
1282	new
1283	new

PART 45 NORTHERN IRELAND

1284	new
1285	new
1286	new
1287	new

PART 46 GENERAL SUPPLEMENTARY PROVISIONS

1288	new
1289	new
1290	new
1291	new
1292	new
1293	1985 s.448A(5) (changed)
1294	new
1295	new
1296	new
1297	new

PART 47 FINAL PROVISIONS

1298	1985 s.747 (changed)
1299	1985 s.745 (changed)
1300(1)	1985 s.746 (changed)
(2)	new

Section of 2006 Act	*Derivation*

SCHEDULES

SCHEDULE 1 CONNECTED PERSONS: REFERENCES TO AN INTEREST IN SHARES OR DEBENTURES

para.1	new
para.2(1)	1985 Sch.13, para.1(1) (changed)
(2)	1985 Sch.13, para.1(1) (changed)
(3)	1985 Sch.13, para.8 (changed)
(4)	1985 Sch.13, para.7
para.3(1)	1985 Sch.13, para.3(1)(a) (changed)
(2)	1985 Sch.13, para.6(1) (changed)
(3)	1985 Sch.13, para.6(2) (changed)
(4)	1985 Sch.13, para.13 (changed)
para.4(1)	1985 Sch.13, para.3(1)(b) (changed)
(2)	1985 Sch.13, para.3(2) (changed)
(3)	1985 Sch.13, para.3(3) (changed)
para.5(1)	1985 Sch.13, para.4 (changed)
(2)	1985 Sch.13, para.5 (changed)
para.6(1)	1985 Sch.13, para.2 (changed)
(2)	1985 Sch.13, para.9 (changed)
(3)	1985 Sch.13, para.10 (changed)
(4)	1985 Sch.13, para.11 (changed)
(5)	1985 Sch.13, para.12 (changed)

SCHEDULE 2 SPECIFIED PERSONS, DESCRIPTIONS OF DISCLOSURES ETC FOR THE PURPOSES OF SECTION 948

paras 1-73	new

SCHEDULE 3 AMENDMENTS OF REMAINING PROVISIONS OF THE COMPANIES ACT 1985 RELATING TO OFFENCES

para.1	amends 1985 s.444
para.2	amends 1985 s.448
para.3	amends 1985 s.449
para.4	amends 1985 s.450
para.5	amends 1985 s.451
para.6	amends 1985 s.453A
para.7	amends 1985 s.451

Section of 2006 Act	Derivation

SCHEDULE 4 DOCUMENTS AND INFORMATION SENT OR SUPPLIED TO A COMPANY

paras 1-8	new

SCHEDULE 5 COMMUNICATIONS BY A COMPANY

paras 1-17	new

SCHEDULE 6 MEANING OF "SUBSIDIARY" ETC: SUPPLEMENTARY PROVISIONS

para.1	1985 Sch.10A, para.1 (changed)
para.2	1985 Sch.10A, para.2(1) (changed)
para.3	1985 Sch.10A, para.3 (changed)
para.4	1985 Sch.10A, para.5
para.5	1985 Sch.10A, para.6
para.6	1985 Sch.10A, para.7
para.7	1985 Sch.10A, para.8
para.8	1985 Sch.10A, para.9 (changed)
para.9	1985 Sch.10A, para.10 (changed)
para.10	1985 Sch.10A, para.11

SCHEDULE 7 PARENT AND SUBSIDIARY UNDERTAKINGS: SUPPLEMENTARY PROVISIONS

para.1	1985 Sch.10A, para.1
para.2	1985 Sch.10A, para.2
para.3	1985 Sch.10A, para.3
para.4	1985 Sch.10A, para.4
para.5	1985 Sch.10A, para.5
para.6	1985 Sch.10A, para.6
para.7	1985 Sch.10A, para.7
para.8	1985 Sch.10A, para.8
para.9	1985 Sch.10A, para.9
para.10	1985 Sch.10A, para.10
para.11	1985 Sch.10A, para.11

SCHEDULE 8 INDEX OF DEFINED EXPRESSIONS

	1985 ss.262A, 744A (changed)

SCHEDULE 9 REMOVAL OF SPECIAL PROVISIONS ABOUT ACCOUNTS AND AUDIT OF CHARITABLE COMPANIES

	New (amends 1985 ss.240, 245, 249A, 249B, 249C, 249D, 249E, 262A, 1986 Order arts 248, 253, 257A, 257B, 257C, 257D, 257E, 270A)

Section of 2006 Act	Derivation
SCHEDULE 10 RECOGNISED SUPERVISORY BODIES	
para.1	CA 1989 Sch.11, para.1 (changed)
para.2	CA 1989 Sch.11, para.2
para.3	CA 1989 Sch.11, para.3
para.4	new
para.5	new
para.6	CA 1989 Sch.11, para.4 (changed)
para.7	CA 1989 Sch.11, para.5 (changed)
para.8	CA 1989 Sch.11, para.6 (changed)
para.9	CA 1989 Sch.11, para.7 (changed)
para.10	CA 1989 Sch.11, para.8 (changed)
para.11	CA 1989 Sch.11, para.9 (changed)
para.12	CA 1989 Sch.11, para.10
para.13	CA 1989 Sch.11, para.10A (changed)
para.14	CA 1989 Sch.11, para.11 (changed)
para.15	CA 1989 Sch.11, para.12 (changed)
para.16	CA 1989 Sch.11, para.12A
para.17	CA 1989 Sch.11, para.13 (changed)
para.18	CA 1989 Sch.11, para.14 (changed)
para.10	CA 1989 Sch.11, para.15
para.20	CA 1989 Sch.11, para.16 (changed)
para.21	CA 1989 Sch.11, para.17
para.22	CA 1989 Sch.11, para.18
para.23	CA 1989 Sch.11, para.19 (changed)
para.24	CA 1989 Sch.11, para.20 (changed)
para.25	CA 1989 Sch.11, para.21
para.26	CA 1989 Sch.11, para.22(1)
para.27	CA 1989 Sch.11, para.22 (2)
SCHEDULE 11 RECOGNISED PROFESSIONAL QUALIFICATIONS	
para.1	CA 1989 Sch.12, para.1 (changed)
para.2	CA 1989 Sch.12, para.2 (changed)
para.3	CA 1989 Sch.12, para.3
para.4	new
para.5	new

Section of 2006 Act	Derivation
para.6(1)-(3)	CA 1989 Sch.12, para.4
(4)	CA 1989 Sch.12, para.6(1)
para.7(1)	CA 1989 Sch.12, para.5
(2)	CA 1989 Sch.12, para.6(1)
para.8	CA 1989 Sch.12, para.7
para.9	CA 1989 Sch.12, para.8
para.10(1)	CA 1989 Sch.12, para.6(2)
(2)	CA 1989 Sch.12, para.6(3)
para.11	CA 1989 Sch.12, para.9

SCHEDULE 12 ARRANGEMENTS IN WHICH REGISTERED THIRD COUNTRY AUDITORS ARE REQUIRED TO PARTICIPATE

paras 1-6	new

SCHEDULE 13 SUPPLEMENTARY PROVISIONS WITH RESPECT TO DELEGATION ORDER

para.1	CA 1989 Sch.13, para.1
para.2	CA 1989 Sch.13, para.2
para.3	CA 1989 Sch.13, para.3
para.4	CA 1989 Sch.13, para.4
para.5	CA 1989 Sch.13, para.5
para.6	CA 1989 Sch.13, para.6
para.7(1)-(3)	CA 1989 Sch.13, para.7(1)-(3)
(4)	new
para.8	CA 1989 Sch.13, para.8
para.9	CA 1989 Sch.13, para.9
para.10	CA 1989 Sch.13, para.10 (changed)
para.11	CA 1989 Sch.13, para.11
para.12	CA 1989 Sch.13, para.12
para.13	CA 1989 Sch.13, para.13

SCHEDULE 14 STATUTORY AUDITORS: CONSEQUENTIAL AMENDMENTS

	new (amends Companies (Audit, Investigations and Community Enterprise) Act 2004, s.16(2), (5))

Section of 2006 Act   *Derivation*

SCHEDULE 15 TRANSPARENCY OBLIGATIONS AND RELATED MATTERS: MINOR AND CONSEQUENTIAL AMENDMENTS

new (amends Financial Services and Markets Act 2000, ss.73, 73A, 90 (heading), 91, 97, 99, 102A, 103, 429, Companies (Audit, Investigations and Community Enterprise) Act 2004, ss.14, 15)

SCHEDULE 16 REPEALS

new

APPENDIX IV

TABLE OF DESTINATIONS

The table below identifies the provisions of the Companies Act 1985 (c.6), the Business Names Act 1985 (c.7) and the extant, substantive (non-amending) provisions in the Companies Act 1989 (c.40) that are repealed and re-enacted (with or without changes) by the Companies Act 2006 and identifies the corresponding provisions in the 2006 Act. The repeals are by s.1295 of and Sch.16 to the 2006 Act although certain provisions also cease to have effect by virtue of ss.1176 and 1177 of the Act and these latter are marked separately. A provision of the Companies Act 1985, Business Names Act 1985 or Companies Act 1989 which is repealed by the Companies Act 2006 but not re-enacted (even in amended form) in the 2006 Act may be listed in this table and described as "repealed", whereas provisions which were repealed by other legislation before the Companies Act 2006 received Royal Assent on November 8, 2006, are not included. Note that Pt XIV (ss.431-453, investigations, and related Sch.15C and 15D) and Pt XV (ss.454-457, orders imposing restrictions on shares) are the main substantive provisions of the Companies Act 1985 that are not repealed by the Companies Act 2006 and remain in force, although s.438 in Pt XIV is repealed. Those provisions in the Companies Act 2006 which are re-enacted in an amended form are marked "(changed)".

There is no entry for Sch.24 to the Companies Act 1985 (punishment of offences) in this table since there is no direct equivalent in the Companies Act 2006, which provides criminal penalties in the relevant sections of the Act rather than in a separate schedule thereto.

The table includes destinations for the remaining provisions in Pt XVIII (ss.462-487) of the Companies Act 1985 (Floating Charges and Receivers (Scotland)) that are re-enacted (subject to amendment) in Pt 2 (ss.37-49) of the Bankruptcy and Diligence etc. (Scotland) Act 2007. Part XVIII of the 1985 Act is repealed by s.46(1) of the Bankruptcy and Diligence etc. (Scotland) Act 2007.

See Appendix II for the remaining substantive provisions of the Companies Act 1985, the Companies Act 1989 and the Companies (Audit, Investigations and Community Enterprise) Act 2004 which are not repealed by the Companies Act 2006 and will continue in force after the Companies Act 2006 is fully operative.

The entries in the table should only be taken as a guide. The table has no official status and has been adapted from a table (relating to the Companies Act 1985 only) prepared by the Department of Trade and Industry which has been considerably amended and extended.

COMPANIES ACT 1985

Provision of Companies Act 1985	*Destination in Companies Act 2006*

PART I FORMATION AND REGISTRATION OF COMPANIES; JURIDICAL STATUS AND MEMBERSHIP

Chapter I Company Formation

s.1 Mode of forming incorporated company

(1)	ss.7(1), (2), 8(1) (changed)
(2)	s.3(1)(4)
(3)	ss.4(1)(3), 9(2)
(3A)	s.7(1) (changed)
(4)	s.5(1), (2)

s.2 Requirements with respect to memorandum

(1)	s.9(2)
(2)	ss.9(2), 88(2)
(3)	s.9(2) (changed)
(4)	s.11(3) (changed)
2(5)	ss.8(1), 10(2), (4)

Provision of Companies Act 1985	Destination in Companies Act 2006
2(6)	ss.8(2), 1146(2) (changed)
2(6A)	ss.8(2), 1146(3) (changed)
2(7)	repealed

s.3 Forms of memorandum

(1)	s.8(2)
(2)	repealed

s.3A Statement of company's objects: general commercial company

	s.31(1) (changed)

s.4 Resolution to alter objects

	repealed

s.5 Procedure for objection to alteration

	repealed

s.6 Provisions supplementing ss. 4, 5

(1)	s.31(2) (changed)
(2)-(5)	repealed

s.7 Articles prescribing regulations for companies

(1)	s.18(2) (changed)
(2)	repealed
(3)	s.18(3) (changed)
(3A)	repealed

s.8 Tables A, C, D and E

(1)	ss.19(1)-(3), 20(2) (changed)
(2)	s.20(1), (2) (changed)
(3)	s.19(4)
(4)	s.19(1)-(3) (changed)
(5)	s.19(5)

s.9 Alteration of articles by special resolution

(1)	s.21(1)
(2)	repealed

s.10 Documents to be sent to registrar

(1)	s.9(1), (5), (6) (changed)
(2)	s.12(1), (2) (changed)
(2A)	repealed
(3)	s.12(3)

Provision of Companies Act 1985	Destination in Companies Act 2006
(4)	s.9(3)
(5)	repealed
(6)	s.9(5)

s.11 Authorised minimum capital (public companies)

	repealed

s.12 Duty of registrar

(1), (2)	s.14
(3), (3A)	s.13(1), (2) (changed)
(3B)	1112

s.13 Effect of registration

(1)	s.15(1)
(2)	s.15(3)
(3)	s.16(2) (changed)
(4)	s.16(3)
(5)	s.16(6)
(6)	s.15(2)(d) (changed)
(7)	s.15(4)

s.14 Effect of memorandum and articles

(1)	s.33(1) (changed)
(2)	s.33(2) (changed)

s.15 Memorandum and articles of company limited by guarantee

(1)	s.37
(2)	s.5(3)

s.16 Effect of alteration on company's members

(1)	s.25(1)
(2)	s.25(2)

s.17 Conditions in memorandum which could have been in articles

	repealed

s.18 Amendments of memorandum or articles to be registered

(1)	s.34(2) (changed)
(2)	ss.26(1), 34(3) (changed)
(3)	ss.26(3), (4), 34(5), (6)

s.19 Copies of memorandum and articles to be given to members

(1)	s.32(1) (changed)

Provision of Companies Act 1985	Destination in Companies Act 2006
(2)	s.32(3), (4) (changed)

s.20 Issued copy of memorandum to embody articles

	repealed

s.22 Definition of "member"

(1)	s.112(1) (changed)
(2)	s.112(2)

s.23 Membership of holding company

(1)	s.136(1)
(2)	s.138(1), (2)
(3)	s.141(1), (2)
(3A)	s.141(3)
(3B)	s.141(4)
(3BA)	s.141(5)
(3C)	s.142(1), (2)
(4), (5)	s.137(1), (2)
(6)	s.137(3), (4)
(7)	s.144
(8)	s.143

s.24 Minimum membership for carrying on business

	repealed

Chapter II Company Names

s.25 Name as stated in memorandum

(1)	s.58(1), (2)
(2)	s.59(1), (2), (3)

s.26 Prohibition on registration of certain names

(1)	ss.53, 65(1)-(5), 66(1)(changed)
(2)	ss.54(1)-(3), 55(1) (changed)
(3)	s.66(2), (3) (changed)

s.27 Alternatives of statutory designations

(1)-(3)	repealed
(4)	ss.58(1), (2), 59(1), (2)

s.28 Change of name

(1)	s.77(1)
(2)	ss.67(1), 68(2), (3)

Provision of Companies Act 1985	*Destination in Companies Act 2006*
(3)	s.75(1), (2), (4)
(4)	ss.68(3), 75(3)
(5)	ss.68(5), (6), 75(5), (6)
(6)	ss.80(1)-(3), 81(1)
(7)	s.81(2), (3)

s.29 Regulations about names

(1)	ss.55(1), 56(1)
(2)	s.56(2)
(3)	s.56(3), (4) (changed)
(4), (5)	repealed
(6)	s.55(2)

s.30 Exemption from requirement of "limited" as part of the name

(1)	repealed
(2), (3)	ss.61(1)-(4), 62(1)-(3) (changed)
(4)	s.60(3)
(5), (5A)	repealed
(5B)	s.60(2)
(5C)-(7)	repealed

s.31 Provisions applying to company exempt under s.30

(1)	s.63(1)
(2)	s.64(1)-(4) (changed)
(3)	s.64(7)
(4)	repealed
(5)	s.63(2), (3)
(6)	s.64(5), (6)

s.32 Power to require company to abandon misleading name

(1)	s.76(1)
(2)	s.76(3)
(3)	s.76(4), (5)
(4)	s.76(6), (7) (changed)
(5)	ss.80(1)-(3), 81(1)
(6)	s.81(2), (3)

s.33 Prohibition on trading under misleading name

(1)	see s.1197 (changed)

Provision of Companies Act 1985	Destination in Companies Act 2006
(2)	s.1197(5)
(3)	s.1197(6), (7)

s.34 Penalty for improper use of "limited" or "cyfyngedig"

	see 1197 (changed)

s.34A Penalty for improper use of community interest company

(1), (2)	s.1197(5) (changed)
(3), (4)	repealed
(5)	s.1197(6), (7) (changed)

Chapter III A Company's Capacity; Formalities of Carrying on Business

s.35 A company's capacity not limited by its memorandum

(1)	s.39(1) (changed)
(2), (3)	repealed
(4)	s.39(2)

s.35A Power of directors to bind the company

(1)	s.40(1)
(2)	s.40(2)
(3)	s.40(3)
(4)	s.40(4)
(5)	s.40(5)
(6)	s.40(6)

s.35B No duty to enquire as to capacity of company or authority of directors

	s.40(2)

s.36 Company contracts: England and Wales

	s.43(1), (2)

s.36A Execution of documents: England and Wales

(1), (2)	s.44(1)
(3)	s.45(1)
(4)	s.44(2), (3), (4)
(4A)	s.44(6)
(6)	s.44(5)
(7)	s.44(8)
(8)	s.44(7)

s.36AA Execution of deeds: England and Wales

(1)	s.46(1)

Provision of Companies Act 1985	Destination in Companies Act 2006
(2)	s.46(2)

s.36B Execution of documents by companies

(1)	s.48(2)
(2)	s.48(3)
(3)	repealed

s.36C Pre-incorporation contracts, deeds and obligations

(1)	s.51(1)
(2)	s.51(2)

s.37 Bills of exchange and promissory notes

	s.52

s.38 Execution of deeds abroad

(1)	s.47(1) (changed)
(2)	s.47(2)
(3)	s.47(1)

s.39 Power of company to have official seal for use abroad

(1)	s.49(1), (2) (changed)
(2), (2A)	s.49(3)
(3)	s.49(4)
(4)	s.49(5)
(5)	s.49(6)

s.40 Official seal for share certificates, etc.

(1)	s.50(1), (2)
(2)	repealed

s.41 Authentication of documents

	repealed

s.42 Events affecting a company's status

(1)	s.1079(1)-(3)
(2)	s.1079(4) (changed)

PART II RE-REGISTRATION AS A MEANS OF ALTERING A COMPANY'S STATUS

s.43 Re-registration of private company as public

(1)	s.90(1), (2) (changed)
(2)	s.90(3)
(3)	ss.92(1), (2), 94(2), (3)

Provision of Companies Act 1985	Destination in Companies Act 2006
(3A)	repealed
(4)	s.92(1)
(5)	s.90(3) (changed)

s.44 Consideration for shares recently allotted to be valued

(1)	s.93(1)
(2)	s.93(2)
(3)	s.93(7)(a)
(4), (5)	s.93(3)-(5)
(6)	s.93(6)
(7)	s.93(6), (7)(b)

s.45 Additional requirements relating to share capital

(1)-(4)	s.91(1)
(5)	s.91(2)
(6)	s.91(3)
(7)	s.91(4)

s.46 Meaning of "unqualified report" in s. 43(3)

(1), (2)	s.92(3)
(3)	s.92(4)
(4)	s.92(5), (6)

s.47 Certificate of re-registration under s. 43

(1)	s.96(1), (2)
(2)	s.94(4)
(3)	s.91(5) (changed)
(4)	s.96(4)
(5)	s.96(5)

s.48 Modification for unlimited company re-registering

(1), (2)	s.90(4)
(3)	s.96(3)

s.49 Re-registration of limited company as unlimited

(1)	s.102(1)
(2)	s.102(2)
(3)	repealed
(4)	s.102(1)
(5)-(7)	s.102(3)

Provision of Companies Act 1985	**Destination in Companies Act 2006**
(8)	ss.102(1), 103(2)-(4) (changed)
(8A)	s.103(3), (4) (changed)
(8B)	s.1112 (changed)
(9)	s.102(4)

s.50 Certificate of re-registration under s. 49

(1)	s.104(1), (2)
(2)	s.104(4)
(3)	s.104(5)

s.51 Re-registration of unlimited company as limited

(1)	s.105(1) (changed)
(2)	s.105(2)
(3)	s.105(3), (4)
(4), (5)	s.106(2)
(6)	repealed

s.52 Certificate of re-registration under s. 51

(1)	s.107(1), (2)
(2)	s.107(4)
(3)	s.107(5)

s.53 Re-registration of public company as private

(1)	ss.97(1), 100(2) (changed)
(2)	s.97(3)
(3)	repealed

s.54 Litigated objection to resolution under s. 53

(1)	s.98(1)
(2), (2A)	ss.98(1), 370(3) (changed)
(3)	s.98(2)
(4)	s.99(1), (2) (changed)
(5)	s.98(3), (4)
(6)	s.98(5), (6)
(7)	s.99(3)
(8)	s.98(6)
(9)	repealed
(10)	s.99(4), (5)

Provision of Companies Act 1985	*Destination in Companies Act 2006*

s.55 Certificate of re-registration under s. 53

(1)	s.101(1), (2)
(2)	s.101(4)
(3)	s.101(5)

PART III CAPITAL ISSUES

s.58 Document offering shares etc. for sale deemed a prospectus

(1), (2)	repealed
(3)	s.755(2)
(4)	repealed

s.62 Meaning of "expert"

	repealed

PART IV ALLOTMENT OF SHARES AND DEBENTURES

s.80 Authority of company required for certain allotments

(1)	ss.549(1), 551(1) (changed)
(2)	ss.549(1)-(3), 551(1), 559
(3)	s.551(2)
(4)	s.551(3), (4)
(5)	s.551(5)
(6)	s.551(6)
(7)	s.551(7)
(8)	s.551(8)
(9)	s.549(4), (5)
(10)	s.549(6) (changed)
(11)	repealed

s.80A Election by private company as to duration of authority

	repealed

s.81 Restriction on public offers by private company

(1)	s.755(1)
(2)	repealed
(3)	s.760

s.84 Allotment where issue not fully subscribed

(1)	s.578(1)
(2)	s.578(2)
(3)	s.578(3) (changed)

Provision of Companies Act 1985	**Destination in Companies Act 2006**
(4)	s.578(4), (5)
(5)	s.578(5)
(6)	s.578(6)

s.85 Effect of irregular allotment

(1)	s.579(1), (2)
(2)	s.579(3)
(3)	s.579(4)

s.88 Return as to allotments, etc.

(1)	s.555(1)
(2)	s.555(2) (changed)
(3)	repealed
(5)	s.557(1), (2)
(6)	ss.557(3), 597(5), (6)

s.89 Offers to shareholders to be on pre-emptive basis

(1)	s.561(1)
(2)	s.568(1)
(3)	s.568(1), (2)
(4)	ss.561(2), 565
(5)	s.566
(6)	s.561(4)

s.90 Communication of pre-emption offers to shareholders

(1)	s.562(1)
(2)	s.568(3)
(3), (4)	repealed
(5)	s.562(3) (changed)
(6)	s.562(4), (5) (changed)

s.91 Exclusion of ss. 89, 90 by private company

(1)	s.567(1), (2)
(2)	s.567(3), (4)

s.92 Consequences of contravening ss 89, 90

(1)	ss.563(1), (2), 568(4)
(2)	ss.563(3), 568(5)

s.93 Saving for other restrictions as to offers

(1)	s.575(1)

Provision of Companies Act 1985	*Destination in Companies Act 2006*
(2)	s.575(2)

s.94 Definitions for ss. 89-96

(2)	ss.560(1), 564, 577
(3)	ss.560(2), 561(3)
(3A)	s.560(2)
(4)	repealed
(5)	s.560(1)
(6)	repealed
(7)	s.574(1), (2)

s.95 Disapplication of pre-emption rights

(1)	ss.570(1), (2), 573(2), (3), (5)
(2)	ss.571(1), (2), 573(4)
(2A)	s.573(1)-(5)
(3)	ss.570(3), 571(3)
(4)	ss.570(4), 571(4), 573(3), (5)
(5)	ss.571(5)-(7), 573(5) (changed)
(6)	572(1)-(3)

s.96 Saving for company's pre-emption procedure operative before 1982

(1), (2)	s.576(1)
(3)	s.576(2)
(4)	s.576(3)

s.97 Power of company to pay commissions

(1)	s.553(1)
(2)	s.553(2)
(3), (4)	repealed

s.98 Apart from s 97, commissions and discounts barred

(1)	s.552(1)
(2)	s.552(2)
(3)	s.552(3)
(4)	s.553(3)

s.99 General rules as to payment for shares on allotment

(1)	s.582(1), (3)
(2)	s.585(1)
(3)	s.585(2)

Provision of Companies Act 1985	Destination in Companies Act 2006
(4)	s.582(2)
(5)	s.585(3)
s.100 Prohibition on allotment of shares at a discount	
(1)	s.580(1)
(2)	s.580(2)
s.101 Shares to be allotted as at least one-quarter paid-up	
(1)	s.586(1)
(2)	s.586(2)
(3), (4)	s.586(3)
(5)	s.586(4)
s.102 Restriction on payment by long-term undertaking	
(1)	s.587(1)
(2)	s.587(2)
(3), (4)	s.587(3)
(5), (6)	s.587(4)
(7)	s.587(5)
s.103 Non-cash consideration to be valued before allotment	
(1)	s.593(1)
(2)	s.593(2)
(3)	s.594(1)-(3)
(4)	s.594(4), (5)
(5)	s.595(1), (2)
(6)	s.593(3)
(7)	ss.594(6), 595(3)
s.104 Transfer to public company of non-cash asset in initial period	
(1)	s.598(1)
(2)	s.598(2)
(3)	s.603
(4)	ss.599(1), (3), 601(1)-(3) (changed)
(5)	s.599(2), (4)
(6)	s.598(4), (5)
s.105 Agreements contravening s. 104	
(1)	s.604(1)
(2)	s.604(2)

Provision of Companies Act 1985	*Destination in Companies Act 2006*
(3)	s.604(3)

s.106 Shares issued to subscribers of memorandum

	s.584

s.107 Meaning of "the appropriate rate"

	ss.592(1), (2), 609(1), (2)

s.108 Valuation and report (s. 103)

(1)	s.1150(1) (changed)
(2)	s.1150(2)
(3)	s.1150(3)
(4)	s.596(2)
(5)	s.1150(4)
(6)	ss.596(3), 600(3)
(7)	s.596(4), (5)

s.109 Valuation and report (s.104)

(1)	s.600(1)
(2)	s.600(2), (3)
(3)	s.600(4), (5)

s.110 Entitlement of valuer to full disclosure

(1)	s.1153(1)
(2)	s.1153(2), (4)
(3)	s.1153(3)

s.111 Matters to be communicated to registrar

(1)	s.597(1), (2)
(2)	s.602(1)
(3)	s.597(3)-(6)
(4)	s.602(2), (3)

s.111A Right to damages, etc. not affected

	s.655

s.112 Liability of subsequent holders of shares allotted

(1)	ss.588(1), 605(1)
(2)	s.605(2)
(3)	ss.588(2), 605(3)
(4)	ss.588(3), 605(4)
(5)	s.588(1), (4)

Provision of Companies Act 1985	Destination in Companies Act 2006
s.113 Relief in respect of certain liabilities under ss. 99 ff.	
(1)	ss.589(1), (2), 606(1)
(2)	ss.589(3), 606(2) (changed)
(3)	ss.589(3), 606(2)
(4)	ss.589(4), 606(3)
(5)	ss.589(5), 606(4)
(6), (7)	ss.589(6), 606(5)
(8)	s.606(6)
s.114 Penalty for contravention	
	ss.590(1), (2), 607(2), (3)
s.115 Undertakings to do work, etc.	
(1)	ss.591(1), (2), 608(1), (2)
(2)	repealed
s.116 Application of s. 99ff. to special cases	
	repealed

PART V SHARE CAPITAL, ITS INCREASE, MAINTENANCE AND REDUCTION

Chapter I General Provisions about Share Capital

s.117 Public company share capital requirements	
(1)	s.761(1)
(2)	s.761(2) (changed)
(3)	s.762(1) (changed)
(3A)	repealed
(4)	s.761(3)
(5)	s.762(3)
(6)	s.761(4) (changed)
(7)	s.767(1), (2)
(7A)	repealed
(8)	s.767(3)
s.118 The authorised minimum	
(1)	ss.763(1), 764(1) (changed)
(2)	s.764(3)
(3)	s.764(4)
s.119 Provision for different amounts to be paid on shares	
	s.581

Provision of Companies Act 1985	Destination in Companies Act 2006

s.120 Reserve liability of limited company

                      repealed

s.121 Alteration of share capital (limited companies)

(1)   s.617(1) (changed)

(2)   ss.617(2), (3), 618(1), 620(1) (changed)

(3)   s.618(2)

(4)   ss.618(3), 620(2) (changed)

(5)   repealed

s.122 Notice to registrar of alteration

(1)   ss.619(1)-(3), 621(1), 663(1), 689(1) (changed)

(2)   ss.619(4), (5), 621(4), (5), 663(4), (5), 689(4), (5)

s.123 Notice to registrar of increased share capital

                      repealed

s.124 Reserve capital of unlimited company

                      repealed

Chapter II Class Rights

s.125 Variation of class rights

(1)   s.630(1)

(2)   s.630(2)-(4) (changed)

(3)-(5)   repealed

(6)   s.334(1)-(4), (6) (changed)

(7)   ss.334(7), 630(5)

(8)   s.630(6)

s.126 Saving for court's powers under other provisions

                      s.632

s.127 Shareholders' right to object to variation

(1)   s.633(1)

(2)   s.633(2), (3)

(2A)   s.633(2)

(3)   s.633(4)

(4)   s.633(5)

(5)   s.635(1)-(3)

(6)   s.633(6)

Provision of Companies Act 1985	Destination in Companies Act 2006
s.128 Registration of particulars of special rights	
(1)	s.556(1)-(3) (changed)
(2)	ss.556(1), (4), 629(2)
(3)	s.637(1) (changed)
(4)	s.636(1) (changed)
(5)	ss.557(1), (2), 636(2), (3), 637(2), (3) (changed)
s.129 Registration of newly created class rights	
(1)	s.638(1) (changed)
(2)	s.640(1) (changed)
(3)	s.639(1) (changed)
(4)	ss.638(2), (3), 639(2), (3), 640(2), (3)
Chapter III Share Premiums	
s.130 Application of share premiums	
(1)	s.610(1)
(2)	s.610(2), (2) (changed)
(3)	s.610(4)
(4)	s.610(5), (6)
s.131 Merger relief	
(1)	s.612(1), (4)
(2)	s.612(2)
(3)	s.612(3)
(4)	s.613(2), (3)
(5)	s.613(4)
(6)	s.613(5)
(7)	s.616(1)
(8)	repealed
s.132 Relief in respect of group reconstructions	
(1)	s.611(1)
(2)	s.611(2)
(3)	s.611(3)
(4)	s.611(4)
(5)	s.611(5)
(6), (7)	repealed
(8)	s.612(4)

Provision of Companies Act 1985	Destination in Companies Act 2006
s.133 Provisions supplementing ss. 131, 132	
(1)	s.615
(2)	s.616(2)
(3)	s.616(3)
(4)	s.616(1)
s.134 Provision for extending or restricting relief from s. 130	
(1)	s.614(1)
(2)	s.1292(1)(a), (b)
(3)	ss.614(2), 1290

Chapter IV Reduction of Share Capital

s.135 Special resolution for reduction of share capital

(1)	s.641(1)-(3) (changed)
(2)	s.641(4)
(3)	repealed

s.136 Application to court for order of confirmation

(1)	s.645(1)
(2)	ss.645(2), (4), 646(4)
(3)	s.646(1)
(4)	s.646(2), (3)
(5)	s.646(4), (5)
(6)	s.645(2), (3)

s.137 Court order confirming reduction

(1)	s.648(1), (2)
(2)	s.648(3), (4)
(3)	s.648(4)

s.138 Registration of order and minute of reduction

(1)	s.649(1) (changed)
(2)	s.649(3) (changed)
(3)	s.649(4) (changed)
(4)	s.649(5), (6) (changed)
(5), (6)	repealed

s.139 Public company reducing capital below authorised minimum

(1)	s.650(1)
(2)	s.650(2)

Provision of Companies Act 1985	Destination in Companies Act 2006
(3)	s.651(1), (2)
(4)	s.651(3) (changed)
(5)	s.651(4), (6), (7)

s.140 Liability of members on reduced shares

(1)	s.652(1) (changed)
(2)	s.653(1)
(3)	s.653(2)
(4)	s.653(3)
(5)	s.653(3)

s.141 Penalty for concealing name of creditor, etc.

	s.647(1), (2) (changed)

Chapter V Maintenance of Capital

s.142 Duty of directors on serious loss of capital

(1)	s.656(1)-(3)
(2)	s.656(4), (5) (changed)
(3)	s.656(6)

s.143 General rule against company acquiring own shares

(1)	s.658(1)
(2)	s.658(2), (3)
(2A)	s.725(4)
(3)	s.659(1), (2)

s.144 Acquisition of shares by company's nominee

(1)	s.660(1), (2) (changed)
(2)	s.661(1), (2) (changed)
(3)	s.661(3)
(4)	s.661(4)

s.145 Exceptions from s. 144

(1)	s.660(3)
(2)	ss.660(3), 661(5)
(3)	s.671

s.146 Treatment of shares held by or for public company

(1)	ss.662(1), 671
(2)	s.662(2), (3)
(3)	s.662(3)

Provision of Companies Act 1985	Destination in Companies Act 2006
(4)	s.662(5), (6)

s.147 Matters arising out of compliance with s. 146(2)

(1)	repealed
(2)	s.664(1), (2)
(3)	s.664(4) (changed)
(4)	s.665(1), (2), (4), (5) (changed)

s.148 Further provisions supplementing ss. 146, 147

(1)	s.668(1), (2)
(2)	s.668(3)
(3)	s.671
(4)	s.669(1), (2)

s.149 Sanctions for non-compliance

(1)	s.666(1), (2)
(2)	s.667(1)-(3)

s.150 Charges of public companies on own shares

(1)	s.670(1)
(2)	s.670(2)
(3)	s.670(3)
(4)	s.670(4)

Chapter VI Financial Assistance by a Company For Acquisition of its Own Shares

s.151 Financial assistance generally prohibited

(1)	ss.678(1), 679(1) (changed)
(2)	ss.678(3), 679(3) (changed)
(3)	s.680(1), (2)

s.152 Definitions for this Chapter

(1)	ss.677(1), 683(1)
(2)	s.677(2), (3)
(3)	s.683(2)

s.153 Transactions not prohibited by s. 151

(1)	ss.678(2), 679(2) (changed)
(2)	ss.678(4), 679(4)
(3)	s.681(1), (2)
(4)	s.682(1), (2)
(5)	s.682(5)

Provision of Companies Act 1985	*Destination in Companies Act 2006*
s.154 Special restriction for public companies	
(1)	s.682(1)
(2)	ss.682(3), (4), 840(4), (5)
s.155 Relaxation of s.151 for private companies	
	repealed
s.156 Statutory declaration under s. 155	
	repealed
s.157 Special resolution under s. 155	
	repealed
s.158 Time for giving financial assistance under s. 155	
	repealed

Chapter VII Redeemable Shares; Purchase by a Company of its Own Shares

s.159 Power to issue redeemable shares	
(1)	s.684(1), (3) (changed)
(2)	s.684(4)
(3)	ss.686(1)-(3) (changed), 691(1), (2)
s.160 Financing, etc. of redemption	
(1)	ss.687(1)-(3), (6), 692(1), (2), (5)
(2)	ss.687(4), (5), 692(3), (4)
(3)	repealed
(4)	ss.688, 706 (changed)
s.162 Power of company to purchase own shares	
(1)	s.690(1) (changed)
(2)	ss.691(1), (2), 692(1)-(5)
(2A)	s.706
(2B)	ss.706, 724(1)
(3)	s.690(2)
(4)	s.724(2)
s.162A Treasury shares	
(1)	s.724(3)
(2)	s.724(4)
(3)	s.724(5)
s.162B Treasury shares: maximum holdings	
(1)	s.725(1)

Provision of Companies Act 1985	Destination in Companies Act 2006
(2)	s.725(2)
(3)	s.725(4)

s.162C Treasury shares: voting and other rights

(1)	s.726(1)
(2), (3)	s.726(2)
(4)	s.726(3)
(5)	s.726(4)
(6)	s.726(5)

s.162D Treasury shares: disposal and cancellation

(1)	ss.727(1), 729(1)
(2)	s.727(2) (changed)
(3)	s.727(3)
(4)	s.729(4)
(5)	s.729(5)

s.162E Treasury shares: mandatory cancellation

(1)	s.729(2)
(2)	s.729(3)
(3)	s.1173(1) (changed)

s.162F Treasury shares: proceeds of sale

(1)	s.731(1)
(2)	s.731(2)
(3)	s.731(3)
(4), (5)	s.731(4)

s.162G Treasury shares: penalty for contravention

	s.732(1), (2) (changed)

s.163 Definitions of "off-market" and "market" purchase

(1)	s.693(2)
(2)	s.693(3)
(3)	s.693(4)
(4), (5)	s.693(5)

s.164 Authority for off-market purchase

(1)	ss.693(1), 694(1)
(2)	s.694(2) (changed)
(3)	ss.694(4), 697(3), 700(3)

Provision of Companies Act 1985	Destination in Companies Act 2006
(4)	ss.694(5), 697(4), 700(4)
(5)	ss.694(1), (3), (4), 698(1), (3), (4), 700(5)
(6)	ss.696(1)-(5), 699(1)-(6), 700(5) (changed)
(7)	ss.697(1)-(4), 698(1), (3), (4), 699(1)-(6), 700(3)-(5)

s.165 Authority for contingent purchase contract

(1)	s.694(3)
(2)	ss.694(2), (4), (5), 695(1), (3), (5), 696(1)-(5)

s.166 Authority for market purchase

(1)	ss.693(1), 701(1)
(2)	s.701(2)
(3)	s.701(3), (5)
(4)	s.701(4), (5)
(5)	s.701(6)
(6)	s.701(7)
(7)	s.701(8)

s.167 Assignment or release of company's right to purchase own shares

(1)	s.704
(2)	s.700(1)-(5)

s.168 Payments apart from purchase price to be made out of distributable profits

(1)	s.705(1)
(2)	s.705(2)

s.169 Disclosure by company of purchase of own shares

(1)	ss.707(1)-(3), 708(1) (changed)
(1A)	ss.707(1)-(3), 708(1) (changed)
(1B)	ss.707(1)-(3), 708(1) (changed)
(2)	s.707(4)
(3)	s.707(5)
(4)	s.702(1)-(4) (changed)
(5)	s.702(6)
(6)	ss.707(6), (7), 708(4), (5)
(7)	s.703(1), (2) (changed)
(8)	s.703(3)
(9)	s.702(7)

Provision of Companies Act 1985	*Destination in Companies Act 2006*

s.169A Disclosure by company of cancellation or disposal of treasury shares

(1)	ss.728(1), 730(1)
(2)	ss.728(2), 730(2)
(3)	ss.728(3), 730(3)
(4)	ss.728(4), (5), 730(6), (7)

s.170 The capital redemption reserve

(1)	s.733(1), (2), (4)
(2), (3)	s.733(3)
(4)	s.733(5), (6)

s.171 Power of private companies to redeem or purchase own shares out of capital

(1)	s.709(1) (changed)
(2)	s.709(2)
(3)	s.710(1), (2)
(4)	s.734(2)
(5)	s.734(3)
(6)	s.734(4)

s.172 Availability of profits for purposes of s. 171

(1)	s.711(1), (2)
(2)	s.712(2)
(3)	s.712(6)
(4)	s.712(3)
(5)	s.712(4)
(6)	s.712(7)

s.173 Conditions for payment out of capital

(1)	s.713(1), (2)
(2)	s.716(1)
(3)	s.714(1)-(3)
(4)	s.714(4) (changed)
(5)	s.714(5), (6) (changed)
(6)	s.715(1), (2)

s.174 Procedure for special resolution under s. 173

(1)	ss.716(2), 723(1)
(2)	s.717(3)
(3)	s.717(4)

Provision of Companies Act 1985	Destination in Companies Act 2006
(4)	s.718(2), (3) (changed)
(5)	s.717(5)

s.175 Publicity for proposed payment out of capital

(1)	s.719(1)
(2)	s.719(2)
(3)	s.719(3)
(4)	ss.719(4), 720(1)
(5)	s.719(4)
(6)	s.720(1), (2), (4) (changed)
(7)	s.720(5), (6)
(8)	s.720(7)

s.176 Objections by company's members or creditors

(1)	s.721(1), (2)
(2)	s.721(2)
(3)	s.722(2), (3)
(4)	s.722(4), (5)

s.177 Powers of court on application under s. 176

(1)	s.721(3)
(2)	s.721(4), (5)
(3)	s.721(6)
(4)	s.721(7)
(5)	repealed

s.178 Effect of company's failure to redeem or purchase

(1)	s.735(1)
(2)	s.735(2)
(3)	s.735(2), (3)
(4)	s.735(4)
(5)	s.735(5)
(6)	s.735(6)

s.179 Power of Secretary of State to modify this Chapter

(1)	s.737(1) (changed)
(2)	repealed
(3)	s.737(2), (3) (changed)
(4)	ss.737(4), 1290

Provision of Companies Act 1985	*Destination in Companies Act 2006*

s.180 Transitional cases arising under this Chapter; and savings

repealed

s.181 Definitions for Chapter VII

s.736

Chapter VIII Miscellaneous Provisions About Shares and Debentures

s.182 Nature, transfer and numbering of shares

(1)	ss.541, 544(1), (2)
(2)	s.543(1), (2)

s.183 Transfer and registration

(1)	s.770(1)
(2)	s.770(2)
(3)	s.773
(4)	s.772
(5), (6)	repealed

s.184 Certification of transfers

(1)	s.775(1), (2)
(2)	s.775(3)
(3)	s.775(4)

s.185 Duty of company as to issue of certificates

(1)	ss.769(1), (2), 776(1), (3)
(2)	s.776(2)
(3)	s.777(1), (2)
(4)	ss.769(2), 776(3), 778(1)
(4A)	s.778(1)
(4B), (4C)	s.778(2)
(4D)	s.778(3)
(5)	ss.769(3), (4), 776(5), (6)
(6)	s.782(1)
(7)	s.782(2), (3)

s.186 Certificate to be evidence of title

(1)	s.768(1), (2)
(2)	s.768(2)

s.187 Evidence of grant of probate or confirmation as executor

s.774

Provision of Companies Act 1985	Destination in Companies Act 2006
s.188 Issue and effect of share warrant to bearer	
(1)	s.779(1)
(2)	s.779(2)
(3)	s.779(3)
s.189 Offences in connections with share warrants (Scotland)	
(1)	s.781(1), (3)
(2)	s.781(2), (4)
s.190 Register of debenture holders	
(1)	s.743(6)
(2)	repealed
(3)	743(1) (changed)
(4)'	repealed
(5)	s.743(2), (6) (changed)
(6)	s.743(3)
s.191 Right to inspect register	
(1)	s.744(1)
(2)	s.744(2)
(3)	s.749(1)
(4)	ss.746(1), (2), 749(2), (3)
(5)	ss.746(3), 749(4)
(6)	s.744(5)
(7)	s.748(1), (2) (changed)
s.192 Liability of trustees of debentures	
(1)	s.750(1), (3)
(2)	s.750(2)
(3)	s.751(1), (2)
(4)	s.751(3), (4)
s.193 Perpetual debentures	
	s.739(1), (2)
s.194 Power to re-issue redeemed debentures	
(1)	s.752(1)
(2)	s.752(2)
(3)	s.753
(4)	s.752(3)

Provision of Companies Act 1985	*Destination in Companies Act 2006*
(5)	s.752(4)

s.195 Contract to subscribe for debentures

	s.740

s.196 Payment of debts out of assets subject to floating charge (England and Wales)

(1)	s.754(1)
(2)	s.754(2)
(3)	s.754(3)
(4)	s.754(4)

s.197 Debentures to bearer (Scotland)

	s.742

PART VI DISCLOSURE OF INTERESTS IN SHARES

s.198 Obligation of disclosure: the cases in which it may arise and "the relevant time"

(2)	s.792(1), (2) (changed)

s.199 Interests to be disclosed

	repealed

s.200 "Percentage level" in relation to notifiable interests

	repealed

s.202 Particulars to be contained in notification

	repealed

s.203 Notification of family and corporate interests

(1)	s.822(1), (2)
(2)	s.823(1)
(3)	s.832(2)
(4)	s.823(3)

s.204 Agreement to acquire interests in a particular company

(1)	s.824(1)
(2)	ss.824(1), (2), 988(4)
(3)	ss.824(3), 988(6)
(4)	s.824(4)
(5)	ss.824(5), 988(7)
(6)	ss.824(6), 988(5)

s.205 Obligation of disclosure arising under s. 204

(1)	s.825(1)
(2)	s.825(2)

Provision of Companies Act 1985	Destination in Companies Act 2006
(3)	s.825(3)
(4)	s.825(4)
(5)	repealed

s.206 Obligations of persons acting together to keep each other informed

	repealed

s.207 Interests in shares by attribution

	repealed

s.208 Interests in shares which are to be notified

(1)	s.820(1)
(2)	s.820(2)
(3)	s.820(3)
(4)	s.820(4)
(5)	s.820(6)
(6)	s.820(5)
(7)	s.820(7)
(8)	s.820(8)

s.209 Interests to be disregarded

	repealed

s.210 Other provisions about notification under this Part

	repealed

s.210A Power to make further provision by regulations

(1)	s.828(1), (2)
(2)-(4)	repealed
(5)	ss.828(3), 1290

s.211 Register of interests in shares

(1), (2)	repealed
(3)	s.808(2)
(4)	s.808(7)
(5)	s.808(4)
(6)	s.810(1)-(3)
(7)	s.819(1)
(8)	ss.809(1), 810(4), 811(1), (2), 813(1)-(3) (changed)
(9)	s.826(1)
(10)	ss.808(5), (6), 819(2), (3)

Provision of Companies Act 1985	**Destination in Companies Act 2006**

s.212 Company investigations

(1)	s.793(1), (2) (changed)
(2)	s.793(3), (4), (6)
(3)	s.793(5)
(4)	s.793(7)
(5)	ss.820(1)-(8), 822(1), (2), 823(1)-(3) 824(1)-(6), 825(1)-(4)
(6)	s.821(1), (2)

s.213 Registration of interests disclosed under s. 212

(1)	s.808(1)-(3) (changed)
(2)	repealed
(3)	ss.808(2), (4)-(7), 809(1), 810(1)-(4), 811(1), (2), 813(1)-(3), 819(1)-(3), 826(1)
(4)	repealed

s.214 Company investigation on requisition by members

(1)	s.803(1), (2) (changed)
(2)	s.803(3) (changed)
(3)	repealed
(4)	s.804(1)
(5)	s.804(2), (3) (changed)

s.215 Company report to members

(1)	s.805(1)
(2)	s.805(2), (3)
(3)	s.805(1), (3)
(4)	s.826(1), (2)
(5)	s.805(6)
(6)	s.805(7)
(7)	ss.805(4), 807(1)-(5)
(8)	s.806(3), (4)

s.216 Penalty for failure to provide information

(1)	s.794(1)
(1A)	s.794(3)
(1B)	s.794(2)
(2)	repealed
(3)	s.795(1), (3)

Provision of Companies Act 1985	**Destination in Companies Act 2006**
(4)	s.795(2)
(5)	s.796(1), (2)

s.217 Removal of entries from register

(1)	s.816 (changed)
(2)	s.817(1) (changed)
(3)	s.817(2), (3)
(4)	s.818(1), (2)
(5)	ss.817(4), 818(3)
(6), (7)	repealed

s.218 Otherwise, entries not to be removed

(1)	s.815(1)
(2)	s.815(2)
(3)	s.815(3), (4)

s.219 Inspection of register and reports

(1)	s.807(1), 811(1)
(2)	s.807(2), 811(2)
(3)	ss.807(3), (4), 813(1), (2) (changed)
(4)	ss.807(5), 813(3)
(5)	repealed

s.220 Definitions for Part VI

(1), (1A)	repealed
(2)	s.827

PART VII ACCOUNTS AND AUDIT

Chapter I Provisions Applying to Companies Generally

s.221 Duty to keep accounting records

(1)	s.386(1), (2)
(2)-(4)	s.386(3)-(5)
(5)	s.387(1), (2)
(6)	s.387(3)

s.222 Where and for how long records to be kept

(1)-(3)	s.388(1)-(3)
(4)	s.389(1), (2), (4)
(5)	s.388(4), (5)
(6)	s.389(3), (4)

Provision of Companies Act 1985	*Destination in Companies Act 2006*
s.223 A company's financial year	
(1)-(5)	s.390(1)-(5)
s.224 Accounting reference periods and accounting reference date	
(1)	s.391(1)
(2), (3)	s.391(2)
(3A)	s.391(4)
(4)-(6)	s.391(5)-(7)
s.225 Alteration of accounting reference date	
(1)	s.392(1)
(3)-(7)	s.392(2)-(6)
s.226 Duty to prepare individual accounts	
(1)	s.394
(2)-(6)	s.395(1)-(5)
s.226A Companies Act individual accounts	
(1), (2)	s.396(1), (2)
(3)	s.396(3) (changed)
(4)	s.396(4)
(5), (6)	s.396(5)
s.226B IAS individual accounts	
	s.397
s.227 Duty to prepare group accounts	
(1)	s.399(2)
(2)-(7)	s.403(1)-(6)
(8)	s.399(2), (3)
s.227A Companies Act group accounts	
(1), (2)	s.404(1), (2)
(3)	s.404(3) (changed)
(4)	s.404(4)
(5), (6)	s.404(5)
s.227B IAS group accounts	
	s.406
s.227C Consistency of accounts	
(1)	s.407(1)
(2)	s.407(2)

Provision of Companies Act 1985	Destination in Companies Act 2006
(3)	s.407(3)
(4)	s.407(4)
(5)	s.407(5)

s.228 Exemption for parent companies included in accounts of larger group

(1), (2)	s.400(1), (2)
(3)	s.400(4)
(4)	s.400(5)
(5)	s.400(3)
(6)	s.400(6)

s.228A Exemption for parent companies included in non-EEA group accounts

(1), (2)	s.401(1), (2)
(3)	s.401(4)
(4)	s.401(5)
(5)	s.401(3)
(6)	s.401(6)

s.229 Subsidiary undertakings included in the consolidation

(1), (2)	s.405(1), (2)
(3)	s.405(3), (4)
(5)	s.402

s.230 Treatment of individual profit and loss account where group accounts prepared

(1)	s.408(1) (changed)
(2)	s.408(2) (changed)
(3), (4)	s.408(3), (4)

s.231 Disclosure required in notes to accounts: related undertakings

(1), (2)	s.409(1), (2) (changed)
(3)	s.409(3), (4) (changed)
(4)	s.409(5)
(5)	s.410(1), (2)
(6)	s.410(3)
(7)	s.410(4), (5)

s.231A Disclosure required in notes to annual accounts: particulars of staff

(1)	s.411(1)
(2)	s.411(3)
(3)	s.411(4)

Provision of Companies Act 1985	*Destination in Companies Act 2006*
(4)	s.411(5)
(5)	s.411(2)
(6)	s.411(7)
(7)	s.411(6)

s.232 Disclosure required in notes to accounts: emoluments and other benefits of directors and others

(1)	repealed
(3)	s.412(5)
(4)	s.412(6)

s.233 Approval and signing of accounts

(1), (2)	ss.414(1), (2), 450(1), (2)
(3)	ss.433(1)-(3), 436(1), (2),
(4)	ss.444(6), 445(5), 446(3), 447(3) (changed)
(5)	ss.414(4), (5) (changed)
(6)(a)	s.433(4), (5)

s.234 Duty to prepare directors' report

(1)	ss.415(1), 417(1), 418(2)
(2), (3)	s.415(2), (3)
(5)	ss.415(4), (5), 419(3), (4)

s.234ZZA Directors' report: general requirements

(1)	s.416(1), (3)
(2)	s.416(2)
(3), (4)	s.416(4) (changed)

s.234ZZB Directors' report: business review

(1), (2)	s.417(3), (4)
(3)	s.417(6)
(4)	s.417(8)
(5)	s.417(6)
(6)	s.417(9)

s.234ZA Statement as to disclosure of information to auditors

(1)	s.418(1)
(2)	s.418(2)
(3)	s.418(3)
(4)	s.418(4)
(5)	repealed

Provision of Companies Act 1985	*Destination in Companies Act 2006*
(6)	s.418(5), (6)

s.234A Approval and signing of directors' report

(1)	s.419(1)
(2)	ss.433(1)-(3), 436(1), (2)
(3)	ss.444(6), 445(5), 446(3), 447(3)
(4)	ss.419(3), (4), 433(4), (5)

s.234B Duty to prepare directors' remuneration report

(1)	ss.420(1), 421(1), (2)
(2)	s.421(1), (2)
(3), (4)	s.420(2), (3)
(5), (6)	s.421(3), (4)

s.234C Approval and signing of directors' remuneration report

(1)	s.422(1)
(2)	ss.433(1)-(3), 436(1), (2)
(3)	s.447(3)
(4)	s.422(2), (3)

s.235 Auditors' report

(1)	ss.475(1), 495(1)
(1A)	s.495(2)
(1B), (2)	s.495(3)
(2A)	s.495(4)
(3)	s.496
(4), (5)	s.497(1), (2)

s.236 Signature of auditors' report

(1)	s.503(1), (2)
(2)	s.505(1), (2) (changed)
(3)	s.444(7) (changed)
(4)	s.505(3), (4)
(5)	s.503(3) (changed)

s.237 Duties of auditors

(1)	s.498(1)
(2)	s.498(2)
(3)	s.498(3)
(4)	s.498(4)

Provision of Companies Act 1985	*Destination in Companies Act 2006*
(4A)	s.498(5)

s.238 Persons entitled to receive copies of accounts and reports

(1), (1A)	ss.423(1), 424(1)-(3) (changed)
(2)	repealed
(3)	s.423(4)
(4)	s.424(4) (changed)
(4A)-(4E)	repealed
(5)	s.425(1), (2)
(6)	s.423(5)

s.239 Right to demand copies of accounts and reports

(1), (2)	ss.431(1), (2), 432(1), (2)
(2A), (2B)	repealed
(3)	ss.431(3), (4), 432(3), (4)
(4)	repealed

s.240 Requirements in connection with publication of accounts

(1)	s.434(1) (changed)
(2)	s.434(2) (changed)
(3)	s.435(1), (2) (changed)
(4)	s.436(1), (2) (changed)
(5)	ss.434(3), 435(3) (changed)
(6)	s.435(5), (6)

s.241 Accounts and reports to be laid before company in general meeting

(1)	s.437(1) (changed)
(2)	ss.437(2), 438(1), (4)
(3), (4)	s.438(2), (3)

s.241A Members' approval of directors' remuneration report

(1)-(3)	s.439(1)
(4)	s.439(2)
(5)	s.439(3)
(6)	s.439(4)
(7)	s.439(3)
(8)	s.439(5)
(9)	s.440(1), (4)
(10)	s.440(2)-(4)

Provision of Companies Act 1985	Destination in Companies Act 2006
(11)	s.440(2), (3)
(12)	s.439(6)

s.242 Accounts and reports to be delivered to the registrar

(1)	ss.441(1), 444(1), (2), 445(1), (2), 446(1), (2), 447(1), (2) (changed)
(2)	s.451(1)
(3)	s.452(1), (2)
(4)	s.451(2)
(5)	s.451(3)

s.242A Civil penalty for failure to deliver accounts

(1)	s.453(1)
(2)	s.453(2) (changed)
(3)	s.453(3)
(4)	s.453(4)

s.242B Delivery and publication of accounts in ECUs

(1)	s.469(1)
(2)	s.469(2)
(3)	s.469(3)
(4)	s.469(4)
(5)	repealed

s.244 Period allowed for laying and delivering accounts and reports

(1)	s.442(2) (changed)
(2)	s.442(3) (changed)
(4)	s.442(4)
(5)	s.442(5)
(6)	s.442(7)

s.245 Voluntary revision of annual accounts or directors' report

(1)	s.454(1)
(2)	s.454(2)
(3)	s.454(3)
(4)	s.454(4) (changed)
(5)	ss.454(5), 1289

s.245A Secretary of State's notice in respect of annual accounts

(1)	s.455(1), (2)
(2)	s.455(3)

Provision of Companies Act 1985	*Destination in Companies Act 2006*
(3)	s.455(4)
(4)	s.455(5)

s.245B Application to court in respect of defective accounts

(1)	s.456(1)
(2)	s.456(2)
(3)	s.456(3)
(3A)	s.456(4)
(4)-(7)	s.456(5)-(8)

s.245C Other persons authorised to apply to court

(1)	s.457(1)
(1A)	s.457(5)
(2), (3)	s.457(2), (3)
(4)	s.457(7)
(4A)	s.457(5)
(4B)	s.457(4)
(5)	s.457(6)

s.245D Disclosure of information held by Inland Revenue to persons authorised to apply to court

(1)	s.458(1)
(2)	s.458(2)
(3)	s.458(1)
(4)	repealed

s.245E Restrictions on use and further disclosure of information disclosed under section 245D

(1), (2)	s.458(3)
(3)	s.458(4), (5)
(4)	s.458(4) (changed)
(5)	ss.1126, 1130

s.245F Power of authorised persons to require documents, information and explanations

(1)	s.459(1)
(2)	s.459(2)
(3)	s.459(3)
(4)	s.459(4)
(5)	s.459(5)
(6)	s.459(6)

Provision of Companies Act 1985	Destination in Companies Act 2006
(7)	s.459(7)
(8)	s.459(8)

s.245G Restrictions on further disclosure of information obtained under section 245F

(1), (2)	s.460(1), (2)
(3)	ss.460(3), 461(1)-(6)
(4)-(6)	s.462(1)-(3)
(7)	s.460(4), (5)
(8)	s.460(4)
(9)	ss.1126, 1130
(10)	s.460(3)
(11)	s.461(7)

Chapter II Exemptions, Exceptions and Special Provisions

s.246 Special provisions for small companies

(1), (2)	repealed
(3)	s.411(1)
(4)	ss.416(3), 417(1)
(5)	s.444(1), (3) (changed)
(6)	s.444(3) (changed)
(7)	ss.444(6), 450(1), (2)
(8)	ss.414(3), 419(2), 444(5), 450(3)

s.246A Special provisions for medium-sized companies

(1)	s.445(1)
(2)	s.445(3) (changed)
(2A)	s.417(7)
(3)	s.445(3) (changed)
(4)	s.450(3)

s.247 Qualification of company as small or medium-sized

(1)(a)	ss.382(1), 465(1)
(1)(b), (2)	ss.382(2), 465(2)
(3), (4)	ss.382(3), (4), 465(3), (4)
(5)	ss.382(5), 465(5) (changed)
(6)	ss.382(6), 465(6)

s.247A Cases in which special provisions do not apply

(1)-(1B)	ss.384(1), 467(1)

Provision of Companies Act 1985	*Destination in Companies Act 2006*
(2)	ss.384(2), 467(2) (changed)
(2A)	ss.384(3), 467(3)
(3)	ss.383(1), 466(1)

s.247B Special auditors' report

(1)	s.449(1)
(2)	ss.444(4), 445(4), 449(2)
(3)	s.449(3)
(4)	s.449(4)
(5)	s.449(5)

s.248 Exemption for small and medium-sized groups

(1), (2)	ss.398, 399(1), (2) (changed)

s.248A Group accounts prepared by small company

	repealed

s.249 Qualification of group as small or medium-sized

(1)(a)	s.466(2)
(1)(b), (2)	s.466(3)
(3)	s.466(4)
(4)	s.466(5), (6)
(5), (6)	s.466(7)

s.249A Exemptions from audit

(1)	s.477(1)
(2)	repealed
(3)	s.477(2), (4)
(3A)	repealed
(4)	repealed
(6)	s.477(3)
(7)	s.477(4)

s.249AA Dormant companies

(1)	s.480(1)
(2)	s.480(2)
(3)	s.481
(4)	s.1169(1)
(5)-(7)	s.1169(2), (3)

Provision of Companies Act 1985	*Destination in Companies Act 2006*
s.249B Cases where exemptions not available	
(1)	ss.478, 479(1)-(3)
(1A)	s.479(3)
(1B)	s.479(1)-(3)
(1C)	s.479(2), (5), (6)
(2), (3)	s.476(1)-(3)
(4)	s.475(2), (3)
(5)	s.475(4)
s.249C The report required for the purposes of section 249A(2)	
	repealed
s.249D The reporting accountant	
	repealed
s.249E Effect of exemptions	
(1)(b)	ss.444(2), 445(2), 446(2) (changed)
(1A), (2)	repealed
s.251 Provision of summary financial statement to shareholders	
(1)	ss.426(1), 427(1)
(2)	s.426(2), (3)
(2A)-(2E)	repealed
(3)	ss.427(2), 428(2)
(3A)	ss.427(3), 428(3)
(4)	ss.427(4), 428(4)
(5)	ss.427(6), 428(6)
(6)	s.429(1), (2)
(7)	ss.434(6), 435(7)
s.252 Election to dispense with laying of accounts and reports before general meeting	
	repealed
s.253 Right of shareholder to require laying of accounts	
	repealed
s.254 Exemption from requirement to deliver accounts and reports	
(1)	s.448(1)
(2)	s.448(2)
(3)	s.448(3)
(4)	s.448(4)

Provision of Companies Act 1985	*Destination in Companies Act 2006*
s.255 Special provisions for banking and insurance companies	
	repealed
s.255A Special provisions for banking and insurance groups	
(1)-(3)	repealed
(4)	s.1164(5)
(5)	s.1165(5)
(5A)	ss.1164(5), 1165(6)
(6A), (6B)	repealed
s.255B Modification of disclosure requirements in relation to banking company or group	
	repealed
s.255D Power to apply provisions to banking partnerships	
(1)	s.470(1)
(2), (2A)	s.470(2)
(4)	s.470(4)
(5)	s.470(3)
Chapter III Supplementary Provisions	
s.256 Accounting standards	
(1), (2)	s.464(1)
(2)	s.464(2)
(4)	s.464(3)
s.257 Power of Secretary of State to alter accounting requirements	
(1)	s.484(1)
(2)	ss.473(1)-(4) (changed), 484(3)
(3)	s.484(4)
(4)(c)	s.484(2)
(4A), (4B), (5)	repealed
s.258 Parent and subsidiary undertakings	
(1)	s.1162(1)
(2)	s.1162(2)
(3)	s.1162(3)
(4)	s.1162(4)
(5)	s.1162(5)
(6)	s.1162(6)

Provision of Companies Act 1985	*Destination in Companies Act 2006*

s.259 Meaning of "undertaking" and related expressions

(1)	ss.1161(1), 1173 "parent company"
(2)	s.1161(2)
(3)	s.1161(3)
(4)	s.1161(4)
(5)	s.1161(5)

s.261 Notes to the accounts

(1)	s.472(1)
(2)	s.472(2)

s.262 Minor definitions

(1)	ss.474(1), 539, 835(6), 1173 "credit institution" (changed)
(2)	s.474(2)
(3)	s.853(4), (5)

s.262A Index of defined expressions

	repealed (see Sch.8)

PART VIII DISTRIBUTION OF PROFITS AND ASSETS

s.263 Certain distributions prohibited

(1)	s.830(1)
(2)	s.829(1), (2)
(3)	s.830(2), (3)
(4)	s.849
(5)	s.850(1)-(3)

s.264 Restriction on distribution of assets

(1)	s.831(1), (6)
(2)	s.831(2), (3)
(3)	s.831(4)
(4)	s.831(5)

s.265 Other distributions by investment companies

(1)	s.832(1)-(3)
(2)	s.832(4)
(3)	s.832(7)
(4)	s.832(5)
(4A)	s.832(6)

Provision of Companies Act 1985	Destination in Companies Act 2006
(5)	s.832(6)
(6)	s.832(5)

s.266 Meaning of "investment company"

(1)	s.833(1)
(2)	ss.833(2), 834(1)
(2A)	s.833(3)
(3)	s.833(4), (5)
(4)	s.834(2)-(5)

s.267 Extension of ss. 265, 266 to other companies

(1)	s.835(1)
(2)	s.835(2)

s.268 Realised profits of insurance company with long term business

(1)	s.843(1), (2), (4), (5)
(2)	s.843(3), (4)
(3)	s.843(6), (7)
(4)	s.843(7)

s.269 Treatment of development costs

(1)	s.844(1)
(2)	s.844(2), (3)

s.270 Distribution to be justified by reference to company's accounts

(1), (2)	s.836(1)
(3)	ss.836(2), 837(1)
(4)	ss.836(2), 838(1), 839(1)
(5)	s.836(3), (4)

s.271 Requirements for last annual accounts

(1), (2)	s.837(2)
(3)	s.837(3), (4)
(4)	s.837(4)
(5)	s.837(5)

s.272 Requirements for interim accounts

(1)	s.838(2)
(2)	s.838(3)
(3)	ss.838(4), (5), 839(4)
(4), (5)	s.838(6)

Provision of Companies Act 1985	Destination in Companies Act 2006

s.273 Requirements for initial accounts

(1)	s.839(2)
(2)	s.839(3)
(3)	s.839(4)
(4)	s.839(5), (6)
(5)	s.839(6)
(6), (7)	s.839(7)

s.274 Method of applying s 270 to successive distributions

(1)	s.840(1)
(2)	s.840(1), (2)
(3)	s.840(3)-(5)
(4)	repealed

s.275 Treatment of assets in the relevant accounts

(1)	s.841(1), (2)
(1A)	s.841(3)
(2)	s.841(5)
(3)	s.842
(4)-(6)	s.841(4)

s.276 Distributions in kind

	s.846(1), (2) (changed)

s.277 Consequences of unlawful distribution

(1)	s.847(1), (2)
(2)	s.847(3), (4)
(3)	repealed

s.278 Saving for provision in articles operative before Act of 1980

	s.848(1), (2)

s.279 Distributions by banking or insurance purposes

	repealed

s.280 Definitions for Part VIII

(1)	s.853(1)
(2)	s.853(2)
(3)	s.853(3)

s.281 Saving for other restraints on distribution

	ss.851, 852 (changed)

Provision of Companies Act 1985	*Destination in Companies Act 2006*

PART IX A COMPANY'S MANAGEMENT; DIRECTORS AND SECRETARIES; THEIR QUALIFICATIONS, DUTIES AND RESPONSIBILITIES

s.282 Directors

(1)	s.154(2) (changed)
(2)	repealed
(3)	s.154(1)

s.283 Secretary

(1)	s.271 (changed)
(2)	repealed
(3)	ss.270(3), 274 (changed)
(4)	repealed

s.284 Acts done by person in dual capacity

	s.280

s.285 Validity of acts of directors

	s.161(1), (2) (changed)

s.286 Qualifications of company secretaries

(1)	s.273(1), (2) (changed)
(2)	s.273(3)

s.287 Registered office

(1)	s.86
(2)	repealed
(3)	s.87(1)
(4)	s.87(2)
(5)	s.87(3)
(6)	s.87(4)
(7)	repealed

s.288 Register of directors and secretaries

(1)	ss.162(1)-(3), 275(1)-(3) (changed)
(2)	ss.167(1), (2), 276(1), (2)
(3)	ss.162(5), 275(5)
(4)	ss.162(6), (7), 167(4), (5), 275(6), (7), 276(3), (4)
(5)	ss.162(8), 275(8)
(5A)	repealed (see s.1141)
(6)	s.162(6), 167(4), 275(6), 276(3)

Provision of Companies Act 1985	Destination in Companies Act 2006

s.289 Particulars of directors to be registered under s 288

(1)	ss.163(1), 164 (changed)
(1A)	repealed (see s.1141)
(2)	ss.163(2), (4), 277(2), (4) (changed)
(3), (4)	repealed

s.290 Particulars of secretaries to be registered under s 288

(1)	ss.277(1), 278(1) (changed)
(1A)	repealed (see s.1141)
(2)	s.278(2)
(3)	s.277(2), (4)

s.292 Appointment of directors to be voted on individually

(1)	s.160(1)
(2)	s.160(2)
(3)	s.160(3)
(4)	s.160(4)

s.293 Age limit for directors

| | repealed |

s.294 Duty of director to disclose his age

| | repealed |

s.303 Resolution to remove director

(1)	s.168(1) (changed)
(2)	s.168(2)
(3)	s.168(3)
(4)	s.168(4)
(5)	s.168(5)

s.304 Director's right to protest removal

(1)	s.169(1), (2)
(2)	s.169(3)
(3)	s.169(4)
(4)	s.169(5)
(5)	s.169(6)

s.305 Directors' names on company correspondence, etc.

| | repealed |

Provision of Companies Act 1985	*Destination in Companies Act 2006*
s.306 Limited company may have directors with unlimited liability	
	repealed
s.307 Special resolution making liability of directors unlimited	
	repealed
s.308 Assignment of office by directors	
	repealed
s.309 Directors to have regard to interests of employees	
(1)	s.172(1)(b)
(2)	repealed
(3)	repealed (see s.170(5))
s.309A Provisions protecting directors from liability	
(1)	s.232(1), (2)
(2)	s.232(1)
(3)	s.232(2)
(4)	s.234(1)
(5)	s.233
(6)	s.232(3) (see s.256)
s.309B Qualifying third party indemnity provisions	
(1), (2)	s.234(2)
(3)	s.234(3)
(4)	s.234(3), (6)
(5)	s.234(4)
(6), (7)	s.234(5)
(8)	repealed (see s.256)
s.309C Disclosure of qualifying third party indemnity provisions	
(1)	s.236(1) (changed)
(2)	s.236(2), (3)
(3)	s.236(4), (5) (changed)
(4)	s.237(1)
(5)	ss.237(1)-(3), (5)-(8), 238(1), (3)-(5)
(6)	repealed (see ss.232(3), 234, 256)
s.310 Provisions protecting auditors from liability	
(1)	s.532(1), (3) (changed)
(2)	s.532(2)

Provision of Companies Act 1985	Destination in Companies Act 2006
(3)	s.533

PART X ENFORCEMENT OF FAIR DEALING BY DIRECTORS

s.311 Prohibition on tax-free payments to directors

	repealed (by s.1177)

s.312 Payment to director for loss of office, etc.

	ss215(1), 217(1), (3) (changed)

s.313 Company approval for property transfer

(1)	ss.215(1), 218(1), (3) (changed)
(2)	s.222(2)

s.314 Director's duty of disclosure on takeover, etc.

(1)	ss.215(1), 219(1) (changed)
(2), (3)	repealed

s.315 Consequences of non-compliance with s. 314

(1)	ss.219(1), (2), 222(3) (changed)
(2)	repealed
(3)	s.219(5)

s.316 Provisions supplementing ss. 312 to 315

(1)	ss.218(5), 219(7)
(2)	s.216(1), (2) (changed)
(3)	s.220(1)
(4)	repealed

s.317 Directors to disclose interest in contracts

(1)	s.182(1) (changed)
(2)	s.182(2) (changed)
(3)	s.185(1), (2) (changed)
(4)	s.185(4)
(5)	s.185(1) (changed)
(7)	s.183(1), (2)
(8)	s.187(1)-(4)
(9)	repealed

s.318 Directors' service contracts to be open to inspection

(1)	ss.228(1), 237(2)
(2), (3)	ss.228(2), 237(3) (changed)
(4)	ss.228(4), 237(5)

Provision of Companies Act 1985	Destination in Companies Act 2006
(6)	s.230
(7)	ss.229(1), 238(1)
(8)	ss.228(5), (6), 229(3), (4), 237(6), (7), 238(3), (4) (changed)
(9)	ss.229(5), 238(5) (changed)
(10)	ss.228(7), 237(8)
(11)	repealed

s.319 Director's contract of employment for more than 5 years

(1)	s.188(1), (3) (changed)
(2)	s.188(4) (changed)
(3)	s.188(2) (changed)
(4)	s.188(6)
(5)	s.188(5)
(6)	s.189
(7)	ss.188(7), 223(1)

s.320 Substantial property transactions involving directors, etc.

(1)	s.190(1), (2) (changed)
(2)	s.191(1)-(5) (changed)
(3)	s.223(1)

s.321 Exceptions from s. 320

(1)	s.190(4)
(2)	ss.192, 193(1), (2) (changed)
(3)	s.192
(4)	s.194(1), (2)

s.322 Liabilities arising from contravention of s. 320

(1)	s.195(1), (2)
(2)	ss.195(2), 196
(3)	s.195(1), (3), (4)
(4)	s.195(3), (5), (8)
(5)	s.195(6)
(6)	s.195(7)

s.322A Invalidity of certain transactions involving directors, etc.

(1)	s.41(1), (2)
(2)	s.41(2)
(3)	s.41(3)

Provision of Companies Act 1985	Destination in Companies Act 2006
(4)	s.41(1)
(5)	s.41(4)
(6)	s.41(5)
(7)	s.41(6)
(8)	s.41(7)

s.322B Contracts with sole members who are directors

(1)	s.231(1), (2) (changed)
(2)	s.231(1)
(3)	s.231(5)
(4)	s.231(3), (4) (changed)
(5)	s.231(7)
(6)	s.231(6)

s.323 Prohibition on directors' dealing in share options

repealed (by s.1177)

s. 324 Duty of director to disclose shareholding in own company

repealed (by s.1177)

s.325 Register of directors' interests notified under s. 324

(1)-(4)	repealed (by s.1177)
(5)	repealed (by s.1177) (see s.809(2), (3))
(6)	repealed (by s.1177)

s.326 Sanctions for non-compliance

repealed (by s.1177)

s.327 Extension of s. 323 to spouses civil partners and children

repealed (by s.1177)

s.328 Extension of s. 324 to spouses civil partners and children

repealed (by s.1177)

s.329 Duty to notify stock exchange of matters notified under preceding sections

repealed (by s.1177)

s.330 General restriction on loans etc to directors and persons connected with them

(1)	repealed
(2)	s.197(1) (changed)
(3)	ss.198(1), (2) (changed), 200(1), (2)
(4)	s.201(1), (2) (changed)
(5)	s.223(1)

Provision of Companies Act 1985	*Destination in Companies Act 2006*
(6)	s.203(1), (6) (changed)
(7)	s.203(1) (changed)

s.331 Definitions for ss. 330 ff.

(1), (2)	repealed
(3)	s.199(1)
(4)	s.199(2), (3)
(6)	ss.198(1), 200(1), 201(1)
(7)	s.202(1)
(8)	s.202(3)
(9)	ss.202(2), 212
(10)	s.202(3)

s.332 Short-term quasi-loans

	repealed

s.333 Inter-company loans in same group

	s.280(1) (changed)

s.334 Loans of small amounts

	s.207(1) (changed)

s.335 Minor and business transactions

(1)	s.207(2) (changed)
(2)	s.207(3)

s.336 Transactions at behest of holding company

	208(1), (2) (changed)

s.337 Funding of director's expenditure on duty to company

(1), (2)	s.204(1) (changed)
(3)	s.204(2) (changed)
(4)	repealed

s.337A Funding of director's expenditure on defending proceedings

(1)	s.205(1) (changed)
(2)	s.205(5)
(3)	s.205(1) (changed)
(4)	s.205(2)
(5)	s.205(3)
(6)	s.205(4)

Provision of Companies Act 1985	*Destination in Companies Act 2006*
s.338 Loan or quasi-loan by money-lending company	
(1)	s.209(1)
(2)	s.209(2)
(3)	s.209(1)
(4), (5)	repealed
(6)	s.209(3), (4)
s.339 "Relevant amounts" for purposes of ss. 334 ff.	
(1)	ss.204(2), 207(1), (2), 210(1)
(2)	ss.204(2), 207(1), (2), 210(2)-(4)
(3)	s.210(3), (4)
(4)	repealed
(5)	s.210(5)
(6)	s.211(1)
s.340 "Value" of transactions and arrangements	
(1)	s.211(1) (changed)
(2)	s.211(2)
(3)	s.211(3)
(4)	s.211(5)
(5)	s.211(6)
(6)	s.211(4)
(7)	s.211(7) (changed)
s.341 Civil remedies for breach of s. 330	
(1)	s.213(1), (2)
(2)	s.213(3), (4)
(3)	s.213(5), (8)
(4)	s.213(6)
(5)	s.213(7)
s.342 Criminal penalties for breach of s. 330	
	repealed
s.343 Record of transactions not disclosed in company accounts	
	repealed (by s.1177)
s.344 Exceptions from s. 343	
	repealed (by s.1177)

Provision of Companies Act 1985	Destination in Companies Act 2006
s.345 Power to increase financial limits	
(1)	s.258(1)
(2)	s.258(2)
(3)	s.258(3)
s.346 "Connected persons", etc.	
(1)	ss.252(1), 254(1), 255(1)
(2), (3)	ss.252(2), (3), 253(2) (changed)
(4)	s.254(2), (5)
(5)	s.255(2), (5)
(6)	ss.254(6), 255(6)
(7)	ss.254(3), 255(3)
(8)	ss.254(4), 255(4)
s.347 Transactions under foreign law	
	s.259

PART XA CONTROL OF POLITICAL DONATIONS

s.347A Introductory provisions	
(1)	s.362 (changed)
(3)	s.379(1)
(4)	s.364(2)
(5)	s.365(1) (changed)
(6)	s.363(1), (2)
(7)	s.363(1), (2) (changed)
(8)	s.379(1)
(9)	s.363(1)
(10)	ss.366(5), 379(2)
(11)	repealed (and see s.1162)
s.347B Exemptions	
(1)	s.375(1)
(2)	s.375(2) (changed)
(3)	s.376(1), (2)
(4)	s.378(1) (changed)
(5)	s.378(3)
(6), (7)	s.378(1) (changed)
(8)	s.377(1)

Provision of Companies Act 1985	Destination in Companies Act 2006
(9)	s.377(3)
(10)	s.377(2)
(11)	s.377(4)

s.347C Prohibition on donations and political expenditure by companies

(1)	s.366(1), (2), (5) (changed)
(2)	s.367(3), (6) (changed)
(3)	s.368(1), (2)
(4)	s.367(5)
(5)	repealed
(6)	s.366(6)

s.347D Special rules for subsidiaries

(1)	s.366(2)
(2)	s.366(2), (5) (changed)
(3)	s.366(2), (3), (5) (changed)
(4)	s.367(3), (6) (changed)
(5)	s.368(1), (2)
(6)	s.367(5)
(7), (8)	repealed
(9)	s.366(6)

s.347E Special rule for parent companies of non-GB subsidiary undertaking

	repealed

s.347F Remedies for breach of prohibitions on company donations etc.

(1)	s.369(1)
(2)	s.369(2), (3) (changed)
(3)	s.369(2), (5)
(4)	s.369(2)
(5)	s.369(6)
(6)	s.369(3) (changed)
(7), (8)	repealed

s.347G Remedy for unauthorised donation or expenditure by non-GB subsidiary

	repealed

s.347H Exemption of directors from liability in respect of unauthorised donation or expenditure

	repealed

Provision of Companies Act 1985	Destination in Companies Act 2006

s.347I Enforcement of directors' liabilities by shareholder action

(1)	s.370(1), (2) (changed)
(2)	s.370(3)
(3)	ss.370(4), 371(1)
(4), (5)	s.371(2)
(6)	s.371(3)
(7)	s.371(4)
(8)	s.371(5)

s.347J Costs of shareholder action

(1)	s.372(1)
(2)	s.372(2)
(3)	s.372(3)
(4), (5)	s.372(4)
(6)	s.372(5)

s.347K Information for purposes of shareholder action

(1)	s.373(1)
(2)	s.373(2)

PART XI COMPANY ADMINISTRATION AND PROCEDURE

Chapter I Company Identification

s.348 Company name to appear outside place of business

(1)	s.82(1), (2)
(2)	s.84(1), (2)

s.349 Company's name to appear in its correspondence, etc

(1)	s.82(1), (2)
(2), (3)	s.84(1), (2)
(4)	repealed

s.350 Company seal

(1)	s.45(2), (3) (changed)
(2)	s.45(4), (5)

s.351 Particulars in correspondence etc

(1), (2)	s.82(1), (2)
(5)	s.84(1), (2)

Provision of Companies Act 1985	**Destination in Companies Act 2006**
Chapter II Register of members	
s.352 Obligation to keep and enter up register	
(1)	s.113(1)
(2)	s.113(2)
(3)	s.113(3), (4)
(3A)	repealed
(4)	s.113(6)
(5)	s.113(7), (8)
(6)	s.121 (changed)
(7)	s.128(1), (2)
s.352A Statement that company has only one member	
(1)	s.123(2) (changed)
(2)	s.123(3) (changed)
(3)	s.123(4), (5)
(3A)	s.124(1), (2)
s.353 Location of register	
(1)	s.114(1) (changed)
(2)	s.114(2)
(3)	s.114(3), (4)
(4)	s.114(5), (6)
s.354 Index of members	
(1)	s.115(1), (2)
(2)	s.115(3)
(3)	s.115(4) (changed)
(4)	s.115(5), (6)
s.355 Entries in register in relation to share warrants	
(1)	s.122(1) (changed)
(2)	s.122(4)
(3)	s.122(5)
(4)	s.122(2), (6)
(5)	s.122(3)
s.356 Inspection of register and index	
(1)	s.116(1) (changed)
(3)	s.116(2)

Provision of Companies Act 1985	Destination in Companies Act 2006
(5)	s.118(1), (2) (changed)
(6)	s.118(3)

s.357 Non-compliance with ss. 353, 354, 356; agent's default

repealed

s.358 Power to close register

repealed

s.359 Power of court to rectify register

(1)	s.125(1)
(2)	s.125(2)
(3)	s.125(3)
(4)	s.125(4)

s.360 Trusts not to be entered on register in England and Wales

s.126

s.361 Register to be evidence

s.127

s.362 Overseas branch registers

(1)	s.129(1)
(2)	s.129(1), (5)
(3)	ss.130(1)-(3), 131(1), (4), 132(1)-(4), 133(1)-(3), 134(1)-(3), 135(1)-(5)
(4), (5)	repealed

Chapter III Annual return

s.363 Duty to deliver annual returns

(1)	s.854(1), (2)
(2)	s.854(3) (changed)
(3)	s.858(1)-(3)
(4)	s.858(1), (2), (4) (changed)
(5)	repealed

s.364 Contents of annual return: general

(1)	s.855(1) (changed)
(2)	s.855(2)
(3)	s.855(3)
(4)-(6)	repealed

s.364A Contents of annual return: particulars of share capital and shareholders

| (1) | s.856(1) |

Provision of Companies Act 1985	Destination in Companies Act 2006
(2)	s.856(2)
(3)	s.856(2) (changed)
(4)	s.856(3)
(5)	s.856(4)
(6)	s.856(5)
(7)	repealed
(8)	s.856(6)

s.365 Supplementary provisions: regulations and interpretation

(1)	s.857(1), (2)
(2)	s.857(3)
(3)	s.859

Chapter IV Meetings and Resolutions

s.366 Annual general meeting

(1)	ss.336(1), 337(1)
(2), (3)	repealed
(4)	s.336(3), (4)

s.366A Election by private company to dispense with annual general meetings

	repealed

s.367 Secretary of State's power to call meting in default

	repealed

s.368 Extraordinary general meeting on members' requisition

(1)	s.303(1), (2)
(2)	s.303(2), (3) (changed)
(2A)	s.303(2)
(3)	s.303(4), (6) (changed)
(4)	ss.304(1), 305(1), (3)
(5)	s.305(4)
(6)	s.305(6), (7)
(7)	s.304(4)
(8)	s.304(1)

s.369 Length of notice for calling meetings

(1), (2)	s.307(2), (3) (changed)
(3)	ss.307(4), 337(2) (changed)
(4)	s.307(5), (6) (changed)

Provision of Companies Act 1985	*Destination in Companies Act 2006*
(4A)	s.308 (changed)
(4B)	ss.308, 309(1), (3) (changed)
(4C)	s.309(2)
(4D)-(4G)	repealed

s.370 General provisions as to meetings and votes

(1)	ss.284(4), 310(4), 318(2), 319(2)
(2)	s.310(1)
(3)	repealed
(4)	s.318(2) (changed)
(5)	s.319(1)
(6)	s.284(1), (3)

s.370A Quorum at meetings of the sole member

	s.318(1), (3) (changed)

s.371 Power of court to order meeting

(1)	s.306(1), (2)
(2)	s.306(3), (4)
(3)	s.306(5)

s.372 Proxies

(1)	s.324(1)
(2)	s.324(2) (changed)
(2A), (2B)	repealed
(3)	s.325(1) (changed)
(4)	s.325(3), (4)
(5)	s.327(1), (2) (changed)
(6)	s.326(1)-(4) (changed)
(6A), (7)	repealed

s.373 Right to demand a poll

(1)	s.321(1), (2) (changed)
(2)	s.329(1), (2) (changed)

s.374 Voting on a poll

	s.322

s.375 Representation of corporations at meetings

(1)	s.323(1)
(2)	s.323(2), (3) (changed)

Provision of Companies Act 1985	Destination in Companies Act 2006
s.376 Circulation of members' resolutions	
(1)	ss.314(1), (4), 315(2), 316(2), 338(1), (4), 339(2), 340(2)
(2)	ss.314(2), (3), 338(3)
(3)	ss.315(1), 339(1)
(4)	repealed
(5)	ss.315(1), 339(1)
(6)	s.339(3)
(7)	ss.315(3), (4), 339(4), (5)
s.377 In certain cases, compliance with s 376 not required	
(1)	ss.314(4), 316(2), 338(4), 340(2) (changed)
(2)	repealed
(3)	s.317(1), (2) (changed)
s.378 Extraordinary and special resolutions	
(1)	s.283(1), (4), (5) (changed)
(2)	s.283(1), (4)-(6) (changed)
(3)	repealed
(4)	s.320(1), (3)
(5)	s.283(5) (changed)
(6)	s.301 (changed)
s.379 Resolution requiring special notice	
(1)	s.312(1)
(2)	s.312(2), (3) (changed)
(3)	s.312(4)
s.379A Elective resolution of private company	
	repealed
s.380 Registration, etc of resolutions and agreements	
(1)	s.30(1)
(2)	s.36(1), (2) (changed)
(3)	repealed
(4)	s.29(1) (changed)
(4A)	s.29(2)
(5)	s.30(2), (3)
(6)	s.36(3), (4) (changed)
(7)	ss.30(4), 36(5)

Provision of Companies Act 1985	*Destination in Companies Act 2006*
s.381 Resolution passed at adjourned meeting	
	s.332
s.381A Written resolutions of private companies	
(1)	ss.288(1), 289(1) (changed)
(2)	s.296(1) (changed)
(3)	repealed
(4)	s.288(5)
(5), (6)	repealed
(7)	s.288(2)
s.381B Duty to notify auditors of proposed written resolution	
	repealed
s.381C Written resolutions: supplementary provisions	
(1)	s.300
(2)	repealed
s.382 Minutes of meetings	
(1)	ss.248(1), 355(1)
(2)	ss.249(1), 356(4)
(3)	repealed
(4)	ss.249(2), 356(5)
(5)	ss.248(3), (4), 355(3), (4) (changed)
s.382A Recording of written resolutions	
(1)	s.355(1) (changed)
(2)	s.356(2), (3)
(3)	repealed (see s.355(4))
s.382B Recording of decisions by the sole member	
(1)	s.357(1), (2)
(2)	s.357(3), (4)
(3)	s.357(5)
s.383 Inspection of minute books	
(1)	s.358(1), (3) (changed)
(3)	s.358(4) (changed)
(4)	s.358(5), (6) (changed)
(5)	s.358(7)

Provision of Companies Act 1985	Destination in Companies Act 2006

Chapter V Auditors

s.384 Duty to appoint auditors

(1)	ss.485(1), 489(1) (changed)
(2)	s.489(2)
(3), (4)	repealed

s.385 Appointment at general meeting at which accounts laid

(1)	repealed
(2)	ss.489(2), (4), 491(1) (changed)
(3)	s.489(3) (changed)
(4)	s.489(4) (changed)

s.385A Appointment by private company which is not obliged to lay accounts

	repealed

s.386 Election by private company to dispense with annual appointment

	repealed

s.387 Appointment by Secretary of State in default of appointment by company

(1)	ss.486(1), 490(1)
(2)	ss.486(2)-(4), 490(2)-(4)

s.388 Filling of casual vacancies

(1)	ss.489(3), 526
(2)	s.526
(3)-(4)	repealed

s.388A Certain companies exempt from obligation to appoint auditors

	repealed

s.389A Rights to information

(1)	s.499(1)
(2)	s.499(2)
(3)	s.500(1)
(4)	s.500(2)
(5)	s.500(3)
(6)	ss.499(3), 500(4)
(7)	ss.499(4) 500(5)

s.389B Offences relating to the provision of information to auditors

(1)	s.501(1), (2)
(2)	s.501(3)

Provision of Companies Act 1985	Destination in Companies Act 2006
(3)	s.501(3) (changed)
(4)	s.501(4), (5)
(5)	s.501(6)

s.390 Right to attend company meetings, etc.

(1)	s.502(2)
(1A)	repealed
(2)	s.502(1)
(3)	s.502(2)

s.390A Remuneration of auditors

(1)	s.492(1)
(2)	s.492(2), (3)
(4)	s.492(4)
(5)	s.492(5)

s.390B Disclosure of services provided by auditors or associates and related remuneration

(1)	ss.494(1), 501(1), (2)
(2)	s.494(2)
(3)	s.494(3)
(4)	s.494(4)
(5)	s.494(5)
(6)	s.1292(1)
(8)	s.494(1)
(9)	ss.494(6), 1289

s.391 Removal of auditors

(1)	s.510(1), (2)
(2)	s.512(1)-(3)
(3)	s.510(3)
(4)	s.513(1), (2)

s.391A Rights of auditors who are removed or not re-appointed

(1)	ss.511(1), 515(1), (2) (changed)
(2)	ss.511(2), 515(3)
(3)	ss.511(3), 515(4)
(4)	ss.511(4), 515(5)
(5)	ss.511(5), 515(6)
(6)	ss.511(6), 515(7)

Provision of Companies Act 1985	**Destination in Companies Act 2006**
s.392 Resignation of auditors	
(1)	s.516(1), (2)
(2)	s.516(3)
(3)	s.517(1)-(3)
s.392A Rights of resigning auditors	
(1)	s.518(1)
(2)	s.518(2)
(3)	s.518(3)
(4)	s.518(4)
(5)	s.518(5)-(7)
(6)	s.518(8)
(7)	s.518(9)
(8)	s.518(10)
s.393 Termination of appointment of auditors not appointed annually	
	repealed
s.394 Statement by person ceasing to hold office as auditor	
(1)	s.519(1)-(3), (7) (changed)
(2)	s.519(4) (changed)
(3)	s.520(2)
(4)	s.520(3)
(5)	s.521(1)
(6)	s.520(4)
(7)	ss.520(5), 521(2) (changed)
s.394A Offences of failing to comply with s.394	
(1)	ss.519(5), 521(3)-(5)
(2)	ss.519(6), 521(4)
(3)	repealed (see s.520(6))
(4)	s.520(6), (8) (changed)

PART XII REGISTRATION OF CHARGES

Chapter I Registration of Charges (England and Wales)

s.395 Certain charges void if not registered	
(1)	ss.860(1), 861(5), 870(1). 874(1), (2)
(2)	s.874(3)

Provision of Companies Act 1985	*Destination in Companies Act 2006*
s.396 Charges which have to be registered	
(1)	ss.860(7), 861(2)
(2)	s.861(3)
(3)	s.861(1)
(3A)	s.861(4)
(4)	s.861(5)
s.397 Formalities of registration (debentures)	
(1)	ss.863(1)-(4), 870(3)
(2)	s.864(1), (3)
(3)	s.864(2)
s.398 Verification of charge on property outside United Kingdom	
(1)	s.866(1)
(2)	s.870(1)
(3)	s.866(2)
(4)	s.867(1), (2)
s.399 Company's duty to register charges it creates	
(1)	ss.860(1), (2), 863(5)
(2)	ss.860(3), 863(5)
(3)	ss.860(4)-(6), s.863(5)
s.400 Charges existing on property acquired	
(1)	ss.861(5), 862(1)
(2)	ss.862(2), (3), 870(2)
(3)	s.870(2)
(4)	s.862(4), (5) (changed)
s.401 Register of charges to be kept by registrar of companies	
(1)	s.869(1), (2), (4)
(2)	s.869(5), (6)
(3)	s.869(7)
s.402 Endorsement of certificate on debentures	
(1)	s.865(1)
(2)	s.865(2)
(3)	s.865(3), (4)
s.403 Entries of satisfaction and release	
(1)	s.872(1), (2) (changed)

Provision of Companies Act 1985	**Destination in Companies Act 2006**
(1A)	repealed
(2)	s.872(3)
(2A)	repealed

s.404 Rectification of register of charges

(1)	s.873(1)
(2)	s.873(2)

s.405 Registration of enforcement of security

(1)	s.871(1), (3)
(2)	s.871(2), (3)
(3)	repealed
(4)	s.871(4), (5)

s.406 Companies to keep copies of instrument creating charges

(1)	ss.875(1), 877(2) (changed)
(2)	s.875(2)

s.407 Company's register of charges

(1)	ss.876(1), 877(2) (changed)
(2)	s.876(2)
(3)	s.876(3), (4)

s.408 Right to inspect instruments which create charges, etc.

(1)	s.877(1), (2), (4) (changed)
(2)	s.877(2) (changed)
(3)	s.877(5), (6)
(4)	s.877(7)

s.409 Charges on Property in England and Wales created elsewhere

	repealed

Chapter II Registration of Charges (Scotland)

s.410 Charges void unless registered

(1)	s.878(1)
(2)	ss.886(1), 889(1)
(3)	s.889(2)
(4)	ss.878(7), 879(1), (3)
(5)	s.879(5), (6)

s.411 Charges on property outside United Kingdom

(1)	s.886(1)

Provision of Companies Act 1985	Destination in Companies Act 2006
(2)	s.884

s.412 Negotiable instrument to secure book debts

	s.879(4)

s.413 Charges associated with debentures

(1)	s.879(2)
(2)	ss.882(1)-(4), 886(3)
(3)	s.883(1)-(3)

s.414 Charge by way of ex facie absolute disposition, etc.

(1)	s.881(1)
(2)	s.881(2), (3)

s.415 Company's duty to register charges created by it

(1)	ss.878(1), (2), 882(5)
(2)	s.878(3), 882(5)
(3)	s.878(4)-(6), 882(5)

s.416 Duty to register charges existing on property acquired

(1)	ss.880(1), (2), 886(2)
(2)	s.886(2)
(3)	s.880(3), (4) (changed)

s.417 Register of charges to be kept by registrar of companies

(1)	s.885(1)
(2)	s.885(2)
(3)	s.885(3)
(4)	s.886(6)

s.418 Certificate of registration to be issued

(1)	s.885(4)
(2)	s.885(4), (5)

s.419 Entries of satisfaction and release

(1)	s.887(1), (3) (changed)
(1A)	repealed
(1B)	s.887(2)
(2)	s.887(4)
(3)	s.887(2) (changed)
(4)	s.887(5)
(5), (5A)	repealed

Provision of Companies Act 1985	**Destination in Companies Act 2006**
s.420 Rectification of register	
	s.888(1), (2)
s.421 Copies of instruments creating charges to be kept by company	
(1)	ss.890(1), 892(2) (changed)
(2)	s.890(2)
s.422 Company's register of charges	
(1)	ss.891(1), 892(2) (changed)
(2)	s.891(2)
(3)	s.891(3), (4)
s.423 Right to inspect copies of instruments, and company's register	
(1)	s.892(1), (2), (4) (changed)
(2)	s.892(4) (changed)
(3)	s.892(5), (6)
(4)	s.892(7)
s.424 Extension of Chapter II	
	repealed
PART XIII ARRANGEMENTS AND RECONSTRUCTIONS	
s.425 Power of company to compromise with creditors and members	
(1)	ss.895(1), 896(1), (2)
(2)	ss.899(1), (3), 907(1), 922(1)
(3)	s.899(4), 901(3), (4) (changed)
(4)	s.901(5), (6)
(5)	repealed
(6)	s.895(2)
s.426 Information as to compromise to be circulated	
(1)	s.897(1)
(2)	s.897(1), (2)
(3)	s.897(1)
(4)	s.897(3)
(5)	s.897(4)
(6)	ss.895(1), 897(5)-(8)
(7)	s.898(1)-(3)
s.427 Provisions for facilitating company reconstruction or amalgamation	
(1)	s.900(1)

Provision of Companies Act 1985	*Destination in Companies Act 2006*
(2)	s.900(1), (2)
(3)	s.900(2)
(4)	s.900(3), (4)
(5)	s.900(6)-(8)
(6)	ss.900(5), 941

s.427A Application of ss. 425-427 to mergers and divisions of public companies

(1)	ss.902(1), 903(1), 907(2), 922(2)
(2)	ss.904(1), 919(1)
(3)	s.938(1), (2)
(4)	s.902(3)
(5)-(7)	repealed
(8)	s.941

PART XIIIA TAKEOVER OFFERS

s.428 Takeover offers

(1)	s.974(1)-(3)
(2)	s.974(4), (5)
(2A)	s.974(6)
(3)	s.976(1)
(4)	s.976(3)
(5)	s.975(1), (2) (changed)
(6)	s.975(3) (changed)
(7)	s.974(7)
(8)	s.991(1)

s.429 Right of offeror to buy out minority shareholders

(1)	s.979(1), (2) (changed)
(2)	s.979(3), (4) (changed)
(3)	s.980(2) (changed)
(4)	s.980(1), (4)
(5)	s.980(5)
(6)	s.980(6), (8)
(7)	s.980(7)
(8)	ss.977(1), 979(8)-(10) (changed)

s.430 Effect of notice under s. 429

(1)	s.981(1)

Provision of Companies Act 1985	Destination in Companies Act 2006
(2)	s.981(2)
(3)	s.981(3)
(4)	s.981(4), (5) (changed)
(5)	s.981(6)
(6)	s.981(7)
(7)	s.981(8)
(8)	s.981(6)
(9)	s.981(9)
(10)	s.982(2), (3)
(11)	s.982(4), (5)
(12)	s.982(6)
(13)	s.982(7)
(14)	s.982(8)
(15)	s.982(9)

s.430A Right of minority shareholder to be bought out by offeror

(1)	ss.983(1)-(3), 984(1)
(1A)	s.983(1)
(2)	s.983(4)
(2A)	s.983(5)
(3)	s.984(3)
(4)	s.984(2)
(5)	s.984(4)
(6)	s.984(5), (7)
(7)	s.984(6)

s.430B Effect of requirement under s. 430A

(1)	s.985(1)
(2)	s.985(2)
(3)	s.985(3)
(4)	s.985(4), (5) (changed)

s.430C Applications to the court

(1)	s.986(1), (2)
(2)	s.986(2)
(3)	s.986(3)
(4)	s.986(5)

Provision of Companies Act 1985	*Destination in Companies Act 2006*
(5)	s.986(9), (10)

s.430D Joint offers

(1)	s.987(1)
(2)	s.987(2), (3) (changed)
(3)	s.987(5), (6)
(4)	s.987(4), (7)
(5)	s.987(8)
(6)	s.987(9)
(7)	s.987(10)

s.430E Associates

(1)	ss.975(4), 977(2) (changed)
(2)	s.979(9)
(3)	s.983(8)
(4)	s.988(1), (4)
(5)	s.988(2)
(6)	s.988(3)
(7)	s.988(3), (5), (7)
(8)	s.988(1)

s.430F Convertible securities

(1)	s.989(1)
(2)	s.989(2)

PART XIV INVESTIGATION OF COMPANIES AND THEIR AFFAIRS; REQUISI-TION OF DOCUMENTS

s.438 Power to bring civil proceedings on company's behalf

repealed (by s.1176(1))

PART XVI FRAUDULENT TRADING BY A COMPANY

s.458 Punishment for fraudulent trading

s.993(1)-(3)

PART XVII PROTECTION OF COMPANY'S MEMBERS AGAINST UNFAIR PREJUDICE

s.459 Order on application of company member

(1)	s.994(1)

Provision of Companies Act 1985	Destination in Companies Act 2006
(2)	s.994(2)
(3)	s.994(3)

s.460 Order on application of Secretary of State

(1)	s.995(2), (3)
(1A)	s.995(1)
(2)	s.995(4)

s.461 Provisions as to petitions and orders under this Part

(1)	s.996(1)
(2)	s.996(2)
(3)	s.996(2)
(4)	repealed
(5)	s.998(1)-(4)
(6)	s.997

PART XVIII FLOATING CHARGES AND RECEIVERS (SCOTLAND)

Provision of Companies Act 1985	Destination in Bankruptcy and Diligence etc. (Scotland) Act 2007

Chapter I Floating Charges

s.462 Power of incorporated company to create floating charge

(1)	BD(S)A 2007, s.38(1), (2)
(4)	BD(S)A 2007, s.38(4) (changed)
(5)	repealed

s.463 Effect of floating charge on winding up

(1)	BD(S)A 2007, s.45(1), (3)
(2)	BD(S)A 2007, s.45(5)
(3)	BD(S)A 2007, s.45(6)
(4)	BD(S)A 2007, s.45(4)

s.464 Ranking of floating charges

(1)	BD(S)A 2007, s.41(1), (4) (changed)
(1A)	repealed
(2)	BD(S)A 2007, s.40(4)
(3)	BD(S)A 2007, s.41(2), (3) (changed)
(4)	BD(S)A 2007, s.40(1)-(3) (changed)
(5)	BD(S)A 2007, s.40(5), (6)
(6)	BD(S)A 2007, s.40(7)

Provision of Companies Act 1985	Destination in Bankruptcy and Diligence etc. (Scotland) Act 2007

s.465 Continued effect of certain charges validated by Act of 1972

(1), (2)	BD(S)A 2007, s.46 (changed)

s.466 Alteration of floating charges

(1)	BD(S)A 2007, s.43(1)-(3) (changed)
(2)-(6)	repealed

Chapter III General

s.486 Interpretation for Part XVIII generally

"company", "fixed security"	BD(S)A 2007, s.47

s.487 Extent of Part XVIII

	repealed

PART XX WINDING UP OF COMPANIES REGISTERED UNDER THIS ACT OR THE FORMER COMPANIES ACTS

Provision of Companies Act 1985	Destination in Companies Act 2006

Chapter VI Matters Arising Subsequent to Winding up

s.651 Power of court to declare dissolution of company void

	repealed

s.652 Registrar may strike defunct company off register

(1)	s.1000(1)
(2)	s.1000(2)
(3)	s.1000(3)
(4)	s.1001(1)
(5)	ss.1000(4)-(6), 1001(2)-(4)
(6)	ss.1000(7), 1001(5)
(7)	s.1002(1)-(3)

s.652A Registrar may strike private company off register on application

(1)	s.1003(1) (changed)
(2)	s.1003(2) (changed)
(3)	s.1003(3)
(4)	s.1003(4)
(5)	s.1003(5)
(6)	s.1003(6)
(7)	s.1003(6)

Provision of Companies Act 1985	Destination in Companies Act 2006

s.652B Duties in connection with making application under s. 652A

(1)	s.1004(1)
(2)	s.1004(2)
(3)	s.1005(1)
(4)	s.1005(2)
(5)	s.1005(3)
(6)	s.1006(1)
(7)	s.1006(2)
(8)	s.1006(3)
(9)	s.1004(3)

s.652C Directors' duties following application under s. 652A

(1)	s.1007(1)
(2)	s.1007(2)
(3)	s.1007(3)
(4)	s.1009(1)
(5)	s.1009(2)
(6)	s.1009(4)
(7)	s.1009(3)

s.652D Sections 652B and 652C: supplementary provisions

(1)	s.1008(1), (2)
(2)	s.1008(3)
(3)	s.1008(3)
(4)	s.1008(4)
(5)(c)	ss.1004(4), 1006(1), 1007(2), 1009(4)
(6)	s.1010
(7)	repealed
(8)	s.1011

s.652E Sections 652B and 652C: enforcement

(1)	ss.1004(5), (7), 1005(4), (6), 1006(4), (6), 1007(4), (6), 1009(5), (7)
(2)	ss.1006(4), (7), 1007(4), (7)
(3)	ss.1004(6), 1005(5)
(4)	s.1006(5)
(5)	ss.1007(5), 1009(6)

Provision of Companies Act 1985	*Destination in Companies Act 2006*
s.653F Other offences connected with s. 652A	
	repealed
s.653 Objection to striking off by person aggrieved	
	repealed
s.654 Property of dissolved company to be bona vacantia	
(1)	s.1012(1)
(2)	s.1012(2)
s.655 Effect on s. 654 of company's revival after dissolution	
(1)	s.1034(1)
(2)	s.1034(2)
(3)	s.1034(4)
(4)	s.1034(5)
(5)	repealed
s.656 Crown disclaimer of property vesting as bona vacantia	
(1)	s.1013(1)
(2)	s.1013(2) (changed)
(3)	s.1013(3)-(5) (changed)
(4)	repealed
(5)	s.1013(6), (7)
(6)	s.1013(8)
s.657 Effect of Crown disclaimer under s. 656	
(1)	s.1014(1)
(2)	ss.1015(1), (2), 1016(1), (2), 1017(1)-(5), 1018(1)-(5), 1019
(3)	repealed (see s.1120)
(4)	s.1020(1), (2)
(5)	s.1021(1), (2)
(6)	s.1021(3)
(7)	repealed
s.658 Liability for rentcharge on company's land after dissolution	
(1)	s.1023(1), (2)
(2)	s.1023(3)

Provision of Companies Act 1985	Destination in Companies Act 2006

PART XXII BODIES CORPORATE SUBJECT, OR BECOMING SUBJECT, TO THIS ACT (OTHERWISE THAN BY ORIGINAL FORMATION UNDER PART I)

Chapter I Companies Formed or Registered under Former Companies Acts

s.675 Companies formed and registered under former Companies Acts

repealed

s.676 Companies registered but not formed under former Companies Acts

repealed

s.677 Companies re-registered with altered status under former Companies Act

repealed

s.678 Companies registered under Joint Stock Companies Acts

repealed

s.679 Northern Ireland and Irish companies

repealed

Chapter II Companies not Formed under Companies Legislation, but Authorised to Register

s.680 Companies capable of being registered under this Chapter

(1)(a), (b)	s.1040(1)
(1) (closing words)	s.1040(2), (3), (6)
(1A)	s.1040(1)
(2)	s.1040(1)
(3)	s.1040(4)
(4)	s.1040(4)
(5)	s.1040(5)

s.681 Procedural requirements for registration

repealed

s.682 Change of name on registration

repealed

s.683 Definition of "joint stock company"

(1)	s.1041(1)
(2)	s.1041(2)

s.684 Requirement for registration by joint stock companies

repealed (to be replaced by regulations: see s.1042)

Provision of Companies Act 1985	*Destination in Companies Act 2006*

s.685 Registration of joint stock company as public company

	repealed (to be replaced by regulations: see s.1042)

s.686 Other requirements for registration

	repealed (to be replaced by regulations: see s.1042)

s.687 Name of company registering

	repealed (to be replaced by regulations: see s.1042)

s.688 Certificate of registration under this Chapter

	repealed (to be replaced by regulations: see s.1042)

s.689 Effect of registration

	repealed (to be replaced by regulations: see s.1042)

s.690 Power to substitute memorandum and articles for deed of settlement

	repealed (to be replaced by regulations: see s.1042)

PART XXIII OVERSEA COMPANIES

Chapter I Registration, etc.

s.690A Branch Registration under the Eleventh Company Law Directive (89/666/EEC)

	repealed (to be replaced by regulations: see Pt 34)

s.690B Scope of sections 691 and 692

	repealed (to be replaced by regulations: see Pt 34)

s.691 Documents to be delivered to registrar

	repealed (to be replaced by regulations: see Pt 34)

s.692 Registration of altered particulars

	repealed (to be replaced by regulations: see Pt 34)

s.692A Change in registration regime

	repealed (to be replaced by regulations: see Pt 34)

Provision of Companies Act 1985	**Destination in Companies Act 2006**

s.693 Obligation to state name and other particulars

	repealed (to be replaced by regulations: see Pt 34)

s.694 Regulation of oversea companies in respect of their names

(1)-(3B)	repealed
(4)	s.1048(1), (2) (changed)
(5)	s.1048(3)-(5)
(6), (7)	

s.694A Service of documents to which section 690A applies

	repealed

s.695 Service of documents on oversea company

(1), (2)	s.1139(2) (changed)

s.695A Registrar to whom documents to be delivered: companies to which s. 690A applies

(1)-(3)	repealed (to be replaced by regulations: see Pt 34)
(4)	s.1059

s.696 Office where documents to be filed

	repealed (to be replaced by regulations: see Pt 34)

s.697 Penalties for non-compliance

	repealed (to be replaced by regulations: see Pt 34)

s.698 Definitions for this chapter

	repealed (to be replaced by regulations: see Pt 34)

s.699 Channel Islands and Isle of Man companies

	repealed (to be replaced by regulations: see Pt 34)

Chapter II Delivery of Accounts and Reports

s.699A Credit and financial institutions to which the Bank Branches Directive (89/117/EEC) applies

(1), (2)	repealed
(3) ("financial institution")	s.1173(1)

s.699AA Credit and financial institutions to which the Eleventh Company Law Directive applies

	repealed (to be replaced by regulations: see Pt 34)

Provision of Companies Act 1985	*Destination in Companies Act 2006*
s.699B Scope of sections 700 to 703	
	repealed (to be replaced by regulations: see Pt 34)
s.700 Preparation of accounts and reports by oversea companies	
	repealed (to be replaced by regulations: see Pt 34)
s.701 Oversea company's financial year and accounting reference periods	
	repealed (to be replaced by regulations: see Pt 34)
s.702 Delivery to registrar of accounts and reports of oversea company	
	repealed (to be replaced by regulations: see Pt 34)
s.703 Penalty for non-compliance	
	repealed (to be replaced by regulations: see Pt 34)
Chapter IV Winding up etc.	
s.703O Scope of Chapter	
	repealed (to be replaced by regulations: see Pt 34)
s.703P Particulars to be delivered to the registrar: winding up	
	repealed (to be replaced by regulations: see Pt 34)
s.703Q Particulars to be delivered to the registrar: insolvency proceedings etc.	
	repealed (to be replaced by regulations: see Pt 34)
s.703R Penalty for non-compliance	
	repealed (to be replaced by regulations: see Pt 34)

PART XXIV THE REGISTRAR OF COMPANIES, HIS FUNCTIONS AND OFFICES

s.704 Registration offices

(1)	repealed
(2)	s.1060(1), (2)
(3)	repealed
(4)	s.1062 (changed)
(5), (6)	repealed
(7), (8)	s.1119(1), (2)

Provision of Companies Act 1985	Destination in Companies Act 2006
s.705 Companies' registered numbers	
(1)	s.1066(1)
(2)	s.1066(2)
(3)	s.1066(3)
(4)	s.1066(4), (5)
(5)(za)	s.1066(6)
s.705A Registration of branches of oversea companies	
(1)	s.1067(1) (changed)
(2)	s.1067(1)
(3)	s.1067(2)
(4)	s.1067(3)
(5)	s.1067(4), (5)
(6)	repealed
s.706 Delivery to the registrar of documents in legible form	
	repealed
s.707A The keeping of company records by the registrar	
(1)	s.1080(4)
(2)	s.1083(1) (changed)
(3)	s.1084(1)-(3) (changed), (5)
(4)	s.1084(4)
s.707B Delivery to the registrar using electronic communications	
	repealed
s.708 Fees payable to registrar	
(1)	s.1063(1)-(3) (changed)
(2), (3)	s.1063(4) (changed)
(4)	s.1063(6)
(5)	s.1063(5) (changed)
s.709 Inspection, etc. of records kept by the registrar	
(1) opening words	s.1085(1), s.1100
(1)(a), (b)	s.1086(1)
(2)	s.1085(2) (changed)
(3)	s.1091(3)
(4)	s.1091(5)
(5)	s.1092(1), (2)

Provision of Companies Act 1985	*Destination in Companies Act 2006*
s.710 Certificate of incorporation	
	s.1065
s.710A Provision and authentication by registrar of documents in non-legible form	
(1)	repealed (see s.1069)
(2)	s.1115(2)
s.710B Documents relating to Welsh companies	
(1)-(3)	s.1104(1), (2)
(4)	s.1104(3)
(5)	s.1104(4)
(6)-(8)	repealed
s.711 Public notice by registrar of receipt and issue of certain documents	
(1)	ss.1064(1)-(3), 1077(1)-(3), 1078(2), (3) (changed)
(2)	s.1079(4) (changed)
s.713 Enforcement of company's duty to make returns	
(1)	s.1113(1)-(3)
(2)	s.1113(4)
(3)	s.1113(5)
s.714 Registrar's index of company and corporate names	
(1)	s.1099(1)-(3) (changed)
(2)	s.1099(4), (5)
s.715A Interpretation	
(1) ("document"), (2)	s.1114(1)
(2), (3)	repealed

PART XXV MISCELLANEOUS AND SUPPLEMENTARY PROVISIONS

s.718 Unregistered companies	
(1)	s.1043(1), (3), (5) (changed)
(2)	s.1043(1)
(3)	s.1043(2), (5) (changed)
(5)	s.1043(4)
(6)	s.1043(6)
s.719 Power of company to provide for employees on cessation or transfer of business	
(1)	s.247(1)
(2)	s.247(2) (changed)
(3)	s.247(4)-(6) (changed)

Provision of Companies Act 1985	**Destination in Companies Act 2006**
(4)	s.247(7) (changed)

s.720 Certain companies to publish periodical statement

	repealed (by s.1177)

s.721 Production and inspection of books where offence suspected

(1)	s.1132(1), (2)
(2)	s.1132(3)
(3)	s.1132(4)
(4)	s.1132(5)

s.722 Form of company registers, etc.

(1)	ss.1134, 1135(1) (changed)
(2)	s.1138(1)
(3)	s.1138(2), (3)

s.723 Use of computers for company records

(1)	s.1135(1) (changed)
(2)	s.1135(5)
(3)-(5)	repealed

s.723A Obligations of company as to inspections of registers, etc.

(1)	s.1137(1), (2)
(2)	s.1137(3)
(3)	s.1137(3)
(4)	s.1137(4)
(5)	s.1292(1)
(6)	s.1137(5)
(7)	ss.1137(6), 1289

s.723B Confidentiality orders

	repealed (see s.1141)

s.723C Effect of confidentiality orders

	repealed (see s.1141)

s.723D Construction of sections 723B and 723C

	repealed (see s.1141)

s.723E Sections 723B and 723C: offences

	repealed (see s.1141)

s.723F Regulations under sections 723B to 723E

	repealed (see s.1141)

Provision of Companies Act 1985	*Destination in Companies Act 2006*
s.725 Service of documents	
(1)	s.1139(1)
(2), (3)	s.1139(4)
s.726 Costs and expenses in actions by certain limited companies	
	repealed
s.727 Power of court to grant relief in certain cases	
(1)	s.1157(1)
(2)	s.1157(2)
(3)	s.1157(3)
s.728 Enforcement of High Court orders	
	repealed
s.729 Annual report by Secretary of State	
	repealed by s.1179
s.730 Punishment of offences	
(1)-(3)	repealed
(4)	s.1125(2)
(5)	ss.1121(1), (3) (changed)
s.731 Summary proceedings	
(1)	s.1127(1), (2)
(2)	s.1128(1)
(3)	s.1128(2)
(4)	s.1128(4)
s.732 Prosecution by public authorities	
(1)	s.1126(1)
(2)	s.1126(2) (changed)
(3)	s.1129 (changed)
s.733 Offences by bodies corporate	
	repealed
s.734 Criminal proceedings against unincorporated bodies	
(1)	s.1130(1), (2) (changed)
(2)	s.1130(3)
(3)	s.1130(2)
(4)	s.1130(2)
(5), (6)	repealed

Provision of Companies Act 1985	**Destination in Companies Act 2006**

PART XXVI INTERPRETATION

s.735 "Company", etc.

(1)(a), (b)	s.1(1)
(1)(c)	s.1171 (changed)
(2)	repealed (see s.4)
(3)	s.1171

s.735A Relationship of this Act to Insolvency Act

	repealed

s.735B Relationship of this Act to Part 6 of the Financial Services and Markets Act 2000

	repealed

s.736 "Subsidiary"; "holding company" and "wholly-owned subsidiary"

(1)	s.1159(1)
(2)	s.1159(2)
(3)	s.1159(4)

s.736A Provisions supplementing s. 736

(1)-(11)	s.1159(3), Sch.6
(12)	s.1159(4)

s.736B Power to amend ss. 736 and 736A

(1)	s.1169(1)
(2)	s.1292(1)
(3)	ss.1160(2), 1289
(4)	s.1160(3)
(5)	s.1160(4)

s.737 "Called-up share capital"

(1), (2)	s.547
(3)	repealed

s.738 "Allotment" and "paid up"

(1)	s.558
(2)	s.583(2)-(3)(d)
(3)	s.583(5)
(4)	s.583(6)

s.739 "Non-cash asset"

(1)	s.1163(1)

Provision of Companies Act 1985	*Destination in Companies Act 2006*
(2)	s.1163(2)

s.740 "Body corporate" and "corporation"

	repealed

s.741 "Director" and "shadow director"

(1)	s.250
(2)	s.251(1), (2)
(3)	s.251(3)

s.742 Expressions used in connection with accounts

(1) ("fixed assets")	s.853(6)
(1) ("parent company")	s.1173(1)
(2)	s.853(4), (5)
(2A)	repealed

s.742A Meaning of "offer to the public"

(1)	s.756(1), (2)
(2)	s.756(3)
(3)	s.756(4), (5)(a)-(d) (changed)
(4)	s.756(4)
(5)	s.756(4)
(6)	s.756(5)(e), (6)
(7), (8)	repealed

s.742B Meaning of "banking company"

(1), (3)	s.1164(1), (2)
(3)	s.1164(3)

s.742C Meaning of "insurance company" and "authorised insurance company"

(1)-(4)	s.1165(1)
(2)	s.1165(2)(b), (c)
(3)	s.1165(4)
(4)	s.1165(2), (3)(a)
(5)	s.1165(8)

s.743 "Employees' share scheme"

	s.1166

s.744 Expressions used generally in this Act

"articles"	s.18(4)
"the Companies Acts"	s.2(1), (2) (changed)

Provision of Companies Act 1985	Destination in Companies Act 2006
"the court"	s.1156(1)-(3) (changed)
"debenture"	s.738
"EEA State"	s.1170
"equity share capital"	s.548
"the Gazette"	s.1173(1)
"hire-purchase agreement"	s.1173(1)
"insurance market activity"	s.1165(7)
"officer"	ss.1121(2), 1173(1)
"oversea company"	s.1044 (changed)
"prescribed"	s.1167
"the registrar of companies", "the registrar"	s.1060(3)
"regulated activity"	s.1173(1)
"share"	s.540(1), (4)

s.744A Index of defined expressions

1262, Sch.8

PART XXVII FINAL PROVISIONS

s.745 Northern Ireland

repealed (and see Pt 45)

s.746 Commencement

repealed (and see s.1300)

SCHEDULES

SCHEDULE 1 PARTICULARS OF DIRECTORS TO BE CONTAINED IN STATEMENT UNDER SECTION 10

repealed

SCHEDULE 2 INTERPRETATION OF REFERENCES TO 'BENEFICIAL INTEREST'

PART 1 References in sections 23, 145, 146 and 148

para.1(1)	ss.139(1), 672(1)
para.1(2)	ss.139(2), 672(2)
para.1(3)	ss.139(3), 672(3)
para.1(4)	ss.139(4), 672(4)
para.2(1)	repealed
para.2(3)	s.672(5)

Provision of Companies Act 1985	Destination in Companies Act 2006
para.2(4)	s.672(6)
para.2(5)	repealed
para.3(1), (2)	ss.140(1), (2), 673(1), (2)
para.4(1)	ss.138(1), (2), 674
para.4(2)	s.138(1)
para.4(3)	s.674
para.5(1)	ss.675(1), (2), 676
para.5(2)	ss.139(5), (6), 140(3), 675(1), (2)
para.5(3)	ss.139(6), 140(4), 676
paras 6-9	repealed

SCHEDULE 4 FORM AND CONTENT OF COMPANY ACCOUNTS

	repealed (to be replaced by accounting standards and regulations: see ss.395-397) subject to: Pt 3 Notes to the accounts
para.56(2), (3)	ss.382(6), 465(6)

PART 7 Interpretation of Schedule

para.94(1), (2)	s.411(6)

SCHEDULE 4A FORM AND CONTENT OF GROUP ACCOUNTS

	repealed (to be replaced by accounting standards and regulations: see ss.403, 404)

SCHEDULE 5 DISCLOSURE OF INFFORMATION: RELATED UNDERTAKINGS

	repealed (to be replaced by regulations: see s.409)

SCHEDULE 6 DISCLOSURE OF INFORMATION: EMOLUMENTS AND OTHER BENEFITS OF DIRECTORS AND OTHERS

	repealed (to be replaced by regulations: see s.412)

SCHEDULE 7 MATTERS TO BE DEALT WITH IN DIRECTORS' REPORT

	repealed (to be replaced by regulations: see s.416)

SCHEDULE 7A DIRECTORS' REMUNERATION REPORT

	repealed (to be replaced by regulations: see s.421)

SCHEDULE 7B SPECIFIED PERSONS, DESCRIPTIONS OF DISCLSOURES ETC. FOR THE PURPOSES OF SECTION 245G

PART 1 Specified persons

	s.461(1)

Provision of Companies Act 1985	**Destination in Companies Act 2006**
PART 2 Specified descriptions of disclosures	
	s.461(4)
PART 3 Overseas regulatory bodies	
	s.461(5), (6)

SCHEDULE 8 FORM AND CONTENT OF ACCOUNTS PREPARED BY SMALL COMPANIES

	repealed (to be replaced by regulations: see ss.396, 404)

SCHEDULE 8A FORM AND CONTENT OF ABBREVIATED ACCOUNTS OF SMALL COMPANIES DELIVERED TO REGISTRAR

	repealed (to be replaced by regulations: see s.444)

SCHEDULE 9 SPECIAL PROVISIONS FOR BANKING COMPANIES AND GROUPS

	repealed (to be replaced by regulations: see ss.396, 404)

SCHEDULE 9A FORM AND CONTENT OF ACCOUNTS OF INSURANCE COMPANIES AND GROUPS

	repealed (to be replaced by regulations: see ss.396, 404)

SCHEDULE 10A PARENT AND SUBSIDIARY UNDERTAKINGS: SUPPLEMENTARY PROVISIONS

para.1	Sch.7 para.1
para.2(1)	Sch.7 para.2(1)
para.2(2)	Sch.7 para.2(2)
para.3(1)	Sch.7 para.3(1)
para.3(2)	Sch.7 para.3(2)
para.3(2)	Sch.7 para.3(3)
para.4(1)	Sch.7 para.4(1)
para.4(2)	Sch.7 para.4(2)
para.4(3)	Sch.7 para.4(3)
para.5(1)	Sch.7 para.5(1)
para.5(2)	Sch.7 para.5(2)
para.6	Sch.7 para.6
para.7(1)	Sch.7 para.7(1)
para.7(2)	Sch.7 para.7(2)
para.8	Sch.7 para.8
para.9(1)	Sch.7 para.9(1)

Provision of Companies Act 1985	Destination in Companies Act 2006
para.9(2)	Sch.7 para.9(2)
para.9(3)	Sch.7 para.9(3)
para.10	Sch.7 para.10
para.11	Sch.7 para.11

SCHEDULE 11 MODIFICATIONS OF PART VIII WHERE COMPANY'S ACCONTS PREPARED IN ACCORDANCE WITH SPECIAL PROVISIONS FOR BANKING OR INSURANCE COMPANIES

repealed (to be replaced by regulations to make amendments)

SCHEDULE 13 PROVISIONS SUPPLEMENTING AND INTERPRETING SECTIONS 324 TO 328

repealed (see Sch.11 and below)

PART 4 Provisions with respect to register of directors' interests to be kept under section 325

para.27	s.809(2), (3)

SCHEDULE 14 OVERSEAS BRANCH REGISTERS

PART 1 Countries and territories in which overseas branch register may be kept

	s.129(2)

PART 2 General provisions with respect to overseas branch registers

para.1(1), (2)	ss.130(1), 135(3)
para.1(3)	ss.130(2), (3), 135(4), (5)
para.2(1)	s.131(1)
para.3(1)	s.134(1), (2) (changed)
para.3(2)	s.134(3)
para.4(1)	s.132(1), (2) (changed)
para.4(2)	s.132(3), (4)
para.5	s.133(1), (2)
para.6	s.135(1), (2)
para.7	s.131(4)

SCHEDULE 15A WRITTEN RESOLUTIONS OF PRIVATE COMPANIES

PART 1 Exceptions

para.1	s.288(2)

PART 2 Adaptation of procedural requirements

para.2	repealed
para.3(1), (2)	ss.571(7), 573(5)
para.5(1), (2)	ss.695(2), 698(2)

Provision of Companies Act 1985	**Destination in Companies Act 2006**
para.5(3), (4)	ss.696(2), 699(2)
para.6(1)	ss.717(2), 718(2)
para.6(2)	s.717(2)
para.6(3)	s.718(2)
para.7	s.188(5)
para.8	repealed

SCHEDULE 15B PROVISIONS SUBJECT TO WHICH SECTIONS 425-427 HAVE EFFECT IN THEIR APPLICATION TO MERGERS AND DIVISIONS OF PUBLIC COMPANIES

para.1	ss.907(1), (2), 922(1), (2)
para.2(1)	ss.905(1), 906(1)-(3), 920(1), 921(1)-(4)
para.2(2)	ss.905(2), (3), 920(2)
para.2(3)	s.920(3)
para.3	ss.908(1). (3), 909(1). (7), 911(1), (2). (4), 912, 923(1) (4), 924(1), (7), 925(5), 926(1), (2), (4), 927(1)-(3), 928
para.4(1)	ss.908(2), 923(2)
para.4(2)	s.923(3)
para.5(1)	ss.909(2), (3), 924(2), (3)
para.5(2)	ss.909(3), 924(3)
para.5(3)	ss.909(4), 924(4)
para.5(4)	s.935(1) (changed)
para.5(6)	s.935(2)
para.5(7)	ss.909(5), 924(5)
para.5(8)	ss.909(6), 924(6)
para.6(1)	ss.910(1), 911(3), 925(1), 926(3)
para.6(2)	ss.910(2), 925(2)
para.6(3)	ss.910(3), 925(3) (changed)
para.6(4)	ss.910(4), 925(4)
para.7	ss.914, 930
para.8(1)	ss.913(1), 929(1)
para.8(2)	ss.913(2), 929(2)
para.9(1)	s.939(1)
para.9(2)	s.939(1), (2)
para.9(3)	s.939(3), (4)
para.9(4)	s.939(5)

Provision of Companies Act 1985	Destination in Companies Act 2006
para.10(1)	ss.918(1), 932(1)
para.10(2)	ss.916(3)-(5), 918(2)-(4), 932(2)-(5)
para.11(1)	s.933(1)-(3), 934(1)
para.11(2)	s.933(1)-(3)
para.11(3)	s.934(1)
para.11(4)	s.934(2)-(4)
para.12(1)	ss.915(1), (6), 917(1), (6)
para.12(2)	s.915(2)
para.12(3)	s.915(3)-(5)
para.12(4)	s.917(2)
para.12(5)	ss.917(3)-(5), 931(3), (5)
para.13(1)	s.931(1)
para.13(2)	s.931(2)
para.13(3)	s.931(3), (4), (6)
para.14(1)	s.916(1)
para.14(2)	s.916(2)
para.14(3)	s.916(3)-(5)
para.15(1)	s.940(1)
para.15(2)	s.940(2)
para.15(3)	s.940(3)

SCHEDULE 20 VESTING OF DISCLAIMED PROPERTY; PROTECTION OF THIRD PARTIES

PART 2 Crown disclaimer under section 656 (Scotland only)

para.5	s.1022(1)
para.6	s.1022(2)
para.7	s.1022(3)
para.8	s.1022(4), (5)
para.9	s.1022(6)

SCHEDULE 21 EFFECT OF REGISTRATION UNDER SECTION 680

repealed (to be replaced by regulations: see s.1042)

SCHEDULE 21A BRANCH REGISTRATION UNDER THE ELEVENTH COMPANY LAW DIRECTIVE (89/666/EEC)

repealed (to be replaced by regulations: see Pt 34)

Provision of Companies Act 1985	Destination in Companies Act 2006

SCHEDULE 21B CHANGE IN REGISTRATION REGIME: TRANSITIONAL PROVISIONS

> repealed (to be replaced by regulations: see Pt 34)

SCHEDULE 21C DELIVERY OF REPORTS AND ACCOUNTS: CREDIT AND FINANCIAL INSTITUTIONS TO WHICH THE BANK BRANCHES DOTECTIVE (89/117/EEC) APPLIES

> repealed (to be replaced by regulations: see Pt 34)

SCHEDULE 21D DELIVERY OF REPORTS AND ACCOUNTS: COMPANIES TO WHICH THE ELEVENTH COMPANY LAW DIRECTIVE APPLIES

> repealed (to be replaced by regulations: see Pt 34)

SCHEDULE 22 PPROVISIONS OF THIS ACT APPLYING TO UNREGISTERED COMPANIES

> repealed (to be replaced by regulations: see s.1043)

SCHEDULE 23 FORM OF STATEMENT TO BE PUBLISHED BY CERTAIN COMPANIES UNDER SECTION 720

> repealed

SCHEDULE 24 PUNISHMENT OF OFFENCES UNDER THIS ACT

> repealed (see note at beginning of this table)

SCHEDULE 25 COMPANIES ACT 1981, SECTION 38, AS ORIGINALLY ENACTED

> repealed

BUSINESS NAMES ACT 1985

Provision of Business Names Act 1985	Destination in Companies Act 2006

s.1 Persons subject to this Act

(1)	ss.1192(1), (2), 1200(1), (2) (changed)
(2)	ss.1192(3), 1200(3) (changed)

s.2 Prohibition of use of certain business names

(1)	ss.1193(1), 1194(1) (changed)
(4)	ss.1193(4), 1194(3) (changed)

s.3 Words and expressions requiring Secretary of State's approval

(1)	repealed
(2)	s.1195(1)-(3) (changed)

s.4 Disclosure required of persons using business names

(1)	ss.1201, 1202(1), 1204(1) (changed)

Provision of Business Names Act 1985	Destination in Companies Act 2006
(2)	s.1202(2) (changed)
(3)	s.1203(1), (2)
(4)	s.1203(3)
(5)	ss.1202(3), 1204(2)
(7)	s.1203(4), (5) (changed)

s.5 Civil remedies for breach of s.4

(1)	ss.83(1), (2), 1206(1), (2)
(2)	ss.1206(4), 83(3)

s.6 Regulations

(1)	ss.1288, 1292(1)(a), (c)
(2)	ss.1193(3), 1194(2), 1197(4), 1290 (changed)
(3)	ss.1202(4), 1204(3), 1289 (changed)

s.7 Offences

(1)	s.1194(5)
(2)	ss.1193(4), (6), 1194(3), (5), 1205(1), (3) (changed)
(3)	ss.84(1), 1193(6), 1194(5) (changed)
(4)	ss.1193(5), 1194(4), 1205(2) (changed)
(6)	s.1207 (changed)

s.8 Interpretation

(1)	ss.1193(2), 1208 (changed)
(2)	repealed

s.9 Northern Ireland

	repealed

s.10 Commencement

	repealed

s.11 Citation

	repealed

COMPANIES ACT 1989

Provision of Companies Act 1989	Destination in Companies Act 2006

PART II ELIGIBILITY FOR APPOINTMENT AS COMPANY AUDITOR

s.24 Introduction

(1)	s.1209 (changed)

Provision of Companies Act 1989	*Destination in Companies Act 2006*
(2)	s.1210(1) (changed)
s.25 Eligibility for appointment	
(1), (2)	s.1212(1) (changed)
(3)	s.1212(2)
s.26 Effect of appointment of partnership	
(1)	s.1216(1)
(2)	s.1216(2)
(3)	s.1216(3)
(4)	s.1216(4)
(5)	s.1216(5)
s.27 Ineligibility on ground of lack of independence	
(1)	s.1214(1)-(3), (5)
(2)	ss.1214(4), 1292(1)(a)
(3)	s.1214(6)
(4)	ss.1214(7), 1289
s.28 Effect of ineligibility	
(1)	s.1213(1)
(2)	ss.1213(2), 1215(1)
(3)	ss.1213(3), (4), 1215(2), (3)
(4)	ss.1213(5)-(7), 1215 (4)-(6)
(5)	ss.1213(8), 1215(7)
s.29 Power of Secretary of State to require second audit	
(1)	s.1248(1)-(3) (changed)
(2)	s.1248(6) (changed)
(3)	s.1248(4), (6) (changed)
(4)	s.1249(2) (changed)
(5)	s.1248(5), (7), (8) (changed)
(6)	s.1249(3) (changed)
(7)	s.1249(1) (changed)
s.30 Supervisory bodies	
(1)	s.1217(1)
(2)	s.1217(2)
(3)	s.1217(3)
(4)	s.1218(4)

Provision of Companies Act 1989	*Destination in Companies Act 2006*
(5)	s.1217(4)

s.31 Meaning of "appropriate qualification"

(1)	s.1219(1)
(2), (3)	repealed
(4)	s.1219(2)
(5)	s.1219(3)
(6)	s.1219(1)

s.32 Qualifying bodies and recognised professional qualifications

(1)	s.1220(1)
(2)	s.1220(2)
(3)	repealed
(4)	s.1220(3)

s.33 Approval of overseas qualifications

(1)	s.1221(1)
(1A)	s.1221(2)
(2)	s.1221(3)
(3)	s.1221(4)
(4)	s.1221(5)
(5)	s.1221(6)
(6)	s.1221(7), (8)

s.34 Eligibility of individuals retaining only 1967 Act authorisation

(1)	s.1222(1)
(2)	s.1222(2)
(3)	repealed
(4)	s.1222(3)

s.35 The register of auditors

(1)	s.1239(1) (changed)
(2)	s.1239(2) (changed)
(3)	s.1239(5) (changed)
(4)	s.1239(6) (changed)
(5)	ss.1239(10), 1289
(6)	s.1239(8)

s.36 Information about firms to be available to public

(1)-(6)	repealed (see CA 2006, s.1240)

Provision of Companies Act 1989	*Destination in Companies Act 2006*
s.37 Matters to be notified to the Secretary of State	
(1)	s.1223(1)
(2)	s.1223(2)
(3)	s.1223(3)
(4)	s.1223(4)
s.38 Power to call for information	
(1)	s.1224(1), (2)
(2)	s.1224(3)
s.39 Compliance orders	
(1)	s.1225(1)
(2)	s.1225(2)
(3)	s.1225(3)
s.40 Directions to comply with international obligations	
(1)	s.1254(1)
(2)	s.1254(2)
(3)	s.1254(3)
s.41 False and misleading statements	
(1)	s.1250(1) (changed)
(2)	s.1250(2) (changed)
(3)	s.1250(4) (changed)
(4)	s.1250(5) (changed)
(5)	s.1250(6), (7) (changed)
(6)	s.1250(8) (changed)
s.42 Offences by bodies corporate, partnerships and unincorporated associations	
(1)	s.1255(1) (changed)
(2)	repealed
(3)	s.1255(2)
(4)	s.1255(3)
s.43 Time limits for prosecution of offences	
(1)	s.1256(1)
(2)	s.1256(2), (3)
(3)	s.1256(5) (changed)
(4)	s.1256(6) (changed)
(5)	s.1256(7) (changed)

Provision of Companies Act 1989	Destination in Companies Act 2006
s.44 Jurisdiction and procedure in respect of offences	
(1)	s.1257(1)
(2)	s.1257(2)
(3)	s.1257(3)
(4)	s.1257(5)
(5)	s.1257(6)
s.45 Fees	
(1)	s.1251(1)
(2)	s.1251(2) (changed)
(3)	s.1251(1) (changed)
(4)	ss.1251(4) (changed), 1288, 1289
(5)	s.1251(3) (changed)
s.46 Delegation of functions of Secretary of State	
(1)	s.1252(1)
(1A)	s.1252(2) (changed)
(2)	s.1252(3), (5) (changed)
(3)	s.1252(4), (6), (7) (changed)
(4)	s.1252(8) (changed)
(5)	s.1252(9)
(6)	s.1252(10)
(7)	s.1288
(8)	ss.1252(11), (12) (changed), 1289, 1290
s.46A Circumstances in which Secretary of State may delegate functions to existing body	
(1)	s.1253(1)
(2)	s.1253(2)
(3)	s.1253(3)
(4)	s.1253(4)
(5)	s.1253(5) (changed)
s.48 Exemption from liability for damages	
(1)	s.1218(1), (2), (5)
(2)	s.1218(3)
s.49 Service of notices	
(1)	s.1258(1)
(2)	s.1258(2)

Provision of Companies Act 1989	*Destination in Companies Act 2006*
(3)	s.1258(3) (changed)
(4)	s.1258(4) (changed)

s.50 Power to make consequential amendments

(1)-(7)	repealed (see CA 2006, s.1264 (changed))

s.51 Power to make provision in consequence of changes affecting accountancy bodies

(1)	s.1263(1) (changed)
(2)	ss.1263(2) (changed), 1288, 1289

s.52 Meaning of "associate"

(1)	s.1260(1)
(2)	s.1260(2)
(3)	s.1260(3)
(4)	s.1260(4)
(5)	s.1260(5)

s.53 Minor definitions

(1)	s.1261(1) (changed)
(2)	s.1261(2)

s.54 Index of defined expressions

	s.1262 (changed)

PART V OTHER AMENDMENTS OF COMPANY LAW

s.130 Company contracts and execution of documents by companies

(6)	s.1045(1), (2) (changed)

PART IX TRANSFER OF SECURITIES

s.207 Transfer of securities

(1)	ss.783(a)-(d), 785(1)
(2)	s.785(2)
(3)	s.785(3)
(4)	s.785(4) (changed)
(5)	s.785(5)
(6)	s.785(6)
(7)	s.788
(8)	s.1292(1)(a)
(9)	s.784(3) (changed)
(10)	s.783(d)

Provision of Companies Act 1989	Destination in Companies Act 2006
SCHEDULES	
SCHEDULE 11 RECOGNITION OF SUPERVISORY BODY	
para.1	Sch.10, para.1 (changed)
para.2	Sch.10. para.2
para.3	Sch.10, para.3
para.4	Sch.10, para.6 (changed)
para.5	Sch.10, para.7 (changed)
para.6	Sch.10, para.8 (changed)
para.7	Sch.10, para.9 (changed)
para.8	Sch.10, para.10 (changed)
para.9	Sch.10, para.11 (changed)
para.10	Sch.10, para.12
para.10A	Sch.10, para.13 (changed)
para.11	Sch.10, para.14 (changed)
para.12	Sch.10, para.15 (changed)
para.12A	Sch.10, para.16
para.13	Sch.10, para.17 (changed)
para.14	Sch.10, para.18 (changed)
para.15	Sch.10, para.19
para.16	Sch.10, para.20 (changed)
para.17	Sch.10, para.21
para.18	Sch.10, para.22
para.19	Sch.10, para.23 (changed)
para.20	Sch.10, para.24 (changed)
para.21	Sch.10, para.25
para.22(1)	Sch.10, para.26
(2)	Sch.10, para.27
SCHEDULE 12 RECOGNITION OF PROFESSIONAL QUALIFICATION	
para.1	Sch.11, para.1 (changed)
para.2	Sch.11, para.2 (changed)
para.3	Sch.11, para.3
para.4	Sch.11, para.6(1)-(3)
para.5	Sch.11, para.7(1)
para.6(1)	Sch.11, para.6(4), 7(2)

Provision of Companies Act 1989	Destination in Companies Act 2006
(2)	Sch.11, para.10(1)
(3)	Sch.11, para.10(2)
para.7	Sch.11, para.8 (changed), s.1289
para.8	Sch.11, para.9
para.9	Sch.11, para.11

SCHEDULE 13 SUPPLEMENTARY PROVISIONS WITH RESPECT TO DELEGATION ORDER

para.1	Sch.13, para.1
para.2	Sch.13, para.2
para.3	Sch.13, para.3
para.4	Sch.13, para.4
para.5	Sch.13, para.5
para.6	Sch.13, para.6
para.7	Sch.13, para.7
para.8	Sch.13, para.8
para.9	Sch.13, para.9
para.10	Sch.13, para.10 (changed)
para.11	Sch.13, para.11
para.12	Sch.13, para.12
para.13	Sch.13, para.13

INDEX

References are to the Companies Act 2006 and exclude the Appendices